THE AMERICAN JOURNEY

THE AMERICAN JOURNEY

A History of the United States

TEACHING AND LEARNING CLASSROOM EDITION

BRIEF FOURTH EDITION

COMBINED VOLUME

David Goldfield
UNIVERSITY OF NORTH CAROLINA, CHARLOTTE

Carl Abbott
PORTLAND STATE UNIVERSITY

Virginia DeJohn Anderson
UNIVERSITY OF COLORADO, BOULDER

Jo Ann E. Argersinger
SOUTHERN ILLINOIS UNIVERSITY

Peter H. Argersinger
SOUTHERN ILLINOIS UNIVERSITY

William L. Barney
UNIVERSITY OF NORTH CAROLINA, CHAPEL HILL

Robert M. Weir
UNIVERSITY OF SOUTH CAROLINA

PEARSON

Prentice
Hall

Upper Saddle River, New Jersey 07458

Library of Congress Cataloging-in-Publication Data
The American journey : a history of the united states   /   David Goldfield . . . [et al.].—
Teaching and learning classroom ed., brief 4th ed.
  p. cm.
 "Combined Volume."
 Includes bibliographical references and index.
 ISBN 0-13-174425-9 (combined : alk. paper)—ISBN 0-13-199247-3 (v. I :
  alk. paper)—ISBN 0-13-199249-X (v. II : alk. paper)
  1. United States—History. I. Goldfield, David R., (Date)
 E178. 1A4925 2006
 973—dc22

                2005035122

VP, Editorial Director: Charlyce Jones Owen
Editorial Assistant: Maureen Diana
Associate Editor: Emsal Hasan
Editor-in-Chief, Development: Rochelle Diogenes
Senior Media Editor: Deborah O'Connell
VP, Director of Production and Manufacturing: Barbara Kittle
Senior Managing Editor: Joanne Riker
Production Liaison: Jan Stephan
Prepress and Manufacturing Manager: Nick Sklitsis
Prepress and Manufacturing Buyer: Ben Smith
Director of Marketing: Brandy Dawson
Marketing Manager: Emily Cleary
Marketing Assistant: Jennifer Lang

Creative Design Director: Leslie Osher
Interior and Cover Designer: Laura Gardner, Amy Rosen, Kathy Mrozek
Director, Image Resource Center: Melinda Reo
Manager, Visual Research: Beth Brenzel
Cover Image Specialist: Karen Sanatar
Image Permission Coordinator: Craig Jones
Photo Researcher: Emily Tietz
Color Scanning Services: Joe Conti, Greg Harrison, Cory Skidds, Rob Uibelhoer, Ron Walko
Composition and Project Management: Jan Pushard/Pine Tree Composition Inc.
Printer/Binder: The Courier Companies, Inc.
Cover Printer: Phoenix Color Corp.

Abraham Lincoln, 1809–1865. 16th President of the United States. (Corbis/Bettmann)

Credits and acknowledgments from other sources and reproduced, with permission, in this textbook appear on appropiate page within text (or on page C-1)

Pearson Education Ltd., London
Pearson Education Australia Pty., Limited, Sydney
Pearson Education Singapore, Pte., Ltd.
Pearson Education North Asia Ltd., Hong Kong

Pearson Education Canada, Ltd., Toronto
Pearson Educación de Mexico, S.A. de C.V.
Pearson Education— Japan, Tokyo
Pearson Education Malaysia, Pte., Ltd.

10 9 8 7 6 5 4 3 2 1

ISBN 0-13-174425-9

CONTENTS

ENGLISH COLONIES IN AN AGE OF EMPIRE   86

IMPERIAL BREAKDOWN, 1763–1774   120

6

Visualizing The Past

7

8

9

10

11

Visualizing The Past

17

A NEW SOUTH: ECONOMIC PROGRESSION AND SOCIAL TRADITION, 1877–1900 480

18

INDUSTRY, IMMIGRANTS, AND CITIES, 1870–1900 510

19

TRANSFORMING THE WEST, 1865–1890 544

POLITICS AND GOVERNMENT, 1877–1900   574

THE PROGRESSIVE ERA, 1900–1917   602

22

CREATING AN EMPIRE, 1865–1917   636

23

AMERICA AND THE GREAT WAR, 1914–1920   664

24

TOWARD A MODERN AMERICA, THE 1920s   692

Visualizing The Past

Advertising and the Modern Woman   720

25

THE GREAT DEPRESSION AND THE NEW DEAL, 1929–1939   722

Voices from the American Journey:
Carlotta Silvas Martine, Eunice Langdon,
and Meridel LeSeur   724

26

WORLD WAR II, 1939–1945   754

Voices from the American Journey: Enrico Fermi   756

THE DILEMMAS OF NEUTRALITY   757
The Roots of War   757

27

THE COLD WAR AT HOME AND ABROAD, 1946–1952   786

28

THE CONFIDENT YEARS, 1953–1964   812

Visualizing The Past

29

SHAKEN TO THE ROOTS, 1965–1980 844

30

THE REAGAN REVOLUTION AND A CHANGING WORLD, 1981–1992 878

31

COMPLACENCY AND CRISIS, 1993–2005 912

American Views

From Then to Now

Maps

SPECIAL FEATURES

Global Perspectives

Visualizing the Past

Overview Tables

PREFACE

The path that led us to *The American Journey* began in the classroom with our students. Our goal is to make American history accessible to students. The key to that goal—the core of the book—is a strong clear narrative. American history is a compelling story and we seek to tell it in an engaging, forthright way. But we also provide students with an abundance of tools to help them absorb that story and put it in context. We introduce them to the concerns of the participants in America's history with primary source documents. The voices of contemporaries open each chapter, describing their own personal journeys toward fulfilling their dreams, hopes, and ambitions as part of the broader American journey. These voices provide a personal window on our nation's history, and the themes they express resonate throughout the narrative.

But if we wrote this book to appeal to our students, we also wrote it to engage their minds. We wanted to avoid academic trendiness, particularly the restricting categories that have divided the discipline of history over the last twenty years or so. We believe that the distinctions involved in the debates about multiculturalism and identity, between social and political history, between the history of the common people and the history of the elite, are unnecessarily confusing.

What we seek is integration—to combine political and social history, to fit the experience of particular groups into the broader perspective of the American past, to give voice to minor and major players alike because of their role in the story we have to tell.

APPROACH

In telling our story, we had some definite ideas about what we might include and emphasize that other texts do not—information we felt that the current and next generations of students will need to know about our past to function best in a new society.

Chronological Organization   A strong chronological backbone supports the book. We have found that the jumping back and forth in time that is characteristic of some American history textbooks confuses students. They abhor dates but need to know the sequence of events in history. A chronological presentation is the best way to be sure they do.

Geographical Literacy   We also want students to be geographically literate. We expect them not only to know what happened in American history, but where it hap-

pened as well. Physical locations and spatial relationships were often important in shaping historical events. The abundant maps in *The American Journey*—all numbered and called out in the text—are an integral part of our story.

Regional Balance   *The American Journey* presents balanced coverage of all regions of the country. In keeping with this balance, the South and the West receive more coverage in this text than in comparable books.

Point of View   *The American Journey* presents a balanced overview of the American past. But "balanced" does not mean bland. We do not shy away from definite positions on controversial issues, such as the nature of early contacts between Native Americans and Europeans, why the political crisis of the 1850s ended in a bloody Civil War, and how Populism and its followers fit into the American political spectrum. If students and instructors disagree, that's great; discussion and dissent are important catalysts for understanding and learning.

Religion   This text stresses the importance of religion in American society both as a source of strength and a reflection of some its more troubling aspects.

Historians mostly write for each other. That's too bad. We need to reach out and expand our audience. An American history text is a good place to start. Our students are not only our future historians, but more important, our future. Let their American journey begin.

FEATURES OF THE TEXT

The American Journey, TLC Edition includes features designed to make American history accessible to students. It provides more learning tools than any other U.S. history text.

- The **Student Tool Kit** that follows this preface helps students get the most out of the text and its features. It introduces students to key conventions of historical writing and it explains how to work with maps, documents, and visuals.
- The **chapter openings** have been expanded to provide a stronger pedagogical map to the content of the chapter.
  - **Chapter-Opening Visual Introductions** provide a pictorial survey of the narrative of the chapter.
  - **Chapter Highlights** provide a preview of the key developments and themes that follow in the chapter.

- **Chapter-opening Questions** ask students to consider carefully the main issues addressed in the narrative.

NEW • **Chapter Outline** introduces the major chapter sections.

- The **Voices from the American Journey** feature, in which brief primary source excerpts, opens each chapter. Consisting of letters, diary entries, and other first-hand accounts, these voices highlight the personal dimension of the American journey and show students the wealth and variety of experiences that make up this country's history. From Olaudah Equiano's narrative of his forced journey to Virginia as a slave, to the ultimate journey Sullivan Ballou made during the Civil War defending the Union, to Cambodian refugee Celia Noup's harrowing journey to California where she took her place as one of the thousands of new immigrants who are reshaping the face of our nation, *Voices from the American Journey* set the stage for the key themes that are explored in each chapter.

- **Overview Tables** summarize complex issues.

- **Quick Reviews,** found at key places in the margins of each chapter, encourage students to review important concepts before moving on.

- **Chapter Chronologies** help students build a framework of key events.

- **Key Terms** are highlighted within each chapter and defined in a running marginal glossary. A list of key terms and relevant page numbers are included at the end of each chapter for reference and review.

- Abundant **maps** help students understand the spatial dimension of history. The fourth edition features over ten new maps. The topographical detail in many of the maps helps students understand the influence of geography on history.

- **Map Explorations** with **Critical Thinking Questions** reinforce geographic literacy and prompt students to engage with maps, often in an interactive fashion. Each *Map Exploration* is found on the *Companion Website*™ for the text.

- **Documents CD-ROM** references are included at appropriate places in the margin of the text.

- **Visualizing the Past** essays, found at the end of selected chapters, analyze important aspects of U.S. history through photographs, fine art, sculpture, woodcuts, and advertisements. Focus questions and a running narrative guide students through a careful examination of the historical implication of each topic in question.

- The **American Views** box in each chapter contains a relevant primary source document. Taken from letters, diaries, newspapers, government papers, and other sources, these bring the people of the past and their concerns vividly alive. An introduction and pre-reading questions relate the documents to the text and direct students' attention to important issues.

- **From Then to Now** features relate important issues and events in each chapter to the issues and events of today, letting students see the relevance of history to their lives. In the fourth edition, this feature has been expanded to include visuals.

NEW • **Global Perspectives** boxes, included in each chapter, make substantive global connections that link the United States to other nations in the world, thereby enhancing students' understanding of America's development. *Global Perspectives* informs students that globalization is not something new because America was part of global trends long before we were a nation. This feature acknowledges that fact and places the American journey within a broader world-wide context. That journey not only influenced other countries and peoples, but we in turn have been shaped by global economic, migratory, technological, and political trends.

- **Chapter Review Questions,** organized by key subtopics in each chapter, help students review material and relate it to broader themes.

- **Where To Learn More** sections listed at the end of each chapter, describe important historical sites (both real and virtual) that students can visit to gain a deeper understanding of the events discussed in the chapter. Icons in the margins within chapters connect the historical sites to relevant content.

- **Illustrations** and **photographs**—tied to the text with detailed captions—provide a visual dimension to history.

CHANGES TO THE FOURTH EDITION

In this edition, there is greater emphasis on diversity, especially women, Native Americans, African Americans, and Hispanic Americans. And more attention is paid to the history of America's environment, highlighting conservation and resource development.

NEW AND EXPANDED COVERAGE INCLUDES:

Chapter 2 A new introductory section highlights experiences of ordinary colonists in New World settlement.

Chapter 14 A new section covers the religious revival of 1857–58, reinforcing the text's comprehensive treatment of religious themes throughout American history.

Chapter 15 The religious and spiritual perceptions of southern soldiers during the Civil War provide material for a new section on Southern Faith to complement the existing discussion on the role of religion in energizing Union troops.

Chapter 19 has expanded coverage of women and new attention to the role of religion and to social violence in the American West.

Chapter 20 provides expanded coverage of the centrality of popular politics and partisanship in American life. The chapter begins with a new *Voices from the American Journey* that provides a description of campaign pageantry in the 1890s.

Chapter 21 includes expanded coverage of the conservation movement and Native Americans and new attention to the interaction of the two. Additional coverage of the role of women in social and political reform, including launching the Progressive Party. New *American Views* on Jane Addams' description of her participation in Progressive politics.

Chapter 22 With the addition of a feature on European imperialism, the American experience is placed into its international context.

Chapter 23 now has expanded coverage of African Americans on the battlefront and homefront and new attention to the impact of total war, the use of gas, and conditions on the frontlines. A new *American Views* features a letter from an American soldier in France in World War I.

Chapter 24 With the addition of a feature on jazz, the importance of American and African-American cultural innovation is placed in an international context.

Chapter 25 provides expanded coverage of the ways women and minorities responded to the Great Depression and the New Deal, especially highlighting the experiences of Native Americans, African Americans, and Hispanic Americans. The new *American Views* in this chapter is an excerpt from John Collier of the Bureau of Indian Affairs, describing the New Deal for Native Americans.

Chapter 28 includes a new section on "Religion and Civil Rights."

Chapter 29 expands the discussion of the origins of the gay rights movement.

Chapter 30 includes a new section on "Mass Media and a Fragmented Culture."

Chapter 31 is updated through the adoption of the Iraqi constitution and Hurricane Katrina and provides a fuller discussion of the globalization of U.S. society and international connections.

INSTRUCTIONAL RESOURCES

The American Journey, TLC edition comes with an extensive package of supplementary print and multimedia materials for instructors and students.

PRINT SUPPLEMENTS FOR THE INSTRUCTOR

Instructor's Resource Binder   A comprehensive instructor resource, this special TLC binder includes the key supplements available with the text, all organized by chapter.

Instructor's Resource Manual   A time-saver in developing and preparing lecture presentations, the *Instructor's Resource Manual* contains chapter outlines, detailed chapter overviews, lecture outlines, topics for discussion, and information about audio-visual resources.

Test Item File   The test item file contains more than 1,500 multiple-choice, identification, matching, true–false, and essay test questions and 10–15 questions per chapter on the maps found in each chapter.

Prentice Hall Test Generator   Suitable for both Windows and Macintosh environments, this commerical-quality, computerized test-management program allows instructors to select items from the test-item file and design their own exams.

Transparency Package   Over 100 full-color transparency acetates of all the maps, charts, and graphs in the text are available as transparency acetates for use in the classroom.

PRINT SUPPLEMENTS FOR THE STUDENT

Reading Critically About History   This brief guide to reading effectively provides students with helpful strategies for reading a history textbook.

Understanding and Answering Essay Questions   This booklet is designed to help students develop analytical tools for understanding different types of essay questions and provides precise guidelines for preparing well-crafted essay answers.

History Notes (Volumes I and II) *History Notes* provides practice tests, essay questions, and map exercises for each chapter to help reinforce key concepts.

American Stories: Biographies in United States History This two-volume collection of 62 biographies in United States history includes introductions, pre-reading questions, and suggested resources.

Documents in United States History (Volumes I and II) This collection of more than 300 primary source documents directly relates to the themes and content of the text. Each document is approximately two pages long and includes a brief introduction and study questions intended to encourage students to analyze the document critically and relate it to the content of the text.

Retrieving the American Past: A Customized U.S. History Reader This collection of documents is an on-demand history database written and developed by leading historians and educators. It offers 86 compelling modules on topics in American history such as "Women on the Frontier," "The Salem Witchcraft Scare," "The Age of Industrial Violence," and "Native American Societies, 1870–1995." Approximately 35 pages in length, each module includes an introduction, several primary documents and secondary sources, follow-up questions, and recommendations for further reading. Instructor-originated material, including other readings and exercises, can be incorporated. Contact your local Prentice Hall representative for more information about this exciting custom-publishing option.

Prentice Hall and Penguin Bundle Program Prentice Hall is pleased to provide adopters of *The American Journey* with an opportunity to receive significant discounts when copies of the text are bundled with Penguin titles in American history. For a list of current titles available for bundling with *The American Journey* contact your local Prentice Hall representative.

MEDIA RESOURCES

Key OneKey Prentice Hall's **OneKey** is a new approach to course management. It is all students need for out-of-class work conveniently organized by chapter to reinforce and apply what they've learned in class and from the text. Among the resources available for each chapter are: a complete media-rich, interactive e-book version of *The American Journey*, quizzes organized by the main topics of each chapter, primary source documents, map labeling and interactive map quizzes. **OneKey** is all instructors need to plan and administer their course. All instructor resources are in one place to maximize effec-

tiveness and minimize time and effort in preparing for class. Instructor material includes: images and maps from *The American Journey*, hundreds of documents, video and audio clips, interactive learning activities, and Power-Point™ presentations.

Instructor's Resource CD-ROM This CD-ROM, like the OneKey website, includes all of the print supplements, multimedia resources, and images and art from *The American Journey*.

Companion Website with Gradetracker www.prenhall.com/goldfield *The American Journey Companion Website* offers students multiple-choice, true-false, essay, identification, map labeling, and document questions based on material from the text, organized by the primary subtopics in each chapter. Additionally, the *Companion Website* provides numerous interactive maps tied to the text, source documents, and other interactive modules related to the content in each chapter. This new version now includes a gradebook option for instructors.

U.S. History Documents CD-ROM Bound in every new copy of *The American Journey*, and organized according to the main periods in American history, the U.S. History Documents CD-ROM contains over 300 primary sources in an easily-navigable PDF file. Each document is accompanied by essay questions that students can answer via the CD-ROM and the Internet.

Exploring America CD-ROM The *Exploring America CD-ROM* features 31 interactive learning activities that drill down to explore the impact of key episodes and developments in U.S. history, including such topics as industrialization, immigration, the women's suffrage movement, the Harlem Renaissance, the American Indian Movement, and globalization.

Prentice Hall OneSearch with Research Navigator™ This brief guide focuses on developing critical thinking skills necessary to evaluate and use online sources. It provides a brief introduction to navigating the Internet with comprehensive references to History web sites. It also includes an access code and instruction on using Research Navigator, a powerful research tool that provides access to three exclusive databases of reliable source material: ContentSelect Academic Journal Database, The New York Times Search by Subject Archive, and Link Library.

Research Navigator™ This unique resource helps your students make the most of their research time. From finding the right articles and journals, to citing sources, drafting and writing effective papers, and completing research assignments, **Research Navigator™** simplifies and streamlines the entire process. Access to this valuable research resource is available with every copy of the *OneSearch* guide and with the *OneKey* website. For more information, contact your local Prentice Hall representative.

ACKNOWLEDGMENTS

All of us are grateful to our families, friends, and colleagues for their support and encouragement. Jo Ann and Peter Argersinger would like in particular to thank Margaret L. Aust, Judy Durbin, B.C. Eady, and Marnie H. Argersinger; William Barney thanks Pamela Fesmire and Rosalie Radcliffe; Virginia Anderson thanks Fred Anderson, Kim Gruenwald, Ruth Helm, Eric Hinderaker, and Chidiebere Nwaubani; and David Goldfield thanks Frances Glenn and Jason Moscato.

We owe a special thanks to John Reisbord for his work on the fourth edition of the *Teaching and Learning Edition*.

Finally, we would like to acknowledge the members of our Prentice Hall family. They are not only highly competent professionals but also pleasant people. We regard them with affection and appreciation. None of us would hesitate to work with this fine group again. We would especially like to thank our editorial team: Charlyce Jones Owen, VP/Editorial Director, and Elaine Silverstein, development editor, for their creativity and skill in crafting the plan for the fourth edition, and for helping us to execute it. Emily Cleary, marketing manager, and Brandy Dawson, Director of Marketing, whose creative and informed marketing strategies demonstrated a unique insight into the textbook market; Joanne Riker and Jan Stephan for keeping the production moving along; Rochelle Diogenes, editor in chief for development, for ensuring that the book had the developmental resources it needed; Nick Sklitsis, manufacturing manager, Benjamin Smith, manufacturing buyer, and Yolanda deRooy, president of Prentice Hall's Humanities and Social Sciences division.

DG

CA

VDJA

JEA

PHA

WLB

RMW

David Goldfield received his Ph.D. in history from the University of Maryland. Since 1982 he has been Robert Lee Bailey Professor of History at the University of North Carolina in Charlotte. He is the author or editor of thirteen books on various aspects of southern and urban history. Two of his works—*Cotton Fields and Skyscrapers: Southern City and Region, 1607-1980 (1982)* and *Black, White, and Southern: Race Relations and Southern Culture, 1940 to the Present* (1990)—received the Mayflower Award for nonfiction and were nominated for the Pulitzer Prize in history. His most recent book is *Still Fighting the Civil War: The American South and Southern History* (2002). When he is not writing history, Dr. Goldfield applies his historical craft to history museum exhibits, voting rights cases, and local planning and policy issues.

Carl Abbott is a professor of Urban Studies and Planning at Portland State University. He taught previously in the history departments at the University of Denver and Old Dominion University, and held visiting appointments at Mesa College in Colorado and George Washington University. He holds degrees in history from Swarthmore College and the University of Chicago. He specializes in the history of cities and the American West and serves as co-editor of the *Pacific Historical Review*. His books include *The New Urban America: Growth and Politics in Sunbelt Cities* (1981, 1987), *The Metropolitan Frontier: Cities in the Modern American West* (1993), *Planning a New West: The Columbia River Gorge National Scenic Area* (1997), and *Political Terrain: Washington, D.C. from Tidewater Town to Global Metropolis* (1999). He is currently working on a comprehensive history of the role of urbanization and urban culture in the history of western North America.

Virginia DeJohn Anderson is Professor of History at the University of Colorado at Boulder. She received her B.A. from the University of Connecticut. As the recipient of a Marshall Scholarship, she earned an M.A. degree at the University of East Anglia in Norwich, England. Returning to the United States, she received her A.M. and Ph.D. degrees from Harvard University. She is the author of *New England's Generation: The Great Migration and the Formation of Society and Culture in the Seventeenth Century* (1991) and several articles on colonial history, which have appeared in such journals as the *William and Mary Quarterly* and the *New England Quarterly*. Her most recent book is *Creatures of Empire: How Domestic Animals Transformed Early America* (2004).

Jo Ann E. Argersinger received her Ph.D. from George Washington University and is Professor of History at Southern Illinois University. A recipient of fellowships from the Rockefeller Foundation and the National Endowment for the Humanities, she is a historian of social, labor, and business policy. Her publications include *Toward a New Deal in Baltimore: People and Government in the Great Depression* (1988) and *Making the Amalgamated: Gender, Ethnicity, and Class in the Baltimore Clothing Industry* (1999).

Peter H. Argersinger received his Ph.D. from the University of Wisconsin and is Professor of History at Southern Illinois University. He has won several fellowships as well as the Binkley-Stephenson Award from the Organization of American Historians, and he is currently president of the Society for Historians of the Gilded Age and Progressive Era. Among his books on political and rural history are *Populism and Politics* (1974), *Structure, Process, and Party* (1992), and *The Limits of Agrarian Radicalism* (1995). His current research focuses on the political crisis of the 1890s.

William L. Barney is Professor of History at the University of North Carolina at Chapel Hill. A native of Pennsylvania, he received his B.A. from Cornell University and his M.A. and Ph.D. from Columbia University. He has published extensively on nineteenth-century U.S. history and has a particular interest in the Old South and the coming of the Civil War. Among his publications are *The Road to Secession* (1972), *The Secessionist Impulse* (1974), *Flawed Victory* (1975), *The Passage of the Republic* (1987), and *Battleground for the Union* (1989). He is currently finishing an edited collection of essays on nineteenth-century America and a book on the Civil War. Most recently, he has edited *A Companion to 19th-Century America* (2001) and finished *The Civil War and Reconstruction: A Student Companion* (2001).

Robert M. Weir is Distinguished Professor of History Emeritus at the University of South Carolina. He received his B.A. from Pennsylvania State University and his Ph.D. from Case Western Reserve University. He has taught at the University of Houston and, as a visiting professor, at the University of Southampton in the United Kingdom. His articles have won prizes from the Southeastern Society for the Study of the Eighteenth Century and the *William and Mary Quarterly*. Among his publications are *Colonial South Carolina: A History*, *"The Last of American Freemen": Studies in the Political Culture of the Colonial and Revolutionary South*, and, more recently, a chapter on the Carolinas in the new *Oxford History of the British Empire* (1998).

When writing history, historians use maps, tables, graphs, and visuals to help their readers understand the past. What follows is an explanation of how to use the historian's tools that are contained in this book.

TEXT

Whether it is a biography of George Washington, an article on the Civil War, or a survey of American history such as this one, the text is the historian's basic tool for discussing the past. Historians write about the past using narration and analysis. Narration is the story line of history. It describes what happened in the past, who did it, and where and when it occurred. Narration is also used to describe how people in the past lived, how they spent their days and even, when the historical evidence makes it possible for us to know, what they thought, felt, feared, or desired. Using analysis, historians explain why they think events in the past happened the way they did and try to offer an explanation. In this book, narration and analysis are interwoven in each chapter.

VISUALS

Visual images embedded throughout the text can provide as much insight into our nation's history as the written word. Within photographs and pieces of fine art lies emotional and historical meaning. Captions provide valuable information, such as in the example below. When studying the images, consider questions such as: "Who are the people?"; "How were they feeling?"; "What event motivated this photograph or painting?"; and "What can be learned from the backdrop surrounding the focal point?" Such analysis allows for a fuller understanding of the people who lived the American journey.

THE WAR FOR INDEPENDENCE: 1774–1783 CHAPTER 6   155

n agreement between the people and their rulers. The people are nd to obey their rulers only so long as the rulers offer them proon. Jefferson's prose transformed what might have been a bland ment into one of history's great statements of human rights.

The Declaration of Independence consists of a magnificently d opening assumption, two premises, and a powerful conclusion. opening assumption is that all men are created equal, that they efore have equal rights, and that they can neither give up these s nor allow them to be taken away. The first premise—that peoestablish governments to protect their fundamental rights to life, ty, and property—is a restatement of contract theory. (With a derful flourish reflecting the Enlightenment's optimism about an potential, Jefferson changed "property" to "the pursuit of hapss.") The second premise is a long list of charges meant to justie Americans' rejection of their hitherto legitimate ruler. Then wed the dramatic conclusion that Americans could rightfully overw King George's rule and replace it with something more satisry to them.

Historians have spilled oceans of ink debating Jefferson's use of expression "all men." In practice, of course, many people were uded from full participation in eighteenth-century American society. Women, pertyless white men, and free black men had no formal political rights and ted legal rights. Slaves enjoyed no rights at all. (Although himself a slaveer, Jefferson was deeply troubled by American slavery. He had wanted to inle a denunciation of the slave trade among the charges against George III in Declaration of Independence, but the Congress took it out, believing that to ne the king for this inhumane business would appear hypocritical.) But if the ds "all men are created equal" had limited practical meaning in 1776, they ever since confronted Americans with a moral challenge to make good on n.

LIGION, VIRTUE, AND REPUBLICANISM

ricans reacted to news of the Declaration of Independence with mixed emos. There was rejoicing as orators read the declaration to great crowds. But many who favored independence worried about how Americans would govthemselves. Most Whigs, animated by the political ideology known as **republiism,** thought a republican government was best suited to American society. Republicanism held that self-government—either directly by the citizens of ntry or indirectly by their elected representatives—provided a more reliable ndation for the good society and individual freedom than did rule by kings. s drawing on contract theory, as in the Declaration of Independence, repubnism called for government by consent of the governed. Drawing on country logy, it was suspicious of excessively centralized government and insistent on need for a virtuous, public-spirited citizenry. Republicanism therefore helped ve the American Revolution a moral dimension.

But other than a state that was not ruled by a hereditary king, what was a relic? And what were the chances that one would survive? Americans had at d a recent example of a republic in the English Civil War of the mid-sevenh century, in which English Puritans had for a time replaced the monarchy a republican "Commonwealth," dedicated to advancing the "common weal," ommon good. Some New Englanders, spiritual descendants of the Puritans,

Thomas Jefferson, author of the Declaration of Independence and future president of the United States. Mather Brown, an American artist living in England, painted this picture of Jefferson for John Adams while the two men were in London on diplomatic missions in 1786. A companion portrait of Adams that Jefferson ordered for himself also survives. Brown's sensitive portrait of a thoughtful Jefferson is the earliest known likeness of him.
Courtesy of Library of Congress

 WHERE TO LEARN MORE
Independence National Historical Park, Philadelphia, Pennsylvania
www.cr.nps.gov

Republicanism A complex, changing body of ideas, values, and assumptions, closely related to country ideology, that influenced American political behavior during the eighteenth and nineteenth centuries.

MAPS

Maps are important historical tools. They show how geography has affected history and concisely summarize complex relationships and events. Knowing how to read and interpret a map is important to understanding history. Map 5–1 from Chapter 5 shows the British colonies on the eastern seaboard of North America in 1763, about twelve years before the American Revolution. It has three features to help you read it: a caption, a legend, and a scale. The **caption** explains the historical significance of the map. Here the caption tells us that in 1763 the British government sought to restrict colonial settlement west of the Appalachian Mountains to prevent conflict between colonists and Indians. Colonial frustration with this policy contributed to the outbreak of the American Revolution.

The legend and the scale appear in the lower right corner of the map. The **legend** provides a key to what the symbols on the map mean. The solid line stretching along the Appalachian Mountains from Maine to Georgia represents the Proclamation Line of 1763. Cities are marked with a dot, capitals with a star, and forts by a black square. Spanish territory west of the Mississippi River is represented in gold; territory settled by Europeans is represented in green. The **scale** tells us that 7/8ths of an inch on the map represents 300 miles (about 480 kilometers) on the ground. With this information, estimates of the distance between points on the map are easily made.

The map also shows the **topography** of the region—its mountains, rivers, and lakes. This helps us understand how geography influenced history in this case. For example, the Appalachian Mountains divide the eastern seaboard from the rest of the continent. The mountains obstructed colonial migration to the west for a long time. By running the Proclamation Line along the Appalachians, the British hoped to use this natural barrier to separate Indians and colonists.

A **critical-thinking question** asks for careful considersation of the spatial connections between geography and history.

MAP EXPLORATION

To explore an interactive versionof this map, go to
http://www.prenhall.com/goldfield3/map5.1

MAP 5–1   Colonial Settlement and the Proclamation Line of 1763   This map depicts the regions claimed and settled by the major groups competing for territory in eastern North America. With the Proclamation Line of 1763, positioned along the crest of the Appalachian Mountains, the British government tried to stop the westward migration of settlers under its jurisdiction and thereby limit conflict with the Indians. The result, however, was frustration and anger on the part of land-hungry settlers.

WHY DO you suppose the Proclamation Line of 1763 was positioned along the crest of the Appalachian Mountains?

MAP EXPLORATIONS

Many of the maps in each chapter are provided in a useful interactive version on the text's *Companion Website*. These maps are easily identified by a bar along the top that reads "Map Exploration." An interactive version of *Colonial Settlements and the Proclamation Line of 1763* can be found at **www.prenhall.com/**

goldfield3/map5.1. The interactive version of this particular map provides an opportunity to pan over an enlarged version of the territory in question. Cities, forts, settlements, and terrain are shown in detail. By moving the cursor north, south, east, or west one can gain a bird's-eye view of the entire region.

STUDY AIDS

Each chapter begins with a **Chapter-Opening Introduction,** a collection of historically significant illustrations that provide visual context for the chapter. Expanded pedagogical support helps students orient themselves to the chapter content: **Chapter Highlights,** mini-summaries that preview key themes and developments, **Questions,** organized by the main subtopics of each chapter, that encourage careful consideration of important themes and developments, and **Chapter Outline,** a brief summary of the main sections wihtin the chapter all provide a road map for study and review. Each of the questions is repeated at the appropriate place in the margin of the text.

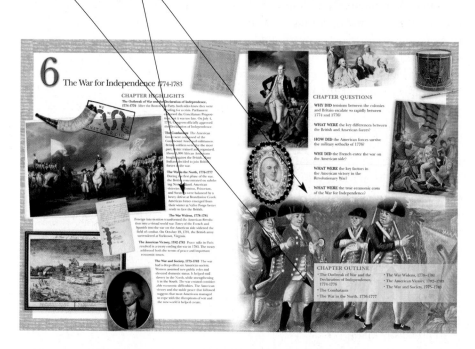

MARGINAL QUESTIONS

The **Questions** that begin each chapter are repeated at the appropriate place in the margin of the text. Students can use these questions as a review test to confirm their understanding of the chapter content.

MARGINAL KEY TERMS/GLOSSARY

Significant historical terms are called out in bold type throughout the text, defined in the margin, and listed at the end of each chapter with appropriate page numbers. All **key terms** in the text are listed alphabetically and defined in a glossary at the end of the book.

WHAT STEPS did Britain and Spain take to block American expansion?

Pilgrims   Settlers of Plymouth Colony, who viewed themselves as spiritual wanderers.

QUICK REVIEWS

The **Quick Reviews,** placed at key locations in the margins of each chapter, provide pinpoint summaries of important concepts, events, or topics in American history and serve as a mini-review resource.

U.S. HISTORY DOCUMENTS CD-ROM

Bound into every new copy of this textbook is a U.S. History Documents CD-ROM. This is a powerful resource for research and additional reading that contains more than 300 primary source documents central to U.S. History. Each document provides essay questions that are linked directly to a website where short-essay answers can be submitted online or printed out. Particularly relevant or interesting documents are called out at appropriate places in the margin throughout the text. A complete list of documents on the CD-ROM is found at the end of the book.

11–3
Sojourner Truth, Address to the Woman's Rights Convention, Akron, Ohio (1851)

OVERVIEW TABLES

The **Overview Tables** in this text are a special features designed to highlight and summarize important topics within a chapter. The Overview Table shown here, for example, summarizes the activities of the organizations and groups of the Progressive Era.

OVERVIEW — MAJOR PROGRESSIVE ORGANIZATIONS AND GROUPS

Group	Activity
Social Gospel movement	Urged churches and individuals to apply Christian ethics to social and economic problems
Muckrakers	Exposed business abuses, public corruption, and social evils through investigative journalism
Settlement House movement	Attempted through social work and public advocacy to improve living and working conditions in urban immigrant communities
National Consumers' League (1898)	Monitored businesses to ensure decent working conditions and safe consumer products
Women's Trade Union League (1903)	United workingwomen and their middle-class "allies" to promote unionization and social reform
National Child Labor Committee (1904)	Campaigned against child labor
Country Life movement	Attempted to modernize rural social and economic conditions according to urban-industrial standards

Chronologies

Each chapter includes a **Chronology,** a list of the key events discussed in the chapter arranged in chronological order. The Chronology for Chapter 16 lists the dates of key events during the Reconstruction era from 1861 to 1877. Chronologies provide a review of important events and their relationship to one another.

Chronology

1861	Tsar Alexander II frees the serfs of Russia
1863	Lincoln proposes his Ten Percent Plan.
1864	Congress proposes the Wade-Davis Bill.
1865	Sherman issues Field Order No. 15.
	Freedmen's Bureau is established.
	Andrew Johnson succeeds to the presidency, unveils his Reconstruction plan.
	Massachusetts desegregates all public facilities.
	Black citizens in several southern cities organize Union Leagues.
	Former Confederate states begin to pass black codes.
1866	Congress passes Southern Homestead Act, Civil Rights Act of 1866.
	Ku Klux Klan is founded.
	Fourteenth Amendment to the Constitution is passed (ratified in 1868).
	Presiden Johnson goes on a speaking tour.
1867	Congress passes Military Reconstruction Acts, Tenure of Office Act.
1868	President Johnson is impeached and tried in the Senate for defying the Tenure of Office Act.
	Republican Ulysses S. Grant is elected president.
1869	Fifteenth Amendment passed (ratified 1870).

1870	Congress passes Enforcement Act.
	Republican regimes topple in North Carolina and Georgia.
1871	Congress passes Ku Klux Klan Act.
1872	Freedmen's Bureau closes down.
	Liberal Republicans emerge as a separate party.
	Ulysses S. Grant is reelected.
1873	Severe depression begins.
	Colfax Massacre occurs.
	U.S. Supreme Court's decision in the *Slaughterhouse* cases weakens the intent of the Fourteenth Amendment.
	Texas falls to the Democrats in the fall elections.
1874	White Leaguers attempt a coup against the Republican government of New Orleans.
	Democrats win off-year elections across the South amid widespread fraud and violence.
1875	Congress passes Civil Rights Act of 1875.
1876	Supreme Court's decision in *United States v. Cruikshank* nullifies Enforcement Act of 1870.
	Outcome of the presidential election between Republican Rutherford B. Hayes and Democrat Samuel J. Tilden is contested.
1877	Compromise of 1877 makes Hayes president and ends Reconstruction.

CONCLUSION AND SUMMARY

The **conclusion** at the end of each chapter puts the subject of the chapter in the broader perspective of U.S. history. The **summary** is organized according to the main subtopics of the chapter and serves as an overview of the content in the chapter. Both of these study aids can be used as a review of important concepts. A thumbnail copy of the chapter-opening introduction is included with an **Image Key** that explains each of the images on the page.

CONCLUSION

All Americans, Whigs and loyalists alike, considered themselves good British subjects. But Americans were a more diverse and more democratic people than the English. A considerably larger percentage of them could participate in government, and for all practical purposes, they had been governing themselves for a long time.

British officials recognized the different character of American society and feared it might lead Americans to reject British control. But the steps they took to prevent this outcome had the opposite effect.

From Britain's perspective the measures taken in the wake of the French and Indian War were a reasonable response to administrative and financial problems in the colonies. Taken one by one from the colonists' perspective, however, they were a rain of blows that finally impelled Americans to rebel.

Attempts to protect their accustomed autonomy first brought the colonial assemblies into conflict with Parliament. Asserting their rights led to greater cooperation between individual colonies. This development, in turn, led to increasingly widespread resistance, then to rebellion, and finally to revolution. Moving imperceptibly from one stage to the next, Americans grew conscious of their common interests and their differences from the English.

SUMMARY

The Colonial Political World During the mid-seventeenth century England began to realize it had limited control over the governance and politics of the colonies in New England. The Dominion of New England was one failed attempt to gain control. English people on both sides of the Atlantic believed that politics ought to reflect social organization. Differing opinions, however, on virtual representation versus actual representation caused greater disagreement. The most direct political confrontations between England and the colonies focused on the role of colonial governors. And, in response to the perceived threat of powerful governors, colonial assemblies asserted themselves as never before.

Expanding Empires During the first half of the eighteenth century, England, Spain, and France all enlarged their North American holdings. The growth in populations was a result of natural increase as well as immigration. Most of the coast from Maine to Georgia was settled by 1760. Colonists who moved to the backcountry often displaced native groups. Spain's empire grew into Texas and California while the French expansion tended to follow major waterways like the Mississippi.

A Century of Warfare The English policy aimed at limiting the expansion of French influence resulted in four wars (King William's War, Queen Anne's War, King George's War, and the French and Indian War) between 1689 and 1763. The conclusion of the final war (the French and Indian War) signaled a dramatic shift in North American history as England would now claim all lands east of the Mississippi, Spain would nominally control the Trans-Mississippi West, and France would lose all of its mainland colonies.

IMAGE KEY
for pages 86–87.

a. A brown patterned neckcloth.
b. New Amsterdam City Hall and Great Dock in the late 17th century.
c. Imported English mahogany clothespress
d. "Español, con India, Mestizo"
e. Dried tobacco leaves.
f. A mounted moth.
g. A half-loom width of oyster silk damask, 18th century.
h. Portrait of Paul Revere
i. Portrait of George Washington
j. A hand-colored woodcut of a settlers' log cabin in the Blue Ridge Mountains (Appalachians).

REVIEW QUESTIONS, KEY TERMS, WHERE TO LEARN MORE, AND ADDITIONAL STUDY RESOURCES

At the end of each chapter there are a number of review and enrichment resources. **Review questions** reconsider the main topics of each chapter. **Key Terms** reference the page within the chapter where the term is defined. The section called **Where to Learn More** lists important historical sites and museums around the country and related Websites (which are also found at appropriate places in the margins of the text) that provide first-hand exposure to historical artifacts and settings. The URL for the *Companion Website*™ is also found at the end of each chapter; this is an excellent resource for additional study aids.

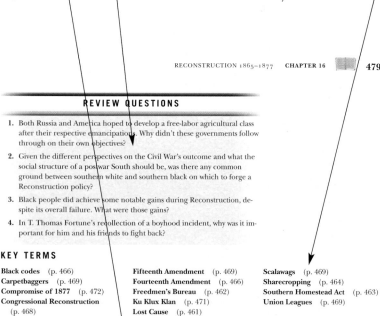

RECONSTRUCTION 1865–1877   **CHAPTER 16**   **479**

REVIEW QUESTIONS

1. Both Russia and America hoped to develop a free-labor agricultural class after their respective emancipations. Why didn't these governments follow through on their own objectives?

2. Given the different perspectives on the Civil War's outcome and what the social structure of a postwar South should be, was there any common ground between southern white and southern black on which to forge a Reconstruction policy?

3. Black people did achieve some notable gains during Reconstruction, despite its overall failure. What were those gains?

4. In T. Thomas Fortune's recollection of a boyhood incident, why was it important for him and his friends to fight back?

KEY TERMS

Black codes (p. 466)
Carpetbaggers (p. 469)
Compromise of 1877 (p. 472)
Congressional Reconstruction (p. 468)
Field Order No. 15 (p. 463)

Fifteenth Amendment (p. 469)
Fourteenth Amendment (p. 466)
Freedmen's Bureau (p. 462)
Ku Klux Klan (p. 471)
Lost Cause (p. 461)
Redeemers (p. 472)

Scalawags (p. 469)
Sharecropping (p. 464)
Southern Homestead Act (p. 463)
Union Leagues (p. 469)

WHERE TO LEARN MORE

Penn Center Historic District, St. Helena Island, South Carolina. The Penn School was a sea-island experiment in the education of free black people established by northern missionaries Laura Towne and Ellen Murray in 1862. They operated it until their deaths in the early 1900s. The Penn School became Penn Community Services in 1948, serving as an educational institution, health clinic, and a social service agency. See its website at **www.penncenter.com**.

Hampton University Museum, Hampton, Virginia. Hampton University was founded by the Freedmen's Bureau in 1868 to provide "practical" training in the agricultural and mechanical fields for former slaves. In addition to a history of the institution, the museum includes one of the oldest collections of African art in the United States. Its website is at **www.hamptonu.edu/museum**.

Beauvoir, Biloxi, Mississippi. The exhibits at Beauvoir, the home of Jefferson Davis, evoke the importance of the Lost Cause for the white survivors of the Confederacy. Especially interesting is the Jefferson Davis Soldiers Home on the premises and the Confederate Veterans Cemetery. Davis spent his retirement in Beauvoir. Go to **www.beauvoir.org**.

Levi Jordan Plantation, Brazoria County, Texas. This site provides an excellent depiction and interpretation of the lives of sharecroppers and tenants during and immediately after the Reconstruction era. The site is especially valuable for demonstrating the transition from slavery to sharecropping. Go to **www .webarchaeology.com**.

 U.S. History Documents CD-ROM
For primary sources related to this chapter, refer to the document CD-ROM.

 www.prenhall.com/goldfield
For study resources related to this chapter, visit the *Companion Website*™.

Historians find most of their information in written records and original documents that have survived from the past. These include government publications, letters, diaries, newspapers—whatever people wrote or printed, including many private documents never intended for publication. Several features in the text highlight the written record so important to understanding historical events.

VOICES FROM THE AMERICAN JOURNEY

Each chapter begins with a brief firsthand account from an individual which powerfully recounts the personal journey he or she took in their lives. Each of these "voices" relates to the themes that follow in the chapter. For example, in Chapter 18 is an excerpt from a letter written by Mary Antin, a Russian-Jewish immigrant who came to America at the turn of the last century.

512 **CHAPTER 18** INDUSTRY, IMMIGRANTS, AND CITIES 1870–1900

IMAGE KEY
for pages 510–511 is on page 540.

We were homeless, houseless, and friendless in a strange place. We had hardly money enough to last us through the voyage for which we had hoped and waited for three long years. We had suffered much that the reunion we longed for might come about; we had prepared ourselves to suffer more in order to bring it about, and had parted with those we loved, with places that were dear to us in spite of what we passed through in them, never again to see them, as we were convinced, all for the same dear end. With strong hopes and high spirits that hid the sad parting, we had started on our long journey. And now we were checked so unexpectedly but surely. . . . When my mother had recovered enough to speak, she began to argue with the gendarme, telling him our story and begging him to be kind. The children were frightened and all but I cried. I was only wondering what would happen. . . . Here we had been taken to a lonely place; . . . our things were taken away, our friends separated from us; a man came to inspect us, as if to ascertain our full value; strange-looking people driving us about like dumb animals, helpless and unresisting; children we could not see crying in a way that suggested terrible things; ourselves driven into a little room where a great kettle was boiling on a little stove; our clothes taken off, our bodies rubbed with a slippery substance that might be any bad thing; a shower of warm water let down on us without warning. . . . We are forced to pick out our clothes from among all the others, with the steam blinding us; we choke, cough, entreat the women to give us time; they persist, "Quick! Quick!, or you'll miss the train!", Oh, so we really won't be murdered! They are only making us ready for the continuing of our journey, cleaning us of all suspicions of dangerous sickness. Thank God! . . .

Oh, what solemn thoughts I had! How deeply I felt the greatness, the power of the scene! The immeasurable distance from horizon to horizon; . . . the absence of any object besides the one ship; . . . I was conscious only of sea and sky and something I did not understand. And as I listened to its solemn voice, I felt as if I had found a friend, and knew that I loved the ocean.
Mary Antin

Mary Antin, *The Promised Land* (Boston: Houghton Mifflin Co., 1912), chap. VIII.

MARY ANTIN, A 13-year-old Jewish girl from Russia, describes her family's perilous journey from persecution in tsarist Russia to the ship that would take her from Hamburg, Germany, to faraway America. In 1894, Mary and her mother and sisters set out from their village to join her father in Boston. Millions of European immigrants made similar journeys across the Atlantic (as did Chinese and Japanese immigrants, across the Pacific), a trip fraught with danger, heartbreak, and the sundering of family ties. So powerful was the promise of American life for the migrants that they willingly risked these obstacles to come to the United States. Mary wrote this letter to her uncle as both a way of conveying the details of her

AMERICAN VIEWS

Each chapter contains a selection from a primary source document. The example shown here is a letter from a Union soldier fighting during the Civil War. Each **American Views** feature begins with a brief introduction followed by several questions—for discussion or written response—on what the document reveals about key issues and events.

AMERICAN VIEWS

WHY THEY FOUGHT ON

s the bloody war dragged on, fatigue and homesickness mounted among the soldiers of both sides, while morale faltered. Still, their letters and diary entries typically indicated a determination to fight on. This was true even for Confederate soldiers after the losses at Gettysburg and Vicksburg in July 1863.

- Soldiers from both sides appealed to the nation's Revolutionary heritage, but in different ways. What are the differences?
- Religion played a major role in motivating troops from both sides. How is this evident in the excerpts presented here?
- How do the writers balance feelings for family with their sense of duty as soldiers?
- Is there irony in the Confederate soldier's fighting "for the sake of liberty"? Would Union soldiers have found it ironic at this stage of the war?

A Pennsylvania officer writing to his wife in 1864: "[A]s sick as I am of this war and bloodshed, as much oh how much I want to be at home with my dear wife and children . . . every day I have a more religious feeling, that this war is a crusade for the good of mankind. . . . I [cannot] bear to think of what my children would be if we were to permit this Hellbegotten conspiracy to destroy this country."

Alfred Lacey Hough to Mary Hough, March 13, 1864, in *Soldier in the West: The Civil War Letters of Alfred Lacey Hough*, ed. Robert G. Athearn (Philadelphia: University of Pennsylvania Press 1957), 178.

An Ohio officer writing to his ten-year old son in 1864: "It tells me that while I am absent from home, fighting the battles of our country, trying to restore law and order, to our once peaceful & prosperous nation, and endeavoring to secure for each and every American citizen of every race, the rights garenteed to us in the Declaration of Independence . . . I have children growing up that will be worthy of the rights that I trust will be left for them."

Ephraim S. Holloway to John W. Holloway, August 7, 1864, Holloway Papers, Ohio Historical Society, Columbus, Ohio.

A Texas officer writing to his wife in 1863: "I am sick of war [and] no gratification could exceed that of my being safe at home with you. . . . [W]ere the contest just commenced I would willingly undergo it again for the sake of . . . our country's independence [so I can] . . . point with pride your children to their father as one who fought for their liberty & freedom."

Edward W. Cade to his wife, January 30, July 9, and November 19, 1863, in *A Texas Surgeon in the C.S.A.*, ed. John Q. Anderon (Tuscaloosa: University of Alabama Press, 1957): 33, 67–68, 81.

A Georgia captain writing to his wife in 1863: "What a calamity! [the losses of Gettysburg and Vicksburg] But let us not despair. . . . We just put forth even greater energy—resolve more fully to conquer or die. Our forefathers were whipped in nearly every battle & lost their capital & yet after seven years of trials and hardships achieved their independence."

William O. Fleming to Georgia Fleming, July 13, 1863, in Fleming Papers, Southern Historical Collection, University of North Carolina, Chapel Hill.

An Alabama lieutenant confiding to his diary in 1864: "We should be proud of [that] noble name [Rebel]. George Washington . . . Thomas Jefferson, Patrick Henry, and 'Light Horse' Harry Lee . . . were all Rebels. . . . Our martyred Saviour was called *seditious*, and I may be pardoned if I rejoice that I am a Rebel."

"War Diary of Captain Robert Emory Park, Twelfth Alabama Regiment," *Southern Historical Society Papers*, II (1876), December 24, 1864, p. 237.

GLOBAL PERSPECTIVES

This feature places the American journey within a broader world-wide context. That journey not only influenced other countries and peoples, but, we in turn have been shaped by global economic, migratory, technological, and political trends.

GLOBAL PERSPECTIVES

THE RACE "PROBLEM" IN EUROPE

L*ike the United States, Europe became more race conscious toward the end of the nineteenth century. A combination of factors, including the misapplication of Charles Darwin's* Origin of Species *(1859) to imply a hierarchy of races, increasing mobility and urbanization, rising nationalism, and imperialist ventures in Asia and Africa, generated a greater awareness of racial differences. Scientists and academics singled out the Nordics, Teutons (Germans), and Anglo-Saxons as the "fittest" of the globe's races; they considered such groups as Jews, Slavs, and southern Europeans to be inferior. Though today we would classify all of these as ethnic groups, Europeans at the time called them races. Some Europeans believed that the "superior" races had an obligation to protect and help the "inferior" ones. For others, the racial hierarchy represented nature's ordering of peoples, and human intervention would therefore serve no purpose. These attitudes justified imperialism abroad and discrimination at home.*

These racial attitudes emerged at a time when many European nations had already granted Jews full legal equality. Freed from occupational, educational, and residential restrictions, the Jewish population flourished as never before, rising and assimilating into European society. Their ascension troubled some Europeans, much as contemporary southern whites felt threatened by African-American mobility. During the 1880s and 1890s, Germany and Austria founded right-wing parties that utilized anti-Semitism to win votes among groups that were wary of modern trends such as urbanization and industrialization. For such people, newly enfranchised Jews were a natural target of hatred and fear. By the 1890s, Europe had a "Jewish problem" that resembled the American South's "Negro problem."

In 1895, Theodor Herzl, an Austrian Jewish journalist, posed an answer to the problem: the voluntary removal of Europe's Jews to Palestine. Surveying the rising tide of European anti-Semitism, Herzl proposed a Jewish nation-state. "Palestine is our ever memorable historic home. . . . the great symbol of the solution of the Jewish Question after eighteen centuries of Jewish suffering."

The first Zionist Congress met in Switzerland in 1897, declaring its aim to create a "home in Palestine secured by public law" for world Jewry. Between 1904 and 1914, about 3,000 Jews per year migrated to the Holy Land. Throughout the first half of the twentieth century, Jewish migration to Palestine was restricted, first by the Ottoman Turks and then by the British. Large numbers of Jews settled instead in the northern cities of the United States.

Blacks in the American South also contemplated separate homelands, either in Africa or in the United States. Back-to-Africa movements appeared periodically in the decades after the Civil War. But as with European Jews, the greatest number of migrants went to the cities of the North, especially after the turn of the twentieth century.

VISUALIZING THE PAST

These essays, found at the end of selected chapters, analyze important aspects of U.S. history through photographs, fine art, sculpture, woodcuts, and advertisements. Focus questions and a running narrative provide a careful examination of the historical implications of each topic in question.

Visualizing The Past...

Mythologizing the "Wild West"

WHAT ELEMENTS do the Remington sculptures, the Curtis photograph, and the "dime novel" illustrations have in common? What, to judge from these images, made the West "wild"? How much do you think these images match up with reality?

One artist, Frederic Remington, deserves much of the credit for creating the West of our imagination. In Montana in 1881 an "old-timer" told him that "there is no more West." Remington decided to "try to record some facts around me." He recorded them first in a series of illustrations, then in paintings, and then in sculpture. Another who determined to "record some facts" was Edward S. Curtis who produced the twenty volume collection, *The North American Indian*, between 1906 and 1930. Curtis persuaded Native American peoples to reenact traditional practices, such as hunting or war parties. Often there was a twenty to fifty year gap between the reenactment and the practice itself. In contrast to Remington and Curtis who sought to (re)capture the truth about the West, "dime novels" sought simply to provide thrills. The "Wild West" is still part of our imaginative landscape.

Edward S. Curtis, "On the Warpath — Atsina," from The North American Indian, v.04; Curtis notes: "These grim-visaged old warriors made a thrilling picture as they rode along, breaking out now and then into wild song of the chase or raid." The image recreates a raiding party. Note the headdress on the party's leader, fourth from left. The photograph was taken in 1908.
▼

▲

Frederick Remington, "The Cheyenne," a 1901 bronze statue, now at the Amon Carter Museum, Fort Worth, Texas. Remington loved to portray action; here a warrior is galloping on his pony into battle.

Frederick S. Remington, "The Cheyenne," 1901, cast 1904. Amon Carter Museum

http://memory.loc.gov/ammem/award98/ienhtml/curthome.html

▲

Frederick Remington, "The Rattlesnake," (1905) Bronze (Height 23 7/8 inches), now at Amon Carter Museum, Fort Worth, Texas. Note how the rattlesnake has reverted from national symbol to natural menace as the cowboy's horse rears up and threatens to throw its rider.

Frederick S. Remington, "The Rattlesnake," 1905. Amon Carter Museum

◄ **"Dime novels" purported to tell true tales of western adventure.** Jesse James was an historical figure, even if the stories in this "Log Cabin Library" edition bore no resemblance to his actual deeds. "The King of the Wild West" was a purely fictional creation.

From the Library of Congress's American Memory site
http://www.loc.gov/exhibits/treasures/tri015.html

FROM THEN TO NOW

This feature connects events and trends in the past to issues that confront Americans today, illustrating the value a historical perspective can contribute to our understanding of the world we live in. The example here, from Chapter 30, compares the roles of women in the American workforce today to those before the Civil War and at the turn of the century.

From Then to Now

IMMIGRATION: AN AMBIVALENT WELCOME

Americans have long extended an ambivalent welcome to newcomers. In the mid-nineteenth century, employment posters often read "Irish Need Not Apply," and today stepped-up border patrols seek to keep out Mexican and other Latin American immigrants. Yet America is a nation settled and built by immigrants whose founding ideals promise equality and opportunity to all. And for much of its history it has offered asylum for the world's oppressed.

In the early years of the republic, Federalists worried that immigrants from Europe might be contaminated by the radical ideas of the French Revolution and sought to make it harder for them to become naturalized citizens. The nation's first naturalization law in the 1790s also barred black immigrants from citizenship. The first sustained attack against newcomers, however, emerged as a result of the surge in immigration during the 1840s and 1850s. It was directed by established immigrant groups, the descendants of settlers from Britain and northwestern Europe, at unfamiliar newcomers, particularly the Irish.

Nativist arguments of that time have found an echo in all subsequent immigration debates. The Irish, it was claimed, would take jobs away from American workers and lower their wages. Taxpayers would have to foot the bill for the strains the newcomers imposed on schools, hospitals, and other civic services. The ignorant immigrants would corrupt the political process. Nativists especially feared religious contamination, claiming that the Catholicism of the Irish was alien to the Protestant values held to be indispensable to the preservation of American liberties. So many Irish arrived so quickly that many nativists were convinced of a papal plot to undermine American freedom. "The bloody hand of the Pope," one wrote, "has stretched itself forth to our destruction."

Eventually the Irish and Germans merged into the

economic and political fabric of American life. But in the late nineteenth century a massive new immigrant surge dominated by people from southern and eastern Europe seeking economic opportunity and fleeing religious oppression transformed American society and renewed nativist fears. This time, race replaced religion as the basis for drawing invidious comparisons between established residents and the newcomers. Pseudoscientific theories relegated Jews, Slavs, and Mediterranean peoples, together with Africans, to an inferior status below people of northern European and especially Anglo-Saxon descent. The newcomers, it was claimed, were unfit for democratic government and would endanger American civilization. Strict anti-immigrant legislation in the 1920s sharply curtailed immigration from outside the Western Hemisphere, banning Asians entirely and setting quotas based on national origin for others.

Recent concerns about immigration result from the unforeseen consequences of a 1965 reform of the immigration law that abolished quotas. Since then, immigration has risen sharply, and the national origins of the immigrants have diverged from previous patterns. By the 1980s, Europeans constituted but 10 percent of the newcomers. The bulk of the remainder continue to come from Asia (40 percent) and Mexico, Central America, and the Caribbean. Once again, anti-immigrant voices worry that alien newcomers are threatening the cohesiveness of the nation's institutions and values. But, once again as well, a more inclusive vision of American identity and ideals seems likely to prevail as the newcomers establish themselves. As Abraham Lincoln expressed it, "There was no exclusively American race entitled to claim liberty by heredity. What held the nation together was an idea of equality that every newcomer could claim and defend by free choice."

EXPLORE THE POWER
OF ONEKEY

OneKey is Prentice Hall's premium exclusive online resource for instructors and students that gives access to the best online teaching and learning tools—available 24/7. Harnessing the power of WebCT, Blackboard, and CourseCompass, Onekey is a new approach to course management that gives abundant teaching and learning resources in one place for maximum convenience, similicity and learning success.

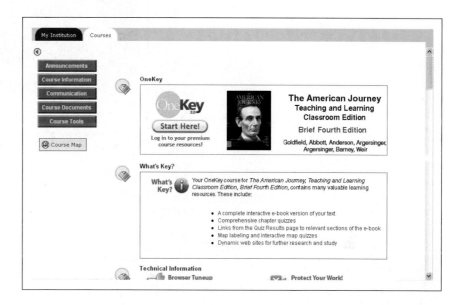

PRESENTATION RESOURCES
FOR INSTRUCTORS

VISUALS

- Images
- Maps, Tables, Figures
- Map Outlines

PowerPoint™ Presentations

- Lecture Aids—Visuals
- Lecture Aids—Text
- Lecture Aids—Lecture Outline

New England

- ※ Puritan congregations governed local communities.
  - ◆ Mix of freedom and repression
- ※ Attempts to introduce religious toleration failed as other denominations practiced their faith openly by 1700.
- ※ New England towns grew rapidly and the expanding population pressed against available land.
- ※ By the mid-eighteenth century New England was reaching the limit of its land supply.

The contrast between the hope and valor of these young southern volunteer soldiers, photographed shortly before the first battle of Bull Run, and the later advertisements for substitutes (at right), is marked. Southern exemptions for slave owners and lavish payment for substitutes increasingly bred resentment among the ordinary people of the South.
SOURCE: (a) First Virginia Regiment,Cook Collection,Valentine Museum Library/Richmond History Center;(b) *Richmond Dispatch*, Library of Congress.

Animations and Activities

- Interactive Maps

Text

- Instructor's Manual

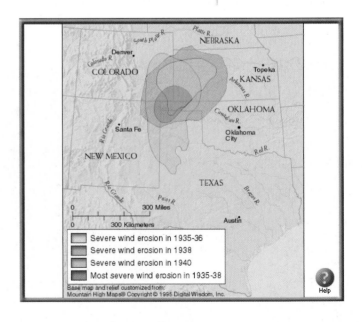

ASSESSMENT RESOURCES FOR STUDENTS

HOMEWORK

- Review Questions
- e-book

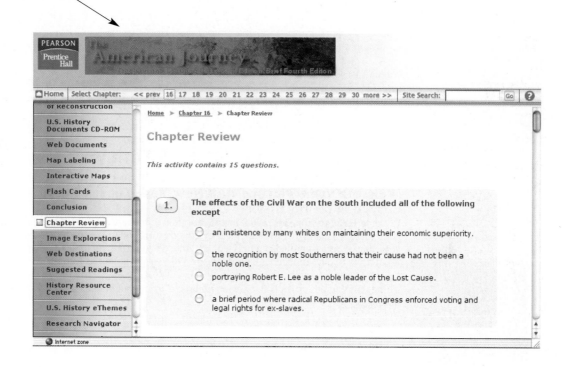

ADDITIONAL STUDENT RESOURCES

LINKS

- Companion Website
- e-themes in U.S. History

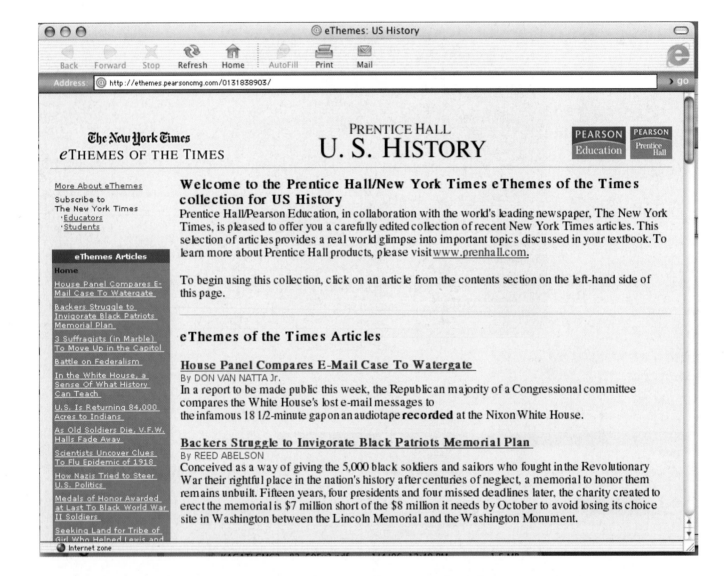

ADDITIONAL RESOURCES

 • Research Navagator

Take a tour at http://researchnavigator.com

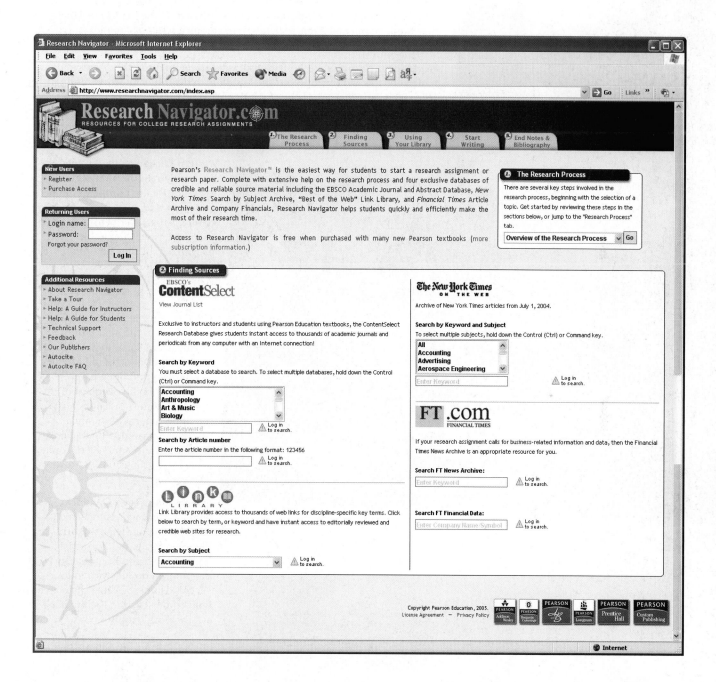

1 Worlds Apart

CHAPTER HIGHLIGHTS

Native American Societies Before 1492 On the eve of contact, Native Americans had developed distinctive cultures based on the regions in which they lived. Mayan and Aztec societies were among a series of complex urban cultures that grew up in Mesoamerica.

West African Societies West African societies developed complex states and trade networks with Europe and the Middle East. Family connections and religious beliefs exerted a powerful influence on African life. Slavery was a part of West African society prior to large-scale European involvement in the slave trade.

Western Europe on the Eve of Exploration In the aftermath of the Black Death, Europe developed a stronger and more productive economy than ever before. European society was hierarchical and patriarchal. By the end of the fifteenth century, a measure of stability had returned to Western Europe.

Contact Motivated by a desire to gain access to the wealth of Asia, Portugal and Spain took the lead in the colonization of the Americas. Technology and disease were key factors in the conquest of the Aztec and Inca empires. In the long run, the Columbian exchange proved to be the most important consequence of contact between Europeans and Native Americans.

Competition for a Continent France and England rejected the division of the New World between Spain and Portugal. Early French and English efforts at colonization met with little success. Domestic issues distracted both countries from the pursuit of New World empires.

CHAPTER QUESTIONS

HOW DID geography shape the development of regional cultures in North America prior to 1492?

WHAT PLACE did the family have in West African society?

WHY DID European princes support voyages of exploration?

WHAT WERE the biological consequences of contact between Europeans and Native Americans?

WHY DID early French and English efforts at colonization falter?

CHAPTER OUTLINE

- Native American Societies Before 1492
- West African Societies
- Western Europe on the Eve of Exploration
- Contact
- Competition for a Continent

IMAGE KEY

for pages xlviii–1 is on page 27.

After a difficult journey of over two hundred miles, the exhausted man arrived at the royal palace in the grand city of Tenochtitlán. He had hurried all the way from the Gulf Coast with important news for the Aztec leader, Moctezuma.

Our lord and king, forgive my boldness. I am from Mictlancuauhtla. When I went to the shores of the great sea, there was a mountain range or small mountain floating in the midst of the water, and moving here and there without touching the shore. My lord, we have never seen the like of this, although we guard the coast and are always on watch.

[When Moctezuma sent some officials to check on the messenger's story, they confirmed his report.]

Our lord and king, it is true that strange people have come to the shores of the great sea. They were fishing from a small boat, some with rods and others with a net. They fished until late and then they went back to their two great towers and climbed up into them. . . . They have very light skin, much lighter than ours. They all have long beards, and their hair comes only to their ears.

Miguel Leon–Portilla, *The Broken Spears: The Aztec Account of the Conquest of Mexico* (Boston, 1962).

MOCTEZUMA WAS FILLED with foreboding when he received the messenger's initial report. Aztec religion placed great emphasis on omens and prophecies, which were thought to foreshadow coming events. Several unusual omens had recently occurred—blazing lights in the sky, one temple struck by lightning and another that spontaneously burst into flames, monstrous beings that appeared and then vanished. Now light-skinned strangers suddenly appeared offshore. Aztec spiritual leaders warned that trouble lay ahead.

The messenger's journey to Tenochtitlán occurred in 1519. The "mountains" he saw were in fact the sails of European ships, and the strange men were Spanish soldiers under the command of Hernán Cortés. Like Columbus's voyage to the Caribbean in 1492, Cortés's arrival in Mexico is considered a key episode in the European discovery of the "New World." But we might just as accurately view the messenger's entry into the Aztec capital as announcing the native Mexicans' discovery of a New World to the east, from which the strangers must have come. Neither the Aztecs nor the Spaniards could have foreseen the far-reaching consequences of these twin discoveries. Before long, a variety of peoples—Native Americans, Africans, and Europeans—who had previously lived worlds apart would come together to create a world that was new to all of them.

This new world reflected the diverse experiences of the many peoples who built it. Improving economic conditions in the fifteenth and early sixteenth centuries propelled Europeans overseas to seek new opportunities for trade and settlement. Spain, Portugal, France, and England competed within Europe, and their conflict carried over into the Americas. Native Americans drew upon their familiarity with the land and its resources, patterns of political and religious authority, and systems of trade and warfare to deal with the European newcomers. Africans

Chronology

c. 40,000–8,000 B.C.	Ancestors of Native Americans cross Bering land bridge.	**1492**	End of *reconquista* in Spain. Columbus's first voyage.
c. 10,000–9000 B.C.	Paleo-Indians expand through the Americas.	**1494**	Treaty of Tordesillas.
c. 9000 B.C.	Extinction of large land mammals in North America.	**1497**	John Cabot visits Nova Scotia and Newfoundland.
c. 8000–1500 B.C.	Archaic Indian era.	**1497–1499**	Vasco da Gama sails around Africa to reach India.
c. 3000 B.C.	Beginnings of agriculture in Mesoamerica.	**1517**	Protestant Reformation begins in Germany.
c. 1500 B.C.	Earliest mound-building culture begins.	**1519–1521**	Hernán Cortés conquers the Aztec empire.
c. 500 B.C.–A.D. 400	Adena-Hopewell mound-building culture.	**1532–1533**	Francisco Pizarro conquers the Inca empire.
c. A.D. 700–1600	Rise of West African empires.	**1534–1542**	Jacques Cartier explores eastern Canada for France.
c. 900	First mounds built at Cahokia.	**1540–1542**	Coronado explores southwestern North America.
	Ancestral Puebloan expansion.	**1542–1543**	Roberval's failed colony in Canada.
c. 1000	Spread of Islam in West Africa.	**1558**	Elizabeth I becomes queen of England.
c. 1000–1015	First Viking voyages to North America.	**1565**	Spanish establish outpost at St. Augustine in Florida.
c. 1000–1500	Last mound-building culture, the Mississippian.	**1560s–1580s**	English renew attempts to conquer Ireland.
c. 1290s	Ancestral Puebloan dispersal into smaller villages.	**1587**	Founding of "Lost Colony" of Roanoke.
1400–1600	Renaissance in Europe.	**1598**	Spanish found colony at New Mexico.
1430s	Beginnings of Portuguese slave trade in West Africa.		

did not come voluntarily to the Americas but were brought by the Europeans to work as slaves. They too would draw on their cultural heritage to cope with both a new land and a new, harsh condition of life.

NATIVE AMERICAN SOCIETIES BEFORE 1492

*I*n 1492, the year Columbus landed on a tiny Caribbean island, perhaps 70 million people—nearly equal to the population of Europe at that time— lived on the continents of North and South America, most of them south of the present border between the United States and Mexico. They belonged to hundreds of groups, each with its own language or dialect, history, and way of life.

From the start, the original inhabitants of the Americas were peoples in motion. The first migrants may have arrived over forty thousand years ago, traveling from central Siberia and slowly making their way to southern South America. These people, and subsequent migrants from Eurasia, probably traveled across a land bridge that emerged across what is now the Bering Strait. Asian seafarers may have crossed the Pacific to settle portions of western North and South America,

HOW DID geography shape the development of regional cultures in North America prior to 1492?

while as recently as eight thousand years ago, a final migration may have brought Siberians to what is now Alaska and northern Canada.

PALEO-INDIANS AND THE ARCHAIC PERIOD

The earliest Americans, called *Paleo-Indians* by archaeologists, traveled in small bands, tracking and killing mammoths, bison, and other large game. The skill of these hunters and the effectiveness of their tools may have contributed to over-hunting, for by about 9000 B.C., mammoths, mastodons, and other large game had become extinct in the Americas. Climatic change also hastened the animals' disappearance. Around twelve thousand years ago, the world's climate began to grow warmer, turning grasslands into deserts and reducing the animals' food supply. This meant that humans too had to find other food sources.

Between roughly 8000 B.C. and 1500 B.C.—what archaeologists call the Archaic period—the Native American population grew and people began living in larger communities. Men and women assumed more specialized roles. Men did most of the hunting and fishing, activities that required travel. Women remained closer to home, gathering and preparing wild plant foods and caring for children. Each group made the tools it used, with men carving fishhooks and arrowheads, and women making such items as bone needles and baskets.

Across the continent, native communities participated in a complex trade network. Trade was not limited to material goods, but also included exchanges of marriage partners, laborers, ideas, and religious practices. Trade networks sometimes extended over great distances. Valuable goods, such as copper from the Great Lakes area and shells from the Gulf of Mexico, have been discovered at archaeological sites far from their places of origin. Ideas about death and the afterlife also passed between groups. So too did certain burial practices, such as the placing of valued possessions in the grave along with the deceased person's body.

THE DEVELOPMENT OF AGRICULTURE

In the latter half of the Archaic period, some Native Americans began farming. Farming in the Americas initially supplemented a diet still largely dependent on hunting and gathering, but gradually assumed a greater role. In addition to maize, the main crop in both South and North America, farmers in Mexico, Central America, and the Peruvian Andes learned to cultivate peppers, beans, pumpkins, squash, avocados, sweet and white potatoes (native to the Peruvian highlands), and tomatoes. Mexican farmers also grew cotton. Maize and bean cultivation spread from Mexico in a wide arc to the north and east. Peoples in what is now the southwestern United States began farming between 1500 and 500 B.C., and by A.D. 200, farmers were tilling the soil in present-day Georgia and Florida.

Wherever agriculture took hold, important social changes followed. Populations grew, because farming produced a more secure food supply than did hunting and gathering. Permanent villages appeared as farmers settled near their fields. In central Mexico, agriculture eventually sustained the populations of large cities. Trade in agricultural surpluses flowed through networks of exchange. In many Indian societies, women's status improved because of their role as the principal farmers. Specialized craft workers produced pottery and baskets to store harvested grains. Even religious beliefs adapted to the increasing importance of farming. In describing the origins of their people, Pueblo Indians of the Southwest compared their emergence from the underworld to a maize plant sprouting from the earth.

QUICK REVIEW

The Earliest Americans

- Paleo-Indians were resourceful hunters.
- During the Archaic period Indians adapted to regional environments.
- Farming began near the end of the Archaic period.

Despite their diversity, certain generalizations can be made about societies that developed within broad regions, or *culture areas* (see Map 1–1).

NONFARMING SOCIETIES

Throughout the North and West, Indians prospered without adopting agriculture. In the challenging environment of the Arctic and Subarctic, small nomadic bands moved seasonally to fish, follow game, and, in the brief summers, gather wild berries. Far to the north, Eskimos and Aleuts hunted whales, seals, and other sea mammals. Farther inland, the Crees and other peoples followed migrating herds of caribou and moose. Northern peoples fashioned tools and weapons of bone and ivory, clothing and boats from animal skins, and houses of whalebones and hides or blocks of sod or snow.

Women were the principal farmers in most Native American societies, growing corn, beans, and other crops that made up most of their food supply. This sixteenth-century French engraving shows Indian men preparing the soil for cultivation and Indian women sowing seeds in neat rows.

David Muench Photography, Inc.

Along the Northwest Coast and the Columbia River Plateau, abundant resources supported one of the most densely populated areas of North America. With rivers teeming with salmon and other fish, and forests full of game and edible plants, people prospered without resorting to farming. Among such groups as the Kwakiutls and Chinooks, extended families lived in large communal houses located in villages of up to several hundred residents.

Farther south, in present-day California, hunter-gatherers lived in smaller villages, several of which might be led by the same chief. These settlements usually adjoined oak groves, where Indians gathered acorns. To protect their access to this important food, chiefs and villagers vigorously defended their territorial claims to the oak groves.

Small nomadic bands in the Great Basin, where the climate was warm and dry, learned to survive on the region's limited resources. Shoshone hunters captured antelope in corrals and trapped small game, such as squirrels and rabbits. In what is now Utah and western Colorado, Utes hunted elk, bison, and mountain sheep and fished in mountain streams. Women gathered pinyon nuts, seeds, and wild berries. In hard times, people ate rattlesnakes, horned toads, and insects.

MESOAMERICAN CIVILIZATIONS

Mesoamerica, the birthplace of agriculture in North America, extends from central Mexico into Central America. A series of complex, literate, urban cultures emerged in this region, beginning with the Olmecs around 1200 B.C., who flourished on Mexico's Gulf Coast until 400 B.C. The Olmecs and other early Mesoamerican peoples built cities featuring large pyramids, developed religious practices that included human sacrifice, and devised calendars and writing systems.

The Mayans.   Mayan civilization followed, reaching its greatest glory between about A.D. 150 and 900 in the southern Yucatán, creating Mesoamerica's most advanced writing and calendrical systems and developing a sophisticated mathematics

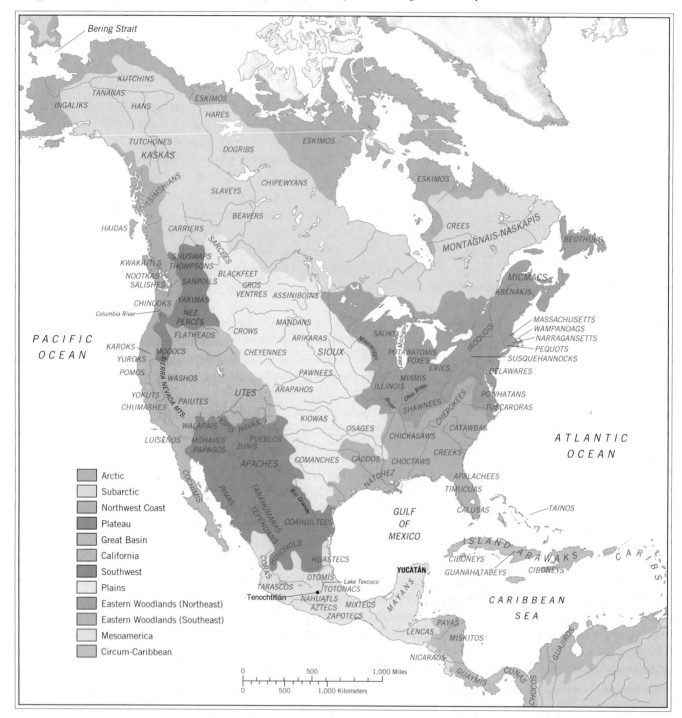

MAP 1–1 North American Culture Areas, c. 1500 Over the course of centuries, Indian peoples in North America developed distinctive cultures suited to the environments in which they lived. Inhabitants of each culture area shared basic patterns of subsistence, craftwork, and social organization. Most, but not all, Indian peoples combined farming with hunting and gathering.

WHAT DOES this map tell you about the role different geographic regions in the Americas played in determining the type of culture (social organization, hunting, farming, etc.) the inhabitants of those regions developed?

that included the concept of zero. The Mayans of the southern Yucatán suffered a decline after 900, but there were still many thriving Mayan centers in the northern Yucatán when Europeans arrived in the Americas. The great city of Teotihuacán dominated central Mexico from the first century to the eighth century A.D. and influenced much of the rest of Mesoamerica through trade and conquest.

The Aztecs.   Some two hundred years after the fall of Teotihuacán, the Toltecs, a warrior people, rose to prominence, dominating central Mexico from about 900 to 1100. In the wake of the Toltec collapse, the **Aztecs,** another warrior people, migrated from the north into the Valley of Mexico and built a great empire that soon controlled much of Mesoamerica. The Aztec capital, Tenochtitlán, was a city of great plazas, broad avenues, magnificent temples and palaces, and busy marketplaces. Built on islands in the middle of Lake Texcoco, it was connected to the mainland by four broad causeways. In 1492, Tenochtitlán was home to some 200,000 people, making it one of the largest cities in the world at the time.

In the great pyramid in Tenochtitlán, Aztec priests sacrificed human victims—by cutting open their chests and removing their still-beating hearts—to offer to the gods to prevent them from destroying the earth. Hundreds, even thousands, of victims died in ceremonies that sometimes lasted for days.

Aztec culture expanded through continuous military conquest, driven by a quest for sacrificial victims and for wealth in the form of tribute payments of gold, food, and handcrafted goods. But as the empire grew, it became increasingly vulnerable to internal division. Neighboring peoples hated the Aztecs and submitted to them out of fear rather than loyalty.

North America's Diverse Cultures

North of Mexico, the introduction of a drought-resistant type of maize around 400 B.C. enabled a series of cultures sharing certain characteristics with Mesoamerica to develop. Beginning about 300 B.C., the Hohokams settled in permanent villages in southern Arizona and devised elaborate irrigation systems that allowed them to harvest two crops of corn, beans, and squash each year. Artisans wove cotton cloth and made goods reflecting Mesoamerican artistic styles out of shell, turquoise, and clay. Extensive trade networks linked the Hohokams to people living as far away as California and Mexico. Their culture endured for over a thousand years but mysteriously disappeared by 1450.

Ancestral Puebloans.   Early in the first century A.D. Ancestral Puebloan peoples (sometimes called Anasazis) began to settle in farming communities where the borders of present-day Colorado, Utah, Arizona, and New Mexico meet. Scarce rainfall, routed through dams and hillside terraces, watered the crops.

Ancestral Puebloans originally lived in villages built on mesas and canyon floors located in New Mexico's Chaco Canyon. The largest town, Pueblo Bonito, covered 3 acres and contained about twelve hundred inhabitants. Its main structure, a four-story-tall complex of over 800 rooms and numerous *kivas,* or ceremonial centers, served as one of several centers of production and exchange throughout the area. But after about 1200, villagers began carving multistoried stone houses into steep canyon walls. Archaeologists suspect that warfare and climate change worked together to force the Puebloans into these precarious homes. Around 1200, a colder climate reduced food supplies, and food scarcity may have

QUICK REVIEW

Mesoamerica

- Mesoamerica was the birthplace of agriculture in North America.
- Olmecs were the first literate urban culture in the region.
- Mayan civilization reached its height between A.D. 150 and 900.

WHERE TO LEARN MORE

Mesa Verde National Park, Colorado. **www.mesa.verde .nationalpark.com**

Aztecs   A warrior people who dominated the Valley of Mexico from 1100–1521.

Cahokia One of the largest urban centers created by Mississippian peoples, containing 30,000 residents in 1250.

encouraged violence. Villagers probably resorted to cliff dwellings for protection. By 1300, most Anasazi surviors had dispersed to villages along the Rio Grande.

Their descendants include the Hopis and Zunis, as well as other Puebloan peoples in the desert Southwest. In many pueblos dispersed throughout the region , men farmed, in contrast to the predominant pattern of women farmers elsewhere in Native America. They established new patterns of exchange with nomadic hunting peoples, such as the Apaches and Navajos, who brought buffalo meat and hides to trade for Pueblo corn, cotton blankets, pottery, and other goods.

Plains Indians. The Great Plains of the continent's interior were much less densely settled than the desert Southwest. Mandans, Pawnees, and other groups settled along river valleys, where women farmed and men hunted bison, whose skin and bones were used for clothing, shelter, and tools. Plains Indians moved frequently, seeking more fertile land or better hunting.

Mound-building Cultures. The gradual spread of agriculture transformed native societies in the Eastern Woodlands, a vast territory extending from the Mississippi Valley to the Atlantic seaboard. Although the process began around 2500 B.C., farming was not firmly established until about A.D. 700. As agriculture spread, several "mound-building" societies—named for the large earthworks their members constructed—developed in the Ohio and Mississippi Valleys. The oldest flourished in Louisiana between 1500 and 700 B.C. The members of the Adena-Hopewell culture, which appeared in the Ohio Valley between 500 B.C. and A.D. 400, built hundreds of mounds, often in the shapes of humans, birds, and serpents. Most were grave sites, where people were buried with valuable goods.

The last mound-building culture, the Mississippian, emerged between 1000 and 1500 in the Mississippi Valley. One of the largest of these was **Cahokia,** located near present-day St. Louis in a fertile floodplain with access to the major river systems of the continent's interior. By 1250, Cahokia had perhaps twenty thousand residents, making it nearly as large as medieval London and the largest American city north of Mexico. Cahokia dominated the Mississippi Valley, linked by trade in food and other products to dozens of villages in the Midwestern region.

Mississippian culture began to decline in the thirteenth century. Archaeologists suspect that an ecological crisis led to Cahokia's fall. Population may have outstripped the food supply, and a series of hot, dry summers created further hardship. By 1400, most of Cahokia's residents were dispersed into scattered farming villages. What followed in the eastern

This artist's rendering, based on archaeological evidence, suggests the size and magnificence of the Mississippian city of Cahokia. By the thirteenth century, it was as populous as medieval London and served as a center of trade for the vast interior of North America. Cahokia Mounds State Historic Site.

Woodlands region was a century or more of warfare and political instability. Similar developments occurred in the southeast, where chronic instability led to regional alliances and the periodic emergence of centers of trade and political power.

Eastern Woodlands peoples were the first to encounter English explorers, and later, English settlers, at the start of the seventeenth century. By that point these native peoples relied on a mixture of agriculture and hunting, fishing, and gathering for their subsistence. Although early colonists sometimes described these Indian groups as nomadic, they in fact inhabited semipermanent villages and moved only when declining soil fertility or, in some instances, warfare compelled them to shift location.

THE CARIBBEAN ISLANDERS

The Caribbean islands were peopled by mainland dwellers who began moving to the islands around 5000 B.C. Surviving at first by hunting and gathering, island peoples began farming perhaps in the first century A.D. They raised manioc, sweet potatoes, maize, squash, beans, peppers, peanuts, and pineapple on clearings made in the tropical forests. Canoes carried trade goods throughout the Caribbean, as well as to Mesoamerica and coastal South America.

By 1492, as many as 4 million people may have inhabited the Caribbean islands. Powerful chiefs ruled over villages, conducted war and diplomacy, and controlled the distribution of food and other goods obtained as tribute from villagers. Elite islanders were easily recognized by their fine clothing, bright feather headdresses, and golden ear and nose ornaments—items that eventually attracted the attention of European visitors.

Long before Europeans reached North America, the continent's inhabitants had witnessed centuries of dynamic change. Empires rose and fell, and new ones took their place. Large cities flourished and disappeared. Periods of warfare occasionally disrupted the lives of thousands of individuals. The Europeans' arrival, at the end of the fifteenth century, coincided with a period of particular instability, as various Native American groups competed for dominance in the wake of the collapse of the centralized societies at Cahokia and Chaco Canyon. Yet at the same time, Native American societies experienced important continuities. These included an ability to adapt to widely varying environmental conditions, the preservation of religious and ceremonial traditions, and an eagerness to forge relationships of exchange with neighboring peoples. Both continuities with past experience and more recent circumstances of political change would shape the ways native peoples would eventually respond to the European newcomers.

WEST AFRICAN SOCIETIES

*I*n the three centuries after 1492, fully six out of seven people who crossed the Atlantic to the Americas were not Europeans but Africans, the vast majority as slaves. Like the Americas, Africa had witnessed the rise of many ancient and diverse cultures (see Map 1–2). They ranged from the sophisticated Egyptian civilization that developed in the Nile Valley over 5000 years ago to the powerful twelfth-century chiefdoms of Zimbabwe to the West African empires that flourished in the time of Columbus and Cortés. Although they were involuntary immigrants, Africans could draw upon their ancient cultural heritages to help shape the New World in which they found themselves.

WHERE TO LEARN MORE

Cahokia Mounds State Historic Site, Collinsville, Illinois.
www.siue.edu/CAHOKIAMOUNDS

WHAT PLACE did the family have in West African society?

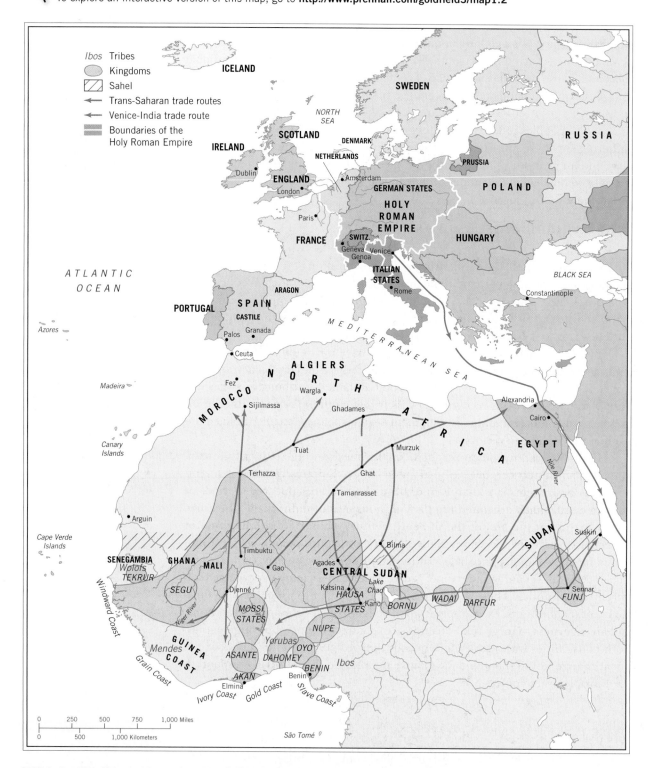

MAP 1–2   West Africa and Europe in 1492   Before Columbus's voyage, Europeans knew little about the world beyond the Mediterranean Basin and the coast of West Africa. Muslim merchants from North Africa largely controlled European traders' access to African gold and other materials.

HOW WERE the routes taken by European and North African traders conducive to the slave trading of the sixteenth, seventeenth, and eighteenth centuries? From what you can see on this map, do you suppose that (in addition to the trading of gold and other materials) the early trading of slaves was also somewhat regulated by North African Muslims?

GEOGRAPHICAL AND POLITICAL DIFFERENCES

Most African immigrants to the Americas came from the continent's western regions. On the whole a sparsely settled region, West Africa nevertheless contained numerous more densely inhabited communities. Many of these settlements clung to the coast, but several important cities lay well inland. Perhaps the greatest of these metropolises was Timbuktu, which had as many as 70,000 residents in the fifteenth century. At that time, Timbuktu served as the seat of the powerful Songhai empire, and was an important center of trade and government.

The Songhai empire was only the latest in a series of powerful states to develop in the region. Songhai, larger and wealthier than its predecessors, dominated the area from around 1450 until it fell to a Moroccan invasion in 1591. Equivalently large empires did not appear in coastal West Africa, although the Asante, Dahomey, Oyo, and Bini kingdoms there grew to be quite powerful. Other coastal peoples, such as the Mendes and Igbos, were decentralized, living in scattered autonomous villages.

In the vast grasslands of the interior, people raised cattle and cultivated millet and sorghum. In the 1500s, European visitors introduced varieties of Asian rice, which soon became another important crop. On the coast—where rain falls nearly every day—people grew yams, bananas, and various kinds of beans and peas in forest clearings. They also kept sheep, goats, and poultry.

Artisans and Merchants.   West Africans were skilled artisans and particularly fine metalworkers. Smiths produced intricate bronze sculptures, designed distinctive miniature gold weights, and forged weapons.

Complex trade networks linked inland and coastal states, and long-distance commercial connections tied West Africa to southern Europe and the Middle East. West African merchants exchanged locally mined gold with traders from North Africa for salt. North African merchants also bought West African pepper, leather, and ivory. The wealth generated by this trans-Saharan trade contributed to the rise of the Songhai and earlier empires.

Farming and Gender Roles.   Most West Africans were farmers, not merchants. West African men and women shared agricultural tasks. Men prepared fields for planting, while women cultivated the crops, harvested them, and dried grain for storage. Men also hunted and, in the grassland regions, herded cattle. Women in the coastal areas owned and cared for other livestock, including goats and sheep. West African women regularly traded goods, including the crops they grew, in local markets.

FAMILY STRUCTURE AND RELIGION

Family connections helped define each person's place in society. While ties between parents and children were of central importance, West Africans also emphasized their links with aunts, uncles, cousins, and grandparents. Groups of families formed clans that further extended an individual's kin ties. Most clans were patrilineal—tracing descent through the father's line—but some, for instance among the Akans and Igbos, were matrilineal.

Religious beliefs magnified the powerful influence of family on African life. Many West Africans believed that their ancestors acted as mediators between the worlds of the living and the dead, they held elaborate funerals for deceased members and continued to perform public rituals at their grave sites, rituals which helped keep the memory of ancestors alive for younger generations.

Craftsman from the West African kingdom of Benin were renowned for their remarkable bronze sculptures. This intricate bronze plaque depicts four African warriors in full military dress. The two tiny figures in the background may be Portuguese soldiers, who first arrived in Benin in the late fifteenth century.

Benin bronze plaque. National Museum of African Art, Smithsonian Institution, Washington, D.C., U.S.A. Aldo Turino, Art Resource, N.Y.

QUICK REVIEW

West African Society
- West Africans were skilled artisans and metalworkers.
- Most West Africans were farmers.
- Most West African clans were patrilineal.

Located in Djenné, Mali, this massive mosque, made of sun-hardened mud, dates from the fourteenth century. At that time, Djenné prospered as a center of trade and Islamic learning.

James Stanfield, National Geographic Image Collection.

Most West Africans believed in a supreme being and several subordinate deities. Like Native Americans, they performed ceremonies to ensure the goodwill of the spiritual forces that suffused the natural world. West African medicine men and women used rituals to protect people from evil spirits and sorcerers. Religious ceremonies were held in sacred places—often near water—but not in buildings that Europeans recognized as churches. And like the Indians, West Africans preserved their faith through oral traditions.

Islam began to take root in West Africa around the eleventh century, probably introduced by Muslim traders from North Africa. By the fifteenth century, the cities of Timbuktu and Djenné had become centers of Islamic learning. Urban dwellers, especially merchants, were more likely to convert to the new religion, as were some rulers. Farmers, however, accustomed to religious rituals that focused on agricultural fertility, were prone to resist Islamic influence more strongly.

EUROPEAN MERCHANTS IN WEST AFRICA AND THE SLAVE TRADE

Before the fifteenth century, Europeans knew little about Africa beyond its Mediterranean coast. Spain, much of which had been subject to Islamic rule before 1492, had stronger ties to North Africa than did most of Europe. But Christian merchants from other European lands had also traded for centuries with North Africans. When stories of West African gold reached European traders, they tried to move deeper into the continent, but they encountered powerful Muslim merchants intent on monopolizing the gold trade.

In the early fifteenth century, the kingdom of Portugal sought to circumvent this Muslim monopoly. Portuguese forces conquered Ceuta in Morocco and gained a foothold on the continent in 1415. Portuguese mariners gradually explored the West African coast, establishing trading posts along the way, where they exchanged horses, clothing, wine, lead, iron, and steel for African gold, grain, animal skins, cotton, pepper, and camels.

By the 1430s, the Portuguese had discovered perhaps the greatest source of wealth they could extract from Africa—slaves. Slavery had long been a part of West African society. In fact, African law recognized slaves (not land, as in Europe) as the only form of private, revenue-producing property. Most slaves within Africa lost their freedom because they were captured in war, but others had been kidnapped or were enslaved as punishment for a crime.

European visitors who observed African slaves in their homeland often described them as "slaves in name only" because they were subject to so little coercion. African slaves at work in the fields appeared little different from other farmers. Slaves might also be employed as soldiers or administrators, fulfilling important duties and enjoying considerable freedom in their daily routines. Slavery in Africa was not necessarily a permanent status and did not automatically apply to the slaves' children. African merchants who sold slaves to European purchasers had no reason to suspect that those slaves would be treated any differently by their new owners, but Africans caught in the web of the transatlantic slave trade entered a much harsher world.

WESTERN EUROPE ON THE EVE OF EXPLORATION

WHY DID European princes support voyages of exploration?

When Columbus sailed from Spain in 1492, he left a continent recovering from the devastating warfare and disease of the fourteenth century and about to embark on the devastating religious conflicts of the sixteenth. Between 1337 and 1453, England and France had exhausted each other in a series of conflicts known as the Hundred Years' War. And between 1347 and 1351, an epidemic known as the Black Death (bubonic plague, and perhaps in some areas a pneumonic form of the disease as well) killed perhaps a third of all Europeans, with results that were felt for more than a century.

The plague left Europe with far fewer workers, but the survivors learned to be more efficient and to rely on technological improvements. Metalworkers built larger furnaces with huge bellows driven by water power. Shipbuilders redesigned vessels with steering mechanisms that could be managed by smaller crews. Innovations in banking, accounting, and insurance also fostered economic recovery. Prosperity was distributed unevenly among social classes, however. In parts of England, France, Sweden, and the German states, peasants and workers protested rising rents and taxes that threatened to absorb most of their wages. Yet on the whole, Europe had a stronger, more productive economy in 1500 than ever before.

In much of Western Europe, economic improvement encouraged an extraordinary cultural movement known as the Renaissance, a "rebirth" of interest in the classical civilizations of ancient Greece and Rome. The Renaissance originated in the city-states of Italy, where a prosperous and educated urban class promoted learning and artistic expression. Wealthy townspeople joined princes in becoming patrons of the arts, offering financial support to painters, sculptors, architects, writers, and musicians.

Most Europeans, however, were peasants living in agricultural communities that often differed in important ways from Native American and West African societies. In European societies, men performed most of the heavy work of farming, while women's labors focused on caring for the family and domestic duties. Europeans lived in states organized into more rigid hierarchies than could be found in many (though not all) parts of North America or West Africa, with the population divided into distinct classes. At the top were the monarchs who, along with the next rank of aristocrats, dominated government and owned most of the land, receiving rents and labor services from peasants and rural artisans. Next, in descending order, came prosperous gentry families, independent landowners, and, at the bottom, landless peasants and laborers.

European society was also patriarchal, with men dominating political and economic life. Europe's rulers were, with few exceptions, men, and men controlled the Catholic Church. Inheritance was patrilineal, and only men could own property.

The Consolidation of Political and Military Authority

By the end of the fifteenth century, after more than a hundred years of incessant conflict, a measure of stability returned to the countries about to embark on overseas expansion. Ferdinand and Isabella of Spain, Louis XI of France, and Henry VII of England successfully asserted royal authority over their previously fragmented realms, creating strong state bureaucracies to control political rivals. They gave special trading privileges to merchants to gain their support, creating links that would later prove important in financing overseas expeditions.

The consolidation of military power went hand in hand with the strengthening of political authority. Portugal developed a strong navy to defend its seaborne merchants. Louis XI of France commanded a standing army, and Ferdinand of Spain created a palace guard to use against potential opponents. Before overseas expansion began, European monarchs exerted military force to extend their authority closer to home. Louis XI and his successors used warfare and intermarriage with the ruling families of nearby provinces to extend French influence. In the early sixteenth century, England's Henry VIII sent soldiers to conquer Ireland. And the Spain of 1492 was forged from the successful conclusion of the *reconquista* ("reconquest") of territory from Muslim control.

Religious Conflict and the Protestant Reformation

Even as these rulers sought to unify their realms, religious conflicts began to tear Europe apart. For more than a thousand years, Catholic Christianity had united western Europeans in one faith. By the sixteenth century, the Catholic Church had accumulated enormous wealth and power. The pope wielded influence not only as a spiritual leader but also as the political ruler of parts of Italy. The church owned considerable property throughout Europe. In reaction to this growing influence, many Christians, especially in Northern Europe, began to criticize the popes and the church itself for worldliness, abuse of power, and betrayal of the legacy of Christ.

In 1517, a German monk, Martin Luther, invited open debate on a set of propositions critical of church practices and doctrines. Luther believed that the

---

Reconquista The long struggle (ending in 1492) during which Spanish Christians reconquered the Iberian peninsula from Muslim occupiers.

church had become too insistent on the performance of good works, such as charitable donations or other actions intended to please God. He called for a return to what he understood to be the purer practices and beliefs of the early church, emphasizing that salvation came not by good deeds but only by faith in God. With the help of the newly invented printing press, his ideas spread widely, inspiring a challenge to the Catholic Church that came to be known as the **Reformation.**

When the Catholic Church refused to compromise, Luther and other critics withdrew to form their own religious organizations, emphasizing the direct, personal relationship of God to the individual believer. Luther urged people to take responsibility for their own spiritual growth by reading the Bible, which he translated for the first time into German. What started as a religious movement, however, quickly acquired an important political dimension.

Sixteenth-century Germany was a fragmented region of small kingdoms and principalities that were officially part of a larger Catholic political entity known as the Holy Roman Empire. Many princes supported Luther for spiritual and secular reasons. When the Holy Roman Empire under Charles V (who was also king of Spain) tried to silence them, the reformist princes protested. From that point on, these princes—and all Europeans who supported religious reform—became known as **Protestants.**

The Protestant movement took a more radical turn under the influence of the French reformer John Calvin, who emphasized the doctrine of **predestination.** Calvin maintained that an all-powerful and all-knowing God chose at the moment of creation which humans would be saved and which would be damned. Each person's fate is thus foreordained, or predestined, by God, although we cannot know our fate during our lifetimes. Good Calvinists struggled to behave as God's chosen, continually searching their souls for evidence of divine grace.

Calvin founded a religious community consistent with his principles in Geneva, a Swiss city-state near the French border. From Germany and Geneva the Protestant Reformation spread to France, the Netherlands, England, and Hungary. The new religious ideas particularly interested literate city-dwellers, such as merchants and skilled artisans, who were attracted to Protestant writings as well as the sermons of Protestant preachers.

The Reformation fractured the religious unity of Western Europe and spawned a century of warfare unprecedented in its bloody destructiveness. Protestants fought Catholics in France and the German states. Popes initiated a "Counter-Reformation" to strengthen the Catholic Church. Europe thus fragmented into warring camps just at the moment when Europeans were coming to terms with their discovery of America.

CONTACT

*P*ortugal, Spain, France, and England competed to establish footholds on other continents in an intense scramble for riches and dominance. The success of these early endeavors was a reflection of Europe's prosperity and of a series of technological breakthroughs that enabled its mariners to navigate beyond familiar waters. By 1600, Spain had emerged as the apparent winner among the European competitors for New World dominance. Its astonishingly wealthy empire included vast territories in Central and South America.

Reformation   Martin Luther's challenge to the Catholic Church, initiated in 1517, calling for a return to what he understood to be the purer practices and beliefs of the early church.

Protestants   All European supporters of religious reform under Charles V's Holy Roman Empire.

Predestination   The belief that God decided at the moment of Creation which humans would achieve salvation.

QUICK REVIEW

Religious Conflict in Europe
- 1517: Martin Luther sparks Reformation.
- John Calvin promotes a more radical vision of Protestantism.
- The Catholic Church launches a "Counter Reformation".

WHAT WERE the biological consequences of contact between Europeans and Native Americans?

GLOBAL PERSPECTIVES

VIKING TRADE ROUTES

One summer day in 1957, two archaeologists working near the Maine coast made a remarkable discovery. The men dug up a small coin buried about five inches deep in the soil. There was a small hole drilled at one edge, which suggested that the coin had been worn as an ornament. When experts examined it closely, they were astonished to learn that it was a silver penny that had been minted in Norway in the eleventh century. How had such an ancient penny made its way to Maine?

Archaeologists now believe that the penny arrived in Maine via a massive intercontinental trade network that linked the Old and New Worlds centuries before Columbus's arrival. The key figures in this long-distance commerce were Viking voyagers from Scandinavia. Between the ninth and eleventh centuries, magnificent ships carried the Vikings over vast distances, from the northernmost reaches of Norway to continental Europe, and westward to Iceland, Greenland, and Canada. Viking expeditions to the British Isles and throughout Europe included violent raids that brought widespread destruction to local populations. In the New World, trade and settlement were the

Vikings' main goals. Evidence of Viking settlements has been found in various sites in Labrador and Newfoundland. An inhabitant from one of those outposts was the likely source of the penny found in Maine. A Viking settler may have accidentally dropped it, or traded it to one of the local native people. From there the coin made its way as much as a thousand miles southward to Maine, passed along through the Native Americans' own channels of trade.

In the Old World, the geographical extent of Viking trade connections was equally impressive. Archaeologists working at an eighth-century site in Sweden, for instance, have unearthed a small bronze statue of Buddha that was cast in northern India. It made its way to the Scandinavian village via trade networks that traversed vast distances, from Russia to the Middle East to the Indian subcontinent. Exotic items like this one discovered in surprising locations offer striking testimony that global trade connections are by no means an invention of the modern era. A thousand years before our own time, people had already found ways to exchange goods across oceans and continents.

THE LURE OF DISCOVERY

Most people, busy making a living, cared little about distant lands. But certain princes and merchants anticipated spiritual and material benefits from voyages of discovery. The spiritual advantages included making new Christian converts and blocking Islam's expansion. On the material side, the voyages would contribute to Europe's prosperity by increasing trade.

Merchants especially sought access to Asian spices like pepper, cinnamon, ginger, and nutmeg that added interest to an otherwise monotonous diet and helped preserve certain foods. But the overland spice trade—and the trade in other luxury goods such as silk and furs—spanned thousands of miles, involved many middlemen, and was controlled at key points by Muslim merchants. One critical center was Constantinople, the bastion of Christianity in the eastern Mediterranean. When that city fell to the Ottomans—the Muslim rulers of Turkey—in 1453, Europeans feared that caravan routes to Asia would be disrupted. This encouraged merchants to turn westward and seek alternative routes. Mariners ventured farther into ocean waters, seeking direct access to the African gold trade and, eventually, a sea route around Africa to Asia.

Advances in Navigation and Shipbuilding.   Ocean voyages required sturdier ships and more reliable navigational tools. In the early fifteenth century, Prince Henry of Portugal, excited by the idea of overseas discovery, sponsored the efforts of shipbuilders, mapmakers, and other workers to solve these practical problems. Iberian shipbuilders perfected the caravel, a ship whose narrow shape and steering rudder suited it for ocean travel. Ship designers combined square sails (good for speed) with triangular lateen sails, which increased maneuverability. European mariners eagerly adopted two important navigational devices—the magnetic compass (first developed in China) and the astrolabe (introduced to Europe by Muslims from Spain), which allowed mariners to determine their position in relation to a star's known location in the sky. As sailors acquired practical experience on the high seas, mapmakers recorded their observations of landfalls, wind patterns, and ocean currents.

Portugal's Bartolomeu Días reached the southern tip of Africa in 1488. Eleven years later, Vasco da Gama brought a Portuguese fleet around Africa to India, opening a sea route to Asia. These initiatives gave Portugal a virtual monopoly on Far Eastern trade for some time.

The Atlantic Islands and the Slave Trade.   The new trade routes gave strategic importance to the islands that lie in the Atlantic off the west coast of Africa and Europe. Spain and Portugal vied for control of the Canary Islands, located 800 miles southwest of the Iberian peninsula. Spain eventually prevailed in 1496 by defeating the islands' inhabitants. Portugal acquired Madeira and the Cape Verde Islands, along with a group of tiny islands off Africa's Guinea Coast.

Sugar, like Asian spices, commanded high prices in Europe, so the conquerors of the Atlantic islands began to cultivate sugar cane on them, on large plantations worked by slave labor. In the Canaries, the Spanish first enslaved the native inhabitants. When disease and exhaustion reduced their numbers, the Spanish brought in African slaves, often purchased from Portuguese traders. On uninhabited islands, the Europeans imported African slaves from the start.

CHRISTOPHER COLUMBUS AND THE WESTWARD ROUTE TO ASIA

Christopher Columbus was not the first European to believe that he could reach Asia by sailing westward. The idea developed logically during the fifteenth century as mariners gained knowledge and experience from their exploits in the Atlantic and around Africa. Most Europeans knew that the world was round, but scoffed at the idea of a westward voyage to Asia in the belief that no ship could carry enough provisions for such a long trip. Columbus's confidence that he could succeed grew from a mathematical error. He mistakenly calculated the earth's circumference as 18,000 (rather than 24,000) miles and so concluded that Asia lay just 3,500 miles west of the Canary Islands. Columbus first sought financial support for a westward voyage from the king of Portugal, whose advisers disputed his calculations and warned him that he would starve at sea before reaching Asia. Undaunted, he turned to Portugal's rival, Spain.

Columbus tried to convince Ferdinand and Isabella that his plan suited Spain's national goals. If he succeeded, Spain could grow rich from Asian trade, send Christian missionaries to Asia (a goal in keeping with the religious ideals of the *reconquista*), and perhaps enlist the Great Khan of China as an ally in the long struggle with Islam. If he failed, the "enterprise of the Indies" would cost little. The Spanish monarchs nonetheless kept Columbus waiting nearly seven years—until

Advances in ship design, including the development of the caravel pictured in this fifteenth-century woodcut, made transoceanic voyages possible. The arrangement of sails allowed the caravel to catch the trade winds and move more quickly across the high seas.

The Granger Collection, New York.

Christopher Columbus by Italian artist Sebastiano del Piombo. The explorer is dressed in the finery of a prosperous Italian Renaissance gentleman including a tricorn hat and sumptuous mantle. 1519 oil on canvas.

Ewing Galloway, Index Stock Imagery, Inc.

WHERE TO LEARN MORE

St. Augustine, Florida.
www.oldcity.com/his2.html

1492, when the last Muslim stronghold at Grenada fell to Spanish forces—before they gave him their support.

After thirty-three days at sea, Columbus and his men made landfall. Although puzzled by his failure to find the fabled cities of China and Japan, Columbus believed that he had reached Asia. Three more voyages, between 1493 and 1504, however, failed to yield clear evidence of an Asian landfall or substantiate Columbus's reports of "great mines of gold and other metals" and spices in abundance.

Obsessed with the wealth he had promised himself and others, Columbus and his men turned violent, sacking the villages of the Tainos and Caribs and demanding tribute in gold. The Spanish forced gangs of Indians to pan rivers for the precious nuggets. Dissatisfied with the meager results, Columbus sought other sources of wealth.

In 1494, Columbus suggested to Ferdinand and Isabella of Spain that the Indies could yield a profit if islanders were sold as slaves. His plan earned him a sharp rebuke from Queen Isabella, who opposed enslaving people she considered to be new Spanish subjects. This royal fastidiousness was short-lived, however. Within a year, the queen agreed that native war captives could be enslaved.

Columbus died in Spain in 1506, still convinced he had found Asia. What he had done was to set in motion a process that would transform both sides of the Atlantic. It would eventually bring wealth to many Europeans and immense suffering to Native Americans and Africans.

THE SPANISH CONQUEST AND COLONIZATION

Of all European nations, Spain was best suited to take advantage of Columbus's discovery. Its experience with the *reconquista* gave it both a religious justification for conquest (bringing Christianity to nonbelievers) and an army of seasoned soldiers—*conquistadores*. In addition, during the *reconquista* and the conquest of the Canary Islands, Spain's rulers had developed efficient techniques for controlling newly conquered lands that could be applied to New World colonies.

The Spanish first established outposts on Cuba, Puerto Rico, and Jamaica (see Map 1–3). The *conquistadores* were more interested in finding gold and slaves than in creating permanent settlements. Leaving a trail of destruction, they attacked native villages and killed or captured the inhabitants.

The End of the Aztec Empire.   In 1519, Hernán Cortés and six hundred soldiers landed on the coast of Mexico. "I and my companions," Cortés announced, "suffer from a disease of the heart which can be cured only with gold." By 1521, Cortés and his men had conquered the powerful Aztec empire. The Spanish soldiers also discovered riches beyond their wildest dreams. They "picked up the gold and fingered it like monkeys," reported one Aztec witness. They were "transported by joy, as if their hearts were illumined and made new."

The swift, decisive Spanish victory depended on several factors. In part, the Spanish enjoyed certain technological advantages. Their guns and horses often enabled them to overwhelm larger groups of Aztec foot soldiers armed with spears and wooden swords edged with obsidian. Cortés benefited from two other factors. First, he exploited divisions within the Aztec empire, acquiring indispensable allies among subject Indians who resented Aztec domination. A second and more important factor was disease. Historians estimate that nearly 40 percent of the inhabitants of central Mexico died of smallpox within a year. Other diseases

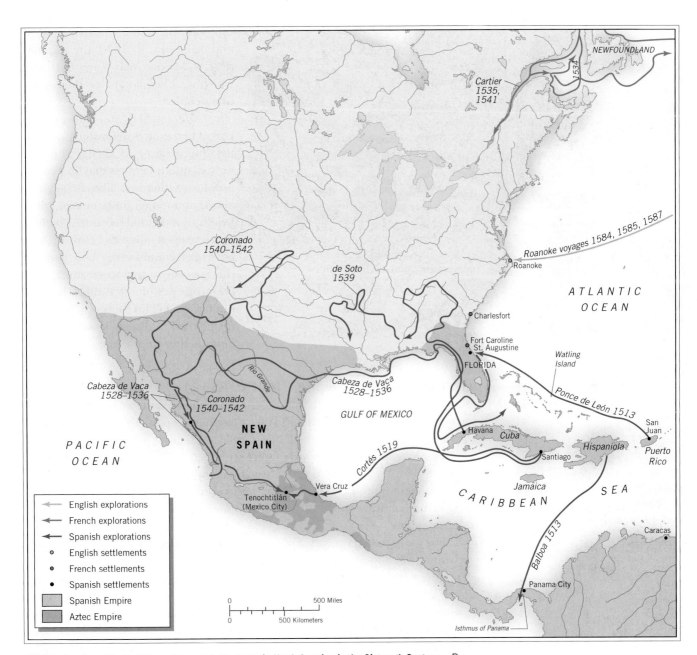

MAP 1–3   Spanish, English, and French Settlements in North America in the Sixteenth Century   By the end of the sixteenth century, only Spain had established permanent settlements in North America. French outposts in Canada and at Fort Caroline, as well as the English settlement at Roanoke, failed to thrive. European rivalries for North America, however, would intensify after 1600.

BASED ON this map, what factors might help to explain why Spain was more successful in the establishment of permanent settlements before 1600 than either France or England? Do you think geographic location (climate, terrain, etc.) may have played a role?

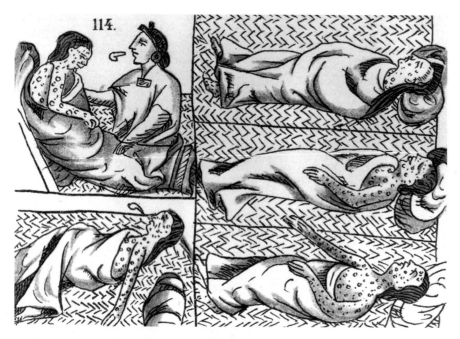

Smallpox wreaked havoc among Native Americans who lacked biological resistance to European diseases. This drawing by Aztec illustrators shows Aztec victims of a smallpox epidemic that struck Tenochtitlán in 1520. Historians estimate that up to 40 percent of the population of central Mexico died within a year. This catastrophic decline weakened the Aztecs' ability to resist the Spanish conquest of their land.

The Granger Collection, New York.

followed, including typhus, measles, and influenza. By 1600, the population of Mexico may have declined from over 15 million to less than a million people.

Aztec society and culture collapsed in the face of appalling mortality. One survivor recalled, "The sick were so utterly helpless that they could only lie on their beds like corpses, unable to move their limbs or even their heads. . . . If they did move their bodies, they screamed with pain." Early in their bid to gain control of the Aztec empire, the Spanish seized Moctezuma, and eventually put him to death. They did not have to kill his successor, however, for he died of disease less than three months after gaining the throne.

The Fall of the Inca Empire. In 1532, Francisco Pizarro and 180 men discovered the Inca empire high in the Peruvian Andes. Taking advantage of a civil war within the empire following its ruler's death, the Spaniards captured Cuzco, the Inca capital, and established a new capital at Lima.

By 1550, Spain's New World empire stretched from the Caribbean through Mexico to Peru. It was administered from Spain by the Council of the Indies. The council aimed to project royal authority into every village in New Spain in order to maintain political control and extract as much wealth as possible from the land and its people.

For more than a century, Spanish ships crossed the Atlantic carrying seemingly limitless amounts of treasure from the colonies. The colonial rulers subjected the native inhabitants of New Spain to compulsory tribute payments and forced labor. Tens of thousands of Indians toiled in silver mines in Peru and Bolivia and on sugar plantations in the Caribbean. When necessary, Spaniards imported African slaves to supplement a native labor force ravaged by disease and exhaustion.

Spanish Incursions to the North. The desire for gold eventually lured Spaniards farther into North America. In 1528, an expedition to Florida ended in disaster when the Spanish intruders provoked an attack by Apalachee Indians.

In 1539, Hernán de Soto led an expedition from Florida to the Mississippi River. Along the way, the Spaniards harassed the native peoples, demanding provisions, burning villages, and capturing women to be servants and concubines. They also exposed the Indians to deadly European diseases. The expedition kept up its rampage for three years, turning toward Mexico only after de Soto died in 1542. In these same years, Francisco Vásquez de Coronado led three hundred troops on an equally destructive expedition through present-day Arizona, New Mexico, and Colorado on a futile search for gold and precious stones.

AMERICAN VIEWS

CABEZA DE VACA AMONG THE INDIANS (1530)

lvar Núñez Cabeza de Vaca came to the New World in 1527 in search of riches, not suffering. But the Spanish expedition of which he was a member met disaster shortly after it arrived in Florida on a mission to conquer the region north of the Gulf of Mexico. Of an original group of three hundred soldiers, only Cabeza de Vaca and three other men (including one African slave) survived. They did so by walking thousands of miles overland from the Gulf Coast to northern Mexico, an eight-year-long ordeal that tested the men's wits and physical endurance. Instead of entering Indian villages as proud conquistadors, Cabeza de Vaca and his companions encountered native peoples from a position of weakness. In order to survive, they had to adapt to the ways of the peoples across whose land they passed. After Cabeza de Vaca made it back to Mexico City, he described his experiences in an official report to the king of Spain. This remarkable document offers vivid descriptions of the territory extending from northern Florida to northern Mexico and the many peoples who inhabited it. It is equally interesting, as this extract suggests, for what it reveals about Cabeza de Vaca himself and the changes he made in the interest of survival.

- While living among the Capoques, what sort of work did Cabeza de Vaca have to do, and why?
- Why did Cabeza de Vaca decide to become a merchant? What advantages did this way of life offer him?
- Why did the Indians welcome Cabeza de Vaca into their communities even though he was a stranger?

[I remained with the Capoques] for more than a year, and because of the great labors they forced me to perform and the bad treatment they gave me, I resolved to flee from them and go to those who live in the forests and on the mainland, who are called those of Charruco, because I was unable to endure the life that I had with these others; because among many other tasks, I had to dig the roots to eat out from under the water and among the rushes where they grew in the ground. And because of this, my fingers were so worn that when a reed touched them it caused them to bleed, and the reeds cut me in many places. . . . And because of this, I set to the task of going over to the others, and with them things were somewhat better for me. And because I became a merchant, I tried to exercise the vocation as best I knew how. And because of this they gave me food to eat and treated me well, and they importuned me to go from one place to another to obtain the things they needed, because on account of the continual warfare in the land, there is little traffic or communication among them. And with my dealings and wares I entered inland as far as I desired, and I went along the coast for forty or fifty leagues. The mainstay of my trade was pieces of snail shell and the hearts of them; and conch shells with which they cut a fruit that is like frijoles [beans], with which they perform cures and do their dances and make celebrations. . . . And in exchange and as barter for it, I brought forth hides and red ocher with which they smear themselves and dye their faces and hair, flints to make the points of arrows, paste, and stiff canes to make them, and some tassels made from deer hair which they dye red. And this occupation served me well, because practicing it, I had the freedom to go wherever I wanted, and I was not constrained in any way nor enslaved, and wherever I went they treated me well and gave me food out of want for my wares, and most importantly because doing that, I was able to seek out the way by which I would go forward. And among them I was very well known; when they saw me and I brought them the things they needed, they were greatly pleased.

Source: Rolena Adorno and Patrick Charles Pautz, eds., *The Narrative of Cabeza de Vaca,* (Lincoln: University of Nebraska Press, 2003), pp. 96–97.

The failure to find gold and silver halted Spain's attempt to extend its empire to the north. By the end of the sixteenth century, the Spanish maintained just two precarious footholds north of Mexico. One was at St. Augustine, on Florida's Atlantic coast. Founded in 1565, this fortified outpost served as a naval base to defend Spanish treasure fleets from raids by English and French privateers. The other settlement was located far to the west in what is now New Mexico. Juan de Oñate, on a futile search for silver mines, claimed the region for Spain in 1598. He and his men proceeded to antagonize the area's inhabitants. Having earned the enmity of the Pueblo people, Oñate barely managed to keep his tiny colony together.

The bloody tactics of men such as Oñate aroused protest back in Spain. The Indians' most eloquent advocate was Bartolomé de Las Casas, a Dominican priest shamed by his own role (as a layman) in the conquest of Hispaniola. Las Casas wrote *In Defense of the Indians,* including graphic descriptions of native sufferings. Instead of eliciting Spanish reforms, however, his work inspired Protestant Europeans to create the "Black Legend," an exaggerated story according to which a fanatical Catholic Spain sought to spread its control at any cost.

1–5
Bartolomé de las Casas, "Of the Island of Hispaniola" (1542)

The Seeds of Economic Decline. Meanwhile, the vast riches of Central and South America glutted Spain's treasury. But this influx of American treasure had unforeseen consequences that would soon undermine Spanish predominance.

In 1492, the Spanish crown, determined to impose religious conformity after the *reconquista,* expelled from Spain all Jews who refused to become Christians. The refugees included many leading merchants who had contributed significantly to Spain's economy. The remaining Christian merchants, now awash in American riches, saw little reason to invest in new trade or productive enterprises that might have sustained the economy once the flow of New World treasure diminished. As a result, Spain's economy eventually stagnated.

The flood of American gold and silver also inflated prices throughout Europe, hurting both workers, whose wages failed to rise as fast, and aristocrats, who were dependent on fixed rents from their estates. Most damaging of all, Spain's monarchs wasted their American wealth fighting expensive wars against their European enemies that ultimately only weakened the nation. By 1600, some disillusioned Spaniards were arguing that the conquest had brought more problems than benefits to their country.

THE COLUMBIAN EXCHANGE

Spain's long-term economic decline was just one of many consequences of the conquest of the New World. In the long run, the biological consequences of contact—what one historian has called the **Columbian exchange**—proved to be the most momentous (see the Overview table, "The Columbian Exchange").

The most catastrophic result of the exchange was the exposure of Native Americans to Old World diseases. Epidemics of smallpox, measles, typhus, and influenza struck Native Americans with great force, killing half, and sometimes as many as 90 percent, of the people in communities exposed to them. The only American disease that may have infected Old World populations was syphilis, which appeared in Spain just after Columbus returned from his first voyage.

Another important aspect of the Columbian exchange was the introduction of Old World livestock to the New World, which began when Columbus brought horses, sheep, cattle, pigs, and goats with him on his second voyage in 1493. Native Americans had few domesticated animals of their own. With few natural predators to limit their numbers, livestock populations boomed in the New World,

1–9
The Columbian Exchange (1590)

Columbian exchange The transatlantic exchange of plants, animals, and diseases that occurred after the first European contact with the Americas.

OVERVIEW   THE COLUMBIAN EXCHANGE

	From Old World to New World	From New World to Old World
Diseases	Smallpox, measles, plague, typhus, influenza, yellow fever, diphtheria, scarlet fever	Sexually transmitted strain of syphilis
Animals	Horses, cattle, pigs, sheep, goats, donkeys, mules, black rats, honeybees, cockroaches	Turkeys
Plants	Wheat, sugar, barley, coffee, rice, dandelion, and other weeds	Maize, beans, peanut, potato, sweet potato, manioc, squash, papaya, guava, tomato, avocado, pineapple, chili pepper, cocoa

Source: Adapted from Alfred Crosby Jr., *The Colombian Exchange: Biological and Cultural Consequences of 1492* (1972).

competing with native mammals for grazing. At least at first, the Indians' unfamiliarity with the use of horses in warfare often gave mounted European soldiers a decisive military advantage. But some native groups adopted these animals for their own purposes. Yaquis, Pueblos, and other peoples in the Southwest began to raise cattle and sheep. By the eighteenth century, Plains Indians had reoriented their culture around the use of horses, which had become essential for travel, hunting buffalo, and carrying burdens. Horses also became a primary object for trading and raiding among Plains peoples.

European ships carried unintentional passengers as well, including the black rat and the honeybee, both previously unknown in the New World. Ships also brought weeds such as thistles and dandelions, whose seeds were often embedded in hay for animal fodder.

Europeans brought a variety of seeds and plants in order to grow familiar foods. Columbus's men planted wheat, chickpeas, melons, onions, and fruit trees on Caribbean islands. Europeans also learned to cultivate native foods, such as corn, tomatoes, squash, beans, and potatoes, as well as nonfood plants such as tobacco and cotton. They carried many of these plants back to Europe, enriching Old World diets with new foods.

CULTURAL PERCEPTIONS AND MISPERCEPTIONS

When members of these societies met for the first time, confusion inevitably resulted. Even simple transactions produced unexpected results. When Columbus showed swords to Caribbean islanders, for example, "they took them by the edge and through ignorance cut themselves" because they had never touched metal weapons. French explorers were similarly taken by surprise when they choked while smoking Iroquois tobacco, which they thought tasted like "powdered pepper." These were relatively minor mishaps and were soon overshadowed by more substantial interactions which seemed to exaggerate the differences between Indians and Europeans.

Religion was extremely important to both Native Americans and Europeans, but differences in forms and practices encouraged misunderstandings. Most Indians believed that the universe contained friendly and hostile spiritual forces in human and other-than-human forms (such as plants, animals, and stars). People interacted with the spirit world through ceremonies that often involved exchanging gifts and performing certain rituals. To Europeans accustomed to worshiping one God in an organized church, Indian traditions were incomprehensible. Indians, in turn, often found Christianity confusing and at first rejected European pressure to convert.

Different understandings of the roles of men and women provided another source of confusion. Europeans assumed that men were naturally superior to women and should dominate them and rule society. They disapproved of the less rigid gender divisions among some Native American peoples. Europeans, accustomed to societies in which men did most agricultural work, also objected to Indian women's dominant role in farming and assumed that men's hunting was more for recreation than subsistence. They often concluded that Indian women lived "a most slavish life." Indians, in turn, sometimes thought that European men failed to make good use of their wives. In Massachusetts, some native men ridiculed colonists "for spoiling good working creatures" by not making their women work in the fields.

These were some of the many cultural differences that separated Indian and European societies. In order for natives and newcomers to get along peaceably with each other, each side would have to adapt to the new circumstances under which both groups now lived. At first, such harmony seemed possible. But it soon became clear that Europeans intended to dominate the lands they discovered. Only three days after he arrived in America, Columbus announced his intention "not to pass by any island of which I did not take possession" and soon speculated on the possibility of enslaving Indians. Such claims to dominance sparked vigorous resistance from native peoples everywhere who strove to maintain their autonomy in a changed world.

COMPETITION FOR A CONTINENT

WHY DID early French and English efforts at colonization falter?

*I*n 1494, the conflicting claims of Portugal and Spain were resolved by the **Treaty of Tordesillas.** The treaty drew a north–south line approximately 1,100 miles west of the Cape Verde Islands. Spain received all lands west of the line, while Portugal held sway to the east. This limited Portugal's New World empire to Brazil, where settlers followed the precedent of the Atlantic island colonies and established sugar plantations worked by slave labor. But the treaty also protected Portugal's claims in Africa and Asia, which lay east of the line.

France and England, of course, rejected the papal grant of the Western Hemisphere to Spain and Portugal. Initially, however, domestic troubles—largely sparked by the Protestant Reformation—distracted the two countries from the pursuit of empire. By the close of the sixteenth century, both France and England insisted on their rights to New World lands, but neither had created a permanent settlement to support its claim.

EARLY FRENCH EFFORTS IN NORTH AMERICA

France was a relative latecomer to New World exploration. Preoccupied with European affairs, France's rulers paid little attention to America until news of Cortés's exploits in Mexico arrived in the 1520s.

In 1524, King Francis I sponsored a voyage by Giovanni da Verrazano, an Italian navigator, who mapped the North American coast from present-day South Carolina to Maine. During the 1530s and 1540s, the French mariner Jacques Cartier made three voyages in search of rich mines to rival those of Mexico and Peru. He explored the St. Lawrence River up to what is now Montreal, hoping to discover a water route through the continent to Asia (the so-called Northwest Passage).

On his third voyage, in 1541, Cartier was to serve under the command of a nobleman, Jean-François de la Rocque, Sieur de Roberval, who was commissioned

Treaty of Tordesillas Treaty negotiated in 1494 to resolve the territorial claims of Spain and Portugal.

by the king to establish a permanent settlement in Canada. Troubles in recruiting colonists delayed Roberval, who—when he finally set sail in 1542—ended up taking convicts as his settlers. Cartier sailed ahead, gathered samples of what he thought were gold and diamonds, and returned to France without Roberval's permission.

Roberval's expedition was poorly organized, and his cruel treatment of the convicts provoked several uprisings. The Iroquois, suspicious of repeated French intrusions on their lands, saw no reason to help them. A year after they arrived in Canada, Roberval and the surviving colonists were back in France. Their return coincided with news that the gold brought back by Cartier was iron pyrite ("fool's gold") and the diamonds were worthless quartz crystals.

Disappointed with their Canadian expeditions, the French made a few brief forays to the south, establishing outposts in what is now South Carolina in 1562 and Florida in 1564. They soon abandoned the Carolina colony, and Spanish forces captured the Florida fort. Then, back in France, a prolonged civil war broke out between Catholics and Protestants. Renewed interest in colonization would have to await the return of peace at home.

ENGLISH ATTEMPTS IN THE NEW WORLD

The English were quicker than the French to stake a claim to the New World but no more successful at colonization. In 1497, King Henry VII sent John Cabot, an Italian mariner, to explore eastern Canada on England's behalf. But neither Henry nor any of his wealthy subjects would invest the funds necessary to follow up on Cabot's discoveries.

The lapse in English activity in the New World stemmed from religious troubles at home. Between 1534 and 1558, England changed its official religion several times. King Henry VIII, who had once defended the Catholic Church against its critics, took up the Protestant cause when the pope refused to annul his marriage to Catherine of Aragon. In 1534, Henry declared himself the head of a separate Church of England and seized the Catholic Church's English property. But in 1553, Mary—daughter of the spurned Catherine of Aragon—became queen and tried to bring England back to Catholicism. She had nearly three hundred Protestants burned at the stake for their beliefs (earning her the nickname "Bloody Mary"), and many others went into exile in Europe.

After Mary's death in 1558, her half-sister Elizabeth I (r. 1558–1603), a committed Protestant, became queen, restoring Protestantism as the state religion, bringing stability to the nation, and renewing England's interest in the New World. She and her subjects saw colonization not only as a way to gain wealth and political advantage but also as a Protestant crusade against Catholic domination.

1–10
Thomas Harriot, The Algonquian Peoples of the Atlantic Coast (1588)

The Colonization of Ireland.   England's first target for colonization, however, was not America but Ireland. Located less than 60 miles west of England and populated by Catholics, Ireland threatened to become a base from which Spain or another Catholic power might invade England. Elizabeth launched a series of brutal expeditions that destroyed Irish villages and slaughtered the inhabitants. Several veterans of these campaigns later took part in New World colonization and drew on their Irish experience for guidance.

The English transferred their assumptions about Irish "savages" to Native Americans. Englishmen in America frequently observed similarities between Indians and the Irish. "When they [the Indians] have their apparel on they look like Irish," noted one Englishman. "The natives of New England," he added, "are accustomed to build their houses much like the wild Irish." When Indians resisted their attempts at conquest, the English recalled the Irish example, claiming that

This image of Jacques Cartier's landing on Labrador in 1534 appears on a sixteenth-century map. The geographical orientation is unusual, with North at the bottom of the picture and South at the top. Note the artist's depiction of well-dressed Europeans meeting fur-clad Indians.

native "savagery" required brutal suppression.

Second, the Irish experience influenced English ideas about colonial settlement. English conquerors set up "plantations" surrounded by palisades on seized Irish lands, importing Protestant tenants from England and Scotland to farm the land. Native Irish people were excluded. English colonists in America followed this precedent when they established plantations that separated English and native peoples.

Expeditions to the New World.
Sir Humphrey Gilbert, a notoriously cruel veteran of the Irish campaigns, composed a treatise to persuade Queen Elizabeth to support such an endeavor. The queen authorized several exploratory voyages, including Martin Frobisher's three trips in 1576–1578 in search of the Northwest Passage to Asia. Frobisher failed to find the elusive passage and sent back shiploads of glittering ore that proved to be fool's gold. Elizabeth had better luck in allowing privateers, such as John Hawkins and Francis Drake, to raid Spanish ships and New World ports for gold and silver.

Meanwhile, Gilbert continued to promote New World settlement, arguing that it would increase England's trade and provide a place for the nation's unemployed people. Like many of his contemporaries, Gilbert believed that England's "surplus" population threatened social order. The population was indeed growing, and economic changes often made it difficult for people to support themselves. Gilbert suggested offering free land in America to English families willing to emigrate.

In 1578, Gilbert received permission to set up a colony along the North American coast. It took him five years to organize an expedition to Newfoundland, which he claimed for England. After sailing southward seeking a more favorable site for a colony, Gilbert headed home, only to be lost at sea during an Atlantic storm. The impetus for English colonization did not die with him, however, for his half-brother, Sir Walter Raleigh (another veteran of the Irish wars), took up the cause.

The Roanoke Colony.
In 1585, Raleigh sent men to build a settlement on Roanoke Island. Most of the colonists were soldiers fresh from Ireland who refused to grow their own food, insisting that the Roanoke Indians should feed them. When the local chief, Wingina, organized native resistance, they killed him. Eventually, the colonists, disappointed not to have found any treasure and exhausted by a harsh winter, returned to England in 1586.

Two members of these early expeditions, however, left a more positive legacy. Thomas Hariot studied the Roanoke and Croatoan Indians and identified plants and animals in the area. John White drew maps and painted a series of watercolors depicting the natives and the coastal landscape. When Raleigh tried once more, in 1587, to found a colony, he chose White to be its leader. This attempt also failed. The ship captain dumped the settlers—who, for the first time, included women and children—on Roanoke Island so that he could pursue Spanish treasure ships. White waited until his granddaughter, Virginia Dare (the first English

child born in America), was safely born and then sailed to England for supplies. But the outbreak of war with Spain delayed his return for three years. Spain had gathered an immense fleet to invade England, and all English ships were needed for defense. Although England defeated the Armada in 1588, White could not obtain a relief ship for Roanoke until 1590.

White found the colony deserted. Digging through the ruins of the village, he found "my books torn from the covers, the frames of some of my pictures and Maps rotten and spoiled with rain." He also saw the word CROATOAN carved on a post and assumed that the colonists had moved to nearby Croatoan Island. But bad weather prevented him from searching there. For years, English and Spanish mariners reported seeing white people along the coast of Chesapeake Bay. But no Roanoke colonists were ever found.

England's interest in colonization did not wane. In 1584, Richard Hakluyt had aroused enthusiasm for America by writing the *Discourse on the Western Planting* for the queen and her advisers. He argued that England would prosper from trade and the sale of New World commodities. Once the Indians were civilized, Hakluyt added, they would eagerly purchase English goods. Equally important, England could plant "sincere religion" (that is, Protestant Christianity) in the New World and block Spanish expansion. Hakluyt's arguments fired the imaginations of many people, and the defeat of the Spanish Armada emboldened England to challenge Spain's New World dominance. The experience of Roanoke should have tempered that enthusiasm. Roanoke's fate underscored the need for adequate funding, the unsuitability of soldiers as colonists, and the need to maintain good relations with the Indians. But the English were slow to learn these lessons. As it was, the sixteenth century ended with no permanent English settlement in the New World.

CONCLUSION

After Columbus's first voyage, Europeans, eager for wealth and power, set out to claim a continent that just a hundred years earlier they had not dreamed existed. African slaves were brought to the Caribbean, Mexico, and Brazil, and forced to labor under extremely harsh conditions for white masters. The Aztec and Incan empires collapsed in the wake of the Spanish conquest. In the Caribbean and parts of Mexico and Peru, untold numbers of native peoples succumbed to European diseases they had never before encountered.

Despite all that had happened, North America was still Indian country. Only Spain had established North American colonies, and even its soldiers struggled to expand north of Mexico. Except in Mexico and the Caribbean, Europeans had merely touched the continent's shores. In 1600, despite the virulent epidemics, native peoples (even in Mexico) still greatly outnumbered European and African immigrants. The next century, however, brought many powerful challenges both to native control and to the Spanish monopoly of settlement.

SUMMARY

Native American Societies Before 1492 On the eve of contact, Native American societies were coexisting much as they had over the centuries before, having developed distinctive cultures based on the regions in which they lived. As many

IMAGE KEY

for pages xlviii–1

a. Dutch colonial officer Peter Minuit purchases Manhattan Island from Man-a-hat-a Native Americans.

b. The meeting of Cortés and Moctezuma at Tenochitlán on November 8, 1519.

c. The coastal Algonquian village of Secoton.

d. A banana blossom.

e. Medicine man ministering to Aztecs who were infected with smallpox by the Spaniards.

f. John White finds no trace of the colony of Roanoke upon his return to Virginia in 1590.

g. Mississippian city of Cahokia.

h. Mosque in Djenné, Mali

i. Pyramid of Kukulcan at Chichen Itza.

Native American societies continued in their development of agriculture, others concentrated on fishing and tracking game. Mayan and Aztec societies were among a series of complex, literate, urban cultures making up Mesoamerican civilizations from central Mexico into Central America.

West African Societies   West African societies, although they had developed trade networks with Europe and the Middle East, still consisted mostly of farmers, not merchants. Family connections helped define each person's place in society, and religious beliefs magnified the powerful influence of family on African life. Though slavery was not yet a major source of export, slavery had long been a part of West African society.

Western Europe on the Eve of Exploration   In Western Europe, recovery from the Hundred Years' War and the Black Death meant a redefinition of labor and productivity. In some parts of Europe, economic improvement encouraged an extraordinary movement known as the Renaissance—a "rebirth" of interest in the classical civilizations of Greece and Rome. European society was patriarchal, with men dominating political and economic life. And, by the end of the fifteenth century, after more than one hundred years of incessant conflict, a measure of stability had returned to Western Europe.

Contact   Portugal, Spain, France, and England were competing to establish footholds on other continents in an intense scramble for riches and dominance as the fifteenth century came to a close. Explorers like Columbus and Ponce de Leon crossed the Atlantic in search of new lands. The dawn of European exploration changed both sides of the Atlantic forever.

Competition for a New Continent   In 1494, the conflicting claims of Portugal and Spain for New World territory were resolved by the Treaty of Tordesillas. France and England, of course, rejected the grant and insisted on their rights to New World land. Although the English were quicker than the French to stake a claim to the New World, neither was very successful at early colonization. However, England's interest in colonization did not wane, and, although the sixteenth century ended with no permanent English settlement in the New World, such a settlement was not far away.

REVIEW QUESTIONS

1. How did the Aztecs who first glimpsed Spanish ships off the coast of Mexico describe to Moctezuma what they had seen? What details most captured their attention?

2. Compare men's and women's roles in Native American, West African, and European societies. What were the similarities and differences? How did differences between European and Native American gender roles lead to misunderstandings?

3. Many of the first European colonizers in North America were military veterans. What impact did this have on their relations with Indian peoples?

4. Why did Spain so quickly become the dominant colonial power in North America? What advantages did it enjoy over France and England?

5. What role did religion play in early European efforts at overseas colonization? Did religious factors always encourage colonization, or did they occasionally interfere with European expansion?

6. In what ways were trade networks important in linking different groups of people in the Old and New Worlds?

KEY TERMS

Aztecs (p. 7)

Cahokia (p. 8)

Columbian exchange (p. 22)

Predestination (p. 15)

Protestants (p. 15)

Reconquista (p. 14)

Reformation (p. 15)

Tordesillas, Treaty of (p. 24)

WHERE TO LEARN MORE

Cahokia Mounds State Historic Site, Collinsville, Illinois. This site, occupied from A.D. 600 to 1500, was the largest Mississippian community in eastern North America. It now includes numerous exhibits, and archaeological excavations continue in the vicinity. The website, **www.siue.edu/CAHOKIAMOUNDS**, contains information and photos of archaeological excavations, as well as a link to a virtual tour.

Mashantucket Pequot Museum, Mashantucket, Connecticut. This tribally owned and operated complex offers a view of eastern Woodlands Indian life, focusing on the Pequots of eastern Connecticut. Exhibits include dioramas, films, interactive programs, and a reconstructed sixteenth-century Pequot village. The homepage for the Mashantucket Pequot Museum and Research Center is **www.mashantucket.com**.

Mesa Verde National Park, Colorado. Occupied by Ancestral Puebloan peoples as early as A.D. 550, the area contains a variety of sites, from early pithouses to spectacular cliff dwellings. The official National Park webpage for Mesa Verde is **www.nps.gov/meve**. Information on individual houses and sites within the park, plus travel and lodging information can be found at **www.mesa.verde.national-park.com**.

National Museum of the American Indian, Washington, D.C. Part of the Smithsonian Institution in the nation's capital, this museum contains excellent exhibits on various aspects of Native American history and culture. There is also a branch, the **George Gustav Heye Museum,** in New York City. The website **www.nmai.si.edu** offers a wealth of information on past and current shows, as well as online exhibitions.

St. Augustine, Florida. Founded in 1565, St. Augustine is the site of the first permanent Spanish settlement in North America. Today the restored community resembles a Spanish colonial town, with narrow, winding streets and seventeenth- and eighteenth-century buildings. The site also contains the restored Castillo de San Marcos, now a national park. The official website for Historic St. Augustine, **www.oldcity.com/his2.html**, provides considerable information about the origins and development of the Spanish settlement.

 U.S. History Documents CD-ROM
For primary sources related to this chapter, refer to the document CD-ROM.

 www.prenhall.com/goldfield
For study resources related to this chapter, visit the *Companion Website*™.

2 Transplantation 1600-1685

CHAPTER HIGHLIGHTS

The French in North America The French established successful colonies in North America in the seventeenth century. The fur trade was the center of the economy of the French colonies. By 1700, New France had about fifteen-thousand settlers.

The Dutch Overseas Empire The Dutch joined the scramble for empire in the early seventeenth century. The Dutch East and West Indies Companies directed Dutch expansion. In 1664, England conquered New Netherland.

English Settlement in the Chesapeake Founded in 1607, Jamestown developed into the prosperous colony of Virginia. The economy of the region was built around tobacco cultivation and tobacco shaped the development of Virginia society.

The Founding of New England Six English colonies were established in New England between 1620 and 1640. Conditions were not as difficult as in Virginia, and colonists lived longer, healthier lives. New Englanders clustered in towns that were the center of their economic, social, and religious lives.

Competition in the Caribbean French, Dutch, and English adventurers challenged the Spanish monopoly in the Caribbean. The first English colonists in the West Indies grew tobacco, but sugar quickly became the primary crop. With sugar cultivation came slavery and the emergence of a biracial society.

The Restoration Colonies Charles II granted a group of supporters the land that became the Carolina colony. Rice cultivation encouraged the importation of slaves, and by 1708, there were more black slaves than white settlers in the colony. William Penn's colony of Pennsylvania was built on Penn's Quaker beliefs. By 1720, Pennsylvania was an economic success.

CHAPTER QUESTIONS

WHAT ROLE did the fur trade and fur traders play in the success of the French colonies?

HOW DID conflict between the English and the Dutch affect Dutch colonization in the Americas?

HOW DID tobacco cultivation shape the development of Virginia society?

WHY WERE the English colonies in New England so different from those in the Chesapeake?

WHAT WAS the connection between sugar cultivation and slavery in the Caribbean?

WHY DID colonists in the Carolinas adopt harsh slave codes?

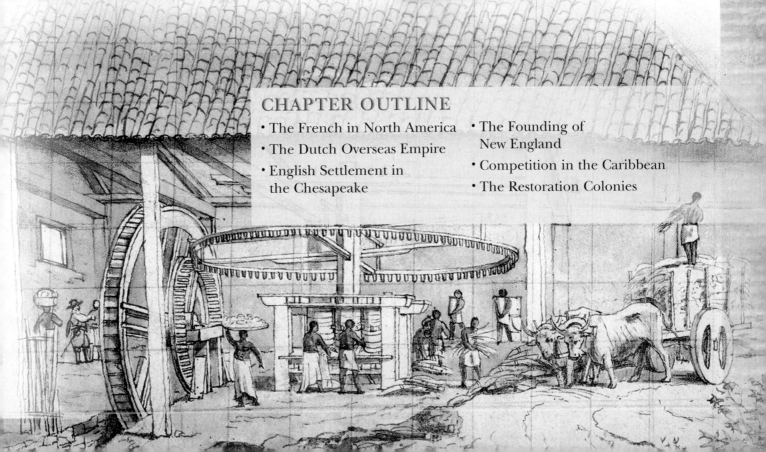

CHAPTER OUTLINE

IMAGE KEY
for pages 30–31 is on page 55.

Martin's Hundred in Virginia, 1623

Loving and kind father and mother:

My most humble duty remembered to you, . . . This is to let you under-stand that I your child am in a most heavy case by reason of the nature of the country, [which] is such that it causeth much sickness, as the scurvy and the bloody flux and diverse other diseases, which maketh the body very poor and weak. . . . [Since] I came out of the ship I never ate anything but peas, and loblollie (that is water gruel). . . . A mouthful of bread for a penny loaf must serve for four men which is most pitiful. . . . [We] live in fear of the enemy every hour . . . for our plantation is very weak by reason of the death and sickness of our company. . . .

But I am not half a quarter so strong as I was in England, and all is for want of victuals, for I do protest unto you that I have eaten more in [one] day at home than I have allowed me here for a week. . . .

[I] saith that if you love me you will redeem me suddenly, for which I do entreat and beg. . . . Good father, do not forget me, but have mercy and pity my miserable case. I know if you did but see me, you would weep to see me. . . .

Richard Frethorne

Susan M. Kingsbury, ed., *The Records of the Virginia Company of London,* 4 vols. (Washington, D.C., 1935), 4:58–62.

RICHARD FRETHORNE HAD crossed the Atlantic to seek his fortune in the new colony of Virginia. Like many of his fellow emigrants, he did so in the hope that one day he would become a prosperous landowner, a status beyond his reach in England. But as his plaintive letter to his parents indicates, life in Virginia was not at all what Frethorne expected it to be. Instead of health and prosperity, Frethorne found sickness and starvation. Fears of an attack by enemy Indians compounded his misery. Yet the starving young Englishman could not simply board the next ship for England. He was under contract to work for the Virginia Company and could not leave until he had completed his term of service. Hence Frethorne's anguished plea to his father to "redeem" him, or buy out the remainder of his contract so that he could return home sooner.

Although his distress was not shared by all colonists, it was sadly typical of many English emigrants to early Virginia. Colonization offered opportunities for advancement, to be sure, but often at the price of sickness, suffering, and danger. Virginia turned out to be England's first permanent colony in the New World, but from Frethorne's perspective in 1623, it was a fragile settlement teetering on the brink of disaster.

Virginia's eventual success, and that of other English colonies, depended upon the willingness of thousands of individuals like Richard Frethorne to face the challenges posed by overseas settlement. Even as their emigration was inspired by hopes of improvement, their quest also reflected England's desire to claim a portion of the New World for itself. Frethorne's journey to Virginia occurred at a time of increased rivalry among European nations eager to replicate Spain's conquest of rich empires. In this scramble for American colonies, England's greatest adversaries were France and the Netherlands. If ordinary colonists were often pre-

Chronology

1581	Northern Provinces of Holland declare independence from Spain.	**1630–1642**	Great Migration to New England.
1589	King Henry IV of France signs Edict of Nantes, granting religious toleration to French Protestants and effectively ending civil war over religion.	**1634**	Lord Baltimore (Cecilius Calvert) founds proprietary colony of Maryland.
1602	Founding of Dutch East India Company.	**1635–1636**	Roger Williams banished from Massachusetts, founds Providence, Rhode Island.
1603–1625	James I reigns as king of England.	**1637**	Anne Hutchinson banished from Massachusetts. Pequot War.
1607	Founding of English colonies at Jamestown and Sagadahoc.	**1638**	New Haven colony founded.
1608	Establishment of French colony at Quebec.	**1640s**	Sugar cultivation and slavery established in West Indies.
1619	First Africans arrive in Jamestown. Virginia's House of Burgesses meets for the first time.	**1642–1660**	English Civil War and Interregnum.
		1649	Maryland's Act for Religious Toleration.
1620	Founding of Plymouth Colony in New England. Mayflower Compact signed.	**1654**	Jewish emigrants from Brazil move to New Amsterdam, creating North America's first permanent Jewish community.
1620s	Tobacco boom in Virginia.	**1660**	Charles II restored to English throne; reigns until 1685.
1624	Dutch found colony of New Netherland.	**1663**	Founding of Carolina colony.
1625	Virginia becomes a royal colony. Fort Amsterdam founded.	**1664**	New Netherland conquered by the English, becomes New York. New Jersey established.
1625–1649	Charles I reigns as king of England.	**1673**	French explorers reach the Mississippi River.
1627	English colony at Barbados founded.	**1681**	Founding of Pennsylvania.
1630	Massachusetts Bay Colony founded.		

occupied with their own tribulations, their leaders could never forget the high stakes involved in the international race for overseas possessions.

THE FRENCH IN NORTH AMERICA

*I*n the mid-sixteenth century, religious warfare between Catholics and Protestants at home had interrupted France's efforts to establish a foothold in North America. But in the early seventeenth century, after King Henry IV restored civil order in France, the situation changed dramatically. With the creation of permanent settlements first along the St. Lawrence River and later in the continent's interior, France staked its claim to an expansive and profitable New World empire.

THE QUEST FOR FURS AND CONVERTS

French fishermen who set up frames on the Newfoundland shore to dry their catch frequently encountered Indians interested in trading beaver pelts for European goods. There was a ready market for these furs in Europe, where beaver hats had become very fashionable. Thus furs joined fish as a source of wealth, and a reason for French explorers and entrepreneurs to establish the colony of New France.

In 1608, Samuel de Champlain led an expedition more than 130 miles up the St. Lawrence River to found a permanent settlement at Quebec. For several decades,

WHAT ROLE did the fur trade and fur traders play in the success of the French colonies?

QUICK REVIEW

The Fur Trade

- Fur traders were critical to New France's success.
- New France was ruled by royal appointees.
- *Coureurs de bois*: independent fur traders living among the Indians.

MAP EXPLORATION

To explore an interactive version of this map, go to
http://www.prenhall.com/goldfield3/map2.1

MAP 2–1 New France, c. 1650 By 1650, New France contained a number of thinly populated settlements along the St. Lawrence River Valley and the eastern shore of Lake Huron. Most colonists lived in Quebec and Montreal; other sites served mainly as furtrading posts and Jesuit missions to the Huron Indians.

WHAT DOES this map tell you about the geographic location of many of the early French colonies in Canada? What do you think were among the critical geographic factors in the decisions France made in colonizing Canada?

Coureur de bois French for "woods runner," an independent fur trader in New France.

Indentured servants
Individuals who contracted to serve a master for a period of four to seven years in return for payment of the servant's passage to America.

the colony was managed by the Company of New France, a private corporation working on its own behalf as well as in France's imperial interests. New France grew slowly; by the 1660s, there were only 3,200 colonists clustered in and around the three main villages (see Map 2–1).

The fur trade supporting the colony's development functioned as a partnership between Indians and Europeans. Indians performed most of the work—trapping beavers, preparing skins, carrying pelts from the interior to trading posts along the St. Lawrence—in return for axes, knives, metal pots, and glass beads. At first, some colonists anticipated that economic ties between the two peoples would be supplemented by marital ones as French traders took Indian wives. Intermarriage, however, was never widespread, occurring mainly among **coureurs de bois** ("woods runners"), independent fur traders who ventured into the forests to live and trade among native peoples. Indian peoples such as the Montagnais and Hurons welcomed the French not only as trading partners, but also as military allies. As a result, the fur trade entangled the French in rivalries among Indian groups that long predated European contact.

For some French colonists, saving Indian souls was even more important than profiting from furs. Beginning in the 1630s, Jesuit missionaries—members of a Catholic religious order founded during the Counter-Reformation—tried to convince Indians to come to the French settlements to hear Christian preaching and learn European ways. When that tactic failed, Jesuits traveled to native villages and learned native languages, bringing Christianity directly to Indian populations.

THE DEVELOPMENT OF NEW FRANCE

After 1663, New France underwent several important changes. First, King Louis XIV disbanded the Company of New France and assumed direct control of the colony. Political reorganization followed. New France was henceforth ruled by two royal appointees: a governor charged with military and diplomatic affairs, and an *intendant* who oversaw colonial finances and the judicial system. The French government also vastly improved Canada's military defenses, investing money in the construction of forts and sending several companies of professional soldiers.

French officials launched a massive campaign to increase migration to the colony. They sent over 700 women—called *filles du roi*, or "king's daughters"—to provide wives in a colony where there were six men of marriageable age for every unmarried French woman. Many male immigrants were *engagés*, or **indentured servants,** who agreed to work for three years in return for food, lodging, a small salary, and a return passage to France. Despite these efforts, only about 250 French immigrants arrived each year. Several factors discouraged prospective colonists, not least of which was Canada's reputation as a distant and inhospitable place. In the end, nearly three out of four immigrants who went to Canada returned home.

By 1700, the population had grown to about 15,000, mostly due to a remarkable level of natural increase. Because land for farms was readily available, couples faced few obstacles in supporting themselves. It was not unknown for some women to bear ten or even fifteen children. As late as 1666, only one out of three French settlers were women, and very few women failed to find husbands.

Many families established farms that produced wheat and other provisions mostly for local consumption. Often the land was technically owned by a gentleman, or *seigneur*, who received a rent payment. Though powerful, these gentlemen never enjoyed anything comparable to the status of aristocrats back in France.

French officials sought to restrict settlement to the St. Lawrence Valley, fearing that further expansion would render the empire impossible to defend. The impetus to move inland, however, could not be restrained. By the 1670s, French traders and missionaries had reached the Mississippi river. In 1681–82, Robert, Sieur de La Salle, followed the Mississippi to the Gulf of Mexico, claiming the entire valley (which he named Louisiana in honor of the king) for France. This expansion of French influence alarmed the English, who had founded colonies along the Atlantic seaboard and feared a growing French presence in the west.

Prosperous and expansive, if not completely manageable from Paris, Canada provided France with a secure foothold on the North American mainland. Its successful establishment contributed to an escalating European competition for land and trade in the New World.

THE DUTCH OVERSEAS EMPIRE

Small but densely populated, the Dutch Republic joined the scramble for empire in the early seventeenth century. The Northern Provinces, sometimes known as Holland, had in 1581 declared their independence from Spain. The new republic, dominated by Protestants, was intent on challenging Catholic Spain's power in the New World as well as the Old. More than any other factor, however, the desire for profit drove the Dutch quest for colonies.

THE DUTCH EAST INDIA COMPANY

The Dutch Republic served as a major center of world trade. Thousands of Dutch ships plied the world's oceans, and the republic's earnings from foreign trade may have surpassed those of the rest of Europe combined. This commercial vitality provided the context for overseas expansion.

The instrument of colonial dominance was the Dutch East India Company, founded in 1602 to challenge what had until then been a virtual Portuguese monopoly of Asian trade. Its first success was the capture of the Spice Islands (now Indonesia and East Timor), followed by the takeover of Batavia (Jakarta), Ceylon (Sri Lanka), and Sumatra. The Company established trading posts on the Gold Coast of West Africa, where it competed with the Portuguese in the slave trade, and at the Cape of Good Hope on Africa's southern tip. Its far-flung commercial net eventually encompassed parts of India and Formosa (Taiwan). These possessions sealed Dutch trading predominance for decades to come.

THE WEST INDIA COMPANY AND NEW NETHERLAND

The Dutch next set their sights on the Americas, creating the West India Company in 1621. Its claim to the Connecticut, Hudson, and Delaware valleys stemmed from the 1609 voyage of Henry Hudson, an Englishman sailing for

HOW DID conflict between the English and the Dutch affect Dutch colonization in the Americas?

The Hartgers View, the earliest known view of New Amsterdam as it appeared c. 1626–1628: colored line engraving, 1651.

The Granger Collection

Champlain's Fight with the Iroquois. This engraving from The Voyages of Samuel de Champlain (1613) is often attributed to Champlain himself, but the inaccuracies in the picture suggest that the artist was not present at the battle. The depiction of this fight in 1609 between Mohawks (right) and Champlain and his Indian allies (left) contains many errors: there are no palm trees on the shores of Lake Champlain, the Indians did not use hammocks, and the boats at the water's edge do not resemble canoes. Nevertheless, the picture does convey the deadly impact of firearms on warriors accustomed to fighting in ranks, using bows and arrows, and protected by wooden or wicker shields.

(National Archives of Canada, Ottawa, Ontario.).

the Dutch, who discovered the river that bears his name.

The first permanent Dutch settlers on mainland North America arrived in 1624 to set up a fur-trading post at Fort Orange (now Albany). Two years later, Peter Minuit and a company of Protestant refugees established New Amsterdam on Manhattan Island. The Hudson River corridor between these two settlements became the heart of the New Netherland colony. Like New France, its economic focus was the fur trade. Dutch merchants forged ties with the Iroquois, who exchanged furs for European tools and weapons.

In the 1630s, to help supply colonial traders, the West India Company offered large landed estates (called patroonships) to wealthy Dutchmen who would be responsible for populating them with tenant farmers. The plan never really worked, and at its peak, New Netherland's colonists only numbered about ten thousand.

What they lacked in numbers the colonists made up for in divisiveness. New Netherland became a magnet for religious refugees from Europe, as well as a destination for Africans acquired through the slave trade. Ethnic differences hindered a sense of community. Among the colony's Dutch, German, French, English, Swedish, Portuguese, and African settlers were Calvinists, Lutherans, Quakers, Catholics, Jews, and Muslims.

The West India Company, more interested in making money than keeping order, dispatched several inept but aggressive governors who provoked conflicts with Indians. Although the colonists generally maintained good relations with their Iroquois trading partners on the upper Hudson River, they had far less friendly dealings with the Algonquian peoples around New Amsterdam. In one particularly gruesome incident in 1645, Governor Willem Kieft ordered a massacre at an encampment of Indian refugees who had refused to pay him tribute. A horrified Dutch witness described Indian children being "thrown into the river, and when the fathers and mothers endeavored to save them, the soldiers would not let them come on land, but made both parents and children drown." Ten years later, Governor Peter Stuyvesant antagonized Susquehannock Indians along the Delaware River by seizing a small Swedish colony where the Susquehannocks had traded.

Such actions provoked retaliatory raids by the Indians, further weakening the colony. Though profitable, the fur trade did not generate the riches to be found in other parts of the Dutch empire. By the 1650s and 1660s, New Netherland increasingly looked like a poor investment to company officials in Europe.

ENGLISH SETTLEMENT IN THE CHESAPEAKE

HOW DID tobacco cultivation shape the development of Virginia society?

When the English again attempted to settle in America in 1607, they chose the lower Chesapeake Bay region. The new settlement, Jamestown, eventually developed into the prosperous colony of Virginia. The reason for Virginia's success was an American plant—tobacco—that commanded good prices from European consumers. Tobacco also underlay the economy of a neighboring colony, Maryland, and had a profound influence on the development of Chesapeake society.

THE ORDEAL OF EARLY VIRGINIA

In 1606, several English merchants, convinced that they could succeed where others had failed, petitioned King James I for a charter incorporating two companies, the *Virginia Company* and the *Plymouth Company,* to attempt New World settlement. James I issued a charter granting the companies two tracts of land along the mid-Atlantic coast. These **joint-stock companies** sold shares to investors (who expected a profit in return) to raise money for colonization.

The Jamestown colony. On a peninsula about 50 miles up a river they named the James in honor of their king, the colonists built a fortified settlement they called Jamestown (see Map 2–2). They immediately began hunting for gold and searching for the Northwest Passage to Asia. But Jamestown was no Mexico. All they found was disappointment and suffering. The swampy region was a perfect breeding area for malarial mosquitoes and parasites carrying other diseases. Spending all their time in search of riches, the settlers neglected to plant crops, and their food supplies dwindled. By January 1608, only thirty-eight colonists were still alive.

The colony's governing council turned to Captain John Smith for leadership. Just 28 years old, Smith had fought against Spain in the Netherlands and the Ottoman Turks in Hungary. He imposed military discipline on Jamestown, organizing settlers into work gangs and decreeing that "he that will not worke shall not eate." His highhanded methods revived the colony but antagonized certain settlers. When a gunpowder explosion wounded Smith in 1609 and forced him to return to England, his enemies had him replaced as leader.

Once again, the colony nearly disintegrated. New settlers arrived, only to starve or die of disease. Of the five hundred people in Jamestown in the autumn of 1609, just sixty remained alive by the spring of 1610—some of whom survived only by eating their dead companions. Facing financial ruin, company officials back in England tried to conceal the state of the colony. They reorganized the company twice and sent more settlers, including glassmakers, winegrowers, and silkmakers, in a desperate effort to find a marketable product. They experimented with harsh military discipline, instructing governors to enforce a legal code—the *Lawes Divine, Morall and Martiall*—that prescribed the death penalty for offenses as trivial as swearing or killing a chicken. When it became clear that such severity discouraged immigration, the company tried more positive inducements.

The first settlers had been expected to work in return for food and other necessities. But the surviving settlers wanted land, so governors began assigning small plots to those who finished their terms of service to the company. In 1616,

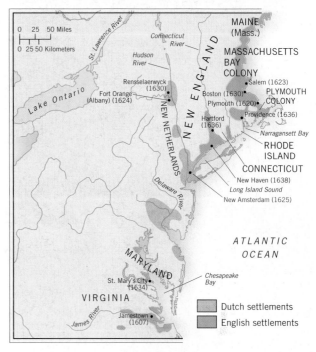

MAP EXPLORATION
To explore an interactive version of this map, go to
http://www.prenhall.com/goldfield3/map2.2

MAP 2–2 English and Dutch Mainland Colonies in North America, c. 1655   Early English colonies clustered in two areas of the Atlantic seaboard—New England and the Chesapeake Bay. Between them lay Dutch New Netherlands, with settlements stretching up the Hudson River. The Dutch also acquired territory at the mouth of the Delaware River in 1655 when they seized a short-lived Swedish colony located there.

ON THE BASIS of this map, what about the geographic location of Dutch colonies was ideal for Dutch colonists? What about their locations might have been problematic?

QUICK REVIEW

Powhatan, Indian Leader
- Chief of a confederacy of about thirty tribes.
- Besieged Jamestown when colonists began stealing corn.
- Father of Pocahontas.

Joint-stock company Business enterprise in which a group of stockholders pooled their money to engage in trade or to fund colonizing expeditions.

C Smith taketh the King of Pamavnkee prisoner 1608

This illustration shows John Smith seizing the scalplock of Opechancanough, Chief Powhatan's brother, during an English raid on an Indian village. Smith released his prisoner only after Indians ransomed him with corn. Thirteen years later, Opechancanough led a surprise attack against the colonists.

Courtesy of the Library of Congress

Headright system   Instituted by the Virginia Company in 1616, this system gave fifty acres to anyone who paid his own way to Virginia and an additional fifty for each person (or "head") he brought with him.

House of Burgesses   The legislature of colonial Virginia. First organized in 1619, it was the first institution of representative government in the English colonies.

the company instituted the **headright system,** giving 50 acres to anyone who paid his own way to Virginia and an additional 50 for each person (or "head") he brought with him.

In 1619, three other important developments occurred. That year, the company began transporting women to become wives for planters and induce them to stay in the colony. It was also the year in which the first Africans arrived in Virginia, and the company created the first legislative body in English America, the **House of Burgesses,** setting a precedent for the establishment of self-government in other English colonies. Landowners elected representatives to the House of Burgesses, which, subject to the approval of the company, made laws for Virginia.

The settlers were still unable to earn the company a profit. To make things worse, the headright system expanded English settlement beyond Jamestown, straining the already tense relations between the English and the Indians.

The English settlement was in the heart of territory ruled by the Indian leader Powhatan, who was then at the peak of his power and chief of a confederacy of about thirty tribes with some fourteen thousand people. After an initial skirmish with English soldiers, he sent gifts of food, assuming that by accepting the gifts, the colonists acknowledged their dependence on him. Further action against the settlers seemed unnecessary, because they seemed fully capable of destroying themselves.

However, armed colonists began seizing corn from Indian villages whenever native people refused to supply it. During one raid in 1609, John Smith held a pistol to the chest of Opechancanough, Powhatan's younger brother, until the Indians ransomed him with corn. Protesting that the English came "to invade my people and possess my Country," Powhatan besieged Jamestown and tried to starve the colony to extinction. The colony was saved by the arrival of reinforcements from England, but war with the Indians continued until 1614.

The marriage of the colonist John Rolfe to Pocahontas, Powhatan's daughter, helped seal the peace in 1614. Pocahontas had briefly been held captive by the English during the war and had been instructed in English manners and religion by Rolfe. Sent to negotiate with Powhatan in the spring of 1614, Rolfe asked the chief for his daughter's hand. Powhatan gave his consent, and Pocahontas—baptized in the Church of England and renamed Rebecca—became Rolfe's wife.

Powhatan died in 1618, and Opechancanough succeeded him as chief. Still harboring intense resentment against the English, the new chief made plans for retaliation. Pocahontas had died on a trip to England in 1617, severing the tie between her family and the English. Early in the morning on March 22, 1622, hundreds of Indian men traveled to the scattered English settlements, as if they meant to visit or trade. Instead, they attacked the unsuspecting colonists, killing 347 by the end of the day—more than one-fourth of the English population.

The English gathered to plot revenge. They struck at native villages, killing the inhabitants and burning cornfields. At peace talks held in April 1623, the English served poisoned wine to their enemies, killing two hundred more. During the ensuing nine years of war, the English treated the Indians with a ferocity that recalled their earlier subjugation of the Irish.

Economic activity ceased as settlers retreated to fortified garrisons. The company went bankrupt, and a royal commission investigating the 1622 attack was shocked to discover that nearly ten times more colonists had died from starvation and disease than at the hands of Indians. King James had little choice but to dissolve the company in 1624, and Virginia became a royal colony the following year. Now the king chose the colony's governor and council, and royal advisers monitored its affairs.

THE IMPORTANCE OF TOBACCO

In their search for a marketable product, settlers had begun growing tobacco after 1610. Initially expensive, it became popular among wealthy consumers. The first cargo of Virginia-grown tobacco arrived in England in 1617 and sold at a highly profitable 3 shillings per pound.

Settlers immediately planted tobacco everywhere—even in the streets of Jamestown. Company officials, unwilling to base the colony's economy on a single crop, tried to restrict annual production. After company rule ended, tobacco planting surged.

Between 1627 and 1669, annual tobacco exports climbed from 250,000 pounds to more than 15 million pounds. As the supply grew, the price per pound plunged from 13 pence in 1624 to a mere penny in the late 1660s, where it remained for the next half-century. The only way colonists could compensate for falling prices was to grow even more, pushing exports to England to more than 20 million pounds per year by the late 1670s.

Tobacco shaped nearly every aspect of Virginia society, from patterns of settlement to the recruitment of colonists. Planters scrambled to claim lands near navigable rivers so that ships could easily reach their plantations and carry their crops to market. As a result, the colonists dispersed into plantations located along waterways. Colonists competed to produce the biggest and best crop and get it to market the fastest, hoping to enjoy even a small price advantage over everyone else.

Tobacco kept workers busy nine months of the year. Planters sowed seeds in the early spring, transplanted seedlings a few weeks later, and spent the summer pinching off the tops of the plants (to produce larger leaves) and removing worms. After the harvest, the leaves were "cured"—dried in ventilated sheds—and packed in large barrels. During the winter, planters cleared and fenced more land and made barrels for next year's crop. Working on his own, one planter could tend two thousand plants, which yielded about 500 pounds of cured tobacco.

The planters turned to England, importing thousands of indentured servants, or contract workers, who (like Richard Frethorne) agreed to a fixed term of labor, usually four to seven years, in exchange for free passage to Virginia. The master provided food, shelter, clothing, and, at the end of the term of service, "freedom dues" paid in corn and clothing. Between 1625 and 1640, an estimated one thousand or more indentured servants arrived each year. Some were orphans; others were condemned criminals given a choice between execution and transportation to Virginia. Most, however, came from the ranks of England's unemployed, who emigrated in hopes of "bettering their condition in a Growing Country."

Most found such hopes quickly dashed. Servants died in alarming numbers from disease, and those who survived faced years of backbreaking labor. Richard

Price punished his servant for pretending to be ill and trying to run away by beating him so severely that the young man died. A jury refused to charge Price with murder, reasoning that the servant deserved punishment and Price had not intended to kill him. The courts (administered by masters) usually favored masters' authority over servants' rights. For every ex-servant who became a landholder, dozens died in poverty. Many ex-servants found land only in places less suitable for tobacco cultivation and more vulnerable to Indian attack.

MARYLAND: A REFUGE FOR CATHOLICS

Encouraged by Virginia's success, in 1632 King Charles I granted 10 million acres of land north of the bay to the nobleman George Calvert, Lord Baltimore. Unlike Virginia, which was founded by a joint-stock company, Maryland was a **proprietary colony**—the sole possession of Calvert and his heirs. They owned all the land, which they could divide up as they pleased, and had the right to set up the colony's government.

Calvert, who was Catholic, intended Maryland to be a refuge for others of his faith. English Catholics were a disadvantaged minority. They paid double taxes and could not worship in public or hold political office. In Maryland, Calvert wanted Catholic colonists to enjoy economic and political power. He intended to divide the land into manors—large private estates like those of medieval England—and distribute them to wealthy Catholic friends. These manorial lords would live on rents collected from tenant farmers, hold the most important governmental offices, and run their own law courts.

Calvert died before settlement began, and his plans unraveled. The majority of colonists, who began arriving in 1634, were Protestants who despised Catholics. Refusing to live as tenants on Catholic estates, they claimed land of their own—a process that accelerated after 1640, when Maryland adopted a headright system like Virginia's as a way to recruit settlers.

Maryland's problems intensified when civil war broke out in England in 1642. For years, political and religious disputes had divided the nation. Charles I, who became king in 1625, clashed with the **Puritans,** who called for further reform of the Church of England. He also antagonized many government leaders by dissolving Parliament in 1629 and ruling on his own for eleven years. Needing funds to suppress a rebellion in Scotland in 1640, however, Charles was forced to recall Parliament, which quickly turned against him. Both king and Parliament recruited armies and went to war in 1642. The parliamentary forces triumphed, and in 1649, they executed Charles. For the next decade, Oliver Cromwell, a Puritan general, ruled until his death in 1658. His son, Richard, proved an inept successor, and in 1660 a group of army officers invited Charles's exiled son to accept the throne.

During the 1640s and 1650s, Maryland Protestants took advantage of the upheaval in England to contest the Calverts' control of the colony. To pacify them, Calvert's son Cecilius established a legislature, assuming that Protestants would dominate the elective lower house while he could appoint Catholics to the upper house. In 1649, Calvert also approved the **Act for Religious Toleration,** the first law in America to call for freedom of worship for all Christians, but the Protestant majority continued to resist Catholic political influence, at one point passing a law that prohibited Catholics from voting.

Instead of the peaceful Catholic refuge Calvert had intended, Maryland soon resembled neighboring Virginia. Its settlers raised tobacco and imported

WHERE TO LEARN MORE

St. Mary's City, Maryland
www.somd.com

Proprietary Colony A colony created when the English monarch granted a huge tract of land to an individual or group of individuals, who became "lords proprietor."

Puritans Individuals who believed that Queen Elizabeth's reforms of the Church of England had not gone far enough in improving the church. Puritans led the settlement of Massachusetts Bay Colony.

Act for Religious Toleration The first law in America to call for freedom of worship for all Christians.

as many indentured servants as possible. Because Maryland initially provided freed servants with 50 acres of land, more became landholders than in Virginia. As in Virginia, however, economic opportunity diminished after 1660 when the price of tobacco dropped. Maryland's settlers enjoyed more peaceful relations with the Indians than the Virginians had, but they fought intensely among themselves.

LIFE IN THE CHESAPEAKE COLONIES

Because of their labor needs, masters preferred to recruit young men in their teens and twenties as indentured servants, importing three or four times as many of them as women. As a result, the populations of Virginia and Maryland were overwhelmingly young and male. Even as late as 1700, Virginia had three English men for every two women. As a consequence of this gender imbalance, many male ex-servants found that marriage was as remote a possibility as landownership. While few unmarried women failed to find husbands, and widows usually remarried soon after their spouses' deaths, their lives were hardly easy.

Malaria and other diseases inflicted hardship on nearly everyone. Few colonists lived past 50, and women's susceptibility to disease during pregnancy meant that many of them barely made it to 40. Such high mortality, combined with late marriages (because servants could not wed until their terms were up), limited the size of families and thus slowed population growth.

Under such conditions, the only way the populations of the Chesapeake colonies could grow during most of the seventeenth century was through continued heavy importation of servants. The number of English settlers rose from about 8,000 in 1640 to 24,000 in 1660.

These conditions hindered colonists from reproducing customary patterns of family life. The frequency of early death produced unusual households, containing various combinations of step-parents and children from different marriages living under the same roof. Many women would be widows at some point in their lives, which gave them temporary control over the family property. Few women received land outright, and if widows remarried, their new spouses usually took control of the estates left by their first husbands. As in England itself, the Chesapeake colonies accorded women little formal authority within society.

The precariousness of life encouraged settlers to invest every penny of profit in land and labor, postponing investment in goods that would bring a more comfortable existence. Early houses were often no larger than 16 by 20 feet, with one or two rooms. Nearly everyone subsisted on a rude diet of pork and corn.

Rough as these conditions were, they far surpassed the circumstances of most native peoples in the Chesapeake. The English population may have been growing slowly, but it still overwhelmed the Indian population, which increasingly suffered high mortality from European diseases. By 1685, there were more than ten colonists for every Indian living in eastern Virginia. By that point, many Native Americans in the Chesapeake had retreated to their own towns, keeping their distance from the colonists in hopes of preserving control over dwindling lands and maintaining a measure of independence from English domination.

THE FOUNDING OF NEW ENGLAND

*T*he first English attempt to settle the northeastern coast of North America was a miserable failure. In 1607, the Plymouth Company sent two ships with 120 Englishmen to found a colony in present-day Maine. The

WHY WERE the English colonies in New England so different from those in the Chesapeake?

colonists alienated the Abenaki Indians who lived there, suffered through a harsh winter, and abandoned their settlement the next summer. However, it was not long before the English renewed their efforts to settle New England.

Six colonies appeared in the region between 1620 and 1640, settled by thousands of people troubled by religious, political, and economic upheavals in England. Between 1616 and 1618, a terrible epidemic swept through coastal New England, killing up to 90 percent of the Indians living there. The devastated survivors were struggling to cope with the consequences of this disaster just as the colonists began to arrive.

THE PILGRIMS AND PLYMOUTH COLONY

Plymouth Colony, the first of the New England settlements, was founded in 1620. Its origins lay in religious disputes that had plagued England since the late sixteenth century. Most of Queen Elizabeth's subjects approved of her efforts to keep England a Protestant nation, but some believed that she had not rid the Church of England of all Catholic practices. The enemies of these reformers, ridiculing them for wanting to purify the Church of England (or **Anglican** Church) of all corruption, called them Puritans.

Following the doctrine of predestination taught by John Calvin and other Protestant reformers, English Puritans believed in an all-powerful God who, at the moment of Creation, determined which humans would be saved and which would be damned. The centerpiece of their spiritual life was conversion: the transforming experience that occurred when individuals felt the stirrings of grace in their souls and began to hope that they were among the saved. Those who experienced conversion were considered saints and acquired new strength to live godly lives.

Puritans rejected the Book of Common Prayer, which regulated Anglican worship, insisting that ministers should pray from the heart and preach from the Bible. They objected when Anglican clergy wore rich vestments that set them apart from ordinary Christians. And they objected to any church organization above the level of the individual congregation, seeing no need for bishops and archbishops. But what they hated most about the Anglican Church was that anyone could be a member. Puritans believed that everyone should attend church services, but they wanted church membership, which conferred the right to partake in the Lord's Supper, or communion, to be limited to saints.

Elizabeth and the rulers who followed her—who as monarchs were the "supreme heads" of the Church of England—disagreed with the Puritans and tried to silence them. Some Puritans, known as **separatists,** were convinced that the Church of England would never change and left it to form their own congregations.

One such group, mainly artisans and middling farmers from the village of Scrooby, in Nottinghamshire, left England in 1607–1608 for Holland, where they stayed for more than a decade. Although they could worship in peace there, many had to struggle to make a living and feared that their children were being tempted by the worldly pleasures of Dutch city life. Some Scrooby separatists gained the backing of the Plymouth Company for a move to America. Called **Pilgrims** because they thought of themselves as spiritual wanderers, they were joined by other separatists and by nonseparatist "strangers" hired to help get the colony started. In all, 102 men, women, and children set sail on the *Mayflower* in September 1620.

After a long and miserable voyage, they landed near Massachusetts Bay. Because this was about 200 miles north of the land their charter permitted them to settle, some of the "strangers" claimed that they were no longer legally bound to obey the expedition's separatist leaders. The leaders responded by drafting the

Anglican Of or belonging to the Church of England, a Protestant denomination.

Separatists Members of an offshoot branch of Puritanism. Separatists believed that the Church of England was too corrupt to be reformed and hence were convinced they must "separate" from it to save their souls.

Pilgrims Settlers of Plymouth Colony, who viewed themselves as spiritual wanderers.

Mayflower Compact, a document that bound all signers to abide by the decisions of the majority.

The Pilgrims settled at Plymouth, the site of a Wampanoag village recently depopulated by disease, where they found abandoned cornfields, Indian graves, and baskets of corn buried underground. Even with this corn, nearly half of the Pilgrims died of starvation and disease that first winter.

Two natives, Squanto and Samoset, emerged from the woods the next spring and approached the Pilgrims on behalf of Massasoit, the Wampanoag leader. The Wampanoags thought the Pilgrims might be useful allies against their enemies, the Narragansetts, who had escaped the recent epidemics.

In 1621, the Wampanoags and the Pilgrims signed a treaty of alliance. The Pilgrims assumed that Massasoit had submitted to the superior authority of King James, whereas Massasoit assumed that he and the English king were equal partners. Until his death in 1622, Squanto offered advice to each side, hoping to achieve honor and influence as a mediator. Economic ties strengthened the alliance. The Indians taught the English how to plant corn and traded corn with them for manufactured goods. The Pilgrims also exchanged corn with northern Indians for furs, which they shipped back to England to help pay off their debts to English investors. In the autumn of 1621, Indians and Pilgrims gathered for a feast celebrating the settlers' first harvest—an event Americans still commemorate as the first Thanksgiving.

Plymouth remained small, poor, and weak, never exceeding about seven thousand settlers and never producing more than small shipments of furs, fish, and timber to sell in England. It took the Pilgrims more than twenty years to repay their English creditors. After 1630, the first New England colony was overshadowed by a new and more powerful neighbor, Massachusetts Bay.

MASSACHUSETTS BAY COLONY AND ITS OFFSHOOTS

The Puritans who founded Massachusetts shared many beliefs with the Pilgrims of Plymouth Colony, but they insisted that the Anglican Church could be reformed and so were not separatists. They went to New England, to create godly churches to serve as models for English reform.

Charles I, who became king in 1625, opposed the Puritans more forcefully than his father had and supported changes in Anglican worship that recalled Catholic practices. England at the time also suffered from economic troubles—including crop failures and a depression in the wool industry—that many Puritans saw as signs of God's displeasure with their country.

In 1629, a group of Puritan merchants and gentlemen received a royal charter for a joint-stock enterprise, the Massachusetts Bay Company, to set up a colony north of Plymouth. John Winthrop, a prosperous lawyer, was selected as the colony's governor. In the spring of 1630, a fleet of eleven ships carried about a thousand men, women, and children across the Atlantic.

Before Winthrop's ship landed, he preached a lay sermon, called "A Model of Christian Charity," to his fellow passengers, reminding them of their goal "to do more service to

WHERE TO LEARN MORE

★ Plimoth Plantation, Plymouth, Massachusetts **pilgrims.net/ plimothplantation/vtour**.

John Winthrop (1588–1649) served as the Massachusetts Bay Colony's governor for most of its first two decades. Throughout his life, Winthrop—like many fellow Puritans—struggled to live a godly life in a corrupt world.

Courtesy American Antiquarian Society.

the Lord" by placing the good of all above private ambitions. Winthrop argued that the Lord had made them his chosen people and that, as a result, "we shall be as a city upon a hill, the eyes of all people are upon us." If they failed to live up to God's expectations, the spectacle of their failure would allow their enemies "to speak evil of the ways of God." With this mingled encouragement and threat ringing in their ears, the emigrants soon landed and founded Boston and six adjoining towns.

Stability, Conformity, and Intolerance. Winthrop described the settlers' mission in New England as a **covenant,** or contract, with God, binding them to meet their religious obligations in return for God's favor. The settlers also created covenants when they founded towns and churches, agreeing to live together in peace.

The desire for peace and purity could breed intolerance. Settlers scrutinized their neighbors for signs of unacceptable behavior. But the insistence on covenants and conformity also created a remarkably stable society, far more peaceable than Virginia's.

That stability was enhanced by the development of representative government. The General Court, which initially included only the shareholders of the joint-stock company, was transformed into a two-house legislature. Freemen—adult males who held property and were church members—could elect representatives to the lower house, as well as eighteen members (called "assistants") to the upper house. They also chose a governor and a deputy governor.

The Connecticut Valley and the Pequot War. At least thirteen thousand settlers came to New England between 1630 and 1642, when the outbreak of the English Civil War halted emigration. The progress of settlement was generally untroubled in coastal Massachusetts, but when colonists moved into the Connecticut River Valley, tensions with Indians grew rapidly. These erupted in 1637 in the brief, tragic conflict called the **Pequot War.**

English settlers from Massachusetts first arrived in the Connecticut Valley in the mid-1630s. For several years, the Pequot Indians had used their partnership with nearby Dutch traders to monopolize the trade in European goods and exert dominance over their native neighbors. In 1633, however, the Dutch invited the Pequots' rivals to trade. The Pequots, suffering terribly from a recent smallpox epidemic, resented losing their special trading rights and approached Massachusetts Bay as an ally against the Dutch. But when English settlers demanded that the Pequots submit to English authority as the price of an alliance, the Pequots turned against them too.

The English settlers allied with the Pequots' enemies, the Narragansetts and Mohegans. In May 1637, English forces surrounded a Pequot village inhabited mainly by women and children, located on the Mystic River. They set it ablaze and shot anyone who tried to escape. Between three hundred and seven hundred Pequots died, a toll that shocked the settlers' Indian allies, who protested that English-style warfare was "too furious, and slays too many men" (see "American Views: Miantonomo's Plea for Indian Unity").

After the surviving Pequots had fled or been sold into slavery, more settlers moved to Connecticut, which soon declared itself a separate colony. In 1639, the settlers adopted the Fundamental Orders, creating a government similar to that of Massachusetts, and the English government granted them a royal charter in 1662.

Roger Williams and the founding of Rhode Island. Massachusetts spun off other colonies as its population expanded in the 1630s and dissenters ran afoul of its intolerant government. Puritan leaders tried to suppress unorthodox reli-

Covenant A contract with God, binding settlers to meet their religious obligations in return for God's favor.

Pequot War Conflict between English settlers and Pequot Indians over control of land and trade in eastern Connecticut.

AMERICAN VIEWS

MIANTONOMO'S PLEA FOR INDIAN UNITY (1642)

*U*ntil European colonization began to force a change in outlook, the native inhabitants of North America never thought of themselves as one people, any more than Europe's residents considered themselves "Europeans." Miantonomo, a Narragansett living in Rhode Island, was one of the first native leaders to call for a unified response to English intrusion. With the gruesome lessons of the Pequot War fresh in his mind, he urged the Montauks of Long Island to put aside their differences with the Narragansetts and join them in opposing the settlers. His appeal, recorded by Lion Gardiner, an English officer during the Pequot War, was uttered in vain. Captured by the English and tried and convicted of the murder of an Indian, Miantonomo was turned over to a Mohegan rival for execution.

- How did Miantonomo describe Indian life before the arrival of the English?
- What changes occurred as a result of their settlement?

Brothers, we must be as one as the English are, or we shall all be destroyed. You know our fathers had plenty of deer and skins and our plains were full of game and turkeys, and our coves and rivers were full of fish.

But, brothers, since these Englishmen have seized our country, they have cut down the grass with scythes, and the trees with axes. Their cows and horses eat up the grass, and their hogs spoil our bed of clams; and finally we shall all starve to death; therefore, stand not in your own light, I ask you, but resolve to act like men. All the sachems both to the east and the west have joined with us, and we are resolved to fall upon them at a day appointed, and therefore I come secretly to you, [be]cause you can persuade your Indians to do what you will.

Source: Steven Mintz, ed., *Native American Voices: A History and Anthology* (1995), pp. 84–85. Reprinted with permission of Brandywine Press.

gious opinions whenever they emerged. Some dissenting colonists, however, refused to conform. Roger Williams, who founded Rhode Island, was one such irrepressible dissenter. Williams was a separatist minister who declared that because the Massachusetts churches had not rejected the Church of England, they shared its corruption. He argued for the separation of church and state, and also attacked the Massachusetts charter, insisting that the king had no right to grant Indian lands to English settlers.

Williams was an immensely likable man; even Governor Winthrop remained on friendly terms with him, but the General Court banished him, intending to ship him back to England. But in the winter of 1635, Williams slipped away with a few followers and found refuge among the Narragansett Indians, from whom he purchased land for the village of Providence, founded in 1636. More towns soon sprang up nearby when a new religious challenge sent additional refugees to Rhode Island from Massachusetts.

Anne Hutchinson's Challenge to the Bay Colony.   Anne Hutchinson arrived in Boston from England with her husband and seven children in 1634. Welcomed by the town's women for her talents as a midwife, she also began to hold religious meetings in her house, where she denounced several ministers.

Many people, including prominent Boston merchants, flocked to Hutchinson's meetings. But her critics believed her to be a dangerous antinomian (someone who claimed to be free from obedience to moral law), because she seemed

2–7
The Trial of Anne
Hutchinson (1638)

QUICK REVIEW

Anne Hutchinson
- Arrived in Boston with her family in 1634.
- Began to hold religious meetings in her house.
- Found guilty of sedition and banished from Massachussetts.

---

to maintain that saints were accountable only to God and not to any worldly authority. Her opponents also objected to her teaching of mixed groups of men and women, a breach of normal gender roles. Colony magistrates arrested her and tried her for sedition—that is, for advocating the overthrow of the government.

During her trial, Hutchinson mounted a lively defense. In the end, however, the court found her guilty and banished her from the colony. With many of her followers, she moved to Rhode Island, where Roger Williams had proclaimed a policy of religious toleration.

At the height of the Hutchinson controversy, a group of zealous Puritan emigrants led by the Reverend John Davenport departed Boston to found New Haven in 1638. Davenport's efforts to impose Puritan conformity in his colony made Massachusetts seem easygoing in comparison. But New Haven failed to thrive, and in 1662, the poor, intolerant, and isolated colony was absorbed into Connecticut.

FAMILIES, FARMS, AND COMMUNITIES IN EARLY NEW ENGLAND

"This plantation and that of Virginia went not forth upon the same reasons," declared one of Massachusetts's founders. Virginians came "for profit," whereas New Englanders emigrated to bear witness to their Puritan faith. Unlike the unmarried young men who moved in great numbers to Virginia, most New Englanders settled with their families.

Even though emigration from England slowed to a trickle after 1642, New England's population continued to grow. With a more balanced sex ratio (about three men to two women) than there was in the early Chesapeake, marriage and childbearing were more common. Families frequently had seven or eight children, compared to the two or three offspring typical of Chesapeake families.

New Englanders were also largely spared from the diseases that ravaged the Chesapeake settlers. Most children survived to reach adulthood and form families of their own. Long-lived parents exercised considerable control over their children's lives. This was especially true for sons, who could not marry until their fathers provided them with sufficient land to support a family. Because fathers depended on their sons for labor, they often postponed granting them the means to economic independence until they were 26 or 27. Daughters, too, contributed their labor to the household economy, but generally married between the ages of 21 and 23. They also depended on the willingness of their fathers to supply them with a dowry (usually livestock and household goods) to bring to their new homes.

Women in Early New England. In New England, as in other colonies and England itself, women were assumed to be legally and economically dependent on the men in their families. Since fewer New England marriages were shortened by the early death of a spouse, fewer New England women experienced widowhood, the one time in their lives when they might enjoy legal independence and exercise control over property.

Women's economic contributions were indeed central to the family's success. In addition to raising the children, women performed essential domestic tasks, including cooking, sewing, gardening, and cleaning. Many engaged in household production and traded the fruits of their labor with other families.

Community and Economic Life. Unlike Chesapeake colonists, who tended to disperse into separate plantations, New Englanders clustered into communities that might contain fifty or a hundred families. The Massachusetts government strongly encouraged town formation by granting tracts of land to groups of families who promised to settle together. The families divided the land among themselves, allotting each family a farm of sufficient size to support its members. People who had higher standing in England received larger farms than those of lower status. Land that the original families could not yet use was held "in common" to be distributed to their children as they grew up. Once they found a town they liked, families tended to stay in place.

At the center of each town stood the meetinghouse, used for both religious and secular purposes. The importance Puritans placed on worship with fellow Christians helped promote communal feeling. At other times, the meetinghouse served as a town hall, where men assembled to discuss matters ranging from local taxes to making sure everyone's fences were mended. Massachusetts law required towns with at least fifty families to support a school (so children could learn to read the Bible). Townsmen tried, not always successfully, to reach decisions by consensus. To oversee day-to-day local affairs, they chose five to seven trusted neighbors to serve as selectmen. Each town could also elect two men to represent it in the colony legislature. New England's stony soil and short growing season offered few ways to get rich, but most people achieved a modest prosperity. They grew corn and other foods and raised livestock to feed their families, selling or trading what they could not use. Without the income generated by a staple crop like tobacco, New England farmers lacked adequate resources to hire large numbers of indentured servants and so relied on family members. Even children as young as five or six contributed their labor to the household economy.

New Englanders regularly traded goods and services with their neighbors. A skilled carpenter might erect a house—usually larger and sturdier than the ramshackle dwellings of Chesapeake settlers—in return for barrels of salted beef. Men with several sons sent them to help neighbors whose children were too young to work. Midwives delivered babies in return for cheese or eggs. Women nursed sick neighbors, whom they might one day call on for similar help.

New England prospered by exploiting a variety of resources, developing a diversified economy that was less vulnerable to depression than Virginia's. Farmers sent livestock and meat to merchants to be marketed abroad. Fishermen caught thousands of pounds of fish to be sold in Europe. New Englanders became such skilled shipbuilders and seafaring merchants that by the 1670s, London merchants were complaining about competition from them. England itself had little use for the products that New England vessels carried, but enterprising merchants found exactly the market they needed in the West Indies.

COMPETITION IN THE CARIBBEAN

*T*he Spanish claimed all the Caribbean islands by right of Columbus's discovery, but during the seventeenth century, French, Dutch, and English adventurers defied them. The French obtained Guadaloupe, Martinique, St. Lucia, St. Vincent, and smaller outposts in the Leeward and Windward Islands. Aruba, Curaçao, St. Martin, Saba, and St. Eustatius became Dutch possessions. England's share of the West Indies included Antigua, Barbados, Montserrat, Nevis, and St. Christopher; in 1655, the English wrested Jamaica from Spain. The West Indies soon became the jewel of England's American empire.

Europeans competed for these islands at first in the hope that they would yield precious metals and provide bases for privateering expeditions. It eventually became clear that the islands would produce treasure of another sort—sugar. In order to reap the enormous profits that sugar could bring, Caribbean planters imported

QUICK REVIEW

Childhood in New England
- Children went to work shortly after their fifth birthday.
- Around age 10 children began doing more complex work.
- Many early teens performed work similar to that of adults.

WHAT WAS the connection between sugar cultivation and slavery in the Caribbean?

enormous numbers of African people to work as slaves under the harshest conditions to be found in the New World.

SUGAR AND SLAVES

The first English colonists who came to the West Indies in the 1620s and 1630s raised tobacco and imported indentured servants to work their fields. By that time, however, tobacco prices were dropping. Moreover, the disease environment of the West Indies proved even harsher than that of the Chesapeake, and settlers died in great numbers.

But by the 1640s, a Barbados planter boasted of "a great change on this island of late from the worse to the better, praised be God." That change was a shift from tobacco to sugar cane. Many English sugar planters grew astonishingly wealthy. In 1646, a 500-acre plantation on Barbados sold for £16,000—more than the whole island had been worth just a few years before. On average, a Caribbean sugar plantation was worth four times as much as a prosperous Chesapeake plantation.

African slaves working at a sugar mill in the West Indies, probably on a Dutch-owned island: line engraving, 17th century.

The Granger Collection, New York

Sugar rapidly transformed the West Indies. Planters deforested whole islands to raise sugar cane. They stopped planting food crops and raising livestock—thereby creating a demand for lumber and provisions that boosted New England's economy.

For some years after the transition to sugar, English planters continued to import white indentured servants, including some kidnapped English and Irish youths, and supplemented the labor force with African slaves. They eventually grew dissatisfied with this labor force. Due to the islands' unhealthy environment and extremely harsh working conditions, servants died in great numbers. The English switched to African laborers, whom they considered better suited to agricultural work in a tropical climate. The planters' choice has been called an "unthinking decision," but it had an enormous impact on English colonial life, first in the islands and then on the mainland.

A BIRACIAL SOCIETY

The English West Indies developed a biracial plantation society—the first in the English colonial world. By 1700, more than 250,000 slaves had been brought to the English islands, and they soon constituted a majority of the population. Slaves lived in wretched conditions, underfed, poorly dressed, and housed in rough huts. They labored six days a week from sunrise to sunset—except at harvest time, when they toiled seven days a week in round-the-clock shifts. Masters considered them property, often branding them like livestock and hunting them with bloodhounds when they ran away.

Laws, sometimes called **slave codes,** declared slavery to be a lifelong condition that passed from slave parents to their children. Slaves had no legal rights and

Slave Codes   A series of laws passed mainly in the southern colonies in the late seventeenth and early eighteenth centuries to define the status of slaves and codify the denial of basic civil rights to them.

were under the complete control of their masters. Only rarely would masters who killed slaves face prosecution, and those who did and were found guilty were subject only to fines. Slaves, in contrast, could be whipped, branded, or maimed for stealing food or harboring a runaway compatriot. Serious crimes such as murder or arson brought execution without trial. Slaves who rebelled were burned to death.

When masters began to import African women as well as men—hoping to create a self-reproducing labor force—slaves formed families and preserved at least some African traditions. They gave their children African names (although masters often gave them English names as well). They celebrated with African music and worked to the rhythm of familiar songs. And they drew on their West African heritage to perform elaborate funeral rituals, often burying their dead with food and other goods to accompany them on the journey to the afterlife.

Some planters, profiting handsomely from their slaves' toil, lived better than many English gentlemen. They indulged in large houses, fine furnishings, and expensive clothing. But sugar production required a heavy investment in land, slaves, mills, and equipment. As great planters took vast amounts of land for themselves, freed servants and small farmers struggled to survive. After 1650, many of these poor men, looking for other places to live, headed for the mainland. They were joined by planters looking for a place to expand their operations once most of the good land on the islands had been brought under cultivation.

THE RESTORATION COLONIES

The initial burst of English colonization ended in 1640 when England tottered on the brink of civil war. With the restoration of Charles II to the throne in 1660, however, interest in North America revived. Charles II rewarded the supporters who had remained loyal to him during his long exile in France with huge grants of American land. Four new colonies—Carolina, Pennsylvania, New Jersey, and New York—resulted from such grants (see Map 2–3). All were proprietary colonies, essentially the private property of the people to whom they had been given. Carolina and Pennsylvania, like the earlier proprietary colony of Maryland, provided their owners the chance to test idealistic social visions. The origins of New York and New Jersey as English colonies, by contrast, lay not in visions of social harmony but in the stern reality of military conquest (see the Overview table, "English Colonies in the Seventeenth Century").

EARLY CAROLINA: COLONIAL ARISTOCRACY AND SLAVE LABOR

In 1663, Charles II granted a group of supporters an enormous tract of land stretching from southern Virginia to northern Florida. The proprietors, who included several Barbados planters, called their colony Carolina, after *Carolus,* the Latin form of the king's name. They envisioned it as growing into a prosperous, orderly society. One of the proprietors, Anthony Ashley Cooper, working closely with his secretary, John Locke, devised the **Fundamental Constitutions of Carolina,** a plan to ensure the colony's stability by balancing property ownership and political rights with a hierarchical social order. It called for the creation of a colonial aristocracy, who would own two-fifths of the land and wield extensive political power. Below them, a large class of freeholders would own small farms and elect representatives to an assembly. At the bottom of the social order would be slaves. This plan never went into effect. People moved in from Virginia and the West

QUICK REVIEW

Slave Codes

- Slavery was a lifelong condition that passed from parents to children
- Slaves had no legal rights
- Masters were all but exempt from prosecution for mistreatment of slaves
- Slaves were subject to punishment at the discretion of masters

WHY DID colonists in the Carolinas adopt harsh slave codes?

Fundamental Constitutions of Carolina   A complex plan for organizing the colony of Carolina, drafted in 1669 by Anthony Ashley Cooper and John Locke.

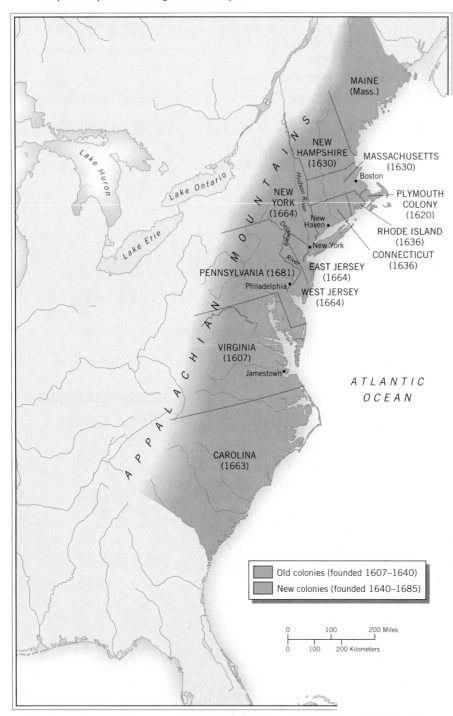

MAP 2–3   English North American Colonies, c. 1685   After the restoration of Charles II in 1660, several large proprietary colonies joined earlier English settlements in New England and the Chesapeake. By 1685, a growing number of English settlers solidified England's claim to the Atlantic coast from Maine (then part of Massachusetts Bay Colony) to the southern edge of Carolina.

EXPLAIN WHY, on the basis of this map, England had such an early stronghold on North America? Why was it difficult by the mid-1680s for other European countries to establish colonies in the New World?

Indies and settled where they pleased. They even voted in the assembly to reject the Fundamental Constitutions. They antagonized the local Indians, who numbered perhaps fifteen thousand when settlers first arrived.

The colonists at first raised livestock to be sold to the West Indies. But the introduction of rice in the 1690s transformed the settlers' economy, making it, as one planter noted, "as much their staple Commodity, as Sugar is to Barbados and Jamaica, or Tobacco to Virginia and Maryland." Rice cultivation in Carolina coincided with an increase in the number of African slaves there, who probably introduced the crop. Ironically, the profits earned from rice persuaded Carolina planters to invest even more heavily in slave labor.

By 1708, there were more black slaves than white settlers in the colony, and two decades after that, black people outnumbered white people by two to one. Rice farming required a substantial investment in land, labor, and equipment, including dikes and dams for flooding fields. Those who could afford such an investment set themselves up as planters in Carolina's coastal rice district, acquiring large estates and forcing poorer settlers to move elsewhere.

Some of these dislocated settlers went to the northern part of Carolina, where the land and climate were unsuited to rice. There they raised tobacco and livestock, and produced pitch, tar, and timber products from the region's pine forests. So different were the two regions that the colony formally split into two provinces—North and South Carolina—in 1729.

Thomas Coram's oil painting (c. 1770) shows the main residence and slave quarters on the Mulberry Plantation near Charleston, South Carolina. The distinctive steep-roofed design of the slave cabins on the left probably reflects African building styles. Slave quarters may not have been located quite as close to the main house as this picture suggests.

Thomas Coram, "View of Mulberry Street, House and Street." Oil on paper, 10 x 17.6 cm, Gibbes Museum of Art/Carolina Art Association. 68.18.01

No colonial proprietor was more idealistic than William Penn, shown here in a
portrait made in about 1698 by Francis
Place. Penn wanted Pennsylvania to be
a place of peace, prosperity, and religious toleration—especially for his
fellow Quakers. The colony eventually
became an economic success but
failed to achieve the social harmony
that Penn had wanted.

AP/Wide World Photos.

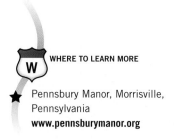

WHERE TO LEARN MORE

★ Pennsbury Manor, Morrisville,
Pennsylvania
www.pennsburymanor.org

Quakers Members of the Society of Friends, a radical religious
group that arose in the mid-seventeenth century. Quakers rejected
formal theology, focusing instead
on the Holy Spirit that dwelt within them.

Frame of Government William
Penn's constitution for Pennsylvania which included a provision allowing for religious freedom.

South Carolina rice planters became some of the wealthiest colonists on the
mainland. But their luxurious style of life came at a price. As Carolina began to
look "more like a negro country than like a country settled by white people,"
planters dreaded the prospect of slave rebellion. To avert this nightmare, they enacted slave codes as harsh as those of the sugar islands.

Carolina would not be a harmonious colony that balanced wealth and power.
It evolved instead into a racially divided society founded on the oppression of a
black majority and permeated by fear.

PENNSYLVANIA: THE DREAM OF TOLERATION AND PEACE

William Penn put his own utopia plans into action in 1681, when Charles II granted
him a huge tract of land north of Maryland. Penn intended his colony to be a
model of justice and peace, as well as a refuge for members of the Society of
Friends, or **Quakers,** a persecuted religious sect to which Penn belonged.

Like the separatists, Quakers abandoned the Church of England as hopelessly corrupt. But they went even further in their beliefs. Rejecting predestination,
they maintained that every soul had a spark of grace and that salvation was possible for all who heeded that "Inner Light." They rejected trained clergy and
church rituals. Instead of formal religious services, Quakers held meetings at which
silence reigned until someone, inspired by the Inner Light, rose to speak.

Quaker beliefs had disturbing social and political implications. Quakers
granted women spiritual equality with men, allowing them to preach, hold separate
prayer meetings, and exercise authority over "women's matters." Arguing that social distinctions were not the work of God, Quakers refused to remove their hats
in the presence of social superiors. And instead of the formal *you,* Quakers addressed superiors with the informal *thee* and *thou.* Because their faith required them
to renounce the use of force, Quakers also refused to perform military service.

When English authorities began harassing Quakers, William Penn, who was
himself jailed briefly, conceived his plan for a New World "holy experiment," a
harmonious society governed by brotherly love. Using his father's connection with
the king, he acquired the land that became Pennsylvania ("Penn's Woods") and
recruited settlers from among Europe's oppressed peoples and persecuted religious sects. By 1700, eighteen thousand emigrants had left England, Wales, Scotland, Ireland, and various German provinces for the new colony.

Many came in families and settled in an area occupied by the Delaware Indians, whose numbers, though still substantial, had recently been reduced by disease and warfare. The "holy experiment" required colonists to live "as Neighbours
and friends" with the Indians as well as with one another. Penn aimed to accomplish this by paying Indians for land and regulating trade. As long as he controlled
the colony, relations between the settlers and the Indians were generally peaceful—
so much so that refugee Indians from nearby colonies moved into Pennsylvania.
Relations between Penn and the settlers, however, were less cordial.

In the **Frame of Government** he devised for Pennsylvania, Penn remained
true to his Quaker principles with a provision allowing for religious freedom. But
true to his aristocratic origins, he designed a legislature with limited powers and
reserved considerable authority for himself. When Penn returned to England
after a brief stay in the colony (1682–1684), the governor and council, both appointed by Penn, fought with elected members of the assembly. Penn's opponents—many of whom were fellow Quakers—objected to his proprietary privileges,
including his control of foreign trade and his collection of fees from landholders.
Settlers on the lower Delaware River gained autonomy for themselves with their
own legislature, in effect creating an unofficial colony that later became Delaware.

OVERVIEW   ENGLISH COLONIES IN THE SEVENTEENTH CENTURY

Colony	Date of Founding	Established Religion	Economy	Government
Virginia	1607	Anglican	Tobacco	Royal (after 1625)
Plymouth	1620	Puritan	Mixed farming	Corporate
St. Christopher	1624	Anglican	Sugar	Royal
Barbados	1627	Anglican	Sugar	Royal
Nevis	1628	Anglican	Sugar	Royal
Massachusetts (including present-day Maine)	1630	Puritan	Mixed farming, fishing, shipbuilding	Corporate
New Hampshire	1630 (first settlement, annexed to Mass. 1643–1679; royal colony after 1679)	Puritan	Mixed farming	Corporate (royal after 1679)
Antigua	1632	Anglican	Sugar	Royal
Montserrat	1632	Anglican	Sugar	Royal
Maryland	1634	None (Anglican after 1692)	Tobacco	Proprietary
Rhode Island	1636	None	Mixed farming	Corporate
Connecticut	1636	Puritan	Mixed farming	Corporate
New Haven	1638	Puritan	Mixed farming	Corporate
Jamaica	1655 (captured from Spanish)	Anglican	Sugar	Royal
Carolina	1663	Anglican	Rice	Proprietary
New York	1664 (captured from Dutch)	None	Mixed farming, furs	Proprietary (royal after 1685)
New Jersey	1664	None	Mixed farming	Proprietary
Pennsylvania	1681	None	Wheat, mixed farming	Proprietary

Settlers continued to fight among themselves and with Penn's heirs after his death. A flood of increasingly aggressive immigrants undermined peaceful relations with the Indians, forcing many native people to move west.

By 1720, Pennsylvania's ethnically and religiously diverse colonists numbered more than thirty thousand. The colony, with some of the richest farmland along the Atlantic coast, was widely known as the "best poor man's country in the world." Growing

GLOBAL PERSPECTIVES

NORTH AMERICA'S FIRST JEWISH COMMUNITY

I n 1654, twenty-three Jews arrived in New Amsterdam after a long voyage from Brazil. The reasons why they ended up in the Dutch colonial town relate to a much larger story of repeated Jewish migrations, undertaken time and again to escape religious persecution. In New Amsterdam these settlers found a home, establishing the first permanent Jewish community in North America.

Many of them could trace their ancestry back to Spain, where there had been a flourishing Jewish community during the Middle Ages. By the fifteenth century, however, the same Christian militancy that inspired the *reconquista* against the Muslims brought trouble for Spain's Jewish population in the form of the Inquisition. Jews who refused to convert to Christianity risked execution as heretics. In 1492, the same year as Columbus's first voyage, Spanish authorities ordered all Jews to leave Spain. Refugee Spanish Jews relocated all over the Mediterranean world, with perhaps a hundred thousand settling in Portugal, Spain's neighbor on the Iberian Peninsula. Many who did so were forced to accept Christian baptism, but continued to follow their own faith in secret. When the authorities threatened to prevent such practices, many Jews chose to leave Por-

tugal. Some sought refuge in the Netherlands, where they found religious toleration and commercial opportunities.

In the early seventeenth century, the same Dutch West India Company that founded New Netherland tried to dislodge the Portuguese from their prosperous sugar-producing colony of Brazil. The company succeeded in capturing the city of Recife in 1630, and for the next 24 years the Dutch ruled over northeastern Brazil. During that time, more than a thousand Jews moved to the colony from the Netherlands. But when the Portuguese regained control of Brazil in 1654, the Jews were forced to move yet again. Most returned to the Netherlands, but a few decided to take their chances in New Amsterdam. At last they found a place where they could stay. When New Netherland became New York in 1664, English authorities continued the Dutch practice of toleration. Even though Jewish colonists were only supposed to worship in private, there was a synagogue in New York City by 1700. Jews eventually settled in other colonies, such as Rhode Island, Pennsylvania, and South Carolina. Wherever they formed their communities, they contributed to the remarkable religious diversity of England's New World empire.

wheat and other crops, the settlers lived mostly on scattered farms rather than in towns. From the busy port of Philadelphia, ships carried much of the harvest to markets in the West Indies and southern Europe. Penn's "holy experiment" in social harmony may have failed, but, as a thriving colony, Pennsylvania succeeded handsomely.

NEW NETHERLAND BECOMES NEW YORK

The proprietary colonies of New York and New Jersey were carved out of the Dutch colony of New Netherland. Competition between the English and the Dutch generated two Anglo-Dutch wars in 1652–1654 and 1665–1667. In the New World, tensions were heightened by the presence of numerous English colonists on Long Island, which the Dutch claimed for themselves.

In 1664, Charles II brought matters to a head by claiming that since the site of New Netherland lay within the bounds of the original charter of Virginia, the land belonged to England. He granted the territory to his brother James, duke of York, who sent ships to back up England's claim. Their arrival provoked a rebellion by the island's English colonists, leading the Dutch governor, Peter Stuyvesant—who commanded just 150 soldiers—to surrender without firing a shot.

The duke of York became proprietor of this new English possession, which was renamed New York. James immediately created another colony, New Jersey, which he granted to his supporters. New York, which James retained for himself, included the port of New York City (the former New Amsterdam) and the Hudson Valley with its fur trade. James encouraged Dutch colonists to remain and promoted immigration from England. By 1700, the settlers numbered twenty thousand.

2–8
A Jesuit Priest
Describes New
Amsterdam (1642)

CONCLUSION

During the seventeenth century, France, the Netherlands, and England competed for land and trade in North America. New France's small and scattered settlements clung to the St. Lawrence River Valley. The profits from the fur trade encouraged the French to maintain friendly relations with their Indian allies and ensured that French kings would closely monitor the colony's affairs. English kings granted charters—sometimes to joint-stock companies (Virginia, Plymouth, Massachusetts), sometimes to proprietors (Maryland, Carolina, New York, New Jersey, Pennsylvania)—and let the colonies develop more or less on their own.

English settlers adjusted to different environments, developed different economies and labor systems, and worshiped in different churches. In South Carolina, New York, Pennsylvania, and the West Indies, most colonists were not even of English origin. What held these colonies together was an overlay of common English institutions of government. By the mid-1680s, all the colonies had legislatures that provided for self-government and laws and judicial institutions based on English models.

The planting of French, Dutch, and English colonies not only ended Spain's monopoly of settlement in North America but also challenged the Indians' hold on the continent. Native peoples had to adapt to rapidly changing circumstances. Transplanted Europeans adapted too, not only in their dealings with native peoples but also in finding and controlling the supply of laborers they needed to make their colonies prosper. For English colonists this meant the widespread adoption of slavery. For millions of Africans, the result was forced migration to the New World.

SUMMARY

The French in North America Although French efforts to found American colonies in the late sixteenth century ended in failure, French fisherman continued to visit the Newfoundland coast. As a result, the French did begin to establish colonies in the early seventeenth century. Quebec, organized by Samuel de Champlain, was the first permanent French settlement in Canada. By 1700, New France had about fifteen thousand settlers.

The Dutch Overseas Empire Small but densely populated, the Dutch Republic joined the scramble for empire in the early seventeenth century. The first permanent Dutch settlers on mainland North America settled at Fort Orange (now Albany) in 1624. Two years later, a company of Protestant refugees established New Amsterdam on Manhattan Island. The Hudson River corridor between these two settlements became the heart of the New Netherland colony.

IMAGE KEY
for pages 30–31.

a. Matoaka, or Pocahontas (c. 1595–1617, the daughter of Native American Chief Powhatan, after her conversion to Christianity and marriage to settler John Rolfe under the new name Rebecca.

b. Map of New Netherland showing a view of New Amsterdam.

c. Beaver

d. John Winthrop, 1588–1649.

e. Several sugarcane stems.

f. New Amsterdam traders bargaining with a view of trade transportation in the background.

g. A tattered historical beaver hat from 1620.

h. Tobacco plant.

i. A Native American exchanges fur pelts for trade goods.

j. African slaves working in a sugar mill in Brazil.

Settlement in the Chesapeake When the English again attempted to settle in America in 1607, they chose the lower Chesapeake Bay region. The new settlement, Jamestown, eventually developed into the prosperous colony of Virginia. It didn't take long before tobacco became the staple crop of this region, supplying much of Western Europe while providing an important source of profit to the Chesapeake Bay area colonies.

The Founding of New England Six English colonies appeared in the New England region between 1620 and 1640. The Pilgrims founded Plymouth in 1620, and, before long, the Massachusetts Bay colony and its offshoots comprised a populous region. The average family in New England had seven or eight children. Unlike Chesapeake colonists who spread out on tobacco lands near navigable rivers, New Englanders clustered in towns, which provided the context for religious, political, and economic activity.

Competition in the Caribbean The Spanish claimed all Caribbean islands by right of Columbus's discovery, but during the early seventeenth century, French, Dutch, and English adventures defied them. The first English colonists who came to the West Indies in the 1630s raised tobacco and imported indentured servants to work their fields. Sugar rapidly transformed the West Indies, and with its boom came the need for labor. Slave labor in the West Indies soon created a biracial society.

The Proprietary Colonies With the accession of Charles II to the English throne in 1660, interest in North American colonies revived. In 1663, Charles II granted a group of supporters a tract of land from southern Virginia to northern Florida. The proprietors called their colony Carolina. By 1708, there were more black slaves than white settlers in the colony. As Carolina continued to grow, William Penn started a colony just north of there. Penn's Quaker beliefs became entrenched in the fabric of the new colony, and his Frame of Government (Penn's constitution for Pennsylvania) included a provision allowing for religious freedom.

REVIEW QUESTIONS

1. To what extent was Richard Frethorne's experience typical of that of English colonists in the New World? What were the causes of his distress?

2. Comparing French, Dutch, and English colonies, which ones attracted the most settlers, and which the fewest? In what colonies were women scarce? What impact did these differences in emigration have on the various colonies' development?

3. Which English settlements were proprietary colonies? Did they share any common characteristics? What plans did the various proprietors have for their colonies, and to what extent were those plans put into effect?

4. When Virginia's settlers first arrived, they encountered a numerous and powerful confederation of Powhatan Indians. New England's colonists, in contrast, began settlement after epidemics had drastically reduced the local native population. In what ways did the presence or absence of substantial Indian populations affect each region's early history?

5. In both Massachusetts and Pennsylvania, religion figured prominently as a motive for settlement. What were the religious beliefs of the settlers in each colony, and how did those beliefs help shape each colony's development?

6. Three colonial regions—the Chesapeake, the West Indies, and Carolina—developed economies dependent on staple crops. What were those crops? In what ways did staple-crop agriculture shape society in each region?

7. In what ways did events in Europe affect the founding of colonies in North America?

KEY TERMS

Act for Religious Toleration   (p. 40)
Anglican   (p. 42)
Coureur de bois   (p. 34)
Covenant   (p. 44)
Frame of Government   (p. 52)
**Fundamental Constitutions
   of Carolina**   (p. 49)

Headright system   (p. 38)
House of Burgesses   (p. 38)
Indentured servants   (p. 34)
Joint-stock company   (p. 37)
Pequot War   (p. 44)
Pilgrims   (p. 42)
Proprietary colony   (p. 40)

Puritans   (p. 40)
Quakers   (p. 52)
Separatists   (p. 42)
Slave codes   (p. 48)

WHERE TO LEARN MORE

Jamestown Settlement, near Williamsburg, Virginia. Site includes replicas of first English passenger ships to Virginia, a reconstructed Powhatan Village, the recreated James Fort, and galleries with Indian and English artifacts. Visitors can also see archaeological excavations of site of the actual James Fort, as well as sample artifacts recovered from the area.

For updated information about archaeological excavations at Jamestown, see **www.apva.org**. At **http:jeffersonvillage.virginia.edu**, you can take a virtual tour of the Jamestown settlement.

St. Mary's City, Maryland. Visitors to this site of the first permanent settlement under the Calvert family may tour the area and view exhibits and living history programs that describe life in early Maryland. The website **www.somd.com** contains information about the historic site of St. Mary's City and has links to a virtual tour of the area.

Plimoth Plantation, Plymouth, Massachusetts. A living history museum, Plimoth Plantation re-creates colony life in the year 1627. There are reproductions of the English village and a Wampanoag settlement. Visitors may also see a replica of the *Mayflower*. For a virtual tour, go to **pilgrims.net/plimothplantation/vtour**. Information on Pilgrims and early years of the colony can be found at **pilgrims.net/plymouth/history**.

Pennsbury Manor, Morrisville, Pennsylvania. A reconstruction of William Penn's seventeenth-century plantation, this site includes furnished buildings and restored gardens. There are also guided tours and demonstrations of colonial crafts. Both **www.bucksnet.com/pennsbury** and **www.pennsburymanor.org** provide information about William Penn, the historic site, and various activities at the manor.

 U.S. History Documents CD-ROM
For primary sources related to this chapter, refer to the document CD-ROM.

 www.prenhall.com/goldfield
For study resources related to this chapter, visit the *Companion Website*™.

3 A Meeting of Cultures

CHAPTER HIGHLIGHTS

Indians and Europeans Although by 1750, European colonists and African slaves together outnumbered Indians north of the Rio Grande, Native Americans continued to dominate much of the continent. More than any other European colonists, the Spanish sought direct control over Indians. The English caused much displacement of Indian tribes through the constant expansion of their land needs. After nearly a century of European settlement, violence erupted in all three North American empires.

Africans and Europeans During the colonial period, virtually all Africans who came to the New World came as slaves. The Spanish and Portuguese first brought Africans to the Americas to replace Indian labor. In the British colonies, economic conditions led to the rapid growth of slavery in the South. By 1750, more slaves in the southern colonies were American-born than African natives, and they had begun to develop a new culture that drew on both their African past and their American present.

European Laborers in Early America Most colonial laborers were, in some measure, unfree. More than half of all white immigrants to the English colonies arrived as indentured servants. Purchasing slaves or the contracts of indentured servants did not make sense for everyone. Northern farmers relied on their children to supply the labor they needed to succeed.

Charleston, July 24th, 1769.

TO BE SOLD,
On THURSDAY the third Day
of AUGUST next,

A CARGO
OF
NINETY-FOUR
PRIME, HEALTHY

NEGROES,
CONSISTING OF
Thirty-nine MEN, Fifteen BOYS,
Twenty-four WOMEN, and
Sixteen GIRLS.
JUST ARRIVED,
In the Brigantine DEMBIA, Francis Bare, Master, from SIERRA-LEON, by
DAVID & JOHN DEAS.

CHAPTER QUESTIONS

WHAT WERE the consequences of trade between Indians and Europeans?

WHAT EFFECT did the development of African American families and communities have on slaves and slave owners?

WHAT METHODS did Europeans employ to acquire and manage labor in colonial America?

CHAPTER OUTLINE

- Indians and Europeans
- Africans and Europeans
- European Laborers in Early America

IMAGE KEY
for pages 58–59 is on page 83.

One day [in 1756], when all our people were gone out to their work as usual, and only I and my sister were left to mind the house, two men and a woman got over our walls, and in a moment seized us both; and without giving us time to cry out, or to make any resistance, they stopped our mouths and ran off with us into the nearest wood. Here they tied our hands, and continued to carry us as far as they could. . . . Thus I continued to travel, both by land and by water, through different countries and various nations, till at the end of six or seven months after I had been kidnapped, I arrived at the sea coast. . . .

The first object that saluted my eyes when I arrived on the coast was the sea, and a slave ship, which was then riding at anchor, and waiting for its cargo. These filled me with astonishment, that was soon converted into terror, which I am yet at a loss to describe. . . . I was immediately handled and tossed up to see if I was sound, by some of the crew; and I was now persuaded that I had got into a world of bad spirits, and that they were going to kill me. Their complexions too, differing so much from ours, their long hair, and the language they spoke, which was very different from any I had ever heard, united to confirm me in this belief. . . . I asked . . . if we were not to be eaten by those white men with horrible looks, red faces, and long hair. . . .

In a little time after, amongst the poor chained men, I found some of my own nation. . . . They gave me to understand we were to be carried to these white people's country to work for them. . . . [Many weeks later] we were landed up a river a good way from the sea, about Virginia county, where we saw few of our native Africans, and not one soul who could talk to me.

Olaudah Equiano, *The Interesting Narrative of the Life of Olaudah Equiano, or Gustavus Vassa, The African.*

OLAUDAH EQUIANO, BORN in 1745 in the African kingdom of Benin, was only a boy when his terrifying journey to America began. The son of an Igbo chief, he was caught in the web of an expanding transatlantic slave trade. Slavery had spread from England's Caribbean colonies to dominate the Chesapeake settlements as well.

At the same time, North American, Indian peoples faced new challenges as they endeavored to maintain their independence despite a flood of immigrants from Europe and Africa. Indians employed different tactics—adaptation, coexistence, diplomacy, resistance—to assert their claims to land and their right to participate in the events and deliberations that affected their lives. The America to which Olaudah Equiano had been forcibly transported remained a place where Indian voices had to be heeded.

Equiano's journey did not end in Virginia. Over the next quarter-century, he visited nearly every part of England's empire and beyond. He worked as the servant of a naval officer, a barber, a laborer, an overseer, saving money to purchase his own freedom. His extraordinary career bore witness to the emergence of an international market for laborers, which—like slavery and Indian relations—shaped the development of North America. Thousands of people from England, Scotland, Ireland, and Germany sought to make their fortunes in America. The interactions of Indians, Africans, and Europeans created not one, but many New Worlds.

INDIANS AND EUROPEANS

Although, by 1750, European colonists and African slaves together outnumbered Indians north of the Rio Grande, Native Americans continued to dominate much of the continent. The colonists remained clustered along the coasts, and some native peoples had scarcely seen any Europeans. Indians living along the northern Pacific coast met their first white men—Russian fur traders—only in the 1740s. By this time, the Pueblos of the Southwest, the Hurons of Canada, and the Algonquians of the Atlantic seaboard had more than a century's experience dealing with Europeans.

The character of the relationship between Indians and Europeans depended on more than relative population size and the length of time they had been in contact. It was also shaped by the intentions of the newcomers—whether they came to extract resources, to trade, to settle, or to gain converts—and by the responses of particular Native American groups intent on preserving their cultures. The result was a variety of regionally distinctive New World communities.

INDIAN WORKERS IN THE SPANISH BORDERLANDS

More than any other European colonists, the Spanish sought direct control over the Indians. The ability to marshal Indian workers for Spanish gain depended on two factors: the existence of sizable Indian communities and Spanish military force. North of the Rio Grande, these conditions could be found in New Mexico and, to a lesser extent, in Florida.

One of the Spaniards' most important methods of labor control was the *encomienda.* Encomiendas, granted to influential Spaniards in New Mexico, gave these colonists the right to collect tribute from the native peoples living on a specific piece of land. It was not supposed to include forced labor, but often it did.

The *repartimiento* was another Spanish technique for exploiting Native American labor. This was a mandatory draft of Indian labor for public projects, such as building forts, bridges, and roads. Laws stated that native workers should be paid and limited the length of their service, but the Spanish often ignored these provisions and sometimes compelled Indians to work on private estates.

Spaniards also acquired laborers by ransoming captives that Indian groups seized from one another. This practice was called *rescate,* and it obliged rescued Indians to work for those who had paid their ransom.

The native peoples strongly resented these Spanish strategies for controlling Indian labor. Spanish demands for labor and tribute remained constant, even when Indian populations declined from disease or crops failed, and workers who resisted were severely punished. Resentments simmered beneath a surface of cooperation until late in the seventeenth century, when long-standing native anger burst forth in rebellion.

THE WEB OF TRADE

Europeans wishing to trade with Indians had to prove their friendship by offering gifts and military aid as well as manufactured goods.

The French were among the most successful in adapting to the Native American understanding of trade, for they knew that good relations were essential to

WHAT WERE the consequences of trade between Indians and Europeans?

The freed slave Olaudah Equiano appears in this 1780 portrait by an unknown artist. After purchasing his freedom, Equiano wrote a vivid account of his capture in Africa and his life in slavery. One of the first such accounts to be published (in 1789), this narrative testified to slavery's injustice and Equiano's own fortitude.

"Portrait of a Negro Man, Olaudah Equiano," 1780s (previously attributed to Joshua Reynolds) by English School (18th c.). Royal Albert Memorial Museum, Exeter, Devon, UK. Bridgeman Art Library, London/New York.

Encomienda   In the Spanish colonies, the grant to a Spanish settler of a certain number of Indian subjects, who would pay him tribute in goods and labor.

Repartimiento   In the Spanish colonies, the assignment of Indian workers to labor on public works projects.

Rescate   Procedure by which Spanish colonists would pay ransom to free Indians captured by rival natives.

Chronology

1440s	Portuguese enter slave trade in West Africa.
c. 1450	Iroquois form Great League of Peace and Power.
1610–1614	First war between English settlers and Powhatan Indians.
1619	First Africans arrive in Virginia.
1622–1632	Second war between English settlers and Powhatan Indians.
1637	Pequot War in New England.
1640s	Slave labor begins to dominate in the West Indies. First phase of the Beaver Wars.
1651	First "praying town" established at Natick, Massachusetts.
1661	Maryland law defines slavery as lifelong, inheritable status.
1670	Virginia law defines status of slaves.
1675–1676	King Philip's War in New England.
1676	Bacon's Rebellion in Virginia.
1680	Pueblo Revolt in New Mexico.
1680s	Second phase of Beaver Wars begins.
1688–1697	England and France fight the War of the League of Augsburg (known in America as King William's War).
1690s	Shift from white indentured servants to black slaves as principal labor force in the Chesapeake.
1701	Iroquois adopt policy of neutrality toward French and English.
1711–1713	Tuscarora War in Carolina.
1713	Beginnings of substantial Scottish, Scots-Irish, and German immigration to colonies.
1715–1716	Yamasee War in Carolina.
1720s	Black population begins to increase naturally in English mainland colonies.
1732	Georgia established.
1739	Stono Rebellion in South Carolina.
1741	Slave conspiracy discovered in New York City.
1750	Slavery legalized in Georgia.
1760–1775	Peak of European and African immigration to English colonies.

This eighteenth-century engraving illustrates, in idealized form, the way Indian peoples traded furs for European goods. The barrel may have contained kettles or other metalware packed in sawdust, while the bale to the left probably held cloth.

Courtesy of the Library of Congress.

keeping New France's fur trade operating smoothly. The fur trade benefited Indians too. "The Beaver does everything perfectly well," noted one native leader, "it makes kettles, hatchets, swords, knives, bread; and, in short, it makes everything."

The benefits of trade were immediate and obvious, but most of the problems were slower to appear. The one exception was the problem of disease, which followed almost immediately from Indians' contacts with European traders. The Huron population declined by half in just six years between 1634 and 1640.

Although Indian hunters enjoyed considerable autonomy in their work, French merchants began to use economic pressure to exert greater control over them. By supplying Indians with trade goods in advance, merchants obligated them to bring in furs as payment. If hunters tried to avoid payment, merchants refused to give them more trade goods. Extending credit in this way allowed the French to control native workers.

The French could control the Indians through credit because native peoples had grown increasingly dependent on European manufactures. In many communities, Indians had abandoned native crafts and instead relied on imported goods. As a result, they had no alternative but to increase their hunting in order to have enough furs to trade for what they needed. "The Cloaths we wear, we cannot make ourselves," a Carolina Cherokee observed in 1753. "We cannot make our Guns. . . . Every necessary Thing in Life we must have from the white People."

Trade with Europeans eventually encouraged violence and warfare. Indians had certainly fought one another before European colonization, but these wars were generally limited in scope and destructiveness. After Europeans arrived, warriors raided their enemies to replace family members lost to disease and fought to avenge losses resulting from the fierce competition for a diminishing supply of fur-bearing animals. The proliferation of firearms made the conflicts deadlier, and more casualties led to further wars.

The **Beaver Wars,** a long struggle between the Hurons and the Iroquois that began in the 1640s, illustrated the ferocity of such contests. The Hurons were trading partners and allies with the French, and the Iroquois had forged ties with Dutch merchants in the Hudson River Valley. To satisfy the European demand for furs, the Hurons and Iroquois both hunted beaver at an unsustainable rate. By the 1630s, they had killed nearly all the beavers on their own lands and began to look elsewhere for furs. The Hurons raised more corn, intending to trade the surplus for furs with Indians living north of the Great Lakes, where beavers were still abundant. The Iroquois, however, began to raid Huron trading parties and then to attack Huron villages.

The Iroquois triumphed in this struggle largely because the Dutch supplied them with guns, whereas the French were reluctant to arm the Hurons. In the end, the Hurons were destroyed. Thousands were killed or captured, and many others fled westward. A French traveler reported seeing no Hurons in "districts which, not ten years ago, I reckoned to contain eight or ten thousand men."

The cycle of warfare did not end with the Hurons' destruction. The victorious Iroquois went on to challenge Indian nations near the Great Lakes and in the Ohio Valley. Although trade brought improvements to native life, cemented alliances with Europeans, and strengthened the economic and diplomatic positions of such successful participants as the Iroquois, over the long run its disadvantages—especially Indians' eventual dependence on Europeans and the escalation of violence—threatened to overshadow its benefits.

Beaver Wars Series of bloody conflicts, occurring between 1640s and 1680s, during which the Iroquois fought the Hurons and French for control of the fur trade in the east and the Great Lakes region.

QUICK REVIEW

Native Americans and English Settlers

- Influx of settlers exposed native peoples to disease.
- Settler's desire for land led to violence between settlers and Indians.
- By 1650 settlers outnumbered Indians in some areas.

DISPLACING NATIVE AMERICANS IN THE ENGLISH COLONIES

In New France and New Netherland, where the fur trade took precedence over farming, Indians always outnumbered Europeans. This numerical superiority and their key role as suppliers of furs allowed native peoples to negotiate with settlers from a position of strength. The situation was much different in the English colonies, whose settlers came to farm and thus competed directly with Indians for land. It did not help matters that, as Indian populations declined because of European diseases, colonial populations burgeoned through immigration and natural increase. As early as 1650, colonists outnumbered Native Americans in coastal Massachusetts and eastern Virginia.

Colonists thrilled at the sight of what they considered vast unoccupied territory. One New England settler declared that the natives "do but run over the grass, as do also the foxes and wild beasts" and therefore that the "spacious and void" land was free for the taking.

Land Use and Property Rights. But the settlers misunderstood how Indians used their territory. Eastern Algonquian peoples cleared areas for villages and planting fields, which native women farmed until the soil grew less fertile. Then they moved to a new location, allowing the former village site to return to forest. In ten to twenty years, they or their descendants might return to that site to clear and farm it again. Indians often built villages near the seacoast or rivers so that they could fish and use reeds and grasses for weaving. In the winter, village communities broke up into small bands to hunt in the forest for deer and other animals.

Thus what the colonists considered "vacant" lands were in fact either being used for nonfarming activities or recovering from human occupation in order to be farmed in years to come. Settlers who built towns on abandoned native village sites deprived the Indians of these future planting fields.

Disputes between Europeans and Indians frequently arose from misunderstandings about the definition of land ownership and property rights. Indian villages claimed sovereignty over a certain territory, which their members collectively used for farming, fishing, hunting, and gathering. For Europeans ownership conferred on an individual the exclusive right to use or sell a piece of land. When Indians transferred land to settlers, the settlers assumed that they had obtained complete rights to the land, whereas the Indians assumed that they had given the settlers not the land itself but only the right to use it.

Settlers' agricultural practices also strained relations with the Indians. Cutting down forests destroyed Indian hunting lands. When colonists dammed rivers, they disturbed Indian fishing. When they surrounded their fields with fences, colonists made trespassers of natives who crossed them. Yet the colonists felt free to let their cattle and pigs loose to graze in the woods and meadows, where they could wander into unfenced Indian cornfields and damage the crops.

Colonial Land Acquisition. The colonists displaced Indian inhabitants, acquiring their lands in various ways. Some colonial leaders, such as Roger Williams in Rhode Island and William Penn of Pennsylvania, insisted on buying land. Settlers, however, sometimes bought land from individual Indians who had no right to sell it. Because land transfers were usually arranged through interpreters and recorded in English, Indians were not always fully informed of the terms of sale. And even Indians who willingly sold land grew resentful as colonists approached them for more. Finally, native peoples could be forced to sell land to settle debts to English creditors.

By the eighteenth century, some colonists simply settled on Indian lands without any legal pretext at all, and appealed to colonial governments for help when the Indians objected. Land speculators amplified this kind of unrest on the edges of settlement as they sought to acquire land as cheaply as possible and sell it for as much as they could.

Finally, colonists often seized Indian lands in the aftermath of war, as befell, among many others, the Pequots in 1637 in Connecticut and, in Carolina, the Tuscaroras in 1713 and the Yamasees in 1715. In each case, settlers moved onto land left vacant after colonial forces killed, captured, and dispersed native peoples. Sometimes colonial leaders contrived for some Indian groups to help them displace others. During the Pequot War, Narragansetts aided Connecticut settlers' efforts to oust the Pequots. Carolina colonists enlisted the help of the Yamasees against the Tuscaroras and then turned to the Cherokees to help them against the Yamasees.

Some Indians who survived warfare and disease staved off the worst effects of English encroachments by forming new native communities just beyond the colonial settlements. But the general trend was hardly encouraging. The colonists' insatiable hunger for land generated relentless pressure on native peoples. Once the pattern of mutual suspicion and territorial competition had been established, it would be difficult to alter.

Bringing Christianity to Native Peoples

In addition to trade and settlement, religion played a powerful role in shaping relations between Native Americans and Europeans in colonial North America. The three major New World empires of Spain, France, and England competed for Indians' souls as well as their lands and riches.

Catholic Missionaries in Spanish Colonies.   Franciscan priests were the driving force behind Spain's efforts to control its colonies of New Mexico and Florida (see Map 3–1). Spain's bases in Florida helped protect Spanish ships bearing treasure from the mines of Mexico and Peru and discouraged the southward spread of English settlement. New Mexico similarly served as a buffer between the silver mines of northern Mexico and roaming Plains Indians. Neither colony attracted many settlers, however, because neither offered much opportunity for wealth. When Franciscan missionaries proposed to move in, Spanish officials agreed and provided financial support.

The priests wore their finest vestments and displayed religious paintings and statues, trying to impress the Indians. They gave away bells, knives, cloth, and food. The natives believed that accepting these gifts obliged them to listen to the priests' Christian message and help the Franciscans build houses and churches.

After brief religious instruction, the missionaries convinced many Indians to accept baptism into the Catholic

This Jesuit missionary, wearing his distinctive Catholic vestments, is baptizing an Indian in New France. French Jesuits proved to be more tolerant than most European missionaries in allowing Indian converts to retain at least some of their own customs.

Courtesy of Library of Congress.

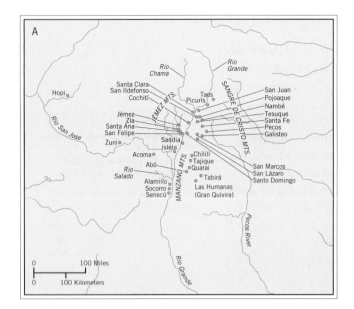

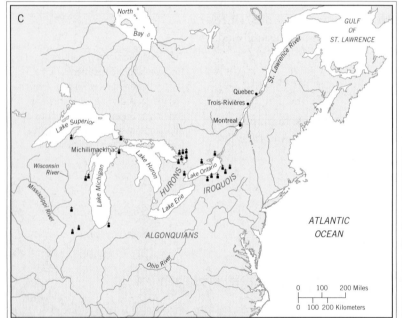

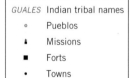

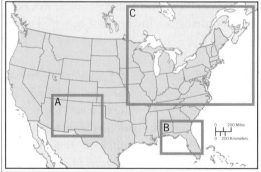

MAP 3–1   Spanish and French Missions in Seventeenth-Century North America   Spanish Franciscans in New Mexico (A) and Florida (B) and French Jesuits in New France (C) devoted considerable effort to converting native peoples to Catholic Christianity.

BASED ON this series of maps, what geographic rationale might have been behind Spanish and French decisions to convert native peoples to Catholic Christianity?

Church. Such conversions often followed epidemics that devastated native villages but spared the Spanish, leading many Indians to wonder if the Christian God might be more powerful than their own gods. In New Mexico, the Spanish offered Pueblo converts protection against Apache raids and access to Franciscan storehouses in times of famine.

The Franciscans insisted that converts abandon their former ways of life and adopt Spanish food, clothing, gender relations, and work routines along with Catholicism. Many Indians preferred to supplement native beliefs and practices with the new teachings. Because the missionaries reacted to this spiritual mixture with horror, inflicting severe punishments that sometimes led to death, native peoples often practiced their own rituals in secret. Christianity had been securely planted in the Spanish borderlands, but not quite as deeply as the missionaries assumed.

French Jesuits in Canada.   To a certain extent, French Jesuits in Canada followed a similar strategy, moving to native villages and seeking to awe Indians with European technology and Catholic rituals. By the 1650s, the Jesuits claimed to have produced thousands of converts, some of whom formed separate native Christian communities.

French missionaries sometimes combined economic pressure with preaching. They persuaded merchants to sell guns only to converted Indians and to offer them other trade goods at a discount. Such tactics doubtless brought some success, but as in New Mexico, the crises engendered by epidemics more often than not sparked an upsurge in conversions. Converts in New France also preferred to meld Catholic teachings with native beliefs. Missionaries hardly condoned this response; one Jesuit complained that Indians "cannot suffer any opposition to their ceremonies." Yet the Jesuits resigned themselves, at least in the short run, to a gradual approach to conversion. The Jesuits reduced the potential for confrontation with the Indians by accepting small changes in converts at first, in hopes of a wholesale transformation to follow.

Missionaries in English Colonies.   The Protestant English were less successful at attracting Native American converts. Puritans frowned on the rituals and religious objects that drew Indians to Catholicism, but Protestant practices held little allure for Indians accustomed to a more ritualistic spiritual life. Even so, Protestant missionaries achieved some success, principally in New England. Beginning in the 1650s and 1660s, Puritan ministers such as John Eliot and Thomas Mayhew, Jr., attracted converts. Eliot helped to establish several "praying towns," where Indians received instruction in Protestant Christianity and English ways. By 1674, about 2,300 Indians resided in these towns.

Elsewhere in the English colonies, missionaries enjoyed little success. Anglican missionaries in the southern colonies did not even begin conversion work until the eighteenth century. Although individual ministers showed genuine interest in conversion, and Anglican officials in England devoted some resources to missionary activities by the eighteenth century, the Protestant English never matched the efforts of Spanish or French Catholics.

AFTER THE FIRST HUNDRED YEARS: CONFLICT AND WAR

After nearly a century of European settlement, violence between colonists and Indians erupted in all three North American empires. Each deadly encounter—King Philip's War in New England, Bacon's Rebellion in Virginia, the Pueblo Revolt in

W WHERE TO LEARN MORE

★ Ste. Marie among the Hurons, near Midland, Ontario, Canada **www** **.saintemarieamongthehurons.on.ca**

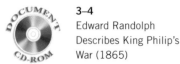

3–4
Edward Randolph
Describes King Philip's
War (1865)

King Philip's War Conflict in New England (1675–1676) between Wampanoags, Narragansetts, and other Indian peoples against English settlers; sparked by English encroachments on native lands.

Bacon's Rebellion Violent conflict in Virginia (1675–1676), beginning with settler attacks on Indians but culminating in a rebellion led by Nathaniel Bacon against Virginia's government.

New Mexico, and the resumption of the Beaver Wars in New France—reflected distinctive features of English, Spanish, and French patterns of colonization.

King Philip's War. The growing frustration of the Wampanoags with the land-hungry settlers whose towns now surrounded them sparked **King Philip's War,** which broke out in 1675. Massasoit's younger son, Metacom—called King Philip by the English—led the Wampanoags in the struggle to preserve their independence against the incursions of the colonists, who now numbered more than fifty thousand.

In the spring of 1675, a colonial court found three Wampanoags guilty of murdering a Christian Indian who had warned the English of Wampanoag preparations for war. Despite Philip's protests, the court sentenced them to be hanged. This act convinced the Wampanoags that they had to strike back against the English before it was too late. The final blow occurred in June 1675, when colonists killed an Indian they found looting an abandoned house and then ignored the Indians' outrage at the murder.

Native warriors attacked outlying villages in Plymouth Colony, moved into the Connecticut River Valley, and then turned eastward again to strike towns within 20 miles of Boston. As the Narragansetts and other groups joined the uprising, Philip successfully eluded the combined forces of Massachusetts, Connecticut, and Plymouth (see "American Views: Mary Rowlandson Among the Indians"). By the summer of 1676, however, the Indians were exhausted, weakened by disease and food shortages. Philip died in an ambush in August 1676, and the war ended soon after.

At least a thousand colonists and perhaps three thousand Indians died in King Philip's War. The Indians succeeded in forcing back the line of settlement but lost what remained of their independence in New England. Philip's head, impaled on a stake, was left for decades just outside Plymouth as a grisly warning of the price to be paid for resisting colonial expansion.

Bacon's Rebellion. As King Philip's War raged in New England, **Bacon's Rebellion** erupted in Virginia and had a similarly devastating effect on that colony's native population. Frustrated by shrinking economic opportunities in eastern Virginia, many settlers, including new arrivals and recently freed indentured servants, moved to Virginia's western frontier. In the summer of 1675, a group of frontier settlers attacked the Susquehannocks to seize their lands. The Indians struck back, prompting Nathaniel Bacon, a wealthy, young planter who had only recently arrived in Virginia, to lead a violent campaign against all Indians, even those at peace with the colonial government. Governor William Berkeley ordered Bacon and his men to stop their attacks. They defied him, turning a war between settlers and Indians into a rebellion of settlers against the colonial authorities.

The rebels believed that Berkeley and the colonial government represented the interests of established tobacco planters. Desperate because of the low price of tobacco, they demanded lower taxes and easier access to land—meaning, in effect, the right to take land from the Indians. Berkeley offered to help protect the settlers from the Indians, but what the rebels wanted was help in exterminating the Indians. They captured and burned the colonial capital at Jamestown, forcing Berkeley to flee. They then burned Indian villages and massacred the inhabitants. Trying to appease the rebels, the House of Burgesses allowed them to seize lands belonging to Indians who had left their villages without permission and legalized the enslavement of Indians.

AMERICAN VIEWS

Mary Rowlandson among the Indians

I n February 1676, in the midst of King Philip's War, Indian warriors attacked the town of Lancaster, Massachusetts. They killed many inhabitants and took 23 colonists captive, including Mary Rowlandson and three of her children. Rowlandson spent the next three months traveling with various groups of Nipmucs, Narragansetts, and Wampanoags. She suffered physically and emotionally, watching her youngest daughter die in her arms and worrying about her other two children, from whom she was frequently separated. During her captivity, Rowlandson survived by accepting her fate and adapting to the Indians' way of life. Finally, with an English victory imminent, Rowlandson was ransomed and rejoined her husband (who had been away at the time of the attack) and family. In 1682, she published an account of her captivity in which she explored the meaning of her experience. Rowlandson's narrative proved so popular that three editions were printed in the first year.

- How did Rowlandson describe the Indians? How did she characterize her encounter with King Philip?
- In what ways did Rowlandson accommodate herself to the Indians' way of life? How did she employ her skills to fit in? Did her gender make a difference in her experience of captivity?
- How did Rowlandson's Puritan faith shape her narrative?

We travelled on till night; and in the morning, we must go over the River to Philip's crew. When I was in the Cannoo, I could not but be amazed at the numerous crew of Pagans that were on the Bank on the other side. When I came ashore, they gathered all about me, I sitting alone in the midst: I observed they asked one another questions, and laughed, and rejoyced over their Gains and Victories. Then my heart began to fail: and I fell a weeping which was the first time to my remembrance that I wept before them. Although I had met with so much Affliction, and my heart was many times ready to break, yet could I not shed one tear in their sight: but rather had been all this while in a maze, and like one astonished: but now I may say as, Psal. 137.1 *By the rivers of Babylon, there we sat down: yea, we wept when we remembered Zion.* There one of them asked me, why I wept, I could hardly tell what to say: yet I answered, they would kill me: No, said he, none will hurt you. Then came one of them and gave me two spoonfulls of Meal to comfort me. . . . Then I went to see King Philip, he bade me come in and sit down, and asked me whether I would smoke (a usual Complement now adayes amongst Saints and Sinners) but this no way suited me. For though I had formerly used Tobacco, yet I had left it ever since I was first taken, *It seems to be a bait, the devil lays to make men loose their precious time.* . . .

During my abode in this place, Philip spake to me to make a shirt for his boy, which I did, for which he gave me a shilling: I offered the money to my master, but he bade me keep it: and with it I bought a piece of Horse flesh. Afterwards he asked me to make a Cap for his boy, for which he invited me to Dinner. I went, and he gave me a Pancake, about as big as two fingers; it was made of parched wheat, beaten, and fryed in Bears grease, but I thought I never tasted pleasanter meat in my life. There was a Squaw who spake to me to make a shirt for her *Sannup* [husband], for which she gave me a piece of Bear. Another asked me to knit a pair of Stockins, for which she gave me a quart of Pease. . . . Hearing that my son was come to this place, I went to see him, and found him lying flat upon the ground: I asked him how he could sleep so? He answered me, *That he was not asleep, but at Prayer;* and lay so, that they might not observe what he was doing. I pray God he may remember these things now he is returned in safety.

Source: Neal Salisbury, ed., *The Sovereignty and Goodness of God, Together with the Faithfulness of His Promises Displayed.* . . . (Boston, 1997), pp. 82–83.

One of the many pueblos scattered along the Rio Grande Valley, Taos served as Popé's headquarters at the start of the Pueblo Revolt in August 1680. Within a few weeks, the Indians drove the Spanish from New Mexico and destroyed most of their settlements. The Spanish did not return until 1693.

TLM Photo

WHERE TO LEARN MORE

Taos Pueblo, Taos, New Mexico
www.cr.nps.gov/worldheritage/taos.htm

Pueblo Revolt Rebellion in 1680 of Pueblo Indians in New Mexico against their Spanish overlords, sparked by religious conflict and excessive Spanish demands for tribute.

By the time troops arrived from England to put down the rebellion, Bacon had died of a fever and most of his men had drifted home. Berkeley arrested and hanged twenty-three rebels, but the real victims of the rebellion were Virginia's Indians. The remnants of the once-powerful Powhatans lost their remaining lands and either moved west or lived in poverty on the edges of English settlement. In the wake of the rebellion, hatred of Indians became a permanent feature of frontier life in Virginia.

The Pueblo Revolt. In 1680, the **Pueblo Revolt** against the Spanish in New Mexico had a very different outcome than did the rebellion in Virginia or the war in New England. Nearly 20,000 Pueblo Indians had grown increasingly restless under the harsh rule of only 2,500 Spaniards. The spark that ignited the revolt was an act of religious persecution. Spanish officials unwisely chose this troubled time to stamp out the Pueblo religion. In 1675, the governor arrested forty-seven native religious leaders on charges of sorcery. The court ordered most of them to be publicly whipped and released but sentenced four to death.

Led by Popé, one of the freed leaders, the outraged Pueblos organized for revenge. A growing network of rebels emerged. By the summer of 1680, Popé commanded an enormous force of rebels drawn from twenty Pueblo villages. On August 10, they attacked the Spanish settlements. Popé urged them to "break up and burn the images of the holy Christ, the Virgin Mary and the other saints, the crosses, and everything pertaining to Christianity" and ordered Indian converts to "plunge into the rivers and wash themselves" to remove the taint of baptism. Within a few weeks, the rebels had destroyed or damaged every Spanish building and killed more than four hundred Spaniards, including twenty-one of the colony's thirty-three missionaries. By October, all the surviving Spaniards had fled New Mexico. They did not return for thirteen years. By then, internal rivalries had split the victorious Pueblo coalition, and Popé had been overthrown as leader. Few Pueblo villages offered much resistance to the new Spanish intrusion. Even so, the Spanish now understood the folly of pushing the Indians too far.

The Iroquois adopt neutrality. Although the Iroquois suffered devastating losses in the Beaver Wars, similar to those inflicted on the Indians in the English colonies, they did not lose their independence. The key to Iroquois survival in the war's aftermath was the adoption of a position of neutrality between the European powers.

Looking for new trading partners to replace the Hurons, the French turned in the 1680s to the Ottawas, Wyandots, and other Indian peoples living near the Great Lakes. But the Iroquois had begun to raid these same peoples for furs and captives. They exchanged the furs for European goods with English traders, who had replaced the Dutch as their partners after the conquest of New Netherland.

When the French moved into the Great Lakes territory, the Iroquois objected to their attempt to "have all the Bevers" for themselves.

The French attacked the Iroquois to prevent them and their English allies from extending their influence in the West. In June 1687, a combined force of French and Christian Indian soldiers invaded the lands of the Senecas, the westernmost of the five nations of the Iroquois League. The Iroquois retaliated by besieging a French garrison at Niagara and killing hundreds of colonists in attacks on French villages along the St. Lawrence River.

The French participated much more directly and suffered greater losses in this renewal of the Beaver Wars than they had in the fighting of the 1640s. The conflict was even more devastating for the Iroquois. The English provided minimal military assistance, and the Iroquois suffered heavy casualties. Perhaps a quarter of their population died from disease and warfare by 1689. The devastation encouraged Iroquois diplomats to find a way to extricate themselves from future English–French conflicts. The result, in 1701, was a pair of treaties, negotiated separately with Albany and Montreal, that recognized Iroquois neutrality and, at least for several decades, prevented either the English or the French from dominating the western lands.

Each of these conflicts grew from a distinctive pattern of contact between colonists and native peoples. English settlers fought for control of land, and the losers were the outnumbered Indians. Spanish colonists clashed with Pueblos over religion, and the more numerous natives won a temporary victory and permanent accommodation with the Spanish Catholic minority. French soldiers battled with the Iroquois over control of the fur trade until both sides agreed to an uneasy truce. In each case, nearly a century of contact culminated in a struggle that revealed the fragility of Indian autonomy.

AFRICANS AND EUROPEANS

*T*he movement of Africans to the Americas was one of the largest forced migrations in world history. By the time New World slavery finally ended, with its abolition in Brazil in 1888, over twelve million Africans had arrived on American shores. Over 350,000 Africans crossed the Atlantic before 1600. More than five times as many, nearly 1.8 million people, arrived in the seventeenth century. In the eighteenth century, another 6.1 million African migrants reached American destinations.

Virtually all Africans arrived as slaves. As one eighteenth-century English observer noted, Africans became "the strength and sinews of this western world," performing much of the labor of colonization. The vast majority of African slaves ended up in Brazil, the West Indies, or New Spain. Only 1 out of 20 Africans came to the British mainland colonies. Their presence transformed English colonial societies everywhere, but particularly in the South. At the same time, Africans were themselves transformed. Out of their diverse African ethnic backgrounds and the experience of slavery itself they gradually forged new identities as African American peoples.

LABOR NEEDS AND THE TURN TO SLAVERY

The scarcity and high cost of labor led some colonial employers to turn to enslaved Africans as a solution. The development of slavery in the colonies was not, however, inevitable. Europeans had owned slaves (both white and black) long before the beginning of American colonization, but slaves formed a small—

WHAT EFFECT did the development of African American families and communities have on slaves and slave owners?

3–12
Alexander Falconbridge, The African Slave Trade (1788)

and shrinking—minority of European laborers. By the fifteenth century, slavery had all but disappeared in northern Europe except as punishment for serious crimes.

Slavery persisted longer in southern Europe and the Middle East. In both regions, religion influenced the choice of who was enslaved. Because neither Christians nor Muslims would hold as slaves members of their own faiths, Arab traders turned to sub-Saharan Africa to find slaves. By the fifteenth century, a durable link between slave status and black skin had been forged in European minds.

Europeans in the New World, however, first attempted to enslave Indians as a way of addressing the labor shortage. Spaniards held Indian slaves in all their New World colonies, as did the Portuguese in Brazil. French Canadians enslaved Pawnee Indians captured in wars in the North American interior. English colonists condemned Indian war captives to slavery as punishment for their opposition to English rule.

Native American slaves, however, could not fill the colonists' labor needs. Everywhere disease and harsh working conditions reduced their numbers. English colonists also discovered practical reasons not to enslave Indians. When traders incited Indian wars to gain slaves, bloodshed often spread to English settlements. Moreover, enslaved Indian men refused to perform agricultural labor, which they considered women's work. Indians could easily escape and make their way back to their own people. By 1700, the Indian slave trade had been largely supplanted by a much larger traffic in Africans.

THE SHOCK OF ENSLAVEMENT

European traders relied on other Africans to capture slaves for them, tapping into a preexisting internal African slave trade. With the permission of local rulers, Europeans built forts and trading posts (called factories) on the West African coast and bought slaves from African traders (see Map 3–2). African rulers occasionally enslaved and sold their own people as punishment for crimes, but most slaves were seized in raids on neighboring peoples. West Africans fought increasingly among themselves to secure captives and began kidnapping individuals from the interior.

Once captured, slaves marched in chains to the coast. Captains examined them to ensure their fitness and branded them like cattle with a hot iron. The slaves then boarded canoes to be ferried to the ships. Slaves brought aboard ships waiting to leave for America sometimes mutinied. These rebellions, fought against great odds, rarely succeeded.

Slaves who could not escape while still in Africa suffered through a horrendous six- to eight-week-long ocean voyage known as the **Middle Passage.** Except for brief excursions on deck for forced exercise, slaves remained below decks, where the air grew foul from the vomit, blood, and excrement in which the terrified victims lay. "The shrieks of the women, and the groans of the dying," recalled Olaudah Equiano, "rendered it a scene of horror almost inconceivable." Some slaves went insane. Others tried to commit suicide by jumping overboard or starving themselves. On many voyages, between 5 and 20 percent of the slaves perished from disease.

Those who survived the dreadful voyage endured the fear and humiliation of sale. Sometimes buyers rushed aboard ship in a scramble to choose slaves. Ship captains also sold slaves at public auctions, where purchasers poked them, looking for signs of disease.

QUICK REVIEW

The Demand for Labor
- Indians first forced into slavery in the Americas.
- By 1700 Indian slave trade replaced by slaves from Africa.
- Over time slaves replaced servants on tobacco plantations.

Middle Passage   The voyage between West Africa and the New World slave colonies

MAP EXPLORATION

To explore an interactive version of this map, go to
http://www.prenhall.com/goldfield3/map3.2

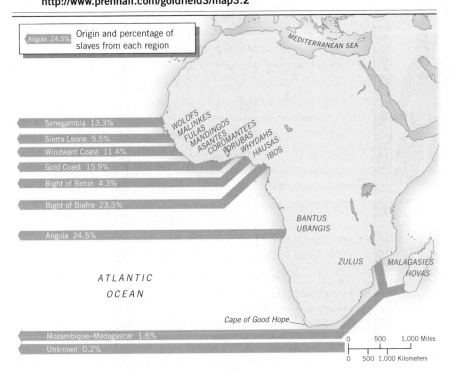

Angola 24.5%   Origin and percentage of slaves from each region

MEDITERRANEAN SEA

WOLOFS
MALINKES
FULAS
MANDINGOS
ASANTES
COROMANTEES
YORUBAS
WHYDAHS
HAUSAS
IBOS

Senegambia 13.3%
Sierra Leone 5.5%
Windward Coast 11.4%
Gold Coast 15.9%
Bight of Benin 4.3%
Bight of Biafra 23.3%
Angola 24.5%

BANTUS
UBANGIS

ZULUS   MALAGASIES
HOVAS

ATLANTIC
OCEAN

Cape of Good Hope

Mozambique–Madagascar 1.6%
Unknown 0.2%

0   500   1,000 Miles
0   500 1,000 Kilometers

MAP 3–2   African Origins of North American Slaves, 1690–1807   Nearly all slaves in English North America were West Africans. Most had been captured or purchased by African slave traders, who then sold them to European merchants.

WHY MIGHT the Bight of Biafra and Angola together have made up nearly 50 percent of all slave trading out of West Africa?

AFRICAN SLAVES IN THE NEW WORLD

The Spanish and Portuguese first brought Africans to the Americas, using them to replace or supplement the dwindling numbers of Indian slaves. The Dutch, who scrambled for a share of the lucrative slave trade, quickly followed suit. English colonists, less familiar with slavery, adopted it more slowly. West Indian planters were the first English settlers to do so on a large scale in the 1640s. In most other English colonies, however, different economic conditions either postponed or prevented slavery's widespread adoption.

Slavery in the Southern Colonies.   The first African immigrants arrived in Virginia in 1619. Yet slavery did not really take hold in Virginia until the end of the seventeenth century, at which point Africans comprised a significant portion of the population. For decades, tobacco planters used white indentured servants because they cost less than slaves, were more readily available, and were familiar. By the 1680s, however, planters in Virginia and Maryland began to shift from servants to slaves.

Two related developments caused this change. First, white indentured servants became harder to find. Fewer English men and women chose to emigrate as servants after 1660 because an improving economy in England provided jobs

QUICK REVIEW

Growth of Slavery
- Slavery grew rapidly in the South.
- The use of slaves made economic sense on tobacco and rice plantations.
- Northern slaves worked as servants, craftsmen, and day laborers.

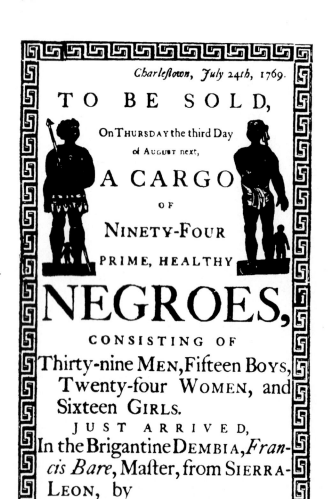

This 1769 broadside advertised the arrival of a cargo of West African slaves in Charleston, South Carolina. By that date, slaves made up over two-thirds of the colony's settlers. Note that nearly equal numbers of men and women have been imported. This practice would eventually contribute to the formation of slave families and communities.

Courtesy of the American Antiquarian Society.

at home, at the same time as competition for white immigrant laborers in the colonies intensified.

Second, as white servants grew scarcer, changes in the slave trade made African slaves more available. Beginning in 1674, England's Royal African Company began shipping slaves to English buyers in the Caribbean and on the mainland. The supply of slaves surged after 1698, when the Royal African Company lost its special trading rights and many English merchants and New Englanders entered the fiercely competitive trade.

Although more expensive than servants, slaves were a better long-term investment. Because slave status passed from slave mothers to their children, buying both men and women gave planters a self-reproducing labor force. Runaway black slaves were more easily recaptured than were escaped servants. And unlike indentured servants, slaves were slaves for life.

Chesapeake planters had already come to see white servants as possessions. This attitude doubtless eased the transition in the 1680s and 1690s to the much harsher system of slavery. In Carolina the introduction of slavery was not gradual. Slaves arrived there right from the start, brought in the 1670s by colony founders accustomed to slavery in Barbados. By 1720, slavery was firmly embedded in all the southern colonies except sparsely settled North Carolina.

Slavery grew rapidly in the southern colonies because it answered the labor needs of planters engaged in the commercial production of tobacco and rice. The demand for slaves became so powerful that it destroyed James Oglethorpe's plan to keep them out of the new colony of Georgia, founded in 1732. Oglethorpe intended Georgia to be a refuge for English debtors. Only rice turned a profit in Georgia, however, and colonists insisted that they needed slaves to keep up with South Carolina's planters. In 1750, Georgia's founders reluctantly legalized slavery; by 1770, slaves made up nearly half of the colony's population.

Slavery in the Northern Colonies. Far fewer slaves lived north of the Chesapeake. They were too expensive for most small northern farmers to use profitably. This was not true, however, for farmers with larger properties in parts of Long Island, the Hudson Valley, Rhode Island, northern New Jersey, and southeastern Pennsylvania. Especially in the eighteenth century, these landowners acquired significant numbers of slaves.

Northern slaves could often be found in cities, especially busy ports such as Newport, Rhode Island, where newly arrived Africans landed. At the start of the eighteenth century, one out of six Philadelphia residents was a slave; by 1740, slaves made up 15 percent of the city's workingmen. In mid-eighteenth-century New York City, slaves comprised between 12 and 14 percent of the population. Urban slaves worked at a variety of occupations. Many were domestic servants in the homes of rich merchants, and professionals. Substantial numbers found employment as artisans.

Changing Race Relations in the Colonies. Before 1700, slaves did not form a majority of the population in any colony, a situation that may have made them seem less threatening to white people. Most seventeenth-century Chesapeake planters did not own slaves. Those who did often held only a few slaves along with white servants. In these households, white and black people lived and worked in close contact. In some areas, free black people—often slaves who had bought their own freedom—prospered in an atmosphere of racial tolerance that would be unthinkable by the eighteenth century.

The career of an ambitious black Virginian named Anthony Johnson, for example, resembled that of many white settlers—a remarkable achievement, given that he arrived in the colony in 1621 as a slave known only as "Antonio a Negro." Johnson's master allowed him to marry and start a family and may even have allowed Anthony to purchase his and his family's liberty. Once free, the Johnsons settled near their former master in eastern Virginia. By 1651, Johnson owned a 250-acre plantation, and his sons eventually acquired even larger estates. He and his sons also owned slaves. When his plantation burned to the ground in 1653, local authorities granted Johnson relief from taxes in recognition of his family's "hard labor and known services" in supporting themselves.

As this nineteenth-century engraving indicates, slaves were often subjected to humiliating physical inspections so that potential buyers could be convinced of their good health and strength.

Courtesy of Library of Congress.

Anthony Johnson belonged to the first or what one historian has called the "charter" generation of American slaves, and his experience reveals how much slavery changed over time. This generation of slaves mainly came from African port towns, where Europeans and Africans had mingled for generations, or by way of the West Indies or New Netherland. Familiar with European ways, often fluent in European languages, they acquired skills and knowledge that enabled them to bargain with their masters in ways their descendants would not be able to replicate. They came in small groups, cultivated their masters as patrons, negotiated for their own property, and often gained their freedom. They enjoyed such advantages because they came to colonies where slavery had not yet become firmly embedded, where the meaning of bondage was still being worked out.

Repressive Laws and Slave Codes.   But Johnson's descendants, and the generations of slaves and free black people who came after them, encountered much harsher conditions. Once slavery became the dominant labor system in the Chesapeake, tobacco planters no longer welcomed free black people, fearing that they might encourage slaves to escape. Black people like the Johnsons, who were already free, suffered under an increasing burden of legal discrimination. Interracial marriages, never common, were prohibited as "shameful Matches."

The condition of slaves was far worse. Slave codes, laws governing slavery, essentially reduced an entire class of human beings to property. In Virginia a series of new laws added to slaves' oppression. A 1662 measure defined slavery as a lifelong and inherited status that passed from slave mothers to their children. A 1667 law stated that baptism would not release slaves from bondage. Two years later, the House of Burgesses gave masters the power of life and death over their slaves. These and other measures were gathered into a comprehensive slave code in Virginia in 1705. Slave codes appeared virtually everywhere, North and South, but were particularly harsh in the southern colonies.

The changing composition of the slave labor force also created tensions. Slaves who arrived in the eighteenth century usually came from the African interior and had had less contact with European customs and language. Worried planters commented on the strange appearance and behavior of these people. Their uneasiness, of course, scarcely compared to the Africans' harrowing experience of being torn away from the only world they knew and thrust into the harsh and unfamiliar condition of slavery.

AFRICAN AMERICAN FAMILIES AND COMMUNITIES

The harshness of the slaves' condition could be relieved somewhat by the formation of close ties with others who shared their circumstances. For such ties to be created, however, several developments had to occur. Slaves had to become sufficiently numerous in specific localities so that black people could have regular contact with one another. Ethnic and language barriers carried over from Africa had to erode so that slaves could communicate with one another. And for family ties to be formed, there had to be adequate numbers of slave women as well as men. Because these conditions were slow to develop, occurring at different rates in different colonies, the formation of African American families and communities was delayed until well into the eighteenth century.

The situation was perhaps most difficult for slaves in the northern colonies. Many slaves there lived alone or in pairs with their master's family. Only in cities and on substantial commercial farms were slaves numerous enough to create their own communities. The formation of families, however, was slowed by a relative scarcity of women. When slave families did appear, husbands and wives often lived in different households as the property of different masters.

The Rise of the Creole Slave Population.   Slaves were far more numerous in the southern colonies, and it is there that African American families and communities emerged with greater success. This fact was especially true in South Carolina and parts of the Tidewater Chesapeake, and it was these regions that witnessed the rise of a creole, or American-born, slave population by about the 1750s.

Creoles lived longer than African immigrants, and creole women usually bore twice as many children as African-born mothers. This circumstance allowed the slave population to grow by natural increase and more closely resemble a normal population of men and women, children and elders. At the same time, creole slaves grew up without personal memories of Africa, and thus African ethnic differences receded in importance. Most creoles knew some English and spoke dialects that mixed English and African words and speech patterns, so that they were able to communicate with other slaves and form African American communities.

Work and Family Life.   Most of a slave's life was structured by work. The vast majority of southern slaves were field hands. On large plantations, masters selected some slave men to be trained as shoemakers, weavers, or tailors and chose others as drivers or leaders of work gangs. Few slave women avoided the drudgery of field labor. If they had families, the end of the day's work in the fields only marked the start of domestic duties back in the slave quarters. Work did not, however, absorb every minute of the slaves' lives, and in the intervals around their assigned duties many slaves nurtured ties of family and community.

This eighteenth-century painting from South Carolina records the preservation of certain African traditions in American slave communities. The dance may be Yoruba in origin, while the stringed instrument and drum were probably modeled on African instruments.

Colonial Williamsburg Foundation, Abby Aldrich Rockefeller Folk Art Center, Williamsburg, VA.

By the late eighteenth century, more than half of Chesapeake and Carolina slaves lived in family groups. These were fragile units, subject to the whims of masters who did not recognize slave marriages as legal, broke up families by sale, and could take slave women as sexual partners at will. Over time, dense kinship networks formed, reflecting West African influences. Slaves placed great emphasis on kin connections, even using familiar terms such as "aunt" and "uncle" to address friends. In naming their children, slaves mingled old and new practices, sometimes giving them the African names of distant kin and sometimes using English names.

Community Life and Religion.   Community life forged ties between slave families and single slaves on the plantations and offered further opportunities to preserve elements of African heritage. Traces of African religious practices endured in America. Reflecting their West African background, slaves placed great emphasis on funerals, in the belief that relatives remained members of kin communities even after death.

Christianity offered little competition to African religious practices during most of the colonial period. Few masters showed much interest in converting their slaves. Evangelical ministers did gain some converts, but the widespread adoption of Christianity by slaves did not occur until after the Revolution.

QUICK REVIEW

Creole Slaves

- Slaves born in America, not Africa
- Lived longer and had more children than African-born slaves
- Played key role in the development of African American identity

WHERE TO LEARN MORE

★ Carter's Grove Slave Quarter, near Williamsburg, Virginia
www.williamsburg.com/plant/carter.html

2–12
James Oglethorpe: The Stono Rebellion (1739)

Stono Rebellion Uprising in 1739 of South Carolina slaves against whites; inspired in part by Spanish officials' promise of freedom for American slaves who escaped to Florida.

African influences shaped aspects of slaves' recreational activity and material life. Slave musicians used African-style instruments to accompany traditional songs and dances. Storytellers entertained audiences with folk tales that may have had African roots. Where slaves were allowed to build their own houses, they often incorporated African elements into the designs. Their gardens frequently contained African foods, such as millet, yams, peppers, and sesame seeds.

Family and community ties gave a sense of belonging and dignity to people whose masters treated them as outcasts. Working and living together, slaves preserved at least some elements of African culture despite the harrowing conditions of their forced migration. Out of their African past and their American experience, they created new identities as African Americans as they coped with the oppressiveness of slavery.

RESISTANCE AND REBELLION

Slaves who resisted their oppression ran the risk of endangering families and friends as well as themselves. But the powerful desire for freedom and the spirit of resistance were not easily suppressed.

Running away from a master was a desperate act, but thousands of slaves did just that. But deciding where else to go posed a problem. Escape out of the South did not bring freedom, because slavery was legal in every colony. After 1733, some runaways went to Florida, where Spanish officials promised them freedom. Others tried to survive on their own in the woods or join the Indians. For slaves with families, running away carried the high emotional cost of separation from loved ones as well as physical danger. Perilous as it was, escape proved irresistible to some slaves, especially young males.

Many slaves chose less perilous ways to resist their bondage. Landon Carter, one of Virginia's wealthiest tobacco planters, once complained that his slaves "seem to be quite dead hearted and either cannot or will not work." He did not realize that he had become the target of forms of resistance more subtle, but every bit as real, as running away. Slaves worked slowly, broke tools, and pretended to be ill in order to exert some control over their working lives. When provoked, they also took more direct action, damaging crops, stealing goods, and setting fire to barns, houses, and fields.

The most serious, as well as the rarest, form of resistance was organized rebellion. South Carolinians and coastal Virginians, who lived in regions where black people outnumbered white people, had a particular dread of slave revolt. But rebellions were extremely hard to organize. No slave rebellion succeeded in the British colonies. Rumors usually leaked out before any action had been taken, prompting severe reprisals against the alleged conspirators.

Two slave revolts did occur in the colonial period, however, and instilled lasting fear in the white colonists. In 1712 in New York City, where black people made up perhaps 20 percent of the population, about twenty slaves set a building on fire and killed nine white men who came to put it out. The revolt was quickly suppressed. The court tried forty-three rebels and sentenced twenty-four to death. The **Stono Rebellion,** colonial America's largest slave uprising, occurred in South Carolina in 1739. It began when about twenty slaves broke into a store and armed themselves with stolen guns. As the rebels marched southward along the Stono River, their ranks grew to perhaps a hundred. Heading for freedom in Spanish Florida, they attacked white settlements along the way. White troops (with Indian help) defeated the rebels within a week, but tensions remained high for months. The death toll, in the end, was about two dozen white people and perhaps twice as many black rebels.

In the wake of the Stono Rebellion, South Carolina's assembly passed a law requiring stricter supervision of slave activities. Other measures encouraged more white immigration to offset the colony's black majority. But the colony continued to rely on the labor system that generated so much fear and brutality, because planters considered slavery indispensable to their economic survival and would not willingly give it up. Their slaves, in turn, obeyed when necessary, resisted when possible, and kept alive the hope that freedom would one day be theirs.

EUROPEAN LABORERS IN EARLY AMERICA

Slavery was one of several responses to the scarcity of labor in the New World. It took hold mainly in areas where the profits from growing export crops such as sugar, rice, and tobacco offset the high purchase price of slaves and where a warm climate permitted year-round work. Elsewhere European masters and employers found various ways to acquire and manage European laborers.

A SPECTRUM OF CONTROL

Most colonial laborers were, in some measure, unfree (see the Overview table, "Predominant Colonial Labor Systems, 1750"). One-half to two-thirds of all white immigrants to the English colonies arrived as indentured servants. But indentured servants carried too high a price for farmers who raised crops mainly for subsistence rather than for sale. Thus, although servants could be found in every colony, they were most common in the Chesapeake and, to a lesser extent, in Pennsylvania, where they produced export crops valuable enough to enable their masters to feed, clothe, and shelter them—and still make a profit.

Slaves replaced white indentured servants in Chesapeake tobacco fields during the eighteenth century. By the middle of the eighteenth century, white servitude, although it still existed in the Chesapeake region as well as in Pennsylvania and New York, was in decline as a dominant labor system.

Eighteenth-century Chesapeake planters also availed themselves of another unfree labor source: transported English convicts. Lawmakers in England saw transportation as a way of getting rid of criminals who might otherwise be executed. Between 1718 and 1775, nearly fifty thousand convicts were sent to the colonies, 80 percent of whom ended up in the Chesapeake. Most were young, lower-class males forced by economic hardship to turn to crime. Labor-hungry planters eagerly bought them for seven-year terms at relatively low prices and exploited them ruthlessly.

An arrangement similar to indentured servitude—the **redemptioner** system—brought many families, especially from German provinces, to the colonies in the eighteenth century. Instead of negotiating contracts for service before leaving Europe, as indentured servants did, redemptioners promised to redeem, or pay, the costs of passage on arrival in America. They often paid part of the fare before sailing. If they could not raise the rest soon after landing, the ship captain who brought them sold them into servitude. The length of their service depended on how much they still owed.

Purchasing slaves, servants, or convicts did not make sense for everyone. Colonists who owned undeveloped land faced many tasks that brought no immediate profit. Rather than buy expensive laborers to accomplish these ends, landowners rented undeveloped tracts to families without property. Both tenants and landlords benefited from this arrangement. Tenants enjoyed greater independence than servants and could save toward the purchase of their own farms. The landlord secured the labor necessary to transform his property into a working farm, thus increasing the land's value. Tenancy worked best in Pennsylvania,

WHAT METHODS did Europeans employ to acquire and manage labor in colonial America?

Redemptioner   Similar to an indentured servant, except that a redemptioner signed a labor contract in America rather than in Europe.

OVERVIEW　PREDOMINANT COLONIAL LABOR SYSTEMS, 1750

	Colony	Labor System
New England	Massachusetts	Family farms
	Connecticut	Family farms
	New Hampshire	Family farms
	Rhode Island	Family farms
Middle Colonies	New York	Family farms, tenancy
	Pennsylvania and Delaware	Indentured servitude, tenancy, family farms
	New Jersey	Family farms, tenancy
South	Maryland	Slavery
	Virginia	Slavery
	North Carolina	Family farms, slavery
	South Carolina	Slavery

WHERE TO LEARN MORE

★ Ephrata Cloister, Ephrata, Pennsylvania **www.cob-net.org/ cloister.htm**

QUICK REVIEW

Child Labor in New England
- Children began work as young as 5 or 6.
- Teenagers took on adult tasks.
- Fathers used ownership of property to tie sons to the land.

New Jersey, and the Hudson and Connecticut River Valleys, where farmers raised wheat and other grains for the market.

Merchants eager to develop New England's fisheries devised other means to fill their labor needs. Because it was fairly easy to get a farm, few New Englanders took on the risky job of fishing. Moreover, few could afford the necessary equipment. Merchants learned to recruit fishermen by advancing credit to coastal villagers so that they could outfit their own boats. To pay off the debt, the fishermen were legally bound to bring their catch to the merchant, who then sold it to Europe and the West Indies. Toward the end of the seventeenth century, as the rising population of coastal villages lowered the cost of labor, merchants abandoned the credit system and paid wages to fishermen instead.

In the northern colonies, the same conditions that made men reluctant to become fishermen deterred them from becoming farm laborers, except perhaps for high wages. Paying high wages, however, or the high purchase cost of servants or slaves was difficult, if not impossible, for New Englanders with farms that produced no export crops. So northern farmers turned to the cheapest and most dependable workers they could find—their children.

Children as young as 5 or 6 years old began with simple tasks and moved on to more complex work as they grew older. By the time they were in their late teens, girls knew how to run households, and boys knew how to farm. Young men could not marry until they could set up their own households and relied on their fathers to provide them with land to do so. Fathers often waited until their sons were in their mid-twenties, compelling them until then to invest their labor in the paternal estate. Thus New England's labor shortage produced strong ties of dependency between generations.

Property owners in all the English colonies found different ways to control the laborers they so desperately needed. But where property owners saw problems—high wages and abundant land—others saw opportunities. For tens of thousands of Europeans, the chance to own or rent a farm or to find steady employment made North America an irresistible magnet.

NEW EUROPEAN IMMIGRANTS

European immigrants flooded into America in the seventeenth and eighteenth centuries. Nearly 250,000 Scots-Irish people came to the colonies after 1718. Tens of thousands of immigrants arrived from Scotland during the same period, some seeking economic improvement and some sent as punishment for rebellions against the king. Thousands of Irish Catholics arrived as servants, redemptioners, and convicts.

Continental Europe contributed another stream of emigrants. Perhaps 100,000 German Protestants left the Rhine Valley. French Protestants (known as Huguenots) began emigrating after 1685, when their faith was made illegal in France. Swiss Protestants likewise fled religious persecution. Even a few Poles, Greeks, Italians, and Jews reached the colonies in the eighteenth century.

Many emigrants responded to pamphlets and newspaper articles that exaggerated the bright prospects of life in America. Others studied more realistic accounts from friends and relatives who had already emigrated. Landowners eager for workers sent agents to port towns to recruit new arrivals to become tenants, often on generous terms.

Streams of emigrants flowed to places where land was cheap and labor most in demand (see Map 3–3). Few went to New England, where descendants of the first settlers occupied the best land. They also avoided areas where slavery predominated—the Chesapeake Tidewater and lowland South Carolina—in favor of the foothills of the Appalachian Mountains, from western Pennsylvania to the Carolinas.

Not all emigrants realized their dreams of becoming independent landowners. The scarcity of labor in the colonies led as easily to the exploitation of white workers as of slaves and Indians. Even so, for many people facing bleak prospects in Europe, the chance that emigration might bring prosperity was too tempting to ignore.

CONCLUSION

By the middle of the eighteenth century, America offered a strikingly diverse mosaic of peoples and communities. Along the St. Lawrence River lay Kahnawake, a village of Mohawks and Abenakis who had adopted Catholicism and French ways under Jesuit instruction. In Andover, Massachusetts, New Englanders tilled fields that their Puritan grandparents had cleared. German immigrants seeking spiritual perfection populated the isolated Pennsylvania settlement of Ephrata. The hundred or so slaves on Robert Carter's Virginia plantation at Nomini Hall gathered on Sunday evenings to nurture ties of community with songs and dances, while the master cultivated his very different sense of community with the neighboring planters. Near St. Augustine, runaway slaves built a town under the protection of Spanish

MAP EXPLORATION

To explore an interactive version of this map, go to
http://www.prenhall.com/goldfield3/map3.3

MAP 3–3   Ethnic Distribution of Settler Population in British Mainland Colonies, c. 1755   Settlers of different ethnic backgrounds tended to concentrate in certain areas. Only New Englanders were predominantly English, while Africans dominated in the Chesapeake Tidewater and South Carolina. German, Scottish, and Scots-Irish immigrants often settled in the backcountry.

DO YOU think colonists from different ethnic backgrounds tended to settle in areas geographically similar to those from which they came?

THE LEGACY OF SLAVERY

As the twenty-first century begins, Americans continue to grapple with the social, economic, and political consequences of the nation's past involvement in the enslavement of Africans. Slavery's roots extend deeply into American history, reaching back before nationhood itself. White colonists, facing a New World labor shortage in the seventeenth century, chose to fill their need for workers by purchasing slaves from Africa. Seeking to produce as much tobacco, rice, or sugar as they could for as little cost as possible, they left a painful legacy that has shaped America's history for centuries.

By the early eighteenth century, slavery was a fixture in every colony, and white colonists had come to associate slave status with black skin. The Revolution, with its rhetoric of freedom, challenged slavery but did not end it. It took another, far bloodier, war in the following century to accomplish that end. But the constitutional amendments outlawing slavery and guaranteeing black people's civil rights that passed after the Civil War—important milestones though they were—still could not eradicate the racism that had become deeply ingrained in American life.

Even today, nearly a century and a half after the Civil War ended, problems persist. Many black Americans have joined the middle class, but many others continue to suffer from discrimination and poverty. Black Americans' average incomes lag behind those of white people, fewer black people attend college, more of them live in impoverished neighborhoods in decaying urban centers. Black victims occasionally become targets of hate crimes merely because of the color of their skin. To a considerable extent, these economic and social dislocations, and the racial attitudes that help to shape them, can be traced to the lingering effects of slavery.

In recent years, while on official visits to Africa, American presidents have acknowledged their nation's historic experience with slavery. In July 2003, President George

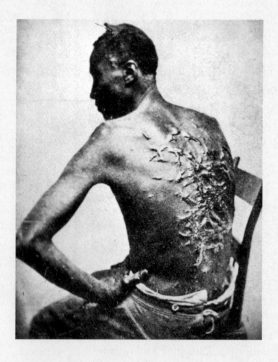

W. Bush made a special trip to the slave-trading post on Senegal's Goree Island, as did Bill Clinton in 1998. Both American leaders took the occasion to express regret for their nation's involvement with slavery and to note its long-standing effects. "The racial bigotry fed by slavery did not end with slavery or with segregation," declared George Bush. "And many of the issues that still trouble America have roots in the bitter experience of other times." Despite occasional calls to do so, neither Congress nor any president has issued a formal apology for American slavery.

The reluctance of political leaders to take on such a sensitive issue may explain the recent search for private remedies. Among these efforts was a federal lawsuit filed in March 2002 against the Aetna Insurance Company, the FleetBoston Financial Corporation, and the CSX Corporation. A group of black plaintiffs charged that these companies had profited from slavery in the past, and ought to make restitution. In the 1850s the Aetna Insurance Company, for example, made money insuring the lives of slaves. A class action suit filed against these and other defendants calling for payment of reparations was dismissed in January 2004. But one of the defendants, JP Morgan Chase, subsequently issued an apology in January 2005 for its subsidiaries' involvement in the slave trade two centuries earlier. The bank also established an initial five-year $5 million college scholarship fund for black students from Louisiana.

How effective reparations would be at ameliorating the condition of poor black Americans, even if ordered by the courts, is unclear. These lawsuits join a host of earlier strategies, including constitutional amendments and civil rights legislation, in seeking to reverse the legacy of slavery and to make equality and justice a reality for all Americans. Even in the first decade of the twenty-first century, the nation is still contending with the consequences of decisions made by some of the earliest colonists almost four hundred years ago.

soldiers. Far to the west, the Spanish, mestizo, and Pueblo residents of Santa Fe warily reestablished ties broken during the Pueblo Revolt. In these and many other communities, peoples from three continents adapted to one another and to American conditions. Indians struggled with the consequences of disease, trade, religious conversion, settlement, and warfare resulting from European immigration. Millions of African slaves suffered under the most repressive labor regime but fought its grip whenever possible. English settlers became landowners in unprecedented numbers and adopted new ways to control laborers, reinventing slavery, unknown in England for centuries. For many European immigrants, the colonies offered the chance for economic improvement. Impoverished servants, transported convicts, and slaves, however, found America to be no land of opportunity

As the eighteenth century wore on, the North American colonies attracted more attention from their home countries. Everywhere the effort to strengthen imperial ties created ambivalence among colonists. Because the English settlers were by far the most numerous, their responses were the most pronounced. As they saw more clearly the differences between themselves and England itself, some colonists began to defend their distinctive habits, while others tried more insistently than ever to imitate English ways. The tension had characterized colonial development from the start. What made the eighteenth century distinctive were the many ways in which the tensions worked themselves out.

SUMMARY

Indians and Europeans Although by 1750 European colonists and African slaves together outnumbered Indians north of the Rio Grande, Native Americans continued to dominate much of the continent. More than any other European colonists, the Spanish sought direct control over Indians. Using the practices of *encomienda, repartimiento,* and *rescate,* Spanish colonists were able to control Indians in use for labor. The English caused much displacement of Indian tribes through their constant expansion of land needs. Through the spread of disease and other means, they managed to push the Indians farther and farther away from prime land once considered theirs. After nearly a century of European settlement, violence between colonists and Indians erupted in all three North American empires. A series of wars and revolts began a period of decades of hostilities between Europeans and Indians.

IMAGE KEY
for pages 58–59.

a. 14 men and 6 women from Guinea arriving on a Dutch ship at Jamestown, Virginia in August 1619, the beginning of slavery in the American colonies.
b. Ball-headed war club.
c. Poster advertising the sale of slaves.
d. The freed slave Olaudah Equiano.
e. Model of the slave ship *Brookes,* showing plain view of slave positions.
f. *Chronicles of Michoacan;* detail from manuscript.
g. The Old Plantation, showing slaves at work.
h. Jesuit missionary baptizing an Indian in New France.
i. Engraving showing humiliating slave inspections.

Africans and Europeans Though many more Africans than Europeans came to the New World during the colonial period, virtually all of them arrived as slaves. The Spanish and the Portuguese first brought Africans to the Americas to supplement the dwindling numbers of Indian slaves. Then, beginning in the 1680s, planters in the Chesapeake colonies began to shift from servants to slaves. Slavery grew most rapidly in the south because of the type of labor needed. European traders relied on other Africans to capture slaves for them. Slaves suffered through a six- to eight-week-long ocean voyage known as the Middle Passage. By about 1750, more slaves in the southern colonies were American-born than African natives.

European Laborers in North America Most colonial laborers were, in some measure, unfree. More than one-half of all white emigrants to the English colonies

GLOBAL PERSPECTIVES

EARLY MODERN EUROPE'S BIGGEST MASS MIGRATION

The stream of German immigrants moving to America in the late seventeenth and eighteenth centuries formed only a small part of a much larger flow of emigrants from the Rhineland to many parts of the globe. The Rhineland was not a single political unit, but a region of small states and principalities located along one of Europe's major rivers. Political fragmentation brought religious diversity, with German Reformed or Lutheran churches dominant in some areas and Catholics in others.

Large-scale emigration of Rhineland inhabitants stemmed from a variety of causes, with warfare a primary motive. During the Thirty Years' War (1618–1648), much of the Rhineland area was devastated by intense religious conflict and famine. In the 1680s and 1690s, Louis XIV of France invaded the region, sparking more turmoil. Almost continual warfare from the 1730s to the 1760s made the lives of Rhineland inhabitants even worse.

Economic hardship and political repression also spurred emigration. Harsh winters in 1708–09 and 1709–10, for instance, destroyed orchards and vineyards, threatening many farmers with impoverishment and even starvation. Harvests failed in many parts of the Rhineland in the 1740s. In addition, religious minorities suffered from persecution, and everyone bore the burden of increasing taxes and arbitrary rule by local princes. For all of these reasons, over the course of the eighteenth century, hundreds of thousands of Rhinelanders decided to flee their homeland.

Many promoters, land speculators, and even governments sought to direct the flow of emigrants to a favored region. Officials from Russia and Prussia, for instance, offered cheap land and tax exemptions to lure migrants to their countries. As a result of this promotional campaign, by far the largest number of Rhineland refugees relocated to various parts of Eastern Europe, including Prussia, Russia, Hungary, and Poland. A smaller flow of emigrants, mostly Protestants, made their way to North America, settling principally in Pennsylvania, New York, and the Carolinas. Still others moved to Cayenne (French Guiana) in South America. The exodus of these German-speaking emigrants to destinations in the Old and New Worlds constituted the most significant mass migration in early modern Europe.

arrived as indentured servants. And, Chesapeake planters tapped another unfree labor source: transported English convicts. Purchasing slaves, servants, and convicts, however, did not make sense for everyone. Northern farmers turned to the cheapest and most dependable workers they could find, their children.

REVIEW QUESTIONS

1. The first phase of Olaudah Equiano's journey into slavery took him from Africa's interior to the coast. What part of this journey most frightened him? Why? How did the development of a transatlantic labor market shape Equiano's experiences in the New World and the Old?

2. English colonists experienced more frequent, and more violent, conflicts with Indians than the settlers of New France did. Why was this so? What factors affected Indian–European relations in the two colonial regions?

3. Why were Catholic missionaries more successful than Protestants in converting Indians to Christianity in early America?

4. When did Chesapeake planters switch from servants to slaves? What factors contributed to their decision to make this change?

5. By about 1750, more slaves in the mainland British colonies were creoles (American-born) than African-born. What effects did this have on the formation of African American communities in America?

6. Different labor systems predominated in various regions of British America. How did the economy of each region help determine its labor system?

7. Tens of thousands of European immigrants came to America in the eighteenth century, but they tended to settle only in certain colonial regions. What destinations did they favor and why?

KEY TERMS

Bacon's Rebellion (p. 68)
Beaver Wars (p. 63)
Encomienda (p. 61)
King Philip's War (p. 68)

Middle Passage (p. 72)
Pueblo Revolt (p. 70)
Redemptioner (p. 79)

Repartimiento (p. 61)
Rescate (p. 61)
Stono Rebellion (p. 78)

WHERE TO LEARN MORE

Ste. Marie among the Hurons, near Midland, Ontario, Canada. This site contains a reconstructed Jesuit mission from the seventeenth century. There is a museum with information about seventeenth-century France as well as life among the Huron Indians. Further information may be found at **www.saintemarieamongthehurons.on.ca.**

Taos Pueblo, Taos, New Mexico. Still a residence for Pueblo Indians, portions of this multistoried pueblo date from the fifteenth century. This was the site from which Popé directed the beginnings of the Pueblo Revolt in 1680. Pictures and other information are available at **www.cr.nps.gov/worldheritage/taos.htm.**

Ephrata Cloister, Ephrata, Pennsylvania. Founded by German immigrants in the eighteenth century, the Ephrata community attracted religious pietists. The site now contains a museum, buildings that reflect medieval German architectural styles, and a collection of decorative art objects. The website **www.cob-net.org/cloister.htm** includes a biography of Ephrata's founder, Johann Conrad Beissel.

Carter's Grove Slave Quarter, near Williamsburg, Virginia. Site includes reconstructed eighteenth-century slave quarters on the original site where slave cabins once stood. Costumed African American interpreters show visitors around and tell stories about actual slaves who lived on the plantation. Information about the house and plantation can be found at **www.williamsburg.com/plant/carter.html.** Pictures of the plantation may also be seen at **www.wise.virginia.edu.**

Anacostia Museum and Center for African American History and Culture, Washington, D.C. Part of the Smithsonian Institution, this museum contains exhibits relating to African American art, culture, and history. Information about current and past exhibitions, as well as online resources, can be found at **anacostia.si.edu.**

 U. S. History Documents CD-ROM
For primary sources related to this chapter, refer to the document CD-ROM.

 www.prenhall.com/goldfield
For study resources related to this chapter, visit the *Companion Website*™.

4 English Colonies in an Age of Empire
1660s–1763

CHAPTER HIGHLIGHTS

Economic Development and Imperial Trade in the British Colonies England, the Netherlands, and France competed vigorously in transatlantic trade. Between 1651 and 1733, Parliament passed laws meant to ensure that more wealth flowed into England's treasury than out of it. The growth of colonial cities mirrored British urban development.

The Transformation of Culture Eighteenth-century Americans sought to emulate the style and culture of Britain. Educated colonists were interested in the ideas of the Enlightenment. For most colonists, religion remained the foundation of their worldview. The Great Awakening drew the colonies closer to England.

The Colonial Political World Late seventeenth-century efforts by the British to take more direct control of the colonies failed. English people on both sides of the Atlantic believed that politics should reflect the social hierarchy. Tensions between Britain and the colonists grew, however, over the issues of virtual representation and the powers of colonial governors.

Expanding Empires During the first half of the eighteenth century, England, France, and Spain all expanded their North American holdings. The British colonies experienced rapid population growth. Spain's empire grew into Texas and California, while French expansion tended to follow major waterways like the Mississippi.

A Century of Warfare The English policy of limiting French expansion resulted in four wars between 1689 and 1763. The decisive British victory in the final war signaled a dramatic shift in North American history. Britain was now the dominant European power on the continent.

CITY HALL AND GREAT DOCK.

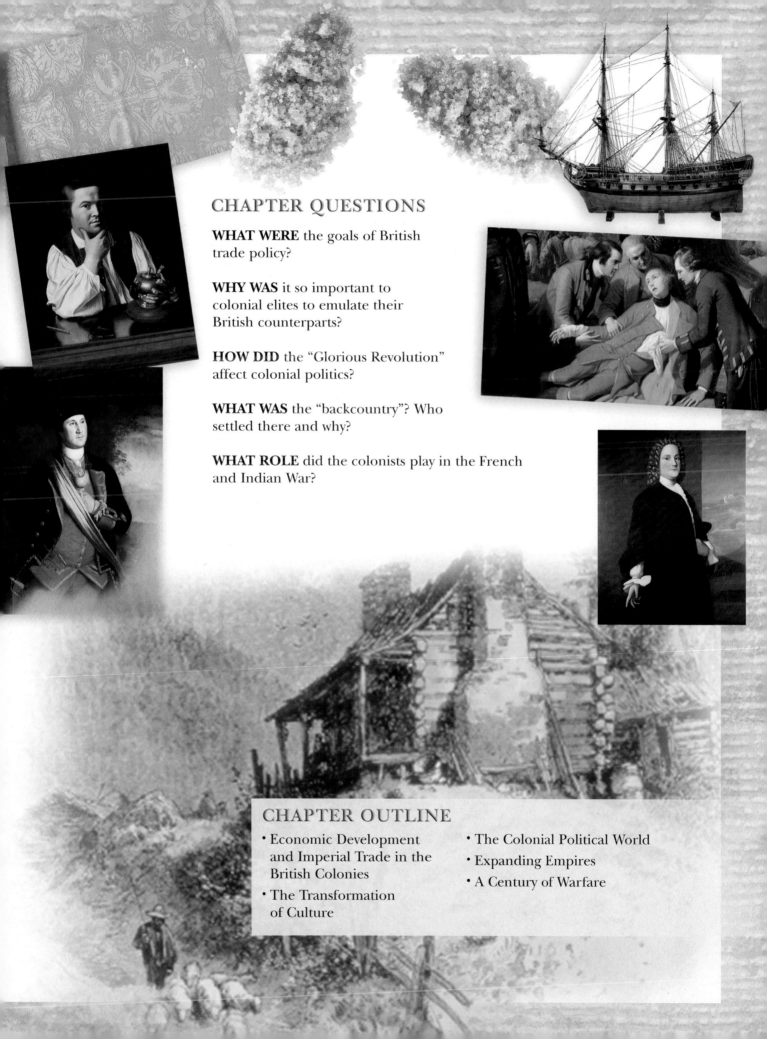

CHAPTER QUESTIONS

WHAT WERE the goals of British trade policy?

WHY WAS it so important to colonial elites to emulate their British counterparts?

HOW DID the "Glorious Revolution" affect colonial politics?

WHAT WAS the "backcountry"? Who settled there and why?

WHAT ROLE did the colonists play in the French and Indian War?

CHAPTER OUTLINE

- Economic Development and Imperial Trade in the British Colonies
- The Transformation of Culture
- The Colonial Political World
- Expanding Empires
- A Century of Warfare

IMAGE KEY

for pages 86–87 is on page 118.

Virginia 26th April 1763

Mr. Lawrence

    Be pleased to send me a genteel sute of Cloaths made of superfine broad Cloth handsomely chosen; I shou[l]d have Inclosed [for] you my measure but in a general way they are so badly taken here that I am convinced it wou[l]d be of very little service; I wou[l]d have you therefore take measure of a Gentleman who wears well made Cloaths of the following size—to wit—Six feet high & proportionably made; if any thing rather Slender than thick for a Person of that highth with pretty long arms & thighs—You will take care to make the Breeches longer than those you sent me last, & I wou[l]d have you keep the measure of the Cloaths you now make by you and if any alteration is required, in my next [letter] it shall be pointed out. Mr Cary will pay your Bill—& I am Sir Yr Very H[um]ble Serv[an]t . . .

George Washington

W.W. Abbot and Dorothy Twohig, eds., *The Papers of George Washington,* Colonial Series, vol. 7 (Charlottesville, 1990).

GEORGE WASHINGTON, ALONG with a few dozen other privileged Virginians, had traveled to Williamsburg for a visit that mixed politics, business, and pleasure. Like Washington, these men had come to the capital to represent their respective counties in the House of Burgesses. When not engaged in government business, they attended to private affairs. Washington was surely not the only one to take the opportunity to write to his London tailor and order the fashionable clothing that advertised his status as a gentleman. He and his fellow burgesses donned their best coats and breeches to attend evening dinner parties and theater performances.

April 1763 marked the fourth time Washington had gone to Williamsburg to take his seat in the legislature. Just 31 years old in 1763, he had recently married Martha Custis, a wealthy widow, and inherited his older brother's plantation at Mount Vernon. He had served his king in battle during the Seven Years' War; now he was eager to exchange his military uniform for the "genteel" broadcloth suits appropriate to his new station. With land and wealth to support his ambitions, he wanted to live, look, and behave like an English country gentleman.

But Washington had never been to England and trusted neither his own judgment nor Williamsburg tailors to know how a proper English gentleman should dress. He had to trust his tailor to make him clothing as suitable for the drawing rooms of London as for the parlors of Williamsburg.

Throughout British America, colonists who had achieved wealth and power tried, like Washington, to imitate the habits and manners of the English gentry. Prosperity and the demand of a growing population for English products tied the colonies ever more tightly into a trade network centered on the imperial metropolis, London. The flow of goods and information between England and America fueled the desires of Washington and other successful colonists for acceptance as transatlantic members of the English elite.

These developments in Britain's American colonies brought them to the attention of European statesmen, who increasingly factored North America into their economic, political, diplomatic, and military calculations. Parliament devised legislation that would channel colonial products into England and away from its European competitors. Spain and France viewed the economic growth and geographic expansion of British North America as a threat to their own colonial possessions. With expansion came conflict, and with conflict a series of four imperial wars, which themselves became powerful engines of change in the New World.

ECONOMIC DEVELOPMENT AND IMPERIAL TRADE IN THE BRITISH COLONIES

Great Britain's greatest assets in its competition with other European nations were a dynamic economy and a sophisticated financial system that put commerce at the service of the state. England's leaders came to see colonies as indispensable to the nation's economic welfare. Colonies supplied raw materials unavailable in the mother country, and colonists and Indians provided a healthy market for English manufactured goods. Parliament knitted the colonies into an empire with commercial legislation, while British merchants traded with and extended credit to growing numbers of colonial merchants and planters. Over time, these developments made colonial societies resemble England and integrated the economies of the colonies with that of the mother country in a vast transatlantic system.

THE REGULATION OF TRADE

England, Holland, and France competed vigorously in transatlantic trade. To improve its competitive position, England adopted a policy of **mercantilism.** The goal was to achieve a favorable balance of trade within the empire as a whole, with exports exceeding imports. Colonies played a crucial role, since they supplied commodities that English consumers would otherwise have to purchase from foreign competitors. Between 1651 and 1733, Parliament passed four types of mercantilist regulations to put this policy into action (see the Overview table, "British Imperial Trade Regulations, 1651–1733").

The first type of regulation aimed at ending Dutch dominance in England's overseas trade. Beginning with the Navigation Act of 1651, all trade in the empire had to be conducted in English or colonial ships, with crews of which at least half were Englishmen or colonists. The act stimulated rapid growth in both England's merchant marine and New England's shipping industry.

The second type of legislation stipulated that certain colonial goods, called **enumerated products,** could be shipped only to England or to another English colony. These goods initially included tobacco, sugar, indigo, and cotton; other products, such as rice, were added later. These laws also required European goods to pass through England before they could be shipped to the colonies. When these goods entered English ports, they were taxed, making them more expensive than English-made items.

The third and fourth types of regulations further enhanced the advantage of English manufacturers who produced for the colonial market. Parliament subsidized certain goods, including linen, gunpowder, and silks. Other laws protected English manufacturers from colonial competition by prohibiting colonists from manufacturing wool, felt hats, and iron on a large scale.

England's commercial goals were largely achieved. The Dutch eventually lost their preeminence in the Atlantic trade. Colonial trade helped the English

---

WHAT WERE the goals of British trade policy?

QUICK REVIEW

British Trade Policy
- All trade in empire to be conducted in English or on colonial ships.
- Colonial trade to be channelled through England or another English colony.
- Subsidization of English goods offered for sale in the colonies.
- Colonists prohibited from large-scale manufacture of certain products.

Mercantilism   Economic system whereby the government intervenes in the economy for the purpose of increasing national wealth.

Enumerated products   Items produced in the colonies and enumerated in acts of Parliament that could be legally shipped from the colony of origin only to specified locations.

This view of the Philadelphia waterfront dates from 1720. It shows how the city had developed into one of British America's principal ports just forty years after its founding.

Peter Cooper "The Southeast Prospect of the City of Philadelphia" ca. 1720. The Library Company of Philadelphia.

Chronology

1651–1733	Parliament passes series of Navigation Acts to regulate imperial trade.
1660	Charles II becomes king of England.
1662	Halfway Covenant adopted by Massachusetts clergy.
1685	James II becomes king of England.
1686–1689	Dominion of New England.
1688	Glorious Revolution in England; James II loses the throne.
1689	William and Mary become English monarchs; Leisler's Rebellion begins in New York.
1689–1697	King William's War in America.
1691–1692	Witchcraft trials in Salem, Massachusetts.
1698	First French settlements near mouth of Mississippi River.
1701	Iroquois adopt policy of neutrality toward France and Britain.
1702–1713	Queen Anne's War in America.
1718	San Antonio, Texas and New Orleans founded.
1734–1735	Jonathan Edwards leads religious revival in Northampton, Massachusetts.
1739	Great Awakening begins in Middle Colonies with George Whitefield's arrival.
1744–1748	King George's War in America.
1754–1763	Seven Years' War in America.
1760s	Spanish begin establishing missions in California.

economy to grow and contributed to London's emergence as Western Europe's largest city. Between 1650 and 1770, the colonial economy expanded twice as fast as England's. Colonists enjoyed protected markets for their staple crops and low prices on English imports. Colonial merchants, operating on equal terms with English traders, took full advantage of commercial opportunities within the empire.

Occasionally, merchants evaded these laws by smuggling. Customs officials, sent over from England, were hard-pressed to stop them. Although they derived much of their income from fines collected from smugglers, officials generally found it easier to accept bribes and look the other way when a suspicious ship arrived in port. By not pushing for perfect compliance, British officials did not put too much pressure on a system that in fact worked remarkably well.

THE COLONIAL EXPORT TRADE AND THE SPIRIT OF ENTERPRISE

By the mid-eighteenth century, the Atlantic had become a busy thoroughfare of international commerce (see Map 4–1). At the heart of Anglo-American trade lay the highly profitable commerce in staple crops, most of which were produced by slave labor.

West Indian sugar far surpassed all other colonial products in importance. West Indian planters joined with the English merchants who marketed their sugar to lobby Parliament for favorable treatment. Because these planters and merchants— known as the sugar interest—wielded so much economic power, politicians listened. In 1733 Parliament passed the Molasses Act, which taxed sugar products from foreign sources, and, in 1739, removed sugar from the list of enumerated items.

Tobacco from the Chesapeake colonies was the second most valuable staple crop. Exports worth about £750,000 arrived each year in England during the late 1760s. Persistent low prices, however, led many tobacco planters to sow some of their land with wheat after about 1750. This change lessened their dependence on tobacco.

MAP EXPLORATION

To explore an interactive version of this map, go to **http://www.prenhall.com/goldfield3/map4.1**

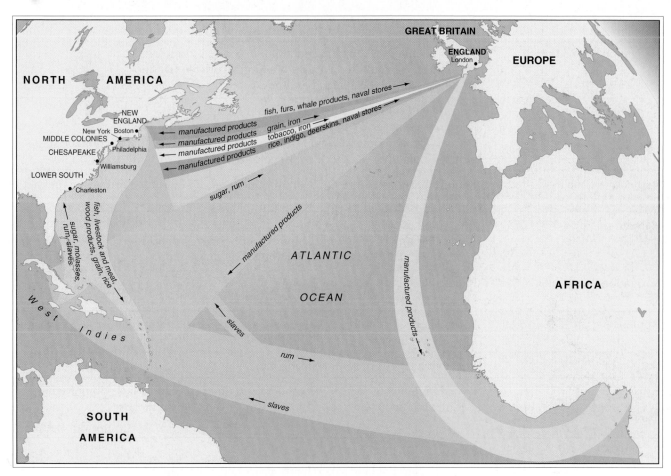

MAP 4–1   Anglo-American Transatlantic Commerce   By the eighteenth century, Great Britain and its colonies were enmeshed in a complex web of trade. Britain exchanged manufactured goods for colonial raw materials, while Africa provided the enslaved laborers who produced the most valuable colonial crops.

ACCORDING TO this map, how did trading between Great Britain and its colonies benefit Great Britain? How did it benefit the colonies? Why was Africa's role so crucial to virtually every aspect of trading between Great Britain and its colonies?

Exports of rice and indigo (a plant that produced an expensive blue dye used in textile manufacture) enriched many South Carolina planters. Parliament encouraged indigo production by granting subsidies to growers and placing stiff taxes on foreign indigo. It also subsidized colonial production of naval stores—such as tar, pitch, and turpentine—to reduce England's dependence on Swedish suppliers.

Wheat exports from the Middle Colonies boomed after 1750, when a combination of poor harvests and warfare in Europe created strong overseas demand. Since farmers in England grew enough wheat to supply the domestic market, ships traveling from Philadelphia or New York to English ports instead carried a variety of other goods, including unrefined iron, potash (used in making soap and glass), salted meats, and wood products.

QUICK REVIEW

Colonial Exports
- Chesapeake colonies: tobacco.
- South Carolina: rice and indigo.
- Middle colonies: wheat.

OVERVIEW BRITISH IMPERIAL TRADE REGULATIONS, 1651–1733

Name of Act	Key Features
Navigation Act of 1651	Aimed to eliminate Dutch competition in overseas trade Required most goods to be carried in English or colonial ships Required crews to be at least half English
Navigation Act of 1660	Required all colonial trade to be carried in English ships Required master and three-quarters of crew to be English Created list of enumerated goods, such as tobacco and sugar, that could be shipped only to England or another English colony
Staple Act of 1663	Required products from Europe, Asia, and Africa to be landed in England before being shipped to the colonies
Plantation Duty Act of 1673	Attempted to reduce smuggling Required captains of colonial ships to post bond that they would deliver enumerated goods to England or pay the "plantation duty" that would be owed in England
Navigation Act of 1696	Plugged loopholes in earlier laws Created vice-admiralty courts in colonies to enforce trade regulations
Woolens Act of 1699	Forbade export of woolen cloth made in the colonies, to prevent competition with English producers
Hat Act of 1732	Prohibited export of colonial-made hats
Molasses Act of 1733	Placed high tax on French West Indian and other foreign molasses imported into colonies to encourage importation of British West Indian molasses

New England's merchants developed a thriving transatlantic trade by carrying other colonies' goods to market. New Englanders built thousands of vessels and eventually dominated shipping within the empire. By 1770, New England's earnings from shipping fees, freight charges, and insurance exceeded the total value of its own exports.

New England merchants also strengthened trade links to the West Indies that had first been forged in the 1650s. By the mid-eighteenth century, more than half of all New England exports went to the islands. Merchants accepted molasses and other sugar by-products in payment, bringing them back to New England to be distilled into cheap rum. Enterprising traders then carried rum to Africa to exchange for slaves. Fewer than 10 percent of New England's population were slaves, but its commercial economy nonetheless depended on slavery.

THE IMPORT TRADE AND TIES OF CREDIT

By the late 1760s, over £4 million worth of English manufactured goods flowed into the colonies each year. Bales of English cloth and leather, crates of glassware and pottery, casks of nails and lead shot piled onto the wharves of Philadelphia and New York. Dockworkers emptied ships' holds of wrought iron, brass, and copper, barrels of refined sugar, and bundles of beaver hats. Some of these goods—ironware, sugar, hats—were made of raw materials from the colonies.

Certain imported items made their way into Indian villages, including weapons, woolen cloth, linen garments, knives, hatchets, and jewelry. Indians

QUICK REVIEW

Colonial Imports

- By late 1760s imports reached annual worth of £4 million.
- Value of imports exceeded exports.
- Over time level of debt in the colonies increased.

were discerning customers and rejected goods not made to their liking. As in the seventeenth century, Indians continued to use such items after their own fashion. An Indian woman might wear a linen shift with an English blanket worn as a mantle, fastened with a beaded belt. The colonists' even heavier consumption of manufactures was vital to British overseas commerce. In terms of value, colonists imported more goods than they exported. This imbalance, however, was remedied in good part by colonial earnings from shipping fees and payments from the British government for colonial military expenses.

British merchants extended credit to colonists on generous terms, making it easy for them to buy British products. These merchants marketed the planters' tobacco and supplied them with English goods, charging the costs of purchase and transportation against the profits they expected the next year's crop to bring.

Easy credit let planters indulge themselves with English goods, and gradually they sank into debt. When trade was brisk and tobacco prices high, neither the planters nor their British creditors worried. But when tobacco prices dropped or an international crisis made overseas trading risky, creditors called in the debts owed to them. At such times, colonial debtors realized how much they depended on goods and credit supplied by distant merchants.

BECOMING MORE LIKE ENGLAND: THE GROWTH OF CITIES AND INEQUALITY

As colonial commerce grew, so did colonial cities. By 1770, Philadelphia's population had reached 30,000, New York's 25,000, Boston's 16,000, and Charleston's 12,000. A fifth city, Baltimore, was rapidly developing at the best harbor on Chesapeake Bay. Only about 5 percent of all mainland colonists lived in cities, but the influence of urban centers far outweighed their size. All colonial cities were seaports, and Europeans took note of the appearance and activity of their dockyards. Oceangoing ships sailed "right up to the town" of Philadelphia on the Delaware River, according to one observer. Boston had "a very fine wharf, at least half a mile long, undertaken at the expense of a number of private gentlemen" to facilitate shipping. New York, then as now, had one of the world's finest harbors, from which it conducted "a more extensive commerce than any town in the English North American provinces."

Indeed, colonial cities resembled English provincial cities more than they did the farming villages of the American countryside. Cities provided all sorts of amenities. Their populations were diverse in ethnic origin and religion. Dr. Alexander Hamilton, a Scottish immigrant, recalled dining at a Philadelphia tavern with "Scots, English, Dutch, Germans, and Irish" and "Roman Catholicks, Church [of England] men, Presbyterians, Quakers, Newlightmen, Methodists, Seventh day men, Moravians, Anabaptists, and one Jew." In addition, the African American population in the northern colonies tended to live in cities. By 1750, slaves made up 20 percent of New York City's population, about 10 percent of Philadelphia's, and nearly 9 percent of Boston's.

Artisans in Colonial Cities. Colonial cities had higher proportions of artisans than did rural villages. Many of them

John Singleton Copley's portrait of the silversmith Paul Revere, painted about 1769, depicts one of Boston's most prominent artisans. As colonists grew wealthier, some commissioned portraits for their homes to serve as emblems of their rising social aspirations. Even so, Copley despaired that America would ever provide a suitable market for his artistic talents and he eventually moved to England.

Paul Revere, c. 1768–70. Copley, John Singleton, U.S., 1738–1815. Oil on canvas, 35 1/2 × 28 1/2 in. (88.9 × 72.3 cm). Gift of Joseph W., William B., and Edward H. R. Revere. Courtesy, Museum of Fine Arts, Boston.

labored at trades directly related to overseas commerce. Others produced pottery, furniture, paper, glassware, iron tools, and various household items. Colonial manufacturing took place in workshops often attached to artisans' houses. Artisans managed a workforce consisting of their wives and children, along with journeymen or apprentices. Apprentices contracted to work for a master for 4 to 7 years in order to learn the "mysteries" of his craft. Like indentured servants, they received no wages but worked for food, clothing, shelter, and a small payment at the end of their service. Once an apprentice finished his training, he became a journeyman, working for a master but now earning wages and saving until he could afford to set up his own shop. Many artisans flourished in colonial cities, but prosperity was by no means guaranteed. Workers at less skilled crafts often earned only a bare living, and ordinary laborers faced seasonal unemployment.

Cities like Philadelphia, New York, and Charleston provided an important setting for some women to support themselves with craft work. Nonetheless, even in cities, women's options were limited. Most employed women were widows striving to maintain a family business until sons grew old enough to take over. Other widows toiled at less prestigious—and less remunerative—jobs as nurses, laundresses, and boardinghouse keepers.

The Growing Gap Between Rich and Poor.   Wherever colonists engaged heavily in commerce—in cities or on plantations—the gap between rich and poor widened during the eighteenth century. In 1687, the richest 10 percent of Boston residents owned 46 percent of the taxable property in the town; by 1771, the top tenth held 63 percent of the taxable wealth. In South Carolina and the Chesapeake, many planters added to the already substantial estates they had inherited, controlling vast amounts of land and numerous slaves. It became increasingly difficult for newcomers to enter their ranks. At the same time, the colonies' growing reliance on slave labor—especially in the South—created a sizeable class of impoverished people denied the chance to better their condition.

To address the growing problem of poverty among white colonists, cities built workhouses, and towns collected funds for poor relief in greater amounts than ever before. Many poor people were aged or ill, without families to help them. Able-bodied workers forced to accept public relief usually owed their misfortune to temporary downturns in the economy, often the result of wartime dislocations.

Even in the worst of times, no more than one out of ten white colonists (mainly city dwellers) depended on public assistance. For free black people who were unemployed and denied public relief, conditions were far worse. A Pennsylvania law went so far as to allow them to be enslaved. And, bad as it was, the problem of poverty among white colonists had not reached anything like the levels seen in England. As much as one-third of England's population regularly received relief, and the numbers swelled during hard times. Eighteenth-century white colonists, on average, enjoyed a higher standard of living than most English residents or other Europeans. So long as land was available colonists could at least eke out a bare subsistence, and many did much better.

Colonial society increasingly resembled Great Britain. The growth of cities mirrored British urban development. The widening gap between rich and poor convinced many colonists that their society had at last matured from its crude beginnings. Eighteenth-century Britons on both sides of the Atlantic believed that societies ought to be organized hierarchically, that God intended for people to be arranged in ranks from rich to poor. The more America resembled Britain, many colonists assumed, the more stable and prosperous it would be.

THE TRANSFORMATION OF CULTURE

D espite the convergence of English and colonial society, many influential settlers worried that America remained culturally inferior to Great Britain. During the eighteenth century, some prosperous colonists strove to overcome this provincial sense of inferiority. They built grand houses and filled them with imported goods, cultivated what they took to be the manners of the British gentry, and followed English and European intellectual developments. Some colonial gentlemen even reshaped their religious beliefs to reflect European notions that God played only an indirect role in human affairs.

These elite aspirations, however, were not shared by most settlers. The majority of colonists had little interest in copying the manners of the English elite, and very few of them altered their spiritual beliefs to fit European patterns. Indeed, familiar religious practices flourished in eighteenth-century America, and when a tremendous revival swept through the colonies beginning in the 1730s, religion occupied center stage in American life.

WHY WAS it so important to colonial elites to emulate their British counterparts?

GOODS AND HOUSES

Eighteenth-century Americans imported more manufactured products from England with every passing year. This practice did not simply reflect the growth of the colonial population, for the rate at which Americans bought British goods exceeded the rate of population increase. Colonists owned more goods, often of better quality, than their parents and grandparents had possessed.

In the less secure economic climate of the seventeenth century, colonists had limited their purchases of goods, investing instead in land to pass on to their children. But by the eighteenth century, prosperous colonists felt secure enough to buy goods to make their lives more comfortable. Benjamin Franklin described such changes in his own household. Accustomed to eating his breakfast of bread and milk with a pewter spoon from an earthenware bowl, he found it one morning "in a China Bowl with a Spoon of Silver" that had cost "the enormous Sum of three and twenty Shillings." His wife, Deborah, justified the purchase by declaring "that she thought her Husband deserved a Silver Spoon & China Bowl as well as any of his Neighbors." To Deborah Franklin, silver and china signified her family's prosperity and good taste.

By the 1760s, nearly every item that George Washington ordered from his London agent could have been purchased in Philadelphia. But Washington wanted the latest English styles and even worried that his agent might take advantage of him by sending goods that were no longer in fashion in England. Washington's desires were hardly unique. One visitor to Maryland, astonished at the speed with which colonists adopted English styles, declared that he was "almost inclined to believe that a new fashion is adopted earlier by the polished and affluent American than by many opulent persons" in London.

Prosperous colonists built grand houses where they lived in greater comfort than ever before. By the 1730s, numerous southern planters had built "great houses" with expensive paneling and marble fireplaces. In the northern colonies, merchants built the most impressive houses, often following architectural pattern books imported from England.

Most settlers lived in one- or two-room dwellings and thus cooked, ate, and slept in the same chamber. But the owners of great houses could devote rooms to specialized uses. Cooking and other domestic work took place in back or in separate outbuildings. Private bedrooms were located upstairs, allowing first-floor rooms to be used for public activities. The most distinctive feature of these grand

Painted at about the time Franklin retired from his printing business, this portrait depicts the one-time craftsman as an aspiring gentleman.

Robert Feke (1707–1752), Portrait of Benjamin Franklin (1706–1790), c. 1746. Oil on canvas, 127 × 102 cm. Courtesy of the Harvard University Portrait Collection. Bequest of Dr. John Collins Warren, 1856.

WHERE TO LEARN MORE

Colonial Williamsburg,
Williamsburg, Virginia
www.colonialwilliamsburg.com/
history/index.cfm

homes was the parlor, an elaborately decorated room used for entertaining guests with music, dancing, and card games.

Prosperous colonists did not build such homes merely to advertise their wealth. They wanted to create the proper setting for a refined way of life, emulating the English gentry in their country estates and London townhouses. But they knew that the true measure of their gentility lay not just in where they lived and what they owned but in how they behaved.

SHAPING MINDS AND MANNERS

Colonists knew that the manners of English gentlefolk set them apart from ordinary people. Many Americans therefore imported "courtesy books," which contained the rules of polite behavior. The young George Washington studied such books carefully. At the age of 13, he copied 110 rules from *Youth's Behaviour; or, Decency in Conversation among Men,* including such advice as "In the Presence of Others Sing not to yourself with a humming Noise, nor Drum with your Fingers or Feet" and "In Company of those of Higher Quality than yourself Speak not till you are ask'd a Question then Stand upright put of[f] your Hat and Answer in few words." Many colonists subscribed to English journals that printed articles describing good manners.

Women, too, cultivated genteel manners. In Charleston, South Carolina, and other colonial cities, girls' boarding schools advertised instruction in "the different branches of Polite Education." Female pupils received only the rudiments of intellectual training in reading, writing, and arithmetic, for it was assumed that women had little need of such accomplishments. The private schools' curricula instead focused on French, music, dancing, and fancy needlework. These were skills that advertised girls' genteel status and prepared them for married lives as mistresses of great houses, mothers of future gentlemen and ladies, and hostesses of grand entertainments.

Such entertainments proliferated in the eighteenth century. Women who could afford to do so invited their neighbors to tea parties, where they could display good manners and fine silver and china at the same time. Robert Carter, one of Virginia's wealthiest gentlemen, once hosted an "elegant" dinner that lasted for nearly eight hours. Such occasions excluded ordinary settlers and reinforced elite colonists' sense of themselves as a separate—and better—class of people.

Some people expressed their gentility through more intellectual pursuits, taking advantage of the relatively high literacy rates among white colonists. In New England, where settlers placed great emphasis on Bible study, about 70 percent of men and 45 percent of women could read and write. Only a third of men in the southern colonies, and even fewer women, could read and write, but even these literacy rates were higher than among England's general population. In 1704, the *Boston News-Letter* became the first continuously published newspaper in British America. By the 1760s nearly every colony had a regularly published newspaper, and booksellers opened shops in several cities. Prominent colonists began to participate in a transatlantic world of ideas.

These colonists, however, were consumers of British and European ideas rather than producers of an American intellectual tradition. They imported thousands of books, subscribed to British journals, and established libraries where borrowing privileges could be purchased for a modest fee. Colonists with literary aspirations emulated their favorite writers. Students at Harvard in Cambridge (founded in 1636) modeled their college newspaper on an English periodical, the *Spectator.* In Virginia, William Byrd II advertised his own genteel pretensions by composing verse in the style of contemporary English poets. The young Thomas Jefferson copied out passages from the English novel *Tristram Shandy.* Benjamin Franklin honed his writing skills by rewriting essays from the *Spectator* and comparing his versions to the originals.

Educated colonists were especially interested in the new ideas that characterized what has been called the **Age of Enlightenment.** The European thinkers of the Enlightenment drew inspiration from recent advances in science that suggested that the universe operated according to natural laws that human reason could discover. They also drew on the work of the English philosopher John Locke, who maintained that God did not dictate human knowledge but rather gave us the power to acquire knowledge through experience and understanding. The hallmark of Enlightenment thought was a belief in the power of human reason to improve the human condition.

This optimistic worldview marked a profound intellectual shift. Enlightenment thinkers rejected earlier ideas about God's unknowable will and continued intervention in human and natural events. They instead assigned God a less active role as the creator of the universe, who had set the world running according to predictable laws, and then let nature—and human beings—shape events. Such ideas inspired a growing international community of scholars to try to discover the laws of nature and to work toward human progress.

Colonial intellectuals sought membership in this scholarly community. A few of them gained election to the Royal Society, the most prestigious learned society in England. Most of their scholarly contributions were unimpressive, but Franklin achieved genuine intellectual prominence. Even as a youth, Franklin hungered after learning and demonstrated a particular gift for science. His experiments with a kite proved that lightning was electricity and gained him an international reputation. Franklin invented the lightning rod, bifocal spectacles, the iron "Franklin stove," and the glass harmonica.

If Franklin's career embodied the Enlightenment ideal of the rational exploration of nature's laws, it also revealed the limited impact of Enlightenment thought in colonial America. Only a few prosperous and educated colonists could afford such intellectual pursuits. Franklin came from humble origins—his father was a maker of candles and soap—but his success as a printer allowed him to retire from business at the age of 42. Only then did he purchase the equipment for his electrical discoveries and have the leisure time to begin his scientific work. Franklin's equipment—and leisure—were as much badges of gentlemanly status as George Washington's London-made suit.

Most colonists remained ignorant of scientific advances and Enlightenment ideas. Unlike aspiring gentlemen and ladies, they had little leisure to devote to literature and polite conversation. When they found time to read, they picked up not a courtesy book or the *Spectator* but the Bible.

COLONIAL RELIGION AND THE GREAT AWAKENING

Church steeples dominated the skylines of colonial cities. By the 1750s, Boston and New York each had eighteen churches, and Philadelphia boasted twenty. Churches and meetinghouses likewise dominated country towns. These buildings bore witness to the diverse and thriving condition of religion in America.

WHERE TO LEARN MORE

Mount Vernon, Virginia
www.mountvernon.org

3–8
Manners and Etiquette in the Eighteenth Century

Age of Enlightenment Major intellectual movement occurring in Western Europe in the late seventeenth and early eighteenth centuries.

In every New England colony except Rhode Island, the Puritan (or Congregationalist) faith was the established religion. The many Congregational churches in the region, headed by ministers trained at Harvard College and Yale (founded in 1701), served the majority of colonists and received financial support from their taxes. Though proud of the Puritan tradition that had inspired New England's origins, ministers and believers nonetheless had to adapt to changing social and religious conditions.

The principal adaptation consisted of a move away from strict requirements for church membership. New England's founders had required prospective members to give convincing evidence that they had experienced a spiritual conversion before they could receive communion and have their children baptized. By the 1660s, however, fewer colonists sought admission under such strict standards. To address this problem, the clergy in 1662 adopted the **Halfway Covenant.** This allowed adults who had been baptized (because their parents were church members), but who had not themselves experienced conversion, to have their own children baptized. By the 1680s, some ministers made church admission even easier, requiring members only to demonstrate knowledge of the Christian faith and to live godly lives.

The Congregational Church also had to accept a measure of religious toleration in New England. Anglicans and Baptists eventually won exemptions from paying taxes to support the Congregational Church. At the same time, some Congregationalist preachers began emphasizing personal piety and good works in their sermons, ideas usually associated with Anglicanism.

In the South, the established Church of England consolidated its authority in the early eighteenth century but never succeeded in exerting effective control over spiritual life. Parishes often lacked trained clergy, and those who did emigrate encountered unexpected obstacles. Anglican clergymen in the southern colonies served parishes that were vast and sparsely settled. Ministers also found that influential planters, accustomed to running parishes when preachers were unavailable, resisted their efforts to take control of churches. Aware that the planters' taxes paid their salaries, many ministers found it easiest simply to preach and behave in ways that offered the least offense. Frontier regions often lacked Anglican churches and clergymen altogether. In such places, dissenting religious groups, such as Presbyterians, Quakers, and Baptists, gained followers among people neglected by the Anglican establishment.

No established church dominated in the Middle Colonies of New York, New Jersey, and Pennsylvania. The region's ethnically diverse population and William Penn's policy of religious toleration guaranteed that a multitude of groups would compete for followers. Yet religion flourished in the Middle Colonies. By the middle of the eighteenth century, the region had more congregations per capita than even New England.

Groups such as the Quakers and the Mennonites, who did not have specially trained ministers, easily formed new congregations in response to local demand. Lutheran and German Reformed churches, however, required European-educated clergy, who were always scarce. When more Lutheran and Reformed clergy arrived in the 1740s and 1750s, they sometimes discovered, as Anglican preachers did in the South, that laymen balked at relinquishing control of the churches. Lutheran and Reformed ministers also learned that their professional training alone could not command respect. Because so many other religious alternatives were available, ministers had to compete for their parishioners' allegiance.

Halfway Covenant Plan adopted in 1662 by New England clergy to deal with problem of declining church membership, allowing children of baptized parents to be baptized whether or not their parents had experienced conversion.

Bewildering spiritual diversity, relentless religious competition, and a comparatively weak Anglican Church all distinguished the colonies from England. Yet in one important way, religious developments during the middle third of the eighteenth century drew the colonies closer to England. A great transatlantic religious revival, originating in Scotland and England, first touched the Middle Colonies in the 1730s. In 1740–1745, it struck the northern colonies with the force of a hurricane, and in the 1760s, the last phase of the revival spread through the South. America had never seen anything like this immense revival, which came to be called the **Great Awakening.**

By 1730, Presbyterians in Pennsylvania had split into factions. One group, led by an immigrant Scottish evangelist, William Tennent, Sr., and his four sons, denounced their opponents as men more interested in regulations than conversion. In the 1730s, Tennent set up the Log College in Neshaminy, Pennsylvania, to train his sons and other young men to be evangelical ministers. What began as a dispute among clergymen eventually blossomed into a broader challenge to religious authority. That challenge gained momentum in late 1739, when one of the most charismatic evangelists of the century, George Whitefield, arrived in the colonies from England.

Whitefield, an Anglican minister who was already famous in Britain as a preacher of great emotional fervor, embarked on a tour of the colonies in the winter of 1739–1740. As soon as Whitefield landed in Delaware, his admirers whipped up local enthusiasm, ensuring that he would preach to huge crowds in Pennsylvania and New Jersey. Whitefield's powerful preaching on the experience of conversion lent support to the Presbyterian faction led by the Tennents and sparked local revivals. Whitefield then moved on to New England, where some communities had already experienced local awakenings.

Whitefield's tour through the colonies knitted these scattered local revivals into the Great Awakening. Crowds gathered in city squares and open fields to listen to his sermons. Whitefield exhorted his audiences to examine their souls for evidence of the "indwelling of Christ" that would indicate that they were saved. He criticized other ministers for emphasizing good works and "head-knowledge" instead of the emotional side of religion.

Settlers normally gathered with family and neighbors in church for formal, structured services. They sat in pews assigned on the basis of social status, reinforcing standards of order and community hierarchy. But Whitefield's sermons were highly dramatic performances. He preached for hours in a booming voice, gesturing wildly and sometimes even dissolving in tears. Thousands of strangers, jostling in crowds that often outnumbered the populations of several villages put together, wept along with him.

Revivals and mass conversions often followed his appearances, to the happy astonishment of local clergy. But their approval evaporated when more extreme revivalists appeared. Gilbert Tennent, William's son, followed Whitefield to Boston and derided the town's ministers as unconverted "dead Drones." James Davenport claimed that God had given him the knowledge of other ministers' spiritual state and routinely denounced by name those he "knew" to be damned. Officials who valued civic order soon tried to silence such extremists by passing laws that prohibited them from preaching in a town without the local minister's permission.

Disputes between individuals converted in the revivals—called **New Lights**—and those who were not (Old Lights) split churches. New Lights insisted that they could not remain in churches with sinful members and unconverted

Great Awakening
Tremendous religious revival in colonial America striking first in the Middle Colonies and New England in the 1740s and then spreading to the southern colonies.

New Lights   People who experienced conversion during the revivals of the Great Awakening.

ministers and so left to form new churches. "Formerly the People could bear with each other in Charity when they differ'd in Opinion," lamented one colonist, "but they now break Fellowship and Communion with one another on that Account."

The Awakening came late to the southern colonies, but it was there, in the 1760s, that it produced perhaps its greatest controversy. Many southern converts became Baptists, combining religious criticism of the Anglicans with condemnation of the wealthy planters' way of life. Plainly dressed Baptists criticized the rich clothes, drinking, gambling, and pride of Virginia's gentry. The planters, in turn, viewed the Baptists as dangerous people who could not "meet a man upon the road, but they must ram a text of Scripture down his throat." Most of all, they hated the Baptists for their willingness to preach to slaves.

Although the revivals themselves gradually waned, the Great Awakening had a lasting impact on colonial society. In addition to introducing colonists to a fervent evangelicalism, it forged new links between Great Britain and the colonies. Evangelical ministers on both sides of the Atlantic exchanged correspondence. Periodicals informed British and American subscribers of advances in true religion throughout the empire.

In the colonies, the Awakening led to the founding of new colleges to serve members of different religious denominations. Middle Colony evangelicals founded the College of New Jersey (now Princeton University) in 1746. In the 1760s, New England Baptists established the College of Rhode Island (now Brown University). An evangelical wing of the Dutch Reformed Church founded Queens College (now Rutgers University) in 1766.

The revivals also brought newcomers into Christian congregations. Chesapeake slaves responded to the evangelists' message and—often contrary to the intent of the white preachers—drew lessons about the equality of humankind. A few black preachers circulated in the slave quarters, spreading the message of salvation and freedom. The impact of revivalism on Indians was less dramatic, but still significant. Evangelicals enjoyed their greatest success in small Native American communities. Native converts often urged fellow Indians to heed the Christian message of self-discipline, not to emulate English colonists, but to revitalize villages beset by alcoholism and other problems linked to European domination.

The Awakening did not greatly increase women's church membership, since women already constituted majorities in many congregations. But by emphasizing the emotional power of Christianity, revivals accorded greater legitimacy to what was thought to be women's more sensitive temperament. Some women, such as Bathsheba Kingsley, were inspired by their conversions to become traveling preachers.

Everywhere, the New Light challenge to established ministers and churches undermined habits of deference to authority. Revivalists urged colonists to think for themselves in choosing which church to join and which minister to follow, not just to conform to what the rest of the community did. As their churches fractured, colonists—particularly New Englanders—faced more choices than ever before in their religious lives.

The exercise of religious choice also influenced political behavior. Voters noticed whether candidates for office were New or Old Lights. Tactics first used to mobilize religious groups—such as organizing committees and writing petitions and letters—also proved useful for political activities. The Awakening thus fostered greater political awareness and participation among colonists.

THE COLONIAL POLITICAL WORLD

*T*he political legacy of the Great Awakening—particularly the emphasis on individual choice and resistance to authority—corresponded to developments in the colonial political world. For most of the seventeenth century, ties within the empire developed from trade rather than governance. But as America grew in wealth and population, king and Parliament sought to manage colonial affairs more directly.

In the late seventeenth century, upheavals on both sides of the Atlantic seemed to confirm for both colonists and Englishmen a common interest in protecting the rights and liberties derived from their shared heritage. The English overthrew King James II, and the people of New England successfully resisted the king's attempt to impose autocratic government in the colonies. But even as colonists and Englishmen asserted their common political culture at the dawn of the eighteenth century, differences in their political practices and ideas began to emerge.

THE DOMINION OF NEW ENGLAND AND THE LIMITS OF BRITISH CONTROL

Before 1650, England made little attempt to exert centralized control in North America. Each colony more or less governed itself, and most political activity occurred at the town or county level. Busy with the routines of daily life, most colonists devoted little time, and even less interest, to politics.

When Charles II became king in 1660, he initially showed little interest in the colonies except as sources of land and government offices with which he could reward his supporters. The grandest prizes, of course, were the great proprietorships, such as Pennsylvania and Carolina, but the creation of a rudimentary imperial bureaucracy also yielded rewards for the king to distribute.

Charles's brother James, the duke of York, envisioned a more tightly controlled empire. He encouraged Charles to appoint military officers with strong ties of loyalty to him as royal governors. In 1675, James convinced Charles to create the Lords of Trade to oversee colonial affairs.

When James II became king in 1685, the whole character of the empire abruptly changed. Seeking to transform it into something much grander and more susceptible to England's control, James set out to reorganize it along the lines of Spain's empire, combining the colonies into three or four large provinces. He appointed powerful governors to carry out policies that he himself would formulate.

James began in the north, creating the **Dominion of New England** out of eight previously separate colonies stretching from Maine (then part of Massachusetts) to New Jersey. He chose Sir Edmund Andros, a former army officer, to govern the vast region with an appointive council but no elective assembly. Andros moved to Boston and initially gained some support from merchants excluded from politics by Massachusetts's insistence that only church members could vote. But he eventually antagonized them and other New Englanders by rigidly enforcing the Navigation Acts, limiting towns to just one annual meeting, remodeling the law courts, challenging property titles, and levying taxes without the colonists' consent.

Events in England ultimately sealed the fate of the Dominion. For years, English Protestants had worried about James's absolutist governing style and his conversion to Catholicism. Their fears increased in 1688, when the queen bore a son to carry on a Catholic line of succession. Parliament's leaders invited James's Protestant daughter, Mary, and her husband, William of Orange, the stadtholder of the Netherlands, to take over the throne. In November 1688, William landed

Dominion of New England James II's failed plan of 1686 to combine eight northern colonies into a single large province, to be governed by a royal appointee with no elective assembly.

in England, and in December, James fled to France, ending a bloodless coup known as the **Glorious Revolution.**

Bostonians overthrew Andros the following April and shipped him back to England. Massachusetts colonists hoped that their original charter of 1629 would be reinstated, but a new one was issued in 1691. It made several important changes. Massachusetts now included the formerly separate Plymouth Colony as well as Maine. Its colonists no longer elected their governor, who would instead be appointed by the monarch. Voters no longer had to be church members, and religious toleration was extended to all Protestants.

The new charter ended exclusive Puritan control in Massachusetts but also restored political stability. During the three years between Andros's overthrow and the arrival of a royal governor in 1692, the colony lacked a legally established government. In this atmosphere of uncertainty, an outbreak of accusations of witchcraft in Salem grew to unprecedented proportions. Over the years, New Englanders had executed a dozen or so accused witches, usually older women. But in the winter of 1691–1692, when several young girls of Salem experienced fits and other strange behavior, hundreds of settlers were accused of witchcraft, and nineteen were hanged. Salem's crisis occurred against a backdrop of local economic change, but it gathered momentum because the Dominion crisis had generated uncertainty about political and legal authority.

The impact of the Glorious Revolution in other colonies likewise reflected local conditions. In New York, after Andros's deputy left, Jacob Leisler, a rich merchant and militia captain, gained power and ruled in a dictatorial fashion. Too slow in relinquishing command to the newly arrived royal governor in 1691, Leisler was arrested for treason and executed. In Maryland, Protestants used the occasion of William and Mary's accession to the throne to lobby for the end of the Catholic proprietorship. They were partly successful. The Calvert family lost its governing powers but retained rights to vast quantities of land. The Anglican Church became the established faith, and Catholics were barred from public office.

The colonists rejected James II, not English authority in general. Their motives (especially in New England) largely reflected powerful anti-Catholic sentiment. William's firm Protestantism reassured them, and most colonists assumed that life would return to normal. But the Glorious Revolution in England and the demise of the Dominion had long-lasting effects that shaped political life in England and America for years to come.

THE LEGACY OF THE GLORIOUS REVOLUTION

In England, the Glorious Revolution signaled a return to political stability after years of upheaval. In 1689, Parliament passed the Bill of Rights, which justified James's ouster and bound future monarchs to abide by the rule of law. They could not suspend statutes, collect taxes, or engage in foreign wars without Parliament's consent, or maintain a standing army in peacetime. Parliamentary elections and meetings would follow a regular schedule, without royal interference. In sum, Parliament claimed to be the crown's equal partner in governing England.

Colonists, too, celebrated the vindication of their rights as Englishmen. Observing the similarity between Parliament and the colonial assemblies, they concluded that their own legislatures had a critical role in governance and in the protection of their rights and liberties. On both sides of the Atlantic, representative government had triumphed.

In fact, Parliament claimed full authority over the colonies and did not recognize their assemblies as its equal. For more than a half-century, however, it did

Glorious Revolution Bloodless revolt that occurred in England in 1688 when parliamentary leaders invited William of Orange, a Protestant, to assume the English throne.

AMERICAN VIEWS

AN ENGLISH MINISTER VISITS THE BACKCOUNTRY

I n 1766, Charles Woodmason, a newly or- dained Anglican minister, embarked on a six- year-long tour to bring religion to backcountry settlers. Born in England, he came to the colonies around 1752, settling first in Charleston, South Car- olina. He lived in the area as a planter and merchant for more than a decade before deciding on a career in the min- istry. Assigned to work in the backcountry, he was shocked to find crude living conditions and ethnically diverse settlers with little or no knowledge of religion. As the following ex- cerpt shows, the journal Woodmason kept during these years contains a fascinating mix of his observations and prejudices.

- How does Woodmason characterize the behavior of backcountry settlers?
- What is Woodmason's opinion of the settlers' religious beliefs?
- How accurately do you think Woodmason's ac- count reflects backcountry society? To what extent did his identity as an English-born gentleman shape his impressions of the region?

In this Circuit of a fortnight I've eaten Meat but thrice, and drank nought but Water—Subsisting on my Bisket and Rice Water and Musk Melons, Cucumbers, Green Apples and Peaches and such Trash. By which am re- duc'd very thin. It is impossible that any Gentleman not season'd to the Clime, could sustain this. . . . Nor is this a Country, or place where I would wish any Gentleman to travel, or settle. . . . [The settlers'] Ignorance and Im- pudence is so very high, as to be past bearing—Very few can read—fewer write. . . . They are very Poor—owing to

their extreme Indolence for they possess the finest Coun- try in America, and could raise but ev'ry thing. They de- light in their present low, lazy, sluttish, heathenish, hellish Life, and seem not desirous of changing it. Both Men and Women will do any thing to come at Liquor, Cloaths, furniture, &c. &c. rather than work for it. . . .

It is very few families whom I can bring to join in Prayer, because most of them are of various Opinions the Husband a Churchman, Wife, a Dissenter, Children nothing at all. . . . Few or no Books are to be found in all this vast Country. . . . Nor do they delight in Histor- ical Books or in having them read to them, as do our Vulgar in England for these People despise Knowledge, and instead of honouring a Learned Person, or any one of Wit or Knowledge be it in the Arts, Sciences, or Lan- guages, they despise and Ill treat them—And this Spir- it prevails even among the Principals of this Province . . . . [At Flatt Creek] I found a vast Body of People as- sembled—Such a Medley! such a mixed Multitude of all Classes and Complexions I never saw. I baptized about 20 Children and Married 4 Couple—Most of these People had never before seen a Minister, or heard the Lords Prayer, Service, or Sermon in their Days. I was a Great Curiosity to them—And they were as great Oddities to me. After Service they went to Revelling Drinking Singing Dancing and Whoring—and most of the Company were drunk before I quitted the Spot— They were as rude in their Manners as the Common Savages, and hardly a degree removed from them.

Source: Richard J. Hooker, ed., *The Carolina Backcountry on the Eve of the Revolution: The Journal and Other Writings of Charles Woodmason, Anglican Itinerant* (Chapel Hill, 1953), pp. 52–56.

not vigorously assert that authority. At the same time, William and his immediate successors lacked James's compulsion to control the colonies, although William did make a few changes to the imperial administration.

During the early eighteenth century, Parliament and royal ministers confined their attention to matters of trade and military defense and otherwise left the colonies on their own. This mild imperial rule, later called the era of "salutary neglect," allowed the colonies to grow in wealth, population, and self-government. It also encouraged colonists to assume equality with the English as members of the empire.

DIVERGING POLITICS IN THE COLONIES AND GREAT BRITAIN

English people on both sides of the Atlantic often compared the state to a family. Just as fathers naturally headed families, adult men led societies. In particular, adult male property holders, who enjoyed economic independence, claimed the right to vote and hold office. Women (who generally could not own property), propertyless men, and slaves had no political role because they, like children, were subordinate to the authority of others. Their dependence on husbands, fathers, masters, or employers—who could influence their political decisions—rendered them incapable of exercising freedom of choice.

States, like families, worked best when all members fulfilled their responsibilities. Rulers ought to govern with the same fairness and benevolence that fathers presumably exercised within their families. In return for protection, the people owed their rulers the same obedience that children accorded their parents.

Eighteenth-century people also believed that government should reflect society's hierarchical organization. In England, this idea was embodied in the monarchy and Parliament. The crown, of course, represented the interests of the royal family. Parliament represented society's two main divisions: the aristocracy in the House of Lords and the common people in the House of Commons. Americans shared the view that government should mirror social hierarchies but found it much more difficult to put the idea into practice.

American society grew closer to the British model during the eighteenth century but was never identical to it. One obvious difference was that America lacked an aristocracy. Elite colonists were often just two or three generations removed from humble beginnings. Hence the acute anxiety that inspired George Washington and other colonial gentlemen to seek refinement, to gain the automatic recognition that England's more secure elites enjoyed.

In both England and America, land ownership was the prerequisite for political participation, because it freed people from dependence on others and gave them a stake in society. In England, this requirement sharply limited participation. Landholding in America, however, was much more widespread. A large majority of white male farmers eventually owned the land they tilled, and in most colonies, 50 to 75 percent of white men were eligible to vote.

Distinctive social conditions in England and America also gave rise to different notions of political representation. Electoral districts for Parliament came in a confusing mixture of shapes, reflecting their status in past centuries. Once-important towns sent representatives on the basis of their former prominence. At the same time, rapidly growing cities, such as Manchester, lacked any representative at all. Some English radicals protested this inequity. Most of their countrymen, however, accepted the idea of **virtual representation,** which held that representatives served the interests of the nation as a whole, not just the locality from which they came. They maintained that since the colonists held interests in common with English people at home, they were virtually represented in Parliament, just like Manchester's residents.

Since the founding of their colonies, however, Americans had experienced **actual representation** and believed that elected representatives should be directly responsive to local interests. They were accustomed to sending written instructions to their legislators, informing them how to vote on important issues. The Americans' experience with actual representation made them extremely skeptical of Parliament's claims to virtual representation. For the first half of the eighteenth century, however, Parliament did not press this claim.

Virtual representation The notion that parliamentary members represented the interests of the nation as a whole, not those of the particular district that elected them.

Actual representation The practice whereby elected representatives normally reside in their districts and are directly responsive to local interests.

The most direct political confrontations between England and the colonies instead focused on the role of colonial governors. In every colony except Connecticut and Rhode Island (where voters chose the executive), either the king or the proprietor appointed the governor. The governors' interests thus lay with their English patrons and not the colonies. More important, governors exercised great power over the colonial assemblies.

In practice, several conditions hampered governors' efforts to exercise their legal authority. Many arrived with detailed instructions on how to govern, a condition that limited their ability to negotiate with colonists over sensitive issues. Governors controlled few offices or other prizes with which to buy the allegiance of their opponents. They struggled to dominate assemblies that grew in size as the colonial population expanded. And in several colonies, including Massachusetts and New York, governors relied on the assemblies to appropriate the money for their salaries—a financial dependence that restrained even the most autocratic executive.

In response to the perceived, if not always realized, threat of powerful governors, colonial assemblies asserted themselves as the guarantors of colonists' liberties. They sent agents (including such prominent figures as Benjamin Franklin) to England to lobby on behalf of colonial interests. Local factions fought for election to the legislature, leading to some of the most contentious politics in the British empire. Governors often stood on the sidelines, either frustrated with their inability to govern or, at times, enlisted on the side of one faction or another.

Despite concerns about the power of governors, most colonists accepted the loose and sometimes contradictory political ties of empire. So long as Parliament treated them as partners in empire and refrained from ruling by coercion, colonists could celebrate British government as "the most perfect combination of human powers in society . . . for the preservation of liberty and the production of happiness."

By the middle of the eighteenth century, the blessings of British government extended to more colonists than ever before. The population of British America grew rapidly and spread out over vast amounts of land. The expansion of British settlement, in turn, alarmed other European powers. Both Spain and France launched new settlements as the competition for the continent entered a new and volatile phase.

EXPANDING EMPIRES

During the first half of the eighteenth century, England, Spain, and France all enlarged their North American holdings according to patterns established during the previous century. Over time, these empires came into closer contact with one another, intensifying the competition for land, trade, resources, and Indian allies.

BRITISH COLONISTS IN THE BACKCOUNTRY

Population growth in British North America during the eighteenth century was truly astonishing. The non-Indian population in the mainland colonies numbered about 260,000 in 1700; by 1760, it had increased to over 1.5 million. Much of this growth stemmed from natural increase. By the mid-eighteenth century, even the slave population, first in the Chesapeake and later in the Lower South, began to reproduce itself, although more slowly than the white population.

Immigration also boosted the population. Thousands of Scots-Irish and German settlers, in addition to thousands of African slaves, helped the population

QUICK REVIEW

Population Growth

- 1700: 265,000 black and white settlers in the mainland colonies.
- 1760: 1.5 million black and white settlers in the mainland colonies.
- Population growth due to natural increase and immigration.

WHAT WAS the "backcountry"? Who settled there and why?

WHERE TO LEARN MORE

Berkeley and Westover Plantations,
Charles City, Virginia
www.jamesriverplantations.org

of the Lower South increase at nearly twice the rate of New England, which attracted few immigrants. Pennsylvania absorbed a continuous stream of immigrants. Indeed, extensive German immigration worried Pennsylvania leaders like Benjamin Franklin. They feared that the newcomers would "never adopt our Language or Customs" and would soon "be so numerous as to Germanize us."

Most of the coast from Maine to Georgia was settled by 1760, forcing new immigrants to move inland. The most dramatic expansion occurred in the foothills and valleys of the Appalachian Mountains from Pennsylvania to Georgia, a region known as the backcountry.

Between 1730 and 1770, nearly a quarter of a million German, Scots-Irish, and English colonists entered the backcountry. For the most part, they raised crops and livestock for subsistence on small, isolated farms. Community life developed slowly, in part because many backcountry settlers moved frequently. In addition, a surplus of men among the first settlers delayed the formation of families.

Contemporary observers derided the crudeness of frontier life. William Byrd scornfully described one backcountry house as a "castle containing of one dirty room with a dragging door to it that will neither open or shut." Genteel observers offered what they considered the most damaging insult by referring to backcountry settlers as "white Indians." These comments reflect emerging tensions between backcountry settlements and older seacoast communities. Coastal planters acquired vast tracts of western land with the intent of selling it to these "crude" settlers. Their interests collided with those of many backcountry settlers, including squatters who occupied the land without acquiring legal title in the hope that their labor in clearing farms would establish their property rights.

Backcountry settlers often complained that the rich eastern planters who dominated the colonial legislatures ignored western demands for adequate representation. Many argued that the crudeness of frontier life was only temporary. Perhaps the best measure of their desire to resemble eastern planters was the spread of slaveholding among prosperous backcountry farmers.

Tensions grew throughout the backcountry as English settlers encroached on Indian lands. Colonists who moved to Pennsylvania's fertile Susquehanna Valley displaced Delawares, Shawnees, and other native peoples who had sought refuge there from earlier white migrations. In South Carolina, the Catawbas moved to ever more remote sites. Indians moving to avoid friction with whites, however, frequently encroached on lands claimed by other tribes—particularly those of the Iroquois Confederacy—leading to conflict among native peoples.

Even where British settlers had not yet appeared, English and Scottish traders could often be found, aggressively pursuing trade with the Indians. Spanish and French observers feared this commercial expansion even more than they did the movement of settlers. In response, the Spanish and French expanded their own territorial claims and tried to strengthen relations with Indian peoples.

THE SPANISH IN TEXAS AND CALIFORNIA

Spain worried that its existing North American colonies would be overwhelmed by its enemies. Florida had become the target of English raiders from South Carolina, who attacked Spanish missions with the help of local Indians. Years of religious persecution and forced labor encouraged Florida's Indians to oppose the Spanish, but the natives also wanted English trade goods, such as guns. Spain maintained a precarious hold on coastal bases at St. Augustine, San Marcos de Apalachee, and Pensacola. By the mid-eighteenth century, however, control of

▼ **MAP EXPLORATION**

To explore an interactive version of this map, go to **http://www.prenhall.com/goldfield3/map4.2**

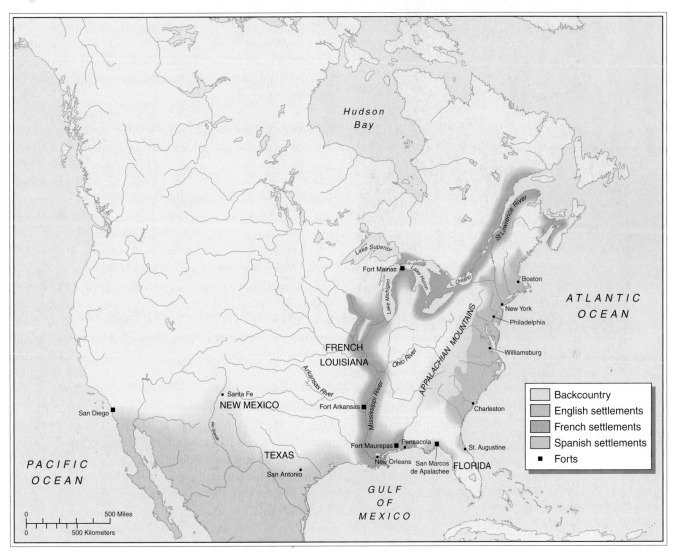

MAP 4–2 Expanding Settlement, c. 1750   Imperial rivalries drove Spain, France, and England to expand their North American empires in the mid-eighteenth century. Once again, this sparked conflict with native peoples as well as with European competitors.

USING THIS map and Map 4–1, explain why Great Britain's victory in the French and Indian War was so crucial to its continued dominance of the western world.

Florida's interior effectively passed to Indian bands allied with English (and, in the west, French) traders.

In 1700, New Mexico was still suffering from the effects of the Pueblo Revolt. Spanish farmers and missionaries slowly moved back up the Rio Grande Valley. Fearful of sparking another revolt, Franciscan priests eased their labor demands and avoided outright religious persecution, allowing the Pueblos to retain many of their customs and religious practices. French traders did not reach Santa Fe until 1739, but persistent rumors of their approach fueled Spanish fears that New Mexico would fall into French hands.

WHERE TO LEARN MORE

Mission Parkway, San Antonio, Texas
http://hotx.com/missions/

This panel of an eighteenth-century painting by an unknown Mexican artist is representative of a genre of portraits illustrating the categories Spanish colonists developed to designate the offspring of various kinds of mixed marriage. This one, labeled "Español, con India, Mestizo," depicts a Spanish father, an Indian mother, and their mestizo child. The scarcity of European women made mixed marriage common in Spanish colonies. Such unions were exceedingly rare in the English colonies, where cultural preferences and the relative abundance of European women discouraged inter-marriage.

Schalkwijlk, Art Resource, N.Y.

To create a buffer zone around their existing colonies, the Spanish moved into Texas and California. The Spanish advance into Texas, however, met with resistance from the French (who also had outposts on the Gulf Coast) and from the Caddos and other Indians armed with French guns. Efforts to fill east Texas with settlers from Spain, Cuba, and the Canary Islands all failed when Spanish officials could not guarantee their safety.

Sixteenth-century Spaniards had considered building outposts in California to supply ships traveling between Mexico and the Philippines but were deterred by the region's remoteness. Spanish interest revived in the 1760s, when it seemed that Russia, which had built fur-trading posts in Alaska, might occupy California. Largely through the efforts of two men—José de Gálvez, a royal official, and Junípero Serra, a Franciscan priest—the Spanish constructed a string of forts and missions from San Diego north to San Francisco between 1769 and 1776.

They initially encountered little opposition from California's Indians, who lived in small, scattered villages and lacked experience with organized warfare. With no European rivals nearby, the Spanish erected an extensive mission system designed to convert and educate Indians and set them to work. Thousands of native laborers farmed irrigated fields and tended horses, sheep, and cattle. They did so under extremely harsh conditions.

According to one observer, Indians who became Christians and settled at the missions endured a fate "worse than that of slaves." The Spanish worked them hard and maintained them in overcrowded, unsanitary dwellings. Native women suffered from sexual exploitation by Spanish soldiers. Epidemics of European diseases swept through the Indian population. Signs of native resistance met with quick and cruel punishment. Despite this, Indians staged several revolts during the eighteenth century, but Spanish soldiers usually suppressed them quickly.

Spain's empire grew, even as it weakened, during the eighteenth century. Its scattered holdings north of the Rio Grande functioned as colonies of another colony—Mexico—shielding it from foreign incursions. From the beginning, Spain's vision of empire had rested not on extensive settlement but on subjugation of native peoples in order to control their labor. After 1700, however, the limitations of this coercive approach to empire became apparent. As their experiences in Florida and Texas vividly demonstrated, the Spanish simply could not compete with the vigorous commercial empires of France and England.

THE FRENCH ALONG THE MISSISSIPPI AND IN LOUISIANA

French expansion followed the major waterways of the St. Lawrence River, the Great Lakes, and the Mississippi into the heart of North America. Explorers reached the Mississippi Valley in the 1670s. Within twenty years, French outposts appeared along the Gulf Coast. New Orleans, the capital and main port of French Louisiana, was founded in 1718. Concerned about defending scattered settlements, French officials forbade colonists to move into the interior. But colonists went anyway, building six villages along the Mississippi in a place they called the *pays des Illinois.*

The first Illinois settlers were independent fur traders (*coureurs de bois,* or "woods runners") unwilling to return to Canada after the French government tried to prohibit their direct trade with Indians. Many found Christian Indian wives and began farming the rich lands along the river. Several hundred emigrants from Canada eventually joined them. The settlers, using the labor of their families and of black and Indian slaves, helped feed the growing population of New Orleans and the lower Mississippi Valley.

French Louisiana contained a remarkably diverse population of Indian peoples, French soldiers and settlers, and German immigrants, as well as African slaves, who by the 1730s outnumbered the European colonists. Louisiana's economy depended mainly on food crops, herding, fishing, and the deerskin trade. Discouraged by the lack of profits, French officials and merchants neglected Louisiana. Significant European emigration to Louisiana essentially ceased after the 1720s.

But the French approach to empire in Louisiana as in Canada depended more on Indian alliances than on settlement. Louisiana's principal allies were the Choctaws. The Choctaws and other native allies offered trade and military assistance in return for guns, trade goods, French help in fighting English raiders seeking Indian slaves, and occasional French mediation of Indian disputes.

French expansion along the Mississippi Valley drove a wedge between Florida and Spain's other mainland colonies; it also blocked the westward movement of English settlers. But France's enlarged empire was only as strong as the Indian alliances on which it rested. When France ordered Louisiana officials to limit expenses and reduce Indian gifts in 1745, the officials objected that the Choctaws "would ask for nothing better than to have such pretexts in order to resort to the English."

The fear of losing Indian favor preoccupied officials in 1745 because at that moment France's empire in America consisted of two disconnected pieces: New France, centered in the St. Lawrence Valley and the Great Lakes basin, and Louisiana, stretching from New Orleans to the *pays des Illinois*. Between them lay a thousand miles of wilderness, through which only one thoroughfare passed— the Ohio River. For decades, communication between the two parts of France's North American empire had posed no problem because Indians in the Ohio Valley allowed the French free passage through their lands. If that policy ended, however, France's New World empire would be dangerously divided.

A Century of Warfare

T he expansion of empires in North America reflected the policies of European states locked in a relentless competition for power and wealth. From the time of the Glorious Revolution, English foreign policy aimed at limiting the expansion of French influence. This, in turn, resulted in a series of four wars. As the eighteenth century wore on, the conflicts between the two countries increasingly involved their American colonies as well as Spain and its colonies. The outcome of each of the wars in America depended no less on the participation of colonists and Indians than on the policies and strategies of the European powers. The conclusion of the final conflict signaled a dramatic shift in North American history (see the Overview table, "The Colonial Wars, 1689–1763").

Imperial Conflict and the Establishment of an American Balance of Power, 1689–1738

When he became king of England in 1688, the Dutch Protestant William of Orange was already fighting the War of the League of Augsburg against France's Catholic king, Louis XIV. Almost immediately, William brought England into the conflict. The war lasted until 1697 and ended, as did the War of the Spanish

W **WHERE TO LEARN MORE**

★ Ste. Genevieve Historic District, Ste. Genevieve, Missouri
www.ste-genevieve.com/histsite.htm

WHAT ROLE did the colonists play in the French and Indian War?

OVERVIEW THE COLONIAL WARS, 1689–1763

Name in the Colonies and Dates	European Name America	Dates in	Results for Britain
King William's War	War of the League of Augsburg, 1688–1697	1689–1697	Reestablished balance of power between England and France
Queen Anne's War	War of the Spanish Succession, 1702–1714	1702–1713	Britain acquired Nova Scotia
King George's War	War of the Austrian Succession, 1739–1748	1744–1748	Britain returned Louisbourg to France British settlers began moving westward Weakening of Iroquois neutrality
French and Indian War	Seven Years' War, 1756–1763	1754–1763	Britain acquired Canada and all French territory east of Mississippi Britain gained Florida from Spain

King William's War The first Anglo-French conflict in North America (1689–1697), the American phase of Europe's War of the League of Augsburg.

Queen Anne's War American phase (1702–1713) of Europe's War of the Spanish Succession.

Country (Real Whig) ideology Strain of thought (focusing on the threat to personal liberty and the taxation of property holders) first appearing in England in the late seventeenth century in response to the growth of governmental power and a national debt.

Grand Settlement of 1701 Separate peace treaties negotiated by Iroquois diplomats at Montreal and Albany that marked the beginning of Iroquois neutrality in conflicts between the French and the British in North America.

Succession (1702–1713) which followed it, in a negotiated peace that reestablished the balance of power.

In America, these two imperial wars—known to British colonists as **King William's War** and **Queen Anne's War,** after the monarchs on the throne at the time—ended with equal indecisiveness. Neither war caused more than marginal changes for the colonies in North America. Both had profound effects, however, on the English state and the Iroquois League.

All European states of the eighteenth century financed their wars by borrowing. But the English were the first to realize that wartime debts did not necessarily have to be repaid during the following peace. The government instead created a funded debt. Having borrowed heavily from large joint-stock corporations, the government used tax revenues to pay the interest on the loans but not to pay off the loans themselves. The corporations accepted this because the interest payments amounted to a steady income that over the long run could amount to more than the original loans.

As the debt grew larger, more taxes were necessary to pay interest on it. Taxes also rose to pay for a powerful navy and a standing army. When the treasury created a larger and more efficient bureaucracy to collect taxes, many Englishmen grew nervous. Their anxiety emerged as a strain of thought known as **Country,** or **"Real Whig," ideology.** Country ideology stressed the threats that a standing army and a powerful state posed to personal liberty. It also emphasized the dangers of taxation to property rights and the need for property holders to retain their right to consent to taxation.

In America, the first two imperial wars transformed the role of the Iroquois League. After the English took over New Netherland in 1664, the Five Nations cultivated trading connections with them and later allied with England during King William's War. But the English offered little help when the French and their Indian allies attacked the Iroquois during that conflict. By 1700, the Iroquois League had suffered such horrendous losses that its leaders sought an alternative to direct alliance with the British.

With the so-called **Grand Settlement of 1701,** the Iroquois adopted a policy of neutrality with regard to the French and British empires. The Iroquois's strategic location between New France and the English colonies allowed them to serve as a geographical and diplomatic buffer. Neutral Iroquois diplomats could play the English against the French, gaining favors from one side in return for promises not to ally with the other. This neutralist policy ensured that for nearly fifty years neither England nor France could gain ascendancy in North America.

Iroquois neutrality offered benefits to the Europeans as well as the Indians. The English, for instance, began to negotiate with them for land. To smooth relations with the English, the Iroquois sold them land formerly occupied by Delawares and Susquehannocks. This transaction simultaneously helped to satisfy the colonists' land hunger and to enrich the Iroquois League.

Meanwhile a neutral Iroquois League claiming control over the Ohio Valley and blocking English access across the Appalachian Mountains helped the French protect the strategic corridor of the Ohio and Mississippi Valleys that linked Canada and Louisiana. The Iroquois remained reasonably effective at keeping the British out of the valley until the late 1740s. The next European war, however, altered these circumstances.

KING GEORGE'S WAR SHIFTS THE BALANCE, 1739–1754

The third confrontation between Britain and France in Europe, the War of the Austrian Succession—**King George's War** to the British colonists—began as a small war between Britain and Spain in 1739. Its immediate cause was British attempts to poach on trade to Spain's Caribbean colonies. But in 1744, France joined in the war against Britain. An Anglo-French conflict once again erupted in North America.

New Englanders saw yet another chance to attack Canada. This time their target was the great fortress of Louisbourg on Cape Breton Island, a naval base that dominated the Gulf of St. Lawrence. An expedition from Massachusetts and Connecticut, supported by a squadron of Royal Navy warships, captured Louisbourg in 1745. This success cut Canada off from French reinforcement. English forces should now have been able to conquer New France.

Instead, politically influential merchants in Albany, New York, chose to continue their profitable trade with the enemy across Lake Champlain, enabling Canada to hold out until the end of the war. When the peace treaty was signed in 1748, Britain, which had fared badly in the European fighting, returned Louisbourg to France. This diplomatic adjustment, routine by European standards, shocked New Englanders. At the same time, New York's illegal trade with the enemy appalled British administrators.

King George's War furnished an equal share of shocks for New France, which had suffered more than in any previous conflict. Even before the war's end, traders from Pennsylvania began moving west to buy furs from Indians who had once traded with the French. The movements of these traders, along with the appearance of Virginians in the Ohio Valley after 1748, gravely concerned the French.

In 1749, the governor general of New France set out to assert direct control over the region by building a series of forts from Lake Erie to the Forks of the Ohio (where the Monongahela and Allegheny Rivers meet to form the Ohio River). This decision signaled the end of France's commitment to Iroquois neutrality. The chiefs of the Iroquois League now found themselves trapped between empires edging closer to confrontation in the Ohio Valley.

The Iroquois, in fact, had never exerted direct power in the Ohio Country. Their control instead depended on their ability to dominate the peoples who actually lived there. The appearance of English traders in the valley offering goods on better

King George's War The third Anglo-French war in North America (1744–1749), part of the European conflict known as the War of the Austrian Succession.

terms than the French or the Iroquois had ever provided undermined Iroquois dominance.

The Ohio Valley Indians increasingly pursued their own independent course. One spur to their disaffection from the Iroquois was the 1744 **Treaty of Lancaster,** by which Iroquois chiefs had sold the rights to trade at the Forks of the Ohio to a group of Virginia land speculators. The Virginians assumed that these trading rights included the right to acquire land for eventual sale to settlers. The Ohio Valley Indians found this situation intolerable, as did the French. When, in 1754, the government of Virginia sent out a small body of soldiers under Lieutenant Colonel George Washington to protect Virginia's claim to the Forks of the Ohio, the French struck decisively to stop them.

THE FRENCH AND INDIAN WAR, 1754–1760: A DECISIVE VICTORY

In April 1754, French soldiers overwhelmed a group of Virginians who had been building a small fort at the Forks of the Ohio. They then erected a much larger fort of their own, Fort Duquesne, on the spot. The French intended to follow up by similarly ousting Washington's weak, untrained troops, who had encamped farther up the Monongahela River. However, at the end of May, Washington's men killed or captured all but one member of a small French reconnaissance party. The French decided to teach the Virginians a lesson. On July 3, they attacked Washington at his encampment, Fort Necessity. The following day, with a quarter of his troops killed or wounded, Washington surrendered.

Even before news of these engagements reached Britain, imperial officials worried that the Iroquois might ally with the French. Britain ordered New York's governor to convene an intercolonial meeting in Albany—known as the Albany Congress—to discuss matters with the Iroquois. Several prominent colonists took advantage of the occasion to put forward the **Albany Plan of Union,** which called for an intercolonial union to coordinate defense, levy taxes, and regulate Indian affairs. But the colonies, too suspicious of one another to see their common interests, rejected the Albany Plan. Meanwhile, events in the west took a turn for the worse.

The French expulsion of the Virginians left the Indians of the region, Delawares and Shawnees, with no choice but to ally with the French in what came to be called the French and Indian War (see Map 4–3). Soon French and Indian attacks fell like hammer blows on backcountry settlements from Pennsylvania to the Carolinas. The Iroquois tried to remain neutral, but their neutrality no longer mattered. Europeans were at last contending directly for control of the Ohio Country.

The **French and Indian War** blazed in America for two years before it erupted as a fourth Anglo-French war in Europe in 1756. Known in Europe as the Seven Years' War (1756–1763), it involved fighting in the Caribbean, Africa, India, and the Philippine Islands as well as in Europe and North America. It was unlike any other eighteenth-century conflict, not only in its immense scope and expense but also in its decisive outcome.

The war had two phases in North America—1754 to 1758 and 1758 through 1760—that corresponded to shifts in European involvement. During the first phase, the French enjoyed a string of successes as they followed their proven strategy—guerrilla war. Relying on Indian allies acting with Canadian soldiers, the French raided English frontier settlements, killing and capturing hundreds of civilians and forcing tens of thousands more to flee. Then they attacked fortified outposts whenever the opportunity arose.

WHERE TO LEARN MORE

★ Johnson Hall, Johnstown, New York
www.johnstown.com/city/johnson.html

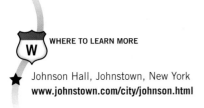

3–9
"The Storm Arising in the West," George Washington Delivers a Warning to the French (1753)

Treaty of Lancaster Negotiation in 1744 whereby Iroquois chiefs sold Virginia land speculators the right to trade at the Forks of the Ohio.

Albany Plan of Union Plan put forward in 1754 calling for an intercolonial union to manage defense and Indian affairs. The plan was rejected by participants at the Albany Congress.

French and Indian War The last of the Anglo-French colonial wars (1754–1763) and the first in which fighting began in North America. The war ended with France's defeat.

The first full campaign of the war, in 1755, saw not only the British colonial frontiers collapsing in terror but also a notable defeat inflicted on the troops Britain had dispatched to attack Fort Duquesne. The British commander in chief, Major General Edward Braddock, marched to within 10 miles of Fort Duquesne, only to have his 1,450-man force surrounded and destroyed by Indians and Canadian militiamen. Braddock's defeat set the tone for virtually every military engagement of the next three years and opened a period of demoralization and internal conflict in the British colonies.

Britain responded to Braddock's defeat by sending a new commander in chief with more trained British soldiers. The new commander, Lord Loudoun, tried to set colonial military affairs on a professional footing. He insisted on managing every aspect of the war effort, not only directing the campaigns but also dictating the amount of support, in men and money, that each colony would provide. Colonial soldiers, who had volunteered to serve under their own officers, objected to Loudoun's command. By the end of 1757, a year of disastrous military campaigns, colonial assemblies were also refusing to cooperate.

Britain's aim had been to "rationalize" the war by making it conform to European professional military standards. Few colonial volunteers met professional standards, and few colonists thought them necessary, especially when British soldiers suffered defeat after defeat at the hands of French and Indian guerrillas. British officers assumed that colonial soldiers were simply lazy cowards. But colonial volunteers, appalled to see men lashed "till the blood came out at the knee" of their breeches, saw British officers as brutal taskmasters.

Despite the astonishing success of their guerrilla tactics, the French, too, began moving toward a more European style of warfare. In the process, they destroyed their strategic and tactical advantages. In 1756, the Marquis de Montcalm, a strong proponent of European professional standards of military conduct, assumed command of French forces. In his first battle, the successful siege of Fort Oswego, New York, Montcalm was horrified by the behavior of his Indian allies, who killed wounded prisoners, took personal captives, and collected scalps as

MAP EXPLORATION

To explore an interactive version of this map, go to **http://www.prenhall.com/ goldfield3/map4.3**

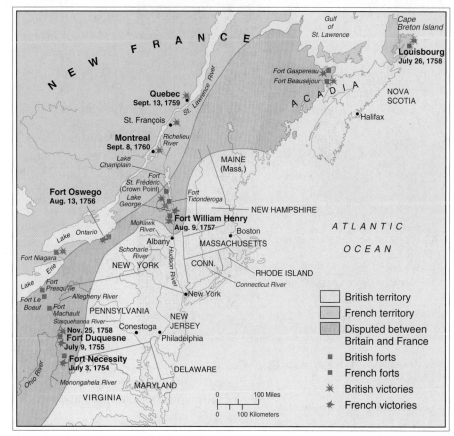

MAP 4–3   The French and Indian War, 1754–1763   Most of the battles of the French and Indian War occurred in the frontier regions of northern and western New York and the Ohio Valley. The influx of settlers into these areas created tensions that eventually developed into war.

WHY WERE efforts by both sides to rationalize and Europeanize the conflict unsuccessful? What role did geography play in dictating the most effective strategies and tactics?

This, the earliest known portrait of George Washington, was painted by Charles Wilson Peale in 1772. It depicts him in his military uniform from the French and Indian War. Military service helped to strengthen Washington's ties with the British Empire.

Washington/Custis/Lee Collection, Washington and Lee University, Lexington, VA.

QUICK REVIEW

Pitt's Policies

- Reimbursements to the colonies in proportion to their contribution.
- De-emphasis of the power of the commander in chief.
- More British troops to fight alongside colonial troops.

---

trophies. He came to regard the Indians—so essential to the defense of New France—as mere savages.

Following his next victory, the capture of Fort William Henry, New York, Montcalm conformed to European practice by allowing the defeated garrison to go home in return for the promise not to fight again. Montcalm's Indian allies, a thousand or more strong, were not to take prisoners, trophies, or plunder. The tragic result came to be known as the Massacre of Fort William Henry. Feeling betrayed by their French allies, the Indians took captives and trophies anyway, killing as many as 185 defenders and capturing about 300 people. This action not only outraged the New England colonies (most of the victims were New Englanders) but also alienated the Indians on whom the defense of Canada depended.

For at the same time that the Europeanization of the war was weakening the French, the British moderated their policies and reached accommodation with the colonists. A remarkable politician came to power in London as England's chief war minister. William Pitt, who as secretary of state directed the British war effort from late 1757 through 1761, realized that friction arose from the colonists' sense that they were bearing all the financial burdens of the war without having any say in how the war was fought. Pitt's ingenious solution was to promise reimbursements to the colonies in proportion to their contribution to the war effort, reduce the power of the commander in chief, and replace the arrogant Loudoun with a less objectionable officer.

Pitt's money and measures restored colonial morale. He sent thousands of British soldiers to America to fight alongside colonial troops. As the Anglo-American forces grew stronger, they operated more successfully, seizing Louisbourg again in 1758. Once more, Canada experienced crippling shortages of supplies. British emissaries persuaded the Delawares and Shawnees to abandon their French alliance, and late in 1758, an Anglo-American force again marched on Fort Duquesne. In command of its lead battalion was Colonel George Washington. The French defenders, abandoned by their native allies and confronted by overwhelming force, blew up the fort and retreated to the Great Lakes.

From this point on, the Anglo-Americans suffered no setbacks, and the French won no victories. Montcalm, forced back to Quebec, decided to risk everything in a European-style, open-field battle against a British force led by General James Wolfe. At the Battle of Quebec (September 13, 1759), Montcalm lost the gamble—and his life (as did the victorious General Wolfe).

But the French had not yet lost the war. What finally decided the outcome of the war in America was not the Battle of Quebec but two other developments: the Battle of Quiberon Bay in France (November 20, 1759) and the Iroquois' decision to join the Anglo-American side in 1760. The sea battle cost the French navy its ability to operate in the Atlantic, preventing it from bringing the reinforcements and supplies Canada needed to survive. At the same time, the Iroquois decision to enter the war on the Anglo-American side tipped the balance irrevocably against the French. The last ragged, hungry defenders of Canada surrendered on September 8, 1760.

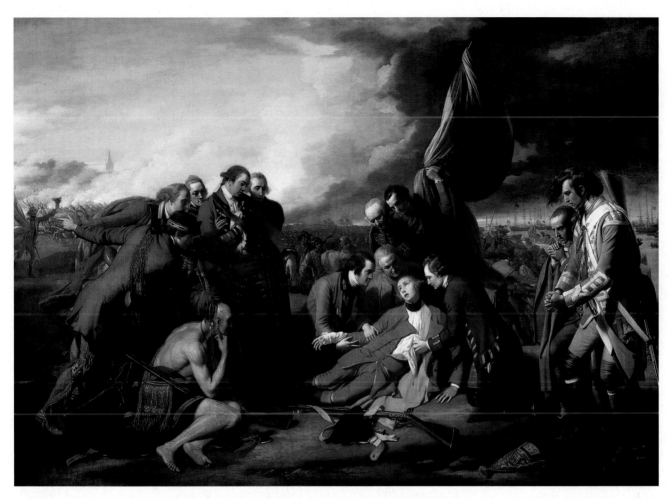

In his most famous painting, American artist Benjamin West depicted the death of the British general James Wolfe at the Battle of Quebec. He portrays Wolfe as a glorious martyr to the cause of British victory. In the left foreground, West added the figure of an Indian, a "noble savage" who contemplates the meaning of Wolfe's selfless sacrifice of his life.

Benjamin West (1738–1820), "The Death of General Wolfe," 1770, oil on canvas, 15.6 4 214.5 cm. Transfer from the Canadian War Memorials, 1921 (Gift of the 2nd Duke of Westminster, Eaton Hall, Cheshire, 1918). National Gallery of Canada, Ottawa, Canada.

THE TRIUMPH OF THE BRITISH EMPIRE, 1763

The war pitting Britain against France and Spain (which had entered the fighting as a French ally in 1762) concluded with an uninterrupted series of British victories. In the Caribbean, where every valuable sugar island the French owned came under British control, the culminating event was the surrender of Havana on August 13, 1762.

These conquests created the unshakable conviction that British arms were invincible. An immense surge of British patriotism spread throughout the American colonies. When news of the conquest of Havana reached Massachusetts, bells rang, cannons fired salutes, and bonfires blazed. General John Winslow of Plymouth, a portly man, rejoiced by becoming "so intoxicated as to jump on the table, and break a great number of bowls."

Hostilities ended formally on February 10, 1763, with the conclusion of the **Treaty of Paris.** France regained its West Indian sugar islands—its most valuable colonial possessions—but lost the rest of its North American empire (see Map 4–4). Britain returned Cuba and the Philippines to Spain and in compensation

Treaty of Paris The formal end to British hostilities against France and Spain in February 1763.

MAP EXPLORATION

To explore an interactive version of this map, go to **http://www.prenhall.com/goldfield3/map4.4**

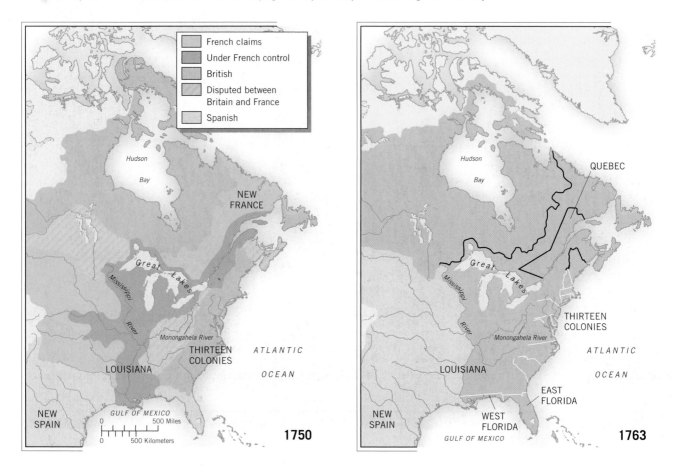

MAP 4–4 **European Empires in North America, 1750–1763** Great Britain's victory in the French and Indian War transformed the map of North America. France lost its mainland colonies, England claimed all lands east of the Mississippi, and Spain gained nominal control over the Trans-Mississippi West.

USING THIS map and Map 4–1, explain why Great Britain's victory in the French and Indian War was so crucial to its continued dominance of the Western world.

received Florida. Now Great Britain owned everything east of the Mississippi, from the Gulf of Mexico to Hudson's Bay. With France and Spain both humbled and on the verge of financial collapse, Britain seemed preeminent in Europe and ready to dominate in the New World.

CONCLUSION

The George Washington who ordered a suit from England in 1763 longed to be part of the elite of the great British empire. If he feared any threat to his position in that elite, it was not Parliament and the king but the uncomfortably large debts he owed to his London agents or perhaps the unruly Baptists who challenged the superiority of the great planters. But such worries, though real, were merely small, nagging doubts, shared by most of his fellow planters.

GLOBAL PERSPECTIVES

THE FIRST WORLD WAR?

The Seven Years' War began in North America's Ohio Valley, but the fighting eventually spread around the globe. The rivalry between England and France sparked conflict wherever the two nations had economic and political interests, including their respective colonies. Before the war ended in 1763, combat had broken out on three continents.

In North America, the theater of war spanned the vast distance between the St. Lawrence Valley and backwoods settlements in western Pennsylvania and Virginia. Numerous naval operations occurred in the Caribbean basin as well. Across the Atlantic, central Europe was hardest hit, with Prussia (which had a treaty of friendship with England) pitted against the allied forces of France, Austria, and Russia. Asia was drawn into the fighting when English forces, led by a British East India Company official named Robert Clive, attacked a French fort near Calcutta.

As would be the case with twentieth-century world wars, diplomatic alliances drew new combatants into the Seven Years' War and further extended its geographic range. In 1762, Spain finally entered the fray in the hope of preventing an overwhelming British victory. That was not to be; instead the powerful British navy seized Spanish possessions in Cuba and the Philippine Islands.

The effects of the Seven Years' War, like the fighting itself, reverberated around the world. Most significantly, France's loss of its North American empire had an Asian parallel with its expulsion from the Indian subcontinent. With the stroke of a pen, the signatories to the 1763 Treaty of Paris ending the war altered the course of history on both sides of the globe.

What was more real to Washington was the great victory that the British empire had just gained over France, a victory that he had helped to achieve. For Washington, as for virtually all other colonial leaders, 1763 was a moment of great promise and patriotic devotion to the British empire. It was a time to rejoice in the fundamental British identity and liberty and rights that seemed to ensure that life in the colonies would be better and more prosperous than ever.

SUMMARY

Economic Development and Imperial Trade in the British Colonies England, the Netherlands, and France competed vigorously in transatlantic trade. Between 1651 and 1733, Parliament passed laws that regulated trade to ensure that more wealth flowed into England's treasury than out of it. By the late 1760s, the colonists imported goods worth nearly £4 million each year, almost all of which came from Great Britain. Nearly two out of every three adult white males living in cities worked at a craft that directly related to overseas commerce. The growth of colonial cities mirrored British urban development, and many colonists assumed the more America resembled Britain, the more prosperous it would be.

The Transformation of Culture Despite the many similarities, many colonists worried that America remained culturally inferior to Britain. Eighteenth-century Americans imported more manufactures from England with every passing year. Many Americans imported "courtesy books," which contained the rules of polite behavior. Educated colonists were especially interested in the new ideas that characterized the Age of Enlightenment. Church steeples dominated the skylines of colonial cities. In all New England colonies except Rhode Island the Puritan faith was the established religion. And it was religion that drew the colonies closer to England through the Great Awakening.

The Colonial Political World During the mid-seventeenth century England began to realize it had limited control over the governance and politics of the colonies in New England. The Dominion of New England was one failed attempt to gain control. English people on both sides of the Atlantic believed that politics ought to reflect social organization. Differing opinions, however, on virtual representation versus actual representation caused greater disagreement. The most direct political confrontations between England and the colonies focused on the role of colonial governors. And, in response to the perceived threat of powerful governors, colonial assemblies asserted themselves as never before.

IMAGE KEY

for pages 86–87.

a. A brown patterned neckcloth.
b. New Amsterdam City Hall and Great Dock in the late 17th century.
c. Imported English mahogany clothespress
d. Image depicting offspring of mixed marriage.
e. Dried tobacco leaves.
f. A mounted moth.
g. A half-loom width of oyster silk damask, 18th century.
h. Portrait of Paul Revere
i. Portrait of George Washington
j. A hand-colored woodcut of a settlers' log cabin in the Blue Ridge Mountains (Appalachians).
k. A small pile of light muscovado sugar.
l. A luxury merchant ship.
m. "The Death of General Wolfe" by American painter Benjamin West. Distraught soldiers huddle around the dying General James Wolfe at the Battle of Quebec.
n. Portrait of Ben Franklin by Robert Feke.

Expanding Empires During the first half of the eighteenth century, England, Spain, and France all enlarged their North American holdings. The growth in populations was a result of natural increase as well as immigration. Most of the coast from Maine to Georgia was settled by 1760. Colonists who moved to the backcountry often displaced native groups. Spain's empire grew into Texas and California while the French expansion tended to follow major waterways like the Mississippi.

A Century of Warfare The English policy aimed at limiting the expansion of French influence resulted in four wars (King William's War, Queen Anne's War, King George's War, and the French and Indian War) between 1689 and 1763. The conclusion of the final war (the French and Indian War) signaled a dramatic shift in North American history as England would now claim all lands east of the Mississippi, Spain would nominally control the Trans-Mississippi West, and France would lose all of its mainland colonies.

REVIEW QUESTIONS

1. Why did George Washington prefer to order a suit from London rather than trust a Virginia tailor to make him one? How does his decision reflect elite colonists' attitudes about American society and culture in the eighteenth century?

2. In what ways did economic ties between Britain and the colonies grow closer in the century after 1660?

3. What was the Great Awakening, and what impact did it have? How did it affect different groups in colonial society?

4. In what ways were colonial and British political ideas and practices similar? In what ways were they different?

5. Why did England, Spain, and France renew their competition for North America in the eighteenth century?

6. What role did warfare play in North America in the eighteenth century? What role did the Iroquois play?

KEY TERMS

Actual representation   (p. 104)
Age of Enlightenment   (p. 97)
Albany Plan of Union   (p. 112)
Country, or "Real Whig," ideology
    (p. 110)
Dominion of New England   (p. 101)
Enumerated products   (p. 89)

French and Indian War   (p. 112)
Glorious Revolution   (p. 102)
Grand Settlement of 1701   (p. 110)
Great Awakening   (p. 99)
Halfway Covenant   (p. 98)
King George's War   (p. 111)
King William's War   (p. 110)

Mercantilism   (p. 89)
New Lights   (p. 99)
Queen Anne's War   (p. 110)
Treaty of Lancaster   (p. 112)
Treaty of Paris   (p. 115)
Virtual representation   (p. 104)

WHERE TO LEARN MORE

- **Mission Parkway, San Antonio, Texas.** Three Spanish missions (Mission Nuestra Señora de la Purisma Concepción, Mission San Francisco de la Espada, Mission San Juan Capistrano) founded in the early eighteenth century are located along this road. Their architecture indicates that they were intended to be fortifications as well as churches. The website **http://hotx.com/missions/** has links to each mission, offering pictures, descriptions, and historical background.

- **Ste. Genevieve Historic District, Ste. Genevieve, Missouri.** This restored site of an early eighteenth-century French settlement in the *pays des Illinois* contains many historic buildings open for tours. A general description of the site is at the website **http://rosecity.net/rhr/stegenevieve.html**. Descriptions and pictures of historic houses can be found at **http://www.ste-genevieve.com/histsite.htm**

- **Colonial Williamsburg, Williamsburg, Virginia.** A reconstruction of the capital of eighteenth-century Virginia, this site covers 173 acres and contains many restored and rebuilt structures, including houses, churches, the House of Burgesses, and the Governor's Palace. Many educational and cultural programs are available. Historical interpreters, dressed in period costume, provide information about eighteenth-century Chesapeake life. The website **www.colonialwilliamsburg .com/history/index.cfm** has a variety of links that include biographical information on eighteenth-century residents of Williamsburg, aspects of colonial life, and material culture. The link to "Electronic Field Trips" has information on how to arrange for an interactive television program and special Internet activities.

- **Mount Vernon, Virginia.** Site of George Washington's much-refurbished home. There is also a reconstructed gristmill and barn, as well as various outbuildings. Exhibits include information on Washington's agricultural experiments. The website **www.mountvernon.org** offers virtual tours of the house and grounds, as well as information on "George Washington, Pioneer Farmer."

- **Johnson Hall, Johnstown, New York.** Eighteenth-century home of William Johnson, who served as superintendent of Indian affairs and directed much of Britain's diplomacy with the Iroquois. Biographical information and pictures can be found at the website **www.johnstown.com/city/johnson.html**

- **Berkeley and Westover Plantations, Charles City, Virginia.** These two eighteenth-century James River plantations suggest the elegance of elite planters' lives. The house and grounds at Berkeley are open to the public, the grounds only at Westover, the home of William Byrd. Pictures, descriptions of the sites, and background on their owners can be found at **www.jamesriverplantations.org** which has links to each plantation.

U.S. History Documents CD-ROM
For primary sources related to this chapter, refer to the document CD-ROM.

www.prenhall.com/goldfield
For study resources related to this chapter, visit the *Companion Website*™.

5 Imperial Breakdown 1763-1774

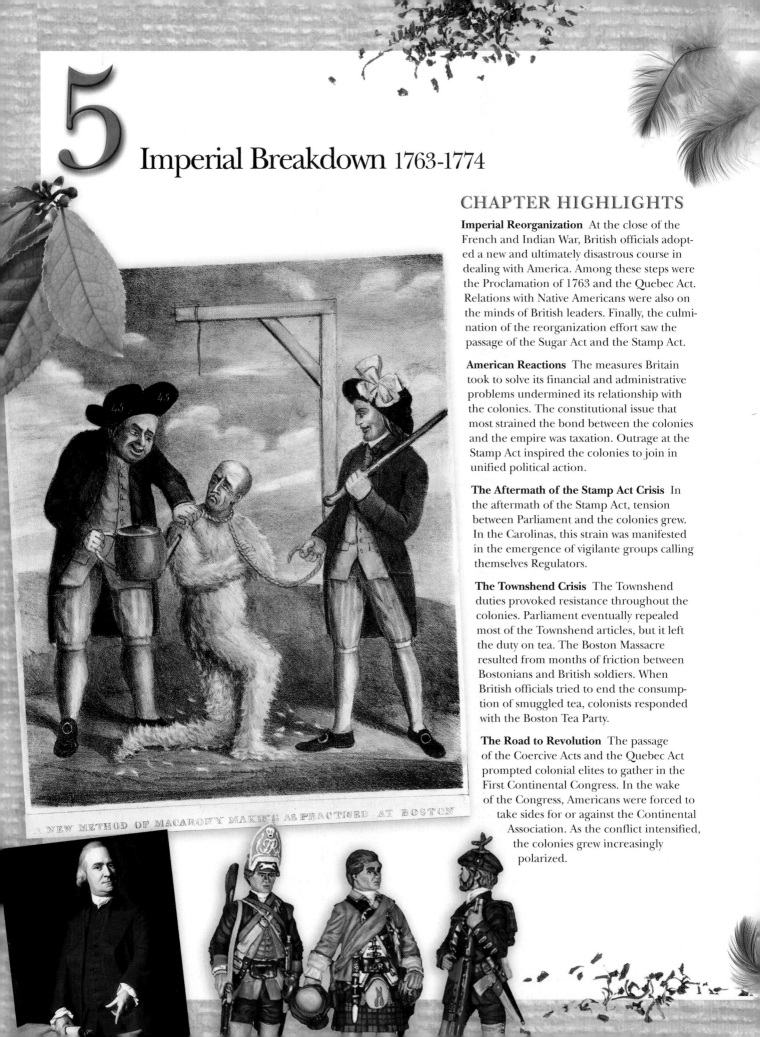

A NEW METHOD OF MACARONY MAKING AS PRACTISED AT BOSTON

CHAPTER HIGHLIGHTS

Imperial Reorganization At the close of the French and Indian War, British officials adopted a new and ultimately disastrous course in dealing with America. Among these steps were the Proclamation of 1763 and the Quebec Act. Relations with Native Americans were also on the minds of British leaders. Finally, the culmination of the reorganization effort saw the passage of the Sugar Act and the Stamp Act.

American Reactions The measures Britain took to solve its financial and administrative problems undermined its relationship with the colonies. The constitutional issue that most strained the bond between the colonies and the empire was taxation. Outrage at the Stamp Act inspired the colonies to join in unified political action.

The Aftermath of the Stamp Act Crisis In the aftermath of the Stamp Act, tension between Parliament and the colonies grew. In the Carolinas, this strain was manifested in the emergence of vigilante groups calling themselves Regulators.

The Townshend Crisis The Townshend duties provoked resistance throughout the colonies. Parliament eventually repealed most of the Townshend articles, but it left the duty on tea. The Boston Massacre resulted from months of friction between Bostonians and British soldiers. When British officials tried to end the consumption of smuggled tea, colonists responded with the Boston Tea Party.

The Road to Revolution The passage of the Coercive Acts and the Quebec Act prompted colonial elites to gather in the First Continental Congress. In the wake of the Congress, Americans were forced to take sides for or against the Continental Association. As the conflict intensified, the colonies grew increasingly polarized.

No Stamp Act.

CHAPTER QUESTIONS

HOW DID conflicts such as the Cherokee War and Pontiac's Rebellion affect relations between Native Americans and colonists?

HOW DID country ideology shape colonial reaction to the Sugar and Stamp Acts?

WHO WERE the Regulators, and what were the Regulator movements?

HOW DID the British respond to the Boston Tea Party?

WHO MADE up the First Continental Congress and what was its purpose?

The BLOODY MASSACRE perpetrated in King Street BOSTON on March 5th 1770 by a party of the 29th Regt.

CHAPTER OUTLINE

- Imperial Reorganization
- American Reactions
- The Aftermath of the Stamp Act Crisis
- The Townshend Crisis
- The Road to Revolution

THE REPEAL, — or the Funeral Procession, of MISS AMERIC-STAMP.

IMAGE KEY
for pages 120–121 on page 143.

Philadelphia, January 1774

My Dear Jack,

Your Uncle wrote the 27 Dec. by Capt. Ayres who brought the Tea. His ship came within four miles of this City on Sunday the 26th where she was stopped, not being suffered to come any farther. . . . The inhabitants sent a Supply of fresh provisions & a Pilot on board [who put them on course for England]. I believe they were glad they came off so well, for at Boston they threw it all into the River, and it would have gone near to have shared the same fate here, but the Capt. had more prudence than to endeavour to force a landing by which means he prevented a great deal of Mischief & Confusion, for they were all determined to oppose it. They think now that the India Company will get the Act which imposes a duty of 3d per pound repealed and then send more over.

Kensington, September 19, 1774

Dear Jack,

The Congress [The First Continental Congress] are now Setting here & have been a fortnight but nothing Transpires. All is kept a profound Secret. There was a [false] report the other day of the Town of Boston being Bombarded by the Men of War lying off the Town. . . . which Occasioned a general consternation along the Continent, and in some parts of the Country they Armed and Marched to the Number of 15,000 & more were getting ready. . . . In Short the Provinces are determined one and all to stand by each other. What the Consequences will be we don't know.

Kensington Nov 1, 1774

My Dear Jack,

Our Congress are broke up and are come to a great Spirited Resolves . . . together with a petition to his Majestie. . . . It is to be published and they have bound themselves to abide by those resolves . . . and if Necessitated to repel force with force. All Importation ceases after the first of December next.

Kensington June 28, 1775

My Dear Jack,

All the Provinces [are] arming and Training in the same Manner, for they are all determined to die or be Free. . . . God knows how it will end but I fear it will be very bad on both sides, and if your drivalish minestry and parliament dont make some concessions and Repeal the Acts, England will lose America for as I said before they are determined to be free.

Eliza Farmar

Pennsylvania Magazine of History and Biography, vol. 40 (1916): 199–207.

ELIZA FARMAR AND her family had recently moved to Kensington, a suburb of Philadelphia, when she wrote these letters, and her ties to relatives in England remained strong. Jack, the recipient of these letters, was her nephew and a clerk in the London office of the East India Company, whose shipment of tea precipitated the Boston Tea Party. Although she hoped that he might come to America, she minced no words in emphasizing the determination of Americans to resist British measures that appeared to infringe upon their freedoms. These letters accordingly chronicle a psychological counterpart to her move to Kensington. She began both journeys as an English subject; she ended them as an American citizen.

Like most colonists, she started out proud to be a British subject and part of Britain's increasingly powerful empire. But over the course of the eighteenth century, Americans had developed a sense of their identity as Americans. Largely governing themselves through their own legislatures, they believed that they enjoyed all the rights of British subjects anywhere.

But in the wake of the French and Indian War, British officials found themselves with a burdensome debt and vastly increased territory to administer. In response, they attempted to change the way they governed the colonies and, for the first time, imposed direct taxes on the colonists.

IMPERIAL REORGANIZATION

At the close of the French and Indian War, British officials adopted a new and ultimately disastrous course in dealing with America. Lacking experience and led by the young and somewhat naive new monarch, George III, they took measures that worked mostly to the disadvantage of the colonies.

BRITISH PROBLEMS

Britain's empire in 1763 was immense, and the problems its rulers faced were correspondingly large. It still faced threats, if diminished ones, from its traditional European enemies. French territory on the North American mainland had been reduced to two tiny islands in the Gulf of St. Lawrence. But France would be eager for revenge, and French inhabitants in the recently acquired territories might prove disloyal to their new rulers in any future war between the two countries.

Spain was less powerful militarily than France but a more significant presence on the North American mainland. Shocked by their inability to defend Cuba and the Philippines during the French and Indian War, Spanish officials stepped up the pace of the reforms they had begun making earlier in the century. Following the efficient French model of colonial government, they appointed *intendants*—generally Spaniards rather than colonials—to ensure better tax collection. Spain also expelled the Jesuit order from its dominions, because Jesuit priests were too independent of royal control to suit Spanish officials. And Spain strengthened its military forces in much of the empire.

Spain began to establish settlements in California in 1769 (see Chapter 4), but these were too weak and too far from the British colonies on the eastern seaboard to worry officials in London. Britain was similarly little concerned about Louisiana, which Spain had acquired from France in compensation for its loss of Florida, though it was closer and more populated. As for Florida, under British control after 1763, the Spanish evacuated it completely.

HOW DID conflicts such as the Cherokee War and Pontiac's Rebellion affect relations between Native Americans and colonists?

QUICK REVIEW

European Territories, 1763

- Britain: territories in North America from Hudson's Bay to the Caribbean, from the Atlantic to the Mississippi.
- France: territory on the mainland reduced to two small islands.
- Spain: Cuba, the Philippines, Louisiana, and California.

Chronology

1759–1761	Cherokee War takes place.
1760	George III becomes king.
1761–1762	Writs of Assistance case in Massachusetts.
1761–1769	British, French, German, Russian, and American astronomers observe transit of Venus across the sun.
1763	Peace of Paris ends French and Indian War.
	Spanish accelerate imperial reforms.
	British troops remain in America.
	Proclamation Line of 1763 limits western expansion of colonial settlement.
	Pontiac's Rebellion begins.
	Paxton Boys murder peaceful Indians.
	Virginia Court decides Parson's Cause.
1764	Sugar Act passed.
	Currency Act passed.
1765	Quartering Act passed.
	Stamp Act passed.
	Stamp Act Congress meets in New York.
1766	Stamp Act repealed; Declaratory Act passed.
	New York Assembly refuses to comply with Quartering Act.
1767	Townshend duties imposed.
	Regulator movements begin in North and South Carolina.
1768	Corsica ceded to France by Genoa.
1769	James Watt, a British inventor, patents a steam engine.
1769–1770	Famine kills one-third of the population in Bengal, India.
1770	Boston Massacre takes place.
	Tea duty retained, other Townshend duties repealed.
1771	North Carolina Regulator movement defeated.
1772	*Gaspee* burned.
	Committees of Correspondence formed.
	First Partition of Poland gives large part of its territory and population to Russia, Austria, and Prussia.
1773	Boston Tea Party takes place.
1774	Coercive Acts passed.
	Quebec Act passed.
	First Continental Congress meets and agrees to boycott British imports.

QUICK REVIEW

Financial Strain on the Empire

- £146-million-pound national debt after French and Indian War
- Many Britons believed Americans should bear more of the burden of empire
- Economic recession increased pressure for new taxes

WHERE TO LEARN MORE

Fort Michilimackinac National Historic Landmark, Mackinaw City, Michigan **www.mackinacparks.com/ michilimackinac/html**

Protecting and controlling the old and new territories in North America as inexpensively as possible presented British officials with difficult questions. How should they administer the new territories? How should they deal with Indians likely to resist further encroachments on their lands? And perhaps most vexing, how could they rein in the seemingly out-of-control colonists in the old territories?

Permitting most of the new areas to have their own assemblies seemed inadvisable but was unavoidable if these areas were to attract settlers. Believing that the increasing power of the legislatures had long since "unhinged" the government of the older colonies, British authorities hoped to avoid similar unruliness in the new territories. In fact, they had long wanted to roll back the power of the old colonial assemblies. But Britain had needed the cooperation of these assemblies during the years of war with France. Now, with France vanquished, imperial officials felt that they could crack down on the local governments.

Resentment against American conduct during the war also colored British thinking. Some of the colonies had failed to enlist their quota of recruits. Worse yet, illicit trade was so common in New England that it cost Britain more to operate the customs service in America than it collected in duties.

England emerged from the war with what was then an immense national debt of approximately £146 million. Alarmed by the unprecedented debt, many

Britons concluded that Americans should bear more of the financial burden of running the empire. An economic recession—triggered by the reduction in spending that followed the war—put further pressure on British officials to reduce taxes in England.

DEALING WITH THE NEW TERRITORIES

In 1763, the British government took several important steps to deal with the new territories, protect the old colonies, and maintain peace with the Indians. One was to keep a substantial body of troops stationed in America even in peacetime—10,000 were initially planned. Another, announced in the royal **Proclamation of 1763,** was to establish civilian governments in East and West Florida. A third, in the same proclamation, was to temporarily forbid white settlement west of the Appalachian Mountains. The purpose of the **Proclamation Line** restricting white settlement was presumably twofold: to keep white settlers and Indians apart, preventing fighting between them, and to hold the colonists closer to the coast, where they would be easier to control (see Map 5–1).

Neither the Proclamation Line nor the stationing of troops in America was particularly wise. The Proclamation Line provoked resentment because it threatened to deprive settlers and speculators in the rapidly developing colonies of the land they coveted. Some who had moved into the Ohio area were removed by force. Other Americans merely ignored the restriction. Moreover, someone had to pay for the troops, forcing the British government to take additional measures that further provoked American resentment. These measures included the imposition of direct taxes and the passage of **Quartering Acts** that required colonial assemblies to provide barracks and certain supplies for the soldiers.

The presence of troops in peacetime alarmed Americans. Sharing the traditional English distrust of standing armies, they wondered whether the soldiers were there to coerce rather than protect them. Given their wariness, Americans would doubtless have objected to the troops and to the taxes necessary to support them even if the troops had done an exemplary job of protecting the frontier. But conflicts with Indians cast doubt on their ability to do even that.

THE STATUS OF NATIVE AMERICANS

If Britain confronted complex problems in North America, Native Americans faced even more difficult ones in dealing with the British. Colonial settlers and their livestock were displacing Indians from their ancient lands, while liquor and rampant cheating by white traders were debasing the fur trade.

Meanwhile British officials no longer found Native American neutrality or military help as important as they once had. Increasingly superfluous as allies and unable to play the European powers off against each other, Native Americans therefore lost much of their former ability to protect themselves by any means short of military resistance.

Two major Indian wars—one breaking out in the late 1750s, during the closing years of the French and Indian War, and the other erupting in its aftermath in the early 1760s—tested British policy toward Native Americans. The first conflict, the **Cherokee War,** took place in the southern Appalachian highlands. In

Cunne Shote, one of three Cherokee chiefs who visited London in 1762, had this portrait painted there by Francis Parsons.

The Granger Collection

Proclamation of 1763 Royal proclamation setting the boundary known as the Proclamation Line.

Proclamation Line Boundary, decreed as part of the Proclamation of 1763, that limited British settlements to the eastern side of the Appalachian Mountains.

Quartering Acts Acts of Parliament requiring colonial legislatures to provide supplies and quarters for the troops stationed in America.

Cherokee War Conflict (1759–1761) on the southern frontier between the Cherokee Indians and colonists from Virginia southward.

MAP EXPLORATION

To explore an interactive version of this map, go to
http://www.prenhall.com/goldfield3/map5.1

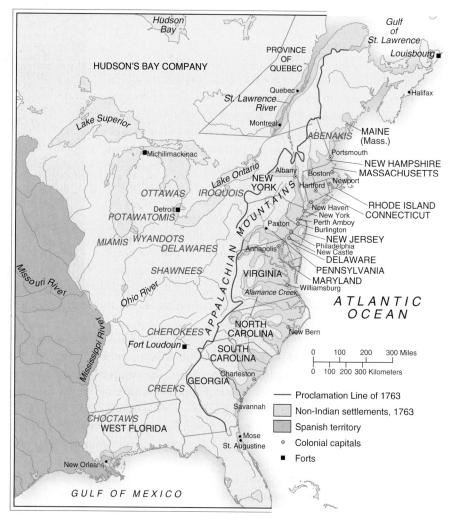

MAP 5–1   Colonial Settlement and the Proclamation Line of 1763   This map depicts the regions claimed and settled by the major groups competing for territory in eastern North America. With the Proclamation Line of 1763, positioned along the crest of the Appalachian Mountains, the British government tried to stop the westward migration of settlers under its jurisdiction and thereby limit conflict with the Indians. The result, however, was frustration and anger on the part of land-hungry settlers.

WHY DO you suppose the Proclamation Line of 1763 was positioned along the crest of the Appalachian Mountains?

1759, Cherokee warriors (who were returning home from a campaign with the British against the French and their Indian allies in western Pennsylvania) may have stolen horses belonging to Virginia colonists. The colonists attacked the Cherokees, killing some of them. The Cherokees retaliated with attacks on western settlements in all of the southern colonies. Three expeditions, manned by British as well as colonial troops, eventually forced the Cherokees to agree, in a 1761 treaty, to surrender land in the Carolinas and Virginia to the colonists.

The second major conflict, **Pontiac's Rebellion,** broke out in 1763 among Indians in the Great Lakes and Ohio Valley regions formerly claimed by France. Many Native American groups feared that the British planned to exterminate them and take their lands now that the French could no longer help them. They also resented the contempt and increased stinginess of British traders and officials. These concerns helped to inspire a united effort to resist the British and revitalize Indian cultures. Neolin, also known as the Delaware Prophet, urged Native Americans to reject European goods and ways. Pontiac, an Ottawa chief, was the most respected leader of at least eight major groups of Native Americans that attacked British forces and American settlers from the Great Lakes to Virginia in 1763.

Pontiac's Rebellion raged until 1766. During intermittent negotiations, Pontiac insisted that British possession of the old French forts in western Pennsylvania and Ohio did not give Great Britain title to the area. The French, he maintained, had been there merely as tenants of the Indians. But the British eventually forced the Indians to give up portions of their territory in return for compensation and guarantees that traditional hunting grounds in the Ohio Valley would remain theirs.

During the war, British commanders sanctioned what would now be regarded as germ warfare against the Indians by giving them blankets that smallpox victims had used. Settlers in Paxton township (near modern Harrisburg, Pennsylvania) lashed out at their peaceful neighbors, the Conestogas. Facing arrest and trial for this outrage, the so-called Paxton Boys marched on Philadelphia, threatening the Pennsylvania Assembly. Benjamin Franklin persuaded them to disperse. Despite the government's efforts, the Paxton Boys were never effectively prosecuted for their acts.

Pontiac's Rebellion and the Cherokee War were costly for both sides. Hoping to prevent such outbreaks, British officials had begun experimenting with centralized control of Indian affairs during the 1750s. The Proclamation of 1763, and the line it established restricting further white settlement, gave officials increased responsibility for protecting the Indians against encroachments by settlers. But land-hungry Americans objected to efforts to keep them off Indian lands, and white traders resented restrictions on their activities. Centralized control of the fur and deerskin trades also proved to be expensive for the British government. British authorities therefore permitted several adjustments in the Indian boundary line and in 1768 returned supervision of the Indian traders to the individual colonies. But such tacit recognition of local autonomy conflicted with imperial plans to restrict the powers of the colonial assemblies.

CURBING THE ASSEMBLIES

As early as the 1750s, in an episode known as the **Parson's Cause,** British officials attempted to curb the American legislatures. Anglican ministers in Virginia drew tax-supported salaries computed in pounds of tobacco. When a drought in the mid-1750s caused a sharp rise in tobacco prices, they expected a windfall. The Virginia House of Burgesses, however, restricted their payment to two pence a pound. Lobbying by the clergy convinced the king to disallow the Two Penny Act, and some Virginia clergymen sued for the unpaid portion of their salaries.

In the most famous of these cases, the Virginia government was defended by Patrick Henry, a previously obscure young lawyer who looked like "a Presbyterian clergyman, used to haranguing the people." Given Henry's eloquence, and its own sense of fair play, the jury found in favor of the suing minister but awarded him only one penny in damages, an award that reflected the hostility many Virginians felt toward the pretensions of the Anglican clergy.

4–2
Declaration of the Injured Frontier Inhabitants [of Pennsylvania] (1764)

Pontiac's Rebellion   Indian uprising (1763–1766) led by Pontiac of the Ottawas and Neolin of the Delawares.

Parson's Cause   Series of developments (1758–1763) that began when the Virginia legislature modified the salaries of Anglican clergymen, who complained to the crown and sued to recover damages. British authorities responded by imposing additional restrictions on the legislature. Virginians, who saw this as a threat, reacted by strongly reasserting local autonomy.

BRITISH STAMPS FOR AMERICA.

These test impressions were the embossments required by the Stamp Act. They were made in Britain in 1765, but, before he understood the depth of American hostility to the act, Benjamin Franklin hoped that in the future someone could "strike the stamps at Philadelphia on all paper for newspapers and almanacs."

North Wind Picture Archives

Currency Act   Law passed by Parliament in 1764 to prevent the colonies from issuing legal tender paper money.

Sugar Act   Law passed in 1764 to raise revenue in the American colonies. It lowered the duty from 6 pence to 3 pence per gallon on foreign molasses imported into the colonies and increased the restrictions on colonial commerce.

Stamp Act   Law passed by Parliament in 1765 to raise revenue in America by requiring taxed, stamped paper for legal documents, publications, and playing cards.

Meanwhile, still in response to the Two Penny Act, the crown further dismayed Virginians by instructing the colony's governor not to sign any new law that modified existing laws unless it contained a clause making it inoperative until the king approved it. This restriction severely hampered the assembly's ability to respond to emergencies such as the drought. The legislators of the colony, Virginians maintained, had the "Right to enact ANY Law they shall think necessary for their INTERNAL Government."

The British administration also sought to restrict the power of colonial legislatures to issue legal tender currency, or paper money. These notes frequently depreciated to only a fraction of their face value in British coin. Parliament had responded in 1751 by forbidding further issues of paper money in New England. In the **Currency Act** of 1764, Parliament extended this restriction to the rest of the colonies, prohibiting them from printing paper money. Because the new restrictions came when most colonies were in an economic recession, Americans considered this step an especially burdensome attempt to curtail the assemblies' powers.

THE SUGAR AND STAMP ACTS

In 1764, the British Parliament, under Prime Minister George Grenville, passed the American Revenue Act, commonly known as the **Sugar Act.** The main purpose of this act, as stated in its preamble, was "for improving the revenue of this kingdom." To generate funds, the Sugar Act and its accompanying legislation combined new and revised duties on colonial imports.

The Sugar Act legislation also lengthened the list of enumerated products—goods that could be sent only to England or destinations within the empire—and required that ships carry elaborate new documents certifying the legality of their cargoes.

To enforce these cumbersome regulations, the British government used the Royal Navy to seize smugglers' ships. It also ordered colonial customs collectors to discharge their duties personally. Previously, the collectors had often lived in England, leaving the work of collection in the colonies to poorly paid deputies. Finally, Parliament gave responsibility for trying violations of the laws to a new vice-admiralty court in Halifax, Nova Scotia. Vice-admiralty courts normally operated without a jury and were therefore more likely to enforce trade restrictions. For this reason, and because of the remote location of the Halifax court, Americans immediately opposed this provision of the Sugar Act. In response, Parliament created three other vice-admiralty courts in the more convenient localities of Boston, Philadelphia, and Charleston, a decision that was not exactly what the colonists had had in mind.

In the spring of 1765, Parliament enacted another tax on Americans, the **Stamp Act.** This legislation required all valid legal documents, as well as newspapers, playing cards, and various other papers, to bear a government-issued stamp, for which there was a charge. The Stamp Act was the first internal tax (as opposed to an external trade duty) that Parliament had imposed on the colonies. Grenville, a lawyer, realized that it raised a constitutional issue: Did Parliament have the right to impose direct taxes on Americans when Americans had no elected representatives in Parliament? Grenville maintained that it did. Americans, he would find, vigorously disagreed.

AMERICAN REACTIONS

*T*he measures Britain took to solve its financial and administrative problems first puzzled, then shocked, and eventually outraged Americans. They expected to be rewarded for their efforts in the French and Indian War and treated with respect. They were certain that as British Americans they shared in the glory and enjoyed all the rights of Englishmen in England.

CONSTITUTIONAL ISSUES

To Americans, it was self-evident that the British measures were unfair. It was difficult to contend, however, that the British authorities had no right to impose them. Then as now, the **British Constitution** was not a single written document. It consisted, rather, of the accumulated body of English law and custom, including acts of Parliament. How, then, could the colonists claim that an act of Parliament was unconstitutional?

Constitutional conflict surfaced early in Massachusetts over the issue of **writs of assistance.** These general search warrants, which gave customs officials in America the power to inspect virtually any building suspected of holding smuggled goods, had to be formally renewed at the accession of a new monarch. When George III became king in 1760, Massachusetts merchants sought to block the reissuance of the writs. Their attorney, James Otis, Jr., maintained that Parliament lacked the authority to empower colonial courts to issue them. Otis lost, but "then and there," a future president of the United States, John Adams, would later write, "the child independence was born."

TAXATION AND THE POLITICAL CULTURE

The constitutional issue that most strained the bond between the colonies and the empire was taxation. Because Parliament had customarily refrained from taxing them, Americans assumed that it could not, and because their own assemblies had taxed them, they believed that those legislatures were in fact their parliaments.

Most Americans believed that to deprive them of the right to be taxed only by their own elected representatives was to deny them one of the most basic rights of Englishmen. British officials, who believed in parliamentary sovereignty, counted the colonists among those constituents. Americans thought otherwise.

American views on taxation and the role of government reflected the influence of country ideology. Country ideology proceeded from two basic assumptions: that human beings are selfish and that they need governments to protect them from one another. But country ideology also held that government power, no matter how necessary or to whom entrusted, is inherently aggressive and expansive. According to the English political philosopher John Locke, rulers have the authority to enforce law "only for the public good." When government exceeds this proper function, the people have the right to change it.

Country ideology stressed that in the English system of government, it was the duty of Parliament, in particular the House of Commons (which represented the people as a whole), to check the executive power of the crown.

HOW DID country ideology shape colonial reaction to the Sugar and Stamp Acts?

British Constitution   The principles, procedures, and precedents that governed the operation of the British government.

Writs of assistance   Documents issued by a court of law that gave British officials in America the power to search for smuggled goods whenever they wished.

Samuel Adams, the leader of the Boston radicals, as he appeared to John Singleton Copley in the early 1770s. In this famous picture, thought to have been commissioned by another revolutionary leader, John Hancock, Adams points to legal documents guaranteeing American rights.

Samuel Adams, about 1772 John Singleton Copley, American, 1738–1815 Oil on canvas 125.73 × 100.33 cm 49 1/2 × 39 1/2 in.) Deposited by the City of Boston L-R 30.76c

Nonimportation movement A tactical means of putting economic pressure on Britain by refusing to buy its exports to the colonies.

Sons of Liberty Secret organizations in the colonies formed to oppose the Stamp Act.

Such an important responsibility required the people's representatives to be men of sufficient property and judgment to make independent decisions. A representative should be "virtuous" (meaning public-spirited), and he should avoid political partisanship. A representative of the appropriate social status who exhibited the proper behavior deserved the deference of his constituents. But if he did not measure up, the people should be able to vote him out.

Country ideology appealed to Americans for a number of reasons. In part, colonists were drawn to it as they were to other English ideas and trends. More important, country ideology's suspicion of those in power suited American politics on the local level, where rivalries and factionalism fostered distrust between those with and without power. Finally, with its insistence on the important political role of the propertied elite, country ideology appealed to America's local gentry. It suggested that it was their duty, as elected political officials, to safeguard the freedom of their constituents.

These ideas have had an enduring influence on American politics, surfacing even today in the suspicion of Washington and "big government." During the eighteenth century, they predisposed Americans to value local control and to expect the worst from remote governments. In so doing, they helped inspire the American Revolution.

PROTESTING THE TAXES

Given this ideological background, the initial American response to the Sugar Act was surprisingly mild. This was because the new taxes it imposed took the form of duties on trade and thus appeared consistent with the earlier Navigation Acts. The actual reaction varied from colony to colony in ways that reflected regional self-interest.

The size of the burden was less important than the principle involved. To Americans steeped in country ideology, direct taxation by London threatened to undercut the elected representatives' power of the purse and thereby remove the traditional first line of defense against a tyrannical executive. Thus all the assemblies eventually passed resolutions flatly maintaining that any parliamentary tax on America, including the Sugar Act, was unconstitutional. By the end of 1764, New York merchants had joined the artisans and merchants of Boston in a **nonimportation movement,** an organized boycott of British manufactured goods.

Unlike the Sugar Act, the Stamp Act had an equal impact throughout the colonies, and the response to it was swift and vociferous. Newspapers and pamphlets were filled with denunciations of the supposedly unconstitutional measure. The colonial legislatures were also quick to condemn the new measure. Virginia's lower house was the first to act, approving Patrick Henry's strong resolutions against the Stamp Act. These were then reprinted in newspapers throughout the colonies, and other legislatures passed similar formal objections.

Popular protests also expressed widespread outrage at the Stamp Act. With a postwar economic slump in some of the colonies, many people now turned to direct action. The **Sons of Liberty,** a collection of loosely organized activists, put pressure on stamp distributors and British authorities. In August 1765, a Boston group led by Ebenezer MacIntosh, a volunteer fireman and shoemaker, demolished property belonging to a revenue agent, and another mob sacked Lieutenant Governor Thomas Hutchinson's house. About a month later, rioters roamed the streets of New York, smashing windows and telling the governor, "[Y]ou'll die a Martyr to your own villany . . . and every man, that assists you, shall be, surely, put to Death."

The Sons of Liberty included people from all ranks of society. The leaders, however, came mostly from the middle and upper classes. Often pushed by more radical common people, some of the elite doubtless joined in the hope of protecting their own positions and interests. How threatened these might be was seen most dramatically in Charleston, where slaves paraded through the streets crying, "Liberty!" Movement leaders were concerned that violence could discredit the American cause.

Partly as a result of the growing unrest, leaders throughout the colonies determined to meet and agree on a unified response to Britain. Nine colonies eventually sent delegates to the **Stamp Act Congress,** which met in New York City in October 1765.

The congress adopted the **Declaration of Rights and Grievances,** which denied Parliament's right to tax the colonies, and petitioned both king and Parliament to repeal the Stamp and Sugar Acts. Parliament, unwilling to acknowledge this challenge to its authority, refused to receive the colonial petitions.

As protests spread, the stamp distributors resigned "for the welfare of the people." In some areas, Americans went about their business as usual without using stamped paper. In other places, they avoided activities that required taxed items. They also stepped up the boycott of British goods that had begun in response to the Sugar Act. British merchants, hurt by this economic pressure, petitioned Parliament for repeal of the Stamp Act, and a new ministry obliged them by rescinding it in March 1766. Modifications in the provisions of the Sugar Act came later in the year.

A satirical British engraving from 1766 showing English politicians burying the Stamp Act, "born 1765 died 1766." The warehouses in the background symbolize the revival of trade with America.

The Granger Collection, N.Y.

THE AFTERMATH OF THE STAMP ACT CRISIS

During the Stamp Act crisis, Benjamin Franklin appeared before Parliament to present American objections to the Stamp and Sugar Acts. Some members apparently concluded from his remarks that the colonists would accept port duties but would oppose direct taxes. They were wrong.

Americans in turn misunderstood the **Declaratory Act** that accompanied the repeal of the Stamp Act. Intended to make Parliament's retreat more acceptable to its members, this act stated that Parliament had the right to "legislate for the colonies in all cases whatsoever." Did *legislate* mean *tax?* Not necessarily, for taxes were traditionally deemed to be a voluntary gift to the king from the people acting through their own representatives. Americans therefore tended to consider the Declaratory Act a mere face-saving gesture. Unfortunately, it was more than that.

A STRAINED RELATIONSHIP

Most members of Parliament continued to believe that they represented everyone in the empire and that they could therefore tax people in the colonies as well as in England. Americans believed just as strongly that "in taxing ourselves and making Laws for our own internal government . . . we can by no means

WHO WERE the Regulators, and what were the Regulator movements?

Stamp Act Congress October 1765 meeting of delegates sent by nine colonies, that adopted the Declaration of Rights and Grievances and petitioned against the Stamp Act.

Declaration of Rights and Grievances Asserts that the Stamp Act and other taxes imposed on the colonists without their consent were unconstitutional.

Declaratory Act Law passed in 1766 to accompany repeal of the Stamp Act that stated that Parliament had the authority to legislate for the colonies "in all cases however."

4–4
"Letters from a Farmer in Pennsylvania"
(1767)

allow our Provincial legislatures to be subordinate to any legislative power on earth."

Relations were never quite the same between England and America after the Stamp Act crisis. Each side became ever more suspicious of the other. March 18, the anniversary of the repeal of the Stamp Act, became an occasion for celebration, giving Americans a national holiday before they had a nation.

In the process Americans also began developing a new conception of their special role in history. Because freedom seemed to be under widespread attack in Europe as well as in the British empire, they increasingly saw themselves as champions in "ONE COMMON CAUSE" that had global dimensions. Thus a struggle for independence on the small island of Corsica in the Mediterranean Sea aroused much interest and sympathy before its failure increased Americans' forebodings about their own plight (see Global Perspectives: Corsica and General Paoli).

Events in America also revealed continuing tensions between Great Britain and the colonies that were cause for concern. When British officials required Massachusetts to compensate those who had suffered losses in the Stamp Act rioting, the legislature complied but pardoned the rioters. In 1767, an irritated Parliament then passed an act suspending the New York legislature because it had not complied with the Quartering Act of 1765. This law required colonial assemblies to provide facilities and certain supplies for royal troops. The New York legislature finally obeyed before the suspending act went into effect and thus remained in business. But such incidents boded ill for the hopes of some colonists that a British government that had repealed the Stamp Act would prove cooperative in other ways.

REGULATOR MOVEMENTS

In 1766, a committee of the South Carolina legislature appointed to consider "the State of the Province" recommended that it establish courts in the rapidly growing backcountry and petition Parliament for repeal of the Currency Act. These suggestions were prompted by mounting unrest in the southern backcountry. Vigilante groups calling themselves **Regulators** had emerged in North Carolina in response to official corruption and in South Carolina in response to lawlessness. High taxes and high court costs in North Carolina oppressed the colony's western farmers. Because the Currency Act reduced the amount of money in circulation, it compounded people's problems. In South Carolina, the devastation and disruptions of the Cherokee War left a legacy of violence. In both colonies, because representation in the assemblies failed to reflect the rapidly growing backcountry populations, legislatures were slow to respond to their needs. As a result, the Regulators did by extralegal action what they could not do through legal channels.

These activities brought the Regulators into conflict with the local elites of both North and South Carolina. The British government, however, only made matters worse. Instead of encouraging the assemblies to increase western representation, the crown sought to curb their power by limiting their size. As for the shortage of currency, Lord Hillsborough, the secretary of state for the colonies, callously informed North Carolinians that "no Consideration of a possible local inconvenience" would prompt Britain to modify the "sound Principles" of the Currency Act. And instead of approving legislation to establish courts in the South

Regulators Vigilante groups active in the 1760s and 1770s in the western parts of North and South Carolina. The South Carolina Regulators attempted to rid the area of outlaws; the North Carolina Regulators were more concerned with high taxes and court costs.

GLOBAL PERSPECTIVES

CORSICA AND GENERAL PAOLI

During the first part of the eighteenth century, the island of Corsica in the Mediterranean Sea belonged to the Italian city-state of Genoa. But Genoese rule was corrupt, and the Corsicans were in almost continual revolt. In 1755 they turned to a remarkable young man, Pasquale Paoli, then only 29 years old, and made him their commanding general. Imposing discipline on his unruly soldiers, Paoli not only drove the Genoese from most of the island but also suppressed traditional blood feuds among his followers, established a democratic representative body, and founded a university. Meanwhile, the Genoese tired of the struggle and sold Corsica to France. A vigorous French attack then defeated Paoli's forces, and he became an exile in London.

Englishmen and Americans followed these events with great interest, and Paoli became a celebrity. He met King George III and joined Samuel Johnson's London literary circle. He also became, quite literally, the toast of the American colonies. In 1769 Philadelphians held a subscription dinner honoring Paoli and the patriots of Corsica. Toasts included the hope that "the spirit of Paoli" would "inhabit every American," that British policy would be just, and that America would be forever free. A popular newspaper, the *New York Journal*, termed Paoli "the greatest man on earth" and his men "sons of liberty in Corsica." Their "glorious struggle" was, according to the paper, extremely "interesting to every friend of liberty and the just rights of mankind." A popular tavern near Philadelphia was called the General Paoli, while the surrounding settlement took his name. British officials were alarmed at the French acquisition of Corsica and the resulting increase in the power of Britain's traditional enemy throughout the Mediterranean Sea, but they were unprepared to counter it and took no significant action. This failure to support the Corsicans increased the doubts of the colonists about the British government's commitment to freedom. America therefore had a special role; if liberty were "extinguished in British realms," a colonist prophesied that America would "open her arms wide to receive" the oppressed friends of freedom.

Carolina backcountry, British officials disallowed it because it specified that judges would hold their positions contingent on good behavior rather than at the pleasure of the crown.

Thus, a crisis confronted local officials by 1767. In South Carolina, the assembly belatedly reapportioned itself, giving the backcountry some representation, and permitted the crown to dictate the terms of judicial appointments. These and other concessions to western residents narrowly averted bloodshed. But in North Carolina, fighting broke out in 1771. Governor William Tryon led the local militia against the Regulators, who had gathered near Alamance Creek. There, he ordered the Regulators to disperse or his men would fire. "Fire and be damned," someone replied, and gunfire erupted, killing 29 men and wounding more than 150 on both sides.

The confrontation in North Carolina was the most serious of its kind, but similar social tensions were apparent in other colonies. To deal with them, colonial leaders had to understand local conditions and be able to act on their knowledge. But British attempts to reform colonial governments threatened to hamstring them.

HOW DID the British respond to the Boston Tea Party?

WHERE TO LEARN MORE

★ Charleston, South Carolina
www.cr.nps.gov/nr/travel/charleston

THE TOWNSHEND CRISIS

Britain had not given up the idea of taxing the colonies with the repeal of the Stamp Act in 1766. Little over a year later, Parliament passed a new set of taxes, the Townshend duties. Another crisis ensued, lasting until an American boycott of British goods forced repeal of most of the new duties. The relatively quiet period that followed ended when Britain made a serious attempt to enforce compliance with the one Townshend duty still on the books, the duty on tea.

TOWNSHEND'S PLAN

Charles Townshend became the leading figure in Britain's government in 1767. He thought he understood the colonies, and he knew that many members of Parliament still wanted to tax Americans. The **Townshend Duty Act** imposed new duties, or external taxes, which Townshend believed the colonists were willing to accept, but no direct, or internal, taxes like the Stamp Tax. The duties covered a number of items the colonists regularly imported—tea, paper, paint, lead, and glass. To make sure that the duties were collected, the British added a new board of customs commissioners for America and located its headquarters in Boston.

The new customs officials were, in fact, far more diligent than their predecessors. One of them, taking advantage of technicalities in the law, entrapped Henry Laurens, a prominent merchant in South Carolina. Other officials harassed the wealthy Boston merchant John Hancock. Seizing his appropriately named vessel *Liberty*, they accused him of smuggling. Hancock may indeed have violated the acts of trade at times, but in this case the accusations were apparently false. The incident sparked a riot in Boston. Britain responded in 1768 by sending troops to Boston. The soldiers would remain there amid mounting hostility for the next year and a half.

AMERICAN BOYCOTT

The Townshend duties, like the stamp tax, provoked resistance throughout the colonies. The purpose of the taxes—to help pay the costs of government in the colonies, including the salaries of governors and judges—also seemed dangerous. Americans believed it was the role of their own assemblies to raise revenues for these costs. By bypassing the assemblies, the Townshend Act threatened to undermine their authority.

There was no equivalent to the Stamp Act Congress in response to the Townshend Act, because British officials barred the assemblies from sending delegates to such a meeting. Even so, Americans gradually organized an effective nonimportation movement. Once again, vigilant laborers and artisans threatened violators of the general boycott with physical violence, but few disturbances occurred. Many Americans signed subscription lists binding themselves, with the other signers, to buy only goods made in the colonies and nothing made in Great Britain. To avoid imported English textiles, American women spun more thread and wove more cloth at home. Wearing homespun became a moral virtue, a sign of self-reliance, personal independence, and the rejection of "corrupting" English luxuries (see "American Views: Social Status and the Enforcement of the Nonimportation Movement").

The nonimportation movement forged a sense of common purpose and trust among all who participated in it, giving them the sense of belonging to a

Townshend Duty Act Act of Parliament, passed in 1767, imposing duties on colonial tea, lead, paint, paper, and glass.

larger community of fellow Americans. Although it was at this point more an imagined community than a political community, it was real enough and large enough to mobilize many ordinary Americans and sharply reduce imports from Britain.

The troubles in America contributed to the king's decision to appoint a new prime minister, Lord North. Thinking remarkably alike, George III and North complemented each other. At the king's insistence, North would remain prime minister until 1782. In 1770, he was prepared to concede that the Townshend duties had been counterproductive because they interfered with British trade. But when Parliament repealed most of them, it left the duty on tea. This symbolic equivalent of the Declaratory Act served to assert Parliament's continuing right to tax the colonies.

THE BOSTON MASSACRE

Ironically, on the same day that North proposed that Parliament rescind most of the Townshend duties—March 5, 1770—British troops fired on American civilians in Boston. This incident, which came to be known to Americans everywhere as the **Boston Massacre,** resulted from months of increasing friction between townspeople and the British troops stationed in the city.

The Boston Massacre occurred when angry and frightened British soldiers fired on a crowd that was pelting them with sticks and stones. Five men died, including Crispus Attucks—subsequently described as "that half Indian, half negro and altogether rowdy"—who has since become the most celebrated casualty of the incident. To preserve order, the troops withdrew from the city. Later two prominent local lawyers successfully defended the soldiers accused of murder.

THE "QUIET PERIOD"

In the so-called Quiet Period that followed, no general grievance united all Americans. But in almost every colony, issues continued to simmer.

Local circumstances produced a confrontation in Rhode Island. The crew of a British revenue schooner, the *Gaspee,* had been patrolling Narragansett Bay, seizing smugglers and, it was said, stealing livestock and cutting down farmers' fruit trees for firewood. When the *Gaspee* ran aground, Rhode Islanders got even. Led by John Brown, a local merchant, they boarded the vessel, shot its captain in the buttocks, and, putting him and his crew ashore, burned the ship. The British government appointed a commission of inquiry with instructions to arrest the culprits and send them to England for trial. Despite its offer of a reward for information about the incident, the commission learned nothing. The British attempt to stamp out smuggling in the colonies was so heavy-handed that it offended the innocent more than it frightened the guilty. Such incidents, and in particular the British threat to send Americans to England for trial, led American leaders to resolve to keep one another informed about British actions. Twelve colonies established **committees of correspondence** for this purpose. Leaders in Boston established similar committees in Massachusetts. There would soon be plenty for these organizations to do, for Boston was about to become the scene of a showdown between imperial authority and colonial resistance.

The Boston Massacre, March 5, 1770, in an engraving by Paul Revere. Copied from an earlier print, Revere's widely circulated version shows—somewhat inaccurately—well-organized soldiers firing on helpless civilians; the names of the dead, including Crispus Attucks, appear below.

Courtesy of Library of Congress.

4–6
The Boston "Massacre" or Victims of Circumstance? (1770)

Boston Massacre After months of increasing friction between townspeople and the British troops stationed in the city, on March 5, 1770, British troops fired on American civilians in Boston.

Committees of correspondence Committees formed in the colonies to keep Americans informed about British measures that would affect them.

AMERICAN VIEWS

SOCIAL STATUS AND THE ENFORCEMENT OF THE NONIMPORTATION MOVEMENT

Many Americans enthusiastically supported the nonimportation movement called in response to the Townshend Duty Act crisis of the late 1760s. A few, however, openly opposed it. Among these was the aristocratic William Henry Drayton of South Carolina, who objected to the composition of the committee chosen to enforce the nonimportation agreement in his region. The committee included artisans and shopkeepers, men who, Drayton claimed, should have no role in public affairs. Their education prepared them only "to cut up a beast in the market to the best advantage, to cobble an old shoe in the neatest manner, or to build a necessary house [privy]," not to make public policy. As the following document makes clear, deference had its limits, and the committeemen emphatically disagreed with him. Drayton was later to reverse himself and actively support the Continental Association's ban on importing British goods in 1775. "The people" wanted it, he would later explain, and "it was our duty, to satisfy our constituents; as we were only servants of the public [at large]."

- Who makes policy in the United States today?
- What qualifications do you think they should have?
- How do your answers to these questions differ from Drayton's? From the "Mechanicks's"?
- How would you explain Drayton's later switch?

THE MECHANICKS OF THE GENERAL COMMITTEE TO WILLIAM HENRY DRAYTON

The gracious Giver of all good things, has been pleased to bestow a certain principle on mankind, which properly may be called common sense: But, though every man hath a natural right to a determined portion of this ineffable ray of the Divinity, yet, to the misfortune of society, many persons fall short of this most necessary gift of God; the want of which cannot be compensated by all the learning of the schools.

The Mechanicks pretend to nothing more, than having a claim from nature, to their share in this inestimable favour, in common with Emperors and Kings, and, were it safe to carry the comparison still higher, they would say with William-Henry Drayton himself; who, in his great condescention, has been pleased to allow us a place amongst human beings: But whether it might have happened from an ill construction of his sensory, or his upper works being damaged by some rough treatment of the person who conducted his birth, we know not; however so it is, that, to us, he seems highly defective in this point, whatever exalted notions he may entertain of his own abilities.

By attending to the dictates of common sense, the Mechanicks have been able to distinguish between

THE BOSTON TEA PARTY

During the Quiet Period, Americans drank smuggled (and therefore untaxed) Dutch tea. Partly as a result, the British East India Company, nearly went bankrupt. Lord North tried to rescue it with the **Tea Act of 1773.** The act permitted the company to ship tea from its warehouses in Britain without paying the duty normally collected there. Because its tea would therefore be cheaper, British authorities assumed that Americans would buy it and simultaneously pay the old Townshend duty. The company selected a few merchants to act as its exclusive agents in the colonies.

This plan angered Americans. Some may have been jealous at being excluded from the tea trade. Most, however, were outraged at the attempt to trick them into paying the tax on tea. Men and women by the thousands decided not to touch the stuff.

Tea Act of 1773 Act of Parliament that permitted the East India Company to sell through agents in America without paying the duty customarily collected in Britain, thus reducing the retail price.

RIGHT and WRONG; in doing which indeed no great merit is claimed, because every man's own feelings will direct him thereto, unless he obstinately, or from a pertinacious opinion of his own superior knowledge, shuts his eyes, and stoickally submits to all the illegal encroachments that may be made on his property, by an ill-designing and badly-informed ministry.

Mr. Drayton may value himself as much as he pleases, on his having had a liberal education bestowed on him, tho' the good fruits thereof have not hitherto been conspicuous either in his public or private life: He ought however to know, that this is not so absolutely necessary to these, who move in the low sphere of mechanical employments. But still, though he pretends to view them with so contemptuous and oblique an eye, these men hope, that they are in some degree useful to society, without presuming to make any comparisons between themselves and him, except with regard to love for their country; for he has amply shewn, that an attachment of this sort is not one of his ruling passions. Nor does he appear in the least to have regarded the peace and good order of that community of which he is a member; otherwise he would not wilfully, and without any cause, have knocked his head against ninety-nine out of every hundred of the people, not only in this province, but of all North-America. . . . After an avowal of principles, incompatible with the essential rights of freemen under the English constitution, surely, no parish in this province, will ever think it prudent, to trust their interests in such hands, for the time to come? Besides, who can say he ever shewed any capacity for business, when he was honoured with a seat in the House of Assembly? . . .

Mr. Drayton may be assured, that so far from being ashamed of our trades, we are in the highest degree thankful to our friends, who put us in the way of being instructed in them; and that we bless God for giving us strength and judgment to pursue them, in order to maintain our families, with a decency suitable to their stations in life. Every man is not so lucky as to have a fortune ready provided to his hand, either by his own or his wife's parents, as has been his lot; nor ought it to be so with all men; and Providence accordingly hath wisely ordained otherwise, by appointing the greatest part of mankind, to provide for their support by manual labour; and we will be bold to say, that such are the most useful people in a community. . . .

We are, Yours, &c.
MECHANICKS of the COMMITTEE.
October 3d, 1769.

Source: *South Carolina Gazette*, October 5, 1769; reprinted in *The Letters of Freeman, etc.: Essays on the Nonimportation Movement in South Carolina* by William Henry Drayton, ed. Robert M. Weir (1977), University of South Carolina Press, pp. 111–114.

Thomas Hutchinson, who had been lieutenant governor of Massachusetts during the Stamp Act riots, was now the colony's royal governor. Two of his sons were among those chosen to be the East India Company's agents. In most other cities, threats from the Sons of Liberty convinced the captains of the tea ships to return to England without landing their cargo. Hutchinson, however, was determined to have the tea unloaded in Boston, and he barred the tea ships there from leaving.

When the Sons of Liberty realized that they could not force the ships to leave, they decided to take dramatic action. On December 16, 1773, Samuel Adams reportedly told a large gathering at Old South Meeting House that it "could do nothing more to preserve the liberties of America." This remark was apparently a prearranged signal for what came to be known as the **Boston Tea Party.** War whoops immediately answered him from the street outside, and a well-organized

Boston Tea Party Incident that occurred on December 16, 1773, in which Bostonians, disguised as Indians, destroyed £9,000 worth of tea belonging to the British East India Company in order to prevent payment of the duty on it.

band of men disguised as Indians raced aboard the *Dartmouth* and two other tea ships, broke open 342 chests of tea, and heaved the contents into the harbor.

THE INTOLERABLE ACTS

Surprised and angry, Britain reacted strongly. Parliament passed a series of repressive measures known as the **Coercive Acts.** The first of these, effective June 1, 1774, was the Boston Port Act, which closed the port of Boston to all incoming and outgoing traffic until the East India Company and the crown received payment for the destroyed tea and lost duties. The Administration of Justice Act, which followed, declared that an official who, while performing his duties, killed a colonist could be tried in England rather than in Massachusetts. The third measure, the Massachusetts Government Act, drastically modified that colony's charter of 1691. Under the old document, the legislature had elected members to the governor's council; henceforth, the crown would appoint them. And appointed, rather than elected, sheriffs would now name juries. In addition, the Massachusetts Government Act limited the number of town meetings that could be held without the governor's prior approval. In another measure, the British government made its commander in chief in America, General Thomas Gage, the governor of Massachusetts and, in the Quartering Act of 1774, declared that the troops under his command could be lodged in virtually any uninhabited building.

On the same day that Parliament enacted these measures, it also passed the **Quebec Act.** This statute enlarged Quebec's boundaries south to the Ohio River and stipulated that the colony was to be governed by an appointed governor and council but no elected assembly (see Map 5–2). The act also provided for the trial of civil cases without a jury and gave the Catholic Church the same privileges that it had enjoyed under the French. The colonists linked the Quebec Act with the Coercive Acts and labeled them the **Intolerable Acts.**

THE ROAD TO REVOLUTION

A mericans throughout the colonies considered the Intolerable Acts so threatening that they organized the First Continental Congress to respond to them. Congress renewed the nonimportation movement and took measures to enforce it strictly. These measures widened the gap between those who supported the British and those who opposed them.

PROTESTANTISM AND THE AMERICAN RESPONSE TO THE INTOLERABLE ACTS

Americans found the territorial, administrative, and religious provisions of the Quebec Act deeply disturbing. The Quebec Act gave Canada jurisdiction over lands north of the Ohio River claimed by Connecticut, Pennsylvania, and Virginia. This deprived settlers of their hoped-for homesteads and land speculators of their hoped-for profits. The administrative provisions of the act—appointed government, no assemblies, no jury for civil cases—also suggested to Americans what Britain might have in store for them.

Americans had similar fears about the religious provisions of the Quebec Act. During the 1760s, some Anglican clergymen had sought to have a bishop ap-

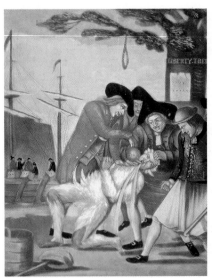

"The Bostonian's Paying the Excise-Man or Tarring & Feathering."

© Christie's Images, Inc.

W WHERE TO LEARN MORE

★ Philadelphia, Pennsylvania
www.ushistory.org/tour/index.html
Boston, Massachusetts www
.thefreedomtrail.org/virtual_tour.html

WHO MADE up the First Continental Congress and what was its purpose?

Coercive Acts Legislation passed by Parliament in 1774; included the Boston Port Act, the Massachusetts Government Act, the Administration of Justice Act, and the Quartering Act of 1774.

Quebec Act Law passed by Parliament in 1774 that provided an appointed government for Canada, enlarged the boundaries of Quebec, and confirmed the privileges of the Catholic Church.

Intolerable Acts American term for the Coercive Acts and the Quebec Act.

pointed for America. Many Americans believed that the British had scrapped the idea. The Quebec Act's concessions to Canadian Catholics, however, seemed to resurrect it in more ominous form. As one Virginian observed, the hierarchical organization of the Anglican Church was "a Relick of the Papal Incroachments" on English law. The Quebec Act accordingly "gave a General Alarm to all Protestants," whose ministers throughout the continent warned their congregations that they might be "bound by Popish chains."

American reactions to the religious provisions of the Quebec Act may have been exaggerated, but some features of the Coercive Acts were cause for real concern. The Boston Port Act arbitrarily punished innocent and guilty Bostonians alike. The Administration of Justice Act—which some with vivid imaginations dubbed the Murder Act—seemed to declare open season on colonists, allowing crown officials to kill them without fear of punishment. The Massachusetts Government Act raised the more realistic fear that no colonial charter was safe.

Nightmarish scenarios filled the colonial newspapers. One clergyman observed that the terms of the Coercive Acts were such that if someone were to "make water" on the door of the royal customs house, an entire colonial city "might be laid in Ashes." Trying to make an example of Boston, the British government had taken steps that united Americans as nothing had ever done before (see the Overview table, "New Restraints and Burdens on Americans, 1759–1774").

THE FIRST CONTINENTAL CONGRESS

Massachusetts wanted to respond to the Intolerable Acts with an immediate renewal of the nonimportation movement. Leaders in other colonies wanted to organize a more coordinated response and called for another meeting like the Stamp Act Congress. The colonies accordingly agreed to send delegates to a meeting in Philadelphia that came to be called the **First Continental Congress.** Because royal governors attempted to prevent the meeting by barring the legislatures from naming delegates, the colonies called extralegal public meetings for the purpose. In the end, all the colonies except Georgia were represented.

The First Continental Congress met at Carpenter's Hall in Philadelphia from September 5 to October 26, 1774, with fifty-five delegates present at one time or another. Some of the more conservative participants favored a compromise with Britain. The speaker of the Pennsylvania Assembly, Joseph Galloway, called for creation of an American "grand council" that would have veto power over parliamentary legislation dealing with America. His plan failed in the Congress by one vote. Instead, those who favored stronger measures—such as Samuel Adams and

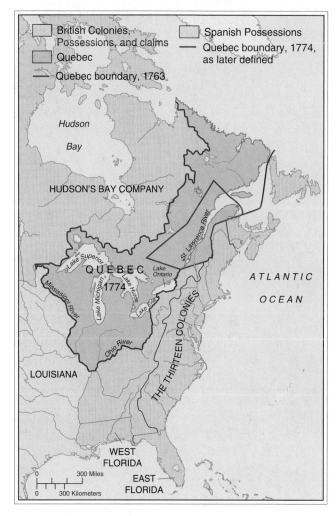

MAP EXPLORATION
To explore an interactive version of this map, go to
http://www.prenhall.com/goldfield3/map5.2

MAP 5–2   The Quebec Act of 1774   The Quebec Act enlarged the boundaries of the Canadian province southward to the Ohio River and westward to the Mississippi, thereby depriving several colonies of claims to the area granted them by their original charters.

WHY WERE SO many American colonists opposed to the Quebec Act? Beyond the expansion of Canada, at the expense of colonies, which provisions of the act provoked the greatest uproar? Why?

First Continental Congress
Meeting of delegates from most of the colonies held in 1774 in response to the Coercive Acts. The Congress endorsed the Suffolk Resolves, adopted the Declaration of Rights and Grievances, and agreed to establish the Continental Association.

OVERVIEW NEW RESTRAINT AND BURDENS ON AMERICANS, 1759–1774

	Limits on Legislative Action	Curbs on Territorial Expansion	Burdens on Colonial Trade	Imposition of New Taxes
1759	Royal instructions restrict ability of Virginia assembly to pass timely legislation.			
1762			Writs of assistance issued. Revenue Act authorizes navy to help enforce customs regulation.	
1763		Proclamation Line keeps white settlement east of the Appalachians.	Peacetime use of navy and new customs officials to enforce Navigation Acts.	
1764	Currency Act limits colonial legislatures' ability to issue paper money.		Vice-admiralty courts strengthened for Sugar Act.	Sugar Act imposes taxes for revenue (modified 1766).
1765				Quartering Act requires assemblies to provide facilities for royal troops. Stamp Act imposes internal taxes on various items (repealed 1766).
	Declaratory Act proclaims Parliament's right to legislate for colonies in all cases whatsoever.			
1767	Royal instructions limit size of colonial assemblies.		Vice-admiralty courts strengthened for Townshend duties. American Customs Service established in Boston.	Townshend duties imposed on some imported goods in order to pay colonial officials. (All but tax on tea repealed, 1770.)
1773				Tea Act reduces duty and prompts Boston Tea Party.
1774 (Intolerable Acts)	Massachusetts Government Act limits town meetings, changes legislature, and violates Massachusetts charter.	Quebec Act enlarges Quebec at expense of colonies with claims in the Ohio River Valley.	Boston Port Act closes harbor until East India Company's tea is paid for.	Quartering Act of 1774 declares that troops could be lodged in virtually any uninhabited building in Boston.

his cousin John, Patrick Henry, and Christopher Gadsden—prevailed. They persuaded most of their colleagues to endorse the **Suffolk Resolves.** These strongly worded resolutions denounced the Coercive Acts as unconstitutional, advised the people to arm, and called for general economic sanctions against Britain.

THE CONTINENTAL ASSOCIATION

The Congress created the **Continental Association** to organize and enforce sanctions against the British. As a first step, the Association pledged Americans to cut off imports from Britain after December 1, 1774. If the dispute with Britain was not resolved by September 1775, the Association called for barring most exports to Britain and the West Indies. All who violated the terms of the Association were to be considered "enemies of American liberty."

Congress also issued a declaration of rights and grievances summarizing its position. This declaration condemned most of the steps taken by Britain authorities since 1763, but "cheerfully" consented to trade regulations for the good of the whole empire. In addition, the Congress sent addresses to the people of America, to the inhabitants of Great Britain, and to the king. The address to the king asked him to use his "royal authority and interposition" to protect his loyal subjects in America. The words were significant, for protection and allegiance were considered the reciprocal duties of a sovereign and his people. After agreeing to convene again on May 10, 1775, if its grievances had not been redressed by then, the First Continental Congress adjourned.

The proceedings of the First Continental Congress revealed division as well as agreement. All the delegates believed that the Coercive Acts were unconstitutional, but they differed on methods to resist them. Only a minority was prepared to take up arms against Britain. Most representatives tried to protect the interests of their own colonies. Those from Virginia and Maryland, for example, insisted that the embargo on exports not begin until planters had finished shipping the current tobacco crop. Even more alarming, some South Carolina delegates threatened to walk out of the meeting unless the nonexportation agreement omitted rice, most of which went to northern Europe by way of Britain. To placate the Carolinians, northerners agreed to the exemption. Gadsden, the most radical of the South Carolina delegates, was disgusted with his colleagues. Their actions, he felt, betrayed the spirit of united purpose Patrick Henry had spoken of so stirringly earlier in the Congress: "The distinctions between Virginians, Pennsylvanians, New Yorkers and New Englanders are no more. I am not a Virginian, but an American."

POLITICAL DIVISIONS

In the wake of the First Continental Congress, Americans were forced to take sides for and against the Continental Association. At this point, not even such well-known radicals as Samuel Adams and Gadsden were advocating independence. English history, Americans believed, was full of instances in which the resolute opposition of a free people forced oppressive ministries and tyrannical kings to back down. They were confident that it could happen again.

As British officials failed, with the passing of time, to accommodate American views of their rights, Americans began in increasing numbers to challenge London's control. The experience of James Wilson, a Pennsylvania lawyer, illustrates this shift. In *Considerations on the Nature and Extent of the Legislative Authority of the British Parliament* (published in 1774), Wilson wrote that he had set out to find

QUICK REVIEW

Congressional Response to the Coercive Acts

- All agreed that Acts were unconstitutional.
- A minority prepared to go to war with Britain.
- Most delegates thought of the interests of their own colony first.

Suffolk Resolves   Militant resolves adopted in 1774 in response to the Coercive Acts by representatives from the towns in Suffolk County, Massachusetts, including Boston.

Continental Association
Agreement, adopted by the First Continental Congress in 1774 in response to the Coercive Acts to cut off trade with Britain until the objectionable measures were repealed.

Whigs   The name used by advocates of colonial resistance to British measures during the 1760s and 1770s.

Tories   A derisive term applied to loyalists in America who supported the king and Parliament just before and during the American Revolution.

a reasonable dividing line between those areas in which Parliament had legitimate authority over the colonies and those in which it did not. But the more he thought, the more he became convinced "that such a line does not exist" and that there can be "no medium between acknowledging and denying that power in all cases." Wilson therefore concluded that Parliament had no authority at all over the colonies, that the colonies' only legal governing bodies were their own assemblies, and that their only link to the British empire was through the king, to whom colonists owed allegiance. British officials and their American supporters strongly disagreed, insisting that Parliament had complete authority over the colonies.

During 1774 and early 1775, as the British–American confrontation grew more heated, lively debates raged in newspapers and pamphlets, and the colonists became increasingly polarized. In the last months before the outbreak of the American Revolution, the advocates of colonial rights began to call themselves **Whigs** and condemned their opponents as **Tories.** These traditional English party labels dated from the late seventeenth century, when the Tories had supported the accession of the Catholic King James II, whereas the Whigs had opposed it. By calling themselves Whigs and their opponents Tories (loyalist was a more accurate label), the advocates of colonial rights cast themselves as champions of liberty and their enemies as defenders of religious intolerance and royal absolutism.

CONCLUSION

All Americans, Whigs and loyalists alike, considered themselves good British subjects. But Americans were a more diverse and more democratic people than the English. A considerably larger percentage of them could participate in government, and for all practical purposes, they had been governing themselves for a long time.

British officials recognized the different character of American society and feared it might lead Americans to reject British control. But the steps they took to prevent this outcome had the opposite effect.

From Britain's perspective, the measures taken in the wake of the French and Indian War were a reasonable response to administrative and financial problems in the colonies. Taken one by one from the colonists' perspective, however, they were a rain of blows that finally impelled Americans to rebel.

Attempts to protect their accustomed autonomy first brought the colonial assemblies into conflict with Parliament. Asserting their rights led to greater cooperation between individual colonies. This development, in turn, led to increasingly widespread resistance, then to rebellion, and finally to revolution. Moving imperceptibly from one stage to the next, Americans grew conscious of their common interests and their differences from the English.

That workingmen and members of the elite dressed as Indians had joined in the dangerous act of defiance known as the Boston Tea Party also foreshadowed coming developments. No one now knows for certain why they adopted that particular disguise, but Indians were a traditional symbol of the new world. And those who were making a new political world were risking much—even, it would shortly turn out, life itself.

SUMMARY

Imperial Reorganization   At the close of the French and Indian War, British officials adopted a new and ultimately disastrous course in dealing with America.

In 1763, the British government took several steps to deal with the new territories, protect the old colonies, and maintain peace with the Indians. Among these steps were the Proclamation of 1763 and the Quartering Acts. Relations with Native Americans were also on the minds of British leaders, as they dealt with both the Cherokee War and Pontiac's Rebellion within a span of three years. Finally, the culmination of the reorganization efforts saw the Sugar Act and Stamp Act passed by Parliament in an effort to collect more taxes from the colonists.

American Reactions The measures Britain took to solve its financial and administrative problems first puzzled, then shocked, and eventually outraged Americans. The constitutional issue that most strained the bond between the colonies and the empire was taxation. With their country ideology, colonists reacted quickly. Shared outrage at the Stamp Act inspired the colonies to join in unified political action. The Sons of Liberty, a collection of protest groups, put pressure on British authorities. Leaders throughout the colonies met and collectively adopted the Declaration of Rights and Grievances, which denied Parliament's right to tax the colonies.

The Aftermath of the Stamp Act Crisis The aftermath of the Stamp Crisis was growing strain between Parliament and the colonies. Growing strain was also evident on the local level with the emergence in 1766 of vigilante groups calling themselves Regulators in response to official corruption in North Carolina and lawlessness in South Carolina.

The Townshend Crisis The Townshend duties, like the stamp tax, provoked resistance throughout the colonies. And, by 1770, Britain was ready to concede that they had been counterproductive. However, in March 1770 British troops fired on American civilians in Boston. This incident, known as the Boston Massacre, resulted from months of increased friction between townspeople and British troops stationed in the city. During the so-called Quiet Period following the Boston Massacre, Americans drank smuggled Dutch tea. When British officials tried to correct this, colonists responded with the Boston Tea Party, during which they heaved 342 chests of tea into the Boston Harbor.

The Road to Revolution Americans found the territorial, religious and constitutional aspects of the Intolerable Acts disturbing. Leaders in most colonies wanted to organize a coordinated response. They agreed to meet in Philadelphia in what was to be called the First Continental Congress. They agreed to endorse the Suffolk Resolves, which strongly denounced the Coercive Acts as unconstitutional. In the wake of the Congress, Americans were forced to take sides for and against the Continental Association. During 1774, as the British-American confrontation grew more heated, the colonies became increasingly polarized.

IMAGE KEY
for pages 120–121

a. Green tea.
b. TARRING & FEATHERING, 1773. A New Method of Macarony Making, as Practiced at Boston. American edition of an English mezzotint satire, 1774, on the treatment given to John Malcom, an unpopular Commisioner of Customs at Boston.
c. Samuel Adams.
d. Three Imrie/Risley by Wilson 1750s 77mm diorama figures, Roger Ranger with two soldiers, French and Indian War, on diorama base.
e. Flank and breast feathers.
f. The first Continental Congress is held in Carpenter's Hall, Philadelphia to define American rights and organise a plan of resistance to the Coercive Acts imposed by the British Parliament as punishment for the Boston Tea Party.
g. American colonials force feed hot tea to an English tax collector after tar and feathering the agent under a Liberty Tree in colonial Boston.
h. English politicians burying the Stamp Act.
i. Dried tea leaves.
j. A "No Stamp Act" teapot.
k. The Boston Massacre.

REVIEW QUESTIONS

1. What do Eliza Farmar's letters tell us about the crisis over dutied tea in 1773 and 1774? What does she think has caused the crisis and who was at fault? What makes her think the colonists have any chance of success in resisting British impositions?

2. How did the British victory and French withdrawal from North America after the French and Indian War affect the relations between Native Americans and white settlers? Between British authorities and Americans?

3. What was the relationship between the French and Indian War and changes in British policy toward America? How did the expectations of Americans and Britons differ in 1763? Why were the new policies offensive to Americans?

4. How was stationing British troops in America related to British taxation of the colonists? Why did the colonists consider taxation by Parliament an especially serious threat to their freedom as well as to their pocketbooks?

5. How did Americans oppose the new measures? Who participated in the various forms of resistance? How effective were the different kinds of resistance? What effect did resistance to British measures have on Americans' internal politics and sense of identity as Americans?

6. What led to the meeting of the First Continental Congress? What steps did the Congress take? What did it expect to achieve? What were the differences between Whigs and Tories?

7. Why was the Corsican patriot General Paoli important to Americans?

KEY TERMS

Boston Massacre   (p. 135)
Boston Tea Party   (p. 137)
British Constitution   (p. 129)
Cherokee War   (p. 125)
Coercive Acts   (p. 138)
Committees of correspondence
   (p. 135)
Continental Association   (p. 141)
Currency Act   (p. 128)
Declaration of Rights
   and Grievances   (p. 131)

Declaratory Act   (p. 131)
First Continental Congress   (p. 139)
Intolerable Acts   (p. 138)
Nonimportation movement
   (p. 130)
Parson's Cause   (p. 127)
Pontiac's Rebellion   (p. 127)
Proclamation Line   (p. 125)
Proclamation of 1763   (p. 125)
Quartering Acts   (p. 125)
Quebec Act   (p. 138)

Regulators   (p. 132)
Sons of Liberty   (p. 130)
Stamp Act   (p. 128)
Stamp Act Congress   (p. 131)
Sugar Act   (p. 128)
Suffolk Resolves   (p. 141)
Tea Act of 1773   (p. 136)
Tories   (p. 142)
Townshend Duty Act   (p. 134)
Whigs   (p. 142)
Writs of assistance   (p. 129)

WHERE TO LEARN MORE

Charleston, South Carolina. Many buildings date from the eighteenth century. Officials stored tea in one of them, the Exchange, to prevent a local version of the Boston Tea Party. The website for Historic Charleston, **http://www .cr.nps.gov/nr/travel/charleston**, provides a map, a list of buildings, and information about them.

Philadelphia, Pennsylvania. Numerous buildings and sites date from the eighteenth century. Independence National Historical Park, between Second and Sixth Streets on Walnut and Chestnut Streets, contains Carpenter's Hall, where the First Continental Congress met, and the Pennsylvania State House (now known as Independence Hall), where the Declaration of Independence was adopted. Philadelphia's Historic Mile, **http://www.ushistory.org/tour/index .html** provides a virtual tour of the great landmarks of the city, including Independence Hall.

 Boston, Massachusetts. Many important buildings and sites in this area date from the seventeenth and eighteenth centuries. They include Faneuil Hall (Dock Square), where many public meetings took place prior to the Revolution, and the Old State House (Washington and State Streets), which overlooks the site of the Boston Massacre. The Freedom Trail, **http://www.thefreedomtrail.org/ virtual_tour.html** provides a well-illustrated virtual tour of the historic sites.

Fort Michilimackinac National Historic Landmark, Mackinaw City, Michigan. Near the south end of the Mackinac Bridge, the present structure is a modern restoration of the fort as it was when Pontiac's Rebellion took a heavy toll of its garrison. The Mackinac State Historic Park's website, **http://www.mackinacparks .com/michilimackinac/html** provides a brief description and photographs of the reconstructed colonial village and fort.

U.S. History Documents CD-ROM
For primary sources related to this chapter, refer to the document CD-ROM.

www.prenhall.com/goldfield
For study resources related to this chapter, visit the *Companion Website*™.

6 The War for Independence 1774-1783

CHAPTER HIGHLIGHTS

The Outbreak of War and the Declaration of Independence, 1774-1776 After the Boston Tea Party, both sides knew they were heading for a crisis. Parliament endorsed the Conciliatory Proposition, but it was too late. On July 4, 1776, Congress officially approved the Declaration of Independence.

The Combatants The American forces were composed of the Continental Army and militiamen. British soldiers were, for the most part, better trained and organized. About 5,000 African Americans fought against the British. Many Indians decided to join British forces in the war.

The War in the North, 1776-1777 During the first phase of the war, the British concentrated on subduing New England. American victories at Trenton, Princeton, and Saratoga were balanced by a heavy defeat at Brandywine Creek. American forces emerged from their winter at Valley Forge better ready to face the British.

The War Widens, 1778-1781 Foreign intervention transformed the American Revolution into a virtual world war. Entry of the French and Spanish into the war on the American side widened the field of combat. On October 19, 1781, the British army surrendered at Yorktown, Virginia.

The American Victory, 1782-1783 Peace talks in Paris resulted in a treaty ending the war in 1783. The treaty addressed both the terms of peace and important economic issues.

The War and Society, 1775-1783 The war had a deep effect on American society. Women assumed new public roles and elevated domestic status. It helped end slavery in the North, while strengthening it in the South. The war created considerable economic difficulties. The American victory and the stable peace that followed suggests that most Americans managed to cope with the disruptions of war and the new world it helped create.

CHAPTER QUESTIONS

WHY DID tensions between the colonies and Britain escalate so rapidly between 1774 and 1776?

WHAT WERE the key differences between the British and American forces?

HOW DID the American forces survive the military setbacks of 1776?

WHY DID the French enter the war on the American side?

WHAT WERE the key factors in the American victory in the Revolutionary War?

WHAT WERE the true economic costs of the War for Independence?

CHAPTER OUTLINE

IMAGE KEY

for pages 146–147 is on page 173.

> *Headquarters, Valley Forge*
>
> *January 14, 1778*
>
> *I barely hinted to you my dearest Father my desire to augment the Continental Forces from an untried Source. . . . I would solicit you to cede me a number of your able bodied men Slaves, instead of leaving me a fortune. I would bring about a twofold good, first I would advance those who are unjustly deprived of the Rights of Mankind to a State which would be a proper Gradation between abject Slavery and perfect Liberty and besides I would reinforce the Defenders of Liberty with a number of gallant Soldiers. . . .*
>
> *Headquarters, Valley Forge*
>
> *February 2, 1778*
>
> *My dear Father,*
>
> *The more I reflect upon the difficulties and delays which are likely to attend the completing our Continental Regiments, the more anxiously is my mind bent upon the Scheme which I lately communicated to you. . . . You seem to think my dear Father, that men reconciled by long habit to the miseries of their Condition would prefer their ignominious bonds to the untasted Sweets of Liberty, especially when offer'd upon the terms which I propose. . . . I am tempted to believe that this trampled people have so much human left in them, as to be capable of aspiring to the rights of men by noble exertions, if some friend to mankind would point the Road, and give them prospect of Success.*
>
> *I have long deplored the wretched State of these men and considered in their history, the bloody wars excited in Africa to furnish America with Slaves. The Groans of despairing multitudes toiling for the Luxuries of Merciless Tyrants. I have had the pleasure of conversing with you sometimes upon the means of restoring them to their rights. When can it be better done than when their enfranchisement may be made conducive to the Public Good.*
>
> *John Laurens*
>
> *Henry Laurens Papers*, vol. 12, pp. 305, 390–392.

JOHN LAURENS WROTE these letters to his father, Henry, at one of the low points of the American Revolution, when victory seemed remote. The letters reveal much about the war and about the aspirations and limitations of the Revolutionary generation. Henry, a wealthy slaveholder from South Carolina, was president of the Continental Congress; his son John was an aide to General Washington.

John, 23 years old in 1778, had been born in South Carolina but educated for the most part in Geneva and London, where he had been exposed to some of the most progressive currents of the Enlightenment. Among these were compassion for the oppressed and the conviction that slavery should be abolished. The war for independence was a cause that appealed deeply to him.

The American version of republicanism combined a New Whig distrust of central authority with a belief in a government rooted in the public spirit of a virtuous citizenry. Clinging fervently to this ideology, Americans at first expected to defeat the British Army with a zealous citizens' militia, but quickly learned that they could prevail only by developing a professional fighting force. With vital French assistance, the new American army eventually overcame the enemy, but the Continental Army was often critically short of soldiers.

Aware of this discrepancy in manpower, Laurens saw an opportunity to solve two problems at once when he returned to America in 1777. Enlisting slaves in the army would provide blacks with a stepping stone to freedom and American forces with desperately needed troops. John, however, tried and failed repeatedly to convince legislatures in the deep south to enroll black troops in exchange for their freedom.

John's idealistic quest for social justice ended in South Carolina, where he died in one of the last skirmishes of the war.

THE OUTBREAK OF WAR AND THE DECLARATION OF INDEPENDENCE, 1774–1776

WHY DID tensions between the colonies and Britain escalate so rapidly between 1774 and 1776?

*A*fter the Boston Tea Party, both the British and the Americans knew that they were approaching a crisis. A British officer in Massachusetts commented in late 1774 that "it is thought by every body here" that British forces would soon have "to take the field." Many Americans also expected a military confrontation but continued to hope that the king would not "reason with us only by the roar of his Cannon."

MOUNTING TENSIONS

In May 1774, General Thomas Gage, the commander in chief of the British army in America, replaced Thomas Hutchinson as governor of Massachusetts. After Gage dissolved the Massachusetts legislature, the General Court, it defied him by assembling anyway. Calling itself the Provincial Congress, the legislature in October 1774 appointed an emergency executive body, the **Committee of Safety,** headed by John Hancock, which began stockpiling weapons and organizing militia volunteers. Some localities had already provided for the formation of special companies of **Minute Men,** who were to be ready at "a minute's warning in Case of an alarm."

Enforcing the Continental Association's boycott of British goods, local committees sometimes assaulted suspected loyalists and destroyed their property. The increasingly polarized atmosphere, combined with the drift toward military confrontation, drove a growing wedge between American loyalists and the patriot anti-British American Whigs.

THE LOYALISTS' DILEMMA

Loyalists and Whigs began to part company in earnest during the fall and winter of 1774–1775 as the threat of war mounted. Most loyalists were farmers, though officeholders and professionals were more numerous among them than in the population at large. Many recent immigrants to the colonies also remained loyal because they felt that the crown offered them some protection against more established Americans. The loyalists numbered close to half a million men and women—some 20 percent of the colonies' free population.

BRITISH COERCION AND CONCILIATION

Britain held parliamentary elections in the fall of 1774, but if Americans hoped that the outcome would change the government's policy toward them, they were disappointed. Lord North's supporters won easily. Under North's direction, in

Committee of Safety Any of the extralegal committees that directed the revolutionary movement and carried on the functions of government at the local level in the period between the breakdown of royal authority and the establishment of regular governments.

Minute Men Special companies of militia formed in Massachusetts and elsewhere beginning in later 1774.

Chronology

1775	April 19: Battles of Lexington and Concord.
	May 10: Second Continental Congress meets.
	June 17: Battle of Bunker Hill.
	December 31: American attack on Quebec.
1776	January 9: Thomas Paine's *Common Sense.*
	July 4: Declaration of Independence.
	September 15: British take New York City.
	December 26: Battle of Trenton.
1777	January 3: Battle of Princeton.
	September 11: Battle of Brandywine Creek.
	October 17: American victory at Saratoga.
	Runaway inflation begins.
	Continental Army winters at Valley Forge.
1778	February 6: France and the United States sign an alliance.
	June 17: Congress refuses to negotiate with British peace commissioners.
	July 4: George Rogers Clark captures British post in the Mississippi Valley.
	December 29: British capture Savannah.
	Death of the great French Enlightenment writer, François-Marie Arouet Voltaire.
1779	June 21: Spain declares war on Britain.
	Americans devastate the Iroquois country.
	September 23: John Paul Jones captures the British ship *Serapis.*
1780	May 12: Fall of Charleston, South Carolina.
	October 7: Americans win Battle of Kings Mountain.
	December 3: Nathanael Greene takes command in the South.
1781	January 17: Americans defeat British at Battle of Cowpens.
	March 15: Battle of Guilford Court House.
	October 19: Cornwallis surrenders at Yorktown.
	Influential German philosopher Immanuel Kant publishes his first major work, *The Critique of Pure Reason.*
1783	March 15: Washington quells the Newburgh "Conspiracy."
	September 3: Peace of Paris signed.
	November 21: British begin evacuating New York.
	First manned balloon flight, in France.
	Quakers present first anti-slavery petition to the British parliament.
1784	United States vessel opens trade with Canton, China.
1788	Britain transports convicts to Australia.

February 1775, Parliament resolved that Massachusetts was in rebellion and prohibited the New England colonies from trading outside the British Empire or sending their ships to the North Atlantic fishing grounds. Similar restrictions on most of the other colonies soon followed.

Meanwhile, in a gesture of appeasement, Parliament endorsed Lord North's **Conciliatory Proposition,** which pledged not to tax the colonies if they would voluntarily contribute to the defense of the empire. British officials, however, would decide what was a sufficient contribution.

Had the Conciliatory Proposition specified a maximum colonial contribution, and had it been offered ten years earlier, the colonists might have found it acceptable. Now it was too late. North's government, in any case, had already sent orders to General Gage to take decisive action against the Massachusetts rebels. These orders triggered the first clash between British and American forces.

THE BATTLES OF LEXINGTON AND CONCORD

On the night of April 18, Gage assembled his men on the Boston Common and marched them toward the little towns of Lexington and Concord (see Map 6–1). Their mission was to arrest rebel leaders Samuel Adams and John Hancock (then

4–8
Address of the Inhabitants of Anson County to Governor Martin (1774)

Conciliatory Proposition Plan whereby Parliament would "forbear" taxation of Americans in colonies whose assemblies imposed taxes considered satisfactory by the British government.

MAP EXPLORATION

To explore an interactive version of this map, go to http://www.prenhall.com/
goldfield3/map6.1

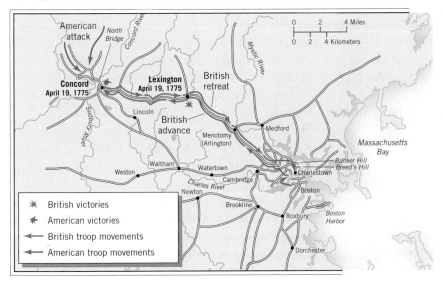

MAP 6–1   The Battles of Lexington and Concord, April 19, 1775   This map shows the area around Boston, where in April 1775 British and American forces fought the first military engagements of the Revolution.

WHY DID COLONIAL resistance to British policies develop into armed conflict in April 1775?

staying in Lexington) and to destroy the military supplies the Committee of Safety had assembled at Concord. Patriots in Boston got wind of the troop movements and sent out riders—one of them the silversmith Paul Revere—to warn their fellows. Adams and Hancock escaped.

When the British soldiers reached Lexington at dawn, they found about 70 armed militiamen drawn up in formation on the village green. Outnumbered ten to one, they probably did not plan to begin a fight. More likely, they were there in a show of defiance, to demonstrate that Americans would not run at the sight of a superior British force.

Months of mounting tension exploded on the Lexington green. A British major ordered the militia to disperse. They were starting to obey when a shot cracked through the dawn stillness. No one now knows who fired. The British responded with a volley that killed or wounded 18 Americans.

The British troops pressed on to Concord and burned what few supplies the Americans had not been able to hide. When their rear guard came under patriot fire at Concord's North Bridge, the British panicked. As they retreated to Boston, patriot Minute Men and other militia harried them from both sides of the road.

News of the fighting at the **Battles of Lexington and Concord** spread quickly. The speed with which distant colonies heard about the outbreak of fighting suggests both the importance Americans attached to it and the extraordinary efforts patriots made to spread word of it. Everywhere, news of Lexington and Concord spurred Whigs into action. The shots fired that April morning would, in the words of the nineteenth-century Concord philosopher and poet Ralph Waldo Emerson, be "heard 'round the world." They signaled the start of the American Revolution.

WHERE TO LEARN MORE

Minute Man National Historical Park, Lexington and Concord, Massachusetts **http://www.cr.nps.gov**

Battles of Lexington and Concord   The first two battles of the American Revolution which resulted in a total of 273 British soldiers dead, wounded, and missing and nearly one hundred Americans dead, wounded, and missing.

Olive Branch Petition Petition adopted by the Second Continental Congress as a last effort of peace that avowed America's loyalty to George III and requested that he protect them from further aggressions.

This fine portrait of George Washington appears in multiple versions depicting the victorious general against different backgrounds, including the battles of Princeton and Yorktown. The painter, Charles Willson Peale, served under Washington at Princeton, and the French commander at Yorktown, the Count de Rochambeau, took an appropriate version home with him in 1783.

Peale, Charles Wilson (1741–1827). (after): George Washington after the battle of Princeton, January 3, 1777. 1779. Oil on canvas, 234.5x155 cm. Inv.:MV 4560. Photo: Gerard Blot. Chateaux de Versailles et de Trianon, Versailles, France. Reunion des Musees Nationaux/Art Resource, NY

THE SECOND CONTINENTAL CONGRESS, 1775–1776

By the time the Second Continental Congress convened in Philadelphia on May 10, 1775, it had a war on its hands. Assuming leadership of the rebellion, the Congress in the succeeding months became, in effect, a national government. It called for the patchwork of local forces to be organized into the Continental Army, authorized the formation of a navy, established a post office, and authorized the printing of paper continental dollars to meet its expenses. Denying Parliament's claim to govern the colonies but not yet ready to declare themselves independent, the delegates sought to preserve their ties to Britain by expressing loyalty to the crown. In the **Olive Branch Petition,** addressed to George III on July 5, they asked the king to protect his American subjects from the military actions ordered by Parliament. The following day, Congress approved the Declaration of the Causes and Necessity of Taking Up Arms, asserting the resolve of American patriots "to die freemen, rather than to live slaves."

COMMANDER IN CHIEF GEORGE WASHINGTON

To take command of the patriot forces around Boston—the newly named Continental Army—Congress turned to George Washington. John Adams, a Whig leader from Massachusetts, first nominated the Virginian. Adams realized this would help transform a local quarrel in New England into a continental conflict. Adams also expected Washington's leadership to help attract recruits from Virginia, then the most populous colony.

Washington was the ideal person for the job. Some of his contemporaries had quicker minds and broader educations; Washington, however, was blessed with good judgment, a profound understanding of both the uses and the limitations of power, and the gift of command. He soon realized that the fate of the patriot cause depended on the survival of the army. The troops in turn revered him. In a crisis, wrote a man who served under him, "his likeness" was more valuable than the large sum the British would have paid for his capture.

EARLY FIGHTING: MASSACHUSETTS, VIRGINIA, THE CAROLINAS, AND CANADA

General Gage, finding himself besieged in Boston after the fighting at Lexington and Concord, decided to seize and fortify territory south of Boston, where his cannons could command the harbor. But the Americans seized the high ground first, entrenching themselves on Breed's Hill north of town. On June 17, 1775, Gage sent 2,200 well-trained soldiers to drive the 1,700 patriot men and boys from their new position. The British succeeded, but at the cost of more than 1,000 casualties. One despondent British officer observed afterward that another such victory "would have ruined us." Misnamed for another hill nearby, this encounter has gone down in history as the Battle of Bunker Hill (see Map 6–2).

During the winter of 1775–1776, the Americans dragged some 60 cannons—the largest weighing as much as a ton—300 miles through snow and over mountains from Fort Ticonderoga to Boston. Mounting them overlooking Boston harbor put the British in an indefensible position. The British then evacuated Boston and moved their troops to Halifax, Nova Scotia. New England was for the moment secure for the patriots. Fighting in the South also went well for the patriots, who defeated loyalist forces (which included slaves who had been promised their freedom if they fought for the loyalist cause), at Great Bridge, near Norfolk, and Moore's Creek Bridge in North Carolina. In June 1776, patriot

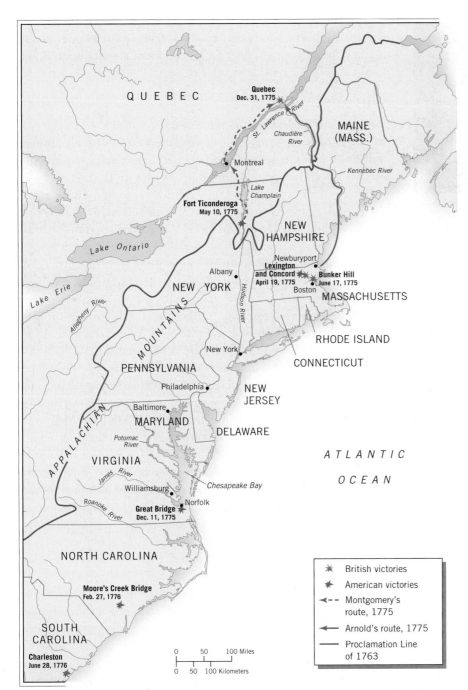

MAP 6–2   Early Fighting, 1775–1776   As this map clearly reveals, even the earliest fighting occurred in widely scattered areas, thereby complicating Britain's efforts to subdue the Americans.

WAS BRITAIN'S early strategy against the colonists effective?

forces successfully repulsed a large British expedition sent to attack Charleston, South Carolina.

In contrast, an attempt to win Canada to the patriot side met with disaster. Two American armies attacked Canada in late 1775. One quickly captured Montreal. The other, under Benedict Arnold, advanced through the Maine wilderness

In this painting of the Battle of Bunker Hill, the artist John Trumbull highlighted the death of Major General Joseph Warren of the Massachusetts militia. Like Trumbull, historians have traditionally emphasized prominent historical figures. More recently, however, they have focused on the common people, such as the militiamen, black and white, who appear at the margins of this picture but who composed the majority of the American forces fighting that day.

The Granger Collection

QUICK REVIEW

Common Sense

- Published by Tom Paine in January 1776.
- Denounced King George and made the case for independence.
- Sold more than 100,000 copies.

Declaration of Independence
The document by which the Second Continental Congress announced and justified its decision to renounce the colonies' allegiance to the British government.

Contract theory of government
The belief that government is established by human beings to protect certain rights—such as life, liberty, and property—that are theirs by natural, divinely sanctioned law and that when government protects these rights, people are obligated to obey it.

in the face of great hardships. The two forces linked up outside heavily fortified Quebec and attacked the city on December 31. The attack and the subsequent siege failed and Canada remained a British province.

INDEPENDENCE

The stunning early successes bolstered the patriots' confidence. In August 1775, King George III rejected the Congress's Olive Branch Petition. Instead, he issued a proclamation declaring the colonies in rebellion and denying them his protection. In December, Parliament barred all exports from the American colonies. These aggressive actions, especially the king's, persuaded many colonists to abandon their loyalty to the crown. More and more, Whigs began to think seriously of declaring full independence from Britain.

At this critical moment, a ne'er-do-well Englishman, recently arrived on American soil, gave the cause of independence a powerful boost. Thomas Paine was by trade a corsetmaker—and twice a fired tax collector. He was also a man of radical ideas—which he expressed forcefully in the everyday English of ordinary people—and he became a powerful polemicist for the American cause. In his pamphlet *Common Sense,* published in Philadelphia in January 1776, Paine denounced King George and made the case for independence. He ridiculed the absurdity of "supposing a continent to be perpetually governed by an island" and described the king as "the Royal Brute" whose tyranny should be thrown off. Simple common sense, Paine concluded, dictated that " 'TIS TIME TO PART."

Common Sense, which sold more than 100,000 copies throughout the colonies, helped predispose Americans toward independence. Tactical considerations also led patriot leaders toward a formal separation from Great Britain. Such a move would make it easier for America to gain desperately needed aid from foreign countries, especially England's ancient enemy, France. Declaring independence would also give American political leaders a solid legal basis for their newly claimed authority. Accordingly, most of the American states (as the rebellious colonies now called themselves) either instructed or permitted their delegates in the Congress to vote for independence.

On June 7, 1776, Virginian Richard Henry Lee introduced in the Congress a resolution stating that the united colonies "are, and of right ought to be, free and independent States." Postponing a vote on the issue, the Congress appointed a committee to draw up a declaration of independence. The committee turned to a young Virginian named Thomas Jefferson to compose the first draft. On June 28, after making revisions in Jefferson's proposed text, the committee presented the document to Congress. When it became clear that the majority favored independence, the Pennsylvania and South Carolina delegations switched sides, and the New York delegation decided to abstain. Thus, when the Congress voted on the resolution for independence on July 2, 1776, all voting delegations approved it. After further tinkering with the wording, the Congress officially adopted the **Declaration of Independence** on July 4, 1776.

Congress intended the declaration to be a justification for America's secession from the British Empire and an invitation to potential allies. Jefferson later maintained that he did not write any more than what everyone was thinking. The political theory that lies behind the declaration is known as the **contract theory of government.** Developed by the late-seventeenth-century English philosopher John Locke and others, the contract theory maintains that legitimate government rests on an agreement between the people and their rulers. The people are bound to obey their rulers only so long as the rulers offer them protection. Jefferson's prose transformed what might have been a bland statement into one of history's great statements of human rights.

The Declaration of Independence consists of a magnificently stated opening assumption, two premises, and a powerful conclusion. The opening assumption is that all men are created equal, that they therefore have equal rights, and that they can neither give up these rights nor allow them to be taken away. The first premise—that people establish governments to protect their fundamental rights to life, liberty, and property—is a restatement of contract theory. (With a wonderful flourish reflecting the Enlightenment's optimism about human potential, Jefferson changed "property" to "the pursuit of happiness.") The second premise is a long list of charges meant to justify the Americans' rejection of their hitherto legitimate ruler. Then followed the dramatic conclusion that Americans could rightfully overthrow King George's rule and replace it with something more satisfactory to them.

Historians have spilled oceans of ink debating Jefferson's use of the expression "all men." In practice, of course, many people were excluded from full participation in eighteenth-century American society. Women, propertyless white men, and free black men had no formal political rights and limited legal rights. Slaves enjoyed no rights at all. (Although himself a slave-owner, Jefferson was deeply troubled by American slavery. He had wanted to include a denunciation of the slave trade among the charges against George III in the Declaration of Independence, but the Congress took it out, believing that to blame the king for this inhumane business would appear hypocritical.) But if the words "all men are created equal" had limited practical meaning in 1776, they have ever since confronted Americans with a moral challenge to make good on them.

Thomas Jefferson, author of the Declaration of Independence and future president of the United States. Mather Brown, an American artist living in England, painted this picture of Jefferson for John Adams while the two men were in London on diplomatic missions in 1786. A companion portrait of Adams that Jefferson ordered for himself also survives. Brown's sensitive portrait of a thoughtful Jefferson is the earliest known likeness of him.

Courtesy of Library of Congress

RELIGION, VIRTUE, AND REPUBLICANISM

Americans reacted to news of the Declaration of Independence with mixed emotions. There was rejoicing as orators read the declaration to great crowds. But even many who favored independence worried about how Americans would govern themselves. Most Whigs, animated by the political ideology known as **republicanism,** thought a republican government was best suited to American society.

Republicanism held that self-government—either directly by the citizens of a country or indirectly by their elected representatives—provided a more reliable foundation for the good society and individual freedom than did rule by kings. Thus drawing on contract theory, as in the Declaration of Independence, republicanism called for government by consent of the governed. Drawing on country ideology, it was suspicious of excessively centralized government and insistent on the need for a virtuous, public-spirited citizenry. Republicanism therefore helped to give the American Revolution a moral dimension.

But other than a state that was not ruled by a hereditary king, what was a republic? And what were the chances that one would survive? Americans had at hand a recent example of a republic in the English Civil War of the mid-seventeenth century, in which English Puritans had for a time replaced the monarchy with a republican "Commonwealth," dedicated to advancing the "common weal," or common good. Some New Englanders, spiritual descendants of the Puritans,

WHERE TO LEARN MORE

Independence National Historical Park, Philadelphia, Pennsylvania
www.cr.nps.gov

Republicanism   A complex, changing body of ideas, values, and assumptions, closely related to country ideology, that influenced American political behavior during the eighteenth and nineteenth centuries.

WHAT WERE the key differences between the British and American forces?

Continental Army The regular or professional army authorized by the Second Continental Congress and commanded by General George Washington during the Revolutionary War.

This British engraving published in 1783 depicts one of the many public readings of the Declaration of Independence that occurred throughout the United States during the weeks following its adoption by the Second Continental Congress on July 4, 1776.

The Granger Collection

considered the Commonwealth to have been a noble experiment. To them, the American Revolution offered another chance to establish a republic of the godly. "When the mere Politician weighs the Danger or Safety of his Country," warned one clergyman, "he computes them in Proportion to its Fortresses, Arms, Money, Provisions, Numbers of Fighting Men, and its Enemies." But, the clergyman continued, the "Christian Patriot" calculates them "by its Numbers of Sinful or praying People, and its Degrees of Holiness or Vice." Such language recalled the Great Awakening; it reached beyond the upper classes who had been directing the resistance to the British and mobilized ordinary people for what their ministers repeatedly assured them was a just war against sin and despotism.

THE COMBATANTS

Republican theory mistrusted professional armies as the instruments of tyrants. A free people, republicans insisted, relied for defense on their own patriotism. When individual or community rights were in danger, free men should grab their muskets from over the fireplace, assemble as the local militia, take care of the problem, and go home (see "American Views: A British Woman Observes an American Militia Exercise in 1775"). But militiamen, as one American general observed, had trouble coping with "the shocking scenes of war" because they were not "steeled by habit or fortified by military pride." In real battles, they often proved unreliable. Americans therefore faced a hard choice: Develop a professional army or lose the war. In the end, they did what they had to do. While state militias continued to offer support, it was the disciplined forces of the Continental Army that won the crucial battles.

PROFESSIONAL SOLDIERS

Washington tightened things up in the new **Continental Army.** Eventually, he prevailed on Congress to adopt stricter regulations and to require enlistments for three years or the duration of the war. Although he used militia effectively, his consistent aim was to turn the Continental Army into a disciplined force that could defeat the British in the large engagements of massed troops characteristic of eighteenth-century European warfare. Guerrilla fighters shooting from behind trees like "savages" had their place in the American war effort, but they could never win a decisive, formal battle. And only such a "civilized" victory would impress the other European powers and establish the legitimacy of the United States.

Many soldiers of fortune, as well as a few idealists, offered their services. France's 19-year-old Marquis de Lafayette was one of the youngest, wealthiest, and most idealistic. Two Poles, Tadeusz Kosciuszko, an engineer, and Kazimierz Pulaski, a cavalry commander who would be mortally wounded at the Battle of Savannah in 1779, also rendered good service. Most useful of all, probably, was Baron von Steuben. His title too was new, but he had experience in the Prussian army, continental Europe's best. He became the Continental Army's drillmaster, and thanks partly to him, Washington's troops increasingly came to resemble their disciplined European counterparts.

The British soldiers—and the nearly 30,000 German mercenaries (Americans called them "Hessians") whom the British government

AMERICAN VIEWS

A BRITISH WOMAN OBSERVES AN AMERICAN MILITIA EXERCISE IN 1775

The following description of North Carolinians preparing for war in 1775 comes from the travel journal of Janet Schaw, a Scotswoman visiting her brother Robert in America. Robert Schaw, although he was appointed a colonel in the North Carolina militia, disapproved of the American cause and eventually refused to take the oath of allegiance to the new state government. His wife, by contrast, according to Janet Schaw, was "so rooted an American, that she detests every thing that is European." Early in June 1775 Janet Schaw saw the militia train outside of Wilmington under their commander, Robert Howe, who later became a major general in the Continental Army. She returned to Scotland in late 1775.

- What does this passage suggest about Janet Schaw's own views of the American cause?
- How accurately do you think it reflects the effectiveness of militia forces?
- What does it suggest about the relationship between patriots and loyalists?

We came down in the morning in time for the review, which the heat made as terrible to the spectators as to the soldiers, or what you please to call them. They had certainly fainted under it, had not the constant draughts of grog supported them. Their exercise was that of bush-fighting, but it appeared so confused and so perfectly different from any thing I ever saw, I cannot say whether they performed it well or not; but this I know that they were heated with rum till capable of committing the most shocking outrages. We stood in

the balcony of Doctor Cobham's [a future loyalist] house and they were reviewed on a field mostly covered with what are called here scrubby oaks which are only a little better than brushwood. They at last however assembled on the plain field, and I must really laugh while I recollect their figures: 2000 men in their shirts and trousers, preceded by a very ill beat-drum and a fiddler, who was also in his shirt with a long sword and a cue at his hair, who played with all his might. They made indeed a most unmartial appearance. But the worst figure there can shoot from behind a bush and kill even a General Wolfe.

Before the review was over, I hear a cry of tar and feather. I was ready to faint at the idea of this dreadful operation. I would have gladly quitted the balcony, but was so much afraid the Victim was one of my friends, that I was not able to move; and he indeed proved to be one, tho' in a humble station. For it was Mr. Neilson's [a loyalist] poor English groom. You can hardly conceive what I felt when I saw him dragged forward, poor devil, frighted out of his wits. However at the request of some of the officers, who had been Neilson's friends, his punishment was changed into that of mounting on a table and begging pardon for having smiled at the regt. He was then drummed and fiddled out of the town, with a strict prohibition of ever being seen in it again.

Source: [Janet Schaw], *Journal of a Lady of Quality: Being the Narrative of a Journey from Scotland to the West Indies, North Carolina, and Portugal, in the Years 1774 to 1776,* ed. Evangeline Walker Andrews in Collaboration with Charles McLean Andrews (1923). Yale University Press.

employed—offered Americans the clearest model of a professional army. Although most of the enlisted men came from the lower classes and from economically depressed areas, many also had skills. Most British troops carried the "Brown Bess" musket. With bayonet attached, it was almost 6 feet long and weighed over 16 pounds. In battle, soldiers usually stood close together in lines three deep. They were expected to withstand bombardment without flinching, fire on command in volleys, and charge with the bayonet.

Military life was tough. On the march, seasoned troops carrying 60-pound packs normally covered about 15 miles a day but could go 30 miles in a "forced"

QUICK REVIEW

Soldiers for Liberty

- France: Marquis de Lafayette
- Poland: Tadeusz Kosciuszko and Kazimierz Pulaski
- Prussia: Baron von Steuben

John Laurens, who hoped to raise black troops in South Carolina as a prelude to the general abolition of slavery, was the only member of George Washington's staff to be killed in battle. This commemorative portrait by Charles Willson Peale bears the Latin inscription "Sweet and proper it is to die for one's country."

Independence National Historic Park

march. In most weather conditions, they wore heavy woolen uniforms dyed bright red for visibility on smoke-filled battlefields (hence their nickname "Redcoats"). They were frequently undernourished, and many more died of disease than of injury in battle. Medical care was, by modern standards, primitive. Treatments for illness included bleeding and purging (induced vomiting and diarrhea). Serious arm or leg wounds usually meant amputation, without antiseptics or anesthetics and often proved fatal.

Severe discipline held soldiers in line. Striking an officer or deserting could bring death; lesser offenses usually incurred a beating. Several hundred lashes, "well laid on" with the notorious cat-o'-nine-tails (a whip with multiple cords, each ending in a nasty little knot or a metal ball), were not uncommon.

Soldiers amused themselves with gambling (despite regulations against it) and drinking. Perhaps two-thirds of the Redcoats were illiterate, and all suffered from loneliness and boredom. Camaraderie and a legendary loyalty to their regiments sustained them.

After the winter of 1777–1778, conditions in the Continental Army came to resemble those in the British army. Like British regulars, American recruits tended to be low on the social scale. The chances for talented enlisted men to win an officer's commission were greater than in the British army. And despite their ragged uniforms, they carried themselves like soldiers. Indeed, Continental soldiers frequently had little more than "their ragged shirt flaps to cover their nakedness," and more than once their bare marching feet left bloody tracks in the snow.

The British and the Americans both had trouble supplying their troops, but for fundamentally different reasons. The British had plenty of hard-coin money with a stable value, which many American merchants and farmers were happy to take in payment for supplies. But they had to rely mostly on supplies shipped to them from the British Isles. The Continental Army, by contrast, had to pay for supplies in paper money, both Continental dollars and state-issued currency, whose value sank steadily as the war progressed.

Feeling themselves outcasts from an uncaring society, the professional soldiers of the Continental Army developed a community of their own. The soldiers were "as strict a band of brotherhood as Masons," one later wrote, and their spirit kept them together in the face of misery. Attempts at mutiny in Washington's camp were few and largely unsuccessful.

Occasionally, American officers let their disgruntlement get out of hand. The most notorious such case was that of Benedict Arnold, a general who compiled a distinguished record during the first three years of the war but then came to feel himself shabbily treated by Congress and his superiors. Seeking better rewards for his abilities, he offered to surrender the strategic fort at West Point (which he commanded) to the enemy. Before he could act, however, his plot was discovered, and he fled to the British, serving with them until the end of the war. Among Americans, his name became a synonym for traitor.

What was perhaps the most serious expression of army discontent—one that threatened the future of republican institutions and civilian government in the United States—occurred near Newburgh, New York, in March 1783, after the fighting was over. During the war, the Congress had promised officers a pension of half-pay for life (the custom in Great Britain), but now many veterans demanded instead full pay for six years. When the Congress failed to grant real assurances that any pay would be forthcoming, hotheaded young officers called a meeting that could have led to an armed uprising and military coup. General Washington, in a dramatic speech, subtly warned the men of all that they might lose by insubordination. A military coup would "open the flood Gates of Civil discord" and "deluge" the nation in blood; loyalty now, he said, would be "one more distinguished proof" of their patriotism. With the fate of the Revolution and the honor of the army hanging in the balance, the movement collapsed. The officers and politicians behind the "conspiracy" were probably only bluffing, using the threat of a discontented army to frighten the states into granting the Congress the power (which it then lacked) to levy taxes so that it could pay the army.

WOMEN IN THE CONTENDING ARMIES

Women accompanied many units on both sides, as was common in eighteenth-century warfare. A few were prostitutes. Most were the married or common-law consorts of ordinary soldiers. These "camp followers" cooked and washed for the troops, occasionally helped load artillery, and provided most of the nursing care. A certain number in a company were subject to military orders and were authorized to draw rations and pay. The role of these women found its way into American folklore in the legend of Molly Pitcher (perhaps Mary Ludwig Hays, the wife of a Continental artillery sergeant), who heroically carried water to gunners to cool them and their overheated guns at the Battle of Monmouth Court House in 1778.

AFRICAN AMERICAN PARTICIPATION IN THE WAR

On June 30, 1779, the British commander in chief, Sir Henry Clinton, promised to allow slaves who fled from rebel owners to join the royal troops to "follow . . . any Occupation" they wished. Hedged as this promise of freedom was, news of it spread quickly among the slave communities, and late in the war, enough black people flocked to the British army in South Carolina and Georgia to make feeding and housing them a serious problem.

The British shared the racial prejudices of many Americans, and despite their efforts to recruit African Americans, were reluctant to arm them. Instead, the British put most of the ex-slaves to work as agricultural or construction workers (many of the free and enslaved blacks accompanying American troops were similarly employed). However, a few relatively well-equipped black British dragoons (mounted troops) did see combat in South Carolina.

Approximately 5,000 African Americans fought against the British and for American independence, hundreds of them in the Continental Army. Many were freemen from Massachusetts and Rhode Island. Several free black men served

During the American Revolution, the Iroquois warrior Cornplanter rose to prominence, becoming a principal Seneca Leader. He was also known as John O'Bail after his Dutch trader father.

The Granger Collection

HOW DID the American forces survive the military setbacks of 1776?

---

among the defenders at Bunker Hill, and at least one distinguished himself sufficiently for his commander to commend him as "an experienced officer as well as an excellent soldier." But the idea of arming African Americans was not well received in the South.

NATIVE AMERICANS AND THE WAR

At first, most Native Americans east of the Mississippi River would probably have preferred to remain neutral, but Indians' skills and manpower were valuable, and by 1776 both sides sought their assistance. Forced to choose, many Native Americans favored the British, hoping thereby to safeguard their lands.

Their prewar experience made them believe that British officials would protect them against white settlers, whereas an American victory would sweep away all restraints on these incursions. The British were also in a better position to provide trade goods and arms. Accordingly, many Indian peoples, including the Cherokees, Creeks, Choctaws, and Chickasaws in the South, decided that it was in their interest to back the British.

In some cases, the pressure to choose sides in the war produced splits within Indian groups. In other cases, though, the war promoted greater unity among Native Americans. Despite factionalism, the Shawnees, Delawares, Miamis, Wyandots, and others in the Ohio Valley eventually forged an alliance to preserve their control of the area with British support.

THE WAR IN THE NORTH, 1776–1777

The Revolutionary War can be divided into three phases. In the first, from the outbreak of fighting in 1775 through 1777, most of the important battles took place in New England, New York, New Jersey, and Pennsylvania. During these years, the Americans faced the British alone. But in 1778, France entered the war on the American side, opening the second phase of the war. Fighting in the second phase would rage from 1778 to 1781, mainly in the South, at sea, and on the western frontier. The third phase of the war, from late 1781 to 1783, saw little actual fighting. With American victory assured, attention shifted to the diplomatic maneuvering leading up to the Peace of Paris (1783).

BRITAIN HESITATES: CRUCIAL BATTLES IN NEW YORK AND NEW JERSEY

During the first phase of the war, the British concentrated on subduing New England, the hotbed of what they saw as "rebellious principles." Replacing General Gage, the government appointed Sir William Howe as commander in chief of British forces and his brother, Richard Howe, as admiral of the naval forces in North American waters. New York City had been the headquarters of the British army during the late colonial period, and the Howes made it their base of operations. In August 1776, the Howes landed troops on Long Island and, in the Battle of Brooklyn Heights, quickly drove the American forces deployed there back to Manhattan Island.

In the ensuing weeks, British forces overwhelmed Washington's forces, driving them out of Manhattan and then, moving north, clearing them from the area around the city at the Battle of White Plains. But the Howes were hesitant to deal a crushing blow, and the Americans were able to retreat across New Jersey into Pennsylvania. The American cause seemed lost, however and the Continental Army almost melted away. On Christmas night, Washington led his forces back across the icy Delaware from Pennsylvania and launched a successful surprise attack on a garrison of Hessian mercenaries at Trenton, New Jersey, on the morning of December 26. A week later, in the Battle of Princeton, Washington overwhelmed a British force at Princeton, New Jersey. Thereafter, Washington withdrew to winter quarters in Morristown, New Jersey, and the Howes made no further effort to pursue him. Both sides suspended operations until the spring. The victories at Trenton and Princeton lifted morale and saved the American cause. But why did the Howes not annihilate the Continental Army while they had the chance? Clearly, they wanted to regain loyal subjects, not alienate them. If they had inflicted a crushing defeat, they would have risked making the Americans permanent enemies of British rule. In short, the British had sound political reasons for not beating the Americans too thoroughly. By the time it became apparent that this cautious strategy was not working, they had lost their best chance to win the war.

THE YEAR OF THE HANGMAN: VICTORY AT SARATOGA AND WINTER AT VALLEY FORGE

Contemporaries called 1777 the Year of the Hangman because the triple sevens suggested a row of gallows. Living up to its ominous name, it was indeed a crucial year for the American cause.

The British began the year by mounting a major effort to end the rebellion. Their strategy was to send a force south from Canada down the Hudson River to link up with the Howes in New York City, isolate New England, and crush the rebellion in that most recalcitrant region. But there was no effort to coordinate strategy between the forces advancing from Canada and the forces in New York. Thus in the end, poorly planned, poorly executed, and unsupported from the south, the campaign ended in disaster for the British.

Some 5,000 Redcoats and 3,000 German mercenaries assembled in Canada during the winter of 1776–1777 under the command of the jaunty, high-living, and popular "Gentleman Johnny" Burgoyne. The army finally set off in June with 1,500 horses hauling its heavy artillery and ponderous supply train. Crossing Lake Champlain, Burgoyne's army recaptured Fort Ticonderoga, but success eluded him after that.

Trouble began as the troops started moving overland through the woods at the southern end of the lake. Forced to clear away huge trees in its path felled by American axmen, the army crawled along at only two or three miles a day. Promised reinforcements never arrived, and a Whig militia force wiped out a force of 800 men that Burgoyne had sent into Vermont to round up badly needed horses.

By October 1777, Burgoyne's army was down to less than 6,000 men and facing disaster. A force of nearly 3,000 Continentals and 9,000 militia, commanded by General Horatio Gates, had now assembled to confront the British. Unable to break through the American lines, Burgoyne surrendered to Gates following the Battle of Saratoga on October 17, 1777.

While Burgoyne was making his way to disaster, General William Howe, rather than moving north to support him, was making plans to destroy

WHERE TO LEARN MORE

Saratoga National Historical Park, New York **www.cr.nps.gov**

(W) **WHERE TO LEARN MORE**

★ Valley Forge National Historical
Park, Valley Forge, Pennsylvania
www.cr.nps.gov

WHY DID the French enter the
war on the American side?

Valley Forge Area of Pennsylvania approximately 20 miles northwest of Philadelphia where General George Washington's Continental troops were quartered from December 1777 to June 1778 while British forces occupied Philadelphia during the Revolutionary War.

Washington's army and capture Philadelphia. In July 1777, Howe's troops sailed from New York to Chesapeake Bay and from there marched on Philadelphia from the south. They met Washington's army on the banks of Brandywine Creek, near the Pennsylvania–Delaware border. The Americans put up a good fight before giving way with a loss of 1,200 killed or captured (twice as many as the British).

Howe occupied Philadelphia, and his men settled down in comfortable winter quarters. The Congress fled to York, Pennsylvania, and the Continental Army established its own winter camp outside Philadelphia at Valley Forge. Here Washington was joined by his wife, Martha, in a small stone farmhouse, surrounded by the log huts that his men built for themselves.

The Continental Army's miserable winter at **Valley Forge** has become famous for its hardships. Suffering from cold, disease, and starvation, as many as 2,500 soldiers died. Yet despite the suffering of the troops, the Continental Army completed its transformation into a disciplined professional force, under the watchful eye of General von Steuben, and with the coming of spring, American prospects improved dramatically.

THE WAR WIDENS, 1778–1781

Since late 1776, Benjamin Franklin and a team of American diplomats had been in Paris negotiating French support for the patriot cause. In the winter of 1777–1778, aware that a Franco-American alliance was close, Parliament belatedly tried to end the rebellion by giving the American colonies full autonomy, including the exclusive right to tax themselves, in return for a resumption of allegiance to the crown. But France and the United States concluded an alliance on February 6, 1778, and news of it reached America before the British commission arrived. Seeing independence within reach, Congress refused to negotiate.

Foreign intervention transformed the American Revolution into a virtual world war, engaging British forces in heavy fighting not only in North America but also in the West Indies and India. In the end, had it not been for French assistance, the American side probably would not have won the clear-cut victory it did.

THE UNITED STATES GAINS AN ALLY

The agreements the United States signed with France included both a commercial treaty and a military alliance. Both sides promised to fight together until Britain recognized the independence of the United States, and France pledged not to seek the return of lands in North America. In turn, France persuaded Spain to declare war on Britain in June 1779. The Spanish fleet augmented the naval power of the countries arrayed against Great Britain.

Meanwhile, Catherine the Great of Russia suggested that the European powers form a League of Armed Neutrality to protect their trade with the United States and other warring countries against British interference. Denmark and Sweden soon joined; Austria, Portugal, Prussia, and Sicily eventually followed. Britain, which wanted to cut off Dutch trade with the United States, used a pretext to declare war on the Netherlands before it could join. Great Britain thus found itself isolated and even, briefly, threatened with invasion. Accordingly, in the spring of 1778, the British replaced the Howes with a tough new commander, Sir Henry Clinton, instructing him to send troops to attack the French West Indies. To replace these troops, Clinton sought closer cooperation with Britain's Indian and loyalist allies. Knowing that he now faced a serious French threat, Clinton also began consolidating his forces. He evacuated Philadelphia and pulled his troops slowly back across New Jersey to New York.

On June 28, 1778, Washington caught up with the British and engaged them at the Battle of Monmouth Court House. The day was hot and the battle hard-fought. For a while, it looked as if the now well-trained Americans might win, but a mix-up in orders cost Washington the victory. This inconclusive battle proved to be the last major engagement in the North. Clinton withdrew to New York, and Continental troops occupied the hills along the Hudson Valley north of the city. The war shifted to other fronts.

FIGHTING ON THE FRONTIER AND AT SEA

Native Americans called Kentucky "a dark and bloody ground," a designation that took on added meaning when Indians began raiding the territory in 1777 on British instructions. The nerve center for coordinating these attacks was the British post of Detroit, and the Americans accordingly made plans to capture it. Two expeditions from Pittsburgh in 1778 failed completely. A third, under Virginian George Rogers Clark, although it never reached Detroit, was more successful (see Map 6–3). In July 1778 Clark's force of 175 frontiersmen captured three key British settlements in the Mississippi Valley: Kaskaskia, Cahokia, and Vincennes. These successes may have strengthened American claims to the West at the end of the war.

Blood also ran on the Pennsylvania and New York frontiers with British and Indian raids on settlers in Pennylvania's Wyoming Valley and New York's Cherry Valley. Both raids became the stuff of legend and stimulated equally savage reprisals against the Indians.

Anglo-American clashes at sea had begun in 1775, shortly after the Battles of Lexington and Concord, and would continue until the end of the war as Americans struggled to break the British navy's blockade. Great Britain was the preeminent sea power of the age, and the United States never came close to matching it. But Congress did its best to challenge the British navy, and the Americans engaged in what was essentially a guerrilla war at sea. Their naval flag, appropriately, pictured a rattlesnake and bore the motto "Don't Tread on Me."

The country's first naval hero, Scottish-born John Paul Jones, was primarily a hit-and-run raider. In the colonies by chance when the war broke out, this adventurer offered his services to the Congress. Benjamin Franklin helped secure Jones an old French merchant ship, which he outfitted for war and renamed the *Bon Homme Richard.* After capturing 17 enemy vessels, he encountered the formidable *H.M.S. Serapis* in the North Sea on September 23, 1779. Completely outgunned, Jones brought his ship close enough to make his small-arms fire more effective. Asked by the British if he was surrendering, Jones reportedly replied, "I have not yet begun to fight." Lashing the two ships together, Jones and his men battled the crew of the *Serapis* for more than four hours. When the *Serapis* finally surrendered, Jones's crew took possession of the British vessel and left the crippled *Bon Homme Richard* to sink.

The Congress and the individual states supplemented America's naval forces by commissioning individual sea captains to outfit their merchant vessels with guns and act as privateers. Some 2,000 American privateers captured more than 600 British ships and forced the British navy to spread itself thin doing convoy duty.

THE LAND WAR MOVES SOUTH

During the first three years of the war, the British made little effort to mobilize what they believed to be considerable loyalist strength in the South. In 1778, however, facing a threat from France and with their forces in the North inactive, they gave

MAP EXPLORATION
To explore an interactive version of this map, go to http://www.prenhall.com/goldfield3/map6.3

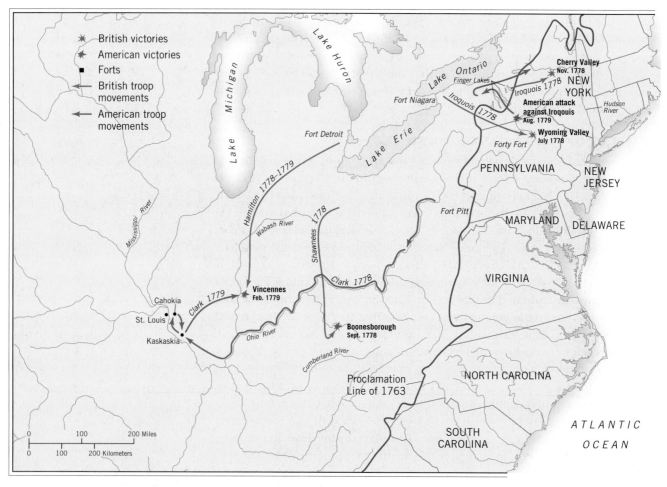

MAP 6–3   The War on the Frontier, 1778–1779   Significant battles in the Mississippi Valley and the frontiers of the seaboard states added to the ferocity of the fighting and strengthened some American claims to western lands.

WERE THE BRITISH at more of a disadvantage the farther from the coast they fought?

southern loyalists a key role in a new strategy for subduing the rebellion. The British southern strategy began to unfold in November 1778, when General Clinton dispatched 3,500 troops to take control of Georgia. Meeting only light resistance, they quickly seized Savannah and Augusta. Indeed, enough inhabitants seemed happy to have the British back for the old colonial government to be restored under civilian control. After their initial success, however, the British suffered some serious setbacks. The Spanish entered the war and seized British outposts on the Mississippi and Mobile rivers. And in February 1779, South Carolina's Whig militia decimated a loyalist militia contingent that was trying to fight its way from the North Carolina backcountry to Georgia to join up with British troops.

But the Americans could not beat the British army. In late September and early October 1779, a combined force of 5,500 American and French troops, supported by French warships, unsuccessfully attacked Savannah. The way was now open for the British to attack Charleston, the military key to the Lower South. In

GLOBAL PERSPECTIVES

AMERICAN INDEPENDENCE ABROAD

The main purpose of the Declaration of Independence was to announce to other nations that the United States had assumed a place among them and was therefore available as a trading partner and military ally. Most countries, however, at first took a wait-and-see approach. As one historian has observed, a "deafening diplomatic silence" greeted the American debut on the world stage.

Unofficial admiration and emulation were quicker and more widespread. As early as 1777, a German newspaper noted that American success would give "new life to the spirit of liberty," and by 1790 at least 26 works on America had been published in three or more European languages. Elsewhere, slaves took direct action. In the West Indies, they celebrated Americans for meriting "Immortal Honour" for "encountering death in every form rather than submit to slavery." Jamaican bondsmen unsuccessfully revolted in 1776, and on islands off the southeastern coast of Africa, slaves likewise rebelled, explaining their actions by observing that "America is free. Could not we be?"

The success of the American Revolution also had profound repercussions in the two most powerful nations of Europe. In France the American example and the depletion of the treasury during the war contributed to a revolution that overthrew the monarchy. In Britain the results were less dramatic but still important. The loss of the North American colonies accelerated an eastward shift in British attention that would make India the crown jewel in the nineteenth-century empire. Whites also began settling Australia in 1788 when Britain started sending convicts there because, unlike the colonies, an independent United States could—and did—refuse to accept them.

Even the abolition of slavery in the British Empire occurred when it did partly as a result of American independence. By tarnishing England's reputation as the model of freedom, the American Revolution prompted a reaction in Britain that helped to stimulate a popular antislavery movement. In addition, the independence of the United States weakened the political influence of the West Indian planters by dividing them from their fellow slaveholders on the mainland. Thus ironically, thanks partly to the American Revolution, Great Britain was able to emancipate its slaves during the 1830s—a full generation before the United States took the same step in a bloody civil war.

December 1779, Clinton sailed through storm-battered seas from New York to the Carolina coast with about 9,000 troops. In the Battle of Charleston, he encircled the city, trapping the patriot forces inside. On May 12, 1780, more than 5,000 Continentals and militia laid down their arms—the worst American defeat of the war and the largest single loss of United States troops to a foreign army until the surrender of American forces in the Philippines to Japan in 1942.

The British were now poised to sweep the entire South. So complete did the British success seem that Clinton tried to force American prisoners to resume their duties as British subjects and join the loyalist militia. Thinking that matters were now well in hand, Clinton sailed back to New York, leaving the southern troops under the command of Lord Cornwallis.

Clinton's confidence that the South had returned securely to the loyalist camp was premature. Atrocities like the slaughter of surrendering Virginians inflamed anti-British feeling. And Clinton's decision to force former rebels into the

W   WHERE TO LEARN MORE

★ Kings Mountain National Military Park and Cowpens National Battlefield, South Carolina
www.cr.nps.gov
www.ilt.columbia.edu/k12/history/aha/battles.html

W   WHERE TO LEARN MORE

★ Yorktown Battlefield, Colonial National Historical Park, Yorktown, Virginia **www.cr.nps.gov**

QUICK REVIEW

Victory at Yorktown

- Summer 1781: Cornwallis marches to Yorktown, Virginia.
- 6,000 British face 8,800 Americans and 7,800 French.
- October 19, 1781: British army surrenders.

loyalist militia backfired, infuriating real loyalists—who saw their enemies getting off lightly—as well as Whigs. Atrocities and reprisals mounted on both sides.

AMERICAN COUNTERATTACKS

After a complete rout of General Horatio Gate's forces near Camden, South Carolina, in the summer of 1780, American morale revived on October 7, 1780, when "over mountain men" (militia) from Virginia, western North Carolina, and South Carolina defeated the British at Kings Mountain, South Carolina. And in December 1780, Nathanael Greene replaced the discredited Gates, bringing competent leadership to the Continentals in the South.

The daring and resourceful Greene realized that he would need an unorthodox strategy to defeat Cornwallis's larger army of seasoned professional troops. He divided his forces, keeping roughly half with him in northeastern South Carolina and sending the other half westward under General Daniel Morgan. At the Battle of Cowpens on January 17, 1781, Morgan cleverly posted his least reliable troops, the militia, in the front line, telling them to run after firing two volleys. When Tarleton attacked, the militia fired and withdrew. Thinking that the American ranks had broken, the Redcoats charged—straight into devastating fire from Morgan's Continentals. Tarleton escaped, but his reputation for invincibility had been destroyed.

Cornwallis now badly needed a battlefield victory. Burning his army's excess baggage, he set off in hot pursuit of Greene and Morgan, who had rejoined forces. The Continentals had the advantage of knowing the country, which was laced with rain-swollen rivers. Finally, on February 13, 1781, Greene's tired men crossed the Dan River into Virginia, and Cornwallis gave up the chase, marching his equally exhausted Redcoats southward. To his surprise, Cornwallis now found himself pursued—though cautiously—by Greene. On March 15, the opposing forces met at Guilford Court House (near present-day Greensboro, North Carolina) in one of the war's bloodiest battles.

By the late summer of 1781, British fortunes were waning in the Lower South. The Redcoats held only the larger towns and the immediately surrounding countryside. With their superior staying power, they won most major engagements, but these victories brought them no lasting gain. As General Greene observed, "We fight, get beat, and rise and fight again." Patriot guerrilla forces, led by such colorful figures as "Gamecock" Thomas Sumter and "Swamp Fox" Francis Marion, disrupted British communications between their Charleston headquarters and outlying garrisons. The loyalist militias that the British had hoped would pacify the countryside proved unequal to the task. Although Greene never defeated the Redcoats outright, his campaign was a strategic success. The British could not hold what they had taken; the Americans had time on their side. Disappointed and frustrated, Cornwallis decided to cut off Greene's supplies and marched north to Yorktown, Virginia, during the summer of 1781.

The final military showdown of the war was at hand. By now, French soldiers were in America ready to fight alongside the Continentals, and a large French fleet in the West Indies had orders to support an attack on the British in North America. Faking preparations for an assault on British-occupied New York, the Continentals (commanded by Washington) and the French headed for the Chesapeake. Cornwallis and his 6,000 Redcoats soon found themselves besieged behind their fortifications at Yorktown by 8,800 Americans and 7,800 French. A French naval victory gave the allies temporary command of the waters around Yorktown. Cornwallis had nowhere to go, and Clinton—still in New York—could not reinforce him quickly enough. On October 19, 1781, the British army surrendered.

THE AMERICAN VICTORY, 1782–1783

*T*he British surrender at Yorktown marked the end of major fighting in North America, though skirmishes continued for another year. But the majority in Parliament now felt that enough men and money had been wasted trying to keep the Americans within the empire. In March 1782, the king accepted Lord North's resignation and appointed Lord Rockingham as prime minister, with a mandate to make peace.

THE PEACE OF PARIS

The peace negotiations, which took place in Paris, were lengthy. The Americans demanded independence, handsome territorial concessions—Franklin, the senior American negotiator, asked for all of Canada—and access to the rich British-controlled fishing grounds in the North Atlantic. The new British prime minister, Lord Shelburne (Rockingham had died in 1782), was inclined to be conciliatory to help British merchants recover their lost colonial trade.

The American negotiators, Franklin, John Adams, and John Jay, masterfully threaded their way among the conflicting interests of the Americans, British, French, and Spanish. With good reason, they feared that the French and Spanish would strike a bargain with the British at the expense of the United States. As a result, the Americans disregarded Congress's instructions to avoid making peace unilaterally. Instead, they secretly worked out their own arrangements with the British that would meet Shelburne's objective of restoring Anglo-American commercial ties. On November 30, 1782, the negotiators signed a preliminary Anglo-American treaty of peace. Its terms were embodied in the final **Peace of Paris,** signed by all the belligerents on September 3, 1783.

The Peace of Paris gave the United States nearly everything it sought except Canada (which was never really a serious issue). Great Britain acknowledged that the United States was "free, sovereign and independent." The northern boundary of the new nation extended west from the St. Croix River (which separated Maine from Nova Scotia) past the Great Lakes to what were thought to be the headwaters of the Mississippi River (see Map 6–4). The Mississippi itself—down to just north of New Orleans—formed the western border. Spain acquired the provinces of East and West Florida from Britain. This territory included parts of present-day Louisiana, Mississippi, Alabama, and Georgia. The treaty did not, however, provide the United States with access to the Gulf of Mexico, a situation that would be a source of diplomatic friction for years.

Several provisions of the treaty addressed important economic issues. Adams, on behalf of his fellow New Englanders, insisted on a provision granting American fishermen access to the waters off eastern Canada. The treaty also required that British forces, on quitting American soil, were to leave behind all American-owned property, including slaves. Another provision declared existing debts between citizens of Britain and the United States still valid, giving British merchants hope of collecting on their American accounts. Congress was to "recommend" that the states restore rights and property taken from loyalists during the war. Nothing was said about the slave trade, which Jay had hoped to ban.

THE COMPONENTS OF SUCCESS

The War for Independence was over. In December 1783, the last British troops left New York. Despite the provisions of the peace treaty and the objections of southern planters, about 3,000 African Americans went with them. Washington's

WHAT WERE the key factors in the American victory in the Revolutionary War?

Peace of Paris   Treaties signed in 1783 by Great Britain the United States, France, Spain, and the Netherlands that ended the Revolutionary War.

MAP EXPLORATION
To explore an interactive version of this map, go to http://www.prenhall.com/goldfield3/map6.4

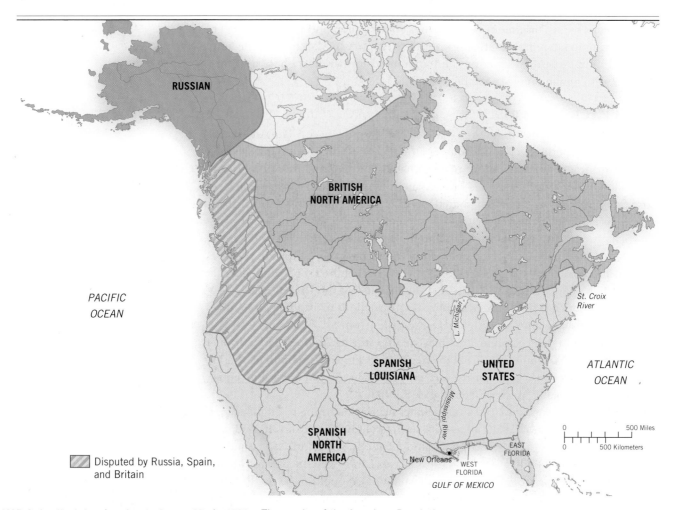

Disputed by Russia, Spain, and Britain

MAP 6–4   North America after the Peace of Paris, 1783   The results of the American Revolution redrew the map of North America, confining Britain to Canada and giving the United States most of the area east of the Mississippi River, though Spain controlled its mouth for most of the next 20 years.

WHAT FACTORS helped determine the territorial settlement reached in the Peace of Paris?

Continental Army had already disbanded in the summer of 1783 (but not, as we have seen, before a dispute over pay came close to provoking a military coup). On December 4, the American commander said an emotional farewell to his officers at New York City's Fraunces Tavern, and on December 23, at Annapolis, Maryland, he resigned his commission to the Congress. Like the legendary citizen-soldier Cincinnatus, who after defending the ancient Roman Republic gave up his power as dictator and went back to plowing his land, Washington went home to Mount Vernon.

Washington's leadership was just one of the reasons why the Americans won the Revolutionary War. French assistance played a crucial role. Some historians contend that without the massive infusion of French men and money in 1781, the Revolution would have failed. The British also contributed heavily to their own downfall with mistakes that included bureaucratic inefficiency, hesitant command, and, worst of all, overconfidence.

Yet it took 175,000 to 200,000 soldiers—Continentals and militia troops—to prevent Great Britain from recovering the colonies. Of these, some 7,000 died in battle. Their casualty rate—30 to 40 percent—may have been the highest of any war in which the United States has been engaged.

WAR AND SOCIETY, 1775–1783

Regular combatants were not the only ones to suffer during the struggle for independence. Eight years of warfare also produced profound dislocations throughout American society. Military service wrenched families apart, sporadic raids brought the war home to vast numbers of people, and everyone endured economic disruptions. As a forge of nationhood, the Revolution tested all Americans, whatever their standing as citizens.

THE WOMEN'S WAR

Everywhere women had to see their husbands, sons, brothers, and fiancés go off to fight and die. Like Mary Silliman in Connecticut, they waited, trying to stay calm until they knew "what tidings God" had for them. At first, with spirits still running high, Mary's letters to her husband, Selleck, reveal an affectionate lightheartedness. Later, the couple's letters grew less playful. Then her husband was captured. The daily round of domestic duties helped to keep her going, but his extended absence increased her burdens and enlarged her responsibilities.

Such circumstances elevated women's domestic status. Women also assumed new public roles during the conflict. The Ladies' Association of Philadelphia was established in 1780 to demonstrate women's patriotism and raise money to buy shirts for the army. Similar associations formed in other states.

Despite their increasing private responsibilities and new public activities, it did not occur to most women to encroach on traditional male prerogatives. When John Adams's wife, Abigail, urged him and the Second Continental Congress to "Remember the Ladies," she was not expecting equal political rights. What she wanted, rather, was some legal protections for women and recognition of their value and need for autonomy in the domestic sphere.

Republican ideology, responding to the changing status of women, assigned them a role that was at once exalted and subordinate. Their job was to nurture wise, virtuous, and public-spirited men. It was this view of women that would prevail in the post-Revolutionary era.

EFFECT OF THE WAR ON AFRICAN AMERICANS

In the northern states, where slavery was already economically marginal and where black men were welcome as volunteers in the Continental Army, the Revolutionary War helped to bring an end to slavery, although it remained legal there for some time (see Chapter 7). In the South, however, slavery was integral to the economy, and white planters viewed it as crucial to their postwar recovery, so the war ultimately strengthened the institution, especially in the Carolinas and Georgia. Of the African Americans who left with the British at the end of the war, many, both slave and free, went to the West Indies. Others settled in Canada, and some eventually reached Africa, where Britain established the colony of Sierra Leone for them.

WHAT WERE the true economic costs of the War for Independence?

5–4
A freelance writer urges his readers to use common sense (1776)

QUICK REVIEW

Women's Roles
- Elevation of women's domestic status.
- New public roles as supporters of independence.
- Limited encroachment on traditional male prerogatives.

OVERVIEW IMPORTANT BATTLES OF THE REVOLUTIONARY WAR

	Battle	Date	Outcome
Early Fighting	Lexington and Concord, Massachusetts	April 19, 1775	Contested
	Fort Ticonderoga, New York	May 10, 1775	American victory
	Breed's Hill ("Bunker Hill"), Boston, Massachusetts	June 17, 1775	Contested
	Great Bridge, Virginia	Dec. 9, 1775	American victory
	Quebec, Canada	Dec. 31, 1775	British repulsed American assault
	Moore's Creek Bridge, North Carolina	Feb. 27, 1776	American victory
The War in the North	Brooklyn Heights, New York	Aug. 27, 1776	British victory
	White Plains, New York	Oct. 28, 1776	British victory
	Trenton, New Jersey	Dec. 26, 1776	American victory
	Princeton, New Jersey	Jan. 3, 1777	American victory
	Brandywine Creek, Pennsylvania	Sept. 11, 1777	British victory (opened way for British to take Philadelphia)
	Saratoga, New York	Sept. 19 and Oct. 17, 1777	American victory (helped persuade France to form an alliance with United States)
	Monmouth Court House, New Jersey	June 28, 1778	Contested

THE WAR'S IMPACT ON NATIVE AMERICANS

Survivors among the approximately 13,000 Native Americans who fought for the British did not have the option of leaving with them at the end of the war. How many died during the conflict is not known, but certainly many did. Not only the Iroquois but other groups lost much. The Americans repeatedly invaded the Cherokees' homeland in the southern Appalachian Mountains.

With the peace treaty of 1783, Britain surrendered its territory east of the Mississippi, shocking and infuriating the Native Americans living there. They had not surrendered, and none of them had been at the negotiations in Paris. With the Americans now claiming their country by conquest, the Revolutionary War was for most Native Americans a disaster that opened the floodgates to a torrent of white settlers.

OVERVIEW   IMPORTANT BATTLES OF THE REVOLUTIONARY WAR (CONTINUED)

	Battle	Date	Outcome
The War on the Frontier	Wyoming Valley, Pennsylvania	June and July 1778	British victory
	Kaskaskia and Cahokia, Illinois; Vincennes, Indiana	July 4, 1778– Feb. 23, 1779	American victories strengthen claims to Mississippi Valley
	Cherry Valley, New York	Nov. 11, 1778	British victory
The War in the South	Savannah, Georgia	Dec. 29, 1778	British victory (took control of Georgia)
	Kettle Creek, Georgia	Feb. 14, 1779	American victory
	Savannah, Georgia	Sept. 3– Oct. 28, 1779	British victory (opened way for British to take Charleston)
	Charleston, South Carolina	Feb. 11– May 12, 1780	British victory
	Camden, South Carolina	Aug. 16, 1780	British victory
	Kings Mountain, South Carolina	Oct. 7, 1780	American victory
	Cowpens, South Carolina	Jan. 17, 1781	American victory
	Guilford Court House, North Carolina	March 15, 1781	Contested
	Yorktown, Virginia	Aug. 30– Oct. 19, 1781	American victory (persuaded Britain to end war)

ECONOMIC DISRUPTION

The British and American armies both needed enormous quantities of supplies. This heavy demand disrupted the normal distribution of goods and drove up real prices seven- or eightfold. The widespread use of depreciating paper money by the American side amplified the rise in prices and triggered severe inflation.

When the British did not simply seize what they needed, they paid for it in hard currency—gold and silver. American commanders, by contrast, had to rely on paper money because the Congress and the states had almost no hard currency at their disposal. The Continental dollar, however, steadily declined in value, and by March 1780, the Congress was forced to admit officially that it was worthless.

Necessity, not folly, drove Congress and the states to rely on the printing press. Rather than alienate citizens by immediately raising taxes to pay for the war, the states printed paper money supposedly redeemable through future tax revenues. By April 1779, as Washington commented, "a wagon load of money will scarcely purchase a wagon load of provisions." Savvy people tried to spend money before its value could drop further, whereas those who had salable commodities such as grain tended to hoard them in the hope that the price would go even higher. Prices also climbed much faster than wages, leaving many working people impoverished.

American soldiers at Yorktown in 1781 as drawn by a young officer in the French army, Jean-Baptiste-Antoine de Verger. The African American on the left is an infantryman of the First Rhode Island Regiment; the next, a musketeer; the third, with the fringed jacket, a rifleman. The man on the right is a Continental artilleryman, holding a lighted match used to fire cannons.

Anne S.K. Brown Military Collection, John Hay Library, Brown University

The rampant inflation was demoralizing and divisive. Lucky speculators and unscrupulous profiteers grew rich, while ordinary and patriotic people suffered. Nevertheless, the successful outcome of the war and the stable peace that followed suggest that most Americans somehow managed to cope. But during the last years of the conflict, their economic and psychological reserves ran low. The total real wealth of private individuals declined by an average of 0.5 percent annually from 1774 to 1805, even with the returning prosperity of the 1790s. Such statistics suggest the true economic cost of the War for Independence.

THE PRICE OF VICTORY

Most American and British commanders tried to keep hostilities "civilized"—if such a characterization can ever be applied to a war—but discipline sometimes broke down among regular troops. Controlling militias or civilians acting on their own was even more difficult. Residents of contested areas near British-occupied cities, such as New York and Charleston, lived in almost constant danger.

Although the British were probably the worse offenders, both sides burned, plundered, and murdered. One can see the results in a returning refugee's description of the area around Beaufort, South Carolina, in the early 1780s: "All was desolation. . . . Robberies and murders are often committed on the public roads. The people that remain have been peeled, pillaged, and plundered. Poverty, want, and hardship appear in almost every countenance . . . , and the morals of the people are almost entirely extirpated."

CONCLUSION

Despite the devastation and divisiveness of the war, many people in Europe and the United States were convinced that it represented something momentous. The *Annual Register*, an influential British magazine, commented accurately in 1783 that the American Revolution "has already overturned those favourite systems of policy and commerce, both in the old and in the new world, which the wisdom of the ages, and the power of the greatest nations, had in vain endeavored to render permanent; and it seems to have laid the seeds of still greater revolutions in the history and mutual relations of mankind."

Americans, indeed, had fired a shot heard round the world. Thanks in part to its heavy investment in the American Revolution, France suffered a grave financial crisis in the late 1780s. This, in turn, ushered in the political crisis that culminated in the French Revolution of 1789.

Once prosperous but distant provinces of a far-flung empire, the North American states had become an independent confederation, a grand experiment in republicanism whose fate mattered to enlightened men and women throughout the Western world. In his written farewell to the rank and file of his troops at the end of October 1783, Washington maintained that "the enlarged prospects of happiness, opened by the confirmation of our independence and sovereignty, almost exceed the power of description." He urged those who had fought with him to maintain their "strong attachments to the union" and "prove themselves not less virtuous and useful as citizens, than they have been persevering and victorious as soldiers." The work of securing the promise of the American Revolution, Washington knew, would now shift from the battlefield to the political arena.

SUMMARY

The Outbreak of War and the Declaration of Independence, 1774–1776 After the Boston Tea Party, both the British and the Americans knew they were heading for a crisis. In a gesture of appeasement, Parliament endorsed the Conciliatory Proposition, pledging not to tax the colonies if they would contribute to the defense of the empire. But, it was too late. General Gage received orders to march to Lexington and Concord to arrest rebels. What ensued were to be the first battles of the Revolutionary War. On July 4, 1776, Congress officially approved the Declaration of Independence.

The Combatants The American forces were composed of a regular Continental Army and militiamen. British soldiers were, for the most part, better trained and organized. For both, military life was tough. And, often only severe discipline would hold soldiers in line. Women accompanied many units on both sides. Approximately 5,000 African Americans fought against the British and for American independence. Many Indians, however, decided it was in their best interest to join British forces in the war.

The War in the North, 1776–1777 During the first phase of the war, the British concentrated on subduing New England. As fighting moved down into New York and New Jersey, Washington won two key battles at Trenton and Princeton. The colonials continued on with a win at the Battle of Saratoga, only to suffer a costly defeat at Brandywine Creek. In the winter of 1777, a large number of colonial fighters camped at Valley Forge. Here, the hard winter and disease set in, but constant training improved their battle-readiness by spring.

The War Widens, 1778–1781 Foreign intervention was to transform the American Revolution into a virtual world war. France allied with America and, Spain with France. Russia, Denmark, Sweden, Austria, the Netherlands, Portugal, Prussia, and Sicily joined a league to protect their trade with the combatants. The expansion of the war prompted the British to attack the southern states in the hope of gaining additional loyalist support. This strategy failed and in the last major battle of the war at Yorktown, Virginia, on October 19, 1781, the British army surrendered.

The American Victory, 1782–1783 The American victory accelerated peace talks, and the Peace of Paris was signed in 1783. Several provisions of the treaty addressed important economic issues such as access to fishing waters in Canada. The War for Independence was over, and British troops began their evacuation of America.

The War and Society, 1775–1783 The war had a great effect on many different aspects of American society. Women everywhere lost husbands, sons, and fathers.

IMAGE KEY
for pages 146–147

a. An 18th-century powderhorn decorated with a map.

b. Engraving printed by Benjamin Franklin in 1754 urging the colonies to unite.

c. The surrender of Lord Cornwallis at Yorktown.

d. The 1783 Treaty of Paris that ended the American Revolution and recognized the independence of the United States.

e. Battle at Lexington, Massachusetts.

f. Portrait of Thomas Jefferson.

g. The Declaration of Independence.

h. Portrait of George Washington.

i. Portrait of John Laurens.

j. A portion of a print depicting the capture of Major John André, the British agent who acted as go-between for the British authorities and Benedict Arnold.

k. Benjamin West's painting of the American commissioners who negotiated the Peace of Paris.

l. Drum and fife belonging to William Diamond (Lexington Historical Society) said to have been played at the battle of Lexington early in the morning of April 19, 1775.

m. An engraving depicting John Paul Jones stopping an American sailor who was attempting to lower the ship's flag as a sign of surrender.

Women also assumed new public roles and increased responsibilities at home. In the Northern states, the war helped bring an end to slavery. In the South, however, slavery was integral to the economy. The successful outcome of the war and the stable peace that followed suggest that most Americans some-how managed to cope with the new world in which they found themselves.

REVIEW QUESTIONS

1. Who were the loyalists, and how many of them were there? What attempts did the British and Americans make in 1775 to avert war? Why did these steps fail?

2. What actions did the Second Continental Congress take in 1775 and 1776? Why did it choose George Washington as the commander of its army? Why was he a good choice?

3. Why did Congress declare independence in July 1776? How did Americans justify their claim to independence?

4. What was republicanism, and why was the enthusiasm that it inspired in-sufficient to win the war?

5. Why were most of the early battles fought in the northern states? What effect did French entry into the war have on British strategy?

6. Why did the initial British victories in the South not win the war for them? Why did the United States ultimately win? What did it obtain by winning?

7. What were the effects of the war on African Americans, women, and American society in general?

8. What were some of the global effects of American independence?

KEY TERMS

Battles of Lexington and Concord (p. 151)
Committee of Safety (p. 149)
Conciliatory Proposition (p. 150)
Continental Army (p. 156)

Contract theory of government (p. 154)
Declaration of Independence (p. 154)
Minute Men (p. 149)

Olive Branch Petition (p. 152)
Peace of Paris (p. 167)
Republicanism (p. 155)
Valley Forge (p. 162)

WHERE TO LEARN MORE

⬡ **Gnadenhutten Monument and Schoenbrunn Village near New Philadelphia, Ohio.** Reconstructed buildings mark the Moravian Indian settlement whose inhabitants were massacred in 1782. The website for the museum and park, **http://www.geocities.com/tusc_hat/gnaden.html**, gives a brief history of the village and Revolutionary War massacre.

- **Independence National Historical Park, Philadelphia, Pennsylvania.** Independence Hall, where Congress adopted the Declaration of Independence, is the most historic building in Philadelphia. The informative website can be accessed through Links to the Past: National Park Service Cultural Resources' comprehensive listing of historic sites in the National Park system, **http://www.cr.nps.gov**

- **Kings Mountain National Military Park and Cowpens National Battlefield, South Carolina.** Situated approximately 20 miles apart, these were the sites of two battles in October 1780 and January 1781 that turned the tide of the war in the South. Both have museums and exhibits. The official site is accessible through Links to the Past: National Park Service Cultural Resources, **http://www.cr.nps.gov**. But see also Battles of the American Revolutionary War, **http://www.ilt.columbia.edu/k12/history/aha/battles.html** for a brief description of the battles and their contexts.

- **Minute Man National Historical Park, Lexington and Concord, Massachusetts.** There are visitors' centers at both Lexington and Concord with explanatory displays. Visitors may also follow the self-guided Battle Road Automobile Tour. The official website is accessible through Links to the Past: National Park Service Cultural Resources, **http://www.cr.nps.gov**

- **Saratoga National Historical Park, New York.** The park preserves and commemorates the American victory that led to French entry into the war. There is a museum with artifacts from the battlefield. Both the explanatory displays and the topography of the area make this an especially illuminating site. The official website is accessible through Links to the Past: National Park Service Cultural Resources, **http://www.cr.nps.gov**

- **Valley Forge National Historical Park, Valley Forge, Pennsylvania.** Reconstructed huts convey a sense of life in the Continental Army camp at Valley Forge during the hard winter of 1777–1778. The official website is accessible through Links to the Past: National Park Service Cultural Resources, **http://www.cr.nps.gov**

- **Yorktown Battlefield, Colonial National Historical Park, Yorktown, Virginia.** The park commemorates the great American victory here. Innovative exhibits enable visitors to follow the course of the war from a multicultural perspective. The official website is accessible through Links to the Past: National Park Service Cultural Resources, **http://www.cr.nps.gov**

 U.S. History Documents CD-ROM
For primary sources related to this chapter, refer to the document CD-ROM.

 www.prenhall.com/goldfield
For study resources related to this chapter, visit the *Companion Website*™.

Visualizing The Past...

The Rattlesnake as a National Symbol

WHAT OTHER characteristics of snakes in general, and rattlesnakes in particular, might have appealed to Revolutionary-era Americans in choosing a national symbol?

One of the tasks facing the Revolutionary generation was to create symbols around which to rally. There was no official flag, no anthem, no Uncle Sam. Benjamin Franklin made perhaps the earliest attempt to create a visual symbol for the prospective nation when he drew "Join, Or Die" to accompany his 1754 Plan of Union. He pictured the colonies as a snake cut into pieces. Why a snake? In mythology, snakes can reattach themselves. Twenty years later, Paul Revere used the snake for the masthead of the revolutionary newspaper, the *Massachusetts Spy*. Once war began, military units adopted the snake as their battle flag. The most famous of these is the Gadsden flag. Christopher Gadsden was a delegate to the Second Continental Congress from South Carolina who played a leading role in creating the U.S. Navy and in appointing Esek Hopkins of Rhode Island as its first commander. He gave the Gadsden flag to Hopkins for his personal standard.

In 1775, pleased with the popular adoption of the snake as a national symbol, Benjamin Franklin noted, that:

> As if anxious to prevent all pretentions of quarrelling with her, the weapons with which nature has furnished her, she conceals in the roof of her mouth, so that, to those who are unacquainted with her, she appears to be a most defenceless animal; and even when those weapons are shewn and extended for her defence, they appear weak and contemptible; but their wounds however small, are decisive and fatal: — Conscious of this, she never wounds till she has generously given notice, even to her enemy, and cautioned him against the danger of treading on her.—Was I wrong, Sir, in thinking this a strong picture of the temper and conduct of America?

◄ The Gadsden flag, used initially by the U.S. Navy. By 1775 the lines indicating the divisions among the colonies have disappeared. The snake has become the rattlesnake, a reptile unique to North America, and one with a highly poisonous venom. "Don't Tread On Me" captured the revolutionaries' insistence that they fought only to defend their liberties.
Corbis/Bettmann

When rotated, Franklin's snake described the North American coastline: He omitted Georgia, only recently founded and inhabited largely by convicts freed from British prisons.

Revere's snake has reattached itself, although the lines where the divisions had been are still visible. Franklin only pictured twelve colonies, but Revere added "G" for Georgia. Further, Revere's snake confronts the British lion. The united serpent is far larger than the lion, something which anticipated Thomas Paine's argument in *Common Sense* that it made no sense for an island to rule a continent.

▲

When rotated, Franklin's snake imitated the North American coastline; he omitted Georgia, which was newly found and inhabited largely by convicts freed from British prisons.

North Wind Picture Archives

7 The First Republic 1776-1789

CHAPTER HIGHLIGHTS

The New Order of Republicanism In May 1776, the Congress called on the colonies to form new state governments. The new state constitutions expanded the power of state legislatures at the expense of state governors. Political power was made the near exclusive province of propertied white men. In 1777, Congress submitted the Articles of Confederation to the states.

Problems at Home 1783 and 1784 were marked by instability and economic problems. Divisions between debtors and creditors sparked political conflict. Congress passed a series of land ordinances opening up western land to development.

Diplomatic Weaknesses While France and the United States remained on good terms, Britain and Spain tried to keep the United States weak and block its expansion. In 1784 Spain closed the Mississippi River to American trade, increasing sectional tension. As the sense of crisis deepened, nationalists grew in influence and number.

Toward a New Union In 1787 the Constitutional Convention met in Philadelphia. Competing plans for Congressional representation proposed by large and small states, resulted in the Great Compromise. Federalists and Anti-federalists clashed during the slow process of ratification.

CHAPTER QUESTIONS

WHAT WERE the most significant weaknesses of the Articles of Confederation?

HOW DID British foreign policy contribute to economic problems in America?

WHAT STEPS did Britain and Spain take to block American expansion?

WHICH GROUPS in American society were most likely to support the Constitution? Why?

CHAPTER OUTLINE

- The New Order of Republicanism
- Problems at Home
- Diplomatic Weaknesses
- Toward a New Union

IMAGE KEY

for pages 178–179 is on page 205.

Springfield Jan. 26, 1787

Sir,

The unhappy time is come in which we have been obliged to shed blood. Shays, who was at the head of about twelve hundred men, marched yesterday afternoon about four o'Clock, towards the public buildings in battle array. He marched his men in an open column by plattoons. I sent several times [through aides] to him to know what he was after, or what he wanted. His reply was, he wanted barracks, and barracks he would have and stores. The answer returned was he must purchase them dear, if he had them. He still proceeded on his march until he approached within two hundred and fifty yards of the arsenal. He then made a halt. I immediately sent Major Lyman, one of my aides, and Capt Buffington to inform him not to march his troops any nearer to Arsenal on his peril, as I was stationed here by order of your Excellency and the Secretary at War, for the defence of the public property, in case he did I should surely fire on him and his men. [After rebuffing Lyman and Buffington,] Shays immediately put his troops in motion, and marched on rapidly near one hundred yards. I then ordered Major Stephens, who commanded the Artillery, to fire upon them. He accordingly did. The two first shott he endeavored to overshoot them, in hopes they would have taken warning without firing among them, but it had no effect on them. Major Stevens then directed his shott thro' the center of his column. The fourth or fifth shot put their whole column into the utmost confusion. Shays made an attempt to display [spread out] the column, but in vain. We had one howitz which was loaded with grape shot, which when fired, gave them great uneasiness. Had I been disposed to destroy them, I might have charged upon their rear and flanks with my Infantry and the two field pieces, and could have killed the greater part of his whole army within twenty five minutes. There was not a single musket fired on either side. I found three men dead on the spot, and one wounded, who is since dead.

I am, Sir, with great respect, Your Excellency's most
Obedient hble Servt
W. Shepard

General Shepard to Governor Bowdoin, Jan. 26, 1787, in *American Historical Review,* vol. 2: July 1897, p. 694.

WILLIAM SHEPARD, the commander of the Hampshire County militia, informed Massachusetts Governor James Bowdoin that the armed insurgents led by Daniel Shays had been routed the previous day in their attempt to seize the federal arsenal at Springfield. Shays, a hitherto obscure Revolutionary War captain, had escaped rural poverty by acquiring his own farm before the outbreak of the Revolution. He enlisted in 1775 and served the patriot cause for five years before returning to his farm in Pelham, a village of small-scale farmers with a tradition of resisting outside authorities. Like many of his fellow farmers in western Massachusetts, Shays faced hard times in the 1780s. A combination of falling farm prices, a shortage of money, heavy taxes, and mounting debts produced an economic crisis that threatened more and more farmers with imprisonment for debt and, worse yet, the loss of their farms. Faced with an unresponsive state legislature controlled by eastern merchants and creditors, angry farmers reacted much as they had during the revolutionary agitation against the British a decade earlier: they organized, protested, and shut down the county courts. By 1786 Shays had emerged as one of their key leaders, and the ragtag army of farmers that he marched against the Springfield arsenal now aimed at nothing less than the overthrow of the state government.

State leaders and eastern merchants were horrified by this armed challenge to their authority. In quickly mobilizing forces to suppress the rebellion, they acted on their belief that the Revolution had been fought to forge a society founded on the rule of law and contract, in which the established order would be upheld. Liberty for them was equated with the right of the individual to pursue wealth and amass property. By contrast, the struggling farmers and artisans supportive of the cause of the rebels defined the liberty won in the Revolution in terms of the right of communities to defend their interests against the threat of moneyed and aristocratic elites.

Driven out of Massachusetts when his army quickly collapsed in 1787, Shays died impoverished in upstate New York in 1825. Still, the movement that bears his name dramatized the fragile nature and conflicting values of America's first republic under the Articles of Confederation. Providing for little more than a loose union of the states, the Articles were ratified in 1781. The years that followed were a period of trial and error marked by a running debate over the meaning of liberty and the extent of power to be entrusted to a national government. Americans favoring a stronger, more centralized government repeatedly cited Shays's Rebellion as an example of the impending chaos that would destroy the republic unless fundamental changes were made. Those changes came with the writing and ratification of the Constitution of the United States in 1788.

THE NEW ORDER OF REPUBLICANISM

As royal authority collapsed during the Revolution, provincial congresses and committees assumed power in each of the former colonies. The Continental Congress, seeking to build support for the war effort, was concerned that these new institutions should have a firm legal and popular foundation. In May 1776, the Congress called on the colonies to form new state governments "under the authority of the people."

This call reflected the political philosophy of republicanism that animated the Revolution (see Chapter 6). To Americans, republicanism meant, first and foremost, that legitimate political authority derives from the people. The people should elect the officials who govern them, and those officials should represent the interests of the people who elected them. Another key aspect of republicanism was the revolutionary idea that the people could define and limit governmental power through written constitutions.

Thus for many Americans, the Congress's call reflected the root purpose of the Revolution—to banish aristocratic tyranny and reconstruct government in the states on republican principles. But if those principles included the idea that legitimate government flowed from the people, it was not always clear just who was included in "the people."

WHAT WERE the most significant weaknesses of the Articles of Confederation?

QUICK REVIEW

Property, Race, Gender, and Citizenship

- Republicans limited political rights to white male property owners.
- 60 to 80 percent of adult white men owned property.
- Revolution did not challenge exclusion of women from politics.

Chronology

1776	States begin writing the first constitutions.
1777	Articles of Confederation proposed.
1780s	English textile production begins to surge with new technological advances.
1781	Articles ratified.
1783	Americans celebrate independence and the peace treaty with Britain.
	British West Indies closed to U.S. traders.
1784	Onset of the postwar depression.
	Opening of China trade by the United States.
	Spain closes the Mississippi.
	Separatist plots in the West.
	Treaty of Fort Stanwix.
1785	Land Ordinance of 1785.
	States begin to issue more paper money.
	Treaty of Fort McIntosh.
1786	Shays's Rebellion breaks out.
	Jay-Gardoqui Treaty defeated.
	Annapolis Convention.
1787	Constitutional Convention at Philadelphia.
	Northwest Ordinance.
1788	Constitution ratified and goes into effect.
	Publication of *The Federalist*.

With the exception of New Jersey, where women meeting the property qualifications were eligible to vote, the state constitutions of the Revolutionary era prohibited women from voting.

Howard Pyle, Corbis/Bettmann

DEFINING THE PEOPLE

When news of the peace treaty with Britain reached New Bern, North Carolina, in June 1783, the citizens held a grand celebration. As reported by Francisco de Miranda, a visiting Spanish officer, "There was a barbecue [a roast pig] and a barrel of rum, from which the leading officials and citizens of the region promiscuously drank with the meanest and lowest kind of people, holding hands and drinking from the same cup. It is impossible to imagine, without seeing it, a more purely democratic gathering."

For Miranda, this boisterous mingling of all citizens as seeming equals confirmed the central tenet of republicanism, the belief that the people were sovereign. But republicanism also taught that political rights should be limited to those who owned private property, because the independent will required for informed political judgment required economic self-sufficiency. This, in effect, restricted political participation to propertied white men. Virtually everyone else was denied political rights. As for Native Americans, they were outside the U.S. body politic and exercised political rights within their own nations.

Because the ownership of property was relatively widespread among white men, some 60 to 85 percent of adult white men could participate in politics. The greatest concentration of the remaining 25 percent or so shut out of the political process were unskilled laborers and mariners living in port cities. The working poor in the cities still included indentured servants. The walking poor—vagrants and transients—might be jailed by local authorities, confined to workhouses, or hired out in public auctions for fixed terms of labor.

Women and the Revolution.   The Revolution did little to change the traditional patriarchal assumption that politics and public life should be the exclusive domain of men. Women, according to republican beliefs, were part of the dependent class and belonged under the control of propertied men, their husbands and fathers. Under common law, women surrendered their property rights at marriage unless they made special arrangements to the contrary. Legally and economically, husbands had complete control over their wives.

To be sure, some women saw in the political and social enthusiasm of the Revolution an opportunity to protest the most oppressive features of their subordination. "I won't have it thought that because we are the weaker sex as to bodily strength we are capable of nothing more than domestic concerns," wrote Eliza Wilkinson of South Carolina. Men, she lamented, "won't even allow us liberty of thought and that is all I want." Such protests, however, had little enduring effect.

Gender-specific language, including such terms as "men," "Freemen," "white male inhabitants," and "free white men," explicitly barred women from voting in almost all state constitutions of the 1770s. Only the New Jersey constitution of 1776 defined **suffrage,** the right to vote, in gender-free terms, extending it to all adults "worth fifty pounds." As a result, until 1807, when the state legislature changed the constitution, propertied women enjoyed the right to vote in New Jersey.

The Revolution did bring women a few limited gains. They benefited from slightly less restrictive divorce laws and gained somewhat greater access to educational and business opportunities. The perception of women's moral status also rose. As the Philadelphia physician Benjamin Rush argued in his *Thoughts upon Female Education* (1787), educated and morally informed women were needed to instruct "their sons in the principles of liberty and government." Often called republican motherhood, this more positive view of women's influence entrusted mothers with the responsibility of passing on republican virtues from one generation to the next.

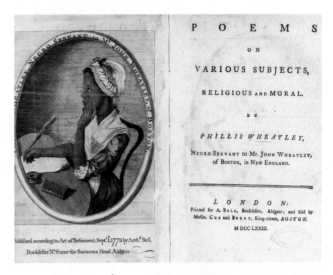

Phillis Wheatley was an acclaimed African-American poet. Kidnapped into slavery as a child in Africa, she was a domestic slave to the Wheatley family of Boston when her first poems were published in 1773.

Scipio Moorhead, Corbis/Bettmann

The Revolution and African Americans in the South.

The Revolution had a more immediate impact on the lives of many African Americans, triggering the growth of free black communities and the development of an African American culture. Changes begun by the Revolution were the main factor in the tremendous increase of free blacks from a few thousand at mid-century to more than 100,000 by 1800. Revolutionary principles of liberty and equality and evangelical notions of human fellowship convinced many whites for the first time to challenge black slavery. In 1784, Virginia Methodists condemned slavery as "contrary to the Golden Law of God on which hang all the Laws and Prophets, and the unalienable Rights of Mankind, as well as every Principle of Revolution." As many whites grew more hostile to slavery, blacks began to seize opportunities for freedom.

5–9
Rights of Women in an Independent Republic

Upwards of 50,000 slaves, or one in ten of those in bondage, gained their freedom as a result of the war. One route was through military service, which generally carried a promise of freedom. All the states except Georgia and South Carolina recruited black regiments. Some 5,000 blacks, mostly slaves, served in the Continental Army. Most of the slaves who gained freedom during the war, however, had fled their owners and made their way to the port cities of the North.

Once freed, blacks tried to break all the bonds of their former servitude. "Negro Soloman," his former owner griped, "now free, prefers to mould bricks rather than serve me." A Delaware mistress felt rejected when a slave she had freed spurned her offer of employment with a friend and found her own job. "I cannot help think," she noted sourly, that "it is too generally the case with all those of colour to be ungrateful." As the number of free blacks increased, those still enslaved grew bolder in their efforts to gain freedom.

QUICK REVIEW

African Americans and the Revolution

- Revolutionary principles sparked some to challenge slavery.
- More than 50,000 slaves gained freedom as results of the war.
- By 1800 free black population reached 100,000.

Northern Blacks and the Revolution.
If the control mechanisms of slavery experienced some strain in the South during the Revolution, in the North, where slaves were only a small percentage of the population, they crumbled. Most northern states ended slavery between 1777 and 1784. New York followed in 1799, and New Jersey in 1804. Nonetheless, although a majority of northern whites now agreed that slavery was incompatible with the Revolution's commitment to **natural rights** and human freedom, they refused to sanction a sudden emancipation. The laws ending slavery in most of the northern states called for only the children of slaves to be freed, and only when they reached adulthood.

Northern blacks had to struggle to overcome white prejudice. Although black males were allowed to vote if they met the property qualifications, most were

Suffrage The right to vote in a political election.

Natural rights Political philosophy that maintains that individuals have an inherent right, found in nature and preceding any government or written law, to life and liberty.

This portrait, sketched in about 1790 by John Trumbull, is the only known likeness of Alexander McGillivray, a Creek leader who effectively played off Spanish and American interests in the Southeast to gain a measure of independence for the Creeks in the 1780s.

Charles Allen Munn Collection, Fordham University Library, Bronx N.Y.

poor and held little property. Facing discrimination in jobs and housing, barred from juries, and denied a fair share of funds for schools, urban blacks had to rely on their own resources. With the help of the small class of property holders among them, they began establishing their own churches and self-help associations.

The Revolution's Impact on Native Americans. Most Indian peoples had stayed neutral during the war or fought for the British (see Chapter 6). Just as the Americans sought to shake off British control, so the Indians, especially the western tribes and most of the Iroquois Confederation, sought to free themselves from American dominance. The British defeat was thus a double blow, depriving the Indians of a valuable ally and exposing them to the wrath of the victorious patriots.

The state governments, as well as the Confederation Congress, treated Indian lands as a prize of war to be distributed to white settlers. Territorial demands on the Indians escalated, and even the few tribes that had furnished troops for the American side struggled to maintain control over their homelands. As they did so, it was clear that white Americans did not consider Native Americans to be part of their republican society.

Most Native Americans did not want or expect equal rights within the new American republic. They viewed themselves as belonging to their own nations, and wanted political rights and control over the land within their nations. Above all, they wanted independence.

In seeking to defend their independence against the growing pressure of white Americans on their lands, Native Americans forged new confederacies in the 1780s that temporarily united them against a common enemy. Thus, the immediate impact of the Revolution on Native Americans was a mixed one. On the one hand, the Revolution had created a new expansionist power in the United States that was intent on settling lands already occupied by Indians. On the other hand, American victory in the Revolution had broken the British monopoly of power in the region west of the Appalachian Mountains. Before the United States could consolidate its claim over the region, new imperial rivalries sprang up that allowed Native Americans to stake out a political middle ground between the competing powers.

THE STATE CONSTITUTIONS

Ten new state constitutions were in place by the end of 1777. In Connecticut and Rhode Island, the new constitutions simply amended the existing colonial charters, which already provided for extensive self-rule, by dropping all references to royal authority. Massachusetts, the only state to hold elections for a special constitutional convention, ratified its constitution in 1780.

All these constitutions were written documents, a striking departure from the English practice of treating a constitution as a collection of customary rights and practices that had evolved over time. In the American view, a constitution was a formal expression of the people's sovereignty, a codification of the powers of government and the rights of citizenship that functioned as a fundamental law to which all public authority was held accountable.

Because Americans had come to associate tyranny with the privileges of royal governors, all the new state constitutions cut back sharply on executive power. Annual elections were now the norm for governors, who were also made subject to impeachment and limited in the number of terms they could serve. Most important, governors lost control over patronage, the power to appoint executive and judicial officials. As the new constitutions curbed the power of governors, they increased that of the legislatures, making them the focal point of government. The legislatures received the power to appoint officials and to oversee military and financial matters.

To make the legislatures more expressive of the popular will, the new constitutions included provisions that lowered property requirements for voting and officeholding, mandated annual elections, increased the number of seats in the legislatures, and made representation more proportional to the geographical distribution of population. Upper houses were made independent of the executive office and opened to popular election.

Americans knew that legislatures, too, could act tyrannically, as they believed Britain's Parliament had done. So in a final check on arbitrary power, each state constitution eventually included some form of a bill of rights that set explicit limits on the power of government to interfere in the lives of citizens. By 1784, the constitutions of all 13 states had provisions guaranteeing religious liberty, freedom of the press, and a citizen's right to such fair legal practices as trial by jury.

Toward Religious Pluralism.   The new constitutions weakened but did not always sever the traditional tie between church and state. Many Americans held, as the Massachusetts Constitution of 1780 put it, that "the happiness of a people, and the good order and preservation of civil government, essentially depend upon piety, religion, and morality." Reflecting this belief, many states, notably in New England, levied taxes for the support of religion. The states of New England also continued to maintain Congregationalism as the established, or state-supported, religion, while allowing dissenting Baptists and Methodists to use funds from the compulsory religious taxes to support their ministers.

The mid-Atlantic region supported several prominent denominations and none was able to dominate the others. This pluralism checked legislative efforts to impose religious taxes or designate any denomination as the established church. In the South, where many Anglican (or Episcopalian) clergymen had been Tories, the Anglican Church lost its former established status.

Radical and Conservative Visions of Republicanism.   Although in general the executive lost power and the legislature gained power under the new state constitutions, the actual structure of each state government reflected the outcome of political struggles between radical and conservative visions of republicanism. The democratically inclined radicals wanted to open government to all male citizens. The conservatives, fearing "mob rule," wanted to limit government to an educated elite of substantial property holders.

In South Carolina, where conservative planters gained the upper hand, the constitution mandated property qualifications that barred 90 percent of the state's white males from holding elective public office. By contrast, Pennsylvania had the most democratic and controversial constitution. Many of Pennsylvania's conservatives had discredited themselves during the Revolution by remaining neutral or loyal to the crown. The Scots-Irish farmers and Philadelphia artisans who stepped into the resulting political vacuum held an egalitarian view of republicanism. The

AMERICAN VIEWS

A French Observer Describes a New Society

In 1782, J. Hector St. John Crevecoeur, a Frenchman who had lived and traveled in British North America, published his impressions of America. The following selection from his Letters from an American Farmer *captures the striking optimism and sense of newness that he found. More so than any other literary work, the* Letters *stamped the new American republic, especially in the minds of Europeans, as the home of the world's freest and most equal people.*

- What is Crevecoeur's image of America? Do you believe it was overly optimistic?
- Why does Crevecoeur put such emphasis on the absence of titles and great disparities of wealth?
- Just what was so new about America to Crevecoeur?
- Why did Crevecoeur ignore African slaves in his definition of the American? What happened to Native Americans in his account of the making of the American?

I wish I could be acquainted with the feelings and thoughts which must agitate the heart and present themselves to the mind of an enlightened Englishman when he first lands on this continent. . . . He is arrived on a new continent; a modern society offers itself to his contemplation, different from what he had hitherto seen. It is not composed, as in Europe, of great lords who possess everything and of a herd of people who have nothing. Here are no aristocratical families, no courts, no kings, no bishops, no ecclesiastical dominion, no invisible power giving to a few a very visible one, no great manufactures employing thousands, no great refinements of luxury. The rich and the poor are not so far removed from each other as they are in Europe. Some few towns excepted, we are all tillers of the earth, from Nova Scotia to West Florida. We are a people of cultivators scattered over an immense territory, communicating with each other by means of good roads and navigable rivers, united by the silken bands of mild government, all respecting the laws without dreading their power, because they are equitable. We are all animated with the spirit of an industry which is unfettered and unrestrained, because each person works for himself. . . . A pleasing uniformity of decent competence appears throughout our habitations. The meanest of our log-houses is a dry and comfortable habitation. Lawyer and merchant are the fairest titles our towns afford; that of a farmer is the only appellation of the rural inhabitants of our country. It must take some time ere he can reconcile himself to our dictionary, which is but short in words of dignity and names of honour. . . . We have no princes for whom we toil, starve, and bleed; we are the most perfect society now existing in the world. Here man is free as he ought to be, nor is this pleasing equality so transitory as many others are. Many ages will not see the shores of our great lakes replenished with inland nations, nor the unknown bounds of North America entirely peopled. . . .

The next wish of this traveller will be to know whence came all these people. They are a mixture of English, Scotch, Irish, French, Dutch, Germans, and Swedes. From this promiscuous breed, that race now called Americans have arisen. . . . What, then, is the American, this new man? He is either an European or the descendant of an European; hence that strange mixture of blood, which you will find in no other country. . . . He is an American, who, leaving behind him all his ancient prejudices and manners, receives new ones from the new mode of life he has embraced, the new government he obeys, and the new rank he holds. He becomes an American by being received in the broad lap of our Alma Mater. Here individuals of all nations are melted into a new race of men, whose labours and posterity will one day cause great changes in the world.

Source: J. Hector St. John Crevecoeur, *Letters from an American Farmer and Sketches of Eighteenth-Century America,* ed. Albert E. Stone (1986), pp. 66–70.

constitution they pushed through in 1776 gave the vote to all free males who paid taxes, regardless of wealth, and eliminated property qualifications for officeholding. In addition, the constitution concentrated power in a unicameral (single-house) legislature, eliminating both the office of governor and the more elite upper legislative house. To prevent the formation of an entrenched class of officeholders, the constitution's framers also required legislators to stand for election annually and barred them from serving more than four years out of seven.

The constitutions of the other states typically enhanced the political influence of ordinary citizens more than the constitution of South Carolina did. Unlike the colonial assemblies, the new bicameral (two-house) legislatures included substantially more artisans and small farmers and were not controlled by men of wealth. The proportion of legislators who came from a common background—those with property valued under £200—more than tripled to 62 percent in the North and more than doubled in the South from the 1770s to the 1780s.

This growing political equality was accompanied by demands that those in government be more responsive to the people. Summing up the prevailing view among Americans about the proper basis for government, William Hooper of North Carolina wrote in 1776, "Rulers must be conceived as the creatures of the people, made for their use, accountable to them, and subject to removal as soon as they act inconsistent with the purposes for which they were formed."

THE ARTICLES OF CONFEDERATION

Once the Continental Congress decided on independence in 1776, it needed to create a legal basis for a permanent union of the states. John Dickinson of Pennsylvania, a reluctant supporter of independence, presented a draft plan for such a union. Dickinson favored a strong central government, but Congress fundamentally altered his original plan to recognize the sovereign power of the individual states. According to the key provision of the **Articles of Confederation** that the Congress finally submitted to the states in November 1777, "Each State retains its sovereignty, freedom and independence, and every power, jurisdiction and right, which is not by this confederation expressly delegated to the United States, in Congress assembled."

The powers the Articles of Confederation delegated to the central government were extremely limited. There were no provisions for a national judiciary or a separate executive branch of government. The Articles made Congress the sole instrument of national authority but restricted it with a series of constitutional safeguards that kept it from threatening the interests of the states. Each state had only one vote in Congress, making it politically equal to the others regardless of its size or population. State legislatures were to choose their congressional delegations and delegates were expected to follow the instructions of their state legislatures and could be recalled at any time. Important measures, such as finances or war and peace, required approval from a majority of nine state delegations voting in the Congress. Amendments to the Articles of Confederation required the unanimous consent of the states.

The Congress had authority primarily in the areas of foreign policy and national defense. It could declare war, make peace, conduct foreign affairs, negotiate with Native Americans, and settle disputes between the states. It had no authority, however, to raise troops or impose taxes.

The central principle behind the Articles was the fear of oppressive, centralized power encroaching on the freedoms for which the Revolution had been fought. In the end, as Edward Rutledge, a delegate from South Carolina to the

Articles of Confederation
Written document setting up the loose confederation of states that comprised the first national government of the United States.

Continental Congress, put it, the new Confederation Congress was vested "with no more Power than is absolutely necessary."

Most states quickly ratified the Articles of Confederation, but Maryland stubbornly held out until March 1781. Because they needed the approval of all 13 states, only then did the Articles officially take effect. Surprisingly, given the prevailing deep suspicion of central power, what caused the delay was the demand of some states to give the Congress a power not included in the Articles submitted for ratification in 1777.

The issue was the unsettled lands in the West between the Appalachian Mountains and the Mississippi River. Some states claimed these lands by virtue of their colonial charter rights, and led by Virginia and Massachusetts, they insisted on maintaining control over these territories. The so-called landless states—those with no claim to the West—insisted that the territories should be set aside as a national domain, a reserve of public land controlled by Congress for the benefit of all the states. Land speculators who had purchased huge tracts of land from the Indians before the Revolution sided with the landless states.

The British threat to the Chesapeake area in early 1781 finally broke the impasse that had delayed final approval of the Articles. Though it retained control of Kentucky, Virginia gave up its claim in the West to a vast area extending north of the Ohio River. In turn, Maryland, agreed to ratify the Articles.

PROBLEMS AT HOME

HOW DID British foreign policy contribute to economic problems in America?

Neither prosperity nor political stability accompanied the return of peace in 1783. The national government struggled to avoid bankruptcy, and in 1784, an economic depression struck. As fiscal problems deepened, creditor and debtor groups clashed angrily in state legislatures. When legislatures passed measures that provided relief to debtors at the expense of creditors, the creditors decried what they saw as the interference of ignorant majorities with the rights of private property. Raising the cry of "legislative despotism," the creditors joined their voices to those who early on had wanted the power of the states curbed by a stronger central government.

THE FISCAL CRISIS

The Continental Congress and the states had incurred heavy debts to finance the Revolutionary War. Unable to impose and collect sufficient taxes to cover the debts and without reserves of gold or silver, they had little choice but to borrow funds and issue certificates, or bonds, pledging repayment. The Congress had the largest responsibility for meeting the war's costs, and to do so, it printed close to $250 million in paper notes. By the end of the war, these Continental dollars were nearly worthless, and the national debt stood at $11 million. As Congress issued new securities to settle claims by soldiers and civilians, the debt rose to $28 million within just a few years.

These fiscal problems ultimately discredited the Articles of Confederation in the eyes of the **nationalists,** a loose bloc of congressmen, army officers, and public creditors who wanted to strengthen the Confederation at the expense of the states. The nationalists first began to organize in the dark days of 1780 and 1781, when inflation was rampant, the army was going unpaid, the Congress had ceased paying interest on the public debt, and the war effort itself seemed in danger of collapsing. Galvanized by this crisis, the nationalists rallied behind Robert Morris, a Philadelphia merchant appointed as superintendent of finance for the Confederation government.

Nationalists Group of leaders in the 1780s who spearheaded the drive to replace the Articles of Confederation with a stronger central government.

Morris sought to enhance national authority through a bold program of financial and political reform. He began by securing a charter from Congress in 1781 for the Bank of North America. Morris wanted it to serve as a national institution, and he used it to hold government funds, make loans to the government, and issue bank notes. Morris was able to resume some specie payments, and he temporarily brought order and economy to the nation's finances. As a result of his reforms, he came to be called the Financier of the Revolution. Nonetheless, he was blocked in his efforts to gain the taxing power that was essential for restoring the shattered credit of the Confederation government.

Morris's larger objective was to create a "bond of union" by having the Congress assume payment of the entire national debt. Settling this debt would lead the propertied classes—the people who had financed the war and held the debt—to identify their economic self-interest with the effective exercise of power by the national government.

But to achieve this political goal, Morris had to gain for the Congress what it had always lacked: the power to tax. In 1781, he proposed a national impost, or tariff, of 5 percent on imported goods. Because this was a national tax, it required an amendment to the Articles of Confederation and the consent of all 13 states. Twelve of the states quickly ratified the impost amendment, but Rhode Island rejected it, sending it down to defeat. When a revised impost plan was considered two years later, New York blocked its passage.

These failures doomed Morris's financial reforms. Morris remained committed to the nationalist cause and would see his ideas resurface under the financial programs of Treasury Secretary Alexander Hamilton in the 1790s (see Chapter 8).

The failure of the impost tax was one of many setbacks that put the nationalists temporarily on the defensive. With the conclusion of peace in 1783, confidence in state government returned, taking the edge off calls to vest the central government with greater authority. Most ominously for the nationalist cause, the states began to assume responsibility for part of the national debt. As Morris had warned in 1781, such a policy entailed "a principle of disunion . . . which must be ruinous." Without the power to tax, the Congress was a hostage to the sovereignty of the individual states with no real authority over the nation's economic affairs. When the economy plunged into a severe depression in 1784, Congress could only look on helplessly.

ECONOMIC DEPRESSION

During the Revolutionary War, Britain closed its markets to American goods. After the war, the British continued this policy, hoping to keep the United States weak and dependent. In the summer of 1783, they excluded Americans from the lucrative trade with the British West Indies, which had been the primary means by which the colonists had built up the credit they needed to offset their imports from Britain.

Meanwhile, British merchants were happy to satisfy America's pent-up demand for consumer goods after the war. Ultimately, however, the British merchants required payment in hard currency, gold and silver coins. Without access to its former export markets, America's only source of hard currency was foreign loans obtained by Congress and what money the French army had spent during the war. This was soon exhausted, and America's trade deficit with Britain ballooned in the early 1780s to $5 million.

The result was an immense bubble of credit that finally burst in 1784, triggering a depression that would linger for most of the decade. As merchants began to press debtors for immediate payment, prices collapsed , and debtors were unable to pay.

QUICK REVIEW

Debt and the Balance of Trade
- Britain sought to keep America weak and dependent.
- Trade imbalance soared in the 1780s.
- Collapse of credit bubble in 1784 led to depression.

Small farmers everywhere had trouble paying their taxes. Rural shopkeepers often could not move goods unless they agreed to barter them for farm produce. Abigail Dwight, who ran a small store in western Massachusetts, reported in 1785 that "most of these People sell on credit for To-Morrow at large—for very little Cash stirring this way—to be pay'd for in old Horses, cows, some Boards, cabbages, turnips, Potatoes etc."

In the cities, wages fell 25 percent between 1785 and 1789, and workers began to organize. They called for tariffs to protect them from cheap British imports and for legislative measures to promote American manufacturers. In the countryside, farmers faced lawsuits for the collection of debts and the dreaded possibility of losing their land.

With insufficient money in circulation to raise prices and reverse the downturn, the depression fed on itself. Congress was powerless to raise cash and was unable to pay off its old debts, including what it owed to the Revolutionary soldiers. Many state governments made things worse by imposing heavy taxes payable in the paper money they had issued during the Revolution. The result was to further reduce the amount of money in circulation, thus increasing deflationary pressures and forcing prices still lower.

Britain's trade policies caused particular suffering among New England merchants. No longer protected under the old Navigation Acts as British vessels, American ships were now barred from most ports in the British Trading Empire. The economy of the mid-Atlantic region held up somewhat better, but even there the loss of the provisioning trade to the British West Indies in grains, livestock, and dairy products cut into the income of merchants and farmers and forced layoffs among artisans who serviced the shipping trade.

In the southern states, British policies compounded the problem of recovering from the physical damage and labor disruptions inflicted by the war. Some 10 percent of the region's slaves had fled during the war, and production levels on plantations fell in the 1780s. Chesapeake planters needed a full decade to restore the prewar output of tobacco, and a collapse in tobacco prices in 1785 left most of them in the same chronic state of indebtedness that had plagued them on the eve of the Revolution.

Farther south, in the Carolina low country, the plantation economy was crippled. War damage had been extensive, and planters piled up debts to purchase additional slaves and repair their plantations and dikes. In spite of these investments, rice production was slow to recover. Burdened by new British duties on American rice, planters saw their rice exports fall by 50 percent. Small farmers in the pine barrens of North Carolina likewise had to adjust to the loss of their formerly protected British market for naval stores.

By the late 1780s, the worst of the depression was over and an upturn was under way in the mid-Atlantic states. Food exports to continental Europe were on the rise, and American merchants were developing new trading ties with India and China. Commercial treaties with the Dutch, Swedes, and Prussians also opened up markets that had been closed to the colonists. Nonetheless, a full recovery had to await the 1790s.

The depression of the 1780s was the culmination of a decade of painful adjustment that followed the wrenching of the American economy from its traditional moorings within the British trading empire. A stagnant economy and burdensome debt combined with a growing population to reduce living standards. With more losers than winners, economic conflict dominated the politics of the states during the Confederation period.

WHERE TO LEARN MORE

South Street Seaport Museum, New York City, New York.
www.southstseaport.org

THE ECONOMIC POLICIES OF THE STATES

The depression had political repercussions in all the states. Merchants, poorly positioned to adjust to the postwar dislocations of trade, led a campaign to slap retaliatory duties on British ships and special taxes on British goods. Likewise artisans and workers, especially in the North, pushed for tariff barriers against cheap British goods as a way to encourage domestic manufacturing and protect their jobs and wages. Most northern states imposed anti-British measures.

State legislatures in the North responded to the protests of artisans by passing tariffs, but the lack of a uniform national policy doomed their efforts. Shippers evaded high tariffs by bringing their cargoes in through states with no tariffs or less restrictive ones. States without ports, such as New Jersey and North Carolina, complained of economic discrimination. When they purchased foreign goods from a neighboring shipping state, they were forced to pay part of the tariff cost, but all the revenue from the tariff accrued to the importing state. James Madison neatly summarized the plight of these states when he noted that "New Jersey, placed between Philadelphia and New York, was likened to a cask tapped at both ends; And North Carolina, between Virginia and South Carolina, to a patient bleeding at both Arms."

Tariff policies also fed sectional tensions between northern and southern states. The agrarian states of the South had interests that differed from those of the states of the North. With the exception of Virginia, they favored free trade policies that encouraged British imports.

The most bitter divisions exposed by the depression of the 1780s, however, were not between states but between debtors and creditors within states. As the value of debt securities the states had issued to raise money dropped during the Revolutionary War, speculators bought them up for a fraction of their face value and then pressured the states to raise taxes and repay the debts in full in hard currency. Wealthy landowners and merchants likewise supported higher taxes and the rapid repayment of debts in hard currency. Arrayed against these creditor groups by the mid-1780s was a broad coalition of debtors: middling farmers, small shopkeepers, artisans, laborers, and people who had overextended themselves speculating in western land. The debtors wanted the states to issue paper money that they could use instead of hard money—gold and silver—to pay their debts. The paper money would have an inflationary effect, raising wages and the prices of farm commodities and reducing the value of debts contracted in hard currency.

Shays's Rebellion.   This was the economic context in which **Shays's Rebellion** exploded in the fall of 1786. Farm foreclosures and imprisonments for failure to pay debts had skyrocketed in western Massachusetts. When the creditor and seaboard interests in the legislature refused to pass any relief measures, some 2,000 farmers took up arms against the state government in Shays's Rebellion.

Outside of western Massachusetts, discontented debtors generally stopped short of armed resistance because of their success in changing the monetary policy of their states. In 1785 and 1786, seven states enacted laws for new paper money issues. In most cases, the result was a qualified success. Combined with laws that prevented or delayed creditors from seizing property from debtors to satisfy debts, the currency issues helped keep a lid on popular discontent.

The most notorious exception to this pattern of fiscal responsibility was in Rhode Island. A rural party that gained control of the Rhode Island legislature in 1786 pushed through a currency law that flooded the state with paper money that

6–7
Divergent Reactions to Shays's Rebellion

Shays's Rebellion An armed movement of debt-ridden farmers in western Massachusetts in the winter of 1786–1787. The rebellion created a crisis atmosphere.

could be used to pay all debts. Creditors who balked at accepting the new money at face value were subject to heavy penalties.

Debtors vs. Conservatives.   The actions of the debtor party in Rhode Island alarmed conservatives everywhere, confirming their fears that legislative bodies dominated by common farmers and artisans rather than, as before the Revolution, by men of wealth and social distinction, were dangerous. Conservatives, creditors, and nationalists alike now spoke of a democratic tyranny that would have to be checked if the republic were to survive and protect its property holders.

CONGRESS AND THE WEST

The Peace of Paris and the surrender of charter claims by the states gave the Congress control of a magnificent expanse of land between the Appalachian Mountains and the Mississippi River. In what would prove the most enduring accomplishment of the Confederation government, the Congress set forth a series of effective provisions for its settlement, governance, and eventual absorption into the Union.

Asserting for the national government the right to formulate Indian policy, the Congress, backed by threats of the use of military force, negotiated a series of treaties with the Indians, beginning in 1784, for the abandonment of their land claims in the West. Against the opposition of states intent on grabbing Indian lands for themselves, Congress resolved in 1787 that its treaties were binding on all the states. And anxious for revenue, Congress insisted on payment from squatters who had filtered into the West before provisions had been made for land sales.

The most pressing political challenge was to secure the loyalty of the West to the new and fragile Union. To satisfy the demands of settlers for self-government, the Congress resolved as early as 1779 that new states would be carved out of the western domain with all the rights of the original states. An early plan for organizing the territories, the Ordinance of 1784, was largely the work of Thomas Jefferson. In it, he proposed to create 10 districts, or territories, each of which could apply for admission as a state when its population equaled that of the free inhabitants in the least populous of the existing states. Jefferson also proposed that settlers be permitted to choose their own officials, and he called for the prohibition of slavery in the West after 1800. Shorn of its no-slavery features, the ordinance passed Congress but was never put into practice.

As settlers and speculators began pouring into the West in 1784, however, the Congress was forced to move quickly to formulate a policy for conveying its public land into private hands. One way or another, settlers were going to get their land, but a pell-mell process of private acquisitions in widely scattered settlements threatened to touch off costly Indian wars, deprive the national government of vitally needed revenue, and encourage separatist movements. The members of Congress had to act on national land policy, warned a western Pennsylvanian, or else "lose the only opportunity they ever will have of extending their power and influence over this new region."

The Congress responded with the **Land Ordinance of 1785.** The crucial feature of this seminal legislation was its stipulation that public lands be surveyed in a rectangular grid pattern before being offered for sale. By requiring that land first be platted into townships of 36 uniform sections of 640 acres each, the ordinance adopted the New England system of land settlement, an approach that promoted compact settlements and produced undisputed land titles. In sharp contrast was

WHERE TO LEARN MORE

Northern Indiana Center for History, South Bend, Indiana.
www.centerforhistory.org/

Land Ordinance of 1785 Act passed by Congress under the Articles of Confederation that created the grid system of surveys by which all subsequent public land was made available for sale.

the typical southern pattern, whereby settlers picked out a piece of land in a large tract ahead of a precise survey and then fought each other in the courts to secure legal title. In an effort to avoid endless litigation, Congress opted for a policy geared to order and regularity.

Congress also attempted to attract a certain type of settler to the West by offering the plots of 640 acres at the then hefty sum of no less than $640, or $1 per acre, payable in hard currency or its equivalent. The goal here was to keep out the shiftless poor and reserve the West for enterprising and presumably law-abiding farm families who could afford the entry cost. Congress also set aside the income from the sale of the sixteenth section in each township for the support of public schools. Support for education, as a congressional report of 1783 put it, would help provide for "security against the increase of feeble, disorderly and dispersed settlements in those remote and extended territories [and] against the depravity of manners which they have a tendency to produce."

Before any land sales occurred under the Ordinance of 1785, impatient settlers continued to push north of the Ohio River and claim homesteads as squatters. They clashed both with local Indian tribes and with the troops sent by the Congress to evict them. Impatient with the slow process of surveying, the Congress sold off 1.5 million acres to a group of New England speculators organized as the Ohio Company. The speculators now pressed their allies in Congress to establish a governmental structure for the West that would protect their investment by bringing the unruly elements in the West under control.

Both the Congress and speculators wanted political stability and economic development in the West and a degree of supervision for settlers. The **Northwest Ordinance of 1787,** the most significant legislative act of the Confederation Congress, filled this need, creating a political structure for the territories and a phased process for achieving statehood that neatly blended public and private interests.

According to the ordinance, controls on a new territory were to be strictest in the early stage of settlement, when Congress would appoint a territorial government consisting of a governor, a secretary, and three judges. When a territory reached a population of 5,000 adult males, those with 50 acres of land or more could elect a legislature. The actions of the legislature, however, were subject to an absolute veto by the governor. Once a territory had a population of 60,000, the settlers could draft a constitution and apply for statehood "on an equal footing with the original states in all respects whatsoever."

The Northwest Ordinance of 1787 stipulated that only three to five states were to be formed out of the Northwest. This was because the admission of new states would weaken the control over Congress that the original 13 states wanted to maintain for themselves as long as possible. Although less democratic in many respects than Jefferson's plan in that it mandated a period of outside control by Congress, the 1787 ordinance provided greater protection for property rights as well as a bill of rights guaranteeing individual freedoms.

Most significant, it prohibited slavery. Southern congressmen agreed to the slavery ban, in part because they feared that planters in the new states would compete with them in the production of slave-produced staples such as tobacco. More important, however, they expected slavery to be permitted in the region south of the Ohio River that was still under the administrative authority of Virginia, North Carolina, and Georgia in the 1780s. Indeed, slavery was allowed in this region when the **Southwest Ordinance of 1790** brought it under national control, a decision that would have grave consequences in the future sectionalization of the United States.

Northwest Ordinance of 1787
Legislation that prohibited slavery in the Northwest Territories and provided the model for the incorporation of future territories into the union as co-equal states.

Southwest Ordinance of 1790
Legislation passed by Congress that set up a government with no prohibition on slavery in U.S. territory south of the Ohio River.

Although the Northwest Ordinance applied only to the national domain north of the Ohio River, it provided the organizational blueprint by which all future territory was brought into the Union. It went into effect immediately and set the original Union on a course of dynamic expansion through the addition of new states.

WHAT STEPS did Britain and Spain take to block American expansion?

DIPLOMATIC WEAKNESSES

Under the Articles of Confederation, the Congress had the authority to negotiate foreign treaties but no economic or military power to enforce their terms. Unable to regulate commerce or set tariffs, Congress had no leverage with which to pry open the restricted trading empires of France, Spain, and most important, Britain.

France and the United States, allies during the Revolutionary War, remained on friendly terms after it. Britain, however, treated its former colonies with contempt, and Spain was also openly antagonistic to the new nation. Both Britain and Spain sought to block American expansion into the trans-Appalachian West. And a dispute with Spain over the West produced the most serious diplomatic crisis of the period, one that spilled over into domestic politics, increasing sectional tensions between northern and southern states and leading many to question the country's chances of survival.

IMPASSE WITH BRITAIN

The Confederation Congress was unable to resolve any of the major issues that poisoned Anglo-American relations in the 1780s. Key among those issues were provisions in the peace treaty of 1783 that concerned prewar American debts to the British and the treatment of Loyalists by the patriots. Britain used what it claimed to be America's failure to satisfy these provisions to justify its own violations of the treaty. The result was a diplomatic deadlock that hurt American interests in the West and in foreign trade.

Article 4 of the peace treaty called for the payment of all prewar debts in gold or silver coin. Among the most numerous of those with outstanding debts to British creditors were tobacco planters in the Chesapeake region of Virginia and Maryland. During the Revolution, the British army had carried off and freed many of the region's slaves without compensating the planters. Still angry, the planters agreed only to pay the face value of their debts to their state treasuries in state or Continental paper money. Since this money was practically worthless, the planters in effect repudiated their debts.

During the Revolution, all the states had passed anti-Loyalist legislation, and many state governments had seized Loyalists' lands and goods, selling them to raise revenue for the war effort. Articles 5 and 6 of the peace treaty pledged the Congress to "recommend" to the states that they stop persecuting Loyalists and restore confiscated Loyalist property. But wartime animosities remained high and the states were slow to rescind their punitive legislation or allow the recovery of confiscated property.

Combined with the matter of the unpaid debts, the continued failure of the states to make restitution to the Loyalists gave the British a convenient pretext to hold on to the forts in the West that they had promised to relinquish in the Treaty of Paris. This was part of an overall strategy to keep the United States weak, divided, and small. The continued British presence in the region effectively shut Americans out of the fur trade with the Indians. It also insulted the sovereignty of the United States and threatened the security of its northern frontier.

Elsewhere, the British, spurred on by Canadian officials, encouraged secession-ist movements in the Northwest and sought out Indian allies to fight for a possi-ble buffer state south of the Great Lakes that would keep Americans hemmed in along the Atlantic seaboard.

Throughout the 1780s, the British also explored the possibility of entering into an economic alliance with Vermont. Created in 1777 out of land claimed by both New York and New Hampshire, Vermont proclaimed itself an inde-pendent republic, free from the control of the British Parliament and the Amer-ican Congress. Ethan Allen and his brothers Ira and Levi held the power in Vermont politics, and their ambitious schemes for profiting from the sale of such raw materials as lumber and naval stores depended on a favorable treaty with Britain. The Allen brothers initiated a series of negotiations with the British in the 1780s in which they offered a treaty of friendship in exchange for recog-nition of Vermont's independence and trading privileges within the British Em-pire. The British were tempted but held back for fear of unduly antagonizing the United States.

Although concerned by British provocations in the West and fears that the British would convert Vermont into a client state, American officials viewed Britain's retaliatory trade policies as the gravest threat to American security and prosperity. John Adams, the American minister to London, concluded that the British would never lift their trading and shipping restrictions until forced to do so by a uniform American system of discriminatory duties on British goods. The problem was that a uniform policy was impossible to achieve under the Articles of Confederation. Retaliatory navigation acts by individual states did little good be-cause they left the British free to play one state off another.

SPAIN AND THE MISSISSIPPI RIVER

At the close of the Revolutionary War, Spain reimposed barriers on American commerce within its empire. Anxious to maintain as large a buffer zone as pos-sible between its Louisiana and Florida possessions and the restless Americans, Spain also refused to recognize the southern and western boundaries of the Unit-ed States as specified in the treaty with Britain in 1783, holding out instead for a more northerly border. And of greatest consequence, it denied the claim of the United States to free navigation of the entire length of the Mississippi River.

The Mississippi question was explosive because on its resolution hinged American settlement and control of the entire western region south of the Ohio River. Southerners were rapidly moving into this area, and the slave South ex-pected to gain new support for an alliance against the commercial North as new slave states were created south of the Ohio. Free navigation of the Mississippi was essential to the realization of these expectations.

In the wake of the Revolution, the settlers of Kentucky, which was still part of Virginia, and Tennessee, which was still part of North Carolina, flirted with the idea of secession. Impatient to secure both political independence and the eco-nomic benefits that would come with access to the Mississippi, the separatists were not particular about whom they dealt with. They became entangled in a web of diplomatic intrigue that included the Spanish, the Indians, and American offi-cials east of the mountains.

Spain sought to use the divided loyalties of American speculators and fron-tier settlers to its advantage, employing some of them as spies and informers. Spain likewise sought to exploit divisions among Indian groups. In a bewildering variety of treaties negotiated by the Congress, individual southern states, and land

Although physically frail, James Madison, shown here in a portrait made in about 1815, was a formidable thinker whose essays in *The Federalist* endure as a lasting contribution to political theory.

The Granger Collection, New York.

speculators, white Americans laid claim to much of the ancestral land of the major Indian nations in the Southeast—the Cherokee, Chickasaw, Choctaw, and Creek. Fraud was rampant, and many Native Americans believed, with good reason, that they had never been consulted in the dispossession of their land. The Spanish responded by recruiting disaffected Indians into an alliance system of their own. Their staunchest allies came from a faction of the Creeks led by Alexander McGillivray, the son of a trader father and a half-French, half-Creek mother. Supplied with arms by the Spanish, these Creeks succeeded in forcing white settlers off their tribal land in Georgia.

Spain stepped up pressure on the West in the summer of 1784, when it closed the Mississippi River within Spanish territory to American trade. Hoping now to benefit from American weakness, Spain also opened negotiations for a long-term settlement with the United States. The Spanish negotiator, Don Diego de Gardoqui, offered a deal that cleverly played the interests of the North against those of the South and West. In exchange for an American agreement to surrender claims to navigate the Mississippi for the next 30 years, Gardoqui proposed to grant the United States significant trading concessions in the Spanish Empire that would open new markets and new sources of hard money to the financially pressed merchants of the northeastern states. John Jay, his American negotiating partner, reluctantly accepted the offer.

When Jay released the terms of the proposed treaty with Spain in 1786, Congress erupted in angry debate. Southerners, who had taken the lead in the settlement of the West, accused Jay of selling out their interests. Vowing that they would not surrender the West, southern congressmen united to defeat the treaty.

The regional antagonisms exposed by the Jay-Gardoqui talks heightened the alarm over the future of the republic provoked by Shays's Rebellion earlier in 1786. Southerners openly calculated the value of remaining in a Union seemingly dominated by the commercial North, and Westerners warned that unless they were upheld on the Mississippi issue, they would consider themselves "relieved from all Federal Obligations and fully at Liberty to exact alliances & Connections wherever they find them." As the sense of crisis deepened in 1786, the nationalists grew in influence and numbers. Led by Alexander Hamilton of New York and James Madison of Virginia, they now argued that only a radical political change could preserve the republic and fulfill the promise of its greatness.

TOWARD A NEW UNION

In June 1786, a worried John Jay wrote to General George Washington that he was "uneasy and apprehensive; more so than during the war. Then we had a fixed object. . . . The case is now altered; we are going and doing wrong, and therefore I look forward to evils and calamities, but without being able to guess at the instrument, nature, or measure of them." Other nationalists fully shared Jay's forebodings. Everywhere they saw unsolved problems and portents of disaster: unpaid debts, social unrest, squabbling states, sectional hostilities, the uncertain status of the West, blocked channels of trade, foreign intrigues, and a paralyzing lack of centralized authority and purpose. They feared that the republic's very survival was now at stake.

In September 1786, delegates from several states met at the **Annapolis Convention,** in Annapolis, Maryland, seeking to devise a uniform system of commercial regulation for the country. While there, a group of nationalist leaders called

WHICH GROUPS in American society were most likely to support the Constitution? Why?

Annapolis Convention
Conference of state delegates at Annapolis, Maryland, that issued a call in September 1786 for a convention to meet at Philadelphia to consider fundamental changes.

on all the states to send delegates to a convention at Philadelphia "to devise such further provisions as shall appear to them necessary to render the constitution of the Federal Government adequate to the exigencies of the Union." The leaders who met at the **Constitutional Convention** in Philadelphia forged an entirely new framework of governance, the **Constitution of the United States,** that called for a federal republic with a powerful and effective national government.

THE ROAD TO PHILADELPHIA

The road to Philadelphia began at Mount Vernon, George Washington's estate in Virginia. Commissioners from Maryland and Virginia met there in March 1785 to resolve jurisdictional and navigational disputes over the Potomac River and Chesapeake Bay, waters shared by the two states. The meeting went so well that the participants invited representatives from Delaware and Pennsylvania to join them at a conference in Annapolis the following year to formulate policies for interstate commerce on the waterways that linked the Chesapeake region and the Ohio Valley. James Madison then broadened the scope of the Annapolis Conference to include representatives from all 13 states for a general discussion of how best to promote and regulate interstate trade.

Only nine states sent delegates to the Annapolis Convention, and only those from five states had actually arrived when the nationalists abruptly adjourned the meeting. They then called on the states and the Congress to approve a full-scale constitutional convention for Philadelphia in May 1787.

The timing of the call for the Philadelphia Convention could not have been better. During the fall and winter of 1786, the agrarian protests unleashed by Shays's Rebellion in Massachusetts spilled over into other states. Coupled with talk of a dismemberment of the Union in the wake of the Jay-Gardoqui negotiations, the agrarian unrest strengthened the case of the nationalists for more centralized authority.

All the states except Rhode Island sent delegates to Philadelphia. Chiefly lawyers by training or profession, most of the 55 men who attended the convention served in the Confederation Congress, and more than one-third had fought in the Revolution. Extremely well educated by the standards of the day, the delegates were members of the intellectual as well as the political and economic elite. As a group, they were far wealthier than the average American. Most had investments in land and the public securities of the United States. At least 19 owned slaves. Their greatest asset as a working body was their common commitment to a nationalist solution to the crisis of confidence they saw gripping the republic. Most of the strong supporters of the Articles of Confederation refused to attend, perhaps because, as Patrick Henry of Virginia remarked, they "smelt a rat."

THE CONVENTION AT WORK

When it agreed to the Philadelphia Convention, Congress authorized only a revision of the Articles of Confederation. Almost from the start, however, the delegates set about replacing the Articles altogether. Their first action was to elect George Washington unanimously as the convention's presiding officer. The most

The federal ship Hamilton was the center of attention in the grand procession staged by supporters of the Constitution in New York City in 1788.

Constitutional Convention
Convention that met in Philadelphia in 1787 and drafted the Constitution of the United States.

Constitution of the United States   The written document providing for a new central government of the United States.

6–9
Patrick Henry Speaks Against Ratification of the Constitution (1788)

W   WHERE TO LEARN MORE

★ Independence National Historical Park, Philadelphia, Pennsylvania.
www.nps.gov/inde/home.htm

Virginia Plan   Proposal calling for a national legislature in which the states would be represented according to population.

New Jersey Plan   Proposal of the New Jersey delegation for a strengthened national government in which all states would have an equal representation in a unicameral legislature.

Great Compromise   Plan proposed at the 1787 Constitutional Convention for creating a national bicameral legislature in which all states would be equally represented in the Senate and proportionally represented in the House.

ardent nationalists then immediately seized the initiative by presenting the **Virginia Plan.** Drafted by James Madison, this plan replaced the Confederation Congress with a truly national government, organized like most of the state governments with a bicameral legislature, an executive, and a judiciary.

Two features of the Virginia Plan stood out. First, it granted the national Congress power to legislate "in all cases in which the separate states are incompetent" and to nullify any state laws that in its judgment were contrary to the "articles of Union." Second, it made representation in both houses of the Congress proportional to population. This meant that the most populous states would have more votes in Congress than the less populous states, giving them effective control of the government. In short, Madison sought to all but eliminate the independent authority of the states while also forcing the smaller states to defer to the more populous ones in national affairs.

Delegates from the small states countered with the **New Jersey Plan,** introduced on June 15 by William Paterson. This plan kept intact the basic structure of the Confederation Congress—one state, one vote—but otherwise amended the Articles by giving the national government the explicit power to tax and to regulate domestic and foreign commerce. In addition, it gave acts of Congress precedence over state legislation, making them "the supreme law of the respective states."

The Great Compromise.   The New Jersey Plan was quickly voted down, and the convention remained deadlocked for another month over how to apportion state representation in the national government. The issue was finally resolved on July 16 with the so-called **Great Compromise.** Small states were given equal footing with large states in the Senate, or upper house, where each would have two votes. In the lower house, the House of Representatives, the number of seats was made proportional to population, giving larger states the advantage. The Great Compromise also settled a sectional dispute over representation between the free (or about to be free) states and the slave states. The southern states wanted slaves counted for apportioning representation in the House but excluded from direct tax assessments. The northern states wanted slaves counted for tax assessments but excluded for apportioning representation. To settle the issue, the Great Compromise settled on an expedient, if morally troubling, formula: free residents were to be counted precisely; to that count would be added three-fifths "of all other persons," excluding Indians not taxed.

The Great Compromise ended the first phase of the convention, which had focused on the general framework of a stronger national government. In its next phase, the convention debated the specific powers to be delegated to the new government. It was at this point that the sectional cleavage between North and South over slavery and other issues came most prominently to the fore.

Regulation of Commerce and the Issue of Slavery.   The sectional clash first erupted over the power of Congress to regulate commerce. At issue was whether Congress could regulate trade and set tariffs by a simple majority vote. Southerners worried that a northern majority would pass navigation acts favoring northern shippers and drive up the cost of sending southern commodities to Europe. To counter this threat, delegates from the Lower South demanded that a two-thirds majority be required to enact trade legislation. A frustrated Madison urged his fellow southerners to remember that "as we are laying the foundation of a great empire, we ought to take a permanent view of the subject."

In the end, Madison had his way; the delegates agreed that enacting trade legislation would require only a simple majority. In return, however, southerners exacted concessions on the slavery issue. Antislavery New Englanders reached a compromise with the delegates from the Lower South: Congress would be barred from acting against the slave trade for 20 years. In addition, bowing to the fears of planters that Congress could use its taxing power to undermine slavery, the convention denied Congress the right to tax exports from any state. And to alleviate southern concerns that slaves might escape to freedom in the North, the new Constitution included an explicit provision calling on the states to return "persons held to Service or Labour" in any other state.

Washington presides over the Constitutional Convention.

The Free Library of Philadelphia

The Office of the Chief Executive.   After settling the slavery question in late August, the convention had one last significant hurdle to clear: the question of the national executive. In large part because of their confidence in George Washington, whom nearly everyone expected to be the first president, the delegates fashioned a chief executive office with broad discretionary powers. The prerogatives of the president included the rank of commander in chief of the armed forces, the authority to conduct foreign affairs and negotiate treaties, the right to appoint diplomatic and judicial officers, and the power to veto congressional legislation. The president's term of office was set at four years, with no limits on how often an individual could be reelected.

Determining how to elect the president proved a thorny problem. The delegates envisioned a forceful, energetic, and independent executive, insulated from the whims of an uninformed public and the intrigues of the legislature. As a result, they rejected both popular election and election by Congress. The solution they hit upon was the convoluted system of an "electoral college." Each state was left free to determine how it would choose presidential electors equal to the number of its representatives and senators. These electors would then cast votes to select a president. If no candidate received a majority of the electoral votes, the election would be turned over to the House of Representatives, where each state would have one vote.

After a style committee polished the wording in the final draft of the Constitution, 39 of the 42 delegates still in attendance signed the document on September 17. The Preamble, which originally began with a list of the states, was reworded at the last minute to begin simply: "We the people of the United States, in order to form a more perfect Union . . ." This subtle change had significant implications. By identifying the people, and not a collection of states, as the source of authority, it emphasized the national vision of the framers and their desire to create a government quite different from a confederation of states.

OVERVIEW OF THE CONSTITUTION

Although not as strong as the most committed nationalists would have liked, the central government outlined in the Constitution was to have far more powers than were entrusted to Congress under the Articles of Confederation (see the Overview table, "The Articles of Confederation and the Constitution Compared.") The

Constitution's provision for a strong, single-person executive had no precedent in the Articles. Nor did the provision for a Supreme Court. The Constitution vested this court, as well as the lower courts that Congress was empowered to establish, with the judicial power of the United States. In addition, the Constitution specifically delegated to Congress the powers to tax, borrow and coin money, regulate commerce, and raise armed forces, all of which the Confederation government had lacked.

Most of the economic powers of Congress came at the expense of the states, which were prohibited from passing tariffs, issuing money, or enacting any law that infringed on the contractual rights of creditors to collect money from debtors. Further curbing the sovereignty of the states was a clause stipulating that the Constitution and all national legislation and treaties were to be "the supreme law of the land." This clause has subsequently been interpreted as giving the central government the power to declare state laws unconstitutional.

A no-nonsense realism, as well as a nationalist outlook, infused the Constitution. Its underlying political philosophy was that, in Madison's wonderful phrase, "ambition must be made to counter ambition." Madison and the other members of the national elite who met at Philadelphia were convinced that self-interest, not disinterested virtue, motivated political behavior. Accepting interest-group politics as inevitable and seeking to prevent a tyrannical majority from forming at the national level, the architects of the Constitution designed a central government in which competing blocs of power counterbalanced one another.

The Constitution placed both internal and external restraints on the powers granted to the central government. The functional division of the government into executive, legislative, and judicial branches, each with ways to keep the others from exercising excessive power, created an internal system of checks and balances. For example, the Senate's authority to approve or reject presidential appointments and to ratify or reject treaties was a curb on the powers of the executive. The president commanded the armed forces, but only Congress could declare war. The president could veto congressional legislation, but Congress could override that veto with a two-thirds vote. To pass in the first place, legislation had to be approved by both the House of Representatives, which, with its membership proportional to population, represented the interests of the people at large, and the Senate, which represented the interests of the states. And as an ultimate check against executive abuse of power, Congress could impeach, convict, and remove from office a president who tried to set himself above the law.

Although the Constitution did not explicitly grant it, the Supreme Court soon claimed the right to invalidate acts of Congress and the president that it found to be unconstitutional. This power of **judicial review** provided another check against legislative and executive authority (see Chapter 9). To guard against an arbitrary federal judiciary, the Constitution empowered Congress to determine the size of the Supreme Court and to impeach and remove federal judges appointed by the president.

The external restraints on the central government were to be found in the nature of its relationship to the state governments. This relationship was based on **federalism,** the division of power between local and central authorities. By listing specific powers for Congress, the Constitution implied that all other powers were to be retained by the states. Thus, while strengthening the national government, the Constitution did not obliterate the sovereign rights of the states, leaving them free to curb the potential power of the national government in the ambiguous areas between national and state sovereignty.

This ambiguity in the federalism of the Constitution was both its greatest strength and its greatest weakness. It allowed both nationalists and advocates of

QUICK REVIEW

Checks on Executive Power.
- Senate given the authority to approve or reject presidential appointments.
- Congress, not the president, given the power to declare war.
- Congress given the power to override presidential vetoes.

Judicial Review   A power implied in the Constitution that gives federal courts the right to review and determine the constitutionality of acts passed by Congress and state legislature.

Federalism   The sharing of powers between the national government and the states.

OVERVIEW   THE ARTICLES OF CONFEDERATION AND THE CONSTITUTION COMPARED

	Articles	Constitution
Sovereign power of central government	No power to tax or raise armies	Power granted on taxes and armed forces
Source of power	Individual states	Shared through federalism between states and national government
Representation in Congress	Equal representation of states in unicameral Congress	Bicameral legislature with equal representation of states in Senate and proportional representation in House
Amendment process	Unanimous consent of states	Consent of three-fourths of states
Executive	None provided for	Office of president
National judiciary	None provided for	Supreme Court

states' rights to support the Constitution. But the issue of slavery, left unresolved in the gray area between state and national sovereignty, would continue to fester, sparking sectional conflict over the extent of national sovereignty that would plunge the republic into civil war three-quarters of a century later.

THE STRUGGLE OVER RATIFICATION

Knowing that they had exceeded their instructions by proposing an entirely new government, and aware that the Articles' requirement of unanimous consent by the state legislatures to any amendment would result in certain defeat, the Philadelphia delegates boldly bypassed both Congress and the state legislatures.

The last article of the Constitution stipulated that it would go into effect when it had been ratified by at least nine of the states acting through specially elected popular conventions. Congress, influenced by the nationalist sentiments of many of its members, one-third of whom had attended the Philadelphia Convention, and perhaps weary of its own impotence, accepted this drastic and not clearly legal procedure, submitting the Constitution to the states in late September 1787.

The delegates in Philadelphia had excluded the public from their proceedings. The publication of the Constitution lifted the veil of secrecy and touched off a great political debate. Although those who favored the Constitution could most accurately have been defined as nationalists, they referred to themselves as **Federalists,** a term that helped deflect charges that they favored an excessive centralization of political authority. By default, the opponents of the Constitution were known as **Antifederalists,** a negative-sounding label that obscured their support of the state-centered sovereignty that most Americans associated with federalism. Initially outmaneuvered in this way, the Antifederalists never did mount an effective campaign to counter the Federalists' pamphlets, speeches, and newspaper editorials (see the Overview table, "Federalists versus Antifederalists"). The Antifederalists did attract some men of wealth and social standing. Most Antifederalists, however, were backcountry farmers who lived far from centers of communication and market outlets for their produce. They distrusted the social and commercial elite, and many Antifederalists saw in the Constitution a sinister plot by this elite "to lord it over the rest of their fellow citizens, to trample the poorer part of the people under

Federalists Supporters of the Constitution who favored its ratification.

Antifederalists Opponents of the Constitution in the debate over its ratification.

OVERVIEW   FEDERALISTS VERSUS ANTIFEDERALISTS

	Federalists	Antifederalists
Position on Constitution	Favored Constitution	Opposed Constitution
Position on Articles of Confederation	Felt Articles had to be abandoned	Felt Articles needed only to be amended
Position on power of the states	Sought to curb power of states with new central government	Felt power of states should be paramount
Position on need for bill of rights	Initially saw no need for bill of rights in Constitution	Saw absence of bill of rights in proposed Constitution as threat to individual liberties
Position on optimum size of republic	Believed large republic could best safeguard personal freedoms	Believed only a small republic formed on common interests could protect individual rights
Source of support	Commercial farmers, merchants, shippers, artisans, holders of national debt	State-centered politicians, most backcountry farmers

their feet that they may be rendered their servants and slaves." The Antifederalists clung to the belief that only a small republic, one composed of relatively homogeneous social interests, could secure the voluntary attachment of the people necessary for a free government. They argued that a large republic, such as the one framed by the Constitution, would inevitably become tyrannical because it was too distant and removed from the interests of common citizen-farmers.

However much the Antifederalists attacked the Constitution as a danger to the individual liberties and local independence that they believed the Revolution had been fought to safeguard, they were no political match for the Federalists. They lacked the wealth, social connections, access to newspapers, and self-confidence of the more cosmopolitan and better-educated Federalists. In addition, the Federalists could more easily mobilize their supporters, who were concentrated in the port cities and commercial farming areas along the coast. The Federalists successfully portrayed the Constitution as the best opportunity to erect a governing structure capable of preserving and extending the gains of the Revolution.

Conservatives shaken by Shays's Rebellion lined up behind the Constitution. So, too, did groups—creditors, merchants, manufacturers, urban artisans, commercial farmers—whose interests would be promoted by economic development. The enhanced powers of the national government held out the promise of protecting the home market from British imports, enlarging foreign markets for American exports, promoting a stable and uniform currency, and raising revenues to pay off the Revolutionary War debt.

In the early stages, the Federalists scored a string of easy victories. Delaware ratified the Constitution on December 7, 1787, and within a month, so too, had Pennsylvania, New Jersey, Georgia, and Connecticut. Except for Pennsylvania, these were small, sparsely populated states that stood to benefit economically or militarily from a stronger central government. The Constitution carried in the larger state of Pennsylvania because of the Federalists' strength in the commercial center of Philadelphia.

The Federalists faced their toughest challenge in the large states that had generally been more successful in going it alone during the 1780s. One of the most telling

MAP EXPLORATION

To explore an interactive version of this map, go to **http://www.prenhall.com/goldfield3/map7.1**

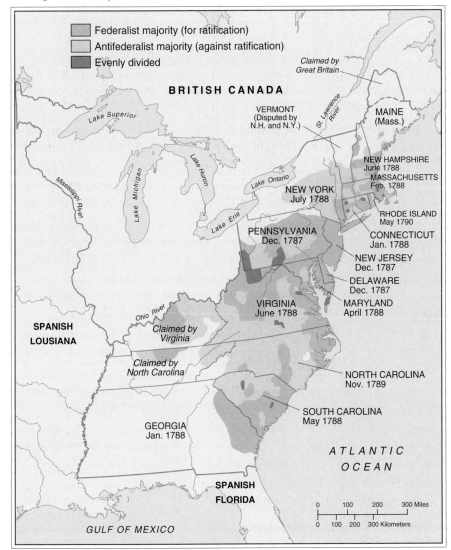

MAP 7–1   The Ratification Vote on the Constitution   Aside from some frontier districts exposed to possible foreign attack, the strongest support for the Constitution came from coastal and interior areas tied into a developing commercial economy.

HOW WOULD you explain the regional pattern of support for the Constitution?

arguments of the Antifederalists in these and other states was the absence of a bill of rights in the Constitution. Realizing the importance of the issue, and citing Article 5 of the Constitution, which provided for an amendment process, the Federalists promised to recommend amending the Constitution with a bill of rights once it was ratified. By doing so, they split the ranks of the Antifederalists in Massachusetts.

After the Federalists gained the support of two venerable heroes of the Revolution, John Hancock and Sam Adams, the Massachusetts convention approved the Constitution by a close vote in February 1788. To win over Hancock, the

GLOBAL PERSPECTIVES

FOREIGN THREATS

"I think I have done all possible to make it possible for the Government of New Orleans to reap benefit from the present situation of the United States. . . . These people intend to live on friendly terms with Spain and we no longer hear the threats we formerly heard . . . we must not neglect them. I think time will bring them to the King."

In this letter of 1788 to the Spanish secretary of state, Don Diego de Gardoqui, the Spanish representative in Philadelphia, outlined Spain's efforts in the 1780s to detach the American settlements in Kentucky from the United States and draw them into an economic alliance with Spanish Louisiana. The goal was to protect Louisiana by both weakening the United States and expanding trading opportunities for the American goods and services desired by the Spanish subjects of Louisiana. Westward expansion by Americans was inevitable, but Spain hoped to control it and turn it to its advantage by offering trading rights on the Mississippi River that would lead to a partnership with the Spanish colony in New Orleans.

The efforts of Spain to draw Kentuckians into its empire, combined with the presence of the British in Canada and the willingness of both of these foreign powers to subsidize Native Americans as they fought to protect their tribal lands against encroachments by white settlers, threatened any effective American control of its trans-Appalachian territory. Meanwhile, British trading restrictions had largely succeeded in reducing the United States to a colonial dependency that furnished British factories with cheap raw materials and purchased British-made goods delivered in British ships. In struggling to establish its sovereign rights in a world of hostile imperial powers, the United States under the Articles of Confederation suffered the crippling disadvantage of lacking any means of formulating or implementing a uniform policy for its defense. More so than any of the other delegates at the Constitutional Convention, Alexander Hamilton drew the obvious conclusion. "You have to protect your rights against Canada in the north, Spain in the south, and your western frontier against the savages. . . . No Government could give us tranquility and happiness at home, which did not possess sufficient strength and stability to make us respectable abroad." Like any new nation confronted with threats to its security, the United States could not afford the luxury or indulge in the utopian hope of dispensing with power politics.

Federalists had played on his vanity, suggesting that they would back him for a top national post. Adams was persuaded to back the Federalists by demonstrations of Boston artisans in favor of national tariff protection.

The major hurdles remaining for the Federalists were Virginia, the most populous state, and strategically located New York. Technically, the Constitution could have gone into effect without them once Maryland, South Carolina, and New Hampshire had ratified it, bringing the total number of states to nine. But without Virginia, which ratified on June 25, and New York, which followed a month later, the new Union would have been weak and the Federalist victory far from assured.

To eke out victory in these crucial states, the Federalists drew on their pragmatism and persuasiveness. As in Massachusetts, they were helped by their promise of a bill of rights. And for the New York campaign, Madison, Jay, and Hamilton wrote an eloquent series of 85 essays known collectively as *The Federalist* to allay fears that the Constitution would so consolidate national power as to menace individual liberties. In the two most original and brilliant essays in *The Federalist*, essays 10 and 51, Madison turned traditional republican doctrine on its head. A large, diverse republic like the one envisaged by the Constitution, he reasoned, not a small and homogeneous one, offered the best hope for safeguarding the rights of all citizens. This was because a large republic would include a multitude of contending interest groups, making it difficult for any combination of them to coalesce into a tyrannical majority that could oppress minority rights. With this argument, Madison had developed a political rationale by which Americans could have both an empire and personal freedom.

North Carolina and Rhode Island did not ratify until after the new government was functioning. North Carolina joined the Union in 1789 once Congress submitted the amendments that constituted the Bill of Rights. The obstinate Rhode Islanders stayed out until 1790, when Congress forced them in with a threat of commercial reprisal.

CONCLUSION

Between 1776 and 1780, Americans developed a unique system of constitutionalism that went far beyond the British model of an unwritten constitution. They proclaimed the supremacy of constitutions over ordinary legislation, detailed the powers of government in a written document, provided protection for individual freedoms in bills of rights, and fashioned a process for framing governments through the election of delegates to a special constitutional convention and the popular ratification of the work of that convention. In all of these areas, Americans were pioneers in demonstrating to the rest of the world how common citizens could create their own governments.

The curbs on centralized power that characterized the state constitutions also applied to what amounted to the first national constitution, the Articles of Confederation. Indeed, the inability of the Confederation Congress to exercise effective power in the areas of taxation and foreign trade was a crippling flaw that thoroughly discredited the Articles in the eyes of the nationalist-minded leaders who had emerged during the Revolution. These leaders overthrew the Articles at the Constitutional Convention in 1787 and engineered a peaceful revolution in securing the ratification of the Constitution. Their victory in creating a new central government with real national powers was built on the foundation of constitutional concepts and mechanisms that Americans had laid down in their state constitutions. The new Constitution rested on the consent of the governed, and it endured because it could be amended to reflect shifts in popular will and to widen the circle of Americans granted the rights of political citizenship.

Accepting as a given that self-interest drove political action, the framers of the Constitution designed the new national government to turn ambition against itself. They created rival centers of power that forced selfish factions to compete in a constant struggle to form a workable majority. The struggle occurred both within the national government and between that government and the states in the American system of federalism. The Constitution thus set the stage for an entirely new kind of national politics.

IMAGE KEY

for pages 178–179

a. Articles of Confederation.

b. The Congress voting Independence.

c. Phyllis Wheatley.

d. Portrait of Alexander McGillivray.

e. The pillars of the "federal edifice" represented by the American colonies in a 1788 cartoon supporting the United States Constitution.

f. Georgia $4 banknote, 1777, issued "for the support of the Continental Troops and other Expences of Government."

g. Women in the State of New Jersey casting their vote.

h. The encounter on 26 January 1787 between Shay's rebels and government troops before the arsenal at Springfield, Massachusetts.

i. The first Stars and Stripes, 1777.

j. Portrait of James Madison.

SUMMARY

The New Order of Republicanism As royal authority collapsed during the Revolution, various provincial congresses and committees assumed power in each of the former colonies. In May 1776, the Congress called on the colonies to form new state governments. Although the role of women was redefined during the Revolution, little changed the traditional patriarchal assumption that politics and public life should be the exclusive domain of men. Ten new state constitutions were in place by 1777. New constitutions curbed the power of governors and increased that of the legislatures, and each state eventually adopted some form of a bill of rights. Also in 1777, Congress submitted to the states the Articles of Confederation.

Problems at Home 1783 and 1784 were marked by instability, near bankruptcy, and an economic depression, much of which was caused by the heavy burden of paying back debts from the war. Bitter divisions formed between debtors and creditors within the states. In 1784 Congress negotiated a series of treaties with the Indians for lands west of the Appalachian Mountains and east of the Mississippi River. A series of land ordinances were passed down from Congress between 1784 and 1790, expanding developed regions into the Midwest.

Diplomatic Weaknesses In the international arena of the 1780s, the United States was a weak and often ridiculed nation. While France and the United States remained on favorable terms, Britain and Spain tried to block American expansion into the West. At the close of the Revolutionary War, Spain reimposed barriers on American commerce with its empire. And, Spain stepped up the pressure on the West in the summer of 1784 when it closed the Mississippi River within Spanish territory to American trade. As the sense of crisis deepened in 1786, the nationalists grew in influence and numbers.

Toward a New Union In September 1786, delegates from several states met at the Annapolis Convention, seeking to devise a uniform system of commercial regulation for the country. While there, another meeting was called in Philadelphia to devise provisions necessary to render the constitution of the government adequate. This second meeting was the Constitutional Convention. Members of the Constitutional Convention proposed the Virginia Plan and the New Jersey Plan, each dealing with representation matters. What came out of both of these plans was the Great Compromise. The convention went on to deal with such issues as slavery and a national executive. Ratification was slow as Federalists and Antifederalists were in direct opposition, but state by state, ratification finally came.

REVIEW QUESTIONS

1. How would you assess the decisions made by Shepard and Shays that resulted in the clash at the Springfield arsenal? Can you imagine any way in which the crisis could have been resolved short of violence?

2. Why do you think that the U.S. Constitution does not cite God or mention religion in any direct way?

3. What was so unprecedented about the new state constitutions, and what principles of government did they embody?

4. What were the problems of the economy in the 1780s, and why did clashes between debtors and creditors become so divisive? Do you think that an

economic recovery could have been achieved under the Articles of
Confederation?

5. Do you feel that the diplomatic weaknesses of the United States under the
   Articles were as serious as its internal problems? What were the sources of
   those weaknesses, and what threat did they pose for national unity?

6. What sorts of men drafted the Constitution in 1787, and how representative
   were they of all Americans? What explains the differences between the
   Federalists and the Antifederalists? Do you think they shared the same vision of what they wanted America to become? How widespread was the popular backing for the Constitution, and what accounts for its ratification?

7. Compare and contrast the options open to the United States in the 1780s
   in developing its economy with those of the new nations that have also
   emerged out of former colonial empires since World War II.

KEY TERMS

Annapolis Convention   (p. 196)
Antifederalists   (p. 201)
Articles of Confederation   (p. 187)
Constitutional Convention   (p. 197)
**Constitution of the United
   States**   (p. 197)
Federalism   (p. 200)
Federalists   (p. 201)

Great Compromise   (p. 198)
Judicial review   (p. 200)
Land Ordinance of 1785   (p. 192)
Nationalists   (p. 188)
Natural rights   (p. 183)
New Jersey Plan   (p. 198)
**Northwest Ordinance
   of 1787**   (p. 193)

Shays's Rebellion   (p. 191)
**Southwest Ordinance
   of 1790**   (p. 193)
Suffrage   (p. 182)
Virginia Plan   (p. 198)

WHERE TO LEARN MORE

South Street Seaport Museum, New York City, New York. Maritime commerce
was the lifeblood of the postrevolutionary economy. The artifacts and exhibits
here offer a fine introduction to the seafaring world of the port city that became
the nation's first capital in the new federal Union. See **www.southstseaport.org**
for more on the impact of trade on the development of New York and information on preservation projects underway in the city.

Independence National Historical Park, Philadelphia, Pennsylvania. Walks
and guided tours through this historic district enable one to grasp much of the
physical setting in which the delegates to the Constitutional Convention met. The
website **www.nps.gov/inde/home.htm** includes a virtual tour of many of the collections at the park, a portrait gallery of leading figures in the Revolution, and
a look at the archaeological projects underway in the park.

Northern Indiana Center for History, South Bend, Indiana. The permanent
exhibition on the St. Joseph River valley of northern Indiana and southern Michigan explains the material world of this region and how it changed as first Europeans and then Americans mingled and clashed with the Native American
population. At **www.centerforhistory.org/** one can learn more about the center
and the variety of programs it offers.

U.S. History Documents CD-ROM
   For primary sources related to this chapter, refer to the document CD-ROM.

www.prenhall.com/goldfield
   For study resources related to this chapter, visit the *Companion Website*™.

8 A New Republic and the Rise of Parties 1789–1800

CHAPTER HIGHLIGHTS

Washington's America According to the national census, there were 4 million Americans in 1790. New Englanders abolished slavery in the 1780s. In many respects, their political culture remained rooted in their Puritan past. The Mid-Atlantic states had the nation's most diverse population, a fact that contributed to the region's political complexity. Climate and soil conditions favored the expansion of slavery and plantation agriculture. Rapid population growth in the West created new political challenges.

Forging a New Government Led by Madison, the first Congress since the Constitutional Congress submitted twelve amendments to the Constitution to the states, ten of which were ratified and became known as the Bill of Rights. Congress also tackled the workings of the cabinet and the court system.

The Emergence of Parties By the end of Washington's first term, two parties had formed: the Federalists and the Republicans. Control of the West remained an elusive goal during the Washington administration. In the nation's first partisan election, Adams was elected over Jefferson in 1796.

The Last Federalist Administration The Adams administration got off to a rocky start from which it never recovered. Despite his many flaws, Adams prevented a war with France and civil war at home. The election of 1800 resulted in the election of Jefferson and marked the end of the Federalist party.

WASHINGTON'S TRIUMPHAL ENTRY INTO NEW YORK IN 1783.

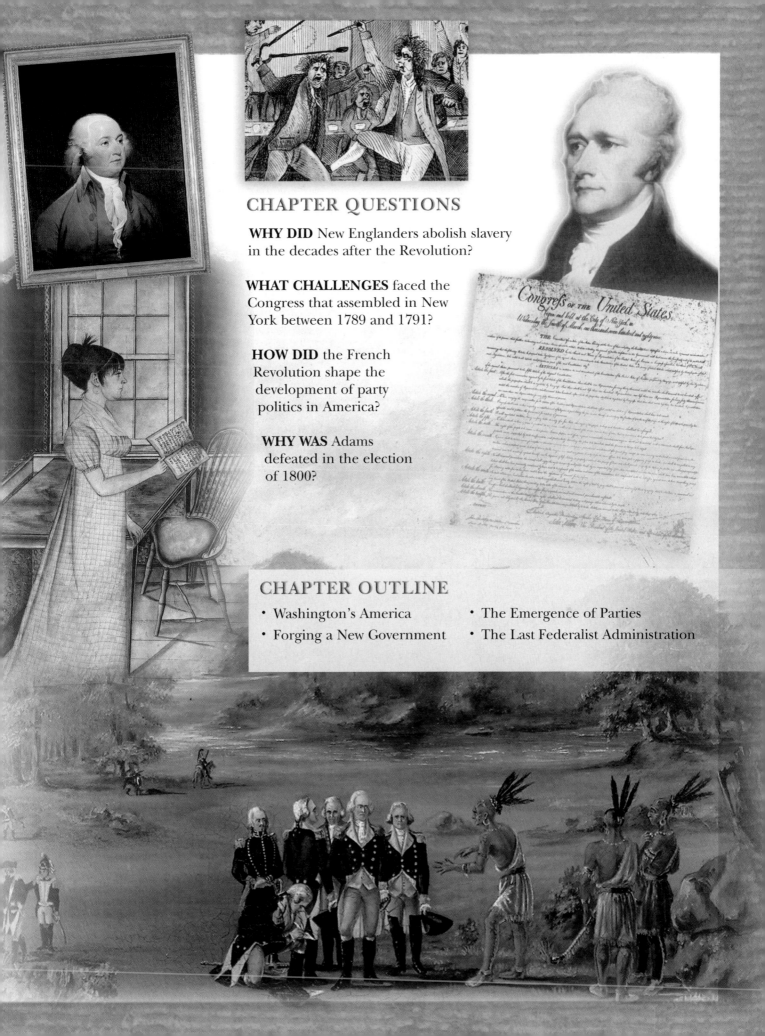

CHAPTER QUESTIONS

WHY DID New Englanders abolish slavery in the decades after the Revolution?

WHAT CHALLENGES faced the Congress that assembled in New York between 1789 and 1791?

HOW DID the French Revolution shape the development of party politics in America?

WHY WAS Adams defeated in the election of 1800?

CHAPTER OUTLINE

- Washington's America
- Forging a New Government
- The Emergence of Parties
- The Last Federalist Administration

IMAGE KEY
for pages 208–209 is on page 233.

April 30, 1789

New York City

    This is the great important day. Goddess of Etiquette assist me while I describe it. . . . The President was conducted out of the middle window into the Gallery [of Federal Hall] and the Oath administered by the Chancellor [Robert R. Livingston, Chancellor of New York]. Notice that the Business was done, was communicated to the Croud by Proclamation . . . who gave three Cheers. . . . As the Company returned into the Senate Chamber, the president took the Chair, and the Senate and representatives their Seats. He rose & all arose also and [he] addressed them [in his inaugural address]. This great Man was agitated and embarrassed more than ever he was by the levelled Cannon or pointed Musket. He trembled and several times could scarce make out to read, tho it must be supposed he had often read it before. He put part of the fingers of his left hand, into the side, of what I think the Taylors call the fall, of his Breetches. Changing the paper into his left hand, after some time, he then did the same with some of the fingers of his right hand. When he came to the Words all the World, *he made a flourish with his right hand, which left rather an ungainly impression. . . . He was dressed in deep brown, with Metal buttons, with an Eagle on them, White Stockings a Bag and Sword— from the Hall there was a grand Procession to St. Pauls Church where prayers were said by the Bishop. The Procession was well conducted and without accident, as far as I have heard. The Militias were all under Arms. [They] lined the Street near the Church, made a good figure and behaved well. The Senate returned to their Chamber after Service, formed & took up the Address. . . . In the Evening there were grand fire Works . . . and after this the People went to bed.*

                                      [William Maclay]

Kenneth R. Bowling and Helen E. Veit, eds., *The Diary of William Maclay and Other Notes on Senate Debates,* March 4, 1789–March 3, 1791 (Baltimore: Johns Hopkins University Press, 1988), pp. 11–13.

SENATOR WILLIAM MACLAY of Pennsylvania wrote this account in his personal journal of the inauguration of George Washington as the first president of the United States at Federal Hall in New York City on April 30, 1789. Born in Pennsylvania in 1737 of Scotch-Irish parents, Maclay held a number of popularly elected offices in the 1780s before his selection by the Pennsylvania legislature in September 1788 as one of the state's first two U.S. senators. He quickly broke with the Washington administration over its fiscal and diplomatic policies. Before his death in 1804, he switched his political allegiance to the opposition party led by Thomas Jefferson.

    Washington's shakiness at his inaugural, which so obviously pained Maclay, reflected the shaky start of the country's new government. Two states, North Carolina and Rhode Island, had not yet ratified the Constitution. The newly elected members of Congress felt no urgency to assume their duties. They had been scheduled to meet in New York on March 4, 1789, to count the ballots of the Electoral College and officially confirm Washington's election, but only one-quarter of them arrived by then. Washington, his dignity ruffled by this show of congressional disinterest, dallied at Mount Vernon until formally notified of his election.

He had every reason to dread taking on the burden of the presidency. As head of the new national government, he would put at risk the legendary status he had achieved during the Revolution. Most Americans intensely feared centralized authority, which is why the framers deliberately left the word *national* out of the Constitution. Washington somehow had to establish loyalty to a new government whose main virtue in the eyes of many was the very vagueness of its defined powers.

The Constitution had created the framework for a national government, but pressing problems demanded the fleshing out of that framework. The government urgently needed revenue to begin paying off the immense debt incurred during the Revolution. It also had to address the unstable conditions in the West. Ultimately, the key to solving these and other problems was to establish the new republic's legitimacy.

The realities of governing would soon shatter the nonpartisan ideal that had prevailed when the Constitution was ratified. By the end of Washington's first term, two political parties had begun to form. The Federalist party, which included Washington and his successor, John Adams, favored a strong central government. The opposition party, the Jeffersonian Republicans, took shape as a result of differences over financial policy and the American response to the French Revolution. Led by Thomas Jefferson, the Republicans were distrustful of excessive central power.

The Federalists, who governed through 1800, succeeded in showing a doubting world ruled by kings and queens that the American experiment in republican government could work. But as inheritors of a political tradition that equated parties with factions the Federalists doubted the loyalty of the Republicans. When the Federalists under President John Adams attempted to suppress the Republicans, the stage was set for the critical election of 1800. Jefferson's victory in that election ended both Federalist rule and the republic's first major internal crisis.

Idealized classical images of women— white, chaste, and pure—were popular emblems in the early republic to portray national ideals of liberty and republican motherhood.

Library of Congress

WASHINGTON'S AMERICA

*I*n 1789, as now, Americans identified and grouped themselves according to many factors, including race, sex, class, ethnicity, religion, and degree of personal freedom. Geographical factors, including climate and access to markets, further divided them into regions and sections. The resulting hodgepodge sorely tested the assumption that a single national government could govern Americans as a whole (see Figure 8–1).

WHY DID New Englanders abolish slavery in the decades after the Revolution?

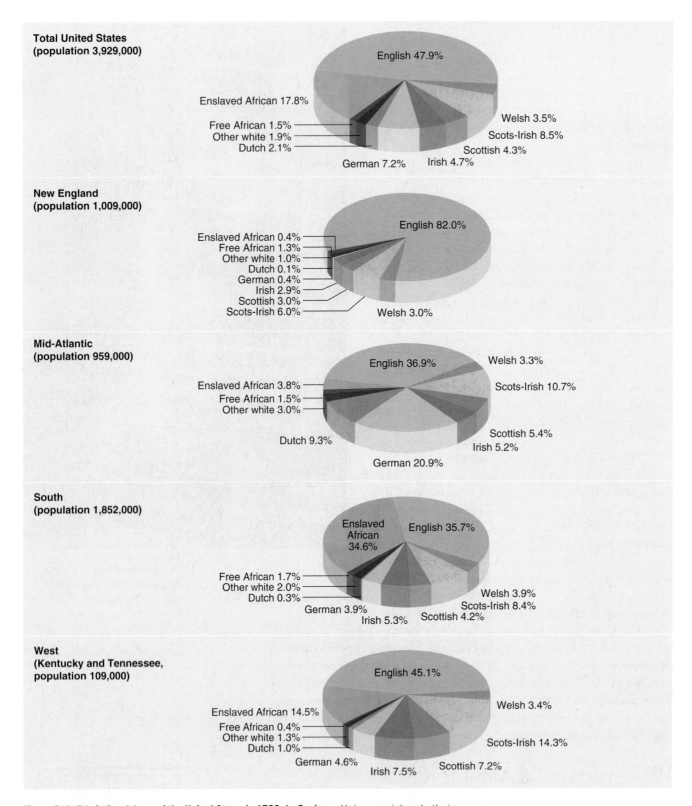

Total United States
(population 3,929,000)

English 47.9%
Enslaved African 17.8%
Free African 1.5%
Other white 1.9%
Dutch 2.1%
German 7.2%
Irish 4.7%
Scottish 4.3%
Scots-Irish 8.5%
Welsh 3.5%

New England
(population 1,009,000)

English 82.0%
Enslaved African 0.4%
Free African 1.3%
Other white 1.0%
Dutch 0.1%
German 0.4%
Irish 2.9%
Scottish 3.0%
Scots-Irish 6.0%
Welsh 3.0%

Mid-Atlantic
(population 959,000)

English 36.9%
Welsh 3.3%
Scots-Irish 10.7%
Enslaved African 3.8%
Free African 1.5%
Other white 3.0%
Scottish 5.4%
Irish 5.2%
Dutch 9.3%
German 20.9%

South
(population 1,852,000)

Enslaved African 34.6%
English 35.7%
Free African 1.7%
Other white 2.0%
Dutch 0.3%
German 3.9%
Irish 5.3%
Scottish 4.2%
Scots-Irish 8.4%
Welsh 3.9%

West
(Kentucky and Tennessee,
population 109,000)

English 45.1%
Welsh 3.4%
Enslaved African 14.5%
Free African 0.4%
Other white 1.3%
Dutch 1.0%
Scots-Irish 14.3%
German 4.6%
Irish 7.5%
Scottish 7.2%

Figure 8–1 Ethnic Breakdown of the United States in 1790, by Region   Unique racial and ethnic patterns shaped each of the nation's four major regions in 1790. New England was most atypical in its lack of racial or ethnic diversity.

Source: *The Statistics of the Population of the United States,* comp. Francis A. Walker (1872), p. 3–7; Thomas L. Purvis, "The European Ancestry of the United States Population, 1790," *William and Mary Quarterly,* 41 (1984), p. 98.

THE UNIFORMITY OF NEW ENGLAND

The national census of 1790 counted nearly 4 million Americans, one in four of whom lived in New England. New England was rather atypical. It alone of the nation's formative regions had largely shut itself off from outsiders. The Puritan notions of religious liberty that prevailed in the region extended only to those who subscribed to the Calvinist orthodoxy of the dominant Congregationalist Church. Geography conspired with this religious exclusiveness to limit population diversity. New England's poor soils and long, cold winters made it an impractical place to cultivate cash crops like the tobacco and rice of the South. As a result, New England farmers had little need of imported white indentured servants or black slaves.

Puritan values and a harsh environment thus combined to make New England the most religiously and ethnically uniform region in the United States. Most of the people living there were descended from English immigrants who had arrived in the seventeenth century. Congregationalism remained the official, state-supported religion in Connecticut and Massachusetts. Blacks and Indians together barely constituted 3 percent of New England's population. The few remaining Indians lived on reservations of inferior land, which they usually left only to find work as servants or day laborers.

New Englanders found slavery incompatible with the natural-rights philosophy that had emerged during the Revolution and gradually began to abolish it in the 1780s. Slavery had, in any case, always been marginal in New England's economy. Owning slaves as domestic servants or artisans had been a status symbol

QUICK REVIEW

New Englanders

- Most of population were descendants of seventeenth-century English immigrants.
- Congregationalism deemed official religion in Connecticut and Massachusetts.
- Women outnumbered men in some parts of the region.
- Slavery abolished in 1780s.

Chronology

1789	Inauguration of Washington.
	Congress establishes the first federal departments.
	French Revolution begins.
1790	Hamilton submits the first of his financial reports to Congress.
1791	Bill of Rights ratified.
	Congress charters the Bank of the United States.
	Slave revolt breaks out in Saint-Domingue (Haiti).
1792	St. Clair's defeat along the Wabash.
	Reelection of Washington.
	Austria and Prussia invade France.
	Execution of King Louis XVI.
1793	France goes to war against Britain, Spain, and Holland.
	Genêt Mission.
	Washington issues Proclamation of Neutrality.
1794	Ohio is opened with the victory of General Anthony Wayne at the Battle of Fallen Timbers.
	Suppression of the Whiskey Rebellion in western Pennsylvania.
1795	Jay's Treaty with Britain ratified.
	Treaty of Greenville with Ohio Indians.
1796	Pinckney's Treaty with Spain ratified.
	Washington's Farewell Address.
	John Adams elected president.
1797	Beginning of the Quasi-War with France.
1798	XYZ Affair.
	Alien and Sedition Acts.
	Provisional army and direct tax.
	Virginia and Kentucky Resolutions.
1799	Fries's Rebellion in Pennsylvania.
	Napoleon assumes power in France.
1800	Franco-American Accord.
	Thomas Jefferson elected president.

This painting of a young woman reading—"General Schumacker's Daughter," by Jacob Maentel—reflects women's increasing access to education in the early years of the nation. Nearly four hundred female academies and seminaries were established between 1790 and 1830.

Jacob Maentel (American, 1778–1863). "General Schumacker's Daughter," c. 1812, pen and watercolor, sight size: 365 × 240 (14⁷⁄₁₆ × 9½). © Board of Trustees, National Gallery of Art, Washington. Gift of Edgar William and Bernice Chrysler Garbisch

for wealthy urban whites in Boston, Portsmouth, and Newport. As a result, about 20 percent of New England's small African-American population lived in cities, where jobs were relatively easy to find.

Women outnumbered men in parts of New England in 1789. This pattern was the result of the pressure of an expanding population and the practice of dividing family farms among male heirs. As farms in the older, more densely settled parts of New England were divided into ever-smaller lots, many young men migrated west in search of cheap, arable land. Thus by 1789, women formed a slight majority in Connecticut, Massachusetts, and Rhode Island.

Despite their superior numbers, women in New England, as elsewhere, remained subordinate to men. Even so, the general testing of traditional authority that accompanied the Revolution led some New England women to question male power. The Massachusetts poet Judith Sargeant Murray, for example, published essays asserting that women were the intellectual equals of men. Murray was the first woman to argue publicly in favor of equal educational opportunities for young women, and she boldly asserted that women should learn how to become economically independent. Republican ideology, emphasizing the need for women to be intellectually prepared to raise virtuous, public-spirited children, led reformers in New England to seek equal access for women to education. In 1789, Massachusetts became the first state to allocate funds specifically for girls' elementary education. And beginning in the 1780s, wealthy residents of eastern cities set up private academies for women that would later provide the foundation for women's higher education. Liberalized divorce laws in New England also allowed a woman to seek legal separation from an abusive or unfaithful spouse.

In other respects, political and social life in New England remained rooted in the Puritan past. Age, property, and reputation determined one's standing in a culture that valued a clearly defined social order. The moral code that governed town life promoted curbs on individual behavior for the benefit of the community as a whole. With their notions of collective liberty, New Englanders subscribed to a version of republicanism that favored strong government, setting themselves apart from most other Americans, who embraced a more individualistic idea of liberty and a suspicion of government power. New Englanders perceived government as a divine institution with a moral responsibility to intervene in people's lives. Acting through town meetings, they taxed themselves for public services at rates two to four times higher than in the rest of the country. Their courts were also far more likely than those elsewhere to punish individuals for crimes against public order and sexual misconduct.

THE PLURALISM OF THE MID-ATLANTIC REGION

The states of the mid-Atlantic region—New York, New Jersey, and Pennsylvania—were the most ethnically and religiously diverse in the nation. People of English descent constituted somewhat less than 40 percent of the population. Other major ethnic groups included the Dutch and Scots-Irish in New York and Germans and

Scots-Irish in New Jersey and Pennsylvania. With ethnic diversity came religious diversity. Among others of English descent, Anglicans predominated in New York, and Quakers in New Jersey and Pennsylvania. The Dutch, concentrated in the lower Hudson Valley, had their own Dutch Reformed Church, and most Germans were either Lutherans or pietists, such as the Mennonites and the Moravians, who stressed personal piety over theological doctrine. The Presbyterian Scots-Irish settled heavily in the backcountry.

This mosaic-like pattern of ethnic and religious groupings was no accident. In contrast to Puritan New England, the Middle Colonies had offered freedom of worship to attract settlers. In addition, economic opportunities for newcomers were much greater than in New England. The region produced surpluses of wheat, flour, and corn that were shipped out of New York and Philadelphia, the two largest cities in North America by 1790. Commercial agriculture fed urban growth and created a greater demand for labor in both rural and urban areas than in New England. The influx of Germans and Scots-Irish into the region in the eighteenth century occurred in response to this demand.

The demand for labor had also been met by importing African slaves. Blacks, both free and enslaved, made up 5 percent of the mid-Atlantic population in 1790, and, as in New England, they were more likely than whites to live in the maritime cities. New York had more slaveholders in 1790 than any other American city except Charleston, South Carolina. About 40 percent of the white families in the city's nearby rural outposts of Queens County, Brooklyn, and Staten Island owned slaves, a rate as high as in Maryland and South Carolina.

Despite its considerable strength in the port cities and adjacent rural areas, slavery was never an economically vital institution in most of the mid-Atlantic region. Commercial agriculture did not rest on a slave base, nor did it produce a politically powerful class of planters. As a result, slavery in the mid-Atlantic region gave way to the demands for emancipation inspired by the natural-rights philosophy of the Revolution.

Pennsylvania in 1780, New York in 1799, and New Jersey in 1804 all passed laws of gradual emancipation. These laws did not free adult slaves but provided that children born of a slave mother were to be freed at ages ranging between 18 and 28. Soon after the laws were passed, however, adult slaves began hastening their own freedom. They ran away, set fires, and pressured their owners to accept cash payments in return for a short, fixed term of labor service. But even as they gained their freedom, African Americans had to confront enduring white racism. The comments of one white New Yorker suggest what they were up against. "We may sincerely advocate the freedom of black men," he wrote, "and yet assert their moral and physical inferiority."

The diversity of the mid-Atlantic region created a complex political environment. Competing cultural and economic interests prevented the kind of broad consensus on the meaning of republicanism that had emerged in New England. Some mid-Atlantic groups favored a strong central government to foster economic development and maintain traditional authority. Others wanted to keep government weak to foster a republican equality that would promote individual freedom.

Those who supported strong government included mercantile and financial leaders in the cities and commercial farmers in the countryside. These people tended to be Anglicans, Quakers, and Congregationalists of English descent. Those opposing them and favoring a more egalitarian republicanism tended to come from the middle and lower classes. They included subsistence farmers in the backcountry and artisans and day laborers in the cities. Fiercely independent and proud of their liberties, they resented the claims of the wealthy to political authority. They resisted government aid to business as a form of political corruption that unfairly enriched those who were already economically powerful.

THE SLAVE SOUTH AND ITS BACKCOUNTRY

In the South—the region from Maryland and Delaware to Georgia—climate and soil conditions favored the production of cash staples for world markets, crops that required backbreaking labor that white immigrants preferred to avoid. Southern planters relied on the coerced labor of African slaves, whose numbers made the South the most populous region in the country.

Just under 40 percent of all southerners were slaves, but their concentration varied within the region. They were a majority in the Chesapeake Tidewater region, where slave ownership was widely distributed among white tobacco planters. Farther south, in the tidal swamps of the South Carolina and Georgia lowcountry, where draining and clearing the land required huge inputs of labor, blacks outnumbered whites five to one. In the lowcountry large planters, the richest men in the country, worked hundreds of slaves in the production of rice, indigo, and sea-island cotton.

Slaves were less numerous in the Piedmont, or foothills, region of the South that lies between the coastal plain and the Appalachian highlands. This was predominantly an area of nonslaveholding farmers. They relied on family labor to raise livestock, corn, and wheat. In the southern mountains, sloping to the southwest from the Blue Ridge in Virginia, the general absence of marketable crops diminished the demand for slave labor.

The free black population in the South had grown rapidly during the 1780s. Thousands of slaves fled behind British lines to win their freedom, and patriots freed others as a reward for enlisting in their forces. The Revolutionary values of liberty and equality also led many slave owners to question the morality of slavery. Legislatures in the Upper South passed laws making it financially easier than before for masters to manumit (free) their slaves. Slavery remained the foundation of the southern economy, however, and whites feared competition from freed blacks. As a result, no southern state embarked on a general program of emancipation, and slavery in the region survived the turbulence of the Revolutionary era.

Economic conditions in the South, where the raw poverty of the backcountry offset the great wealth of the lowcountry, stamped the region's politics and culture. Tidewater planters were predominantly Anglican and of English descent. Piedmont farmers were more likely to be Scots-Irish Presbyterians and Baptists. More evangelical in their religion, and with simpler habits and tastes, the backcountry Baptists denounced the lowcountry planters for their luxury and arrogance. The planters retaliated by trying unsuccessfully to suppress the backcountry evangelicals.

7–6
An African American Calls for an End to Slavery (1791)

The planters were indeed proud, domineering, and given to ostentatious displays of wealth. Planters understood liberty to mean the power of white males, unchecked by any outside authority, to rule over others. The only acknowledged check on this power was the planter's sense of duty, his obligation to adhere to an idealized code of conduct befitting a gentleman and a man of honor.

Backcountry farmers also jealously guarded their liberties. "They are," noted a late-eighteenth-century traveler, "extremely tenacious of the rights and liberties of republicanism. They consider themselves on an equal footing with the best educated people of the country, and upon the principles of equality they intrude themselves into every company." Backcountry farmers shared with the planters a disdain for government and restraints on the individual. But they opposed the planters' belief in a social hierarchy based on wealth and birth that left both poor whites and black slaves in a subordinate position.

THE GROWING WEST

Between the Appalachian Mountains and the Mississippi River stretched the most rapidly growing region of the new nation, the West. Land-hungry settlers poured across the mountains once the British recognized the American claim to the region in the Treaty of Paris. During the 1780s, the white population of the West exploded from less than 10,000 to 200,000. The region's Native American population was about 150,000.

Indians strongly resisted white claims on their lands. A confederation of tribes in the Ohio Valley, led by the Miamis and supplied with firearms by the British in exchange for furs, kept whites out of the Old Northwest territory, the area north of the Ohio River. South of the Ohio, white settlements were largely limited to Kentucky and Tennessee. In what is today Alabama and Mississippi, the Creeks and their allies blocked American expansion.

Most white migrants in Kentucky and Tennessee were the young rural poor from the seaboard slave states. The West offered them the opportunity to claim their own farms and gain economic independence, free from the dominance of planters and the economic competition of slave labor. But planters also saw the West as a land of opportunity. Many planters' sons migrated to the West with a share of the family's slaves to become planters in their own right. This process laid the foundation for the extension of slavery into new regions. As early as 1790, slaves made up more than 10 percent of the population of Tennessee and Kentucky.

Life in the western settlements was harsh and often cruel. Mortality was high, especially among infants. Travelers from the East described settlers living in crudely built log cabins with squalid, filthy interiors infested with fleas and lice. Easterners also found an appallingly casual acceptance of violence.

Isolation and uncertainty haunted frontier life. The Appalachians posed a formidable barrier to social and economic intercourse with the East. Few settlers had the labor resources to produce an agricultural surplus for shipment to market down the Ohio and Mississippi rivers. Most farmers lived at a semisubsistence level. Many of them, mostly Scots-Irish, did not own the land they cultivated. These squatters, as they were called, occupied the land hoping someday to obtain clear title to it.

In Kentucky, squatters, aligned with a small class of middling landowners, spearheaded the movement for political separation from Virginia that gained statehood for the territory in 1792. The settlers wanted to break the control that Tidewater planters had gained over most of the land and lucrative government offices in Kentucky. In their minds, planters, officeholders, land speculators, and gentlemen of leisure were all part of an aristocracy tied to the distant government in Richmond and intent on robbing them of their liberty.

Despite the movement in Kentucky for statehood, the ultimate political allegiance of the West was uncertain. Westerners wanted the freedom to control their own affairs and outlets for their crops. Apparently, they were willing to strike a deal with any outside power offering to meet these needs. The British, contrary to the terms of the Treaty of Paris, had not abandoned their military posts in the

QUICK REVIEW

Westerners

- White population of West 200,000 by end of 1780s.
- Relationship between whites and Indians tense and sometimes violent.
- Most white migrants to Kentucky and Tennessee were young, rural poor from seaboard slave states.

Old Northwest. Using their military position and close ties with the Indians as leverage, the British encouraged separatist movements north of the Ohio River.

Spain posed a more serious threat. It asserted that most of the area south of the Ohio and east of the Mississippi was Spanish territory. Most important, Spain controlled New Orleans and thus the main outlet on the Mississippi River for western produce. Washington had warned in 1784 that the political loyalties of the West wavered "on a pivot," and the future of the region loomed as a major test for his administration.

FORGING A NEW GOVERNMENT

The Congress that assembled in New York (the temporary capital) from 1789 to 1791 faced a daunting challenge, it had to give form and substance to the framework of the new national government outlined in the Constitution. Executive departments had to be established, a federal judiciary organized, sources of revenue found, terms of international trade and foreign policy worked out, and the commitment to add a bill of rights to the Constitution honored.

Staunch supporters of the new government had easily carried the first national elections in 1788 and enjoyed large majorities in both houses of Congress. These people brought superb administrative talents to the task of governing. Many, however, were clumsy politicians and unsympathetic to the egalitarian sensibilities of the electorate. By 1792, they faced growing political opposition.

"MR. PRESIDENT" AND THE BILL OF RIGHTS

The first problem for Washington and Congress was to decide just how the chief executive of the new republic should be addressed. In a debate that tied up Congress for a month, the more democratically inclined members of the House argued that "His Highness," the title Vice President John Adams and many in the Senate preferred, smacked of a longing for monarchical rule. Adams and the others grudgingly agreed to accept "Mr. President."

Whatever his title, Washington was intent on surrounding the presidency with an aura of respectability. He set down strict rules for his interactions with the public and at all times he carried himself with stern reserve. After a dinner with the president, one senator remarked that "as usual the company was as grave as at a funeral."

Meanwhile Congress got down to business. James Madison, now a representative from Virginia, early emerged as the most forceful leader in the House. He pushed for speedy action on the bill of rights. To allay the fears of Antifederalists that the Constitution granted too much power to the national government, the Federalists had promised to consider amendments that protected both individual rights and liberties and the rights of states. But Madison astutely kept the focus of the amendments on personal liberties. He submitted 19 amendments, and Congress soon settled on 12. Ten of these, known collectively as the **Bill of Rights,** were ratified by the states and became part of the Constitution as of December 15, 1791.

The Bill of Rights is one of the most enduring legacies of the first Congress. Most of the first eight amendments are concerned with individual rights. They guarantee religious freedom, freedom of expression, and the safeguarding of individuals and their property against arbitrary legal proceedings. Only three amendments speak of state interests. Citing the necessity of a "well regulated Militia" for

WHAT CHALLENGES faced the Congress that assembled in New York between 1789 and 1791?

WHERE TO LEARN MORE

Federal Hall National Memorial, New York, New York
www.nps.gov/feha/

7–5
Opposing Visions for the New Nation (1791)

Bill of Rights A written summary of inalienable rights and liberties.

"the security of a free State," the Second Amendment guarantees "the right of the people to keep and bear Arms." This assured the states that they could rely on their militias for protection against federal tyranny. The Ninth and Tenth Amendments stipulate that the powers not granted to the national government in the Constitution are retained by the people and the states.

The Bill of Rights broadened the government's base of popular support. Once Congress submitted the amendments to the states for ratification, North Carolina (1789) and Rhode Island (1790) overcame their lingering objections and joined the Union. The Bill of Rights also assured Americans that the central government would not try to impose a uniform national culture.

DEPARTMENTS AND COURTS

In the summer of 1789, Congress authorized the first executive departments: the State Department for foreign affairs, the Treasury for finances, and the War Department for the nation's defense. The only debate about them concerned the extent of presidential control over the officials who would head them. The Constitution gave the president the right to nominate public officials but required the consent of the Senate to confirm their appointments. The Constitution was silent, however, on whether the president could dismiss an official without the Senate's consent. Congress decided that the president could do so, setting an important precedent that bolstered presidential power. Department heads would now be closely bound to the president. As a group, they would evolve into the cabinet, the president's chief advisory body.

Greater controversy attended the creation of the federal judiciary. The Constitution called for "one Supreme Court" but left it up to Congress to authorize lower federal courts. The framers were deliberately vague about the federal judiciary, because Antifederalists and proponents of states' rights feared that national courts would be far removed from the people and would act as engines of oppression.

The **Judiciary Act of 1789** represented an artful compromise. It created a hierarchical national judiciary based on 13 federal district courts, one for each state. Appeals from these courts were to be heard in one of three circuit courts, and the Supreme Court was to have the final say in contested cases. In a major concession to the Antifederalists, however, the act limited jurisdiction in federal courts to legal issues stemming from the Constitution and the laws and treaties of the national government. The distinctive legal systems and customs of the states remained intact. State courts would continue to hear and rule on the vast majority of civil and criminal cases.

REVENUE AND TRADE

Aware that Congress under the Articles of Confederation had been crippled by its inability to secure a reliable source of income, Madison acted to put the finances of the new federal government on a firm footing. Nearly everyone agreed that the government's chief source of income should be a tariff on imported goods and tonnage duties (fees based on cargo capacity) on ships entering American ports.

The **Tariff Act of 1789** was designed primarily to raise revenue, not to protect American manufacturers by keeping out foreign goods with high duties. It levied a duty of 5 percent on most imported goods but imposed tariffs as high as 50 percent on a limited number of items, such as steel, salt, cloth, and tobacco. The debate on the Tariff Act provoked some sectional sparring. Manufacturers, who were concentrated in the North, wanted high tariffs for protection against

Judiciary Act of 1789   Act of Congress that implemented the judiciary clause of the Constitution by establishing the Supreme Court and a system of lower federal courts.

Tariff Act of 1789   Apart from a few selected industries, this first tariff passed by Congress was intended to raise revenue and not protect American manufactures from foreign competition.

W WHERE TO LEARN MORE

Hamilton Grange National
Memorial, New York, New York
www.nps/gov/hagr/

QUICK REVIEW

Madison's Fiscal Policies

- Hoped to use tonnage duties to raise revenue.
- Tariffs also meant to punish countries that had not signed commercial deals with the United States.
- Madison's proposals defeated by a coalition of Congressional opponents.

Tonnage Act of 1789 Duty levied on the tonnage of incoming ships to U.S. ports; tax was higher on foreign-owned ships to favor American shippers.

foreign competition. In contrast, farmers and southern planters wanted low tariffs to keep down the cost of the manufactured goods they purchased.

Madison originally hoped to use tonnage duties not only to raise revenue but also to strike at foreign nations like Britain that had not signed a commercial treaty with the United States. Since the Revolution, Britain had kept its trading empire closed to American merchants while at the same time exploiting the United States as a market for its manufactured goods. In contrast, France, America's ally during the Revolution, had a commercial treaty with the United States that recognized the American position on equal trading relations and the rights of neutral shippers during war.

Madison wanted to punish the British with a duty of 60 cents per ton on British ships entering American ports, twice the proposed duty on French ships. He hoped to dislodge the British from their dominant position in American markets and to open up overseas trade for American and French shippers.

Madison's duties failed to pass Congress, defeated by an unlikely coalition of sectional interests. Southerners voted against them because they feared their result would be to give New England merchants a monopoly on the carrying trade and raise the cost of shipping tobacco to Europe. But northern merchants, presumably the beneficiaries of the duties, also opposed them. They were leery of disrupting their profitable trade with Britain, especially with the economic slump of the 1780s abating. The **Tonnage Act of 1789,** as finally passed, treated all foreign ships equally.

HAMILTON AND THE PUBLIC CREDIT

The Treasury was the largest and most important new department. To its head, Alexander Hamilton of New York, fell the task of bringing order to the nation's ramshackle finances. The basic problem was the huge debt left over from the Revolution. With interest going unpaid, the debt was growing, and by 1789, it had reached $52 million. In addition, state governments had debts totaling close to $25 million. Until the government set up and honored a regular schedule for paying interest, the nation's public credit would be worthless. Unable to borrow, the government would collapse.

Hamilton was ambitious, egotistical, and overbearing. But he also had a brilliant financial mind and a sweeping vision of national greatness. He was convinced that the economic self-interests of the wealthy and well-born offered the only sound foundation for the success of the new government.

At the request of Congress, Hamilton prepared a series of reports on the nation's finances and economic condition. In the first, issued in January 1790, Hamilton proposed a bold plan to address the Revolutionary War debt. The federal government, he maintained, should fund the national debt at full face value. To do this, he proposed exchanging the old debt, including accrued interest, for new government bonds bearing interest at about 4 percent. In addition, Hamilton maintained that the federal government should assume the remaining war debt of the state governments. The intent of this plan was to give the nation's creditors an economic stake in the stability of the new nation and to subordinate state financial interests to those of the central government.

In his second report, issued in December 1790, Hamilton called for an excise tax (a tax on the production, sale, or consumption of a commodity) on distilled whiskey produced within the United States. The purpose of the tax was to raise additional revenue for interest payments on the national debt and establish the government's authority to levy internal taxes on its citizens.

The third report recommended the chartering of a national bank, the Bank of the United States. Hamilton patterned his proposed bank after the Bank of England and intended it to meet a variety of needs. Jointly owned by the federal government and private investors, it would serve as the fiscal (financial) and depository agent of the government and make loans to businesses. Through a provision that permitted up to three-fourths of the value of bank stock to be purchased with government bonds, the bank would create a market for public securities and hence raise their value. Most important, the bank would provide the nation with a stable currency.

Hamilton's final report, issued in December 1791, recommended government actions to promote industry. Looking, as always, to the British model of economic development, he argued that the United States would never become a great power as long as the nation imported most of its manufactured goods. Hamilton advocated aid to American manufacturers in the form of protective tariffs (high tariffs meant to make imported goods more expensive than domestic goods) for such industries as iron, steel, and shoemaking—which had already begun to establish themselves—and direct subsidies to assist with start-up costs for other industries. Hamilton believed that such "patronage," as he called it, would ultimately foster interregional economic dependence. Thus, in Hamilton's vision, manufacturing, like a national currency, would be a great national unifier.

REACTION AND OPPOSITION

The breadth and boldness of Hamilton's program invited opposition. About half the members of Congress owned some of the nation's debt, and nearly all of them agreed with Hamilton that it should be paid off. Some opponents, however, were concerned that Hamilton's plan was unfair. Hard times had forced most of the original holders of the debt—by and large, ordinary citizens—to sell their certificates to speculators at a fraction of their face value.

Others objected, on republican grounds, that Hamilton had no intention of actually eliminating the government's debt. He envisioned instead a permanent debt, with the government making regular interest payments as they came due. The debt, in the form of government securities, would serve as a vital prop for the support of moneyed groups.

Opposition to Hamilton's proposal to have the federal government assume state debts reflected sectional differences. With the exception of South Carolina, the southern states had already paid back a good share of their war debts. Thus Hamilton's plan stood to benefit the northern states disproportionately. Because Hamilton had linked the funding of the national debt with the assumption of state debts, southern opposition threatened funding as well. Tensions mounted as the deadlock continued into the summer of 1790.

Tempers cooled when a compromise was reached in July. Southerners agreed to accept funding in its original form. Assumption passed after Hamilton cut a deal with Virginians James Madison and Thomas Jefferson. In exchange for southern support of assumption, Hamilton agreed to line up northern votes for locating the nation's permanent capital on the banks of the Potomac River, where it would be surrounded by the slave states of Maryland and Virginia.

Hamilton's alliance with Madison and Jefferson proved short-lived, dissolving when Madison led the congressional opposition to Hamilton's proposed bank. Madison and most other southerners viewed the bank as evidence of a willingness to sacrifice the interests of the agrarian South in favor of the financial and industrial interests of the North. They argued that the Constitution did not explicitly authorize Congress to charter a bank or any other corporation.

QUICK REVIEW

Hamilton's Reports
- Plan to address Revolutionary War debt.
- Call for an excise tax on distilled whiskey.
- Proposal to charter a national bank.
- Recommendation for government to promote industry.

The bank bill passed Congress on a vote that divided along sectional lines. Madison's objections, however, left Washington concerned that the bank might not be constitutional. He sought the cabinet's opinion, provoking the first great debate over how the Constitution should be interpreted. Thomas Jefferson, the secretary of state, sided with Madison and for the first time openly clashed with Hamilton. Taking a strict-constructionist position, he argued that all powers the Constitution had not expressly delegated to the national government were reserved to the states under the Tenth Amendment. Hamilton, in a brilliant rejoinder, argued that Article 1, Section 8, of the Constitution, which declares that Congress has the right "to make all laws which shall be necessary and proper" to exercise its powers and those of the federal government, gives Congress implicit authority beyond its explicitly enumerated powers. With this broad-constructionist position, he won Washington to his side.

With Washington's signature on the bill, Hamilton's bank was chartered for 20 years. Congress also passed a hefty 25 percent excise tax on distilled liquor. Little, however, of Hamilton's plan to promote manufacturing survived.

THE EMERGENCE OF PARTIES

HOW DID the French Revolution shape the development of party politics in America?

By the end of Washington's first term, Americans were dividing into two camps. On one side stood those who still called themselves **Federalists.** These were the supporters of Hamilton's program—speculators, creditors, merchants, manufacturers, and commercial farmers. They were the Americans most fully integrated into the market economy and in control of it. In both economic and cultural terms, the Federalists were drawn from the more privileged segments of society. Jefferson and Madison shrewdly gave the name **Republican** to the party that formed in opposition to the Federalists, thus identifying it with individual liberties and the heritage of the Revolution. The Republicans accused Hamilton and the Federalists of attempting to impose a British system of economic privilege and social exploitation. The initial core of the party consisted of southern planters and backcountry Scots-Irish farmers, Americans outside the market economy or skeptical of its benefits. The Republicans were committed to an agrarian America in which power remained in the hands of farmers and planters.

In 1792, parties were still in a formative stage. The political divisions that had appeared first in Congress and then spread to Washington's cabinet did not yet extend very deeply into the electorate. However, a series of crises in Washington's second term deepened and broadened the incipient party divisions. By 1796, rival parties were contesting the presidency and vying for the support of an increasingly politically organized electorate.

THE FRENCH REVOLUTION

The French Revolution began in 1789, and in its early phase, most Americans applauded it. France had been an ally of the United States during the Revolutionary War and now seemed to be following the example of its American friends in shaking off monarchical rule. By 1792, however, the French Revolution had turned violent and radical. Its supporters confiscated the property of aristocrats and the church, slaughtered suspected enemies, and executed the king, Louis XVI. In early 1793, republican France was at war with Britain and the European powers.

The excesses of the French Revolution and the European war that erupted in its wake touched off a bitter debate in America. Federalists drew back in hor-

Federalists Supporters of Hamilton's program; they were American's most fully integrated into the market economy—and in control of it.

Republican (Jeffersonian) party Party headed by Thomas Jefferson that formed in opposition to the financial and diplomatic policies of the Federalist party; favored limiting the powers of the national government and placing the interests of farmers over those of financial and commercial groups.

OVERVIEW   FEDERALIST PARTY VERSUS REPUBLICAN PARTY

Federalists	Republicans
Favored strong central government	Wanted to limit role of national government
Supported Hamilton's economic program	Opposed Hamilton's economic program
Opposed French Revolution	Generally supported French Revolution
Supported Jay's Treaty and closer ties to Britain	Opposed Jay's Treaty and favored closer ties to France
In response to threat of war with France, proposed and passed Direct Tax of 1798, Alien and Sedition Acts, and legislation to enlarge army	Opposed Alien and Sedition Acts and enlarged army as threats to individual liberties
Drew strongest support from New England; lost support in mid-Atlantic region after 1798	Drew strongest support from South and West

ror from France's new regime. They insisted that the terror unleashed by the French was far removed from the reasoned republicanism of the American Revolution. For the Republicans, however, the French remained the standard-bearers of the cause of liberty for common people everywhere.

Franco-American Relations.   When the new French ambassador, Edmond Genêt, arrived in the United States in April 1793—just as the debate in America over the French Revolution was heating up—Franco-American relations reached a turning point. The two countries were still bound to one another by the Franco-American Alliance of 1778. The alliance required the United States to assist France in the defense of its West Indian colonies and to open American ports to French privateers if France were attacked. Genêt, it soon became clear, hoped to embroil the United States in the French war against the British.

Genêt's actions forced Washington to call a special cabinet meeting. The president feared that Genêt would stampede Americans into the European war, with disastrous results for the nation's finances. Hamilton urged Washington to declare American neutrality in the European war, maintaining that the president could commit the nation to neutrality on his own authority when Congress, as was then the case, was not in session. Jefferson, although he too wanted to avoid war, opposed Hamilton on these issues. Disputing Washington's power to act on his own, Jefferson maintained that the warmaking powers of Congress reserved for it alone the right to issue a declaration of neutrality.

Washington steered a middle course. He granted Genêt a formal reception and took no action to suspend the Franco-American treaties. But he accepted Hamilton's argument on his authority to declare neutrality and issued a proclamation on April 22, 1793, stating that the United States would be "friendly and impartial toward the belligerent powers."

The Growth of Democratic-Republican Societies.   American politics became more open and aggressive in the wake of Genêt's visit. Pro-French enthusiasm lived on in a host of grass-roots political organizations known as the

WHERE TO LEARN MORE

Cincinnati Historical Society, Cincinnati, Ohio
www.cincymuseum.org/

This painting by an officer on General Wayne's staff shows Little Turtle, a Miami chief, speaking through an interpreter to General Wayne (with one hand behind his back) during the negotiations that led to the Treaty of Greenville.

Source: Painting; P & S, 1914.0001; *The Treaty of Fort Greenville, Ohio,* 1795. Artist unknown, member of Gen. Anthony Wayne's staff.

Treaty of Greenville Treaty of 1795 in which Native Americans in the Old Northwest were forced to cede most of the present state of Ohio to the United States.

Democratic-Republican societies. As their name suggests, these societies reflected a belief that democracy and republicanism were one and the same. This was a new concept in American politics. The members of the new societies argued that only democracy—meaning popular participation in politics and direct appeals by politicians to the people—could maintain the revolutionary spirit of 1776, because the people were the only true guardians of that spirit. As a letter writer to the *Newark Gazette* put it: "It must be the mechanics and farmers, or the poorer class of people (as they are generally called), that must support the freedom which they and their fathers purchased with their blood—the nobility will never do it—they will be always striving to get the reins of government into their own hands, and then they can ride the people at pleasure."

The Democratic-Republican societies attacked the Washington administration for failing to assist France, and they expressed the popular feeling that Hamilton's program favored the rich over the poor. For the first time, Washington himself was personally assailed in the press.

SECURING THE FRONTIER

Control of the West remained an elusive goal throughout Washington's first term. Indian resistance in the Northwest Territory initially prevented whites from pushing north of the Ohio River. The powerful Miami Confederacy, led by Little Turtle, routed two ill-trained American armies in 1790 and 1791. The southern frontier was quieter, but the Spanish continued to use the Creeks and Cherokees as a buffer against American penetration south of the Tennessee River.

By 1793, many western settlers felt abandoned by the national government. They believed that the government had broken a promise to protect them against Indians and foreigners. Much of the popularity of the Democratic-Republican societies in the West fed off these frustrations. Westerners also demanded free and open navigation on the Mississippi River. This, in the minds of Westerners, was their natural right. Without it, they would be forever impoverished. "If the interest of Eastern America requires that we should be kept in poverty," argued the Mingo Creek society of western Pennsylvania, "it is unreasonable from such poverty to exact contributions. The first, if we cannot emerge from, we must learn to bear, but the latter, we never can be taught to submit to."

Submission to national authority, however, was precisely what the Federalists wanted from both the Indians and the western settlers. In the summer of 1794, the Washington administration sent into the Ohio region not the usual ragtag crew of militia and unemployed city dwellers but a force built around veterans from the professional army. The commander, General Anthony Wayne, was a savvy, battle-hardened war hero.

Wayne's victory on August 4, 1794, at the Battle of Fallen Timbers, near present-day Toledo, broke the back of Indian military resistance in Ohio. In the resulting **Treaty of Greenville,** signed in August 1795, 12 tribes ceded most of the

AMERICAN VIEWS

LITTLE TURTLE DEFENDS THE MIAMI LANDS

The climax of what had become a 30-year war between Native Americans and white settlers for control of the Ohio country came in 1794 with the American victory at the Battle of Fallen Timbers. The most innovative and successful of the Indian leaders who had emerged in the conflict was the Miami war chief Mishikinakwa, or Little Turtle as he was known by whites. The following is from one of Little Turtle's speeches during the peace negotiations with the victorious Americans at Greenville, Ohio, in July, 1795.

- How would you characterize Little Turtle's stance during the negotiations and his attitude toward Wayne?
- On what basis did Little Turtle justify the land claims of the Miamis in the Ohio country? How would this differ from the way in which whites staked their claim to the land?
- How did Little Turtle explain his leadership of the Miamis, and how did this differ from white notions of leadership?
- What might account for the divisions among the Indians that were cited by Little Turtle?

General Wayne: I hope you will pay attention to what I now say to you. I wish to inform you where your younger brothers, the Miamies, live, and, also, the Pottawatamies of St. Joseph's, together with the Wabash Indians. You have pointed out to us the boundary line between the Indians and the United States, but I now take the liberty to inform you, that the line cuts off from the Indians a large portion of country, which has

been enjoyed by my forefathers time immemorial, without molestation or dispute. The prints of my ancestors' houses are every where to be seen in this portion. . . . It is well known by all my brothers present, that my forefathers kindled the first fire at Detroit; from thence, he extended his lines to the head waters of Scioto; from thence, down the Ohio, to the mouth of the Wabash, and from thence to Chicago, on Lake Michigan. . . . I have now informed you of the boundaries of the Miami nation, where the Great Spirit placed my forefathers a long time ago, and charged him not to sell or part with his lands, but to preserve them for his posterity. This charge has been handed down to me. . . . I was much surprised to find that my other brothers differed so much from me on this subject: for their conduct would lead one to suppose, that the Great Spirit, and their forefathers, had not given them the same charge that was give[n] to me, but, on the contrary, had directed them to sell their lands to any white man who wore a hat, as soon as he should ask it of them. Now, elder brother, your younger brothers, the Miamies, have pointed out to you their country, and also to our brothers present. When I hear your remarks and proposals on this subject [of Miami lands], I will be ready to give you an answer; I came with an expectation of hearing you say good things, but I have not heard what I have expected.

Source: Documents, Legislative and Executive, of the Congress of the United States, From the First Session of the First to the Third Session of the Thirteenth Congress, Inclusive: commencing March 3, 1789, and ending March 3, 1815 vol. IV (Washington: Gales and Seaton, 1832), pp. 570–571.

present state of Ohio to the U.S. government in return for an annual payment of $9,500. The Ohio country was now open to white settlement (see American Views).

THE WHISKEY REBELLION

Within a few months of Wayne's victory at Fallen Timbers, another American army was on the move. Its target was the so-called whiskey rebels of western Pennsylvania, who were openly resisting Hamilton's excise tax on whiskey. Hamilton was determined to enforce the tax and assert the supremacy of national laws. Although resistance to the tax was widespread, he singled out the Pennsylvania rebels.

Washington was convinced that the Democratic-Republican societies of western Pennsylvania were behind the defiance of federal authority there. He welcomed the opportunity to chastise these organizations, which he identified with the dangerous doctrines of the French Revolution.

Washington called on the governors of the mid-Atlantic states to supply militia forces to crush the **Whiskey Rebellion.** The 13,000-man army that assembled at Harrisburg and marched into western Pennsylvania in October 1794 was larger than any Washington had commanded during the Revolution. But the rebellion, as Jefferson sardonically noted, "could never be found." The army met no resistance and expended considerable effort rounding up 20 prisoners. Still, the Federalists had made their point: when its authority was openly challenged, the national government would use military force to compel obedience.

The Whiskey Rebellion starkly revealed the conflicting visions of local liberty and national order that divided Americans of the early republic. The non-English majority on the Pennsylvania frontier, Irish, Scots-Irish, German, and Welsh, justified resistance to the whiskey tax with the same republican ideology that had fueled the American Revolution. In putting down the Pennsylvania rebels, Washington and Hamilton acted on behalf of more English and cosmopolitan groups in the East who valued central power as a check on any local resistance movement that might begin unraveling the still fragile republic.

TREATIES WITH BRITAIN AND SPAIN

Washington's government had the resources to suppress Indians and frontier dissidents but lacked sufficient armed might to push Spain and especially Britain out of the West.

The British, embroiled in what they saw as a life-or-death struggle against revolutionary France, clamped a naval blockade on France and its Caribbean colonies in the fall of 1793. The French countered by opening their colonial trade to neutral shippers. American merchants stepped in and reaped profits by supplying France. The British retaliated by seizing American ships involved in the French trade. They further claimed the right to search American ships and impress, or forcibly remove, sailors they suspected of having deserted from the British navy. Desperate to avert a war, Washington sent John Jay, the chief justice of the United States, to London to negotiate an accord.

From the American point of view, the resulting agreement, known as **Jay's Treaty,** was flawed but acceptable. Jay had to abandon the American insistence on the right of neutrals to ship goods to nations at war without interference. He also had to grant Britain "most favored nation" status, giving up the American right to discriminate against British shipping and merchandise. And he had to reconfirm the American commitment to repay in full pre-Revolutionary debts owed to the British. In return, Britain pledged to compensate American merchants for the ships and cargoes it had seized in 1793 and 1794, to abandon the six forts it still held in the American Northwest, and to grant the United States limited trading rights in India and the British West Indies.

Signed in November 1794, Jay's Treaty caused an uproar in the United States when its terms became known in March 1795. Southerners saw in it another sellout of their interests. Republicans, joined now by urban artisans, were infuriated that Jay had stripped them of their chief weapon, economic retaliation, for breaking free of British commercial dominance. The Senate ratified the treaty in June 1795, but only because Washington backed it.

Jay's Treaty, combined with a string of French victories in Europe in 1795, convinced Spain to adopt a more conciliatory attitude toward the United States.

Whiskey Rebellion   Armed uprising in 1794 by farmers in western Pennsylvania who attempted to prevent the collection of the excise tax on whiskey.

Jay's Treaty   Treaty with Britain negotiated in 1794 in which the United States made major concessions to avert a war over the British seizure of American ships.

In the **Treaty of San Lorenzo** in 1795 (also known as Pinckney's Treaty), Spain accepted the American position on the 31st parallel as the northern boundary of Spanish Florida and granted American farmers the right of free transit through the port of New Orleans.

THE FIRST PARTISAN ELECTION

Partisanship, open identification with one of the two parties, steadily rose in the 1790s, fueled in large measure by a new print culture. Circulated and discussed in taverns and coffeehouses, newspapers helped draw ordinary Americans into the political process. Ongoing involvement in the raucous, celebratory political culture that Americans fashioned also politicized them. Through festivals on July 4 honoring the nation's independence, street parades, and demonstrations favoring or opposing such events as the French Revolution or Jay's Treaty, various groups publicly proclaimed and acted out their version of what it meant to be an American. National self-identity varied by class, race, sex, and region, but as newspaper reports of local activities were copied and disseminated across the country, Americans could feel that they were joined in a collective effort to define what the nation meant to them. As a national identity was being forged and contested, lines of partisanship were marked and deepened.

Although denied formal political rights, women wrote and attended plays with explicit political messages, joined in patriotic rituals, and organized their own demonstrations. To show their support for the French Revolution, women in Menetomy, Massachusetts, wore liberty caps and cockades, the symbols of the French cause. Two widows in Charleston, South Carolina, one American, the other French, went further in July 1793, when they staged a clever form of street theater in front of a large crowd. As reported by a Charleston newspaper, "after having repudiated their husbands on account of their ill-treatment, [they] conceived the design of living together in the strictest union and friendship in order to give a pledge of their fidelity [and] requested that their striped gowns should be penned together, that their children should be looked upon as one family, while their mothers showed them an equal affection." Here was a double-edged message. Just as a union of the French and the Americans could dispense with the need for Britain, so, it appeared, two women could enjoy domestic bliss without the need for husbands. By the late 1790s, both parties were seeking to broaden their popular appeal by including women in their partisan rallies.

As partisanship spread, no symbol of traditional authority, Washington included, was safe from challenge. He announced his decision to retire from public life in his Farewell Address of September 1796. Devoting most of this address to a denunciation of partisanship, he invoked the republican ideal of disinterested, independent statesmanship as the only sure and virtuous guide for the nation. He warned against any permanent foreign alliances and cautioned that the Union itself would be endangered if parties continued to be characterized "by geographical discriminations, *Northern* and *Southern*, *Atlantic* and *Western*, whence designing men may endeavor to excite a belief that there is a real difference of local interests and views."

Confirming Washington's fears, the election of 1796 was the first openly partisan election in American history. John Adams was the Federalist candidate, and Thomas Jefferson, the Republican candidate. As a result of disunity in the Federalist ranks, the election produced the anomaly of a Federalist president (Adams) and a Republican vice president (Jefferson). The result was a new administration badly divided from the start.

Despite the election's confused outcome, the sectional pattern in the voting was unmistakable. Only the solid support of regional elites in New England and

7–8
George Washington, Farewell Address (1796)

Treaty of San Lorenzo (Pickney's Treaty) Treaty with Spain in 1795 in which Spain recognized the 31st parallel as the boundary between the United States and Spanish Florida.

With the horrors of the French Revolution forming a backdrop, this cartoon depicts France as a five-headed monster demanding a bribe from the three Americans sent by Adams. The Federalists hoped that such anti-French sentiments would lead to an open war.

The Granger Collection

WHY WAS Adams defeated in the election of 1800?

WHERE TO LEARN MORE

Adams National Historic Site, Quincy, Massachusetts
www.nps.gov/adam/

XYZ Affair Diplomatic incident in 1798 in which Americans were outraged by the demand of the French for a bribe as a condition for negotiating with American diplomats.

Quasi-War Undeclared naval war of 1797 to 1800 between the United States and France.

the mid-Atlantic states enabled the Federalists to retain the presidency. Adams received all the northern electoral votes, with the exception of Pennsylvania's. Jefferson was the overwhelming favorite in the South.

THE LAST FEDERALIST ADMINISTRATION

*T*he Adams administration got off to a rocky start from which it never recovered. Adams had been a lawyer before the Revolution; he was a veteran of both Continental Congresses, had been a diplomat in Europe for a decade, and had served as Washington's vice president for eight years. But despite this extraordinarily rich background in public affairs, he was politically naive. Scrupulously honest but quick to take offense, he lacked the politician's touch for inspiring personal loyalty and crafting compromises based on a realistic recognition of mutual self-interest. But putting the interests of the country before those of his party, he almost single-handedly prevented a nearly certain war with France and a possible civil war at home. The price he paid was a badly split Federalist Party that refused to unite behind him when he sought reelection in 1800.

THE FRENCH CRISIS AND THE XYZ AFFAIR

An aggressive coalition known as the Directory gained control of revolutionary France in 1795 and denounced the Jay treaty as evidence of an Anglo-American alliance against France. The French annulled the commercial treaty of 1778 with the United States, ordered the seizure of American ships carrying goods to the British, and declared that any American sailors found on British ships, including those forcibly pressed into service, would be summarily executed.

In the fall of 1797, Adams sent three commissioners to Paris in an effort to avoid war. The French treated the three with contempt. Having just conquered the Netherlands and detached Spain from its British alliance, France was in no mood to compromise. Through three intermediaries, identified by Adams only as X, Y, and Z when he informed Congress of the negotiations, the French foreign minister demanded a large bribe to initiate talks and an American loan of $12 million.

In April 1798, the Senate published a full account of the insulting behavior of the French in what came to be called the **XYZ Affair.** The public was indignant, and war fever swept the country. By the fall of 1798, American ships were waging an undeclared war against the French in Caribbean waters, a conflict that came to be known as the **Quasi-War.**

The Federalists in Congress, dismissing Republican objections, also voted to create a vastly expanded army. They tripled the size of the regular army to 10,000 men and authorized a special provisional army of 50,000. Congress put the provisional army under Washington's command, with Hamilton as his second in command. To pay for the expanded army, the Federalists pushed through the Direct Tax of 1798, a levy on land, slaves, and dwellings.

CRISIS AT HOME

The thought of Hamilton in charge of a huge army convinced many Republicans that their worst nightmares were about to materialize. Adams shared such fears. As the Republicans immediately sensed and Adams came to realize, Hamilton's supporters, known as the High Federalists, saw the war scare with France as an opportunity to stamp out dissent, cement an alliance with the British, and strengthen and consolidate the powers of the national government.

The Federalists passed four laws in the summer of 1798, known collectively as the **Alien and Sedition Acts,** that confirmed the Republicans' fears. Three of these acts were aimed at immigrants. The Alien Enemies Act empowered the president to deport foreigners who came from countries at war with the United States. The more sweeping Alien Friends Act authorized the president to expel any alien resident he suspected of subversive activities. The Naturalization Act extended the residency requirement for American citizenship from five to fourteen years. The most dangerous of the four acts in the minds of Republicans was the Sedition Act, a measure that made it a federal crime to engage in any conspiracy against the government or to utter or print anything "false, scandalous and malicious" against the government. Federalist judges were blatantly partisan in their enforcement of the Sedition Act. Twenty-five individuals, mostly Republican editors, were indicted under the act, and ten were convicted.

Jefferson and Madison turned to the safely Republican legislatures of Kentucky and Virginia for a forum from which to attack the constitutionality of the Alien and Sedition Acts. Taking care to keep their authorship secret, they each drafted a set of resolutions that challenged the entire centralizing program of the Federalists. In doing so, they produced the first significant articulation of the southern stand on **states' rights.**

The resolutions—adopted in the fall of 1798—proposed a compact theory of the Constitution. They asserted that the states had delegated specific powers to the national government for their common benefit. If a state decided that the national government had exceeded its powers, it could "interpose" its authority to shield its citizens from a tyrannical law. In a second set of resolutions, the Kentucky legislature introduced the doctrine of **nullification,** the right of a state to render null and void a national law it deemed unconstitutional.

Jefferson and Madison hoped that these resolutions would rally voters to the Republican Party as the defender of threatened American liberties. In the end, however, what aroused popular rage against the Federalists was not legislation directed against aliens and subversives but the high cost of Federalist taxes.

The Direct Tax of 1798 fell on all owners of land, dwellings, or slaves and provoked widespread resentment. Enforcing it required an army of bureaucrats—more than 500 for the state of Pennsylvania alone. In February 1799, a group of men led by an auctioneer named John Fries released tax evaders from prison in Bethlehem. President Adams responded to Fries's Rebellion with a show of force. Fries and two other men were arrested, convicted of treason, and sentenced to be

Short and pudgy, Adams had little of Hamilton's physical presence as a natural leader. But he had a first-rate mind and the political courage to place the nation's needs above those of his Federalist party when he peacefully ended the Quasi-War with France.

John Trumbull; White House Historical Association (White House Collection). (25)

Alien and Sedition Acts
Collective name given to four acts passed by Congress in 1798 that curtailed freedom of speech and the liberty of foreigners resident in the United States.

States' rights Favoring the rights of individual states over rights claimed by the national government.

Nullification A constitutional doctrine holding that a state has a legal right to declare a national law null and void within its borders.

REPUBLICANS

Turn out, turn out and save your Country from ruin !

From an *Emperor*—from a *King*—from the iron grasp of a *British Tory Faction*—an unprincipled banditti of British speculators. The hireling tools and emissaries of his majesty king George the 3d have thronged our city and diffused the poison of principles among us.

DOWN WITH THE TORIES, DOWN WITH THE BRITISH FACTION,

Before they have it in their power to enslave you, and reduce your families to distress by heavy taxation. Republicans want no Tribute-liars—they want no ship Ocean-liars—they want no Rufus King's for Lords —they want no Varick to lord it over them—they want no Jones for senator, who fought with the British against the Americans in time of the war.—But they want in their places such men as

Jefferson & Clinton,

who fought their Country's Battles in the year '76

By associating their Federalist opponents with the hated Tories of the American Revolution, the Republicans appealed to the voters as the true defenders of American liberation.

Collection of the New York Historical Society, Negative #35609.

Franco-American Accord of 1800 Settlement reached with France that brought an end to the Quasi-War and released the United States from its 1778 alliance with France.

executed. (Adams later pardoned them.) But the Federalists had now lost much of their support in Pennsylvania.

THE END OF THE FEDERALISTS

The events in Pennsylvania reflected the air of menace that gripped the country as the campaign of 1800 approached. The army was chasing private citizens whose only crime was resisting hateful taxes—in the eyes of many, a continuation of an honorable Revolutionary ideal. Federal soldiers also roughed up Republican voters at polling places. Southern Republicans talked in private of the possible need to resist Federalist tyranny by force and, failing in that, to secede from the Union. Hamilton and the High Federalists saw in the Kentucky and Virginia resolutions "a regular conspiracy to overturn the government."

No one did more to defuse the charged atmosphere than President Adams. The Federalists depended for their popular support on the expectation of a war with France. Adams refrained from asking for a declaration of war. Adams believed that, after a series of setbacks, the French would now be more open to conciliation. Of greater importance, Adams recognized that war with France could trigger a civil war at home. Hamilton and the High Federalists, he realized, would use war as an excuse to crush the Republican opposition in Virginia. Fearful of Hamilton's intentions and unwilling to run the risk of militarizing the government and saddling it with a huge war debt, Adams broke with his party and decided to reopen negotiations with France in February 1799.

The **Franco-American Accord of 1800** that resulted from Adams's initiative released the United States from its 1778 alliance with France. It also obligated the United States to surrender all claims against the French for damages done to American shipping during the Quasi-War. The negotiations in Paris dragged on through the election of 1800, but for the Hamiltonian Federalists, the political damage had already been done. Although rumors of possible violence continued to circulate, the Republicans grew increasingly confident that they could peacefully gain control of the government.

The Federalists nonetheless ran a competitive race in 1800. Adams's peace policy bolstered his popularity. And because American merchants had profited from supplying both sides in the European war, the country was enjoying a period of prosperity that benefited the president and his party. But the wounds opened by Adams's decision to broker a peace with France continued to fester. Hamilton and his friends felt that Adams had betrayed them, and Hamilton wrote a scathing attack on the president in a letter that fell into the hands of Aaron Burr. Burr published the letter, airing the Federalists' squabbling in public.

The Federalists, hampered by party disunity, could not counter the Republicans' aggressive organizational tactics. They found it distasteful to appeal to common people. One party member lamented that the Republicans sent spokesmen "to every class of men, and even to every individual man, that can be gained. Every threshing floor, every husting, every party at work on a house-frame or raising a building, the very funerals are infected with bawlers or whisperers against government."

Wherever they organized, the Republicans attacked the Federalists as monarchists plotting to undo the gains of the Revolution. The Federalists responded with emotional appeals that depicted Jefferson as a godless revolutionary whose election would usher in a reign of terror. "The effect," intoned the Reverend William Linn, "would be to destroy religion, introduce immorality, and loosen all bonds of society."

Attacks like Linn's reflected the fears of Calvinist preachers that a tide of disbelief was about to submerge Christianity in the United States. Church attendance had declined in the 1790s. **Deism,** an Enlightenment religious philosophy popular among the leaders of the Revolutionary era, was now beginning to make inroads among ordinary citizens. Deists viewed God as a kind of master clockmaker who created the laws by which the universe runs but otherwise leaves it alone. They rejected revelation for reason, maintaining that the workings of nature alone reveal God's design.

These developments convinced Calvinist ministers, nearly all of them Federalists, that the atheism of the French Revolution was infecting American republicanism. They lashed out at the Republicans as perverters of religious and social order.

The Republicans won the election by mobilizing voters through strong party organizations. Voter turnout in 1800 was twice what it had been in the early 1790s, and most of the new voters were Republicans. The Direct Tax of 1798 cost the Federalists the support of commercial farmers in the mid-Atlantic states. Artisans in port cities had already switched to the Republicans in protest over Jay's Treaty. Adams carried New England and had a smattering of support elsewhere. With New York added to their solid base in the South and the backcountry, the Jeffersonians gained an electoral majority (see Map 8–1).

Party unity among Republican electors was so strong that Jefferson and Burr each received 73 electoral votes. Consequently the election was thrown into the House of Representatives, which, until the newly elected Congress was seated, was still dominated by Federalists. Hoping to deny Jefferson the presidency, the Federalists in the House backed Burr. The result was a deadlock that persisted into the early months of 1801. On February 16, 1801, the Federalists yielded. Informed through intermediaries that Jefferson would not dismantle Hamilton's fiscal system, enough Federalists cast blank ballots to give Jefferson the majority he needed for election. The Twelfth Amendment to the Constitution, ratified in 1804, prevented a similar impasse from arising again by requiring electors to cast separate ballots for president and vice president.

Deism   Religious orientation that rejects divine revelation and holds that the workings of nature alone reveal God's design for the universe.

QUICK REVIEW

Presidential Election of 1800
- Federalists could not overcome party disunity.
- Federalists attacked as disbelievers in Christianity.
- Strong part organization won election for Republicans Jefferson and Burr.

MAP EXPLORATION
To explore an interactive version of this map, go to
http://www.prenhall.com/goldfield3/map8.1

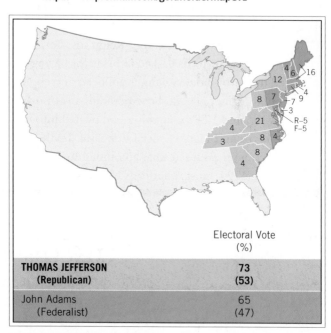

	Electoral Vote (%)
THOMAS JEFFERSON (Republican)	**73** **(53)**
John Adams (Federalist)	65 (47)

MAP 8–1   The Election of 1800   The sharp erosion of Federalist strength in New York and Pennsylvania after 1798 swung the election of 1800 to the Republicans.

WHAT DOES this map show you about the interests of Jeffersonian Republicans versus those of the Federalists? Based on geographic regions, which party was more likely to represent farmers?

GLOBAL PERSPECTIVES

NEUTRALITY IN AN AGE OF REVOLUTION

"**W**hereas it appears that a state of war exists between Austria, Prussia, Sardinia, Great Britain, and the United Netherlands on the one part and France on the other, and the duty and interest of the United States require that they should with sincerity and good faith adopt and pursue a conduct friendly and impartial toward the belligerent powers:

I have therefore thought fit . . . to exhort and warn the citizens of the United States carefully to avoid all acts and proceeding whatsoever which may in any manner tend to contravene such disposition."

In these words President Washington proclaimed the neutrality of the United States in the European war spawned by the French Revolution. He realized, as did most Americans, that the new and still weak nation had far more to lose than gain by embroiling itself in the European war. Still, before the French Revolution turned to regicide and the Reign of Terror in 1793–1794, Americans basked in pride for having first raised the revolutionary banner of liberty and equality that their former ally was now spreading over Europe. But by the mid-1790s exultation had turned into disillusionment and fears of social upheaval. By the time that Napoleon assumed what amounted to dictatorial powers in 1799, most Americans had reverted to their earlier belief in the uniqueness of the American Revolution. As Madison observed when reflecting on the French experience, America remained as "the only Theatre in which true liberty can have a fair trial."

Despite believing that the French had discredited the cause of liberty, Americans clung to the hope that the contagion of liberty they had first unleashed in their Revolution would topple autocratic regimes across the world. And spread it did in a wide arc of revolutionary movements that stretched across the Western world. The French colony of Saint-Domingue (Haiti) exploded in unrest in 1791 once the French Revolution had outlawed slavery. Touissant L'Ouverture, the slave grandson of an African king, led black armies in a ten-year war of liberation that resulted in the independence of Haiti in 1804. Napoleon's invasion of the Iberian Peninsula in 1809 created a power vacuum in Spain's American empire. A host of revolutions broke out to fill the vacuum, and Mexico, Argentina, Bolivia, Chile, Colombia, Ecuador, Peru, and Venezuela all gained their freedom from Spanish rule. None of these revolutions closely followed the American or French model. All, however, were united by a common political language of liberty, popular self-rule, and constitutionalism that the Americans and the French had bequeathed to global politics.

CONCLUSION

*I*n 1789, the American republic was little more than an experiment in self-government. The Federalists provided a firm foundation for that experiment. Hamilton's financial program, neutrality in the wars of the French Revolution, and the diplomatic settlement with Britain in Jay's Treaty bequeathed the young nation a decade of peace and prosperity.

Federalist policies, however, provoked strong opposition rooted in conflicting economic interests and contrasting regional views over the meaning of liberty and government in the new republic. The Federalist coalition split during Washington's second term when southern planters joined urban artisans and backcountry Scots-Irish farmers in opposing Jay's Treaty and the commercially oriented program of the Federalists. During John Adams's administration, Quaker and

German farmers in the mid-Atlantic states defected from the Federalists over the tax legislation of 1798, and three of the four regions of the country lined up behind the Republicans. The new Republican majority was united by the belief that the actions of the New England Federalists threatened individual liberty and regional autonomy.

The openly partisan politics of the 1790s surprised the country's founders, who equated parties with the evils of factionalism. They had not foreseen that parties would forge a necessary link between the rulers and the ruled and create a mechanism by which group values and regional interests could be given a political voice. Party formation climaxed in the election of 1800, when the Republicans ended the Federalists' rule. The Republicans won by embracing the popular demand for a more egalitarian social and political order.

To the credit of the Federalists, they relinquished control of the national government peacefully. The importance of this precedent can scarcely be exaggerated. It marked the first time in modern political history that a party in power handed over the government to its opposition. It now remained to be seen what the Republicans would do with their newfound power.

SUMMARY

Washington's America The national census of 1790 counted nearly four million Americans, one in four of whom lived in New England. New Englanders found slavery incompatible with the natural rights philosophy that had emerged during the Revolution and abolished it in the 1780s. In other respects, though, politics in New England remained rooted in the Puritan past. The states in the Mid-Atlantic region were the most diverse in the nation, which created a complex political environment. In the South climate and soil conditions favored the production of cash staples for world markets and the use of slavery. And, between the Appalachian Mountains and the Mississippi River stretched the most rapidly growing region of the new nation, the West. Life in the West was harsh and often cruel, and Westerners were willing to strike a deal with almost any outside power to meet their needs.

Forging a New Government The Congress that assembled in New York from 1789 to 1791 faced a challenge scarcely less daunting than that of the Constitutional Convention of 1787. Led by Madison, the Congress submitted twelve amendments to the Constitution to the states of which ten were ratified. These ten are known as the Bill of Rights. Congress was also busy working out the cabinet and the court system.

The Emergence of Parties Two parties formed by the end of Washington's first term: the Federalists and the Republicans. In 1792, still in their formative stages, the parties re-elected an unopposed Washington. Control of the West remained an elusive goal throughout Washington's presidency. Among the distractions were wars with the Indians (the Battle of Fallen Timbers) and a Whiskey Rebellion in western Pennsylvania. The first partisan election was the election of 1796, with a divided nation electing Adams over Jefferson.

IMAGE KEY
for pages 208–209

a. Manhattan end of the Brooklyn Ferry, c. 1790.

b. Washington's Triumphal Entry Into New York. A tapestry, of George Washington and his retinue riding into New York amid cheering crowds standing on a street and balconies.

c. American political button from the 18th century.

d. John Adams wears a brown suit with a high folded collar over a white cravat in a framed painting by John Trumbull.

e. Painting depicting women's increasing access to education.

f. Little Turtle and General Wayne.

g. Congressional Pugilists: American cartoon engraving, 1798, on the fight in Congress between Roger Griswold (weilding cane) the Matthew Lyon, the most notable victim of the Sedition Act of 1798.

h. American politician Alexander Hamilton (1757 - 1804), after service as *aide de camp* to George Washington during the War of Independence, wrote the majority of the Federalist Papers in support of acceptance of the constitution. Painting by John Trumbull (1756-1843).

i. The twelve amendments submitted by the Congress of the United States in 1790 to safeguard the rights of individuals from the interference of the federal government. Ten of these articles were adopted in 1791 as the Bill of Rights - the first ten amendments of the US Constitution. This document bears the signature of John Adams, then vice president of the United States.

The Last Federalist Administration   The Adams administration got off to a rocky start from which it never recovered. His administration dealt with the XYZ Affair, the Quasi-War with France, the Alien and Sedition Acts, and Fries's Rebellion. With Adams's many failed policies and the turmoil surrounding his presidency, the election of 1800 saw Jefferson narrowly elected president and the end of the Federalist party.

REVIEW QUESTIONS

1. What role did the "people" play in Washington's inauguration in 1789? What was the purpose of the grand procession, and why was the militia present?

2. What was distinctive about the four regions of the United States in 1790? What were the common values and goals that brought white Americans together?

3. What were the major problems confronting the Washington administration, and how effectively were they resolved? Why was Washington so cautious when confronted with the outbreak of war in Europe?

4. Who were the Federalists and the Republicans, and how did they differ over the meaning of liberty and the power of the national government? What were the major steps in the formation of two distinct parties in the early United States?

5. Why did regional differences tend to pit the North against the South by the late 1790s?

6. How did the XYZ Affair lead to a political crisis in the United States? Why did the Federalists believe that they would benefit from a war against France?

7. Jefferson called his election in 1800 the "revolution of 1800." What do you think he meant? Would you agree with him?

KEY TERMS

Alien and Sedition Acts   (p. 229)
Bill of Rights   (p. 218)
Deism   (p. 231)
Federalists   (p. 222)
Franco-American Accord of 1800   (p. 230)
Jay's Treaty   (p. 226)

Judiciary Act of 1789   (p. 219)
Nullification   (p. 229)
Quasi-War   (p. 228)
Republican (Jeffersonian)   (p. 222)
States' rights   (p. 229)
Tariff Act of 1789   (p. 219)

Tonnage Act of 1789   (p. 220)
Treaty of Greenville   (p. 224)
Treaty of San Lorenzo   (p. 227)
Whiskey Rebellion   (p. 226)
XYZ Affair   (p. 228)

WHERE TO LEARN MORE

◌ **Cincinnati Historical Society, Cincinnati, Ohio.** Collections include written and visual materials on the history of the Old Northwest Territory. Visit its website, **www.cincymuseum.org/** for information on its programs and the accessibility of its printed and audiovisual collections.

🖰 **Federal Hall National Memorial, New York, New York.** This museum and historic site holds artifacts relating to President Washington's inauguration. Its website, **www.nps.gov/feha/** includes a printable travel guide to various sites in Manhattan administered by the National Parks Service.

🖰 **Hamilton Grange National Memorial, New York, New York.** The home of Alexander Hamilton contains materials on his life. A brief history of the home and Hamilton's life can be found at its website, **www.nps/gov/hagr/**

🖰 **Adams National Historic Site, Quincy, Massachusetts.** This site preserves buildings and manuscripts associated with four generations of the Adams family. See its website, **www.nps.gov/adam/** for information on guided tours and the various homes that are part of the site.

 U.S. History Documents CD-ROM
For primary sources related to this chapter, refer to the document CD-ROM.

 www.prenhall.com/goldfield
For study resources related to this chapter, visit the *Companion Website*™.

9 The Triumph and Collapse of Jeffersonian Republicanism 1800–1824

CHAPTER HIGHLIGHTS

Jefferson's Presidency Jeffersonian Republicans wanted an agrarian republic based on widespread economic equality for yeoman farmers. The Louisiana Purchase increased the size of the United States dramatically. Jefferson's Embargo Act of 1807 crippled his presidency in its final year.

Madison and the Coming of War A variety of factors pushed Madison toward war with Britain. On the eve of the war, Madison was faced with the pan-Indian resistance movement. The War Hawks kept up the pressure for armed conflict with Britain.

The War of 1812 The United States was unprepared to fight the War of 1812. The war devolved into a stalemate and the Treaty of Ghent re-established the pre-war status quo. American victory in the Battle of New Orleans ended British influence in Louisiana and dealt a death blow to Federalism.

The Era of Good Feelings The postwar years were characterized by a spirit of political harmony and sectional unity. The Republicans promoted a program of economic nationalism. America expanded and consolidated its empire. The Monroe Doctrine declared the Americas off-limits to European colonization.

The Breakdown of Unity Economic depression and renewed conflict over slavery ended the Era of Good Feelings. The slavery controversy was partly quelled by the Missouri Compromise. The election of 1824, won by John Quincy Adams, marked the end of Republican unity.

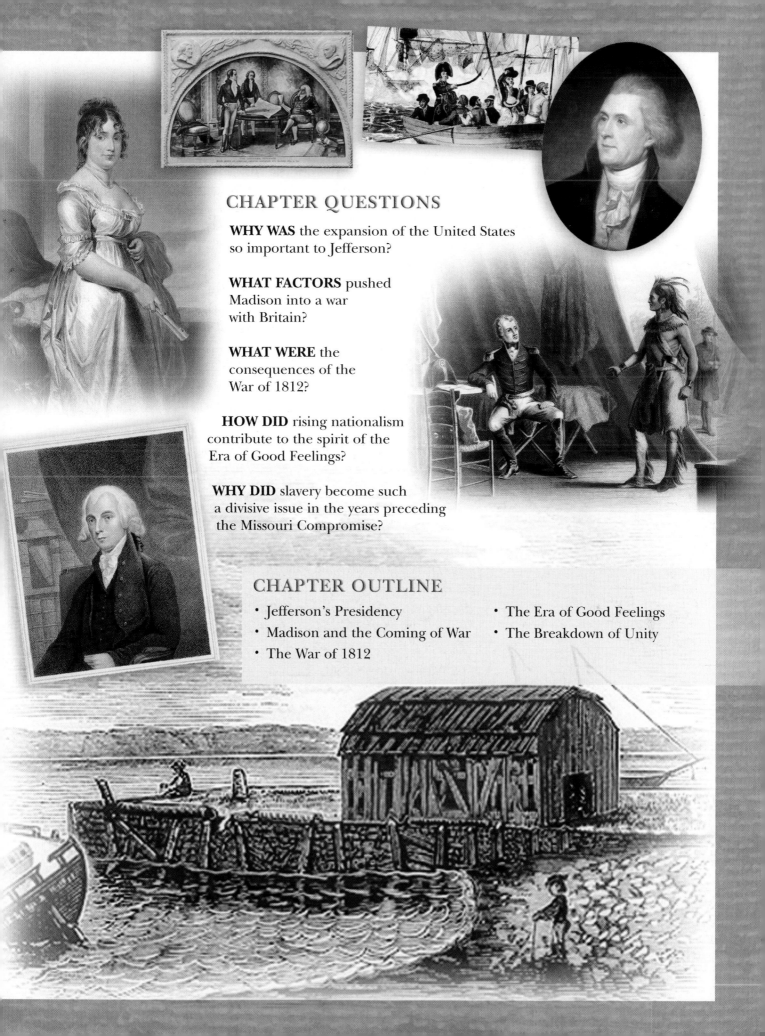

CHAPTER QUESTIONS

WHY WAS the expansion of the United States so important to Jefferson?

WHAT FACTORS pushed Madison into a war with Britain?

WHAT WERE the consequences of the War of 1812?

HOW DID rising nationalism contribute to the spirit of the Era of Good Feelings?

WHY DID slavery become such a divisive issue in the years preceding the Missouri Compromise?

CHAPTER OUTLINE

- Jefferson's Presidency
- Madison and the Coming of War
- The War of 1812
- The Era of Good Feelings
- The Breakdown of Unity

IMAGE KEY

for pages 236–237 is on page 261.

Riversdale, 30 August 1814

My dear Sister,

Since I started this letter [on Aug. 9] we have been in a state of continual alarm, and now I have time to write only two or three lines to ask you to tell Papa that we are alive, in good health, and I hope safe from danger. I am sure that you have heard the news of the battle of Bladensburg where the English defeated the American troops with Madison 'not at their head, but at their rear.'

From there they went to Washington where they burned the Capitol, the President's House, all the public offices, etc. During the battle I saw several cannonballs with my own eyes, and I will write all the details to your husband. At the moment the English ships are at Alexandria which is also in their possession.

I don't know how all this will end, but I fear very badly for us. It is probable that it will also bring about a dissolution of the union of the states, and in that case, farewell to the public debt. You know I have predicted this outcome for a long time. Wouldn't it be wise to send your husband here without delay, in order to plan with me the best course to pursue for Papa's interests as well as yours?

This letter will go, I think, by a Dutch ship. If I have time with the confusion we are in, I will write again in a few days, perhaps by the same vessel. At present my house is full of people every day and at night my bedroom is full of rifles, pistols, sabers, etc. Many thanks to your husband for the information in his letter of 27 April, and tell him that I invested all his money in the May loan [of the U.S. Treasury]. Please give many greetings to my dear Father and to Charles [her brother]. Embrace your children for me and believe me,

Your affectionate sister,

Rosalie E. Calvert

Margaret Law Callcott, ed., *Mistress of Riversdale: The Plantation Letters of Rosalie Stier Calvert, 1795–1821* (Baltimore: Johns Hopkins University Press, 1991), pp. 271–272.

ROSALIE CALVERT WROTE to her sister in Europe with news of the British attack on Washington, D.C. in August 1814, the low point of the American cause in the War of 1812. The youngest of the three children of a wealthy Belgian family that had fled the advancing armies of revolutionary France, Rosalie was 16 when her family arrived in Philadelphia in the summer of 1794. Her father, Henri J. Stier, brought with him a sizable fortune in gold, U.S. currency, and paintings. The family lived off the income from Henri's investments in U.S. securities and, unsurprisingly, was strongly Federalist in its political leanings. After resettling in Annapolis, most of the Stiers returned to Europe in 1803 when political conditions had stabilized. Left behind was Rosalie, entrusted with the management of the family's financial holdings. In 1799, Rosalie had married George Calvert, a descendant of the proprietors of the Maryland colony and a kinsman of the Washingtons.

Rosalie's wealth and elite social standing deepened her political conservatism. Moreover, the coming to power of the Jeffersonian Republicans in 1801 triggered bitter memories of the revolutionary turmoil she had experienced as a young woman in Belgium. In her eyes, Jefferson and his followers were demagogues who catered to the poor and threatened to infect America with the political radicalism of the French Revolution. She blamed the War of 1812 on ignorant, ill-conceived Republican policies and feared that the war would unleash massive unrest. Thus the sense of "continual alarm" that runs through her letter in August 1814, at a time when the war had spilled over into her home.

Her fears were overblown. Rosalie, however, survived the war by only six years. Her great wealth could not shield her from the duties of a wife, most notably frequent childbearing. The strain of ten pregnancies in 21 years of marriage likely contributed to her death at the age of 43 from congestive heart failure. Despite her denunciations of the Republicans, Jefferson and his Republican successors, James Madison and James Monroe, succeeded in promoting the growth and independence of the United States in the first quarter of the nineteenth century. Expansionist policies to the south and west more than doubled the size of the republic and fueled the westward spread of slavery. The war against Britain from 1812 to 1815, if less than a military triumph, nonetheless freed Americans to look inward for economic development.

At the height of Republican success just after the War of 1812, the Federalist party collapsed. Without an organized opposition to enforce party discipline, the Republicans soon followed the Federalists into political oblivion. The nation's expansion produced two crises—a financial panic and a battle over slavery in Missouri—that shattered the facade of republican unity. By the mid-1820s, a new party system was emerging.

JEFFERSON'S PRESIDENCY

*T*homas Jefferson believed that a true revolution had occurred in 1800. In his eyes, the defeat of the monarchical Federalists reconfirmed the true political legacy of the Revolution by restoring the republican majority to its rightful control of the government.

Unlike the Hamiltonian Federalists, whose commercial vision of America accepted social and economic inequalities as inevitable, the Jeffersonians wanted a predominantly agrarian republic based on widespread economic equality for white yeomen families to counter any threat posed by the privileged few to the people's liberties. Thus they favored territorial expansion as a means of adding enough land to maintain self-reliant farmers as the guardians of republican freedoms.

Jefferson's first administration was a solid success. A unified Republican party reduced the size and scope of the federal government, allowed the Alien and Sedition Acts to lapse, and celebrated the Louisiana Purchase. His second term, however, was a bitter disappointment, marked by the massive unpopularity of Jefferson's embargo on American foreign trade. As a result, Jefferson left his successor, James Madison, a divided party, a revived Federalism, and an unresolved crisis in foreign affairs.

WHY WAS the expansion of the United States so important to Jefferson?

CHAPTER 9

Chronology

1801	Thomas Jefferson is inaugurated, the first Republican president.
	John Marshall becomes chief justice.
1802	Congress repeals the Judiciary Act of 1801.
1803	*Marbury v. Madison* sets the precedent of judicial review by the Supreme Court.
	Louisiana Purchase.
	Lewis and Clark expedition begins.
	Britain and France resume their war after a brief peace.
1804	Vice President Aaron Burr kills Alexander Hamilton in a duel.
	Judges John Pickering and Samuel Chase impeached by Republicans.
1806	Britain and France issue orders restricting neutral shipping.
	Betrayal of the Burr conspiracy.
1807	*Chesapeake* affair.
	Congress passes the Embargo Act.
	Congress prohibits the African slave trade.
1808	James Madison elected president.
1809	Repeal of the Embargo Act.
	Passage of the Nonintercourse Act.
1810	Macon's Bill No. 2 reopens trade with Britain and France.
	United States annexes part of West Florida.
	Georgia state law invalidated by the Supreme Court in *Fletcher* v. *Peck*.
1811	Battle of Tippecanoe and defeat of the Indian confederation.
	Charter of the Bank of the United States expires.
1812	Congress declares war on Britain.
	American loss of Detroit.
	Napoleon invades Russia.
1813	Perry's victory at Battle of Put-in-Bay.
	Battle of the Thames and death of Tecumseh.

1814	Jackson crushes the Creeks at the Battle of Horseshoe Bend.
	British burn Washington, D.C., and attack Baltimore.
	Macdonough's naval victory on Lake Champlain turns back a British invasion.
	Hartford Convention meets.
	Treaty of Ghent signed.
1815	Jackson routs British at the Battle of New Orleans.
	Congress of Vienna arranges a peace settlement for Europe after Napoleon's defeat at Waterloo.
1816	Congress charters the Second Bank of the United States and passes a protective tariff.
	James Monroe elected president.
1817	Rush-Bagot Treaty demilitarizes the Great Lakes.
1818	Anglo-American Accords on trade and boundaries.
	Jackson's border campaign in Spanish East Florida.
1819	Trans-Continental Treaty between United States and Spain.
	Beginning of the Missouri controversy.
	Financial panic sends economy into a depression.
	McCulloch v. *Maryland* upholds constitutionality of the Bank of the United States.
1820	Missouri Compromise on slavery in the Louisiana Purchase.
	Monroe reelected.
1821	Greek revolt against the Turks.
1822	The United States extends diplomatic recognition to the new nations of Latin America.
1823	Monroe Doctrine proclaims Western Hemisphere closed to further European colonization.
1825	John Quincy Adams elected president by the House of Representatives.

REFORM AT HOME

Jefferson set the style and tone of his administration from the beginning. He was the first president to be inaugurated in Washington, D.C., and his inauguration was as unpretentious as the raw and primitive capital city itself. Jefferson walked from his lodgings to the Capitol building to be sworn in. His dress was neat but shorn of such gentlemanly refinements as a wig. He emphasized in his inaugural address the overwhelming commitment of Americans to the "republican form" of government and affirmed his own support of civil liberties as an American principle.

Believing that the Federalists had promoted aristocratic pretensions and courtly intrigue through such practices as weekly levees for presidential guests, Jefferson replaced the levees with small, men-only dinners, where he aired his political views. This effort to achieve republican purity in governance, one that denied women any political role, created a void in the capital's social life that was filled by the wives of cabinet members and women drawn from the social elite. It was their dinner parties and receptions that enabled politically minded women and men to come together, lobby on behalf of friends and relatives, and build the networks that influenced how political offices and favors were distributed. Influential Washington hostesses such as Dolley Madison soon wielded a good deal of informal political power as they helped make possible a national political culture.

Dolley Madison, the engaging young wife of James Madison, Jefferson's secretary of state, served as the unofficial social hostess in the White House during the administration of Jefferson, a widower.

The Granger Collection

The cornerstone of Republican domestic policy was retrenchment, a return to the frugal, simple federal establishment the Jeffersonians believed to be the original intent of the Constitution. Determined to root out what they viewed as Federalist corruption and patronage, the Republicans began by reforming fiscal policy. Jefferson's secretary of the treasury, Albert Gallatin, convinced Jefferson that the Bank of the United States was essential for financial stability and blocked efforts to dismantle it. Unlike Hamilton, however, Gallatin thought that a large public debt was a drag on productive capital and an unfair burden on future generations. He succeeded in reducing the national debt from $83 million in 1800 to $57 million by 1809.

The Republicans eliminated all internal taxes, including the despised tax on whiskey. Slashes in the military budget kept government expenditures below the level of 1800. The cuts in military spending, combined with soaring revenues from customs collections, left Gallatin with a surplus in the budget that he could devote to debt repayment.

Jefferson moved to break the Federalist stranglehold on federal offices by appointing officials with sound Republican principles. Arch-Federalists, those Jefferson deemed guilty of misusing their offices for openly political reasons, were immediately replaced, and Republicans filled other posts opened up by attrition. By the time Jefferson left the presidency in 1809, Republicans held nearly all the appointive offices.

Jefferson moved most aggressively against the Federalists in the judiciary. Just days before they relinquished power, the Federalists passed the Judiciary Act

WHERE TO LEARN MORE

Monticello, Charlottesville, Virginia
www.monticello.org/

of 1801, legislation that both enlarged the judiciary and packed it with more Federalists appointed by Adams, the outgoing president.

The Republicans fought back, quickly repealing the Judiciary Act of 1801. Frustrated Federalists now turned to John Marshall, the chief justice and a staunch Federalist, hoping that he would rule that Congress had acted unconstitutionally in removing the recently appointed federal judges. Marshall moved carefully to avoid an open confrontation. He was aware that the Republicans contended that Congress and the president had at least a coequal right with the Supreme Court to decide constitutional questions.

The issue came to a head in the case of *Marbury* **v.** *Madison* (1803), which centered on Secretary of State James Madison's refusal to deliver a commission to William Marbury, one of Adams's "midnight appointments" (so-called because Adams made them on his next-to-last day in office) as a justice of the peace for the District of Columbia. Marshall held that although Marbury had a legal right to his commission, the Court had no jurisdiction in the case. The Court ruled that the section of the Judiciary Act of 1789 granting it the power to order the delivery of Marbury's commission was unconstitutional because it conferred on the Court a power not specified in Article 3 of the Constitution on cases of original jurisdiction. Stating that it was "emphatically the province and duty of the judicial department to say what the law is," Marshall created the precedent of judicial review, the power of the Supreme Court to rule on the constitutionality of federal law. This doctrine was of pivotal importance for the future of the Court. Marshall's assertion of the Court's power deepened Republican suspicions of judicial tyranny. Demanding popular election for all judges, radical Republicans rejected the entire notion of an appointed judiciary. Jefferson did not want to go that far, but he believed that judges should be accountable to the popular will.

THE LOUISIANA PURCHASE

In foreign affairs, fortune smiled on Jefferson during his first term. The European war that had almost sucked in the United States in the 1790s subsided. Britain and France agreed on a truce in 1802. Meanwhile, Jefferson, despite his distaste for a strong navy, ordered a show of force in the Mediterranean to punish the Barbary pirates who were preying on American shipping and taking American sailors hostage. For years, the North African states of Morocco, Algeria, Tunis, and Tripoli had demanded cash tribute from foreigners trading in the Mediterranean. Jefferson stopped the payments in 1801, and when attacks on American shipping resumed, he retaliated by sending warships and marines to the Mediterranean. The tribute system continued until 1815, but on much more favorable terms for the United States.

The Anglo-French peace removed any immediate threat of war, but the return of peace also allowed Spain and France to reclaim their colonial trade in the Western Hemisphere. Of greater long-range concern, the new ruler of France, Napoleon Bonaparte, was now free to develop his plans for reviving the French empire in America. In a secret treaty with Spain in 1800, Napoleon reacquired the Louisiana Territory.

Unconfirmed reports of the treaty reached Jefferson in the spring of 1801. He had long believed that Spain would be powerless to stem the spread of the expanding American population into its territories in western North America. France, by contrast, was a formidable opponent. French control of the Mississippi Valley, combined with the British presence in Canada, threatened to hem in the United States and deprive Jefferson's farmers of their empire of liberty.

QUICK REVIEW

Judiciary Act of 1801

- Enlarged the judiciary and packed it with Adams' appointees.
- Repealed by Republican Congress.
- Conflict came to head in case of *Marbury* v. *Madison* (1803).

8–8
Sacagawea Interprets for Lewis and Clark (1804)

Marbury **v.** *Madison* Supreme Court decision of 1803 that created the precedent of judicial review by ruling as unconstitutional part of the Judiciary Act of 1789.

Jefferson was prepared to reverse his party's traditional foreign policy to eliminate this threat. He opened exploratory talks with the British on an Anglo-American alliance to drive the French out of Louisiana. He also strengthened American forces in the Mississippi Valley and secured congressional approval for the Lewis and Clark expedition through upper Louisiana. Although best known for its scientific discoveries, this expedition was designed initially as a military mission. Jefferson applied diplomatic and military pressure to induce Napoleon to sell New Orleans and a small slice of coastal territory to its east to the United States. To his surprise, Napoleon suddenly decided in early 1803 to sell all of the immense Louisiana Territory to the United States.

This **Federalist cartoon** satirizes Jefferson, in the form of a prairie dog, coughing up the $2 million bribe to Napoleon for the acquisition of West Florida, while a French diplomat stands by dancing and taunting Jefferson.

Library of Congress

9.2
A Matter of Honor or Vengeance? (1804)

Napoleon had envisioned the rich sugar island of Saint-Domingue (modern-day Haiti) as the jewel of his new empire and intended to use the Louisiana Territory as a granary to supply the island. During the upheavals of the French Revolution, the slaves on the island, led by Touissant L'Ouverture, rebelled in a bloody and successful bid for independence.

Without firm French control of Saint-Domingue, Louisiana was of little use to Napoleon. And when the U.S. Congress passed resolutions threatening an American attack on New Orleans, he realized that he was likely to have to fight to keep it. With a renewed war against Britain looming, he had better use for his troops in Europe and wanted to keep Americans neutral. For $15 million, he offered to part with the whole of Louisiana.

Despite the lack of any specific authorization in the Constitution for the acquisition of foreign territory or the incorporation as American citizens of the 50,000 French and Spanish descendants then living in Louisiana, Jefferson accepted Napoleon's deal. The Louisiana Purchase doubled the size of the United States, offered seemingly endless space to be settled by yeoman farmers, and opened up another frontier for slaveholders in the lower Mississippi Valley.

Jefferson was willing, as the Federalists had been when they were in power, to stretch the Constitution to support his definition of the national good. Conversely, it was now the Federalists who relied on a narrow reading of the Constitution in a futile attempt to block the Louisiana acquisition.

FLORIDA AND WESTERN SCHEMES

The magnificent prize of Louisiana did not satisfy Republican territorial ambitions. Still to be gained were river outlets on the Gulf Coast essential for the development of plantation agriculture in Alabama and Mississippi. The boundaries of the Louisiana Purchase were so vague that Jefferson felt justified in claiming Spanish-held Texas and the Gulf Coast eastward from New Orleans to Mobile Bay, including the Spanish province of West Florida. Against stiff Spanish opposition, he pushed ahead with his plans to acquire West Florida. This provoked the first challenge to his leadership of the party.

Once it was clear that Spain did not want to sell West Florida to the United States, Jefferson accepted Napoleon's offer to act as a middleman in the acquisition. Napoleon's price was $2 million. He soon lost interest in the project, however, and Jefferson lost prestige in 1806, when he pushed an appropriations bill through Congress to pay for Napoleon's services. Former Republican stalwarts in Congress denounced the bill as bribe money and staged a party revolt against the president's devious tactics.

Jefferson's failed bid for West Florida emboldened Westerners to demand that Americans seize the territory by force. In 1805 and 1806, Aaron Burr, Jefferson's first vice president, apparently became entangled in an attempt at just such a land grab.

Republicans had been suspicious of Burr since his dalliance with the Federalists in their bid to make him, rather than Jefferson, president in 1800. He further alienated the party when he involved himself with the efforts of a minority of die-hard Federalists who feared that incorporation of the vast Louisiana Purchase into the United States would leave New England powerless in national affairs. They concocted a plan for a northern confederacy. New York was central to their scheme. Rebuffed by Hamilton, they turned to Burr and backed him in the New York gubernatorial race of 1804. Burr lost, largely because Hamilton denounced him. The enmity between the two men reached a tragic climax in July 1804, when Burr killed Hamilton in a duel at Weehawken, New Jersey. Although indicted for murder in the state of New Jersey, Burr was able to return to Washington where he both resumed his duties as vice-president and hatched a separatist plot for the west.

The Burr conspiracy remains mysterious. He may have been thinking of carving out a separate western confederacy in the lower Mississippi Valley. Whatever he had in mind, he blundered in relying on General James Wilkinson as a co-conspirator. Wilkinson, the military governor of the Louisiana Territory and also a double agent for Spain, betrayed Burr. Jefferson made extraordinary efforts to secure his conviction, but Burr was acquitted when the government failed to prove its case for treason in 1807.

EMBARGO AND A CRIPPLED PRESIDENCY

Concern about a possible war against Britain in 1807 soon quieted the uproar over Burr's trial. After Britain and France had resumed their war in 1803, the United States became enmeshed in the same quarrels over neutral rights, blockades, ship seizures, and impressment of American sailors that had almost dragged the country into war in the 1790s. Caught in the middle of the conflict between Britain and France, but eager to supply both sides, was the American merchant marine, the world's largest carrier of neutral goods.

During the flush years from 1793 to 1807, American ship tonnage tripled, and the value of exports soared fivefold. American merchants dominated commerce, not only between Britain and the United States, but also between the European continent and the French and Spanish colonies in the West Indies.

In June 1807, however, the **Chesapeake Incident** nearly triggered an Anglo-American war. A British ship, the *Leopard,* ordered a U.S. frigate, the *Chesapeake,* to submit to a search in coastal waters off Norfolk, Virginia. When the commander of the *Chesapeake* refused, the *Leopard* opened fire, and three Americans were killed. Jefferson resisted the popular outcry for revenge. Instead, he barred Amer-

***Chesapeake* Incident** Attack in 1807 by the British ship *Leopard* on the American ship *Chesapeake* in American territorial waters.

ican ports to British warships and called both for monetary compensation and an end to impressments, not only because the country was woefully unprepared for war but also because he passionately believed that international law should settle disputes between nations.

In a last burst of the idealism that had animated the republicanism of the Revolution, Jefferson resorted to a trade embargo as a substitute for war. The **Embargo Act of 1807,** an expression of Jefferson's policy of "peaceable coercion," prohibited American ships from leaving port to any nation until Britain and France repealed their trading restrictions on neutral shippers.

The premise of the embargo was that Europe was so dependent on American foods and raw materials that it would do America's bidding if faced with a cutoff. This premise was not so much wrong as unrealistic. The embargo did hurt Europe, but the people who first felt the pain were British textile workers and slaves in the colonies, hardly those who wielded the levers of power.

The American export trade and its profits dried up with Jefferson's self-imposed blockade. Nearly all economic groups suffered under the embargo. Especially hard hit were New England shippers and merchants, and they accused the Republicans of near-criminal irresponsibility for forcing a depression on the country. Jefferson responded to these criticisms and to widespread violations of the embargo with a series of enforcement acts that consolidated executive powers far beyond what the Federalists themselves had been able to achieve while in power.

As the embargo tightened and the 1808 presidential election approached, the Federalist party revived. The Federalist presidential candidate, Charles C. Pinckney, running against Secretary of State James Madison, Jefferson's hand-picked successor, polled three times as many votes as he had in 1804. Madison won only because he carried the South and the West, the Republican heartland.

Before Madison took office, the Republicans abandoned Jefferson's embargo, replacing it with the Nonintercourse Act, a measure that prohibited American trade only with Britain and France.

The caption on this 1807 illustration of a deserted pier in Portland, Maine— "And the grass literally grew upon the wharves."—reflects the hardship Jefferson's embargo caused as it choked off the American export trade.

North Wind Picture Archives

QUICK REVIEW

Economic Warfare

- June 1807: *Chesapeake* Incident provokes calls for war.
- Jefferson responds with Embargo Act of 1807.
- Embargo Act replaced with less restrictive Nonintercourse Act of 1809.

MADISON AND THE COMING OF WAR

Frail-looking and short, Madison struck most contemporaries as an indecisive and weaker version of Jefferson. Yet in intellectual toughness and resourcefulness he was at least Jefferson's equal. He failed because of an inherited foreign policy that was partly of his own making as Jefferson's secretary of state. The Republicans' idealistic stand on neutral rights was ultimately untenable unless backed up by military and political force. Madison concluded as much when he decided on war against Britain in the spring of 1812. A war against America's old enemy also promised to restore unity to a Republican party increasingly divided over Madison's peaceful diplomacy. Thus did Madison and his fellow Republicans push for a war they were eager but unprepared to fight.

THE FAILURE OF ECONOMIC SANCTIONS

Early in his administration, Madison convinced himself that the impasse in Anglo-American relations was about to be broken. Britain benefited from the Nonintercourse Act at the expense of France, and the British began to relax their restrictions on neutral shipping, known as the Orders in Council, in favor of U.S. commerce. At the same time, the British minister in Washington, David Erskine, reached an agreement with Madison that called for completely rescinding the Orders in Council as they applied to the United States. In return, Madison pledged

WHAT FACTORS pushed Madison into a war with Britain?

Embargo Act of 1807 Act passed by Congress in 1807 prohibiting American ships from leaving for any foreign port.

The Prophet Tenkswatawa was the spiritual leader of the pan-Indian movement that sought to revitalize native culture and block the spread of white settlement in the Old Northwest.

Courtesy of Library of Congress

WHERE TO LEARN MORE

Montpelier, Montpelier Station, Virginia **www.montpelier.org/**

Pan-Indian resistance movement Movement calling for the political and cultural unification of Indian tribes in the late eighteenth and early nineteenth centuries.

to terminate nonintercourse against Britain while maintaining it against France.

Unfortunately, Erskine had exceeded his instructions, and the Madison-Erskine agreement was disavowed as soon as news of it reached London. With Madison floundering, Congress stepped in with its own policy in 1810. Macon's Bill No. 2 threw open American trade to everyone but stipulated that if either France or England lifted its restrictions, the president would resume trading sanctions against the other. Madison now looked even more foolish when he accepted Napoleon's duplicitous promises in 1810 to withdraw his decrees against American shipping on the condition that if Britain did not follow suit, Madison would force the British to respect American rights. Madison was under no illusion as to Napoleon's honesty, but he was desperate to apply pressure on the British to match the apparent French concessions. By the time Napoleon's duplicity became clear, he had already succeeded in worsening Anglo-American tensions. In November 1810, Madison reimposed nonintercourse against Britain, putting the two nations on a collision course.

THE FRONTIER AND INDIAN RESISTANCE

Mounting frustrations in the South and West also pushed Madison toward a war against Britain. Farm prices, including those for the southern staples of cotton and tobacco, plunged when Jefferson's embargo shut off exports, and they stayed low after the embargo was lifted. Blame for the persistent agricultural depression focused on the British and their stranglehold on overseas trade after 1808. As a glut of American goods piled up in English ports, prices remained depressed. Western settlers also accused the British of inciting Indian resistance. The British did seek alliances with Indians in the Old Northwest. However, it was the unceasing demand of Americans for ever more Indian land, not any British incitement, that triggered the **pan-Indian resistance movement** that so frightened western settlers on the eve of the War of 1812.

In the Treaty of Greenville (1795) (see Chapter 8), the American government had promised that any future acquisitions of Indian land would be approved by all native peoples in the region. Nonetheless, government agents continued to play one group against another and encouraged the division of groups from within. By such means, William Henry Harrison, the governor of the Indiana Territory, procured most of southern Indiana in the Treaty of Vincennes of 1804. Two extraordinary leaders, the Shawnee chief Tecumseh and his brother, the Prophet Tenkswatawa, channeled Indian outrage over this treaty into a movement to unify tribes throughout the West for a stand against the white invaders.

The message of pan-Indianism was unwavering: white encroachments had to be stopped and tribal and clan divisions submerged in a return to native rituals and belief systems. Indian land could be saved and self-respect regained only through tribal cooperation and a spiritual rebirth. Tenkswatawa had undergone such a rebirth when he saved himself from alcoholism, and much of the passion he brought to preaching reflected his own sense of redemption. With the assistance of Tecumseh, Tenkswatawa established the Prophet's Town in 1808. At the confluence of the Wabash and Tippecanoe rivers in north-central Indiana, this encampment became headquarters of an intertribal confederation. As he tried to explain to the worried Governor Harrison, his goals were peaceful. He admonished his followers, "[Do] not take up the tomahawk, should it be offered by the British, or by the long knives: do not meddle with any thing that does not belong to you, but mind your own business, and cultivate the ground, that your women and your children have enough to live on."

That ground, of course, was the very reason the Indians could not live in peace and dignity. White settlers wanted it and would do anything to get it. In November 1811, Harrison marched an army to Prophet's Town and provoked the Battle of Tippecanoe. While Tecumseh was absent on a recruiting mission among the southern tribes, impetuous young braves attacked Harrison's army. Losses were heavy on both sides, but Harrison's forces prevailed. Harrison's victory came at a high cost: Tecumseh now joined forces with the British, leaving the frontier more unsettled than ever.

While Harrison's aggressiveness was converting fears of a British-Indian alliance into a self-fulfilling prophecy, expansionist-minded southerners struck at Britain through Spain, now its ally against Napoleon. With the covert support of President Madison, American adventurers staged a bloodless revolt in Spanish West Florida between Louisiana and the Pearl River.

Hatred of Native Americans, expansionist pressures, the lingering agricultural depression, and impatience with the administration's policy of economic coercion, all pointed in the same direction, a war against Britain coupled with an American takeover of British Canada and Spanish Florida. This was the rallying cry of the **War Hawks,** the 40 or so prowar congressmen swept into office in 1810. Generally younger men from the South and West, the War Hawks were led by Henry Clay of Kentucky. Along with other outspoken nationalists, such as John C. Calhoun of South Carolina, Clay played a key role in building congressional support for Madison's growing aggressiveness on the British issue.

DECISION FOR WAR

In July 1811, deceived by Napoleon and dismissed by the British as the head of a second-rate power, Madison had run out of diplomatic options and was losing control of his party.

When Congress met, Madison tried to lay the groundwork for war. But the Republican-controlled Congress balked at strengthening the military or raising taxes to pay for war, citing their party's traditional view of high taxes and a strong military as the tools of despots. Madison secretly asked Congress on April 1, 1812, for a 60-day embargo, a move designed to give American merchant ships time to return safely to their homeports. On June 1, he sent a war message to Congress in which he laid out the stark alternative of submission or resistance to British control of American commerce.

For Madison and most other Republicans, the impending conflict was a second war for independence. Free and open access to world markets was certainly at stake, but so was national pride. The arrogant British policy of impressment was a humiliating affront to American honor and headed the list of grievances in Madison's war message.

A divided Congress declared war on Britain. Support for the war was strongest in regions whose economies had been damaged the most by the British blockade and control of Atlantic commerce. Thus the South and the West favored war. Conversely, mercantile New England, a region that had, ironically, prospered as a result of British interference with ocean commerce, opposed the war.

FEDERALIST ANTIWAR RESOLUTIONS

 s the policies of the Madison administration in the spring of 1812 increasingly pointed toward war against Great Britain, New England Federalists mounted protest meetings in an effort to preserve peace. Passed at a meeting in Providence, Rhode Island, on April 7, 1812, the following resolutions make the Federalist case for the disastrous consequences of a war against Britain and reveal the depths of the party's division over foreign policy.

- On what grounds did the Federalists accuse the Republicans of an anti-British bias?
- What did the Federalists argue would be the results of a war against Britain?
- How could the Federalists now depict France, America's ally during the Revolutionary War, as a greater threat to American freedoms than Britain?

Voted and Resolved unanimously,

That, in our opinion, the peace, prosperity and happiness of these United States, are in great jeopardy; inasmuch as, we have the strongest reasons to believe, the general government have determined to make war on Great-Britain. . . . We are further confirmed in our apprehensions . . . by the evident partiality [the Republicans] have for a long time manifested towards one of the belligerents; and their deep-rooted enmity towards the other. The decrees of both nations equally violate our neutral rights; but France by her Berlin Decree, was the first aggressor; and still persists in capturing and burning our vessels on the high seas; and in robbing, imprisoning, and insulting our citizens; yet all these atrocities have been either palliated, or excused; while every effort has been made to excite the prejudices and animosities of our people against Great Britain. British vessels are excluded from our harbors; and our citizens are forbidden to import goods of the growth and manufacture of Britain and her dependencies; at the same time that French privateers are suffered to refit in American ports; and French goods are received, and protected, by our government. . . . All this, too, is done, when our trade to France, is of little value; and that to England, and her dependence is, of more importance to the United States, than with all the world besides.

Resolved, That . . . believing as we most sincerely do, that a war with England, at this time, is neither necessary, nor expedient, we deem it a duty which we owe to our families, and to our country, to use our utmost efforts to avert so great a calamity; and . . . we are of opinion that this expression ought to be given in the approaching elections. If we choose Democratic [Republican] State Rulers, we choose war; if we choose Federal State Rulers, we choose peace. . . .

But should we, forgetful of our duties, elect democratic rulers, and thereby let loose this wild spirit of war, what calamities, and horrors must spread themselves over those devoted States! All the taxes proposed must fall upon us; our foreign and coasting commerce be cut off; our fisheries be destroyed; our agriculture neglected. . . . The destruction of our navigation would interrupt, and we fear, ruin our numerous, and flourishing manufactories; for, when the enemies['] ships cover our coasts, we can neither obtain the necessary materials, nor export the manufactured goods.

But these evils are only the beginning of sorrows. When war arrives, what will give protections to our harbours and maritime towns? [The enemy] will . . . make a war of frequent, and sudden descent on our long, and defenceless sea-coast. Ships manned, and now moored on the other side of the Atlantic Ocean, can, in forty days, be riding on the waters of our bay and river. What could then save our sea-port towns, together with all the vessels in our harbours from conflagration, pillage, and military exaction?

Dreadful are these consequences of war: but more dreadful will await us. A war with England will bring us into alliance with France. This alliance would make the last page of our history as a nation. All the horrors of war might be endured; but who can endure to become a Slave?; If we are allied to that putrid pestilence of tyranny; our laws, freedom, independence, national name and glory, are blotted out from the memory of man; If Bonaparte sends to this country, ships, and French soldiers, and French generals, we shall soon be like Holland, and Italy, and Switzerland, and every other country where this scourge of nations has been permitted to set his foot.

The votes that carried the war declaration came from northern Republicans, who saw the impending struggle as a defense of America's experiment in self-government. Nine-tenths of the congressional Republicans voted for war, but not a single Federalist did so. For the Federalists, the real enemy was France, which had actually seized more American ships than had the British.

The Federalists' anger increased when they learned that the British had been prepared to yield on one of the most prominent issues. On June 23, the British government revoked for one year its Orders in Council against the United States. This concession, however, did not address impressment or monetary compensation, and news of it reached America too late to avert a war.

THE WAR OF 1812

The Republicans led the nation into a war it was unprepared to fight. Still, the apparent vulnerability of Canada to invasion made it possible to envision an American victory. Yet bungled American invasions verged on tragicomedy, and British-Canadian forces and their Indian allies stymied American advances. Likewise, the British failed to secure their strategic objective—naval control of the Great Lakes—and their counterinvasions of the United States bogged down. By the fall of 1814, both sides were eager for an end to the military stalemate.

Internal dissent endangered the Union as much as did British troops. Nearly all Federalists believed that pro-French fanatics and slaveholding agrarians in the Republican party had consistently sacrificed the commercial interests of New England. A minority of Federalists was convinced that New England could never regain its rightful place in shaping national policy and was prepared to lead a secession movement. Although blocked by party moderates, the secessionists tarred Federalism with the brush of treason. Consequently, the Republicans, the party that brought the country to the brink of a military disaster, emerged from the war more powerful than ever.

SETBACKS IN CANADA

The **War of 1812** unleashed deep emotions that often divided along religious lines. From their strongholds in the Congregationalist churches in New England, the Federalists preached that all true Christians opposed a war "against the nation from which we are descended, and which for many generations has been the bulwark of the religion we profess." Such antiwar sentiments, however, outraged the Baptists and Methodists. They believed, as resolved by the Georgia Baptist Association in 1813, that the British government was "corrupt, arbitrary, and despotic" and that the war was "just, necessary, and indispensable."

Fiercely loyal to Madison, who had championed religious freedom in Virginia, these Methodists and Baptists harbored old grudges against the established churches of both Britain and New England for suppressing their religious rights. Madison hoped to channel this Christian anti-British patriotism into the conquest of Canada. Two out of three Canadians were native-born Americans who, it was assumed, would welcome the United States Army with open arms. Only 5,000 British troops were initially stationed in Canada, and Canadian militia were outnumbered nine to one by their American counterparts. No wonder Madison and his advisers felt that Canada was ripe for the taking, "a mere matter of marching," as Jefferson put it.

Canada was also the only area where the United States could strike directly against British forces. Although officially a war to defend America's neutrality on

GLOBAL PERSPECTIVES

THE U.S. RESPONSE TO INDEPENDENCE MOVEMENTS

"America . . . proclaimed to mankind the inextinguishable rights of human nature, and the only lawful foundations of government. . . . Wherever the standard of freedom and Independence has been or shall be unfurled, there will her heart, her benedictions and her prayers be. But she goes not abroad, in search of monsters to destroy. . . . She well knows that by once enlisting under other banners than her own, were they even the banners of foreign independence, she would involve herself beyond the power of extrication, in all the wars of interest and intrigue, of individual avarice, envy, and ambition, which assume the colors and usurp the standards of freedom. The fundamental maxims of her policy would insensibly change from *liberty* to *force*. . . . She might become the dictatress of the world. She would no longer be the ruler of her spirit. . . . [America's] glory is not *dominion,* but *liberty*. Her march is the march of the mind."

Drawn from the Independence Day speech of Secretary of State John Quincy Adams in 1821, these words gave classic expression to an enduring tension in America's relations with the outside world: Should the United States promote liberty and independence by the force of its example or the force of its arms? Adams was responding to political opponents who were demanding that the United States involve itself in the independence movements in Latin America and Greece. Adams refused to do so. The United States had no vital interests at stake in Greece, and aid to the rebels or premature recognition of the government they were struggling to form carried the risk of embroiling the United States in a conflict with their enemies, the Turks and Russians. Moreover, direct United States involvement in a European affair would set a dangerous precedent that Europeans could cite to intervene in the Western Hemisphere, where Adams wanted the United States to have a free hand.

As for the Latin American revolutionaries, Adams noted their disregard of the civil rights for which Americans had contended during the Revolution. He had no doubt that the independence movements to the south would eventually succeed, but he believed that the United States could best support them and the cause of liberty by championing and vindicating its own freedom and independence. To intervene abroad in an effort to transform foreign societies was to endanger liberty at home.

At the insistence of President Monroe, Adams extended diplomatic recognition to the new Latin American nations in 1822. In so doing, he insisted that the United States would recognize only governments that promised to adhere to all of their international obligations. Recognition, he stressed, carried no moral approval. This was the recognition policy followed by the United States government for 90 years, until President Woodrow Wilson committed it to a policy of liberal interventionism abroad.

the high seas, the War of 1812 was largely a land war. The United States simply did not have enough ships to do more than harass the powerful British navy.

Madison's strategic vision was clear, but its execution was pathetic. Three offensives against Canada in 1812 were embarrassing failures. In the first, in July, General William Hull crossed into Canada from Detroit and invited Canadians to join the American cause. He found few takers. Meanwhile, Fort Michilimackinac fell, and Tecumseh's warriors cut Hull's communications. Hull hurried back to Detroit, only to surrender his army on August 16 to the smaller British-Indian force.

The loss of Detroit, preceded a day earlier by the abandonment of Fort Dearborn (present-day Chicago) and the massacre of its inhabitants, exposed western settlements to the full fury of frontier warfare. Americans in the Indiana Territory fled outlying areas for the safety of forts in the interior. By the end of the year, the British controlled half of the Old Northwest.

Farther east, the Americans botched two offensives in 1812. In October, an American thrust across the Niagara River was defeated when the New York state militia refused to cross the river to join the regular army troops on the Canadian side. This left the isolated forces under General Stephen Van Rensselaer easy prey for the British at the Battle of Queenston Heights. Then the long-delayed third offensive, aimed at Montreal, the center of British operations in Canada, ended in a bloodless fiasco.

All the Republicans had to show for the first year of the war were morale-boosting but otherwise insignificant naval victories. In individual combat between ships, the small American navy acquitted itself superbly. Early in the war, American privateers harassed British merchant vessels, but the easy pickings were soon gone. British naval squadrons were redeployed to protect shipping, and other warships kept up a blockade that stifled American commerce.

Military setbacks and antiwar feeling in much of the Northeast hurt the Republicans in the election of 1812. Madison won only narrowly. Federalists and other disaffected northerners rallied behind DeWitt Clinton, an antiadministration Republican from New York. The now familiar regional pattern in voting repeated itself. Madison swept the electoral vote of the South and West. He ran poorly in the Northeast and won only because his party held on to Pennsylvania.

Creek war leader Red Eagle surrenders to Andrew Jackson after the Battle of Horseshoe Bend in 1814.

© Corbis

WESTERN VICTORIES AND BRITISH OFFENSIVES

American forces fared better in 1813. In September, the navy won a major engagement on Lake Erie that opened up a supply line in the western theater. Commodore Oliver Hazard Perry attacked the British fleet in the **Battle of Put-in-Bay,** on the southwestern shore of the lake, and forced the surrender of all six British ships.

With the loss of Lake Erie, the British were forced to abandon Detroit. General William Henry Harrison caught up with the British garrison and their Indian allies on the banks of the Thames River in southern Ontario. Harrison won a decisive victory. Tecumseh, the most visionary of the Indian warriors, was killed, and the backbone of the Indian resistance was broken. The Old Northwest was again safe for American settlement.

The Battle of the Thames ended British plans for an Indian buffer state. But by 1814, Britain had bigger goals in mind. A coalition of European powers forced Napoleon to abdicate in April 1814, thus freeing Britain to focus on the American war. British strategy in 1814 called for two major offensives—an invasion south from Montreal down Lake Champlain in upstate New York, and an attack on Louisiana aimed at seizing New Orleans with a task force out of

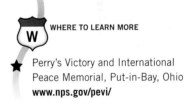

WHERE TO LEARN MORE

Perry's Victory and International Peace Memorial, Put-in-Bay, Ohio
www.nps.gov/pevi/

Battle of Put-in-Bay American naval victory on Lake Erie in September 1813 in the War of 1812 that denied the British strategic control over the Great Lakes.

This is how an artist depicted the American victory at the Battle of the Thames on October 5, 1833. Shown on horseback is Colonel Richard M. Johnson of the Kentucky mounted volunteers, who claimed to have killed Tecumseh during the battle.

Library of Congress

WHERE TO LEARN MORE

★ Fort McHenry National Monument, Baltimore, Maryland
www.nps.gov/fomc/archeology/ overview.html

Treaty of Ghent Treaty signed in December 1814 between the United States and Britain that ended the War of 1812.

Jamaica. The overall objective was nothing less than a reversal of America's post-1783 expansion.

The British attacks could hardly have come at a worse time for the Madison administration. The Treasury was nearly bankrupt. Against the wishes of Treasury Secretary Gallatin, Congress had refused to preserve the Bank of the United States when its charter expired in 1811. Lacking both a centralized means of directing wartime finances and any significant increase in taxes, the Treasury was forced to rely on makeshift loans. Inflation also became a problem when state banks, no longer restrained by the control of a national bank, overissued paper money in the form of bank notes.

As the country's finances tottered toward collapse, political dissent in New England was reaching a climax. In 1814, the British extended their blockade of American commerce northward to include New England. Cries for resistance against "Mr. Madison's war" culminated in a call issued by the Massachusetts legislature for a convention to consider "a radical reform of the national compact."

The darkest hour came in August 1814. A British amphibious force occupied and torched Washington, D.C. The defense of Washington was slipshod at best. Still, the British actions stiffened American resistance, and the failure of a follow-up attack on Baltimore deprived the British of any strategic gain. Baltimore's defenses held, stirring Francis Scott Key, a young lawyer who viewed the bombardment from a British prisoner-of-war ship, to write the Star-Spangled Banner.

The Chesapeake campaign was designed to divert American attention from the major offensive General George Prevost was leading down the shores of Lake Champlain. Prevost commanded the largest and best-equipped army the British had yet assembled, but he was forced to turn back when Commodore Thomas McDonough defeated a British fleet on September 11 at the Battle of Plattsburgh. The British were ready for peace, but one of their trump cards had yet to be played—the southern offensive against New Orleans. The outcome of that campaign could still upset whatever was decided at Ghent.

THE TREATY OF GHENT AND THE BATTLE OF NEW ORLEANS

By the fall of 1814, the British were eager to redraw the map of post-Napoleonic Europe, restore profitable relations with America, and reduce their huge war debt. The British negotiators at Ghent agreed to a peace treaty on terms the Americans were delighted to accept. The **Treaty of Ghent,** signed on Christmas Eve, 1814, simply restored relations to their status at the start of the war. The ink had barely dried on the Treaty of Ghent when the British government sent reinforcements to General Edward Pakenham, the commander of the Louisiana invasion force. The British had always held that the Louisiana Purchase was fraudulent, and they were prepared to install a new government in Louisiana if Pakenham succeeded. Far from being an anticlimax to a war that was already over, the showdown between British and American forces at the **Battle of New Orleans** in January 1815 had immense strategic significance for the United States.

The hero of New Orleans, in song and legend, was Andrew Jackson. A planter-politician from Tennessee, Jackson rose to prominence during the war as a ferocious Indian fighter. As a general in the Tennessee militia, Jackson crushed Indian resistance in the Old Southwest at the Battle of Horseshoe Bend in March 1814. Supported by 600 Indian allies, Jackson's militia virtually slaughtered some 1,000 Creek warriors. Jackson then forced the vanquished Creeks to cede two-thirds of their territory to the United States. On the southern frontier as well as the northern, Native Americans emerged as the major losers of the war.

After his Indian conquests, Jackson was promoted to general in the regular army and given command of the defense of the Gulf Coast. The overconfident British frontally attacked Jackson's lines on January 8, 1815. The result was a massacre.

Strategically, Jackson's smashing victory at New Orleans ended any possibility of a British sphere of influence in Louisiana. Politically, it was a deathblow to Federalism. Set against the revived nationalism that marked the end of the war, the Federalists now seemed to be parochial sulkers who put regional interests above the national good. Worse yet, they struck many Americans as quasi-traitors who had been prepared to desert the country in the face of the enemy. As a significant political force, Federalism was dead.

THE ERA OF GOOD FEELINGS

*I*n 1817, on the occasion of a presidential visit by James Monroe, a Boston newspaper proclaimed the **Era of Good Feelings,** an expression that nicely captured the spirit of political harmony and sectional unity that washed over the republic in the immediate postwar years. National pride surged with the humbling of the British at New Orleans, the demise of the Federalists lessened political tensions, and the economy was booming. The Republicans had been vindicated, and for a short time they enjoyed de facto status as the only governing party.

In 1819, however, an economic depression and a bitter controversy over slavery shattered the harmony. The nationalist tide set in motion by the end of the war had run its course, and the Republicans divided on sectional and economic issues.

ECONOMIC NATIONALISM

The War of 1812 had taught the Republicans to appreciate the old Federalist doctrines on centralized national power. For Henry Clay and John C. Calhoun, the most prominent of the new generation of young, nationalist-minded Republicans, the first order of business was to create a new national bank. Fiscal stability required the monetary coordination and restraint that only a new Bank of the United States could provide. Introduced by Calhoun, the bank bill passed Congress in 1816. Modeled after Hamilton's original bank and also headquartered in Philadelphia, the **Second Bank of the United States** was capitalized at $35 million, making it by far the nation's largest bank. Its size and official status as the depository and dispenser of the government's funds gave the bank tremendous economic power.

After moving to repair the fiscal damage of the war, the Republicans then acted to protect what the war had fostered. Embargoes followed by three years of war had forced American businessmen to manufacture goods they previously had imported. In 1815 and again in 1816, the British inundated the American market

HOW DID rising nationalism contribute to the spirit of the Era of Good Feelings?

Battle of New Orleans
Decisive American War of 1812 victory over British troops in January 1815 that ended any British hopes of gaining control of the lower Mississippi River Valley.

Era of Good Feelings   The period from 1817 to 1823 in which the disappearance of the Federalists enabled the Republicans to govern in a spirit of seemingly nonpartisan harmony.

Second Bank of the United States   A national bank chartered by Congress in 1816 with extensive regulatory powers over currency and credit.

with cheap imports to strangle American industry in its infancy. Responding to this challenge to the nation's economic independence, the Republicans passed the Tariff of 1816, the first protective tariff in American history. The act levied duties of 20 to 25 percent on imported goods that could be produced in the United States.

Responding to pressure from the War Department and western states, Congress earmarked revenue from the tariff and $1.5 million from the Bank of the United States for transportation projects. The lack of a road system in the trans-Appalachian region had severely hampered troop movements during the war. Also, western congressmen demanded improved outlets to eastern markets.

In early 1817, an internal-improvements bill passed Congress. Despite the soaring rhetoric of John C. Calhoun, the bill's sponsor, seeking to "bind the republic together with a perfect system of roads and canals," President Madison remained unmoved. Though in agreement with the bill's objectives, he was convinced that the Constitution did not permit federal financing of primarily local projects. He vetoed the bill just before he left office.

Congressional passage of Calhoun's internal-improvements bill marked the pinnacle of the Republicans' economic nationalism. Frightened by the sectional disunity of the war years, a new generation of Republicans jettisoned many of the ideological trappings of Jefferson's original agrarian party. Their program was a call for economic, and therefore political, unity. Such unity was to be achieved through a generous program of national subsidies consisting of tariffs for manufacturers in the Northeast and transportation funds for planters and farmers in the South and West. Support for this program was strongest in the mid-Atlantic and western states, the regions that stood to gain the most economically. Opposition centered in the Southeast. This opposition took on an increasingly hard edge in the South as the Supreme Court outlined an ever more nationalist interpretation of the Constitution.

JUDICIAL NATIONALISM

Under Chief Justice John Marshall, the Supreme Court had long supported the nationalist perspective Republicans began to champion after the war. Two principles defined Marshall's jurisprudence: the primacy of the Supreme Court in all matters of constitutional interpretation and the sanctity of contractual property rights. In *Fletcher* v. *Peck* (1810), for example, the Court ruled that a Georgia law voiding a land grant made by an earlier legislature—on the grounds that it had involved massive fraud—violated the constitutional provision barring any state from "impairing the obligation of contracts." Marshall held that despite the fraud, the original land grant constituted an unbreakable legal contract.

In *Dartmouth College* v. *Woodward*, the Court ruled that Dartmouth's original royal charter of 1769 was a contract protected by the Constitution. Therefore the state of New Hampshire could not alter the charter without the prior consent of the college. By sanctifying charters, or acts of incorporation, as contracts, the Court prohibited states from interfering with the rights and privileges they had bestowed on private corporations.

In *McCulloch* v. *Maryland* (1819), a unanimous Court, in language similar to but even more sweeping than that used by Alexander Hamilton in the 1790s, upheld the constitutional authority of Congress to charter a national bank and thereby regulate the nation's currency and finances. As long as the end was legitimate "within the scope of the Constitution," Congress had full power to use any means not expressly forbidden by the Constitution to achieve that end. Here was the boldest statement to date of the loose, or "implied powers," interpretation of the Constitution.

QUICK REVIEW

Economic Nationalism
- Second Bank of the United States established.
- Tariff of 1816 protected American manufacturers.
- Revenue from the tariff earmarked for transportation projects.

Fletcher **v. Peck** Supreme Court decision of 1810 that overturned a state law by ruling that it violated a legal contract.

Dartmouth College **v. Woodward** Supreme Court decision of 1819 that prohibited states from interfering with the privileges granted to a private corporation.

TOWARD A CONTINENTAL EMPIRE

Marshall's legal nationalism paralleled the diplomatic nationalism of John Quincy Adams, secretary of state from 1817 to 1825. Convinced in his Puritan soul that God and nature had ordained that America stretch from the Atlantic to the Pacific as a beacon of liberty to the world, Adams used whatever tactics were necessary to realize that vision. Adams shrewdly exploited Britain's desire for friendly and profitable relations after the War of 1812.

The **Rush-Bagot Agreement** of 1817 signaled the new pattern of Anglo-American cooperation. The agreement strictly limited naval armaments on the Great Lakes, thus effectively demilitarizing the border with Canada. The **Anglo-American Accords** of the following year resolved several issues left hanging after the war. The British once again recognized American fishing rights off Labrador and Newfoundland, a concession that was of great importance to New England. The boundary of the Louisiana Territory abutting Canada was set at the 49th parallel, and both nations agreed to the joint occupation of Oregon, the territory in the Pacific Northwest that lay west of the Rocky Mountains.

Having secured the northern flank of the United States, Adams was now free to deal with the South and West. Adams wanted all of Florida and an undisputed American window on the Pacific. The adversary here was Spain. In March 1818, Jackson led his troops across the border into Spanish Florida. He destroyed encampments of the Seminole Indians, seized two Spanish forts, and executed two British subjects on the grounds that they were selling arms to the Seminoles for raids on the Alabama-Georgia frontier. Despite later protestations to the contrary, Jackson had probably exceeded his orders. He might well have been censured by the Monroe administration had not Adams supported him, telling Spain that Jackson was defending American interests and warning that he might be unleashed again.

Spain yielded to the American threat in the **Trans-Continental Treaty of 1819.** The United States annexed East Florida, and Spain recognized the prior American seizures of West Florida in 1810 and 1813. Adams secured an American hold on the Pacific Coast by drawing a boundary between the Louisiana Purchase and the Spanish Southwest that ran stepwise up the Sabine, Red, and Arkansas rivers to the Continental Divide and then due west along the 42nd parallel to the Pacific. Spain renounced any claim to the Pacific Northwest; the United States in turn renounced its shaky claim to Texas under the Louisiana Purchase and assumed $5 million in Spanish debts to American citizens.

Adams's success in the Spanish negotiations turned on the British refusal to threaten war or assist Spain in the wake of Jackson's high-handed actions in Florida. Spanish possessions and the lives of two British subjects were worth little when weighed against the economic advantages of retaining close trading ties with the United States. Moreover, Britain, like the United States, had a vested interest in developing trade with the newly independent Latin American countries. Recognizing this common interest, George Canning, the British foreign minister, proposed in August 1823 that the United States and Britain issue a joint declaration opposing any European attempt to recolonize South America or to assist Spain in regaining its colonies.

President Monroe rejected the British overture, but only at the insistence of Adams. Canning's offer had a string attached to it: a mutual pledge by the British and Americans not to annex former Spanish territory. But Adams was confident that within a generation, the United States would acquire California, Texas, and perhaps Cuba as well. He wanted to maintain the maximum freedom of action for

Rush-Bagot Agreement Treaty of 1817 between the United States and Britain that effectively demilitarized the Great Lakes by sharply limiting the number of ships each power could station on them.

Anglo-American Accords Series of agreements reached in the British-American Conventions of 1818 that fixed the western boundary between the United States and Canada, allowed for joint occupation of Oregon, and restored American fishing rights.

Trans-Continental Treaty of 1819 Treaty between the United States and Spain in which Spain ceded Florida to the United States, surrendered all claims to the Pacific Northwest, and agreed to a boundary between the Louisiana Purchase territory and the Spanish Southwest.

Monroe Doctrine In December 1823, Monroe declared to Congress that the Americas "are henceforth not to be considered as subjects for future colonization by any European power."

future U.S. policy and avoid any impression that America was beholden to Britain. He also wanted to cement relations with the new nations of Latin America that he had refused to recognize formally until 1822. Thus originated the most famous diplomatic statement in early American history, the **Monroe Doctrine.**

In his annual message to Congress in December 1823, Monroe declared that the Americas "are henceforth not to be considered as subjects for future colonization by any European power." In turn, Monroe pledged that the United States would not interfere in the internal affairs of European states.

THE BREAKDOWN OF UNITY

WHY DID slavery become such a divisive issue in the years preceding the Missouri Compromise?

For all the intensity with which he pursued his continental vision, John Quincy Adams worried in early 1819 that "the greatest danger of this union was in the overgrown extent of its territory, combining with the slavery question." His words were prophetic. A sectional crisis flared in 1819 over slavery and its expansion when the territory of Missouri sought admission to the Union as a slave state. Simultaneously, a financial panic ended postwar prosperity and crystallized regional discontent over banking and tariff policies. Party unity cracked under these pressures, and each region backed its own presidential candidate in the wide-open election of 1824.

This 1830 painting shows Chief Justice John Marshall in the full robes of his office. Marshall's leadership molded the Supreme Court into an effective instrument of the national government.

John Marshall by Chester Harding (1792–1886), Oil on canvas, 1830. U.R. 106.1830. Collection of the Boston Athenaeum.

THE PANIC OF 1819

From 1815 to 1818, Americans enjoyed a wave of postwar prosperity. European markets were starved for American goods after a generation of war and trade restrictions, so farmers and planters expanded production and brought new land into cultivation. The availability of public land in the West on easy terms of credit sparked a speculative frenzy, and land sales soared. State banks and, worse yet, the Bank of the United States fed the speculation by making loans in the form of bank notes far in excess of their hard-currency reserves. Before the bubble burst, cotton prices doubled to 30 cents a pound and real-estate values became wildly inflated.

European markets for American cotton and food supplies returned to normal by late 1818. In January 1819, cotton prices sank in England, and the Panic of 1819 was on. Cotton was the most valuable American export, and expected returns from the staple were the basis for an intricate credit network anchored in Britain. The fall in cotton prices triggered a credit contraction that soon engulfed the overextended American economy. Commodity prices fell across the board, and real-estate values collapsed, especially in and around western cities.

A sudden shift in policy by the Bank of the United States virtually guaranteed that the economic downturn would settle into a depression. The Bank stopped all loans, called in all debts, and refused to honor drafts drawn on its branches in the South and West. Bankruptcies mush-

roomed as creditors forced the liquidation of farms and real estate. For westerners, the Bank of the United States now became "the Monster," a ruthless institution controlled by eastern aristocrats who callously destroyed the hopes of farmers.

Southern resentment over the hard times brought on by low cotton prices
focused on the tariff. Planters charged that the Tariff of 1816 unfairly raised their
costs and amounted to an unconstitutional tax levied for the sole benefit of northern manufacturers. Unreconstructed Jeffersonians, now known as the Old Republicans, spearheaded a sharp reaction against the South's flirtation with
nationalist policies in the postwar period by demanding a return to strict states'-
rights doctrines.

THE MISSOURI COMPROMISE

Until 1819, slavery was not a major divisive issue in American politics. The Northwest Ordinance of 1787, which banned slavery in federal territories north of the
Ohio River, and the Southwest Ordinance of 1790, which permitted slavery south
of the Ohio, represented a compromise that had allowed slavery in areas where
climate and soil conditions favored slave-based agriculture. What was unforeseen
in the 1780s, however, was the explosive demand for slave-produced cotton
generated by the English textile industry in the early nineteenth century (see
Chapter 11).

Despite the prohibition of the African slave trade in 1807, all hopes for the
natural death of slavery were gone by 1819. Kentucky, Tennessee, Louisiana, Mississippi, and Alabama had all been added to the Union as slave states since 1787.
Florida had just been annexed and surely would be another slave state. A thriving cotton market was underwriting slavery's expansion across the South, and
even Missouri, a portion of the Louisiana Purchase that northerners initially assumed would be inhospitable to slavery, had fallen under the political control of
slaveholders.

The Missouri issue increased long-simmering northern resentment over the
spread of slavery and the southern dominance of national affairs under the Virginia presidents. In February 1819, James Tallmadge, a Republican congressman
from New York, introduced an amendment in the House mandating a ban on future slave imports and a program of gradual emancipation as preconditions for
the admission of Missouri as a state. Missourians, as well as southerners in general,
rejected the Tallmadge Amendment. The states, they argued, had absolute sovereignty in the drafting of their constitutions, and any attempt by Congress to set
conditions for statehood was unconstitutional.

Without a two-party system in which each party had to compromise to protect its interests, voting followed sectional lines. The amendment passed in the
northern-controlled House, but it was repeatedly blocked in the Senate, which
was evenly divided between free and slave states. The debates were heated, and
southerners spoke openly of secession if Missouri were denied admission as a slave
state.

The stalemate over Missouri persisted into the next session of Congress. Finally,
Speaker of the House Henry Clay engineered a compromise in March 1820. Congress put no restrictions on slavery in Missouri, and the admission of Missouri as a
slave state was balanced by the admission of Maine (formerly part of Massachusetts)
as a free state. In return for their concession on Missouri, northern congressmen
demanded a prohibition on slavery in the remainder of the Louisiana Purchase north
of the 36°30′ parallel, the southern boundary of Missouri (see Map 9–1). With the

9–5
Thomas Jefferson
Reacts to the
"Missouri Question"
(1820)

QUICK REVIEW

Tallmadge Amendment

- Tallmadge Amendment (1819: ban
  on future slave importations and
  imposition of program of gradual
  emancipation as condition of
  Missouri statehood.)
- Passed by the House but rejected by
  the Senate.
- Voting broke down on regional
  lines.

MAP EXPLORATION

To explore an interactive version of this map, go to **http://www.prenhall.com/goldfield3/map9.1**

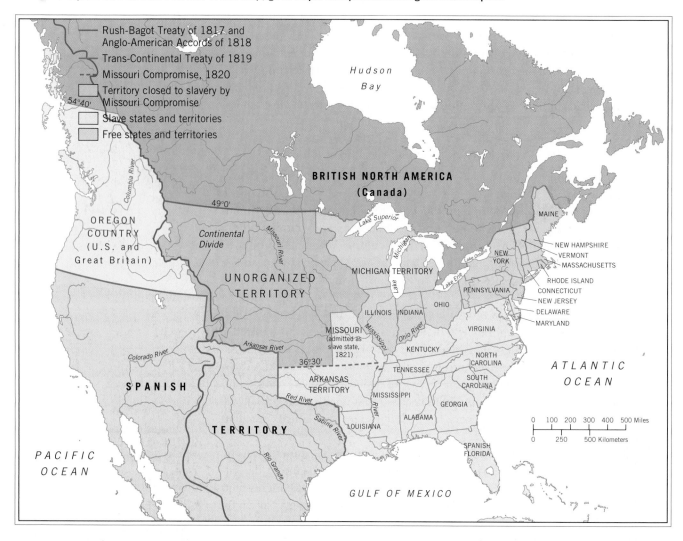

MAP 9–1   **The Missouri Compromise of 1820 and Territorial Treaties with Britain and Spain, 1818–1819**   Treaties with Britain and Spain in 1818 and 1819 clarified and expanded the nation's boundaries. Britain accepted the 49th parallel as the boundary between Canada and the United States in the Trans-Mississippi West to the Oregon Country; Spain ceded Florida to the United States and agreed to a boundary stretching to the Pacific between the Louisiana Purchase territory and Spanish possessions in the Southwest. Sectional disputes over slavery led to the drawing of the Missouri Compromise line of 1820 that prohibited slavery in the Louisiana Territory north of 36°30.

HOW DID the treaties with Spain and Britain of 1818 and 1819 and the Missouri Compromise of 1820 geographically change the United States?

Missouri Compromise

Sectional compromise in Congress in 1820 that admitted Missouri to the Union as a slave state and Maine as a free state and prohibited slavery in the northern Louisiana Purchase territory.

Missouri Compromise, the Louisiana Purchase was closed to slavery in the future, except for the Arkansas Territory and what would become the Indian Territory of Oklahoma. The compromise almost unraveled when Missouri submitted a constitution the following November that required the state legislature to bar the entry of free black people. This mandate violated the guarantee in the U.S. Constitution that "the citizens of each State shall be entitled to all privileges and im-munities of citizens in the several States." Missouri's restric-tionist policy obviously denied African-American citizens the constitutional right to move from one state to any other state. Southerners were quick to point out, however, that free states as well as slave states already restricted the right of free black people to vote or to serve in the militia.

The nearly universal acceptance by white Americans of second-class citizenship for free black Americans permit-ted Clay to dodge the issue. Missouri's constitution was ac-cepted with the proviso that it "shall never be construed" to discriminate against citizens in other states. By sacrificing the claims of free black citizens for equal treatment, the Union survived its first great sectional crisis over slavery.

The Missouri crisis made white southerners aware that they were now a political minority within the Union. More rapid population growth in the North had reduced south-ern representation in the House to just over 40 percent. Of greater concern was the crystallization in Congress of a northern majority arrayed against the expansion of slavery. Southern threats of secession died out in the aftermath of the Missouri Compromise, but it was an open question whether the sectional settlement really solved the inter-twined issues of slavery and expansion or merely side-stepped them for a day of final reckoning.

THE ELECTION OF 1824

The election of 1820 made Monroe, like both his Repub-lican predecessors, a two-term president. Republican unity, however, was more apparent than real. Voters had no choice in 1820, and without two-party competition, no outlets existed for expressing popular dissatisfaction with the Republicans. Instead, the Republicans split into fac-tions as they began jockeying almost immediately for the election of 1824 (see Map 9–2).

Five candidates competed to replace Madison. All of them were nominal Republicans, and three were members of his cabinet. Secretary of War John C. Cal-houn soon dropped out. He preferred to accept a nomination as vice president, confident that his turn would come in 1828. The other candidates, Secretary of the Treasury William Crawford from Georgia, Secretary of State John Quincy Adams from Massachusetts, Henry Clay from Kentucky, and Andrew Jackson from Tennessee, each had a strong regional following. As the Republican Party frag-mented, sectional loyalties were replacing partisan allegiances.

As the "official" party nominee, Crawford was the early favorite. Clay, Jack-son, and Adams were nominated by their state legislatures. None of the candi-dates ran on a platform, but Crawford was identified with states' rights, and Clay and Adams with centralized government. Clay in particular was associated with the national bank, protective tariffs, and federally funded internal improvements, a package of federal subsidies he called the **American System.** Jackson took no stand on any of the issues.

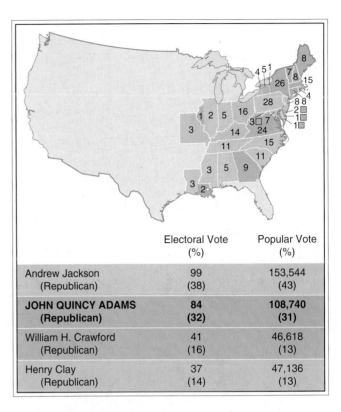

	Electoral Vote (%)	Popular Vote (%)
Andrew Jackson (Republican)	99 (38)	153,544 (43)
JOHN QUINCY ADAMS (Republican)	**84 (32)**	**108,740 (31)**
William H. Crawford (Republican)	41 (16)	46,618 (13)
Henry Clay (Republican)	37 (14)	47,136 (13)

MAP 9–2   The Election of 1824   The regional appeal of each of the four presidential candidates in the election of 1824 prevented any candidate from receiving a majority of the electoral vote. Consequently, and as set forth in the Constitution, the House of Representatives had to choose the president from the three lead-ing candidates. Its choice was John Quincy Adams.

WHAT DOES this map suggest about the political climate in the United States in 1824?

American System   The pro-gram of government subsidies fa-vored by Henry Clay and his followers to promote American economic growth and protect do-mestic manufacturers from foreign competition.

Jackson's noncommittal stance turned out to be a great asset. It helped him to project the image of a military hero, fresh from the people, who was unsullied by any connection with Washington politicians, whom the public associated with hard times and sectional controversies. He was the highest vote-getter (43 percent of the popular vote), but none of the four candidates had a majority in the electoral college.

As in 1800, the election was thrown into the House of Representatives. Each state had one vote. Clay, who had received the fewest electoral votes, was eliminated. Crawford had suffered a debilitating stroke and was no longer a viable candidate. Thus it came down to Adams or Jackson. Anxious to undercut Jackson, his chief rival in the West, Clay used his influence as speaker of the House to line up support for Adams, a fellow advocate of a strong centralized government.

Adams won the election, and he immediately named Clay as his secretary of state, the office traditionally viewed as a stepping-stone to the presidency. Jackson and his followers were outraged. They smelled a "corrupt bargain" in which Clay had bargained away the presidency to the highest bidder. Vowing revenge, they began building a new party that would usher in a more democratic era of mass-based politics.

CONCLUSION

In 1800, the Republicans were an untested party whose rise to power frightened many Federalists into predicting the end of the Union and constitutional government. The Federalists were correct in sensing that their days of power had passed, but they underestimated the ideological flexibility the Republicans would reveal once in office and the imaginative ways in which Jefferson and his successors would wield executive power to expand the size of the original Union. The Republicans were shrewd empire builders astute enough to add to their base of political support in the South and West. They also paved the way for the nation to evolve as a democratic republic rather than the more aristocratic republic preferred by the Federalists.

Most Federalists never did learn the art of popular electioneering, and they were too elitist to have any desire to do so. Although foreign-policy issues arising out of Jefferson's and Madison's attempts to assert American neutral rights during the Anglo-French war kept the Federalists alive and even briefly revived the party, the British posed the greatest test of Republican leadership. The Republicans chose war rather than surrender their claims of American rights. Jackson's victory at the Battle of New Orleans ended the war in a burst of American glory, and the Federalists were swept aside by the postwar surge of nationalism.

By the mid-1820s, the Republicans were about to join the Federalists as political dinosaurs. With no Federalist threat to enforce party discipline, the Republicans lost their organizational strength. Embracing economic nationalism after the war made the party's original focus on states' rights all but meaningless. Ideologically and organizationally adrift, the party split into regional coalitions in the wake of the Missouri controversy and the panic of 1819. But before it dissolved, the party left as its most enduring legacy the foundations of a continental empire.

SUMMARY

Jefferson's Presidency Thomas Jefferson believed that a true revolution had occurred in 1800, a peaceful overthrow of the Federalist party. Unlike Federalists, Jeffersonian Republicans wanted an agrarian republic based on widespread economic equality for white yeomen farmers. The cornerstone of his Republican policy was retrenchment, a return to the frugal, simple federal establishment. His foreign policy successes included the Louisiana Purchase; however, his Embargo Act of 1807 crippled his presidency in its final year.

Madison and the Coming of War Early in his administration, Madison became convinced that the impasse in Anglo-American relations was about to be broken. Mounting frustrations in the South and West also pushed Madison toward a war against Britain. On the eve of war Madison had to deal with the pan-Indian resistance movement and the Battle of Tippecanoe. And, as war with Britain seemed imminent, the war cries of the War Hawks pushed the nation ever closer to the brink.

The War of 1812 In 1812, Republicans in a divided Congress led the nation into a war it was unprepared to fight. Internal dissent endangered the Union almost as much as the British. Early losses to the British in Canada were embarrassing defeats for Madison; however, later battles saw U.S. victories despite a successful British naval blockade. The final and decisive battle (the Battle of New Orleans) came in 1815 as Andrew Jackson led the United States to victory in the war.

The Era of Good Feelings In 1817 a Boston newspaper proclaimed the Era of Good Feelings, a spirit of political harmony in the postwar years. Henry Clay and John Calhoun, having learned to appreciate old Federalist doctrines on centralized national power, created the Second Bank of the United States. And, after moving to repair the fiscal damage of the War of 1812, Republicans then acted to protect what the war had fostered through tariffs. Nationalism also took hold in the form of judicial nationalism in several landmark Supreme Court rulings. Finally, diplomatic nationalism paved the way for expanding the United States through treaties with Britain and Spain.

The Breakdown of Unity In 1819, an economic depression and a bitter controversy over slavery shattered the harmony, and Republicans divided on sectional and economic issues. Sinking prices for American products overseas led to the Panic of 1819. Soon the economic panic led Southerners to worry about the North's emancipation powers. The slavery controversy was partly quelled by the Missouri Compromise. And, in 1824, John Quincy Adams became president in an election that effectively ended the unity in the Republican party.

IMAGE KEY
for pages 236–237

a. Thomas Jefferson.
b. "Burning of the White House" by Leslie Saalburg.
c. Map of the Great Lakes.
d. James Monroe and Robert R. Livingstone completing negotiations with Comte Talleyrand for the Louisiana Purchase.
e. Portrait of Dolley Madison.
f. Portrait of James Madison.
g. The caption on this 1807 illustration of a deserted pier in Portland, Maine—"And the grass literally grew upon the warves."—reflects the hardship Jefferson's embargo caused as it choked off the American export trade.
h. War of 1812, Battle of Lake Erie.
i. Portrait of Thomas Jefferson.
j. Red Eagle surrenders to Andrew Jackson.

REVIEW QUESTIONS

1. What changes did the Republicans bring to the federal government? How did their policies differ from those of their Federalist predecessors?

2. Why were the Republicans so intent on expanding the boundaries of the United States, and why did the Federalists oppose an expansionist program?

3. What factors accounted for the Federalists' inability to regain national power after they lost the election of 1800?

4. What external and internal factors drew the United States into war against Britain? Could the war have been avoided?

5. What accounted for the difficulties of the United States in waging the War of 1812, and why was the war widely viewed as a great American victory? How did the war lead to an increasing pattern of diplomatic cooperation between the United States and Britain?

6. Why was Rosalie Calvert so critical of the Republican party and U.S. entry into the War of 1812? To what extent would New England Federalists have shared her views?

7. What explains the upsurge of nationalism that underlay the Era of Good Feelings? Why were the Republicans unable to maintain their party unity after 1819?

8. What accounted for the noninvolvement of the United States in the revolutionary movements in Latin America and the long delay in extending formal recognition to the new governments established there?

KEY TERMS

American System (p. 259)
Anglo-American Accords (p. 255)
Battle of New Orleans (p. 253)
Put-in-Bay, Battle of (p. 251)
Chesapeake **Incident** (p. 244)
Dartmouth College v. Woodward (p. 254)
Embargo Act of 1807 (p. 245)

Era of Good Feelings (p. 253)
Fletcher v. Peck (p. 254)
Marbury v. Madison (p. 242)
Missouri Compromise (p. 258)
Monroe Doctrine (p. 256)
Pan-Indian resistance movement (p. 246)
Rush-Bagot Agreement (p. 255)

Second Bank of the United States (p. 253)
Trans-Continental Treaty of 1819 (p. 255)
Treaty of Ghent (p. 252)
War Hawks (p. 247)
War of 1812 (p. 249)

WHERE TO LEARN MORE

Fort McHenry National Monument, Baltimore, Maryland. This historic site preserves the fort that was the focal point of the British attack on Baltimore and contains a museum with materials on the battle and the writing of the Star-Spangled Banner. For the military history of the fort and the archaeological work at the site, see **www.nps.gov/fomc/archeology/overview.html**

- **Tippecanoe Battlefield Museum, Battle Ground, Indiana.** This museum includes artifacts from the Indian and white settlement of Indiana and visual materials on the Battle of Tippecanoe of 1811. The museum's website at **www.tcha.mus.in.us/battlefield.htm** includes an account of the battle and its aftermath.

- **Monticello, Charlottesville, Virginia.** The architecturally unique home of Thomas Jefferson and the headquarters for his plantation serves as a museum that provides insights into Jefferson's varied interests. Information on educational programs and upcoming events at Monticello, as well as the new Jefferson Library in Charlottesville, can be found at **www.monticello.org/**

- **Montpelier, Montpelier Station, Virginia.** The museum here was the home of James Madison, and it includes material on his life as a politician and planter. Its website at **www.montpelier.org/** provides information on tours and programs and a look at the archaeological findings at Montpelier.

- **Perry's Victory and International Peace Memorial, Put-in-Bay, Ohio.** At the site of Perry's decisive victory on Lake Erie in 1813 now stands a museum that depicts the role of the Old Northwest in the War of 1812. For a printable travel guide and information on the new visitor center, see **www.nps.gov/pevi/**

- **Lewis and Clark Expedition.** This site provides a wealth of information and resources, including photo essays, interactive maps, web resources, a list of planned events, the journals of the expedition, and a bibliography of recent works. **http://www.time.com/time/2002/lewis_clark**

 U.S. History Documents CD-ROM
For primary sources related to this chapter, refer to the document CD-ROM.

 www.prenhall.com/goldfield
For study resources related to this chapter, visit the *Companion Website*™.

10 The Jacksonian Era
1824–1845

CHAPTER HIGHLIGHTS

The Egalitarian Impulse By the end of the 1820s, universal white male suffrage was the norm almost everywhere. Between 1800 and 1840 the Second Great Awakening transformed the religious landscape. The same egalitarian impulse drove these twin democratic revolutions.

Jackson's Presidency Jackson portrayed himself as the embodiment of the people's will. Jackson promoted policies that forced most Indians out of the Eastern United States. Jackson's stands in the Nullification Crisis and the Bank War demonstrated that he tolerated no opposition to his positions.

Van Buren and Hard Times The Panic of 1837 set the tone for Van Buren's presidency. Van Buren's Independent Treasury reestablished the Democrat's reputation as the party of limited government. Van Buren's reputation as a vacillator undermined his support.

The Rise of the Whig Party The Whigs based their mass appeal on the claim they could best defend the republican liberties of the people. Whigs believed in social progress and interventionist government. In 1840 they took control of both the Congress and the presidency.

The Whigs in Power William Henry Harrison's death made John Tyler president. He blocked Whig legislation and was expelled from the party. The Texas issue played a major role in the election of 1844, an election won by James K. Polk.

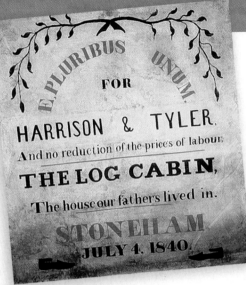

CHAPTER QUESTIONS

WHAT WERE the political consequences of the Second Great Awakening?

HOW DID the Jacksonian Democrats capitalize on the new mass politics?

WHAT CHALLENGES did Van Buren face during his presidency?

WHAT WAS the basis of Whig popularity? What did they claim to stand for?

WHY WAS William Henry Harrison's death such a blow to the Whig agenda?

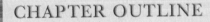

CHAPTER OUTLINE

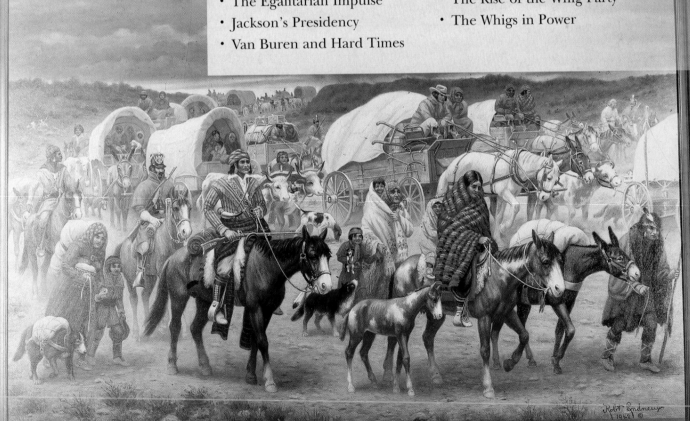

IMAGE KEY
for pages 264–265 is on page 291.

Newport, New Hampshire

September, 1828

Wherever a person may chance to be in company, he will hear nothing but politicks discussed. In the ballroom, or at the dinner table, in the Stage-coach & in the tavern; even the social chitchat of the tea table must yield up to the everlasting subject.

How many friendships are broken up! With what rancor the political war is carried on between the editorial corps! To what meanness[,] vulgarity & abuse is that champion of liberty, in proper hands, the press prostituted! With what lies and scandal does the columns of almost every political paper abound! I blush for my country when I see such things, & I often tremble with apprehension that our Constitution will not long withstand the current which threatens to overwhelm it. Our government is so based that an honest difference between American citizens must always exist. But the rancorous excitement which now threatens our civil liberties and a dissolution of this Union does not emanate from an honest difference of opinion, but from a determination of an unholy league to trample down an Administration, be it ever so pure, & be its acts ever so just. It must not be. There is a kind Providence that overlooks the destinies of this Nation and will not suffer it to be overthrown by a party of aspiring office seekers & political demagogues.

Benjamin B. French

Donald B. Cole and John J. McDonough, eds., *Witness to the Young Republic: A Yankee's Journal, 1828–1870* (Hanover, N.H.: University Press of New England, 1989), pp. 15–16.

BENJAMIN BROWN FRENCH, a young editor and county clerk in Newport, New Hampshire, penned these words in his journal in September 1828. Like most other Americans, he was amazed, indeed, shocked, by the intense, seemingly all-pervasive partisanship stirred up in the presidential election of 1828 between Andrew Jackson and John Quincy Adams. Whether measured by the vulgar personal attacks launched by a partisan press, the amount of whiskey and beef consumed at political barbecues, or the huge increase in voter turnout, this election marked the entrance of ordinary Americans onto the political stage.

The partisanship that French found so disturbing in 1828 quickly became the basis of his livelihood. After joining the Democrats in 1831, he spent most of his subsequent years as a political officeholder in Washington, holding a variety of appointive jobs. His own fortunes initially depended on the political success of the Democratic party. Then, after breaking with the Democrats in the 1850s over the slavery issue, he succeeded in finding government employment in Republican administrations until his death in 1870.

What made French's career possible was the ongoing democratization of American politics in the early decades of the nineteenth century. The number and potential power of the voters expanded, and professional politicians realized that party success now depended on reaching and organizing this enlarged electorate. The "Jacksonian Democrats," named for their leader, Andrew Jackson, were the first party to learn this fundamental lesson. Trumpeting Andrew Jackson as the friend of the common man and the foe of aristocratic privilege, they won a landslide victory in 1828 and held national power through the 1830s.

By the mid-1830s, the Whig party had formed in opposition to the Jacksonians. The Whigs offered an ordered vision of American progress and liberty, anchored in the use of governmental power to expand economic opportunities and promote morality. By embracing electoral techniques of popular appeal first used by the Democrats, the Whigs captured the presidency in 1840. Their triumph heralded a new party system, one based on massive voter turnouts and two-party competition in every state.

The luckless Whigs failed to capitalize on their victory, however. Their newly elected president, William Henry Harrison, died shortly after entering office, and Vice President John Tyler, his successor, blocked the Whigs' economic program. Spurned by the Whigs as a traitor, Tyler then reopened the explosive question of slavery and territorial expansion by pushing to annex the independent republic of Texas, where slavery was legal.

The Democrats regained power in 1844 by skillfully exploiting the Texas issue, but they set an ominous precedent. The debate over the expansion of slavery became embedded in the political system, and the greatest strength of the mass-based parties, their ability to tap and unleash popular emotions, now became their greatest weakness. The slavery issue began to take on a life of its own beyond the control of party leaders. The seeds of the Civil War were being sown.

THE EGALITARIAN IMPULSE

WHAT WERE the political consequences of the Second Great Awakening?

Political democracy, defined as the majority rule of white males, was far from complete in early nineteenth-century America. Acting on the belief that only property owners with a stake in society should have a voice in governing it, the landed and commercial elites of the Revolutionary era erected legal barriers against the full expression of majority sentiments. These barriers came under increasing attack after 1800 and were all but eliminated by the 1820s.

As politics opened to mass participation, popular styles of religious leadership and worship emerged in a broad reaction to the formalism and elitism of the dominant Protestant churches. The same egalitarian impulse drove these twin democratic revolutions, and both represented an empowerment of the common man. Popular movements now spoke his language and appealed to his quest for republican equality. (Women would have to wait longer.)

THE EXTENSION OF WHITE MALE DEMOCRACY

In 1816 Congress thought itself prudent and justified when it voted itself a hefty raise to $1,500 a year. The public thought otherwise. So sharp was the reaction against the Salary Act of 1816 that 70 percent of the members of Congress were turned out of office at the next election. Congress quickly repealed the salary increase, but not before John C. Calhoun spoke for many in Congress when he plaintively asked, "Are we bound in all cases to do what is popular?" The answer was apparently yes.

The uproar over the Salary Act marked a turning point in the transition from the deferential politics of the Federalist-Republican period to the egalitarianism of the coming Jacksonian era. Individual states, not the federal government, defined who could vote. Six states, Indiana, Mississippi, Illinois, Alabama,

QUICK REVIEW

Salary Act of 1816
- Congress voted itself a pay raise.
- Outraged public rejects 70 percent of incumbents at next election.
- Conflict represents turn toward the politics of Jacksonian era.

Chronology

1826	Disappearance of William Morgan.	1833	Congress passes the Force Act and the Compromise Tariff.
1827	Emergence of the Anti-Masons, the first third party.		American Anti-Slavery Society established.
1828	Andrew Jackson elected president.	1834	Whig party begins to organize.
	John C. Calhoun writes *The South Carolina Exposition and Protest.*	1836	Texas War of Independence and establishment of the Republic of Texas.
1830	Congress passes the Indian Removal Act.		Congress passes first gag rule on abolitionist petitions.
	Greek independence established.		Van Buren elected president.
	July Revolution in France.	1837	Panic of 1837 sets off a depression.
	Revolutions break out in Belgium, Poland, and Italian states.	1840	Independent Treasury Act passes.
1831	William Lloyd Garrison starts publication of the *Liberator.*		William Henry Harrison elected first Whig president.
	Nat Turner leads a slave uprising in Virginia.	1841	John Tyler succeeds to presidency on death of Harrison.
1832	Jackson vetoes bill for rechartering the Second Bank of the United States; Bank War begins.	1842	United States and Britain sign the Webster-Ashburton Treaty.
	South Carolina nullifies the Tariffs of 1828 and 1832.	1844	James K. Polk elected president.
	Jackson reelected.		Gag rule repealed.
	Election reform bill passes in Britain.	1845	Texas admitted to the Union.

Missouri, and Maine, entered the Union between 1816 and 1821, and none of them required voters to own property. Meanwhile, proponents of suffrage liberalization won major victories in the older states. By the end of the 1820s, universal white male suffrage was the norm everywhere except Rhode Island, Virginia, and Louisiana.

Extending the Suffrage and Democratic Reform.   Broadening the suffrage was part of a general democratization of political structures and procedures in the state governments. Representation in most state legislatures was made more equal by giving more seats to newer, rapidly growing regions. States removed or reduced property qualifications for officeholding. The selection of local officials and, in many cases, judges was taken out of the hands of governors and executive councils and given to the voters. Written ballots were the norm by the 1820s. Most significant for national politics, voters acquired the power to choose presidential electors. (see Map 10–1).

Several currents swelled the movement for democratic reform. Limiting voting rights to those who owned landed property seemed increasingly elitist when economic changes were producing new classes—workers, clerks, and small tradesmen—whose livelihoods were not tied directly to the land. At the same time, the middling and lower ranks of society demanded the ballot and access to offices to protect themselves from the commercial and manufacturing interests that benefited most from economic change.

Of greatest importance, however, was the incessant demand that all white men be treated equally. The logical extension of the ideology of the American

QUICK REVIEW

Expansion of the Franchise

- Opposition to land ownership as qualification for voting.
- Demands that all white men be treated equally.
- As political rights for white men expanded, political opportunities shrunk for women and free black people.

MAP EXPLORATION

 To explore an interactive version of this map, go to **http://www.prenhall.com/goldfield3/ map10.1**

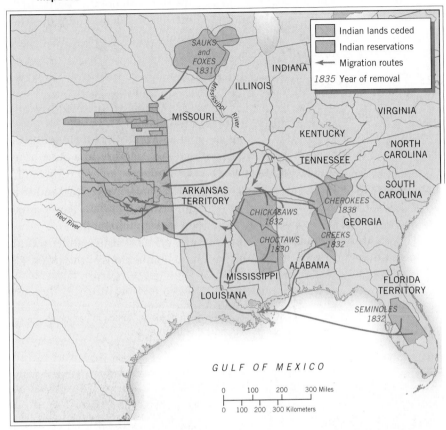

MAP 10–1   Indian Removals   The fixed policy of the Jackson administration and pressure from the states forced Native Americans in the 1830s to migrate from their eastern home-lands to a special Indian reserve west of the Mississippi River.

WHY DO you think the Indian reservations are located west of the Mississippi?

Revolution, this demand for equality made republicanism by the 1820s synony-mous with simple majority rule.

The Disfranchisement of Free Blacks and Women.   As political opportuni-ties expanded for white males, they shrank for women and free black people. By the early 1800s, race and gender began to replace wealth and status as the basis for defining the limits of political participation. In state after state, the same con-stitutional conventions that embraced universal suffrage for white men deprived black men of the vote or burdened them with special property qualifications. Moreover, none of the 10 states that entered the Union from 1821 to 1861 al-lowed black suffrage. African Americans protested in vain. "Foreigners and aliens to the government and laws," complained black New Yorkers in 1837, "strangers to our institutions, are permitted to flock to this land and in a few years are en-dowed with all the privileges of citizens; but we native born Americans . . . are most of us shut out." By the 1850s, black males could vote only in certain New England states.

Advocates of greater democratization explicitly argued that only white males had the intelligence and love of liberty to be entrusted with political rights. In denouncing distinctions drawn on property as artificial and demeaning, the white egalitarians simultaneously erected new distinctions based on race and sex that were supposedly natural and hence immutable.

THE POPULAR RELIGIOUS REVOLT

Second Great Awakening
Series of religious revivals in the first of the nineteenth century characterized by great emotionalism in large public meetings.

In religion as well as politics, ordinary Americans demanded a greater voice in the early nineteenth century. Insurgent religious movements rejected the formalism and traditional Calvinism of the Congregational and Presbyterian churches, the dominant Protestant denominations in Washington's America. In a blaze of fervor known as the **Second Great Awakening,** evangelical sects led by the Methodists and Baptists radically transformed the religious landscape between 1800 and 1840. A more popularly rooted Christianity moved outward and downward as it spread across frontier areas and converted marginalized and common folk.

The Baptists and Methodists, both spinning off numerous splinter groups, grew spectacularly and were the largest religious denominations by the 1820s. The

The Second Great Awakening originated on the frontier. Preachers were adept at arousing emotional fervor, and women in particular responded to the evangelical message of spiritual equality open to all who would accept Christ into their lives.

Collection of the New York Historical Society, Negative # 26275

key to their success was their ability to give religious expression to the popular impulse behind democratic reform. Especially in the backcountry of the South and West, where the first revivals occurred, itinerant preachers reshaped religion to fit the needs and values of ordinary Americans.

Evangelical Christianity emphasized personal, heartfelt experience that would produce a spiritual rebirth. The emotional force unleashed at the mass revivals known as camp meetings astounded observers. "The scene that then presented itself to my mind was indescribable," recalled James Finley of the camp meeting at Cane Ridge, Kentucky, in 1801. "At one time I saw at least five hundred swept down in a moment, as if a battery of a thousand guns had been opened upon them, and then immediately followed shrieks and shouts that rent the very heavens."

The evangelical religion of the traveling preachers was democratic in its populist rejection of traditional religious canons and its encouragement of organizational forms that gave a voice to popular culture. Salvation was no longer simply bestowed by an implacable God, as taught by the Calvinist doctrine of individual predestination (see Chapter 1). Ordinary people could now actively choose salvation, and this possibility was exhilarating. "Why, then, I can be saved!" exclaimed Jesse Lee upon hearing a Methodist preacher in Massachusetts. "I have been taught that only a part of the race could be saved, but if this man's singing be true, all may be saved." Evangelical churches bound the faithful into tightly knit communities that expressed and enforced local values and standards of conduct.

Evangelicalism and Minority Rights.

Evangelicalism was especially appealing to women and African Americans. Excluded from most areas of public life, women found strength and comfort in the evangelical message of Christian love and equality. As the wife of a Connecticut minister explained, church membership offered women a welcome release from "being treated like beasts of burden [and] drudges of domineering masters." In the first flush of evangelical excitement, female itinerant preachers spread the gospel up and down the East Coast. By thus defying social convention, these women offered a model of independent action. Other women organized their own institutions within denominations still formally controlled by men. Women activists founded and largely directed hundreds of church-affiliated charitable societies and missionary associations.

Evangelicalism also empowered black Americans. African American Christianity experienced its first sustained growth in the generation after the Revolutionary War. As a result of their uncompromising commitment to convert slaves, the Baptists and Methodists led the way. They welcomed slaves at their revivals, encouraged black preachers, and above all else, advocated secular and spiritual equality. Many of the early Baptist and Methodist preachers directly challenged slavery. In converting to Methodism, one slave stated that "from the sermon I heard, I felt that God had made all men free and equal, and that I ought not be a slave." Perceiving in it the promise of liberty and deliverance, the slaves received the evangelical gospel in loud, joyous, and highly emotional revivals. They made it part of their own culture, fusing Christianity with folk beliefs from their African heritage.

The Limits of Equality.

But for all its liberating appeal to women and African Americans, evangelicalism was eventually limited by race and gender in much the same way as the democratic reform movement. Denied positions of authority in white-dominated churches and resentful of white opposition to integrated worship, free black northerners founded their own independent churches.

As increasing numbers of planters embraced evangelicalism after the 1820s, southern evangelicals first muted their attacks on slavery and then developed a full-blown religious defense of it based on the biblical sanctioning of human bondage. They similarly cited the Old Testament patriarchs to defend the unquestioned authority of fathers over their households, the masters of slaves, women, and children. Many popular religious sects in the North also used a particularist reading of the Bible to exalt the independence of white males at the expense of everyone else.

In religion as well as politics, white men retained the power in Jacksonian America. Still, the Second Great Awakening removed a major intellectual barrier to political democracy. Traditional Protestant theology viewed the mass of humanity as sinners predestined to damnation and hence was loath to accept the idea that those same sinners, by majority vote, should make crucial political decisions. In rejecting this theology, ordinary Americans made a fundamental intellectual breakthrough. "Salvation open to all" powerfully reinforced the legitimacy of "one man, one vote."

THE RISE OF THE JACKSONIANS

The Jacksonian Democrats were the first party to mold and organize the democratizing impulse in popular culture. Much like the revivalists and the democratic reformers, the Jacksonians fashioned communications techniques that tapped into the hopes and fears of ordinary Americans. In so doing, they built the first mass-based party in American history.

In Andrew Jackson the new **Democratic party** that formed between 1824 and 1828 had the perfect candidate for the increasingly democratic temperament of the 1820s. Born of Scots-Irish ancestry on the Carolina frontier in 1767, Jackson was a self-made product of the southern backcountry. Lacking any formal education, family connections, or inherited wealth to ease his way, he relied on his own wits and raw courage to carve out a career as a frontier lawyer and planter in Tennessee. He won fame as the military savior of the republic with his victory at the Battle of New Orleans. Conqueror of the British, the Spanish, and the Indians, all of whom had blocked frontier expansion, he achieved incredible popularity in his native South. His strengths and prejudices were those most valued by the restless, mobile Americans to whom he became a folk hero.

Jackson lost the election of 1824, but his defeat turned out to be a blessing in disguise. The wheeling and dealing in Congress that gave the presidency to John Quincy Adams enveloped his administration in a cloud of suspicion from the start. It also enhanced Jackson's appeal as the honest tribune of the people whose rightful claim to the presidency had been spurned by intriguing politicians in Washington. His supporters now claimed that the people, as well as Jackson, had been swindled by the "corrupt bargain" between Adams and Clay. Moreover, the ill-fated Adams presidency virtually destroyed itself. Adams seemed frozen in an eighteenth-century past. Uncomfortable with the give-and-take of politics or the idea of building a coalition to support himself, Adams was out of touch with the political realities of the 1820s.

Just how out of touch was revealed when Adams delivered his first annual message to Congress in 1825. He presented a bold vision of an activist federal government promoting economic growth, social advancement, and scientific progress. Such a vision might have received a fair hearing in 1815, when postwar nationalism was in full stride. By 1825, postwar nationalism had dissolved into sectional bickering and burning resentments against banks, tariffs, and the political establishment. The Jacksonians charged that an administration born in corruption now wanted to waste the people's money by promoting more corruption and greed. And when Adams urged Americans not "to proclaim to the world that we are palsied by the will of our constituents," the Jacksonians attacked him as an arrogant aristocrat contemptuous of the common man.

Little of Adams's program passed Congress, and his nationalist vision drove his opponents into the Jackson camp. Southern planters jumped onto the Jackson bandwagon out of fear that Adams might use federal power against slavery; westerners joined because Adams revived their suspicions of the East. The most important addition came from New York, where Martin Van Buren had built the **Albany Regency,** a tightly disciplined state political machine.

Van Buren belonged to a new breed of professional politicians. As a young lawyer, he quickly grasped how politics could open up career opportunities. The discipline and regularity of strict party organization gave him and others from the middling ranks a winning edge in competition against their social betters. Van Buren redefined parties as something good in and of themselves. Indeed, he and his followers argued that parties were indispensable instruments for the successful expression of the popular will against the dominance of elites.

State leaders such as Van Buren organized the first national campaign that relied extensively on new techniques of mass mobilization. In rallying support for Jackson against Adams in 1828, these state leaders put together chains of party-subsidized newspapers and coordinated a frantic schedule of meetings and rallies. Grassroots Jackson committees reached out to voters. Politics became a folk spectacle as torchlight parades awakened sleepy towns and political barbecues doled out whiskey and food to farmers from the surrounding countryside.

The election of 1828 centered on personalities, not issues. This in itself was a victory for Jackson's campaign managers. Although each side tried to depict the other's candidate as morally unfit, the Jackson men were more in tune with public sentiment, which identified Adams's call for a strong government with special privileges for the favored few. Thus for many voters, Adams personified a discredited elite and Jackson the voice of the people.

Jackson carried every state south and west of Pennsylvania in 1828 and polled 56 percent of the popular vote. Voter turnout shot up to 55 percent from the apathetic 25 percent of 1824. Adams ran well only in New England and in commercialized areas producing goods for outside markets. Aside from the South, where he was virtually untouchable, Jackson's appeal was strongest among ordinary Americans who valued their local independence and felt threatened by outside centers of power beyond their control. He rolled up heavy majorities from Scots-Irish farmers in the Baptist-Methodist evangelical belt of the backcountry and from unskilled workers with an Irish Catholic background.

Jackson's Presidency

Once in office, Jackson proved to be the most forceful and energetic president since Jefferson. Jackson dominated his presidency with the sheer force of his personality. At one time or another, his administration angered southern planters, frightened eastern bankers and commercial interests, and outraged New England reformers. Nonetheless, Jackson remained popular because he portrayed himself as the embodiment of the people's will.

The Jacksonians had no particular program in 1828. Apart from removing Indians to areas west of the Mississippi River, Jackson's first term was notable primarily for its political infighting. Two political struggles that came to a head in

HOW DID the Jacksonian Democrats capitalize on the new mass politics?

Albany Regency   The tightly disciplined state political machine built by Martin Van Buren in New York.

JACKSON.

New Orleans Jan.ʸ 8.ᵗʰ 1815.

This bust portrait of Jackson in uniform, issued as a print during the 1832 presidential race, invokes his military image and especially his victory at New Orleans in 1815.

Library of Congress

WHERE TO LEARN MORE

★ The Hermitage, Hermitage, Tennessee **www.thehermitage.com/**

10–4
The "Commoner"
Takes Office (1828)

Spoils system The awarding of government jobs to party loyalists.

1832–1833, the Bank War and the nullification crisis, stamped the Jacksonians with a lasting party identity. By destroying the Second Bank of the United States and rejecting the attempt of South Carolina to nullify (or annul) a national tariff, Jackson firmly established the Democrats as the enemy of special privilege, the friend of the common man, and the defender of the Union.

JACKSON'S APPEAL

Jackson's inauguration struck many conservatives as ushering in a vulgar new order in national affairs. A vast crowd poured into Washington to applaud the people's hero. They cheered loudly when Jackson took his oath of office and then rushed to the White House for a postinauguration reception, where they pressed in on waiters trying to serve refreshments. Bowls of liquor-laced punch went flying, and glass and china crashed to the floor as a seeming mob surged through the White House.

Ordinary Americans identified with Jackson as with no earlier president, and he convinced them that he was using his office as the instrument of their will. Although they were led by wealthy planters and entrepreneurs, the Jacksonians skillfully depicted themselves as the champions of the common man against aristocratic interests that had enriched themselves through special privileges granted by the government. Jackson proclaimed his task as one of restoring the federal government to the ideal of Jeffersonian republicanism, in which farmers and artisans could pursue their individual liberty free of any government intervention that favored the rich and powerful.

Jackson began his assault on special privilege by proclaiming a reform of the appointment process for federal officeholders. Accusing his predecessors, especially Adams, of having created a social elite of self-serving bureaucrats, he vowed to make government service more responsive to the popular will.

Jackson's reform of the federal bureaucracy had more style than substance. He removed only about one-fifth of the officeholders he inherited, and most of his appointees came from the same relatively high-status groups as the Adams people. But by providing a democratic rationale for government service, he opened the way for future presidents to move more aggressively against incumbents. Thus emerged the **spoils system,** in which the victorious party gave government jobs to its supporters and removed the appointees of the defeated party, tying party loyalty to the reward of a federal appointment.

When Jackson railed against economic privilege, he most often had in mind Henry Clay's American System (see Chapter 9). Clay's program called for a protective tariff, a national bank, and federal subsidies for internal improvements; his goal was to bind Americans together in an integrated national market. To the Democrats, Clay's system represented government favoritism at its worst, a set of costly benefits at the public's expense for special-interest groups. In 1830, Jackson struck a blow for the Democratic conception of the limited federal role in economic development. He vetoed the Maysville Road Bill, which would have provided federal money for a road to be built entirely within Kentucky. The bill was unconstitutional, he claimed, because it benefited only the citizens of Kentucky and not the American people as a whole. Moreover, since the Maysville project was within Clay's congressional district, Jackson had the added delight of embarrassing his most prominent political enemy.

Jackson's Maysville veto did not rule out congressional appropriations for projects deemed beneficial to the general public. This pragmatic loophole gave Democrats all the room they needed to pass more internal-improvement projects during Jackson's presidency than during all of the previous administrations together. Having built a mass party, the Democrats soon discovered that they had to funnel federal funds to their constituents back home.

INDIAN REMOVAL

Some 125,000 Indians lived east of the Mississippi when Jackson became president. The largest concentration was in the South, where five Indian nations, the Cherokees, Creeks, Choctaws, Chickasaws, and Seminoles, controlled millions of acres of land in what soon would become the great cotton frontiers of southwestern Georgia and central Alabama and Mississippi.

Pressure from the states to remove the Indians had been building since the end of the War of 1812. It was most intense in Georgia. In early 1825, Georgia authorities finalized a fraudulent treaty that ceded most of the Creek Indians' land to the state.

In 1828, Georgia moved against the Cherokees, the best-organized and most advanced (by white standards) of the Indian nations. By now a prosperous society of small farmers with their own newspaper and schools for their children, the Cherokees wanted to avoid the fate of their Creek neighbors. In 1827, they adopted a constitution declaring themselves an independent nation with complete sovereignty over their land. The Georgia legislature reacted by placing the Cherokees directly under state law, annulling Cherokee laws and even the right of the Cherokees to make laws, and legally defining the Cherokees as tenants on land belonging to the state of Georgia. By also prohibiting Indian testimony in cases against white people, the legislature stripped the Cherokees of any legal rights. They were now easy prey for white settlers, who scrambled onto Cherokee land after gold was discovered in northern Georgia in 1829. Alabama and Mississippi followed Georgia's lead in denying Indians legal rights.

Thus the stage was set for what Jackson always considered the most important measure of the early days of his administration, the **Indian Removal Act.** Jackson had no qualms about allowing state officials to override federal protection of Native Americans. In his first annual message, Jackson sided with state officials in the South and advised the Indians "to emigrate beyond the Mississippi or submit to the laws of those States." This advice enabled Jackson to pose as the friend of the Indians, the wise father who would lead them out of harm's way and save them from rapacious white people.

Congress acted on Jackson's recommendation in the Indian Removal Act of 1830. The act appropriated $500,000 for the negotiation of new treaties under which the southern Indians would surrender their territory and be removed to land in the trans-Mississippi area (primarily present-day Oklahoma). Although force was not authorized and Jackson stressed that removal should be voluntary, no federal protection was provided for Indians harassed into leaving by land-hungry settlers. Ultimately, Jackson did deploy the U.S. Army, but only to

10–5
Andrew Jackson, First Annual Message to Congress (1829)

QUICK REVIEW

Georgia and the Cherokees

- Georgia stole land of Creek Indians in 1825.
- Georgia moved against Cherokees in 1828, stripping them of all legal rights.
- Stage was set for Indian Removal Act.

Indian Removal Act   President Andrew Jackson's measure that allowed state officials to override federal protection of Native Americans.

For the Cherokees, the *Trail of Tears* stretched 1,200 miles from the homeland in the East to what became the Indian Territory in Oklahoma.
The Granger Collection, New York

Trail of Tears   The forced march in 1838 of the Cherokee Indians from their homelands in Georgia to the Indian Territory in the West.

Black Hawk's War   Short 1832 war in which federal troops and Illinois militia units defeated the Sauk and Fox Indians led by Black Hawk.

round up and push out Indians who refused to comply with the new removal treaties.

And so most of the Indians left the eastern United States. The government was ill prepared to supervise the removal. The private groups that won the federal contracts for transporting and provisioning the Indians were the ones that had entered the lowest bids Thousands of Indians, perhaps as many as one-fourth of those who started the trek, died on the way to Oklahoma, the victims of cold, hunger, disease, and the general callousness of the white people they met along the way. It was indeed, as recalled in the collective memory of the Cherokees, a **Trail of Tears.**

Tribes that resisted removal were attacked by white armies. Federal troops joined local militias in 1832 in suppressing the Sauk and Fox Indians of Illinois and Wisconsin in what was called **Black Hawk's War.** More a frantic attempt by the Indians to reach safety on the west bank of the Mississippi than an actual war, this affair ended in the slaughter of 500 Indian men, women, and children by white troops and their Sioux allies. The Seminoles held out in the swamps of Florida for seven years between 1835 and 1842 in what became the longest Indian war in American history. Their resistance continued even after their leader, Osceola, was captured while negotiating under a flag of truce.

Jackson forged ahead with his removal policy despite the opposition of eastern reformers and Protestant missionaries. Aligned with conservatives concerned by Jackson's cavalier disregard of federal treaty obligations, they came within three votes of defeating the removal bill in the House of Representatives. Jackson ignored their protests (see American Views: "Memorial and Protest of the Cherokee Nation, 1836" pages 278–79) as well as the legal rulings of the Supreme Court. In *Cherokee Nation v. Georgia* (1831) and *Worcester v. Georgia* (1832), the Court ruled that Georgia had violated the U.S. Constitution in extending its jurisdiction over the Cherokees. Chief Justice John Marshall defined Indian tribes as "dependent domestic nations" subject only to the authority of the federal government. Marshall may have won the legal argument, but he was powerless to enforce his decisions without Jackson's cooperation. Aware that southerners and westerners were on his side, Jackson ignored the Supreme Court rulings and pushed Indian removal to its tragic conclusion.

THE NULLIFICATION CRISIS

Jackson's stand on Indian removal confirmed the impression of many of his followers that when state and national power conflicted, he could be trusted to side with the states. But when states' rights forces in South Carolina, known as the nullifiers, directly challenged Jackson in the early 1830s over tariff policy, they precipitated the nullification crisis, the most serious sectional crisis since the Missouri debates of 1819–1820. And Jackson revealed himself to be an ardent nationalist on the issue of majority rule in the Union. He won the showdown with South Carolina and established the nationalist credentials of his Democratic party. In reaction to his strong stand, however, the solid front of Democratic power in the South began to crack.

After the first protective tariff in 1816, rates increased further in 1824 and then jumped to 50 percent in 1828 in what was denounced as the "Tariff of Abominations." Southerners were especially angry over the 1828 tariff, because it had been contrived by northern Democrats to win additional northern support for Jackson in his presidential campaign. The outcry was loudest in South Carolina, an old cotton state losing population to the West in the 1820s as cotton prices remained low after the Panic of 1819. What fueled antitariff sentiment was not just the economic argument that high tariffs worsened the agricultural depression by raising the cost of manufactured goods purchased by farmers and planters and lowering the foreign demand for agricultural exports. Protective tariffs were also denounced as an unconstitutional extension of national power over the states; many southern planters feared that they were only a prelude to forced emancipation of the slaves.

South Carolina was the only state where African Americans made up the majority of the population. In the marshes and tidal flats south of Charleston, the lowcountry district of huge rice plantations black people outnumbered, white people ten to one in the summer months. Nat Turner's Rebellion, a bloody slave uprising in Virginia in 1831, and earlier aborted rebellions in the 1820s (see Chapter 11), left fearful planters convinced that growing antislavery agitation in the North and in England was feeding slave unrest. The disturbances so far would be "nothing to what we shall see," warned the South Carolina planter James Hamilton, Jr., "if we do not stand manfully at the Safety Valve of Nullification."

Led by the lowcountry planters, the antitariff forces in South Carolina controlled state politics by 1832. They called themselves the nullifiers, a name derived from the constitutional theory developed by John C. Calhoun. Pushing to its logical extreme the states'-rights doctrine first outlined in the Kentucky and Virginia Resolutions of 1798, Calhoun argued that a state, acting through a popularly elected convention, had the sovereign power to declare an act of the national

WHERE TO LEARN MORE

Rice Museum, Georgetown, South Carolina **www.ricemuseum.com/**

QUICK REVIEW

Fear of Rebellion and Northern Intentions

- African Americans were majority of South Carolina's population.
- Rebellions convinced planters that anti-slavery movement was feeding slave unrest.
- Southerners feared that protective tariffs were a prelude to emancipation.

AMERICAN VIEWS

MEMORIAL AND PROTESTS OF THE CHEROKEE NATION, 1836

O*f the major tribes in the Southeast, the Chero-kees fought longest and hardest against the Jacksonian policy of Indian removal. Led by their principal chief, John Ross, the son of a Scot and a mixed-blood Cherokee woman, they submitted the following protest to Congress against the fraudulent 1835 Treaty of New Echota forced on them by the state of Georgia. Although clearly opposed by an overwhelming majority of the Cherokees, this treaty provided the legal basis for the forced removal of the Cherokee people from Georgia to the Indian Territory.*

- On what legal grounds did the Cherokees base their protest? What pledges had been made to them by the U.S. government?
- What did the Cherokees mean when they said they had been "taught to think and feel as the American citizen"? If the Cherokees had become "civilized" by white standards, why did most whites still insist on their removal?
- Why would President Jackson have allowed white intruders to remain on land reserved by treaties for the Cherokees?
- Do you feel that the Cherokees were justified in believing that they had been betrayed by the American government?

The undersigned representatives of the Cherokee nation, east of the river Mississippi, impelled by duty, would respectfully submit . . . the following statement of facts: It will be seen, from the numerous treaties between the Cherokee nation and the United States, that from the earliest existence of this government, the United States, in Congress assembled, received the Cherokees and their nation into favor and protection; and that the chiefs and warriors, for themselves and all parts of the Cherokee nation, acknowledged themselves and the said Cherokee nation to be under the protection of the United States of America, and of no other sovereign whatsoever: they also stipulated, that the said Cherokee nation will not hold any treaty with any foreign power, individual State, or with individuals of any State: that for, and in consideration of, valuable concessions made by the Cherokee nation, the United States solemnly guaranteed to said nation all their lands not ceded, and pledged the faith of the government, that "all white people who have intruded, or may hereafter intrude, on the lands reserved for the Cherokees, shall be removed by the United States, and proceeded against, according to the provisions of the act, passed 30th March, 1802," entitled "An act to regulate trade and intercourse with the Indian tribes, and to preserve peace on the frontiers." It would be useless to recapitulate the numerous provisions for the security and protection of the rights of the Cherokees, to be found in the various treaties between their nation and the United States. The Cherokees were happy and prosperous under a scrupulous observance of treaty stipulations by the government of the United States, and from the fostering hand extended over them, they made rapid advances in civilization, morals, and in the arts and sciences. Little did they anticipate, that when taught to think and feel as the American citizen, and to have with him a common interest, they were to be despoiled by their guardian, to become strangers and wanderers in the land of their fathers, forced to return to the savage life, and to seek a new home in the wilds of the far west, and that without their consent. An instrument purporting to be a treaty with the Cherokee people, has recently been made public by the President of the United States, that will have such an operation, if carried into effect. This instrument, the delegation ever before the civilized world, and in the presence of Almighty God, is fraudulent, false upon its face, made by unauthorized individuals, without the sanction, and against the wishes, of the great body of the Cherokee people. Upwards of fifteen thousand of those people have protested against it, solemnly declaring they will never acquiesce.

Source: U.S. Congress, *Executive Documents* (1836)

THE MILITANT CONSCIOUSNESS OF WILLIAM APESS

Although virtually erased in the historical record, the Native Americans of New England had not vanished by the nineteenth century. They persisted, both as individuals and as a culture. Numbering no more than a few thousand, most lived impoverished on reservations where they were denied the local self-governance extended to whites. The young left early, searching for whatever paying jobs they could find. One of these marginalized, transient Indians, the Pequot William Apess, produced a remarkable collection of autobiographical and protest writings that he began publishing in pamphlet form in 1829. The following excerpts reveal the anger, passion, and eloquence he brought to his indictment of white injustices to his people in Massachusetts.

> Why does Apess link the plight of Indians in Massachusetts with that of Indians in Georgia?
> How does he use the military contributions of Indians on the patriot side in the American Revolution to stake a claim for himself and his people to the liberties of republicanism?
> In what way does does his condemnation of the dispossession of Indian lands by whites change or complicate the traditional approach to American history as an unfolding story of freedom and opportunity?

Perhaps you have heard of the oppression of the Cherokees and lamented over them much, and thought the Georgians were hard and cruel creatures; but did you ever hear of the poor, oppressed and degraded Marshpee Indians in Massachusetts and lament over them? . . . And we do not know why the people of this Commonwealth want to cruelize us any longer, for we are sure that our fathers *fought, bled, and died for the liberties* of their now weeping and suffering children. . . . *Oh, white man! white man!* The blood of our fathers, spilt in the Revolutionary War, cries from the ground of our native soil, to break the chains of oppression, and let our children *go free!*" . . .

No doubt there are many good people in the United States who would not trample upon the rights of the poor, but there are many others who are willing to roll in their coaches upon the tears and blood of the poor and unoffending natives—those who are ready at all times to speculate on the Indians and defraud them out of their rightful possessions. Let the poor Indian attempt to resist the encroachments of his white neighbors, what a hue and cry is instantly raised against him. It has been considered as a trifling thing for the whites to make war on the Indians for the purpose of driving them from their country and taking possession thereof. This was, in their estimation, all right, as it helped to extend the territory and enriched some individuals. But let the thing be changed. Suppose an overwhelming army should march into the United States for the purpose of subduing it and enslaving the citizens; how quick would they fly to arms, gather in multitudes around the tree of liberty, and contend for their rights with the last drop of their blood. And should the enemy succeed, would they not eventually rise and endeavor to regain their liberty? And who would blame them for it?

Source: Barry O'Connell, ed., *On Our Own Ground: The Complete Writings of Willaim Apess, a Pequot* (University of Massachusetts Press, 1992).

government null and inoperative. Once a state nullified a law, it was to remain unenforceable within that state's borders unless three-fourths of all the states approved a constitutional amendment delegating to the national government the power that was challenged. If such an amendment passed, the nullifying state had the right to leave the Union.

Calhoun, who had been elected vice president in 1828, openly embraced nullification after he broke with Jackson in 1830. Just as the president learned that Calhoun, while secretary of war in 1818, had wanted to censure Jackson for his raid into Spanish Florida, a curious episode known as the Eaton Affair was reaching a climax. When the wives of Jackson's cabinet members, led by Floride Calhoun, pointedly snubbed Peggy Eaton, the wife of Jackson's secretary of war, on the grounds that she was a "loose woman" who had driven her first husband to suicide, Jackson was convinced that Calhoun was plotting to discredit his administration. The political consequences of the Eaton Affair included not only Calhoun's fall from Jackson's favor but also the resignation of the entire cabinet.

With Calhoun's approval, a South Carolina convention in November 1832 nullified the tariffs of 1828 and 1832 (a compromise tariff that did not reduce rates to a low enough level to satisfy the nullifiers). The convention decreed that customs duties were not to be collected in South Carolina after February 1, 1833.

Calhoun always insisted that nullification was not secession. He further defended his doctrine as a constitutional means of protecting minority rights within a Union dominated by a tyrannical national majority. Jackson considered nullification a dangerous and nonsensical perversion of the Constitution, and he vowed to crush any attempt to block the enforcement of federal laws.

In January 1833, Jackson, in the Force Bill, received from Congress full authorization to put down nullification by military force. Simultaneously, he worked to defuse nullification by supporting a new tariff that would cut duties by half within two years. Because Jackson's opponents in Congress did not want him to get political credit for brokering a compromise, they pushed through their own tariff measure. The Compromise Tariff of 1833 lowered duties to 20 percent but extended the reductions over a 10-year period. Up against this combination of the carrot and the stick, the nullifiers backed down.

Jackson's stand established the principle of national supremacy grounded in the will of the majority. Despite his victory, however, states'-rights doctrines remained popular both in the South and among many northern Democrats. By dramatically affirming his right to use force against a state in defense of the Union, Jackson drove many planters out of the Democratic party. In the shock waves set off by the nullification crisis, a new anti-Jackson coalition began to form in the South.

THE BANK WAR

What amounted to a war against the Bank of the United States became the centerpiece of Jackson's presidency and a defining event for the Democratic Party. Like most westerners, Jackson distrusted banks. Because gold and silver coins were scarce and the national government did not issue or regulate paper currency, money consisted primarily of notes issued as loans by private and state banks. These bank notes fluctuated in value according to the reputation and creditworthiness of the issuing banks. In the credit-starved West, banks were particularly unreliable. Many bankers made quick profits by issuing notes without the gold or silver reserves to redeem them and then skipping town when they were on the verge of being found out. Even when issued by honest bankers, notes often could not be redeemed at face value because of market conditions. All of this struck

QUICK REVIEW

Jackson and the Bank of the United States

- Jackson and most Westerners distrusted banks.
- Jackson talked about not rechartering the Bank of the United States.
- Struggle over future of Bank ended with victory for Jackson at expense of Democrats image.

many Americans, and especially farmers and workers, as inherently dishonest. They wanted to be paid in "real" money, gold or silver coin, and they viewed bankers as parasites who did nothing but fatten their own pockets by manipulating paper money. The largest and most powerful bank was the Bank of the United States, and citizens who were wiped out or forced to retrench drastically by the Panic of 1819 never forgave the Bank for saving itself at the expense of its debtors. Still, prosperous times had returned, and the Bank underwrote the economic expansion with its healthy credit reserves and stable bank notes. By 1832, the Bank was as popular as it ever would be.

Beginning with his first annual message, Jackson had been making noise about not rechartering the

This Democratic cartoon portrays Jackson as the champion of the people attacking the Bank of the United States, a many-headed monster whose tentacles of corruption spread throughout the states.

Collection of The New York Historical Society, Negative # 42459

Bank, at least in its present form. Searching for an issue to use against Jackson in the presidential campaign of 1832, Clay forced Jackson's hand. Clay convinced bank president Nicholas Biddle to apply to Congress for a new charter. Clay reasoned that he had Jackson trapped. If Jackson went along with the new charter, Clay could take credit for the measure. If he vetoed it, Clay could attack Jackson as the enemy of a sound banking system.

Clay's clever strategy backfired. Jackson turned on him and the Bank with a vengeance. On July 10, 1832, Jackson vetoed the rechartering bill for the Bank in a message that appealed both to state bankers and to foes of all banks. He took a ringing "stand against all new grants of monopolies and exclusive privileges, against any prostitution of our Government to the advancement of the few at the expense of the many."

The business community and eastern elites lashed out at Jackson's veto as the demagogic ravings of an economic fool. In rejecting Jackson's claims that the Bank had fostered speculative and corrupt financial practices, the pro-Bank forces had the better of the economic argument. But Jackson won the political battle, and he went to the people in the election of 1832 as their champion against the banking aristocracy. Although his support was no stronger than it had been in 1828, he easily defeated Clay, the candidate of the short-lived National Republican party, which had also backed Adams in 1828.

Having blocked the rechartering of the Bank when Congress failed to override his veto, Jackson then set out to destroy it. In Roger B. Taney he finally found a secretary of the treasury (his first two choices refused) who agreed to sign the order removing federal deposits from the Bank in 1833. Drained of its lifeblood, the deposits, the Bank was reduced by 1836 to seeking a charter as a private corporation in the state of Pennsylvania. In the meantime, the government's money was deposited in "pet banks," state banks controlled by loyal Democrats. Jackson won the Bank War, but he left the impression that the Democrats had played fast and loose with the nation's credit system. The economy overheated in his second

term. High commodity prices and abundant credit, both at home and abroad, propelled a buying frenzy of western lands. Prices soared, and inevitably the speculative bubble had to burst. When it did, the Democrats would be open to the charge of squandering the people's money by shifting deposits to reckless state bankers who were part of a corrupt new alliance between the government and private economic interests. Jackson was out of office when the Panic of 1837 hit; Van Buren, his successor, paid the political price for Jackson's economic policies.

VAN BUREN AND HARD TIMES

WHAT CHALLENGES did Van Buren face during his presidency?

WHERE TO LEARN MORE

Martin Van Buren National Historic Site, Kinderhook, New York
www.nps.gov/mava/home.htm

Facing a sharp economic downturn, Van Buren appeared indecisive and unwilling to advance a bold program. When the rise of a radical abolitionist movement in the North revived sectional tensions over slavery, he awkwardly straddled the divisive issue. In the end, he undermined himself by failing to offer a compelling vision of his presidency.

THE PANIC OF 1837

For over a decade, the economy had benefited from a favorable business cycle. Easy credit and the availability of territories opened up by Jackson's Indian removal policy generated a stampede to buy land in the West. As in 1817 and 1818, Americans piled up debt on the assumption that the good times would never end.

Broken families and demoralized workers were among the litany of evils blamed on the Panic of 1837.
Library of Congress

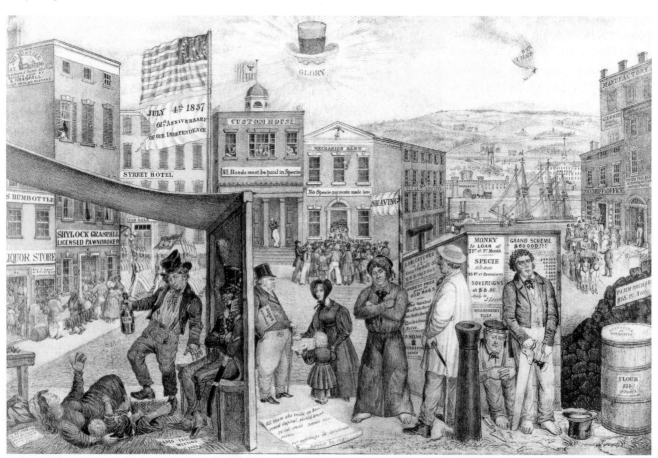

Even as it expanded, the American economy had remained vulnerable to disruptions in the supply of foreign capital and the sale of agricultural exports that underpinned prosperity. In late 1836, the Bank of England tightened its credit policies. Concerned about the large outflow of specie to the United States, it raised interest rates and reduced the credit lines of British merchants heavily involved in the American trade. Consequently, the British demand for cotton fell and with it the price of cotton (see Figure 10–1). Because cotton, as the leading export, was the main security for most loans issued by American banks and mercantile firms, its drop in value set off a chain reaction of contracting credit and falling prices. When panic-stricken investors rushed to the banks to redeem their notes in specie, the hard-pressed banks suspended specie payments.

What began as a bank panic soon dragged down the entire economy. Bankruptcies multiplied, investment capital dried up, and business stagnated. Nine states in the South and West defaulted (stopped making payments) on their bonds. Workers in the shoe, textile, mining, and construction industries suddenly found themselves without jobs. After a brief recovery in 1838, another round of credit contraction drove the economy into a depression that did not bottom out until 1843. In the manufacturing and commercial centers of the Northeast, unemployment reached an unheard-of 20 percent. The persistence of depressed agricultural prices meant that farmers and planters who had incurred debts in the 1830s faced the constant threat of losing their land or their slaves.

THE INDEPENDENT TREASURY

The Democrats' political opponents, now coalescing as the **Whig party,** claimed that Jackson's destruction of the Bank of the United States had undermined business confidence. In their view, Jackson had then compounded his error by trying to force a hard-money policy on the state banks that had received federal deposits.

Jackson had taken his boldest step against paper money when he issued the **Specie Circular** of 1836, which stipulated that large tracts of public land could be bought only with specie. The Specie Circular contributed to the Panic of 1837 by requiring the transfer of specie to the West for land transactions just when eastern banks were strapped for specie reserves. Bankers and speculators denounced Jackson for interfering with the natural workings of the economy and blundering into a monetary disaster.

The Democrats were caught in a dilemma. By dramatically politicizing the banking issue and removing federal money from the national bank, the Democrats had in effect assumed the burden of protecting the people from the banking and business community. Once they shifted treasury receipts to selected state banks, they had to try to regulate these banks. Otherwise they would be accused of creating a series of little "monsters" and feeding the paper speculation they so decried. But any regulatory policy contradicted the Democratic commitment to limit governmental power.

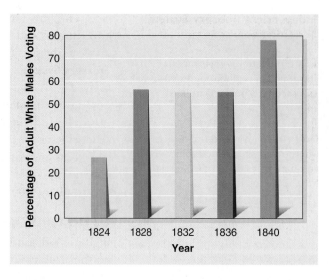

Figure 10–1 Voter Turnout in Presidential Elections, 1824–1840
The creation of mass-based political parties dramatically increased voter turnout in presidential elections. Voting surged in 1828 with the emergence of the Jacksonian Democratic party and again in 1840 when the Whig party learned to appeal to the mass electorate.
Data Source: Richard P. McCormick, "New Perspectives on Jacksonian Politics," in *The Nature of Jacksonian America,* ed. Douglas T. Miller (1972), p. 103.

QUICK REVIEW

The Panic of 1837
- American debt increased in the early 1830s.
- 1836: Bank of England tightened its credit policies.
- Falling cotton prices set off a chain reaction.
- Banking crisis led to a general economic downturn.

Whig party   Political party, formed in the mid-1830s in opposition to the Jacksonian Democrats, that favored a strong role for the national government for promoting economic growth.

Specie Circular   Proclamation issued by President Andrew Jackson in 1836 stipulating that only gold or silver could be used as payment for public land.

Independent Treasury System
Fiscal arrangement first instituted by President Martin Van Buren in which the federal government kept its money in regional vaults and transacted its business in hard money.

Gag rule   A procedural device whereby antislavery petitions were automatically tabled in Congress with no discussion.

10–11
A French Traveler Reports on American Society (1835)

WHAT WAS the basis of Whig popularity? What did they claim to stand for?

The only way out of the dilemma was to make a clean break between the government and banking. Van Buren reestablished the Democrats' tarnished image as the party of limited government when he came out for the **Independent Treasury System.** Under this plan, the government would dispense with banks entirely. The Treasury would conduct its business only in gold and silver coin and would store its specie in regional vaults or subtreasuries.

The Independent Treasury System restored the ideological purity of the Democrats as the friends of honest money, but it prolonged the depression. Specie locked up in government vaults was unavailable for loans in the private banking system that could have expanded the credit needed to revive the economy. The end result was to reduce the money supply and further depress prices.

UPROAR OVER SLAVERY

In 1831, William Lloyd Garrison of Boston inaugurated a radical new phase in northern attacks on slavery with the publication of his abolitionist paper the *Liberator*. The abolitionists embraced the doctrine of immediatism, an immediate moral commitment to begin the work of emancipation. Inspired by the wave of religious revivals sweeping the North in the late 1820s, they seized on slavery as the greatest sin of all. (For more on the abolitionists, see Chapter 12.)

The abolitionists touched off a political uproar when they launched a propaganda offensive in 1835. They produced over a million pieces of antislavery literature, much of which was sent to the South through the U.S. mail. Alarmed white southerners vilified the abolitionists as fanatics intent on enticing the slaves to revolt. Abolitionist tracts were burned, and, with the open approval of Jackson, southern postmasters violated federal law by censoring the mail to keep out antislavery materials.

Unable to receive an open hearing in the South, the abolitionists now focused on Congress. Beginning in 1836 and continuing through Van Buren's presidency, hundreds of thousands of antislavery petitions, some with thousands of signatures, flooded into Congress. Most called for the abolition of slavery in the District of Columbia. Southern congressmen responded by demanding that free speech be repressed in the name of southern white security. This censorship took the form of the **gag rule,** a procedural device whereby antislavery petitions were automatically tabled with no discussion.

With Van Buren's reluctant support, the gag rule became a Democratic Party measure, and it identified the Democrats as a prosouthern party in the minds of many northerners. Ironically, while Van Buren was attacked in the North as a lackey of the slave interests, he was damned in the South as being unsafe on the slavery issue. In short, tensions over slavery and the economy doomed Van Buren to be cast as a vacillating president fully trusted by neither section.

THE RISE OF THE WHIG PARTY

The Bank War and Jackson's reaction to nullification shook loose pro-Bank Democrats and many southern states' righters from the original Jacksonian coalition, and these groups joined the opposition to Jackson. By 1834, the anti-Jacksonians started to call themselves Whigs, a name associated with eighteenth-century American and British opponents of monarchical tyranny.

By 1840, the Whigs had mastered the techniques of political organization and mobilization pioneered by the Democrats in the late 1820s. They ran William

THE SECOND PARTY SYSTEM

	Democrats	Whigs
Ideology	Favor limited role of federal government in economic affairs and in matters of individual conscience; support territorial expansion	Favor government support for economic development and controls over individual morality; opposed to expansion
Voter support	Mainly subsistence farmers, unskilled workers, and Catholic immigrants	Mainly manufacturers, commercial farmers, skilled workers, and northern evangelicals
Regional strength	South and West	New England and Upper Midwest

Henry Harrison, their own version of a military hero, and swept to victory. The **second party system** of intense national competition between Whigs and Democrats was now in place (see the Overview table, "The Second Party System").

THE PARTY TAKING SHAPE

The Whig party was born in the congressional reaction to Jackson's Bank veto and his subsequent attacks on the national bank. Led by the unlikely trio of Henry Clay and Daniel Webster, nationalists from the West and New England, and John C. Calhoun, a states' righter from the South, the congressional opposition accused Jackson of demagogic appeals to the poor against the rich. What upset them, apart from the specific content of Jackson's policies, was how he enforced his will. Jackson wielded his executive power like a bludgeon. Whereas all earlier presidents together had used the veto only 10 times, Jackson did so a dozen times. He openly defied the Supreme Court and Congress, and unlike his predecessors, he took each case directly to the people. It seemed to his opponents that Jackson was threatening to undermine the constitutional system of checks and balances.

Local and state Whig coalitions sent an anti-Jackson majority to the House of Representatives in 1835. The most powerful of these coalitions was in New York, where a third party, the **Anti-Masons,** joined the Whigs. The party had originated in western New York in the late 1820s as a grassroots response to the sudden disappearance and presumed murder of William Morgan, an itinerant artisan who threatened to expose the secrets of the Order of Freemasons. When efforts to investigate Morgan's disappearance ran into a legal dead end, rumors spread that the exclusivist Masons constituted a vast conspiracy that conferred special privileges and legal protection on its members. To combat this "monster," farmers and townspeople flocked to the new Anti-Masonic party.

Although it spread into New England and the neighboring mid-Atlantic states, the Anti-Mason party was unable to sustain itself. Recognizing that the opponents of the Anti-Masons were usually the entrenched local interests of the Democratic Party, shrewd politicians, led by Thurlow Weed and William Seward of New York, took up the movement and absorbed most of it into the anti-Jackson coalition. They thus broadened the Whigs' base and added an egalitarian message to their appeal.

By 1836, the Whigs were strong enough to mount a serious challenge for the presidency. However, they still lacked an effective national organization that

Second Party System The national two-party competition between Democrats and Whigs from the 1830s through the early 1850s.

Anti-Masons Third party formed in 1827 in opposition to the presumed power and influence of the Masonic order.

could unite their regional coalitions behind one candidate. They ran three candidates, Daniel Webster of Massachusetts, William Henry Harrison of Ohio, and Hugh Lawson White of Tennessee, and some Whigs hoped that the regional popularity of these candidates would siphon off enough votes from Van Buren to throw the election into the House of Representatives. But Van Buren won an electoral majority by holding on to the populous mid-Atlantic states and improving on Jackson's showing in New England. Still, the Whigs were encouraged by the results. Compared to Jackson, Van Buren did poorly in what had been the overwhelmingly Democratic South, which was now open to further Whig inroads.

WHIG PERSUASION

The Whigs, like the Democrats, based their mass appeal on the claim that they could best defend the republican liberties of the people. Whereas the Democrats attributed the threat to those liberties to privileged monopolies of government-granted power, the Whigs found it in the expansive powers of the presidency as wielded by Jackson and in the party organization that put Jackson and Van Buren into office. In 1836, the Whigs called for the election of "a president of the nation, not a president of party." Underlying this call was the persistent Whig belief that parties undermined individual liberties and the public good by fostering and rewarding the selfish interests of the party faithful. The Whigs always insisted that Congress should be the locus of power in the federal system.

The Whigs were quicker than the Democrats to embrace economic change in the form of banks and manufacturing corporations. Most Whigs viewed governmental power as a positive force to promote economic development. They favored the spread of banking and paper money, chartering corporations, passing protective tariffs to support American manufacturers, and opening up new markets for farmers through government-subsidized transportation projects.

The Whigs' economic program appealed mostly to Americans who were benefiting from economic change or expecting to do so. They drew heavily from commercial and planting interests in the South. They were also the party of bankers, manufacturers, small-town entrepreneurs, farmers prospering from the market outlets of canals and railroads, and skilled workers who valued a high tariff as protection from the competition of goods produced by cheap foreign labor. These Whig groups also tended to be native-born Protestants of New England or Yankee ancestry, particularly those caught up in the religious revivals of the 1820s and 1830s. The strongest Whig constituencies comprised an arc of Yankee settlements stretching from rural New England through central New York and around the southern shores of the Great Lakes.

Whigs believed in promoting social progress and harmony through an interventionist government. The Whigs favored such social reforms as prohibiting the consumption of alcohol; preserving the sanctity of the Protestant Sabbath through bans on business activities on Sundays; caring for orphans, the physically handicapped, and the mentally ill in state-run asylums and hospitals; and teaching virtuous behavior and basic knowledge through a centralized system of public education. Much of the Whigs' reform impulse was directed against non-English and Catholic immigrants, those Americans who the Whigs believed most needed to be taught the virtues of self-control and disciplined work habits. Not coincidentally, these groups, the Scots-Irish in the backcountry, the Reformed Dutch, and Irish and German Catholics, were the most loyal Democrats. These Democrats were typically subsistence farmers on the periphery of market change and un-skilled workers forced by industrial change to abandon their hopes of ever open-ing their own shops. They equated an activist government with special privileges for the economically and culturally powerful and identified with the Democrats' desire to keep the government out of the economy and individual religious practices.

The Election of 1840

Aside from the Independent Treasury Act and legislation establishing a 10-hour workday for federal employees, the Van Buren administration had no program to combat the Whig charge of helplessness in the face of economic adversity. Henry Clay, who promised that his American System would revive the economy with gov-ernment aid, appeared the most likely Whig candidate for president against Van Buren in 1840. Yet Whig power brokers, placing victory above principle, dumped Clay, who represented the party's ideological heart, for a popular military hero, William Henry Harrison of Ohio.

Harrison had run surprisingly well as one of the Whigs' regional candidates in 1836 and had revealed a common touch with the voters. Unlike Clay, he was un-tainted by any association with the Bank of the United States, the Masonic Order, or slaveholding. As the victor at the Battle of Tippecanoe and a military hero in the War of 1812, he enabled Whig image-makers to cast him, like Jackson, as the honest, patriotic soldier worthy of the people's trust. In a decision that came back to haunt them, the Whigs geographically balanced their ticket by selecting John Tyler, a planter from Virginia, as Harrison's running mate. Tyler was an advocate of states' rights and a former Democrat who had broken with Jackson over the Force Bill.

The Democrats inadvertently gave the Whig campaign a tremendous boost. A Democratic editor wisecracked that "Old Granny" Harrison (he was 67) was such a simpleton that he would like nothing better than to retire to a log cabin with a government pension and a barrel of hard cider. Pouncing on this sneer, the Whigs created a Harrison who never was, a yeoman farmer of humble origins and homespun tastes, whose rise to prominence was a democratic model of success for other Americans to follow. Thus Harrison, who was descended from the Virginia slaveholding aristocracy, became a symbol of the common man. Indeed, they pinned the label of the dandified and elitist aristocrat on Van Buren, whom they called "Martin Van Ruin."

The Whigs beat the Democrats at their own game of mass politics in 1840. They reversed the roles and symbolism of the Jackson-Adams election of 1828 and seized the high ground as the party of the people. In a further adaptation of ear-lier Democratic initiatives, the Whigs put together a frolicking campaign of slo-gans, parades, and pageantry. Politics became a carnival in which voters were shamelessly wooed with food, drink, and music in huge rallies complete with live animals and gigantic buckskin balls that were triumphantly rolled from one rally to another.

The Whigs gained control of both Congress and the presidency in 1840. Harrison won 53 percent of the popular vote (see Map 10–2). Turnout surged to an unprecedented 78 percent of eligible voters, a whopping increase over the av-erage of 55 percent in the three preceding presidential elections. As the new ma-jority party, the Whigs finally had the opportunity, or so they thought, to implement their economic program.

QUICK REVIEW

William Henry Harrison of Ohio
- Untainted by association with Bank of the United States, Masonic Order, or slaveholding.
- Hero of War of 1812.
- Selected John Tyler of Virginia as his running mate.

THE WHIGS IN POWER

*T*he Whigs expected that Clay would move quickly on Whig economic policies by marshaling his forces in Congress and trying to dominate a pliant Harrison. But Harrison died from pneumonia in April 1841, barely a month after his inauguration, ruining Clay's plans.

WHY WAS William Henry Harrison's death such a blow to the Whig agenda?

HARRISON AND TYLER

Harrison was the type of president the Whigs wanted. He had pledged to follow the dictates of party leaders in Congress and defer to the judgment of his cabinet. Bowing to Clay's demands, he agreed to call Congress into special session to act on Whig party measures. Thus his death was a real blow to Whig hopes of establishing the credibility of their party as an effective agent for positive change.

Just how serious that blow was soon became apparent when Tyler became president, the first vice president to succeed on the death of a president. This stiff, unbending planter subscribed to a states'-rights agrarian philosophy that put him at odds with the urban and commercial elements of the Whig party. Clay's economic nationalism struck him as a program of rank corruption that surrendered the constitutional rights of the South to power-hungry politicians and manufacturers in the North. Clay forged ahead with the party agenda, the repeal of the Independent Treasury System and its replacement by a new national bank, a protective tariff, and the distribution of the proceeds of the government's public land sales to the states as funds for internal improvements.

Tyler used the negative power of presidential vetoes to stymie the Whig program. He twice vetoed bills to reestablish a national bank. The second veto led to the resignation of the cabinet he had inherited from Harrison, save for Secretary of State Daniel Webster, who was in the midst of negotiations with the British. Enraged congressional Whigs then expelled Tyler from the party.

A now desperate Clay sought to salvage what was left of his American System. He lined up southern votes for the distribution of federal funds to the states by agreeing to a ceiling of 20 percent on tariff rates. Westerners were won over by Clay's support for the Preemption Act of 1841, a measure that allowed squatters to purchase up to 160 acres of public land at the minimum government price of $1.25 per acre.

Clay's legislative wizardry got him nowhere. When the Whigs passed a higher tariff in 1842 with a provision for distribution, Tyler vetoed it and forced them to settle for a protective tariff with no distribution. In the end, Clay had no national bank, no funds for internal improvements, and only a slightly higher tariff.

THE TEXAS ISSUE

In 1842, Webster wrapped up his negotiations with the British over a long-standing boundary dispute. The **Webster-Ashburton Treaty** of that year established the boundary between British Canada and Maine and parts of the Upper Midwest. An agreement was also reached to cooperate in suppressing the African slave trade. Webster now resigned from the cabinet to join his fellow Whigs, allowing Tyler to follow

Webster-Ashburton Treaty
Treaty signed by the United States and Britain in 1842 that settled a boundary dispute between Maine and Canada.

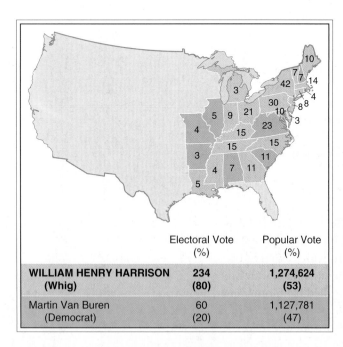

	Electoral Vote (%)	Popular Vote (%)
WILLIAM HENRY HARRISON (Whig)	**234 (80)**	**1,274,624 (53)**
Martin Van Buren (Democrat)	60 (20)	1,127,781 (47)

MAP 10–2 The Election of 1840 Building upon their strength in the commercializing North, the Whigs attracted enough rural voters in the South and West to win the election of 1840.

WHY WERE Southerners not unified in their support for a party in the election of 1840?

a pro-southern policy of expansion that he hoped would gain him the Democratic nomination for the presidency in 1844. His goal was the annexation of Texas.

Texas had been a slaveholding republic since 1836, when rebellious Americans, joined by some *tejanos* (Texans of Mexican descent), declared their independence from Mexico. Jackson extended diplomatic recognition before leaving office, but he refused the new nation's request to be annexed to the United States out of fear of provoking a war with Mexico. But he was also aware that the addition of Texas, a potentially huge area for the expansion of plantation slavery, would inflame sectional tensions and endanger Van Buren's chances in the upcoming presidential election. In private, however, he urged Texans to seize harbors on the Pacific Coast from Mexican control and thus make annexation more attractive to the commercial interests of the Northeast.

For the sake of sectional harmony, party leaders sidestepped the Texas issue after 1836. Tyler renewed the issue in 1843 to curry favor among southern and western Democrats. He replaced Webster as secretary of state with a proannexationist Virginian, Abel P. Upshur, and secretly opened negotiations with the Texans. After Upshur's death in an accidental explosion on the battleship *Princeton*, John C. Calhoun completed the negotiations and dramatically politicized the slavery issue. In the spring of 1844, Calhoun and Tyler submitted to the Senate a secretly drawn up treaty annexing Texas to the United States. Calhoun also made public his correspondence with Richard Pakenham, the British minister in Washington. Calhoun accused the British of seeking to force emancipation on Texas in return for economic aid and a British-brokered Mexican recognition of Texan independence. Calhoun concluded that the security and preservation of the Union demanded the annexation of Texas.

The Pakenham letter hit the Senate like a bombshell, convincing antislavery Northerners that the annexation of Texas was a slaveholders' conspiracy to extend slavery and swell the political power of the South. In June 1844, the Senate rejected Calhoun's treaty of annexation by a two-to-one margin. Still, the issue dominated the election of 1844.

THE ELECTION OF 1844

The Whig and Democratic National Conventions met in the spring of 1844 in the midst of the uproar over Texas. Both Clay, who had the Whig nomination locked up, and Van Buren, who was the strong favorite for the Democratic one, came out against immediate annexation. Clay's stand was consistent with Whig fears that territorial expansion would disrupt the party's plans for ordered economic development. But Van Buren's anti-Texas stand cost him his party's nomination. In a carefully devised strategy, western and southern Democrats united to deny him the necessary two-thirds vote of convention delegates. A deadlocked convention turned to James K. Polk of Tennessee, a confirmed expansionist who had the blessing of Jackson, the party's patriarch.

To counter the charge that they were a prosouthern party, the Democrats ran in 1844 on a platform that linked Oregon to Texas as a territorial objective. Glowing reports from Protestant missionaries of the boundless fertility of Oregon's Willamette Valley triggered a migration to the new promised land. At the same time, the report of a naval expedition sent to explore the Pacific aroused the interest of New England merchants in using Oregon as a jumping-off point for expanded trade with China.

Some 6,000 Americans were in Oregon by the mid-1840s, and demands mounted, especially from northern Democrats, that the United States lay exclusive

GLOBAL PERSPECTIVES

AN AGE OF REFORM

"Turn where we may—within, around—the voice of great events is proclaiming to us, 'Reform, that you may preserve.' Now, therefore . . . take counsel . . . of the signs of this most portentous time. . . . The danger is terrible. The time is short. If this Bill should be rejected, I pray to God that none of those who concur in rejecting it may ever remember their votes with unavailing regret, amidst the wreck of laws, the confusion of ranks, the spoliation of property, and the dissolution of social order."

Thomas Babington Macaulay used this argument in the British Parliament to support the Reform Bill of 1832, legislation that extended the vote to Britain's industrial middle classes. Social changes produced by the Industrial Revolution had resulted in massive inequities and corruption in an electoral system that traditionally had consolidated power in the hands of wealthy conservative landowners. Events on the European continent gave greater weight to Macaulay's warning that England must reform or face revolution at home. The July Revolution of 1830 in France had deposed a conservative king and replaced him with one acceptable to the upper middle class. In the same year the Belgians succeeded in establishing their independence, but Austrian troops crushed a nationalist revolution in Italy, and Russian troops did likewise in Poland.

The revolutions of 1830 made it clear that the conservative order imposed on Europe at the Congress of Vienna in 1815 could not withstand the demands for political change unleashed by the wars of the French Revolution or the economic change associated with the Industrial Revolution. Revolutionary ideals of legal equality and the right of cultural communities to determine their own fate as independent nations intersected with demands by the new middle and working classes for access to political power. The result was a continuing challenge to the status quo that periodically erupted into uprisings and revolutions. The next great wave of unrest that spilled over Europe after 1830 was the revolutions of 1848.

With the glaring exception of slavery, the United States by the 1830s was already a reformed society by the standards of Europe and the rest of the world. Liberal notions of individualism and self-improvement were wedded to mass democratic politics and a vibrant nationalism. But as long as slavery remained, America's national purpose would be tainted and tragically flawed.

---

claim to Oregon. The Polk Democrats seemed to endorse them when they asserted an American claim "to the whole of the Territory of Oregon."

Polk's expansionist program united the Democrats and enabled them to campaign with much more enthusiasm than in 1840. Acquiring Texas and Oregon not only held out the hope of cheap, abundant land to debt-burdened farmers in the North and planters in the South but also played on the anti-British sentiments of many voters. In contrast, the Whig campaign was out of focus. Clay sensed that his opposition to the immediate annexation of Texas was hurting him in the South, and he started to waver. This wavering, however, failed to stem the defection of proslavery southern Whigs to the Democrats and cut into his support among antislavery Whigs in the North. Clay lost to Polk by less than 2 percent of the popular vote.

Tyler claimed Polk's victory as a mandate for the immediate annexation of Texas. He knew that it would still be impossible to gain the two-thirds majority in the Senate necessary for the approval of a treaty. Thus he resorted to the constitutionally unprecedented expedient of a joint resolution in Congress inviting Texas to join the Union. Tyler signed the joint resolution on March 1, 1845.

Although Tyler had failed to secure the Democratic nomination in 1844, he had gained Texas. He also had the satisfaction of getting revenge against the Whigs, the party that had disowned him. Texas, more than any other issue, defeated Clay and the Whigs in 1844.

CONCLUSION

*T*he Jacksonian era ushered in a revolution in American political life. Politicians learned how to appeal to a mass electorate and to build disciplined parties that channeled popular desires into distinctive party positions. In the two decades after 1824, voter participation in national elections tripled, and Democrats and Whigs competed on nearly equal terms in every region.

Politics did not fully enter the mainstream of American life until the rise of the second party system of Democrats and Whigs. The election of 1824 revived interest in presidential politics, and Jackson's forceful style of leadership highlighted the presidency as the focal point of American politics. Voters in favor of government aid for economic development and a social order based on Protestant moral controls turned to the Whigs. Conversely, those who saw an activist government as a threat to their economic and cultural equality turned to the Democrats.

The national issues around which the Democrats and Whigs organized and battled down to 1844 were primarily economic. Slavery, in the form of the Texas question, replaced the economy as the decisive issue in the election of 1844. With this shift, party appeals began to focus on the place of slavery in American society, creating an escalating politics of sectionalism. Within a decade, the slavery issue would rip apart the second party system.

IMAGE KEY
for pages 264–265

a. A Cherokee Indian newspaper.
b. Andrew Jackson speaking to a crowd after his election.
c. $5 note of the Second Bank of the United States.
d. A banner for William Henry Harrison and John Tyler features political slogans of the Log Cabin campaign above the date of the rally.
e. Americans endure poverty and unemployment by drinking, begging, and rioting in the streets of a city during the Panic of 1837.
f. Trail of Tears.
g. Cartoon portrayal of Jackson attacking the Bank of the United States.
h. General Andrew Jackson portrait by Thomas Sully.
i. An old, antique Bible bound in leather with a gold cross on the front cover.

SUMMARY

The Egalitarian Impulse As politics opened to mass participation in the early nineteenth century, popular styles of religious leadership and worship erupted in broad reaction against the dominant Protestant churches. The Second Great Awakening further transformed the religious landscape between 1800 and 1840. In politics, longstanding property requirements for voting were dropped by many states, and the rise of Jacksonian Democrats resulted in the election and reelection of Andrew Jackson as president.

Jackson's Presidency Once in office, Jackson tolerated no interference from his subordinates. His dealings in such crises as the Bank War and the nullification movement further showed his intolerance for interference in any form. And, in his dealings with the Native Americans, as shown through the Indian Removal Act, the Trail of Tears, and Black Hawk's War, Jackson further illustrated his unwillingness to compromise.

Van Buren and Hard Times Where Jackson forged ahead regardless of consequences, Martin Van Buren tended to hang back, carefully calculating all of the political angles. Early in his presidency he was forced to deal with the economic Panic of 1837. Following this crisis, Van Buren reestablished the Democrats tarnished

image as the party of limited government when he came out for the Independent Treasury System. His support, though reluctant, of the gag rule in 1836 damaged his reputation among Northern reformers. Burdened by a depression, he was beaten handily in electoral votes by William Henry Harrison in the election of 1840.

The Rise of the Whig Party   The Whig party was born in the congressional reaction to Jackson's Bank veto and his subsequent attacks on the national bank. By 1836, the Whigs were strong enough to mount a serious challenge for the presidency. The Whigs, like the Democrats, based their mass appeal on the claim that they could best defend the republican liberties of the people. Whigs believed in promoting social progress and harmony through an interventionist government. By 1840, Whigs had mastered the techniques of political organization and mobilization, and in 1840 they gained control of both Congress and the presidency.

The Whigs in Power   William Henry Harrison's death was a real blow to Whig hopes of establishing the credibility of their party as an effective agent for positive change. John Tyler, the first vice president to succeed on the death of a president, was cut from a different cloth than Harrison. Tyler used the negative power of presidential vetoes to stymie the Whig program. Enraged congressional Whigs then expelled Tyler from the party. In the 1844 election, the Whigs ran Henry Clay as their candidate, losing in a close race to James K. Polk.

REVIEW QUESTIONS

1. Explain the democratic movements of the early nineteenth century. What role did race and gender play in these movements? What evidence is there for the existence of similar democratic sentiments in Europe?

2. What distinguished Jackson's presidency from those of his predecessors? How did he redefine the role of the president?

3. How was the Bank War central to the development of the Democratic and Whig parties? Why did the political debates of the 1830s focus on financial issues?

4. In terms of ideology and voter appeal, how did the Democrats and Whigs differ? How did each party represent a distinctive response to economic and social change?

5. How would you describe the changes in American politics between 1824 and 1840? What accounted for these changes?

6. How did the annexation of Texas emerge as a political issue in the early 1840s? Why were the Democrats more in favor of territorial expansion than the Whigs?

7. What do you think accounted for the sense of shock, even outrage, with which Benjamin Brown French reacted to the partisanship of the election of 1828?

KEY TERMS

Albany Regency   (p. 273)
Anti-Masons   (p. 285)
Black Hawk's War   (p. 276)
Democratic party   (p. 272)
Gag rule   (p. 284)

Independent Treasury System
   (p. 284)
Indian Removal Act   (p. 275)
Second Great Awakening   (p. 270)
Second party system   (p. 285)

Specie Circular   (p. 283)
Spoils system   (p. 274)
Trail of Tears   (p. 276)
Webster-Ashburton Treaty   (p. 288)
Whig party   (p. 283)

WHERE TO LEARN MORE

 Rice Museum, Georgetown, South Carolina. Rice planters were the leaders of the nullification movement, and the interpretive materials here on the history of rice cultivation help one understand how slave labor was employed to produce their great wealth. Maps to the museum and news of special events can be found at **www.ricemuseum.com/.**

 The Hermitage, Hermitage, Tennessee. This site, the plantation home of Andrew Jackson, includes a museum with artifacts of Jackson's life. Its website, **www.thehermitage.com/,** lists events and programs and examines the archaeological projects undertaken at the Hermitage.

Martin Van Buren National Historic Site, Kinderhook, New York. The site preserves Lindenwald, Van Buren's home after he left the presidency, and includes a library with materials on Van Buren and his political era. Its recently expanded website, **www.nps.gov/mava/home.htm,** discusses the history of Lindenwald and includes a virtual tour of its art collection.

U.S. History Documents CD-ROM
For primary sources related to this chapter, refer to the document CD-ROM.

www.prenhall.com/goldfield
For study resources related to this chapter, visit the *Companion Website*™.

11 Slavery and the Old South 1800–1860

CHAPTER HIGHLIGHTS

The Lower South Cotton was king in the Lower South and provided an economic basis for Southern sectionalism. The plantation system, relying on the labor of slaves, provided cotton for the world's textile mills. While cotton was profitable, the Lower South lagged behind in industrialization and urbanization.

The Upper South Climate and geography distinguished the Upper South from the Lower South. The Upper South emerged from an economic slump in the 1850s with a more diverse economy and increased urbanization. The Upper South exported slaves to the Lower South, giving the region a greater stake in slavery.

Slave Life and Culture African Americans developed a culture of their own centered on family and religion. Resistance to slavery took a variety of forms, ranging from day-to-day passive resistance to open revolt. Escape attempts were common, but relatively few escaped slaves managed to remain free.

Free Society The influence of planters on the South was disproportionate to their actual numbers. The majority of Southern white people owned no slaves. A small number of free blacks lived precariously between slave and white society.

The Proslavery Argument By the 1830s, with slavery under attack, Southerners were making the argument that slavery was a positive good. Some Protestant churches split into Northern and Southern branches, foreshadowing future sectional divisions. Even Southern white people who opposed slavery feared emancipation.

A SLAVE AUCTION IN VIRGINIA.—FROM A SKETCH BY OUR SPECIAL ARTIST.

SLAVE COLLAR
RICHMOND VIRGINIA
SLAVE MARKET

THIS ANTE-BELLUM SLAVE COLLAR HAS AN
OLD TAG ATTACHED FROM AN EARLY
HISTORICAL SOCIETY COLLECTION. A RARE
AND CHOICE RELIC FROM EARLY VIRGINIA

CHAPTER QUESTIONS

HOW DID the increasing demand for cotton shape the
development of slavery in the Lower South?

WHAT CAUSED the decline of slavery after 1800
in the Upper South?

WHAT FORMS of resistance were available
to slaves?

WHAT PLACE did free blacks have in
Southern society?

HOW DID the southern defense of
slavery change between the early nineteenth
century and the 1850s?

CHAPTER OUTLINE

- The Lower South
- The Upper South
- Slave Life and Culture
- Free Society
- The Proslavery Argument

IMAGE KEY

for pages 294–295 is on page 317.

Had Mrs Wheeler condemned me to the severest corporal punishment, or exposed me to be sold in the public slave market in Wilmington [North Carolina] I should probably have resigned myself with apparent composure to her cruel behests. But when she sought to force me into a compulsory union with a man whom I could only hate and despise it seemed that rebellion would be a virtue, that duty to myself and my God actually required it, and that whatever accidents or misfortunes might attend my flight nothing could be worse than what threatened my stay.

Marriage like many other blessings I considered to be especially designed for the free, and something that all the victims of slavery should avoid as tending essentially to perpetuate that system. Hence to all overtures of that kind from whatever quarter they might come I had invariably turned a deaf ear. I had spurned domestic ties not because my heart was hard, but because it was my unalterable resolution never to entail slavery on any human being. And now when I had voluntarily renounced the society of those I might have learned to love should I be compelled to accept one, whose person, and speech, and manner could not fail to be ever regarded by me with loathing and disgust. Then to be driven in to the fields beneath the eye and lash of the brutal overseer, and those miserable huts, with their promiscuous crowds of dirty, obscene and degraded objects, for my home I could not, I would not bear it.

Hannah Crafts

Henry Louis Gates, Jr., ed., *The Bondwoman's Narrative* (New York: Warner Books, 2002), pp. 206–207.

HANNAH CRAFTS WAS the name an African-American woman adopted after she escaped from slavery in the late 1850s. This passage is from *The Bondwoman's Narrative*, the only known novel written by a female black slave. Although the precise identity of Crafts remains uncertain, the evidence strongly suggests that she was a house slave of John Hill Wheeler of North Carolina who fled north in the spring of 1857, married a Methodist clergyman, and merged into the black middle class of southern New Jersey. As a fugitive slave in the North, Crafts risked recapture at any time prior to the outbreak of the Civil War. Her decision not to publish her autobiographical slave narrative might well have been based on the fear that its detailed portrayal of the Wheeler family would reveal her whereabouts to an owner intent on reclaiming her.

Knowing from firsthand experience that masters frequently violated the sanctity of slave marriages and, under the law, could keep any resulting children as slaves, she believed that all slaves should remain celibate: "Marriage can only be filled with profit, and honor, and advantage by the free." Triggering her decision to flee was Mrs. Wheeler's demand that she "marry" the field hand Bill, that is, submit to being raped by a man she despised and to living in the squalor of the huts in the slave quarters.

Only the system of slavery that Crafts described with revulsion makes it possible to speak of the antebellum South as a single region despite its geographical and cultural diversity. It was black slavery that created a bond among white Southerners and cast them in a common mold.

Not only did slavery make the South distinctive, it was also the source of the region's immense agricultural wealth, the foundation on which planters built their fortunes, the basis for white upward mobility, and the means by which white people controlled a large black minority. Slavery also frightened white southerners with a vision of what might happen to them should they not protect their own personal liberties, including, paradoxically, the liberty to enslave African Americans. Southern white men were thus quick to take offense at any challenge to their honor or independence. Precisely because slavery was so deeply embedded in southern life and customs, white leadership reacted to the mounting attacks on slavery after 1830 with an ever more defiant defense of the institution, which, in turn, reinforced a growing sense among white southerners that their values divided them from their fellow citizens in the Union.

The South of 1860 was geographically much larger and more diverse than it had been in 1800. It was also more uniformly committed to a single cash crop, cotton. Cotton became king, as contemporaries put it, and it provided the economic basis for southern sectionalism. During the reign of King Cotton, however, regional differences emerged between the Lower South, where the linkage between cotton and slavery was strong, and the Upper South, where slavery was relatively less important and the economy was more diversified.

Chronology

1790s	Large-scale conversions of slaves to Christianity begin.
1793	Eli Whitney patents the cotton gin.
1800	Gabriel Prosser leads a rebellion in Richmond, Virginia.
1807	Britain abolishes the slave trade.
1808	Congress prohibits the African slave trade.
1811	Slaves rebel in Louisiana.
1816–1819	First cotton boom in the South.
1822	Denmark Vesey's Conspiracy fails in Charleston, South Carolina.
1831	Nat Turner leads a rebellion in Southampton County, Virginia.
1831–1832	Virginia legislature debates and rejects gradual emancipation.
1832	Thomas R. Dew publishes the first full-scale defense of slavery.
1837–1845	Slavery issue divides Presbyterians, Methodists, and Baptists into separate sectional churches.
1845	Florida and Texas, the last two slave states, are admitted to the Union.
1850s	Cotton production doubles.
1857	Hinton R. Helper publishes *The Impending Crisis of the South.*

THE LOWER SOUTH

*A*long growing season, adequate rainfall, navigable rivers, and untapped fertility gave the Lower South—consisting, in 1850, of South Carolina, Georgia, Florida, Alabama, Mississippi, Louisiana, and Texas—incomparable natural advantages for growing cotton. Ambitious white southerners exploited these advantages by extending slavery to the newer cotton lands that opened up in the Lower South after 1800 (see Map 11–1). Cotton production and slavery thus went hand in hand.

HOW DID the increasing demand for cotton shape the development of slavery in the Lower South?

COTTON AND SLAVES

Once the cotton gin removed the technical barrier to its commercial production, upland, or short-staple, cotton could be planted far inland, and small farmers could grow it profitably because it required no additional costs for machinery or drainage systems (see Chapter 12).

As a result, after the 1790s, the production of short-staple cotton boomed. Moreover, like the South's other cash crops, upland cotton was well suited for slave labor because it required fairly continuous tending throughout the year.

W **WHERE TO LEARN MORE**

★ Cottonlandia Museum, Greenwood, Mississippi **www.gcvg.com/CL.html**.

MAP EXPLORATION
To explore an interactive version of this map, go to
http://www.prenhall.com/goldfield3/map11.1

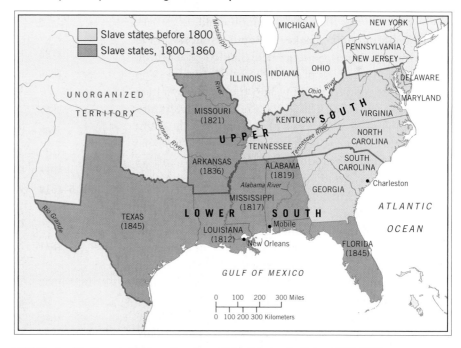

MAP 11–1   The Spread of Slavery: New Slave States Entering the Union, 1800–1850
Seven slave states entered the Union after 1800 as cotton production shifted westward.

WHY WAS cotton production especially suited to slave labor?

13–1
State v. Boon (1801)

Once the harvest was in, the slaves cleared land, cut wood, and made repairs. The long work year maximized the return on capital invested in slave labor.

Despite the care required, the cultivation of cotton left plenty of time for slaves to grow food. The major grain in the southern diet was corn, which needed little attention while cotton was being harvested and could be planted earlier or later than cotton during the long growing season. Surplus corn could be fed to hogs and converted into pork. Because almost all cotton farms and plantations also raised corn and hogs, the South virtually fed itself.

The linkage of cotton and slaves was at the heart of the plantation system that spread westward after the War of 1812. As wasteful agricultural practices exhausted new lands, planters moved to the next cotton frontier farther west. Cotton output exploded from 73,000 bales (a bale weighed close to 500 pounds) in 1800 to more than 2 million bales by midcentury, thanks to the fertility of virgin land and to technological changes, such as improved seed varieties and steam-powered cotton gins. Slave labor accounted for more than 90 percent of cotton production.

Plantations, large productive units specializing in a cash crop and employing at least 20 slaves, were the leading economic institution in the Lower South. Planters were the most prestigious social group, and, though less than 5 percent of white families were in the planter class, they controlled more than 40 percent of the slaves, cotton output, and total agricultural wealth. Most had inherited or married into their wealth, but they could stay at the top of the South's class structure only by continuing to profit from slave labor.

Planters had the best land and were more likely than farmers to belong to agricultural reform societies and to learn about superior seed varieties and progressive growing techniques. The ownership of 20 or more slaves enabled planters to use gangs to do both routine and specialized agricultural work. This **gang system,** a crude version of the division of labor that was being introduced in northern factories, permitted a regimented work pace. Teams of field hands, made up of women as well as men, had to work at a steady pace or else feel the lash. They were supervised by white overseers and black drivers, slaves selected for their managerial skills and agricultural knowledge.

By 1850, the plantations of the Lower South were larger and more specialized than those elsewhere in the South, and the wealth of their owners was more ostentatiously displayed. The plantation districts of the Lower South stifled the growth of towns and economic enterprise. Planters, as well as ordinary farmers, strove to be self-sufficient. The most significant economic exchange, exporting cotton, took place in international markets and was handled by specialized commission merchants in Charleston, Mobile, and New Orleans. The Lower South had amassed great wealth, but most outsiders saw no signs of progress there.

THE PROFITS OF SLAVERY

Most modern studies indicate that the average rate of return on capital invested in a slave was about 10 percent a year, a rate that at least equaled that of alternative investments in the South or the North. Not surprisingly, the newer regions of the cotton kingdom in the Lower South, with the most productive land and the greatest commitment to plantation agriculture, consistently led the nation in per capita income.

The profitability of slavery ultimately rested on the enormous demand for cotton outside the South. Demand grew at about 5 percent a year during the first half of the nineteenth century. Demand was so strong that prices held steady at around 10 cents a pound in the 1850s, even as southern production of cotton doubled. Textile mills in Britain were always the largest market, but demand in continental Europe and the United States grew even faster after 1840.

The Slave Trade.   Prices for a male field hand rose from $250 in 1815 to $900 by 1860. Prices at any given time varied according to the age, sex, and skills of the slave, as well as overall market conditions, but the steady rise in prices meant that slave owners could sell their human chattel and realize a profit over and above what they had already earned from the slaves' labor. This was especially the case with slave mothers; the children they bore increased the capital assets of their owners.

Slaves flowed from the older areas of the Upper South to the newer plantation districts in the Lower South. Indeed, after Congress ended the African slave trade in 1807, it became difficult to smuggle in significant numbers of African slaves, so planters in the Deep South had to depend on the internal trade for the bulk of their labor supply. More than 800,000 slaves were moved between regions

Labor demands on a plantation peaked during the harvesting of cotton.

Courtesy Library of Congress

QUICK REVIEW

Economy of Slavery

- Prices for average male field hand: $250 in 1815, $900 in 1860.
- Female slaves of childbearing age valued almost as highly as male field hands.
- Large and profitable regional market in slaves.

Gang System   The organization and supervision of slave field hands into working teams on Southern plantations.

GLOBAL PERSPECTIVES

THE SUPPRESSION OF THE AFRICAN SLAVE TRADE

"Who durst have hoped that when we abolished the Slave Trade last spring we should be so soon in a situation to compel all other Powers to renounce it too? & that merely by the use of a maritime system, which are own interest & self-preservation prescribe to us, which every party in the country is prepared to acquiesce in, if not loudly applaud, & which even the British West Indies will be the first to rejoice in & commend. . . ."

James Stephen, a British abolitionist who played a key role in the passage of legislation that prohibited slave-trading within the British empire beginning in 1808, deftly combined idealism and national self-interest in the above argument calling on the British navy to put an end to the Atlantic slave trade. He was writing against the backdrop of the Napoleonic Wars in the early nineteenth century when the British were deploying their naval power to interdict all neutral shipping to Napoleonic Europe. By seizing ships trading with the French, Dutch, Spanish, and Portuguese colonies, the British were also choking off supplies of slaves and provisions to these colonies. For Stephen, the British now had a providentially ordained opportunity to liberate Africa from the curse of the slave trade while simultaneously furthering their strategic objectives in the war against Napoleon. As he emphasized, a British decision to abolish the slave trade during peacetime would only have benefited rival nations willing to continue the trade and reap its profits.

With the British taking the lead (and the U.S. followed in 1808), most of the countries of Europe had prohibited the slave trade by 1815. The major exceptions were Spain and Portugal, which were intent on maintaining a flow of African slaves into Spanish Cuba and Portuguese Brazil. Only unrelenting British pressure that forced Spain, Portugal, and, Brazil, following its independence in the 1820s, to sign treaties suppressing the slave trade finally brought an end to the legal shipment of slaves out of Africa to the Western Hemisphere. The smuggling of slaves, especially into Cuba and Brazil, continued until the 1860s, but by the end of the American Civil War, the trade had finally been closed off. Long before it had, slaveholders in the American South relied on the natural increase of their slaves and the sale of slaves from the Upper to the Lower South to meet their labor needs. And now, once they had to rely exclusively on native-born slaves, many slaveholders convinced themselves that they had transformed slavery into a progressive, paternalistic institution.

in the South from 1790 to 1860, and professional slave traders transported at least 60 percent of them. Drawing on lines of credit from banks, the traders paid cash for slaves, most of whom they bought from plantations in the Upper South. By selling these slaves in regional markets where demand had driven up the price, they turned a tidy profit.

The sheer size of the internal slave trade indicates just how profit-driven slave owners were. Few of them hesitated to break up slave families for sale when market conditions were right. Slave children born in the Upper South after 1820 stood a one-in-three chance of being sold during their lifetime. Most of the profits from slave labor and sales went into buying more land and slaves. Because slave owners had little economic incentive to shift their capital resources into manufacturing or urban development, industrialization and urbanization fell far behind the levels in the free states. The South had one-third of the nation's population in 1860 but produced by value only 10 percent of the nation's manufacturing output. Fewer than one in ten Southerners lived in a city, compared to more than one in three northeasterners and one in seven midwesterners.

Nowhere was the indifference of planters to economic diversification more evident than in the Lower South, which had the smallest urban population and the fewest factories. Planters here were not opposed to economic innovations that promised greater profits, but they feared social changes that might undermine the stability of slavery. Most planters suspected that the urban environment weakened slavery. An editorial in the *New Orleans Crescent* charged that slaves in the city were "demoralized to a deplorable extent, all owing to the indiscriminate license and indulgence extended them by masters, mistresses, and guardians, and to the practice of forging passes, which has now become a regular business in New Orleans." For a white person, a "demoralized" slave was one who behaved as if free.

Urban Slavery.   Urban slaves were artisans, semiskilled laborers, and domestics, and, unlike their rural counterparts, they usually lived apart from their owners. They had much more freedom than field hands to move around, interact with white people and other black people, and experiment with various social roles. Many of them, especially if they had a marketable skill, such as carpentry or tailoring, could hire out their labor and retain some of their wages for themselves after reimbursing their owners.

Urban slavery declined from 1820 to 1860, a decline that reflected both doubts about the stability of slavery in an urban setting and the large profits that slave labor earned for slave owners in the rural cotton economy.

Industrial Slavery.   The ambivalence of planters toward urban slavery also characterized their attitudes toward industrialization and industrial slavery. If based on free labor, industrialization risked promoting an antislavery class consciousness among manufacturing laborers that would challenge the property rights of slave owners. Many planters considered free workers potential abolitionists.

But the use of slaves as factory operatives threatened slave discipline because an efficient level of production required special incentives. A Virginian noted of slaves that he had hired out for industrial work, "They were worked hard, and had too much liberty, and were acquiring bad habits. They earned money by overwork, and spent it for whisky, and got a habit of roaming about and *taking care of themselves;* because, when they were not at work in the furnace, nobody looked out for them."

Thus, planters supported industrialization only as an adjunct, not an alternative, to the plantation economy. Planters invested in railroads and factories, but their holdings remained concentrated in land and slaves. They augmented their incomes by renting slaves to manufacturers and railroad contractors but were quick to recall them when they were needed on the plantation.

No more than 5 percent of the slaves in the Lower South ever worked in manufacturing, and most of these were in rural enterprises serving local markets too small to interest northern manufacturers.

THE UPPER SOUTH

*T*he eight slave states of the Upper South lay north of the best growing zones for cotton. The northernmost of these states—Delaware, Maryland, Kentucky, and Missouri—bordered on free states and were known as the Border South. The four states south of them—Virginia, North Carolina, Tennessee, and Arkansas—constituted a middle zone. Slavery was entrenched in all these states, but it was less dominant than in the cotton South.

QUICK REVIEW

Urban Slavery
- 1820–1860: slaves decreased from 22 percent to 10 percent of urban population.
- Planters had a general ambivalence toward industrialization.
- Many planters saw factory work as a threat to slave discipline.

WHAT CAUSED the decline of slavery after 1800 in the Upper South?

WHERE TO LEARN MORE

Appalachian Museum of Berea College, Berea, Kentucky
www.museum.appstate.edu/exhibits/exhibits.shtml

The key difference between the Upper and Lower South was the suitability of the Lower South for growing cotton with gangs of slave laborers. Except for a few prime cotton districts, the Upper South lacked the fertile soil and long growing season necessary for the commercial production of cotton, rice, or sugar (see Map 11–2). Consequently, the demand for slaves was smaller than in the Lower South.

While the Lower South was undergoing a cotton boom after the War of 1812, the Upper South was mired in a long economic slump, from which it did not emerge until the 1850s. The improved economy of the Upper South in the late antebellum period increasingly relied on free labor, a development that many cotton planters feared would diminish southern unity in defense of slavery.

A PERIOD OF ECONOMIC ADJUSTMENT

To inhabitants and visitors alike, vast stretches of the Upper South presented a dreary spectacle of exhausted fields and depopulation in the 1820s and 1830s. Land values fell as farmers dumped their property and headed west. "Emigration

MAP EXPLORATION

To explore an interactive version of this map, go to
http://www.prenhall.com/goldfield3/map11.2

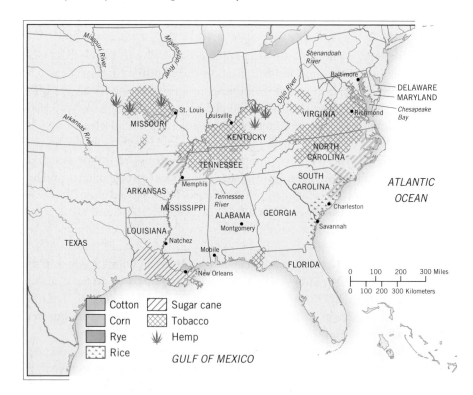

MAP 11–2   Cotton and Other Crops in the South, 1860   Most of the Upper South was outside the cotton belt, where the demand for slave labor was greatest.

WHY WAS the increasing dominance of cotton cultivation in the Lower South accompanied by a growing concentration of slaves in that region? What agricultural trends help explain the relative decline of slavery in the Upper South?

is here raging with all the strength of fanaticism," wrote a Virginian in 1837, "and nothing else can be talked of but selling estates, at a great sacrifice, and '*packing off*' for the '*far west.*'"

Agricultural reform emerged in the 1830s as one proposed solution to this economic crisis. Its leading advocate was Edmund Ruffin, a Virginia planter who tirelessly promoted the use of marl (calcium-rich seashell deposits) to neutralize the overly acidic and worn-out soils of the Upper South. He also called for deeper plowing, systematic rotation of crops, and upgrading the breeding stock for animal husbandry.

Ruffin's efforts, and those of the agricultural societies and fairs spawned by the reform movement, met with some success, especially in the 1840s, when the prices of all cash staples fell. Still, only a minority of farmers ever embraced reform. These were generally the well-educated planters who read the agricultural press and could afford to change their farming practices.

Although soil exhaustion and wasteful farming persisted, agriculture in the Upper South had revived by the 1850s. A rebound in the tobacco market accounted for part of this revival, but the growing profitability of general farming was responsible for most of it.

Particularly in the Border South, the trend was toward agricultural diversification. Farmers and planters lessened their dependence on slave labor or on a single cash crop and practiced a thrifty, efficient agriculture geared to producing grain and livestock for urban markets. Western Maryland and the Shenandoah Valley and northern sections of Virginia grew wheat, and in the former tobacco districts of the Virginia and North Carolina Tidewater, wheat, corn, and garden vegetables became major cash crops.

Expanding urban markets and a network of internal improvements facilitated the transition to general farming. Both these developments were outgrowths of the movement for industrial diversification launched in the 1820s in response to the heavy outflow of population from the Upper South.

Growing Urbanization.   Although not far advanced by northern standards, urbanization and industrialization in the Upper South were considerably greater than in the Lower South. By 1860, the Upper South accounted for three-fourths of the South's manufacturing capital and output and nearly all of its heavy industry. Canals and railroads linked cities and countryside in a denser transportation grid than in the Lower South.

With an economy more balanced among agriculture, manufacturing, and trade than a generation earlier, the Upper South at midcentury was gradually becoming less tied to plantation agriculture and slave labor. The rural majority increasingly prospered by growing foodstuffs for city-dwellers and factory workers. The labor market for railroad construction and manufacturing work attracted northern immigrants, helping to compensate for the loss of the native-born population through migration to other states.

The economic adjustment in the Upper South converted the labor surplus of the 1820s into a labor scarcity by the 1850s. "It is a fact," noted Edmund Ruffin in 1859, "that labor is greatly deficient in all Virginia, and especially in the rich western counties, which, for want of labor, scarcely yet yield in the proportion of one tenth of their capacity." Like many planters in the cotton states, Ruffin feared that free labor was about to replace scarce and expensive slave labor in Virginia and much of the Upper South.

THE DECLINE OF SLAVERY

Slavery was clearly growing weaker in the Upper South by the 1850s. The decline was most evident along the northern tier of the Upper South, where the proportion of slaves to the overall population fell steadily after 1830.

Elsewhere in the Upper South, slavery was holding its own by the 1850s. Only in Arkansas, whose alluvial lands along the Mississippi River offered a new frontier for plantation agriculture, was slavery growing rapidly. Slaves, however, still made up only 25 percent of the population of Arkansas in 1860 and were confined mainly to the southeastern corner of the state.

In every decade after 1820, the internal slave trade drained off about 10 percent of the slaves in the Upper South, virtually the entire natural increase. The sale of surplus slaves was a windfall for planters whose slaves had become an economic burden. This same windfall gave planters the capital to embark on agricultural reform and shift out of tobacco production. Investment capital in the Upper South was not flowing into slave property but into economic diversification that expanded urban manufacturing. Both of these structural changes increasingly put slavery at a competitive disadvantage against free labor.

The wheat, corn, oats, and fodder crops that replaced tobacco in much of the Upper South did not require continuous attention. Unlike tobacco, wheat needed intensive labor only at planting and harvest. Thus, as planters abandoned tobacco, they kept fewer slaves and relied on cheap seasonal workers to meet peak labor demand.

Urban manufacturers likewise wanted workers who could be hired and fired at a moment's notice. Immigrant workers displaced slaves in most of the factories in the Border South. By 1860, slaves made up just 1 percent of the population in St. Louis and Baltimore, the South's major industrial cities.

Slavery was in economic retreat across the Upper South after 1830. There were still plantation districts with large concentrations of slaves, and slave owners retained enough political power to defeat all challenges to their property interests. Nevertheless, the gradual turn to free labor was unmistakable. As Alfred Iveson, a Georgia planter, noted with alarm in 1860, "Those border States can get along without slavery. Their soil and climate are appropriate to white labor; they can live and flourish without African slavery; but the cotton States cannot."

QUICK REVIEW

Forces Behind Decline
- Agriculture reform.
- Economic diversification.
- Expansion of urban manufacturing.

SLAVE LIFE AND CULTURE

WHAT FORMS of resistance were available to slaves?

Nearly 4 million slaves lived in the South by 1860, a more than fivefold increase since the ratification of the Constitution. This population gain was overwhelmingly due to an excess of births over deaths. Despite some smuggling of slaves into the United States, the British-led effort to suppress an African slave trade after 1808 was successful in closing off fresh supplies from Africa.

Almost all southern slaves were thus native-born by the mid-nineteenth century. They were not Africans but African Americans, and they shared the common fate of bondage. By resisting an enslavement they could not prevent, they shaped a culture of their own that eased their pain and raised their hopes of someday being free. They retained their dignity in the face of continual humiliation and relied on their family life and religious beliefs as sources of strength under nearly intolerable circumstances.

WORK ROUTINES AND LIVING CONDITIONS

Each southern state had its own **slave code,** laws defining the status of slaves and the rights of masters; the codes gave slave owners near-absolute power over their human property.

"The right of personal liberty in the slave is utterly inconsistent with the idea of slavery," wrote Thomas R. R. Cobb of Georgia in a legal treatise on slavery. Slaves could not own property, make contracts, possess guns or alcohol, legally marry (except in Louisiana), leave plantations without the owner's written permission, or testify against their masters or any other white person in a court of law. Many states also prohibited teaching a slave to read or write. The murder of a slave by a master was illegal, but in practice, the law and community standards looked the other way if a disobedient slave was killed while being disciplined.

The slave codes penalized any challenge to a master's authority or any infraction of plantation rules. Whippings were the most commonly authorized punishment. Striking a master, committing arson, or conspiring to rebel were punishable by death. Most masters recognized that it made good business sense to feed, clothe, and house their slaves well enough to ensure productive labor and to encourage a family life that would enable the slave population to reproduce itself.

However, planters rarely provided their slaves with more than the bare necessities. The slaves lived mainly on rations of cornmeal and salt pork, supplemented with vegetables they grew on the small garden plots that many planters permitted and with occasional catches of game and fish. This diet provided ample calories but often insufficient vitamins and nutrients to protect slaves against such diseases as beriberi and pellagra. Intestinal disorders were chronic, and dysentery and cholera were common. According to one study, the life expectancy for slaves at birth was 21 to 22 years, roughly half the white life expectancy.

Planters furnished slaves with two sets of coarse clothing, one for summer and one for winter. Their housing, typically a 15-by-15-foot one-room cabin for five or six occupants, provided little more than basic shelter against the elements. "They were built of logs," a traveler noted of slave cabins in South Carolina, "with no windows—no opening at all, except the doorway, with a chimney of sticks and mud; with no trees about them, no porches, or shades, of any kind. Except for the chimney . . . I should have conjectured that it had been built for a powder-house, or perhaps an ice-house, never for an animal to sleep in."

Large planters placed these cabins in a row, an arrangement that projected precision and undifferentiated order. Slaves expressed their individuality by furnishing their cabins with handmade beds and benches and by pushing for the right to put in gardens.

Working Conditions. The diet and housing of most slaves may have been no worse than that of the poorest whites in both the North and the South, but their workload was undoubtedly heavier. Just over half of the slave population at mid-century was concentrated on plantation units with 20 or more slaves, and most of these slaves worked as field hands in gang labor. Overseers freely admitted that they relied on whippings to make slaves in the gangs keep at their work.

The fear of the whip on a bare back set the pace. At daybreak, recalled Solomon Northrup of his enslavement on a Louisiana plantation, "the fears and labors of another day begin; and until its close there is no such thing as rest. [The slave] fears he will be caught lagging through the day; he fears to approach the

---

W WHERE TO LEARN MORE

★ The Anacostia Museum Center for African American History
www.si.edu/anacostia/

QUICK REVIEW

Health and Welfare

- Planters provided the bare necessities.
- Slave diets were insufficient in vitamins and nutrients.
- Clothing and shelter were rudimentary.
- Life expectancy at birth for slaves was roughly half that of whites.

Slave Codes A series of laws passed mainly in the Southern colonies in the late seventeenth and early eighteenth centuries to defend the status of slaves and codify the denial of basic civil rights to them.

Especially on large plantations, slave nursemaids cared for the young children in the white planter's family.

From the Collection of the Louisiana State Museum.

gin-house with his basket-load of cotton at night; he fears, when he lies down, that he will oversleep himself in the morning."

Some 15 to 20 percent of plantation slaves were house servants or skilled artisans who had lighter and less regimented workloads than field hands. Some planters used the prospect of transfer to these relatively privileged positions as an incentive to field hands to work harder. Extra rations, time off on weekends, passes to visit a spouse on a nearby plantation, and the right to have a garden plot were among the other incentives planters used to keep labor productivity high. However, what a planter viewed as privileges, benevolently bestowed, slaves quickly came to see as customary rights. Despite the power of the whip, if planters failed to respect these "rights," slave morale would decline, and the work routine would be interrupted.

Nearly three-fourths of the slaves worked on plantations and medium-sized farms. Most of the remainder, those in units with fewer than 10 slaves, worked on small farms in close contact with the master's family. Slave couples on smallholdings were more likely to live on separate farms. Owners with only a few slaves were also more vulnerable than planters to market downturns that could force them to sell slaves and further divide families.

Of all slaves, 10 percent were not attached to the land, laboring instead at jobs that most white workers shunned. Every southern industry, but most particularly extractive industries such as mining and lumbering, relied heavily on slaves. Racial tensions often flared in southern industry, and when the races worked together, skilled white laborers typically insisted on being placed in supervisory positions.

Industrial slaves worked at least as hard as field hands. Compared to plantation slaves, however, they had more independence off the job and greater opportunities to earn money of their own. By undertaking extra factory work, known as "overwork," industrial slaves could earn $50 or more a month, money they could use to buy goods for their families or, in rare cases, to purchase their freedom.

FAMILIES AND RELIGION

The core institution of slave life was the family. Despite all the obstacles arrayed against them, many slave marriages produced enduring commitments and a supportive moral code for family members. Most slave unions remained intact until the death or, frequently, the sale of one spouse. Close to one-third of slave marriages were broken up by sales or forced removals.

Both parents were present in about two-thirds of slave families, the same ratio as in contemporary peasant families in western Europe. Most slave fathers struggled to help feed their families by hunting and fishing, and they risked beating and death to defend their wives against sexual abuse by the overseer or master. Besides their field labors, slave mothers had all the burdens of pregnancy, child care, laundry, and cooking.

No anguish under slavery was more heartrending than that of a mother whose child was sold away from her. "Oh, my heart was too full!" recalled Charity

Bowery on being told that her boy Richard had been sold. "[My mistress] had sent me away on an errand, because she didn't want to be troubled with our cries. I hadn't any chance to see my poor boy. I shall never see my poor boy. I shall never see him again in this world. My heart felt as if it was under a great load."

Charity Bowery's experience was hardly unique. Most parents could only teach their children the skills of survival in a world in which white people had a legal monopoly on violence. The most valuable of these skills was the art of hiding one's true feelings from white people and telling them what they wanted to hear.

Extensive kinship ties provided a support network for the vulnerable slave family. Thickest on the older and larger plantations, these networks included both blood relatives and other significant people. Children were taught to address elders as "Aunt" and "Uncle" and fellow slaves as "sister" and "brother." If separated from a parent, a child could turn to relatives or the larger slave community for care and assistance.

Slaves followed West African customs by prohibiting marriage between cousins and by often naming their children after departed grandparents. They also drew on their African heritage to create a religion that fit their needs. The ancestors of nineteenth-century slaves brought no common religion with them when they were taken to the New World. However, beliefs common to a variety of African religions survived. Once slaves began to embrace Christianity in the late eighteenth century, they blended these beliefs into an African Christianity.

In keeping with African traditions, the religion of the slaves fused the natural and spiritual worlds, accepted the power of ghosts over the living, and relied on an expressive form of worship in which the participants shouted and swayed in rhythm with the beat of drums and other instruments.

By most estimates, no more than 20 percent of slaves ever converted to Christianity. Those who did found in Christianity a message of deliverance rooted in the liberation of Moses's people from bondage in Egypt. The Jesus of the New Testament spoke to them as a compassionate God who had shared their burden of suffering, so that all peoples could hope to find the Promised Land of love and justice.

The initial exposure of slaves to Christianity usually came from evangelical revivalists, and slaves always favored the Baptists and Methodists over other denominations. The evangelical message of universal spiritual equality confirmed the slaves' sense of personal worth. Less formal in both their doctrines and organization than the Presbyterians and Episcopalians, the evangelical sects allowed the slaves more leeway to choose their own preachers and engage in their physical call-and-response pattern of worship. Perhaps because they baptized by total immersion, which evoked the purifying power of water so common in African religions, the Baptists gained the most slave converts.

Most planters were pragmatic about encouraging Christianity among their slaves. They wished to control religion, as they did other aspects of slaves' lives. Worried that abolitionist propaganda might attract the slaves to Christianity as a religion of secular liberation, some planters in the late antebellum period tried to convert their slaves to their own version of Christianity, one that preached a gospel of passivity and obedience, centered on Paul's call for servants to "obey in all things your Masters."

Although most slaves viewed the religion of their owners as hypocritical and the sermons of white ministers as propaganda, they attended the special slave chapels some masters built and sat in segregated galleries in white churches on Sunday mornings. But in the evening, out of sight of the master or overseer, they

QUICK REVIEW

Religion and Slavery

- A variety of African religions survived in America.

- No more than 20 percent of slaves converted to Christianity.

- Most planters favored Christianity among slaves only if the planters had control.

held their own services in the woods and listened to their own preachers. As much as they could, the slaves hid their religious life from white people. Many slaves experienced religion as a spiritual rebirth that gave them the inner strength to endure their bondage. As one recalled, "I was born a slave and lived through some hard times. If it had not been for my God, I don't know what I would have done."

RESISTANCE

Open resistance to slavery was futile. The persistently disobedient slave would be sold "down river" to a harsher master or, in extreme cases, killed.

Although the odds of succeeding were infinitesimal, slaves did plot rebellions. Four major uprisings occurred in the nineteenth century. The first, **Gabriel Prosser's Rebellion** in 1800, involved about 50 armed slaves around Richmond, though perhaps as many as 1,000 slaves knew about Prosser's plans. The rebels' failure to seize a key road to Richmond and a slave informer's warning to white authorities doomed the rebellion before it got under way. State authorities executed Prosser and 25 of his followers.

A decade later, in what seems to have been a spontaneous bid for freedom, several hundred slaves in the river parishes (counties) above New Orleans marched on the city. More than 60 slaves died, and the heads of the leading rebels were posted on poles along the Mississippi River to warn others of the fate that awaited rebellious slaves.

The most carefully planned slave revolt, **Denmark Vesey's Conspiracy,** like Prosser's, failed before it got started. Vesey, a literate carpenter and lay preacher in Charleston who had purchased his freedom, planned the revolt in the summer of 1822. He assigned teams of rebels specific targets, such as the municipal guardhouse and arsenal. Once Charleston was secured, the rebels apparently planned to flee to Haiti. The plot collapsed when two domestic servants betrayed it. White authorities responded swiftly and savagely. They hanged 35 conspirators, including Vesey, and banished 37 others from the state.

One slave revolt, **Nat Turner's Rebellion,** in Southampton County, Virginia, did erupt before it could be suppressed. Turner was a literate field hand driven by prophetic visions of black vengeance against white oppressors. Convinced by what he called "signs in heaven" that he should "arise and prepare myself and slay my enemies with their own weapons," he led a small band of followers on a murderous rampage in late August 1831. The first white man to be killed was Joseph Travis, Turner's owner, known for his lenient treatment of slaves. In the next two days, the rebels killed 60 other white people. An enraged posse, aided by slaves, captured or killed most of Turner's party. Turner and more than 30 other slaves were executed, and panicky white people killed more than 100 other slaves.

Slaves well understood that the odds against a successful rebellion were insurmountable. They could see who had all the guns. Moreover, they lacked the numbers to overwhelm the white population. Surveillance by mounted white patrols, part of the police apparatus of slavery, limited organized rebellion by slaves to small, local affairs that were quickly suppressed.

Nor could many slaves escape to freedom. The **Underground Railroad,** a secret network of stations and safe houses organized by Quakers and other black and white antislavery activists, provided some assistance. However, fellow slaves or free black people, especially in the cities of the Border South, provided the only help most runaways could count on. Out of more than 3 million slaves in the 1850s, only about 1,000 a year permanently escaped. (see American Views: A Letter from an Escaped Slave to His Former Master.)

13–3
Nat Turner, Confession (1831)

Gabriel Prosser's Rebellion
Slave revolt that failed when Gabriel Prosser, a slave preacher and blacksmith, organized a thousand slaves for an attack on Richmond, Virginia, in 1800.

Denmark Vesey's Conspiracy
The most carefully devised slave revolt in which rebels planned to seize control of Charleston in 1822 and escape to freedom in Haiti, a free black republic, but they were betrayed by other slaves, and seventy-five conspirators were executed.

Nat Turner's Rebellion
Uprising of slaves in Southampton County, Virginia, in the summer of 1831 led by Nat Turner that resulted in the death of 55 white people.

Underground Railroad
Support system set up by antislavery groups in the Upper South and the North to assist fugitive slaves in escaping the South.

Running away was common, but most runaways fled no farther than to nearby swamps and woods. Most voluntarily returned or were tracked down by bloodhounds within a week. Aside from those who were protesting a special grievance or trying to avoid punishment, slaves who ran away usually did so to visit a spouse or loved one. Occasionally, runaways could bargain for lenient treatment in return for faithful service in the future. Most were severely punished.

Slaves resisted complete domination by their masters in less overt ways. They mocked white people in folktales like those about B'rer Rabbit, for example, in which weak but wily animals cunningly outsmart their stronger enemies. Slave owners routinely complained of slaves malingering at work, abusing farm animals, losing tools, stealing food, and committing arson. These subversive acts of protest never challenged the system of slavery itself, but they did help slaves to maintain a sense of dignity and self-respect.

After fleeing from slavery in Maryland in 1849, Harriet "Moses" Tubman, standing on the left, risked re-enslavement by returning to the South on several occasions to assist in the escapes of other slaves. She is photographed here with some of those she helped free.

Smith College, Sophia Smith Collection, Northampton, Massachusetts.

FREE SOCIETY

The abolitionists and the antislavery Republican Party of the 1850s portrayed the social order of the slave South as little more than haughty planters lording it over shiftless poor white people. The reality was considerably more complex. Southern cities, though small by northern standards, provided jobs for a growing class of free workers who increasingly clashed with planters over the use of slave labor. These same cities, notably in the Upper South, were also home to the nation's largest concentration of free black people. Their freedom, though restricted, contradicted the racial justification of slavery. They competed with white workers for jobs, and by the 1850s pressure was mounting on them to leave the South or be enslaved. The free society in the South was surely more diverse than its antislavery critics charged, but overriding racism bonded most white people together to defend the prerogatives of white supremacy.

WHAT PLACE did free blacks have in Southern society?

THE SLAVEHOLDING MINORITY

The white-columned plantation estate approached from a stately avenue of shade trees and framed by luxuriant gardens remains the most popular image of the slave South. In fact, such manorial estates were utterly unrepresentative of the lifestyle of the typical slaveholder. Only the wealthiest planters could live in such splendor, and they constituted less than 1 percent of southern white families in 1860.

Large Planters.   Only in the rice districts of the South Carolina lowcountry and in the rich sugar- and cotton-growing areas of the Mississippi Delta were large planters more than a small minority of the slaveholding class. Fewer than one out of five planter families, less than 1 percent of all families, owned more than

AMERICAN VIEWS

A Letter from an Escaped Slave to His Former Master

I n 1859, Jackson Whitney was one of 6,000 fugitive slaves living in Canada, a sanctuary of freedom beyond the reach of the Fugitive Slave Act of 1850. Like most fugitives, he was male, and he had been forced to leave his family behind in Kentucky. His letter, as well as other direct testimony by African Americans about their experiences and feelings while enslaved, gives us information about slavery that only the slaves could provide.

- How would you characterize the tone of Whitney's letter? How did he express his joy at being a free man?
- How did Whitney feel that Riley, his former owner, had betrayed him?
- What did Whitney mean by the phrase "a slave talking to 'massa'"? How did he indicate that he had been hiding his true feelings as a slave?
- How did Whitney contrast his religious beliefs and those of Riley? How did he expect Riley to be punished?
- What pained Whitney about his freedom in Canada, and what did he ask of Riley?

March 18, 1859

Mr. Wm. Riley, Springfield, Ky.,
Sir:

I take this opportunity to dictate a few lines to you, supposing you might be curious to know my whereabouts. I am happy to inform you that I am in Canada, in good health, and have been here several days. Perhaps, by this time, you have concluded that robbing a woman of her husband, and children of their father does not pay, at least in your case; and I thought, while lying in jail by your direction, that if you had no remorse or conscience that would make you feel for a poor, broken-hearted man, and his worse-than-murdered wife and child, . . . and could not by any entreaty or permission be induced to do as you promised you would, which was to let me go with my family for $800, but contended for $1,000, when you had promised to take the same you gave for me (which was $660.) at the time you bought me, and let me go with my dear wife and children! but instead would render me miserable, and lie to me, and to your neighbors . . . and when you was at Louisville trying to sell me! then I thought it was time for me to make my feet feel for Canada, and let

---

WHERE TO LEARN MORE

Jarrell Plantation, Juliette, Georgia
www.mylink.net/~jarrell/.

50 slaves. Most planters wanted to acquire wealth, not display it. They were restlessly eager to move on and abandon their homes when the allure of profits from a new cotton frontier promised to relieve them of the debts they had incurred to purchase their slaves.

Planters' Wives. Besides raising her children, the plantation mistress managed the household staff, oversaw the cooking and cleaning, gardened, dispensed medicine and clothing to the slaves, and often assisted in their religious instruction. When guests or relatives came for an extended visit, the wife had to make all the special arrangements that such occasions entailed. When the master was called off on a business or political trip, she kept the plantation accounts. In many respects, she worked harder than her husband.

Planters' wives often complained in their journals and letters of their isolation from other white women and the physical and mental toil of managing slaves. Their deepest anger stemmed from their humiliation by husbands who kept slave mistresses or sexually abused slave women. Bound by their duties as wives not to express this anger publicly, white women tended to vent their frustrations on black

your conscience feel in your pocket. Now you cannot say but that I did all that was honorable and right while I was with you, although I was a slave. I pretended all the time that I thought you, or some one else had a better right to me than I had to myself, which you know is rather hard thinking.

You know, too, that you proved a traitor to me in the time of need, and when in the most bitter distress that the human soul is capable of experiencing; and could you have carried out your purposes there would have been no relief. But I rejoice to say that an unseen, kind spirit appeared for the oppressed, and bade me take up my bed and walk, the result of which is that I am victorious and you are defeated. I am comfortably situated in Canada, working for George Harris [another fugitive slave from Kentucky who had bought a farm in Canada]. . . .

There is only one thing to prevent me being entirely happy here, and that is the want of my dear wife and children, and you to see us enjoying ourselves together here. I wish you could realize the contrast between Freedom and slavery; but it is not likely that we shall ever meet again on this earth.

But if you want to go to the next world and meet a God of love, mercy, and justice, in peace; who says, "Inasmuch as you did it to the least of them my little ones, you did it unto me", making the professions that you do, pretending to be a follower of Christ, and tormenting me and my little ones as you have done, [you] had better repair the breaches you have made among us in this world, by sending my wife and children to me; thus preparing to meet your God in peace; for, if God don't punish you for inflicting such distress on the poorest of His poor, then there is no use of having any God, or talking about one. . . .

I hope you will consider candidly, and see if the case does not justify every word I have said, and ten times as much. You must not consider that it is a slave talking to 'massa' now, but one as free as yourself.

I subscribe myself one of the abused of America, but one of the justified and honored of Canada.

Jackson Whitney

Source: John W. Blassingame, ed., *Slave Testimony: Two Centuries of Letters, Speeches, Interviews, and Autobiographies* (Louisiana State University Press, 1977).

women whose alleged promiscuity they blamed for the sexual transgressions of white males.

Small Slaveholders.   Generally younger than the planters, small slaveholders were a diverse lot. About 10 percent were women, and another 20 percent or so were merchants, businessmen, artisans, and urban professionals. Most were farmers trying to acquire enough land and slaves to become planters.

Small slaveholders had scant economic security. A deadly outbreak of disease among their slaves or a single bad crop could destroy their credit and force them to sell their slaves to clear their debts. Nor could small holders hope to compete directly with the planters. In any given area suitable for plantations, they were gradually pushed out as planters bought up land to raise livestock or more crops. In general, only slave owners who had established themselves in business or the professions had the capital reserves to rise into the planter elite.

Especially in the Lower South, owning slaves was a necessary precondition for upward mobility, but it was hardly a sufficient one. As a Baptist opponent of slavery put it, "Without slaves a man's children stand but poor chance to marry in

OVERVIEW   STRUCTURE OF FREE SOCIETY IN THE SOUTH, C. 1860

Group	Size	Characteristics
Large planters	Less than 1 percent of white families	Owned 50 or more slaves and plantations in excess of 1,000 acres; the wealthiest class in America
Planters	About 3 percent of white families	Owned 20 to 49 slaves and plantations in excess of 100 acres; controlled bulk of southern wealth and provided most of the political leaders
Small slaveholders	About 20 percent of white families	Owned fewer than 20 slaves and most often fewer than five; primarily farmers, though some were part of a small middle class in towns and cities
Nonslaveholding whites	About 75 percent of white families	Mostly yeomen farmers who owned their own land and stressed production for family use; one in five owned neither slaves nor land and squatted on least desirable land where they planted some corn and grazed some livestock; in cities they worked as artisans or, more typically, day laborers
Free blacks	About 3 percent of all free families	Concentrated in the Upper South; hemmed in by legal and social restrictions; mostly tenants or farm laborers; about one-third lived in cities and generally were limited to lowest-paying jobs

reputation." Aside from conferring status, owning a few slaves could relieve a white household of much hard domestic labor. "I wish to God every head of a family in the United States had one [slave] to take the drudgery and menial service off his family," proclaimed Andrew Johnson of Tennessee in the U.S. Senate. (Johnson succeeded Abraham Lincoln as president in 1865.)

THE WHITE MAJORITY

Three-fourths of southern white families owned no slaves in 1860. Although most numerous in the Upper South, nonslaveholders predominated wherever the soil and climate were not suitable for plantation agriculture. Most were yeoman farmers who worked their own land with family labor.

These farmers were quick to move when times were bad and their land was used up, but once settled in an area, they formed intensely localized societies in which fathers and husbands held sway over their families. Networks of kin and friends provided labor services when needed, fellowship in evangelical churches, and staple goods that an individual farm could not produce. The yeomanry aimed to be self-sufficient and limited their market involvement to the sale of livestock and an occasional cotton crop that could bring in needed cash.

Yeoman farmers jealously guarded their independence and they demanded that planters treat them as social equals. Rather than risk financial ruin by buying slaves on credit to grow cotton, they grew food crops and depended on their families to work the fields. Far longer than most northern farmers, they continued to make their own clothes, shoes, soap, and other consumer items.

In areas where there were both small farms and scattered plantations, the interests of the yeomen and the planters were often complementary. Planters provided local markets for the surplus grain and livestock of nonslave-holders and, for a small fee, access to gristmills and gins for grinding corn and cleaning cotton. They lent small sums to poorer neighbors in emergencies or to pay taxes. The yeomen staffed the slave patrols and became overseers on the plantations. Both groups sought to protect property rights from outside interference and to maintain a system of racial control in which white liberties rested on black degradation.

When yeomen and planters clashed, it was usually over economic issues. Large slaveholders needing better credit and marketing facilities gravitated toward the Whig party, which called for banks and internal improvements. Nonslaveholding farmers, especially in the Lower South, tended to be Democrats who opposed banks and state-funded economic projects. These partisan battles, however, rarely involved a debate about the merits of slavery. As long as planters deferred to the egalitarian sensibilities of the yeomen by courting them at election time and promising to safeguard their liberties, the planters were able to maintain broad support for slavery across class lines. Around 15 percent of rural white families owned neither land nor slaves. These were the so-called poor whites, stigmatized by both abolitionists and planters as lazy and shiftless. Planters habitually complained that poor whites demoralized their slaves by showing that a person could survive without steady labor.

Most landless white people were resourceful and enterprising enough to supply themselves with all the material comforts they wanted. Back in the swamps and pine barrens, shunned by planters and yeomen alike, they squatted on a few acres of land, put up crude cabins for shelter, planted some corn, and grazed livestock in the surrounding woods. Although poor by most standards, they were also defiantly self-reliant.

Nonslaveholders were a growing majority in southern cities, especially among the working classes. These urban workers shared no agricultural interests or ties with the planters. Nor were most of them, especially in the unskilled ranks, southern-born. Free workers, especially Irish and German immigrants, increasingly replaced slaves in urban labor markets. These white workers bitterly resented competition from black slaves, and their demands to exclude slaves from the urban workplace reinforced planters' belief that cities bred abolitionism.

A yeoman farmstead in New Braufels, Texas. The yeomanry strove for self-sufficiency by growing food crops and grazing livestock.

Daughters of the Republic of Texas Library. Yanaguana Society Collection.

FREE BLACK PEOPLE

A few southern black people, 6 percent of the total in 1860, were "free persons of color." They constituted 3 percent of the free population in the South. These free black people occupied a precarious and vulnerable position between degraded enslavement and meaningful freedom. White intimidation and special legal provisions known as **black codes** (found throughout the North as well) denied them

Black codes Laws passed by states and municipalities denying many rights of citizenship to free black people before the Civil War.

Barbering was one of the skilled trades open to black men during the antebellum years. Several wealthy African Americans began their careers as barbers.

The Granger Collection, New York.

nearly all the rights of citizenship. Because of the legal presumption in the South that all black people were slaves, they had to carry freedom papers, official certificates of their freedom. They were shut out of the political process and could not testify against white people in court. Many occupations, especially those involved in the communication of ideas, such as the printing trades, were closed to them.

Every slave state forbade the entry of free black people, and every municipality had rules and regulations that forced them to live as an inferior caste. Any sign of upward mobility or intimation of equal standing was ruthlessly suppressed. More than four-fifths of the southern free black population lived in the Upper South. Most were the offspring of slaves freed by private manumissions between 1780 and 1800, when slavery temporarily loosened in the Chesapeake region in the wake of the Revolutionary War.

As in the North, legal barriers and white prejudice generally confined free black people to the poorest-paying and most menial work. In rural areas, a handful became independent farmers, but most worked as farm laborers or tenants. The best economic opportunities were in the cities, where some found factory jobs and positions in the skilled trades. Because the South had a general shortage of skilled labor, free black artisans could earn a respectable income. Indeed, the percentage of black people in the skilled trades was generally higher in the South than in the North.

One-third of the free black people in the Upper South lived in cities. Cities offered black people not only jobs but also enough social space to found their own churches and mutual-aid associations. Especially after 1840, urban African-American churches became the center of black community life. Church Sunday schools and day schools provided black people practically their only access to education, which they persisted in pursuing despite white opposition. A "good education," declared a black schoolmaster in Baltimore, "is the *sine qua non* as regards the elevation of our people."

Less than 2 percent of the black people in the Lower South were free in 1860. Most of the Lower South's free black population descended from black emigrants who fled the revolutionary unrest in Haiti in the 1790s. These refugees were artisans, shopkeepers, and farmers who settled primarily in Charleston and New Orleans. Able to secure a solid economic footing, they left their descendants wealthier than any other free black people in the United States. Free black people in the Lower South were more likely than those in the Upper South to have a marketable skill, and two-thirds of them lived in cities.

A light skin enhanced the social standing of free black people among color-conscious whites in the Lower South. Nearly 70 percent of free black people in 1860 were mulattoes. Mulattoes could count on greater white patronage, and they monopolized the best jobs available to free black people. A mulatto elite emerged in Charleston, Mobile, and New Orleans that carefully distanced itself from most black people, slave or free. In New Orleans, where a tradition of racially mixed unions dated back to French and Spanish rule, mulattoes put on lavish "octoroon balls," attended by freewomen of color and by white men.

Despite the emergence of a three-tiered racial hierarchy in the port cities of the Lower South, white officialdom insisted on maintaining a white and black racial dichotomy. As the racial defense of slavery intensified in the 1850s, more calls were made for laws to banish or enslave free black people.

Despised and feared by white people as a subversive element in a slave society, free black Southerners were daily reminded that their freedom rested on the whims of the white majority. As white attitudes turned uglier in the late antebellum period, that freedom became ever less secure.

THE PROSLAVERY ARGUMENT

In the early nineteenth century, most white people would have called slavery a necessary evil, an unfortunate legacy from earlier generations that was needed to maintain racial peace.

The 1830s marked a turning point. After the twin shocks of Nat Turner's Rebellion and the onset of the abolitionist crusade (for more on this crusade, see Chapter 12), white mobs emerged to stifle any open criticism of slavery in the Lower South. By the 1850s, politicians, intellectuals, and evangelical ministers were arguing that slavery was an institution ordained by God as the foundation of southern prosperity, white democracy, and Christian instruction for heathen Africans. Slavery, they insisted, was a mild, paternalistic, and even caring institution.

HOW DID the southern defense of slavery change between the early nineteenth century and the 1850s?

RELIGIOUS ARGUMENTS

Evangelical Protestantism dominated southern religious expression by the 1830s, and its ministers took the lead in combating abolitionist charges that slavery was a moral and religious abomination. The support of southern churches for slavery grew more pronounced and articulate once the abolitionists stepped up their attacks on slavery in the mid-1830s.

Southern evangelicals accepted the Bible as God's literal word, and through selective reading they found abundant evidence to proclaim slavery fully in accord with His moral dictates. Southern evangelicals also turned to the Bible to support their argument that patriarchal authority, the unquestioned power of the father, was the basis of all Christian communities. Part of that authority extended over slaves, and slavery thus became a matter of family governance, a domestic institution in which Christian masters of slaves, unlike capitalist masters of free "wage slaves" in the North, accepted responsibility for caring for their workers in sickness and old age. Far from being a moral curse, therefore, slavery was part of God's plan to Christianize an inferior race and teach its people how to produce raw materials that benefited the world's masses.

The growing commitment of southern evangelicals to slavery as a positive good clashed with the anti-slavery position and the generally more liberal theology of northern evangelicals. In 1837, the Presbyterians split along sectional lines in part because of differences over slavery. In 1844, as a direct result of the slavery issue, the Methodist Episcopal Church, the nation's largest, divided into northern and southern churches. The Baptists did the same a year later. These religious schisms foreshadowed the sectionalized political divisions of the

As this cartoon reflects, a staple of proslavery propaganda was the contrast between the allegedly contented and healthy lot of slaves and the condition of starving factory workers exploited by the system of wage labor.

Courtesy of Library of Congress

1850s; they also severed one of the main emotional bonds between whites in the North and the South. The religious defense of slavery was central to the slave-holding ethic of paternalism that developed after 1830. By the 1850s, planters commonly described slaves as members of an extended family who were treated better than free workers in the North. This language often reflected the planters' psychological need to feel appreciated, even loved, as caring parents by their slave dependents. Some evangelical masters tried to act as moral stewards to their slaves and to curb the worst features of their bondage. Such slaveholders, however, were a minority, and efforts to reform slavery failed largely because masters would accept no limits on their power to control and work their slaves as they saw fit.

RACIAL ARGUMENTS

13–7
George Fitzhugh, "The Blessings of Slavery" (1857)

More common than the biblical defense of slavery was the racial argument that black people were unfit for freedom. If freed, so went the argument, they would turn to crime and sexually assault white women. Only the controls of slavery enabled the races to coexist in the South. Slavery as necessary racial control was a central theme in Thomas R. Dew's *Review of the Debates in the Virginia Legislature of 1831 and 1832*, the first major justification of slavery by a southerner. Concerned by the introduction of a proposal for gradual emancipation into the Virginia legislature, Dew, a Tidewater planter, tried to unite white people on the issue of race.

The racial argument resonated powerfully among white people because nearly all of them, including those otherwise opposed to slavery, dreaded emancipation. Unable to conceive of living in a society with many free black people, most white people could see no middle ground between slavery and the presumed social chaos of emancipation.

Despite its apparent success in forging white solidarity, the racial argument could be turned on its head and used to weaken slavery. Most white northerners were about as racist as their southern counterparts, but they were increasingly willing to end slavery on the grounds that the stronger white race should help black people improve themselves as free persons. The same arguments also encouraged some white southerners to challenge the economic prerogatives of slaveholders. Why, for example, should any white people, as members of the master race, be forced into economic competition against skilled slave artisans? Why should not all nonagricultural jobs be legally reserved for white people? Doctrines of black inferiority could not prevent white unity from cracking when the economic interests of nonslaveholders clashed with those of planters.

CONCLUSION

Slavery and a biracial social order defined the South as a distinctive region. The spread of plantation agriculture across the Lower South after 1830 deepened the involvement of white southerners in cotton and slavery. At the same time, the abolitionist movement in the North attacked slavery on moral grounds and demanded that it be abolished. As southern interests became more enmeshed in an institution that outsiders condemned, religious and intellectual leaders portrayed slavery as a Christian institution and a positive good necessary for white democracy and harmonious race relations. Proslavery ideologues stridently insisted that the South was separate from and superior to the rest of the nation.

The proslavery argument depicted a nearly ideal society blessed by class and racial harmony. In reality, social conditions in the slave South were contradictory

WHERE TO LEARN MORE

★ Meadow Farm Museum, Richmond, Virginia **www.co.henrico.va.us/rec/kmfarm.html**.

and conflict-ridden. Slaves were not content in their bondage. Relations between masters and their slaves were antagonistic, not affectionate, and wherever the system of control slackened, slaves resisted their owners. The publication in 1857 of Hinton Rowan Helper's *The Impending Crisis of the South*, a scathing indictment by a white North Carolinian of slavery's harmful effect on economic opportunities for average white people, vividly showed that not all were convinced by the proslavery argument.

Planters were not fooled by the public rhetoric of white unity. They knew that slavery was increasingly confined to the Lower South, and that elsewhere in the South white support for it was gradually eroding. Planters feared the double-edged challenge to their privileged position posed by outside interference with slavery and internal white disloyalty. By the 1850s, many of them were concluding that the only way to resolve their dilemma was to make the South a separate nation.

SUMMARY

The Lower South Cotton was king in the Lower South and provided an economic basis for Southern sectionalism. The Lower South had incomparable natural advantages for growing cotton and short-staple cotton expanded westward after the invention of the cotton gin. The plantation system, relying on the labor of slaves, provided cotton to the world's textile mills. While cotton was economically profitable, the Lower South lagged behind in industrialization and urbanization. Slavery was not confined to agriculture; slaves lived in cities and towns with a few more freedoms, including the ability to earn wages.

The Upper South Climate and geography distinguished the Upper South from the Lower South; the eight slave states lay north of the best growing zones for cotton. The Upper South emerged from an economic slump in the 1850s with diversified agriculture, urbanization, and an expansion of manufacturing and trade. The region served as a slave exporter to the Lower South and had an economic stake in slavery although the institution was not as widespread in the Upper South or as profitable.

Slave Life and Culture By the mid-nineteenth century Southern slaves were native-born; their number had increased more than five times. African-American slaves had shaped a culture of their own to deal with the humiliations and difficulties of their lives; in their family life and religious beliefs they found the strength to sustain themselves with hope. In addition to day to day resistance, slave uprisings occurred; the only real opportunity for escape was the Underground Railroad, but only a relatively small number were able to permanently escape northward or to Canada.

Free Society While the planter society of the South was numerically small, their influence was extensive. The majority of Southern white people owned no slaves; they were farmers who worked their own land with family labor. This group sometimes clashed with the planters; however, all white southerners sought to maintain their status through the degradation and intimidation of African Americans. A

IMAGE KEY
for pages 294–295

a. Fluffy white, mature cotton bolls on the stem of a plant.
b. "The Shadow" Plantation of Louisiana.
c. "Slavery and the Old South, 1800–1860." A slave auction in Virginia, 1861. English engraving.
d. A whip of coiled rope with a wooden handle; used on slaves.
e. An advertisement promoting the auction of eight black slaves together with miscellaneous inanimate property belonging to a North Carolina gentleman.
f. A chain used to tie together gangs of slaves.
g. African American slaves / farm workers carry sacks of cotton on their heads while leaving a South Carolina plantation field. "Returning from the Cotton Fields in South Carolina," ca. 1860.
h. A slave collar with an attached tag from the slave market in Richmond, Virginia.
i. A runaway slave is depicted on the frontispiece of the Anti Slavery Record of 1837.
j. A yeoman farmstead
k. Colonel and Mrs. James A. Whiteside, son Charles, and servants by James Cameron. A wealthy colonial family and two servants sit on a posh veranda with a checkered floor overlooking an expansive rugged landscape.
l. Pro slavery cartoon, 1841.

small number of free blacks lived precariously between slave and white society, their freedoms growing less secure as the 1800s progressed.

The Proslavery Argument By the 1830s, slavery was under attack, and Southerners countered by defending slavery as a positive good and used Biblical examples to support their arguments. Some Protestant churches split between Northern and Southern branches foreshadowing the sectional political divisions that were to come. Even Southern white people opposed to slavery feared emancipation; they could see no middle ground between slavery and freedom.

REVIEW QUESTIONS

1. What factors accounted for the tremendous expansion of cotton production in the South? How was this expansion linked to slavery and westward movement?

2. What differentiated the Upper South from the Lower South? What role did slavery play in each region after 1815?

3. How would you characterize the life of a plantation slave? What insights does Hannah Crafts's opening account provide into the special vulnerability of slave women? Why were religion and family such key features of the world that slaves built for themselves? What evidence is there of resistance and rebellion among the slaves?

4. How did most nonslaveholding white southerners live? What values did they prize most highly? Why did most nonslaveholders accept slavery or at least not attack it directly?

5. What was the position of free black southerners in southern society? How were their freedoms restricted?

6. How did white southerners attempt to defend slavery and reconcile it with Christianity?

7. How was the development of the Old South linked to the international cotton market?

KEY TERMS

Black codes (p. 313)
Denmark Vesey's Conspiracy (p. 308)

Gabriel Prosser's Rebellion (p. 308)
Gang system (p. 299)

Nat Turner's Rebellion (p. 308)
Slave codes (p. 305)
Underground Railroad (p. 308)

WHERE TO LEARN MORE

⬡ **The Anacostia Museum Center for African American History.** This museum of the Smithsonian Institution explores American history and cultures from an African-American perspective. Go to **www.si.edu/anacostia/** for information on its exhibits and a calendar of events.

⬡ **Appalachian Museum of Berea College, Berea, Kentucky.** This museum is an excellent source for understanding the lifestyle and material culture of the nonslaveholding farmers in the Appalachian highlands. For an overview of its exhibits, see **www.museum.appstate.edu/exhibits/exhibits.shtml**.

 Cottonlandia Museum, Greenwood, Mississippi. The library and museum depict the history of cotton in the Mississippi Delta. Special collections include some Native American artifacts. Information on its displays can be found at **www.gcvg.com/CL.html**.

 Jarrell Plantation, Juliette, Georgia. This state historic site consists of a 15-building farm complex that conveys a good sense of the physical dimensions of a nineteenth-century Georgia plantation. For a visual tour of the plantation, go to **www.mylink.net/~jarrell/**.

Meadow Farm Museum, Richmond, Virginia. The archives and museum are especially strong on southern farm life in the mid-nineteenth century. A description of the museum is at **www.co.henrico.va.us/rec/kmfarm.html**.

U.S. History Documents CD-ROM
For primary sources related to this chapter, refer to the document CD-ROM.

www.prenhall.com/goldfield
For study resources related to this chapter, visit the *Companion Website*™.

12 The Market Revolution and Social Reform 1815–1850

CHAPTER HIGHLIGHTS

Industrial Change and Urbanization In the 1800s the United States experienced a transportation and manufacturing revolution. Urbanization brought new work patterns as manufacturing moved from the home to factories. The Northeast experienced the most dramatic growth and most profound social change.

Reform and Moral Order Social and economic change frightened religious and business leaders in the East. Their benevolent empire was made up of a host of societies that targeted individual vices, especially the consumption of alcohol. Women played key roles in these reform movements.

Institutions and Social Improvement Reformers created new schools, prisons, and asylums that operated on the basis of the Enlightenment assumption that the proper environment could reform deviants and produce virtuous citizens. Utopians sought perfection by withdrawing from society.

Abolitionism and Women's Rights Abolitionism emerged from the same religious impulse that energized other reform movements in the North. Abolitionists attacked slavery and all of its supporters. The abolitionist movement split over the issue of women's rights. Abolitionists brought their cause into the political mainstream by focusing attention on the pernicious influence of "Slave Power" on the rights of all white people.

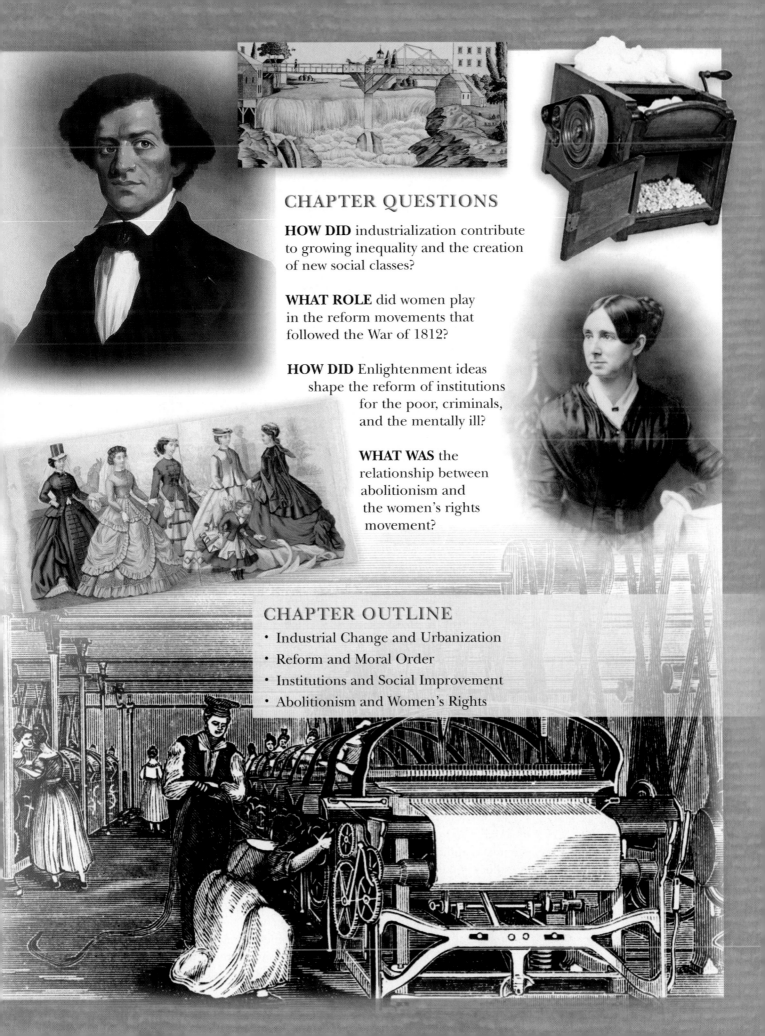

CHAPTER QUESTIONS

HOW DID industrialization contribute to growing inequality and the creation of new social classes?

WHAT ROLE did women play in the reform movements that followed the War of 1812?

HOW DID Enlightenment ideas shape the reform of institutions for the poor, criminals, and the mentally ill?

WHAT WAS the relationship between abolitionism and the women's rights movement?

CHAPTER OUTLINE

- Industrial Change and Urbanization
- Reform and Moral Order
- Institutions and Social Improvement
- Abolitionism and Women's Rights

IMAGE KEY
for pages 320–321 is on page 354.

East Boylston, Mass.
10th mo. 2d, 1837

Dear Friend: . . .

The investigation of the rights of the slave has led me to a better understanding of my own. I have found the Anti-Slavery cause to be the high school of morals in our land—the school in which human rights *are more fully investigated, and better understood and taught, than in any other. Here a great fundamental principle is uplifted and illuminated, and from this central light, rays innumerable stream all around. Human beings have* rights, *because they are* moral *beings: the rights of* all *men grow out of their moral nature; and as all men have the same moral nature, they have essentially the same rights. These rights may be wrested from the slave, but they cannot be alienated: his title to himself is as perfect* now, *as is that of Lyman Beecher [a prominent minister]: it is stamped on his moral being, and is, like it, imperishable. Now if rights are founded on the nature of our moral being, then the* mere circumstance of sex *does not give to man higher rights and responsibilities, than to woman. To suppose that it does, would be to deny the self-evident truth, that the "physical constitution is the mere instrument of the moral nature." To suppose that it does, would be to break up utterly the relations, of the two natures, and to reverse their functions, exalting the animal nature into a monarch, and humbling the moral into a slave; making the former a proprietor, and the latter its property. When human beings are regarded as* moral *beings, sex, instead of being enthroned upon the summit, . . . sinks into insignificance and nothingness. My doctrine then is, that whatever it is morally right for man to do, it is morally right for woman to do. Our duties originate, not from difference of sex, but from the diversity of our relations in life, the various gifts and talents committed to our care, and the different eras in which we live.*

Angelina Emily Grimké

Aileen S. Kraditor, ed., *Up From the Pedestal: Selected Writings in the History of American Feminism* (New York: Quadrangle, 1968), pp. 62–63.

ANGELINA GRIMKÉ wrote the above as part of a public letter to Catherine Beecher, a pioneer in women's education and the daughter of the evangelical preacher Lyman Beecher mentioned in the letter. In 1837, on an abolitionist lecture tour in New England with her sister Sarah, Angelina had become the first American woman to defy the social taboo against women speaking in public to a mixed audience of men and women. Catherine Beecher was among the many critics of the Grimké sisters, and Angelina publicly responded to her attacks.

Born in 1805 to a wealthy slaveholding family in Charleston, Angelina passionately rejected slavery when she became a young adult. As was also true for her sister, this rejection was part of a religious conversion to Quakerism. Angelina left her home in Charleston in 1829 and joined Sarah in Philadelphia. The sisters joined the abolitionist movement in 1835, and within two years had become the crusade's most celebrated (and notorious) platform lecturers.

Soon after her marriage in 1838 to the abolitionist Theodore Weld, Angelina compiled much of the firsthand documentation on slavery for his *American Slavery as It Is*, a popular antislavery tract that appeared in 1839. She resumed her reform activities in the 1850s and worked for the emancipation of the slaves during the Civil War, although she only rarely spoke in public.

Although Angelina, in her commitment to radical reform, was hardly typical of antebellum American women, let alone women of the planter class, her journey from a privileged life in Charleston to one of social activism in the North speaks to the radicalizing potential of the reform impulse that swept over the nation after the War of 1812.

This reform impulse was strongest in the North, where traditional social and economic relations were undergoing wrenching changes as a market revolution accelerated the spread of cities, factories, and commercialized farms. New middle and working classes evolved in response to such changes, which were the most pronounced in the Northeast. The North was also the area where the emotional fires of evangelical revivals burned the hottest.

The religious message of the Second Great Awakening, which began in the early 1800s, provided a framework for responding to the changes that accompanied the market revolution. Social evils, and the sinful consequences of economic and social changes, could be cleansed only if good Christians helped others find the path of righteousness.

The first wave of reform after the War of 1812 focused on individual behavior, targeting drinking, gambling, sexual misconduct, and Sabbath-breaking. By the 1830s, a second phase of reform turned to institutional solutions for crime, poverty, and social delinquency. The third phase of the reform cycle rejected the social beliefs and practices that prescribed fixed and subordinate positions to certain Americans based on race and also on sex. This radical phase culminated in the abolitionist and women's rights movement.

INDUSTRIAL CHANGE AND URBANIZATION

In 1820, 80 percent of the free labor force worked in agriculture, and manufacturing played a minor role in overall economic activity. Over the next three decades, however, the United States joined England as a world leader in industrialization. By 1850, manufacturing accounted for one-third of total commodity output, and 45 percent of the labor force were nonfarm workers.

The most direct cause of this rapid and sustained surge in manufacturing was increased consumption within the United States of the goods the country was producing. The **transportation revolution** dramatically reduced transportation costs and shipping times, opened up new markets for farmers and manufacturers alike, and provided an incentive for expanding production (see Table 12–1). As

HOW DID industrialization contribute to growing inequality and the creation of new social classes?

WHERE TO LEARN MORE

Baltimore Center for Urban Archaeology, Baltimore, Maryland

Transportation Revolution
Dramatic improvements in transportation that stimulated economic growth after 1815 by expanding the range of travel and reducing the time and cost of moving goods and people.

Table 12–1   Impact of the Transportation Revolution on Traveling Time

Route	1800	1830	1860
New York to Philadelphia	2 days	1 day	Less than 1 day
New York to Charleston	More than 1 week	5 days	2 days
New York to Chicago	6 weeks	3 weeks	2 days
New York to New Orleans	4 weeks	2 weeks	6 days

Chronology

1790	Samuel Slater opens the first permanent cotton mill in Rhode Island.
1793	Eli Whitney patents the first cotton gin.
1807	Robert Fulton's steamboat, the *Clermont,* makes its pioneering voyage up the Hudson River.
1814	The Boston Associates opens its Waltham mill, the first textile factory to mechanize all phases of production.
1817	Construction of the Erie Canal begins.
	American Colonization Society is founded.
1819–1823	Economic depression.
1820s	The new nations of Latin America commit themselves to policies of gradual emancipation.
1824	In *Gibbons v. Ogden,* the Supreme Court strikes down a state monopoly over steamboat navigation.
1825	Erie Canal is completed.
1826	American Temperance Society launches its crusade.
1828	The Baltimore and Ohio, the most important of the early railroads, is chartered.
1829	David Walker publishes *Appeal to the Colored Citizens of the World.*
1830	Joseph Smith founds the Church of Jesus Christ of Latter-day Saints.
1830–1831	Evangelical revivals are held in northern cities.
1831	William Lloyd Garrison begins publishing the *Liberator.*
1833	Slaves in the British Empire are emancipated.
	American Anti-Slavery Society is organized.

1834	New York Female Reform Society is founded.
	Female workers at the Lowell Mills stage their first strike.
1836	Congress passes gag rule.
1837	Horace Mann begins campaign for school reform in Massachusetts.
	Antiabolitionist mob kills Elijah P. Lovejoy.
	In *Charles River Bridge v. Warren Bridge,* the Supreme Court encourages economic competition by ruling that presumed rights of monopolistic privileges could not be used to block new economic enterprises.
1839–1843	Economic depression.
1840	Abolitionists split into Garrisonian and anti-Garrisonian societies.
	Political abolitionists launch the Liberty party.
1841	Brook Farm is established.
	Dorothea Dix begins her work to improve conditions for the mentally ill.
1842	Massachusetts Supreme Court in *Commonwealth v. Hunt* strengthens the legal right of workers to organize trade unions.
1845	Potato famine in Ireland sets off a mass migration of Irish to the United States.
1846–1848	Mormons migrate to the West.
1847	John Humphrey Noyes establishes the Oneida Community.
1848	Seneca Falls Convention outlines a program for women's rights.

agricultural and manufactured goods were exchanged more efficiently, a growing home market continually stimulated the development of American manufacturing.

THE TRANSPORTATION REVOLUTION

In 1815 the cost of moving goods by land transportation was prohibitively high. It cost just as much to haul heavy goods by horsedrawn wagons 30 miles into the interior as to ship them 3,000 miles across the Atlantic Ocean. Water transportation was much cheaper, but it was limited to the coast or navigable rivers. Thus, only farmers located near a city or a river could grow surplus crops for sale in an outside market.

Steamboats and Canals.   Steamboats provided the first transportation breakthrough. By the 1820s, steamboats had reduced the cost and the time of upriver shipments by 90 percent. As steamboats spread to western waters, more and more farmers could reap the economic benefits of exporting corn, pork, and other foodstuffs.

Western trade did not start to flow eastward until the completion of the Erie Canal in 1825, the first and most successful of the artificial waterways designed to link eastern seaboard cities with western markets (see Map 12–1). An immediate success, the Erie Canal reduced the cost of sending freight from Buffalo to New York City by more than 90 percent, and by the 1840s, it was pulling in more western trade than was being sent to New Orleans on the Mississippi River.

Anxious to match the Erie's success, other states launched plans for competing canals to the West, but no other canal could overcome the tremendous advantage of the Erie's head start in fixing trading patterns along its route. Before the Panic of 1837 abruptly ended the canal boom, three broad networks of canals had been built. One set linked seaboard cities on the Atlantic with their agricultural hinterlands, another connected the Mid-Atlantic states with the Ohio River Valley, and a third funneled western grain to ports on the Great Lakes.

Railroads.   Railroads were the last and ultimately the most important of the transportation improvements that spurred economic development in Jacksonian America. The railroads of the 1830s were a radically new technology that overturned traditional notions of time and space. "I cannot describe the strange sensation produced on seeing the train of cars come up. And when I started in them . . . it seemed like a dream," exclaimed Christopher Columbus Baldwin of Massachusetts when he saw his first railroad car in 1835.

The construction of the first American railroads began in the late 1820s, and they all pushed outward from seaboard cities eager to connect to the western market. By 1840, the railroads had become the most dynamic booster of inter-regional trade.

The rail network in place by mid-century was already altering the North-South sectional balance. The bulk of western trade no longer went downriver to New Orleans but was shipped east by rail. Moving in the opposite direction, to the West, were northern-born settlers, manufactured goods, and cultural values that increasingly unified the free states east of the Mississippi into a common economic and cultural unit. As the distinctions between them blurred, the Northeast and the Old Northwest were becoming just the North. Significantly, no direct rail connection linked the North and the South.

Government and the Transportation Revolution.   Both national and state government promoted the transportation revolution. State legislatures furnished some 70 percent of the funding for canals and about half of all railroad capital. By the 1830s, the states were also making it easier for private businesses, and especially those in transportation, to receive the legal privileges of incorporation. These included the protection of limited liability, that is, the limiting of investors' liability to their direct financial stake in the company, and the power of eminent domain, the legal right to purchase whatever land was needed for rights-of-way. The federal government provided engineers for railroad surveys, lowered tariffs on iron used in rail construction, and granted subsidies to the railroads in the form of public land. Most important, however, were two Supreme Court decisions that helped open up the economy to competition. In *Gibbons v. Ogden* (1824), the Court overturned a New York law that had given Aaron Ogden a monopoly on steamboat service between New York and New Jersey. Thomas Gibbons, Ogden's competitor, had a federal license for the coastal trade. The right to compete under the national

W WHERE TO LEARN MORE

★ Erie Canal Museum, Syracuse, New York **www.eriecanalmuseum.org/**

19–3
The Case for the Erie Canal

QUICK REVIEW

Railroads
- Most important link in Jacksonian transportation revolution.
- 1825: first general-purpose railroad opened in England.
- By mid-century, railroads were a vital part of American economy.

Gibbons v. Ogden   Supreme Court decision of 1824 involving coastal commerce that overturned a steamboat monopoly granted by the state of New York on the grounds that only Congress had the authority to regulate interstate commerce.

MAP EXPLORATION

To explore an interactive version of this map, go to **http://www.prenhall.com/goldfield3/map12.1**

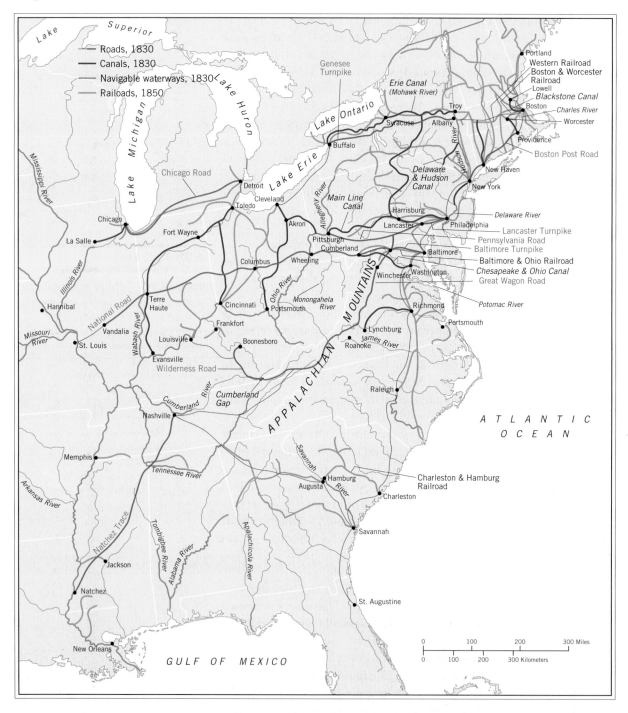

MAP 12–1 The Transportation Revolution   By 1830, a network of roads, canals, and naviga-ble rivers was spurring economic growth in the first phase of the transportation revolution. By 1850, railroads, the key development in the second phase of the transportation revolution, were opening up additional areas to commercial activity.

WHICH CITIES probably benefited the most from the new transportation infrastructure and why?

license, the Court ruled, took legal precedence over Ogden's monopoly. The decision affirmed the supremacy of the national government to regulate interstate commerce.

A new Court, presided over by Roger B. Taney, who became chief justice when John Marshall died in 1835, struck a bolder blow against monopoly in the landmark case of *Charles River Bridge v. Warren Bridge* in 1837. Taney ruled that the older Charles River Bridge Company had not received a monopoly from Massachusetts to collect tolls across the Charles River. Any uncertainties in the charter rights of corporations, reasoned Taney, should be resolved in favor of the broader community interests that would be served by free and open competition.

Canal boats below a lock at the Junction of the Erie with the Northern (Champlain) Canal. Aquatint by John Hill.

Collection of the New York Historical Society, Negative # 34684

CITIES AND IMMIGRANTS

Barely one in 20 Americans in the 1790s lived in an urban area. By 1850, more than one in seven Americans was a city-dweller, and the nation had 10 cities whose population exceeded 50,000 (see Map 12–2). The transportation revolution triggered this surge in urban growth. The cities that prospered were those with access to the expanding network of cheap transport on steamboats, canals, and railroads. A huge influx of immigrants after the mid-1840s and simultaneous advances in steam engines provided the cheap labor and sources of power that increasingly made cities focal points of manufacturing production.

The Port Cities.   America's largest cities in the early nineteenth century were its Atlantic ports: New York, Philadelphia, Baltimore, and Boston. By 1810, New York had become the largest American city, and by the 1850s its population exceeded 800,000. Between 1820 and 1860 one-third of the nation's exports and more than three-fifths of its imports passed through New York. No wonder the poet Walt Whitman trumpeted this metropolis as "the heart, the brain, the focus, the main spring, the pinnacle, the extremity, the no more beyond of the new world."

New York's harbor gave oceangoing ships direct, protected access to Manhattan Island, and from there, the Hudson River provided a navigable highway flowing 150 miles north to Albany, deep in the state's agricultural interior. No other port was so ideally situated for trade. And no other had the advantage of access to the Erie Canal. New York City benefited, not only from the increased volume of western foodstuffs sent east across the Erie and then down the Hudson River for export to Europe, but also from the swelling flow of finished goods shipped out of New York for sale to western farmers. The city's banks brought together the capital that made New York the country's chief financial center.

As they grew, the Atlantic ports pioneered new forms of city transportation. Omnibuses, horsedrawn coaches carrying up to 20 passengers, and steam ferries were in common use by the 1820s. The first commuter railroad, the Boston and Worcester, began service in 1838. At mid-century, horsedrawn street railway lines moved at speeds of about 6 miles an hour, overcoming some of the limitations of the

Charles River Bridge v. Warren Bridge   Supreme Court decision of 1837 that promised economic competition by ruling that the broader rights of the community took precedence over any presumed right of monopoly granted in a corporate charter.

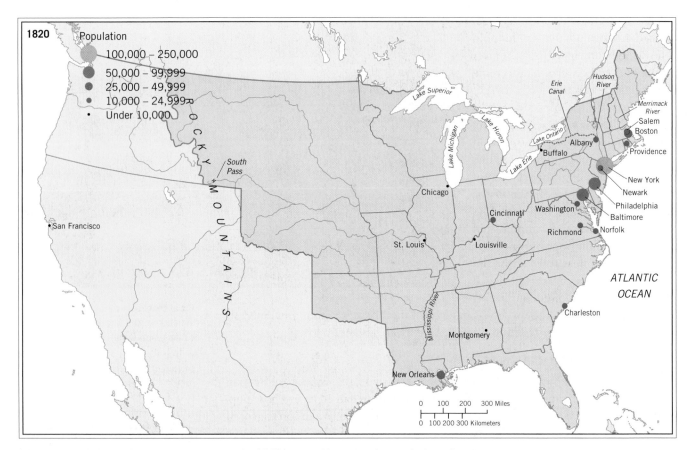

MAP 12–2A   **The Growth of Cities, 1820–1860**   In 1820, most cities were clustered along the Atlantic seaboard. By 1860, new transportation outlets—canals and railroads—had fostered the rapid growth of cities in the interior, especially at trading locations with access to navigable rivers or to the Great Lakes. Much of this growth occurred in the 1850s.

Data Source: Statistical Abstract of the United States.

WHY WAS the growth of cities the slowest in the South?

"walking cities" of the early nineteenth century. Accompanying this growth were the first slums, the most notorious of which was the Five Points district of New York City.

Small, flimsy wooden structures, often crammed into back alleys, housed the working poor in cramped, fetid conditions. Backyard privies, supplemented by chamber pots, were the standard means of disposing of human waste. These outhouses overflowed in heavy rain and often contaminated private wells, the source of drinking water. Garbage and animal wastes simply accumulated on streets, scavenged by roving packs of hogs.

Inland Cities.   The fastest-growing cities were in the interior. Pittsburgh, at the head of the Ohio River, was the first western city to develop a manufacturing sector to complement its exchange function. With access to the extensive coalfields of western Pennsylvania, Pittsburgh had a cheap fuel that provided the high heat needed to manufacture iron and glass. It emerged as America's best-known and

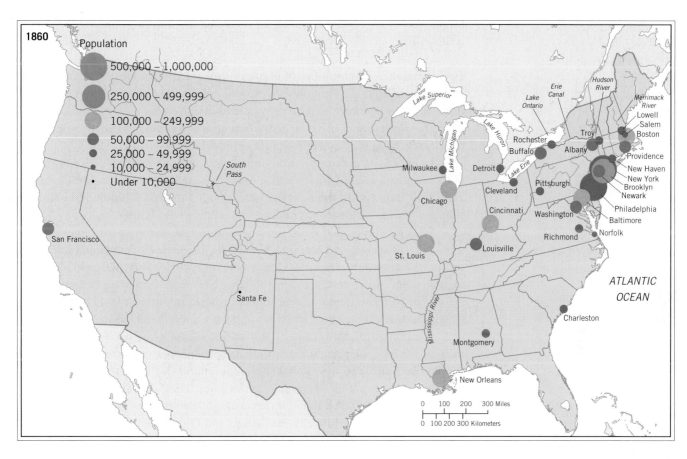

MAP 12–2B

most polluted manufacturing city. Cincinnati, downstream on the Ohio, soon became famous for its hogs. "Porkopolis," as it was called, was the West's first meat-packing center. St. Louis, just below the merger of the Missouri and Mississippi rivers, prospered by servicing American trade with the trans-Mississippi West.

By the 1840s, the Great Lake ports of Cleveland, Detroit, Milwaukee, and Chicago were the dynamic centers of western urbanization. Their combined population increased twenty-five-fold between 1830 and 1850. The Great Lakes served as an extension of the Erie Canal, and cities on the lakes where incoming and outgoing goods had to be unloaded for transshipment benefited enormously.

New Industrial Cities.   The only other cities growing as fast as the Great Lakes ports were the new industrial towns. The densest cluster of these was in rural New England along the fall line of rivers, where the rapidly falling water provided cheap power to drive the industrial machinery of factories and machine shops. Each town was tied to a transportation network that brought in raw cotton for the textile mills from the mercantile centers of Boston and Providence and shipped out the finished goods.

Lowell, Massachusetts, was America's first large-scale planned manufacturing city. Founded in 1822 by Boston businessmen, Lowell was built around the falls of the Merrimack River. Lowell's success became a model for others to

QUICK REVIEW

Immigration at Mid-century

- Surge of immigrants fueled growth of cities after the 1830s.
- Economic and political upheaval spurred mass migration from Europe.
- Famine drove 1.5 million Irish to America.

follow, and by 1840, New England led the North in both urbanization and industrialization.

Immigration. The number of immigrants from 1840 to 1860, 4.2 million, represented a tenfold increase over the number that had come in the two preceding decades. At mid-century, most of the population of New York was foreign-born, and in all the port cities of the Northeast, immigrants dominated the manufacturing work force. Most of these immigrants were Irish and German.

In the 1840s, economic and political upheavals in Europe spurred mass migration, mostly to the United States. A blight wiped out the Irish potato crop in 1845 and 1846, and in the next five years about 1 million Irish died of malnutrition and disease. Another 1.5 million fled, many to the United States.

Without marketable skills, the Irish had to take the worst and lowest-paying jobs. Still, cash wages and access to food made the American city preferable to the prospect of starvation in Ireland. Urging her parents to join her, Margaret McCarthy, an Irish domestic servant, wrote in 1850 that New York was a place "where no man or woman ever Hungered or ever will and where you will not be Seen Naked . . . where you would never want or be at a loss for a good Breakfast and Dinner."

German immigrants came to America to escape poor harvests and political turmoil. Far more Germans than Irish had owned property as farmers, artisans, and shopkeepers and had the capital to purchase land in the West and the skills to join the ranks of small businessmen in the cities. They were also more likely than the Irish to have entered the country through Baltimore or New Orleans. From there they fanned out into the Mississippi and Ohio valleys. With the Irish, they made up over half of the population of St. Louis by the 1850s and were close to a majority in the other large cities of the Midwest and Northeast. About four in five of all the immigrants arriving after 1840 settled in the New England and mid-Atlantic states. Their sheer numbers transformed the size and ethnic composition of the working class, especially in the cities of the Northeast. And their cheap labor provided the final ingredient in the expansion of industrialization that began after the War of 1812.

Lowell was the nation's leading textile center and the second-largest city in Massachusetts by 1850. The building with the cupola and the structure with dormers and chimneys were part of the mill complex. The two detached buildings were boardinghouses for the young women who worked in the mills.

American Textile History Museum

THE INDUSTRIAL REVOLUTION

In 1815, the Northeast had the largest cities, the most developed capital markets, the readiest access to the technological skills of artisans, and the greatest supply of available labor. The first large-scale factories, the textile mills, were erected in New England in the 1820s. For the next 30 years, the United States had the most rapidly developing industrial economy in the world.

The household and the small workshop were the sites of manufacturing in Jefferson's America. Wider markets for household manufactures began to develop in the late eighteenth century with the coming of the **putting-out system.** Local merchants furnished ("put out") raw materials to rural households and paid at a piece rate for the labor that converted the raw materials into manufactured products. The supplying merchant then marketed and sold these goods.

In the cities and larger towns, most manufacturing was done by artisans. Working in their own shops and with their own tools, they produced small batches of finished goods. Each artisan had a specific skill that set him above common laborers. These skills came from hands-on experience and craft traditions that were handed down from one generation to the next.

Master craftsmen taught the "mysteries of the craft" to the journeymen and apprentices who lived with them and worked in their shops. Journeymen had learned the skills of their craft but lacked the capital to open their own shops. Apprentices were adolescent boys legally sent by their fathers to live with and obey a master craftsman in return for being taught a trade. By the terms of the contract, known as an indenture, the master also provided for the apprentice's schooling and moral upbringing. An apprentice could reasonably expect to be promoted to journeyman in his late teens and begin advancement toward his competency, a secure income from an independent trade that would enable him to support a family.

The factory system of production that would undercut both household and artisanal manufacturing after 1815 could produce goods far more quickly and cheaply per worker than could artisans or rural households. Factories subdivided the specialized skills of the artisan into a series of semiskilled tasks, a process foreshadowed by the putting-out system. Factories also put workers under systematic controls. And in the final stage of industrialization, they boosted workers' productivity through the use of power-driven machinery.

Britain pioneered the technological advances that drove early industrialization. Despite attempts to prohibit the emigration of artisans who knew how the machinery worked, some British mechanics made it to the United States. Samuel Slater was one of them, and he took over the operation of a fledging mill in Providence, Rhode Island. With his knowledge of how to build the water-powered spinning machinery, he converted the mill into the nation's first permanent cotton factory in 1790.

Slater's factory, and those modeled on it, manufactured yarn that was put out to rural housewives to be woven into cloth. The first factory to mechanize the operations of spinning and weaving and turn out finished cloth was incorporated in Waltham, Massachusetts, in 1813. The Waltham factory was heavily capitalized, relied on the latest technology, and recruited its work force from rural farm families.

The first real spurt of factory building came with the closing off of British imports during the Embargo and the War of 1812. But the great test of American manufacturing came after 1815, when peace with Britain brought a flood of cheap British manufactured goods.

Sources of Labor.   Industrial labor was more expensive in America than in England, where the high cost of land forced the rural poor into the cities to find work. In contrast, land was cheap and plentiful in the United States, and Americans preferred the independence of farm work to the dependence of factory labor. Consequently, the first mill workers were predominantly children. The owners set up the father on a plot of company-owned land, provided piecework for the mother, and put the children to work in the mills.

Although this so-called **Rhode Island system** of family employment sufficed for small mills, it was inadequate for the larger, more mechanized factories that

Putting-out System   System of manufacturing in which merchants furnished households with raw materials for processing by family members.

Rhode Island System   During the industrialization of the early nineteenth century, the recruitment of entire families for employment in a factory.

At mid-century most industrial work was still done by hand. Shown here are two foundry workers holding floor rammers used for packing sand against molds.

Courtesy Library of Congress

Waltham System During the industrialization of the early nineteenth century, the recruitment of unmarried young women for employment in factories.

were built in New England after the War of 1812. The owners of these mills recruited unmarried, adolescent daughters of farmers from across New England as their laborers in the **Waltham system.** Although factory wages were low, they were more than these young women could earn doing piecework in the home or as domestics. The wages also brought a liberating degree of financial independence. "When they felt the jingle of silver in their pockets," recalled Harriet Hanson Robinson of her fellow workers at Lowell in the 1830s, "there for the first time, their heads became erect and they walked as if on air."

To overcome parental fears that their daughters might be exposed to morally corrupting conditions in the mills and mill towns, New England manufacturers set up paternalistic moral controls. Single female workers had to live in company-owned boardinghouses that imposed curfews, screened visitors, and mandated church attendance. The mill women worked six days a week from dawn to dusk for low wages. There were limits to what the women would endure, and in 1834 and 1836 the female hands at Lowell "turned out" to protest wage reductions in demonstrations that were the largest strikes in American history up to that time.

After the economic downturn of the late 1830s, conditions in the mills grew worse. By the mid-1840s, however, the Irish, desperate for work, sent their children into the mills at an earlier age than Yankee families. These workers did not leave after two or three years of building up a small dowry for marriage, as many New Englanders did. By the early 1850s, more than half the textile operatives were Irish women.

In the mid-Atlantic region, where the farm population was more prosperous than in New England and fewer young women were available for factory work, immigrants were an important source of manufacturing workers as early as the 1820s. They played an especially crucial role in urban manufacturing. The port cities lacked usable waterpower, but by drawing on a growing pool of cheap, immigrant labor, manufacturers could expand production while driving down the cost.

Except in New England textile factories and the smaller factories and shops in the seaboard cities, native-born males were the largest group of early manufacturing workers. They came from poor rural families that lacked enough land to pass on to male heirs. As late as 1840, women, including those working at home, made up about half of the manufacturing work force and one-quarter of the factory hands. Regardless of their sex, few of these workers brought any specific skills to their jobs, and thus they had little bargaining power. Economic necessity forced them to accept low wages and harsh working conditions. The sheer increase in their numbers, as opposed to any productivity gains from technological innovations, accounted by 1850 for two-thirds of the gains in manufacturing output.

Technological Gains. After 1815, American manufacturers began to close the technological gap with Britain by drawing on the skills of American mechanics. Mechanics experimented with new designs, improved old ones, and patented inventions that found industrial applications outside their own crafts.

The most famous early American invention was Eli Whitney's cotton gin. By cheaply and quickly removing the seeds from cotton fibers, the cotton gin spurred the cultivation of cotton across the South.

Whitney also pushed the idea of basing production on interchangeable parts. After receiving a federal contract to manufacture muskets, he designed new milling machines and turret lathes that transformed the technology of machine tool production. The federal arsenal at Harpers Ferry, Virginia, developed machine tools that could manufacture standardized, interchangeable parts. The new techniques were first applied in 1815 to the manufacture of wooden clocks and by the 1840s to sewing machines, farm machinery, and watch parts. The **American system of manufacturing,** low-cost, standardized mass production, built around interchangeable parts stamped out by machines, was America's unique contribution to the industrial revolution.

The 1840s registered the highest rate of expansion in the manufacturing sector of the economy in the nineteenth century. The adoption of the stationary steam engine in urban manufacturing fueled much of this expansion. High-pressure steam engines enabled power-driven industry to locate in the port cities of the Northeast and the booming cities on the Great Lakes. By turning to steam power and new machine tools, western manufacturers after 1840 enlarged their region's industrial base and created a new industry, the mass production of agricultural implements.

To provide their mills with a steady, reliable source of water, one that would not be affected by the whims of nature, the Boston Associates constructed a series of dams and canals that extended to the headwaters of the Merrimack River in northern New Hampshire. Inevitably, the ecology of the region changed. Farmers protested when their fields and pastures were submerged, but lawyers for the Boston Associates successfully argued that water, like other natural resources, should be treated as a commodity that could contribute to economic progress. Increasingly, the law treated nature as an economic resource to be engineered and bought and sold.

GROWING INEQUALITY AND NEW CLASSES

In the first half of the nineteenth century, the economy grew three times faster than in the eighteenth century, and per capita income doubled. Living standards for most Americans improved. Houses, for those who could afford them, became larger, better furnished, and better heated. Nonetheless, half of the adult white males were propertyless at mid-century. Wealth had become more concentrated, and extremes of wealth and poverty eroded the Jeffersonian ideal of a republic of independent proprietors who valued liberty because they were economically free.

The gap between the rich and the poor widened considerably in the early phases of industrialization. In 1800, the richest 10 percent of Americans owned 40 to 50 percent of the national wealth. By the 1850s, their share was about 70 percent. The most glaring discrepancies in wealth appeared in the large cities. Most of the urban rich had been born wealthy, the offspring of old-

WHERE TO LEARN MORE

Hanford Mills Museum, East Meredith, New York
www.hanfordmills.org/

American system of manufacturing   A technique of production pioneered in the United States in the first half of the nineteenth century that relied on precision manufacturing with the use of interchangeable parts.

Shown here working at power looms under the supervision of a male overseer, young single women constituted the bulk of the labor force in the first textile factories of New England.
Corbis

QUICK REVIEW

A Growing Gap between Rich and Poor

- 1800: Richest 10 percent of Americans owned 40–50 percent of national wealth
- 1850s: Richest 10 percent of Americans owned 70 percent of national wealth

QUICK REVIEW

Class Consciousness

- Separation of home and work first step in evolving class consciousness.
- Home a place of material comfort for rising middle class.
- Having servants a sign of status.
- Middle class shaped by evangelical religion.

money families who had married and invested wisely. They belonged to exclusive clubs, attended lavish balls and dinners, were waited on by a retinue of servants in their mansions, and generally recoiled from what they considered the "mob government" ushered in by the Jacksonian Democrats. As one of the urban elite noted, it was a society "characterized by a spirit of exclusiveness and persecution unknown in any other country. Its gradations not being regulated according to rank and titles, selfishness and conceit are its principal elements; and its arbitrary distinctions the more offensive, as they principally refer to fortune."

The New Middle Class.   The faster pace of economic growth that enabled the urban rich to increase their wealth also created opportunities for a rapidly expanding new middle class. This class grew as the number of nonmanual jobs increased. The result by mid-century was a new middle class superimposed on the older one of independent farmers, artisans, shopkeepers, and professionals. The separation of work and home constituted the first step in an evolving sense of class consciousness. As the market revolution advanced, the workplace increasingly became a specialized location of production or selling. Middle-class fathers now left for work in the morning, while mothers governed households that were primarily residential units and places of material comfort, where growing quantities of consumer goods were on display. Having servants became a status symbol. Shunned as degrading by most native-born white women, these low-paying jobs were filled by African-American and young immigrant (especially Irish) women.

Besides turning to etiquette books for advice on proper manners in public and in the home, the middle class also tried to shape its behavior by the tenets of evangelical religion. Revivals swept northern cities in the late 1820s. Charles G. Finney led the most dramatic and successful ones in the cities along the Erie Canal in upstate New York. Finney preached that salvation was available to those who willed it. He also stressed that both economic and moral success depended on the virtues of sobriety, self-restraint, and hard work. Aggressiveness and ambition at work were not necessarily sinful so long as businessmen reformed their own moral lives and helped others do the same. This message was immensely reassuring to employers and entrepreneurs, for it confirmed and sanctified their own pursuit of economic self-interest. It also provided them with a religious inspiration for attempting to exert moral control over their communities and employees. **Temperance,** the prohibition of alcoholic beverages, was the greatest of the evangelically inspired reforms, and abstinence from alcohol became the most telling evidence of middle-class respectability.

Women and the Cult of Domesticity.   The evangelical ministers of the northern middle class enshrined women as the moral superiors of men. Though considered weak and passive, women were also held to be uniquely pure and pious. Women, who easily outnumbered men at Sunday services and weeknight prayer meetings, were now responsible for converting their homes into loving, prayerful centers of domesticity, and the primary task of motherhood became the Christian nurturing of souls entrusted to a mother's care.

This sanctified notion of motherhood reflected and reinforced shifting patterns of family life. Families became smaller as the birthrate fell by 25 percent in the first half of the nineteenth century. The decline was greatest in the urban middle class after 1820. Children were no longer an economic asset as they had been on a family farm. Middle-class couples consciously limited the size of their families, and women stopped having children at an earlier age. As a result, parents devoted more care and financial resources to child rearing.

Temperance   Reform movement originating in the 1820s that sought to eliminate the consumption of alcohol.

Beginning in the 1820s, ministers and female writers elevated the family role of middle-class women into a **cult of domesticity.** This idealized conception of womanhood insisted that the biological differences of God's natural order determined separate social roles for men and women. Characterized as strong, aggressive, and ambitious, men naturally belonged in the competitive world of business and politics. Women's providential task was to preserve religion and morality in the home and family. Held to be innately weak, nurturing, and selfless, only they possessed the moral purity necessary for rearing virtuous children and preserving the home as a refuge from the outside world.

The Working Classes.   In the preindustrial United States, the working class was predominantly native-born and of artisan origins. By mid-century, most urban workers were immigrants or the children of immigrants and had never been artisans in a skilled craft.

Job skills, sex, race, and ethnicity all divided workers after 1840. Master craftsmen were the most highly skilled and best-paid workers. As industrialization proceeded, the unity of the old artisan class splintered. Ambitious master craftsmen with access to capital rose into the ranks of small businessmen and manufacturers.

By the 1830s, journeymen were becoming permanent wage earners with little prospect of opening their own shops. This new wage-earning class denounced the new industrial relations as a "system of mental and physical slavery." To protect their liberties from what they considered a new aristocracy of manufacturers, they organized workingmen's parties in the 1830s, centered in the eastern cities. At the top of these parties' lists of reforms were free public education, the abolition of imprisonment for debt, and a 10-hour workday. But the depression of 1839–1843 forced mechanics to concentrate on their economic survival, and the Democrats siphoned off many of their political leaders.

Early Trade Unions.   Journeymen also turned to trade union activity in the 1820s and 1830s to gain better wages, shorter hours, and enhanced job security. Locals from various trades formed the National Trades Union, the first national union, in 1834. The new labor movement launched more than 150 strikes in the mid-1830s.

Although the Panic of 1837 decimated union membership, the early labor movement did achieve two notable victories. First, by the late 1830s, it had forced employers to accept the 10-hour day as the standard for most skilled workers. Second, in a landmark decision handed down in 1842, the Massachusetts Supreme Court ruled in *Commonwealth* v. *Hunt* that a trade union was not necessarily subject to laws against criminal conspiracies and that a strike could be used to force employers to hire only union members.

The unions defended artisanal rights and virtues, and they ignored workers whose jobs had never had craft status. As massive immigration merged with industrialization after 1840, this basic division between workers widened. On one side was the male, Protestant, and native-born class of skilled artisans. On the other side was the working-class majority of factory laborers and unskilled workers, predominantly immigrants and women who worked for a wage as domestics or factory hands.

Increasingly fearing these workers as a threat to their job security and Protestant values, in the 1840s American-born artisans joined **nativist organizations** that sought to curb mass immigration from Europe and limit the political rights of Catholic immigrants. One of the few issues that brought immigrants and nativists together was the nearly universal demand of white workers that black workers be confined to the most menial jobs.

Cult of domesticity   The belief that women, by virtue of their sex, should stay home as the moral guardians of family life.

Nativist organizations   Joined by American-born artisans in the 1840s which sought to curb mass immigration from Europe and limit the political rights of Catholic immigrants.

OVERVIEW   CHANGES PROMOTING GROWTH IN THE TRANSFORMED ECONOMY

Sector	1815	1850
Travel and transportation	By foot and horsedrawn wagon	Cheaper and faster with canals, steamboats, and railroads opening up new markets
Population	Overwhelmingly native-born, rural, and concentrated east of Appalachian Mountains	Four times larger as a result of natural increase and surge of immigration after 1840; settlement of West and growth of cities
Wage labor	Native-born, primarily women and children in manufacturing	Expanding as rural poor and immigrants enter manufacturing work force
Power	Water-driven mills	Steam-driven engines
Farming	Subsistence-oriented; surplus sold in localized markets	Commercialized agriculture spreading in response to improvements in transportation
Manufacturing	Small-scale production in household units and artisan shops	Large-scale production in eastern cities and factories

Gender also divided workers. Working-class men shared the dominant ideology of female dependence. They measured their own status as husbands by their ability to support their wives and daughters. Beginning in the 1830s, male workers argued that their wages would be higher if women were barred from the labor force. A report of the National Trades Union in 1836 insisted that a woman's "efforts to sustain herself and her family are actually the same as tying a stone around the neck of her natural protector, Man, and destroying him with the weight she has brought to his assistance."

With these views, male workers helped lock wage-earning women into the lowest-paying and most exploited jobs. Women workers tried to organize, but the male labor movement refused to lend much support, generally restricting their assistance to pushing for legislation that would limit the hours worked by women and children, a stand that enhanced their male image as protectors of the family.

REFORM AND MORAL ORDER

The rapidity and extent of the social and economic changes that accompanied the market revolution were disorienting, even frightening, to many Americans, particularly religious leaders and wealthy businessmen in the East. Alarmed by what they perceived as a breakdown in moral authority, they sought to impose moral discipline on Americans.

These eastern elites, with the indispensable support of their wives and daughters, created a network of voluntary church-affiliated reform organizations known collectively as the **benevolent empire.** Revivals in the 1820s and 1830s broadened the base of reform to include the newly evangelicalized middle class in northern cities and towns.

WHAT ROLE did women play in the reform movements that followed the War of 1812?

Benevolent empire   Network of reform associations affiliated with Protestant churches in the early nineteenth century dedicated to the restoration of moral order.

THE BENEVOLENT EMPIRE

For the Reverend Lyman Beecher, the United States in 1814 presented "a scene of destitution and wretchedness." From his Presbyterian pulpit in Litchfield, Connecticut, and then in Boston, he became the leader of a clerical drive to restore morality to America.

Evangelical businessmen in the seaboard cities backed the call to restore moral order. Worried by the increasing number of urban poor, wealthy merchants contributed vital financial support for a network of reform associations.

The reform societies built on the Second Great Awakening's techniques of organization and communication. The Protestant reformers sent out speakers on regular schedules along prescribed routes. They developed organizations that maintained a constant pressure for reform. National and local boards of directors supervised the work of salaried managers, who inspired volunteers to combat sin among the unconverted. When steam presses and stereotype plates halved the cost of printing and dramatically increased its speed, the American Bible Society was the first organization to exploit this revolution in the print media. By 1830 religious presses were churning out more than 1 million Bibles and 6 million tracts a year.

A host of local societies targeted individual vices. Their purpose, as summed up by a Massachusetts group, the Andover South Parish Society for the Reformation of Morals, was "to discountenance [discourage] immorality, particularly Sabbath-breaking, intemperance, and profanity, and to promote industry, order, piety, and good morals." These goals linked social and moral discipline, appealing both to churchgoers concerned about godlessness and profit-oriented businessmen eager to curb their workers' unruly behavior.

With volunteers drawn largely from the teenage daughters of evangelical businessmen, Sunday interdenominational schools combined elementary education with the teaching of the Bible and Protestant principles. By 1832, nearly 10 percent of all American children aged 5 to 14 were attending Sunday schools.

The boldest expression of the drive to enhance Protestant Christian power was the **Sabbatarian movement.** In 1828, evangelicals led by Lyman Beecher formed the General Union for Promoting the Observance of the Christian Sabbath. Their immediate goal was the repeal of a law passed by Congress in 1810 directing post offices to deliver mail on Sunday. Their broader mission was to enforce local statutes that shut down business and leisure activities on Sundays.

In 1829, insisting on the separation of church and state, the Democratic Congress upheld the postal law of 1810. Businessmen, workingmen, southern evangelicals, and religious conservatives all felt that the Sabbath purists had gone too far in a movement now seen as a threat to civil liberties and the rights of private property.

The General Union disbanded in 1832, but it left an important legacy for future reform movements. On the one hand, it developed techniques that converted the reform impulse into direct political action. On the other hand, the failure of the Sabbatarians revealed that a new approach was needed that encouraged individuals to reform themselves without coercive controls. It soon emerged in the temperance movement.

THE TEMPERANCE MOVEMENT

Temperance, the drive against the consumption of alcohol, had the greatest impact on the most people of any reform movement. Its success rested on what Lyman Beecher called "a new moral power." Dismayed by popular resistance to the coercive moralism of the first wave of Protestant reform, evangelicals concluded

Sabbatarian movement
Reform organization founded in 1828 by Congregationalist and Presbyterian ministers that lobbied for an end to the delivery of mail on Sundays and other Sabbath violations.

11–2
Lyman Beecher,
Six Sermons on
Intemperance (1828)

that reform had to rest on persuasion, and it had to begin with the voluntary decision of individuals to free themselves from sin.

In 1826, evangelicals founded the **American Temperance Society.** Their goal was to bring about a radical change in American attitudes toward alcohol and its role in social life. By 1830, American consumption of alcohol had reached an all-time high of 7.1 gallons of pure alcohol per year for every American aged 14 and over (about three times present-day levels). Taverns easily outnumbered churches as gathering places. Alcohol was used to pay common laborers and itinerant preachers on the early Methodist circuit. Masters and journeymen shared a drink as a customary way of taking a break from work, and no wedding, funeral, or meeting of friends was complete without alcohol.

For the temperance crusade to succeed, the reformers had to finance a massive propaganda campaign and link it to an organization that could mobilize and energize thousands of people. They built such a mass movement by merging temperance into the network of churches and lay volunteers that the benevolent empire had developed and by adopting the techniques of revivals to win converts.

Evangelical reformers denounced intemperance as the greatest sin of the land. Alcohol represented all that was wrong in America: crime, poverty, insanity, broken families, boisterous politicking, Sabbath-breaking.

This message thundered from the pulpit and the public lectern. Thanks to the generous financial subsidies of wealthy benefactors, it was also broadcast in millions of tracts printed on the latest high-speed presses. Like revivals, temperance rallies combined emotionally charged sermons with large, tearful prayer meetings to evoke guilt among sinners, who would then seek release by taking the pledge of abstinence.

Within a decade, the American Temperance Society had more than 5,000 local chapters and statewide affiliates, most in the Northeast. A million members had pledged abstinence by 1833. Women constituted one-third to more than one-half of the members in local temperance societies. As the moral protectors of the family, they pressured their husbands to take the teetotaler's pledge and stick by it, raised sons to shun alcohol, and banished liquor from their homes. By the 1840s, temperance and middle-class domesticity had become synonymous.

Businessmen welcomed temperance as a model of self-discipline in their efforts to regiment factory work. Many of them presumably agreed with the *Temperance Recorder* that "the enterprise of this country is so great, and competition so eager in every branch of business . . . , that profit can only result from . . . *temperance.*"

Temperance made its first significant inroads among the working classes during the economic depression of 1839–1843. Joining together in what they called Washington Temperance Societies, small businessmen and artisans, many of them reformed drunkards, carried temperance into working-class districts. In a telling measure of the temperance movement's success, per capita alcohol consumption fell to less than 2 gallons per year by 1845.

WOMEN'S ROLE IN REFORM

The first phase of women's reform activities represented an extension of the domestic ideal promoted in the Cult of Domesticity. Assumptions about women's unique moral qualities permitted, and even encouraged, them to assume the role of "social mother" by organizing on behalf of the orphaned and the widowed.

The revivalist call in the 1820s for moral action inspired middle-class women to join voluntary female groups. They founded maternal associations, where they prayed and fasted for the moral strength to save the souls of their children. Other associations sponsored revivals, visited the poor, established Sunday schools, and

American Temperance Society
National organization established in 1826 by evangelical Protestants that campaigned for total abstinence from alcohol and was successful in sharply lowering per capita consumption of alcohol.

distributed Bibles and religious tracts. These reformers widened the public role of women, but their efforts also reinforced cultural stereotypes of women as nurturing helpmates who deferred to males.

A second phase in the reform efforts by women developed in the 1830s. Unlike their benevolent counterparts, the reformers now began to challenge male prerogatives and move beyond moral persuasion. The crusade against prostitution exemplified the new militancy. Women seized leadership of the movement in 1834 with the founding of the New York Female Moral Reform Society. In the pages of their journal, *Advocate for Moral Reform,* members identified male greed and licentiousness as the causes for the fallen state of women. Identified, too, were the male patrons of the city's brothels. The society blamed businessmen for the low wages that forced some women to resort to prostitution and denounced lustful men for engaging in "a regular crusade against [our] sex."

In 1839, this attack on the sexual double standard became a national movement with the establishment of the **American Female Moral Reform Society.** With 555 affiliates throughout the evangelical heartland of the North, female activists mounted a lobbying campaign that reached out to a mass audience. By the 1840s, such unprecedented political involvement enabled women to secure the first state laws criminalizing seduction and adultery.

Other women's groups developed a more radical critique of American society and its male leadership. The Boston Seamen's Aid Society, founded in 1833 by Sarah Josepha Hale, a widow with five children, soon rejected the benevolent tradition of distinguishing between "respectable" and "unworthy" poor. Hale discovered that her efforts to guide poor women toward self-sufficiency flew in the face of the low wages and substandard housing that trapped her clients in poverty. She concluded in 1838 that "it is hardly possible for the hopeless poor to avoid being vicious." Hale attacked male employers for exploiting the poor. "Combinations of selfish men are formed to beat down the price of female labor," she wrote in her 1836 annual report, "and then they call the diminished rate the market price."

BACKLASH AGAINST BENEVOLENCE

Some of the benevolent empire's harshest critics came out of the populist revivals of the early 1800s. They considered the Protestant reformers' program a conspiracy of orthodox Calvinists from old-line denominations to impose social and moral control on behalf of a religious and economic elite.

These criticisms revealed a profound mistrust of the emerging market society. In contrast to the evangelical reformers, drawn from the well-educated business and middle classes who were benefiting from economic change, most evangelical members of the grass-roots sects and followers of the itinerant preachers were unschooled, poor, and hurt by market fluctuations that they could not control. Socially uprooted and economically stranded, they found a sense of community in their local churches and resisted control by wealthier, better-educated outsiders. Above all, they clung to beliefs that shored up the threatened authority of the father over his household.

With the elevation of women to the status of moral guardians of the family and agents of benevolent reform outside the household, middle-class evangelicalism in the Northeast was becoming feminized. This new social role for women was especially threatening, indeed, galling, for men who were the casualties of the more competitive economy. Raised on farms where the father had been the unquestioned lawgiver and provider, these men attacked feminized evangelicalism for undermining their paternal authority.

American Female Moral Reform Society Organization founded in 1839 by female reformers that established homes of refuge for prostitutes and petitioned for state laws that would criminalize adultery and the seduction of women.

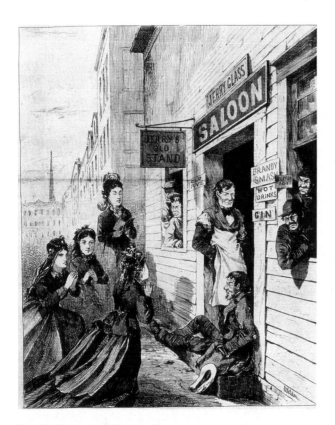

The temperance crusade brought women out of their homes and into the streets to pray in front of taverns filled with drunken men.

Getty Images Inc.—Hulton Archive Photo

HOW DID Enlightenment ideas shape the reform of institutions for the poor, criminals, and the mentally ill?

Church of Jesus Christ of Latter-day Saints (Mormon Church) Church founded in 1830 by Joseph Smith and based on the revelations in a sacred book he called the Book of Mormon.

The **Church of Jesus Christ of Latter-day Saints** (also known as the **Mormon Church**) represented the most enduring religious backlash of economically struggling men against the aggressive efforts of reforming middle-class evangelicals. Joseph Smith, who established the church in upstate New York in 1830, came from a New England farm family uprooted and impoverished by market speculations gone sour. He and his followers were alienated not only from the new market economy but also from what they saw as the religious and social anarchy around them.

Based on Smith's divine revelations as set forth in the Book of Mormon (1830), their new faith offered converts both a sanctuary as a biblical people and a release from social and religious uncertainties. They believed that the mainstream evangelical churches had corrupted Christ's original gospel.

Mormonism assigned complete spiritual and secular authority to men. Only through subordination and obedience to their husbands could women hope to gain salvation. To be a Mormon was to join a large extended family that was part of a shared enterprise. Men bonded their labor in a communal economy to benefit all the faithful. Driven by a strong sense of social obligation, the Mormons forged the most successful alternative vision in antebellum America to the individualistic Protestant republic of the benevolent reformers. (For the Mormons' role in the westward movement, see Chapter 13.)

INSTITUTIONS AND SOCIAL IMPROVEMENT

*A*lthough evangelical Protestantism was its mainspring, antebellum reform also had its roots in the European Enlightenment. Like the evangelicals inspired by religious optimism, reformers drawing on Enlightenment doctrines of progress had unbounded faith in social improvement. They saw in America an unlimited potential to fashion a model republic of virtuous, intelligent citizens.

Studies published in the 1820s that documented increasing urban poverty, crime, and teenage delinquency created a sense of urgency for many reformers. Guided by the Enlightenment belief that environmental conditions shaped human character, reformers created a new system of public schooling in the North. They also prodded state legislatures to fund penitentiaries for criminals, asylums for the mentally ill, reformatories for the delinquent, and almshouses for the poor.

As reformers were implementing new institutions for shaping individual character after 1820, a host of utopian communities also tapped into an impulse for human betterment. Most of these communities were short-lived because the new forms of social and economic organization they promoted were far too radical for all but a handful of Americans.

SCHOOL REFORM

Before the 1820s, schooling in America was an informal, haphazard affair. Private tutors and academies for the wealthy, a few charitable schools for the urban poor, and rural one-room schoolhouses open for a few months each year constituted formal education at the primary level.

The first political demands for free tax-supported schools originated with the **Workingmen's movement** in eastern cities in the 1820s. Decrying what the Philadelphia Working Men's Committee in 1830 described as "a monopoly of talent, which consigns the multitude to comparative ignorance, and secures the balance of knowledge on the side of the rich and the rulers," workers called for free public education. In pushing for "equal republican education," they sought to guarantee that all citizens, no matter how poor, could achieve meaningful liberty and equality. Their proposals, however, met stiff resistance from wealthier property holders, who refused to pay taxes to support the education of working-class children.

The breakthrough in public education came in New England, where the disruptive forces of industrialization and urbanization were felt the earliest. Increased economic inequality, growing numbers of impoverished Irish Catholic immigrants, and the emergence of a mass democracy based on nearly universal white male suffrage convinced reformers of the need for state-supported schools.

In 1837, the Massachusetts legislature established the nation's first state board of education. The head of the board for the next 12 years, Horace Mann, demanded that the state government assume centralized control over Massachusetts schools. All schools should have the same standards of compulsory attendance, strict discipline, common textbooks, professionally trained teachers, and graded, competitive classes of age-segregated students.

Once this system was in place, Mann promised, the schools would become "the great equalizer of the conditions of men, the balance-wheel of the social machinery." Education, Mann stated, "does better than disarm the poor of their hostility against the rich; it prevents being poor."

Democrats in the Massachusetts legislature denounced Mann's program and the laboring poor, who depended for economic survival on the wages their children could earn, resisted compulsory-attendance laws and a longer school year. Farmers fought to maintain local control over schooling and to block the higher taxes needed for a more comprehensive and professionalized system. The Catholic Church protested the thinly veiled attempts of the reformers to indoctrinate all students in the moral strictures of middle-class Protestantism.

Mann and his allies nonetheless prevailed in most of the industrializing states. Manufacturers hoped that the schools would turn out a more obedient and punctual labor force, and the more skilled and prosperous workers saw in public education a key to upward mobility for their children.

Most important for its political success, school reform appealed to the growing northern middle class. Schools would instill the moral and economic discipline that the middle class deemed essential for a progressive and ordered society.

Out of the northern middle class also came the young female teachers who increasingly staffed elementary schools. Presumed by their nature to be more nurturing than men, women now had an entry into teaching, the first profession open to them. Besides, women could also be paid far less than men; school boards assumed that they would accept low wages while waiting to be married.

Just over 50 percent of the white children between 5 and 19 years of age in the United States were enrolled in school in 1850, the highest percentage in the world at the time. Working-class parents pulled their children out of school at an earlier age than higher-income middle-class parents. Planters continued to rely on private tutors or academies, and southern farmers saw little need for public education. The slave states, especially in the Lower South, lagged behind the rest of the nation in public education.

PRISONS, WORKHOUSES, AND ASYLUMS

Up to this time, Americans had depended on voluntary efforts to cope with crime, poverty, and social deviance. Convinced that these efforts were inadequate, reformers turned to public authorities to establish a host of new institutions, penitentiaries, workhouses, mental hospitals, orphanages, and reformatories, to deal with social problems.

All these public institutions reflected a new attitude toward conditions that until then had been regarded as inevitable and irreversible. For example, eighteenth-century Americans never thought of rehabilitating criminals. Prisons were simple structures used to hold criminals before they were fined, whipped, mutilated, or executed. But the institutional reformers of the Jacksonian era believed that criminals, as well as the poor and other deviants, could be morally redeemed. The reformers held that people's environments shaped their character for good or evil. Samuel Gridley Howe, a prison reformer, proclaimed: "Thousands of convicts are made so in consequence of a faulty organization of society. . . . They are thrown upon society as a sacred charge; and that society is false to its trust, if it neglects any means for their reformation." In the properly ordered environment of new institutions, discipline and moral character would be instilled in criminals and other deviants.

Reformers had particularly high expectations for the penitentiary systems pioneered in Pennsylvania and New York in the 1820s. Unlike earlier prisons, the penitentiaries were huge, imposing structures that isolated the prisoners from each other and the outside world. Cut off from all corrupting influences, forced to learn that hard work teaches moral discipline, and uplifted by religious literature, criminals would be guided toward becoming law-abiding, productive citizens.

Workhouses. The same philosophy of reform provided the rationale for asylums to house the poor and the insane. The number of transient poor and the size of urban slums increased as commercial capitalism uprooted farmers from the land and undercut the security of craft trades. Believing that the poor, much like criminals, had only themselves to blame, public officials and their evangelical allies prescribed a therapeutic regimen of discipline and physical labor to cure the poor of their moral defects.

The custodians of the workhouses banished drinking, gambling, and idleness. Their prime responsibility was to supervise the inmates in a tightly scheduled daily routine built around manual labor. Once purged of their laziness and filled with self-esteem as the result of work discipline, the poor would be released to become useful members of society.

Asylums for the Mentally Ill. Reformers believed that too many choices in a highly mobile, materialistic, and competitive society drove some people insane. Following the lead of New York and Massachusetts in the 1830s, 28 states had established mental hospitals by 1860. These facilities set rigid rules and work assignments to teach patients how to order their lives.

While the reformers did provide social deviants with cleaner, safer living conditions, their penitentiaries and asylums succeeded more in classifying and segregating inmates than in reforming them. Witnessing the rigorous control of every movement of the isolated prisoners at the Eastern State Penitentiary in Philadelphia, the English novelist Charles Dickens declared "this slow and daily tampering with the mysteries of the brain to be immeasurably worse than any torture of the body." Penitentiaries, reformatories, and workhouses failed to eliminate or noticeably check poverty, crime, and vice. Refusing to question their basic premise that repressive institutions could promote individual responsibility, reformers abandoned

In the concern etched in her face, this photograph captures the compassion that Dorothea Dix brought to her crusade for mental health reform.

Courtesy of Library of Congress

their environmental explanations for deviance. By mid-century, they were defining deviants and dependents as permanent misfits with ingrained character defects.

UTOPIAN ALTERNATIVES

Unlike the reformers, who aimed to improve the existing order by guiding individuals to greater self-discipline, the utopians sought perfection by withdrawing from society and its confining institutions.

Though following different religious and secular philosophies of communitarian living, all the utopians wanted to fashion a more rational and personally satisfying alternative to the competitive materialism of antebellum America. Nearly all the communities sought to transform the organization and rewards of work, thus challenging the prevailing dogmas about private property.

The most successful utopian communities were religious sects whose reordering of both sexual and economic relations departed sharply from middle-class norms. The **Shakers,** at their height in the 1830s, attracted some 6,000 followers. The Shakers traced their origins to the teachings of Ann Lee ("Mother Lee"). An illiterate factory laborer in mid-eighteenth-century England, Lee had a revelation in 1770 that the Second Coming of Christ was to be fulfilled in her own womanly form, the embodiment of the female side of God. Fired by another vision in 1774, Lee led eight of her followers to America, where, after her death in 1784, her disciples established the first Shaker community in New Lebanon, New York.

Organized around doctrines of celibate **communism,** Shaker communities held all property in common. The sexes worked and lived apart from each other. Dancing during religious worship brought men and women together and provided an emotional release from enforced sexual denial. In worldly as well as spiritual terms, women enjoyed an equality in Shaker life that the outside world denied them. For this reason, twice as many women as men joined the Shakers.

The Shakers gradually dwindled. Their rule of celibacy meant, of course, that they could propagate themselves only by recruiting new members, and few new converts joined the movement after 1850.

John Humphrey Noyes, a graduate of Dartmouth who studied for the ministry at Yale, established the **Oneida Community** in upstate New York in 1847. He attracted over 200 followers with his perfectionist vision of plural marriage, community nurseries, group discipline, and common ownership of property. Charged with adultery, Noyes fled to Canada in 1879, but the Oneida Community survived into the twentieth century.

Secular utopians aspired to perfect social relations through rationally designed planned communities. Bitter critics of the social evils of industrialization, they tried to construct models for a social order free from poverty, unemployment, and inequality. They envisioned cooperative communities that balanced agricultural and industrial pursuits in a mixed economy that recycled earnings to the laborers who actually produced the wealth.

Despite their high expectations, nearly all the planned communities ran into financial difficulties and soon collapsed. The pattern was set by the first of the controversial socialist experiments, **New Harmony** in Indiana, the brainchild of the wealthy Scottish industrialist and philanthropist Robert Owen. A proponent of utopian **socialism,** Owen promised to create a new order where "the degrading and pernicious practices in which we are now well trained, of buying cheap and selling dear, will be rendered unnecessary" and "union and co-operation will supersede individual interest." But within two years of its founding in 1825, New Harmony fell victim to inadequate financing and internal bickering.

WHERE TO LEARN MORE

Shaker Museum at South Union, Kentucky **www.shakermuseum.com/**

Shakers   The followers of Mother Ann Lee, who preached a religion of strict celibacy and communal living.

Communism   A social structure based on the common ownership of property.

Oneida Community   Utopian community established in upstate New York in 1848 by John Humphrey Noyes and his followers.

New Harmony   Short-lived utopian community established in Indiana in 1825, based on the socialist ideas of Robert Owen, a wealthy Scottish manufacturer.

Socialism   Political and economic theory advocating that land, natural resources, and the chief industries should be owned by the community as a whole.

Brook Farm A utopian community and experimental farm established in 1841 near Boston.

Transcendentalism A philosophical and literary movement centered on an idealistic belief in the divinity of individuals and nature.

WHERE TO LEARN MORE

Historic New Harmony, New Harmony, Indiana
www.newharmony.org/

WHAT WAS the relationship between abolitionism and the women's rights movement?

The economic misery of the depression of the 1840s revived interest in utopian ventures and helped popularize the ideas of Charles Fourier, a French utopian who proposed to restore dignity to labor and end poverty by dividing society into phalanxes, cooperative units of workers who lived communally. Scores of Fourierist communities were set up, but few survived into the 1850s.

About the only secular cooperative that gained lasting fame was **Brook Farm** in West Roxbury, Massachusetts (today part of Boston). Established in 1841, Brook Farm was a showcase for the transcendentalist philosophy of Ralph Waldo Emerson. A former Unitarian minister in Boston, Emerson taught that intuition and emotion could grasp a truer ("transcendent") reality than could the senses alone. Although disbanded after six years as an economic failure, Brook Farm inspired intellectuals such as Nathaniel Hawthorne, who briefly lived there. In turn, his writings and those of other writers influenced by **transcendentalism** flowed into the great renaissance of American literature in the mid-nineteenth century.

A DISTINCTLY NATIONAL LITERATURE

In an 1837 address at Harvard titled "The American Scholar," Emerson called for a distinctly national literature devoted to the democratic possibilities of American life. "The literature of the poor, the feelings of the child, the philosophy of the street, the meaning of household life, are the topics of the time," he proclaimed.

Walt Whitman, whose *Leaves of Grass* (1855) foreshadowed modern poetry in its use of free verse, shared Emerson's faith in the possibilities of individual fulfillment, and his poems celebrated the democratic variety of the American people. Henry David Thoreau, Emerson's friend and neighbor, embodied the transcendentalist fascination with nature and self-discovery by living in relative isolation for 16 months at Walden Pond, near Concord, Massachusetts. His *Walden; or, Life in the Woods* (1854) became an American classic.

Nathaniel Hawthorne and Herman Melville, the greatest novelists of the American renaissance, focused on the existence of evil and the human need for community. In *The Scarlet Letter* (1850) and *The House of the Seven Gables* (1851), Hawthorne probed themes of egoism and pride to reveal the underside of the human soul. Melville's *Moby-Dick* (1851) depicted the consequences of a competitive individualism unchecked by a social conscience. In his relentless pursuit of the great white whale, Captain Ahab destroys himself and his crew.

Much of the appeal of the utopian communities flowed from the same concern about the splintering and selfishness of antebellum society that animated Hawthorne and Melville. Promising economic security and social harmony to buttress a threatened sense of community, the utopians failed to lure all but a few Americans from the acquisitiveness and competitive demands of the larger society.

ABOLITIONISM AND WOMEN'S RIGHTS

Abolitionism emerged from the same religious impulse that energized reform throughout the North. What distinguished the abolitionists was their insistence that slavery was *the* great national sin, an evil that mocked American ideals of liberty and Christian morality. Under the early leadership of William Lloyd Garrison, the abolitionists uncompromisingly attacked not only slaveholders but also all others whose moral apathy helped support slavery. After provoking a storm of protest in both the North and the South, the abolitionist movement split in 1840. Crucial in this division was Garrison's support of women's rights. Most abolitionists broke with him and founded their own antislavery organization. Female abolitionists took the lead in organizing a separate women's rights movement.

REJECTING COLONIZATION

In the early nineteenth century, when slavery was expanding westward, almost all white Americans regardless of class or region were convinced that emancipation would lead either to a race war or the debasement of their superior status through racial interbreeding. This paralyzing fear of general emancipation, rooted in pervasive racism, long shielded slavery from sustained attack.

In 1817, antislavery reformers from the North and the South founded the **American Colonization Society.** Slaveholding politicians from the Upper South, notably Henry Clay, James Madison, and President James Monroe, were the leading organizers of the society. Gradual emancipation accompanied by the removal of black people from America to Africa was the only solution these white reformers could imagine for ridding the nation of slavery and avoiding a racial bloodbath. Their goal was to make America all free *and* all white.

The American Colonization Society had no real chance of success. No form of emancipation, no matter how gradual, could appeal to slaveowners who could profit from the labor of their slaves. Moreover, the society could never afford to purchase the freedom of any significant number of slaves. Almost all the African Americans it transported to Liberia, the West African colony it helped found, were already free. At the height of its popularity in the 1820s, the society sent only 1,400 colonists to Africa. During that same decade, the American slave population increased by more than 450,000.

Free African Americans bitterly attacked the colonizers' central assumption that free black people were unfit to live as citizens in America. Typical of the colonizers' racist thinking was the claim by Henry Clay in 1827 that the "free coloured" were the "most vicious" of all Americans. "Contaminated themselves, they extend their vices to all around them, to the slaves and to the whites."

Most free African Americans were native-born, and they considered themselves Americans with every right to enjoy the blessings of republican liberty. As a black petition in 1817 stated, banishment from America "would not only be cruel, but in direct violation of the principles, which have been the boast of this republic."

Organizing through their own churches in northern cities, free African Americans founded some 50 abolitionist societies, offered refuge to fugitive slaves, and launched the first African-American newspaper in 1827, *Freedom's Journal.* David Walker, a free black man who had moved from North Carolina to Massachusetts, published his ***Appeal to the Colored Citizens of the World*** in 1829. In a searing indictment of white greed and hypocrisy, he rejected colonization and insisted that "America is more our country, than it is the whites', we have enriched it with our *blood and tears.*" He warned white America that "wo, wo, will be to you if we have to obtain our freedom by fighting."

As if in response to this call for revolutionary resistance by the enslaved, Nat Turner's Rebellion exploded in the summer of 1831 (see Chapter 11). Both alarmed and inspired by the increased tempo of black militancy, a small group of antislavery white people abandoned all illusions about colonization and embarked on a radically new approach for eradicating slavery.

ABOLITIONISM

William Lloyd Garrison, a Massachusetts printer and the leading figure in early abolitionism, became coeditor of an antislavery newspaper in Baltimore in 1829. Before the year was out, Garrison was arrested and convicted of criminal libel for

American Colonization Society Organization, founded in 1817 by antislavery reformers, that called for gradual emancipation and the removal of freed blacks to Africa.

Appeal to the Colored Citizens of the World Written by David Walker, a published insistence that "America is more our country, than it is the whites'—we have enriched it with our *blood and tears.*"

OVERVIEW   TYPES OF ANTISLAVERY REFORM

Type	Definition	Example
Gradualist	Accepts notions of black inferiority and attempts to end slavery gradually by purchasing the freedom of slaves and colonizing them in Africa	American Colonization Society
Immediatist	Calls for immediate steps to end slavery and denounces slavery and racial prejudice as moral sins	Abolitionists
Political Antislavery	Recognizes slavery in states where it exists but insists on keeping slavery out of the territories	Free-Soilers

his editorials against a Massachusetts merchant engaged in the domestic slave trade. Recognizing that his lack of freedom in jail paled against that of the slave, Garrison emerged with an unquenchable hatred of slavery. Returning to Boston, he launched his own antislavery newspaper, the *Liberator*, in 1831. A year later, he was instrumental in founding the New England Anti-Slavery Society.

As militant as the free African Americans who comprised the bulk of the early subscribers to the *Liberator*, Garrison committed abolitionism to the twin goals of immediatism, an immediate moral commitment to end slavery, and racial equality. Only by striving toward these goals, he insisted, could white America ever hope to end slavery without massive violence.

The abolitionists' demand for the legal equality of black people was as unsettling to public opinion as their call for immediate, uncompensated emancipation. Discriminatory laws restricted the political and civil liberties of free African Americans in every state.

Garrison, harsh and uncompromising in denouncing slavery and advocating black rights, instilled the antislavery movement with moral urgency. But without the organizational and financial resources of a national society, the message of the early Garrisonians rarely extended beyond free black communities in the North. The success of British abolitionists in 1833, when gradual, compensated emancipation was enacted for Britain's West Indian colonies, inspired white and black abolitionists to gather at Philadelphia in December 1833 and form the **American Anti-Slavery Society.**

Arthur and Lewis Tappan, two wealthy merchants who dominated the abolitionist movement in New York City, provided financial backing for the Anti-Slavery Society. The young evangelical minister Theodore Dwight Weld, fusing abolitionism with the moral passion of religious revivalism, brought the antislavery message of the eastern radicals to the West in 1834 with the revivals he preached at Lane Theological Seminary in Cincinnati. The "Lane rebels," students gathered by Weld, fanned out as itinerant agents to seek converts for abolitionism throughout the Yankee districts of the rural North. Weld's *American Slavery as It Is: Testimony of a Thousand Witnesses*, a massively documented indictment of slavery, became a bestseller in 1839.

Revivalist exhortations were just one of the techniques the abolitionists exploited to mobilize public opinion against slavery. They spread their message through rallies, paid lecturers, children's games and toys, and the printed word. They distributed millions of antislavery tracts, and by the late 1830s, abolitionist sayings ap-

American Anti-Slavery Society
The first national organization of abolitionists, founded in 1833.

peared on posters, emblems, song sheets, and even candy wrappers.

Women were essential in all of these activities. From the very beginning of the movement, they established their own antislavery societies as auxiliaries to the national organizations run and dominated by men. Initially, their role was limited to raising funds, circulating petitions, and visiting homes to gain converts. Often operating out of local churches, women were grass-roots organizers of a massive petition campaign launched in the mid-1830s. Women signed more than half of the antislavery memorials sent to Congress.

The abolitionists focused their energies on mass propaganda because they saw their role as social agitators who had to break through white apathy and change public opinion. By 1840 they had succeeded in enlisting nearly 200,000 northerners in 2,000 local affiliates of the American Anti-Slavery Society. Most whites, however, remained unmoved, and some violently opposed the abolitionists.

Antiabolitionist mobs in the North went on a rampage in the mid-1830s. They disrupted antislavery meetings, beat and stoned speakers, destroyed printing presses, burned the homes of the wealthy benefactors of the movement, and vandalized free black neighborhoods in a wave of terror that drove many black people from several northern cities. Local elites, especially those with profitable ties to the slave economy of the South, often incited the mobs, whose fury expressed the anxiety of semiskilled and common laborers that they might lose their jobs if freed slaves moved north.

In the South, the hostility to abolitionism took the form of burning and censoring antislavery literature, offering rewards for the capture of leading abolitionists to stand trial for allegedly inciting slave revolts, and tightening up slave codes and the surveillance of free black people. Meanwhile, Democrats in Congress yielded to slaveholding interests in 1836 by passing a gag rule that automatically tabled antislavery petitions with no debate.

The hostility and violence abolitionism provoked convinced Garrison and some of his followers that American institutions and values were fundamentally flawed. In 1838, Garrison helped found the New England Non-Resistant Society, dedicated to the belief that a complete moral regeneration, based on renouncing force in all human relationships, was necessary if America were ever to live up to its Christian and republican ideals. The Garrisonian nonresistants rejected all coercive authority, whether expressed in human bondage, clerical support of slavery, male dominance in the patriarchal family, the racial oppression of back people, or the police power of government.

Garrison's opponents within the abolitionist movement accused him of alienating the public by identifying the antislavery cause with radical attacks on traditional authority. His support for the growing demand of antislavery women to be treated as equals in the movement brought the factional bickering to a head and split the American Anti-Slavery Society. In turn, the opposition of most male abolitionists to the public activities of their female counterparts provoked a militant

The illustration on the masthead of this 1831 issue of the *Liberator* condemns the relegation of slaves to the legal status of chattel, mere livestock to be bought and sold, no different from cattle or horses. Revulsion at the treatment of human beings as property was central to the abolitionist indictment of slavery.

The Library Company of Philadelphia

AMERICAN VIEWS

APPEAL OF A FEMALE ABOLITIONIST

ydia Maria Child's Appeal, *published in Boston in 1833, was a landmark in abolitionist literature for both the thoroughness of its attack on slavery and its refutation of racist ideology and discrimination. This condemnation of racial prejudice was the most radical feature of abolitionist ideology. It directly challenged the deeply held beliefs and assumptions of nearly all white Americans, in the North as well as the South. Racism and slavery, as Child shows in this excerpt from her Appeal, fed off one another in the national curse of slavery.*

- How does Child argue that northern white people must bear some of the responsibility for perpetuating slavery?
- What arguments does Child make against racial discrimination in northern society?
- What did Child mean when she wrote that "the Americans are peculiarly responsible for the example they give"? Do you agree with her?
- How does Child deal with the charge that the abolitionists threatened the preservation of the Union?

While we bestow our earnest disapprobation on the system of slavery, let us not flatter ourselves that we are in reality any better than our brethren of the South. Thanks to our soil and climate, and the early exhortions of the Quakers, the form of slavery does not exist among us; but the very spirit of the hateful and mischievous thing is here in all its strength. . . . Our prejudice against colored people is even more inveterate than it is at the South. The planter is often attached to his negroes, and lavishes caresses and kind words upon them, as he would on a favorite hound: but our cold-hearted, ignoble prejudice admits of no exception, no intermission.

The Southerners have long continued habit, apparent interest and dreaded danger, to palliate the wrong they do; but we stand without excuse. . . . If the free States wished to cherish the system of slavery forever, they could not take a more direct course than they now do. Those who are kind and liberal on all other subjects, unite with the selfish and the proud in their unrelenting efforts to keep the colored population in the lowest state of degradation; and the influence they unconsciously exert over children early infuses into their innocent minds the same strong feelings of contempt. . . .

The state of public feeling not only makes it difficult for the Africans to obtain information, but it prevents them from making profitable use of what knowledge they have. A colored man, however intelligent, is not allowed to pursue any business more lucrative than that of a barber, a shoeblack, or waiter. These,

---

faction of these women into founding their own movement to achieve equality in American society.

THE WOMEN'S RIGHTS MOVEMENT

Feminism grew out of abolitionism because of the parallels many women drew between the exploited lives of the slaves and their own subordinate status in northern society. Considered biologically inferior to men, women were denied the vote, deprived of property or control of any wages after marriage, and barred from most occupations and advanced education. "In striving to cut [the slave's] irons off, we found most surely that we were manacled *ourselves*," argued Abby Kelley, a Quaker abolitionist.

Antislavery women demanded an equal voice in the abolitionist movement. Despite strong opposition from many of his fellow male abolitionists, Garrison helped Abby Kelley win a seat on the business committee of the American Anti-Slavery Society at its convention in 1840. The anti-Garrisonians walked out of the convention and formed a separate organization, the American and Foreign Anti-Slavery Society.

11–3
Sojourner Truth, Address to the Woman's Rights Convention, Akron, Ohio (1851)

and all other employments, are truly respectable, whenever the duties connected with them are faithfully performed; but it is unjust that a man should, on account of his complexion, be prevented from performing more elevated uses in society. Every citizen ought to have a fair chance to try his fortune in any line of business, which he thinks he has ability to transact. Why should not colored men be employed in the manufactories of various kinds? If their ignorance is an objection, let them be enlightened, as speedily as possible. If their moral character is not sufficiently pure, remove the pressure of public scorn, and thus supply them with motives for being respectable. All this can be done. It merely requires an earnest wish to overcome a prejudice, which . . . is in fact opposed to the spirit of our religion, and contrary to the instinctive good feelings of our nature. . . . When the majority heartily desire a change, it is effected, be the difficulties what they may. The Americans are peculiarly responsible for the example they give; for in no other country does the unchecked voice of the people constitute the whole of government. . . .

The strongest and best reason that can be given for our supineness on the subject of slavery, is the fear of dissolving the Union. The Constitution of the United States demands our highest reverence. . . . But we must not forget that the Constitution provides for any change that may be required for the general good. The great machine is constructed with a safety valve, by which any rapidly increasing evil may be expelled whenever the people desire it.

If the Southern politicians are determined to make a Siamese question of this also, if they insist that the Union shall not exist without slavery, it can only be said that they join two things, which have no affinity with each other, and which cannot permanently exist together. They chain the living and vigorous to the diseased and dying; and the former will assuredly perish in the infected neighborhood.

The universal introduction of free labor is the surest way to consolidate the Union, and enable us to live together in harmony and peace. If a history is ever written entitled "The Decay and Dissolution of the North American Republic," its author will distinctly trace our downfall to the existence of slavery among us.

Source: Lydia Maria Child, *An Appeal in Favor of That Class of Americans Called Africans* (originally published 1833), ed. Carolyn L. Karcher (University of Massachusetts Press, 1996).

What was rapidly becoming known as the "woman question" also disrupted the 1840 World Anti-Slavery Convention in London. The refusal of the convention to seat the American female delegates was the final indignity that transformed the discontent of women into a self-conscious movement for women's equality. Two of the excluded delegates, Lucretia Mott and Elizabeth Cady Stanton, vowed to build an organization to "speak out for *oppressed* women."

Their work went slowly. Early feminists were dependent on the abolitionists for most of their followers, and they were unable to do more than hold local meetings and sponsor occasional speaking tours. Many women sympathetic to the feminist movement hung back lest they be shunned in their communities. A minister's wife in Portsmouth, New Hampshire, wrote to a feminist friend, "There are but few here who think of women as anything more than slave or plaything, and they think I am different from most women."

In 1848, Stanton and Mott were finally able to call the first national convention ever devoted to women's rights at Seneca Falls, in upstate New York. The **Seneca Falls Convention** issued the **Declaration of Sentiments,** a call for full female

Seneca Falls Convention The first convention for women's equality in legal rights, held in upstate New York in 1848.

Declaration of Sentiments The resolutions passed at the Seneca Falls Convention in 1848 calling for full female equality, including the right to vote.

Mobs of angry men often broke up meetings organized by women seeking the right to vote. Shown here is a male escort offering protection to Lucretia Mott and another suffragette at one such meeting.

WHERE TO LEARN MORE

Women's Rights Historical Park, Seneca Falls, New York
www.nps.gov/wori/wrnhp.htm

Liberty party The first antislavery political party, formed in 1840.

equality. It identified male patriarchy as the source of women's oppression and demanded the vote for women as a sacred and inalienable right of republican citizenship.

The Seneca Falls agenda defined the goals of the women's movement for the rest of the century. The call for the vote met the stiffest opposition, and male legislators refused to budge. The feminists' few successes before the Civil War came in economic rights. By 1860, 14 states had granted women greater control over their property and wages, most significantly under New York's Married Women's Property Act of 1860. Largely the result of the intense lobbying of Susan B. Anthony, the act established women's legal right to control their own wage income and to sue fathers and husbands who tried to deprive them of their wages.

Despite such successes, the feminist movement did not attract broad support. Most women found in the doctrine of separate spheres a reassuring feminine identity that they could express either at home or in benevolent and reform societies. Within the reform movement as a whole, women's rights were always a minor concern.

POLITICAL ANTISLAVERY

Political abolitionism had its roots in the petition campaign of the late 1830s. Congressional efforts to suppress the discussion of slavery backfired when John Quincy Adams, the former president who had become a Massachusetts congressman, resorted to an unending series of parliamentary ploys to get around the gag rule (see Chapter 10). Adams became a champion of the constitutional right to petition Congress for redress of grievances. White northerners who had shown no interest in abolitionism as a moral crusade for black people now began to take a stand against slavery when the issue involved the civil liberties of whites and the dominant political power of the South. By the hundreds of thousands, they signed abolitionist petitions in 1837 and 1838 to protest the gag rule and the admission of Texas as a slave state.

In 1840, anti-Garrisonian abolitionists tried to turn this new antislavery constituency into an independent political party. They formed the **Liberty Party** and ran James G. Birney, a former slaveholder converted by Weld to abolitionism, as their candidate for the presidency. He failed to draw even 1 percent of the popular vote, but antislavery districts dominated by evangelical New Englanders elected several antislavery congressmen.

The Liberty Party opposed any expansion of slavery in the territories, condemned racial discrimination in the North as well as slavery in the South, and won the support of most black abolitionists. In 1843, a national African-American convention in Buffalo endorsed the Liberty Party.

This political activism was part of a concerted effort by African Americans to assert leadership in an antislavery movement that rarely treated them as equals. Frederick Douglass was their most dynamic spokesman. After escaping from slavery in 1838, Douglass became a spellbinding lecturer for abolitionism and in 1845 published his classic autobiography, *Narrative of the Life of Frederick Douglass, an American Slave*. Increasingly dissatisfied with Garrison's Christian pacifism and his stand against political action, Douglass broke with Garrison in 1847 and founded a black abolitionist newspaper, the *North Star*. The break became irreparable in 1851 when

Douglass publicly denied the Garrisonian position that the Constitution was a proslavery document. If properly interpreted, Douglass insisted, "the Constitution is a *glorious liberty document*," and he called for a political war against slavery.

Although the Liberty Party elected only one of its candidates to Congress (Gerrit Smith of New York), it kept slavery in the forefront of national politics. Led by Joshua R. Giddings, a small but vocal bloc of antislavery politicians began to popularize the frightening concept of "the Slave Power," a vast conspiracy of planters and their northern lackeys that controlled the federal government and was plotting to spread slavery and subvert any free institutions that opposed it.

The specter of the Slave Power made white liberties, and not black bondage, central to northern concerns about slavery. This shift redefined the evil of slavery to appeal to the self-interest of white northerners who had rejected the moral appeals of the Garrisonians. White people who had earlier been apathetic now began to view slavery as a threat to their rights of free speech and self-improvement.

Birney again headed the Liberty Party ticket in 1844, but he ran only marginally stronger than in 1840. Nonetheless, the image of the Slave Power predisposed many Northerners to see the expansionist program of the incoming Polk administration as part of a southern plot to secure more territory for slaveholders at the expense of northern farmers. Northern fears that free labor would be shut out of the new territories won in the Mexican War provided the rallying cry for the Free-Soil Party of 1848, which foreshadowed the more powerful Republican Party of the late 1850s.

CONCLUSION

*W*ith surprising speed after 1815, transportation improvements, technological innovations, and expanding markets drove the economy toward industrialization. Wealth inequality increased, old classes were reshaped, and new ones formed. These changes were most evident in the Northeast, where capital, labor, and growing urban markets spurred the acceleration of manufacturing. The reform impulse that both reflected and shaped these changes was also strongest in the Northeast.

The new evangelical Protestantism promised that human perfectibility was possible if individuals strove to free themselves from sin. Influenced by this promise, the northern middle class embraced reform causes that sought to improve human character. Temperance changed American drinking habits and established sobriety as the cultural standard for respectable male behavior. Middle-class reform also emphasized institutional solutions for what were now defined as the social problems of ignorance, crime, and poverty.

The most radical of the reform movements focused on women's equality and the elimination of slavery. The women's rights movement emerged out of women's involvement in reform, especially in abolitionism. Feminism and abolitionism triggered a backlash from the more conservative majority. This backlash prevented women from gaining legal and political equality, the major demand of the feminists, and convinced most abolitionists that they had to switch from moral

WHERE TO LEARN MORE

★ Oberlin College Library, Oberlin, Ohio www.oberlin.edu/library/

WHERE TO LEARN MORE

★ Slater Hill Historic Site, Pawtucket, Rhode Island www.artcom.com/museums/vs/sz/02862-06.htm

After escaping to freedom in 1838, Frederick Douglass became a commanding figure in the abolitionist movement. His speeches denouncing slavery were fiery and eloquent.

Frederick Douglass (1817?–1895). Oil on canvas, c. 1844, attr. to E. Hammond. The Granger Collection.

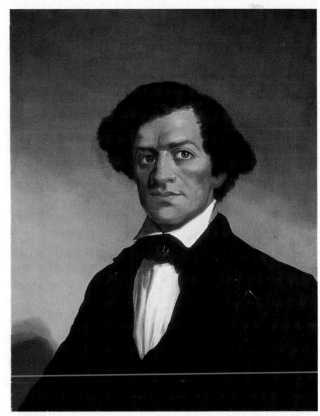

GLOBAL PERSPECTIVES

THE INTERNATIONAL DIMENSIONS OF ABOLITION

"The trumpet has sounded through all the colonial dependencies of our country, which proclaims 'liberty to the captives.' O! what heart is there so cold, so seared, so dead, as to feel no thrill of exulting emotion at the thought, that on the morning of this day, eight hundred thousand fellow-men and fellow-subjects, who, during the past night, slept bondmen, awoke freemen! [British emancipation will be] but the first day of a Jubilee year,—of a period of successive triumphs . . . of continuous and rapidly progressive prosperity, to the cause of freedom. [Once America joins Britain in the work of emancipation] the world will be shamed into imitation:— and in no long period, there will not be found on a earth a remnant of it."

On August 1, 1834, the day that the British Emancipation Act of 1833 took effect, the Reverend Ralph Wardlaw of Glasgow, Scotland, spoke these words of millennial joy and hope for the future. It was a day of exultation for reformers on both sides of the Atlantic. The spark of freedom was first struck in Britain by the creation in 1787 of the Quaker-inspired Society for the Abolition of the Slave Trade. It exploded into a revolutionary conflagration when the slaves in St.

Domingue rose up in rebellion in 1791 and unleashed the greatest slave revolt in the Western Hemisphere. By 1808, reformers in Britain and the United States had prohibited the African slave trade. When the Spanish Empire in Latin America began to break up after 1810, the independence movements in the former colonies committed themselves to emancipation. In a startling reversal from the situation in 1800, only Brazil and Cuba remained as major slave areas in Latin America by the 1820s. Then, as the result of a massive grass-roots campaign that inundated Parliament with 5,000 petitions and half a million signers, Britain passed the Emancipation Act of 1833, which emancipated the slaves in its colonies as of August 1, 1834.

British emancipation buoyed the abolitionist cause in the United States and was a major factor in emboldening the abolitionists to organize a national society in 1833. It also convinced them, as the Reverend Wardlaw had argued, that Protestant Christianity was poised to take the lead in an epic struggle for human betterment. That was the vision that inspired the abolitionists as they set out to redeem America's revolutionary heritage by cleansing the nation of slavery.

agitation to political persuasion. The political abolitionists soon found that the most effective approach in widening the antislavery appeal was their charge that a Slave Power conspiracy threatened the freedoms of white northerners.

SUMMARY

Industrial Change and Urbanization In the 1800s the United States experienced a transportation and manufacturing revolution; this accelerated the spread of cities, factories, and commercial farming. Urbanization brought new work patterns as manufacturing moved from the home to factories. The Northeast experienced the greatest growth; swelling the size of all cities were immigrants, most coming from Ireland and Germany. The new middle class was the product of the changes in employment opportunities; the new working classes contained native-born artisans competing for jobs with immigrants and women.

Reform and Moral Order The changes to society that accompanied this market revolution frightened religious leaders and businessmen in the East. The benevolent empire responded with a host of societies targeted at individual vices, especially the consumption of alcohol. Women played a significant role in

IMMIGRATION: AN AMBIVALENT WELCOME

Americans have long extended an ambivalent welcome to newcomers. In the mid-nineteenth century, employment posters often read "Irish Need Not Apply," and today stepped-up border patrols seek to keep out Mexican and other Latin American immigrants. Yet America is a nation settled and built by immigrants whose founding ideals promise equality and opportunity to all. And for much of its history it has offered asylum for the world's oppressed.

In the early years of the republic, Federalists worried that immigrants from Europe might be contaminated by the radical ideas of the French Revolution and sought to make it harder for them to become naturalized citizens. The nation's first naturalization law in the 1790s also barred black immigrants from citizenship. The first sustained attack against newcomers, however, emerged as a result of the surge in immigration during the 1840s and 1850s. It was directed by established immigrant groups, the descendants of settlers from Britain and northwestern Europe, at unfamiliar newcomers, particularly the Irish.

Nativist arguments of that time have found an echo in all subsequent immigration debates. The Irish, it was claimed, would take jobs away from American workers and lower their wages. Taxpayers would have to foot the bill for the strains the newcomers imposed on schools, hospitals, and other civic services. The ignorant immigrants would corrupt the political process. Nativists especially feared religious contamination, claiming that the Catholicism of the Irish was alien to the Protestant values held to be indispensable to the preservation of American liberties. So many Irish arrived so quickly that many nativists were convinced of a papal plot to undermine American freedom. "The bloody hand of the Pope," one wrote, "has stretched itself forth to our destruction."

Eventually the Irish and Germans merged into the economic and political fabric of American life. But in the late nineteenth century a massive new immigrant surge dominated by people from southern and eastern Europe seeking economic opportunity and fleeing religious oppression transformed American society and renewed nativist fears. This time, race replaced religion as the basis for drawing invidious comparisons between established residents and the newcomers. Pseudoscientific theories relegated Jews, Slavs, and Mediterranean peoples, together with Africans, to an inferior status below people of northern European and especially Anglo-Saxon descent. The newcomers, it was claimed, were unfit for democratic government and would endanger American civilization. Strict anti-immigrant legislation in the 1920s sharply curtailed immigration from outside the Western Hemisphere, banning Asians entirely and setting quotas based on national origin for others.

Recent concerns about immigration result from the unforeseen consequences of a 1965 reform of the immigration law that abolished quotas. Since then, immigration has risen sharply, and the national origins of the immigrants have diverged from previous patterns. By the 1980s, Europeans constituted but 10 percent of the newcomers. The bulk of the remainder continue to come from Asia (40 percent) and Mexico, Central America, and the Caribbean. Once again, anti-immigrant voices worry that alien newcomers are threatening the cohesiveness of the nation's institutions and values. But, once again as well, a more inclusive vision of American identity and ideals seems likely to prevail as the newcomers establish themselves. As Abraham Lincoln expressed it, "There was no exclusively American race entitled to claim liberty by heredity. What held the nation together was an idea of equality that every newcomer could claim and defend by free choice."

these reform movements, not always with the approval of males who saw their authority being undermined.

IMAGE KEY
for pages 320–321

a. An abolitionist freeing a slave from his shackles: colored woodcut, c. 1840, from an American antislavery almanac.

b. A map of western New York State in 1811 including the proposed Erie Canal route, the Finger Lakes, Lake Ontario, and Lake Erie.

c. Pages from an American Pictorial Primer, c. 1845.

d. Frederick Douglass (1817?–1895). Oil on canvas, c. 1844, attr. to E. Hammond.

e. Six females model American Victorian fashion in Godey's *Lady's Book for April, 1867.* Colored, painted lithograph.

f. Young single women constituted the bulk of the labor force in the first textile factories of New England.

g. Pawtucket Bridge and Falls, watercolor and ink on paper, 15 × 19 1/2.

h. The original cotton gin of inventor Eli Whitney.

i. Dorothea Dix.

Institutions and Social Improvement Based in the Enlightenment belief that people and society could be improved, the reformers implemented new institutions to shape individual character. Free, tax-supported public education was one of their most lasting achievements; prisons and asylums for the mentally ill were also targeted. Utopian reformers sought self-improvement by withdrawing into communitarian societies; the intellectuals who were drawn to Brook Farm had a lasting impact, as these transcendentalists were the catalyst for the nineteenth-century renaissance of American literature.

Abolitionism and Women's Rights Abolitionism emerged from the same religious impulse that energized reform throughout the North. Believing slavery was the great national sin, abolitionists attacked the institution and all its supporters. After provoking a storm of protests in the North and the South, the abolitionist movement divided, with women expanding their efforts into a women's rights movement. Abolitionists moved their cause into the political mainstream and focused attention on what they called the growing "Slave Power" threatening the nation.

REVIEW QUESTIONS

1. Why were improvements in transportation so essential to the growth of the economy after 1815? What were the nature and scope of these improvements?

2. What is an industrial revolution? How can we explain the surge in manufacturing in the United States from 1815 to 1850?

3. What was the religious impulse behind the first wave of reform? What innovations in reaching a mass audience did the benevolent reformers pioneer?

4. What drew women into reform? Why did many of them feel a special affinity for abolitionism?

5. Why was abolitionism the most radical reform of all? How was it linked to an international movement calling for the end of slavery?

6. Why do you think so few Southern women of the plantation class followed Angelina Grimké on her journey from social privilege to social activism?

KEY TERMS

American Anti-Slavery Society (p. 346)

American Colonization Society (p. 345)

American Female Moral Reform Society (p. 339)

American system of manufacturing (p. 333)

American Temperance Society (p. 338)

Appeal to the Colored Citizens of the World (p. 345)

Benevolent empire (p. 336)

Brook Farm (p. 344)

Charles River Bridge v. Warren Bridge (p. 327)

Church of Jesus Christ of Latter-day Saints (Mormon Church) (p. 340)

Communism (p. 343)

Cult of domesticity (p. 335)

Declaration of Sentiments (p. 349)

Gibbons v. Ogden (p. 325)

Liberty Party (p. 350)

WHERE TO LEARN MORE

Baltimore Center for Urban Archaeology, Baltimore, Maryland. Operated by Baltimore City Life Museum, the center has a large collection of artifacts depicting urban life in the eighteenth and nineteenth centuries and a working archaeological library.

Hanford Mills Museum, East Meredith, New York. This museum preserves and interprets water-powered machinery and explains the role played by local mills in the community life of the nineteenth century. For a map and links to events, workshops, and education programs, visit **www.hanfordmills.org/**.

Slater Hill Historic Site, Pawtucket, Rhode Island. The Sylvanus Brown House of 1758, the Slaren Mill of 1793, and the Wilkinson Mill of 1810 are on the site. An extensive library and holdings provide insight into the social and economic world of the early industrial revolution. Information on hours, collections, and exhibits can be found at **www.artcom.com/museums/vs/sz/02862-06.htm**.

Erie Canal Museum, Syracuse, New York. The museum houses extensive collections on the building and maintenance of the Erie Canal, and its photo holdings visually record much of the history of the canal. In addition to information on exhibits, tours, and school programs, its website, **www.eriecanalmuseum.org/**, includes pictures of a replica of an Erie Canal line boat.

Historic New Harmony, New Harmony, Indiana. The tours and museum holdings at this preserved site offer a glimpse into the communal living that Robert Owen tried to promote in his utopian plan. For a brief history of New Harmony and links to special events and programs at the site, go to **www .newharmony.org/**.

Oberlin College Library, Oberlin, Ohio. Oberlin was a hotbed of reform agitation, and the tracts, broadsides, photographs, and other memorabilia here are especially rich on the activities of white evangelicals and black abolitionists. For an introduction to the library and its holdings, visit **www.oberlin.edu/library/**.

Shaker Museum at South Union, Kentucky. The exhibits, artifacts, and archives are a superb source for understanding the history and material culture of the Shakers and other radical sects. Its website, **www .shakermuseum.com/**, includes a brief history of the Shakers, photographs of restored buildings, and an overview of the museum's holdings.

Women's Rights Historical Park, Seneca Falls, New York. The park provides an interpretive overview of the first women's rights convention and includes among its historical sites the restored home of Elizabeth Cady Stanton. Go to **www.nps.gov/wori/wrnhp.htm** for links to the museum's summer calendar of events and information on programs.

U.S. History Documents CD-ROM
For primary sources related to this chapter, refer to the document CD-ROM.

www.prenhall.com/goldfield
For study resources related to this chapter, visit the *Companion Website*™.

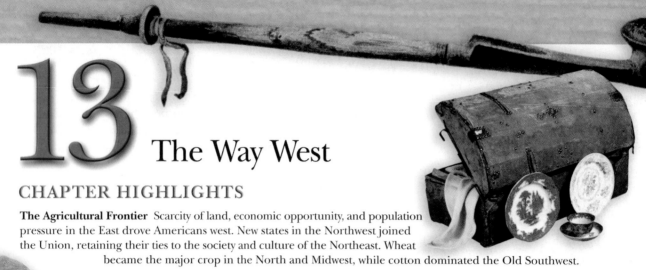

13 The Way West

CHAPTER HIGHLIGHTS

The Agricultural Frontier Scarcity of land, economic opportunity, and population pressure in the East drove Americans west. New states in the Northwest joined the Union, retaining their ties to the society and culture of the Northeast. Wheat became the major crop in the North and Midwest, while cotton dominated the Old Southwest.

The Frontier of the Plains Indians The Great Plains were dominated by the Sioux and the Comanche. The first Americans to venture into the West were the mountain men in the 1820s. Farm families making the long trek to Oregon and California followed them in the 1840s.

The Mexican Borderlands Native Americans made up the majority of the population of the Mexican borderlands. The Mexican government invited Americans to settle in Texas in the 1820s. Armed conflict between Mexico and American settlers resulted in independence for Texas. Mexico's grip on California and New Mexico was weakened by the appearance of American traders and settlers. Fleeing persecution in the East, the Mormons made a home for themselves in Utah.

The Americanization of Texas In the late 1820s and early 1830s, a flood of immigrants entered Texas, many of whom ignored Mexican laws. The policies of the Mexican dictator General Santa Ana sparked clashes between Mexican troops and rebellious Texans. The Texans' victory resulted in Texas's independence and the ascendance of Anglo elites at the expense of *Tejanos*.

Politics, Expansion, and War President Polk hoped to add California, Texas, Oregon, and New Mexico to the United States. Many Americans believed in Manifest Destiny, the God-given right to settle the entire continent. Polk provoked a war with Mexico. The American victory resulted in the addition of California and the present-day Southwest to the United States.

CHAPTER QUESTIONS

HOW DID economic and demographic pressures in the East spur Western migration?

WHAT STRATEGIES did the Sioux use to maintain their power on the Great Plains?

WHICH PEOPLES lived in the Southwest?

WHAT FORCES contributed to the Americanization of Texas?

WHY WAS James K. Polk so eager to provoke a war with Mexico?

CHAPTER OUTLINE

- The Agricultural Frontier
- The Frontier of the Plains Indians
- The Mexican Borderlands
- The Americanization of Texas
- Politics, Expansion, and War

IMAGE KEY
for pages 356–357 is on page 382.

On an occasion when I had interrogated a Sioux chief, on the upper Missouri, about their Government, their punishments and tortures of prisoners, for which I had freely condemned them for the cruelty of the practice, he took occasion, when I had got through, to ask me some questions relative to modes in the civilized world, which, with his comments upon them, were nearly as follows: and struck me, as I think they must every one, with great force.

He . . . told me he had often heard that white people hung their criminals by the neck, and choked them to death like dogs, and those their own people; to which I answered, "yes." He then told me he had learned that they shut each other up in prisons, where they keep them a great part of their lives because they can't pay money! I replied in the affirmative to this, which occasioned great surprise and excessive laughter, even among the women. . . . He said . . . that he had been along the Frontier, and a good deal amongst the white people, and he had seen them whip their little children, a thing that is very cruel, he had heard also, from several white medicine-men, that the Great Spirit of the white people was the child of a white woman, and that he was at the last put to death by the white people! This seemed to be a thing that he had not been able to comprehend, and he concluded by saying, "the Indians' Great Spirit got no mother—the Indians no kill him, he never die." He put me a chapter of other questions as to the trespasses of the white people on their lands, their continual corruption of the morals of their women, and digging open the Indians' graves to get their bones, &c. To all of which I was compelled to reply in the affirmative, and quite glad to close my note-book, and quietly to escape from the throng that had collected around me, and saying (though to myself and silently), that these and an hundred other vices belong to the civilized world, and are practiced upon (but certainly, in no instance, reciprocated by) the "cruel and relentless savage."

George Catlin

Virgil J. Vogel, ed., *A Documentary History of the American Indian* (New York: Harper & Row, 1972), pp. 138–139.

GEORGE CATLIN, ONE of the great illustrators of the American Indians, recorded these words in the 1830s when he traveled over the trans-Mississippi West painting and sketching, in his words, "the looks and customs of the vanishing races of native man in America." Unlike most whites of his generation, he approached Indian cultures with respect, and he realized that native peoples had a valid critique of the culture and values of white America. Born in 1796 in the Wyoming Valley of northeastern Pennsylvania, he was raised among memories of Indians and their warfare. After briefly practicing law, he turned to painting and portraiture as a career in the 1820s. He was so taken with the physical grace and dignity of a group of Indians visiting Philadelphia in 1824 that he committed his life's work to a visual recording of Indian history and customs before their way of life was engulfed by a surging tide of white settlement.

Some 300,000 Americans traveled the Oregon Trail in the 1840s and 1850s in a trek that eventually made the United States a nation that spanned the continent. These overlanders were part of a restless tide of white migration that eventually saw more than 50,000 Americans a year migrate west of the Appalachians after the War of 1812.

After settling the area between the Appalachian Mountains and the Mississippi River, the American West of the early nineteenth century, migrants headed beyond the Mississippi River in the 1840s. The broad expanse of the trans-Mississippi region (stretching from the Mississippi Valley to the Pacific Coast) had become the new American West by mid-century. The West became a meeting ground of people from diverse cultures as Anglo-Americans came into contact and conflict with the Indians of the Plains and the Mexicans of the Southwest. Convinced of the superiority of their political and cultural values, Anglo-Americans asserted a God-given right to spread across the continent and impose their notions of liberty and democracy on peoples whose land they coveted. In the process, they defeated and subjugated those who stood in their way.

Manifest Destiny was the label for this presumed providential right, and it provided a justification for the aggressively expansionist Democratic administration of James K. Polk, which came to power in 1845. The most dramatic result of these policies was the Mexican War of 1846–1848, which made California and the present-day Southwest part of the American continental empire.

The Agricultural Frontier

The U.S. population ballooned from 5.3 million in 1800 to more than 23 million by 1850. As the population expanded, it shifted westward. Fewer than one in ten Americans lived west of the Appalachians in 1800; by 1850, about half did (see Map 13–1).

Through purchase and conquest, the land area of the United States more than tripled in the first half of the nineteenth century. Here was space where Americans could raise the large families of a rural society.

Declining soil fertility and rising population pressure in the rural East propelled these migrations. A common desire for greater economic opportunity, however, resulted in two distinct western societies by the 1840s. North of the Ohio River, in the Old Northwest, free labor and family farms defined the social order. South of the Ohio was the Old Southwest, a society dominated by slave labor and the plantation.

The Crowded East

Looking back at his rural youth, Omar H. Morse recalled, "My Parents were in very limited circumstances financially yet blessed with a large family of children which is a poor man's capital though capital of this kind is not considered very available in case of financial Depression." Born in 1824 in the upstate New York village of Hastings, Morse had no prospect of inheriting land from his father, so he moved in the 1840s to Wisconsin. Bad luck and too many debts prevented Morse from ever achieving landed independence. He lost three farms and eventually settled in Minnesota, where he worked at odd jobs and built houses. Heading west did not guarantee economic success, but it was the best option open to land-starved easterners who dreamed of leaving a productive farm to their children.

By the early nineteenth century, land was scarce in the East, especially in New England. After generations of population growth and subdivisions of landholdings to male heirs, most New England communities no longer had enough arable land to satisfy all the young men who wanted their own farms.

HOW DID economic and demographic pressures in the East spur Western migration?

WHERE TO LEARN MORE

Living History Farms, Des Moines, Iowa **www.lhf.org/**

Manifest Destiny   Doctrine, first expressed in 1845, that the expansion of white Americans across the continent was inevitable and ordained by God.

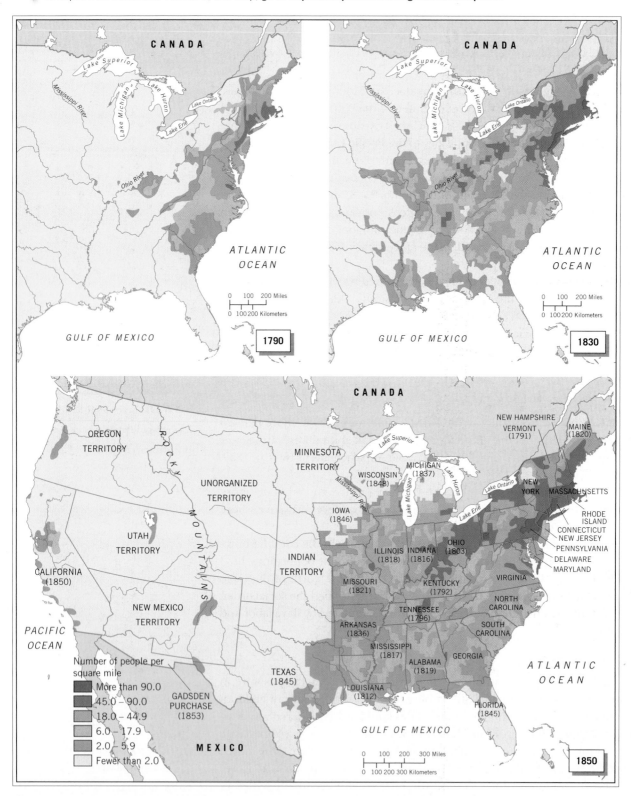

MAP 13–1   The Westward Shift of the United States Population, 1790–1850 With a speed that was unimaginable in 1790, the United States quickly became a continental nation that stretched from the Atlantic to the Pacific by 1850. Particularly dramatic was the population growth in what became the Midwest.

WHAT CHANGES occurred between 1830 and 1850 to encourage the settlement of territories in the West?

Land was more productive and expensive farther south, in the Mid-Atlantic States. Agriculture was more commercialized than in New England, and economic inequality was thus higher. Successful farmers became wealthy by specializing in wheat and hiring the rural poor to work their fields. One-third to one-half of the young men in the commercialized agricultural districts of New Jersey and Pennsylvania were landless by the end of the eighteenth century. These men and their families, many of whom were recently arrived Scots-Irish and German immigrants, led the western migration from Pennsylvania.

The pressure to move west was greatest in the slave states along the eastern seaboard. Although population density here was just two-thirds of that in New England, landholdings were more concentrated and the soil more exhausted than in the Northeast. Tenants who wanted their own land and small farmers tired of competing against slave labor were forced west across the mountains. They were joined by the sons of planters. Despite marriages arranged to keep land within the wealthy families, there was no longer enough good land left to carve out plantations for all the younger sons.

By the early 1800s, the young and the poor in the rural East had every incentive to head west. Land was the basis of wealth and social standing, and its ownership separated the independent from the dependent, the rooted from the rootless.

The western settler, observed a traveler on the Missouri frontier in the 1820s, wanted "to be a freeholder, to have plenty of rich land, and to be able to settle his children around him." Government policy under the Jeffersonian Republicans and Jacksonian Democrats attempted to promote these goals. Central to the land policy of the federal government after 1800 was the conviction that political liberties rested on the broadest possible base of land ownership. Thus public policy and private aspirations merged in the belief that access to land was the key to preserving American freedom.

When Jefferson took office in 1801, the minimum price for public land was $2 per acre, and a block of 320 acres had to be purchased at one time. By the 1830s, the price was down to $1.25 per acre, and the minimum purchase was only 80 acres. Congress also protected squatters, who had settled on public land before it was surveyed, from being outbid by speculators at land sales. The Preemption Act of 1841 guaranteed the right to purchase up to 160 acres at the minimum price of $1.25 when the public auction was held.

THE OLD NORTHWEST

The number of Americans who settled in the heartland of the Old Northwest, Ohio, Indiana, and Illinois, rose tenfold from 1810 to 1840. Ohio had already entered the Union in 1803; Indiana joined in 1816, Illinois in 1818. The end of the

Chronology

1803–1806	Lewis and Clark travel up the Missouri River in search of a water route to the Pacific.
1816	Settlers surge into the trans-Appalachian region.
1821	Mexico gains its independence from Spain.
	Santa Fe Trail opens.
	Stephen F. Austin establishes the first American colony in Texas.
1824	Rocky Mountain Fur Company begins the rendezvous system.
1830	Congress creates the Indian Territory.
1834	Protestant missions are established in Oregon.
	Santa Anna seizes power in Mexico.
1836	Texas wins its independence from Mexico.
1837	Smallpox epidemic hits the Plains Indians.
1842	First large parties of migrants set out on the Oregon Trail.
1845	United States annexes Texas.
	Democrats embrace Manifest Destiny.
	The Great Irish Famine begins.
1846	Mexican War breaks out.
	United States and Britain reach an agreement in Oregon.
1847	Mormons begin settlement of Utah.
1848	Oregon Territory is organized.
	Treaty of Guadalupe Hidalgo ends the Mexican War.
	Revolutions sweep across Europe.
1851	Fort Laramie Treaty with the Plains Indians is signed.

QUICK REVIEW

Why Go West?

- Scarcity of land in the East.
- Exhausted soil.
- Competition with slave labor.
- Cheap and abundant land in the West.

WHERE TO LEARN MORE

★ Conner Prairie, Noblesville, Indiana
www.connerprairie.org

War of 1812 and the abandonment by the British of their former Indian allies opened the region to a flood of migrants.

Two streams of migrants, one predominantly northern and the other southern, met in the lower Midwest and viewed each other as strangers. Lucy Maynard, a New Englander living in south-central Illinois, noted that her neighbors were "principally from Indiana and Kentucky, some from Virginia, all friendly but very different from our people in their manners and language and every other way."

A Mosaic of Settlements.   The Old Northwest was less a melting pot in which regional cultures merged than a mosaic of settlements in which the different values and folkways of regional cultures from throughout the East took root and expanded. Belts of migration generally ran along a line from east to west as settlers sought out soil types and ecological conditions similar to those they had left behind. Thus the same North-South cultural differences that existed along the Atlantic seaboard in 1800 were to be found half a century later in the Mississippi Valley.

A transplanted Yankee culture from New England and upstate New York spread over the upper Midwest, northern Ohio, Indiana, and Illinois, as well as Michigan and Wisconsin. These westerners were Whiggish in their politics, tended to be antislavery, and valued a communal sense of responsibility that regulated moral behavior and promoted self-improvement. The highland southerners who settled the lower Midwest, southern Ohio, Indiana, and Illinois, as well as Kentucky, were Democrats: they fiercely distrusted any centralized authority, political or moral, and considered Yankees intolerant do-gooders. Holding the balance of cultural and political power were the migrants from Pennsylvania and New Jersey, who were accustomed to ethnic diversity and the politics of competing economic groups. They settled principally in central Ohio, Indiana, and Illinois. By emphasizing economic growth and downplaying the cultural politics that pitted Yankees against southerners, they built a consensus around community development.

It took about ten years of backbreaking labor to create an 80-acre farm in heavily wooded sections. The work of women was essential for the success of the farm and the production of any salable surplus. Charlotte Webb Jacobs, from the Sugar Creek community on the Illinois prairie, proudly recalled, "I made everything that we wore; I even made my towels and table cloths, sheets and everything in the clothing line."

Because outside labor was scarce and expensive, communities pooled their efforts for such tasks as raising a cabin. Groups of settlers also acted as cooperative units at public land auctions. Local associations known as **claims clubs** enforced the extralegal right of squatters to enter noncompetitive bids on land they had settled and improved. The high cost of hauling goods to outside markets kept the early frontier economy barely above self-sufficiency. This initial economy, however, soon gave way to a more commercially oriented agriculture when steamboats, canals, and railroads opened up vast new markets (see Chapter 12).

The first large market was in the South, down the corridor of the Ohio and Mississippi rivers, and its major staples were corn and hogs. By the 1830s, the Erie Canal and its feeder waterways in the upper Midwest began to reorient much of the western farm trade to the Northeast. Wheat, because of its ready marketability for milling into flour, became the major cash crop for the northern market.

Wheat production skyrocketed when settlers overcame their initial reluctance to farm in a treeless terrain and moved into the prairies of Indiana and Illinois in the 1840s. New plows helped break the thick prairie sod. The plows were followed

Claims clubs   Groups of local settlers on the nineteenth-century frontier who banded together to prevent the price of their land claims from being bid up by outsiders at public land auctions.

in the 1840s by horsedrawn mechanical harvesters. Once railroads provided direct access to eastern markets, the Midwest became the nation's breadbasket.

The commercialization of agriculture in the West contributed to the growth of eastern manufacturing. Western farms supplied eastern manufacturers with inexpensive raw materials for processing into finished goods. By flooding national markets with corn and wheat, western produce not only supplied eastern workers with cheap food but also forced noncompetitive eastern farmers either to move west or to work in factories in eastern cities. In turn, the West itself became an ever-growing market for eastern factory goods.

The combination of favorable farm prices and steadily decreasing transportation costs generated a rise in disposable income that was spent on outside goods or invested in internal economic development. A network of canals and railroads was laid down, and manufacturing cities grew from towns favorably situated by water or rail transport. There was still room for subsistence farming, but the West north of the Ohio was now economically specialized and socially diverse.

THE OLD SOUTHWEST

"The *Alabama Feaver* rages here with great violence and has carried off vast numbers of our Citizens," wrote a North Carolina planter in 1817 about the westward migration from his state. "I am apprehensive, if it continues to spread as it has done, it will almost depopulate the country." By 1850, more than 600,000 white settlers from Maryland, Virginia, and the Carolinas lived in slave states to the south and west, and many of them had brought their slaves with them. Indeed, from 1790 to 1860, more than 800,000 slaves were moved from the South Atlantic region into the Old Southwest.

Soaring cotton prices after the War of 1812 and the smashing of Indian confederations during the war propelled the first surge of migration into the Old Southwest (see Map 13–1). Before cotton prices plunged in the Panic of 1819, planters flooded into western Tennessee and the Black Belt, a crescent-shaped band of rich, black loamy soil arcing westward from Georgia through central Alabama and Mississippi. Migration surged anew in the 1830s when cotton prices were again high and the Chickasaws and Choctaws had been forced out of the incredibly fertile Delta country between the Yazoo and Mississippi rivers (see Chapter 10). The 1840s brought Texas fever to replace the Alabama fever of the 1810s, and a steady movement to the Southwest rounded out the contours of the cotton South. In less than 30 years, six new slave states—Mississippi (1817), Alabama (1819), Missouri (1821), Arkansas (1836), Florida (1845), and Texas (1845)—joined the Union (see the Overview table, Westward Expansion and the Growth of the Union, 1815–1850).

The southwestern frontier attracted both slaveholding planters and small independent farmers. The planters, though a minority, had the capital or the credit to acquire the best lands and the slave labor to

QUICK REVIEW

Commercialization of Agriculture
- New technology spurred production.
- Commercialization of agriculture contributed to growth of eastern manufacturing.
- West became a market for eastern factory goods.

Cyrus McCormick pioneered the development of horsedrawn mechanical reapers. Shown here demonstrating his reaper to potential customers, McCormick helped revolutionize American agriculture with labor-saving machinery that made possible far larger harvests of grain crops.

The Old Print Shop

OVERVIEW

WESTWARD EXPANSION AND THE GROWTH OF THE UNION, 1815–1850

New Free States	New Slave States	Territories (1850)
Indiana, 1816	Mississippi, 1817	Minnesota
Illinois, 1818	Alabama, 1819	Oregon
Maine, 1820	Missouri, 1821	New Mexico
Michigan, 1837	Arkansas, 1836	Utah
Iowa, 1846	Florida, 1845	
Wisconsin, 1848	Texas, 1845	

make those lands productive. The slaveholders were responding both to the need for fresh land and to the extraordinary demand for short-staple cotton. More typical settlers on the southern frontier were the small independent yeomen farmers who generally owned no slaves. Usually settling in the valleys, on the ridges, and in the hill country, they often soon sold out to neighboring planters and headed west again. Like the yeoman farmer Gideon Linecum, they relished "the pleasure of frequent change of country."

The yeomanry moved onto the frontier in two waves. The first consisted of stockmen-hunters, a restless, transient group that spread from the pine barrens in the Carolina backcountry to the coastal plain of eastern Texas. These pioneers prized unfettered independence and measured their wealth in the livestock left to roam and fatten on the sweet grasses of uncleared forests. They were quick to move on when farmers, the second wave, started to clear the land for crops.

Like the stock herders, the yeoman farmers valued self-sufficiency and the leisure to hunt and fish. In pursuit of these goals, they practiced a diversified agriculture aimed at feeding their families. The more ambitious farmers, usually those who owned one or two slaves, grew some cotton, but most preferred to avoid the economic risks of cotton production.

Measured by per capita income, and as a direct result of the profits from slave-produced cotton on virgin soils, the Old Southwest was a wealthier society than the Old Northwest in 1850. In the short term, the settlement of the Old Southwest was also more significant for national economic development. Cotton accounted for more than half the value of all American exports after the mid-1830s. More than any other commodity, cotton paid for American imports and underpinned national credit. But southern prosperity was not accompanied by the same economic development and social change as in the Old Northwest. Compared to the slave West in 1860, the free-labor West was twice as urbanized, and far more of its workforce was engaged in nonagricultural pursuits.

The Southwest Ordinance, enacted by Congress in 1790, opened all territories south of the Ohio River to slavery. Slaves, land, and cotton were the keys to wealth on the southern frontier, and agricultural profits were continually plowed back into more land and slaves to produce more cotton. In contrast, prosperous farmers in the Old Northwest had no slaves to work additional acres. Hence they were much more likely to invest their earnings in promotional schemes designed to attract settlers whose presence would raise land values and increase business for local merchants and entrepreneurs. As early as the 1840s, rural communities in the Old Northwest were supporting bustling towns that offered jobs in trade and manufacturing on a scale far surpassing anything in the slave West. By the 1850s, the Midwest was almost as urbanized as the Northeast had been in 1830, and nearly half its labor force no longer worked on farms.

The Old Southwest remained overwhelmingly agricultural. Once the land was settled, the children of the first generation of slaveholders and yeomen moved west to the next frontier. Relatively few newcomers took their place. By the 1850s, Kentucky, Tennessee, Alabama, and Mississippi, the core states of the Old Southwest, were all losing more migrants than they were gaining.

THE FRONTIER OF THE PLAINS INDIANS

Few white Americans had ventured west of the Mississippi by 1840. Reports of explorations of the southern plains by Zebulon Pike in 1806 and Stephen Long in 1819 dismissed the area as the Great American Desert, an arid, treeless landscape with little agricultural potential.

Moreover, Americans had no legal claim to much of the trans-Mississippi West, or merely the paper title of the Louisiana Purchase, to which none of the native inhabitants had acquiesced. Beyond Texas and the boundary line drawn by the Trans-Continental Treaty of 1819 lay the northern possessions of Mexico. Horse-mounted Indian tribes dominated by the Sioux were a formidable power throughout the central Plains.

Before the 1840s, only fur trappers and traders had pushed across the Great Plains and into the Rockies. The 1840s brought a sudden change, a large migration westward that radically altered the ecology of the Great Plains. Farm families trapped in an agricultural depression and enticed by Oregon's bounty turned the trails blazed by the fur traders into ruts on the **Oregon Trail,** the route that led to the first large settlement of Americans on the Pacific Coast.

TRIBAL LANDS

At least 350,000 Native Americans lived in the plains and mountains of the trans-Mississippi West in 1840. They were loosely organized into tribal groups, each with its own territory and way of life. Most inhabited the Great Plains region, which lay north and west of the Indian Territory reserved for eastern tribes in the present state of Oklahoma. The point where the prairies of the Midwest gave way to the higher, drier plains marked a rough division between predominantly agricultural tribes to the east and nomadic, hunting tribes to the west.

In the 1830s, the U.S. government set aside a broad stretch of country between the Platte River to the north and the Red River to the south (most of what is now Oklahoma and eastern Kansas) exclusively for tribes resettled from the East under the Indian Removal Act of 1830 and for village-living groups native to the area. However, even as Congress was debating the idea of a permanent Indian reserve, the pressure on native peoples in the Mississippi Valley both from raiding parties of Plains Indians and the incessant demands of white farmers and speculators for land was rendering a stable Indian-white boundary meaningless.

On the eve of Indian removal in the East, the Sauks, Foxes, Potawatomis, and other Indian peoples inhabited Iowa. The defeat of the Sauks and Foxes in what white Americans called Black Hawk's War in 1832 opened Iowa to white settlement and forced tribes to cede land (see Chapter 10). In 1838, Congress created the Territory of Iowa, which encompassed all the land between the Mississippi

WHAT STRATEGIES did the Sioux use to maintain their power on the Great Plains?

QUICK REVIEW

The Pawnees
- By 1830s, Pawnees primarily an agricultural people.
- Agreed in 1833 treaty to move north.
- Attacked by Sioux in the north and white settlers in the south.

W WHERE TO LEARN MORE

Indian Museum of North America, Crazy Horse, South Dakota
www.crazyhorse.org/museum.shtml

Oregon Trail Overland trail of more than two thousand miles that carried American settlers from the Midwest to new settlements in Oregon, California, and Utah.

and Missouri rivers north of the state of Missouri. The remaining Indians were now on the verge of being pushed completely out of the region. Throughout the upper Mississippi Valley in the 1830s, other groups suffered a similar fate, and the number of displaced Indians swelled.

The first to be displaced were farming peoples whose villages straddled the woodlands to the east and the open plains to the west. These border tribes were caught in a vise between the loss of their land to advancing white people and the seizure of their horses and agricultural provisions by Indian raiders from the plains. The Pawnees were among the hardest hit.

By the 1830s, the Pawnees were primarily an agricultural people who embarked on seasonal hunts for game in the Platte River Valley. In 1833, they signed a treaty with the U.S. government in which they agreed to withdraw north of the Platte in return for subsidies and military protection from the hostile Indians on the plains. Once the Pawnees moved north of the Platte, Sioux attacked them and seized control of the prime hunting grounds. When the Pawnees in desperation filtered back south of the Platte, in violation of the treaty of 1833, they encountered constant harassment from white settlers. Forced back north of the Platte by the U.S. government, the Pawnees were eventually driven out of their homeland by the Sioux.

The Sioux were the dominant power on the northern and central Great Plains, more than able to hold their own against white Americans in the first half of the nineteenth century. Armed with guns they had acquired from the French, the western Sioux dominated the prairies east of the Missouri River by 1800.

The Sioux learned to use the horse from the Plains Indians. Introduced to the New World by the Spanish, horses had revolutionized the lives of native peoples on the Great Plains. The Sioux were the most successful of all the tribes in melding two facets of white culture, the gun and the horse, into an Indian culture of warrior-hunters.

Although the Sioux frequently fought other tribes, casualties from these encounters were light. The Sioux and other Plains Indians fought not to kill the greatest number of the enemy, but rather to dominate hunting grounds and to win individual honor by "counting coup" (touching a live foe). When an Army officer in 1819 urged the Sioux to make peace with the Chippewas, Little Crow, a Santee Sioux, explained why war was preferable: "Why, then, should we give up such an extensive country to save the life of a man or two annually?"

When the United States acquired title to the Great Plains in the Louisiana Purchase of 1803, the western Sioux economy was based on two seasonally restricted systems of hunting. In summer, the Sioux hunted buffalo on horseback on the plains. In winter, on foot, they trapped beaver. In great spring trading fairs, the western Sioux exchanged their buffalo robes and beaver pelts for goods acquired by the Santee Sioux from European traders.

As the supply of beaver dwindled and the demand for buffalo hides from American and European traders increased in the early 1800s, the Sioux extended their buffalo hunts. In a loose alliance with the Cheyennes and Arapahos, Sioux war parties pushed aside or subjugated weaker tribes to the south and west of the Missouri River basin.

Because they lived in small wandering bands, the Sioux were less susceptible to the epidemics brought by the white traders than were the more sedentary village peoples. The Sioux were also one of the first tribes to be vaccinated against smallpox by doctors sent up the Missouri River by the Bureau of Indian Affairs in the early 1830s. Smallpox reached the plains in the 1780s, and a major epidemic in 1837 probably halved the region's Indian population. Particularly hard hit were tribes attempting to resist the Sioux advance.

Some 25,000 strong by 1850, the western Sioux had increased in power and numbers since they first encountered American officials during the Lewis and Clark Expedition in 1804 and 1805. "These are the vilest miscreants of the savage race," Lewis and Clark wrote of the Sioux, "and must ever remain the pirates of the Missouri, until such measures are pursued by our government as will make them feel a dependence on its will for their supply of merchandise."

Words were one thing, gaining power over the Sioux another. Americans could vilify the Sioux, but they could not force them into dependence in the first half of the nineteenth century.

THE FUR TRADERS

"Curiosity, a love of wild adventure, and perhaps also a hope of profit, for times are hard, and my best coat has a sort of sheepish hang-dog hesitation to en-counter fashionable folk, combined to make me look upon the project with an eye of favour." As best he could recollect, these were the motives that induced Warren A. Ferris, a New York civil engineer, to join the American Fur Company in 1829 at the age of 19 and go west as a fur trapper and mountain man. During their golden age in the 1820s and 1830s, the trappers blazed the trails that far greater numbers of white settlers would follow in the 1840s.

The western fur trade originated in the rivalry between British and American companies for profitable furs, especially beaver pelts. Until the early 1820s, the Hudson's Bay Company, a well-capitalized British concern, dominated the trans-Mississippi fur trade. A breakthrough for American interests came in 1824 when two St. Louis businessmen, William Henry Ashley and Andrew Henry of the Rocky Mountain Fur Company, developed the rendezvous system, which eliminated the need for permanent and costly posts deep in Indian territory. In keeping with Indian traditions of periodic intertribal meetings, the rendezvous system brought together trappers, Indians, and traders in a grand annual fair at a designated site in the high mountain country of Wyoming.

Except for the annual fairs, the mountain men lived isolated, hard lives in the wilderness. Their closest relations were with Indians, and about 40 percent of the trappers married Indian women, unions that often linked them economically and diplomatically to their bride's tribe.

Living conditions in the wilderness were primitive, even brutal. Mortality rates among trappers ran as high as 80 percent a year. Death could result from an accidental gunshot wound, an encounter with a grizzly, or an arrow from an Indian whose hunting grounds a trapper had transgressed.

For all its dangers, the life of a trapper appealed to unattached young men like Warren Ferris. They were fleeing the confinements, as well as the comforts, of white civilization and were as free as they could be. When on a hunt with the Indians, they were part of a spectacle unknown to other white Americans, one that was already passing into history. "Fancy to yourself," Ferris asked readers of his published journals, "three thousand horses of every variety of size and colour, with trappings almost as varied as their appearance . . . ridden by a thousand souls . . . their persons fantastically ornamented. . . . Listen to the rattle of numberless lodgepoles [trailed] by packhorses. . . . Yonder see a hundred horsemen pursuing a herd of antelopes."

Shown here is a Lakota shirt, c. 1850, that was specially woven for those Sioux warriors who had distinguished themselves in battle. The blue and yellow dyes symbolize sky and earth, and the strands of human hair represent acts of bravery performed in defense of the Lakota people.

Shirt, about 1860s, unknown Sioux artist. Deer skin, hair, quills, feathers, paint, 1947.235. Denver Art Museum Collection, Native Arts Acquisitions Funds. © Photo by Denver Art Museum. All Rights Reserved.

  WHERE TO LEARN MORE

Museum Association of American Frontier and Fur Trade, Chadron, Nebraska
www.stepintohistory.com/states/NE/Fur_Trade.htm

12-3
Across the Plains with
Catherine Sager
Pringle in 1844

QUICK REVIEW

The Oregon Trail

- First large party overlanders left Missouri in 1842.
- Most overlanders were young farm families.
- In the 1840s, five thousand of the ninety thousand people who attempted the trip died.

 MAP EXPLORATION

To explore an interactive version of this map, go to
http://www.prenhall.com/goldfield3/map13.2

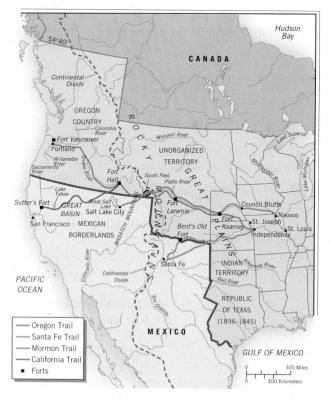

MAP 13–2 Western Overland Trails The great overland trails to the West began at the Missouri River. The Oregon Trail crossed South Pass in Wyoming and then branched off to Oregon, California, or Utah. The Santa Fe Trail carried American goods and traders to the Mexican Southwest.

WHAT ROLE did geography play in determining overland trails?

Such spectacles were increasingly rare after 1840, the year of the last mountain men's rendezvous on the Green River in Wyoming. The most exploitative phase of the fur trade in the 1830s had ravaged the fur-bearing animals and accelerated the spread of smallpox among the tribes. Whiskey, the most profitable item among the white man's trading goods, had corrupted countless Indians and undermined the vitality of tribal cultures.

The mountain men explored every trail and path from the front (or eastern) range of the Rockies to the Pacific. The main trading corridor of the fur trade became the main overland route to the West in the 1840s. The mountain men had removed the mystery of western geography, and in so doing they hastened the end of the frontier conditions that had made their unique way of life possible.

THE OREGON TRAIL

The ruts are still there. One can follow them to the horizon in the Platte River Valley of Nebraska and the dry tablelands of Wyoming, Idaho, and Nevada. They were put there by the wheels of wagons hauled by oxen on a jolting 2,000-mile journey across plains, mountains, and deserts from Missouri to Oregon, Utah, and California (see Map 13–2). Some 150,000 Americans made this overland trek in the heyday of the Oregon Trail in the 1840s and early 1850s (see Figure 13–1). Most of them walked alongside their wagons. They covered up to 15 miles a day on a journey that lasted close to six months.

Before the 1830s, few Americans had heard of Oregon, and practically none lived there. Protestant missionaries established the first permanent white settlements in the 1830s. Reports of Oregon's fertility that the missionaries sent east sparked the first popular interest in the region.

The missionaries repeatedly failed in their efforts to convert the Indians of the region to Christianity. Unlike the trappers, the missionaries sought to change the entire structure of Indian life and beliefs. But with their numbers already thinned by the diseases brought in by the trappers, Oregon tribes such as the Cayuses refused to abandon their traditional culture based on hunting and fishing to work for white farmers. During a measles epidemic in 1847, the Cayuses killed two of the most prominent missionaries, Marcus and Narcissa Whitman. In retaliation, white Americans, who now numbered more than 5,000, virtually exterminated the Cayuses.

The first large party of overlanders on the Oregon Trail left Independence, Missouri, for the Willamette Valley in 1842. Independence and St. Joseph in Missouri and, by the 1850s, Council Bluffs in Iowa were the jumping-off points for the Oregon Trail. Merchants profited from supplying, usually at inflated prices, wagons, mules, oxen, guns, ammunition, and staples like flour, bacon, and sugar.

Most overlanders were young farm families from the Midwest who had moved at least once before in their restless search for the perfect farm that would keep them out of debt. Usually the male head of a household made the decision to move. Women often regretted giving up ties with kin and friends. Besides their usual work of minding the children and cooking and cleaning, they would now have to help drive wagons and tend livestock. Still, many women were also optimistic about the journey. "Ho—for California, at last we are on the way," exclaimed Helen Carpenter in 1857, "and with good luck may some day reach the 'promised land.'" A study of 159 women's trail diaries indicates that about one-third of the women strongly favored the move. Margaret Frink, for example, recalled that she "never had occasion to regret the prolonged hardships of the toilsome journey."

In the 1840s, some 5,000 of the 90,000 men, women, and children who set out on the Oregon Trail died along the way. But although the overlanders were terrified of encountering Indians, who they assumed would be hostile, few died from Indian attacks. Indians killed only 115 migrants in the 1840s, and trigger-happy white migrants provoked most of the clashes. Disease and accidents were the great killers.

Cooperation between families was the key to a successful overland crossing. The men in a party often drew up a formal, written constitution at the start of a trip spelling out the assignments and work responsibilities of each wagon. Timing was crucial. A wagon train had to leave late enough in the spring to get good grass in Nebraska for the oxen and mules. Too early a departure, and the wagon train risked getting bogged down in spring mud; too late, and it risked being trapped in the snows of the Pacific coastal ranges.

Before "Oregon fever" had run its course, the flow of white settlers across the continent radically changed the economy and ecology of the Great Plains. Pressure mounted on plants and animals, reducing the land's ability to support all the tribes accustomed to living off it. Intertribal warfare intensified as the supply of buffalo and other game dwindled. Far from being separated from white people by a permanent line of division, the Plains Indians now stood astride the main path of white migration to the Pacific.

In response, officials in the Bureau of Indian Affairs organized a great gathering of the tribes in 1851. At this conference they pushed through the Fort Laramie Treaty. In exchange for accepting limitations on their movements and for the loss of game, the tribes were to receive annual compensation of $50,000 a year for 50 years (later reduced by the U.S. Senate to 10 years).

Most of the Indians at the Fort Laramie conference were the Sioux and their allies. The Sioux viewed the treaty as confirming their dominance on the Great Plains. When American negotiators tried to restrict Sioux hunting to north of the Platte, the Sioux demanded and received treaty rights to lands south of the Platte as well. "These lands once belonged to the Kiowas and the Crows," argued a western Sioux, "but we whipped those nations out of them, and in this we did what the white men do when they want the lands of the Indians."

The Fort Laramie Treaty represented a standoff between the Sioux and the U.S. government, the two great powers on the Plains. If neither yielded its claim to the region, war between them would be inevitable.

The Mexican Borderlands

*B*y the mid-1840s, parties of emigrant Americans were beginning to branch off the main Oregon Trail on their way to Utah and California, which were then part of Mexico's northern borderlands (see Map 13–2). Mostly

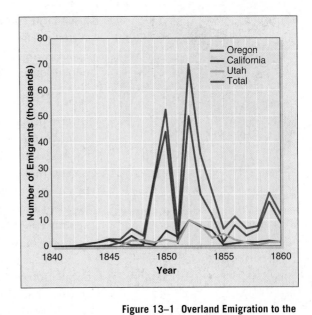

Figure 13–1 Overland Emigration to the West, 1840–1860   Immigration to the trans-Mississippi West steadily increased in the 1840s as farm families moved to Oregon or Utah. After the discovery of gold in California in 1849, California attracted the bulk of the emigrants, many of whom were single men hopeful of striking it rich.

Data Source: John D. Unruh, Jr., *The Plains Across: The Overland Emigrants and the Trans-Mississippi West, 1840–60* (1982), pp. 84–85.

WHERE TO LEARN MORE

Scotts Bluff National Monument, Gering, Nebraska **www.nps.gov/scbl/**

WHICH PEOPLES lived in the Southwest?

In trunks such as this one, women transported their fine pieces of china to the West on the Oregon Trail.

W   WHERE TO LEARN MORE

Indian Pueblo Cultural Center, Albuquerque, New Mexico
www.indianpueblo.org

This painting by Alfred James Miller depicts the busy interior of Fort Laramie in 1837.

Alfred Jacob Miller, *The Interior of Fort Laramie*, 1858–60. The Walters Art Museum, Baltimore.

a semiarid and thinly populated land of high plateaus, dry basins, and desert bisected north to south by mountain ranges, the borderlands had been part of the Spanish empire in North America. Mexico inherited this territory when it won independence from Spain in 1821.

THE PEOPLES OF THE SOUTHWEST

Diverse peoples lived in the Southwest. Imperial Spain had divided them into four main groupings: Indians, full-blooded Native Americans who retained their own languages and customs; *mestizos*, people of racially mixed ancestry, usually Spanish and Indian; *criollos*, American-born whites of Spanish ancestry; and Spaniards. By far the smallest group was the Spaniards. Despite their small numbers, the Spanish, along with the *criollos*, monopolized economic and political power. This wealthy elite controlled the labor of the *mestizos* in the predominantly ranching economy of the borderlands.

The largest single group in the borderlands were the Indians, about half the population in the 1820s. Most had not come under direct Spanish or Mexican control. Those who had were part of the mission system.

Spanish missions, most of them established by the Franciscan order, aimed both to Christianize and "civilize" the Indians, making them loyal imperial subjects. Mission Indians were forced to abandon their native economies and culture and settle in agricultural communities under the tight supervision of the friars (see Chapter 1). Spanish soldiers and royal officials, who lived in military garrisons known as *presidios*, accompanied the friars.

The largest concentration of Indians, some 300,000 when the Spanish friars arrived in the 1760s, was in California. Most of these, the Paiutes, Chumashes, Pomos, Shastas, and a host of smaller tribes, occupied their own distinct ecological zones where they gathered and processed what the rivers, forests, and grasslands provided. The Paiutes in the Owens Valley perfected an intricate system for irrigating wild grasses, but only the Yumans along the Colorado River in southeastern California practiced full-scale agriculture. The Spanish marveled at their lush fields of wheat, maize, beans, tobacco, and melons.

The major farming Indians east of California were the Pueblo peoples of Arizona and New Mexico. The Pueblo Indians were a peaceful people closely bound to small, tightly knit communities. Formally a part of the Spanish mission system, they had incorporated the Catholic God and Catholic rituals into their own polytheistic religion, which stressed the harmony of all living things with the forces of nature.

Once the Pueblos made their peace with the Spaniards after their great revolt in 1680 (see Chapter 3), their major enemies were the nomadic tribes that lived by hunting and raiding. These tribes outnumbered the Pueblos four to one and controlled most of the Southwest until the 1850s. Horses gave these nomadic tribes enormous mobility and the means of ranging far and wide for the economic resources that sustained their transformation into societies of mounted warriors.

Other tribes in the Mexican borderlands included the Navajos, the Apaches, the Comanches, and the Kiowas. The Comanches, a branch of the mountain Shoshonis who moved to the plains when horses became available, were the most feared of the nomadic peoples. Utterly fearless, confident, and masterful horsemen, they gained a reputation of mythic proportions for their prowess as mounted warriors. For food

and clothing, they relied on the immense buffalo herds of the southern
plains. For guns, horses, and other
trading goods, they lived off their
predatory raids. When the Santa Fe
Trail opened in the early 1820s, their
shrewdness as traders gave them a new
source of firearms that strengthened
their raiding prowess.

The three focal points of white
settlement in the northern borderlands of Mexico, Texas, New Mexico,
and Alta California (as distinguished
from Lower, or Baja, California), were
never linked by an effective network
of communications or transportation.
Each of these settlements was an iso-

lated offshoot of Hispanic culture with a semiautonomous economy based on ranching and a mostly illegal trade with French, British, and American merchants that
brought in a trickle of needed goods.

Mexico's most pressing problem in the 1820s was protecting its northern
states from the Comanches. To serve as a buffer against the Comanches, the Mexican government in 1821 invited Americans into Texas, opening the way to the
eventual American takeover of the territory.

THE AMERICANIZATION OF TEXAS

*T*he Mexicans faced the same problems governing Texas that the Spanish
had. Sparsely populated and economically struggling, Mexican Texas shared
a border with the United States along the Sabine River in Louisiana and
the Red River in the Arkansas Territory (see Map 13–2). The threat that the nearby
Americans posed to Mexico's security was obvious to Mexican officials. As one of
them early noted with alarm: "If we do not take the present opportunity to people
Texas, day by day the strength of the United States will grow until it will annex Texas,
Coahuila, Saltillo, and Nuevo León like the Goths, Visigoths, and the other tribes
that assailed the Roman Empire." However, attempts to promote Mexican immigration into Texas failed. Reasoning that the Americans were going to come in any
event and anxious to build up the population of Texas against Indian attacks, the
Mexican government encouraged Americans to settle in Texas by offering huge
grants of land in return for promises to accept Mexican citizenship, convert to
Catholicism, and obey the authorities in Mexico City.

The first American *empresario,* the recipient of a large grant in return for a
promise to bring in settlers, was Stephen F. Austin. The Austin grant encompassed
18,000 square miles. Other grants were smaller but still lavish. The *empresarios* stood
to grow wealthy by leasing out land, selling parcels to settlers, and organizing the
rest into large-scale farms that produced cotton with slave labor. For the Americans who followed in their wake, Texas offered good land that was so cheap it was
almost free. As early as 1830, eastern and south-central Texas was becoming an extension of the plantation economy of the Gulf coastal plain (see American Views:
Mexican Views of the U.S. Expansion).

More Americans moved into Texas with slaves than the Mexicans had anticipated. Many settlers simply ignored Mexican laws, especially the Emancipation

The paintings by George Catlin are
among the best visual sources for understanding the material culture of the
Plains Indians. This painting, c. 1834,
shows how central was the buffalo in
the life of the Comanches, the most
powerful tribe on the Southern Plains.

Art Resource, N.Y.

WHAT FORCES contributed to
the Americanization of Texas?

QUICK REVIEW

Peoples of the Southwest
• Indians
• Spanish
• *Mestizos:* those of racially mixed
ancestry
• *Criollos:* American-born whites of
Spanish ancestry

Empresarios   Agents who received a land grant from the Spanish or Mexican government in
return for organizing settlements.

MAP EXPLORATION

To explore an interactive version of this map, go to
http://www.prenhall.com/goldfield3/map13.3

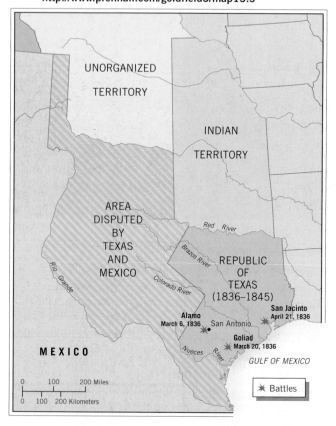

MAP 13–3 **Texas and Mexico after the Texas Revolt** The Battle of San Jacinto was the decisive American victory that gained the independence of Texas, but the border dispute between Texas and Mexico would not be resolved until the Mexican War a decade later.

HOW WAS the border dispute between Texas and Mexico resolved, and how did its resolution affect each geographically?

Alamo Franciscan mission at San Antonio, Texas that was the site in 1836 of a siege and massacre of Texans by Mexican troops.

Proclamation of 1829 that forbade slavery in the Republic of Mexico. In 1830, the Mexican government attempted to assert its authority. It levied the first taxes on the Americans, prohibited the further importation of slaves, and closed the international border to additional immigration. Still, another 10,000 Americans spilled across the border in the early 1830s, and they continued to bring in slaves.

Unlike the *empresarios,* many of whom became Catholic and married into elite *Tejano* (Spanish-speaking Mexicans born in Texas) families, these newcomers lived apart from Mexicans and rejected Mexican citizenship. Cultural tensions escalated. A clash became inevitable in 1835 when General Santa Anna, elected president of Mexico in 1833, overturned the liberal Mexican constitution of 1824. He established himself as a dictator in 1834, and his centralist rule ended any hope of the Americans *empresarios* and their *Tejano* allies that Texas might become an autonomous state within a federated Mexico. Skirmishing between Mexican troops and rebellious Texans began in the fall of 1835.

At first, the Anglo-*Tejano* leadership sought to overthrow Santa Anna, restore the constitution of 1824, and win separate statehood for Texas within a liberal Mexican republic. Santa Anna, however, refused to compromise. When he raised a large army to crush the uprising, he radicalized the rebellion and pushed its leaders to declare complete independence on March 2, 1836. Four days later, a Mexican army of 4,000 annihilated the 187 defenders of the **Alamo,** an abandoned mission in San Antonio. A few weeks later at Goliad, another 300 Texans were killed after they had agreed to surrender (see Map 13–3).

"Remember the Alamo!" and "Remember Goliad!" were powerful rallying cries for the beleaguered Texans. Volunteers from the American South rushed to the aid of the main Texan army, commanded by Sam Houston. Houston's victory in April 1836 at the Battle of San Jacinto established the independence of Texas. Captured while trying to flee, Santa Anna signed a treaty in May 1836, recognizing Texas as an independent republic with a boundary on the south and west at the Rio Grande. However, the Nueces River to the north of the Rio Grande had been the administrative border of Texas under Mexican rule. The Mexican Congress rejected the treaty, and the boundary remained in dispute.

In part because Mexico refused to recognize the Texas Republic, Anglos feared *Tejanos* as a subversive element. Pressure mounted on them to leave, especially after Santa Anna launched a major counterattack in 1842, capturing San Antonio. Those who stayed lost much of their land and economic power as Anglos used their knowledge of American law or just plain chicanery to reduce the *Tejanos* to second-class citizens.

More difficult to subordinate were the Comanches. By the early 1840s, Texans and Comanches were in a state of nearly permanent war. Only the force of the federal army after the Civil War ended the Comanches' long reign over the high, dry plains of northern and western Texas.

THE PUSH INTO CALIFORNIA AND THE SOUTHWEST

California. Mexican rule in California was always weak. For *Californios,* Californians of Spanish descent, Mexico was literally *la otra banda,* "the other shore." In trying to strengthen its hold on this remote and thinly populated region, the Mexican government relied on a program of economic development.

The centerpiece of the Mexican program was the secularization of the missions, opening up the landholdings of the Catholic Church to private ownership and releasing the mission Indians from paternalistic bondage. Small allotments of land were set aside for the Indians, but most returned to their homelands. Those who remained became a source of cheap labor for the *rancheros* who carved up the mission lands into huge cattle ranches. Thus by the 1830s, California had entered what is called the *rancho* era. The main beneficiaries of this process, however, were not the Mexican authorities who had initiated it but the American traders who responded to the economic opportunities presented by the privatization of the California economy.

New England merchants had been trading in California since the 1780s. Ships from New England and New York sailed around Cape Horn to California ports, where they unloaded trading goods. Servicing this trade in California was a resident colony of American agents, some 300 strong by the mid-1840s.

Whereas Yankees dominated the American colonies in coastal California, it was mostly midwestern farm families who filtered into the inner valleys of California from the Oregon Trail in the 1830s and 1840s (see Map 13–2). Nearly a thousand Americans had arrived by 1846.

California belonged to Mexico in name only by the early 1840s. The program of economic development had strengthened California's ties to the outside world at the expense of Mexico. American merchants and California *rancheros* ran the economy, and both groups had joined separatist movements against Mexican rule. Unlike the *Californios,* who were ambivalent about their future political allegiance, the Americans wanted to be part of the United States.

New Mexico. Except for Utah, the American push into the interior of the Mexican Southwest followed the California pattern of trade preceding settlement. When Mexico liberalized the formerly restrictive trading policies of Spain, American merchants opened up the 900-mile-long **Santa Fe Trail** from Independence, Missouri, to Santa Fe, New Mexico. Starved for mercantile goods, the New Mexicans were a small but highly profitable market.

Brent's Old Fort, built on the Arkansas River at the point where the Santa Fe Trail turned to the southwest, was the fulcrum for the growing economic influence of Americans over New Mexican affairs. Completed in 1832, the fort enabled the Brent brothers from Missouri to control a flourishing and almost monopolistic trade with Indians, trappers, caravans on the Santa Fe Trail, and the large landowners and merchants of New Mexico. This trade pulled New Mexico

THE MEXICAN RULERS,
migrating from Matamoras, with their Treasures —

This anti-Catholic lithograph sarcastically depicts the "rulers" of Mexico as lecherous Catholic clerics who were quick to desert the Mexican town of Matamoras when U.S. troops arrived in May 1846. The priest and monk ride out of Matamoras accompanied by young women, bottles of wine, and other booty.

Library of Congress

QUICK REVIEW

Mexican Rule in California

- Mexican rule in California weak.
- Government initiated program of economic development to help strengthen its control over region.
- Centerpiece of program: secularization of missions.

Californios Californians of Spanish descent.

Santa Fe Trail The 900-mile trail opened by American merchants for trading purposes following Mexico's liberalization of the formerly restrictive trading policies of Spain.

AMERICAN VIEWS

MEXICAN VIEWS OF THE U.S. EXPANSION

A MEXICAN VIEW OF THE TEXANS, 1828

By the late 1820s, Mexico was reassessing its policy of encouraging American immigration to Texas. Concerned over the large numbers and uncertain loyalties of the American settlers, the government appointed a commission in 1827 ostensibly to survey the boundary between Louisiana and the province of Texas. The real purpose of the commission was to recommend policy changes that would strengthen Mexico's hold on Texas. The following excerpt is from a journal kept by José María Sánchez, the draftsman of the boundary commission.

- Why was the Mexican government so ineffective in maintaining control over Texas?
- What was the appeal of Texas for Americans? How did most of them enter Texas and take up land?
- Why did Sánchez have such a low opinion of the Americans in the Austin colony? What did he think of Stephen Austin?
- Why did the Mexicans fear that they would lose Texas?

The Americans from the north have taken possession of practically all the eastern part of Texas, in most cases without the permission of the authorities. They immigrate constantly, finding no one to prevent them, and take possession of the *sitio* [location] that best suits them without either asking leave or going through any formality other than that of building their homes. Thus the majority of inhabitants in the Department are North Americans, the Mexican population being reduced to only Bejar, Nacogdoches, and La Bahía del Espíritu Santo, wretched settlements that between them do not number three thousand inhabitants, and the new village of Guadalupe Victoria that has scarcely more than seventy settlers. The government of the state, with its seat at Saltillo, that should watch over the preservation of its most precious and interesting department, taking measures to prevent its being stolen by foreign hands, is the one that knows the least not only about actual conditions, but even about its territory. . . . Repeated and urgent appeals have been made to the Supreme Government of the Federation regarding the imminent danger in which this interesting Department is of becoming the prize of the ambitious North Americans, but never has it taken any measures that may be called conclusive. . . .

[Sánchez goes on to describe the village of Austin and the American colony founded by Stephen Austin.]

Its population is nearly two hundred persons, of which only ten are Mexicans, for the balance are all Americans from the North with an occasional European. Two wretched little stores supply the inhabitants of the colony: one sells only whiskey, rum, sugar, and coffee; the other, rice, flour, lard, and cheap cloth. . . . The Americans from the North, at least the great part of those I have seen, eat only salted meat, bread made by themselves out of corn meal, coffee, and home-made cheese. To these the greater part of those who live in the village add strong liquor, for they are in general, in my opinion, lazy people of vicious character. Some of them cultivate their small farms by planting corn; but this task they usually entrust to their negro slaves, whom they treat with considerable harshness. Beyond the village

into the cultural and economic orbit of the United States and undermined what little sovereign power Mexico held in the region.

Ties of blood and common economic interests linked a small group of American businessmen with the local elite. After thwarting an 1841 Texan attempt to occupy Santa Fe, the leaders of New Mexico increasingly looked to the United States to protect their local autonomy. They quickly decided to cooperate with the American army of invasion when the Mexican War got under way. Over the opposition of the clergy and ranchers still loyal to Mexico, this group was instrumental in the American takeover of New Mexico.

WHERE TO LEARN MORE

W

★ Fort Union National Monument, Watrous, New Mexico **www.nps .gov/foun/**

in an immense stretch of land formed by rolling hills are scattered the families brought by Stephen Austin, which today number more than two thousand persons. The diplomatic policy of this empresario, evident in all his actions, has, as one may say, lulled the authorities into a sense of security, while he works diligently for his own ends. In my judgment, the spark that will start the conflagration that will deprive us of Texas, will start from this colony. All because the government does not take vigorous measures to prevent it. Perhaps it does not realize the value of what it is about to lose.

A MEXICAN REBEL IN 1859

The U.S. victory in the Mexican War intensified cultural conflict along the now expanded Hispanic frontier. The Anglos (as Mexicans called white Americans) quickly assumed positions of political and economic dominance. They broke treaties designed to protect the property rights and land titles of Mexican-Americans and under the cover of legality bullied peoples of Mexican descent. The resulting anger and resentment flared up in a brief revolt in 1859 in the lower Rio Grande valley led by Juan Cortina, a ranch owner who had fought for Mexico in the Mexican War. The following is from one of the proclamations issued by Cortina.

> What was Cortina's opinion of the Anglos?
> What reasons did he cite for the uprising?
> How did he attempt to rally support for his cause?

Mexicans! When the State of Texas [became] an integrant part of the Union, flocks of vampires, in the guise of men, came and scattered themselves in the settlements, without any capital except the corrupt heart and the most perverse intentions. Some, brimful of laws, pledged to us their protection against the attacks of the rest; others assembled in shadowy councils, attempted and excited the robbery and burning of our relatives on the other side of the river Bravo; while others, to the abusing of our unlimited confidence, when we intrusted them with our titles [to land], which secured the future of our families, refused to return them under false and frivolous pretexts. . . . Many of you have been robbed of your property, incarcerated, chased, murdered, and hunted like wild beasts, because your labor was fruitful, and because your industry excited the vile avarice which led them.

Mexicans! Is there no remedy for you? . . . Mexicans! My part is taken; the voice of revelation whispers to me that to me is entrusted the work of breaking the chains of your slavery, and that the Lord will enable me, with powerful arm, to fight against our enemies, in compliance with the requirements of that Sovereign Majesty [God], who, from this day forward, will hold us under His protection. On my part, I am ready to offer myself as a sacrifice for your happiness; and counting upon the means necessary for the discharge of my ministry, you may count upon my cooperation, should no cowardly attempt put an end to my days.

Source: José María Sánchez, excerpted from "A Trip to Texas in 1828," trans. Carlos E. Castaneda from *Southwestern Historical Quarterly*, vol. 29 Copyright 1926. Reprinted courtesy of Texas State Historical Association, Austin, Texas. All rights reserved.

Source: House Executive Documents, No. 52, 36st Congress, 1st session, 1860, pp. 80–82.

Utah.   At the extreme northern and inner reaches of the Mexican borderlands lay Utah. Aside from trade with the Utes, Spain and Mexico had largely ignored this remote region. Its isolation and lack of white settlers, however, were precisely what made Utah so appealing to the Mormons, the Church of Jesus Christ of Latter-day Saints. For the Mormons in the 1840s, Utah became the promised land in which to build a new Zion.

Founded by Joseph Smith in upstate New York in the 1820s, Mormonism grew rapidly within a communitarian framework that stressed hard work and economic cooperation under the leadership of patriarchal leaders (see Chapter 12).

The economic success of close-knit Mormon communities, combined with the righteous zeal of their members, aroused the fears and hostility of non-Mormons. Harassed out of New York, Ohio, and Missouri, the Mormons thought they had found a permanent home by the late 1830s in Nauvoo, Illinois. But the murder of Joseph Smith and his brother by a mob in 1844 convinced the beleaguered Mormons that they had to leave the settled East for a refuge in the West. In 1846 a group of Mormons migrated to the Great Basin in Utah. Under the leadership of Brigham Young, they established a new community in 1847 at the Great Salt Lake on the western slopes of the Wasatch Mountains.

The Mormons succeeded by concentrating their farms along the fertile and relatively well-watered Wasatch Front. They dispensed land and organized an irrigation system that coordinated water rights with the amount of land under production. To their dismay, however, they learned in 1848 that they had not left the United States after all. The Union acquired Utah, along with the rest of the northern borderlands of Mexico, as a result of the Mexican War.

POLITICS, EXPANSION, AND WAR

WHY WAS James K. Polk so eager to provoke a war with Mexico?

The Democrats viewed their victory in the election of 1844 (see Chapter 10) as a popular mandate for expansion. They had campaigned on a platform that boldly demanded both Texas and the "reoccupation" of Oregon up to 54°40′.

James K. Polk, the new Democratic president, fully shared this expansionist vision. The greatest prize in his eyes was California. When he was stymied in his efforts to purchase California and New Mexico, he tried to force concessions from the Mexican government by ordering American troops to the mouth of the Rio Grande, far within the territory claimed by Mexico. When the virtually inevitable clash of arms occurred in late April 1846, war broke out between the United States and Mexico.

Victory resulted in the **Mexican Cession of 1848,** which added a half-million square miles to the United States. Polk's administration also finalized the acquisition of Texas and reached a compromise with the British on the Oregon Territory that recognized American sovereignty in the Pacific Northwest up to the 49th parallel. The United States was now a nation that spanned a continent.

MANIFEST DESTINY

With a phrase that soon entered the nation's vocabulary, John L. O'Sullivan, editor and Democratic politician, proclaimed in 1845 America's "manifest destiny to overspread and to possess the whole of the continent which Providence has given us for the development of the great experiment of Liberty and federated self-government entrusted to us." Central to Manifest Destiny was the assumption that white Americans were a special people. Evangelical revivals in the early nineteenth century then added an aggressive sense of urgency to America's presumed mission to spread the benefits of Protestantism and Christian civilization.

What distinguished the special American mission as enunciated by Manifest Destiny was its explicitly racial component. Caucasian Anglo-Saxon Americans, as the descendants of ancient Germanic tribes that had purportedly brought the seeds of free institutions to England, were now said to be the foremost race in the world. The superior racial pedigree they claimed for themselves gave white Americans the natural right to expand westward, a chosen people carrying the blessings of democracy and progress.

Advocates of Manifest Destiny were not warmongers calling for conquest. Still, the doctrine was undeniably a self-serving justification for what other peoples

Mexican Cession of 1848 The addition of half a million square miles to the United States as a result of victory in the 1846 war between the United States and Mexico.

would see as territorial aggrandizement. Manifest Destiny and popular stereotypes lumped Indians and Mexicans together as inferior peoples. An emigrant guide of 1845 spoke of the Mexican Californians as "scarcely a visible grade in the scale of intelligence, above the barbarous tribes by whom they are surrounded." For Waddy Thompson, an American diplomat in Mexico in the early 1840s, the Mexicans in general were "lazy, ignorant, and, of course, vicious and dishonest." This alleged Mexican inferiority was attributed to racial intermixture with the Indians, who, it was said, were hopelessly unfit for civilization.

Manifest Destiny was closely associated with the Democratic party. For Democrats, expansionism would counterbalance the debilitating effects of industrialization and urbanization. As good Jeffersonians, they stressed the need for more land to realize the ideal of a democratic republic rooted in the virtues and rough equality of independent farmers. For their working-class Irish constituency, the Democrats touted the broad expanses of the West as the surest means to escape the misery of wage slavery.

Manifest Destiny captured the popular imagination when the country was still mired in depression after the Panic of 1837. The way out of the depression, according to many Democrats, was to revive the export trade. Thomas Hart Benton, a Democratic senator from Missouri, was the leading spokesman for the vast potential of an American trade with India and China, a trade to be secured by American possession of the harbors on the Pacific Coast.

THE MEXICAN WAR

Once in office, Polk was willing to compromise on Oregon because he dreaded the possibility of a two-front war against both the Mexicans and the British.

In the spring of 1846, after Polk had abrogated the agreement on the joint occupation of Oregon, the British agreed to a boundary at the 49th parallel if they were allowed to retain Vancouver Island in Puget Sound. The Senate quickly approved the offer in June 1846. British-American trade continued to flourish, Mexico lost a potential ally, and, most important, Polk could now concentrate on the Mexican War, which had erupted a month earlier.

Polk refused to budge on the American claim that the Rio Grande was the border between Texas and Mexico. The Mexicans insisted that the Nueces River, 100 miles north of the Rio Grande, was the border, as it had been when Texas was part of Mexico. A boundary on the Rio Grande would more than double the size of Texas.

Polk sent 3,500 troops under General Zachary Taylor to the Nueces River in the summer of 1845. Polk also stepped up his efforts to acquire California. He instructed Thomas Larkin, the American consul in Monterey, California, to inform the *Californios* and Americans that the United States would support them if they revolted against Mexican rule. Polk also

12–5
Thomas Corwin, Against the Mexican War (1847)

In this late-1872 evocation of the spirit of Manifest Destiny, Indians retreat westward as white settlers, guided by a diaphanously clad America, spread the benefits of American civilization.

©Christie's Images, Inc.

Following a brief siege, the Mexican fortress of Vera Cruz fell to the invading U.S. troops in March 1847. The way was now clear for Scott's army to march on Mexico City.

Courtesy Library of Congress

QUICK REVIEW

War with Mexico

- Polk sought a war that would give United States control of California.
- Mexico fought bravely but could not match American military.
- Treaty of Guadalupe Hidalgo (1848): Mexico gave up claim to Texas north of Rio Grande, Alta California, and New Mexico.

Taos Revolt   Uprising of Pueblo Indians in New Mexico that broke out in January 1847 over the imposition of American rule during the Mexican War; the revolt was crushed within a few weeks.

secretly ordered the U.S. Pacific naval squadron to seize California ports if war broke out with Mexico. Polk's final effort at peaceful expansion was the Slidell mission in November 1845. He sent John L. Slidell to Mexico City to offer $30 million to purchase California and New Mexico and to secure the Rio Grande boundary.

When Polk learned that the Mexican government had refused to receive Slidell, he set out to draw Mexico into a war that would result in the American acquisition of California. In early 1846, he ordered General Taylor to advance to the Rio Grande, deep in the disputed border region. Taylor blockaded the mouth of the Rio Grande (an aggressive act even if the river had been an international boundary) and built a fort on the northern bank across from the Mexican town of Matamoros. The Mexicans attacked and were repulsed on April 24.

Even before the news reached Washington, Polk had decided on war. Informed of the clash between Mexican and American troops in early May (it took ten days for the news to reach Washington), he sent a redrafted war message to Congress on May 9 asserting that Mexico "has invaded our territory, and shed American blood on American soil." Congress declared war on May 13, 1846.

The war was a stunning military success for the United States (see Map 13–4). An army sent west under Colonel Stephen W. Kearny occupied New Mexico. The conquest was relatively bloodless, because most of the local elite cooperated with the American forces. Sporadic resistance was largely confined to poorer Mexicans and the Pueblo Indians, who feared that their land would be confiscated. The largest uprising, ruthlessly suppressed, was the **Taos Revolt** in January 1847, led by Jesús Trujillo and Tomasito, a Pueblo chieftain.

Kearny's army then moved to Tucson and eventually linked up in southern California with pro-American rebels and U.S. forces sent ashore by the Pacific squadron. Despite the loss of its northern provinces, Mexico refused to concede defeat. After Taylor had established a secure defensive line in northeastern Mexico with a victory at Monterrey in September 1846 and repulsed a Mexican counterattack at Buena Vista in February 1847, Polk directed General Winfield Scott to invade central Mexico. Following an amphibious assault on Vera Cruz in March 1847, Scott captured Mexico City in September.

Peace talks concluded in the Treaty of Guadalupe Hidalgo, signed on February 2, 1848. Mexico surrendered its claim to Texas north of the Rio Grande and ceded Alta California and New Mexico (including present-day Arizona, Utah, and Nevada). The United States paid $15 million, assumed over $3 million in claims of American citizens against Mexico, and agreed to grant U.S. citizenship to Mexicans resident in its new territories.

Polk had gained his strategic goals, but the cost was 13,000 American lives (most from diseases such as measles and dysentery), 50,000 Mexican lives, and the poisoning of Mexican-American relations for generations. The war also, as will be seen in Chapter 14, heightened sectional tensions over slavery and weakened the political structure that was vital to preserving the Union.

MAP EXPLORATION

To explore an interactive version of this map, go to **http://www.prenhall.com/goldfield3/map13.4**

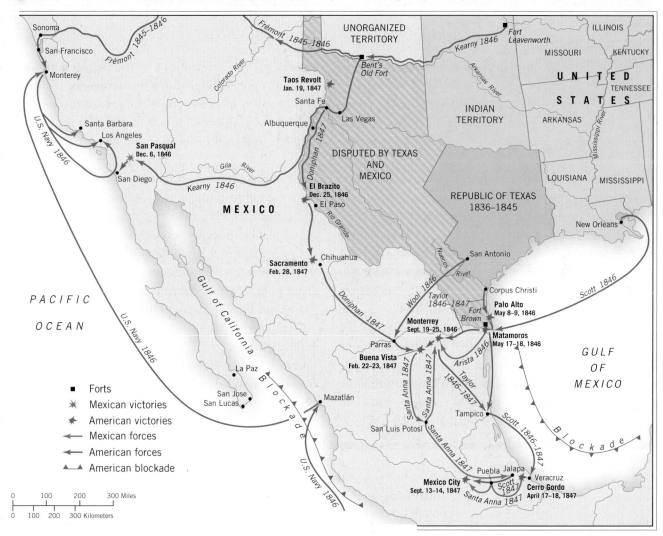

MAP 13–4   The Mexican War   Victories by General Zachary Taylor in northern Mexico secured the Rio Grande as the boundary between Texas and Mexico. Colonel Stephen Kearny's expedition won control of New Mexico, and reinforcements from Kearny assured the success of American troops landed by the Pacific Squadron in gaining Alta California for the United States. The success of General Winfield Scott's amphibious invasion at Vera Cruz and his occupation of Mexico City brought the war to an end.

WHY DID the United States feel the need to employ naval blockades to the east and west of Mexico?

CONCLUSION

Population pressure on overworked farms in the East impelled much of this westward migration, but by the 1840s, expansion had seemingly acquired a momentum all its own, one that increasingly rejected the claims of other peoples to the land. Far from being a process of peaceful, evolutionary, and democratic change, expansion involved the spread of slavery, violent confrontations, and the uprooting and displacement of native peoples. By 1850, the earlier notion of re-

GLOBAL PERSPECTIVES

The Great Famine in Ireland

"W e] saw sights that will never wholly leave the eyes that beheld them—cowering wretches, almost naked in the savage weather, prowling in turnip-fields, and endeavoring to grub up roots which had been left, but running to hide as the mail-coach rolled by . . . ; and sometimes I could see in front of the cottages little children leaning against a fence when the sun shone out—for they could not stand—their limbs fleshless, their bodies half naked, their faces bloated yet wrinkled, and of a pale greenish hue,—children who would never, it was too plain, grow up to be men and women."

Such were the scenes of hunger and despair witnessed by the Irish nationalist John Mitchel as he traveled through western Ireland in 1847. In the half-century before 1845, the Irish population doubled to 8 million. The high nutritional yield from the potato, up to three times as much per acre as grain, made this surge of population possible. The yield from one or two acres planted in potatoes enabled a family to survive, but just barely, on a small plot of land subject to ever greater subdivisions by the British landlord. When the potato fungus hit in the summer of 1845 and continued to spread in succeeding years, the roughly half of the population directly dependent on the potato lost its precarious margin for survival. Piecemeal British efforts at food relief were totally inadequate to cope with the crisis. Starvation and emigration carried off 3 million Irish in the next decade.

Similar agricultural crises, though none as disastrous, struck other impoverished, landless peasants across Europe in the middle of the nineteenth century. The result was an ongoing series of emigrations from poor, overpopulated rural areas to the United States and the industrial centers of Europe. These uprooted peasants furnished the cheap labor for the rapid industrialization of England and parts of the European continent. In the United States the proponents of Manifest Destiny welcomed them as adding to the numbers of the white race that would spread American values and liberties ever westward.

serving the trans-Mississippi West as a permanent Indian country had been abandoned. The derogatory stereotypes of Mexican-Americans that were a staple of both popular thought and expansionist ideology showed clearly that American control after the Mexican War would relegate Spanish-speaking people to second-class status. However misleading and false much of it was, the rhetoric of Manifest Destiny did highlight a central truth. Broad, popular support existed for expanding across the continent. As the Mexican War made clear, the United States was now unquestionably the dominant power in North America. The only serious threat to its dominance in the near future would come from inside, not outside, its domain.

Summary

The Agricultural Frontier The American population boomed in the 1800s; by 1850 about half of all Americans lived west of the Appalachian Mountains. The amount of available land, the economic opportunities associated with land ownership, and population pressure in the East propelled these migrants westward. New states in the Northwest joined the Union; while culturally tied to the Northeast, this area experienced migration from all sections of the country. Wheat was the major crop grown by Northern and Midwestern farmers; in the expanding Old Southwest it was cotton as slaveholding planters and independent farmers moved westward.

The Frontier of the Plains Indians Knowledge of the Trans-Mississippi West in the early 1800s was scanty and incorrect. The Great Plains were dominated by native

MANIFEST DESTINY AND AMERICAN FOREIGN POLICY

From the birth of the nation in 1776 to the U.S. war on terrorism in the wake of the attacks on September 11, 2001, a sense of mission has often imbued American foreign policy. Manifest Destiny was one expression of that sense of mission.

Thomas Paine, in *Common Sense,* declared that America had the "power to begin the world over again." The shining force of the American republic's free government, Paine believed, would redeem those suffering under despotic monarchies. According to the lofty rhetoric of Manifest Destiny, America would fulfill this divinely ordained mission by absorbing all the people of North America, at least those deemed capable of self-government, into the republic.

Manifest Destiny helped inspire the American surge to the Pacific and justify the Mexican War. But the war also provoked a contrary fear: Was the United States guilty of an imperial conquest that threatened liberty rather than promoting it? When expansionists pushed for the acquisition of all of Mexico, opponents objected. Mexicans, they claimed, were unfit to join Anglo-Saxon Americans in assuming the responsibilities of self-rule. At the same time, to subject Mexico to colonial rule would deny it the democratic liberty that Manifest Destiny promised. Consequently, the All-Mexico movement soon collapsed.

After cresting in the 1840s, Manifest Destiny lost its appeal. Expansionists in the late nineteenth century invoked Manifest Destiny to justify America's acquisition of an overseas empire following the Spanish-American War, but the new empire did not really fit the model. The advocates of Manifest Destiny had envisioned neighboring peoples in North America voluntarily joining the republic. According to critics, the new empire, on the contrary, rested on the once-despised imperialist doctrines of Old World Europe.

For former president Grover Cleveland, the annexation of the Hawaiian Islands in 1898 was "a perversion of our national mission," a signal that the nation was prepared to "abandon old landmarks and . . . follow the lights of monarchical hazards."

Cleveland and the other anti-imperialists lost the turn-of-the-century debate over whether the nation should acquire dependent possessions abroad. Still, by insisting, with Thomas Paine, that America's true mission must be to serve as the "model republic" for others to follow, they established the theme that characterized at least the public face of American diplomacy in the twentieth century. President Woodrow Wilson, for example, justified American intervention in World War I as a moral crusade to save democracy in Europe, and he sought in vain to bring the United States into a new international body, the League of Nations, designed to curb aggressive nations and prevent future wars. Wilsonian idealism infused the foreign policy of President Franklin D. Roosevelt during World War II and inspired the formation of the United Nations. Throughout the Cold War, America identified itself as the protector of democratic freedoms from the threat of international communism. In the post–Cold War world, Presidents George H. W. Bush and Bill Clinton cited the need to uphold human rights as grounds for U.S. military intervention abroad. President George W. Bush has gone further by claiming that the United States has the right to use preemptive force against any "evil power" deemed a threat to world peace and the future security of the United States.

Critics have charged that the mantle of human rights cloaks the pursuit of less noble U.S. interests in other nations. Whether or not this critique is valid, it is clear that as the twenty-first century dawns, any interventionist foreign policy must present itself in the idealistic terms of a special American mission if it is to have public support.

tribes, especially the Sioux in the north and Comanche in the south. The first Americans to venture into the West were the mountain men in the 1820s, followed by farm family pioneers from the Midwest trekking toward the Oregon Country and California on the overland trails in the 1840s.

The Mexican Borderlands Northern Mexico's borderlands were semiarid and thinly populated by diverse ethnic groups, the majority Native American. Mexico's hold on the region was weak; in the 1820s Americans, at the invitation of the Mexican government, began settling Texas. The eventual clash between the settlers and Mexico resulted in warfare and independence for Texas. Mexico's grip on California and New Mexico was weakened by the appearance of American traders who were soon followed by settlers. In Mexican-held Utah, the Mormons, led by Brigham Young, found a home free from the threat of persecution.

Politics, Expansion, and War President Polk's expansionist vision included adding California, Texas, New Mexico, and the Oregon Country to the United States. Americans believed in their Manifest Destiny to possess the continent; this philosophy was not welcomed by those occupants already living in the West. Conflict over the southern border of Texas provided an excuse for declaring war; the Mexican War was a one-sided conflict, and the American victory resulted in California and the present day Southwest being added to the United States.

IMAGE KEY

for pages 356–357

a. Cactus with thick green stem with thick glossy spines and a large pinkish coloured flower near the top of the plant.

b. Albert Bierstadt (1830–1902), "The Oregon Trail" (oil on canvas).

c. A long wooden pipe of the Mandan tribe drawn by Swiss artist Karl Bodmer.

d. The type of trunk often seen on the Oregon Trail.

e. A scale model of a Native American Plains Indian tepee, with an accompanying figure of a man for perspective.

f. Lakota shirt, c. 1850.

g. John Gast (Active 1870's). "American Progress", c. 1872. Depicts the diaphanously clad America floating over a variety of American people and animals heading westward. The emblematic figure carries a school book and a telegraph wire.

h. George Catlin, "Commanche Village Life," 1834.

i. Alfred Jacob Miller, "The Interior of Fort Laramie," 1858–60.

j. Nathaniel Currier, "General Winfield Scott at the Siege of Vera Cruz, March 1847."

REVIEW QUESTIONS

1. What accounted for the westward movement of Americans? How did the presence or absence of slavery affect developmental patterns in the new settlements?

2. How was the West of the Plains Indians transformed after 1830 as peoples migrated both within the region and into it from various directions? Why were the Sioux so powerful? How did they interact with other Native Americans and the U.S. government?

3. Who lived in the Mexican borderlands of the Southwest? Why was it so difficult for the Mexican government to maintain effective control of the region? What role did trade play in the American penetration of the Southwest?

4. What did Americans mean by Manifest Destiny? Why was territorial expansion so identified with the Democratic Party?

5. Who was responsible for the outbreak of the Mexican War? Were Mexicans the victims of American aggression? Why did the British make no effort to intervene?

6. How valid was the Sioux chief's indictment of the pretensions of white civilization as related to George Catlin?

KEY TERMS

Alamo (p. 372)
Californios (p. 373)
Claims clubs (p. 362)

Empresarios (p. 371)
Manifest Destiny (p. 359)
Mexican Cession of 1848 (p. 376)

Oregon Trail (p. 365)
Santa Fe Trail (p. 373)
Taos Revolt (p. 378)

WHERE TO LEARN MORE

◯ **Indian Pueblo Cultural Center, Albuquerque, New Mexico.** This center provides an excellent orientation to the culture, crafts, and community life of the Pueblo and southwestern Indians. It also includes much material on archaeological findings. Visit **www.indianpueblo.org/** for a calendar of events and an introduction to the history of the nineteen pueblos.

◯ **Museum Association of American Frontier and Fur Trade, Chadron, Nebraska.** The library in the museum holds archives, maps, and some photographs dealing with the western fur trade. In addition to an event calendar, its website, **www.stepintohistory.com/states/NE/Fur_Trade.htm**, provides links to other museums and preservation sites.

◯ **Indian Museum of North America, Crazy Horse, South Dakota.** This is one of the best sources for learning about the culture of the Teton Sioux and other American and Canadian tribes on the Great Plains. Holdings include outstanding examples of Indian art and artifacts. For information on exhibits, educational and cultural programs, and special collections of Native American art, go to **www.crazyhorse.org/museum.shtml**.

◯ **Living History Farms, Des Moines, Iowa.** This site includes several working farms, operated as they were at different points in the nineteenth century, as well as a mid-twentieth-century farm. A vintage town with a general store, church, and other buildings has also been re-created. Its website, **www.lhf.org/**, lists events and provides a look at four farm sites.

◯ **Scotts Bluff National Monument, Gering, Nebraska.** Scotts Bluff was a prominent landmark on the Oregon Trail, and the museum exhibits here have interpretive material on the trail and the western phase of expansion. Go to **www.nps.gov/scbl/** to print a park travel guide and to access a website devoted to the frontier photographer and artist William Henry Jackson.

◯ **Conner Prairie, Noblesville, Indiana.** The museum and historic area re-create a sense of life on the Indiana frontier during the period of the Old Northwest. **www.connerprairie.org**.

◯ **Fort Union National Monument, Watrous, New Mexico.** Fort Union was a nineteenth-century military post, and the holdings and exhibits in the museum relate to frontier military life and the Santa Fe Trail. For a printable travel guide and a history of the park that includes bibliographical aids, go to **www.nps.gov/foun/**.

 U.S. History Documents CD-ROM
For primary sources related to this chapter, refer to the document CD-ROM.

 www.prenhall.com/goldfield
For study resources related to this chapter, visit the *Companion Website*™.

14 The Politics of Sectionalism
1846–1861

CHAPTER HIGHLIGHTS

Slavery in the Territories As new territories were added to the United States, the issue of slavery became more pressing and the debate intensified. The admission of California to the Union triggered a political crisis. The resulting Compromise of 1850 pleased neither side. The publication of Uncle Tom's Cabin galvanized opposition to slavery in the North.

Political Realignment By the 1850s, all policies were interpreted in the light of their impact on slavery. Conflicts over slavery and immigration contributed to political realignment in the North, with the Republican Party emerging as a powerful new player. Events in Kansas and the Dred Scott decision further polarized the nation.

The Road to Disunion The South saw itself as increasingly victimized by the North. The election of Abraham Lincoln in 1860 was the signal for secession for many in the South. The attack on Fort Sumter was the spark that ignited the Civil War.

THE FAMOUS JARRETT & PALMER LONDON COMPY CONSOLIDATED WITH SLAVINS ORIGINAL AMERICAN TROUPE

UNCLE TOM'S CABIN.

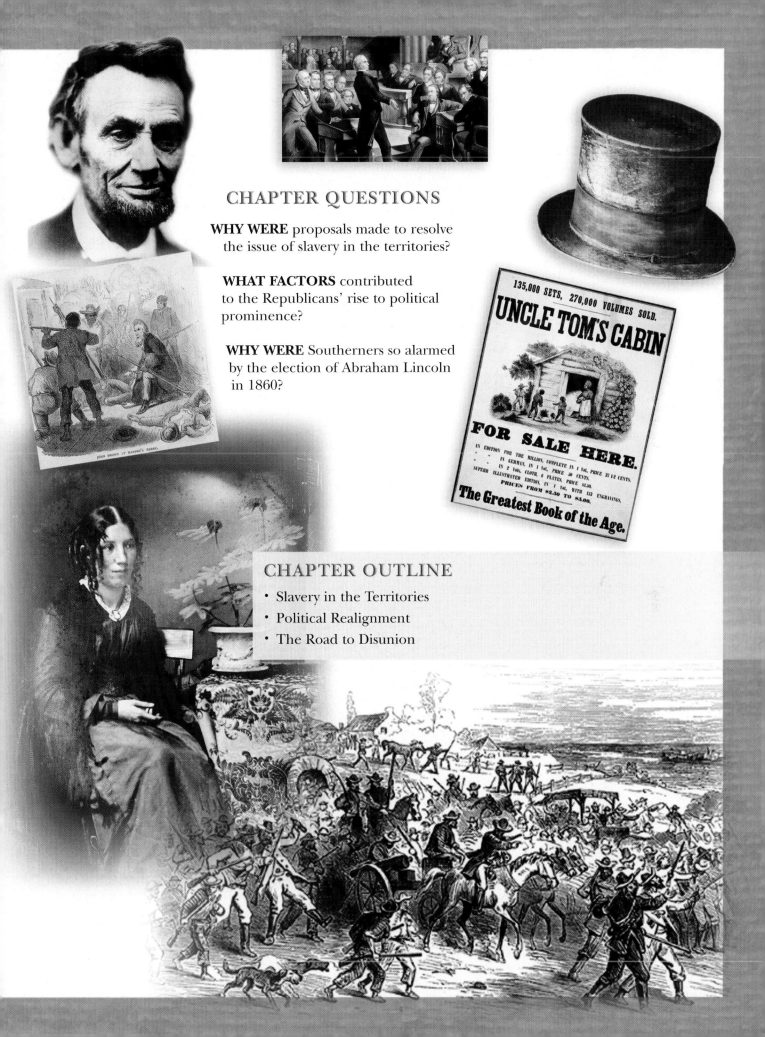

CHAPTER QUESTIONS

WHY WERE proposals made to resolve the issue of slavery in the territories?

WHAT FACTORS contributed to the Republicans' rise to political prominence?

WHY WERE Southerners so alarmed by the election of Abraham Lincoln in 1860?

135,000 SETS, 270,000 VOLUMES SOLD.

UNCLE TOM'S CABIN

FOR SALE HERE.

AN EDITION FOR THE MILLION, COMPLETE IN 1 Vol., PRICE 37 1-2 CENTS.
IN GERMAN, IN 1 Vol., PRICE 50 CENTS.
IN 2 Vols., CLOTH, 6 PLATES, PRICE $1.50.
SUPERB ILLUSTRATED EDITION, IN 1 Vol., WITH 153 ENGRAVINGS,
PRICES FROM $2.50 TO $5.00.

The Greatest Book of the Age.

CHAPTER OUTLINE

* Slavery in the Territories
* Political Realignment
* The Road to Disunion

IMAGE KEY
for pages 384–385 is on page 416.

December 16, 1852
My Dear Madam,

So you want to know what sort of woman I am! Well, if this is any object, you shall have statistics free of charge. To begin, then, I am a little bit of a woman, somewhat more than forty, about as thin and dry as a pinch of snuff, never very much to look at in my best days and looking like a used up article now.

I was married when I was twenty-five years old to a man rich in Greek and Hebrew and Latin and Arabic, and alas, rich in nothing else. . . . But then I was abundantly furnished with wealth of another sort. I had two little curly headed twin daughters to begin with and my stock in this line has gradually increased, till I have been the mother of seven children, the most beautiful and the most loved of whom lies buried near my Cincinnati residence. It was at his dying bed and at his grave that I learned what a poor slave mother may feel when her child is torn away from her. In those depths of sorrow which seemed to me immeasurable, it was my only prayer to God that such anguish might not be suffered in vain. There were circumstances about his death of such peculiar bitterness, of what seemed almost cruel suffering that I felt that I could never be consoled for it unless this crushing of my own heart might enable me to work out some great good to others.

I allude to this here because I have often felt that much that is in that book had its root in the awful scenes and bitter sorrow of that summer. It has left now, I trust, no trace on my mind except a deep compassion for the sorrowful, especially for mothers who are separated from their children. . . .

This horror, this nightmare abomination! Can it be in my country! It lies like lead on my heart, it shadows my life with sorrow; the more so that I feel, as for my own brothers, for the South, and am pained by every horror I am obliged to write, as one who is forced by some awful oath to disclose in court some family disgrace. . . .

Yours affectionately,
H. B. Stowe

Harriet Beecher Stowe to Eliza Cabot Follen, December 16, 1852; from Jeanne Boydston, Mary Kelley, and Anne Margolis, *The Limits of Sisterhood* (Chapel Hill: University of North Carolina Press, 1988), 178–180.

HARRIET BEECHER STOWE, in her letter to the poet and fellow abolitionist Eliza Cabot Follen, revealed how being a wife and a mother had influenced her perception of slavery and inspired her writing. The deep piety and self-effacement expressed in the letter, as well as her transparent grief over the loss of her son, typified mid-nineteenth-century correspondence between women.

Slavery was an abstract concept to most white northerners at the time. Stowe personalized it in a way that made them see it as an institution that did not just oppress black people but also destroyed families and debased well-meaning Christian masters.

Stowe had grown up in a family of evangelical Protestant ministers and abolitionists. Her father, Lyman Beecher, was a prominent evangelical reformer. All six of his sons became ministers. Two of his three daughters, Catharine and Harriet, became accomplished writers. In Beecher's view, personal and societal salvation were closely connected, a principle that is apparent in Harriet's letter.

As slavery took on a personal and tragic meaning for Stowe, so it would move from being just another political issue to a moral crusade. Stowe's personal journey transformed it into a political passion; for the millions who read her book, the political became personal. Yet the anguish she expressed in her writing and the outrage it generated among her readers was hardly prefigured when a relatively obscure congressman from Pennsylvania stepped forward in 1846 with a modest proposal that not only placed slavery front and center as a national political issue, but would shake the Union to its very core.

Slavery was not, of course, a new political issue: the debate over the Missouri Compromise, the nullification controversy, and the battles in Congress over abolitionist mailings and petitions had roiled the political waters for nearly a generation prior to 1846. But after 1846, the clashes between northern and southern congressmen over issues relating to slavery became more frequent and more difficult to resolve. In the coming years, several developments, including white southerners' growing consciousness of themselves as a minority, the mixture of political issues with religious questions, and the rise of the Republican Party, would aggravate sectional antagonism. But the flash point that first brought it to the fore was the issue of slavery in the territories acquired from Mexico.

SLAVERY IN THE TERRITORIES

Whatever its boundaries over the years, the West symbolized the hopes and dreams of white Americans. It was the region of fresh starts, of possibilities. To exclude slavery from the western territories was to exclude white southerners from pursuing their vision of the American dream. Exclusion, an Alabamian declared, meant "that a free citizen of Massachusetts was a better man and entitled to more privileges than a free citizen of Alabama." Northern politicians disagreed. They argued that exclusion preserved equality, the equality of all white men and women to live and work without competition from slave labor or rule by despotic slaveholders. From the late 1840s until 1861, northern and southern leaders attempted to fashion a solution to the problem of slavery in the territories. Four proposals dominated the debate:

- Outright exclusion
- Extension of the Missouri Compromise line to the Pacific
- Popular sovereignty, allowing the residents of a territory to decide the issue
- Protection of the property of slaveholders (meaning their right to own slaves) even if few lived in the territory

The first major debate on these proposals occurred during the early days of the Mexican War and culminated in the Compromise of 1850.

WHY WERE proposals made to resolve the issue of slavery in the territories?

Chronology

1846	Wilmot Proviso is submitted to Congress but is defeated.
1848	Gold is discovered in California.
	Whig Party candidate Zachary Taylor defeats Democrat Lewis Cass and Free-Soiler.
	Martin Van Buren for the presidency.
	Revolutions in Europe; publication of Karl Marx and Friedrich Engels's *Communist Manifesto*.
1850	California applies for statehood.
	President Taylor dies; Vice President Millard Fillmore succeeds him.
	Compromise of 1850 is passed.
1851	Harriet Beecher Stowe publishes *Uncle Tom's Cabin*.
1852	Democrat Franklin Pierce is elected president in a landslide over Whig candidate Winfield Scott.
	Whig Party disintegrates.
1853	National Black Convention convenes in Rochester, New York, to demand repeal of the Fugitive Slave Act.
	Crimean War erupts between Russia and Turkey over Russian demand to protect Christian shrines in Palestine; soon engulfs Britain and France eventually leads to the unification of Germany and Italy.
1854	Ostend Manifesto is issued.
	Kansas-Nebraska Act repeals the Missouri Compromise.
	Know-Nothing and Republican parties are formed.
1855	Civil war erupts in "Bleeding Kansas."
	William Walker attempts a takeover of Nicaragua.
1856	"Sack of Lawrence" occurs in Kansas; John Brown makes a retaliatory raid at Pottawatomie Creek.
	Democratic congressman Preston Brooks of South Carolina canes Massachusetts senator Charles Sumner in the U.S. Senate.

	Democrat James Buchanan is elected president over Republican John C. Frémont and American (Know-Nothing) candidate Millard Fillmore.
1857	Supreme Court issues *Dred Scott* decision.
	Kansas territorial legislature passes the proslavery Lecompton Constitution.
	Panic of 1857 begins.
1858	Senatorial candidates Abraham Lincoln and Stephen A. Douglas hold series of debates in Illinois.
1859	John Brown's Raid fails at Harpers Ferry, Virginia.
1860	Constitutional Union Party forms.
	Democratic Party divides into northern and southern factions.
	Republican candidate Abraham Lincoln is elected president over southern Democratic candidate John C. Breckinridge, northern Democratic candidate Stephen A. Douglas, and Constitutional Unionist candidate John Bell.
	South Carolina secedes from the Union.
1861	The rest of the Lower South secedes from the Union.
	Crittenden Plan and Tyler's Washington peace conference fail.
	Jefferson Davis assumes presidency of the Confederate States of America.
	Lincoln is inaugurated.
	Fort Sumter is bombarded; Civil War begins.
	Several Upper South states secede.
	Tsar Alexander II of Russia frees the serfs.

Wilmot Proviso The amendment offered by Pennsylvania Democrat David Wilmot in 1846 which stipulated that "as an express and fundamental condition to the acquisition of any territory from the Republic of Mexico . . . neither slavery nor involuntary servitude shall ever exist in any part of said territory."

THE WILMOT PROVISO

In August 1846, David Wilmot, a Pennsylvania Democrat, offered an amendment to an appropriations bill for the Mexican War. The language of the **Wilmot Proviso** stipulated that "as an express and fundamental condition to the acquisition of any territory from the Republic of Mexico . . . neither slavery nor involuntary servitude shall ever exist in any part of said territory." The proviso did not apply to Texas, which had become a state before the war began.

Wilmot explained that he wanted only to preserve the territories for "the sons of toil, of my own race and own color." By thus linking the exclusion of slavery in the territories to freedom for white people, he hoped to generate support across the

North, regardless of party, and even in some areas of the Upper South. Linking freedom for white people to the exclusion of slaves infuriated southerners. It implied that the mere proximity of slavery was degrading and that white southerners were therefore a degraded people, unfit to join other Americans in the territories.

Northern lawmakers, a majority in the House of Representatives, passed more than 50 versions of the proviso between 1846 and 1850. In the Senate, however, where each state had equal representation, the proviso was consistently rejected and never became law. Religious differences also sharpened the sectional conflict over the proviso. By the late 1840s, growing numbers of northern evangelicals advocated political action. During the debate on the Wilmot Proviso, a Boston minister wrote, "The great problem for the Christian world now to accomplish is to effect a closer union between religion and politics. . . . We must make men to do good and be good." Southern evangelicals recoiled from such mixing of church and state, charging northerners with abandoning the basic tenets of evangelical Christianity.

THE ELECTION OF 1848

Both Democrats and Whigs wanted to avoid identification with either side of the Wilmot Proviso controversy, and they selected their 1848 presidential candidates accordingly. The Democrats nominated Michigan senator Lewis Cass, a party stalwart, who understood the destructive potential of the slavery issue. In 1847, he suggested that territorial residents, not Congress, should decide slavery's fate. This solution, **popular sovereignty,** had a do-it-yourself charm: Keep the politicians out of it, and let the people decide. Cass was deliberately ambiguous, however, on when the people should decide. The timing was important. If residents could decide only when applying for statehood, slavery would be legal up to that point. The ambiguity aroused more fears than it allayed.

The Whigs were silent on the slavery issue. They selected General Zachary Taylor of Mexican War fame. If the Whigs were looking for someone with no political record, they found him in the squat and craggy-faced Taylor. Taylor belonged to no party and had never voted. His background provided some clues to his views. He lived in Louisiana in the Lower South, he owned a hundred-slave plantation, and his now-deceased daughter had been married to Jefferson Davis, Mississippi's staunch proslavery senator.

Taylor's background disturbed many antislavery northern Whigs who, along with remnants of the old Liberty Party and a scattering of northern Democrats, bolted their parties and formed the Free-Soil Party. Its slogan, "Free soil, free speech, free labor, free men," was a catalog of white liberties that the South had allegedly violated over the previous decade.

The Free-Soilers' appeal centered on their opposition to slave labor in the territories. Free labor, they believed, could not compete with bonded labor. The party nominated former president Martin Van Buren.

Chalking up one out of seven northern votes, Van Buren ran strongly enough in 11 of the 15 northern states to deny the winning candidate in those states a majority of the votes cast. But he could not overcome Taylor's strength in the South. Taylor was elected, giving the nation its first president from the Lower South.

THE GOLD RUSH

Events in distant California, recently acquired from Mexico, would leave Taylor little time to savor his victory. By the time he took office in March 1849, a gold rush was under way there. Through 1849 and 1850, more than 100,000 hopefuls flooded

Popular Sovereignty   A solution to the slavery crisis suggested by Michigan senator Lewis Cass by which territorial residents, not Congress, would decide slavery's fate.

The California Gold Rush attracted a multi-national population. Here, Chinese miners relax at their camp. The placid scene masks the occasionally-violent confrontations between different racial and ethnic groups drawn to the gold fields.

Courtesy of Elliot Koeppel

into California. Anarchy and geology combined to form a volatile mixture in appropriately named settlements like Hangtown, Gouge Eye, and Whiskeytown. One unfortunate miner wrote back east to his family in 1850: "I take this opportunity of writing these few lines to you hoping to find you in good health. Me and Charley is sentenced to be hung at five o/clock for robbery. Give my best to Frank and Sam."

The rush also attracted migrants from around the world. California soon became a polyglot empire of Chinese, Chileans, Mexicans, Irish, Germans, and Turks. Blacks, mostly slaves brought by southern masters, also roamed the gold fields.

Almost overnight, San Francisco was transformed from a modest port to a cosmopolitan metropolis. By the mid-1850s, a half-billion dollars in gold money had passed through the city, and a good bit of it stayed. The image of California, and of the West in general, as wild or golden, dates from this era. But the romance of California and the wealth it generated loomed more troubling back east as the territory filled up with people in 1849. For the western dream would soon become ensnared in the conflict over slavery.

THE COMPROMISE OF 1850

When the California territory's new residents began asking for statehood and drafted a state constitution, the document contained no provision for slavery. The constitution reflected antiblack rather than antislavery sentiment. If Congress accepted the residents' request for statehood, California would enter the Union as a free state. The Union at the time consisted of 15 free states and 15 slave states. The admission of California would tip the balance and give free states a majority in the Senate. California, with its rapidly growing population, would also add to the 61 vote majority the North enjoyed in the House of Representatives. New Mexico appeared poised to follow suit and enter the Union as the seventeenth free state. Southerners saw their political power slipping away. Northern leaders saw an opportunity to stop the extension of slavery and reduce southern influence in the federal government.

When Congress confronted the issue of California statehood in December 1849, partisans on both sides began marshaling forces for what promised to be a long and bitter struggle. No one, at first, knew where Taylor stood. He supported, it turned out, a version of popular sovereignty and favored allowing California and the other territories acquired from Mexico to decide the slavery issue for themselves. Under normal circumstances, the residents of a new territory organized a territorial government under the direction of Congress. When the territory's population approached 30,000 or so, residents could draft a constitution and petition Congress for statehood. Taylor proposed bypassing the territorial stage, and congressional involvement in it, and having California and New Mexico admitted as states directly. The result would be to bring both into the Union as free states.

Taylor was a nationalist and a strong believer in Manifest Destiny. He did not oppose slavery, but he abhorred the slavery issue because it threatened his vision of a continental empire. Southerners were certain to object strongly. But the president had a chilling message for them: "Whatever dangers may threaten [the Union] I shall stand by it and maintain it in its integrity."

Southerners resisted Taylor's plan, and Congress deadlocked on the territorial issue. Henry Clay then stepped forward with his last great compromise. To break the impasse, Clay urged that Congress should take four steps:

- Admit California as a free state, as its residents clearly preferred.
- Allow the residents of the New Mexico and Utah territories to decide the slavery issue for themselves.
- End the slave trade in the District of Columbia.
- Pass a new fugitive slave law to enforce the constitutional provision stating that a person "held to Service or Labor in one state . . . escaping into another . . . shall be delivered upon Claim of the party to whom such Service or Labor may be due."

Clay's proposal provoked a historic Senate debate that began in February 1850, featuring America's three most prominent statesmen, Clay, Calhoun, and Daniel Webster. Calhoun argued that the compromise did not resolve the slavery issue to the South's satisfaction, and he proposed to give southerners in Congress the right to veto legislation as a way to safeguard their minority rights. Webster stood up to support the compromise, at deep political peril to himself. His Massachusetts constituents detested the fugitive slave provision, which gave southern slaveholders the right to "invade" northern states to reclaim escaped slaves.

After tumultuous deliberation that lasted into the summer of 1850, the Senate rejected the compromise. President Taylor, who had vowed to veto any compromise, died unexpectedly of a stomach ailment after overindulging in cherries and milk in the hot sun at a July 4 celebration in Washington. Vice President Millard Fillmore, a pro-Clay New Yorker, assumed the presidency after Taylor's death. Compared with Taylor, who had stormed around the White House daring southerners to attempt secession, Fillmore was a back-room man. Fillmore let it be known that he favored Clay's package and would sign it if passed.

Although the Senate had rejected the compromise, Illinois senator Stephen A. Douglas kept it alive. Douglas envisioned an urban, industrial West linked to the East by a vast railroad network eventually extending to the Pacific. Above all, Douglas professed an unbending nationalism. To him, according to a biographer, "the Union was sacred, the symbol of all human progress."

Like Webster, Douglas feared for the Union if the compromise failed. Realizing that it would never pass as a package, he proposed to break it up into its components and hold a separate vote on each. With a handful of senators voting for all parts, and with different sectional blocs supporting one provision or another, Douglas engineered a majority for the compromise, and Fillmore signed it.

The **Compromise of 1850** (see Map 14-1) was not a compromise in the sense of each opposing side consenting to certain terms desired by the other. The North gained California but would have done so in any case. Southern leaders looked to the West and saw no slave territories awaiting statehood. They gained the **Fugitive Slave Act,** which reinforced their right to seize and return to bondage slaves who had fled to free territory, but it was slight consolation. Few slave owners from the Lower South would bear the expense and uncertainty of chasing an escaped slave into free territory. And the North's hostile reception to the law made southerners doubt its commitment to the compromise.

14–4
A Dying Statesman Speaks Out Against the Compromise of 1850

Compromise of 1850 The four-step compromise which admitted California as a free state, allowed the residents of the New Mexico and Utah territories to decide the slavery issue for themselves, ended the slave trade in the District of Columbia, and passed a new fugitive slave law to enforce the constitutional provision stating that a slave escaping into a free state shall be delivered back to the owner.

Fugitive Slave Act Law, part of the Compromise of 1850, that required the authorities in the North to assist Southern slave catchers and return runaway slaves to their owners.

MAP EXPLORATION
To explore an interactive version of this map, go to **http://www.prenhall.com/goldfield3/map14.1**

MAP 14–1   The Compromise of 1850   Given the unlikely prospect that any of the western territories would opt for slavery, the compromise sealed the South's minority status in the Union.

WHAT WERE the results of the Compromise of 1850, and how did the country react to the news of the Compromise?

WHERE TO LEARN MORE

The Underground Railroad Freedom
Center, Cincinnati, Ohio
www.undergroundrailroad.org

RESPONSE TO THE FUGITIVE SLAVE ACT

Nonetheless, except for a few publicized cases, northern authorities typically cooperated with southern slave owners to help them retrieve their runaway property. The effect of the Fugitive Slave Act on public opinion, however, was to polarize North and South even further.

The strongest reaction to the act was in the black communities of the urban North. The Fugitive Slave Act brought the danger of slavery much closer to home. No black person was safe under the new law. Mistaken identity, the support of federal courts for slaveholders' claims, and the presence of informants made reenslavement a real possibility. The lives that 400,000 black northerners had constructed, often with great difficulty, appeared suddenly uncertain.

Black northerners formed associations to protect each other and repel, violently if necessary, any attempt to capture and reenslave them. Boston's black leaders created the League of Freedom. Black Chicagoans organized the Liberty Association, with teams assigned to "patrol the city, spying for possible slave-hunters." Similar associations appeared in Cleveland and Cincinnati. Some black people left the United States. As many as 20,000 African Americans may have found their way across the border into Canada during the 1850s in response to fears over capture and reenslavement. Another solution was proposed by Martin Delany, a prominent black abolitionist. He argued for the establishment of a black homeland at several potential sites in Central or South America or on the west coast of Africa. "Go we must," he wrote in 1852. "To remain here in North America and be crushed to the earth in vassalage and degradation, we never will."

During the early 1850s, black northerners gathered in conventions to demand the repeal of the Fugitive Slave Act. Frederick Douglass convened the National Black Convention in Rochester, New York, in July 1853, at which he established a national council of black leaders to address issues of political and civil rights. Although the council was short-lived, it reflected a growing militancy. How much of this militancy filtered down to slaves in the South is difficult to say. Slaveholders noted an increase in black resistance during the early 1850s. A white Virginian noted in 1852 that "it is useless to disguise the fact, its truth is undeniable, that a greater degree of insubordination has been manifested by the negro population within the last few months, than at any previous period in our history as a state."

UNCLE TOM'S CABIN

Sectional controversy over the Fugitive Slave Act was relatively modest compared to the firestorm ignited by abolitionist writer Harriet Beecher Stowe with the publication of a novel about southern slavery. *Uncle Tom's Cabin*, which first appeared in serial form in 1851, moved many northern white people from the sidelines of the sectional conflict to more active participation.

At the beginning of *Uncle Tom's Cabin*, a Kentucky slave owner is reluctantly forced by financial ruin to sell some of his slaves. Among them are the son of two mulatto slaves, George and Eliza Harris, and an older slave, Tom. Eliza escapes across the ice-choked Ohio River, clutching her son to her breast as slave catchers and their bloodhounds pursue them. Tom submits to sale to a New Orleans master. When that master dies, Tom is sold to Simon Legree, who owns a plantation on the Red River in Louisiana. Legree is vicious and sadistic—the only major slaveholding character in the book whom Stowe portrays in this manner. Tom, a devout Christian, remains loyal and obedient until Legree asks him to whip another slave. When Tom refuses, Legree beats him to death.

Aiming to evoke strong emotions in the reader, Stowe offered not abstractions but characters who seemed real. The broken family, the denial of freedom, and the Christian martyr were emotional themes. The presence of mulattoes in the book testified to widespread interracial and extramarital sex, which northerners, then in the midst of a religious revival, viewed as an abhorrent sin destructive to family life. And the depiction of southern masters struggling unsuccessfully with their consciences focused public attention on how slavery subverted Christianity.

Stowe's book gave slavery a face; it changed people's moral perceptions about the institution in an era of deep Protestant piety; it was a Sermon on the Mount

CAUTION!!
COLORED PEOPLE
OF BOSTON, ONE & ALL,

You are hereby respectfully CAUTIONED and advised, to avoid conversing with the
Watchmen and Police Officers
of Boston,

For since the recent ORDER OF THE MAYOR & ALDERMEN, they are empowered to act as
KIDNAPPERS
AND
Slave Catchers,

And they have already been actually employed in KIDNAPPING, CATCHING, AND KEEPING SLAVES. Therefore, if you value your LIBERTY, and the *Welfare of the Fugitives* among you, *Shun* them in every possible manner, as so many *HOUNDS* on the track of the most unfortunate of your race.

Keep a Sharp Look Out for KIDNAPPERS, and have TOP EYE open.
APRIL 24, 1851.

The Fugitive Slave Act threatened the freedom of escaped slaves living in the North, and even of free black northerners. This notice, typical of warnings posted in northern cities, urged Boston's African American population to take precautions.
Courtesy Library of Congress

14–2
Harriet Beecher Stowe, from *Uncle Tom's Cabin* (1852)

Harriet Beecher Stowe, the daughter of a prominent Northern evangelist, catapulted to international fame with the publication of *Uncle Tom's Cabin*. The novel helped raise the debate over slavery from a political to a moral level.

Southworth, Albert Sands (1811–1894), and Hawes, Josiah Johnson (1808–1901), Harriet Beecher Stowe. Daguerreotype, 4½ 3½ in. The Metropolitan Museum of Art, Gift of I. N. Phelps Stokes, Edward S. Hawes, Alice May Hawes, and Marion Augusta Hawes, 1937

for a generation of northerners seeking witness for their Christianity and a crusade on behalf of their faith. It transformed abolitionism, bringing the movement, whose extreme rhetoric many northerners had previously viewed with disapproval, to the edge of respectability.

For southerners, *Uncle Tom's Cabin* was a damnable lie, a political tract disguised as literature. One southerner denounced the book as a "criminal prostitution of the high functions of the imagination to the pernicious intrigues of sectional animosity." Some Southerners retaliated with crude plays and books of their own. In these versions of slavery, no slave families were broken up, no slaves were killed, and all masters were models of Christian behavior.

Black northerners embraced *Uncle Tom's Cabin*. Frederick Douglass's National Black Convention resolved that the book was "a work plainly marked by the finger of God" on behalf of black people. Some black people hoped that the book's popularity would highlight the hypocrisy of white Northerners who were quick to perceive evil in the South but were often blind to discrimination against African Americans in the North.

THE ELECTION OF 1852

While the nation was reading and reacting to *Uncle Tom's Cabin,* a presidential election campaign took place. The Compromise of 1850 had divided the Whigs deeply. Although the Whigs nominated Mexican War hero and Virginian Winfield Scott for president, few southern Whigs viewed the nonslaveholding general as a friend of their region.

The Democratic Party entered the campaign more united. Despite reservations, the northern and southern wings of the party both announced their support for the Compromise of 1850. Southern Democrats viewed the party's nominee, Franklin Pierce of New Hampshire, as safe on the slavery issue despite his New England heritage. Pierce satisfied northerners as a nationalist devoted to the idea of Manifest Destiny. His service in the Mexican War and his good looks and charm won over doubters from both sections.

Given the disarray of the Whigs and the relative unity of the Democrats, the election results were predictable. Pierce won overwhelmingly with 254 electoral votes to Scott's 42. But Pierce's landslide victory could not obscure the deep fissures in the American party system. The Whigs were finished as a national party. And the Democrats, despite their electoral success, emerged frayed from the election. In the Lower South, conflicts within the party between supporters and opponents of the Compromise of 1850 had overshadowed the contests between Democrats and Whigs.

POLITICAL REALIGNMENT

WHAT FACTORS contributed to the Republican's rise to political prominence?

*F*ranklin Pierce hoped to duck the slavery issue by focusing on Young America's dreams of empire. Americans were still susceptible to nationalist fervor. For all their sectional, religious, ethnic, and racial differences, they shared a common language and political institutions. New technologies like the railroad and the telegraph were working to bind them together physically as well.

The country was optimistic, and its possibilities for advancement seemed limitless. But President Pierce's attempts to forge national sentiment around an aggressive foreign policy failed. And his administration's inept handling of a new territorial controversy in Kansas forced him to confront the slavery debate. As Missouri senator Thomas Hart Benton, a Democrat, had realized during the debates over the Wilmot Proviso in 1848, no matter what policies a president pursued, Congress and the American people would interpret them in the light of their impact, real or potential, on slavery.

Franklin Pierce lacked the skilled leadership the times demanded. Troubled by alcoholism, worried about his chronically ill wife, and grief-stricken over the death of three young sons, Pierce presided weakly over the nation and increasingly deferred to proslavery interests.

YOUNG AMERICA'S FOREIGN MISADVENTURES

Pierce's first missteps occurred in pursuit of Young America's foreign ambitions. The administration turned a greedy eye toward Spanish-ruled Cuba, just 90 miles off the coast of Florida. Spanish authorities were harassing American merchants exporting sugar from Cuba and the American naval vessels protecting the merchants' ships. Southerners supported an aggressive Cuba policy, seeing the island as a possible new slave state. And nationalists saw great virtue in replacing what they perceived as a despotic colonial regime with a democratic government under the guidance of the United States.

In October 1854, three American diplomats met in Ostend, Belgium, to discuss Cuba. The group composed a document on Cuba called the **Ostend Manifesto** that claimed that the island belonged "naturally to the great family of states of which the Union is the Providential Nursery." The implication was that Spain's control of Cuba was unnatural. The United States would offer to buy Cuba from Spain, but if Spain refused to sell, the authors warned, "by every law, human and Divine, we shall be justified in wresting it from Spain."

The Ostend Manifesto caused an uproar and embarrassed the Pierce administration when it became public. Other nations quickly denounced it as a "buccaneering document" and a "highwayman's plea." It provoked a similar reaction in the United States, raising suspicions in the North that the South was willing to provoke a war with Spain to expand the number of slaveholding states.

Meanwhile, the Pierce administration's aggressive foreign policy encouraged private citizens to pursue Young America's goals in Latin America. Such was the case of self-styled "General" William Walker and his private army, "the immortals." Walker moved from Tennessee to California, and in 1853, after amassing arms and men, he invaded Mexican-owned Baja California and proclaimed a republic. Before he could establish a permanent government and legalize slavery, the Mexicans tossed him out. Undaunted, Walker and his followers plunged into the civil war that had erupted in Nicaragua in May 1855. He gained control of the country by the end of the year, proclaimed himself president, and invited southern slaveholders to take up residence. The Pierce administration immediately recognized Walker's government; the people of Nicaragua did not. Backed by other Central American countries, they fought to oust the little general. Congressional pressure forced the Pierce administration to cool its support for Walker, and his financial resources dried up. His foes overthrew him in 1857, and he fled Nicaragua on an American naval vessel. After two more abortive attempts at conquest in Central America, he was executed by a Honduran firing squad in 1860.

Ostend Manifesto   Message sent by U.S. envoys to President Pierce from Ostend, Belgium, in 1854, stating that the United States had a "divine right" to wrest Cuba from Spain.

These and other setbacks frustrated Pierce's hope that foreign adventures would mute the angry debate over slavery. Instead, the proslavery overtones of the Cuban fiasco and Walker's open courting of southern support sharpened sectional conflict. While Pierce fumbled in the area of foreign policy, Senator Stephen A. Douglas of Illinois was developing a national project that also promised to draw the country together, the construction of a transcontinental railroad.

STEPHEN DOUGLAS'S RAILROAD PROPOSAL

Douglas, the supreme nationalist, understood that a transcontinental railroad would tie the nation together. Not only would it physically link East and West, it would also help spread American democracy. In short, a transcontinental railroad made good economic and political sense.

Douglas had in mind a transcontinental route extending westward from Chicago through the Nebraska Territory. Unfortunately for his plans, Indians already occupied this region, many of them on land the U.S. government had set aside as Indian Territory and barred to white settlement. Once again, and not for the last time, the federal government responded by reneging on earlier promises and forcing Indians to move. With the Indian "obstacle" removed, Douglas sought congressional approval to establish a government for the Nebraska Territory.

THE KANSAS-NEBRASKA ACT

Douglas's Kansas-Nebraska Bill split the Nebraska Territory into two territories, Kansas and Nebraska, with the implicit understanding that Kansas would become a slave state and Nebraska a free state. Consistent with Douglas's belief in popular sovereignty, it left the actual decision on slavery to the residents of the territories. But because it allowed southerners to bring slaves into an area formerly closed to slavery, it repealed the Missouri Compromise.

Northerners of all parties were outraged. The Missouri Compromise had endured for 34 years as a basis for sectional accord on slavery. Now it was threatened, northern leaders charged, by the South's unquenchable desire to spread slavery and expand its political power. Using language indicative of the way religious and conspiratorial imagery had infected political debate, transforming it into a contest of good against evil, of liberty against oppression, they said it was "a gross violation of a sacred pledge," "a criminal betrayal of precious rights," and "part and parcel of an atrocious plot" to make a free territory a "dreary region of despotism, inhabited by masters and slaves." President Pierce, however, backed the bill, assuring the support of enough northern Democrats to secure it a narrow victory. The **Kansas-Nebraska Act** was law.

In August 1854, shortly after Congress adjourned, Douglas left Washington for his home in Chicago, to rest and mend political fences. He did not enjoy a pleasant journey home. "I could travel," he later recalled, ". . . by the light of my own effigy on every tree we passed." Arriving in Chicago, he addressed a large hostile crowd outside his hotel balcony. As he departed, he lost his temper and blurted, "It is now Sunday morning. I'll go to church; you can go to hell."

"BLEEDING KANSAS"

Because of its fertile soil, favorable climate, and location adjacent to the slave state of Missouri, Kansas was the most likely of the new territories to support slavery. As a result, both southerners and antislavery northerners began an intensive drive to recruit settlers and establish a majority there.

WHERE TO LEARN MORE

Adair Cabin and John Brown Museum, John Brown Memorial Park, Osawatomie, Kansas
www.kshs.org/places/adair.htm

Kansas-Nebraska Act Law passed in 1854 creating the Kansas and Nebraska Territories but leaving the question of slavery open to residents, thereby repealing the Missouri Compromise.

In March 1855, proslavery forces, relying on the ineligible votes of Missouri residents, fraudulently elected a territorial legislature. This legislature promptly passed a series of harsh measures, including a law mandating the death penalty for aiding a fugitive slave and another making it a felony to question slaveholding in Kansas. For good measure, the proslavery majority expelled the few free-staters elected to the assembly. In response, free-staters established their own government in Topeka and vowed to make Kansas white.

Armed Missourians cross the border into Kansas to vote illegally for a proslavery government in 1855.

The Newberry Library

A sporadic civil war erupted in Kansas in November 1855 and reached a climax in the spring of 1856. Journalists dubbed the conflict **"Bleeding Kansas."** On May 21, a group of proslavery officials attacked the free-state stronghold of Lawrence, subjecting it to a heavy artillery barrage. No one was killed, but the town suffered substantial damage. Eastern newspapers, exaggerating the incident, called it "the sack of Lawrence." Three days later, antislavery agitator John Brown, originally from Connecticut, went with several sympathizers to Pottawatomie Creek south of Lawrence in search of proslavery settlers. Armed with razor-sharp broadswords, they split the skulls and hacked the bodies of five men.

Kansans were not the only Americans bleeding over slavery. Five days before the "sack of Lawrence," Massachusetts senator Charles Sumner delivered a long-winded diatribe, "The Crime Against Kansas," full of personal insults against several southerners, especially elderly South Carolina senator Andrew P. Butler. Two days later, Butler's cousin, South Carolina congressman Preston Brooks, entered the mostly vacant Senate chamber, where Sumner sat working on a speech. Seeking to defend his cousin's honor, Brooks raised his walking cane and beat Sumner over the head. Sumner recovered but did not return to the Senate for over three years. His empty chair offered northerners' mute confirmation of their growing conviction that southerners were despotic. Southerners showered Brooks with new walking canes.

KNOW-NOTHINGS AND REPUBLICANS: RELIGION AND POLITICS

The Sumner incident, along with the Kansas-Nebraska Bill and the civil war in Kansas, further polarized North and South, widening sectional divisions within the political parties. From 1854 to 1856, northerners moved into new political parties that altered the national political landscape and sharpened sectional conflict.

Although the slavery issue was mainly responsible for the party realignment in the North, other factors played a role as well. Nearly 3.5 million immigrants entered the United States between 1848 and 1860. Some of these newcomers, especially the Germans, were escaping failed democratic revolutions in Europe. They were predominantly middle-class Protestants who, along with the smaller number of German Catholics and Jews, settled mostly in the cities. More than

"Bleeding Kansas" Violence between pro- and antislavery forces in Kansas Territory after the passage of the Kansas-Nebraska Act in 1854.

1 million of the immigrants, however, were poor Irish Roman Catholics, fleeing their homeland to avoid starvation.

The Irish immigrants made their homes in northern cities, which were in the midst of Protestant revivals and reform. They also competed for jobs with native-born Protestant workers. Because the Irish would work for lower wages, the job competition bred animosity and sometimes violence. But it was their Roman Catholic religion that most concerned some urban Protestants, who associated Catholicism with despotism and immorality, the same evils they attributed to southerners. For their part, the Irish made it clear that they had little use for Protestant reform, especially temperance and abolitionism. The clash of cultures would soon further disturb a political environment increasingly in flux over the slavery issue.

New parties emerged from this cauldron of religious, ethnic, and sectional strife. Anti-immigrant, anti-Catholic sentiment gave rise to the **Know-Nothing Party,** which began as a secret organization in July 1854. Its name derived from the reply that members gave when asked about the party: "I know nothing." In addition to their biases against Catholics and foreigners, the Know-Nothings shared a fear that the slavery issue could destroy the Union.

Know-Nothing candidates fared surprisingly well in local and congressional elections during the fall of 1854, carrying 63 percent of the statewide vote in Massachusetts and making strong showings in New York and Pennsylvania. In office, Know-Nothings achieved some notable reforms. In Massachusetts, where they pursued an agenda similar to that of the Whigs in earlier years, they secured administrative reforms and supported public health and public education programs.

The Know-Nothings' anti-Catholicism, however, overshadowed their reform agenda. Ethnic and religious bigotry were weak links to hold together a national party. Southern and northern Know-Nothings soon fell to quarreling over slavery despite their vow to avoid it, and the party split. Many northern Know-Nothings soon found a congenial home in the new **Republican Party.** The Republican Party formed in the summer of 1854 from a coalition of antislavery Conscience Whigs and Democrats disgusted with the Pierce administration's Kansas policy. Like the Know-Nothings, the Republicans advocated strong state and federal governments to promote economic and social reforms. But the new party did not espouse the Know-Nothings' anti-Catholic and anti-immigrant positions. The overriding bond among Republicans was their opposition to the extension of slavery in the territories.

Reflecting its opposition to slavery, the Republican Party was an anti-southern sectional party. Northern Whig merchants and entrepreneurs who joined the party were impatient with southern obstruction in Congress of federal programs for economic development and high tariffs to protect American industries from foreign competition. In a bid to keep slavery out of the territories, the Republicans favored limiting homesteads in the West to 160 acres. Not incidentally, populating the territories with northern whites would ensure a western base for the new party.

Heightened sectional animosity laced with religious and ethnic prejudice fueled the emergence of new parties and the weakening of old political affiliations in the early 1850s. As the nation prepared for the presidential election of 1856, the Democrats had become a party top-heavy with southerners; the Know-Nothings splintered along sectional lines; some Whigs remained active under the old party name, mainly on the state and local levels in North and South; and the Republican Party was becoming an important political force in the North and, to southerners, the embodiment of evil.

Know-Nothing Party Anti-immigrant party formed from the wreckage of the Whig Party and some disaffected Northern Democrats in 1854.

Republican Party Party that emerged in the 1850s in the aftermath of the bitter controversy over the Kansas-Nebraska Act, consisting of former Whigs, some Northern Democrats, and many Know-Nothings.

THE ELECTION OF 1856

The presidential election of 1856 proved to be one of the strangest in American history. The Know-Nothings and the Republicans faced a national electorate for the first time. The Democrats were deeply divided over the Kansas issue. Rejecting both Pierce and Douglas, they turned instead to a longtime insider, James Buchanan. This Pennsylvanian's major asset was that he had been absent from the country the previous three years as ambassador to Great Britain and was thus untainted by the Kansas controversy. The Republicans passed over their most likely candidate, the New York senator and former Whig William H. Seward. Instead, they nominated a military hero, John C. Frémont, a handsome, dark-haired soldier of medium height and medium intelligence. His wife, Jessie Benton, the daughter of Missouri senator Thomas Hart Benton, was his greatest asset. In effect, she ran the campaign and wisely encouraged her husband to remain silent. The Know-Nothings split into "South Americans" and "North Americans." The South Americans nominated Millard Fillmore, although he was not a Know-Nothing. The North Americans eventually and reluctantly embraced Frémont.

The overall result pleased southerners, but the details left them uncomfortable. Buchanan won by carrying every southern state and the Lower North, Pennsylvania, New Jersey, Illinois, Indiana, and California. But Frémont, a political novice running on his party's first national ticket, carried 11 free states, and the rest he lost by scant margins to Buchanan. It was a remarkable showing for a two-year-old party.

Buchanan, who brought more than a generation of political experience to the presidency, would need every bit and more. He had scarcely settled into office when two major crises confronted him: a Supreme Court decision that challenged the right of Congress to regulate slavery in the territories, and renewed conflict over Kansas.

THE DRED SCOTT CASE

Dred Scott was a slave owned by an army surgeon based in Missouri. In the 1830s and early 1840s, he had traveled with his master to the state of Illinois and the Wisconsin Territory before returning to Missouri. In 1846, Scott sued his master's widow for freedom on the grounds that the laws of Illinois and the Wisconsin Territory barred slavery. After a series of appeals, the case reached the Supreme Court. Chief Justice Roger Taney of Maryland, joined by five other justices of the nine-member Supreme Court (five of whom came from slave states), dismissed Scott's suit two days after Buchanan's inauguration in March 1857.

Taney's opinion contained two bombshells. First, he argued that black people were not citizens of the United States. Because Scott was not a citizen, he could not sue. In reaching this conclusion, Taney noted that the framers of the Constitution had never intended citizenship for slaves. The framers, according to Taney, respected a long-standing view that slaves were "beings of an inferior order . . . so far inferior that they had no rights which the white man was bound to respect."

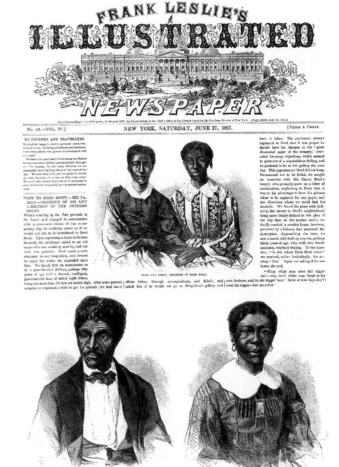

Dred Scott and his wife, Harriet, are portrayed here with their children as an average middle-class family, an image that fueled northern opposition to the Supreme Court's 1857 decision that denied both Scott's freedom and citizenship.

Courtesy of Library of Congress

Second, Taney held that even if Scott had standing in court, his residence in the Wisconsin Territory did not make him a free man. This was because the Missouri Compromise, which was still in effect in the 1840s, was, in Taney's view, unconstitutional. The compromise, the chief justice explained, deprived citizens of their property (slaves) without the due process of law granted by the Fifth Amendment to the U.S. Constitution. In effect, Taney ruled that Congress could not bar slavery from the territories.

Black Americans reacted bitterly to the **Dred Scott Decision.** Throughout the urban North, African Americans held meetings to denounce the decision. One gathering in Philadelphia in April 1857 resolved "that the only duty the colored man owes to a constitution under which he is declared to be an inferior and degraded being . . . is to denounce and repudiate it." A statewide black convention in Ohio objected in even stronger language: "If the Dred Scott dictum be the true . . . law of the land, then are the founders of the American Republic convicted by their descendants of base hypocrisy, and colored men absolved from all allegiance to a government which withdraws all protection." The gap between American ideals as stated and their application to black Americans had never been wider or more apparent.

The decision also shocked Republicans. The right of Congress to ban slavery from the territories, which Taney had apparently voided, was one of the party's central tenets. Republicans responded by ignoring the implications of the decision for the territories while promising to abide by it so far as it affected Dred Scott himself. Once in office, Republicans vowed, they would seek a reversal. This position allowed them to attack the decision without appearing to defy the law.

The *Dred Scott* decision boosted Republican fortunes in the North even as it seemed to undercut the party. Fears of a southern Slave Power conspiracy, which some had dismissed as fanciful and politically motivated, now seemed justified.

THE LECOMPTON CONSTITUTION

Establishing a legitimate government in Kansas was the second major issue to bedevil the Buchanan administration. The president made a good start, sending his friend and fellow Pennsylvanian Robert Walker (then a resident of Mississippi) to Kansas as territorial governor to oversee the election of a constitutional convention in June 1857.

But free-staters, fearing that the slavery forces planned to stuff the ballot box with fraudulent votes, announced a boycott of the June election. As a result, proslavery forces dominated the constitutional convention, which was held in Lecompton. And Walker, although a slaveholder, let it be known that he thought Kansas would never be a slave state, putting himself at odds with proslavery residents.

Walker persuaded the free-staters to vote in October to elect a new territorial legislature. The returns gave the proslavery forces a narrow victory, but Walker discovered irregularities. In McGee, Kansas, 20 voters somehow had cast 1,200 votes for proslavery candidates. And in Oxford, a community of a mere six houses, 1,601 names appeared on the voting rolls, all in the same handwriting and all copied from the Cincinnati city directory. Walker threw out these returns, and the free-staters took control of the territorial legislature for the first time.

Undeterred, the proslavery forces drafted a proslavery constitution at the constitutional convention in Lecompton. Buchanan, who had promised southerners a proslavery government in Kansas, submitted the **Lecompton Constitution** to the Senate for approval even though it clearly sidestepped the popular sovereignty requirement of the Kansas-Nebraska Act.

WHERE TO LEARN MORE

Constitution Hall, Lecompton, Kansas
www.kshs.org/places/constit.htm

Dred Scott Decision Supreme Court ruling, in a lawsuit brought by Dred Scott, a slave demanding his freedom based on his residence in a free state, that slaves could not be U.S. citizens and that Congress had no jurisdiction over slavery in the territories.

Lecompton Constitution
Proslavery draft written in 1857 by Kansas territorial delegates elected under questionable circumstances; it was rejected by two governors, supported by President Buchanan, and decisively defeated by Congress.

Like the Kansas-Nebraska Act, the Lecompton Constitution outraged many northerners. Northern Democrats facing reelection refused to support a president of their own party, and, though the constitution passed in the Senate, Democratic opposition killed it in the House. Among Lecompton's opponents was Stephen A. Douglas.

Douglas knew that the *Dred Scott* decision and Buchanan's support of the Lecompton Constitution would help the Republicans and hurt him and his fellow northern Democrats in the 1858 congressional elections. The **Panic of 1857,** a severe economic recession that lingered into 1858, also worked to the advantage of the Republicans. Republicans claimed that government intervention, specifically, Republican-sponsored legislation to raise certain tariffs, give western land to homesteaders, and fund transportation projects, if passed by Congress, could have prevented the panic. The Democrats' inaction, they said, reflected the southern Slave Power's insensitivity to northern workers.

Southerners disagreed. The panic had scarcely touched them. Cotton prices were high, and few southern banks failed. The Republicans' proposed legislative remedies, in their view, would enrich the North and beggar the South.

THE RELIGIOUS REVIVAL OF 1857–1858

In the midst of economic depression and sectional controversy, a religious revival swept across the nation's cities in the winter of 1857–1858. Beginning with lunch time prayer meetings among businessmen in New York City, the phenomenon spread throughout the country, though concentrating in the larger urban centers of the Northeast. Ministers and lay leaders of the movement encouraged men to turn away from the reform "isms" of the era—feminism, abolitionism, and socialism among them. Men, they suggested, should not worship secular ideologies, but should make the Bible the foundation of their behavior and thought. And they should reestablish their leadership both in spiritual and family matters.

Although the revival peaked by the spring of 1858, its long-range impact was significant. The event marked the first major national forum for the Young Men's Christian Association (YMCA), an organization dedicated to improving the spiritual life of urban men. The revival also provided an early opportunity for a young Boston minister, D. L. Moody, to hone his evangelical skills. After the Civil War, Moody became the nation's first prominent evangelist, preaching to immense crowds and offering a message that transcended individual Protestant denominations.

Finally, the revival highlighted the growing importance of the urban middle class in the cultural and religious life of the nation. As the revival highlighted, some feared that the growing integration of religion and politics could harm the nation's religious life and burden the political process with sharper divisions than were necessary. But by 1858, it became increasingly difficult to distinguish the political from the spiritual. The Illinois senatorial contest between Democrat Stephen A. Douglas and Abraham Lincoln of the Republican Party proved a case in point.

THE LINCOLN-DOUGLAS DEBATES

Douglas faced a forceful opponent in his 1858 reelection campaign. The Republicans had nominated Abraham Lincoln, a 49-year-old lawyer and former Whig congressman. The Kentucky-born Lincoln had risen from modest circumstances to become a prosperous lawyer in the Illinois state capital of Springfield. Lincoln had developed a reputation as an excellent stump speaker with a homespun sense

Panic of 1857 Banking crisis that caused a credit crunch in the North; it was less severe in the South, where high cotton prices spurred a quick recovery.

Abraham Lincoln making a point at Coles County (Illinois) Fairgrounds, 1858. His U.S. Senate opponent, Stephen A. Douglas, sitting at Lincoln's right, waits his turn. The Lincoln-Douglas debates captivated Illinois voters, who turned out in great numbers to witness the rhetorical fireworks.

Illinois State Historical Library

14–9
Abraham Lincoln, "A House Divided" (1858)

QUICK REVIEW

The Freeport Doctrine

• Proclaimed by Steven Douglas during Lincoln-Douglas debates.

• Slavery could exist in a territory only if the people passed a law to protect it.

• Without such a law, slavery could not exist and slaves could not enter that territory.

Lincoln-Douglas Debates
Series of debates in the 1858 Illinois senatorial campaign during which Douglas and Lincoln staked out their differing opinions on the issue of slavery.

of humor, a quick wit, and a self-deprecating style that fit well with the small-town residents and farmers who composed the majority of the Illinois electorate.

But substance counted more than style with Illinois voters. Most of them opposed the extension of slavery into the territories, although generally not out of concern for the slaves. Few voters would support dissolving the Union over the slavery issue. Douglas, who knew his constituents well, branded Lincoln a dangerous radical for warning, in a biblical paraphrase, that the United States, like "a house divided against itself," could not "endure permanently half slave and half free." Lincoln could not allow the charge of radicalism to go unanswered. So, in July 1858, he challenged Douglas to a series of debates across the state. Douglas was reluctant to provide exposure for his lesser-known opponent, but he could not reject Lincoln's offer outright, lest voters think he was dodging his challenger. He agreed to debates in seven of the state's nine congressional districts.

The **Lincoln-Douglas debates** put the differences between Lincoln and Douglas, Republicans and Democrats, and North and South into sharp focus. At Freeport, Lincoln asked Douglas to reconcile popular sovereignty, which Douglas had long championed, with the *Dred Scott* decision, which seemed to outlaw it by prohibiting a territorial legislature from excluding slavery before statehood. Douglas replied with what came to be known as the Freeport Doctrine. Slavery, he argued, could exist in a territory only if residents passed a law to protect it. Without such a law, no slaveholders would move in, and the territory would be free. Thus, if residents did nothing, there could be no slavery in the territory.

For Douglas, slavery was not a moral issue. What mattered was what white people wanted. Lincoln and many Republicans had a very different view. For them, slavery was a moral issue. As such, it was independent of what the residents of a territory wanted. In the final Lincoln-Douglas debate, Lincoln turned to his rival and explained: "The real issue in this controversy . . . is the sentiment on the part of one class that looks upon the institution of slavery *as a wrong,* and of another class that does not look upon it as a wrong. . . . The Republican party . . . look upon it as being a moral, social and political wrong . . . and one of the methods of treating it as a wrong is to make provision that it shall grow no larger. . . . That is the real issue. . . . It is the eternal struggle between these two principles, right and wrong, throughout the world."

Lincoln tempered his moralism with practical politics. He took care to distance himself from the abolitionists, asserting that he abided by the Constitution and did not seek to interfere in places where slavery existed. Privately, he prayed for its demise. To Lincoln, slavery was immoral, but inequality was not. The Republican Party was antislavery, but it did not advocate racial equality. Lincoln lost the senatorial contest but won national respect and recognition.

Despite Lincoln's defeat in Illinois, the Republicans made a strong showing in the 1858 congressional elections across the North. The increased Republican presence and the sharpening sectional divisions among Democrats portended a bitter debate over slavery in the new Congress. *Northern* and *Southern* took on meanings that expressed a great deal more than geography.

THE ROAD TO DISUNION

*I*n 1859 abolitionist John Brown, who had avenged the "sack of Lawrence" in 1856, led a raid against a federal arsenal at Harpers Ferry, Virginia, in the vain hope of sparking a slave revolt. This event brought the frustrations of both sides of the sectional conflict to a head. The presidential election campaign of 1860 began before the uproar over the raid had subsided. In the course of that contest, one of the last nationally unifying institutions, the Democratic Party, broke apart. The election of Abraham Lincoln, an avowedly sectional candidate, triggered a crisis that defied peaceful resolution.

WHY WERE Southerners so alarmed by the election of Abraham Lincoln in 1860?

Although the crisis spiraled into a civil war, this outcome did not signal the triumph of sectionalism over nationalism. Ironically, in defending their stands, both sides appealed to time-honored nationalist and democratic sentiments. Southern secessionists believed they were the true keepers of the ideals that had inspired the American Revolution. They were merely re-creating a more perfect Union. It was not they, but the Republicans, who had sundered the old Union by subverting the Constitution's guarantee of liberty. Lincoln similarly appealed to nationalist themes, telling northerners that the United States was "the last best hope on earth."

Northerners and Southerners both appealed to nationalism and democracy but applied different meanings to these concepts. The differences underscored how far apart the sections had grown. When southerners and northerners looked at each other, they no longer saw fellow Americans; they saw enemies.

NORTH-SOUTH DIFFERENCES

Economic Differences.   Behind the ideological divide that separated North and South lay real and growing social and economic differences (see the Overview Table, South and North Compared in 1860). As the North became increasingly urban and industrial, the South remained primarily rural and agricultural. The urban population of the free states increased from 10 to 26 percent between 1820 and 1860. In the South, in the same period, it increased only from 5 to 10 percent. Likewise the proportion of the northern workforce in agriculture declined from 68 percent to 40 percent between 1800 and 1860, whereas in the South it increased from 82 percent to 84 percent.

The need of city-dwellers for ready-to-wear shoes and clothing, household iron products, processed foods, homes, workplaces, and public amenities boosted industrial production in the North. In contrast, in the South, the slower rate of urbanization, the lower proportion of immigrants, and the region's labor-intensive agriculture kept industrial development modest. The proportion of U.S. manufacturing capital invested in the South declined from 31 to 16 percent between 1810 and 1860. In 1810, per capita investment in industrial enterprises was 2.5 times greater in the North than in the South; in 1860, it was 3.5 times greater.

The rate of urban and industrial growth in the North was greater than anywhere else in the world in the early nineteenth century. Even when compared to the West, however, the South was falling behind. The South and West had about the same levels of manufacturing investment and urban population in the 1850s, but the rate of growth was even greater in the West than in the North.

These economic developments generated communities of innovation in the North, especially in the rapidly expanding cities, where people traded ideas and technical information and skills. One of the most important innovations of the era was the telegraph, pioneered by Samuel F. B. Morse. As information became a

valuable currency for a new age, such improvements in communications and transportation tended to reinforce the economic dominance of the Northeast.

Social and Religious Differences. More subtle distinctions between North and South became evident as well by midcentury. Southerners tended to be more violent than northerners. The slave states had a higher homicide rate than the free states, and more southerners carried weapons. Southern values stressed courtesy, honor, and courage. Southerners were more inclined to military service than northerners. They had proportionately more cadets enrolled in the United States Military Academy at West Point; more than 60 percent of the volunteer soldiers for the Mexican War hailed from the South; and, excluding West Point and the Naval Academy at Annapolis, seven of the nation's eight military colleges were located in the South.

The South had a high illiteracy rate, nearly three times greater than the North, eight times greater if black southerners are included. In the South, education was barred by law to slaves and limited for most white people. Many white leaders viewed education more as a privilege for the well-to-do than a right for every citizen.

Evangelical Protestantism attracted increasing numbers in both North and South, but its character differed in the two regions. The Methodist Church divided along sectional lines over slavery in 1844, and the Baptists split the following year. The Presbyterians splintered in 1837 over mainly doctrinal issues, but the rupture became complete in 1861. In the North, evangelical Protestants viewed social reform as a prerequisite for the Second Coming of Christ. As a result, they were in the forefront of most reform movements. Southern evangelicals generally defended slavery.

The Effects of Slavery. Slavery accounted for many of the differences between the North and the South. Investment in land and slaves limited investment in manufacturing. The availability of a large slave labor force reduced the need for farm machinery and limited the demand for manufactured products. Slaves were relatively immobile. They did not migrate to cities in massive numbers as did northern farmers. Nor could they quickly fill the labor demands of an expanding urban economy. Agriculture usually took precedence.

Slavery contributed to the South's martial tradition and its lukewarm attitude toward public education. Fully 95 percent of the nation's black population lived in the South in 1860, and 90 percent of these were slaves. As a result, the South was often a region on edge. Fearful of revolt, especially in the 1850s, when rumors of slave discontent ran rampant, white people felt compelled to maintain patrols and militias in constant readiness. The South was also determined to keep slaves as ignorant as possible. Educated slaves would be susceptible to abolitionist propaganda and more inclined to revolt.

The South's defense of slavery and the North's attack on it fostered an array of stereotypes that exaggerated the real differences between the sections.

Southerners saw northerners as crass and materialistic but themselves as generous and compassionate. Northerners saw southerners as brutal and backward, themselves as progressive and temperate. Southerners perceived themselves as honorable and chaste and saw northerners as corrupt and loose living. Northerners saw southerners as perverse and lazy, themselves as righteous and hardworking. The South, according to southerners, was the land of moonlight and magnolias (an image that actually originated in the North), while the North was the region of muggings and mudslinging. Northerners saw southerners as lords of the lash and themselves as angels of mercy.

Ironically, although slavery increasingly defined the character of the South in the 1850s, a growing majority of white southerners did not own slaves. Slavery nonetheless implicated nonslaveholders in ways that ensured their support for it. By satisfying the demand for labor on large plantations, it relieved many rural white southerners from serving as farmhands and enabled them to work their own land. Slaveholders also recruited nonslaveholders to suppress slave violence or rebellion. Some nonslaveholders hoped to purchase slaves someday. Many dreamed of migrating westward to the next cotton frontier where they might find greater opportunity to own land and slaves. This dream not only bound white Southerners together on slavery but also prompted their strong support for southern access to the western territories. Finally, regardless of a white man's social or economic status, as long as racial slavery existed, the color of his skin made him a member of a privileged class that could never be enslaved.

While white southerners were more united on slavery than on other issues, their defense of slavery presented them with a major dilemma. It left them vulnerable to moral condemnation because, in the end, slavery was morally indefensible. A minority in their own country and a lonely voice for a despised institution that was for them a significant source of wealth, southerners were understandably jittery.

JOHN BROWN'S RAID

Shortly after he completed his mayhem at Pottawatomie Creek, John Brown left Kansas and approached several New England abolitionists for funds to continue his private war in the territory. After several failed businesses, more than 20 lawsuits for nonpayment of debts, and a brush with horse rustling, he had at last found his life's calling: He had become a moderately successful fund-raiser for his own violent frontier exploits.

But when Brown returned to Kansas in late 1857, he discovered that peace had settled over that troubled territory. Residents now cared more about making money than about making war. Leaving Kansas for the last time, he went east with a new plan. He proposed to attack and capture the federal arsenal at Harpers Ferry, Virginia, a small town near the Maryland border. The assault, Brown imagined, would spark a slave uprising that would eventually spread to the rest of the state. With funds from his New England friends, he equipped a few dozen men and hired an English army officer to train them.

When Brown outlined his scheme to Frederick Douglass, the noted black abolitionist warned him against it. But his white New England friends were less cautious, and a

John Brown, wounded during his raid on the federal arsenal at Harpers Ferry, lies on a cot during his trial for murder and treason in Charlestown, Virginia in 1859.

The Granger Collection, New York

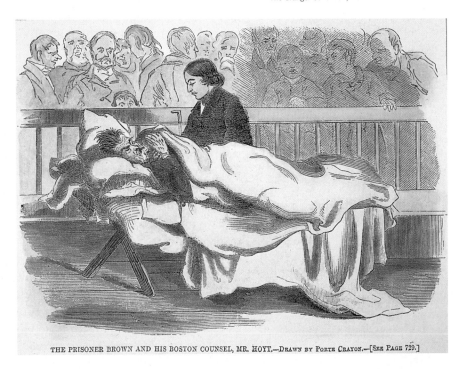

THE PRISONER BROWN AND HIS BOSTON COUNSEL, MR. HOYT.—DRAWN BY PORTE CRAYON.—[SEE PAGE 729.]

OVERVIEW   SOUTH AND NORTH COMPARED IN 1860

	South	North
Population	Biracial; 35 percent African American	Overwhelmingly white; less than 2 percent African American
Economy	Growing, though relatively undiversified; 84 percent of workforce in agriculture	Developing through industrialization and urbanization; 40 percent of workforce in agriculture
Labor	Heavily dependent on slave labor, especially in Lower South	Free wage labor
Factories	15 percent of national total	85 percent of national total; concentrated in the Northeast
Railroads	Approximately 10,000 miles of track; primarily shorter lines, with fewer links to trunk lines	Approximately 20,000 miles of track; more effectively linked to trunk lines connecting east and west
Literacy	17 percent illiteracy rate for free population	6 percent illiteracy rate

group of six prominent abolitionists (the "Secret Six") gave Brown additional funds for his project.

On the night of October 16, 1859, Brown and 22 followers captured the federal arsenal at Harpers Ferry and waited for the slaves to rally to his banner. Meanwhile, the townspeople alerted outside authorities. The Virginia militia and a detachment of United States Marines under the command of Colonel Robert E. Lee arrived and put a quick end to **John Brown's Raid.** They wounded Brown and killed or captured most of his force.

Although the primary goal of the attack had been to inspire a slave insurrection, no one had bothered to inform the local slaves. And despite the secret nature of the expedition, Brown had left behind a mountain of documents. He had tried to conquer the state of Virginia with 22 men and an ill-conceived plan.

The raid, though foolish and unsuccessful, played on southerners' worst fears of slave rebellion, adding a new dimension: Here was an attack engineered not from within the South but from the North. Some southern white people may have dismissed the ability or even the desire of slaves to mount revolts on their own, but they less easily dismissed the potential impact of outside white agitators. The state of Virginia tried Brown on the charge of treason to the state. Brown, recovering from his wounds, attended most of the trial on a stretcher. The trial was swift but fair. The jury sentenced Brown to hang. Speaking to the court after his sentencing, Brown suggested that he was God's agent in a holy war: "I believe that to have interfered as I have done . . . in behalf of [God's] despised poor, is no wrong, but right. Now, if it is deemed necessary that I should forfeit my life for the furtherance of the ends of justice, and mingle my blood further with the blood of my children and with the blood of millions in this slave country whose rights are disregarded by wicked, cruel, and unjust enactments, I say, let it be done."

Some northerners compared Brown's execution with the death of a religious martyr. The abolitionist William Lloyd Garrison asked readers of the *Liberator* to "let the day of [Brown's] execution . . . be the occasion of such a public moral

John Brown's Raid   New England abolitionist John Brown's ill-fated attempt to free Virginia's slaves with a raid on the federal arsenal at Harper's Ferry, Virginia, in 1859.

demonstration against the bloody and merciless slave system as the land has never witnessed." Most northerners, however, including many Republicans, had condemned the raid. Still, the dignity of Brown's death touched many. Condemning the deed, they nevertheless embraced the cause.

The outpouring of northern grief over Brown's death convinced white southerners that the threat to their security was not over. John Brown's Raid significantly changed southern public opinion. However much they defended slavery, most southerners were for the Union. The northern reaction to John Brown's trial and death, however, troubled them. The *Richmond Whig*, a newspaper that reflected moderate Upper South opinion, observed in early 1860 that "recent events have wrought almost a complete revolution in the sentiments, the thoughts, the hopes, of the oldest and steadiest conservatives in all the southern states. . . . There are thousands upon . . . thousands of men in our midst who, a month ago, scoffed at the idea of a dissolution of the Union as a madman's dream, but who now hold the opinion that its days are numbered, its glory perished."

It was one thing to condemn slavery in the territories but another to attack it violently where it was long established. Southerners now saw in the Republican party the embodiment of John Brown's ideals and actions. So, in their view, the election of a Republican president would be a death sentence for the South.

THE ELECTION OF 1860

In April 1860, the Democratic Party, the sole surviving national political organization, held its convention in Charleston, South Carolina. Northern Democrats arrived in Charleston united behind Stephen A. Douglas. Although they constituted a majority of the delegates, they could not muster the two-thirds majority necessary to nominate their candidate. Other issues, however, were decided on a simple majority vote, permitting northern Democrats to defeat a platform proposal for a federal slave code in the territories.

Southern extremists who favored secession hoped to disrupt the convention and divide the party. They reasoned that the Republicans would then win the presidency, providing the South with the justification to secede. The platform vote gave them the opportunity they were seeking. Accompanied by spectators' cheers, delegates from five Lower South states, South Carolina, Florida, Mississippi, Louisiana, and Texas, walked out. The Arkansas and Georgia delegations joined them the following day.

Still without a nominee, the Democrats agreed to reconvene in Baltimore in June. This time, the Upper South delegations marched out when Douglas Democrats, in a commanding majority, refused to seat the Lower South delegations that had walked out in Charleston. The remaining delegates nominated Douglas for president. The bolters, who included almost all the southern delegates plus a few northerners loyal to President Buchanan, met in another hall and nominated John C. Breckinridge of Kentucky. In the previous month, former Whigs, mainly from the Upper South, who would not support Breckinridge and could not support Douglas, together with Whig allies in the North who had not defected to the Republican Party, formed the **Constitutional Union Party** and nominated John Bell of Tennessee for president.

Sensing victory, the Republicans convened in Chicago. If they could hold the states won by Frémont in 1856, add Minnesota (a new Republican-leaning state), and win Pennsylvania and one of three other Lower North states, Illinois, Indiana, or New Jersey, their candidate would win. These calculations dictated a

Constitutional Union Party
National party formed in 1860, mainly by former Whigs, that emphasized allegiance to the Union and strict enforcement of all national legislation.

RELIGION AND POLITICS

When evangelical Protestantism first emerged in the late eighteenth century, its adherents advocated the separation of church and state. By the 1850s, however, the social landscape of America had changed. A wave of immigrants, many of them Roman Catholic, threatened Protestant dominance. Growing cities and rapid technological and economic change strained the traditional moral and social order. Alarmed by these changes, evangelicals entered the political arena. Their convictions, as we saw in Chapter 12, helped drive the antebellum reform movement.

The give and take of politics, however, posed a challenge to the evangelical belief in an absolute truth grounded in the Bible. Eventually the two great evangelical crusades of the 1850s—anti-Catholicism and abolitionism—were subsumed within the Republican Party. And after the Civil War, the Republican Party gradually lost its radical fervor.

By the twentieth century, the evangelical movement had begun to turn away from politics and revert to its traditional focus on saving souls. In 1950, Jerry Falwell, an emerging evangelical leader, declared himself "a soul-winner and a separatist," meaning he wanted little involvement with society at large, much less with politics. But then came the upheavals of the 1960s and 1970s that challenged traditional morality and authority, including the Supreme Court's decision in *Roe v. Wade* to legalize abortion. In addition, the Internal Revenue Service began questioning the tax-exempt status of various religious groups. Once again, a changing social landscape compelled evangelicals to enter the political arena, this time to defend themselves against what they perceived to be an encroaching government. Organizations emerged to mobilize evangelical voters, including Jerry Falwell's Moral Majority in the late 1970s and Pat Robertson's Christian Coalition in 1989.

In the 1850s the Northeast was the center of evangelical politics. Now evangelical political organizations speak with a mostly Southern accent. In the 1850s opposition to slavery was the focus of evangelical politics. Now it is opposition to abortion and other social issues that have risen to prominence with the end of the

Cold War and the nation's growing prosperity. Evangelical activists have once again found a home in the Republican Party. The Democrats, they believe, are too permissive and too committed to abortion rights, just as nineteenth century Democrats had been committed to the defense of slavery.

And again, as in the 1850s, evangelical involvement has heated political discourse with the language of righteousness. In 1992, Randall Terry, founder of Operation Rescue, a militant antiabortion organization, wrote in his newsletter that "to vote for Bill Clinton is to sin against God." In a similar if more flowery declaration, a New England evangelical journal proclaimed the 1856 presidential contest a choice between "the bloodstained ticket of the Democratic party, responsible for the murder of your brothers and mine on the plains of Kansas," and a Republican ticket designated by "the God of peace and purity as the one that shall smile upon you."

Most Americans today, as in the 1850s, recoil from the overt intrusion of religion into politics, and groups like the Christian Coalition have had only limited success in electing their favored candidates. Despite these disappointments, they have been as wary of compromise as their nineteenth-century predecessors. As one evangelical leader explained in 1999: "I would rather go to bed with a clear conscience after losing."

But if evangelical political organizations cannot gain control of Congress and the presidency, it is unlikely that their social agenda—which, in addition to antiabortion legislation, includes prayer in school, the posting of the Ten Commandments in public places, and laws restricting the rights of homosexuals—will be enacted. Today, some evangelical strategists call for a "popular front" approach, allying themselves with candidates not openly associated with the evangelical agenda. Abolitionists in the 1850s faced the same quandary between ideological purity and political pragmatism. Their support of Abraham Lincoln in 1860 reflected a bow toward pragmatism, a course that ultimately proved successful for their cause, but not without a bloody civil war.

platform and a candidate who could appeal to the four Lower North swing states, where antislavery sentiment was not so strong.

In selecting an appropriate presidential nominee, the Republicans faced a dilemma. Senator William H. Seward came to Chicago as the leading candidate. But his immoderate condemnation of southerners and slavery worried moderate northern voters—precisely the voters the party needed for victory.

Reservations about Seward benefited Abraham Lincoln. When Seward faltered, Lincoln rose and won the Republican nomination.

The presidential campaign of 1860 actually comprised two campaigns. In the South, the contest was between Breckinridge and Bell; in the North, it was Lincoln against Douglas. Lincoln did not even appear on the ballot in most southern states.

In those days, states did not hold gubernatorial elections on the same day, or even in the same month, as the national presidential election. When, in mid-October, Republicans swept the statehouses in two crucial states, Pennsylvania and Indiana, Douglas made an extraordinary decision, but one consistent with his ardent nationalism. He abandoned his campaign and headed south at great personal peril to urge southerners to remain in the Union now that Lincoln's election was inevitable. Lincoln became the nation's sixteenth president, with 40 percent of the popular vote. He took most northern states by significant margins and won all the region's electoral votes except three in New Jersey. This gave him a substantial majority of 180 electoral votes.

SECESSION BEGINS

Four days after Lincoln's victory, the South Carolina legislature called on the state's citizens to elect delegates to a convention to consider secession. Meeting on December 20, the delegates voted unanimously to leave the Union. By February 1, six other states had all held similar conventions and decided to leave the Union. Representatives from the seven seceding states met to form a separate country, the **Confederate States of America.** On February 18, Jefferson Davis was sworn in as its president.

The secessionists mounted an effective propaganda campaign, deftly using the press to persuade voters to elect their delegates to the state conventions. Framing the issue as a personal challenge to every southern citizen, they argued that it would be cowardly to remain in the Union, a submission to despotism and enslavement. Southerners, they maintained, were the true heirs to the spirit of 1776. Lincoln and the Republicans meant to deny southerners the right to life, liberty, and the pursuit of happiness.

PRESIDENTIAL INACTION

Because Lincoln would not take office until March 4, 1861, the Buchanan administration had to cope with the secession crisis during the critical months of December and January. The president's failure to work out a solution with Congress as secession fever swept the Lower South undermined Unionist forces in the seceding states.

When Buchanan lost the support of northern Democrats over the Lecompton Constitution, he turned to the South for support and filled his cabinet with southerners. Now, facing the secession crisis, he proposed holding a constitutional convention to amend the Constitution in ways that would satisfy the South's demands on slavery. This outright surrender to southern demands, however, had no chance of passing in Congress.

Buchanan's administration quickly fell apart. As the Lower South states left the Union, their representatives and senators left Washington, and with them went Buchanan's closest advisers and key cabinet officials. Buchanan, a lame duck,

WHERE TO LEARN MORE

★ "A House Divided," mounted by the Chicago Historical Society, Chicago, Illinois www.chicagohs.org

Confederate States of America
Nation proclaimed in Montgomery, Alabama, in February 1861, after the seven states of the Lower South seceded from the United States.

QUICK REVIEW

Buchanan and Secession

• Buchanan had to deal with secession crisis in the months between Lincoln's election and inauguration.

• Buchanan failed to work with Congress to find a solution.

• Buchanan hoped waiting would bring the South to its senses.

bereft of friends and advisers, did little more than condemn secession. He was reluctant to take action that would limit the options of the incoming administration or, worse, tip the balance in the Upper South toward secession. He hoped that waiting might bring an isolated Lower South to its senses and give efforts to mediate the sectional rift a chance to succeed.

PEACE PROPOSALS

Previous sectional conflicts, dating from the Missouri Compromise of 1820, had brought forth the ingenuity and good will of political leaders to effect compromise and draw the Union back from the brink of disintegration. Both ingenuity and good will were scarce commodities in the gray secession winter of 1860–1861. The two conflicting sides had little trust in each other, and the word "compromise" was viewed as more a synonym for capitulation than salvation.

Kentucky senator John J. Crittenden chaired a Senate committee that proposed a package of constitutional amendments in December 1860 designed to solve the sectional crisis. The central feature of the Crittenden Plan was the extension of the Missouri Compromise line through the territories all the way to California. Meanwhile, ex-president John Tyler emerged from retirement to lead an effort by the border states, the Upper South and the Lower North, to forge a peace. Delegates from these states met in February 1861, but their plan differed little from Crittenden's. Both plans got nowhere in Congress.

LINCOLN'S VIEWS ON SECESSION

President-elect Lincoln monitored the secession of the Lower South states and the attempts to reach a compromise from his home in Springfield. Although he said nothing publicly, he made it known that he did not favor compromises like those proposed by Crittenden and Tyler.

Lincoln counted on Unionist sentiment to keep the Upper South from seceding. Like Buchanan, he felt that the longer the Lower South states remained isolated, the more likely they would be to return to the fold. For a while, events seemed to bear him out. In North Carolina, the *Wilmington Herald* responded to South Carolina's secession by asking readers, "Will you suffer yourself to be spit upon in this way? Are you submissionists to the dictation of South Carolina . . . are you to be called cowards because you do not follow the crazy lead of that crazy state?"

One by one, Upper South states registered their support for the Union. A closer look, however, reveals that there were limits to the Upper South's Unionism. Most voters in the region went to the polls assuming that Congress would eventually reach a compromise based on the Crittenden proposals, Tyler's peace conference, or some other remedy. Leaders in the Upper South saw

MAP EXPLORATION

To explore an interactive version of this map, go to
http://www.prenhall.com/goldfield3/map14.2

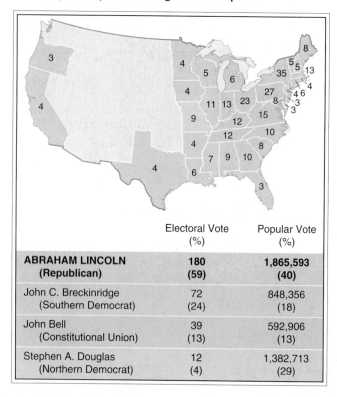

	Electoral Vote (%)	Popular Vote (%)
ABRAHAM LINCOLN (Republican)	**180 (59)**	**1,865,593 (40)**
John C. Breckinridge (Southern Democrat)	72 (24)	848,356 (18)
John Bell (Constitutional Union)	39 (13)	592,906 (13)
Stephen A. Douglas (Northern Democrat)	12 (4)	1,382,713 (29)

MAP 14–2   The Election of 1860   The election returns from 1860 vividly illustrate the geography of sectionalism.

BASED ON the geographic sectionalism shown in this map, what issues were important to voters in the election of 1860?

themselves as peacemakers, but it was unlikely that the Upper South would abide the use of federal force against its southern neighbors.

Lincoln believed that the slavery issue had to come to a crisis before the nation could solve it. Although he said in public that he would never interfere with slavery in the slave states, the deep moral revulsion he felt toward the institution left him more ambivalent in private. As he confided to a colleague in 1860, "The tug has to come, and better now, than any time hereafter" (see American Views: Lincoln on Slavery).

FORT SUMTER: THE TUG COMES

In his inaugural address on March 4, 1861, Abraham Lincoln denounced secession and vowed to uphold federal law but tempered his firmness with a conciliatory conclusion. Addressing southerners specifically, he assured them, "We are not enemies but friends. . . . Though passion may have strained, it must not break our bonds of affection. The mystic chords of memory, stretching from every battlefield, and patriot grave, to every living heart and hearthstone, all over this broad land, will yet swell the chorus of the Union, when again touched, as surely they will be, by the better angels of our nature."

Southerners wanted concessions, not conciliation, however. The new president said nothing about slavery in the territories, nothing about the constitutional amendments proposed by Crittenden and Tyler, and nothing about the release of federal property in the South to the Confederacy. Even some northerners hoping for an olive branch were disappointed. But Lincoln was hoping for time—time to get the Lower South states quarreling with one another, time to allow Union sentiment to build in the Upper South, and time to convince northerners that the Union needed preserving. He did not get that time.

One day after Lincoln's inauguration, Major Robert Anderson, the commander of **Fort Sumter** in Charleston harbor, informed the administration that he had only four to six weeks' worth of provisions left. Sumter was one of three southern forts still under federal control. Confederate batteries had ringed the fort, and Anderson estimated that only a force of at least 20,000 troops could provision and defend the fort. Anderson assumed that Lincoln would understand the hopeless arithmetic and order him to evacuate Fort Sumter.

News of Anderson's plight changed the mood in the North. The Slave Power, some said, was holding him and his men hostage. Frustration grew over Lincoln's silence and inaction. The Confederacy's bold resolve seemed to contrast sharply with the federal government's confusion and inertia. By the end of March, nearly a month after Anderson had informed Lincoln of the situation at Fort Sumter, the president finally moved to provision Major Anderson.

Hoping to avoid a confrontation, the president did not send the troops that Anderson had requested. Instead he ordered unarmed ships to proceed to the fort, deliver the provisions, and leave. Only if the Confederates fired on them were they to force their way into the fort with the help of armed reinforcements. Lincoln notified South Carolina authorities that he intended to do nothing more than "feed the hungry."

At Charleston, Confederate general P. G. T. Beauregard had standing orders to turn back any relief expedition. But President Davis wanted to take Sumter before the provisions arrived to avoid fighting Anderson and the reinforcements at the same time. He also realized that the outbreak of fighting could compel the Upper South to join the Confederacy. But his impatience to force the issue placed the Confederacy in the position of firing, unprovoked, on the American flag and at Major Anderson, who had become a national hero.

Fort Sumter   A fort located in Charleston, South Carolina, where President Lincoln attempted to provision federal troops in 1861, triggering a hostile response from on-shore Confederate forces, opening the Civil War.

AMERICAN VIEWS

LINCOLN ON SLAVERY

I n the weeks after the 1860 election, northern and southern leaders sought out President-elect Abraham Lincoln for his views on slavery. But Lincoln had spoken often on the institution in the years immediately preceding the election. His speech two years earlier, excerpted here, offered an unequivocal statement of his moral and philosophical opposition to slavery. Implied in the speech was the belief that the contradiction between American ideals and slavery could not be brokered, compromised, or ignored.

- How do Lincoln's actions from his election in November 1860 to the firing on Fort Sumter in April 1861 reflect the principles enunciated in his Springfield address?
- The two letters, one to fellow Illinois Republican Lyman Trumbull and the other to Virginia Democrat John A. Gilmer, indicate Lincoln's firm opposition to the extension of slavery into the territories. Are they consistent with the views expressed in Springfield two years earlier?
- Despite the difference in tone, do you think the letters both say essentially the same thing?

SPEECH OF HON. ABRAHAM LINCOLN
Springfield, Illinois, June 17, 1858

We are now far into the fifth year since policy was initiated with the avowed object and confident promise of putting an end to slavery agitation. Under the operation of that policy, that agitation has not only not ceased, but has constantly augmented. In my opinion, it will not cease until a crisis shall have been reached and passed. "A house divided against itself cannot stand." I believe this government cannot endure permanently half slave and half free. I do not expect the Union to be dissolved; I do not expect the house to fall; but I do expect it will cease to be divided. It will become all one thing, or the other. . . . So I say in relation to the principle that all men are created equal, let it be as nearly reached as we can. If we cannot give free-

dom to every creature, let us do nothing that will impose slavery upon any other creature. . . . I leave you, hoping that the lamp of liberty will burn in your bosoms until there shall no longer be a doubt that all men are created free and equal.

Springfield, Ills. Dec. 10, 1860
Hon. L. Trumbull

My dear Sir: Let there be no compromise on the question of extending slavery. If there be, all our labor is lost, and ere long, must be done again. The dangerous ground, that into which some of our friends have a hankering to run, is Pop[ular] Sov[ereignty]. Have none of it. Stand firm. The tug has to come, & better now, than any time hereafter. Yours as ever,

A. Lincoln

Springfield, Ill. Dec. 15, 1860
Hon. John A. Gilmer:

My dear Sir: . . . I have no thought of recommending the abolition of slavery in the District of Columbia, nor the slave trade among the slave states . . . and if I were to make such recommendation, it is quite clear Congress would not follow it. As to the use of patronage in the slave states, where there are few or no Republicans, I do not expect to inquire for the politics of the appointee, or whether he does or not own slaves. . . . In one word, I never have been, am not now, and probably never shall be, in a mood of harassing the people, either North or South. On the territorial question, I am inflexible. . . . On that, there is a difference between you and us; and it is the only substantial difference. You think slavery is right and ought to be extended; we think it is wrong and ought to be restricted. For this, neither has any just occasion to be angry with the other.

Your obt. Servt.
A. Lincoln

Source: John G. Nicolay and John Hay, eds., *Works of Abraham Lincoln*, vol. 6 (New York, Century Co.,1905).

OVERVIEW   THE EMERGING SECTIONAL CRISIS

Event	Year	Effect
Wilmot Proviso	1846	Congressman David Wilmot's proposal to ban slavery from territories acquired from Mexico touched off a bitter sectional dispute in Congress.
Compromise of 1850	1850	Law admitted California as a free state, granted the population of Utah and New Mexico Territories the right to decide on slavery, and established a new and stronger Fugitive Slave Act, all of which "solved" the territorial issue raised by the Wilmot Proviso but satisfied neither North nor South and planted the seeds of future conflict.
Election of 1852	1852	Results confirmed demise of the Whig Party, initiating a period of political realignment.
Kansas-Nebraska Act	1854	Law created the Kansas and Nebraska Territories and repealed the Missouri Compromise of 1820 by leaving the question of slavery to the territories' residents. Its passage enraged many northerners, prompting some to form the new Republican Party.
"Bleeding Kansas"	1855–1856	Sometimes violent conflict between pro- and antislavery forces in Kansas further polarized the sectional debate.
Election of 1856	1856	Presidency was won by Democrat James Buchanan of Pennsylvania, but a surprisingly strong showing by the recently formed Republican Party in the North set the stage for the 1860 election.
Dred Scott Case	1857	The Supreme Court ruling that slaves were not citizens and that Congress had no authority to ban slavery from the territories boosted Republican prospects in the North.
Lecompton Constitution	1857	Proslavery document, framed by a fraudulently elected constitutional convention in Kansas and supported by President Buchanan, further convinced northerners that the South was subverting their rights.
John Brown's Raid	1859	Unsuccessful attempt to free the South's slaves, this attack on a federal arsenal in Harpers Ferry, Virginia, increased sectional tension.
Election of 1860	1860	Republican Abraham Lincoln won a four-way race for the presidency. The last major national party, the Democrats, disintegrated. Lower South states seceded.
Fort Sumter	1861	Confederate forces attacked the fort in April 1861, Lincoln called for troops, and several Upper South states seceded. The Civil War was underway.

On April 10, Davis ordered Beauregard to demand the immediate evacuation of Fort Sumter. Anderson refused. Before dawn on April 12, 1861, the first Confederate shell whistled down on the fort. After more than a day of shelling, during which more than 5,000 artillery rounds struck Fort Sumter, Anderson surrendered.

When the verdict of Fort Sumter reached President Lincoln, he called on the southern states still in the Union to send troops to put down the rebellion. Refusing to make war on South Carolina, the Upper South states of Virginia, North Carolina, Tennessee, and Arkansas seceded, and the Confederacy expanded to 11 states.

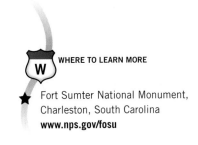

WHERE TO LEARN MORE

Fort Sumter National Monument, Charleston, South Carolina
www.nps.gov/fosu

GLOBAL PERSPECTIVES

THE REVOLUTIONS OF 1848

New Yorkers greeted the "Magnificent Magyar," Hungarian patriot Louis Kossuth, as a conquering hero in December 1851. Supporters rushed the stage from which he was to deliver a speech, and one female admirer tore off a section of his coat as a prized souvenir. To New Yorkers, Kossuth embodied the democratic ideals of their nation founded on the principles of liberty and equality.

Fueled by rapid industrial and urban transformation, democratic sentiment spread over the European continent among the new working and middle classes in the 1840s. France showed the way. When the government of King Louis-Philippe failed to respond to demands for economic and political reforms, these groups banded together to overthrow the monarchy in February 1848. But the resulting government and new constitution under Charles Louis Napoleon Bonaparte, the nephew of the famous ruler, offered only superficial change, as reformers squandered their advantage with internal bickering between radicals and moderates.

When students at the University of Bonn heard the news of Louis-Philippe's downfall, they rushed into the town square to demand civil and religious liberties and the formation of a German national state. "We were dominated by a vague feeling," one student recalled, "as if a great outbreak of elemental forces had begun, as if an earthquake was impending of which we had felt the first shock." But the authoritarian rulers of the nine German states, while they allowed the formation of an all-German parliament and the drafting of a republican constitution, ignored both and the revolution failed.

A similar scenario played out in the Austrian Empire, a conglomeration of 11 different ethnic peoples, including Kossuth's Hungary. The ruling Hapsburg monarchy initially accepted some of the reformers' demands but then ruthlessly suppressed uprisings in Prague, Vienna, and Buda (Hungary). The Austrians also reestablished their control over portions of Italy, successfully overcoming a movement for Italian unity and reform.

These setbacks troubled Americans. Their initial enthusiasm for the revolutionary movements of 1848 was rooted in the belief that mankind naturally prefers liberty and equality and that the American experiment was exportable to other peoples. President James K. Polk hailed developments in Europe in 1848: "The great principles of popular sovereignty which were proclaimed in 1776 by the immortal author of our Declaration of Independence, seem now to be in the course of rapid development throughout the world."

The failure of these revolutionary movements made the American experiment that much more precious, and it also highlighted some contradictions in American democratic life. Frederick Douglass wondered how Americans could lionize a Hungarian freedom fighter, but hunt down Americans with the same aspirations. Events of the 1850s would sorely test that experiment.

CONCLUSION

When David Wilmot submitted his amendment to ban slavery from the territories gained from Mexico, he could not have foreseen that the debate he unleashed would end in civil war just 15 years later. But by the 1850s the slavery issue had become weighted with so much moral and political freight that it defied easy resolution.

The political conflict over slavery coalesced around northern efforts to curtail southern expansion and power and southern attempts to maintain power and influence in the federal government by planting the institution in the western territories.

Northerners and southerners eventually interpreted any incident or piece of legislation as an attempt by one side to gain moral and political advantage at the other's expense. Northerners viewed the *Dred Scott* decision, the Lecompton Constitution, and the southern reaction to John Brown's Raid as evidence of a Slave Power conspiracy to deny white northerners their constitutional rights. Southerners interpreted the northern reaction to these same events as evidence of a conspiracy to rob them of security and equality within the Union.

By 1861, the national political parties that had muted sectional animosities were gone, and so were national church organizations and fraternal associations. The ideals that had inspired the American Revolution remained in place, especially the importance of securing individual liberty against encroachment by government. But with each side interpreting them differently, these ideals served more to divide than to unite. Southerners viewed the North and the Republican Party as threats to their individual liberties. Northerners believed that the South was conspiring to rob them of their individual rights as well and that only the federal government stood between their freedom and the despotism of the Slave Power. Both sides claimed for themselves the role of guardian of the Revolutionary tradition. Lincoln's election left northerners feeling vindicated and southerners feeling vulnerable.

Ironically, as Americans in both sections talked of freedom and self-determination, the black men and women in their midst had little of either. Lincoln went to war to preserve the Union; Davis, to defend a new nation. Slavery was the spark that ignited the conflict, but white America seemed more comfortable embracing abstract ideals than real people. Northerners and southerners would confront this irony during the bloodiest war in American history, but they would not resolve it.

IMAGE KEY

for pages 384–385

a. Dredd Scott and his wife. ca. 1857.

b. The slave Eliza is attacked by vicious dogs while crossing ice floes of a frozen river with her baby in a poster advertising a production of *Uncle Tom's Cabin*.

c. John Brown portrait photo (1800–1859).

d. Gold ore and gravel in a shallow pan.

e. President Abraham Lincoln, Washington D.C., April 10, 1865.

f. Inside the Armory at Harper's Ferry, Virginia, where John Brown and his men were trapped by the fire of the U.S. Marines under the command of Colonel Robert E Lee, 18 October 1859 in a contemporary colored engraving.

g. Harriet Beecher Stowe.

h. Armed Missourians cross border into Kansas to vote illegally.

i. A thoughtful Henry Clay addresses attentive senators on the floor of the US Senate in 1850.

j. An old fashioned black stovepipe hat with a narrow brim like the one worn by Abe Lincoln.

k. A poster for *Uncle Tom's Cabin*.

SUMMARY

Slavery in the Territories As Americans expanded westward and new territories were added, the nation's attention became focused on the expansion of slavery. Clashes between the North and the South became more frequent and shrill; the existing political parties seemed unable to resolve the issue. The admission of California triggered a new crisis; the resulting Compromise of 1850 and Fugitive Slave Act left both sides unhappy. The publication of *Uncle Tom's Cabin* brought the evils of slavery to ordinary Americans and galvanized opposition to slavery in the North. The presidential election of 1852 revealed an increasingly divided nation.

Political Realignment By the 1850s, all policies were interpreted in the light of their impact on slavery. Expansionist plans involving Cuba, the building of a transcontinental railroad, and organization of the Kansas and Nebraska Territories were all tied to either expanding or limited slavery. Political parties in the North realigned over slavery and immigration with a new party, the Republican

Party, emerging in 1854. The *Dred Scott* case and Lecompton Constitution caused bitter reactions; the Lincoln-Douglas debates put the divisions and moral issue of slavery in sharp focus.

The Road to Disunion Ideological, economic, and social differences separated North and South. The South saw itself as increasingly victimized by the North; the raid of John Brown and its aftermath convinced Southerners their security in the Union was in jeopardy. The election of a Republican president would be a death sentence in Southern eyes; extremists believed it would give them the justification to secede. The election of Abraham Lincoln, the Republican candidate in 1860, was the signal for secession and formation of a separate nation. Lincoln initially took no action against the South, but when Fort Sumter was fired upon, Lincoln responded.

REVIEW QUESTIONS

1. How do you account for the great success of Harriet Beecher Stowe's *Uncle Tom's Cabin?*

2. How did the failure of democratic revolutions in Europe affect Americans' perspectives on their own system of government?

3. Discuss the role of evangelical religion in sharpening the sectional conflict between North and South.

4. Between the time he was elected president in November and his inauguration in March, what options did Abraham Lincoln have for resolving the sectional crisis?

5. Northerners and southerners appealed to the same American ideals in support of their respective positions. Could they both have been correct?

KEY TERMS

"Bleeding Kansas" (p. 397)
Compromise of 1850 (p. 391)
Confederate States of America
  (p. 409)
Constitutional Union Party
  (p. 407)
Dred Scott Decision (p. 400)

Fort Sumter (p. 413)
Fugitive Slave Act (p. 391)
John Brown's Raid (p. 406)
Kansas-Nebraska Act (p. 396)
Know-Nothing Party (p. 398)
Lecompton Constitution (p. 400)
Lincoln-Douglas debates (p. 402)

Ostend Manifesto (p. 395)
Panic of 1857 (p. 401)
Popular Sovereignty (p. 389)
Republican Party (p. 398)
Wilmot Proviso (p. 388)

WHERE TO LEARN MORE

⬭ **The Underground Railroad Freedom Center, Cincinnati, Ohio.** The Center provides information on the Northern response to the Fugitive Slave Act. See its websit at **www.undergroundrailroad.org**.

⬭ **Adair Cabin and John Brown Museum, John Brown Memorial Park, Osawatomie, Kansas.** Maintained by the Kansas Historical Society, the cabin (which once belonged to John Brown's sister) and the museum are located on the site of the Battle of Osawatomie, one of the critical events of "Bleeding Kansas." Its website is **www.kshs.org/places/adair.htm**.

- **Constitution Hall, Lecompton, Kansas.** This site, also run by the Kansas State Historical Society, is where proslavery delegates framed the controversial Lecompton Constitution that increased sectional discord. Go to **www.kshs .org/places/constit.htm**.

- **Harpers Ferry National Historical Park, West Virginia.** Exhibits interpret John Brown's Raid and re-create some of the atmosphere and structures of the 1850s village and the federal arsenal. Its website is **www.nps.gov/hafe**.

- **"A House Divided," mounted by the Chicago Historical Society, Chicago.** This exhibit depicts the major events of the sectional crisis during the 1850s, the election of 1860, and the coming of the Civil War. It continued until 2001 and is now available online. Go to **www.chicagohs.org**.

- **Fort Sumter National Monument, Charleston, South Carolina.** This historic site interprets the bombardment of the fort and the events that immediately preceded the Civil War. Go to **www.nps.gov/fosu**.

 U.S. History Documents CD-ROM
For primary sources related to this chapter, refer to the document CD-ROM.

 www.prenhall.com/goldfield
For study resources related to this chapter, visit the *Companion Website*™.

15 Battle Cries and Freedom Songs: The Civil War 1861–1865

CHAPTER HIGHLIGHTS

Mobilization, North and South Both sides thought the war would be short and neither side was well prepared. The North had superior resources and political leadership. The Confederacy sought to fight a defensive war that would wear down Northern public opinion.

The Early War, 1861–1862 The North's offensive strategy dictated the course of the war for the first two years. Southern victories in the East were balanced by setbacks in the West. At the end of 1862, the outcome of the war was still in doubt.

Turning Points, 1862–1863 Battlefield defeats ended the Confederate hope of attracting foreign allies and gave the North new momentum. Lincoln used the North's victories as an opportunity to issue the Emancipation Proclamation. By the end of 1863, the tide of battle had turned decidedly in the North's favor.

War Transforms the North The war required a strong and active central government. It also stimulated the Northern economy, although wages did not keep up with prices. Racial and ethnic tensions in the North sparked the New York draft riots.

The Confederacy Disintegrates Battlefield losses combined with economic hardship undermined morale in the South. After 1864, President Davis could not keep the Confederacy from disintegrating. In desperation, the South considered arming slaves.

The Union Prevails, 1864–1865 Grant and Sherman launched offensives that destroyed the South's remaining forces. Victories in the field led to the reelection of Abraham Lincoln and the passage of the Thirteenth Amendment. Northern joy at the war's end was tempered by Lincoln's assassination.

CHAPTER QUESTIONS

WHAT WERE the North's key advantages at the outset of the war?

HOW DID the two side's objectives dictate their strategies in the early years of the war?

WHAT CONVINCED Lincoln to issue the Emancipation Proclamation?

WHAT IMPACT did the war have on the North's economy?

HOW DID the war affect the lives of Southern women?

WHAT WAS Grant's strategy for ending the war?

CHAPTER OUTLINE

- Mobilization, North and South
- The Early War, 1861–1862
- Turning Points, 1862–1863
- The War Transforms the North
- The Confederacy Disintegrates
- The Union Prevails, 1864–1865

IMAGE KEY

for pages 418–419 is on page 453.

July 14, 1861

Camp Clark, Washington, DC

My very dear Sarah:

The indications are very strong that we shall move in a few days, perhaps tomorrow. And lest I should not be able to write you again I feel impelled to write a few lines that may fall under your eye when I am no more. Our movement may be one of a few days' duration and be full of pleasure. And it may be one of severe conflict and death to me. "Not my will but thine O God be done." If it is necessary that I should fall on the battle-field for my Country I am ready. I have no misgivings about, or lack of confidence in the cause in which I am engaged, and my courage does not halt or falter. I know how American Civilization now leans upon the triumph of the government and how great a debt we owe to those who went before us through the blood and suffering of the Revolution. And I am willing, perfectly willing, to lay down all my joys in this life, to help maintain this government, and to pay that debt. But my dear wife, when I know that with my own joys I lay down nearly all of yours, . . . is it weak or dishonorable that while the banner of my purpose floats calmly and proudly in the breeze, underneath, my unbounded love for you my darling wife and children should struggle in fierce though useless contest with my love of country? . . .

Sarah, my love for you is deathless, it seems to bind me with mighty cables that nothing but omnipotence can break; and yet my love of Country comes over me like a strong wind and bears me irresistibly with all those chains to the battle-field.

The memories of the blissful moments I have enjoyed with you come crowding over me, and I feel most deeply grateful to God and you, that I have enjoyed them for so long. And how hard it is for me to give them up and burn to ashes the hopes and future years, when, God willing, we might still have lived and loved together, and see our boys grown up to honorable manhood around us. . . . If I do not [return], my dear Sarah, never forget how much I loved you, nor that when my last breath escapes me on the battle-field, it will whisper your name.

Forgive my many faults, and the many pains I have caused you. How thoughtless, how foolish I have sometimes been! . . .

But, O Sarah, if the dead can come back to this earth and flit unseen around those they love, I shall be with you, in the gladdest days and the darkest nights . . . always, always, and if there be a soft breeze upon your cheek, it shall be my breath[;] as the cool air fans your throbbing temple, it shall be my spirit passing by. Sarah do not mourn me dead; think I am gone and wait for thee, for we shall meet again. . . .

Sullivan

Sullivan Ballou to Sarah Ballou, July 14, 1861. Geoffrey C. Ward et al., eds., *The Civil War: An Illustrated History* (New York: Alfred A. Knopf, 1990), 82–83.

SULLIVAN BALLOU'S letter to his wife on the eve of the First Battle of Bull Run typified the sentiments of the civilian armies raised by both North and South.

Just a few months earlier, Major Sullivan Ballou of the Second Regiment, Rhode Island Volunteers, was a 32-year-old attorney with a wife and two young sons. But the events of the 1850s stoked Ballou's interest in politics, and he became a dedicated Republican and devoted supporter of Abraham Lincoln. When the war came, he volunteered and was sent to Washington, D.C. He wrote this letter from his camp. A few days later, his company marched to Manassas, Virginia, where they engaged Confederate troops on July 21 at the First Battle of Bull Run. Sullivan Ballou was killed in the battle.

The Civil War preserved the Union, abolished slavery, and killed at least 620,000 soldiers, more than in all the other wars the country fought combined. To come to terms with this is to try to reconcile the war's great accomplishments with its awful consequences. When the war began, only a small minority of northerners linked the preservation of the Union with the abolition of slavery. By 1863, Union and freedom had become inseparable federal objectives. The Confederacy fought for independence and the preservation of slavery. The Confederate objectives dictated a defensive military strategy; the Union objectives dictated an offensive strategy.

Black southerners seized the initiative in the war against slavery, especially in the months after the Emancipation Proclamation, eventually joining Union forces in combat against their former masters. Soon, another war to secure the fruits of freedom would begin.

MOBILIZATION, NORTH AND SOUTH

Neither side was prepared for a major war. The Confederacy lacked a national army. Each southern state had a militia, but by the 1850s, these companies had become more social clubs than fighting units. The Union had a regular army of only 16,000 men, most of whom were stationed west of the Mississippi River.

Each government augmented these meager military reserves with thousands of new recruits and developed a bureaucracy to mount a war effort. At the same time, the administrations of Presidents Lincoln and Davis secured the loyalty of their civilian populations and devised military strategies for a war of indeterminate duration.

WAR FEVER

The day after Major Robert Anderson surrendered Fort Sumter, President Lincoln moved to enlarge his small, scattered army by mobilizing state militias for 90 days. Four states—Virginia, Arkansas, North Carolina, and Tennessee—refused the call and seceded from the Union. About one-third of the officer corps of the regular army, including some of the highest-ranking officers, resigned their commissions to join the Confederacy.

Both North and South believed that the war would end quickly. Some southerners believed that the Yankees would quit after the first battle. "Just throw three or four shells among those blue-bellied Yankees," a North Carolinian blustered, "and they'll scatter like sheep."

Northerners closed ranks behind the president after the Confederacy's attack on Fort Sumter. Stephen A. Douglas, a leading Democrat, called on the

WHAT WERE the North's key advantages at the outset of the war?

Chronology

1861	**January**	Benito Juarez becomes President of Mexico dedicated to restoring national unity.
	March	Tsar Alexander II emancipates Russia's serfs.
		Kingdom of Italy proclaimed.
	April	Confederates fire on Fort Sumter; Civil War begins.
	July	First Battle of Bull Run.
1862	**February**	Forts Henry and Donelson fall to Union forces.
	March	Peninsula Campaign begins.
		Battle of Glorieta Pass, New Mexico.
	April	Battle of Shiloh.
		New Orleans falls to Federal forces.
	May	Union captures Corinth, Mississippi.
	July	Seven Days' Battles end.
		Congress passes the Confiscation Act.
	August	Second Battle of Bull Run.
	September	Battle of Antietam.
	December	Battle of Fredericksburg.
1863	**January**	Emancipation Proclamation takes effect.
	May	Battle of Chancellorsville; Stonewall Jackson is mortally wounded.
	June	French forces capture Mexico City.
	July	Battle of Gettysburg.
		Vicksburg falls to Union forces.

		New York Draft Riot occurs.
		Black troops of the 54th Massachusetts Volunteer Infantry Regiment assault Fort Wagner outside Charleston.
	September	Battle of Chickamauga.
	November	Battle of Chattanooga.
1864	**May**	Battle of the Wilderness.
	June	Battle of Cold Harbor.
		Ferdinand Maximilian Joseph, archduke of Austria, crowned emperor of Mexico with support of French troops.
	September	Sherman captures Atlanta.
	November	President Lincoln is reelected.
		Sherman begins his march to the sea.
1865	**January**	Congress passes Thirteenth Amendment to the Constitution, outlawing slavery (ratified December 1865).
	February	Charleston surrenders.
	March	Confederate Congress authorizes enlistment of black soldiers.
	April	Federal troops enter Richmond.
		Lee surrenders to Grant at Appomattox Court House.
		Lincoln is assassinated.

15–2
The "Cornerstone" Speech (1861)

Republican Lincoln to offer his and his party's support. "There can be no neutrals in this war," Douglas said, "only patriots, or traitors." American flags flew everywhere. Southerners were equally eager to support their new nation. They punctuated stirring renditions of "Dixie" with the high-pitched piercing sounds that would later be known as the "rebel yell." Enlistment rallies, wild send-offs at train stations, and auctions and balls to raise money for the troops were staged throughout the Confederacy.

The feeling that a holy war was unfolding energized recruits. A Union soldier expressed his feelings in a letter home at the beginning of the war: "I believe our cause to be the cause of liberty and light . . . the cause of God, and holy and justifiable in His sight, and for this reason, I fear not to die in it if need be." Equally convinced of the righteousness of his cause, a Confederate soldier wrote: "Our

Cause is Just and God is Just and we shall finally be successful whether I live to see the time or not."

As war fever gripped North and South, volunteers on both sides rushed to join, quickly filling the quotas of both armies. The initial enthusiasm, however, wore off quickly. After four months of war, a young Confederate soldier admitted, "I have seen quite enough of a soldier's life to satisfy me that it is not what it is cracked up to be."

The South in particular faced a contradiction between its ideology and the demands of full-scale war. Southerners were loyal to their localities, counties, and states. Southern leaders had been fighting for decades to defend states' rights against national authority. Now these same leaders had to forge the states of the Confederacy into a nation. By early spring of 1862, the Confederate government was compelled to order the first general draft in American history.

The Confederate draft law allowed several occupational exemptions. Among them was an infamous provision that allowed one white man on any plantation with more than 20 slaves to be excused from service. The reason for the exemption was to ensure the security and productivity of large plantations, not to protect the privileged, but it led some southerners to conclude that the struggle had become "a rich man's war but a poor man's fight."

The initial flush of enthusiasm faded in the North as well. Responding to a call for additional troops, some northern states initiated a draft during the summer of 1862. In March 1863, Congress passed the Enrollment Act, a draft law that, like the Confederate draft, allowed for occupational exemptions. A provision that allowed a draftee to hire a substitute aroused resentment among working-class northerners. Anger at the draft, as well as poor working conditions, sparked several riots during 1863. But the North was less dependent on conscription than was the South.

The armies of both sides included men from all walks of life, from common laborers to clerks to bankers. An undetermined number of women, typically disguised as men, also served in both armies. They joined for the same reasons as men: adventure, patriotism, and glory.

THE NORTH'S ADVANTAGE IN RESOURCES

The resources of the North, including its population, industrial and agricultural capacity, and transportation network, greatly exceeded those of the South. The 2.1 million men who fought for the Union represented roughly half the men of military age in the North. The 900,000 men who fought for the Confederacy, by contrast, represented fully 90 percent of its eligible population. Nearly 200,000 African Americans, most of them ex-slaves from the South, took up arms for the Union. Not until the last month of the war did the Confederacy consider arming slaves.

The Confederacy compensated somewhat for its numerical disadvantage by requiring long tours of duty, which meant that its forces tended to be more experienced than those of the Union. But the Union's greater numbers left the South vulnerable to a war of attrition.

At the beginning of the war, the North controlled 90 percent of the nation's industrial capacity. The North had dozens of facilities for producing war matériel; the South had only one munitions plant, the Tredegar Iron Works in Richmond. Northern farms, more mechanized than their southern counterparts, produced record harvests of meat, grains, and vegetables. Southern farms were productive, but the South lacked the North's capacity to transport and distribute food

QUICK REVIEW

Northern Advantages
- Twice the number of soldiers.
- North controlled 90 percent of nation's industrial capacity.
- Naval superiority.

efficiently. The railroad system in the North was more than twice the size of the South's.

Thanks to the North's abundance of resources, no soldier in any previous American army had ever been outfitted as well as the blue-uniformed Union trooper. The official color of the Confederate uniform was gray, although a dusty brown shade was more common. Most southern soldiers, however, did not wear distinguishable uniforms, especially toward the end of the war. They also often lacked proper shoes or any footwear at all. Still, the South never lost a battle because of insufficient supplies or inadequate weaponry. New foundries opened, and manufacturing enterprises in Augusta, Georgia; Selma, Alabama; and elsewhere helped keep the Confederate armies equipped.

Unstable finances proved more of a handicap for the Confederacy than its relatively low industrial capacity. The Confederate economy, and its treasury, depended heavily on cotton exports. But a Union naval blockade and the ability of textile manufacturers in Europe to find new sources of supply restricted this crucial source of revenue. The imposition of taxes would have improved the Confederacy's finances, but southerners resisted taxation. The government sold interest-bearing bonds to raise money, but as Confederate fortunes declined, so did bond sales. With few other options, the Confederacy financed more than 60 percent of the $1.5 billion it spent on the war with printing-press money. Inflation spiraled out of control, demoralizing civilians.

The Union had more abundant financial resources than the Confederacy, and the federal government was more successful than the Confederate government at developing innovative ways to meet the great cost of the war. Like the Confederacy, the federal government issued paper money, bills derisively known as "greenbacks," that was not backed by gold or silver. But the federal government also offset its expenses with the country's first income tax, which citizens could pay in greenbacks, a move that bolstered the value and credibility of the paper currency. These financial measures eliminated the need for wage and price controls and rationing and warded off ruinous inflation in the North.

LEADERS, GOVERNMENTS, AND STRATEGIES

Leadership ability, like resources, played an important role in the war. It was up to the leaders of the two sides to determine and administer civilian and military policy, to define war objectives, and to inspire a willingness to sacrifice in both citizens and soldiers.

The Confederate president, Jefferson Davis, had to build a government from scratch during a war. Although Davis's career qualified him for the prodigious task of running the Confederacy, aspects of his character compromised his effectiveness. He had a sharp intellect but, colleagues found him aloof. He was inclined to equate compromise with weakness and interpreted any opposition as a personal attack.

Southerners viewed themselves as the genuine heirs of the American Revolution and the true defenders of the United States Constitution. If the South were to establish itself as a separate country, however, southerners had to renounce their American identity and develop one of their own. But on what distinctive aspects of southern life could the Confederacy build such an identity? Slavery was distinctively Southern, but most white southerners, even if they believed that slavery served their interests, did not own slaves. Southerners had forcefully advanced the ideology of states' rights, but, with its emphasis on the primacy of state sovereignty over central authority, states' rights, too, was a weak foundation on which to build a national consciousness.

QUICK REVIEW

Jefferson Davis and the Southern Cause

- Davis not a leader by personality.
- Southerners saw themselves as true heirs of the Revolution.
- Davis needed to provide Southerners with a vision of their future state.

15–4
Why They Fought
(1861)

Northerners, like southerners, needed a convincing reason to endure the prolonged sacrifice of the Civil War. Lincoln and other northern leaders secured support by convincing their compatriots of the importance of preserving the Union. Lincoln eloquently articulated this view, framing the war as more than a military conquest. The president viewed the conflict in global terms, its results affecting the hopes for democratic government around the world. He concluded that the war "presents to the whole family of man, the question, whether a constitutional republic . . . can or cannot maintain its territorial integrity, against its own domestic foes."

The secession of Virginia, Arkansas, North Carolina, and Tennessee left four border slave states, Maryland, Delaware, Kentucky, and Missouri, hanging in the balance. Were Maryland and Delaware to secede, the federal capital at Washington, D.C., would be surrounded by Confederate territory. The loss of Kentucky and Missouri would threaten the borders of Iowa, Illinois, Indiana, and Ohio and remove the Deep South from the threat of imminent invasion. Lincoln viewed Kentucky as the key to retaining the three other border states: "I think to lose Kentucky is nearly to lose the whole game. Kentucky gone, we cannot hold Missouri, nor, as I think, Maryland. . . . We would as well consent to separation at once, including the surrender of this capital."

Lincoln adopted a "soft" strategy to secure the border states, stressing the restoration of the Union as the sole objective of Federal military operations and assuring border residents that his government would not interfere with slavery. But early reports from the four states were troubling. The four governors displayed polite indifference or overt hostility to the federal government.

Maryland's strategic location north of Washington, D.C., rendered its loyalty to the Union vital. Lincoln dispatched Federal troops to monitor the fall elections in the state, placed its legislature under military surveillance, and arrested officials who opposed the Union cause, including the mayor of Baltimore. This show of force guaranteed the pro-Union candidate for governor an overwhelming victory and saved Maryland for the Union. Delaware, although nominally a slave state, remained staunchly for the Union.

Missourians settled their indecision by combat. The fighting culminated with a Union victory in March 1862 at the Battle of Pea Ridge, Arkansas. Pro-Confederate Missourians refused to concede defeat and waged an unsuccessful guerrilla war over the next two years.

Kentucky never seceded but attempted to remain neutral at the outset of the war. The legislature was pro-Union, the governor pro-southern. Both sides actively recruited soldiers in the state. In September 1861, when Confederate forces invaded Kentucky and Union forces moved to expel them, the state became one of the war's battlegrounds.

Although Virginia went with the Confederacy, some counties in the western part of the state opposed secession and, as early as the summer of 1861, took steps to establish a pro-Union state. In June 1863, West Virginia became the nation's thirty-fifth state.

The North's goal of preserving the union required conquest. Federal forces had to invade the South, destroy its armies, and rout its government. The Confederacy, for its part, did not need to conquer the North. Fighting a defensive battle in its own territory, the South had only to hang on until growing northern opposition to the war or some decisive northern military mistake convinced the Union to stop fighting.

But the South's strategy had two weaknesses. First, it demanded more patience than the South had shown in impulsively attacking Fort Sumter. Second, the

South might not have sufficient resources to draw out the war long enough to swing northern public opinion behind peace.

THE EARLY WAR, 1861–1862

HOW DID the two sides'
objectives dictate their strategies in
the early years of the war?

The North's offensive strategy dictated the course of the war for the first two years. In the West, the federal army's objectives were to hold Missouri, Kentucky, and Tennessee, to control the Mississippi River, and eventually to detach the area west of the Appalachians from the rest of the Confederacy. In the East, Union forces sought to capture Richmond, the Confederate capital. The U.S. Navy imposed a blockade along the Confederate coast and pushed into inland waterways to capture southern ports.

The Confederates defended strategic locations throughout their territory or abandoned them when prudence required. By the end of 1862, the result remained in the balance. Although Union forces had attained some success in the West, the southern armies there remained intact. In the East, where resourceful Confederate leaders several times stopped superior Union forces, the southerners clearly had the best of it.

FIRST BULL RUN

By July 1861 President Lincoln ordered General Irvin McDowell to move his forces into Virginia to take Richmond (see Map 15–1). Confronting McDowell 20 miles southwest of Washington at Manassas was a Confederate army under General P. G. T. Beauregard. The two armies clashed on July 21 at the First Battle of Bull Run (known to the Confederacy as the First Battle of Manassas). The Union troops seemed at first on the verge of winning. But Beauregard's forces, along with General Joseph E. Johnston's reinforcements, repulsed the assault.

Bull Run dispelled some illusions and reinforced others. It boosted southerners' confidence and seemed to confirm their boast that one Confederate could whip ten Yankees, even though the opposing armies were of relatively equal strength when the fighting began. The Union rout planted the suspicion in northern minds that perhaps the Confederates were invincible and destroyed the widespread belief in the North that the war would be over quickly.

THE WAR IN THE WEST

Federal forces may have retreated in Virginia, but they advanced in the West. Two Confederate forts on the Tennessee-Kentucky border, Fort Henry on the Tennessee River and Fort Donelson on the Cumberland River, guarded the strategic waterways that linked Tennessee and Kentucky to the Mississippi Valley (see Map 15–2). In February 1862, Union general Ulysses S. Grant coordinated a land and river campaign against the forts.

Grant's combined river and land campaign caught the southerners unprepared and outflanked. The Union victory drove a wedge into southern territory and closed the Confederacy's quickest path to the West from Virginia and the Carolinas. The Confederacy's only safe link across the Appalachians was now through Georgia. The Confederacy never recovered its strategic advantage in the West.

Grant next moved his main army south to Pittsburgh Landing on the Tennessee River, to prepare for an assault on the key Mississippi River port and rail center of Vicksburg. After blunting a surprise Confederate attack at Shiloh Church near Pittsburgh Landing, Grant pushed the southerners back to Corinth, Mississippi.

QUICK REVIEW

The First Battle of Bull Run

- July 21, 1861: Beauregard (Confederacy) and McDowell (Union) meet at Manassas.
- Confederate troops repulse a strong Union attack.
- Colonel Thomas J. Jackson earns his nickname "Stonewall."

Federal forces complemented their victories at Shiloh and Corinth with another important success at New Orleans. Admiral David G. Farragut blasted the Confederate river defenses protecting New Orleans and sailed a federal fleet onto the city in April 1862. The result was to open 200 miles of the Mississippi River, the nation's most vital commercial waterway, to Union traffic. With the fall of Memphis to Union forces in June, Vicksburg remained the only major river town still in Confederate hands. The western losses exposed a major problem in the Confederates' defensive strategy: their military resources were stretched too thin to defend their vast territory.

REASSESSING THE WAR: THE HUMAN TOLL

The fierce fighting at Shiloh wrought unprecedented carnage. Each side suffered more than 10,000 casualties. "Too shocking, too horrible," a Confederate survivor of Shiloh wrote. "God grant that I may never be the partaker in such scenes again . . . when released from this I shall ever be an advocate of peace." A Union soldier wrote of "the dead and dying lying in masses, some with arms, legs, and even their jaws shot off, bleeding to death, and no one to wait upon them to dress their wounds."

Women on both sides played a major role in caring for the wounded and sick. In the North, members of the U.S. Sanitary Commission attempted to upgrade hospital and medical care. This voluntary organization, founded in April 1861, was staffed mainly by women volunteers who collected and distributed medical supplies and clothing and advised on cleaning hospitals and camps. The commission made some headway during the first year of the war, but in the months after Shiloh and with the resumption of fighting in the East, the extent of casualties often overwhelmed the dedicated volunteers.

Advanced weaponry combined with outdated military tactics to increase the death toll. Only late in the war did tactics change, but even then, the problems of communication and the inability to precisely coordinate attacks continued to favor the packed ranks of men advancing forward at a trot, often in the face of withering fire.

Even if a soldier escaped death on the battlefield and survived a hospital stay, he still faced the possibility of death from disease. Roughly twice as many men died from disease as on the battlefield during the Civil War. Typhoid, commonly and appropriately known as "camp fever," claimed the most lives.

Many soldiers turned to religion for consolation in response to the growing carnage. Soldiers often gathered with their comrades to sing hymns before retiring for the night. Stories circulated of a Bible carried in a pocket that stopped a bullet whistling toward a soldier's heart.

MAP EXPLORATION
To explore an interactive version of this map, go to
http://www.prenhall.com/goldfield3/map15.1

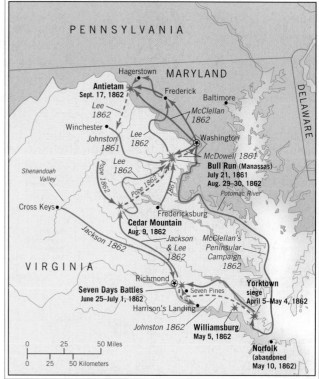

MAP 15–1   From First Bull Run to Antietam: The War in the East, 1861–1862   The early stages of the war demonstrated the strategies of the Confederacy and the Union. Federal troops stormed into Virginia hoping to capture Richmond and bring a quick end to the war. Through a combination of poor generalship and Confederate tenacity, they failed. Confederate troops hoped to defend their territory, prolong the war, and eventually win their independence as northern patience evaporated. They proved successful initially, but, with the abandonment of the defensive strategy and the invasion of Maryland in the fall of 1862, the Confederates suffered a political and morale setback at Antietam.

WHY DID the South abandon its defensive strategy in the fall of 1862?

MAP EXPLORATION

To explore an interactive version of this map, go to **http://www.prenhall.com/goldfield3/map15.2**

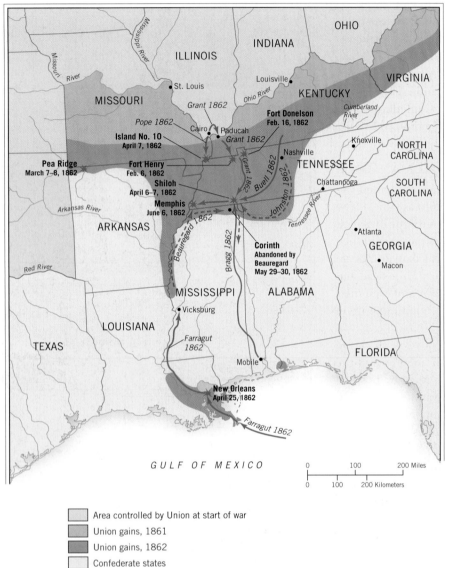

Area controlled by Union at start of war
Union gains, 1861
Union gains, 1862
Confederate states
◄— Union advances
◄— Confederate advances
◄- - Confederate retreats
✴ Union victories

MAP 15–2   The War in the West, 1861–1862   Because of the early Union emphasis on capturing Richmond, the war in the West seemed less important to northerners. But from a strategic standpoint, the victories at Forts Henry and Donelson, which drove a wedge into southern territory and closed the Confederacy's quickest path to the West from Virginia and the Carolinas, and the capture of New Orleans and its Mississippi River port were crucial and set the stage for greater federal success in the West in 1863.

BASED ON this map, what was the Union's overall strategy in these campaigns?

THE WAR IN THE EAST

With Grant and Farragut squeezing the Confederacy in the West, Lincoln ordered a new offensive against Richmond in the East that he believed would end the war. Following the defeat at Bull Run, he had shaken up the Union high command and appointed General George B. McClellan to lead what was now called the Army of the Potomac. McClellan succeeded in transforming it into a disciplined fighting force. He was well liked by his soldiers, who referred to him affectionately as "Little Mac." McClellan returned their affection, perhaps too much. A superb organizer, he would prove overly cautious on the field of battle.

In March 1862, at the outset of the Peninsula Campaign, McClellan moved his 112,000-man army out of Washington and maneuvered his forces by boat down the Potomac River and Chesapeake Bay to the peninsula between the York and James rivers southeast of the Confederate capital (see Map 15–1). Union forces took Yorktown, Williamsburg, and Norfolk. Confederate general Joseph E. Johnston withdrew his forces up the peninsula toward Richmond, preparing for what most felt would be the decisive battle of the war. McClellan, moving ponderously up the peninsula, clashed with Johnston's army inconclusively at Seven Pines in late May 1862. Johnston was badly wounded in the clash, and President Davis replaced him with General Robert E. Lee, who renamed the forces under his command the Army of Northern Virginia.

A career army officer who resigned his commission to serve his state and new country, General Robert E. Lee's quiet courage and sense of duty inspired his men.

Corbis/Bettman

Refusing an offer from Winfield Scott to take command of the federal forces, he resigned from the U.S. Army and went with Virginia after it left the Union. Lee's reserved and aristocratic bearing masked a gambler's disposition. A fellow officer noted, "his name might be Audacity. He will take more chances, and take them quicker than any other general in this country." Under his daring leadership, the Confederacy's defensive strategy underwent an important shift.

Lee seized the initiative on June 25, 1862, attacking McClellan's right flank. For a week, the armies sparred in a series of fierce engagements known collectively as the Seven Days' Battles. More than 30,000 men were killed or wounded on both sides, the deadliest week of the war so far. Although McClellan prevailed in these contests, the carnage so shocked him that he withdrew to Harrison's Landing on the James River. An exasperated Lincoln replaced McClellan with John Pope. Although Lee had saved Richmond, he had lost one-fourth of his 80,000-man army. Nonetheless, he remained convinced of the wisdom of his offensive-defensive strategy.

Lee went to work to vindicate these tactics. A series of inconclusive skirmishes brought Union and Confederate armies together once more near Manassas Junction. The Second Battle of Bull Run was as much a disaster for the Union as the first had been. Lee's generalship befuddled Pope and again saved Richmond.

TURNING POINTS, 1862–1863

Having stymied the Union war machine, Lee contemplated a bold move, a thrust into northern territory to bring the conflict to the North and stoke northerners' rising hostility to the war. President

WHAT CONVINCED Lincoln to issue the Emancipation Proclamation?

Lincoln also harbored a bold plan. Gradually, during the spring and summer of 1862, the president had concluded that emancipation of the Confederacy's slaves was essential for preserving the Union. But Lincoln was reluctant to take this step before the Union's fortunes on the battlefield improved. As the fall of 1862 approached, the Union and Confederate governments both prepared for the most significant conflicts of the war to date.

THE NAVAL AND THE DIPLOMATIC WAR

The Union's naval strategy was to blockade the southern coast and capture its key seaports and river towns. The intention was to prevent arms, clothing, and food from reaching the Confederacy and keep cotton and tobacco from leaving. This vital trade raised much needed money and brought the Confederacy into contact with European nations, a connection its leaders hoped to reinforce on the diplomatic front.

Understandably, the Confederate naval strategy was to break the blockade and defend the South's vital rivers and seaports. The Confederacy built several warships to serve as blockade runners and as privateers to attack Union merchant ships, and they briefly disrupted federal operations before Union vessels regained the advantage. Historians disagree about the effectiveness of the Union naval blockade, but any restriction in the flow of trade hurt the Southern cause.

The Diplomatic Front. The Davis administration did chalk up some minor diplomatic victories early in the war. Great Britain declared itself neutral and allowed British merchants to sell arms and supplies to both the Confederacy and the Union. France followed with a similar concession.

In the end, the Confederacy's hopes for diplomatic recognition depended on its ability to show that it could secure its independence on the battlefield. After Lee's victories in Virginia in the spring of 1862 and his subsequent decision to invade the North, British intervention in the war grew more likely. The British government had more or less decided that if Lee emerged victorious from his planned invasion, it would press for mediation.

ANTIETAM

In September 1862, Lee crossed the Potomac into Maryland (see Map 15–1). He was on his way to cut the Pennsylvania Railroad at Harrisburg.

Luck intervened for the North when a Union corporal found a copy of Lee's orders for the disposition of his army. But even with this information, "Little Mac" moved so cautiously that Lee had time to retreat to defensive positions at Sharpsburg, Maryland, along Antietam Creek. There Lee's army of 39,000 men came to blows with McClellan's army of 75,000.

The Battle of Antietam saw the bloodiest single day of fighting in American history. About 2,100 Union soldiers and 2,700 Confederates died, and another 18,500, equally divided, were wounded. McClellan squandered his numerical superiority with uncoordinated and timid attacks. Although the armies had fought to a tactical draw, the battle was a strategic defeat for the Confederacy.

Antietam marked a major turning point in the war. It kept Lee from directly threatening northern industry and financial institutions. It prompted Britain and France to abandon plans to grant recognition to the Confederacy. And it provided Lincoln with the victory he needed to announce the abolition of slavery.

QUICK REVIEW

The War at Sea
- Union naval blockade strengthened over time.
- Confederate ships had limited success running the blockade.
- Restriction of trade hurt the Southern cause.

WHERE TO LEARN MORE

Antietam National Battlefield, Sharpsburg, Maryland
www.nps.gov/anti/

QUICK REVIEW

Turning Point: Antietam
- Kept Lee from directly threatening the North.
- Prompted Britain and France to abandon plans to recognize the Confederacy.
- Provided Lincoln with the opportunity to announce the abolition of slavery.

EMANCIPATION

President Lincoln despised slavery, but he had always maintained that preserving the Union was his primary war goal. An astute politician, Lincoln realized that he had to stress Union and equivocate on slavery to keep the northern public united in support of the war. But from the war's outset, the possibility of emancipation as a war objective was considered in the Republican Congress, in the Union army, and among citizens throughout the Northern states.

Lincoln had said in his inaugural address that he had "no purpose, directly or indirectly, to interfere with the institution of slavery in the states where it exists." By March 1862, however, his moral repugnance for slavery, and the military arguments for abolition, led him to propose a resolution, which Congress adopted, supporting the compensated emancipation of slaves. The measure died, however, when Congress failed to appropriate funds for it and slaveholders in the border states expressed no interest in the plan.

Pressure from northern civilians, Union soldiers, and Congress for some form of emancipation mounted in the spring of 1862. In response, the Republican Congress prohibited slavery in the territories and abolished slavery in the District of Columbia. The act emancipating the district's slaves called for compensating slave owners and colonizing the freed slaves in black republics, such as Haiti and Liberia. Then, in July 1862, Congress passed the **Confiscation Act,** which ordered the seizure of land from disloyal southerners and the emancipation of their slaves.

Although support for emancipation had grown both in the army and among civilians, it was still not favored by a majority in the North, especially not in the border states. But other considerations favored emancipation. Freeing the slaves would appeal to the strong antislavery sentiment in Britain and gain support for the Union cause abroad. And it would weaken the Confederacy's ability to wage war by removing a crucial source of labor.

By mid-1862, the president had resolved to act on his moral convictions and proclaim emancipation. Taking the advice of Secretary of State Seward, however, he decided to wait for a battlefield victory. Antietam gave the president his opening, narrow though it was, and on September 22, 1862, he announced his intention to issue the **Emancipation Proclamation,** to take effect January 1, 1863, in all states still in rebellion. The proclamation exempted slaves in the border states loyal to the Union and in areas under federal occupation. By raising the stakes of the war, President Lincoln hoped to shorten it. And, by leaving slaves in the border states untouched, he maintained their loyalty, or at least their neutrality.

But it would be a mistake to attribute Lincoln's motives primarily to military necessity. Secretary of the Navy Gideon Welles took notes on the cabinet meeting that followed the victory at Antietam. According to Welles's account, Lincoln made little reference to political or military strategy at the meeting. Instead, the president explained that he "had made a vow, a covenant, that if God gave us the victory in the approaching battle, he would consider it an indication of Divine will, and that it was his duty to move forward in the cause of emancipation."

Southerners reacted to the Emancipation Proclamation with outrage. Jefferson Davis, taking a positive view, thought that the proclamation would invigorate the Southern war effort.

Northerners generally approved of the Emancipation Proclamation. Although abolitionists comprised a minority of the northern population, most civilians and soldiers recognized the military advantages of emancipation. A private in

Confiscation Act Second confiscation law passed by Congress, ordering the seizure of land from disloyal Southerners and the emancipation of their slaves.

Emancipation Proclamation Decree announced by President Abraham Lincoln in September 1862 and formally issued on January 1, 1863, freeing slaves in all Confederate states still in rebellion.

the Army of the Potomac wrote home his support for "putting away any institution if by so doing it will help put down the rebellion."

The Emancipation Proclamation represented far more than its qualified words and phrases expressed. Lincoln had freed the slaves. What had begun as a war to save the Union was now a holy war of deliverance. Freedom and Union entwined in the public consciousness of the North. As Lincoln noted in his December 1862 message to Congress, "[I]n giving freedom to the slave, we assure freedom to the free."

As word of the Emancipation Proclamation raced through the slave grapevine, slaves rejoiced. But the proclamation only continued a process that had begun when the first Union armies invaded the South. In the months before freedom came, many slaves had run away to Union camps, dug Union trenches, and scouted for federal troops.

Even before the Emancipation Proclamation, slaves throughout the South "stole" their freedom. After the Proclamation, the trickle of black slaves abandoning their masters became a flood as they sought freedom behind Union lines.

Theo Kaufman, *On to Liberty,* 1867, oil on canvas, 36″ × 56″. The Metropolitan Museum of Art. Gift of Irving and Joyce Wolf, 1982 (1982.443.3). Photograph © 1982 The Metropolitan Museum of Art.

The 1862 Confiscation Act included slaves with other Confederate property as "contraband" of war and subject to confiscation. As they helped the Union cause, contrabands also sought to help fellow slaves "steal" their freedom. When Union forces occupied part of the Georgia coast in April 1862, for example, March Haynes, a slave who had worked as a river pilot in Savannah, began smuggling slaves to the Union lines. Federal general Quincy Adams Gilmore provided a swift boat for Haynes's missions. In return, Haynes supplied Gilmore with "exact and valuable information" on the strength and location of Confederate defenses. The Emancipation Proclamation accelerated the slaves' flight from bondage. After 1863, ex-slaves served in increasing numbers in the Union army.

More than 80 percent of the roughly 180,000 black soldiers and 20,000 black sailors who fought for the Union were slaves and free black men from the South. President Lincoln strongly advocated enlisting former slaves. In March 1863, he wrote, with exaggerated enthusiasm, that "the bare sight of 50,000 armed and drilled black soldiers on the banks of the Mississippi would end the rebellion at once." On the contrary, the appearance of black Union troops infuriated the Confederates.

The Confederate government formally labeled white officers leading black troops as instigators of slave rebellion and punished them accordingly, presumably by hanging. Black soldiers, when captured, were returned to slavery. The Lincoln administration retaliated by suspending prisoner exchanges, which resulted in horrible conditions in Confederate and Union prisons.

On some occasions, Confederate treatment of African-American prisoners of war was worse than a return to bondage. In April 1864, General Nathan Bedford Forrest, a slave-trader prior to the war and a founder of the Ku Klux Klan after the war, overran federal positions at Fort Pillow, Tennessee. Though the black Union defenders surrendered, Forrest's men shouted, "Kill the damn niggers, shoot them down!" More than 100 surrendered black soldiers were murdered, along with some white officers.

But for black volunteers, the promise of freedom and redemption outweighed the dangers of combat. Frederick Douglass, whose son Lewis distinguished himself in the all-black 54th Massachusetts Volunteer Infantry Regiment, explained in early 1863, "Once let the black man get upon his person the brass letters, 'U.S.,' let him get an eagle on his buttons and a musket on his shoulder and bullets in his pockets, and there is no power on earth which can deny that he has earned the right to citizenship in the United States." Sojourner Truth, a former slave who saw many of her 13 siblings sold into slavery, canvassed northern cities to rally public opinion for the deployment of black troops.

Although black soldiers were eager to engage the enemy and fought as ably as their white comrades, they received lower pay and performed the most menial duties in camp.

Despite discrimination, black soldiers fought valiantly at Port Hudson, Louisiana; near Charleston; and, late in the war, at the siege of Petersburg, Virginia. The most celebrated black encounter with Confederate troops occurred in July 1863, during a futile assault by the 54th Massachusetts Regiment on Fort Wagner outside Charleston. The northern press, previously lukewarm toward black troops, heaped praise on the effort. "Through the cannon smoke of that dark night," intoned a writer in the *Atlantic Monthly*, "the manhood of the colored race shines before many eyes that would not see."

If only President Lincoln could find such gallantry among his generals! George McClellan had failed to follow his advantage at Antietam in September

W **WHERE TO LEARN MORE**

★ Gettysburg National Military Park, Gettysburg, Pennsylvania
www.nps.gov/gett/

MAP EXPLORATION

To explore an interactive version of this map, go to
http://www.prenhall.com/goldfield3/map15.3

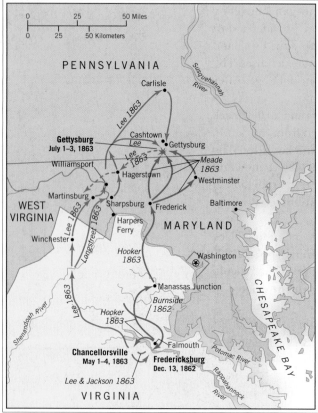

Area controlled by Union
Area controlled by Confederacy
← Union advances
← Confederate advances
◄--- Confederate retreats
✳ Union victories
✳ Confederate victories

MAP 15–3   From Fredericksburg to Gettysburg: The War in the East, December 1862–July 1863   By all logic, the increasingly outgunned and outfinanced Confederacy should have been showing signs of faltering by 1863. But bungling by Union generals at Fredericksburg and Chancellorsville sustained southern fortunes and encouraged Robert E. Lee to attempt another invasion of the North.

HOW WAS Robert E. Lee able to press on, outgunned and outfinanced, into 1863 and beyond?

1862, allowing Lee's army to escape to Virginia and remain a formidable fighting force. And despite Union successes in the West, the Confederate forces massed there remained largely intact.

FROM FREDERICKSBURG TO GETTYSBURG

In late 1862, after Antietam, the president replaced McClellan with General Ambrose E. Burnside. Despite his commanding stature, Burnside was shy and insecure. Claiming incompetence, he had twice refused the command. His judgment proved better than Lincoln's.

Moving swiftly against Lee's dispersed army in northern Virginia, Burnside reached the Rappahannock River opposite Fredericksburg in November 1862 (see Map 15–3). But the pontoon bridges to ford his 120,000 soldiers across the river arrived three weeks late, giving Lee an opportunity to gather his 78,000 men. On December 13, the Union forces launched a poorly coordinated and foolish frontal assault that the Confederates repelled, inflicting heavy federal casualties. Burnside, having performed to his own expectations, was relieved of command, and Major General Joseph Hooker was installed in his place.

The hard-drinking Hooker lacked Burnside's humility but not his incompetence. Resuming the offensive in the spring of 1863, Hooker hoped to outflank Lee. But the Confederate commander surprised Hooker by sending Stonewall Jackson to outflank the Union right. Between May 1 and May 4, Lee's army delivered a series of crushing attacks on Hooker's forces at Chancellorsville. Outnumbered two to one, Lee had pulled off another stunning victory, but at a high cost. Lee lost some 13,000 men, fewer than Hooker's 17,000, but more than the Confederacy could afford.

Still, Lee appeared invincible. Chancellorsville thrust Lincoln into another bout of despair. Meanwhile, Lee, to take advantage of the Confederacy's momentum and the Union's gloom, planned another bold move. On June 3, 1863, the 75,000-man Army of Northern Virginia broke camp and headed north once again (see American Views: Why They Fought On).

President Lincoln sent the Union Army of the Potomac after Lee. But General Hooker dallied, requested more troops, and allowed the Confederates to march from Maryland into Pennsylvania. An infuriated Lincoln replaced Hooker with George Gordon Meade.

Lee's Army of Northern Virginia occupied a wide swath of Pennsylvania territory from Chambersburg to Wrightsville along the Susquehanna River, across from the state capital at Harrisburg. When Lee learned of Meade's movements, he ordered his troops to consolidate in a defensive position at Cashtown, 45 miles from Harrisburg. That the greatest battle of the war

AMERICAN VIEWS

WHY THEY FOUGHT ON

s the bloody war dragged on, fatigue and home-sickness mounted among the soldiers of both sides, while morale faltered. Still, their letters and diary entries typically indicated a determination to fight on. This was true even for Confederate soldiers after the losses at Gettysburg and Vicksburg in July 1863.

- Soldiers from both sides appealed to the nation's Revolutionary heritage, but in different ways. What are the differences?

- Religion played a major role in motivating troops from both sides. How is this evident in the excerpts presented here?

- How do the writers balance feelings for family with their sense of duty as soldiers?

- Is there irony in the Confederate soldier's fighting "for the sake of liberty"? Would Union soldiers have found it ironic at this stage of the war?

A Pennsylvania officer writing to his wife in 1864: "[A]s sick as I am of this war and bloodshed, as much oh how much I want to be at home with my dear wife and children . . . every day I have a more religious feeling, that this war is a crusade for the good of mankind. . . . I [cannot] bear to think of what my children would be if we were to permit this Hellbegotten conspiracy to destroy this country."

Alfred Lacey Hough to Mary Hough, March 13, 1864, in *Soldier in the West: The Civil War Letters of Alfred Lacey Hough,* ed. Robert G. Athearn (Philadelphia: University of Pennsylvania Press 1957), 178.

An Ohio officer writing to his ten-year old son in 1864: "It tells me that while I am absent from home, fighting the battles of our country, trying to restore law and order, to our once peaceful & prosperous nation, and endeavoring to secure for each and every American citizen of every race, the rights garenteed to us in the Declaration of Independence . . . I have children growing up that will be worthy of the rights that I trust will be left for them."

Ephraim S. Holloway to John W. Holloway, August 7, 1864, Holloway Papers, Ohio Historical Society, Columbus, Ohio.

A Texas officer writing to his wife in 1863: "I am sick of war [and] no gratification could exceed that of my being safe at home with you. . . . [W]ere the contest just commenced I would willingly undergo it again for the sake of . . . our country's independence [so I can] . . . point with pride your children to their father as one who fought for their liberty & freedom."

Edward W. Cade to his wife, January 30, July 9, and November 19, 1863, in *A Texas Surgeon in the C.S.A.,* ed. John Q. Anderson (Tuscaloosa: University of Alabama Press, 1957): 33, 67–68, 81.

A Georgia captain writing to his wife in 1863: "What a calamity! [the losses of Gettysburg and Vicksburg] But let us not despair. . . . We just put forth even greater energy—resolve more fully to conquer or die. Our forefathers were whipped in nearly every battle & lost their capital & yet after seven years of trials and hardships achieved their independence."

William O. Fleming to Georgia Fleming, July 13, 1863, in Fleming Papers, Southern Historical Collection, University of North Carolina, Chapel Hill.

An Alabama lieutenant confiding to his diary in 1864: "We should be proud of [that] noble name [Rebel]. George Washington . . . Thomas Jefferson, Patrick Henry, and 'Light Horse' Harry Lee . . . were all Rebels. . . . Our martyred Saviour was called *seditious,* and I may be pardoned if I rejoice that I am a Rebel."

"War Diary of Captain Robert Emory Park, Twelfth Alabama Regiment," *Southern Historical Society Papers,* II (1876), December 24, 1864, p. 237.

MAP EXPLORATION

To explore an interactive version of this map, go to
http://www.prenhall.com/goldfield3/map15.4

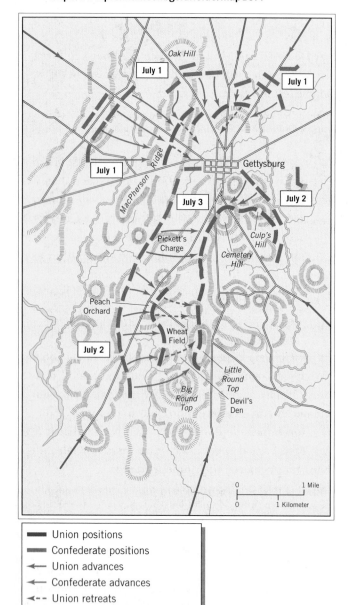

Union positions
Confederate positions
Union advances
Confederate advances
Union retreats

MAP 15–4   The Battle of Gettysburg, July 1–3, 1863   In a war that lasted four years, it is difficult to point to the decisive battle. But clearly, the outcome during those hot July days at Gettysburg set the tone for the rest of the war. The result was unclear until the final day of battle, and even then it might have gone either way. Winning by a whisker was enough to propel Union armies to a string of victories over the next year and to throw Confederate forces back on their defenses among an increasingly despairing population. Gettysburg marked the last major southern invasion of the North.

WHY WAS the Battle of Gettysburg so crucial?

erupted at nearby Gettysburg was pure chance. A Confederate brigade left Cashtown to confiscate much-needed shoes from a factory in Gettysburg. Meeting federal cavalry resistance near the town, the brigade withdrew. On July 1, 1863, a larger Confederate force advanced toward Gettysburg to disperse the cavalry and seize the shoes. What the Confederates did not realize was that the entire Army of the Potomac was coming up behind the cavalry (see Map 15–4).

During the first day of battle, July 1, the Confederates appeared to gain the upper hand, forcing Union forces back from the town to a new position on Cemetery Hill. On the second day, the entire Union army was in place, but the Confederates took several key locations along Cemetery Ridge before federal forces pushed them back to the previous day's positions. On July 3, the third day of the battle, Lee made a fateful error. Believing that the center of Meade's line was weak, he ordered an all-out assault against it.

The key battle of the day occurred at three in the afternoon at Cemetery Ridge, preceded by a fierce artillery duel. When the Union guns suddenly went silent, the Confederates, thinking they had knocked them out, began a charge led by General George Pickett. As the Confederate infantry marched out with battle colors flying, the Union artillery opened up again and tore apart the charging southerners.

After Pickett's charge, Lee rode among his troops and urged them to brace for a final Union assault. The attack never came. Meade allowed Lee to withdraw into Maryland and cross the Potomac to Virginia.

Gettysburg was the bloodiest battle of the war. The Union suffered 23,000 casualties; the Confederacy, 28,000. The battle's outcome boosted morale in the North and drained Lee's army of men and matériel.

The Union victory at Gettysburg lifted the veil of gloom in the North. President Lincoln, in his address dedicating the cemetery at Gettysburg in November of that year, used the evangelical metaphor of rebirth to comment on the importance of the sacrifice on that battlefield. On this consecrated ground, he declared, from the "honored dead," will come "a new birth of freedom."

VICKSBURG, CHATTANOOGA, AND THE WEST

As Union forces thwarted Confederate dreams in Pennsylvania, other federal troops bore down on strategic Rebel strongholds in the western theater of the war. Union military success in the West would seriously compromise the South's ability to move goods and men across rail lines and over waterways and leave vulnerable the ultimate western prize, the Confederate bread basket, Georgia.

Vicksburg presented Ulysses S. Grant with several strategic obstacles (see Map 15–5). In 1862, the formidable defenses on the city's western edge, which overlooked and controlled the Mississippi, had thwarted a Union naval assault, and the labyrinth of swamps, creeks, and woods protecting the city from the north had foiled General Sherman. By March 1863, Grant had devised a brilliant plan to take Vicksburg that called for rapid maneuvering and expert coordination. Grant had his 20,000 Union troops ferried across the Mississippi from the Louisiana side at a point south of Vicksburg. Then he marched them quickly into the interior of Mississippi. They moved northeastward, captured the Mississippi state capital at Jackson, and turned west toward Vicksburg. On May 22, 1863, Grant settled down in front of the city, less than 600 yards from Confederate positions. Grant's tight siege and the Union navy's bombardment from the river cut the city off completely. Their situation hopeless, General John Pemberton and his 30,000-man garrison surrendered on July 4.

The Union and Confederate dead at Gettysburg represent the cost of the war, the price of freedom. President Lincoln transformed the battleground from a killing field to a noble symbol of sacrifice for American ideals. Gettysburg continues to occupy a special place in our nation's history and in the memory of its citizens.

National Archives and Records Administration

As Grant was besieging Vicksburg in June 1863, Union general William S. Rosecrans, commanding the Army of the Cumberland, advanced against Confederate general Braxton Bragg, whose Army of the Tennessee held Chattanooga, a "doorway" on the railroad that linked Richmond to the lower South. The capture of the city would complete the uncoupling of the West from the eastern Confederacy.

At Rosecrans's approach, Bragg abandoned Chattanooga and took up positions at nearby Chickamauga Creek. When the two armies clashed at Chickamauga on September 19, Bragg pushed Rosecrans back to Chattanooga. Bragg seized the railroad leading into Chattanooga and bottled up Rosecrans there, much as Grant had confined Pemberton at Vicksburg. Both sides had suffered heavily. Suddenly, the Union's careful strategy for the conquest of the western Confederacy seemed in jeopardy.

The Confederate position on the heights overlooking Chattanooga appeared impregnable. But the Confederate camp was plagued by dissension, with some officers openly questioning Bragg's ability. President Davis ordered General James Longstreet (along with one-third of Bragg's army) on a futile expedition against Union forces at Knoxville, Tennessee. Converging on Chattanooga with reinforcements, Union generals Grant, Sherman, and Hooker took advantage of the divided Confederate army to break the siege and force Bragg's army to retreat into Georgia. The Union now dominated most of the West and faced an open road to the East.

The Confederacy's reverses at Vicksburg and Chattanooga mirrored its misfortunes farther west of the Mississippi River. Although a relatively minor theater of war, the territory west of the Mississippi provided supplies and strategic advantages for the Confederate West.

Native American tribes in the Trans-Mississippi West, such as the Navajos, Dakotas, and Lakotas, spent a good deal of the Civil War battling federal troops for territory and resources, quite apart from the sectional conflict. Three regiments of Cherokee Indians, however, led by Colonel (later Brigadier General) Stand Watie,

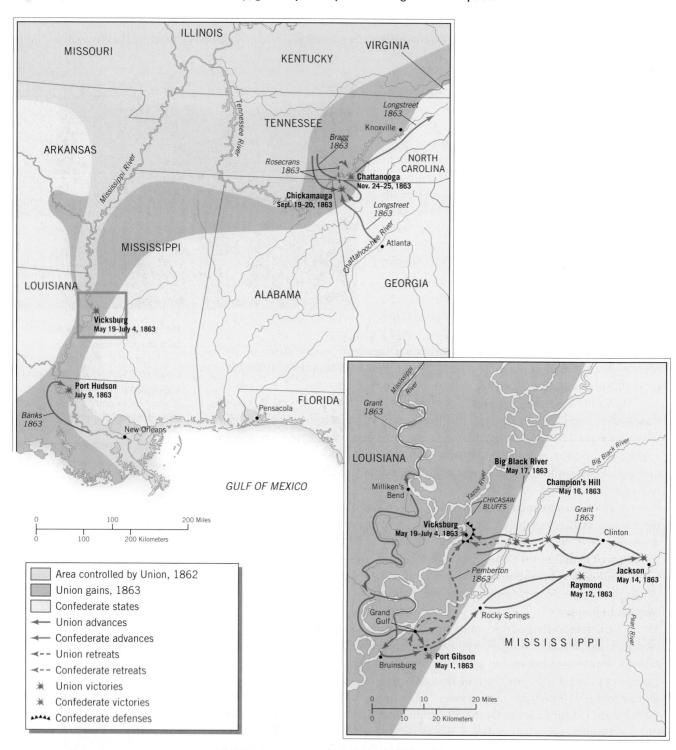

MAP 15–5 Vicksburg and Chattanooga: The War in the West, 1863 Devising a brilliant strategy, Union General Ulysses S. Grant took the last major Mississippi River stronghold from Confederate hands on July 4, 1863, dealing a significant economic and morale blow to the South. Coupled with the defeat at Gettysburg a day earlier, the fall of Vicksburg portended a bitter finale to hopes for southern independence. Grant completed his domination of the West by joining forces with several Union generals to capture Chattanooga and push Confederate forces into Georgia, setting the stage for the capture of that key southern state in 1864.

BASED ON this map, how was Grant able to take the last major Mississippi stronghold from Confederate hands?

fought for the South at the Battle of Pea Ridge in 1862. The Union won the battle and, with it, control of Missouri and northern Arkansas. Texas was critical to Confederate fortunes, both as a source of supply for the East and as a base for the conquest of the Far West.

Texas, however, was far from secure. It suffered from internal dissent and violence on its borders. In the east and along the southern frontier in the lower Rio Grande Valley, Union gunboats and troops disrupted Confederate supply lines. By 1864, with the Union in control of the Mississippi, and federal troops along the Mexican border, Texas had lost its strategic importance.

WAR TRANSFORMS THE NORTH

The Union successes in 1863 had a profound impact on both sides. For the North, hopes of victory and reunion increased. The federal government expanded its bureaucracy to wage war efficiently, and a Republican-dominated Congress passed legislation that broadened federal power and furthered the war effort. Boosted by federal economic legislation and wartime demand, the northern economy boomed. Women entered the workforce in growing numbers. But labor unrest and class and racial tensions suggested that prosperity had a price.

WARTIME LEGISLATION AND POLITICS

Before the Civil War, the federal government rarely affected citizens' lives directly. But raising troops, protecting territory, and mobilizing the economy for war required a strong and active central government. With the departure of the South from the Union, Republicans dominated all branches of the federal administration. This left them in a position to test the constitutional limits of federal authority.

Suppressing Dissent.   President Lincoln began almost immediately to use executive authority to suppress opposition to the war effort in the North. In one of his most controversial actions, he issued a temporary suspension of the writ of habeas corpus, the constitutional protection against illegal imprisonment. Suspending it allowed the government to arrest suspected Confederate agents and hold them indefinitely, a procedure sanctioned by the Constitution "when in cases of rebellion or invasion the public safety may require it." The suspension became permanent in September 1862.

Despite the suspension of habeas corpus, Lincoln compiled a fairly good record for upholding basic American civil liberties. Although the authorities shut down a handful of newspapers temporarily, the administration made no attempt to control the news or subvert the electoral process. Two major elections were held during the war. In the first, the off-year election in 1862, Republicans retained control of Congress but lost several seats to Democrats. In the presidential election of 1864, Lincoln won reelection in a hard-fought contest.

There was dissent in the Republican Party, and it had an effect on national policy. **Radical Republicans** hounded Lincoln from early in his administration, establishing the Joint Committee on the Conduct of the War to examine and monitor military policy. They also pressed Lincoln for quicker action on emancipation, though they supported the president on most crucial matters.

Republicans used the federal government to enhance individual opportunities, especially in the West. The **Homestead Act,** passed in May 1862, granted

Radical Republicans   A shifting group of Republican congressmen, usually a substantial minority, who favored the abolition of slavery from the beginning of the Civil War and later advocated harsh treatment of the defeated South.

Homestead Act   Law passed by Congress in May 1862 providing homesteads with 160 acres of free land in exchange for improving the land within five years of the grant.

160 acres free to any settler in the territories who agreed to improve the land (by cultivating it and erecting a house) within five years of the grant.

Other legislation to boost the nation's economy and the fortunes of individual manufacturers and farmers included the **Land Grant College Act** of 1862, a protective tariff that same year, and the National Banking Act of 1863. The Land Grant Act awarded the proceeds from the sale of public lands to the states for the establishment of colleges offering instruction in "agriculture and mechanical arts." The tariff legislation protected northern industry from foreign competition while raising revenue for the Union. The National Banking Act of 1863 replaced the bank notes of individual states with a uniform national currency. These measures helped sustain the Union war effort and enjoyed widespread support. The expansion of government into other areas, however, aroused opposition in some quarters, none more than the draft laws.

Congress passed the first national conscription law in 1863. Almost immediately, evasion, obstruction, and weak enforcement threatened to undermine it. Conflicts between citizens and federal officials over the draft sometimes erupted in violence. The worst draft riot occurred in New York City in July 1863.

The **New York Draft Riot** began when a mostly Irish mob, protesting conscription, burned the federal marshal's headquarters. Racial and class antagonisms quickly joined antidraft anger as the mob went on a rampage through the city's streets. The rioters hanged two black New Yorkers who wandered into their path and burned the Colored Orphan Asylum. City officials and the police stood by, unable or unwilling to stem the riot, which claimed more than 100 lives. It was finally quelled by army units fresh from Gettysburg, along with militia and naval units. The draft resumed a month later.

THE NORTHERN ECONOMY

After an initial downturn during the uncertain months preceding the war, the northern economy picked up quickly. High tariffs and massive federal spending soon made up for the loss of southern markets and the closing of the Mississippi River. Profits skyrocketed for some businesses. New industries boomed, and new inventions increased manufacturing efficiency, as in the sewing machine industry, which was first commercialized in the 1850s. Technological advances there greatly increased the output of the North's garment factories. Production of petroleum, used as a lubricant, increased from 84,000 gallons to 128 million gallons during the war.

Despite the loss of manpower to the demands of industry and the military, the productivity of northern agriculture grew during the war. As machines replaced men on the farm, manufacturers of farm machinery became wealthy. Crop failures in Europe dramatically increased the demand for American grain.

Trade Unions and Strikebreakers.
With men off to war and immigration down, labor was in short supply. Although wages increased, prices rose more. The trade union movement, which suffered a serious setback in the depression of 1857, revived. By 1865, more than 200,000 northern workers belonged to labor unions.

Employers struck back at union organizing by hiring strikebreakers, usually African Americans. Labor conflicts between striking white workers and black strikebreakers sparked riots in New York City and Cincinnati. The racial antagonism accounted in part for workers' opposition to Lincoln's Emancipation Proclamation and for the continued strength of the Democratic Party in northern cities.

Land Grant College Act Law passed by Congress in July 1862 awarding proceeds from the sale of public lands to the states for the establishment of agricultural and mechanical colleges.

New York Draft Riot A mostly Irish-immigrant protest against conscription in New York City in July 1863 that escalated into class and racial warfare that had to be quelled by federal troops.

Deep social and ethical problems were emerging in northern society and would become more pronounced in the decades after the Civil War. For the time being, the benefits of economic development for the Union cause outweighed its negative consequences. The thriving northern economy fed, clothed, and armed the Union's soldiers and kept most civilians employed and well fed. Prosperity and the demands of a wartime economy also provided northern women with unprecedented opportunities.

NORTHERN WOMEN AND THE WAR

More than 100,000 northern women took jobs in factories, sewing rooms, and arsenals during the Civil War. Stepping in for their absent husbands, fathers, and sons, they often performed tasks previously reserved for men but at lower pay.

Women also had the opportunity to serve the war effort directly in another profession previously dominated by men—nursing. Physicians and officers, however, although they tolerated women nurses as nurturing morale boosters, thought little of their ability to provide medical care. Clara Barton, one of the most notable nurses of the war, treated soldiers on the battlefield at great peril to her own safety and to the consternation of officers. A British journalist, impressed by Barton and the thousands of women like her, commented that no conflict in history was so much "a woman's war" as the Civil War.

The new economic opportunities the war created for women left northern society more open to a broader view of women's roles. One indication of this change was the admission of women to eight previously all-male state universities after the war. Like the class and racial tensions that surfaced in northern cities, the shifting role of women during the Civil War hinted at the promises and problems of postwar life. The changing scale and nature of the American economy, the expanded role of government, and the shift in class, racial, and gender relations are all trends that signaled what historians call the "modernization" of American society.

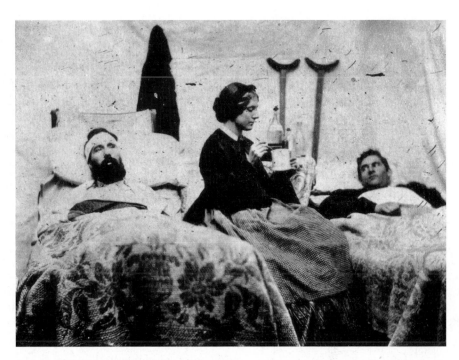

Nurse Ann Bell tends a fallen Union soldier. Although medical practices were primitive and many young men died from poorly treated wounds or disease, the U.S. Sanitary Commission attempted to improve care in Union hospitals during the war. The war helped open nursing as a respectable occupation for women.

Corbis/Bettman

THE CONFEDERACY DISINTEGRATES

As battlefield losses mounted, the Confederacy disintegrated. After 1863, defeat infected Confederate politics, ruined the southern economy, and eventually invaded the hearts and minds of the southern people. What is remarkable is that such losses did not demoralize the Confederacy sooner. Disillusionment against the Confederate government did not erode support for Lee and his army. The South pinned its waning hopes on its defensive military strategy.

HOW DID the war affect the lives of Southern women?

SOUTHERN POLITICS

As the war turned against the Confederacy, southerners increasingly turned against each other. Some joined peace societies, which emerged as early as 1861. Other southerners preferred quieter dissent. They refused to join the army, pay taxes, or obey laws prohibiting trade with the enemy.

States' rights, a major principle of the seceding states, proved an obstacle to the Davis administration's efforts to exert central authority. The governors of Georgia and North Carolina gave the Richmond government particular difficulty, hoarding munitions, soldiers, supplies, food, and money. Even cooperative governors refused to allow state agents to collect taxes for the Confederacy.

Unlike Abraham Lincoln, Jefferson Davis could not appeal to party loyalty to control dissent because the Confederacy had no parties. Davis's frigid personality, his insistence on attending to minute details, and his inability to accept even constructive criticism gracefully, also set him apart from Lincoln and worsened political tensions within the Confederacy.

Several parts of the South began clamoring for peace during the fateful summer of 1863. By November 1864, the Confederacy was suffering as much from internal disaffection as from the attacks of Union armies. Confederate authorities could not suppress civilian unrest in Virginia, North Carolina, and Tennessee, and Union spies operated openly in Mobile, Wilmington, and Richmond.

Davis and other Confederate leaders might have averted some of these political problems had they succeeded in building a strong sense of Confederate nationalism among soldiers and civilians. They tried several strategies to do so. For example, Davis tried to identify the Confederacy's fight for independence with the American Revolution of 1776. But egalitarian revolutionary ideals quickly lost their appeal in the face of poverty, starvation, and defeat.

THE SOUTHERN ECONOMY

By 1863, the Confederacy was having a difficult time feeding itself. Destruction of farms by both sides and growing Union control of waterways and rail lines restricted the distribution of food. Bread riots erupted in Mobile, Atlanta, and Richmond. In Mobile, a group of women marched under banners reading "Bread or Blood" and "Bread and Peace." Armed with hatchets, they looted stores for food and clothing.

Southern soldiers had marched off to war in neat uniforms with shiny buttons, many leaving behind self-sustaining families. But in August 1863, diarist Mary Chesnut, wife of a Confederate official in Richmond, watched 10,000 men marching near Richmond and commented, "Such rags and tags as we saw now. Most garments and arms were . . . taken from the enemy." The soldiers' families were threadbare as well. The prohibitive cost of new clothing prompted a group of women in northern Georgia to raid a textile mill for calico cloth in 1863.

The predations of both Union and Confederate soldiers further threatened civilians in the South. The women and children left alone on farms and plantations were vulnerable to stragglers and deserters from both armies who sometimes robbed, burned houses, raped, and murdered. Southerners also feared that slaves on isolated plantations would rise up against their masters. Most slaves, however, were more intent on escape than revenge.

Some slaves felt genuine affection for the families they served and stayed on with them even after the war. Some protected white southerners from Union soldiers and hid valuables for them. But women forced to manage plantations alone could never be sure where their slaves stood. Mary Chesnut wrote in her diary

WHERE TO LEARN MORE

Museum of the Confederacy, Richmond, Virginia **www.moc.org**

about her mother's butler, "He looks over my head, he scents freedom in the air."

As Confederate casualties mounted, more and more southern women and children, like their northern counterparts, faced the pain of grief. Funeral processions became commonplace in the cities and black the color of fashion.

SOUTHERN WOMEN AND THE WAR

In the early days of the Civil War, southern white women continued to live their lives according to antebellum conventions. Magazine articles urged them to preserve themselves as models of purity for men debased by the violence of war. Women flooded newspapers and periodicals with patriotic verses and songs that stressed the need to suppress grief and fear for the good of the men at the front. A Virginia woman confided to her diary, "We must learn the lesson which so many have to endure, to struggle against our feelings."

By the time of the Civil War, such emotional concealment had become second nature to planters' wives. They had long had to endure their anguish over their husbands' nocturnal visits to the slave quarters. They were used to the condescension of men who assumed them to be intellectually inferior. And they accepted in bitter, self-sacrificing silence the contradiction between the myth of the pampered leisure they were presumed to enjoy and the hard demands their lives actually entailed. But some southern women chafed at their supporting role and, as Confederate manpower and matériel needs became acute, took on new productive responsibilities.

The needs of the Confederacy drew women outside the home to fill positions vacated by men. They managed plantations. They worked in the fields alongside slaves. They worked in factories to make uniforms and munitions. They worked in government offices as clerks and secretaries. They taught school. And many, like their northern counterparts, served as nurses. Eventually, battlefield reverses and economic collapse undermined all these roles, leaving women and men alike struggling simply to survive.

As the war dragged on and the southern economy and social order deteriorated, even the patriots suffered from resentment and doubt. By 1864, many women were helping their deserting husbands or relatives elude Confederate authorities. In Randolph County, North Carolina, two women torched a barn belonging to a state official in charge of rounding up deserters. Incidents like these convinced authorities that women were mainly responsible for desertion in the last years of the war.

By 1864, many southern white women had tired of the war. Some devoutly religious women concluded that it was God, not the Yankees, who had brought destruction on the South for its failure to live up to its responsibilities to women and children. Others blamed their men. Women greeted defeated troops retreating from Vicksburg with shouts of "We are disappointed in you!" However, despite hardship and privation, support for the Confederacy persisted among some women, accompanied by fierce hatred of the enemy. One woman displayed the

Wartime food shortages, skyrocketing inflation, and rumors of hoarding and price-gouging drove women in several southern cities to protest violently. Demonstrations like the 1863 food riot shown here reflected a larger rending of southern society as Confederate losses and casualties mounted on the battlefield. Some southern women placed survival and providing for their families ahead of boosting morale and silently supporting a war effort that had taken their men away. Their defection hurt the Confederate cause.

Corbis/Bettman

QUICK REVIEW

Confederate Women

- As war dragged on, Southern women took more active role at home and in the workplace.
- Some served as spies and nurses.
- Near the end of the war, many women helped their husbands desert.

bones of a federal soldier in her yard and another hoped for a "Yankee skull" to use as a jewelry box.

THE UNION PREVAILS, 1864–1865

WHAT WAS Grant's strategy for ending the war?

Despite the Union's dominant military position after Vicksburg and Gettysburg and the Confederacy's mounting home-front problems, three obstacles to Union victory remained. Federal troops under General William T. Sherman controlled Chattanooga and the gateway to Georgia, but the Confederate Army of Tennessee, commanded by Joseph E. Johnston, was still intact, blocking Sherman's path to Atlanta. Robert E. Lee's formidable Army of Northern Virginia still protected Richmond. And the Confederacy still controlled the rich Shenandoah Valley, which fed Lee's armies and supplied his cavalry with horses. In March 1864, President Lincoln brought General Ulysses S. Grant to Washington and appointed him commander of all Union armies. Grant set about devising a strategy to overcome these obstacles.

GRANT'S PLAN TO END THE WAR

Grant brought two innovations to the final campaign. First, he coordinated the Union war effort, directing the Union's armies in Virginia and the Lower South to attack at the same time, keeping steady pressure on all fronts. Second, Grant changed the tempo of the war. Before, long periods of rest had intervened between battles. Grant, with the advantage of superior numbers, proposed nonstop warfare.

Although Grant's strategy ultimately worked, several problems and miscalculations undermined its effectiveness. With Sherman advancing in Georgia, Grant's major focus was Lee's army in Virginia. But Grant underestimated Lee. The Confederate general thwarted him for almost a year and inflicted horrendous casualties on his army. Confederate forces under Jubal Early drove Union forces from the Shenandoah Valley in June 1864, depriving Grant of troops and allowing the Confederates to maintain their supply lines. And the incompetence of General Benjamin Butler, charged with advancing up the James River to Richmond in May 1864, further eroded Grant's plan. Finally, many of Grant's officers felt enduring loyalty to General George McClellan, whom Lincoln had dismissed in 1862, and considered Grant a mediocrity who had triumphed in the West only because his opposition there had been third-rate.

Lee's only hope was to make Grant's campaign so costly and time-consuming that the northern general would abandon it before the southerners ran out of supplies and troops. But despite problems and setbacks, Grant kept relentless pressure on Lee.

Grant and General George Meade began their campaign against Lee in May 1864, crossing the Rapidan River near Fredericksburg, Virginia, and marching toward an area known as the Wilderness (see Map 15–6). Lee attacked the Army of the Potomac, which outnumbered his forces 118,000 to 60,000, in the thickets of the Wilderness on May 5 and 6 before it could reach open ground. Much of the fighting involved fierce hand-to-hand combat. The toll was frightful, 18,000 casualties on the Union side, 10,000 for the Confederates.

In the past, Union commanders would have pulled back and rested after such an encounter, but Grant pushed on. Marching and fighting, his casualties always higher than Lee's, Grant continued southward. Attacking the entrenched Confederate army at Spotsylvania, his army suffered another 18,000 casualties to the Confederates' 11,000. Undeterred, Grant moved on toward

QUICK REVIEW

Grant's Strategy
- Better coordination of Union effort and the application of steady pressure.
- The waging of nonstop warfare.
- Grant's plan worked in the long run, but at a high cost.

MAP EXPLORATION
To explore an interactive version of this map, go to **http://www.prenhall.com/goldfield3/map15.6**

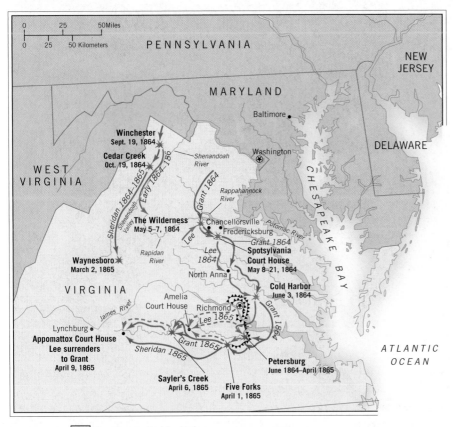

MAP 15–6   Grant and Lee in Virginia, 1864–1865   The engagements in Virginia from May 1864 to April 1865 between the two great generals proved decisive in ending the Civil War. Although Lee fared well enough in the Wilderness, Spotsylvania, and Cold Harbor campaigns, the sheer might and relentlessness of Grant and his army wore down the Confederate forces. When Petersburg fell after a prolonged siege on April 2, 1865, Richmond, Appomattox, and dreams of southern independence soon fell as well.

WHAT HAPPENED at Cold Harbor? What did this battle reveal about the Union's population advantage over the Confederacy?

Cold Harbor, where Lee's troops again awaited him in entrenched positions. Flinging his army against withering Confederate fire on June 3, he lost 7,000 men in eight minutes.

In less than a month of fighting, the Army of the Potomac had lost 55,000 men. The slaughter undermined Grant's support in northern public opinion and

General Ulysses S. Grant had the pews from a local church moved to a grove of trees where he and his officers planned the following day's assault on Confederate troops at Cold Harbor, Virginia. Grant appears at the left of the photograph, leaning over a bench and studying a map.

Library of Congress. Artist: Mathew Brady

15–3
General William Tecumseh Sherman on War (1864)

led peace advocates to renew their quest for a cease-fire. With antiwar sentiment growing in the North as the presidential elections approached in November, Lee's defensive strategy seemed to be working.

Grant decided to change his tactics. Abandoning his march on Richmond from the north, he shifted his army south of the James River to approach the Confederate capital from the rear. Wasting no time, he surprised the Confederates with an attack on Petersburg, a critical rail junction 23 miles south of Richmond. It was a brilliant maneuver, but the hesitant actions of Union corps commanders gave Lee time to reinforce the town's defenders. Both armies dug in for a lengthy siege.

While Grant engaged Lee in Virginia, Union forces under William T. Sherman in Georgia engaged in a deadly dance with the Army of Tennessee under the command of Joseph E. Johnston as they began the campaign to take Atlanta.

Hoping to lure Sherman into a frontal assault, Johnston settled his forces early in May at Dalton, an important railroad junction 75 miles north of Atlanta. Sherman declined to attack and instead made a wide swing around the Confederates, prompting Johnston to abandon Dalton, rush south, and dig in again at Resaca to prevent Sherman from cutting the railroad. Again Sherman swung around without an assault, and again Johnston rushed south to cut him off, this time at Cassville.

This waltz continued for two months, until Johnston had retreated to a strong defensive position on Kennesaw Mountain, barely 20 miles north of Atlanta. At this point, early in July, Sherman launched a disastrous attack. The Union suffered 3,000 casualties, the Confederates only 600. Sherman would not make such a mistake again. He resumed his maneuvering and by mid-July had forced Johnston into defensive positions on Peachtree Creek just north of Atlanta. Fearing that Johnston would let Sherman take Atlanta without a fight, President Davis dismissed Johnston and installed John Bell Hood of Texas in his place. This was a grave error. Hood, in the opinion of those who fought for him, had a "lion's heart" but a "wooden head."

In late July, Hood began a series of attacks on Sherman, beginning at Peachtree Creek on July 20, and was thrown back each time with heavy losses. Sherman launched a series of flanking maneuvers around the city in late August that left Hood in danger of being surrounded. The Confederate general had no choice but to abandon Atlanta and, on the night of September 1, Hood evacuated the city, burning everything of military value.

The loss of Atlanta was a severe blow to the Confederacy. Several of the South's major railroads converged at the city, and its industries helped arm and clothe the armies. Atlanta's fall also left Georgia's rich farmland at the mercy of Sherman's army. Most significant, the fall of Atlanta revived the morale of the war-weary North and helped ensure Lincoln's reelection in November. The last hope of the Confederacy, that a peace candidate would replace Lincoln and end the war, had faded.

THE ELECTION OF 1864 AND SHERMAN'S MARCH

Before Sherman's victory at Atlanta, northern dismay over Grant's enormous losses and his failure to take Richmond raised the prospect of a Democratic election victory. Nominating George B. McClellan, the former commander of the Union's armies, as their presidential candidate, the Democrats appealed to voters as the party of peace. They also appealed to the anti-emancipation sentiment that was strong in some parts of the North.

The fall of Atlanta and the Union's suddenly improved military fortunes undermined Democratic prospects. Another Union victory three weeks before the elections gave Lincoln a further boost and diminished McClellan's chances.

In the voting on November 8, Lincoln captured 55 percent of the popular vote, losing only New Jersey, Delaware, and Kentucky. Republicans likewise swept the congressional elections, retaining control of both the Senate and the House of Representatives.

The Republican victory reinforced the Union commitment to emancipation. A proposed constitutional amendment outlawing slavery everywhere in the United States, not just those areas still in rebellion, passed Congress and was ratified as the **Thirteenth Amendment** to the U.S. Constitution in 1865.

After Sherman took Atlanta, he proposed to break Confederate resistance once and for all by marching his army to the sea and destroying everything in its

Thirteenth Amendment
Constitutional amendment ratified in 1865 that freed all slaves throughout the United States.

path. Sherman's March got under way on November 15. His force of 60,000 men, encountering little resistance, entered Savannah on December 22, 1864. Just a few weeks earlier, Union forces in Tennessee had routed Hood's army at the Battle of Franklin and then crushed it entirely at the Battle of Nashville. Hood's defeat removed any threat to Sherman's rear.

Sherman resumed his march in February 1865, heading for South Carolina, the heart of the Confederacy and the state where the Civil War had begun. Sherman's troops pushed aside the small force that assembled to oppose them, wreaked greater destruction in South Carolina than they had in Georgia, and burned the state capitol at Columbia. Sherman sent the colonel of a black regiment to receive the surrender of Charleston and ordered black troops to be the first to take possession of the city. The soldiers marched in singing "John Brown's Body," to the cheers of the city's black population.

Sherman ended his march in Goldsboro, North Carolina, in March 1865. Behind the Union army lay a barren swath 425 miles long from Savannah to Goldsboro.

When Abraham Lincoln took the oath of office for a second time on March 4, 1865, the result of the war was a foregone conclusion. In a brief but inspirational address, the president provided the spiritual blueprint for reconciliation. Lincoln declared that God had cursed both sides and had visited a destructive war on the nation because of the sin of slavery, a sin, he stressed, that was national, not regional. Once the bloody conflict was over, Lincoln wanted reconciliation rather than retribution to inform the national policy: "With malice toward none; with charity for all; with firmness in the right, as God gives us to see the right, let us strive on to finish the work we are in; to bind up the nation's wounds; to care for him who shall have borne the battle, and for his widow, and his orphan—to do all which may achieve and cherish a just, and a lasting peace, among ourselves, and with all nations." In the meantime, the bitter struggle would continue.

In March 1865, in a move reflecting their desperation, Confederate leaders revived a proposal that they had previously rejected: to arm and free slaves. President Davis hoped this action would gain the Confederacy not only a military benefit but also diplomatic recognition from countries that had balked because of slavery. Not surprisingly, slaves themselves greeted the proposal with little enthusiasm. They might have found service in the Confederate army an acceptable alternative to bondage earlier in the war, but not now, with Union victory imminent.

On March 13, 1865, a reluctant Confederate Congress passed a bill to enlist black soldiers, but without offering them freedom. Ten days later, President Davis and the War Office issued a general order that promised immediate freedom to slaves who enlisted. The war ended before the order could have any effect. The irony was that in the summer of 1864, a majority of northerners probably would have accepted reunion without emancipation had the Confederacy abandoned its fight.

THE ROAD TO APPOMATTOX AND THE DEATH OF LINCOLN

With Sherman's triumph in Georgia and the Carolinas and Sheridan's rout of the Confederates in the Shenandoah Valley, Lee's army remained the last obstacle to Union victory. On April 1, Sheridan's cavalry seized a vital railroad junction on Lee's right flank, forcing Lee to abandon Petersburg and the defense of Rich-

WHERE TO LEARN MORE

Appomattox Court House,
Appomattox, Virginia
www.nps.gov/apco/

mond. Lee tried a daring run westward toward Lynchburg, hoping to secure much-needed supplies and to join Johnston's Army of Tennessee in North Carolina to continue the fight.

President Davis fled Richmond with his cabinet and headed toward North Carolina. Richard Gill Forrester, a 17-year-old black youth, awoke to find the evacuation underway. He reached under his bed and pulled out an American flag. Maneuvering through the chaotic streets, young Forrester reached the state capitol building, climbed to the top, and affixed the banner to the flagpole. Union troops occupied the Confederate capital on April 3, and two days later, President Lincoln walked through its streets to the cheers of his army and an emotional reception from thousands of black people. "I know I am free," shouted one black spectator, "for I have seen Father Abraham and felt him."

Grant's army of 60,000 outran Lee's diminishing force of 35,000 and cut off his escape at Appomattox Court House, Virginia, on April 7. Convinced that further resistance was futile, the Confederate commander met Grant on April 9, 1865, in the McLean house at Appomattox to sign the documents of surrender. The Union general offered generous terms, allowing Lee's men to go home unmolested and to take with them horses or mules "to put in a crop."

Joseph E. Johnston surrendered to Sherman near Durham, North Carolina, on April 26. On May 10, Union cavalry captured President Davis in southern Georgia. On May 26, Texas general Kirby Smith surrendered his trans-Mississippi army, and the Civil War came to an end.

On April 11, President Lincoln addressed a large crowd from the White House balcony and spoke briefly of his plans to reconstruct the South with the help of persons loyal to the Union, including recently freed slaves. At least one listener found the speech disappointing. A sometime actor and full-time Confederate patriot, John Wilkes Booth, muttered to a friend in the throng, "That means nigger citizenship. Now, by God, I'll put him through. That is the last speech he will ever make."

On the evening of April 14, Good Friday, the president went to Ford's Theatre in Washington to view a comedy, *Our American Cousin.* During the performance, Booth shot the president, wounding him mortally, then jumped from Lincoln's box to the stage shouting *"Sic semper tyrannis"* ("Thus ever to tyrants") and fled the theater. Union troops tracked him down to a barn in northern Virginia and killed him. Investigators arrested eight accomplices who had conspired with Booth to murder other high officials in addition to Lincoln. Four of the accomplices were hanged.

Southerners reacted to Lincoln's assassination with surprisingly mixed emotions. Many saw some slight hope of relief for the South's otherwise bleak prospects. But General Johnston and others like him were aware of Lincoln's moderating influence on the radical elements in the Republican Party that were pressing for harsh terms against the South. The president's death, Johnston wrote, was "the greatest possible calamity to the South."

This photograph of Abraham Lincoln was taken four days before John Wilkes Booth assassinated him in Ford's Theatre.

Courtesy Library of Congress

WHERE TO LEARN MORE

Ford's Theatre National Historical Site, Washington, D.C.
www.nps.gov/foth/index2.htm

 MAJOR BATTLES OF THE CIVIL WAR, 1861–1865

Battle or Campaign	Date	Outcome and Consequences
First Bull Run	July 21, 1861	Confederate victory, destroyed the widespread belief in the North that the war would end quickly, fueled Confederate sense of superiority
Forts Henry and Donelson	February 6–16, 1862	Union victory, gave the North control of strategic river systems in the western Confederacy and closed an important link between the eastern and western Confederacy
Shiloh Church	April 6–7, 1862	Union victory, high casualties transformed attitudes about the war on both sides
Seven Days' Battles	June 25–July 1, 1862	Stand-off, halted McClellan's advance on Richmond in the Peninsula Campaign
Second Bull Run	August 29–30, 1862	Confederate victory, reinforced Robert E. Lee's reputation for invincibility
Antietam	September 17, 1862	Stand-off, halted Lee's advance into the North, eliminated Confederacy's chance for diplomatic recognition, encouraged Lincoln to issue the Emancipation Proclamation
Fredericksburg	December 13, 1862	Confederate victory, revived morale of Lee's army
Chancellorsville	May 2–6, 1863	Confederate victory, Stonewall Jackson killed, encouraged Lee to again invade North
Gettysburg	July 1–3, 1863	Union victory, halted Confederate advance in the North, major psychological blow to Confederacy
Vicksburg	November 1862–July 1863	Union victory; closed the key Confederate port on the Mississippi, also dealt a severe blow to Confederate cause
Chattanooga	August–November 1863	Union victory, solidified Union dominance in the West
Wilderness and Cold Harbor	May and June 1864	Two Confederate victories, inflicted huge losses on Grant's army; turned public opinion against Grant but failed to force him to withdraw
Atlanta	May–September 1864	Union victory; Confederacy lost key rail depot and industrial center
Sherman's March	November 1864–March 1865	Nearly unopposed, Sherman's army cut a path of destruction through Georgia and South Carolina, breaking southern morale
Battles of Franklin and Nashville	November and December 1864	Union victories in Tennessee; effectively destroyed Army of Tennessee
Siege of Petersburg	June 1864–April 1865	Long stalemate ended in Union victory; led to fall of Richmond and surrender of Lee's army at Appomattox Court House

GLOBAL PERSPECTIVES

FRENCH INTERVENTION IN MEXICO

Europeans held ambivalent attitudes toward the Civil War. Most British workers, recoiling from the concept of slave labor, generally sympathized with the Union cause, but textile workers supported intervention on behalf of the Confederacy. British merchants and manufacturers, while calculating that the disintegration of the American republic would remove a major competitor, profited immensely from Union orders during the war. British leaders may have privately rejoiced at the seeming demise of the American experiment, but they worried that a federal defeat would lead to a European free-for-all in Latin America.

And then there was France. The French (and the Russians as well) held some affection for the Union cause if for no other reason than that a strong, united America stood as a counterweight to British power. But even as they professed their neutrality, they cheered Confederate successes as clearing the way for French ambitions in Latin America.

In the wake of another of its brutal civil wars, Mexico established a democratic government committed to civil and religious freedom under Benito Juárez in 1860. When the United States plunged into its own bloody civil war, Mexico, still recovering from the conflict that brought Juárez to power, became vulnerable to foreign intrigue.

Mexico's frequent civil wars generated a huge debt to several European nations and small hope for repayment. France seized on the debt issue as a pretext for intervention. Joined by British and Spanish forces, the French seized the customs house at Veracruz, a major source of revenue for Mexico. That French designs involved more than money became apparent when their allies left and France consolidated its grip on Mexico, installing Archduke Ferdinand Maximilian, an Austrian, as emperor. Napoleon III thus cemented an alliance with the powerful Hapsburgs, rulers of the Austro-Hungarian Empire, as he advanced his own ambitions in North America.

Maximilian remained in power only because he was backed by French troops. The Lincoln administration could do little to help Mexican patriots during the Civil War. Confederate leaders adopted a more opportunistic view of French intervention, hoping to exchange their recognition of Maximilian's government for France's recognition of the Confederacy.

Benito Juárez, now deposed, led a dogged resistance to Maximilian. In 1865, as the Union triumphed, Napoleon III faced the prospect of 1 million Union soldiers available to cross the border to support Juárez's claim to the government. He withdrew his troops in 1867, and Juárez captured and executed Maximilian in June.

France was not the only European power trolling in Latin American waters during the Civil War. Spain re-annexed the Dominican Republic in 1861, but in 1865 the Dominicans, emboldened by the end of the American Civil War, expelled the Spanish. By 1870, the United States made it clear to Europe that the Monroe Doctrine was very much alive and that any incursions into the Western Hemisphere would result in a swift American reaction. By the 1880s, the United States was moving ambitiously into Latin America, beginning a long and sometimes stormy relationship with this region.

CONCLUSION

Just before the war, William Sherman had warned a friend from Virginia, "You people of the South don't know what you are doing. This country will be drenched in blood. . . . [W]ar is a terrible thing." He was right. More than 365,000 Union soldiers died during the war, 110,000 in battle, and more than 256,000 Confederate soldiers, 94,000 in battle. Total casualties on both sides, including wounded, were more than 1 million.

Compounding the suffering of the individuals behind these gruesome statistics was the incalculable suffering, in terms of grief, fatherless children, women who never married, families never made whole, of the people close to them.

The war devastated the South. The region lost one-fourth of its white male population between the ages of 20 and 40. It also lost two-fifths of its livestock and half of its farm machinery. Union armies destroyed many of the South's railroads and shattered its industry. Between 1860 and 1870, the wealth of the South declined by 60 percent, and its share of the nation's total wealth dropped from more than 30 percent to 12 percent. The wealth of the North, in contrast, increased by half in the same period.

The Union victory solved the constitutional question about the right of secession and sealed the fate of slavery. The issue that dominated the prewar sectional debate had vanished. Now, when politicians intoned Independence Day orations or campaign speeches about the ideals of democracy and freedom, the glaring reality of human bondage would no longer mock their rhetoric.

The Civil War stimulated societal changes that grew more significant over time. It did not make the Union an industrial nation, but it taught the effectiveness of centralized management, new financial techniques, and the coordination of production, marketing, and distribution. Likewise, the war did not revolutionize gender relations in American society, but by opening new opportunities to women in fields such as nursing and teaching, it helped lay the foundation for the woman's suffrage movement of the 1870s and 1880s.

The war was not responsible for every postwar change in American society, and it left many features of American life intact. The experience of pulling together in a massive war effort, for example, did not soften class antagonisms. Capitalism, not labor, triumphed during the war. And it was industrialists and entrepreneurs, not working people, who most benefited from the war's bonanza.

For black southerners, emancipation was the war's most significant achievement. The war to end slavery changed some American racial attitudes, especially in the North. At the outset of the Civil War, only a small minority of northerners considered themselves abolitionists. After the Emancipation Proclamation, every northern soldier became a liberator. By the end of the war, perhaps a majority of northerners supported granting freedmen the right to vote and to equal protection under the law, even if they believed (as many did) that black people were inferior to white people. The courage of black troops and the efforts of African-American leaders to link the causes of reunion and freedom were influential in bringing about this shift.

Most white southerners did not experience a similar enlightenment. Some were relieved by the end of slavery, but most greeted it with fear, anger, and regret. For them, the freed slaves would be living reminders of the South's defeat and the end of a way of life grounded in white supremacy.

If the Civil War resolved the sectional dispute of the 1850s by ending slavery and denying the right of the southern states to secede, it created two new equally troubling problems: how to reunite South and North and how to deal with the legacy of slavery.

In November 1863, President Lincoln was asked to say a few words at the dedication of the federal cemetery at Gettysburg. There, surrounded by a somber scene of fresh graves, Lincoln bound the cause of the Union to that of the country's founders: "Fourscore and seven years ago our fathers brought forth upon this continent a new nation, conceived in liberty and dedicated to the proposition that all men are created equal. Now we are engaged in a great civil war, testing whether that nation, or any nation so conceived and so dedicated can long endure." A Union victory, Lincoln hoped, would not only honor the past but also call forth a new nation, cleansed of its sins, to serve as an inspiration to oppressed peoples around the world. He called on the nation to resolve "that the nation shall, under God, have a new birth of freedom; and that government of the people, by the people, for the people, shall not perish from the earth." The two-minute Gettysburg Address captured what Union supporters were fighting for and connected their sacrifices to the noble causes of freedom and democratic government. That would be both the hope and the challenge of the peace that followed a hard war.

IMAGE KEY
for pages 418–419

a. Gray cap of a Confederate solider from the American Civil War.

b. Blue Union soldier hat with a bugle emblem embroidered on the front.

c. Slaves seek freedom behind union lines.

d. President Abraham Lincoln, Washington D.C., April 10, 1865.

e. Southern bread riots.

f. Photo of engineers of the 8th New York State Militia in front of a tent, 1861.

g. American President Abraham Lincoln presents the Emancipation Proclamation to grateful black slaves and white peasants in a political cartoon about education, freedom, and equality.

h. Robert E. Lee (1807–1870). Commander in chief of the Confederate armies during the Civil War.

i. Federal flag that flew over Ft. Sumter.

j. Battle flag of the Second Battalion Hilliard's Alabama Legion. This flag was pierced 83 times during the charge up Snod Grass Hill, at Chickamauga, Georgia.

SUMMARY

Mobilization, North and South In the initial rush of enthusiasm, both the North and South believed the Civil War would be short. While neither side was well prepared, the North's resources for fighting a lengthy conflict greatly exceeded the South's. The North also had the leadership of Abraham Lincoln who eloquently articulated the goal of preserving the Union. The Confederacy's tactic was to wage a defensive war and wear down Northern public opinion; sufficient patience and resources would be necessary for success.

The Early War, 1861–1862 The North's offensive strategy dictated the course of the war for the first two years. The first battle of the war at Bull Run was a Confederate victory, but as Union forces retreated in the East, they had made some advances in the West under General Ulysses S. Grant. The carnage in 1862 at Shiloh blunted the initial enthusiasm of both sides with the realization that much bloody fighting lay ahead. A new Union offensive in Virginia aimed at the Confederate capital Richmond was halted by Robert E. Lee's generalship. By the end of 1862, the outcome of the war remained in the balance.

Turning Points, 1862–1863 Could the South overcome its human and economic shortcomings by victory on the battlefield? Would the Confederacy gain a valuable ally in Great Britain or France? Diplomatic recognition never came; Lee was defeated at Antietam as he attempted a Northern invasion. Lincoln used this victory to issue the Emancipation Proclamation making the war to save the Union also a war to free the slaves. Confederate defeats at Gettysburg and Vicksburg in July 1863 marked key turning points; Union forces were becoming dominante in the East and the West.

War Transforms the North Such a large-scale war called for a strong and active central government. Constitutional limitations were tested; new economic measures were passed; racial and ethnic tensions erupted in the New York draft riots. The thriving Northern economy fed, clothed, and armed the Union's soldiers and kept most civilians employed and well fed.

The Confederacy Disintegrates Battlefield losses increased discontent over the unequal sharing of hardships including the draft, food shortages, and inflation, but support for Lee and the Confederate army remained high. After 1864, President Davis could not keep the Confederacy from fracturing; with food scarce and money worthless, many, especially the South's women, wanted the war to end.

The Union Prevails, 1864–1865 Lincoln's appointment of General Grant as commander of all Union armies meant that relentless pressure would now be on Lee and the Southern armies. After Union victories in Virginia, the capture of Atlanta, and Sherman's "march to the sea," the capture of the Confederate capital Richmond would result in Lee's surrender at Appomattox. The Union wave of victories had brought the reelection of Lincoln and the passage of the Thirteenth Amendment; joy over the war's end was tempered by the assassination of President Lincoln by a Southern sympathizer.

REVIEW QUESTIONS

1. How did the Union and the Confederacy compare in terms of resources, leadership, and military strategies in the period 1861–1863? What impact did these factors have on the course of the war?

2. What was the significance of the battles of Antietam and Gettysburg? In what ways were they turning points in the Civil War?

3. Given that the federal government was fighting a civil war, why did not European powers, other than France, take advantage of that distraction and meddle in Latin American affairs?

4. What effects did the Emancipation Proclamation have on the Union and Confederate causes?

5. Compare and contrast the roles played by women, in the North and in the South, during the Civil War, and explain how their actions and activities aided or hindered the war effort of their respective nations.

6. Sullivan Ballou made the ultimate sacrifice for his cause. Why did he fight?

KEY TERMS*

Confiscation Act (p. 431)
Emancipation Proclamation (p. 431)
Homestead Act (p. 439)

Land Grant College Act (p. 440)
New York Draft Riot (p. 440)
Radical Republicans (p. 439)
Thirteenth Amendment (p. 447)

* See the Overview table, on p. 450 for major battles of the Civil War.

WHERE TO LEARN MORE

Museum of the Confederacy, Richmond, Virginia. This museum has rotating exhibits on various aspects of the Confederate effort during the Civil War, both on the home front and on the battlefield. The Confederate White House, which is open to the public, is next door to the museum. Visit its website at **www.moc.org**.

Gettysburg National Military Park, Gettysburg, Pennsylvania. An excellent and balanced interpretation awaits the visitor at this national park. See its website, **www.nps.gov/gett/**.

Antietam National Battlefield, Sharpsburg, Maryland. Also an excellent and balanced interpretation at this battlefield site. Go to **www.nps.gov/anti/**.

Ford's Theatre National Historical Site, Washington, D.C. The place where John Wilkes Booth assassinated President Abraham Lincoln not only depicts those events, including artifacts from the assassination, but also presents period plays. Its website is **www.nps.gov/foth/index2.htm**.

Appomattox Court House, Appomattox, Virginia. What historian Bruce Catton termed "a stillness at Appomattox" can be felt at the McLean house in this south-central Virginia town. The house is much as it was when Confederate General Robert E. Lee surrendered his forces to General Ulysses S. Grant on April 9, 1865. An almost reverential solitude covers the house and the well-maintained grounds today. Its website is at **www.nps.gov/apco/**.

 U.S. History Documents CD-ROM
For primary sources related to this chapter, refer to the document CD-ROM.

 www.prenhall.com/goldfield
For study resources related to this chapter, visit the *Companion Website*™.

Visualizing The Past...

The Civil War

WHAT DID the photographer include that is missing from the illustrations? What did the illustrators include that is missing from the photograph? What did war look like to the civilian who saw only the illustrations? To the civilian who saw only the photograph? To the civilian who saw both?

Two new media drastically altered the ways in which people on the home front experienced war. One was photography. Mathew B. Brady and other pioneering photographers took thousands of pictures of battlefield scenes, which were then shown in weekly exhibits. For a small fee, the spectator could see photographs of battles fought just days before. The images themselves are of very good quality and quite large. The major drawback was technical. The photographer had to expose his glass plate to the light for a full minute, any movement during that time, created a blur. So, Brady's and other photographic images captured the look of the battlefield after the fighting was over.

The other new medium was the illustrated magazine. *Harper's Illustrated Weekly*, only a few years old at the outbreak of the war, was the biggest with a circulation running into the hundreds of thousands. Its illustrators drew battles as they were happening capturing the charges and the hand-to-hand fighting that the photographer could not. Below is a stereopticon photograph of a *Harper's* artist at Gettysburg, taken for the Brady Company. Viewers looked through a special device which fused the two images. As you examine the images included in this essay, consider these questions.

Courtesy of Library of Congress

"Dead at Gettysburg," a photograph taken for the Brady Company. The dead included both Union soldiers and a Confederate. For the vast majority of those paying admission to see this and other images, this was the first time they witnessed the carnage of battle.

Courtesy of Library of Congress

◄ "The Battle of Gettysburg—Longstreet's Attack Upon Our Left Center—Blue Ridge In the Distance" appeared in *Harper's Weekly* for July 22, 1863. Note the use of "our" to describe the position of the Union troops. Note too that the viewer is positioned behind the Union lines.

American Antiquary Society

► "The Harvest of Death—Gettysburg, July 4, 1863" appeared in *Harper's Weekly* for July 22, 1863. It shows only Union dead along with dead horses and overturned wagons.

American Antiquary Society

THE HARVEST OF DEATH—GETTYSBURG, July 4, 1863.—[Photographed by A. Gardner, Washington.]

16

Reconstruction 1865–1877

CHAPTER HIGHLIGHTS

White Southerners and the Ghosts of the Confederacy, 1865 Many Southerners came to see the Civil War as the Lost Cause and would not let its memory die. The Lost Cause was used to justify the war, resistance to Reconstruction, and the reversal of gains by African-Americans.

More than Freedom: African-American Aspirations in 1865 Former slaves wanted to be free of white supervision. They also wanted land, voting and civil rights, and education. The Freedmen's Bureau was a first step by the federal government towards the achievement of those goals. Most former slaves did not become independent landowners, but instead worked as sharecroppers or migrated to the cities.

Federal Reconstruction, 1865-1870 The two great issues of Reconstruction were the position of African Americans in American society and how to reform the former Confederate states. Presidential Reconstruction gave way to Congressional Reconstruction. Federal efforts brought mixed results and by 1870 white Southerners were regaining control of their states.

Counter-Reconstruction, 1870-1874 Depression and scandal held the attention of Northerners, while white Southerners regained control of the South. Groups like the Ku Klux Klan used violence to erode the gains of African Americans.

Redemption, 1874-1877 By 1877 all the former Confederate states had rejoined the Union and the Redeemers had triumphed. Northerners were no longer interested in Reconstruction. African Americans had few of the rights and privileges enjoyed by other Americans.

The Failed Promise of Reconstruction With the tacit agreement of Northern whites, Southern whites were free to work out their own resolution to race relations. The price of sectional reconciliation was the independence and equality of African Americans. Despite the passage of the Fourteenth and Fifteenth Amendments, for most African Americans Reconstruction was a failure.

VICKSBURG, MISSISSIPPI.—[SEE PAGE 398.]

DECEMBER 19,

HARPER'S WEEKLY.

813

Edmund Commander

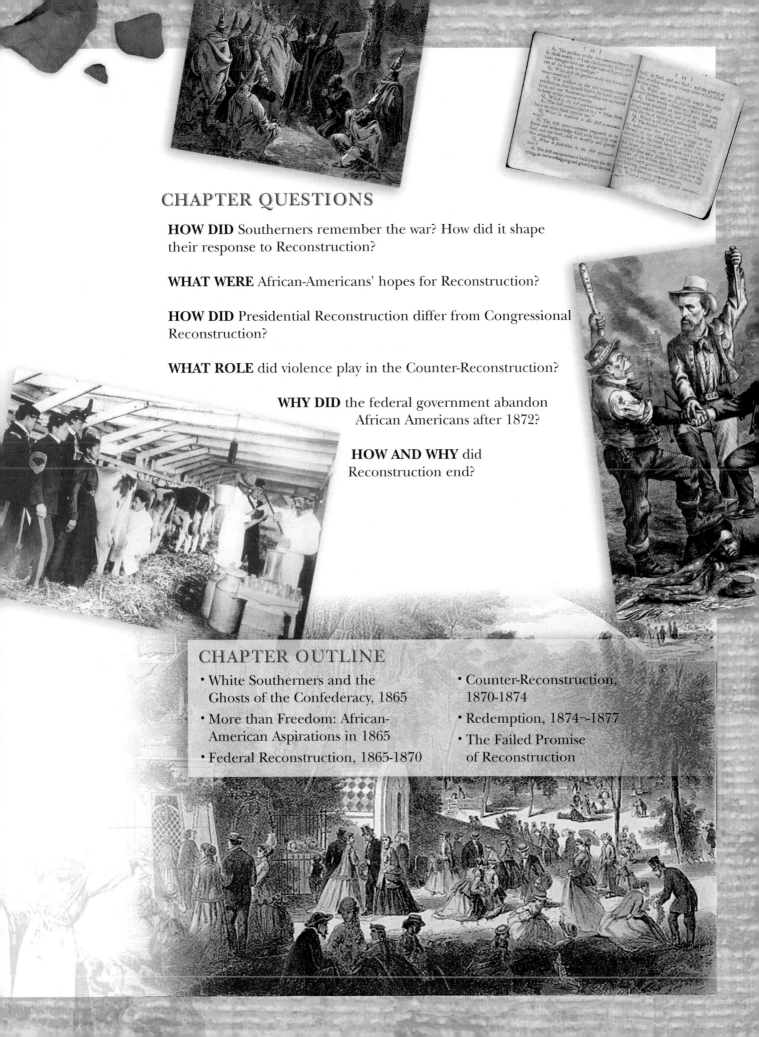

CHAPTER QUESTIONS

HOW DID Southerners remember the war? How did it shape their response to Reconstruction?

WHAT WERE African-Americans' hopes for Reconstruction?

HOW DID Presidential Reconstruction differ from Congressional Reconstruction?

WHAT ROLE did violence play in the Counter-Reconstruction?

WHY DID the federal government abandon African Americans after 1872?

HOW AND WHY did Reconstruction end?

CHAPTER OUTLINE

- White Southerners and the Ghosts of the Confederacy, 1865
- More than Freedom: African-American Aspirations in 1865
- Federal Reconstruction, 1865-1870
- Counter-Reconstruction, 1870-1874
- Redemption, 1874–1877
- The Failed Promise of Reconstruction

IMAGE KEY
for pages 458–459 is on page 478.

Marianna, Florida 1866

The white academy opened about the same time the church opened the school for the Negro children. As the colored children had to pass the academy to reach the church it was easy for the white children to annoy them with taunts and jeers. The war passed from words to stones which the white children began to hurl at the colored. Several colored children were hurt and, as they had not resented the rock-throwing in kind because they were timid about going that far, the white children became more aggressive and abusive.

One morning the colored children armed themselves with stones and determined to fight their way past the academy to their school. [They] approached the academy in formation whereas in the past they had been going in pairs or small groups. When they reached hailing distance, a half dozen white boys rushed out and hurled their missiles. Instead of scampering away, the colored children not only stood their ground and hurled their missiles but maintained a solemn silence. The white children, seeing there was no backing down as they expected, came rushing out of the academy and charged the colored children.

During some fifteen minutes it was a real tug of war. In the close fighting the colored children got the advantage gradually and began to shove the white children back. As they pressed the advantage the white children broke away and ran for the academy. The colored fighters did not follow them but made it hot for the laggards until they also took to their heels. There were many bruises on both sides, but it taught the white youngsters to leave the colored ones alone thereafter. T. Thomas Fortune, Norfolk Journal and Guide

T. Thomas Fortune, "Norfolk Journal and Guide," August 20, 1927, reprinted in Dorothy Sterling, ed., *The Trouble They Seen: Black People Tell the Story of Reconstruction* (Garden City, N.Y.: Doubleday, 1976): 22–24.

T. Thomas Fortune, felt that this incident encapsulated the dilemma of Reconstruction. In the journey from slavery to freedom, education emerged as an important element of full citizenship for African Americans. The eagerness with which black children (and adults) flooded schools was matched by the hostility of the white community, which resented any social advance or pretense of equality in the former bondsmen.

Reconstruction was not merely a series of white aggressions against African-American aspirations, followed by black retreats. The violence and disorder that punctuated southern society after the Civil War was due in part to the refusal of blacks to relinquish their dreams of equal citizenship, including the right to a decent education.

Thomas did not back down, though by 1878 he understood that the promise of his schoolboy days could not be realized in the South. Thomas left for New York City, where he obtained a job as a printer for the *New York Sun*. New York's gain was the South's loss, a process repeated many times over as talented young black men and women migrated north. It was a double tragedy for the South: losing people who could have rebuilt a shattered region, and missing the opportunity to create a society based on racial equality.

The position of African Americans in American society and how and under what terms to readmit the former Confederate states were the two great issues of the Reconstruction era.

Between 1865 and 1867, under President Andrew Johnson's Reconstruction plan, white southerners pretty much had their way with the former slaves and with their own state governments. Congressional action between 1867 and 1870 attempted to balance black rights and home rule, with mixed results. After 1870, white Southerners gradually regained control of their states and localities, denying black southerners their political gains while Republicans in Washington lost interest in policing their former enemies.

WHITE SOUTHERNERS AND THE GHOSTS OF THE CONFEDERACY, 1865

The casualties of war in the South continued long after the hostilities ceased. Cities such as Richmond, Atlanta, Savannah, Charleston, and Columbia lay in ruins; farmsteads were stripped of everything but the soil; infrastructure, especially railroads were damaged or destroyed; factories and machinery were demolished; and at least 5 million bales of cotton, the major cash crop, had gone up in smoke.

Their cause lost and their society destroyed, white southerners lived through the summer and fall of 1865 surrounded by ghosts, the ghosts of lost loved ones, joyful times, bountiful harvests, self-assurance, and slavery. Defeat shook the basic tenets of their religious beliefs. But many other white southerners refused to accept their defeat as a divine judgment. Instead, they insisted, God had spared the South for a greater purpose. They came to view the war as the **Lost Cause** and interpreted it, not as a lesson in humility, but as an episode in the South's journey to salvation.

This view, in which the war became the Lost Cause, and Reconstruction became the Redemption, served to forge a community among white southerners at a time of great unrest. The Lost Cause also enabled white southerners to move on with their lives and concentrate on rebuilding their shattered region. Moreover, this new history implied a stainless Old South and required the return of the freedmen, if not to the status of slaves, then at least to a lowly place in society.

The Lost Cause would not merely exist as a memory, but also as a three-dimensional depiction of southern history, in rituals and celebrations, and as the educational foundation for future generations. The statues of the Confederate common soldier erected typically on the most important site in a town, the commemorations of Confederate Memorial Day, the birthdays of prominent Confederate leaders, the reunions of veterans, and the textbooks implanting the white history of the South in young minds—all of these ensured that the Lost Cause would not only be an interpretation of the past, but also the basic reality of the present and the foundation for the future.

Most white southerners approached the great issues of freedom and reunification with unyielding views. They saw African Americans as adversaries whose attempts at self-improvement were a direct challenge to white people's belief in their own racial superiority. White southerners saw outside assistance to black southerners as another invasion.

Lost Cause   The phrase many white Southerners applied to their Civil War defeat. They viewed the war as a noble cause but only a temporary setback in the South's ultimate vindication.

HOW DID Southerners remember the war? How did it shape their response to Reconstruction?

This engraving shows southerners decorating the graves of rebel soldiers at Hollywood Memorial Cemetery in Virginia in 1867. Northerners and southerners alike honored their war dead. But in the South, the practice of commemorating fallen soldiers became an important element in maintaining the myth of the Lost Cause that colored white southerners' view of the war.

The Granger Collection, New York

Chronology

1861	Tsar Alexander II frees the serfs of Russia.
1863	Lincoln proposes his Ten Percent Plan.
1864	Congress proposes the Wade-Davis Bill.
1865	Sherman issues Field Order No. 15.
	Freedmen's Bureau is established.
	Andrew Johnson succeeds to the presidency, unveils his Reconstruction plan.
	Massachusetts desegregates all public facilities.
	Black citizens in several southern cities organize Union Leagues.
	Former Confederate states begin to pass black codes.
1866	Congress passes Southern Homestead Act, Civil Rights Act of 1866.
	Ku Klux Klan is founded.
	Fourteenth Amendment to the Constitution is passed (ratified in 1868).
	President Johnson goes on a speaking tour.
1867	Congress passes Military Reconstruction Acts, Tenure of Office Act.
1868	President Johnson is impeached and tried in the Senate for defying the Tenure of Office Act.
	Republican Ulysses S. Grant is elected president.
1869	Fifteenth Amendment passed (ratified 1870).

1870	Congress passes Enforcement Act.
	Republican regimes topple in North Carolina and Georgia.
1871	Congress passes Ku Klux Klan Act.
1872	Freedmen's Bureau closes down.
	Liberal Republicans emerge as a separate party.
	Ulysses S. Grant is reelected.
1873	Severe depression begins.
	Colfax Massacre occurs.
	U.S. Supreme Court's decision in the *Slaughterhouse* cases weakens the intent of the Fourteenth Amendment.
	Texas falls to the Democrats in the fall elections.
1874	White Leaguers attempt a coup against the Republican government of New Orleans.
	Democrats win off-year elections across the South amid widespread fraud and violence.
1875	Congress passes Civil Rights Act of 1875.
1876	Supreme Court's decision in *United States v. Cruikshank* nullifies Enforcement Act of 1870.
	Outcome of the presidential election between Republican Rutherford B. Hayes and Democrat Samuel J. Tilden is contested.
1877	Compromise of 1877 makes Hayes president and ends Reconstruction.

MORE THAN FREEDOM: AFRICAN-AMERICAN ASPIRATIONS IN 1865

WHAT WERE African Americans' hopes for Reconstruction?

Black southerners had a quite different perspective on the Civil War and Reconstruction, seeing the former as a great victory for freedom and the latter as a time of great possibility.

The former slaves did not initially even dream of social equality. They did harbor two potentially contradictory aspirations. The first was to be left alone, free of white supervision. But the former slaves also wanted land, voting and civil rights, and education. To secure these, they needed the intervention and support of the white power structure.

In 1865, African Americans had reason to hope that their dreams of full citizenship might be realized. They enjoyed a reservoir of support for their aspirations among some Republican leaders.

The first step Congress took beyond emancipation was to establish the Bureau of Refugees, Freedmen, and Abandoned Lands in March 1865. Congress envisioned the **Freedmen's Bureau,** as it came to be called, as a multipurpose agency to provide

Freedmen's Bureau Agency established by Congress in March 1865 to provide social, educational, and economic services, advice, and protection to former slaves and destitute whites; lasted seven years.

social, educational, and economic services, advice, and protection to former slaves and destitute white southerners. Congress also authorized the bureau to rent confiscated and abandoned farmland to freedmen in 40-acre plots, with an option to buy. This auspicious beginning belied the great disappointments that lay ahead.

EDUCATION

The greatest success of the Freedmen's Bureau was in education. The bureau coordinated more than 50 northern philanthropic and religious groups, which, in turn, established 3,000 freedmen's schools in the South, serving 150,000 men, women, and children.

At the end of the Civil War, only about 10 percent of black southerners were literate, compared with more than 70 percent of white southerners. Within a decade, black literacy had risen above 30 percent. Some black southerners went on to one of the 13 colleges established by the American Missionary Association and black and white churches. Between 1860 and 1880 more than 1,000 black southerners earned college degrees.

Many white southerners condemned efforts at "Negro improvement." They viewed the time spent on education as wasted. White southerners also harassed white female teachers, questioning their morals and threatening people who rented rooms to them. After the Freedmen's Bureau folded in 1872 and many of the northern societies that supported freedmen's education collapsed or cut back their involvement, education for black southerners became more haphazard.

"FORTY ACRES AND A MULE"

An overwhelmingly agricultural people, freedmen looked to farm ownership as a key element in their transition from slavery to freedom. Even before the war's end, rumors circulated through black communities in the South that the government would provide each black family with 40 acres and a mule. These rumors were fueled by General William T. Sherman's **Field Order No. 15** in January 1865, which set aside a vast swath of abandoned land along the South Atlantic coast from the Charleston area to northern Florida for grants of up to 40 acres.

By June 1865, about 40,000 former slaves had settled on Sherman land along the southeastern coast. In 1866, Congress passed the **Southern Homestead Act,** giving black people preferential access to public lands in five southern states. Two years later, the Republican government of South Carolina initiated a land-redistribution program financed by the sale of state bonds. By the late 1870s, more than 14,000 African-American families had taken advantage of this program.

The highest concentration of black land ownership was in the Upper South and in areas of the Lower South with better economic conditions and less white hostility toward black people. By 1890, one out of three black farmers in the Upper South owned his land, compared to one out of five for the South as a whole.

The vast majority of former slaves, however, especially those in the Lower South, never fulfilled their dreams of land ownership. Rumors to the contrary, the federal government never intended to implement a land-redistribution program in the South. General Sherman viewed his field order as a temporary measure to support freedmen for the remainder of the war. President Andrew Johnson nullified the order in September 1865, returning confiscated land to its former owners. Most of the land-redistribution programs that emerged after the war, including government-sponsored programs, required black farmers to have capital, something that was difficult for them to acquire.

Republican Party rhetoric of the 1850s extolled the virtues and dignity of free labor over the degradation of slave labor. Unlike slaves, according to the then

WHERE TO LEARN MORE

Penn Center Historic District, St. Helena Island, South Carolina **www.penncenter.com**.

WHERE TO LEARN MORE

Hampton University Museum, Hampton, Virginia **www.hamptonu.edu/museum**.

Field Order No. 15   Order by General William T. Sherman in January 1865 to set aside abandoned land along the southern Atlantic coast for forty-acre grants to freedmen, rescinded by President Andrew Johnson later that year.

Southern Homestead Act
Largely unsuccessful law passed in 1866 that gave black people preferential access to public lands in five southern states.

Milk sampling Hampton Institute. Hampton, which opened in Virginia in 1868, was one of the first of several schools established with the help of northern philanthropic and missionary societies to allow freedmen to pursue a college education. Hampton stressed agricultural and vocational training. The military uniforms were typical for male students, black and white, at agricultural and mechanical schools.

Courtesy of Hampton University archives

Sharecropping Labor system that evolved during and after Reconstruction whereby landowners furnished laborers with a house, farm animals, and tools and advanced credit in exchange for a share of the laborers' crop.

prevailing view, free laborers could enjoy the fruits of their work and might someday become owners or entrepreneurs themselves. It was self-help, not government assistance, that guaranteed individual success. After the war, many white northerners envisioned former slaves assuming the status of free laborers, not necessarily of independent landowners.

Most of the officials of the Freedmen's Bureau shared these views and therefore reviving the southern economy was a higher priority than helping former slaves acquire farms. Thus they encouraged freedmen to work for their former masters under contract and to postpone their quest for land.

By the late 1870s, most former slaves in the rural South had been drawn into a subservient position in a new labor system called **sharecropping.** The premise of this system was relatively simple: The landlord furnished the sharecroppers with a house, a plot of land to work, seed, some farm animals, and farm implements and advanced them credit at a store the landlord typically owned. In exchange, the sharecroppers promised the landlord a share of their crop, usually one-half. In theory, a sharecropper could save enough to secure economic independence.

But white landlords perceived black independence as both contradictory and subversive. Black sharecroppers found that the proceeds from their share of the crop never left them very far ahead. Southern states passed crop-lien laws, which gave the storeowner the right to the following year's crop in exchange for the current year's credit. Some sharecroppers found themselves in perpetual debt and worked as virtual slaves.

Migration to Cities

Before the war, the city had offered slaves and free black people a measure of freedom unknown in the rural South. After the war, African Americans moved to cities to find families, seek work, escape the tedium and supervision of farm life, or simply to test their right to move about.

Between 1860 and 1870, the African-American population in every major southern city rose significantly. In Atlanta, for example, black people accounted for one in five residents in 1860 and nearly one in two by 1870.

Rather than developing one large ghetto, as happened in many northern cities, black southerners lived in small concentrations in and around cities. Many found work serving white families, as guards, laundresses, or maids, for very low wages.

Most rural black southerners, however, worked as unskilled laborers. In both Atlanta and Nashville, black people comprised more than 75 percent of the unskilled workforce in 1870. Their wages were at or below subsistence level.

Faith and Freedom

Religious faith framed and inspired the efforts of African Americans to test their freedom on the farm and in the city. Black southerners saw emancipation in biblical terms as the beginning of an exodus from bondage to the Promised Land.

The church became a primary focus of African-American life. It gave black people the opportunity to hone skills in self-government and administration that white-dominated society denied them. The church also operated as an educational institution.

The desire to read the Bible inspired thousands of former slaves to attend the church school. The church also spawned other organizations that served the black community, such as burial societies, Masonic lodges, temperance groups, trade unions, and drama clubs. The church and the congregation were a cohesive force in black communities.

The efforts of former slaves in the classroom, on the farm, in cities, and in the churches reflect the enthusiasm and expectations with which black southerners greeted freedom. But the majority of white southerners were unwilling to see those expectations fulfilled. For this reason, African Americans could not secure the fruits of their emancipation without the support and protection of the federal government.

FEDERAL RECONSTRUCTION, 1865–1870

When the Civil War ended in 1865, no acceptable blueprint existed for reconstituting the Union. President Lincoln favored a conciliatory policy toward the South. As early as 1863, Lincoln had proposed to readmit a seceding state if 10 percent of its prewar voters took an oath of loyalty to the Union and it prohibited slavery in a new state constitution. But this Ten Percent Plan did not require states to grant equal civil and political rights to former slaves, and many Republicans in Congress thought it was not stringent enough. In 1864, a group of them responded with the Wade-Davis Bill, which required a majority of a state's prewar voters to pledge their loyalty to the Union and demanded guarantees of black equality before the law. The bill was passed at the end of a congressional session, but Lincoln kept it from becoming law by refusing to sign it (an action known as a "pocket veto").

The controversy over the plans introduced during the war reflected two obstacles to Reconstruction that would continue to plague the ruling Republicans after the war. First, neither the Constitution nor legal precedent offered any guidance on whether the president or Congress should take the lead on Reconstruction policy. Second, there was no agreement on what that policy should be.

President Andrew Johnson, some conservative Republicans, and most Democrats believed that because the Constitution made no mention of secession, the southern states had been in rebellion but had never left the Union, and therefore that there was no need for a formal process to readmit them. Moderate and radical Republicans disagreed, arguing that the defeated states had forfeited their rights. Moderates and radicals parted company, however, on the conditions necessary for readmission to the Union. The radicals wanted to treat the former Confederate states as territories, or "conquered provinces," subject to congressional legislation. Moderates wanted to grant the seceding states more autonomy and limit federal intervention in their affairs while they satisfied the conditions of readmission.

PRESIDENTIAL RECONSTRUCTION, 1865–1867

The responsibility for developing a Reconstruction policy initially fell on Andrew Johnson, who succeeded to the presidency upon Lincoln's assassination.

Most northerners and many Republicans approved Johnson's Reconstruction plan when he unveiled it in May 1865. Johnson extended pardons and restored property rights, except in slaves, to southerners who swore an oath of allegiance to the Union and the Constitution. Southerners who had held prominent posts in the Confederacy, however, and those with more than $20,000 in taxable property, had to petition the president directly for a pardon, a reflection of Johnson's disdain for wealthy whites. The plan said nothing about the voting rights or civil rights of former slaves.

HOW DID Presidential Reconstruction differ from Congressional Reconstruction?

16–2
Carl Schurz, Report on the Condition of the South (1865)

QUICK REVIEW

Johnson's Reconstruction Plan

- Johnson extended pardons to Southerners who swore an oath of allegiance.
- He restored property rights to Southerners who swore an oath of allegiance.
- His plan had nothing to say about the voting and civil rights of former slaves.

The black church was the center of African-American life in the postwar urban South. Most black churches were founded after the Civil War, but some, such as the first African Baptist Church in Richmond, shown here in an 1874 engraving, traced their origins to before 1861.

The Granger Collection, New York

Northern Democrats applauded the plan's silence on these issues and its promise of a quick restoration of the southern states to the Union. Republicans approved the plan because it restored property rights to white southerners, although some wanted it to provide for black suffrage. Republicans also hoped that Johnson's conciliatory terms might attract some white southerners to the Republican Party.

White southerners, however, were not so favorably impressed by Johnson's plan, and their response turned northern public opinion against the president. Although most states accepted President Johnson's modest requirements, several objected to one or more of them. When Johnson ordered special congressional elections in the South in the fall of 1865, the all-white electorate returned many prominent Confederate leaders to office.

In late 1865, the newly elected southern state legislatures revised their antebellum slave codes. The updated **black codes** allowed local officials to arrest black people who could not document employment and residence or who were "disorderly" and sentence them to forced labor on farms or road crews. The codes also restricted black people to certain occupations, barred them from jury duty, and forbade them to possess firearms. Apprenticeship laws permitted judges to take black children from parents who could not, in the judges' view, adequately support them. Given the widespread poverty in the South in 1865, the law could apply to almost any freed black family. (See American Views: "Mississippi's 1865 Black Codes".)

A consensus formed among radical Republicans, who comprised nearly half of the party's strength in Congress, that to gain readmission, a state would have to extend suffrage to black citizens, protect freedmen's civil rights, and have its white citizens officially acknowledge these rights.

But the radicals could not unite behind a program, and it fell to their moderate colleagues to take the first step toward a congressional Reconstruction plan. The moderates shared the radicals' desire to protect the former slaves' civil and voting rights. But they would not support land-redistribution schemes or punitive measures against prominent Confederates. The moderates' first measure, passed in early 1866, extended the life of the Freedmen's Bureau and authorized it to punish state officials who failed to extend equal civil rights to black citizens. But President Johnson vetoed the legislation.

Undeterred, Congress passed the Civil Rights Act of 1866 in direct response to the black codes. The act specified the civil rights to which all U.S. citizens were entitled. In creating a category of national citizenship with rights that superseded state laws, the act changed federal-state relations (and in the process overturned the *Dred Scott* decision). President Johnson vetoed the act, but it became law when Congress mustered a two-thirds majority to override his veto.

To keep freedmen's rights safe from presidential vetoes, state legislatures, and federal courts, the Republican-dominated Congress moved to incorporate some of the provisions of the 1866 Civil Rights Act into the Constitution. The **Fourteenth Amendment,** which Congress passed in June 1866, addressed the issues of civil and voting rights. It guaranteed every citizen equality before the law. The two key sections of the amendment prohibited states from violating the civil rights of their citizens, thus outlawing the black codes.

President Johnson encouraged southern white intransigence by openly denouncing the Fourteenth Amendment. The president's diatribes against the Republican Congress won him followers in those northern states with a reservoir of opposition to black suffrage. But the tone and manner of his campaign offended many as undignified. In the 1866 elections, the Democrats suffered embarrassing defeats in the North as Republicans managed better than two-thirds majorities in both the House and Senate, sufficient to override presidential vetoes. Radical Republicans, joined by

QUICK REVIEW

Thaddeus Stevens

- Stevens of Pennsylvania led the radical forces in the House of Representatives.

- Stevens envisioned a South with no large plantations and few landless farmers.

- Stevens found few supporters for his ideas.

Black Codes Laws passed by states and municipalities denying many rights of citizenship to free blacks after the Civil war.

Fourteenth Amendment Passed by Congress in 1866, guaranteed every citizen equality before the law by prohibiting states from violating the civil rights of their citizens, thus outlawing the black codes.

AMERICAN VIEWS

MISSISSIPPI'S 1865 BLACK CODES

W*hite southerners, especially landowners and business owners, feared that emancipation would produce a labor crisis; freedmen, they expected, would either refuse to work or strike hard bargains with their former masters. White southerners also recoiled from the prospect of having to treat their former slaves as full social equals. Thus, beginning in late 1865, several southern states, including Mississippi, enacted laws designed to control black labor, mobility, and social status. Northerners responded to the codes as a provocation, a bold move to deny the result of the war and its consequences.*

- How did the black codes fit into President Andrew Johnson's Reconstruction program?
- Some northerners charged that the black codes were a backdoor attempt at reestablishing slavery. Do you agree?
- If southern states enacted black codes to stabilize labor relations, how did the provisions below effect that objective?

From An Act to Confer Civil Rights on Freedmen, and for other Purposes

Section 1. All freedmen, free negroes and mulattoes may sue and be sued, implead and be impleaded, in all the courts of law and equity of this State, and may acquire personal property, and choose in action, by descent or purchase, and may dispose of the same in the same manner and to the same extent that white persons may: Provided, That the provisions of this section shall not be so construed as to allow any freedman, free negro or mulatto to rent or lease any lands or tenements except in incorporated cities or towns, in which places the corporate authorities shall control the same.

Section 7. Every civil officer shall, and every person may, arrest and carry back to his or her legal employer any freedman, free negro, or mulatto who shall have quit the service of his or her employer before the expiration of his or her term of service without good cause; and said officer and person shall be entitled to receive for arresting and carrying back every deserting employee aforesaid the sum of five dollars, and ten cents per mile from the place of arrest to the place of delivery; and the same shall be paid by the employer, and held as a set off for so much against the wages of said deserting employee: Provided, that said arrested party, after being so returned, may appeal to the justice of the peace or member of the board of police of the county, who, on notice to the alleged employer, shall try summarily whether said appellant is legally employed by the alleged employer, and has good cause to quit said employer. Either party shall have the right of appeal to the county court, pending which the alleged deserter shall be remanded to the alleged employer or otherwise disposed of, as shall be right and just; and the decision of the county court shall be final.

From An Act to Amend the Vagrant Laws of the State

Section 2. All freedmen, free negroes and mulattoes in this State, over the age of eighteen years, found on the second Monday in January, 1866, or thereafter, with no lawful employment or business, or found unlawfully assembling themselves together, either in the day or night time, and all white persons assembling themselves with freedmen, free negroes or mulattoes, or usually associating with freedmen, free negroes or mulattoes, on terms of equality, or living in adultery or fornication with a freed woman, freed negro or mulatto, shall be deemed vagrants, and on conviction thereof shall be fined in a sum not exceeding, in the case of a freedman, free negro or mulatto, fifty dollars, and a white man two hundred dollars, and imprisonment at the discretion of the court, the free negro not exceeding ten days, and the white man not exceeding six months.

Source: "Laws in Relation to Freedmen," 39 Congress, 2 Session, Senate Executive Document 6, Freedmen's Affairs, 182–86.

MAP EXPLORATION

To explore an interactive version of this map go to
http://www.prenhall.com/goldfield3/map16.1

— Boundaries of the five military districts

☐ Former Confederate states

1868 Date of readmission to Union

(1874) Date of reestablishment of conservative Democratic party control

MAP 16–1   Congressional Reconstruction, 1865–1877
When Congress wrested control of Reconstruction policy from President Andrew Johnson, it divided the South into the five military districts depicted here. The commanding generals for each district held the authority both to hold elections and to decide who could vote.

WHAT DID each of the former Confederate states have to do to be eligible for readmission to the Union?

QUICK REVIEW

Radical Republican Objectives

• Secure freedmen's right to vote.

• Make it likely that southern states would have Republican governments.

• Require the South to accept preeminence of the federal government and the end of slavery.

Congressional Reconstruction
Name given to the period 1867–1870 when the Republican-dominated Congress controlled Reconstruction era policy.

Fifteenth Amendment   Passed by Congress in 1869, guaranteed the right of American men to vote, regardless of race.

moderate colleagues, seized the initiative when Congress reconvened.

CONGRESSIONAL RECONSTRUCTION, 1867–1870

The radicals' first salvo in their attempt to take control of Reconstruction occurred with the passing, over President Johnson's veto, of the Military Reconstruction Acts. The measures, passed in March 1867, inaugurated a period known as **Congressional Reconstruction** or Radical Reconstruction. With the exception of Tennessee, the only southern state that had ratified the Fourteenth Amendment and been readmitted to the Union, Congress divided the former Confederate states into five military districts, each headed by a general (see Map 16–1). The commanders' first order of business was to conduct voter-registration campaigns to enroll black people and bar white people who had held office before the Civil War and supported the Confederacy. The eligible voters would then elect delegates to a state convention to write a new constitution that guaranteed universal manhood suffrage. Once a majority of eligible voters ratified the new constitution and the Fourteenth Amendment, their state would be eligible for readmission to the Union.

To limit presidential interference with their policies, Republicans passed the Tenure of Office Act, prohibiting the president from removing certain officeholders without the Senate's consent. Johnson, angered at what he believed was an unconstitutional attack on presidential authority, deliberately violated the act by firing Secretary of War Edwin M. Stanton, a leading radical, in February 1868. The House responded by approving articles of impeachment against a president for the first time in American history. That set the stage for the next step prescribed by the Constitution: a Senate trial to determine whether the president should be removed from office.

Johnson had indeed violated the Tenure of Office Act, a measure of dubious constitutionality even to some Republicans, but enough Republicans felt that his actions fell short of the "high crimes and misdemeanors" standard set by the Constitution for dismissal from office. Seven Republicans deserted their party, and Johnson was acquitted. The outcome weakened the radicals and eased the way for Ulysses S. Grant, a moderate Republican, to gain the party's nomination for president in 1868.

The Republicans viewed the 1868 presidential election as a referendum on Congressional Reconstruction. Republicans "waved the bloody shirt," reminding voters of Democratic disloyalty, the sacrifices of war, and the peace only Republicans could redeem. Democrats denounced Congressional Reconstruction as federal tyranny and, in openly racist appeals, warned white voters that a Republican victory would mean black rule. Grant won the election, but his margin of victory was uncomfortably narrow. Black voters' overwhelming support for Grant probably provided his margin of victory.

The Republicans retained a strong majority in both houses of Congress and managed to pass another major piece of Reconstruction legislation, the **Fifteenth Amendment,** in February 1869. The amendment guaranteed the right of American men to vote, regardless of race.

The Fifteenth Amendment allowed states to keep the franchise a male prerogative, angering many in the woman-suffrage movement more than had the Fourteenth Amendment. The resulting controversy severed the ties between the movement and Republican politics. Susan B. Anthony broke with her abolitionist colleagues and opposed the amendment. Women who supported the amendment formed the New England Woman Suffrage Association, challenging Anthony's American Equal Rights Association.

SOUTHERN REPUBLICAN GOVERNMENTS, 1867–1870

Away from Washington, the first order of business for the former Confederacy was to draft state constitutions. The documents embodied progressive principles new to the South. They mandated the election of numerous local and state offices. The constitutions committed southern states, many for the first time, to public education. Lawmakers enacted a variety of reforms, including social welfare, penal reform, legislative reapportionment, and universal manhood suffrage.

The Republican regimes that gained control in southern states promoted vigorous state government and the protection of civil and voting rights. Three Republican constituencies supported these governments. The native white group was mostly made up of yeomen farmers. Residing mainly in the upland regions of the South and long ignored by lowland planters and merchants in state government, they were left devastated by the war. They struggled to keep their land and hoped for an easing of credit and for debt-stay laws to help them escape foreclosure. They wanted public schools for their children and good roads to get their crops to market. Some urban merchants and large planters also called themselves Republicans. Collectively, opponents called these native white southerners **scalawags.**

Northern transplants, or **carpetbaggers,** as many southern whites called them, constituted a second group of southern Republicans. Thousands of northerners came south during and after the war.

African Americans constituted the Republican Party's largest southern constituency. In three states, South Carolina, Mississippi, and Louisiana, they also constituted the majority of eligible voters. They viewed the franchise as the key to civic equality and economic opportunity and demanded an active role in party and government affairs.

Black people began to take part in southern politics even before the end of the Civil War, especially in cities occupied by Union forces. In April 1865, black people in Norfolk, Virginia created the Colored Monitor Union club, modeled after regular Republican Party organizations in northern cities, called **Union Leagues.** Despite white threats, black southerners thronged to Union League meetings in 1867, even forging interracial alliances in states such as North Carolina and Alabama. Focusing on political education and recruitment, the leagues successfully mobilized black voters. In 1867, more than 90 percent of eligible black voters across the South turned out for elections.

Black southerners were not content just to vote; they also demanded political office. The number of southern black congressmen in the U.S. House of Representatives increased from two in 1869 to seven in 1873, and more than 600 African Americans, most of them former slaves from plantation counties, were elected to southern state legislatures between 1867 and 1877.

African Americans generally did not promote race-specific legislation. Rather, they supported measures such as debt relief and state funding for education that benefited all poor and working-class people. Like all politicians, however, black officials in southern cities sought to enact measures beneficial to their constituents, such as roads and sidewalks.

WHERE TO LEARN MORE

Beauvoir, Biloxi, Mississippi
www.beauvoir.org.

Scalawags Southern whites, mainly small landowning farmers and well-off merchants and planters, who supported the Southern Republican party during Reconstruction.

Carpetbaggers Northern transplants to the South, many of whom were Union soldiers who stayed in the South after the war.

Union Leagues Republican party organizations in Northern cities that became an important organizing device among freedmen in Southern cities after 1865.

Cartoonist Thomas Nast's interpretation of emancipation as a transformative experience for African Americans. Released from the brutality and limitations of slavery, the freed men and women now have the opportunity for work, education, and a family and home life just like white, middle-class Americans.

E. Sachse and Company, *The Shackle Broken by the Genius of Freedom,* Baltimore, Md.; 1874.

WHAT ROLE did violence play in the Counter-Reconstruction?

16–8
Albion W. Tourgee,
Letter or Ku Klux Klan
Activities (1870)

During the first few years of Congressional Reconstruction, Republican governments walked a tightrope, attempting to lure moderate Democrats and unaffiliated white voters into the party without slighting the black vote. They used the lure of patronage power and the attractive salaries that accompanied public office.

Republicans also gained support by expanding the role of state government to a degree unprecedented in the South. Southern Republican administrations appealed to hard-pressed upland white constituents by prohibiting foreclosure and passing stay laws that allowed farm owners additional time to repay debts. They undertook building programs that benefited black and white citizens, erecting hospitals, schools, and orphanages. Stepping further into social policy than most northern states at the time, Republican governments in the South expanded women's property rights, enacted legislation against child abuse, and required child support from fathers of mulatto children.

Despite these impressive policies, southern Republicans were unable to hold their diverse constituency together. The excesses of some state governments, high taxes, contests over patronage, and conflicts over the relative roles of white and black party members opened rifts in Republican ranks. Patronage triggered intraparty warfare. Every office secured by a Democrat created a disappointed Republican. Class tensions erupted in the party as economic development policies sometimes superseded relief and social service legislation supported by small farmers. There were differences among black voters too. In the Lower South, divisions that had developed in the prewar era between urban, lighter-skinned free black people and darker, rural slaves persisted into the Reconstruction era. In many southern states, black clergy, because of their independence from white support and their important spiritual and educational role, became leaders. But most preached salvation in the next world rather than equality in this one.

COUNTER-RECONSTRUCTION, 1870–1874

Republicans might have survived battles over patronage, policy, expenditures, and taxes. But they could not overcome racism and the violence it generated. Racism killed Republican rule in the South because it deepened divisions within the party, encouraged white violence, and eroded support in the North. Southern Democrats discovered that they could use race baiting and racial violence to create solidarity among white people that overrode their economic and class differences.

Northerners responded to the persistent violence in the South, not with outrage, but with a growing sense of tedium. They came to accept the arguments of white southerners that it was folly to allow black people to vote and hold office. Racism became respectable.

THE USES OF VIOLENCE

Racial violence preceded Republican rule. As African Americans moved about, attempted to vote, haggled over labor contracts, and carried arms as part of the occupying Union forces, they tested the patience of white southerners, to whom any black assertion of equality seemed threatening. Cities, where black and white people competed for jobs and where black political influence was most visible, became flashpoints for interracial violence.

White paramilitary groups were responsible for much of the violence directed against African Americans. Probably the best-known of these groups was the **Ku Klux Klan.** The Klan directed much of its violence toward subverting the electoral process. One historian has estimated that roughly 10 percent of all black delegates to the 1867 state constitutional conventions in the South became victims of political violence during the next decade.

Not all Klan attacks had political objectives. Klansmen struck against anyone, black or white, who they believed had violated racial boundaries. A Georgia Klansman murdered a freedman because he could read and write. Klansmen in Florence, South Carolina, killed a black man who rented a plantation "because such a thing ought not to be."

The federal government responded with a variety of legislation. One example was the Fifteenth Amendment, ratified in 1869, which guaranteed the right to vote. Another was the Enforcement Act of 1870, which authorized the federal government to appoint supervisors in states that failed to protect voting rights. When violence and intimidation persisted, Congress followed with a second, more sweeping measure, the Ku Klux Klan Act of 1871. This law permitted federal authorities, with military assistance, if necessary, to arrest and prosecute members of groups that denied a citizen's civil rights if state authorities failed to do so. The Klan Act was not successful in curbing racial violence, but with it, Congress, by claiming the right to override state authority to bring individuals to justice, established a new precedent in federal-state relations.

THE FAILURE OF NORTHERN WILL

The success of political violence after 1871 reflected less the inadequacy of congressional legislation than a failure of will on the part of northern Republicans to follow through on commitments to southern Republican administrations. The erosion of northern support for Congressional Reconstruction began as early as the presidential election of 1868. Republican candidate Ulysses S. Grant's campaign theme that year was "Let Us Have Peace," a reference to the political turmoil in the South.

The commitment to voting rights for black southerners, widespread among Republicans in 1865 and affirmed in the Fifteenth Amendment, faded as well. American politics in the 1870s seemed increasingly corrupt and irresponsible. Scandal abounded. The Democratic boss William M. Tweed and his associates transformed Tammany Hall, a Democratic club, into a full-fledged political machine that robbed New York City of an astounding $100 million. Federal officials allowed private individuals to manipulate the stock market for spectacular gains. Several members of Congress and President Grant's vice president exchanged government favors for railroad stock.

A growing number of Americans attributed the debacle to the expansion of the right to vote. Voting was a privilege to be earned, they maintained, not a basic right of citizenship. And black people, according to some Republicans, had not earned that right.

The racist assumption behind this view found growing support among intellectuals. Racism gained an aura of scientific respectability in the late nineteenth century. White racial theorists held that it was folly to grant suffrage to African

Ku Klux Klan Perhaps the most prominent of the vigilante groups that terrorized black people in the South during the Reconstruction era, founded by the Confederate veterans in 1866.

The Klan directed violence at African Americans primarily for political activity. Here a black man, John Campbell, vainly begs for mercy in Moore County, North Carolina, in August 1871.

The Granger Collection, New York

Americans because an inferior race (black) could not hold power over a superior race (white). The perpetual turmoil in the South, the extravagances of some Republican southern administrations, and their persistent inability to attract sufficient numbers of white voters all reinforced the view that these governments were unnatural.

Concerns about the quality of the electorate reflected the rising stakes of public office in post–Civil War America. The urban industrial economy boomed in the five years after the war. Republicans promoted and benefited from the boom, and it influenced their priorities. While the federal government denied land to the freedman, it doled out millions of acres to corporations. Issues of fiscal responsibility, tariffs, and hard money replaced freedom and reunion as party priorities.

Not all Republicans approved of the party's promotion of economic development. Some questioned the prudence of government intervention in the "natural" operation of the economy. The emerging scandals of the Grant administration led to calls for reform. Republican governments, North and South, were condemned for their lavish spending and high taxes.

LIBERAL REPUBLICANS AND THE ELECTION OF 1872

Liberal Republicans, as the reformers called themselves, put forward an array of suggestions to improve government and save the Republican Party. They advocated civil service reform to reduce reliance on patronage and the abuses that accompanied office seeking. To limit government and reduce artificial economic stimuli, the reformers called for tariff reduction and an end to federal land grants to railroads. For the South, they recommended a general amnesty for white people and a return to "local self-government" by men of "property and enterprise."

When the Liberals failed to convince other Republicans to adopt their program, they broke with the party. Taking advantage of this split, the Democrats forged an alliance with the Liberals. Together, they nominated journalist Horace Greeley to challenge Ulysses S. Grant for the presidency in the election of 1872. Grant won resoundingly, helped by high turnout among black voters in the South.

WHY DID the federal government abandon African-Americans after 1872?

REDEMPTION, 1874–1877

For southern Democrats, the Republican victory in 1872 underscored the importance of turning out larger numbers of white voters and restricting the black vote. They accomplished these goals over the next four years with a surge in political violence, secure in the knowledge that federal authorities would not intervene against them. The elections of 1876 affirmed the triumph of white southerners. Reconstruction did not end; it was overthrown.

In a religious metaphor that matched their view of the Civil War as a lost crusade, southern Democrats called their victory "Redemption" and depicted themselves as **Redeemers,** holy warriors who had saved the South from the hell of black Republican rule. Generations of American boys and girls would learn this interpretation of the Reconstruction era, and it would affect race relations for nearly a century.

THE DEMOCRATS' VIOLENT RESURGENCE

Redeemers   Southern Democrats who wrested control of governments in the former Confederacy, often through electoral fraud and violence, from Republican, beginning in 1870.

The violence between 1874 and 1876 differed in several respects from earlier attempts to restore white government by force. Attackers operated more openly and more closely identified themselves with the Democratic Party. Mounted, gray-clad ex-Confederate soldiers flanked Democratic candidates at campaign rallies and "visited" black neighborhoods afterward to discourage black people from voting. With black people intimidated and white people already prepared to vote, election days were typically quiet.

Democrats swept to victory across the South in the 1874 elections. The successful appeal to white supremacy inspired a massive white turnout to unseat Republicans in Virginia, Florida (legislature only), and Arkansas. Texas had fallen to the Democrats in 1873. Only South Carolina, Mississippi, and Louisiana, states with large black populations, survived the debacle. But the relentless tide of terror would soon overwhelm them as well.

In Louisiana, a group of elite Democrats in New Orleans organized a military organization, known as the White League, in 1874 to challenge the state's Republican government. In September 1874, more than 8,000 White Leaguers staged a coup to overthrow the Republican government of New Orleans. The city's police, and the intervention of nearby federal troops, saved the government and prevented a wholesale slaughter. But the incident only inspired White Leaguers to redouble their efforts. Unrest such as events in Louisiana also plagued Mississippi and South Carolina.

THE WEAK FEDERAL RESPONSE

Congress responded to the violence with the Civil Rights Act of 1875. The act prohibited discrimination against black people in public accommodations, such as theaters, parks, and trains, and guaranteed freedmen's rights to serve on juries. It had no provision for voting rights, which Congress presumed the Fifteenth Amendment protected. The only way to enforce the law was for individuals to bring grievances related to it before federal courts in the South.

When black people tested the law by trying to use public accommodations, they were almost always turned away. Some filed suit, with disappointing results. Most judges either interpreted the law narrowly or declared it unconstitutional. In 1883, the U.S. Supreme Court agreed and overturned the act, declaring that only the states, not Congress, could redress "a private wrong, or a crime of the individual."

THE ELECTION OF 1876 AND THE COMPROMISE OF 1877

Reconstruction officially ended with the presidential election of 1876, in which the Democrat Samuel J. Tilden ran against the Republican Rutherford B. Hayes. The scandals of the Grant administration, northern weariness with southern Republican governments, and the persisting economic depression worked in the Democrats' favor.

When the ballots were counted, it appeared that Tilden, a conservative New Yorker respectable enough for northern voters and Democratic enough for white southerners, had won. But despite a majority in the popular vote, disputed returns in three southern states left him with only 184 of the 185 electoral votes needed to win.

Southern Democrats wanted Tilden to win, but they wanted control of their states more. Hayes intended to remove federal support from the remaining southern Republican governments anyway. It thus cost him nothing to promise to do so in exchange for the contested electoral votes. The so-called **Compromise of 1877** installed Hayes in the White House and gave Democrats control of every state government in the South. In practical terms, the Compromise signaled the revocation of civil rights and voting rights for black southerners. The Fourteenth and Fifteenth Amendments would be dead letters in the South until well into the twentieth century. On the two great issues confronting the nation at the end of the Civil War, reunion and freedom, the white South had won. It reentered the Union largely on its own terms with the freedom to pursue a racial agenda consistent with its political, economic, and social interests.

As this Thomas Nast cartoon makes clear, the paramilitary violence against black southerners in the early 1870s threatened not only the voting rights of freedmen, but their dreams of education, prosperity, and family life. In this context, the slogan "The Union As It Was" is highly ironic.

Courtesy of Library of Congress

QUICK REVIEW

Civil Rights Act of 1875

- Introduced by Charles Sumner, the bill passed in a watered-down version.

- Prohibited discrimination in public accommodations.

- Overturned by the U.S. Supreme Court in 1883.

Compromise of 1877 The Congressional settling of the 1876 election which installed Republican Rutherford B. Hayes in the White House and gave Democrats control of all state governments in the South.

CONSTITUTIONAL AMENDMENTS AND FEDERAL LEGISLATION OF THE RECONSTRUCTION ERA

Amendment or Legislation	Purpose	Significance
Thirteenth Amendment (passed and ratified in 1865)	Prevented southern states from reestablishing slavery after the war	Final step toward full emancipation of slaves
Freedmen's Bureau Act (1865)	Oversight of resettlement, labor for former slaves	Involved the federal government directly in relief, education, and assisting the transition from slavery to freedom; worked fitfully to achieve this objective during its seven-year career
Southern Homestead Act (1866)	Provided black people preferential access to public lands in five southern states	Lack of capital and poor quality of federal land thwarted the purpose of the act
Civil Rights Act of 1866	Defined rights of national citizenship	Marked an important change in federal-state relations, tilting balance of power to national government
Fourteenth Amendment (passed 1866; ratified 1868)	Prohibited states from violating the rights of their citizens	Strengthened the Civil Rights Act of 1866 and guaranteed all citizens equality before the law
Military Reconstruction Acts (1867)	Set new rules for the readmission of former-Confederate states into the Union and secured black voting rights	Initiated Congressional Reconstruction
Tenure of Office Act (1867)	Required congressional approval for the removal of any official whose appointment had required Senate confirmation	A congressional challenge to the president's right to dismiss cabinet members; led to President Andrew Johnson's impeachment trial
Fifteenth Amendment (passed 1869; ratified 1870)	Guaranteed the right of all American male citizens to vote regardless of race	The basis for black voting rights
Civil Rights Act of 1875	Prohibited racial discrimination in jury selection, public transportation, and public accommodations	Rarely enforced; Supreme Court declared it unconstitutional in 1883

THE MEMORY OF RECONSTRUCTION

Southern Democrats used the memory of Reconstruction to help maintain themselves in power. As white southerners elevated Civil War heroes into saints and battles into holy struggles, they equated Reconstruction with Redemption. For white southerners, white Democrats in particular, had rescued the South from a purgatory of black rule and federal oppression. Whenever southern Democrats felt threatened over the next century, they reminded their white constituents of the sacrifices and heroism of the war, the "horrors of Reconstruction," the menace of black rule, and the cruelty of the Yankee occupiers. The southern view of Reconstruction permeated textbooks, films, and standard accounts of the period. By the early 1900s, professional historians at the nation's finest institutions concurred in this view, ignoring contrary evidence and rendering the story of African Americans invisible.

The national historical consensus grew out of a growing national reconciliation concerning the war, a mutual agreement that both sides had fought courageously and that it was time to move on. Immediately after the Civil War, a number of prominent white southerners urged their neighbors to work on rebuilding the South rather than hating the Yankees. But general reconciliation remained on hold until the end of Reconstruction, when white southerners reclaimed both their governments and their dominance over African Americans. Once that recovery occurred, joint battlefield commemorations stressed mutual bravery and shared sacrifice. Hidden in all the good will was the tacit agreement between southern and northern whites that the South was now free to work out its own resolution to race relations.

Ideally, Americans could have had *both* healing and justice, but instead they settled for the former.

THE FAILED PROMISE OF RECONSTRUCTION

*I*f the demise of Reconstruction elicited a sigh of relief from most white Americans, black southerners greeted it with frustration. Still, the former slaves were better off in 1877 than in 1865. They were free, however limited their freedom. Some owned land; some held jobs in cities. They raised their families in relative peace and experienced the spiritual joys of a full religious life. They socialized freely with relatives and friends, and they moved about. But by 1877, the "golden moment," an unprecedented opportunity for the nation to live up to its ideals by extending equal rights to all its citizens, black and white alike, had passed.

MODEST GAINS AND FUTURE VICTORIES

Black southerners experienced some advances in the decade after the Civil War, but these owed little to Reconstruction. Black families functioned as economic and psychological buffers against unemployment and prejudice. Black churches played crucial roles in their communities. Self-help and labor organizations offered mutual friendship and financial assistance.

Black people also scored some modest economic successes during the Reconstruction era. In the Lower South, black per capita income increased 46 percent between 1857 and 1879, compared with a 35 percent decline in white per capita income. Collectively, black people owned more than $68 million worth of property in 1870, a 240 percent increase over 1860, but the average worth of each was only $408. The overwhelming majority of black people, however, were landless agricultural laborers eking out a meager income that merchants and landlords often snatched to cover debts.

The Fourteenth and Fifteenth Amendments to the Constitution are among the few bright spots in Reconstruction's otherwise dismal legacy. The Fourteenth Amendment guaranteed former slaves equality before the law; the Fifteenth Amendment protected their right to vote. Both amendments elevated the federal government over the states by protecting freedmen from state attempts to deny them their rights. But the benefits of these two landmark amendments did not accrue to African Americans until well into the twentieth century.

In the late nineteenth century, the Supreme Court would uphold the legality of racial segregation and black disfranchisement, in effect declaring that the Fourteenth and Fifteenth Amendments did not apply to African Americans.

CONCLUSION

*W*hite southerners robbed black southerners of their gains and sought to reduce them again to servitude and dependence, if not to slavery. But in the process, the majority of white southerners lost as well.

HOW AND why did Reconstruction end?

WHERE TO LEARN MORE

Levi Jordan Plantation, Brazoria County, Texas
www.webarchaeology.com.

QUICK REVIEW

Advances
- Black families and institutions played a crucial role in Reconstruction Era.
- Fourteenth Amendment guaranteed equality before the law.
- Fifteenth Amendment protected the right to vote.

GLOBAL PERSPECTIVES

EMANCIPATION AND FREEDOM IN THE UNITED STATES AND RUSSIA

*T*sar Alexander II (1855–1881) freed Russia's serfs in 1861, two years before Abraham Lincoln's Emancipation Proclamation. Although Russian serfs had more rights than American slaves, both were tied to the land and to their landlords/masters. The liberation of the serfs was part of a broader reform plan designed to help modernize Russia.

On becoming tsar in 1855, Alexander II had relaxed the speech, travel, and press restrictions imposed by his predecessors, resulting in an influx of Western ideas into Russia. These ideas helped create widespread public support for the liberation of the serfs. The tsar couched his emancipation proclamation in the ideals of God and country, but its origin lay primarily in Russia's economic aspirations and the tsar's political strategy. While most Americans perceived their liberated slaves as forming an agricultural working class, Alexander made land ownership one of the major attractions of emancipation. The government divided farms equally between the landlords and the former serfs, compensating the owners for the divided property.

In theory at least, Russian serfs seemed in a better position than the southern freedmen to secure economic independence, given the land they received. One Russian official exulted, "The people are erect and transformed; the look, the walk, the speech, everything is changed." But the Russian serfs found their economic situation little improved. The land chosen for redistribution was marginal, and redistribution came with a major catch: the former serfs were required to repay the state on the installment plan. Given the quality of the land, the relatively high interest rates attached to the loans, and the vast numbers of serfs and their families, repayment was unrealistic even in the longterm. To ensure that the former serfs would pay up, the tsar allowed local governments to keep the peasants on their land until they fulfilled their financial obligations. In other words, they were as much tied to the land after emancipation as before. And, as a method to improve the quality of agricultural cultivation, the multiplicity of small plots and impoverished peasants was also a failure.

As in the United States, violence marred the transition from bondage to freedom. Rebellions flared in several parts of Russia, but the tsar's armies put these uprisings down quickly. Some of the former serfs managed to escape to towns and cities and become part of the growing laboring class, much as freedmen went to southern cities. In the cities, both former serfs and slaves came closer to the free-labor ideal posited but not supported by their respective governments. In rural areas, reform broke down through a lack of planning and a failure of will.

Yeoman farmers missed an opportunity to break cleanly from the Old South and establish a more equitable society. Instead, they allowed the old elites to regain power and gradually ignore their needs. They preserved the social benefit of a white skin at the cost of almost everything else.

As federal troops left the South, an era of possibility for American society ended, and a new era began. "The southern question is dead," a Charleston newspaper proclaimed in 1877. "The question of labor and capital, work and wages" had moved to the forefront. The chance to redeem the sacrifice of a bloody civil war with a society that fulfilled the promise of the Declaration of Independence and the Constitution for all citizens slipped away.

SUMMARY

White Southerners and the Ghosts of the Confederacy, 1865 While some white Southerners saw the destruction of the Confederacy as punishment, others came

AFRICAN-AMERICAN VOTING RIGHTS IN THE SOUTH

Right from the end of the Civil War, white southerners resisted African-American voting rights. Black people, with equal determination, used the franchise to assert their equal right to participate in the political process. Black voting rights proved so contentious that Congress sought to secure them with the Fourteenth and Fifteenth Amendments to the U.S. Constitution. But U.S. Supreme Court decisions in *United States v. Cruikshank* (1876) and in the Civil Rights Cases (1883) undermined federal authority to protect the rights of freedmen, including voting rights. A combination of violence, intimidation, and legislation effectively disfranchised black southerners by the early twentieth century.

During the 1960s, a period some historians have referred to as the Second Reconstruction, Congress passed legislation designed to override state prohibitions and earlier court decisions limiting African-American voting rights. The key measure, the 1965 Voting Rights Act, not only guaranteed black southerners (and later, other minorities) the right to register and vote but also protected them from procedural subterfuges, many of which dated from the first Reconstruction era, that would dilute their votes. These protections proved necessary because of the extreme racial polarization of southern elections: White people rarely voted for black candidates.

To ensure African-American candidates an opportunity to win elections, the federal government after 1965 insisted that states and localities establish procedures to increase the likelihood of such a result. As part of this process, the federal government also monitored state redistricting for congressional elections, which occurs every decade in response to population shifts recorded in the national census.

By the early 1990s, states were being directed to draw districts with majority-black voting populations to ensure African-American representation in the

U.S. Congress and in state legislatures. The federal government cited the South's history of racial discrimination and racially polarized voting to justify these districts. But white Southerners challenged such claims, as they had more than a century earlier, and their challenges proved successful in federal court.

In 1993, the U.S. Supreme Court issued a decision in a North Carolina redistricting case, *Shaw v. Reno*, that struck down a majority-black congressional district in that state. Subsequent decisions in other southern districts produced similar rulings. The general principle followed by the Court has been that if race is a key justification for drawing these districts, then they violate the Fourteenth Amendment, which, according to the Court majority, demands color-blind electoral procedures. But as Supreme Court Justice William Brennan noted, "to read the Fourteenth Amendment to state an abstract principle of color-blindness is itself to be blind to history." The framers of the Reconstruction Amendments had the protection of the rights of the freedmen in mind (including and especially voting rights) when they wrote those measures. One voting rights expert has charged that the Court rulings have ushered in a "Second Redemption."

But it is also true that beginning in 1998 and continuing through the 2004 elections, black congressional incumbents in Georgia and North Carolina, running in redrawn districts in which black voters were in the minority (and less than 40 percent, at that) won reelection. These results may indicate that racially polarized voting is diminishing in the South, although they may also reflect the power of incumbency and the weak campaigns of the challengers. In any case, the issue of African-American voting rights in the South and the degree to which the federal government may or may not intercede to protect those rights remains as much at issue as it was more than a century ago.

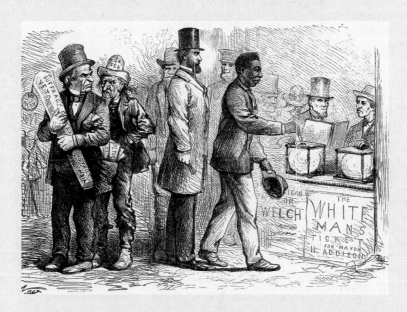

to view the war as the "Lost Cause" and would not allow the memory of the Civil War to die. The myth of the Lost Cause was a need to rationalize and justify the devastation and loss of life; the Reconstruction era became the Redemption and forged community in a time of uncertainty about the future. In this mythology, African Americans were cast in the role of adversaries who challenged whites' belief of their own racial superiority.

More than Freedom: African-American Aspirations in 1865 Former slaves wanted to be free of white supervision; they also desired land, voting and civil rights, and education. At the end of the Civil War, African Americans had reason to hope their dreams might be achieved through such actions as the establishment of the Freedmen's Bureau. The vast majority of former slaves was never able to realize their dreams of independent land ownership and continued to work as farm laborers; others migrated to cities. Their religious faith inspired them; they saw their emancipation in biblical terms and the church became the primary focus of the African-American community.

Federal Reconstruction, 1865–1870 The federal government had two great challenges following the Civil War; supporting the freedom of former slaves and rejoining the Confederacy to the Union. No blueprint for Reconstruction existed; the Constitution was silent on the issue and there was no agreement on policy. Presidential Reconstruction and Congressional Reconstruction brought mixed results. The Civil Rights Act and the Fourteenth and Fifteenth Amendments were key legislative acts during this period; however, by 1870, white Southerners were gradually regaining control of their states and using violence and intimidation to erode gains made by African Americans.

Counter-Reconstruction, 1870–1874 While most of the nation was distracted by political scandals and a serious economic depression, white Southerners regained control of the South. Racial violence through groups like the Ku Klux Klan subverted the electoral process; the success of political violence reflected the erosion of Northern support for Congressional Reconstruction.

Redemption, 1874–1877 After more than fifteen years of Reconstruction, Republicans lost interest in policing their former enemies. By 1877 the Redeemers had triumphed, and all the former Confederate states had returned to the Union in the Compromise of 1877 following the disputed 1876 presidential election. Southern states now had all of their rights and many of their leaders restored to pre-Civil War conditions. Freed slaves remained in mostly subservient positions with few of the rights and privileges enjoyed by other Americans.

The Failed Promise of Reconstruction The tacit agreement between Southern and Northern whites was that the South was now free to work out its own resolution to race relations. The price of sectional reconciliation was that the dream that former slaves held of economic independence and equality would not materialize. The Fourteenth and Fifteenth Amendments were bright spots in the legacy of Reconstruction; the overwhelming majority of African Americans had become landless agricultural workers, eking out a meager income that merchants and landlords often snatched to cover debts. For most, Reconstruction was a failed promise.

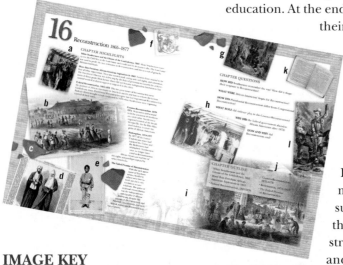

IMAGE KEY
for pages 458–459

a. Freedmen (freed black slaves) vote in 1867.
b. Noon at the primary school for Freedmen at Vicksburg, Mississippi: colored engraving, 1866.
c. Rocks and stones like those used to hurl at former slaves.
d. Two members of the Ku Klux Klan holding guns and wearing hoods and long robes, pictured in Harper's Weekly.
e. A young African American boy with new clothes and a book provided by the Freedmen's Bureau.
f. Thomas Nast cartoon.
g. Klan violence.
h. Milking cows at Hampton.
i. African-American worshippers during a tumultuous church service on New Year's Eve. Sketch by Joseph Becker.
j. White Southerners memorializing Confederate dead, Hollywood Cemetary, Richmond, VA. 1867.
k. Pages 44 and 45 from the New England Primer show the religious content of the Primer.
l. Three white men decry the Reconstruction Acts of Congress as "usurpations and unconstitutional, revolutionary, and void" while clasping hands above the fallen body of a black man.

REVIEW QUESTIONS

1. Both Russia and America hoped to develop a free-labor agricultural class after their respective emancipations. Why didn't these governments follow through on their own objectives?

2. Given the different perspectives on the Civil War's outcome and what the social structure of a postwar South should be, was there any common ground between southern white and southern black on which to forge a Reconstruction policy?

3. Black people did achieve some notable gains during Reconstruction, despite its overall failure. What were those gains?

4. In T. Thomas Fortune's recollection of a boyhood incident, why was it important for him and his friends to fight back?

KEY TERMS

Black codes   (p. 466)
Carpetbaggers   (p. 469)
Compromise of 1877   (p. 473)
Congressional Reconstruction
   (p. 468)
Field Order No. 15   (p. 463)

Fifteenth Amendment   (p. 468)
Fourteenth Amendment   (p. 466)
Freedmen's Bureau   (p. 462)
Ku Klux Klan   (p. 471)
Lost Cause   (p. 461)
Redeemers   (p. 472)

Scalawags   (p. 469)
Sharecropping   (p. 464)
Southern Homestead Act   (p. 463)
Union Leagues   (p. 469)

WHERE TO LEARN MORE

Penn Center Historic District, St. Helena Island, South Carolina. The Penn School was a sea-island experiment in the education of free black people established by northern missionaries Laura Towne and Ellen Murray in 1862. They operated it until their deaths in the early 1900s. The Penn School became Penn Community Services in 1948, serving as an educational institution, health clinic, and a social service agency. See its website at **www.penncenter.com**

Hampton University Museum, Hampton, Virginia. Hampton University was founded by the Freedmen's Bureau in 1868 to provide "practical" training in the agricultural and mechanical fields for former slaves. In addition to a history of the institution, the museum includes one of the oldest collections of African art in the United States. Its website is at **www.hamptonu.edu/museum**

Beauvoir, Biloxi, Mississippi. The exhibits at Beauvoir, the home of Jefferson Davis, evoke the importance of the Lost Cause for the white survivors of the Confederacy. Especially interesting is the Jefferson Davis Soldiers Home on the premises and the Confederate Veterans Cemetery. Davis spent his retirement in Beauvoir. The grounds and some structures suffered significant damage from Hurricane Katrina. Go to **www.beauvoir.org**

Levi Jordan Plantation, Brazoria County, Texas. This site provides an excellent depiction and interpretation of the lives of sharecroppers and tenants during and immediately after the Reconstruction era. The site is especially valuable for demonstrating the transition from slavery to sharecropping. Go to **www.webarchaeology.com**

 U.S. History Documents CD-ROM
For primary sources related to this chapter, refer to the document CD-ROM.

 www.prenhall.com/goldfield
For study resources related to this chapter, visit the *Companion Website*™.

17

A New South: Economic Progress and Social Tradition 1877–1900

CHAPTER HIGHLIGHTS

The Newness of the South The newness of the New South was to be found in its industrialization and urbanization, not in social relations. The Democratic party dominated Southern politics after 1877. Economically, the South remained behind the booming North.

The Southern Agrarian Revolt
Cotton was the basis of the South's agricultural economy. As cotton prices fell, Southern farmers organized to support each other and promote their collective interests. Southern Populists failed to gain significant political power.

Women in the New South
Southern women were active in reform, using churches and clubs as vehicles for their activities. Middle-class women's reform in the New South was essentially conservative.

Settling the Race Issue
The generation of black people who came of age in the 1890s demanded full participation in Southern society. White Southerners responded to such aspirations with violence. Between 1882 and 1903, 2,000 black Southerners were lynched. Key Supreme Court rulings and Northern indifference cleared the way for segregation by law and the disfranchisement of blacks. In the 1890s most white Americans, in both the North and South, believed that black people were inferior and deserved second-class status.

Ida B. Wells

Black Heritage USA 25

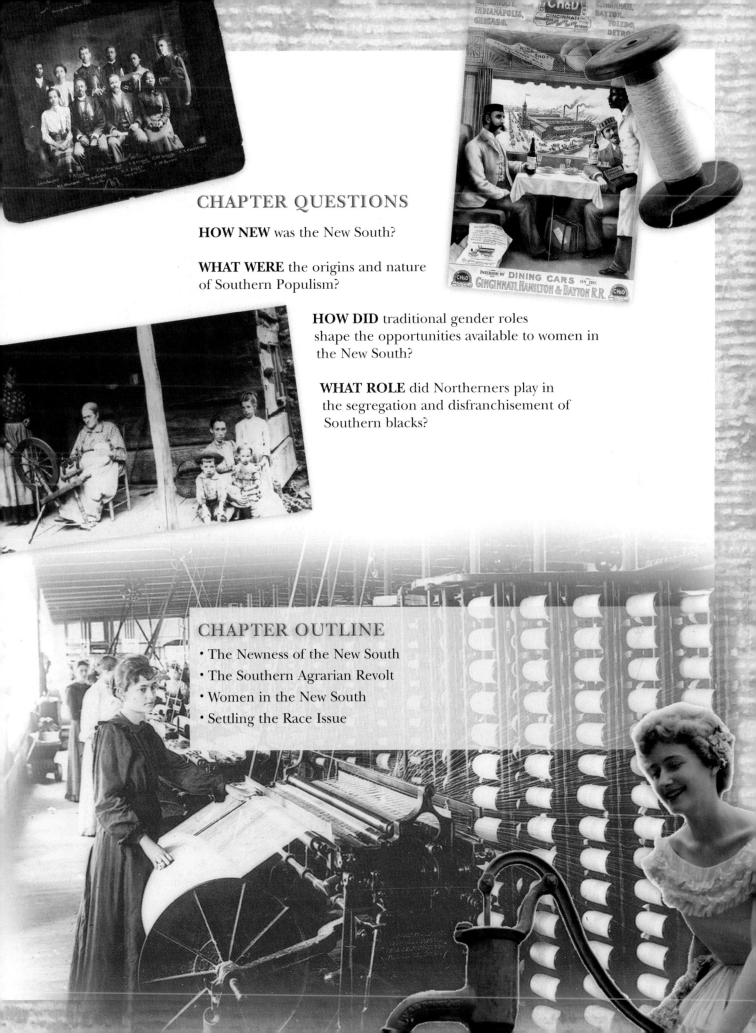

CHAPTER QUESTIONS

HOW NEW was the New South?

WHAT WERE the origins and nature of Southern Populism?

HOW DID traditional gender roles shape the opportunities available to women in the New South?

WHAT ROLE did Northerners play in the segregation and disfranchisement of Southern blacks?

CHAPTER OUTLINE

- The Newness of the New South
- The Southern Agrarian Revolt
- Women in the New South
- Settling the Race Issue

IMAGE KEY
for pages 480–481 is on page 508.

The colored woman of to-day occupies . . . a unique position in this country. . . . She is confronted by both a woman question and a race problem. . . . While the women of the white race can with calm assurance enter upon the work they feel by nature appointed to do [including reform efforts both inside and outside the home], while their men give loyal support and appreciative countenance to [these] efforts, recognizing in most avenues of usefulness the propriety and the need of woman's distinctive co-operation, the colored woman too often finds herself hampered and shamed by a less liberal sentiment . . . on the part of those for whose opinion she cares most. . . .

You do not find the colored woman selling her birthright for a mess of pottage. . . . It is largely our women in the South to-day who keep the black men solid in the Republican Party. The black woman can never forget, however lukewarm the party may to-day appear, that it was a Republican president who struck the manacles from her own wrists and gave the possibilities of manhood to her helpless little ones; and to her mind a Democratic Negro is a traitor and a time-server.

To be a woman in a . . . [new] age carries with it a privilege and an opportunity never implied before. But to be a woman of the Negro race in America, and to be able to grasp the deep significance of the possibilities of the crisis, is to have a heritage, it seems to me, unique in the ages. In the first place, the race is young and full of the elasticity and hopefulness of youth. All its achievements are before it. . . . Everything to this race is new and strange and inspiring. There is a quickening of its pulses and a glowing of its self-consciousness. Aha, I can rival that! I can aspire to that! I can honor my name and vindicate my race! Something like this, it strikes me, is the enthusiasm which stirs the genius of young Africa in America; and the memory of past oppression and the fact of present attempted repression only serve to gather momentum for its irrepressible power. . . . What a responsibility then to have the sole management of the primal lights and shadows! Such is the colored woman's office. She must stamp weal or woe on the coming history of this people. May she see her opportunity and vindicate her high prerogative.

Anna J. Cooper,
A Voice from the South, 1892

Anna Julia Cooper, *A Voice from the South* (Xenia, Ohio: The Aldine Printing House, 1892): 134–135, 138–140, 142–145. The book may be accessed from the Internet: http://docsouth.unc.edu/church/cooper/cooper.html.

ANNA J. COOPER undertook an incredible journey that took her from slavery at her birth in Raleigh, North Carolina, in 1858 to a doctoral degree at the Sorbonne in Paris, France, and to a prominent career as an educator. Throughout her life she remained a firm believer in the role women, especially black women, should play in striking down both white supremacy and male domination. In 1892, Cooper published *A Voice from the South,* excerpted here. The book appeared at a time when the first African-American generation raised in freedom generated a relatively prosperous, educated middle class intent on challenging the limits of race in the New South. The assertiveness of this generation alarmed their white counterparts, who launched a campaign of violence and repression, mainly directed at black men.

Cooper's tone reflects the optimism of the New South and an enthusiasm for the expanding public role of women. At the same time, her critical assessment of black men is scarcely concealed. She implies that black men have held black women back, unlike their white counterparts. Cooper also suggests that black men share at least some of the blame for the white assault on their political rights. Her solution for racial advancement and, presumably, for white hostility to black aspirations is to increase the public profile of black women. But however "new" the New South may have been, traditional views of southern whites on race and gender rendered that solution untenable.

Cooper lived to see the dawn of a new racial and gender era in the South and in America, but the journey would take many years and many lives. She died at the age of 106 in 1964.

The Newness of the New South

Southerners of both races and genders shared Anna J. Cooper's optimism in the decades after Reconstruction. They did what other Americans were doing between 1877 and 1900; they built railroads, erected factories, and moved to towns and cities, only on a smaller scale and with more modest results. The changes, nonetheless, brought political and social turmoil, emboldening black people like Cooper to assert their rights, encouraging women to work outside the home and pursue public careers, and frightening some white men.

By 1900, southern white leaders, urban and rural, had used the banner of white supremacy to stifle dissent. They removed African Americans from political life and constricted their social and economic role.

Thus, the New South's "newness" was to be found primarily in its economy, not in its social relations, though the two were complementary. After Reconstruction, new industries absorbed tens of thousands of first-time industrial workers from impoverished rural areas. Southern cities grew faster than those in any other region of the country. A burst of railroad construction linked these cities to one another and to the rest of the country, giving them increased commercial prominence. Growing in size and taking on new functions, cities extended their influence into the countryside with newspapers, consumer products, and new values. But this urban influence had important limits. It did not bring electricity, telephones, public health services, or public schools to the rural South. It did not greatly broaden the rural economy with new jobs. And it left the countryside without the daily contact with the outside world that fostered a broader perspective.

The Democratic Party dominated southern politics after 1877, significantly changing the South's political system. Through various deceits, Democrats purged most black people and some white people from the electoral process and suppressed challenges to their leadership. The result was the emergence by 1900 of the **Solid South,** a period of white Democratic Party rule that lasted into the 1950s.

Although most southern women remained at home or on the farm, piecing together families shattered by war, some enjoyed new options after 1877. Middle-class women in the cities, both white and black, became increasingly active in civic

HOW NEW was the New South?

Solid South   The one-party (Democratic) political system that dominated the South from the 1890s to the 1950s.

Chronology

1872   Texas and Pacific Railway connects Dallas to eastern markets.

1880   First southern local of the Women's Christian Temperance Union is formed in Atlanta.

1881   Booker T. Washington establishes Tuskegee Institute.

1882   Agricultural Wheel is formed in Arkansas.

1883   Laura Haygood founds the home mission movement in Atlanta.

1884   James B. Duke automates his cigarette factory.

1886   Dr. John Pemberton creates Coca-Cola.

     Southern railroads conform to national track gauge standards.

1887   Charles W. Macune expands the Southern Farmer's Alliance from its Texas base to the rest of the South.

1888   The Southern Farmers' Alliance initiates a successful boycott of jute manufacturers.

1890   Mississippi becomes the first state to restrict black suffrage with literacy tests.

1892   The Populist Party forms.

1894   United Daughters of the Confederacy is founded.

     Populist and Republican fusion candidates win control of North Carolina.

1895   Booker T. Washington delivers his "Atlanta Compromise" address.

1895   Publication of Theodor Herzl's *The Jewish State* outlining his ideas for a Jewish homeland in Palestine in response to rising anti-Semitism in Europe.

1896   Populists endorse the Democratic presidential candidate and fade as a national force.

     In *Plessy v. Ferguson*, the Supreme Court permits segregation by law.

1897   First Zionist Congress meets in Switzerland.

1898   North Carolina Mutual Life Insurance is founded.

     Democrats regain control of North Carolina.

1899   Publication of *Die Grundlagen des neunzehnten Jahrhunderts* ["The Foundations of the Nineteenth Century"] by British scientist Houston Stewart Chamberlain, promoting the superiority of the German "race."

1903   W. E. B. Du Bois publishes *The Souls of Black Folk*.

1905   James B. Duke forms the Southern Power Company.

     Thomas Dixon publishes *The Clansman*.

1906   Bloody race riots break out in Atlanta.

1907   Pittsburgh-based U.S. Steel takes over Birmingham's largest steel producer.

QUICK REVIEW

Southern Women: 1877-1900
- Most Southern women remained at home or on the farm.
- Middle-class women increasingly active in civic work and reform.
- Young white women found work in mills, factories, and as servants.

QUICK REVIEW

Southern Industries
- Iron and steel
- Textiles
- Tobacco
- Timber

---

work and reform. Tens of thousands of young white women from impoverished rural areas found work in textile mills, in city factories, or as servants.

The status of black southerners changed significantly between 1877 and 1900. The members of the first generation born after Emancipation sought more than just freedom as they came of age. They also expected dignity and self-respect and the right to work, to vote, to go to school, and to travel freely. White southerners responded with the equivalent of a second Civil War, and they won. By 1900, black southerners found themselves more isolated from white southerners and with less political power than at any time since 1865. Despite these setbacks, they succeeded, especially in the cities, in building a rich community life and spawning a vibrant middle class.

AN INDUSTRIAL AND URBAN SOUTH

Southerners manufactured very little in 1877, less than 10 percent of the national total. By 1900, however, they boasted a growing iron and steel industry, textile mills that rivaled those of New England, a world-dominant tobacco industry, and a timber-processing industry that helped make the South a leading furniture-manufacturing center. A variety of regional enterprises also rose to prominence, among them the maker of what would become the world's favorite soft drink, Coca-Cola.

Steel Mills and Textiles.   Birmingham, barely a scratch in the forest in 1870, exemplified one aspect of what was new about the New South. Within a decade, its iron and steel mills were belching the smoke of progress across the northern Alabama hills. By 1889, Birmingham had surpassed the older southern iron center of Chattanooga, Tennessee, and was preparing to challenge Pittsburgh, the nation's preeminent steelmaking city.

Although the South had manufactured cotton products since the early decades of the nineteenth century, chronic shortages of labor and capital kept the industry small. In the 1870s, however, several factors drew local investors into textile enterprises. The population of the rural South was rising, but farm income was low, ensuring a steady supply of cheap labor. Cotton was plentiful and cheap. The center of the industry was in the Carolina Piedmont, a region with good railroads, plentiful labor, and cheap energy. By 1900, the South had surpassed New England to become the nation's foremost textile-manufacturing center.

Tobacco and Coca-Cola.   The South's tobacco industry, like its textile industry, predated the Civil War. The discovery of bright-leaf tobacco, a strain suitable for smoking in the form of cigarettes, changed Americans' tobacco habits. In 1884, James B. Duke installed the first cigarette-making machine in his Durham, North Carolina, plant. By 1900, Duke's American Tobacco Company controlled 80 percent of all tobacco manufacturing in the United States.

Although not as important as textiles or tobacco in 1900, a soft drink developed by an Atlanta pharmacist, Dr. John Pemberton, eventually became the most renowned southern product worldwide. Pemberton developed the drink, a mixture of oils, caffeine, coca leaves, and cola nuts, in his backyard in an effort to find a good-tasting cure for headaches. He called his concoction Coca-Cola. By the mid-1890s, Coca-Cola enjoyed a national market. Southerners were such heavy consumers that the Georgia Baptist Association felt compelled to warn its members "The more you drink, the more you want to drink." The Baptists may have been on to something, as Coca-Cola's original formula did, in fact, include chemically active coca leaves.

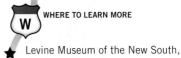

WHERE TO LEARN MORE

Levine Museum of the New South, Charlotte, North Carolina. **www.museumofthenewsouth.org**

Railroads and Growth.   Southern railroad construction boomed in the 1880s, outpacing the rest of the nation (see Map 17–1). In 1886, the southern railroads agreed to conform to a national standard for track width, firmly linking the region into a national transportation network and ensuring quick and direct access for southern products to the booming markets of the Northeast.

The railroads connected many formerly isolated small southern farmers to national and international agricultural markets. Drawn into commercial agriculture, the farmers were now subject to market fluctuations, their fortunes rising and falling with the market prices for their crops. To an extent unknown before the Civil War, the market now determined what farmers planted, how much credit they could expect, and on what terms.

The railroad also opened new areas of the South to settlement and economic development. In 1892, according to one guidebook, Florida was "in the main inaccessible to the ordinary tourist, and unopened to the average settler." But railroad construction boomed in the state in the 1890s, and by 1912 there were tourist hotels as far south as Key West. Railroads also penetrated the Appalachian Mountains, expanding markets for farmers but also opening the area to outside timber and coal-mining interests.

MAP EXPLORATION

To explore an interactive version of this map, go to **http://www.prenhall.com/goldfield3/map17.1**

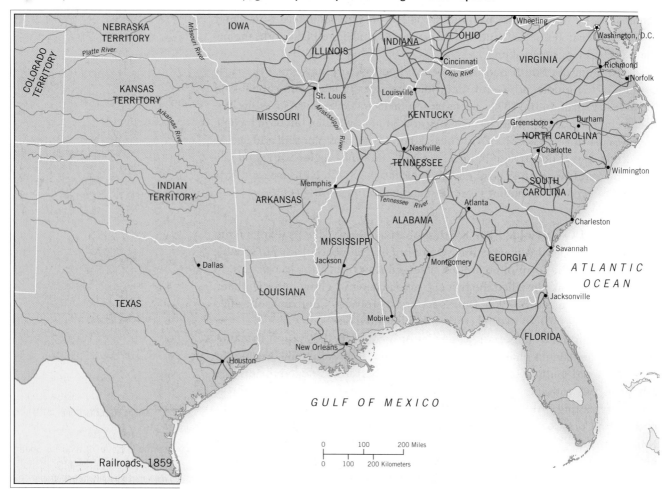

Railroads, 1859

MAP 17–1A   Railroads in the South, 1859 and 1899   A postwar railroad construction boom promoted commercial agriculture and industry in the South. Unlike the railroads of the prewar South, uniform gauges and connections to major trunk lines in the North linked southerners to the rest of the nation. Northern interests, however, owned the major southern railroads in 1899, and most of the products flowing northward were raw materials to be processed by northern industry or shipped elsewhere by northern merchants.

The railroad increased the prominence of interior cities at the expense of older coastal cities. Antebellum ports such as New Orleans, Charleston, and Savannah declined as commerce took to the rails. Cities such as Dallas, Atlanta, Nashville, and Charlotte, astride great railroad trunk lines, emerged to lead southern urban growth.

Railroads also spurred the growth of smaller towns that marketed and processed farm products for the surrounding countryside. A town on a rail line that invested in a cotton press and a cottonseed-oil mill would become a marketing hub for the surrounding countryside within a day's wagon ride away. The number of towns with fewer than 5,000 people doubled between 1870 and 1880 and doubled again by 1900.

MAP EXPLORATION

To explore an interactive version of this map, go to **http://www.prenhall.com/goldfield3/map17.1**

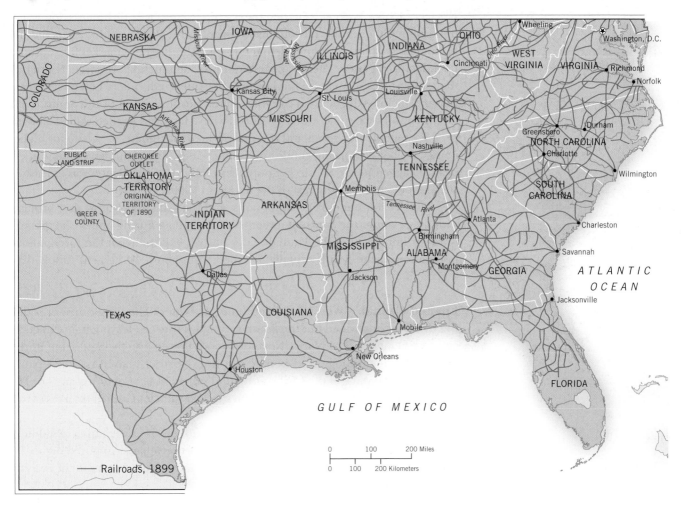

MAP 17–1B

WHAT EFFECT did railroads have on the Southern workforce?

THE LIMITS OF INDUSTRIAL AND URBAN GROWTH

Rapid as it was, between 1860 and 1900, the South's share of the nation's manufacturing increased only marginally from 10.3 percent to 10.5 percent, and its share of the nation's capital declined slightly from 11.5 percent to 11 percent. About the same percentage of people worked in manufacturing in the southern states east of the Mississippi in 1900 as in 1850. Between 1860 and 1880, the per capita income of the South declined from 72 percent of the national average to 51 percent, and by 1920 it had recovered to only 62 percent.

A weak agricultural economy and a high rural birthrate depressed wages in the South. Southern industrial workers earned roughly half the national average manufacturing wage during the late nineteenth century. In 1904, a Memphis

QUICK REVIEW

Railroads and the South

- Connected small Southern farmers to national and international markets.
- Opened new areas in the South to settlement and development.
- Increased the importance of interior cities at the expense of older cities.

businessman boasted that his city "can save the northern manufacturer . . . who employs 400 hands, $50,000 a year on his labor bill."

Effects of Low Wages. Despite their attractiveness to industrialists, low wages undermined the southern economy in several ways. Poorly paid workers did not buy much, keeping consumer demand low and limiting the market for southern manufactured goods. They also could not provide much tax revenue, restricting the southern states' ability to fund services like public education. Low wages meant that mostly low-skilled, labor-intensive industries flourished in the South. Well-educated workers would either go north, where factories needed skilled labor to produce high-quality goods and run complicated machinery, or agitate for higher wages and better working conditions in the South. As a result, investment in education lagged in the South. Per-pupil expenditure in the region was at least 50 percent below that of the rest of the nation in 1900.

Finally, low wages kept immigrants, and the skills and energy they brought with them, out of the South. Between 1860 and 1900, during one of the greatest waves of immigration the United States has yet experienced, the foreign-born population of the South actually declined from about 10 percent to less than 2 percent.

Limited Capital. Why did the South not do better? The simple answer is that the Civil War had wiped out the South's capital resources, leaving it, in effect, an economic colony of the North. Northern goods flowed into the South, but northern capital, technology, and people did not. Northern-based national banks emerged in the wake of the Civil War to fund northern economic expansion. The South, in contrast, had few banks, and they lacked sufficient capital reserves to fuel an equivalent expansion.

Investment in the South seemed riskier and less promising than investment in the vibrant northern economy. As a result, northern banks imposed higher interest rates and shorter terms on loans to southerners than on loans to their northern customers.

With limited access to other sources of capital, the South's textile industry depended on thousands of small investors in towns and cities. These investors avoided risk and shunned innovation. Most textile operations remained small-scale.

The lumber industry, the South's largest, typified the shortcomings of southern economic development in the late nineteenth century. It required little capital, relied on unskilled labor, and processed its raw materials on site. After clear-cutting, (i.e., felling all the trees) in one region, sawmills moved quickly to the next stand of timber, leaving behind a bare landscape, rusting machinery, and a workforce no better off than before.

Birmingham's iron and steel industry also suffered from financial weakness. Part of the fault lay with the mill owners, who relied on cheap black labor rather than investing in expensive technology. Another problem was the limited market for steel in the mostly agricultural South. Southern farmers compounded this problem by relying on people and mules instead of farm machinery.

The tobacco industry, however, avoided the problems that plagued other southern enterprises. James B. Duke's American Tobacco Company was so immensely profitable that he became, in effect, his own bank. With more than enough capital to install the latest technology in his plants, Duke bought out his competitors. He then diversified into electric power generation, investing in an en-

WHERE TO LEARN MORE

Sloss Furnaces National Historical Landmark, Birmingham, Alabama. www.slossfurnaces.com

terprise that became the Southern Power Company in 1905 (and later the Duke Power Company). He also endowed what became Duke University.

Southern industry fit into a narrow niche of late-nineteenth-century American industrialization. With an unskilled and uneducated work force, poor access to capital and technology, and a weak consumer base, the South processed raw agricultural products and produced cheap textiles, cheap lumber products, and cheap cigarettes. "Made in the South" became synonymous with bottom-of-the-line goods. In the South, textile mills were typically located in the countryside, often in mill villages where employers could easily recruit families and keep them isolated from the distractions and employment alternatives of the cities. The timber industry similarly remained a rural-based enterprise. Tobacco manufacturing helped Durham and Winston, North Carolina, grow, but they remained small compared to northern industrial cities. Duke moved his corporate headquarters to New York to be near that city's financial, advertising, and communications services.

FARMS TO CITIES: IMPACT ON SOUTHERN SOCIETY

If industrialization in the South was limited compared to the North, it nonetheless had an enormous impact on southern society. In the southern Piedmont, failed farmers moved to textile villages to earn a living. Entire families secured employment and often a house in exchange for their labor. Widows and single young men also moved to the mills, usually the only option outside farm work in the South. Nearly one-third of the textile-mill labor force by 1900 consisted of children under the age of 14 and women. They worked 12 hours a day, six days a week, although some firms allowed a half-day off on Saturday.

Southern urban growth, which also paled in comparison with that of the North, had a similarly disproportionate impact on southern society.

By the 1890s, textile mills were a common sight in towns throughout the South. The mills provided employment for impoverished rural families, especially women and children.

T.E. Armistead Collection, University of South Alabama Archives

In 1880, southern towns often did not differ much from the countryside in appearance, economy, religion, and outlook. Over the next 20 years, the gap between town and country widened. By 1900, a town in the New South would boast a business district and more elegant residences than before. It would have a relatively prosperous economy and more frequent contact with other parts of the country. Its influence would extend into the countryside. Mail, the telegraph, the railroad, and the newspaper brought city life to the attention of farm families. In turn, farm families visited nearby towns and cities more often. Many never returned to the farm.

The urban South drew the region's talented and ambitious young people. White men moved to cities to open shops or take jobs as bank clerks, bookkeepers, merchants, and salesmen. White women worked as retail clerks, telephone operators, and office personnel. Black women filled the growing demand for laundresses and domestic servants. And black men also found prospects better in towns than on the farm, despite a narrow and uncertain range of occupations available to them. The excitement that drew some southerners to their new cities repelled others. To them, urbanization and the emphasis on wealth, new technology, and display represented a second Yankee conquest. The cities, they feared, threatened to infect the South with northern values, undermining southern grace, charm, faith, and family. Ministers warned against trafficking with the urban devil, whose temptations could overcome even the most devout individual.

Country people held ambivalent views of the city. Farm children looked forward to the Saturday excursion to town, when they would gaze into shop windows, watch people rushing about, wonder at the workings of electricity, and drink a "Coka Cola" at the drugstore. Their parents shared some of this excitement but experienced apprehension as well. They were disturbed by the easy blurring of class and racial distinctions in town and offended by the scorn with which town folk sometimes treated them.

White southerners in town and country, who not long before had lived similar lives, grew distant. Small landholding white farmers and their families had fallen on hard times. The market that lured them into commercial agriculture threatened to take away their independence. They faced the loss of their land and livelihood. Their way of life no longer served as the standard for the South. New South spokesmen promoted cities and industries and ordered farmers to get on board the train of progress before it left the station without them.

THE SOUTHERN AGRARIAN REVOLT

WHAT WERE the origins and nature of Southern Populism?

Even more than before the Civil War, cotton dominated southern agriculture between 1877 and 1900. And the economics of cotton brought despair to cotton farmers. Those who grew two other traditional southern cash crops, rice and tobacco, fared better. Steady demand allowed rice and tobacco growers to maintain a decent standard of living. Cotton was another matter. The size of the cotton crop continued to set annual records after 1877. But the price of cotton fell while the price of fertilizers, agricultural tools, food, and most other necessities went up. As a result, the more cotton the farmers grew, the less money they made.

Before the Civil War, the South fed itself. After the war, with railroads providing direct access to major cotton-marketing centers, farmers produced more cotton and less food. The South became an importer of food. As a common lament went in 1893, "Five-cent cotton, forty-cent meat, how in the world can a poor man eat?"

COTTON AND CREDIT

The solution to this agrarian dilemma seemed simple: Grow less cotton. But that course was not possible for several reasons. In a cash-poor economy, credit ruled. Cotton was the only commodity instantly convertible into cash and thus the only commodity accepted for credit. Food crops generated less income per acre than cotton. Local merchants, themselves bound in a web of credit to merchants in larger cities, accepted cotton as collateral. As cotton prices plummeted, the merchants required their customers to grow more cotton to make up the difference.

Trapped in debt by low cotton prices and high interest rates, small landowning farmers lost their land in record numbers. Both black farmers and white farmers were affected. But white farmers were more likely than black farmers to own their farms, so the effect on them was more dramatic. Just after the Civil War, less than one-third of white farmers in the South were tenants or sharecroppers. By the 1890s, nearly half were.

Some areas were able to diversify. Good rail connections in Georgia, for example, made peach farming profitable for some farmers. Railroads likewise helped cattle ranching spread in Texas. But few crops or animals had the geographical range of cotton. Soil type, rainfall, animal parasites, and frost made alternatives unfeasible. Moreover, cotton required no machinery or irrigation system.

SOUTHERN FARMERS ORGANIZE, 1877–1892

As their circumstances deteriorated, southern farmers fought back. They lobbied for debt-stay laws and formed farmer organizations. They widened the circle of their community to include other farmers sharing the same plight. They wanted to make the market fairer, to lower interest rates and ease credit, to regulate railroad freight rates, and to keep the prices of necessities in check.

But these goals required legislation that neither the federal government nor southern state governments were inclined to support. Therefore, southern farmers joined their colleagues nationwide to address common grievances related to pricing, credit, and tax policies. By 1875, nearly 250,000 southern landowners had joined the National Grange of the Patrons of Husbandry or, more popularly, simply the **Grange** (see Chapter 20). The leaders of the Grange, however, were large landowners. They did not have the same interests as the small farmers who made up the organization's rank and file.

Salvation and Cooperation. The most powerful agricultural reform organization, the **Southern Farmers' Alliance,** originated in Texas in the late 1870s. Alliance-sponsored farmers' cooperatives provided their members with discounts on supplies and credit. Members also benefited from marketing their cotton crops collectively.

The faces of this white sharecropper family in North Carolina reflect the harshness of farm life in the late nineteenth- and early twentieth-century South, a period when thousands of southerners, white and black alike, slipped from land ownership to sharecropping.

Courtesy of North Carolina Division of Archives and History

Grange The National Grange of the Patrons of Husbandry, a national organization of farm owners formed after the Civil War.

Southern Farmer's Alliance The largest of several organizations that formed in the post-Reconstruction South to advance the interests of beleaguered small farmers.

The Alliance was still very much a Texas organization in 1887 when Charles W. Macune, a Wisconsin native, became its driving force. Macune sent a corps of speakers to create a network of southern cooperatives. Within two years, the Alliance had spread throughout the South and into the North and West. By 1890, it claimed more than a million members. With the exception of a few large landowners and some tenant farmers, almost all were small farmers who owned their own land.

The Alliance operated like a religious denomination. Its leaders preached a message of salvation through cooperation to audiences of as many as 20,000 people at huge revival-like rallies. Qualifications for membership included a belief in the divinity of Jesus and the literal truth of the Bible. Alliance speakers, many of them rural ministers, often held meetings in churches. They urged members to visit "the homes where lacerated hearts are bleeding, to assuage the suffering of a brother or a sister, bury the dead, care for the widows and educate the orphans." The Alliance lobbied state legislatures to fund rural public schools. To increase the sense of community, the Alliance sponsored picnics, baseball games, and concerts.

The Alliance became for many small farmers a surrogate government and church in a region where public officials and many mainline Protestant ministers ignored their needs. Alliance leaders criticized the many Baptist, Methodist, and Presbyterian ministers who had strayed from the traditional emphasis on individual salvation and were defending a status quo that benefited large planters and towns.

Some Alliance members left their churches for new religious groups. The new churches promoted a vision of an egalitarian South. They accepted women on an equal basis, and occasionally black people as well. As many as a third of Holiness preachers were women.

Women also found an active role as officers and speakers in the Alliance. As a Texas woman declared, "The Alliance has come to redeem woman from her enslaved condition. She is admitted into the organization as the equal of her brother, and the ostracism which has impeded her intellectual progress in the past is not met with."

However, the Alliance did not accept black members. Black farmers formed the first **Colored Farmers' Alliance** in Texas in 1886. The Colored Alliance had fewer landowners and more tenants and sharecroppers in its ranks than the white organization. It concerned itself with issues relevant to this constituency, such as higher wages for cotton pickers. In 1891, the Colored Alliance attempted a region-wide strike over farm wages but was unable to enforce it in the worsening southern economy.

The white Alliance had better results with a protest over price fixing. To protect cotton shipped to market, farmers wrapped it in a burlap-like material called jute. In 1888, jute manufacturers combined to raise the price from 7 cents to as much as 14 cents a yard. The Alliance initiated a jute boycott throughout the South, telling farmers to use cotton bagging as an alternative. The protest worked, forcing the chastened jute manufacturers to offer farmers their product at a mere 5 cents per yard.

Storing Cotton.   This success encouraged Macune to pursue a more ambitious project, his **subtreasury plan.** Alliance members were to store their crops in a subtreasury (i.e., warehouse), keeping their cotton off the market until the price rose. In the meantime, the government would loan the farmers up to 80 percent of the

Colored Farmers' Alliance   An organization of Southern black farmers formed in Texas in 1886 in response to the Southern Farmer's Alliance, which did not accept black people as members.

Subtreasury Plan   A program promoted by the Southern Farmer's Alliance in response to low cotton prices and tight credit. Farmers would store their crop in a warehouse until prices rose, in the meantime borrowing up to 80 percent of the value of the stored crops from the government at a low interest rate.

value of the stored crops at a low interest rate of 2 percent per year. This arrangement would free farmers from merchants' high interest rates and crop liens.

Macune urged Alliance members to endorse political candidates who supported the subtreasury scheme. Many Democratic candidates for state legislatures throughout the South did endorse it and were elected, with Alliance backing, in 1890. Once in office, however, they failed to deliver.

The failure of the subtreasury plan, combined with a steep drop in cotton prices after 1890, undermined the Alliance. In 1891, Alliance membership declined by two-thirds in Georgia. Desperate Alliance leaders merged their organization with a new national political party in 1892, the People's Party, better known as the **Populist Party.** The Populists appropriated the Alliance program and challenged Democrats in the South and Republicans in the West. The merger reflected desperation more than calculation.

SOUTHERN POPULISTS

Northern farmers, like their southern counterparts, faced growing financial pressure. Just as southern farmers had turned to the Democratic Party to redress their grievances, northern farmers turned to the dominant party in the northern farming states, the Republican Party, to redress theirs. Like the Democrats, the Republicans failed to respond. In 1890, disillusioned farmers in Kansas founded the Populist Party. The Populists held their first national nominating convention in Omaha in July 1892.

The Populists supported a wide range of reforms, many adopted from the Alliance, including the direct election of United States senators by popular vote rather than by state legislatures, an income tax, woman suffrage, government ownership of railroads, and various proposals to ease credit. In the South, they challenged the Democratic Party, sometimes courting Republicans, including black voters.

Southern populists were ambivalent about African Americans. On the one hand, black people constituted a voting bloc the Populists could ill afford to ignore. On the other hand, appealing to black voters would expose Populists to demagogic attacks from Democrats for undermining white supremacy, frightening away potential white backers. Many southern Populists, including former members of the Alliance, supported segregation and never made the gesture of racial reconciliation.

Despite the risks, Populists in at least two southern states, Texas and Georgia, openly appealed for black votes. The Texas Populist platform called for "equal justice and protection under the law to all citizens without reference to race, color or nationality." In Georgia, the Populist leader Tom Watson supported a biracial party organization and counseled white people to accept black people as partners in their common crusade. "You are kept apart," Watson told black and white Georgians, "that you may be separately fleeced of your earnings. You are made to hate each other because upon that hatred is rested the keystone of the arch of financial despotism which enslaves you both."

Most black people, though, remained loyal to the Republican Party. Black people also suspected the Populists' motives. The party appealed mainly to small landowning farmers, not, as most black southerners were, unpropertied tenants and sharecroppers. And even the Texas Populists, while appealing for black support, opposed black officeholding and jury service.

Unwilling or unable to mobilize black voters and unsuccessful in dislodging white voters from the Democratic Party, the Populists finished a distant third in

17–9
The Omaha Platform of the Populist Party (1892)

QUICK REVIEW

Political Affiliation of African Americans

- Some populists made appeals to African Americans.
- Most African Americans remained loyal to the Republican party.
- Many blacks were suspicious of the populists' motives.

Populist Party   A major third party of the 1890s, formed on the basis of the Southern Farmers' Alliance and other organizations, mounting electoral challenges against Democrats in the South and the Republicans in the West.

the 1892 presidential election. In the South, their only significant inroads were in the state legislatures of Texas, Alabama, and Georgia.

The Populists had only a few additional successes in the South after 1892, even in the midst of an economic depression. Their major victory was in North Carolina in 1894. Republicans had remained a political force in the state's mountain counties and among black people in its eastern part. Adopting a fusion strategy, the Populists ran candidates on a combined ticket with Republicans. The fusion candidates captured the governorship and state legislature. Once in office, they overhauled the state electoral machinery, simplified voter-registration procedures, and established nonpartisan electoral panels to monitor elections. Reflecting Populist influence, they also imposed limits on interest rates, increased expenditures for education, and raised taxes on railroads.

Higher cotton prices and returning prosperity in the late 1890s, however, undermined Populist support in North Carolina, as in the rest of the South. In 1896, the Populists assisted in their own nationwide demise by merging with the Democrats for the presidential election of 1896. In 1898, Democrats surged back into office in North Carolina on the strength of a virulent white supremacy campaign and promptly undid the work of the fusionists.

WOMEN IN THE NEW SOUTH

HOW DID traditional gender roles shape the opportunities available to women in the New South?

In the late-nineteenth-century North, women became increasingly active in reform movements, including woman suffrage, labor legislation, social welfare, and city planning. Building on their antebellum activist traditions, northern women, sometimes joining with men, sought to improve the status of women.

Because the antebellum reform movements included abolitionism, they had made little headway in the South. As a result, southern women had a meager reform tradition to build on. The war also left them ambivalent about independence. With husbands, fathers, and brothers dead or incapacitated, many women had to care for themselves and their families in the face of defeat and deprivation. Some determined never again to depend on men.

The response of southern white men to the war also complicated women's efforts to improve their status. Southern men had been shaken by defeat. To regain their self-esteem, they recast the war as a noble crusade rather than a defeat. And they imagined southern white women as paragons of virtue and purity who required men to defend them. Demands for even small changes in traditional gender roles would threaten this image. Southern women understood this and never mounted an extensive reform campaign like their sisters in the North.

Despite such limitations, middle-class southern women found opportunities to broaden their social role and enter the public sphere in the two decades after 1880. They found these opportunities primarily in the cities, where servants, stores, and schools freed them of many of the productive functions, such as making clothing, cooking, and child care, that burdened their sisters in the country and kept them tied to the home.

CHURCH WORK AND PRESERVING MEMORIES

Southern women waded warily into the public arena, using channels men granted them as natural extensions of the home, such as church work. The movement to found home mission societies, for example, was led by single white women in the Methodist Church. Home missions promoted industrial education among the

QUICK REVIEW

Southern Women and Reform

- Southern women played an active role in the public arena.
- Laura Haygood started the movement to found home mission societies.
- Lily Hammond opened settlement houses in Atlanta in the 1890s.

poor and helped working-class women become self-sufficient. Lily Hammond, an Atlantan, extended the mission concept when she opened settlement houses in black and white neighborhoods in Atlanta in the 1890s. **Settlement houses,** pioneered in New York in the 1880s, promoted middle-class values in poor neighborhoods and provided them with a permanent source of services.

Religion also prompted southern white women to join the **Women's Christian Temperance Union (WCTU).** Women framed temperance and the prohibition of alcohol as a family issue—alcohol ruined families, victimizing innocent women and children. WCTU members visited schools to educate children about the evils of alcohol, addressed prisoners, and blanketed men's meetings with literature. As a result, they became familiar with the South's abysmal school system and its archaic criminal justice system. They soon began advocating education and prison reform as well as legislation against alcohol.

By the 1890s, many WCTU members realized that they could not achieve their goals unless women had the vote. Rebecca Latimer Felton, an Atlanta suffragist and WCTU member, reflected the frustration of her generation of southern women in an address to working women in 1892: "But some will say, you women might be quiet, you can't vote, you can't do anything! Exactly so, we have kept quiet for nearly a hundred years hoping to see relief come to the women of this country, and it hasn't come. How long must our children be slain? If a mad dog should come into my yard, and attempt to bite my child or myself, would you think me out of my place, if I killed him with a dull meat axe? . . . [You] would call that woman a brave woman . . . and yet are we to sit by while drink ruins our homes?"

Despite the WCTU's roots in southern churches, the activism of its members alarmed some southern men. Few women, however, had really radical objectives in mind. Rebecca Felton's own career highlighted the essentially conservative nature of the reform movement among middle-class women in the New South. Born in 1835 to a wealthy planter family, she attended college and married Dr. William H. Felton, a physician and minister 12 years her senior. Felton threw herself into a variety of reform activities, ranging from woman suffrage to campaigns against drinking, smoking, and Coca-Cola. She fought for child-care facilities and sex education, as well as compulsory school attendance, and she pushed for the admission of women to the University of Georgia. But she strongly supported textile operators over textile workers and defended white supremacy. She had no qualms about the lynching of black men, executing them without trial "a thousand times a week if necessary" to preserve the purity of white women. In 1922, she became the first woman member of the U.S. Senate.

The dedication of southern women to commemorating the memory of the Confederate cause also indicates the conservative nature of middle-class women's reform in the New South. Ladies' Memorial Associations formed after the war to ensure the proper burial of Confederate soldiers and suitable markings for their graves. The associations joined with men to erect monuments to Confederate leaders and, by the 1880s, to the common soldier. These activities reinforced white solidarity and constructed a common heritage for all white southerners regardless

The Confederate battle flag on this parade float reflects its emerging status as an icon of the Lost Cause in the late nineteenth century.

Courtesy of Library of Congress

Settlement House A multipurpose structure in a poor neighborhood that offered social welfare, educational, and homemaking services to the poor or immigrants usually under private auspices and directed by middle-class women.

Women's Christian Temperance Union (WCTU) Women's organization whose members visited schools to educate children about the evils of alcohol, addressed prisoners, and blanketed men's meetings with literature.

of class or location. Work for the Lost Cause reflected traditional roles, but it also offered a way for women to hone leadership and organizational skills, preparing them for less traditional public activities in the 1890s.

WOMEN'S CLUBS

A broader spectrum of southern middle-class women joined women's clubs than joined church-sponsored organizations or memorial associations. Most women's clubs began in the 1880s as literary or self-improvement societies that had little interest in reform. By 1890, most towns and cities boasted at least several women's clubs and perhaps a federated club organization. But by that time, some clubs and their members had also begun to discuss political issues, such as child labor reform, educational improvement, and prison reform. Southern women's club members sought out their sisters in the North. As Georgia's federated club president, Mrs. A. O. Granger, wrote in 1906, "Women of intellectual keenness in the South could not be left out of the awakening of the women of the whole country to a realization of the responsibility which they properly had in the condition of their fellow-women and of the children."

The activities of black women's clubs paralleled those of white women's clubs. Only rarely, however, as at some meetings of the Young Women's Christian Association (YWCA) or occasional meetings in support of prohibition, did black and white club members interact. Some white clubwomen expressed sympathy for black women privately, but publicly they maintained white solidarity. Most were unwilling to sacrifice their own reform agenda to the cause of racial reconciliation.

The primary interest of most southern white women's clubs was the plight of young white working-class and farm women. This interest reflected the growing number of such women in the workforce. Single and adrift in the city, many worked for low wages, and some slipped into prostitution. The clubs sought to help them make the transition from rural to urban life or to improve their lives on the farm. To this end, they focused on child labor reform and on upgrading public education.

SETTLING THE RACE ISSUE

WHAT ROLE did Northerners play in the segregation and disfranchisement of Southern blacks?

The assertiveness of a new generation of African Americans in the 1880s and 1890s, especially in urban areas, provided the impetus and opportunity for white leaders to secure white solidarity. To counter black aspirations, white leaders enlisted the support of young white southerners, convincing them that the struggle for white supremacy would place them beside the larger-than-life heroes of the Civil War generation. African Americans resisted the resulting efforts to deprive them of their remaining freedoms. Though some left the South, many more built new lives and communities within the restricted framework white southerners allowed them.

THE FLUIDITY OF SOUTHERN RACE RELATIONS, 1877–1890

Race relations remained remarkably fluid in the South between the end of Reconstruction and the early 1890s. Despite the departure of federal troops and the end of Republican rule, many black people continued to vote and hold office. Some Democrats even courted the black electorate. Though segregation ruled in churches, schools, and in some organizations and public places after the Civil War, black people and white people continued to mingle, do business with each other, and often maintain cordial relations.

In 1885, T. McCants Stewart, a black journalist from New York, traveled to his native South Carolina, expecting a rough reception once his train headed south from Washington, D.C. To his surprise, the conductor allowed him to remain in his seat while white riders sat on baggage or stood. He provoked little reaction among white passengers when he entered the dining car. Some of them struck up a conversation with him. Stewart, who admitted he had begun his journey with "a chip on my shoulder . . . [daring] any man to knock it off," now observed that "the whites of the South are really less afraid to [have] contact with colored people than the whites of the North." In Columbia, South Carolina, Stewart found that he could move about with no restrictions. "I can ride in first-class cars. . . . I can go into saloons and get refreshments even as in New York. I can stop in and drink a glass of soda and be more politely waited upon than in some parts of New England."

During the 1880s, black people joined interracial labor unions and continued to be active in the Republican Party. They engaged in business with white people. African Americans and white people hunted and fished together, worked side by side at sawmills, and traded with each other. Cities were segregated more by class than by race, and people of both races sometimes lived in the same neighborhoods. To be sure, black people faced discrimination in employment and voting and random retaliation for perceived violations of racial barriers. But the barriers were by no means fixed.

THE WHITE BACKLASH

The black generation that came of age in this environment demanded full participation in American society. As the young black editor of Nashville's *Fisk Herald* proclaimed in 1889, "We are not the Negro from whom the chains of slavery fell a quarter of a century ago. . . . We are now qualified, and being the equal of whites, should be treated as such."

For many in the generation of white southerners who came of age in the same period, this assertiveness rankled. These young white people, raised on the myth of the Lost Cause, were continually reminded of the heroism and sacrifice of their fathers during the Civil War. For them, black people replaced the Yankees as the enemy; they saw it as their mission to preserve white purity and dominance. Echoing these sentiments, David Schenck, a Greensboro, North Carolina, businessman, wrote in 1890 that "the breach between the races widens as the young free negroes grow up and intrude themselves on white society and nothing prevents the white people of the South from annihilating the negro race but the military power of the United States Government." Using the Darwinian language popular among educated white people at the time, Schenck concluded, "I pity the Negro, but the struggle is for the survival of the fittest race."

The South's deteriorating rural economy and the volatile politics of the late 1880s and early 1890s exacerbated the growing tensions between assertive black people and threatened white people. So too did the growth of industry and cities in the South. In the cities, black and white people came into close contact, competing for jobs and jostling each other for seats on streetcars and trains. Racist rhetoric and violence against black people accelerated in the 1890s.

LYNCH LAW

In 1892, three prominent black men, Tom Moss, Calvin McDowell, and William Stewart, opened a grocery on the south side of Memphis, an area with a large African-American population. The People's Grocery prospered, while a white-owned store

Lynching became a public spectacle, a ritual designed to reinforce white supremacy. Note the matter-of-fact satisfaction of the spectators at this gruesome murder of a black man.

Courtesy Library of Congress

Lynching   Execution, usually by a mob, without trial.

across the street struggled. The proprietor of the white-owned store, W. H. Barrett, secured an indictment against Moss, McDowell, and Stewart for maintaining a public nuisance. Outraged black community leaders called a protest meeting at the grocery, during which two people made threats against Barrett. Barrett learned of the threats, notified the police, and warned the gathering at the People's Grocery that white people planned to attack and destroy the store. Nine sheriff's deputies, all white, approached the store to arrest the men who had threatened Barrett. Fearing Barrett's threatened white assault, the people in the grocery fired on the deputies, unaware who they were, and wounded three. When the deputies identified themselves, 30 black people surrendered, including Moss, McDowell, and Stewart, and were imprisoned. Four days later, deputies removed the three owners from jail, took them to a deserted area, and shot them dead.

The men at the People's Grocery had violated two of the unspoken rules that white southerners imposed on black southerners to maintain racial barriers: They had prospered, and they had forcefully challenged white authority. During 1892, a year of political agitation and economic depression, 235 **lynchings** occurred in the South. White mobs lynched nearly 2,000 black southerners between 1882 and 1903. Most lynchers were working-class whites with rural roots, who were struggling in the depressed economy of the 1890s and enraged at the fluidity of urban race relations.

The silence or tepid disapproval of white leaders condoned this orgy of violence. The substitution of lynch law for a court of law seemed a cheap price to pay for white solidarity at a time when political and economic pressures threatened entrenched white leaders. In 1893, Atlanta's Methodist bishop, Atticus G. Haygood, usually a spokesman for racial moderation, objected to the torture some white lynchers inflicted on their victims but added, "Unless assaults by Negroes on white women and little girls come to an end, there will most probably be still further displays of vengeance that will shock the world."

Haygood's comments reflect the most common justification for lynching, the presumed threat posed by black men to the sexual virtue of white women. Sexual "crimes" could include remarks, glances, and gestures. Yet only 25 percent of the lynchings that took place in the 30 years after 1890 had an alleged sexual connection. Certainly, the men of the People's Grocery had committed no sex crime. Lynchers did not carry out their grisly crimes to end a rape epidemic; they killed to keep black men in their place and to restore their own sense of manhood and honor.

Ida B. Wells, who owned a black newspaper in Memphis, used her columns to publicize the People's Grocery lynchings. The great casualty of the lynchings, she noted, was her faith that education, wealth, and upright living guaranteed black people the equality and justice they had long sought. The reverse was true.

The more black people succeeded, the greater was their threat to white people. She investigated other lynchings, countering the claim that they were the result of assaults on white women. When she suggested that, on the contrary, perhaps some white women were attracted to black men, the white citizens of Memphis destroyed her press and office. Exiled to Chicago, Wells devoted herself to the struggle for racial justice.

SEGREGATION BY LAW

Southern white lawmakers sought to cement white solidarity and ensure black subservience in the 1890s by instituting **segregation** by law and the **disfranchisement** of black voters. Racial segregation restricting black Americans to separate and rarely equal public facilities had prevailed nationwide before the Civil War. After 1870, the custom spread rapidly in southern cities.

During the same period, many northern cities and states, often in response to protests by African Americans, were ending segregation. Roughly 95 percent of the nation's black population, however, lived in the South. Integration in the North, consequently, required white people to give up very little to black people. And as African-American aspirations increased in the South during the 1890s while their political power waned, they became more vulnerable to segregation by law at the state level. At the same time, migration to cities, industrial development, and technologies such as railroads and elevators increased the opportunities for racial contact and muddled the rules of racial interaction.

Much of the new legislation focused on railroads, a symbol of modernity and mobility in the New South. Local laws and customs could not control racial interaction on interstate railroads. White passengers objected to black passengers' implied assertion of economic and social equality when they sat with them in dining cars and first-class compartments. Black southerners, by contrast, viewed equal access to railroad facilities as a sign of respectability and acceptance. When southern state legislatures required railroads to provide segregated facilities, black people protested.

Segregation laws required the railroads to provide "separate but equal" accommodations for black passengers. Railroads balked at the expense involved in doing so and provided black passengers with distinctly inferior facilities. In 1890, Homer Plessy, a black Louisianan, refused to leave the first-class car of a railroad traveling through the state. Arrested, he filed suit, arguing that his payment of the first-class fare entitled him to sit in the same first-class accommodations as white passengers. He claimed that under his right of citizenship guaranteed by the Fourteenth Amendment, neither the state of Louisiana nor the railroad could discriminate against him on the basis of color.

The U.S. Supreme Court ruled on the case, *Plessy v. Ferguson,* in 1896. In a seven-to-one decision, the Court held that Louisiana's railroad segregation law did not violate the Constitution as long as the railroads or the state provided equal accommodations for black passengers. The only justice to vote against the decision was John Marshall Harlan, a Kentuckian and former slave owner. In a stinging

Ida B. Wells, an outspoken critic of lynching, fled to Chicago following the People's Grocery lynchings in Memphis in 1892 and became a national civil-rights leader.

The Granger Collection, New York

Segregation A system of racial control that separated the races, initially by custom but increasingly by law, during and after Reconstruction.

Disfranchisement The use of legal means to bar individuals or groups from voting.

Plessy* v. *Ferguson Supreme Court decision holding that Louisiana's railroad segregation law did not violate the Constitution as long as the railroads or the state provided equal accommodations.

GLOBAL PERSPECTIVES

THE RACE "PROBLEM" IN EUROPE

Like the United States, Europe became more race conscious toward the end of the nineteenth century. A combination of factors, including the misapplication of Charles Darwin's Origin of Species *(1859) to imply a hierarchy of races, increasing mobility and urbanization, rising nationalism, and imperialist ventures in Asia and Africa, generated a greater awareness of racial differences. Scientists and academics singled out the Nordics, Teutons (Germans), and Anglo-Saxons as the "fittest" of the globe's races; they considered such groups as Jews, Slavs, and southern Europeans to be inferior. Though today we would classify all of these as ethnic groups, Europeans at the time called them races. Some Europeans believed that the "superior" races had an obligation to protect and help the "inferior" ones. For others, the racial hierarchy represented nature's ordering of peoples, and human intervention would therefore serve no purpose. These attitudes justified imperialism abroad and discrimination at home.*

These racial attitudes emerged at a time when many European nations had already granted Jews full legal equality. Freed from occupational, educational, and residential restrictions, the Jewish population flourished as never before, rising and assimilating into European society. Their ascension troubled some Europeans, much as contemporary southern whites felt threatened by African-American mobility. During the 1880s and 1890s, Germany and Austria founded right-wing parties that utilized anti-Semitism to win votes among groups that were wary of modern trends such as urbanization and industrialization. For such people, newly enfranchised Jews were a natural target of hatred and fear. By the 1890s, Europe had a "Jewish problem" that resembled the American South's "Negro problem."

In 1895, Theodor Herzl, an Austrian Jewish journalist, posed an answer to the problem: the voluntary removal of Europe's Jews to Palestine. Surveying the rising tide of European anti-Semitism, Herzl proposed a Jewish nation-state. "Palestine is our ever memorable historic home. . . . the great symbol of the solution of the Jewish Question after eighteen centuries of Jewish suffering."

The first Zionist Congress met in Switzerland in 1897, declaring its aim to create a "home in Palestine secured by public law" for world Jewry. Between 1904 and 1914, about 3,000 Jews per year migrated to the Holy Land. Throughout the first half of the twentieth century, Jewish migration to Palestine was restricted, first by the Ottoman Turks and then by the British. Large numbers of Jews settled instead in the northern cities of the United States.

Blacks in the American South also contemplated separate homelands, either in Africa or in the United States. Back-to-Africa movements appeared periodically in the decades after the Civil War. But as with European Jews, the greatest number of migrants went to the cities of the North, especially after the turn of the twentieth century.

17–10
From *Plessy v. Ferguson* (1896)

dissent, he predicted that the decision would result in an all-out assault on black rights. "The destinies of the two races . . . are indissolubly linked together," Harlan declared, "and the interests of both require that the common government of all shall not permit the seeds of race hate to be planted under the sanction of law."

Harlan's was a prophetic dissent. Both northern and southern states enacted new segregation laws in the wake of *Plessy v. Ferguson*. In practice, the separate facilities for black people these laws required, if provided at all, were rarely equal. Protests in the press, appeals to white leaders, and occasional boycotts failed to stem the rising tide. By 1900, segregation by law extended to public conveyances, theaters, hotels, restaurants, parks, and schools.

The segregation statutes came to be known collectively as **Jim Crow laws,** after the blackface stage persona of Thomas Rice, a white northern minstrel-show performer in the 1820s. Reflecting white stereotypes of African Americans, Rice had caricatured Crow as a foolish, elderly, lame slave who spoke in an exaggerated dialect.

Economic segregation followed social segregation. Before the Civil War, black men had dominated such crafts as carpentry and masonry. By the 1890s, white men were replacing them in these trades and excluding them from new ones, such as plumbing and electrical work. Trade unions, composed primarily of craft workers, began systematically to exclude African Americans. Confined increasingly to low or unskilled positions in railroad construction, the timber industry, and agriculture, black people underwent deskilling, a decline in workforce expertise, after 1890. With lower incomes from unskilled labor, they faced reduced opportunities for better housing and education.

DISFRANCHISEMENT

With economic and social segregation came political isolation. The authority of post-Reconstruction Redeemer governments had rested on their ability to limit and control the black vote. Following the political instability of the late 1880s and the 1890s, however, white leaders determined to disfranchise black people altogether, thereby reinforcing white solidarity and eliminating the need to consider black interests. Support for disfranchisement was especially strong among large landowners in the South's plantation districts, where heavy concentrations of black people threatened their political domination. Urban leaders, especially after the turmoil of the 1890s, looked on disfranchisement as a way to stabilize politics and make elections more predictable.

The movement to reduce or eliminate the black vote in the South began in the 1880s and continued through the early 1900s (see the Overview table, The March of Disfranchisement across the South, 1889–1908). Democrats enacted a variety of measures to attain their objectives without violating the letter of the Fifteenth Amendment. They complicated the registration and voting processes. States enacted **poll taxes,** requiring citizens to pay to vote. They adopted the secret ballot, which confused and intimidated illiterate black voters accustomed to using ballots with colors to identify parties. States set literacy and educational qualifications for voting or required prospective registrants to "interpret" a section of the state constitution. To avoid disfranchising poor, illiterate white voters with these measures, states enacted **grandfather clauses,** granting the vote automatically to anyone whose grandfather could have voted prior to 1867 (the year Congressional Reconstruction began). The grandfathers of most black men in the 1890s had been slaves, ineligible to vote.

Lawmakers sold white citizens on franchise restrictions with the promise that they would apply only to black voters and would scarcely affect white voters. This promise proved untrue. Alarmed by the Populist uprising, Democratic leaders used disfranchisement to gut dissenting parties. During the 1880s, minority parties in the South consistently polled an average of 40 percent of the statewide vote; by the mid-1890s, the figure had diminished to 30 percent despite the Populist insurgency. Turnout dropped even more dramatically. In Mississippi, for example, voter turnout in gubernatorial races during the 1880s averaged 51 percent; during the 1890s, it was 21 percent. Black turnout in Mississippi, which averaged 39 percent in the 1880s, plummeted to near zero in the 1890s.

Black people protested disfranchisement vigorously. When 160 South Carolina delegates gathered to amend the state constitution in 1895, the six black

WHERE TO LEARN MORE

Atlanta History Center, Atlanta, Georgia.
www.atlhist.org/exhibitions/html/ metropolitan_frontiers.htm

Jim Crow Laws Segregation laws that became widespread in the South during the 1890s.

Poll Taxes Taxes imposed on voters as a requirement for voting.

Grandfather Clause Rule that required potential voters to demonstrate that their grandfathers had been eligible to vote; used in some Southern states after 1890 to limit the black electorate.

OVERVIEW   THE MARCH OF DISFRANCHISEMENT ACROSS THE SOUTH, 1889–1908

Year	State	Strategies
1889	Florida	Poll tax
1889	Tennessee	Poll tax
1890	Mississippi	Poll tax, literacy test, understanding clause
1891	Arkansas	Poll tax
1893, 1901	Alabama	Poll tax, literacy test, grandfather clause
1894, 1895	South Carolina	Poll tax, literacy test, understanding clause
1894, 1902	Virginia	Poll tax, literacy test, understanding clause
1897, 1898	Louisiana	Poll tax, literacy test, grandfather clause
1899, 1900	North Carolina	Poll tax, literacy test, grandfather clause
1902	Texas	Poll tax
1908	Georgia	Poll tax, literacy test, understanding clause, grandfather clause

delegates among them mounted a passionate but futile defense of their right to vote. Black delegate W. J. Whipper noted the irony of white people clamoring for supremacy when they already held the vast majority of the state's elected offices. Robert Smalls, the state's leading black politician, urged delegates not to turn their backs on the state's black population (see American Views: "Robert Smalls Argues against Disfranchisement"). Such pleas fell on deaf ears.

A NATIONAL CONSENSUS ON RACE

How could the South get away with it? How could southerners openly segregate, disfranchise, and lynch African Americans without a national outcry? Apparently, the majority of Americans in the 1890s subscribed to the notion that black people were inferior to white people and deserved to be treated as second-class citizens. Contemporary depictions of black people show scarcely human stereotypes: black men with bulbous lips and bulging eyes, fat black women wearing turbans and smiling vacuously, and black children contentedly eating watermelon or romping with jungle animals. Popular theater of the day featured white men in blackface cavorting in ridiculous fashion and singing songs such as "All Coons Look Alike to Me" and "I Wish My Color Would Fade." Among the widely read books of the era was *The Clansman*, a glorification of the rise of the Ku Klux Klan. D. W. Griffith transformed *The Clansman* into an immensely popular motion picture epic under the title *Birth of a Nation*.

So-called scientific racism purported to establish white superiority and black inferiority on biological grounds. Northern-born professional historians reinterpreted the Civil War and Reconstruction in the white South's favor. Historian William A. Dunning, the generation's leading authority on Reconstruction, wrote in 1901 that the North's "views as to the political capacity of the blacks had been irrational." Respected journals openly supported disfranchisement and

AMERICAN VIEWS

ROBERT SMALLS ARGUES AGAINST DISFRANCHISEMENT

Born in Beaufort, South Carolina, in 1839, Robert Smalls worked as a slave pilot in Charleston harbor. In 1862, he emancipated himself, with his family and friends, when he delivered a Confederate steamer, The Planter, to the Union fleet blockading the harbor. He entered politics in 1864 as a delegate from his state to the Republican National Convention. He helped write South Carolina's Reconstruction constitution, which, among its provisions, guaranteed the right of former slaves to vote and hold office. Smalls won election to the state house of representatives in 1869, the state senate in 1871, and the U.S. House of Representatives in 1875. With opportunities for African Americans to hold public office declining following Reconstruction, Smalls secured appointment as collector of the port of Beaufort, a federal post he occupied until his death in 1915. In the speech excerpted here, delivered to the South Carolina Constitutional Convention of 1895, he bitterly assails the state's plan to disfranchise black voters.

- From the white perspective, what is Smalls's most telling argument against the disfranchisement and the planned strategies to implement it?
- How does Smalls depict the black citizens of South Carolina?
- Why were white political leaders unmoved by Smalls's plea?

Mr. President, this convention has been called for no other purpose than the disfranchisement of the negro. . . .

The negroes are paying taxes in the south on $263,000,000 worth of property. In South Carolina, according to the census, the negroes pay tax on $12,500,000 worth of property. That was in 1890. You voted down without discussion . . . a proposition for a simple property and education qualification [for voting]. What do you want? . . . In behalf of the 600,000 negroes in the State and the 132,000 negro voters all that I demand is that a fair and honest election law be passed. We care not what the qualifications imposed are, all that we ask is that they be fair and honest, and honorable, and with these provisos we will stand or fall

by it. You have 102,000 white men over 21 years of age, 13,000 of these cannot read nor write. You dare not disfranchise them, and you know that the man who proposes it will never be elected to another office in the State of South Carolina. . . . Fifty-eight thousand negroes cannot read nor write. This leaves a majority of 14,000 white men who can read and write over the same class of negroes in this State. We are willing to accept a scheme that provides that no man who cannot read nor write can vote, if you dare pass it. How can you expect an ordinary man to "understand and explain" any section of the Constitution, to correspond to the interpretation put upon it by the manager of election, when by a very recent decision of the supreme court, composed of the most learned men in the State, two of them put one construction upon a section, and the other justice put an entirely different construction upon it. To embody such a provision in the election law would be to mean that every white man would interpret it aright and every negro would interpret it wrong. . . . Some morning you may wake up to find that the bone and sinew of your country is gone. The negro is needed in the cotton fields and in the low country rice fields, and if you impose too hard conditions upon the negro in this State there will be nothing else for him to do but to leave. What then will you do about your phosphate works? No one but a negro can work them; the mines that pay the interest on your State debt. I tell you the negro is the bone and sinew of your country and you cannot do without him. I do not believe you want to get rid of the negro, else why did you impose a high tax on immigration agents who might come here to get him to leave?

Now, Mr. President we should not talk one thing and mean another. We should not deceive ourselves. Let us make a Constitution that is fair, honest and just. Let us make a Constitution for all the people, one we will be proud of and our children will receive with delight.

Source: *The Columbia State*, October 27, 1895.

Racial stereotypes permeated American popular culture by the turn of the twentieth century. Images like this advertisement for Pullman railroad cars, which depicts a deferential black porter attending to white passengers, reinforced racist beliefs that black people belonged in servile roles. Immersed in such images, white people assumed they depicted the natural order of things.

Collection of The New York Historical Society. Negative number 51391.

segregation. The progressive journal *Outlook* hailed disfranchisement because it made it "impossible in the future for ignorant, shiftless, and corrupt negroes to misrepresent their race in political action." Harvard's Charles Francis Adams, Jr. chided colleagues who disregarded the "fundamental, scientific facts" that, he claimed, demonstrated black inferiority. The *New York Times*, summarizing this national consensus in 1903, noted that "practically the whole country" supported the "southern solution" to the race issue, because "there was no other possible settlement."

These views permeated Congress, which made no effort to block the institutionalization of white supremacy in the South after 1890, and the courts, which upheld discriminatory legislation. As a delegate at the Alabama disfranchisement convention of 1901 noted, "The race problem is no longer confined to the States of the South, [and] we have the sympathy instead of the hostility of the North."

By the mid-1890s, Republicans were so entrenched in the North and West that they did not need southern votes to win presidential elections or to control Congress. Their attention, diverted by economic problems and labor unrest, no longer rested on the South. The emerging consensus on the meaning of the Civil War and Reconstruction, part of the national reconciliation discussed in the preceding chapter, also worked against a federal response to the elimination of black rights in the South.

As the white consensus on race emerged, the status of African Americans slipped in the North as well as the South. Although no northern states threatened to deny black citizens the right to vote, they did increase segregation. The booming industries of the North generally did not hire black workers. Antidiscrimination laws on the books since the Civil War went unenforced. In 1904, 1906, and 1908, race riots erupted in Springfield, Ohio; Greensburg, Indiana; and Springfield, Illinois, matching similar disturbances in Wilmington, North Carolina; and Atlanta, Georgia.

RESPONSE OF THE BLACK COMMUNITY

How could African Americans respond to the growing political, social, and economic restrictions on their lives? Given white America's hostility, protest proved ineffective, even dangerous. African Americans organized more than a dozen boycotts of streetcar systems in the urban South between 1896 and 1908 in an effort to desegregate them, but not one succeeded. The Afro-American Council, formed in 1890 to protest the deteriorating conditions of black life, accomplished little and disbanded in 1908. W. E. B. Du Bois organized an annual Conference on Negro Problems at Atlanta University beginning in 1896, but it produced no effective plan of action.

A few black people chose to leave the South. Most black people who moved in the 1890s stayed within the South, settling in places like Mississippi, Louisiana, and Texas, where they could find work with timber companies or farming new lands that had opened to cotton and rice cultivation.

An Urban Middle Class. More commonly, black people withdrew to develop their own rich community life within the restricted confines white society permitted them. Particularly in the cities of the South, they could live relatively free of white surveillance and even white contact. In 1890, fully 70 percent of black city dwellers lived in the South; and between 1860 and 1900, the proportion of black people in the cities of the South rose from one in six to more than one in three. The institutions, businesses, and families that black people had begun painstakingly building during Reconstruction continued to grow, and in some cases flourish, after 1877.

By the 1880s, a new black middle class had emerged in the South. Urban-based, professional, business-oriented, and serving a primarily black clientele, its members fashioned an interconnected web of churches, fraternal and self-help organizations, families, and businesses. Black Baptists, AME, and AME Zion churches led reform efforts that sought to eliminate drinking, prostitution, and other vices in black neighborhoods.

African-American fraternal and self-help groups, led by middle-class black people, functioned as surrogate welfare organizations for the poor. More than 50 percent of Nashville's black men, for example, belonged to fraternal associations in the city. Fraternal orders also served as the seedbed for such business ventures as the North Carolina Mutual Life Insurance Company, founded in Durham in 1898. Within two decades, North Carolina Mutual became the largest black-owned business in the nation and helped transform Durham into the "capital of the black middle class." Durham's thriving black business district included several black-owned insurance firms, banks, and a textile mill. Most southern cities boasted active black business districts by the 1890s.

The African-American middle class worked especially hard to improve black education. Declining black political power encouraged white leaders to reduce funding for black public education. By the early 1900s, the student-teacher ratio in Nashville's segregated school system was 33 to one for white schools but 71 to one for black schools. To improve these conditions, black middle-class leaders solicited educational funds from northern philanthropic organizations.

The pride of accomplishment is evident in this photograph of the Georgia State College class of 1900. By this time, black institutions of higher education in the South were turning out ambitious and talented graduates who faced an increasingly grim future in their native region.

Shivery Family Photograph Collection, Photographs and Prints Division, Schomburg Center of Research in Black Culture, The New York Public Library, Astor, Lenox, and Tilden Foundations

Black Women's Roles.   Black women played an increasingly active and prominent role in African-American communities after 1877, especially in cities. Black women's clubs evolved to address the new era in race relations. Black women's clubs supported day-care facilities for working mothers and settlement houses in poor black neighborhoods modeled after those in northern cities. Atlanta's Neighborhood Union, founded by Lugenia Burns Hope in 1908, provided playgrounds and a health center and obtained a grant from a New York foundation to improve black education in the city. Black women's clubs also established homes for single black working women to protect them from sexual exploitation.

After disfranchisement, middle-class black women assumed an even more pivotal role in the black community. They often used their relations with prominent white women and organizations such as the WCTU and the Young Women's Christian Association (YWCA) to press for public commitments to improve the health and education of African Americans. Absent political pressure from black men, and given the danger of African-American males asserting themselves in the tense racial climate after 1890, black women became critical spokespersons for their race.

The extension of black club work into rural areas of the South, where the majority of the African-American population lived, to educate families about hygiene, nutrition, and childcare, anticipated similar efforts among white women after 1900. They nurtured a self-help strategy to improve the conditions of the people they sought to help. One of the most prominent African-American leaders of the late nineteenth and early twentieth centuries, Booker T. Washington, adopted a similar approach to racial uplift.

Booker T. Washington's Accommodation.

Born a slave in Virginia in 1856, Washington and his family worked in the salt and coal mines of West Virginia after the Civil War. Ambitious and flushed with the postwar enthusiasm for advancement that gripped freedmen, he enrolled in Hampton Normal and Agricultural Institute, the premier black educational institution in the South. Washington worked his way through Hampton, graduated, taught for a time, and then, in 1881, founded the Tuskegee Institute for black students in rural Alabama. Washington thought that his students would be best served if they learned a trade and workplace discipline. By learning industrial skills, he maintained, black people could acquire self-respect and economic independence. As a result, Tuskegee emphasized vocational training over the liberal arts.

Washington argued that African Americans should accommodate themselves to segregation and disfranchisement until they could prove their economic worth to American society. In exchange for this accommodation, however, white people should help provide black people with the education and job training they would need to gain their independence. This position was known as the **Atlanta Compromise.** Despite his conciliatory public stance, Washington secretly helped to finance legal challenges to segregation and disfranchisement. The social and economic realities of the South, meanwhile, frustrated his educational mission. Increasingly, black people were shut out of the kinds of jobs for which Washington hoped to train them. Facing a depressed rural economy and growing racial violence, they had little prospect of advancement.

17–11
W.E.B. Du Bois, from "Of Mr. Booker T. Washington and Others"

W. E. B. Du Bois Attacks the Atlanta Compromise.

Another prominent African-American leader, W. E. B. Du Bois, challenged Washington's acceptance of black social inequality. Born in Massachusetts in 1868, Du Bois was the first African American to earn a doctorate at Harvard. Du Bois promoted self-help, education, and black pride. In *The Souls of Black Folk,* published in 1903, he described the strengths of black culture and attacked Washington's Atlanta Compromise. Du Bois was a cofounder, in 1910, of the **National Association for the Advancement of Colored People (NAACP),** an interracial organization dedicated to restoring African-American political and social rights.

Despite their differences, Washington and Du Bois agreed on many issues. Both had reservations about allowing illiterate black people to vote, and both believed that black success in the South required some white assistance. As Du Bois wrote in *The Souls of Black Folk,* "Any movement for the elevation of the Southern Negro needs the cooperation, the sympathy, and the support of the best white people in order to succeed." But it became apparent to Du Bois that "the best white people" did not care to elevate black southerners. In 1906, after a bloody race riot in Atlanta, Du Bois left the South, a decision millions of black southerners would make over the next two decades.

A curtain had descended between black and white, in both the North and the South, on the issue of race. Northerners did not care to look behind that curtain to acknowledge the injustice of southern treatment of black people. As long

Atlanta Compromise Booker T. Washington's policy accepting segregation and disfranchisement for African Americans in exchange for white assistance in education and job training.

National Association for the Advancement of Colored People (NAACP) Interracial organization co-founded by W. E. B. Du Bois in 1910 dedicated to restoring African-American political and social rights.

as it provided the raw materials for the North's new urban industrial economy and maintained the peace, the South could count on the rest of the country not to interfere in its solution to race relations. Indeed, to the extent that most white Americans concerned themselves with race, they agreed with the southern solution.

Conclusion

In many respects, the South was more like the rest of the nation in 1900 than at any other time since 1860. Southern cities hummed with activity, and industries from textiles to steel dotted the southern interior. Young men and women migrated to southern cities to pursue opportunities unavailable to their parents. Advances in the production and marketing of cigarettes and soft drinks would soon make southern entrepreneurs and their products household names. Southerners ordered fashions from Sears, Roebuck catalogs and enjoyed electric lights, electric trolleys, and indoor plumbing as much as other urban Americans.

Americans idealized the South—not the urban industrial South, but a mythical South of rural grace and hospitality. It was this fantasy South that white people in both the North and the South imagined as they came to a common view on race and reconciled their differences. White southerners cultivated national reconciliation but remained fiercely dedicated to preserving the peculiarities of their region: a one-party political system, disfranchisement of African Americans, and segregation by law. The region's urban and industrial growth, impressive from the vantage of 1865, paled before that of the North. The South remained a colonial economy characterized more by deep rural poverty than urban prosperity.

How one viewed the New South depended on one's vantage point. White northerners accepted at face value the picture southerners painted for them of a chastened and prosperous, yet still attractive, region. Middle-class white people in the urban South enjoyed the benefits of a national economy and a secure social position. Middle-class white women enjoyed increased influence in the public realm, but not to the extent of their northern sisters. And the institutionalization of white supremacy gave even poor white farmers and factory workers a place in the social hierarchy a rung or two above the bottom.

For black people, the New South proved a crueler ruse than Reconstruction. No one now stepped forward to support their cause and stem the erosion of their economic independence, political freedom, and civil rights. Yet they did not give up the American dream, nor did they give up the South for the most part. They built communities and worked as best they could to challenge restrictions on their freedom.

The New South was thus both American and southern. It shared with the rest of the country a period of rapid urban and industrial growth. But the legacy of war and slavery still lay heavily on the South, manifesting itself in rural poverty, segregation, and black disfranchisement.

The northern-born W. E. B. Du Bois challenged segregation and pinned his hopes for improving the condition of African Americans on a talented elite.

The Granger Collection

Summary

The Newness of the New South   The "newness" of the New South was to be found primarily in its economic shift toward industrialization and urbanization rather than its social relations. Urban and rural white leaders had used the banner of

white supremacy to constrict African-American social and economic roles; the Solid South, a white Democratic voting bloc emerged. Industry from textiles to steel dotted the Southern landscape, young men and women migrated to cities, and railroads connected the growing urban centers. Economically, the South remained behind the booming North; a weak agricultural economy, high birthrate, and low wages were some of the undermining factors.

The Southern Agrarian Revolt More than even before the Civil War, cotton dominated Southern agriculture; the price of cotton was low, and the prices of fertilizer, tools and necessities rose. Curtailing production to raise prices was not an option; the credit-based economy of the South was dependent upon cotton. Black and white sharecroppers and tenant farmers fought back by organizing, scoring limited successes; it took higher cotton prices and returning prosperity in the late 1890s to bring relief to farmers.

IMAGE KEY
for pages 480–481

a. Students and a teacher work in a laboratory at the Tuskegee Institute in Alabama. c. 1900.
b. Railway map of Florida.
c. Ida B. Wells.
d. An ad for Juliet chewing tobacco.
e. Ida B. Wells (1862–1931) pictured on a United States postage stamp from 1989.
f. E. A. Overstreet and members of the class of 1900 of the Georgia State Independent College.
g. Women spin yarn and tend children on the porch of a log cabin in North Carolina in 1907.
h. Southern textile mill in towns throughout the South.
i. Racial stereotypes permeated advertising.
j. Thread on a large spool.
k. A woman in a hoop skirt grips gently the handle of an old fashioned water pump.

Women in the New South White women in the South were cast in the roles of paragons of virtue and purity who needed men to defend them. With these limitations, middle-class women entered the public arena slowly. Women's involvement in church organizations, temperance, and as protectors of Southern history allowed them involvement without challenging the class and racial inequalities of the New South, while women's club activities addressed their self-improvement and allowed them to help other women.

Settling the Race Issue The generation of black people who had come of age by the 1890s demanded full participation; white Southerners raised on the myth of the Lost Cause resented the changed status of black people. Economic and political violence worsened the tensions, and violence, including lynchings, accelerated. Segregation and disfranchisement laws were passed; the U.S. Supreme Court condoned separate accommodations in the case *Plessy* v. *Ferguson*. The majority of white Americans, North and South, ascribed to the notion of black inferiority; no national debate resulted in response to the new restrictions. African Americans responded by creating their own community life within these new confines. Booker T. Washington and W. E. B. Du Bois differed on the approaches black people should take to accommodate and improve themselves.

REVIEW QUESTIONS

1. In what ways did the growing activism of white middle-class women, the increasing assertiveness of young urban black people, and the persistence of the agricultural depression affect the politics of the South in the late 1880s and early 1890s?

2. We associate segregation and disfranchisement with reactionary political and social views. Yet many white people who promoted both seriously believed them to be reforms. How could white people hold such a view?

3. What strategies did black southerners employ in response to the narrowing of economic and political opportunities in the New South?

4. What accounted for Anna J. Cooper's optimism for African-American women in the South at a time when southern whites were beginning an extensive legal and physical assault on black civil rights?

5. Why did racial "problems" emerge as a major issue in Europe and the United States in the late nineteenth century?

KEY TERMS

Atlanta Compromise   (p. 506)
Colored Farmer's Alliance   (p. 492)
Disfranchisement   (p. 499)
Grandfather clause   (p. 501)
Grange   (p. 491)
Jim Crow laws   (p. 501)
Lynching   (p. 498)

National Association for the Advancement of Colored People (NAACP)   (p. 506)
Plessy v. Ferguson   (p. 499)
Poll taxes   (p. 501)
Populist Party   (p. 493)
Segregation   (p. 499)

Settlement house   (p. 495)
Solid South   (p. 483)
Southern Farmers' Alliance   (p. 491)
Subtreasury Plan   (p. 492)
Women's Christian Temperance Union (WCTU)   (p. 495)

WHERE TO LEARN MORE

 Levine Museum of the New South, Charlotte, North Carolina. The museum has exhibits on various New South themes and a permanent exhibit on the history of Charlotte and the Carolina Piedmont. **www.museumofthenewsouth.org**.

 Atlanta History Center, Atlanta, Georgia. The major exhibit, "Metropolitan Frontiers, 1835–2000," includes a strong segment on the New South era, including the development of separate black and white economies in Atlanta. The Herndon home, also on the grounds of the center, has an exhibit on black upper-class life in Atlanta from 1880 to 1930. **www.atlhist.org/exhibitions/html/metropolitan_frontiers.htm**.

Sloss Furnaces National Historical Landmark, Birmingham, Alabama. The site recalls the time when Birmingham challenged Pittsburgh as the nation's primary steel-producing center. **www.slossfurnaces.com**.

U.S. History Documents CD-ROM
For primary sources related to this chapter, refer to the document CD-ROM.

www.prenhall.com/goldfield
For study resources related to this chapter, visit the *Companion Website*™.

18 Industry, Immigrants, and Cities
1870–1900

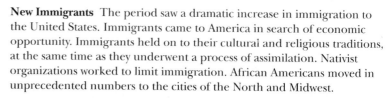

CHAPTER HIGHLIGHTS

New Industry The Gilded Age of the late 1800s saw America transformed into the world's foremost industrial power. Technology, industrialization, and the development of the modern corporation transformed both work and urban living. Immigrants, women, and children were drawn into the workplace. Industrial tensions led to unionization and confrontations between employers and employees.

Chinese Primary Public School, 920 Clay St., Chinatown, San Francisco

New Immigrants The period saw a dramatic increase in immigration to the United States. Immigrants came to America in search of economic opportunity. Immigrants held on to their cultural and religious traditions, at the same time as they underwent a process of assimilation. Nativist organizations worked to limit immigration. African Americans moved in unprecedented numbers to the cities of the North and Midwest.

New Cities An urban-industrial core extended from New England to the Great Lakes. Cities expanded upward and outward. Urban dwellers sorted themselves by social class and ethnic group. The new middle class transformed America into a consumer society and leisure activities, spectator sports, and amusement parks became hallmarks of urban life.

CHAPTER QUESTIONS

HOW DID workers respond to the changing demands of the workplace in the late nineteenth century?

WHAT IMPACT did new immigration have on cities in the North?

WHO MADE UP the new middle class?

CHAPTER OUTLINE
- New Industry
- New Immigrants
- New Cities

IMAGE KEY
for pages 510–511 is on page 541.

> *We were homeless, houseless, and friendless in a strange place. We had hardly money enough to last us through the voyage for which we had hoped and waited for three long years. We had suffered much that the reunion we longed for might come about; we had prepared ourselves to suffer more in order to bring it about, and had parted with those we loved, with places that were dear to us in spite of what we passed through in them, never again to see them, as we were convinced, all for the same dear end. With strong hopes and high spirits that hid the sad parting, we had started on our long journey. And now we were checked so unexpectedly but surely. . . . When my mother had recovered enough to speak, she began to argue with the gendarme, telling him our story and begging him to be kind. The children were frightened and all but I cried. I was only wondering what would happen. . . . Here we had been taken to a lonely place; . . . our things were taken away, our friends separated from us; a man came to inspect us, as if to ascertain our full value; strange-looking people driving us about like dumb animals, helpless and unresisting; children we could not see crying in a way that suggested terrible things; ourselves driven into a little room where a great kettle was boiling on a little stove; our clothes taken off, our bodies rubbed with a slippery substance that might be any bad thing; a shower of warm water let down on us without warning. . . . We are forced to pick out our clothes from among all the others, with the steam blinding us; we choke, cough, entreat the women to give us time; they persist, "Quick! Quick!, or you'll miss the train!", Oh, so we really won't be murdered! They are only making us ready for the continuing of our journey, cleaning us of all suspicions of dangerous sickness. Thank God! . . .*
>
> *Oh, what solemn thoughts I had! How deeply I felt the greatness, the power of the scene! The immeasurable distance from horizon to horizon; . . . the absence of any object besides the one ship; . . . I was conscious only of sea and sky and something I did not understand. And as I listened to its solemn voice, I felt as if I had found a friend, and knew that I loved the ocean.*
> *Mary Antin*
>
> Mary Antin, *The Promised Land* (Boston: Houghton Mifflin Co., 1912), chap. VIII.

MARY ANTIN, A 13-year-old Jewish girl from Russia, describes her family's perilous journey from persecution in tsarist Russia to the ship that would take her from Hamburg, Germany, to faraway America. In 1894, Mary and her mother and sisters set out from their village to join her father in Boston. Millions of European immigrants made similar journeys across the Atlantic (as did Chinese and Japanese immigrants, across the Pacific), a trip fraught with danger, heartbreak, and the sundering of family ties. So powerful was the promise of American life for the migrants that they willingly risked these obstacles to come to the United States. Mary wrote this letter to her uncle as both a way of conveying the details of her family's exodus and of maintaining contact with a world and a family she had left behind.

For Mary, America did indeed prove to be *The Promised Land*, as she titled her emigration memoir, published in 1912. At the age of 15, she published her first poem in the *Boston Herald* and, after attending Barnard College in New York City, she wrote on immigrant issues, lectured widely, and worked for Theodore Roosevelt's Progressive Party. She fought against immigration-restriction legislation and promoted public education as the main channel of upward mobility for immigrants.

Mary and her family were part of a major demographic and economic transformation in the United States between 1870 and 1900. Rapid industrial development changed the nature of the workforce and the workplace. Large factories staffed by semiskilled laborers displaced the skilled artisans and small shops that had dominated American industry before 1870. Industrial development also accelerated urbanization. Between the Civil War and 1900, the proportion of the nation's population living in cities, swelled by migrants from the countryside and immigrants from Europe and Asia, increased from 20 to 40 percent.

New opportunities opened as old opportunities disappeared. Vast new wealth was created, but poverty increased. New technologies eased life for some but left others untouched. It would be the great dilemma of early-twentieth-century America to reconcile these contradictions and satisfy the American quest for a decent life for all within the new urban industrial order.

Few locations encapsulated this dilemma better than Philadelphia during the Centennial Exposition of 1876, marking the nation's hundredth birthday. Visitors to the Exposition witnessed the ingenuity of the world's newest industrial power. Thomas Edison explained his new automatic telegraph, and Alexander Graham Bell demonstrated his telephone to the wonder of onlookers. A giant Corliss steam engine loomed over the entrance to Machinery Hall, dwarfing the other exhibits and providing them with power. "Yes," a visitor concluded, "it is in these things of iron and steel that the national genius most freely speaks."

For many Americans, however, the fanfare of the exposition rang hollow. The country was in the midst of a depression that had begun in 1873 and would not bottom out until 1877. Tens of thousands were out of work, and countless others had lost their savings in bank failures and sour investments. With the typical daily wage a dollar, most Philadelphians could not afford the exposition's 50-cent admission price. They celebrated instead at "Centennial City," a ragtag collection of cheap bars, seedy hotels, small restaurants, and circus sideshows hurriedly constructed of wood and tin along a muddy mile-long strip across the street from the exposition's sturdy halls and manicured lawns.

This small area of Philadelphia reflected the promise and failure of late-nineteenth-century America, a period often called the **Gilded Age.** The term is taken from the title of a novel by Mark Twain that satirizes the materialistic excesses of the day. It serves as a shorthand description of the shallow worship of wealth, and the veneer of respectability and prosperity covering deep economic and social divisions, that characterized the period.

Gilded Age   Term applied to late-nineteenth-century America that refers to the shallow display and worship of wealth characteristic of that period.

New Industry

Between 1870 and 1900, the United States transformed itself from an agricultural nation, a nation of farmers, merchants, and artisans, into the world's foremost industrial power, producing more than one-third of the world's manufactured goods. By the early twentieth century, factory workers

HOW DID workers respond to the changing demands of the workplace in the late nineteenth century?

Chronology

1869	The Knights of Labor is founded in Philadelphia.
1870	John D. Rockefeller organizes the Standard Oil Company.
	Congress passes the Naturalization Act barring Asians from citizenship.
1871	Unification of Germany in the wake of rising nationalism following the Franco-Prussian War.
1876	The Centennial Exposition opens in Philadelphia.
	Beginning of the rule of dictator Porfirio Diaz in Mexico, whose regime is ended by the Mexican Revolution.
1877	Execution of ten Molly Maguires in Pennsylvania.
	The Great Uprising railroad strike, the first nationwide work stoppage in the United States, provokes violent clashes between workers and federal troops.
1879	Thomas Edison unveils the electric light bulb.
1880	Founding of the League of American Wheelmen helps establish bicycling as one of urban America's favorite recreational activities.
1881	Assassination of Tsar Alexander II begins a series of pogroms that triggers a wave of Russian Jewish immigration to the United States.
1882	Congress passes the Chinese Exclusion Act.
	First country club in the United States founded in Brookline, Massachusetts.
1883	National League merges with the American Association and opens baseball to working-class fans.
1884	Berlin Conference on Africa to set rules for competing European powers annexing African territory.
1886	The Neighborhood Guild, the nation's first settlement house, opens in New York City.
	Riot in Chicago's Haymarket Square breaks the Knights of Labor.
	American Federation of Labor is formed.
1887	Anti-Catholic American Protective Association is formed.
1888	Wanamaker's department store introduces a "bargain room," and competitors follow suit.
1889	Jane Addams opens Hull House, the nation's most celebrated settlement house, in Chicago.
1890	Jacob A. Riis publishes *How the Other Half Lives*.
1891	African-American Chicago physician Daniel Hale Williams establishes Provident Hospital, the nation's first interracially staffed hospital.
1892	General Electric opens the first corporate research and development division in the United States.
	Strike at Andrew Carnegie's Homestead steelworks fails.
1894	Pullman Sleeping Car Company strike fails.
	Immigration Restriction League is formed.
1895	American-born Chinese in California form the Native Sons of the Golden State to counter nativism.
1897	George C. Tilyou opens Steeplechase Park on Coney Island in Brooklyn, New York.
	First Zionist Congress meets in Switzerland proclaiming its aim to create a home in Palestine for the Jewish people.
1898	Congress passes the Erdman Act to provide for voluntary mediation of railroad labor disputes.

made up one-fourth of the workforce, and agricultural workers had dropped from a half to less than a third.

Although the size of the industrial workforce increased dramatically, the number of firms in any given industry shrank. Mergers, changes in corporate management and the organization of the workforce, and a compliant government left a few companies in control of vast segments of the American economy. Workers, reformers, and eventually government challenged this concentration of economic power.

INVENTING TECHNOLOGY: THE ELECTRIC AGE

Technology played a major role in transforming factory work and increasing the scale of production. Steam engines and, later, electricity, freed manufacturers from dependence on water power. Factories no longer had to be located by rivers.

They could be built anywhere accessible to the transportation system and a concentration of labor. Technology also enabled managers to substitute machines for workers, skewing the balance of power in the workplace toward employers. And it transformed city life, making available a host of new conveniences. By the early twentieth century, electric lights, appliances, ready-made clothing, and store-bought food eased middle-class life. Electric trolleys whisked clerks, salespeople, bureaucrats, and bankers to new urban and suburban subdivisions. Electric streetlights lit up city streets at night. As the historian and novelist Henry Adams put it at the turn of the century, "In the essentials of life . . . the boy of 1854 stood nearer [to] the year one than to the year 1900."

For much of the nineteenth century, the United States was dependent on the industrial nations of Europe for technological innovation. In the late nineteenth century, the United States changed from a technology borrower to a technology innovator. By 1910, a million patents had been issued in the United States, 900,000 of them after 1870.

Nothing represented this shift better than Thomas A. Edison's development of a practical electric light bulb and electric generating system. Edison's invention transformed electricity into a new and versatile form of industrial energy. It also reflected a change in the relationship between science and technology. Until the late nineteenth century, advances in scientific theory usually followed technological innovation, rather than the other way around. Techniques for making steel, for example, developed before scientific theories emerged to explain how they worked. In contrast, a theoretical understanding of electricity preceded its practical use as a source of energy. Edison's research laboratory at Menlo Park, New Jersey, also established a model for corporate-sponsored research and development that would rapidly increase the pace of technological innovation.

Scientists had already discovered that passing an electric current through a filament in a vacuum produced light. They had not yet found a filament, however, that could last for more than a few minutes. Edison tried a variety of materials, from grass to hair from a colleague's beard, before succeeding with charred thread. In 1879, he produced a bulb that burned for an astounding 45 hours. Then he devised a circuit that provided an even flow of current through the filament. After thrilling a crowd with the spectacle of 500 lights ablaze on New Year's

A humorous view of Thomas Edison's laboratories in Menlo Park, New Jersey, around 1880. There was no joking, however, about the potential of Edison's incandescent bulb and his other practical adaptations of electricity for everyday use. Electricity would soon transform life for millions of people. Edison's methods set the precedent for corporate research and development that would accelerate the pace of new discoveries with practical applications.

National Park Service, Edison National Historic Site

WHERE TO LEARN MORE

Edison National Historic Site,
West Orange, New Jersey
www.nps.gov/edis

Eve in 1879, Edison went on to build a power station in New York City to serve businesses and homes by 1882. The electric age had begun.

Edison's initial success touched off a wave of research and development in Germany, Austria, Great Britain, France, and the United States. Whoever could light the world cheaply and efficiently held the key to an enormous fortune. Ultimately, the prize fell not to Edison but to Elihu Thomson, a high school chemistry teacher in Philadelphia. Leaving teaching to devote himself to research full-time, Thomson founded his own company and in 1883 moved to Connecticut. Thomson purchased Edison's General Electric Company in 1892 and established the country's first corporate research and development division. His scientists produced what was then the most efficient light bulb design, and by 1914, General Electric was producing 85 percent of the world's light bulbs.

Following this precedent, other American companies established research and development laboratories. Standard Oil, U.S. Rubber, the chemical giant DuPont, and the photographic company Kodak all became world leaders in their respective industries because of innovations their laboratories developed.

The process of invention that emerged in the United States gave the country a commanding technological lead. But the modernization of industry that made the United States the world's foremost industrial nation after 1900 reflected organizational as well as technological innovation.

THE CORPORATION AND ITS IMPACT

The modern corporation provided the structural framework for the transformation of the American economy. A corporation is an association of individuals that is legally authorized to act as a fictional person and thus relieve its individual members of certain legal liabilities. This form of business organization had existed since colonial times but became a significant factor in the American economy with the growth of railroad companies in the 1850s. A key feature of a corporation is the separation of ownership from management. A corporation can raise capital by selling ownership shares, or stock, to people who have no direct role in running it. The shareholders benefit from dividends drawn on profits and, if the corporation thrives, from the rising value of its stock.

The corporation had two major advantages over other forms of business organization that made it attractive to investors. First, unlike a partnership, which dissolves when a partner dies, a corporation can outlive its founders. This durability permits long-term planning. Second, a corporation's officials and shareholders are not personally liable for its debts. If it goes bankrupt, they stand to lose only what they have invested in it.

As large corporations emerged in major American industries, they had a ripple effect on the economy. To build plants, merge with or acquire other companies, develop new technology, and hire workers, large corporations needed huge supplies of capital. They turned to the banks to help meet these needs, and the banks grew in response. The corporations stimulated technological change as they looked for ways to speed production, improve products, and lower costs. As they grew, they generated jobs.

Large industrial corporations also changed the nature of work. Into the late nineteenth century, well-paid skilled artisans, typically native-born, dominated the industrial workplace. Operating alone or in groups, they controlled the pace of their work, their output, and even the hiring and firing of coworkers. By the early twentieth century, control of the workplace was shifting to managers, and semiskilled and unskilled workers were replacing skilled artisans.

QUICK REVIEW

Corporations

• Corporation: an association with legal rights and liabilities separate from those of its members.

• Became a significant factor with the growth of railroads in the 1850s.

• Key feature of the corporation is the separation of ownership and management.

Because corporations usually located factories in cities, they stimulated urban growth. Large industrial districts sprawled along urban rivers and rail lines. There were exceptions, but nonetheless, by 1900, fully 90 percent of all manufacturing occurred in cities.

Two organizational strategies, vertical integration and horizontal integration, helped successful corporations reduce competition and dominate their industries. **Vertical integration** involved the consolidation of all functions related to a particular industry, from the extraction and transport of raw materials to manufacturing and finished-product distribution and sales. Vertical integration reduced a company's dependence on outside suppliers, cutting costs and delays. Geographical dispersal went hand in hand with vertical integration. Different functions, a factory and its source of raw materials, for example, were likely to be in different places, a development made possible by such advances in communication as the telephone.

The meatpacking industry provides a good example of vertical integration. Meat is perishable and cannot be transported long distances without refrigeration. To reach eastern markets, cattlemen had to ship live animals in cattle cars from western ranges to major rail centers like Chicago. Since only 40 percent of a steer is edible, shippers were paying freight charges for a lot of commercially useless weight.

Gustavus Swift, a Boston native who moved to Chicago in 1875, realized that refrigerated railway cars would make it possible to ship butchered meat, eliminating the need to transport live cattle. He invented a refrigerated car but could not sell it to the major railroads because they feared losing their substantial investment in cattle cars and pens. Swift had the cars built himself and convinced a Canadian railroad with only a small stake in cattle shipping to haul them to eastern markets. He established packinghouses in Omaha and Kansas City near the largest cattle markets, built refrigerated warehouses at key distribution points, and hired a sales force to convince eastern butchers of the quality of his product. He now controlled the production, transportation, and distribution of his product, the essence of vertical integration. By 1881, he was shipping $200,000 worth of beef a week. Competitors soon followed his example.

Horizontal integration involved the merger of competitors in the same industry. John D. Rockefeller's Standard Oil Company pioneered horizontal integration in the 1880s.

He began investing in Cleveland oil refineries by his mid-twenties and formed Standard Oil in 1870. Using a variety of tactics, including threats, deceit, and price wars, Rockefeller rapidly acquired most of his competitors. Standard Oil controlled 90 percent of the nation's oil refining by 1890. Acquiring oil fields and pipelines as well as refineries, it achieved both vertical and horizontal integration.

The invention of the internal combustion engine and the growth of automobile and truck manufacturing after 1900 suddenly made an inconsequential byproduct of the refining process, gasoline, an indispensable fuel. By that time, the refining and production of oil had spread to Texas and Oklahoma. The Texas oil fields dwarfed the Pennsylvania basin and soon surpassed their eastern rivals in output, spawning towns from the Gulf Coast to the Permian Basin in West Texas, and new companies such as the Texas Oil Company (Texaco) and Gulf Oil, breaking Rockefeller's near-monopoly. The petroleum industry represented one of the earliest shifts of industrial wealth from the Northeast and Midwest to the South and Southwest.

Other entrepreneurs achieved similar dominance in other industries and amassed similarly enormous fortunes. James B. Duke, who automated cigarette manufacturing, gained control of most of the tobacco industry. Andrew Carnegie

Vertical Integration The consolidation of numerous production functions, from the extraction of the raw materials to the distribution and marketing of the finished products, under the direction of one firm.

Horizontal Integration The merger of competitors in the same industry.

consolidated much of America's steel industry within his Carnegie Steel Company (later U.S. Steel). By 1900, Carnegie's company was producing one-quarter of the country's steel.

The concentration of industry in the hands of a few powerful corporations alarmed many Americans. In the words of one historian, the corporations "seemed to signal the end of an open, promising America and the beginning of a closed, unhappier society." Impersonal and governed by profit, the modern corporation challenged the ideal of the self-made man and the belief that success and advancement would reward hard work. These concerns eventually prompted the federal and state governments to respond with antitrust and other regulatory laws (see Chapters 20 and 21).

Tabloid newspapers reinforced distrust of the corporations with exposés of the sharp business practices of corporate barons such as Rockefeller and Carnegie and accounts of the sumptuous lifestyles of the corporate elite. Public concern notwithstanding, however, the giant corporations helped increase the efficiency of the American economy, raise the national standard of living, and transform the United States into a major world power. Corporate expansion generated jobs that attracted rural migrants and immigrants by the millions from Europe and Asia to American cities.

THE CHANGING NATURE OF WORK

From the perspective of the workers, immigrant and native-born alike, the growth of giant corporations was a mixed blessing. The corporations provided abundant jobs, but they firmly controlled working conditions. A Pennsylvania coal miner spoke for many of his fellows in the 1890s when he remarked, "The working people of this country . . . find monopolies as strong as government itself. They find capital as rigid as absolute monarchy. They find their so-called independence a myth."

Since the mid-nineteenth century, industrialists had been introducing ways to simplify manufacturing processes so that they could hire low-skilled workers. This deskilling process accelerated in the 1890s in response to new technologies, new workers, and workplace reorganization. By 1906, according to a U.S. Department of Labor report, industrial labor had been reduced to minute, low-skilled operations, making skilled artisans obsolete.

Mechanization and technological innovation did not reduce employment, although they did eliminate some jobs, most of them skilled. On the contrary, the birth of whole new industries created a huge demand for workers. Innovations in existing industries, like railroads, similarly spurred job growth.

Ironically, it was a shortage of skilled workers as much as other factors that encouraged industrialists to mechanize. Unskilled workers cost less than the scarce artisans. And with massive waves of immigrants arriving from Europe and Asia between 1880 and 1920 (joined after 1910 by migrants from the American South), the supply of unskilled workers seemed limitless.

Low Salaries and Long Hours. The new workers shared little of the wealth generated by industrial expansion and enjoyed few of the gadgets and products generated by the new manufacturing. Nor did large corporations put profits into improved working conditions. In 1881, on-the-job accidents maimed or killed 30,000 railroad workers. At a U.S. Steel plant in Pittsburgh, injuries or death claimed one out of every four workers between 1907 and 1910. In Chicago's meat plants, injuries were commonplace. Upton Sinclair wrote in his novel *The Jungle* (1906), a chronicle of the killing floors of meatpacking plants in Chicago, "It was to be counted as a wonder that there were not more men slaughtered than cattle"

Factory workers typically worked 10 hours a day, six days a week in the 1880s. Steel workers put in 12 hours a day. The mills operated around the clock, so once every two weeks, when the workers changed shifts, one group had to take a "long turn" and stay on the job for 24 hours.

Long hours affected family life. By Sunday, most factory workers were too tired to do more than sit around home. During the week, they had time only to eat and sleep. As one machinist testified before a U.S. Senate investigative committee in 1883: "They were pretty well played out when they come home, and the first thing they think of is having something to eat and sitting down, and resting, and then of striking a bed. Of course when a man is dragged out in that way he is naturally cranky, and he makes all around him cranky . . . and staring starvation in the face makes him feel sad, and the head of the house being sad, of course the whole family are the same, so the house looks like a dull prison."

Workers lived as close to the factory as possible, to reduce the time and expense of getting to work. The environment around many factories, however, was almost as unwholesome as the conditions inside. Industrial wastes fouled streams and rivers around many plants. The factories along the Cuyahoga River in Cleveland turned that waterway into an open sewer by the turn of the century.

Big factories were not characteristic of all industries after 1900. In some, like the "needle," or garment, trade, operations remained small scale. But salaries and working conditions in these industries were, if anything, worse than in the big factories. The garment industry was dominated by small manufacturers who assembled clothing for retailers from cloth provided by textile manufacturers. The manufacturers squeezed workers into small, cramped, poorly ventilated **sweatshops.** A government investigator in Chicago in the 1890s described one sweatshop in a three-room tenement where the workers, a family of eight, both lived and worked: "The father, mother, two daughters, and a cousin work together making trousers at seventy-five cents a dozen pairs. . . . They work seven days a week. . . . Their destitution is very great."

Child Labor.   Child labor was common in the garment trade and other industries. Shocked reformers in the 1890s told of the devastating effect of factory labor on children's lives, citing cases like that of a 7-year-old girl whose legs were paralyzed and deformed because she toiled "day after day with little legs crossed, pulling out bastings from garments."

Industries that employed many children were often dangerous, even for adults. In the gritty coal mines of Pennsylvania, breaker boys, youths who stood on ladders to pluck waste matter from coal tumbling down long chutes, breathed harmful coal dust all day. Girls under 16 made up half the workforce in the silk mills of Scranton and Wilkes-Barre, Pennsylvania. Girls with missing fingers from mill accidents were a common sight in those towns.

By 1900, Pennsylvania and a few other states had passed legislation regulating child labor, but enforcement of these laws was lax. Parents desperate for income often lied about their children's age, and government officials were often sympathetic toward mill or mine owners, who paid taxes and provided other civic benefits.

WORKING WOMEN

Women accompanied children into the workforce outside the home in increasing numbers after 1870. The comparatively low wages of unskilled male workers often required women family members to work as well. Between 1870 and 1920, the number of women and children in the workforce more than doubled.

Sweatshops Small, poorly ventilated shops or apartments crammed with workers, often family members, who pieced together garments.

Noted urban photographer Lewis Hine captures the cramped working conditions and child labor in this late-nineteenth-century canning factory. Women and children provided a cheap and efficient workforce for labor-intensive industries.

George Eastman House

QUICK REVIEW

Working Women in 1900

- 85 percent of wage-earning women unmarried and under 25.
- Typical female factory worker earned $6 per week.
- Some working-class women turned to prostitution.

Like child labor, the growing numbers of women in the workforce alarmed middle-class reformers. They worried about the impact on family life and on the women themselves. Working-class men were also concerned. The trend toward deskilling favored women. Employers, claiming that women worked only for supplemental money, paid them less than men. A U.S. Department of Labor commissioner asserted that women worked only for "dress or pleasure." In one St. Louis factory in 1896, women received $4 a week for work for which men were paid $16 a week. Women chafed under this wage system but had no recourse other than to quit.

Most women worked out of economic necessity. In 1900, fully 85 percent of wage-earning women were unmarried and under the age of 25. They supported siblings and contributed to their parents' income. A typical female factory worker earned $6 a week in 1900. On this wage, a married woman might help pull her family up to subsistence level. For a single woman on her own, however, it allowed little more, in the writer O. Henry's words, "than marshmallows and tea."

Over time, more work options opened to women, but low wages and poor working conditions persisted. Women entered the needle trades after widespread introduction of the sewing machine in the 1870s. Factories gradually replaced sweatshops in the garment industry after 1900, but working conditions improved little.

The downtown department store became a significantly female place in the late nineteenth century, as shopping increasingly held a feminine connotation.

These emporiums also provided employment opportunities for working-class young women. Store managers staffed the sales floor with workers who would be both deferential and knowledgeable. The salesgirls enjoyed a latitude in their positions that factory girls could not approach. Management felt some compulsion toward fair treatment of the sales staff, fearing that employees might turn their anger toward the customer. Despite the long hours and low pay, the lure of working in a glittering showplace and wielding at least a little autonomy rendered this job the most coveted for working-class young women.

On the factory floor, young women had less room for negotiation because the customer was far removed from the manufacturing process, but they banded together, sometimes in labor unions after 1900, to demand and receive concessions from management. Working women, no less than working men, refused to be inanimate recipients of bosses' decrees and working conditions. The factory, though less so than the department store, was a space for negotiation between worker and management. And if a young woman could obtain some basic skills, other opportunities loomed as well.

The introduction of the typewriter transformed office work, dominated by men until the 1870s, into a female preserve. Women were alleged to have the dexterity and tolerance for repetition that the new technology required. But they earned only half the salary of the men they replaced. Middle-class parents saw office work as clean and honorable compared with factory or sales work. Consequently, clerical positions drew growing numbers of native-born women into the urban workforce after 1890. A top-paid office worker in the 1890s earned as much as $900 a year. Teaching, another acceptable occupation for middle-class women, typically paid only $500 a year.

By the turn of the century, women were gaining increased access to higher education. Coeducational colleges were rare, but by 1900 there were many women-only institutions. By 1910, women comprised 40 percent of all American college students, compared to 20 percent in 1870. Despite these gains, many professions, including those of physician and attorney, remained closed to women.

Most women college graduates found employment in such "nurturing" professions as nursing, teaching, and library work. Between 1900 and 1910, the number of trained women nurses increased sevenfold. In response to the growing problems of urban society, a relatively new occupation, social work, opened to women. There were 1,000 women social workers in 1890 and nearly 30,000 by 1920. Reflecting new theories on the nurturing role of women, school boards after 1900 turned exclusively to female teachers for the elementary grades. Despite these gains, women's work remained segregated. More than 90 percent of all wage-earning women in 1900 worked at occupations in which women comprised the great majority of workers. Some reforms meant to improve working conditions for women reinforced this state of affairs. Protective legislation restricted women to "clean" occupations and limited their ability to compete with men in other jobs.

Women also confronted negative stereotypes. Most Americans in 1900 believed a woman's proper role was to care for home and family. The system of "treating" on dates reinforced stories about loose salesgirls, flirtatious secretaries, and easy factory workers. Newspapers and magazines published exposés of working girls descending into prostitution. These images encouraged sexual harassment at work, which was rarely punished.

Working women faced a difficult dilemma. To justify their desire for education and training, they had to argue that these would enhance their roles as wives and mothers. To gain improved wages and working conditions, they increasingly

QUICK REVIEW

Stereotypes

- Most Americans believed that a woman's proper role was to care for her home and her family.
- Stereotypes reinforced notion that working women were promiscuous.
- Sexual harassment at work was rarely punished.

supported protective legislation that restricted their opportunities in the workplace.

RESPONSES TO POVERTY AND WEALTH

Concerns about working women merged with larger anxieties about the growing numbers of impoverished workers in the nation's cities during the 1890s and the widening gap between rich and poor. While industrial magnates flaunted their fabulous wealth, working men and women led hard lives on meager salaries and in crowded dwellings. In his exposé of poverty in New York, *How the Other Half Lives* (1890), the Danish-born urban reformer Jacob Riis wrote that "the half that is on top cares little for the struggles, and less for the fate of those who are underneath so long as it is able to hold them there and keep its own seat."

The urban poor included workers as well as the unemployed, aged, widowed, and disabled. The industrial economy strained working-class family life. Workplace accidents and deaths left many families with only one parent. Infant mortality among the working poor was nearly twice the citywide norm in 1900. Epidemic diseases, especially typhoid, an illness spread by impure water, devastated crowded working-class districts.

Inadequate housing was the most visible badge of poverty. Crammed into four- to six-story buildings on tiny lots, **tenement** apartments in urban slums were notorious for their lack of ventilation and light. Authorities did nothing to enforce laws prohibiting overcrowding for fear of leaving people homeless. The population density of New York's tenement district in 1894 was 986.4 people per acre, the highest in the world at the time.

One early attempt to deal with these conditions was the settlement house. The settlement house movement, which originated in England, sought to moderate the effects of poverty through neighborhood reconstruction. New York's Neighborhood Guild, established in 1886, was the first settlement house in the country; Chicago's **Hull House,** founded in 1889 by Jane Addams, a young Rockford (Illinois) College graduate, became the most famous. Addams had visited settlement houses in England and thought the idea would work well in American cities.

The Gospel of Wealth.   Late-nineteenth-century political ideology discouraged more comprehensive efforts to remedy urban poverty until the Progressive Era (discussed in Chapter 21). According to the **Gospel of Wealth,** a theory popular among industrialists, intellectuals, and some politicians, any intervention on behalf of the poor was of doubtful benefit. Hard work and perseverance, in this view, led to wealth. Poverty, by implication, resulted from the flawed character of the poor.

A flawed attempt to apply Charles Darwin's theory of biological evolution to human society emerged as a more common justification than the Gospel of Wealth for the growing gap between rich and poor. According to the theory of **Social Darwinism,** the human race evolves only through competition. The fit survive, the weak perish, and humanity moves forward. Wealth reflects fitness; poverty, weakness. For governments or private agencies to interfere with this natural process is futile. Thus, Columbia University president Nicholas Murray Butler, claiming that "nature's cure for most social and political diseases is better than man's," warned against charity for the poor in 1900. Standard Oil's John D. Rockefeller concurred, asserting that the survival of the fittest is "the working out of a law of nature and a law of God."

Tenements   Four- to six-story residential dwellings, once common in New York, built on tiny lots without regard to providing ventilation or light.

Hull House   Chicago settlement house that became part of a broader neighborhood revitalization project led by Jane Addams.

Gospel of Wealth   Thesis that hard work and perseverance lead to wealth, implying that poverty is a character flaw.

Social Darwinism   The application of Charles Darwin's theory of biological evolution to society, holding that the fittest and wealthiest survive, the weak and the poor perish, and government action is unable to alter this "natural" process.

The new industrial age created great wealth and abject poverty, and the city became the stage upon which these hard economic lessons played out. Here a "modest" Fifth Avenue mansion in turn-of-the-century New York City; farther downtown, Jacob Riis found this tenement courtyard.

Getty Images Inc., Hulton Archive Photos

Photograph by Jacob A. Riis, The Jacob A. Riis Collection, Museum of the City of New York

WORKERS ORGANIZE

The growing power of industrial corporations and the declining power of workers generated social tensions reminiscent of the sectional crisis that triggered the Civil War. Wild swings in the business cycle, the fluctuation between periods of growth and contraction in the economy, aggravated these tensions. Two prolonged depressions, one beginning in 1873 and the other in 1893, threw as many as 2 million laborers out of work. Skilled workers, their security undermined by deskilling, were hit particularly hard. They saw the nation "drifting," as a carpenter put it in 1870, "to that condition of society where a few were rich, and the many very poor."

Beginning after the Civil War and continuing through World War I, workers fought their loss of independence to industrial capital by organizing and striking (see the Overview table, "Workers Organize"). Violence often accompanied these actions.

Such was the case with the railroad strike of 1877, sometimes referred to as the **Great Uprising.** The four largest railroads, in the midst of a depression and in the wake of a series of pay cuts over the preceding four years, agreed to slash wages yet again. When Baltimore & Ohio Railroad workers struck in July to protest the cut, President Rutherford B. Hayes dispatched federal troops to protect the line's property. The use of federal troops infuriated railroad workers throughout the East and Midwest, and they stopped work. Violence erupted in Pittsburgh when the state militia opened fire on strikers and their families, killing 25, including a woman and three children. As news of the violence spread, so did the

Great Uprising Unsuccessful railroad strike of 1877 to protest wage cuts and the use of federal troops against strikers; the first nationwide work stoppage in American history.

Organization	History	Strategies
Knights of Labor	Founded in 1869; open to all workers; declined after 1886	Disapproved of strikes; supported an array of labor reforms, including cooperatives; favored broad political involvement
American Federation of Labor	Founded in 1886; open only to craft workers and organized by craft; hostile to blacks and women; became the major U.S. labor organization after 1880s	Opposed political involvement; supported a limited number of labor reforms; approved of strikes

Knights of Labor Labor union founded in 1869 that included skilled and unskilled workers irrespective of race or gender.

American Federation of Labor (AFL) Union formed in 1886 that organized skilled workers along craft lines and emphasized a few workplace issues rather than a broad social program.

Collective Bargaining Representatives of a union negotiating with management on behalf of all members.

strike. Over the next two weeks, police and federal troops continued to clash with strikers. By the time this first nationwide work stoppage in American history ended, more than 100 had been killed. The wage cuts remained.

Despite its ultimate failure, the Great Uprising was notable for the way workers cooperated with one another across ethnic and, in some cases, racial lines. The experience proved important in the next major upheaval, nine years later.

The **Knights of Labor,** a union of craft workers founded in Philadelphia in 1869, grew dramatically after the Great Uprising under the leadership of Terence V. Powderly. Remarkably inclusive for its time, the Knights welcomed black workers and women to its ranks. Victories in several small railroad strikes in 1884 and 1885 boosted its membership to nearly one million workers by 1886.

In that year, the Knights led a movement for an eight-hour workday. Ignoring the advice of the national leadership to avoid strikes, local chapters staged more than 1,500 strikes involving more than 340,000 workers. Employers fought back. They persuaded the courts to order strikers back to work and used local authorities to arrest strikers for trespassing or obstructing traffic. In early May 1886, police killed four unarmed workers during a skirmish with strikers in Chicago. Rioting broke out when a bomb exploded at a meeting in Haymarket Square to protest the slayings. The bomb killed seven policemen and four strikers and left 100 people wounded. Eight strike leaders were tried for the deaths, and despite a lack of evidence linking them to the bomb, four were executed.

The Haymarket Square incident, and a series of disastrous walkouts that followed it, weakened the Knights of Labor. By 1890, it had fewer than 100,000 members. Thereafter, the **American Federation of Labor** (AFL), founded in 1886, became the major organizing body for skilled workers.

The AFL was much less ambitious, and less inclusive, than the Knights of Labor. Led by a British immigrant, Samuel Gompers, it emphasized **collective bargaining,** negotiations between management and union representatives, to secure workplace concessions. The AFL also discouraged political activism. With this business unionism, the AFL proved more effective than the Knights of Labor at meeting the needs of skilled workers, but it left out the growing numbers of unskilled workers, black workers, and women workers, to whom the Knights had given a glimmer of hope.

Rather than including all workers in one large union, the AFL organized skilled workers by craft. It then focused on a few basic workplace issues important to each craft. This organizing technique ensured that rank-and-file members in a union shared similar objectives. The result was greater cohesion and discipline. In 1889 and 1890, more than 60 percent of AFL-sponsored strikes were successful, a remarkable record in an era when most strikes failed.

Responding to this success, employers determined to break the power of craft unions just as they had destroyed the Knights. In 1892, Andrew Carnegie dealt the steelworkers' union a major setback in the Homestead strike. Carnegie's manager, Henry Clay Frick, announced to workers at Carnegie's Homestead plant in Pennsylvania that he would negotiate only with workers individually and not renew the union's collective bargaining contract. Expecting a strike, Frick locked the union workers out of the plant and hired 300 armed guards to protect the nonunion ("scab") workers he planned to hire in their place. Union workers, with the help of their families and unskilled workers, seized control of Homestead's roads and utilities. In a bloody confrontation, they drove back Frick's forces. Nine strikers and seven guards died. But Pennsylvania's governor called out the state militia to open the plant and protect the nonunion workers. After four months, the union capitulated.

In 1894, workers suffered another setback in the Pullman strike, against George Pullman's Palace Sleeping Car Company. The strike began when the company cut wages for workers at its plant in the "model" suburb it had built outside Chicago, without a corresponding cut in the rent it charged workers for their company-owned housing. When Pullman rejected their demands, the workers appealed for support to the American Railway Union (ARU), led by Eugene V. Debs. On behalf of the Pullman strikers, Debs ordered a boycott of any trains with Pullman cars, disrupting train travel in several parts of the country. The railroads claimed to be innocent victims of a local dispute, and with growing public support, they fired workers who refused to handle trains with Pullman cars. Debs called for all ARU members to walk off the job, crippling rail travel nationwide. When Debs refused to honor a federal court injunction against the strike, President Cleveland, at the railroads' request, ordered federal troops to enforce it. Debs was arrested, and the strike and the union were broken.

These setbacks, and the depression that began in 1893, left workers and their unions facing an uncertain future. But growing public opposition to the use of troops, the high-handed tactics of industrialists, and the rising concerns of Americans about the power of big business sustained the unions. Workers would call more than 22,000 strikes over the next decade, the majority of them union-sponsored. Still, no more than 7 percent of the American workforce was organized by 1900.

NEW IMMIGRANTS

*T*he late nineteenth century was a period of unprecedented worldwide population movements. The United States was not the only New World destination for the migrants of this period. Many also found their way to Brazil, Argentina, and Canada. The scale of overseas migration to the United States after 1870, however, dwarfed all that preceded it. Between 1870 and 1910, the country received more than 20 million immigrants. Before the Civil War, most immigrants came from northern Europe. Most of the new immigrants, by contrast, came from southern and eastern Europe. Swelling their ranks were migrants from Mexico and Asia, as well as internal migrants moving from the countryside to American cities (see Map 18–1).

WHAT IMPACT did new immigration have on cities in the North?

MAP EXPLORATION

To explore an interactive version of this map, go to **http://www.prenhall.com/goldfield3/map18.1**

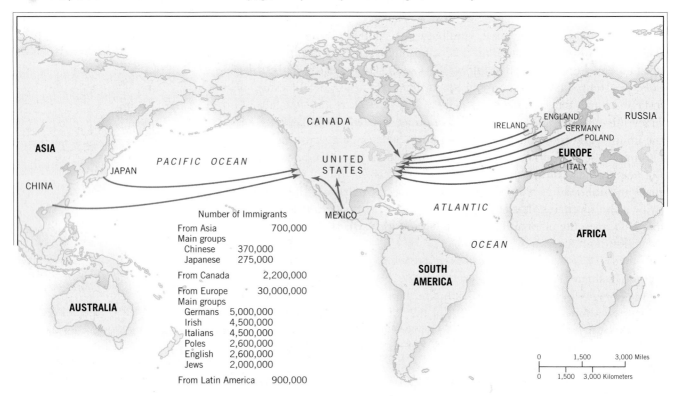

MAP 18–1 Patterns of Immigration, 1820–1914 The migration to the United States was part of a worldwide transfer of population that accelerated with the industrial revolution and the accompanying improvement in transportation.

WHAT FORCES propelled so many people to emigrate from European countries?

OLD WORLD BACKGROUNDS

The people of southern and eastern Europe had long been accustomed to migrating within Europe on a seasonal basis to find work to support their families. In the final quarter of the nineteenth century, however, several factors drove migrants beyond the borders of Europe and into the Western Hemisphere.

A growing rural population combined with unequal land distribution to create economic distress in late-nineteenth-century Europe. With land ownership concentrated in increasingly fewer hands, more and more people found themselves working ever smaller plots as laborers rather than owners.

For Russian Jews, religious persecution compounded economic hardship. After the assassination of Tsar Alexander II in 1881, which was falsely blamed on Jews, the government sanctioned a series of violent attacks on Jewish settlements; these attacks were known as **pogroms.** At the same time, the government forced Jews into fewer towns, deepening their poverty and making them easier targets for violence.

Sometime during the 1880s, an agent from the Hamburg-American Line, a German steamship company, visited a village in the Russian Ukraine where the great-grandparents of one of this book's authors lived. Shortly after his visit, they boarded a train to Austrian-occupied Poland and Hamburg. There they boarded a Hamburg-American steamer emblazoned with a large banner proclaiming *Willkommen* ("Welcome"). Like Mary Antin, whose recollection begins this chapter, just boarding that ship, they felt that they were entering the United States. Millions of others like them sailed on ocean liners from Germany, Italy, and Great Britain over the next 30 years.

Chinese and Japanese immigrants also came to the United States in appreciable numbers for the first time during the late nineteenth century. Most Chinese immigrants came from Canton in South China, a region of great rural poverty. They worked on railroads and in mines throughout the West and as farm laborers in California. Many eventually settled in cities such as San Francisco, where they established residential enclaves referred to as Chinatowns. Japanese began immigrating to the United States in the late 1880s, driven by a land shortage even more acute than the one in Europe. The first wave came by way of Hawaii to work on farms in California, taking the place of Chinese workers who had moved to the cities.

Some immigrants came from right on our borders. In the late nineteenth century, Mexicans came across the border to work on the ranches and cotton farms of South and West Texas. Whether on farms, in squalid quarters in the *barrios* of El Paso or San Antonio, or in the smaller urban centers in South Texas, such as Laredo, living and working conditions were harsh. By the turn of the century, Mexican laborers in urban areas began to organize into unions.

Most migrants intended to stay only a year or two, long enough to earn money to buy land or, more likely, to start a business back home and improve life for themselves and their families. Roughly half of all immigrants to the United States between 1880 and World War I returned to their country of origin. Some made several round trips. Jews, unwelcome in the lands they left, were the exception. No more than 10 percent of Jewish immigrants returned to Europe, and very few Jews from Russia, who accounted for almost 80 percent of Jewish immigrants after 1880, went back home.

Most of the newcomers were young men. (Jews, again, were the exception: reflecting their intention to stay in their new home, they tended to migrate in families.) Immigrants easily found work in large urban factories, with their voracious demands for unskilled labor. Except for the Japanese, few immigrants came to work on farms after 1880.

By 1900, women began to equal men among all immigrant groups as young men who had decided to stay sent for their families. In a few cases, entire villages migrated, drawn by the good fortune of one or two compatriots, a process called **chain migration.** The success of Francesco Barone, a Buffalo tavern owner, induced 8,000 residents of his former village in Sicily to migrate to that city, many arriving on tickets Barone purchased.

Immigrants tended to live in neighborhoods among people from the same homeland. Their native culture helped shape their response to their new home.

Hope for a new generation. Victoria de Ortiz came to Nebraska with her family around 1915 to escape the turmoil in Mexico and, like millions of other immigrants of that era, to make a better life for herself and her family. The black lines are part of the photograph.
Courtesy of the Nebraska State Historical Society

WHERE TO LEARN MORE

★ Strawbery Banke, Portsmouth, New Hampshire **www.strawberybanke.org**

WHERE TO LEARN MORE

★ Japanese American National Museum, Los Angeles, California **www.janm.org**

Chain Migration Process common to many immigrant groups whereby one family member brings over other family members, who in turn bring other relatives and friends and occasionally entire villages.

19–12
Mary Antin, *The Promised Land* (1912)

The desire of the new immigrants to retain their cultural traditions led contemporary observers to doubt their ability to assimilate into American society. Even sympathetic observers, such as social workers, marveled at the utterly foreign character of immigrant districts. In 1900, a Philadelphia social worker, Emily Dinwiddie, visited an Italian neighborhood and described "black-eyed children, rolling and tumbling together, the gaily colored dresses of the women and the crowds of street vendors, that give the neighborhood a wholly foreign appearance."

THE NEIGHBORHOOD

Immigrants did not live in homogeneous communities isolated from the rest of society. Rarely did a particular ethnic group comprise more than 50 percent of a neighborhood. The Chinese were the exception, but even the borders of Chinatowns usually overlapped with other neighborhoods.

In smaller cities and in the urban South, where foreign-born populations were smaller, ethnic groups were more geographically dispersed, though occasionally they might inhabit the same neighborhood. In turn-of-the-century Memphis, for example, Irish, Italian, and Jewish immigrants lived in a single immigrant district (called the Pinch), sharing schools and recreational space even as they led their singular institutional, religious, and family lives.

Immigrants maintained their cultural traditions through the establishment of religious and communal institutions. Charitable organizations were frequently connected to religious institutions. The church or synagogue became the focal point for immigrant neighborhood life. Much more than a place of worship, it was a school for transmitting Old World values and language to American-born children. The church or synagogue also functioned as a recreational facility and a gathering place for community leaders. In Jewish communities, associations called *landsmanshaften* arranged for burials, jobs, housing, and support for the sick, poor, and elderly.

Religious institutions played a less formal role among Chinese and Japanese neighborhoods. For them, the family functioned as the source of religious activity and communal organization. Chinatowns were organized in clans of people with the same surname. An umbrella organization called the Chinese Consolidated Benevolent Association emerged; it functioned like the Jewish *landsmanshaften*. Perhaps most important, the association shipped the bones of deceased members back to China for burial in ancestral cemeteries. A similar association, the Japanese Association of America, governed the Japanese community in the United States. This organization was sponsored by the Japanese government, which was sensitive to mistreatment of its citizens abroad and anxious that immigrants set a good example. The Japanese Association, unlike other ethnic organizations, actively encouraged assimilation and stressed the importance of Western dress and learning English.

Ethnic newspapers, theaters, and schools supplemented associational life for immigrants. These institutions reinforced Old World culture while informing immigrants about American ways. Thus, the *Jewish Daily Forward*, first published in New York in 1897, reminded readers of the importance of keeping the Sabbath while admonishing them to adopt American customs.

THE JOB

If the neighborhood provided a familiar and supportive environment for the immigrant, work offered the ultimate reward for coming to America. All immigrants perceived the job as the way to independence and as a way out, either back to the Old World or into the larger American society.

AMERICAN VIEWS

TENEMENT LIFE

In 1890, the Danish immigrant Jacob A. Riis published How the Other Half Lives, *an exposé of living conditions among immigrants in New York City's Lower East Side neighborhood. The book, complete with vivid photographs, caused a sensation. At a time when newspapers and magazines competed for readers with lurid tales of urban life, Riis's detailed and gruesome depictions shocked readers and provided an impetus for housing reform in New York and, eventually, across the urban nation. Riis's scientific tone, devoid of sensationalism, rendered the scenes that much more dramatic. For a nation that valued family life and the sanctity of childhood, Riis's accounts of how the environment, inside and outside the tenement, destroyed young lives provided moving testimony that for some and perhaps many immigrants, the "promise" had been taken out of the Promised Land.*

- What is Jacob Riis's attitude toward the tenement dwellers?
- Considering the destitute character of the family Riis describes, what sort of assistance do you think they receive?
- Why do you suppose the authorities were reluctant to enforce sanitary, capacity, and building regulations in these neighborhoods?

Look into any of these houses, everywhere the same piles of rags, of malodorous bones and musty paper all of which the sanitary police flatter themselves they have banished. . . . Here is a "parlor" and two pitch-dark coops called bedrooms. Truly, the bed is all there is room for. The family teakettle is on the stove, doing duty for the time being as a wash-boiler. By night it will have returned to its proper use again, a practical illustration of how poverty . . . makes both ends meet. One, two, three beds are there, if the old boxes and heaps of foul straw can be called by that name; a broken stove with crazy pipe from which the smoke leaks at every joint, a table of rough boards propped up on boxes, piles of rubbish in the corner. The closeness and smell are appalling. . . .

Well do I recollect the visit of a health inspector to one of these tenements on a July day when the thermometer outside was climbing high in the nineties; but inside, in that awful room, with half a dozen persons washing, cooking, and sorting rags, lay the dying baby alongside the stove, where the doctor's thermometer ran up to 115 degrees! Perishing for the want of a breath of fresh air in this city of untold charities! . . .

A message came one day last spring summoning me to a Mott Street tenement in which lay a child dying from some unknown disease. With the "charity doctor" I found the patient on the top floor, stretched upon two chairs in a dreadfully stifling room. She was gasping in the agony of peritonitis [abdominal infection] that had already written its death-sentence on her wan and pinched face. The whole family, father, mother, and four ragged children, sat around looking on with the stony resignation of helpless despair that had long since given up the fight against fate as useless. A glance around the wretched room left no doubt as to the cause of the children's condition. "Improper nourishment," said the doctor, which translated to suit the place, meant starvation. The father's hands were crippled from lead poisoning. He had not been able to work for a year. A contagious disease of the eyes, too long neglected, had made the mother and one of the boys nearly blind. The children cried with hunger. . . . For months the family had subsisted on two dollars a week from the priest, and a few loaves and a piece of corned beef which the sisters sent them on Saturday. The doctor gave direction for the treatment of the child, knowing that it was possible only to alleviate its sufferings until death should end them, and left some money for food for the rest. An hour later, when I returned, I found them feeding the dying child with ginger ale, bought for two cents a bottle at the pedlar's cart down the street. A pitying neighbor had proposed it as the one thing she could think of as likely to make the child forget its misery.

The type of work available to immigrants depended on their skills, the local economy, and local discrimination. Mexican migrants to southern California, for example, concentrated in railroad construction. Mostly unskilled, they replaced Chinese laborers when the federal government prohibited Chinese immigration after 1882. Mexicans built the interurban rail lines of Los Angeles in 1900 and established communities at their construction camps. Los Angeles businessmen barred Mexicans from other occupations. Similarly, Chinese immigrants were confined to work in laundries and restaurants within the boundaries of Los Angeles's Chinatown.

The Japanese who came to Los Angeles around 1900 were forced into sectors of the economy that native-born white people had either shunned or failed to exploit. The Japanese turned this discrimination to their benefit when they transformed the cultivation of market-garden crops into a major agricultural enterprise. By 1904, Japanese farmers owned more than 50,000 acres in California.

Other ethnic groups in other parts of the country had to conform to similar constraints. Greeks in Chicago, for example, restricted to food services, established restaurants, fruit distributorships, and ice-cream factories throughout the city.

Stereotypes also channeled immigrants' work options, sometimes benefiting one group at the expense of another. Jewish textile entrepreneurs, for example, sometimes hired only Italians because they thought them less prone to unionization than Jewish workers. Other Jewish bosses hired only Jewish workers, hoping that ethnic loyalty would overcome the lure of the unions. Pittsburgh steelmakers preferred Polish workers to the black workers who began arriving in northern cities in appreciable numbers after 1900.

Jews, alone among European ethnic groups, found work almost exclusively with one another. Among the factors contributing to this pattern may have been the discrimination Jews faced in eastern Europe, the existence of an established Jewish community when they arrived, and their domination of the needle trades. Jews comprised three-quarters of the more than half-million workers in New York City's garment industry in 1910. Jews were also heavily concentrated in the retail trade.

Like their native-born counterparts, few married immigrant women worked outside the home, but unlike the native-born, many Italian and Jewish women did piecework for the garment industry in their apartments. Unmarried Polish women often worked in factories or as domestic servants. Japanese women, married and single, worked with their families on farms. Until revolution in China in 1911 began to erode traditional gender roles, married Chinese immigrant women typically remained at home.

The paramount goal for many immigrants was to work for themselves rather than for someone else. Some immigrants parlayed their skills and a small stake into successful businesses. Most new arrivals, however, had few skills, and no resources beyond their wits, with which to realize their dreams. Family members and small ethnic-based community banks provided the initial stake for most immigrant businesses. Many of these banks failed, but a few prospered. For example, the Bank of Italy, established by Amadeo Pietro Giannini in San Francisco in 1904, eventually grew into the Bank of America, today one of the nation's largest financial institutions.

Immigrants could not fully control their own destinies in the United States, any more than native-born Americans could. Hard work did not always ensure success. Almost all immigrants, however, faced an obstacle that by its nature white native-born Americans did not: the antiforeign prejudice of American nativism.

WHERE TO LEARN MORE

Pasa al Norte, El Paso, Texas
http://dmc.utp.edu/test/norte

NATIVISM

Despite the openness of America's borders in the nineteenth century, and contrary to the nation's reputation as a refuge from foreign persecution and poverty, immigrants did not always receive a warm reception. Ben Franklin groused about the "foreignness" of German immigrants during the colonial era. From the 1830s to 1860, nativist sentiment, directed mainly at Irish Catholic immigrants, expressed itself in occasional violence and job discrimination.

When immigration revived after the Civil War, so did antiforeign sentiment. But late-nineteenth-century **nativism** differed in two ways from its antebellum predecessor. First, the target was no longer Irish Catholics, but the even more numerous Catholics and Jews of southern and eastern Europe. Second, late-nineteenth-century nativism had a pseudoscientific underpinning. As we saw in Chapter 17, the "scientific" racism of the period maintained that there was a natural hierarchy of race. At the top, with the exception of the Irish, were northern Europeans, especially those of Anglo-Saxon ancestry. Below them in descending order were French, Slavs, Poles, Italians, Jews, Asians, and Africans. Social Darwinism, which justified the class hierarchy, reinforced scientific racism.

When the "inferior" races began to arrive in the United States in significant numbers after 1880, nativists sounded the alarm. The director of the U.S. census warned that eastern and southern Europeans were "beaten men from beaten races. They have none of the ideas and aptitudes which fit men to take up readily and easily the problem of self-care and self-government." The result of unfettered migration would be "race suicide."

The popular press translated these scientific pronouncements into blunter language. In the mid-1870s, a Chicago newspaper described recently arrived immigrants from Bohemia (the present-day Czech Republic) as "depraved beasts, harpies, decayed physically and spiritually, mentally and morally, thievish and licentious." The rhetoric of the scientific press was scarcely less extreme. *Scientific American* magazine warned immigrants to "assimilate" quickly or "share the fate of the native Indians" and face "a quiet but sure extermination."

Such sentiments generated proposals to restrict foreign immigration. The treatment of the Chinese provided a precedent. Chinese immigrants had long worked for low wages, under harsh conditions, in mining and railroad construction in the West. Their different culture and their willingness to accept low wages provoked resentment among native- and European-born workers. Violence against Chinese laborers increased during the 1860s and 1870s. In 1870, the Republican-dominated Congress passed the Naturalization Act, which limited citizenship to "white persons and persons of African descent." The Chinese Exclusion Act of 1882, passed following another decade of anti-Chinese pressure, made the Chinese the only ethnic group in the world that could not immigrate freely into the United States.

Labor competition also contributed to the rise of another anti-immigrant organization. A group of skilled workers and small businessmen formed the American Protective Association (APA) in 1887 and claimed half a million members a year later. The APA sought to limit Catholic civil rights in the United States to protect the jobs of Protestant workingmen.

The Immigration Restriction League (IRL), formed in 1894 in the midst of a depression, took a more modest and indirect approach. The IRL proposed to require prospective immigrants to pass a literacy test that most southern and eastern Europeans would presumably fail. Cynically reaching out to native-born

Nativism   Favoring the interests and culture of native-born inhabitants over those of immigrants.

workers, the IRL vowed that its legislation would protect "the wages of our workingmen against the fatal competition of low-price labor."

The IRL ultimately failed to have its literacy requirement enacted. The return of prosperity and the growing preference of industrialists for immigrant labor put an end to calls for formal restrictions on immigration for the time being.

Immigrants and their communal associations fought attempts to restrict immigration. The Japanese government even hinted at violent retaliation if Congress ever enacted restrictive legislation on Japanese similar to that imposed on the Chinese. But most immigrants believed that the more "American" they became, the less prejudice they would encounter. Accordingly, leaders of immigrant groups stressed the importance of assimilation.

In 1895, a group of American-born Chinese in California formed a communal association called the Native Sons of the Golden State. Stressing the need to assimilate, the association's constitution declared, "It is imperative that no members shall have sectional, clannish, Tong [a secret fraternal organization] or party prejudices against each other. . . . Whoever violates this provision shall be expelled." A handbook written at the same time for immigrant Jews recommended that they "hold fast," calling that attitude "most necessary in America. Forget your past, your customs, and your ideals. . . . A bit of advice to you: do not take a moment's rest. Run, do, work, and keep your own good in mind."

Assimilation connotes the loss of one culture in favor of another. The immigrant experience of the late nineteenth and early twentieth centuries might better be described as a process of adjustment between old ways and new. It was a dynamic process that resulted in entirely new cultural forms. The Japanese, for example, had not gone to Los Angeles to become truck farmers, but circumstances led them to that occupation, and they used their cultural heritage of hard work, strong family ties, and sober living to make a restricted livelihood successful. Sometimes economics and the availability of alternatives resulted in modifications of traditions that nonetheless maintained their spirit. In the old country, Portuguese held *festas* every Sunday honoring a patron saint. In New England towns, they confined the tradition to their churches instead of parading through the streets.

Despite the antagonism of native-born white people toward recent immigrants, the greatest racial divide in America remained that between black and white. Newcomers quickly caught on to this distinction and sought to assert their "whiteness" as a common bond with other European immigrant groups and a badge of acceptance into the larger society. For immigrants, therefore, becoming "white," distancing themselves from African-American culture and people, was often part of the process of adjusting to American life, especially as increasing numbers of black southerners began moving to northern cities.

ROOTS OF THE GREAT MIGRATION

Nearly 90 percent of African Americans still lived in the South in 1900, most in rural areas. Between 1880 and 1900, however, black families began to move into the great industrial cities of the Northeast and Midwest. They were drawn by the same economic promise that attracted overseas migrants and were pushed by growing persecution in the South. Job opportunities probably outweighed all other factors in motivating what became known as the **Great Migration.**

In most northern cities in 1900, black people typically worked as common laborers or domestic servants. They competed with immigrants for jobs, and in most cases they lost. Immigrants even claimed jobs that black workers had once

WHERE TO LEARN MORE

Angel Island State Park,
San Francisco Bay
www.Angelisland.org

Great Migration The mass movement of African Americans from the rural South to the urban North, spurred especially by new job opportunities during World War I and the 1920s.

dominated, such as barbering and service work in hotels, restaurants, and transportation. Fannie Barrier Williams, a turn-of-the-century black activist in Chicago, complained that between 1895 and 1905, "the colored people of Chicago have lost . . . nearly every occupation of which they once had almost a monopoly."

Black women had very few options in the northern urban labor force outside of domestic service. The retail and clerical jobs that attracted young working-class white women remained closed to black women. Employers rejected them for any job involving direct contact with the public. Addie W. Hunter, who qualified for a civil-service clerical position in Boston, could not find work to match her training. She concluded in 1916, "For the way things stand at present, it is useless to have the requirements. Color . . . will always be in the way."

The lack of options black migrants confronted in the search for employment matched similar frustrations in their quest for a place to live. Even more than foreign immigrants, they were restricted to segregated urban ghettos. Small black ghettos existed in antebellum northern cities. In 1860, four out of every five black residents of Detroit lived in a clearly defined district, for example. After the Civil War, black ghettos emerged in southern and border cities. The black districts in northern cities were more diverse than those in southern cities. Migration brought rural southerners, urban southerners, and West Indians together with the black northerners already living there. People of all social classes lived in these districts.

The difficulties that black families faced to make ends meet paralleled in some ways those of immigrant working-class families. Restricted job options, however, limited the income of black families, even with black married women five times more likely to work than married white women. In black families, moreover, working teenage children were less likely to stay home and contribute their paychecks to the family income.

Popular culture reinforced the marginalization of African Americans. Vaudeville and minstrel shows, popular urban entertainments around 1900, featured songs belittling black people and black characters with names like Useless Peabody and Moses Abraham Highbrow. Immigrants frequented these shows and absorbed the culture of racism from them. The new medium of film perpetuated the negative stereotypes.

In the North as in the South, African Americans sought to counter the hostility of the larger society by building their own communal institutions. An emerging

An African-American religious meeting, New York City, early 1900s. Black migrants from the South found vibrant communities in northern cities typically centered around black churches and their activities. Like immigrants from Asia and Europe, who sought to transplant the culture of their homelands within the urban United States, black migrants reestablished southern religious and communal traditions in their new homes.

WHERE TO LEARN MORE

★ Statue of Liberty National Monument and Ellis Island, New York, New York
www.nps.gov/stli

GLOBAL PERSPECTIVES

THE ERA OF GLOBAL MIGRATIONS

The massive wave of immigration from Europe and Asia to the United States was part of a worldwide migration in the late nineteenth century. Italian peasants, for example, migrated to major cities in their newly unified country, to Berlin and London, to South America, and to Canada and Australia as well as to the United States. A major objective of the migrants was to improve their lot so that they and their families would have a better life. Countries that were undergoing industrialization, particularly those in the Western Hemisphere, provided opportunities that did not exist in China, Japan, Italy, and Eastern Europe.

In Italy, too little land, too many people, and the lack of educational and social opportunities aided the migration stream. Italy experienced a sudden surge in fertility in the 1880s. That, combined with a declining mortality rate, resulted in sharply reduced resources and land, especially in the mostly rural regions of southern Italy and Sicily. It was a region where tax policies favored the wealthy landlords. High tariffs protected northern Italian industry but not southern enterprises, resulting in high unemployment. Adding to the misery, a blight eradicated vineyards in southern Italy, and, in 1905, a series of earthquakes rattled the region. In 1908, a tsunami in the Straits of Messina between Sicily and the Italian mainland leveled the city of Messina. None of these economic, political, and natural misfortunes by themselves caused people to pull up roots in a very rooted society. But in combination, their effect was powerful.

The same combination spurred immigration from other countries. Economic policies that ruined farm workers in southern China touched off migrations to the West Coast of the United States. In Japan, soaring inflation and unemployment during the 1870s and 1880s, worsened by a destructive typhoon in 1884, prompted nearly 30,000 Japanese to leave for Hawaii. Russian Jewish migrants feared not only for their livelihoods but their lives. Emigration was more of a necessity than a choice in these cases.

While opportunities provided the attraction, and economic, political, and religious oppression at home provided the push, technology enhanced the means to get to far-flung places. The migration of labor was something that had gone on since ancient times. But by the late nineteenth century, the advent of railroads and steamships shrunk the world, making jobs accessible anywhere. These new modes of transportation, combined with inexpensive newspapers, letters from countrymen, and the telegraph, also spread information quickly and more widely than ever before. As Mary Antin wrote about her Russian town in the early 1890s, "America was in everybody's mouth."

middle-class leadership sought to develop black businesses. Despite these efforts, chronic lack of capital kept black businesses mostly small and confined to the ghetto. Immigrant groups often pooled extended-family capital resources or tapped ethnic banks. With few such resources at their disposal, black businesses failed at a high rate. Most black people worked outside the ghetto for white employers. Economic marginalization often attracted unsavory businesses—dance halls, brothels, and bars—to black neighborhoods. One recently arrived migrant from the South complained that in his Cleveland neighborhood, his family was surrounded by loafers, "gamblers [and] pocket pickers; I can not raise my children here like they should be."

Other black institutions proved more lasting than black businesses. In Chicago in 1891, black physician Daniel Hale Williams established Provident Hospital, the nation's first interracially staffed hospital, with the financial help of wealthy white Chicagoans. Although it failed as an interracial experiment, the hospital thrived, providing an important training ground for black physicians and nurses.

Black branches of the Young Men's and Young Women's Christian Association provided living accommodations, social facilities, and employment information for black young people. Many black migrants to northern cities, perhaps a majority, were single, and the "Y" provided them with guidance and a "home." By 1910, black settlement houses modeled on the white versions appeared in several cities.

NEW CITIES

Despite the hardships associated with urban life, the American city continued to act, in the words of the contemporary novelist Theodore Dreiser, as a "giant magnet." Immigration from abroad and migration from American farms to the cities resulted in an urban explosion during the late nineteenth century (see Map 18–2). In 1850, six cities had a population exceeding 100,000; by 1900, thirty-eight did. In 1850, only 5 percent of the nation's population lived in cities of more than 100,000 inhabitants; by 1900, the figure was 19 percent. The nation's population tripled between 1860 and 1920, but the urban population increased ninefold.

In Europe, a few principal cities, such as Paris and Berlin, absorbed most of the urban growth during this period. In the United States, by contrast, growth was more evenly distributed among many cities. In 1820, about 18 percent of the urban population of the United States lived in New York, the nation's largest city; by 1890, its share had fallen to 7 percent.

Despite the relative evenness of growth, a distinctive urban system had emerged by 1900, with New York and Chicago anchoring an urban-industrial core extending in a crescent from New England to the cities bordering the Great Lakes. Western cities like Denver, San Francisco, and Los Angeles emerged as dominant urban places in their respective regions but did not challenge the urban core for supremacy. Southern cities, limited in growth by low consumer demand, low wages, and weak capital formation, were drawn into the orbit of the urban core. Atlanta, an offspring of the railroad, prospered as the region's major way station for funneling wealth into the urban North (see Chapter 17).

Urban growth highlighted the growing divisions in American society. The crush of people and the emergence of new technologies expanded the city outward and upward as urban dwellers sorted themselves by social class and ethnic group. While the new infrastructure of water and sewer systems, bridges, and trolley tracks kept steel mills busy, it also fragmented the urban population by allowing settlements well beyond existing urban boundaries. The way people satisfied their needs for food, clothing, and shelter stimulated the industrial economy while distinguishing one class from another. Although urban institutions emerged to counter these divisive trends, they could not overcome them completely.

CENTERS AND SUBURBS

The centers of the country's great cities changed in scale and function in this era, achieving a prominence they would eventually lose in the twentieth century. Downtowns expanded up and out as tall buildings arose, monuments to business and finance, creating towering urban skylines. Residential neighborhoods were pushed out, leaving the center dominated by corporate headquarters and retail and entertainment districts.

WHO MADE up the new middle class?

MAP EXPLORATION

To explore an interactive version of this map, go to **http://www.prenhall.com/goldfield3/map18.2**

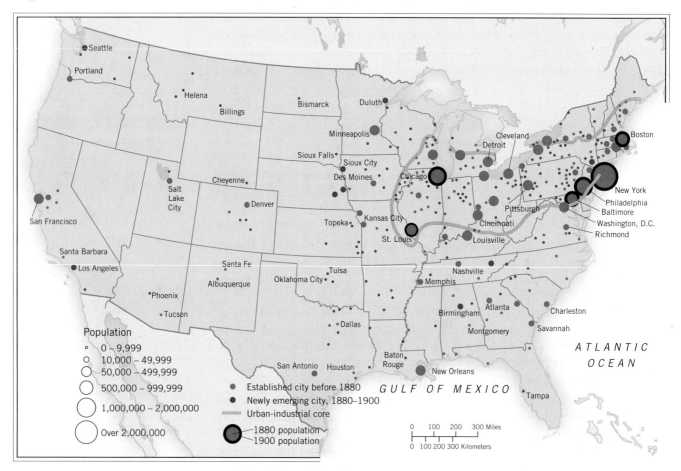

MAP 18–2   The Growth of American Cities, 1880–1900   Several significant trends stand out on this map. First is the development of an urban-industrial core, stretching from New England to the Midwest, where the largest cities were located. And second is the emergence of relatively new cities in the South and West, reflecting the national dimensions of innovations in industry and transportation.

WHAT WERE the economic forces that contributed to the growth of some cities and the decline of others?

WHERE TO LEARN MORE

Missouri Historical Society, St. Louis, Missouri **www.mohistory.org**

Corporate heads administered their empires from downtown, even if their factories were located on the urban periphery or in other towns and cities. Banks and insurance companies clustered in such financial centers as Atlanta's Five Points district to service the corporations. Department stores and shops clustered in retail districts in strategic locations along electric trolley lines.

As retail and office uses crowded out dwellings from the city center, a new phenomenon emerged: the residential neighborhood. Advances in transportation technology, first the horsedrawn street railway and, by the 1890s, the electric trolley, eased commuting for office workers. Some in the growing and increasingly affluent middle class left the crowded, polluted city altogether to live in new residential suburbs. These people did not abandon the city; they still looked to it for its jobs, schools, libraries, and entertainment, but they rejected it as a place to live.

The suburb emerged as the preferred place of residence for the urban middle class after 1870. The ideals that had promoted modest suburban growth earlier in the nineteenth century—privacy, aesthetics, and home ownership—became increasingly important to the growing numbers of middle-class families after 1880. Consider the Russells of Short Hills, New Jersey. Short Hills lay 18 miles by railroad from New York City. William Russell; his wife, Ella Gibson Russell; and their six children moved there from Brooklyn in the late 1880s, seeking a "pleasant, cultured people whose society we could enjoy" and a cure for Russell's rheumatism. Russell owned and managed a small metal brokerage in New York and enjoyed gardening, reading, and socializing with his new neighbors. Ella Russell cared for their six children with the help of a servant and also found time for several clubs and charities.

The design of the Russells's home reflected the principles Catharine Beecher and Harriet Beecher Stowe outlined in their suburban home bible, *American Woman's Home* (1869). The kitchen, according to Beecher and Stowe, should be organized for expedience and hygiene. The home's utilities should be confined to a central core, freeing wall areas for other functions. The new technology of central heating made it unnecessary to divide a house into many small rooms, each with its own fireplace or stove. Taking advantage of this change, Beecher and Stowe recommended that a home's ground floor have fewer but larger rooms, to encourage the family to pursue their individual activities in a common space.

The once-prevailing view that women were too frail for vigorous exercise was changing. Thus, the entire Russell family was to be found enjoying the tennis, swimming, and skating facilities at the Short Hills Athletic Club. The emphasis on family togetherness also reflected the changing role of men in late-nineteenth-century society. Women's roles also broadened, as Ella Russell's club work attested.

Suburbs differed, not only from the city, but also from one another. With the growth after 1890 of the electric trolley, elevated rail lines, and other relatively inexpensive forms of commuter travel, suburbs became accessible to a broader spectrum of the middle class. The social structure, architecture, and amenities of suburbs varied, depending on the rail service and distance from the city.

The suburb underscored the growing fragmentation of life in and around American cities in the late nineteenth century. Residence, consumer habits, and leisure activities reflected growing social and class divisions. Yet, at the same time, the growing materialism of American society promised a common ground for its disparate ethnic, racial, and social groups.

THE NEW MIDDLE CLASS

From the colonial era, America's urban middle class had included professionals, physicians, lawyers, ministers, educators, editors, as well as merchants, shopkeepers, and skilled artisans (until they dropped from the middle class in the late nineteenth century). In the late nineteenth century, industrial technology and urban growth expanded the urban middle class to include salespeople, factory supervisors, managers, civil servants, technicians, and a broad range of "white-collar" office workers, such as insurance agents, bank tellers, and legal assistants. This newer middle class set national trends in residential patterns, consumption, and leisure.

The more affluent members of the new middle class, like the Russells, repaired to new subdivisions within and outside the city limits. Simple row houses sheltered the growing numbers of clerks and civil servants who remained in the city. These dwellings contrasted sharply with the crowded one- or two-room apartments that confined the working class.

A CONSUMER SOCIETY

The new middle class transformed America into a consumer society. In earlier times, land had been a symbol of prestige. Now it was consumer goods. And the new industries obliged with a dazzling array of merchandise and technologies. By 1910, the new middle class lived in all-electric homes with indoor plumbing. A typical kitchen might include an electric coffeepot, a hot plate, a chafing dish, and a toaster. The modern city dweller worked by the clock, not by the sun. Eating patterns changed: cold packaged cereals replaced hot meals at breakfast; fast lunches of Campbell's soup, "a meal in itself," or canned stews weaned Americans from the heavy lunch. Jell-O appeared in the 1890s, touted as America's "most quick and easy" dessert.

Advertising played an important role in the consumer society. Advertisers created demand and developed loyalty for brand-name products. In early-twentieth-century New York, a six-story-high Heinz electric sign was a sensation, especially the 40-foot-long pickle at its top.

The middle class liked anything that saved time: trolleys, trains, electric razors, vacuum cleaners. By 1900, some 1.4 million phones were in service, and many middle-class homes had one.

The middle class liked its news in an easy-to-read form. Urban tabloids multiplied after 1880, led by Joseph Pulitzer's *New York World* and William Randolph Hearst's *New York Journal*. The newspapers organized the news into topical sections, used bold headlines and graphics to catch the eye, ran human interest stories to capture the imagination, inaugurated sports pages to attract male readers, and offered advice columns for women.

As the visual crowded out the printed in advertising, newspapers, and magazines, these materials became accessible to a wider urban audience. Immigrants, who might have had difficulty reading small-type newspapers, received their initiation into the mainstream of American society through the tabloids.

In a similar manner, the department store, essentially a middle-class retail establishment, became one of the city's most democratic forums and the focus of the urban downtown after 1890. Originating in the 1850s and 1860s, with the construction of retail palaces such as Boston's Jordan Marsh, Philadelphia's Wanamaker & Brown, New York's Lord & Taylor, and Chicago's Marshall Field, the department store came to epitomize the bounty of the new industrial capitalism. They exuded limitless abundance with their extensive inventories, items for every budget, sumptuous surroundings, and efficient, trained personnel.

At first, most department-store customers were middle-class married women. Not expected to work and with disposable income and flexible schedules, these women had the means and time to wander department store aisles. The stores catered to their tastes, and the current emphasis on home and domesticity. Industry churned out uniform, high-quality products in abundance, and middle-class salaries absorbed them. Department stores maintained consumers' interest with advertising campaigns arranged around holidays like Easter and Christmas, the seasons, and the school calendar. Each event required new clothing and accessories, and the ready-made clothing industry changed fashions accordingly.

Soon the spectacle and merchandise of the department store attracted shoppers from all social strata, not just the middle class. Though many less affluent women came merely to "window-shop," some came to buy. After 1890, department stores increasingly hired young immigrant women to cater to their growing foreign-born clientele.

The department store, the turn-of-the-century shopping mall, provided inexpensive amusement for young working-class people, especially immigrants. Mary Antin recalled how she and her teenage friends and sister would spend their Saturday nights patrolling "a dazzlingly beautiful palace called a 'department store.'" It was there that Mary and her sister "exchanged our hateful homemade European costumes . . . for real American machine-made garments, and issued forth glorified in each other's eyes."

By 1900, department stores had added sporting goods and hardware sections and were attracting customers from a wide social spectrum.

THE GROWTH OF LEISURE ACTIVITIES

The expanding floor space devoted to sporting goods reflected the growth of leisure in urban society. And like other aspects of that society, leisure and recreation both separated and cut across social classes. The leisure activities of the wealthy increasingly removed them from the rest of urban society. As such sports as football became important extracurricular activities at Harvard, Yale, and other elite universities, intercollegiate games became popular occasions for the upper class to congregate and, not incidentally, to discuss business. The elite also gathered at the athletic clubs and country clubs that emerged as open spaces disappeared in the city. The clubs offered a suburban retreat, away from the diverse middle- and working-class populations, where the elite could play in privacy.

Middle-class urban residents could not afford country clubs, but they rode electric trolleys to the end of the line to enjoy suburban parks and bicycle and skating clubs. Reflecting the emphasis on family togetherness in late-nineteenth-century America, both men and women participated in these sports. Bicycling in particular became immensely popular.

Baseball was the leading middle-class spectator sport. Organized baseball originated among the urban elite before the Civil War. The middle class took over the sport after the war. Baseball epitomized the nation's transition from a rural to an urban industrial society. Reflecting rural tradition, it was played on an expanse of green, usually on the outskirts of the city. It was leisurely; unlike other games, it had no time limit. Reflecting industrial society, however, it had clearly defined rules and was organized into leagues. Professional leagues were profit-making enterprises, and, like other enterprises, they frequently merged. Initially, most professional baseball games were played on weekday afternoons, making it hard for working-class spectators to attend. After merging with the American Association in 1883, the National League adopted some of its innovations to attract more fans, including beer sales, cheap admission, and, despite the objections of Protestant churches, Sunday games.

The tavern, or saloon, was the workingman's club. Typically an all-male preserve, the saloon provided drink, cheap food, and a place to read a newspaper, socialize, and learn about job opportunities. Alcoholism was a severe problem in cities, especially, though not exclusively, among working-class men, fueling the prohibition movement of the late nineteenth century.

Amusement parks, with their mechanical wonders, were another hallmark of the industrial city. Declining trolley fares made these parks accessible to the working class around 1900. Unlike taverns, they provided a place for working-class men and women to meet and date.

The most renowned of these parks was Brooklyn's Coney Island. In 1897, George C. Tilyou opened Steeplechase Park on Coney Island. He brought an invention by George Washington Ferris, a giant rotating vertical wheel, equipped with swinging carriages, to the park from Chicago, and the Ferris Wheel quickly became a Coney Island signature. Together with such attractions as mechanical horses and 250,000 of Thomas Edison's light bulbs, Steeplechase dazzled patrons with its technological wonders. It was quickly followed by Luna Park and Dreamland, and the Coney Island attractions became collectively known as "the poor man's paradise." Immigrant entrepreneurs, seeing a good thing, flocked to Coney Island to set up sideshows, pool halls, taverns, and restaurants. One German immigrant opened a small café serving sausages that he named "frankfurters" after his native Frankfurt. Locals called them "Coney Island hots" or "hot dogs" because they resembled the dachshund, a German-bred dog.

After 1900, the wonders of Coney Island began to lure people from all segments of an increasingly diverse city. In much the same manner, baseball was becoming a national pastime as games attracted a disparate crowd of people with little in common but their devotion to the home team.

Increasing materialism had revealed great fissures in American urban society by 1900. Yet places like department stores, baseball parks, and amusement parks provided democratic spaces for some interaction. Newspapers and schools also offered diverse groups the vicarious opportunity to share similar experiences.

CONCLUSION

The new industrial order, the changing nature of work, the massive migrations of populations from the countryside and abroad, and the rise of great cities changed the American landscape in the late nineteenth century. By 1900, the factory worker and the department store clerk were more representative of the new America than the farmer and small shopkeeper. Industry and technology had created thousands of new jobs, but they also eliminated the autonomy many workers had enjoyed and limited their opportunities to advance.

Immigrants thronged to the United States to realize their dreams of economic and religious freedom. They found both to varying degrees but also discovered a darker side to the promise of American life. The great cities thrilled newcomers with their possibilities and their abundance of goods and activities. But the cities also bore witness to the growing divisions in American society.

Still, it would be wrong to depict the nation in 1900 as merely a larger and more divided version of what it had been in 1876. Although sharp ethnic, racial, and class differences persisted, the nation seemed better poised to address them in 1900 than it had a quarter-century earlier. Labor unions, ethnic organizations, government legislation, and new urban institutions promised ways to remedy the worst abuses of the new urban, industrial economy.

SUMMARY

New Industry The Gilded Age of the late 1800s saw America transformed into the world's foremost industrial power. Technological and scientific advances, the modernization of industry, and the development of the modern corporation created changes in work life and urban living. The demand for workers drew immigrants to America and women and children into the work place. In the new urban landscape poverty abounded; the growing gap between rich and poor was seen as a result of Social Darwinism and survival of the fittest. Industrial tensions resulted in workers organizing into unions, and labor strikes, some violent, resulted as employers fought back to break the power of the unions.

New Immigrants The period saw a dramatic rise in immigration to the United States, as the number of people moving to America from northern and western Europe slackened, the numbers from southern and eastern Europe, Latin America, and Asia increased. Work, and the resulting independence it would bring, was the goal; immigrants maintained their religious and cultural traditions while some Americans attempted to restrict their numbers through legislation. African Americans moved into the industrial cities of the North and Midwest drawn by the same promise that attracted overseas immigrants.

New Cities Cities acted like giant magnets; an urban-industrial core extended from New England to the Great Lakes; the crush of people and the emergence of new technologies expanded the city outward and upward. Urban dwellers sorted themselves by social class and ethnic groups; residential neighborhoods, downtowns, and suburbs became fixtures of the modern city. The new middle class transformed America into a consumer society and leisure activities, spectator sports, and amusement parks became hallmarks of urban life.

IMAGE KEY
for pages 510–511

a. A classroom in the Chinese Public Primary School in Chinatown, San Francisco, with a white teacher.

b. A crowd of children at work in a nineteenth century canning factory. The children sit on overturned baskets while poring over their work under the gaze of an adult male supervisor in their midst.

c. A replica of the first light bulb.

d. A family rides in a historic Ford Model T automobile.

e. Abject poverty created by the new industrial age.

f. A humorous view of Thomas Edison's laboratories in Menlo Park, New Jersey.

g. The Sixth Maryland militia in Baltimore fires into a hostile crowd of laborers throwing rocks during the Great Railroad Strike of 1877.

h. Great wealth created by the new industrial age.

i. Fashionable people crowded the boardwalk in Atlantic City each Easter Sunday in the early twentieth century to see and be seen.

REVIEW QUESTIONS

1. Were there ways to achieve the benefits of industrialization without its social costs, or did the nation's political and economic systems make that impossible?

2. How did working-class women respond to the new economy? How did their participation and responses differ from that of working-class men?

3. What factors accounted for immigration becoming a global phenomenon during the late nineteenth century?

4. The growing fragmentation of urban life reflected deep divisions in modern urban industrial society. At the same time, there were forces that tended to overcome these divisions. What were these forces, and were they sufficient to bridge the divisions?

5. How did Old World conditions influence Mary Antin's adjustment to American life? Would individuals from other immigrant groups have expressed similar sentiments, or was Mary's reaction specific to her Jewish background?

KEY TERMS

American Federation of Labor (p. 524)

Chain migration (p. 527)

Collective bargaining (p. 524)

Gilded Age (p. 513)

Gospel of Wealth (p. 522)

Great Migration (p. 532)

Great Uprising (p. 523)

Horizontal integration (p. 517)

Hull House (p. 522)

Knights of Labor (p. 524)

Nativism (p. 531)

Pogroms (p. 526)

Social Darwinism (p. 522)

Sweatshops (p. 519)

Tenements (p. 522)

Vertical integration (p. 517)

WHERE TO LEARN MORE

Edison National Historic Site, West Orange, New Jersey. The site contains the Edison archives, including photographs, sound recordings, and industrial and scientific machinery. Its 20 historic structures dating from the 1880–1887 period include Edison's home and laboratory. **www.nps.gov/edis.**

Japanese American National Museum, Los Angeles, California. Housed in a converted Buddhist temple, this museum includes artifacts and photographs of early Japanese immigration and settlement. The core exhibit is "Issei Pioneers: Japanese Immigration to Hawaii and the Mainland from 1885 to 1924." **www.janm.org.**

Paso al Norte. This museum, located in El Paso, Texas, serves as the Mexico–United States International Immigration History Center. Its exhibits focus on the importance of El Paso ("the Southwest Ellis Island") as a port-of-entry between the United States and Mexico from the late sixteenth century to the present. **http://dmc.utp.edu/test/norte.**

Missouri Historical Society, St. Louis, Missouri. The Society displays a long-term exhibition accompanied by public programs called "St. Louis in the Gilded Age," which focuses on the changes generated by industrialization and urban development in St. Louis from 1865 to 1900. **www.mohistory.org.**

Senator John Heinz Pittsburgh Regional History Center, Pittsburgh, Pennsylvania. Through its long-term exhibition, "Points in Time: Building a Life in Western Pennsylvania, 1750–Today," the Center explores the growth of the Pittsburgh metropolitan area, especially its expansion during the great industrial boom at the turn of the twentieth century. **www.pghhistory.org.**

Angel Island State Park, San Francisco Bay. Angel Island served as a detention center from 1910 to 1940 for Asian immigrants who were kept there for days, months, and, in some cases, years while immigration officials attempted to ferret out illegal entries. Exhibits depict the era through pictures and artifacts. **www.Angelisland.org.**

Strawbery Banke, Portsmouth, New Hampshire. This museum includes an exhibit and audiovisual presentations on the adjustment of one immigrant family to American life: "Becoming Americans: The Shapiro Story, 1898–1929" presents the story of an immigrant Jewish family in the context of immigration to the small, coastal city of Portsmouth at the turn of the twentieth century. **www.strawberybanke.org.**

Statue of Liberty National Monument and Ellis Island, New York, New York.
More than 12 million immigrants were processed at Ellis Island between 1892 and 1954. The exhibits provide a fine overview of American immigration history during this period. There is an ongoing oral history program as well. **www.nps.gov/stli**.

 U.S. History Documents CD-ROM
For primary sources related to this chapter, refer to the document CD-ROM.

 www.prenhall.com/goldfield
For study resources related to this chapter, visit the *Companion Website*™.

19 Transforming the West
1865–1890

CHAPTER HIGHLIGHTS

Subjugating Native Americans Native Americans adapted their customs and activities to fit their environment. As whites moved westward they attempted to subjugate Indians, displace them from their land, and strip them of their culture. Indians were forced onto reservations, but efforts at "Americanization" were largely unsuccessful.

Exploiting the Mountains: The Mining Bonanza The first stage of economic development in the West focused on mining. Individual prospectors gave way to mining companies as mining practices changed. Miners' unions tried to protect the interests of miners, but met fierce and sometimes violent resistance from mining companies and their political allies.

Using the Grass: The Cattle Kingdom Railroads connected the cattle industry to its markets in the East. Cow towns served as shipping points for cattle. The entry of large companies into the cattle industry led to overgrazing and an economic and ecological disaster. Corporations turned cowboys into wage laborers.

Working the Earth: Homesteaders and Agricultural Expansion Agricultural growth boosted the Western economy and bound it to national and world markets. Advertising and the Homestead Act stimulated settlement of the Great Plains. Farmers and their families faced a difficult life. The investment in technology, materials, and transportation costs involved in farming the West made farmers dependent on other people and the impersonal forces of the market.

CHAPTER QUESTIONS

WHAT WERE the main objectives of federal Indian policy in the late nineteenth century?

WHAT WERE the environmental consequences of the expansion of mining in the nineteenth century?

WHAT FACTORS contributed to the development of the range cattle industry?

HOW DID new technology contribute to the growth of Western agriculture?

CHAPTER OUTLINE

- Subjugating Native Americans
- Exploiting the Mountains: The Mining Bonanza
- Using the Grass: The Cattle Kingdom
- Working the Earth: Homesteaders and Agricultural Expansion

IMAGE KEY
for pages 544–545 is on page 569.

WHERE TO LEARN MORE

Golden Spike National Historic Site, near Promontory, Utah
www.nps./gov/gosp.

After a pleasant ride of about six miles we attained a very high elevation, and, passing through a gorge of the mountains, we entered a level, circular valley, about three miles in diameter, surrounded on every side by mountains. The track is on the eastern side of the plain, and at the point of junction extends in nearly a southwest and northeast direction. Two lengths of rails are left for today's work. . . . At a quarter to nine A.M. the whistle of the C.P. [Central Pacific Railroad] is heard, and soon arrives, bringing a number of passengers. . . . Two additional trains arrive from the East. At a quarter to eleven the Chinese workmen commenced leveling the bed of the road with picks and shovels, preparatory to placing the ties. . . . At a quarter past eleven the Governor's train arrived. The engine was gayly decorated with little flags and ribbons, the red, white, and blue. At 12 M. the rails were laid, and the iron spikes driven. The last tie that was laid is 8 feet long, 8 inches wide, and 6 inches thick. It is of California laurel, finely polished, and is ornamented with a silver escutcheon bearing the following inscription: "The last tie laid on the Pacific Railroad, May 10th, 1869." . . .

The point of contact is 1,085 4/5 miles from Omaha, leaving 690 miles for the C.P. portion of the work. The engine Jupiter, of the C.P., and engine 119, of the U.P.R.R. [Union Pacific Railroad] moved up within thirty feet of each other. . . . Three cheers were given for the Government of the United States, for the railroad, for the President, for the Star Spangled Banner, for the laborers, and for those who furnished the means respectively. The four spikes, two gold and two silver, were furnished by Montana, Idaho, California, and Nevada. They were about seven inches long, and a little larger than the iron spike. Dr. Harkness, of Sacramento, on presenting to Governor Stanford a spike of pure gold, delivered a short and appropriate speech. The Hon. F.A. Tuttle, of Nevada, presented Dr. Durant with a spike of silver, saying: 'To the iron of the East, and the gold of the West, Nevada adds her link of silver to span the continent and wed the oceans.' . . . The two locomotives then moved up until they touched each other, . . . and at one P.M., under an almost cloudless sky, and in the presence of about one thousand one hundred people, the completion of the greatest railroad on earth was announced.

Andrew J. Russell, "The Completion of the Pacific Railroad," Frank Leslie's Illustrated Newspaper, June 5, 1869.

ANDREW J. RUSSELL'S short journey on the morning of May 10, 1869, from Ogden to Promontory Summit, Utah, enabled him to document what he called "the completion of the greatest work of the age, by which this vast continent is spanned, from ocean to ocean, by the iron path of travel and commerce." The transcontinental railroad symbolized the classic American journey, a people and a nation moving westward.

Its construction also set a precedent for western development. The two railroads that met in a desolate sagebrush basin were huge corporate enterprises, not individual efforts, and corporations would dominate western growth as much as they did eastern industrialization. The crowd of onlookers had good reason to give three cheers for the federal government, for by providing land grants and financial subsidies it played a crucial role in railroad construction, as in virtually all aspects of western development.

The railroads' dependence on capital investment, engineering knowledge, technological innovations, and labor skills also typified western development. Their labor forces both reflected and reinforced the region's racial and ethnic diversity. European immigrants, Mexicans, Paiute Indians, both male and female, and especially Chinese, recruited in California and Asia, chiseled the tunnels through the mountains, built the bridges over the gulches, and laid the ties and rails across the plains. But Russell had the Chinese workers step back so as not to appear in the famous photographs he took at Promontory, an indication of the racism that marred so many western achievements.

Laying track as quickly as possible to collect the subsidies awarded by the mile, the railroad corporations adopted callous and reckless construction tactics, resulting in waste, deaths (perhaps as many as a thousand Chinese), and environmental destruction, all consequences that would similarly characterize other forms of economic development in the West. And as with most American undertakings in the West, the construction provoked conflict with the Cheyenne, Sioux, and other tribes.

The most important feature of the railroad, however, was that traffic moved in both directions. The transcontinental and subsequent railroads helped move soldiers, miners, cattle raisers, farmers, merchants, and other settlers into the West, but they also enabled the West to send precious metals, livestock, lumber, and wheat to the growing markets in the East. Thus the railroad both integrated the West into the rest of the nation and made it a crucial part of the larger economic revolution that transformed America after the Civil War.

17–3
Horace Greeley,
An Overland Journey
(1860)

SUBJUGATING NATIVE AMERICANS

*T*he initial obstacle to exploiting the West was the people already living there, who used its resources in their own way and held different concepts of progress and civilization. For despite easterners' image of the West as an unsettled wilderness, Native Americans had long inhabited it and had developed a variety of economies and cultures. As whites pressed westward, they attempted to subjugate the Indians, displace them from their lands, and strip them of their culture. Conquest gradually forced Indians onto desolate reservations, but efforts to destroy their beliefs and transform their way of life were less successful.

TRIBES AND CULTURES

Throughout the West, Indians had adapted to their environment, developing subsistence economies ranging from simple gathering to complex systems of irrigated agriculture. Each activity encouraged their sensitivity to the natural world, and each had social and political implications.

In the Northwest, abundant food from rich waters and dense forests gave rise to complex and stable Indian societies. During summer fishing runs, the Tillamooks, Chinooks, and other tribes caught salmon that, after being dried in smokehouses, sustained them throughout the year. During the mild winters, they developed artistic handicrafts, elaborate social institutions, and a satisfying religious life.

WHAT WERE the main objectives of federal Indian policy in the late nineteenth century?

WHERE TO LEARN MORE

National Museum of the American Indian, Washington, D.C.
www.nmai.si.edu

Chronology

1858	Gold is discovered in Colorado, Nevada, and British Columbia.
1860	Gold is discovered in Idaho.
1862	Homestead Act is passed.
	Gold is discovered in Montana.
1864	Militia slaughters Cheyennes at Sand Creek, Colorado.
1867	Cattle drives make Abilene the first cow town.
1868	Fort Laramie Treaty is signed.
1869	First transcontinental railroad is completed.
1872	Canada enacts homestead law.
1874	Gold is discovered in the Black Hills.
	Turkey Red wheat is introduced in Kansas.
	Barbed wire is patented.
1876	Indians devastate U.S. troops in the Battle of the Little Bighorn.
1879	Defeat of Araucanian Indians opens the pampas to settlement in Argentina.
	"Exodusters" migrate to Kansas.
1885	Chinese massacred at Rock Springs, Wyoming.
1887	Dawes Act is passed.
1890	Government troops kill 200 Sioux at Wounded Knee, South Dakota.
1892	Mining violence breaks out at Coeur d'Alene, Idaho.
1893	Western Federation of Miners is organized.

QUICK REVIEW

Indians in the West
- Desert tribes had to contend with a harsh environment.
- The cultures of many Southwest tribes emphasized communal solidarity.
- The most numerous Indian groups in the West lived on the Great Plains.

At the opposite environmental extreme, in the dry and barren Great Basin of Utah and Nevada, Shoshones and Paiutes ate grasshoppers and other insects to supplement their diet of rabbits, mice, and other small animals. Such harsh environments restricted the size, strength, and organizational complexity of societies.

In the Southwest, the Pueblos dwelled in permanent towns of adobe buildings and practiced intensive agriculture. Because tribal welfare depended on maintaining complex irrigation systems, the Zunis, Hopis, and other Pueblos emphasized community solidarity rather than individual ambition. Town living encouraged social stability and the development of effective governments, elaborate religious ceremonies, and creative arts.

The most numerous Indian groups lived on the Great Plains. The largest of these tribes were the Lakotas, or Sioux, who ranged from western Minnesota through the Dakotas; the Cheyennes and Arapahos, who controlled much of the central plains between the Platte and Arkansas rivers; and the Comanches, preeminent on the southern plains. Two animals dominated the lives of these peoples: the horse, which enabled them to move freely over the plains and to use the energy stored in the valuable grasses, and the buffalo, which provided meat, hides, bones and horns for tools, and a focus for spiritual life.

Clashing Values. Despite their diversity, all tribes emphasized community welfare over individual interest. Their economies were based on subsistence rather than profit. They tried to live in harmony with nature to ward off sickness, injury, death, or misfortune. And they were intensely religious, absorbed with the need to establish proper relations with supernatural forces that linked human beings with all other living things. The connections among these basic values appeared in the frequent religious rituals regulating hunting and in the Indians' attitude toward land, which they regarded, like air and water, as part of nature to be held and used communally, not as an individual's personal property from which others could be excluded.

Disdaining Native Americans and their religion, white people condemned them as "savages" to be converted or exterminated. Rejecting the concept of communal property, most settlers demanded land for the exclusive use of ambitious individuals. Ignoring the need for natural harmony, they followed their own culture's goal of extracting wealth from the land for a market economy.

No one expressed these cultural differences better than the great Sioux leader Sitting Bull. Referring to the forces of the spirit world, he declared: "It is through this mysterious power that we too have our being and we therefore yield to our neighbors, even our animal neighbors, the same right as ourselves, to inhabit this land. Yet . . . [w]e have now to deal with another race. . . . Possession is a disease with them. These people have made many rules that the rich may break but the poor may not. . . . They claim this mother of ours, the earth, for their own and fence their neighbors away; they deface her with their buildings. . . . That nation is like a spring freshet that overruns its banks and destroys all who are in its path. We cannot dwell side by side."

FEDERAL INDIAN POLICY

The government had in the 1830s adopted the policy of separating whites and Indians (see Chapter 13). Eastern tribes were moved west of Missouri and resettled on land then scorned as "the Great American Desert," unsuitable for white habitation and development. This division collapsed in the 1840s, when the United States acquired Texas, California, and Oregon, and migrants crossed Indian lands to reach the West Coast. Mormons developed a trail through Indian country in 1847 and settled on Indian lands; gold and silver discoveries beginning in 1848 prompted miners to invade Indian lands. Rather than curbing white entry into Indian country, the government built forts along the overland trails and ordered the army to punish Indians who threatened travelers.

White migration devastated the Indians, already competing among themselves for the limited resources of the Plains. Migrants' livestock destroyed crucial timber and pastures along streams in the semiarid region; trails disrupted buffalo grazing patterns and eliminated buffalo from tribal hunting ranges. The Pawnees in particular suffered from the violation of their hunting grounds. One observer reported that "their trail could be followed by the dead bodies of those who starved to death." The Plains Indians also suffered from diseases the white migrants introduced. Smallpox, cholera, measles, whooping cough, and scarlet fever swept through the tribes killing up to 40 percent of their population.

Recognizing that the Great American Desert could support agriculture, white settlers pressed on the eastern edge of the plains and demanded the removal of the Indians. Simultaneously, railroad companies developed plans to lay tracks across the plains. To promote white settlement, the federal government decided to relocate the tribes to separate and specific reserves. In exchange for accepting such restrictions, the government would provide the tribes with annual payments of livestock, clothing, and other materials. To implement this policy, the government negotiated treaties extinguishing Indian rights to millions of acres (see Map 19–1), and ordered the army to keep Indians on their assigned reservations.

The commissioner of Indian affairs aptly described the Indians' lot: "By alternate persuasion and force these tribes have been removed, step by step, from mountain to valley, and from river to plain, until they have been pushed halfway across the continent. They can go no further; on the ground they now occupy the crisis must be met, and their future determined."

WARFARE AND DISPOSSESSION

Most smaller tribes accepted the government's conditions, but larger tribes resisted. From the 1850s to the 1880s, warfare engulfed the advancing frontier. Indians sometimes initiated conflict, especially in the form of small raids, but invading Americans bore ultimate responsibility for these wars. As General Philip Sheridan declared of the Indians: "We took away their country and their means of support, broke up their mode of living, their habits of life, introduced disease and decay among them, and it was for this and against this that they made war. Could anyone expect less?"

One notorious example of white aggression occurred in 1864, at Sand Creek, Colorado. Gold discoveries had attracted a flood of white miners and settlers onto land only recently guaranteed to the Cheyennes and Arapahos. Rather than

MAP EXPLORATION

To explore an interactive version of this map, go to **http://www.prenhall.com/goldfield3/map19.1**

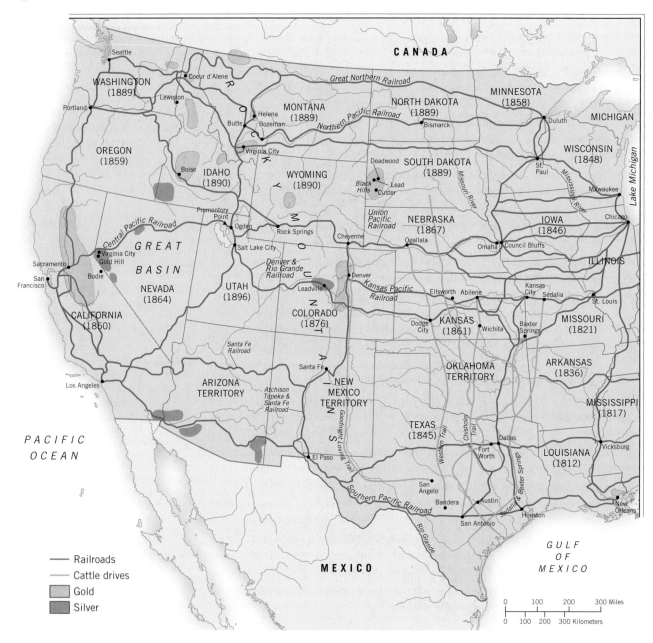

MAP 19–1   Indian Land Cessions, 1860–1894

HOW DID federal Indian policy change over the course of the nineteenth century? How did the government respond to Indian efforts to resist dispossession?

enforcing the Indians' treaty rights, however, the government compelled the tribes to relinquish their lands, except for a small tract designated as the Sand Creek reservation. But white settlers wanted to eliminate the Indian presence altogether. John Chivington, a Methodist minister who had organized Denver's first Sunday school, led a militia force to the Sand Creek camp of a band of Cheyennes under Black Kettle, an advocate of peace and accommodation. The militia attacked Black Kettle's sleeping camp without warning. With howitzers and rifles, the soldiers fired into the camp and then assaulted any survivors with swords and knives. One white trader later described the helpless Indians: "They were scalped, their brains knocked out; the [white] men used their knives, ripped open women, clubbed little children, knocked them in the head with their guns, beat their brains out, mutilated their bodies in every sense of the word."

The **Sand Creek Massacre** appalled many easterners. The Cheyennes, protested the commissioner of Indian affairs, were "butchered in cold blood by troops in the service of the United States." Westerners, however, justified the brutality as a means to secure their own opportunities. One western newspaper demanded, "Kill all the Indians that can be killed. Complete extermination is our motto."

Other tribes were more formidable. None was more powerful than the Sioux, whose military skills had been honed in conflicts with other tribes. An army offensive against the Sioux in 1866 failed completely. Entire units deserted in fear and frustration; others were crushed by the Sioux. On the Bozeman Trail, in what the Lakotas called the Battle of One Hundred Slain, the Sioux wiped out an army detachment led by a captain who had boasted that he would destroy the Sioux nation.

With the army unable to defeat the Sioux and their allies, and with many easterners shocked by both the military's indiscriminate aggression and the expense of the fighting, the government sued for peace. Describing white actions as "uniformly unjust," a federal peace commission in 1868 negotiated the **Second Treaty of Fort Laramie,** in which the United States abandoned the Bozeman Trail and other routes and military posts on Sioux territory, one of the few times Indians forced the whites to retreat. The United States also guaranteed the Sioux permanent ownership of the western half of South Dakota and the right to inhabit and hunt in the Powder River country in Wyoming and Montana, an area to be henceforth closed to all white people.

For several years, peace prevailed on the northern plains, but in 1872, the Northern Pacific Railroad began to build westward on a route that would violate Sioux territory. General William T. Sherman drew up plans for the war that he expected the construction to provoke. He regarded railroad expansion as the most important factor in defeating the Indians, for it would allow troops to travel as far

This photograph, taken by A. J. Russell, records the celebration at the joining of the Central Pacific and Union Pacific railroads on May 10, 1869, at Promontory Summit, Utah. Railroads transformed the American West, linking the region to outside markets, spurring rapid settlement, and threatening Indian survival.

Union Pacific Historical Collection

 **WHERE TO LEARN MORE**

Fort Laramie, National Historic Site, near Guernsey, Wyoming
www.nps.gov/fola/.

Sand Creek Massacre The near annihilation in 1864 of Black Kettle's Cheyenne band by Colorado troops under Colonel John Chivington's orders to "kill and scalp all, big and little."

Second Treaty of Fort Laramie
The treaty acknowledging U.S. defeat in the Great Sioux War in 1868 and supposedly guaranteeing the Sioux perpetual land and hunting rights in South Dakota, Wyoming, and Montana.

W WHERE TO LEARN MORE

★ Little Bighorn Battlefield National Monument, Crow Agency, Montana **www.nps.gov/libi/home.htm**.

17–7
Tragedy at Wounded Knee (1980)

QUICK REVIEW

Americanization

- Government policy required Indians to adopt white values and beliefs.
- Protestant reformers played an active role in the implementation of this policy.
- A variety of coercive methods were used to achieve "Americanization".
- These efforts at forced assimilation failed.

Battle of the Little Bighorn
Battle in which Colonel George A. Custer and the Seventh Cavalry were defeated by the Sioux and Cheyennes under Sitting Bull and Crazy Horse in Montana in 1876.

in a day as they could march in weeks. Other technological developments, from the telegraph to rapid-fire weapons, also undercut the skills of the Indian warrior.

The destruction of the buffalo also threatened Native Americans. From 1872 to 1874, white hunters killed 4 million buffalo, often taking only the hides and leaving the bodies to rot. Reporters found vast areas covered with "decaying, putrid, stinking remains." Federal officials encouraged the buffalo's extermination because it would destroy the Indians' basis for survival.

The climactic provocation of the Sioux began in 1874, when Colonel George A. Custer led an invasion to survey the Black Hills for a military post and to confirm the presence of gold. Thousands of white miners then illegally poured onto Sioux land. Ignoring Sioux demands that the government enforce the Fort Laramie treaty, the army insisted that the Indians leave their Powder River hunting grounds. When the Sioux refused, the army attacked. The Oglala Sioux, under Crazy Horse, repulsed one prong of this offensive at the Battle of the Rosebud in June 1876 and then joined a larger body of Sioux under Sitting Bull and their Cheyenne and Arapaho allies to overwhelm a second American column, under Custer, at the **Battle of the Little Bighorn.**

But the Indians could not follow up their dramatic victory. They had to divide their forces to find fresh grass for their horses and to hunt for their own food. The U.S. Army relentlessly pursued the separate bands to exhaustion. In the end, the conquest of the northern plains came, not through any decisive victory, but through attrition and the inability of the traditional Indian economy to support resistance to the technologically and numerically superior white forces.

The defeat of the Sioux nearly completed the Indian Wars. In the Northwest, the Nez Percé resisted in 1877 when the government reneged on its agreement to protect their land. Outwitting and outfighting the larger forces of the U.S. Army over a 1,500-mile retreat toward Canada, the exhausted Nez Percé surrendered after being promised a return to their own land. But the government refused to honor that pledge, too, and imprisoned the tribe in Oklahoma, where more than a third perished within a few years.

In the Southwest, the Navajos and the Comanches were subdued, as the Sioux had been, by persistent pursuit that prevented them from obtaining food. The last to submit were the Apaches, under Geronimo. In 1886, he and 36 followers, facing 5,000 U.S. troops, finally surrendered. Geronimo and other Apaches were sent to a military prison in Florida; the tribes were herded onto reservations. The Oglala chief Red Cloud concluded of the white invasion: "They made us many promises, more than I can remember, but they never kept but one. They promised to take our land, and they took it."

LIFE ON THE RESERVATION: AMERICANIZATION

Conquering the tribes and taking their land were only the initial objectives of government policy. The next goal was to require Indians to adopt white ways. This goal did not involve assimilation but merely "Americanization," an expression of cultural conquest.

The government received aid from many Christian denominations, which had long proposed nonviolent methods of controlling Indians. They helped staff reservations as agents, missionaries, or civilian employees. Protestant philanthropists controlled several private organizations that worked to shape Indian policy, including the Indian Rights Association and the Women's National Indian Association. Reformers wanted to change Indian religious and family life, train Indian children in

Protestant beliefs, and force Indians to accept private ownership and market capitalism.

Confined to reservations, Indians were a captive audience for white reformers. Furthermore, with their very survival dependent on government rations and annual payments stipulated by treaties, Indians were "compelled by sheer necessity," as one federal official said, to accept government orders "or starve." Government agents of the Bureau of Indian Affairs used their power to undermine tribal authority and destroy traditional Indian government, prohibiting tribal councils from meeting and imprisoning tribal leaders.

White activists sought to destroy Indian religion because it was "pagan" and because it helped Indians resist assimilation. Protestant religious groups persuaded the Bureau of Indian Affairs to frame a criminal code prohibiting tribal religious practices. Established in 1884, the code remained in effect until 1933. To enforce the ban, the government withheld rations and disrupted the religious ceremonies that transmitted traditional values. In 1890, to suppress the Ghost Dance religion, the army even used artillery and killed at least 200 Sioux men, women, and children at Wounded Knee, South Dakota, in what became known as the **Wounded Knee Massacre.**

Red Cloud, Oglala Lakota chief in the 1880s. In the 1860s, he led the Sioux to military victory over the United States, forcing the government, in the Treaty of Fort Laramie, to abandon army posts and withdraw from Sioux territory.

The Denver Public Library

The government and religious groups also used education to eliminate Indian values and traditions. They isolated Indian children from tribal influences at off-reservation boarding schools. Troops often seized Indian children for these schools, where they were confined until after adolescence. The schoolchildren were forced to speak English, attend Christian services, and profess white American values (see American Views: "Zitkala-Sa's View of Americanization").

Finally, the government and the religious reformers imposed the economic practices and values of white society on Indians. Government agents taught Indian men how to farm; Indian women were taught household tasks. These tactics reduced the status of Indian women, whose traditional responsibility for agriculture had guaranteed them respect and authority. Nor could men farm successfully on reservation lands that whites had already rejected as unproductive. Whites, however, believed that the real obstacle to economic prosperity for the Indians was their rejection of private property. The Indians' communal values, the reformers argued, inhibited the pursuit of personal success that lay at the heart of capitalism As one official declared Indians must be taught to be more "mercenary and ambitious to obtain riches."

To force such values on Indians, Congress in 1887 passed the **Dawes Act,** which divided tribal lands among individual Indians and opened the remainder to white settlement. Under this "reform," the amount of land held by Indians declined by more than half by 1900. White acquisition and exploitation of Indian land seemed to be the only constant in the nation's treatment of Native Americans. Assimilation failed, because most Indians clung to their own values and rejected those favored by whites. As Big Bear, a chief of the Otoe-Missouria, defiantly declared, "You cannot make white men of us. That is one thing you can't do." But if it was not yet clear what place Native Americans would have in America, it was at least clear by 1900 that they would no longer stand in the way of western development.

Wounded Knee Massacre
The U.S. Army's brutal winter massacre in 1890 of at least two hundred Sioux men, women, and children as part of the government's assault on the tribe's Ghost Dance religion.

Dawes Act   An 1887 law terminating tribal ownership of land and allotting some parcels of land to individual Indians with the remainder opened for white settlement.

AMERICAN VIEWS

ZITKALA-SA'S VIEW OF AMERICANIZATION

itkala-Sa, or Red Bird, was an eight-year-old Sioux girl when she was taken from her South Dakota reservation in 1884 and placed in a midwestern missionary school, where she encountered what she called the "iron routine" of the "civilizing machine." Here she recalls her first day at the school.

- What lessons were the missionaries trying to teach Zitkala-Sa by their actions?
- What lessons did Zitkala-Sa learn?

Soon we were being drawn rapidly away by the white man's horses. When I saw the lonely figure of my mother vanish in the distance, a sense of regret settled heavily upon me. . . . I no longer felt free to be myself, or to voice my own feelings. The tears trickled down my cheeks, and I buried my face in the folds of my blanket. Now the first step, parting me from my mother, was taken, and all my belated tears availed nothing. . . . Trembling with fear and distrust of the palefaces . . . I was as frightened and bewildered as the captured young of a wild creature. . . .

[At the missionary school,] the constant clash of harsh noises, with an undercurrent of many voices murmuring an unknown tongue, made a bedlam within which I was securely tied. And though my spirit tore itself in struggling for its lost freedom, all was useless. . . .

We were placed in a line of girls who were marching into the dining room. . . . A small bell was tapped, and each of the pupils drew a chair from under the table. Supposing this act meant they were to be seated, I pulled out mine and at once slipped into it from one side. But when I turned my head, I saw that I was the only one seated, and all the rest at our table remained standing. Just as I began to rise, looking shyly around to see how chairs were to be used, a second bell was sounded. All were seated at last, and I had to crawl back into my chair again. I heard a man's voice at one end of the hall, and I looked around to see him. But all others hung their heads over their plates. As I glanced at the long chain of tables, I caught the eyes of a paleface woman upon me. Immediately I dropped my eyes, wondering why I was so keenly watched by the strange woman. The man ceased his mutterings, and then a third bell was tapped. Every one picked up his knife

and fork and began eating. I began crying instead, for by this time I was afraid to venture anything more.

But this eating by formula was not the hardest trial in that first day. Late in the morning, my friend Judewin gave me a terrible warning. Judewin knew a few words of English; and she had overheard the paleface woman talk about cutting our long, heavy hair. Our mothers had taught us that only unskilled warriors who were captured had their hair shingled by the enemy. Among our people, short hair was worn by mourners, and shingled hair by cowards!

. . . I remember being dragged out, though I resisted by kicking and scratching wildly. In spite of myself, I was carried downstairs and tied fast in a chair. I cried aloud, shaking my head all the while until I felt the cold blades of the scissors against my neck, and heard them gnaw off one of my thick braids. Then I lost my spirit. . . . My long hair was shingled like a coward's. In my anguish I moaned for my mother, but no one came to comfort me. Not a soul reasoned quietly with me, as my own mother used to do; for now I was only one of many little animals driven by a herder. . . .

I blamed the hard-working, well-meaning, ignorant [missionary] woman who was inculcating in our hearts her superstitious ideas. Though I was sullen in all my little troubles, as soon as I felt better I was . . . again actively testing the chains which tightly bound my individuality like a mummy for burial. . . .

Many specimens of civilized peoples visited the Indian school. The city folks with canes and eyeglasses, the countrymen with sunburnt cheeks and clumsy feet, forgot their relative social ranks in an ignorant curiosity. Both sorts of these Christian palefaces were alike astounded at seeing the children of savage warriors so docile and industrious. . . .

In this fashion many [whites] have passed idly through the Indian schools during the last decade, afterward to boast of their charity to the North American Indian. But few there are who have paused to question whether real life or long-lasting death lies beneath this semblance of civilization.

Source: Zitkala-Sa, "The School Days of an Indian Girl" (1900). Reprinted in *American Indian Stories* (Glorieta, N.Mex.: Rio Grande Press, 1976).

554

EXPLOITING THE MOUNTAINS: THE MINING BONANZA

Migrants to the American West exploited the region's natural resources in pursuit of wealth and success. The challenges they confronted and the ventures they initiated gave rise to romantic images: the West as a land of adventure, opportunity, and freedom. All too often, however, reality differed from legend.

In the later nineteenth century, the West experienced several stages of economic development that transformed the environment, produced economic and social conflict, and integrated the region into the modern national economy. The first stage of development centered on mining, which attracted eager prospectors into the mountains and deserts in search of gold and silver. They founded communities, stimulated the railroad construction that brought further development, and contributed to the disorderly heritage of the frontier. But few gained the wealth they expected.

RUSHES AND MINING CAMPS

The first important gold rush in the Rocky Mountains came in Colorado in 1859. More than 100,000 prospectors crowded into Denver and the nearby mining camps. Simultaneously, the discovery of the famous Comstock Lode in Nevada produced an eastward rush of miners from California. Strikes in the northern Rockies followed in the 1860s. Boise City and Lewiston in Idaho and Helena in Montana became major mining centers, and other camps prospered briefly before fading into ghost towns. Later, other minerals shaped frontier development: silver in Nevada, silver and lead in Colorado and Idaho, silver and copper in Arizona and Montana.

Mining camps were often isolated by both distance and terrain. They frequently consisted only of flimsy shanties, saloons, crude stores, dance halls, and brothels. Such towns reflected the speculative, exploitive, and transitory character of mining. And yet they did contribute to permanent settlement by encouraging agriculture, industry, and transportation in the surrounding areas.

The camps had an unusual social and economic structure. Their population was overwhelmingly male. Women found far fewer economic opportunities than men did on the mining frontier. Some became prospectors, but most stayed within conventional domestic spaces. Several opened lodging houses or hotels. Those with less capital worked as seamstresses and cooks and took in washing. The few married women often earned more than their husbands by boarding other miners willing to pay for the trappings of family life.

Prostitution.   But the largest source of paid employment for women was prostitution, a flourishing consequence of the gender imbalance and the limited economic options for women. As one Denver prostitute later noted, "I went into the sporting life for business reasons and no other. It was a way for a woman in those days to make money and I made it." Many who entered brothels already suffered from economic hardship or a broken family. Prostitution then usually worsened their distress. By the 1890s, as men gained control of the vice trade from the madams, violence, suicide, alcoholism, disease, drug addiction, and poverty overcame most prostitutes.

WHAT WERE the environmental consequences of the expansion of mining in the nineteenth century?

WHERE TO LEARN MORE

Bodie State Historic Park, Bodie, California www.bodie.net/

QUICK REVIEW

Prostitution
- Largest source of paid employment for women in the West.
- Most women entered prostitution as a result of economic or familial hardship.
- Authorities showed little interest in welfare of prostitutes.

One Methodist missionary expressed his horror of early mining town saloons and their patrons: "The utter recklessness, the perfect 'Abandon' with which they drink, gamble, and swear is altogether astounding." By the 1890s, when a photographer took this carefully posed picture of Crapper Jack's Saloon in Cripple Creek, Colorado, saloon society was still popular but seemed more restrained.

The Denver Public Library

Public authorities showed little concern for the abuse and even murder of prostitutes, although they fined and taxed "sporting women" to raise revenue. Condemning such moral indifference, middle-class Protestant women in Denver and other cities established "rescue homes" to protect or rehabilitate prostitutes and dance-hall girls from male vice and violence.

Saloon Society.   The gender imbalance in the mining camps also made saloons prevalent among local businesses. An 1879 business census of Leadville, Colorado, reported 10 dry-goods stores, 4 banks, and 4 churches, but 120 saloons, 19 beer halls, and 118 gambling houses. Saloons were social centers in towns where most miners lived in crowded and dirty tents and rooming houses. As Mark Twain wrote in *Roughing It* (1872), his account of Virginia City, "The cheapest and easiest way to become an influential man and be looked up to by the community at large, was to stand behind a bar, wear a cluster-diamond pin, and sell whiskey."

One observer of the Montana camps reported that men, "unburdened by families, drink whenever they feel like it, whenever they have money to pay for it, and whenever there is nothing else to do. . . . Bad manners follow, profanity becomes a matter of course. . . . Excitability and nervousness brought on by rum help these tendencies along, and then to correct this state of things the pistol comes into play." Disputes over mining claims could become violent, adding to the disorder. The California mining town of Bodie experienced 29 killings between 1877 and 1883, a homicide rate higher than that of any U.S. city a century later. But such killings occurred only within a small group of males, young, single, surly, and armed, who were known as the Badmen of Bodie. Daily life for most people was safe.

Collective Violence.   Indeed, personal and criminal violence, which remains popularly associated with the West, was less pervasive than collective violence. This, too, affected mining camps and was aggravated by their ethnic and racial diversity. Irish, Germans, English, Chinese, Australians, Italians, Slavs, and Mexicans, among others, rushed into the mining regions. In many camps, half the population was foreign-born and another fourth consisted of first-generation Americans.

The European immigrants who sometimes encountered nativist hostility in the East experienced less animosity in the West, but nonwhite minorities often suffered. In particular, white people frequently drove Mexicans and Chinese from their claims or refused to let them work in higher-paid occupations in the mining camps. The Chinese had originally migrated to the California gold fields and thereafter spread to the new mining areas of the Rockies and the Great Basin. In 1870, more than a quarter of Idaho's population and nearly 10 percent of Montana's was Chinese. Where they were numerous, the Chinese built their own communities and maintained their customs.

But racism and fear of economic competition sparked hostility and violence against the Chinese almost everywhere. The worst anti-Chinese violence occurred in Rock Springs, Wyoming, in 1885 when white miners killed 28 unresisting Chinese miners and drove away all 700 residents from the local Chinatown. Although the members of the mob were well known, the grand jury found no cause for legal action. Such community sanction for violence against racial minorities made mob attacks one of the worst features of the mining camps.

LABOR AND CAPITAL

New technology had dramatic consequences for both miners and the mining industry. Initially, mining was an individual enterprise in which miners used simple tools, such as picks and shovels, wash pans, and rockers, to work shallow surface deposits. More complex and expensive operations were needed to reach the precious metal buried in the earth. Hydraulic mining, for example, required massive capital investment to build reservoirs, ditches, and troughs to power high-pressure water cannons that would pulverize hillsides and uncover the mineral deposits. Still more formidable was quartz, or lode, mining, sometimes called hard-rock mining. Time, money, and technology were required to sink a shaft into the earth, timber underground chambers and tunnels, install pumps to remove underground water and hoists to lower men and lift out rock, and build stamp mills and smelters to treat the ore.

Chinese miners in Idaho operate the destructive water cannons used in hydraulic mining. Technological changes made most miners wage workers for companies.

Idaho State Historical Society

Such complex, expensive, and permanent operations necessarily came under corporate control. Often financed with eastern or British capital, the new corporations integrated the mining industry into the larger economy. Hard-rock mining produced more complex ores than could be treated in remote mining towns, but with the new railroad network, they were shipped to smelting plants as far away as Kansas City and St. Louis and then to refineries in eastern cities. Western ores thus became part of national and international business.

Effects of Corporate Mining.   Quartz mining thus helped usher the mining frontier into a more stable period. But the new corporate mining had disturbing effects. Its impact on the environment was horrendous. Hydraulic mining washed away hillsides, depositing debris in canyons and valleys to a depth of 100 feet or more, clogging rivers and causing floods, and burying thousands of acres of farmland. Such damage provoked an outcry and eventually led to government regulation.

Corporate mining also hurt miners, transforming them into wage workers with restricted opportunities. "It is useless to say that here all have an equal chance," conceded a Colorado newspaper in 1891. Miners' status declined as new machinery, such as power drills, reduced the need for skilled laborers and enabled employers to hire cheaper workers from eastern and southern Europe. Mining corporations, moreover, did little to protect miners' health or safety. Miners called power hoists "man killers" because they frequently crushed and

QUICK REVIEW

Technology and Mining
- Mining began as an individual enterprise.
- Deeper mining required expensive equipment.
- As mining became more complex and costly, it came under corporate control.

dismembered workers. Investigating the new machinery in 1889, the Montana inspector of mines concluded that "death lurks even in the things which are designed as benefits."

Unions and Union Busting. To protect themselves, miners organized unions. These functioned as benevolent societies, using members' dues to pay benefits to injured miners or their survivors. Several unions established hospitals. Union halls offered an alternative to the saloons by serving as social and educational centers. Unions also promoted miners' interests by striking against wage cuts and campaigning for mine safety. They convinced states to pass mine safety laws and, beginning in the 1880s, to appoint mine inspectors. The chief role of these state officials was, in the words of a Colorado inspector, to decide "How far should an industry be permitted to advance its material welfare at the expense of human life?"

The industry itself, however, often provided the answer to this question, for mining companies frequently controlled state power and used it to crush unions. Thus, in 1892, in the Coeur d'Alene district of Idaho, mining companies locked out strikers and imported a private army, which battled miners in a bloody gunfight. Management next persuaded the governor and the president to send in the state militia and the U.S. Army. State officials then suppressed the strike and the union by confining all union members and their sympathizers in stockades.

When mining companies in Utah, Colorado, and Montana pursued the same aggressive tactics of lockouts and wage cuts, the local miners' unions in the West united for strength and self-protection. In 1893, they formed one of the nation's largest and most militant unions, the Western Federation of Miners.

Violence and conflict were attributable not to frontier lawlessness but to the industrialization of the mines. Both management's tactics and labor's response mirrored conditions in the industrial East. In sum, western mining, reflecting the industrialization of the national economy, had been transformed from a small-scale prospecting enterprise characterized by individual initiative and simple tools into a large-scale corporate business characterized by impersonal management, outside capital, advanced technology, and wage labor.

USING THE GRASS: THE CATTLE KINGDOM

*T*he development of the range-cattle industry opened a second stage of exploitation of the late-nineteenth-century West. It reflected the needs of an emerging eastern urban society, the economic possibilities of the grasslands of the Great Plains, the technology of the expanding railroad network, and the requirements of corporations and capital. It also brought "cow towns" and urban development to the West.

CATTLE DRIVES AND COW TOWNS

The cattle industry originated in southern Texas, where the Spanish had introduced cattle in the eighteenth century. As industrial expansion in the East and Midwest enlarged the urban market for food, the potential value of Texas steers increased. And the extension of the railroad network into the West opened the possibility of tapping that market. The key was to establish a shipping point on the railroads west of the settled farming regions, a step first taken in 1867 by Joseph McCoy, who selected Abilene, Kansas. Abilene was the western railhead of the Kansas Pacific Railroad and was ringed by lush grasslands for cattle. Texans opened

GLOBAL PERSPECTIVES

THE WEST ABROAD

Americans have always liked to think of the American West as a distinctive region whose prospectors, cowboys, and homesteaders helped shape an exceptional national experience. In fact, however, other countries also experienced comparable developments in the late nineteenth century. While the United States and other countries romanticized their frontier experiences, common environmental, economic, and social forces diminished their distinctiveness.

An obvious demonstration that the frontier was not uniquely American was the interlocking western development in the United States and Canada. The mining frontier crossed the border and included gold rushes in British Columbia from 1858 to 1867 and the Yukon in the 1890s. Canadian goldfields imported California's mining regulations and also followed the pattern of corporate supplanting placer mining. As for cattle raising, one Alberta rancher said in 1884: "We adopted pretty much the same system as was carried on across the border." Ranchers used Canada's public domain for pasture, while cowboys had familiar clothing, work, and wages. Stock associations developed to safeguard ranchers' interests, and gradually big eastern Canadian and British firms dominated the industry.

Like its American counterpart, the Canadian government promoted the construction of a transcontinental railroad, the Canadian Pacific, with land grants and subsidies. It enacted a homestead law providing free land in 1872. It encouraged European immigrants to settle and then witnessed land booms, commercial wheat production, and falling crop prices.

Canada experienced less violence and disorder than the United States, largely because of its Indian policy. Although it too established reservations, Canada treated Indians with respect, created a system of incorruptible agents, and used the North West Mounted Police to prevent the exploitation of Indians by settlers. The Mounted Police also maintained law and order on the mining and ranching frontiers.

While Canada most closely paralleled the American experience, Australia, too, had similarities. Its gold rush began in 1851, attracted miners, technology, and capital from California, and saw violence against Chinese. As in North America, corporate mining soon replaced the original "diggers." In 1861 Australia enacted homestead-type laws to assist small farmers who eventually developed into major wheat producers. And in the 1870s a large-scale pastoral economy, though based on sheep, not cattle, emerged in its vast arid region.

Argentina had no mining frontier, but after suppressing the Araucanian Indians in 1879 to open the pampas to settlement, it developed first a cattle ranching and then an agricultural frontier. Argentine gauchos, like American cowboys, came to symbolize the national character, though they too soon became ranch hands dependent on wages. The government promoted railroad construction in the 1880s, and European immigration helped people the prairies, spurring wheat production and the adoption of the new farming technologies.

the **Chisholm Trail** through Indian Territory to drive their cattle northward to Abilene. Within three years, a million and a half cattle reached Abilene, divided into herds of several thousand, each directed by a dozen cowhands on a "long drive" taking two to three months.

Cow Town Life.   The cattle trade attracted other entrepreneurs who created a bustling town. As both railroads and settlement advanced westward, a series of other cow towns—Ellsworth, Wichita, Dodge City, Cheyenne—attracted the long drives, cattle herds, and urban development.

Chisholm Trail   The route followed by Texas cattle raisers driving their herds north to markets at Kansas railheads.

17–4
Joseph G. McCoy, Historic Sketches of the Cattle Trade of the West and Southwest (1874)

As with the mining camps, the cow towns' reputation for violence was exaggerated. They adopted gun-control laws, prohibiting the carrying of handguns within city limits, and established police forces to maintain order. The cow towns regulated, rather than prohibited, prostitution and gambling, for merchants viewed these vices as necessary to attract the cattle trade.

Most cow towns dwindled into small towns serving farm populations. But cow towns, again like mining camps, contributed to the growth of an urban frontier. Railroads often determined the location and growth of western cities, providing access to markets for local products, transporting supplies and machinery for residents, and attracting capital for commercial and industrial development. The West, in fact, had become the most urban region in the nation by 1890, with two-thirds of its population living in communities of at least 2,500 people.

RISE AND FALL OF OPEN-RANGE RANCHING

The significance of the long drive to the cow towns faded as cattle raising expanded beyond Texas. Indian removal and extension of the railroads opened land for ranching in Kansas, Nebraska, Wyoming, Colorado, Montana, and the Dakotas. Cattle reaching Kansas were increasingly sold to stock these northern ranges rather than for shipment to the packinghouses. Ranches soon spread across the Great Plains and into the Great Basin, the Southwest, and even eastern Oregon and Washington. This expansion was helped by the initially low investment that ranching required. Calves were cheap, and grass was mostly free. Ranchers did not buy, but merely used, the grazing lands of the open range, which was public land. Moreover, their labor costs were minimal: they hired cowboys in the spring to round up new calves for branding and in the fall to herd steers to market.

By the early 1880s, the high profits from this enterprise and an expanding market for beef attracted speculative capital and reshaped the industry. Eastern and European capital flooded the West, with British investors particularly prominent. Some investors went into partnership with existing ranchers, providing capital in exchange for expertise and management. Wisconsin investors formed the Three Rivers Land and Cattle Company of New Mexico, for example, by buying into a ranch owned and operated by Susan Barber, whom they then employed as general manager. Barber was unusual in the male-dominated industry, but the managerial skills she demonstrated were necessary for success. On a larger scale, British and American corporations acquired, expanded, and managed huge ranches.

Effects of Corporate Control. Large companies soon dominated the industry, just as they had gained control of mining. They worked together to enhance their power, especially by restricting access to the range and by intimidating small competitors. Some large companies illegally enclosed the open range, building fences to exclude newcomers and minimize labor costs by reducing the number of cowboys needed to control the cattle. One Wyoming newspaper complained: "some morning we will wake up to find that a corporation has run a wire fence about the boundary lines of Wyoming, and all within the same have been notified to move."

Such tensions sometimes exploded in instances of social violence as serious as those that disrupted the mining frontier. Attempts by large ranchers to fence off public lands in Texas provoked the Fence-Cutters War of 1883–84. Montana's largest cattlemen organized an armed force known as "Stuart's Stranglers" and, in America's worst vigilante violence, killed over a hundred people they viewed as challenging their power. Less deadly but more famous was the Johnson County War in Wyoming, when large ranchers, their foremen, and hired Texas gunmen set out with a death list of 70 people to eliminate. They murdered three people but met such popular resistance that the U.S. Army had to be called in to save them.

The corporate cattle boom overstocked the range and threatened the industry itself. Overgrazing replaced nutritious grasses with sagebrush, Russian thistle, and other plants that livestock found unpalatable. Droughts in the mid-1880s further withered vegetation and enfeebled the animals. Millions of cattle starved or froze to death in terrible blizzards in 1886 and 1887. These ecological and financial disasters destroyed the open-range cattle industry. The surviving ranchers reduced their operations, restricted the size of their herds, and tried to ensure adequate winter feed by growing hay. To further reduce their dependence on natural vegetation, they introduced drought-resistant sorghum and new grasses; to reduce their dependence on rainfall, they drilled wells and installed windmills to pump water.

COWHANDS AND CAPITALISTS

One constant in the cattle industry was the cowboy, but his working conditions and opportunities changed sharply over time and corresponded little to the romantic image of a dashing individual free of social constraints. Cowboys' work was hard, dirty, seasonal, tedious, sometimes dangerous, and poorly paid. Many early cowboys were white southerners unwilling or unable to return home after the Civil War. Black cowhands made up perhaps 25 percent of the trail-herd outfits. Many others, especially in Texas and the Southwest, were Mexicans. Indeed, Mexicans developed most of the tools, techniques, and trappings that characterized the cattle industry: from boots, chaps, and the "western" saddle to roundups and roping. Black and Mexican cowboys were often relegated to the more lowly jobs, such as wrangler, a "dust-eater" who herded horses for others to use, but most served as ordinary hands on ranch or trail. As the industry expanded northward, more cowboys came from rural Kansas, Nebraska, and neighboring states.

Initially, in the frontier-ranching phase dominated by the long drive, cowboys were seasonal employees who worked closely with owners. Often the sons or neighbors of ranchers, they frequently expected to become independent stock raisers themselves. They typically enjoyed the rights to "maverick" cattle, or put their own brand on unmarked animals they encountered, and to "run a brand," or to own their own cattle while working for a ranch. These informal rights provided opportunities to acquire property and move up the social ladder.

As ranching changed with the appearance of large corporate enterprises, so did the work and work relationships of cowhands. The power and status of employer and employees diverged, and the cowboys' traditional rights disappeared. Employers redefined mavericking as rustling and prohibited cowhands from running a brand of their own.

Employees of the Prairie Cattle Company at the ranch headquarters in Dry Cimarron, New Mexico, in 1888. The company, a British corporation, held 8,000 square miles of land.

The Denver Public Library

One cowboy complained that these restrictions deprived a cowhand of his one way "to get on in the world." But that was the purpose: Cowboys were to be workers, not potential ranchers and competitors.

Unions and Strikes. Cowboys sometimes responded to these structural transformations the same way skilled workers in the industrial East did, by forming unions and striking. The first strike occurred in Texas in 1883, when the Panhandle Stock Association, representing large operators, prohibited ranch hands from owning their own cattle and imposed a standard wage. More than 300 cowboys struck seven large ranches. Ranchers evicted the cowboys, hired scabs, and brought in the Texas Rangers to drive the strikers from the region.

Other strikes also failed because corporate ranches and their stock associations had the power, and cowhands faced long odds in their efforts to organize. They were isolated across vast spaces and had little leverage in the industry. Members of the Northern New Mexico cowboys union, formed in 1886, recognized their weakness and conceded to their employees "we are dependent on you."

The transformation of the western cattle industry and its integration into a national economy dominated by corporations thus made the cherished image of cowboy independence and rugged individualism more myth than reality. One visitor to America in the late 1880s commented: "Out in the fabled West, the life of the 'free' cowboy is as much that of a slave as is the life of his Eastern brother, the Massachusetts mill-hand. And the slave-owner is in both cases the same, the capitalist."

HOW DID new technology contribute to the growth of Western agriculture?

WORKING THE EARTH: HOMESTEADERS AND AGRICULTURAL EXPANSION

Even more than ranching and mining, agricultural growth boosted the western economy and bound it tightly to national and world markets. In this process, the government played a significant role, as did the railroads, science and technology, eastern and foreign capital, and the dreams and hard work of millions of rural settlers. The development of farming produced remarkable economic growth, but it left the dreams of many unfulfilled.

SETTLING THE LAND

To stimulate agricultural settlement, Congress passed the most famous land law, the **Homestead Act** of 1862 (see the Overview table, "Government Land Policy"). The measure offered 160 acres of free land to anyone who would live on the plot and farm it for five years. The act promised opportunity and independence to ambitious farmers. The governor of Nebraska exclaimed, "What a blessing this wise and humane legislation will bring to many a poor but honest and industrious family."

Limits of the Homestead Act. However, prospective settlers found less land open to public entry than they expected. Federal land laws did not apply in much of California and the Southwest, where Spain and Mexico had previously transferred land to private owners. Elsewhere, the government had given away millions of acres to railroads or authorized selling millions more for educational and other purposes. Moreover, other laws provided for easy transfer of public lands to cattle companies, to other corporations exploiting natural resources, and to land speculators.

Homestead Act 1862 law providing 160 acres of free land to anyone who would live on and farm the land for five years.

OVERVIEW   GOVERNMENT LAND POLICY

Legislation	Result
Railroad land grants (1850–1871)	Granted 181 million acres to railroads to encourage construction and development
Homestead Act (1862)	Gave 80 million acres to settlers to encourage settlement
Morrill Act (1862)	Granted 11 million acres to states to sell to fund public agricultural colleges
Other grants	Granted 129 million acres to states to sell for other educational and related purposes
Dawes Act (1887)	Allotted some reservation lands to individual Indians to promote private property and weaken tribal values among Indians and offered remaining reservation lands for sale to whites (by 1906, some 75 million acres had been acquired by whites)
Various laws	Permitted direct sales of 100 million acres by the Land Office

Thus, settlers in Kansas, Nebraska, Minnesota, and the Dakotas in the late 1860s and early 1870s often found most of the best land unavailable for homesteading and much of the rest remote from transportation facilities and markets. As much as 40 percent of the land in Kansas, for example, was closed to homesteading, which prompted the editor of the *Kansas Farmer* to complain that "the settlement of the state is retarded by land monopolists, corporate and individual." Although 375,000 farms were claimed by 1890 through the Homestead Act, a success by any measure, most settlers had to purchase their land.

The Homestead Act also reflected traditional eastern conceptions of the family farm, which were inappropriate in the West. A farm of 160 acres would have suited conditions in eastern Kansas or Nebraska, but farther west, larger-scale farming was necessary. And the law ignored the need for capital—for machinery, buildings, livestock, and fencing—that was required for successful farming on the Great Plains.

Promoting Settlement.   Thus, other forces assumed responsibility for promoting settlement. Newspaper editors trumpeted the prospects of their region. Land companies, eager to sell their speculative holdings, sent agents through the Midwest and Europe to encourage migration. Steamship companies, hoping to sell transatlantic tickets, advertised the opportunities in the American West across Europe. Religious and ethnic groups encouraged immigration.

Most important, railroad advertising and promotional campaigns attracted people to the West. In 1882 alone, the Northern Pacific distributed more than 630,000 pieces of promotional literature in English, Swedish, Dutch, Danish, and Norwegian. "The glowing accounts of the golden west sent out by the R.R. companies," one pioneer later recalled, had convinced her that "they were doing a noble work to let poor people know there was such a grand haven they could reach." Only later did she realize the railroads' selfish motive. Not only would they profit from selling their huge land reserves to settlers, but a successful agricultural economy would produce crops to be shipped east and a demand for

WHERE TO LEARN MORE

American Historical Society of Germans from Russia Museum, Lincoln, Nebraska

manufactured goods to be shipped west on their lines. The railroads therefore advanced credit to prospective farmers, provided transportation assistance, and extended technical and agricultural advice.

Thus encouraged, migrants poured into the West, occupying and farming more acres between 1870 and 1900 than Americans had in the previous 250 years. Farmers settled in every region. Most, however, streamed into the Great Plains states, from the Dakotas to Texas. White migrants predominated in the mass migration, but African Americans initiated one of its most dramatic episodes, a millenarian folk movement they called the Exodus. Seeking to escape the misery and repression of the post-Reconstruction South, these poor "Exodusters" established several dozen black communities in 1879 in Kansas and Nebraska on the agricultural frontier. The Exodusters, said one observer, "regarded Kansas as a modern Canaan."

Many of the new settlers came from Europe, sometimes in a chain migration of entire villages, bringing with them not only their own attitudes toward the land but also special crops, skills, settlement patterns, and agricultural practices. Peasants from Norway, Sweden, and Denmark flocked to Minnesota. Germans, Russians, and Irish put down roots across Texas, Kansas, Nebraska, and the Dakotas. French, Germans, and Italians developed vineyards, orchards, and nurseries in California, where laborers from Japan and Mexico also arrived to work in fields and canneries. Immigrants often settled in separate ethnic communities, held together by their church, and attempted to preserve their language and customs.

Hispanic Losses. Migrants moved into the West in search of opportunity, which they sometimes seized at the expense of others already there. In the Southwest, Hispanics had long lived in village communities largely outside a commercial economy, farming small tracts of irrigated land and herding sheep on communal pastures. As Anglos, or white Americans, arrived, their political and economic influence undermined traditional Hispanic society. Congress restricted the original Hispanic land grants to only the villagers' home lots and irrigated fields, throwing open most of their common lands to newcomers. Hispanic title was confirmed to only 2 million of the 37.5 million acres at stake. Anglo ranchers and settlers manipulated the federal land system to control these lands. The notorious Santa Fe Ring, a group of lawyers and land speculators, seized millions of acres through fraud and legal chicanery.

Spanish Americans resisted these losses in court or through violence. *Las Gorras Blancas* ("the White Caps") staged night raids to cut fences erected by Anglo ranchers and farmers and to attack the property of railroads, the symbol of the encroaching new order. "Our purpose," they announced, "is to protect the rights of the people in general and especially those of the helpless classes." Such resistance, however, had little success.

As their landholdings shrank, Hispanic villagers could not maintain their pastoral economy. Many became seasonal wage laborers in the Anglo-dominated economy, sometimes working as stoop labor in the commercial sugar-beet fields that emerged in the 1890s, sometimes working on the railroads or in the mines. Women also participated in the new labor market. Previously crucial to the subsistence village economy, they now sought wage labor as cooks and domestic servants in railroad towns and mining camps. Hispanics retained some cultural autonomy, but they had little influence over the larger processes of settlement and development.

HOME ON THE RANGE

Farm families encountered many difficulties, especially on the Great Plains, where they had to adapt to a radically new environment. The scarcity of trees on the plains meant that there was little wood for housing, fuel, and fencing. Until they had reaped several harvests and could afford to import lumber, pioneer families lived in houses made of sod. Though inexpensive and sturdy, sod houses were also dark and dirty. Snakes, mice, and insects often crawled out of the walls and roofs.

Women's Work.   Within these rough houses, women worked to provide food, clothing, and medicine to ensure the family's survival. Their efforts were greatly constrained by the harsh environment. For fuel, families often had to rely on buffalo or cattle "chips," dried dung, which repelled some newcomers. The scarcity of water also complicated women's domestic labor. They often had to transport water over long distances, pulling barrels on "water sleds" or carrying pails on neck yokes. They melted snow on the stove for wash water and used the same water over again for different chores. Where possible, they also helped to dig wells by hand.

Some women farmed the land themselves. Single women could claim land under the Homestead Act, and in some areas, women claimants made up 18 percent of the total and succeeded more frequently than men in gaining final title. At times, married women operated the family farm by themselves while their husbands worked elsewhere to earn the money needed for seeds, equipment, and building supplies. In the 1870s, one Dakota woman recounted the demands women faced: "I had lived on a homestead long enough to learn some fundamental things: that while a woman had more independence here than in any other part of the world, she was expected to contribute as much as a man, not in the same way, it is true, but to the same degree; that people who fought the frontier had to be prepared to meet any emergency; that the person who wasn't willing to try anything once wasn't equipped to be a settler."

Isolation and Community.   Isolation and loneliness troubled many early settlers on the plains. Women especially suffered because they frequently had less contact with other people than farm men, who conducted their families' business in town and participated in such public activities as political meetings. One woman complained that "being cut off from everybody is almost too much for me."

Over time, conditions improved. "It does beet all how fast this country is getting up," wrote one South Dakota woman in 1886. "I'm looking round and see two new houses been put up since yesterday." As population increased, women in particular worked to bind isolated households into communities by organizing social activities and institutions. They held fairs, dances, and picnics and established churches, schools, and libraries, thereby gaining both companionship and a sense of purpose.

Churches, in turn, also promoted community. Indeed, many were "union" churches, open to people of all denominations. In addition to holding religious services, revivals, and camp meetings, churches were often the center of social life, especially by sponsoring sociables and children's organizations. "However great may have been the need for salvation," one plains woman recalled, "the need for recreation was given preference." Nondenominational Sunday schools helped bind together differing nationalities and church preferences, and because they did not require the services of an ordained minister they often enabled women to initiate and lead community activities.

Other institutions also encouraged community action. Rural families created their own agricultural cooperatives and other economic and social organizations, like local Grange lodges. External developments also served the rural population. Few were more important than Rural Free Delivery, which eventually brought letters, newspapers, magazines, and advertisements to farm families' doorsteps, or mail-order houses, which made available to farm people such helpful goods as stoves, sewing machines, and shoes. After acquiring her first Montgomery Ward catalog in 1885, one Wyoming woman declared it "impossible to exaggerate the importance of . . . this book of wonder." Such changes helped incorporate westerners into the larger society.

FARMING THE LAND

Pioneer settlers had to make daunting adjustments to develop the agricultural potential of their new land. Advances in science, technology, and industry made such adjustments possible. The changes not only reshaped the agricultural economy but also challenged traditional rural values and expectations.

Growing Crops. Fencing was an immediate problem, for crops needed protection from livestock. But without timber, farmers could not build wooden fences. Barbed wire, developed in the mid-1870s, solved the problem. By 1900, farmers were importing nearly 300 million pounds of barbed wire each year from eastern and midwestern factories.

The aridity of most of the West also posed difficulties. In California and Colorado, settlers used streams fed by mountain snow packs to irrigate land. Elsewhere, enterprising farmers developed variants of the "dry farming" practices that the Mormons had introduced in Utah to maximize the limited rainfall. Some farmers erected windmills to pump underground water. The scarce rainfall also discouraged the cultivation of many of the crops that supported traditional general agriculture and encouraged farmers to specialize in a single cash crop for market. Gradually, many plains farmers turned from corn to wheat, especially the drought-resistant Turkey Red variety introduced into Kansas by immigrants from Russia. Government agencies and agricultural colleges contributed to the success of such adaptations, and private engineers and inventors also fostered agricultural development. Related technological advancements included grain elevators that would store grain for shipment and load it into rail cars mechanically and mills that used corrugated, chilled-iron rollers rather than millstones to process the new varieties of wheat.

Mechanization and technological innovations made possible the large-scale farming practiced in semiarid regions. Farmers required special

Many Mexican Americans turned to mining as the Southwest was developed. But they suffered from a dual wage system that discriminated in favor of Anglos and were often restricted to segregated housing areas.

Division of Cultural Resources, Wyoming Department of Commerce.

THE LEGACY OF INDIAN AMERICANIZATION

The assumptions, objectives, and failures of the Americanization policies of the nineteenth century continue to affect American Indians more than a century later. Although periodically modified (see Chapter 25), these policies long persisted, as did their consequences. In the 1970s official investigations reported that the continuing attempts of the Bureau of Indian Affairs to use education to force Indians into an Anglo-American mold "have been marked by near total failure, haunted by prejudice and ignorance."

Similarly, the economic problems on reservations in the nineteenth century foreshadowed conditions a century later. Today, Indians rank at the bottom on almost all measures of economic well-being. Lack of economic opportunity leaves isolated reservations with unemployment rates averaging 40 percent. Off the reservation, discrimination, limited skills, and inadequate capital further restrict Indians' job prospects. The U.S. Commission on Civil Rights reported in 2003 that Indians endured a "quiet crisis" of poverty, discrimination, and unmet promises.

Indians also continue to suffer from poor health conditions. They have the highest rates of infant mortality, pneumonia, hepatitis, tuberculosis, and suicide in the nation and a life expectancy 25 years less than the national average. The federal government has failed its legal obligation to provide Indians with decent health care. In 2004 it spent twice as much per capita on health care for federal prisoners as for Indians, and its Indian Health Service has crumbling facilities, obsolete equipment, and too few physicians and nurses.

Indian culture, however, did not succumb to either the pressure to Americanize or these miserable conditions. In the words of a Shoshone writer, "Indian history didn't end in the 1800s. Indian cultures . . . evolve, grow, and continually try to renew themselves."

In recent decades, Indian peoples have begun to reclaim their past and assert control over their future. Dramatic protests, most notably a confrontation in 1973 between Indian activists and the FBI at Wounded Knee, the site of the notorious 1890 massacre, have called attention to Indian grievances. But Indians have also moved effectively to regain control of the institu-

tions that define their cultural identity. They have established community schools and tribal community colleges that provide a bilingual, bicultural education, seeking to preserve traditions while opening new opportunities. They have built tribal museums and visitor centers in order to shape the presentation of their histories and cultures. There are now more than 200 such institutions, from the Seneca-Iroquois museum in upstate New York to the Makah Tribal Museum on the Olympic Peninsula.

Indians have also won legal recognition of their right to their cultural patrimony. The Native American Graves Protection and Repatriation Act of 1990 gives Indian communities the right to reclaim, or "repatriate," material artifacts and skeletal remains from museums and historical societies. The Native American Religious Freedom Act of 1978 affirmed their right to practice their traditional religions and have access to sacred sites. Indian dance, once suppressed by white authorities, has revived, and the powwow has become a national Indian institution and symbol of Indian identity.

With the help of historians and lawyers, Indians are also winning enforcement of long-ignored treaty provisions guaranteeing them land ownership and water, hunting, and fishing rights. Court decisions have recognized the right of tribes to permit gambling on their reservations, and some tribes have built profitable casinos, attracting economic development that creates new job opportunities for their people and permits them to stay on their land.

Indians still confront hostility and condescension reminiscent of attitudes a century ago. A white museum official, for example, seeking to prevent the repatriation of Pawnee artifacts, claimed recently that Indians do not have a real religion. But Indians have proved resilient in preserving their cultural heritage and keeping it vibrant for future generations. Dramatically symbolizing that resilience was the 2004 opening of the National Museum of the American Indian on the Mall in Washington, D.C. "What we really want visitors to understand," said its director, a Cheyenne, "is that we survived" both conquest and Americanization. "We are still here, making vital contributions."

plows to break the tough sod, new harrows to prepare the soil for cultivation, grain drills to plant the crop, and harvesting and threshing machines to bring it in. Thanks to more and better machines, agricultural efficiency and productivity shot up. So did farmers' costs.

Growing Tensions. These developments reflected both the expansion of agriculture and its increasing dependence on the larger society. Western commercial farmers needed the high demand of eastern and midwestern cities and the expanding world market. The rail network provided essential transportation for their crops; the nation's industrial sector produced necessary agricultural machinery. Banks and loan companies extended the credit and capital that allowed farmers to take advantage of mechanization and other new advances; and many other businesses graded, stored, processed, and sold their crops. In short, because of its market orientation, mechanization, and specialization, western agriculture relied on other people or impersonal forces as it was incorporated into the national and international economy.

When conditions were favorable—good weather, good crops, and good prices—western farmers prospered. Too often, however, they faced adversity. In the late 1880s, drought coincided with a slump in crop prices. The large European market that had encouraged agricultural expansion in the 1870s and early 1880s contracted after 1885, when several nations erected trade barriers to U.S. commodities. More important, America's production competed with that from Argentina, Canada, Australia, and Russia, and a world surplus of grain drove prices steadily downward.

Squeezed between high costs for credit, transportation, and manufactured goods and falling agricultural prices, western farmers faced disaster. They responded by lashing back at their points of contact with the new system. They especially condemned the railroads, believing that the companies charged excessive and discriminatory freight rates. Luna Kellie complained of the railroads, "The minute you crossed the Missouri River your fate both soul and body was in their hands. What you should eat and drink, what you should wear, everything was in their hands and they robbed us of all we produced except enough to keep body and soul together and many many times not that."

Farmers censured the grain elevators in the local buying centers. Often owned by eastern corporations, including the railroads, elevators allegedly exploited their local monopoly to cheat farmers by fixing low prices or misrepresenting the quality of wheat. A Minnesota state investigation found that systematic fraud by elevators cost farmers collectively a massive sum.

Farmers also denounced the bankers and mortgage lenders who had provided the credit for them to acquire land, equipment, and machinery. With failing crops and falling prices, many western farms were foreclosed.

Stunned and bitter, western farmers concluded that their problems arose because they had been incorporated into the new system, an integrated economy directed by forces beyond their control. And it was a system that did not work well. "There is," one of them charged, "something radically wrong in our industrial system. There is a screw loose."

Sunday school meeting in Custer County, Nebraska, in 1888. Sunday schools were important social as well as religious institutions on the Great Plains, where, as one newspaper reported, rural families often felt like "strangers in a strange land."

Nebraska State Historical Society

CONCLUSION

*I*n a few decades, millions of people had migrated westward in search of new opportunities. With determination, ingenuity, and hard work they had settled vast areas, made farms and ranches, built villages and cities, brought forth mineral wealth, and imposed their values on the land. These were remarkable achievements, though tempered by the shameful treatment of Indians and the often destructive exploitation of natural resources. But if most westerners took pride in their accomplishments, and a few enjoyed wealth and power, many also grew discontented with the new conditions they encountered as the "Wild" West receded.

Railroad expansion, population movements, eastern investment, corporate control, technological innovations, and government policies had incorporated the region fully into the larger society. Indians experienced this incorporation most thoroughly and most tragically, losing their lands, their traditions, and often their lives; the survivors were dependent on interlopers determined to "Americanize" them. Cowboys and miners also learned that the frontier merely marked the cutting edge of eastern industrial society. Both groups were wageworkers, often for corporations controlled by eastern capital; neither could escape integration into the national economy by managerial decisions, transportation links, and market forces. Most settlers in the West were farmers, but they too learned that their distinctive environment did not insulate them from assimilation into larger productive, financial, and marketing structures.

The processes of incorporation drained away westerners' hopes along with their products, and many of the discontented would demand a serious reorganization of relationships and power. Led by angry farmers, they turned their attention to politics and government, where they encountered new obstacles and opportunities.

IMAGE KEY
for pages 544–545

a. "The Cheyenne" by Frederick Remington.

b. Passengers and train crew shooting buffalo on the line of the Kansas-Pacific Railroad: color line engraving, 1871.

c. A feather fan carried by Yuchi dancers. American Museum of Natural History.

d. "The Rattlesnake" by Frederick Remington.

e. Chief Wooly Head's wife and child.

f. Thirty-three horse team harvester, cutting, threshing, and sacking wheat, c. 1902.

g. An old fashioned steam locomotive engine with an attached coal car.

h. A Chinese mine worker steadies a water cannon in a shallow riverbed in Idaho with a fellow laborer standing nearby.

SUMMARY

Subjugating Native Americans As white people pressed westward, the initial obstacle to exploiting the West was the people who already lived there. The native peoples used the land in their own way, had different concepts of progress and civilization, and had developed a variety of economies and cultures. From the 1850s to the 1880s, warfare engulfed the advancing frontier; railroad expansion, the destruction of the buffalo, and technological development undercut the ability of the Native Americans to resist. The conquest gradually forced Indians onto reservations, but efforts to "Americanize" the Indian way of life were less successful.

Exploiting the Mountains: The Mining Bonanza The first stage of the economic development of the West centered on mining as swarms of eager prospectors were attracted into the mountains and deserts in search of gold and silver. The male-dominated saloon society of the mining camps generated violence and social conflicts. Mining was transformed from an individual effort into a corporate one; as minerals became more difficult to uncover, mining became technologically complex and expensive. Corporate mining permanently changed the landscape of the West through its environmental impact.

Using the Grass: The Cattle Kingdom The development of the range cattle industry opened a second stage in the exploitation of the West. It reflected the needs of the Eastern urban society for food and the ability of the expanding rail network to deliver it. The cattle kingdom spread from Texas throughout the Great Plains; after the era of the long drives, cattle ranching became an increasingly corporate endeavor. While the romantic image of the cowboy is one of a rugged individualist freed of societal constraints, the actual work was hard, dirty, seasonal, dangerous, and poorly paid.

Working the Earth: Homesteaders and Agricultural Expansion Even more than ranching and mining, agricultural growth boosted the West's economy and bound it to national and world markets. Government played a significant role in the expansion of farming, as did railroads, science and technology, Eastern capital, and hard work. The Homestead Act, along with land, railroad, and steamship companies, encouraged Western migration. Settlers encountered many difficulties: a radically new environment, the need for new farming techniques, weather conditions, loneliness, and isolation. These were combined with farmers becoming part of a global economic system; farmers reached the conclusion that something was terribly wrong with the system, and that bankers, grain elevator operators, and the railroads were to blame.

REVIEW QUESTIONS

1. Why was the completion of the first transcontinental railroad, described by Andrew J. Russell, celebrated from Boston to San Francisco? How did western railroads shape the settlement and development of the West and affect the East as well?

2. What factors were most influential in the subjugation of American Indians?

3. What were the major goals of federal Indian policy, and how did they change?

4. How did technological developments affect Indians, miners, and farmers in the West?

5. How did the federal government help transform the West?

6. In what ways did European investors, markets, and migrants influence the development of the American West?

KEY TERMS

Chisholm Trail (p. 558)
Dawes Act (p. 552)
Homestead Act (p. 562)

Battle of the Little Bighorn (p. 551)
Sand Creek Massacre (p.550)

Second Treaty of Fort Laramie (p. 550)
Wounded Knee Massacre (p. 552)

WHERE TO LEARN MORE

Bodie State Historic Park, Bodie, California. The largest authentic ghost town in the West, Bodie was an important mining center from the 1860s to the 1880s. About 170 buildings remain, including a museum with mining equipment and artifacts of everyday life. **www.bodie.net/**

Little Bighorn Battlefield National Monument, Crow Agency, Montana. The site of Custer's crushing defeat includes a monument to the Seventh Cavalry atop Last Stand Hill. A newly authorized Indian Memorial will include sacred texts, artifacts, and pictographs of the Plains Indians. **www.nps.gov/libi/home.htm**

American Historical Society of Germans from Russia Museum, Lincoln, Nebraska. This unique museum, consisting of a complex of restored homes, exhibitions, and archives, preserves the history and culture of Germans who emigrated to Russia and then to the American Great Plains, where they contributed importantly to the development of a multicultural society and an agricultural economy.

National Museum of the American Indian, Smithsonian Institution, Washington D.C. This spectacular new museum opened in 2004 and reflects the world view of Native Americans, from exhibits on Indian spirituality and identity to performances of traditional dances and important lecture series. **www.nmai.si.edu**

National Cowboy Hall of Fame, Oklahoma City, Oklahoma. This large institution contains an outstanding collection of western art, displays of cowboy and Indian artifacts, and both kitschy exhibitions of the mythic Hollywood West and serious galleries depicting the often hard realities of the cattle industry. Its many public programs also successfully combine fun with learning. **www.cowboyhalloffame.org/index2.html**

Golden Spike National Historic Site, near Promontory, Utah. The completion of the transcontinental railroad here in 1869 is reenacted from May to October, using reproductions of the original locomotives. Visitors can drive the route of the railroad, now a National Backway Byway through abandoned mining and railroad towns, from Promontory to Nevada. Virtual tour, history, and tourist links on **www.nps./gov/gosp**

Fort Laramie, National Historic Site, near Guernsey, Wyoming. A fur-trading post, stop on the Oregon Trail, site of treaty negotiations with the Plains Indians, and staging area for military campaigns, Fort Laramie is now a living-history museum with many original buildings. For a virtual tour of the fort and information about visiting, see **www.nps.gov/fola/**

 U.S. History Documents CD-ROM
For primary sources related to this chapter, refer to the document CD-ROM.

 www.prenhall.com/goldfield
For study resources related to this chapter, visit the *Companion Website*™.

Visualizing The Past...

Mythologizing the "Wild West"

WHAT ELEMENTS do the Remington sculptures, the Curtis photograph, and the "dime novel" illustrations have in common? What, to judge from these images, made the West "wild"? How much do you think these images match up with reality?

One artist, Frederic Remington, deserves much of the credit for creating the West of our imagination. In Montana in 1881 an "old-timer" told him that "there is no more West." Remington decided to "try to record some facts around me." He recorded them first in a series of illustrations, then in paintings, and then in sculpture. Another who determined to "record some facts" was Edward S. Curtis who produced the twenty volume collection, *The North American Indian,* between 1906 and 1930. Curtis persuaded Native American peoples to reenact traditional practices, such as hunting or war parties. Often there was a twenty to fifty year gap between the reenactment and the practice itself. In contrast to Remington and Curtis who sought to (re)capture the truth about the West, "dime novels" sought simply to provide thrills. The "Wild West" is still part of our imaginative landscape.

Edward S. Curtis, "On the Warpath — Atsina," from The North American Indian, v.04; Curtis notes: "These grim-visaged old warriors made a thrilling picture as they rode along, breaking out now and then into wild song of the chase or raid." The image recreates a raiding party. Note the headdress on the party's leader, fourth from left. The photograph was taken in 1908.

▼

Frederick Remington, "The Cheyenne," a 1901 bronze statue, now at the Amon Carter Museum, Fort Worth, Texas. Remington loved to portray action; here a warrior is galloping on his pony into battle.

Frederick S. Remington, "The Cheyenne," 1901, cast 1904. Amon Carter Museum

http://memory.loc.gov/ammem/award98/ienhtml/curthome.html

Frederick Remington, "The Rattlesnake," (1905) Bronze (Height 23 7/8 inches), now at Amon Carter Museum, Fort Worth, Texas. Note how the rattlesnake has reverted from national symbol to natural menace as the cowboy's horse rears up and threatens to throw its rider.

Frederick S. Remington, "The Rattlesnake," 1905. Amon Carter Museum

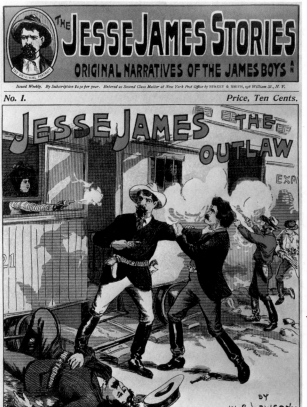

◀ **"Dime novels" purported to tell true tales of western adventure.** Jesse James was an historical figure, even if the stories in this "Log Cabin Library" edition bore no resemblance to his actual deeds. "The King of the Wild West" was a purely fictional creation.

From the Library of Congress's American Memory site
http://www.loc.gov/exhibits/treasures/tri015.html

20 Politics and Government
1877—1900

CHAPTER HIGHLIGHTS

The Structure and Style of Politics Politics was dominated by the two major parties. Virtually all men participated in politics. Religious, ethnic, and regional factors determined party ties, but third parties emerged around issues. Women gained full or partial suffrage in some states.

The Limits of Government By present standards, government was neither productive nor efficient. A weak president, closely matched parties, and a small and inefficient bureaucracy combined to limit government action.

Public Policy and National Elections The national political arena was dominated by several issues, including civil service reform, tariffs, and business and financial regulations. Despite the passion they evoked, these issues divided both parties and therefore played only a small role in determining elections and were seldom solved by government action.

The Crisis of the 1890s In the 1890s, a third-party challenge generated by agricultural discontent disrupted the party system. A depression added to the crisis. Changing public attitudes led to new demands on government and the realignment of parties and voters.

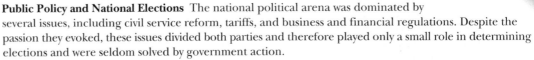

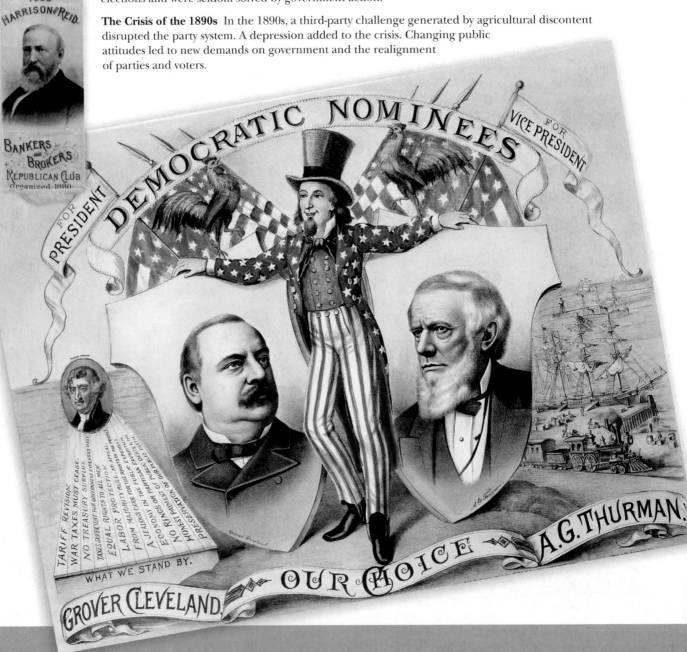

CHAPTER QUESTIONS

HOW DID parties mobilize voters in the late nineteenth century?

HOW EFFECTIVE was the federal government in addressing the problems of America's industrializing economy?

WHY WERE monetary issues so important to so many Americans at the end of the nineteenth century?

WHAT FACTORS contributed to the rise and fall of the Populist party?

CHAPTER OUTLINE

- The Structure and Style of Politics
- The Limits of Government
- Public Policies and National Elections
- The Crisis of the 1890s

IMAGE KEY
for pages 574–575 is on page 599.

The largest political procession of the season in Fort Wayne, so far, was that of the Republicans Saturday night. They turned out in very large numbers and paraded on the principal streets preparatory to the speaking which came later at the Rifles' armory. The following were in line:

First Regiment Band

Railroad Men's Club

Soldiers' and Sons' Union Club

Tippecanoe Club

Chase Club

Lincoln Club

McKinley Club

Colored Drum Corps

Colored Republicans' Club

Republican Voters

The McKinley Club wore tin hats and the Tippecanoe Club carried torches that spouted fire at intervals. One of the prettiest illuminations was the railroad lantern light of the Railroad Men's Republican club. The numerous lights of the colors used in the railway service make as pretty a sight as can be seen anywhere.

Most of the clubs were in fine uniforms and made a grand appearance. Numerous banners and transparencies announcing mottoes of the campaign were carried. One banner bore the words, "Cleveland's record—Glad Lincoln was shot—Pronounced the war a failure."

The great parade was viewed by thousands of people who thronged the streets all along the line of march.

The hall was crowded and the meeting was most enthusiastic. Music was furnished by the band and Emerson quartette of Huntington. . . . The quartette just took the cake. Anything more enjoyable and mirth-provoking than their glees rendered as they render them would be hard to find. After music by the quartette, which was enthusiastically encored, Dr. Stemen, the presiding officer, introduced the speaker of the evening, Hon. L.R. Stookey, of Warsaw, Ind. Mr. Stookey is a ready and rapid speaker. He paid a glowing tribute to the soldiers, and referred in scathing terms to Grover Cleveland's treatment of them and his insulting vetoes of pension bills. He spoke . . . [of a law providing for election supervisors at the polls] and what we ask is that it shall apply without limitation north and south whenever there is an attempt or danger of attempt, to deny equal rights of all to cast their free ballot and have it counted as cast.

When he concluded the Emerson quartette gave another selection and responded to an encore. The audience then began to call loudly for "You," "You." Mr. A.J. You, our candidate for congress, was then introduced and made a stirring address. Mr. You has been speaking nearly every day and

evening and is holding out first rate and proving himself one of the most pop-
ular candidates in the field.

  He was repeatedly and enthusiastically cheered during his speech. An-
other selection by the quartette, and the house resounded with calls for
"Brown," "Brown." Rev. W.H. Brown, for years the pastor of the A.M.E.
church, of this city, took the platform and though he protested that the hour
was too late to permit another speech made it clearly evident in the course of a
twenty minute speech that the colored people of the country understand the sit-
uation and intend to stand by the party that broke the chains and gave free-
dom to the slave. The meeting then adjourned to music by the Glee club.

  Source: Fort Wayne (Ind.) *Weekly Gazette,* October 20, 1892.

THE *Fort Wayne Weekly Gazette,* a fiercely Republican newspaper, proudly reported on the activities of the local Republicans in Indiana during the political campaign in 1892. Parites used these activities to mobilize ardently partisan voters into a politics of participation. The pageantry and hoopla made politics a major source of popular entertainment for Republicans and Democrats alike. But the extreme campaign rhetoric and outright misrepresentation of opponents—the Republican insistence that the Democratic presidential candidate, Grover Cleveland, had been pleased by the assassination of Abraham Lincoln— indicated the intensity of partisan emotions. So did the military-style campaign, with uniformed marchers organized into companies, brigades, and divisions; with signs, slogans, and speeches referring to soldiers and the Civil War. These campaign features also pointed to the enduring importance of the Civil War as a basis for partisan divisions and loyalties and marked electoral politics as a masculine business.

  At the same time, contemporary issues did matter. The marchers' tin hats were an unmistakable and favorable reference to a controversial Republican tariff law that had so prohibitively taxed foreign tin plate that an American tin-plate-manufacturing industry emerged. Stookey's stump appeal for election supervisors to protect voters' rights at the polls similarly pointed to an important policy issue while hinting at the sometimes violent nature of elections.

  The prominent role of Rev. Brown, the content of his speech, and the participation of the Colored Drum Corps and the Colored Republicans' Club in the parade show that partisan divisions in the United States overlapped with racial, religious, and other social divisions. Black voters, for instance, would "stand by the party that broke the chains and gave freedom to the slave." The journey to the polls, symbolized by the parade through Fort Wayne, invoked the most basic beliefs and values of Americans.

  While the *Gazette* lavished praise on the Republican campaign and ridiculed the opposition, its Democratic counterpart, the *Fort Wayne Sentinel,* extolled the success of the Democratic campaign, the enthusiasm of Democratic crowds, the integrity of Democratic candidates, and the despicable nature of the Republican Party. Such partisanship permeated journalism as well as nearly all aspects of public life, including government agencies.

  These features of late-nineteenth-century politics would eventually be transformed in significant ways. But while they endured, they shaped not only campaigns and elections but also the form and role of government. Only a national crisis in the

Chronology

1867	Patrons of Husbandry (the Grange) is founded.
1869	Massachusetts establishes the first state regulatory commission.
1873	Silver is demonetized in the "Crime of '73."
1874	Woman's Christian Temperance Union is organized.
1875	U.S. Supreme Court, in *Minor v. Happersett,* upholds denial of suffrage to women.
1876	Greenback Party runs presidential candidate.
1877	Rutherford B. Hayes becomes president after disputed election.
	Farmers' Alliance is founded.
	Supreme Court, in *Munn v. Illinois,* upholds state regulatory authority over private property.
1878	Bland-Allison Act obliges the government to buy silver.
1880	James A. Garfield is elected president.
1881	Garfield is assassinated; Chester A. Arthur becomes president.
1883	Pendleton Civil Service Act is passed.
1884	Grover Cleveland is elected president.
1886	Supreme Court, in *Wabash v. Illinois,* rules that only the federal government, not the states, can regulate interstate commerce.
1887	Interstate Commerce Act is passed.

1888	Benjamin Harrison is elected president.
1890	Sherman Antitrust Act is passed.
	McKinley Tariff Act is passed.
	Sherman Silver Purchase Act is passed.
	National American Woman Suffrage Association is organized.
	Wyoming enters the Union as the first state with woman suffrage.
1892	People's Party is organized.
	Cleveland is elected to his second term as president.
1893	Depression begins.
	Sherman Silver Purchase Act is repealed.
1894	Coxey's Army marches to Washington.
	Pullman strike ends in violence.
1895	Supreme Court, in *Pollock v. Farmers' Loan and Trust Company,* invalidates the federal income tax.
	Supreme Court, in *United States v. E. C. Knight Company,* limits the Sherman Antitrust Law to commerce, excluding industrial monopolies.
1896	William Jennings Bryan is nominated for president by Democrats and Populists.
	William McKinley is elected president.
1900	Currency Act puts U.S. currency on the gold standard.

1890s would finally cause some Americans to demand more of their political leaders and institutions.

HOW DID parties mobilize voters in the late nineteenth century?

THE STRUCTURE AND STYLE OF POLITICS

Political parties dominated political life. They organized campaigns, controlled balloting, and held the unswerving loyalty of most of the electorate. While the major parties worked to maintain a sense of unity and tradition among their followers, third parties sought to activate those the major parties left unserved. Other Americans looked outside the electoral arena to fulfill their political goals.

CAMPAIGNS AND ELECTIONS

Political campaigns and elections generated remarkable public participation and constituted a major form of entertainment. In cities and towns across the nation, as in Fort Wayne, thousands of men in elaborate uniforms marched in massive torchlight parades to demonstrate partisan enthusiasm. Political picnics and camp meetings served a comparable function in rural areas.

The excitement of political contests prompted the wife of Chief Justice Morrison Waite to write longingly on election day, 1876, "I should want to vote all day." But women, though they often identified with and endorsed a political party, could not vote at all in national elections. Justice Waite himself had just a year earlier written the unanimous opinion of the Supreme Court (in *Minor v. Happersett*) that the Constitution did not confer suffrage on women.

Virtually all men participated in politics. In many states, even immigrants not yet citizens were eligible to vote and flocked to the polls. African Americans voted regularly in the North and irregularly in the South before being disfranchised at the end of the century. Overall, turnout was remarkably high, averaging nearly 80 percent of eligible voters in presidential elections between 1876 and 1900.

Political parties mobilized this huge electorate. They kept detailed records of voters, transported them to the polls, and sometimes even paid their poll taxes or naturalization fees to make them eligible. With legal regulations and public machinery for elections negligible, parties dominated the campaigns and elections. Until the 1890s, most states had no laws to ensure secrecy in voting, and ballots were printed by the parties.

Because they had only the names of the candidates of the party issuing them and often varied in size and color ballots revealed the voters' party allegiance. Paid party workers, known as peddlers or hawkers, stationed themselves near the polls, each trying to force his ticket on prospective voters.

The open and partisan aspects of the electoral process did not necessarily lead to election fraud, however much they shaped the nature of political participation. In these circumstances, campaigns and elections provided opportunities for men to demonstrate publicly their commitment to their party and its values, thereby reinforcing their partisan loyalties.

Nonvoting women, too, often exhibited their partisanship in this exciting political environment. Women wrote partisan literature and gave campaign speeches. Sometimes partisan women acted together with men; other times they worked through separate women's organizations such as the Woman's Natoinal Republican Association. In these partisan groups women discussed and circulated party literature and devised plans to influence elections. Their partisanship was so deeply embedded that they remained loyal Republicans even when the party repudiated woman suffrage. "What discourages me about women," noted suffragist Susan B. Anthony, was that they care more for "[their] political party . . . than for [their] own political rights."

PARTISAN POLITICS

A remarkably close balance prevailed between the two major parties in the elections of this era. Democrats and Republicans had virtually the same level of electoral support, one reason they worked so hard to get out the vote (see Map 20–1). Control of the presidency and Congress

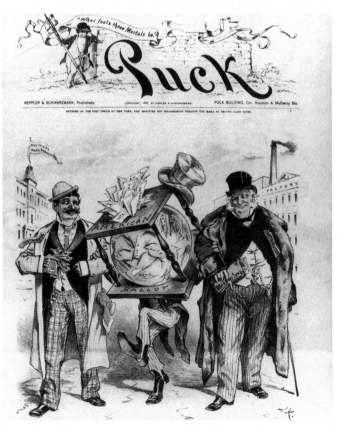

The lack of public controls over party-dominated elections led some Americans to fear that shady politicians and powerful special interests could corrupt the ballot box and thwart popular will.

Stock Montage, Inc./Historical Pictures Collection

WHERE TO LEARN MORE

Rest Cottage, Evanston, Illinois
www.wctu.org/house.html

MAP EXPLORATION
To explore an interactive version of this map, go to
http://www.prenhall.com/goldfield3/map20.1

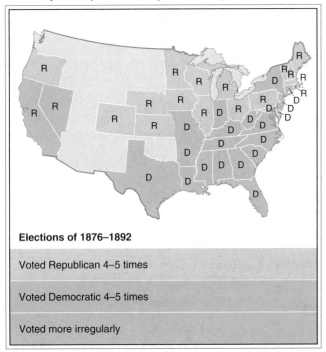

Elections of 1876–1892

Voted Republican 4–5 times

Voted Democratic 4–5 times

Voted more irregularly

MAP 20–1   **The Two-Party Stalemate of the Late Nineteenth Century**
Strong parties, staunch loyalties, and an evenly divided electorate
made for exciting politics but often stalemated government in the
late nineteenth century. Most states voted consistently for one of
the major parties, leaving the few swing states like New York and
Indiana the scenes of fierce partisan battles.

WHAT WAS the geographical pattern of Republican
versus Democratic voting during this time period?

shifted back and forth. Rarely did either party control both
branches of government at once.

The party balance gave great influence to New York,
New Jersey, Ohio, and Indiana, whose evenly divided voters
controlled electoral votes that could swing an election either
way. Both parties tended to nominate presidential and vice
presidential candidates from those states to woo their voters. The parties also concentrated campaign funds and
strategy on the swing states. Thus the Republican presidential candidate James Garfield of Ohio commented in
1880: "Nothing is wanting except an immediate and liberal
supply of money for campaign expenses to make Indiana
certain. With a victory there, the rest is easy." Garfield narrowly carried Indiana by 6,000 votes, and the nation by 9,000
out of 9.2 million cast. His victory was not the outcome of
a contest over great issues but of carefully organized, tightly
balanced parties mobilizing their supporters.

Party Loyalty.   Interrelated regional, ethnic, religious,
and local factors determined the party affiliations of most
Americans. Economic issues, although important to the
politics of the era, generally did not decide party ties.
Farmers, for example, despite their many shared economic concerns, affiliated with both major parties. Like
religious belief and ethnic identity, partisan loyalty was
largely a cultural trait passed from parents to children.

Republicans were strongest in the North and Midwest, where they benefited from their party's role as the
defender of the Union in the Civil War. "Republicanism
in [Iowa] is not a logical conviction," reported one journalist in 1884; "it is a baleful fanaticism. . . . The war is
still in progress in this region. . . . The women are worse
than the men; they are intolerant, ferocious, implacable."
The Republican Party appealed primarily to old-stock Americans and other Protestants, including those of German and Scandinavian descent. African Americans,
loyal to the party that had emancipated and enfranchised the slaves of the South,
also voted the Republican wherever possible. Democrats were strongest in the
South, where they stood as the defenders of the traditions of the region's white
population. But Democrats also drew support in the urban Northeast, especially
from Catholics and recent immigrants.

Party Identities.   Each major party consisted of a complex coalition of groups
with differing traditions and interests. One observer of the Democratic Party in California described it as "a sort of Democratic happy family, like we see in the prairie-
dog villages, where owls, rattlesnakes, prairie dogs, and lizards all live in the same
hole." To hold its coalition together, each party identified itself with a theme that appealed broadly to all its constituents.

Republicans identified their party with nationalism and national unity and
attacked the Democrats as an "alliance between the embittered South and the

slums of the Northern cities." They combined a "bloody shirt" appeal to the memories of the Civil War with campaigns for immigration restriction and cultural uniformity. Seeing a threat to American society in efforts by Catholic immigrants to preserve their ethnic and cultural traditions, for example, Republican legislatures in several states in the 1880s and 1890s enacted laws regulating parochial schools, the use of foreign languages, and alcohol consumption.

Democrats portrayed themselves as the party of limited government and "personal liberties," a theme that appealed to both the racism of white southerners and the resentment immigrants felt about the nativist meddling of Republicans. The Democrats' commitment to personal liberties had limits. They supported the disfranchisement of African Americans, the exclusion of Chinese immigrants, and the dispossession of American Indians.

The partisan politics of both major parties culminated in party machines, especially at the local level. Led by powerful bosses, such as the Democrat Richard Croker of New York and the Republican George Cox of Cincinnati, the machines controlled not only city politics but also municipal government. Party activists used well-organized ward clubs to mobilize working-class voters, who were rewarded with municipal jobs and baskets of food or coal doled out by the machine. Public contracts and franchises were peddled to businesses whose high bids covered kickbacks to the machine.

Third Parties.   The partisan politics of the era left room for several third parties, organized around specific issues or groups. The **Prohibition Party** persistently championed the abolition of alcohol but also supported electoral reforms such as woman suffrage, economic reforms such as railroad regulation and income taxes, and social reforms including improved race relations. Some farmers and workers formed larger but shorter-lived third parties, charging that Republicans and Democrats had failed to respond to economic problems caused by industrialization or, worse still, had deliberately promoted powerful business interests at the expense of ordinary Americans. The **Greenback Party** of the 1870s denounced "the infamous financial legislation which takes all from the many to enrich the few." Its policies of labor reform and currency inflation (to stimulate and democratize the economy) attracted supporters from Maine to Texas. The most significant third party was the People's or **Populist Party** of the 1890s.

ASSOCIATIONAL POLITICS

Associations of like-minded citizens, operating outside the electoral arena, played an increasingly important role in late-nineteenth-century politics. These organizations worked to achieve public policies beneficial to their members. Farmers organized many such groups, most notably the Patrons of Husbandry, known familiarly as the Grange (see Chapter 17). Its campaign for public regulation of the rates charged by railroads and grain elevators helped convince midwestern states to pass the so-called **Granger laws.**

To the Grangers' dismay, industrialists also formed pressure groups. Organizations such as the American Iron and Steel Association and the American Protective Tariff League lobbied Congress for high tariff laws and made campaign contributions to friendly politicians of both parties.

A small group of conservative reformers known derisively as **Mugwumps** (the term derives from the Algonquian word for "chief") devoted most of their efforts to campaigning for honest and efficient government through civil service reform.

A meeting in 1880 of the National Woman Suffrage Association protested the exclusion of women from electoral politics. Susan B. Anthony noted with regret that "to all men woman suffrage is only a side issue."

The Granger Collection, New York

WHERE TO LEARN MORE

Susan B. Anthony House National Historic Landmark, Rochester, New York www.susanbanthonyhouse .org/main.html

National American Woman Suffrage Association The organization, formed in 1890, that coordinated the ultimately successful campaign to achieve women's right to vote.

HOW EFFECTIVE was the federal government in addressing the problems of America's industrializing economy?

They organized the National Civil Service Reform League to publicize their cause and lobby Congress. Other pressure groups focused on cultural politics. The rabidly anti-Catholic American Protective Association, for example, agitated for laws restricting immigration, taxing church property, and inspecting Catholic religious institutions.

Women as Activists. Women were also active in associational politics. Susan B. Anthony and others formed groups to lobby Congress and state legislatures for constitutional amendments extending the right to vote to women. The leading organizations merged in 1890 as the **National American Woman Suffrage Association.** Despite the opposition of male politicians of both major parties, suffragists had succeeded by the mid-1890s in gaining full woman suffrage in four western states—Wyoming, Colorado, Idaho, and Utah—and partial suffrage (the right to vote in school elections) in several other states, east and west.

With petition campaigns, demonstrations, and lobbying, women's social service organizations sought to remedy poverty and disease, improve education and recreation, and provide day nurseries for the children of working women. The Illinois Woman's Alliance—organized in 1888 by suffragists, women assemblies of the Knights of Labor, and middle-class women's clubs—investigated the conditions of women and children in workshops and factories—and campaigned successfully for protective labor legislation and compulsory school-attendance laws.

The Woman's Christian Temperance Union (WCTU) gained a massive membership by campaigning for restrictive liquor laws. Under the leadership of Frances Willard, the WCTU built on traditional women's concerns to develop an important critique of American society. Reversing the conventional view, Willard argued that alcohol abuse was a result, not a cause, of poverty and social disorder. Under the slogan of "Home Protection," the WCTU inserted domestic issues into the political sphere with a campaign for social and economic reforms far beyond temperance. It particularly sought to strengthen and enforce laws against rape. Willard bitterly noted that 20 states fixed the age of consent at ten and that "in Massachusetts and Vermont it is a greater crime to steal a cow" than to rape a woman. The WCTU also pushed for improved health conditions, reached out to the Knights of Labor to support workplace reforms, and lobbied for federal aid to education, particularly as a means to provide schooling for black children in the South. It eventually supported woman suffrage as well, on the grounds that women needed the vote to fulfill their duty to protect home, family, and morality.

THE LIMITS OF GOVERNMENT

Despite the popular enthusiasm for partisan politics and the persistent pressure of associational politics, government in the late nineteenth century was neither active nor productive by present standards. The receding governmental activism of the Civil War and Reconstruction years coincided with a resurgent belief in localism and **laissez-faire** policies. In addition, a Congress and presidency divided between the two major parties, a small and inefficient bureaucracy, and judicial restraints joined powerful private interests to limit the size and objectives of the federal government.

THE WEAK PRESIDENCY

The presidency was a weak and restricted institution. The impeachment of President Johnson at the outset of Reconstruction had undermined the office. President Grant clearly subordinated it to the legislative branch by deferring to Congress on appointments and legislation. Other factors contributed as well. The men who filled the office between 1877 and 1897—Republicans Rutherford B. Hayes (1877–1881), James A. Garfield (1881), and Chester A. Arthur (1881–1885); Democrat Grover Cleveland (1885–1889 and 1893–1897); and Republican Benjamin Harrison (1889–1893)—were all honest and generally capable. Each had built a solid political record at the state or federal level. But they were all conservatives, with a narrow view of the presidency, and proposed few initiatives. The most aggressive of them, Cleveland, used his energy in a singularly negative fashion, vetoing two-thirds of all the bills Congress passed, more than all his predecessors combined.

The presidents of this era viewed their duties as chiefly administrative and made little effort to reach out to the public or to exert legislative leadership. (See Global Perspectives: "Why Great Men Are Not Chosen Presidents.") In 1885, Woodrow Wilson, at the time a professor of history and government, described "the business of the president" as "not much above routine" and concluded that the office might "not inconveniently" be made purely administrative, its occupant a sort of tenured civil servant.

The presidency was also hampered by its limited control over bureaus and departments, which responded more directly to Congress, and by its small staff. As Cleveland complained, "If the President has any great policy in mind or on hand he has no one to help him work it out."

THE INEFFICIENT CONGRESS

Congress was the foremost branch of the national government. It exercised authority over the federal budget, oversaw the cabinet, debated public issues, and controlled legislation. Its members were often state and national party leaders, who were strong-willed and, as one senator conceded, "tolerated no intrusion from the President or from anybody else."

But Congress was scarcely efficient. The repeated shifts in party control impeded effective action. So, too, did the loss of experienced legislators to rapid turnover. In some Congresses, a majority of members were first-termers. Procedural rules, based on precedents from a simpler time and manipulated by determined partisans, hindered congressional action. The most notorious rule required that a quorum be not only present but voting. When the House was narrowly divided along party lines, the minority could block all business simply by refusing to answer when the roll was called.

But as a nationalizing economy required more national legislation, the amount of business before Congress grew relentlessly. The expanding scale of congressional work prompted a gradual reform of procedures and the centralization of power in the Speaker of the House and the leading committees. These changes did not, however, create a coherent program for government action.

18–3
The Gilded Age (1880)

Laissez-faire   The doctrine that government should not intervene in the economy, especially through regulation.

GLOBAL PERSPECTIVES

"WHY GREAT MEN ARE NOT CHOSEN PRESIDENTS"

American politics and government were subjects of great interest to Europeans. Accustomed to monarchs, prime ministers, parliaments, and efficient civil service bureaucracies, they found perplexing the decentralized American system of federalism, the emphasis on localism and laissez-faire, and the popular frenzy and organizational thrust of partisan politics. Nothing was more fascinating than the character of American political leaders, who seemed to Europeans to be consistently unimaginative and dull. As one noted, "The only thing remarkable about them is that being so commonplace they should have climbed so high."

Lord James Bryce of Great Britain provided the classic European perspective on the American presidency in 1888. "Europeans often ask," Bryce observed, "how it happens that this great office . . . is not more frequently filled by great and striking men?" This seemed particularly puzzling given that the United States boasted of an open society which rewarded ability, not one bound by the hereditary distinctions of aristocracy.

Most important in explaining the absence of "brilliancy" among American presidents, Bryce ventured, was the political system of the United States, with its party-dominated politics and its limited government.

"In America party loyalty and party organization have been hitherto so perfect that any one put forward by the party will get the full party vote if his character is good and his "record," as they call it, unstained. . . . Even those who admit his mediocrity will vote straight when the moment for voting comes. Besides, the ordinary American voter does not object to mediocrity. He has a lower conception of the qualities requisite to make a statesman than those who direct public opinion in Europe have. He likes his candidates to be sensible, vigorous, and, above all, what he calls "magnetic," and does not value, because he sees no need for, originality or profundity, a fine culture or a wide knowledge. . . .

After all, . . . a President need not be a man of brilliant intellectual gifts. Englishmen, imagining him as something like their prime minister, assume that he ought to be a dazzling orator, able to sway legislatures or multitudes, possessed also of the constructive powers that can devise a great policy or frame a comprehensive piece of legislation. They forget that the President does not sit in Congress, . . . submit bills nor otherwise influence the action of the legislature. His main duties are to be prompt and firm in securing the due execution of the laws and maintaining the public peace. . . . Eloquence, . . . imagination, profundity of thought or extent of knowledge . . . are not necessary."

THE FEDERAL BUREAUCRACY AND THE SPOILS SYSTEM

Reflecting presidential weakness and congressional inefficiency, the federal bureaucracy remained small and limited in the late nineteenth century. There were little more than 50,000 government employees in 1871, and three-fourths of them were local postmasters scattered across the nation. The number of federal employees grew to 157,000 in 1891 but it was still the postal service that absorbed most of this increase.

The system for selecting and supervising federal officials had developed gradually in the first half of the century. Known as the spoils system, its basic principle was that victorious politicians awarded government jobs to party workers, with little regard for qualifications, and ousted the previous employees. Appointees then typically promised part of their salary and time to the political interests of their patron or party. The spoils system played a crucial role in all aspects of politics.

It enabled party leaders to strengthen their organizations, reward loyal party service, and attract the political workers needed to mobilize the electorate.

Critics, however, charged that the system was riddled with corruption, abuse, and inefficiency. Rapid turnover bred instability; political favoritism bred incompetence. Even worse, the spoils system absorbed the president and Congress in unproductive conflicts over patronage.

INCONSISTENT STATE GOVERNMENT

Considered closer and more responsible to the people, state governments had long exercised police power and regulatory authority. They collected taxes for education and public works, and they promoted private enterprise and public health. Still, they did little by today's standards. Few people thought it appropriate for government at any level to offer direct help to particular social groups.

Nonetheless, state governments gradually expanded their role in response to the stresses produced by industrialization. Following the lead of Massachusetts in 1869, most states had by the turn of the century created commissions to investigate and regulate industry. Public intervention in other areas of the economy soon followed, as one observer noted, in "utter disregard of the laissez-faire principle." In Minnesota, for example, the state helped farmers by establishing a dairy commission, prohibiting the manufacture or sale of margarine, creating a bureau of animal industry, and employing state veterinarians. Other laws regulated railroads, telegraphs, and dangerous occupations, prohibited racial discrimination in inns, and otherwise protected the public welfare.

Not all such agencies and laws were effective, nor were all state governments as diligent as Minnesota's. Southern states, especially, lagged, and one midwesterner complained that his legislature "meets in ignorance, sits in corruption, and dissolves in disgrace every two years." Still, the widening scope of state action represented a growing acceptance of public responsibility for social welfare and economic life.

PUBLIC POLICIES AND NATIONAL ELECTIONS

Several great issues dominated the national political arena in the late nineteenth century, including civil service reform, tariffs, and business and financial regulation. Rarely, however, did these issues clearly and consistently separate the major political parties. Instead, they divided each party into factions along regional, interest, and economic lines. As a consequence, these leading issues often played only a small role in determining elections and were seldom resolved by government action.

CIVIL SERVICE REFORM

Reform of the spoils system emerged as a prominent issue during the Hayes administration. The Mugwumps and other reformers wanted a professional civil service, based on merit and divorced from politics. They expected such a system to promote efficiency, economy, and honesty in government. But they also expected it to increase their own influence. As one Baltimore Mugwump said, civil service reform would replace ignorant and corrupt officeholders with "gentlemen . . . who need nothing and want nothing from government except the satisfaction of using their talents," or at least with "sober, industrious . . . middle-class persons who have taken over . . . the proper standards of conduct."

WHY WERE monetary issues so important to so many Americans at the end of the nineteenth century?

WHERE TO LEARN MORE

Rutherford B. Hayes Presidential Center, Fremont, Ohio
www.rbhayes.org/

WHERE TO LEARN MORE

James A. Garfield Home,
Mentor, Ohio **www.nps**
.gov/jaga/index.htm

18–7
The Assassination
of President Garfield
(1889)

Although not fully renouncing the spoils sytem, President Hayes struck a blow for civil service reform by firing Chester A. Arthur from his post as New York customs-house collector after an investigation found Arthur's patronage system characterized by ignorance, inefficiency, and corruption."

But the weakness of the civil service reformers was dramatically underscored in 1880 when the Republicans, to improve their chances of carrying the crucial state of New York, nominated Arthur for vice president on a ticket headed by James Garfield of Ohio. They won, and Garfield immediately found himself enmeshed in the demands of the unreformed spoils system. He once complained to his wife, "I had hardly arrived before the door-bell began to ring and the old stream of office-seekers began to pour in. . . . All day long it has been a steeple chase, I fleeing and they pursuing." Within a few months of his inauguration in 1881, Garfield was assassinated by a disappointed and crazed office seeker, and Arthur became president.

Public dismay over this tragedy finally spurred changes in the spoils system. Arthur himself urged Congress to act, and in 1883, it passed the **Pendleton Civil Service Act.** This measure prohibited federal employees from soliciting or receiving political contributions from government workers and created the Civil Service Commission to administer competitive examinations to applicants for government jobs. A professional civil service free from partisan politics gradually emerged, strengthening the executive branch's ability to handle its increasing administrative responsibilities.

The new emphasis on merit and skill rather than party ties opened new opportunities to women. By the early 1890s, women held a third of the clerical positions in the executive departments in Washington. Their work in public life challenged the conventional belief that a woman's ability and personality limited her to the domestic sphere. One woman described her "brain work" as an examiner of accounts in the Interior Department in 1893 as "demanding the closest and most critical attention, together with a great deal of legal and business knowledge."

THE POLITICAL LIFE OF THE TARIFF

Tariffs on imported goods provided revenue for the federal government and protected American industry from European competition. They promoted industrial growth but often allowed favored industries to garner high profits. By the 1880s, tariffs covered 4,000 items and generated more revenue than the government needed to carry on its limited operations.

Reflecting its commitment to industry, the Republican Party vigorously championed protective tariffs. Party leaders also claimed that American labor benefited from tariff protection. "Reduce the tariff, and labor is the first to suffer," declared William McKinley of Ohio. Most Democrats, by contrast, favored tariff reduction, a position that reflected their party's relatively laissez-faire outlook. They argued that lower tariffs would encourage foreign trade, lower the cost of living, and, by reducing the treasury surplus, minimize the temptation for the government to pursue activist policies (see the Overview table, "Arguments in the Tariff Debates").

The differences between the parties, however, were often more rhetorical than substantial. They disagreed only about how high tariffs should be and what interests they should protect. California Democrats called for protective duties on wool and raisins, products produced in California; Massachusetts Republicans, to aid their state's shoe manufacturers, supported tariffs on shoes but opposed

---

QUICK REVIEW

Tariffs and Politics

• Tariffs provided revenues and protected American industries from competition.

• Republicans were strong supporters of protective tariffs.

• Congressmen voted for tariffs that benefited their home districts.

Pendelton Civil Service Act
A law of 1883 that reformed the spoils system by prohibiting government workers from making political contributions and creating the Civil Service Commission to oversee their appointment on the basis of merit rather than politics.

OVERVIEW   ARGUMENTS IN THE TARIFF DEBATES

Area Affected	High-Tariff Advocates	Low-Tariff Advocates
Industry	Tariffs promote industrial growth.	Tariffs inflate corporate profits.
Employment	Tariffs stimulate job growth.	Tariffs restrict competition.
Wages and prices	Tariffs permit higher wages.	Tariffs increase consumer prices.
Government	Tariffs provide government revenue.	Tariffs violate the principle of laissez-faire and produce revenues that tempt the government to activism.
Trade	Tariffs protect the domestic market.	Tariffs restrict foreign trade.

tariffs on leather. A Democratic senator from Indiana, elected on a campaign pledge to reduce tariffs, summed up the prevailing rule succinctly: "I am a protectionist for every interest which I am sent here by my constituents to protect."

In the 1884 campaign, the Republican presidential candidate, James G. Blaine, maintained that prosperity and high employment depended on high tariffs. The Democrats' platform endorsed a lowered tariff, but their candidate, Grover Cleveland, generally ignored the issue. Unable to address this and other important issues, both parties resorted to scandal mongering. The Democrats exploited Blaine's image as a beneficiary of the spoils system. Republicans responded by exposing Cleveland as the father of an illegitimate child.

Cleveland continued to avoid the tariff issue for three years after his election, until the growing treasury surplus and rising popular pressure for tariff reduction prompted him to act. He devoted his entire 1887 annual message to attacking the "vicious, inequitable, and illogical" tariff, apparently making it the dominant issue of his 1888 reelection campaign. Once again, however, the distinctive political attribute of the period—intense and organized campaigning between closely balanced parties—forced both Democrats and Republicans to blur their positions. Cleveland proposed a Democratic platform that ignored his recent message and did not even use the word *tariff*. Cleveland won slightly more popular votes than his Republican opponent, Benjamin Harrison of Indiana, but Harrison carried the electoral college, indicating the decisive importance of strategic campaigning, local issues, and large campaign funds rather than great national issues.

The triumphant Republicans raised tariff rates to prohibitive levels with the McKinley Tariff Act of 1890. The law provoked a popular backlash that helped return the Democrats to power. Still, the Democrats made little effort to push tariff reform.

WHERE TO LEARN MORE

President Benjamin Harrison's Home, Indianapolis, Indiana
www.presidentbenjaminharrison.org/

THE BEGINNINGS OF FEDERAL REGULATION

While business leaders pressed for protective tariffs and other public policies that promoted their interests, they otherwise used their great political influence to ensure governmental laissez-faire. Popular pressure nonetheless compelled Congress to take the first steps toward the regulation of business with the passage of the Interstate Commerce Act in 1887 and the Sherman Antitrust Act in 1890.

The rapid growth of great industrial corporations and their disruptive effects on traditional practices and values profoundly alarmed the public (see

Chapter 18). Farmers condemned the power of corporations over transportation facilities and their monopolization of industries affecting agriculture. Small business owners suffered from the destructive competition of corporations, workers were exploited by their control of the labor market, and consumers felt victimized by high prices.

Popular concern focused first on the railroads, the preeminent symbol of big business. The resulting pressure was responsible for the Granger laws enacted in several midwestern states in the 1870s to regulate railroad freight and storage rates. At first, the Supreme Court upheld this legislation, ruling in *Munn v. Illinois* (1877) that state governments had the right to regulate private property when it was "devoted to a public use." But in 1886, the Court ruled in *Wabash, St. Louis, and Pacific Railway Company v. Illinois* that only the federal government could regulate interstate commerce. This decision effectively ended state regulation of railroads but simultaneously increased pressure for congressional action. With the support of both major parties, Congress in 1887 passed the **Interstate Commerce Act.**

The act prohibited rebates, discriminatory rates, and pooling and established the **Interstate Commerce Commission (ICC)** to investigate and prosecute violations. The ICC was the first federal regulatory agency. But its powers were too limited to be effective. Senator Nelson Aldrich of Rhode Island, a leading spokesman for business interests, described the law as an "empty menace to great interests, made to answer the clamor of the ignorant." Railroads continued their objectionable practices. They frustrated the commission by refusing to provide required information and endlessly appealing its orders to a conservative judiciary. In its first 15 years, only one court case was decided in favor of the ICC. Not surprisingly, popular dissatisfaction with the railroads continued into the twentieth century.

Many people saw railroad abuses as indicative of the dangers of corporate power in general and demanded a broader federal response. Exposés of the monopolistic practices of such corporations as Standard Oil forced both major parties to endorse national antitrust legislation during the campaign of 1888. In 1890, Congress enacted the **Sherman Antitrust Act** with only a single vote in opposition. But this near-unanimity concealed real differences over the desirability and purpose of the law. Although it emphatically prohibited any combination in restraint of trade (any attempt to restrict competition), the law was vaguely written and too weak to prevent abuses. The courts further weakened the act, and presidents of both parties made little effort to enforce it. Corporations remained as ominous threat in the eyes of many Americans.

THE MONEY QUESTION

President Garfield suggested the complexities of monetary policy when he wryly declared that a member of Congress had been committed to an asylum after "he devoted himself almost exclusively to the study of the currency, became fully entangled with the theories of the subject, and became insane." Despite the sometimes arcane and difficult nature of the money question, millions of Americans adopted positions on it and defended them with religious ferocity.

Creditors, especially bankers, as well as conservative economists and many business leaders favored limiting the money supply. They called this a **sound money** policy and insisted that it would ensure economic stability, maintain property values, and retain investor confidence. Farmers and other debtors complained that this deflationary monetary policy would depress already low crop prices, drive debtors further into debt, and restrict economic opportunities. They favored ex-

Interstate Commerce Act The 1887 law that expanded federal power over business by prohibiting pooling and discriminatory rates by railroads and establishing the first federal regulatory agency, the Interstate Commerce Commission.

Interstate Commerce Commission (ICC) The first federal regulation agency, established in 1887 to oversee railroad practices.

Sherman Antitrust Act The first federal antitrust measure, passed in 1890; sought to promote economic competition by prohibiting business combinations in restraint of trade or commerce.

Sound money Misleading slogan that referred to a conservative policy of restricting the money supply and adhering to the gold standard.

panding the money supply to match the country's growing population and economy. They expected this inflationary policy to raise prices, stimulate the economy, reduce debt burdens, and increase opportunities.

The conservative leadership of both major parties supported the sound money policy, but their rank-and-file membership included many inflationists. As a result, the parties avoided confronting each other on the money issue.

The conflict between advocates of sound money and inflation centered on the use of paper money, or "greenbacks," and silver coinage. The greenback controversy had its roots in the Civil War. To meet its expenses during the war, the federal government issued $450 million in greenbacks, paper money backed only by the credit of the United States, not by gold or silver, the traditional basis of currency. In 1875, sound money advocates in Congress enacted a deflationary law that withdrew some greenbacks from circulation and required that the remainder be convertible into gold after 1878. Outraged inflationists organized the Greenback Party. They charged that the major parties had "failed to take the side of the people" and instead supported the "great moneyed institutions." The Greenbackers polled more than a million votes in 1878 and elected 14 members of Congress. As the depression faded, however, so did interest in the greenback issue, and the party soon withered.

The Silver Issue.   Inflationists then turned their attention to the silver issue, which would prove more enduring and disruptive. Historically, the United States had been on a bimetallic standard, using both gold and silver as the basis of its currency. In 1873, Congress passed a law "demonetizing" silver, thereby making gold the only standard for American currency. Gold-standard supporters hoped that the law would promote international trade by aligning U.S. financial policy with that of Great Britain, which insisted on gold-based currency. But they also wanted to prevent new silver discoveries in the American West from expanding the money supply.

Indeed, silver production soon boomed, flooding the commercial market and dropping the value of the metal. Rural debtor groups, seeing renewed silver coinage as a means to reverse the long deflationary trend in the economy, denounced the "Crime of '73" and demanded a return to the bimetallic system.

Again, both major parties equivocated. Eastern conservatives of both parties denounced silver; southerners and westerners demanded **free silver,** meaning unlimited silver coinage. One New York Democrat complained that western and southern members of his party were "mad as wild Texas steers on this silver dollar business. As we pass each other in the streets they seem to sneer, and hiss through their teeth the words 'gold bug,' and look as if they would like to spit upon [us]." By 1878, a bipartisan coalition succeeded in passing the Bland-Allison Act. This compromise measure required the government to buy and coin at least $2 million of silver a month. However, the government never exceeded the minimum, and the law had little inflationary effect.

As hard times hit rural regions in the late 1880s, inflationists secured passage of the Sherman Silver Purchase Act of 1890. The Treasury now had to buy a larger volume of silver and pay for it with treasury notes redeemable in either gold or silver. But this, too, produced little inflation. Debtors of both parties remained convinced that the government favored the "classes rather than the masses." Gold-standard advocates (again, of both parties) were even less happy with the law and planned to repeal it at their first opportunity. The division between the two groups was deep and bitter.

Free silver   Philosophy that the government should expand the money supply by purchasing and coining all the silver offered to it.

WHAT FACTORS contributed
to the rise and fall of the
Populist Party?

THE CRISIS OF THE 1890s

*I*n the 1890s, social, economic, and political pressures created a crisis for both the political system and the government. A third-party political challenge generated by agricultural discontent disrupted traditional party politics. A devastating depression spawned social misery and labor violence. Changing public attitudes led to new demands on the government and a realignment of parties and voters.

FARMERS PROTEST INEQUITIES

The agricultural depression that engulfed the Great Plains and the South in the late 1880s brought misery and despair to millions of rural Americans. "At the age of 52 years, after a long life of toil, economy, and self-denial, I find myself and family virtual paupers," lamented one Kansan. His family's farm, rather than being "a house of refuge for our declining years, by a few turns of the monopolistic crank has been rendered valueless." To a large extent, the farmers' plight stemmed from bad weather and international overproduction of farm products. Seeking relief, however, the farmers naturally focused on the inequities of railroad discrimination, tariff favoritism, a restrictive financial system, and apparently indifferent political parties.

Credit Inequities.   Angry farmers particularly singled out the systems of money and credit that worked so completely against agricultural interests. Government rules for national banks directed credit into the urbanized North and East at the expense of the rural South and West and prohibited loans on farm property and real estate. As a result, farmers had to turn to other sources of credit and pay higher interest rates. Declining crop prices made it difficult for them to pay their debts, and mortgage foreclosures crushed the hopes of many. The government's policies of monetary deflation worsened the debt burden for all farmers.

Freight Rates and Tariffs.   Farmers protested other features of the nation's economic system as well. Railroad freight rates were two or three times higher in the West and South than in the North and East. Protective tariffs on agricultural machinery and other manufactured goods further raised their costs. By the 1890s, many farmers were convinced that the nation's economic and political institutions were aligned against them.

Farmers Organize.   In response, farmers turned to the **Farmers' Alliance,** a popular movement of protest and reform which spread across the South and West. The Farmers' Alliance restricted its membership to men and women of the "producing class" and urged them to stand "against the encroachments of monopolies and in opposition to the growing corruption of wealth and power." At first, the Alliance organized farmers' cooperatives to market crops and purchase supplies. Although some co-ops worked well, most soon failed because of the opposition of established business interests. The Alliance also developed ingenious proposals to remedy rural credit and currency problems. In the South, the Alliance pushed the subtreasury system, which called on the government to warehouse farmers' cotton and advance them credit based on its value (see Chapter 17). In the West, the Alliance proposed a system of federal loans to

Farmers' Alliance   A broad mass movement in the rural South and West during the late nineteenth century, encompassing several organizations and demanding economic and political reforms.

farmers, using land as security. These proposals were immensely popular among farmers, but the major parties and Congress rejected them. The Alliance also took up earlier calls for free silver, government control of railroads, and banking reform, again to no avail. Denouncing the indifference of the major parties and the institutions of government, William A. Peffer, the influential editor of the Alliance newspaper the *Kansas Farmer*, declared that the "time has come for action. The people will not consent to wait longer. . . . The future is full of retribution for delinquents."

THE PEOPLE'S PARTY

In the West, discontented agrarians organized independent third parties to achieve reforms the major parties had ignored. State-level third parties appeared in the elections of 1890 under many names. All eventually adopted the labels "People's" or "Populist," which were first used by a Kansas party in June 1890. The new party's campaign, marked by grim determination and fierce rhetoric, set the model for Populist politics and introduced many of the movement's leaders. One was *Kansas Farmer* editor Peffer. Others included "Sockless Jerry" Simpson, Annie Diggs, and Mary E. Lease.

When hostile business and political leaders attacked the Populist program as socialistic, Lease retorted, "You may call me an anarchist, a socialist, or a communist. I care not, but I hold to the theory that if one man has not enough to eat three times a day and another has $25,000,000, that last man has something that belongs to the first." Lease spoke as clearly against the colonial status experienced by the South and West: "The great common people of this country are slaves, and monopoly is the master. The West and South are bound and prostrate before the manufacturing East."

The Populist parties proved remarkably successful. They gained control of the legislatures of Kansas and Nebraska and won congressional elections in Kansas, Nebraska, and Minnesota. Their victories came at the expense of the Republicans, who had traditionally controlled politics in these states, and contributed to a massive defeat of the GOP in the 1890 midterm elections. Thereafter, Populists won further victories throughout the West as miners, railroad workers and small stockraisers. rallied to the cause.

In the South, the Alliance did not initially form third parties but instead attempted to seize control of the dominant Democratic Party by forcing its candidates to pledge support to the Alliance platform. The rural southern electorate then swept these "Alliance Democrats" into office, electing four governors, several dozen members of Congress, and a majority of legislators in eight states.

With their new political power, farmers enacted reform legislation in many western states. New laws regulated banks and railroads and protected debtors by capping interest rates and restricting mortgage foreclosures. Others protected unions and mandated improved workplace conditions. Still others made the political system more democratic. Populists were instrumental, for example, in winning woman suffrage in Colorado and Idaho. In the South, however, the Democratic Party frustrated reform, and most Alliance Democrats repudiated their Alliance pledges and remained loyal to their party and its traditional opposition to governmental activism.

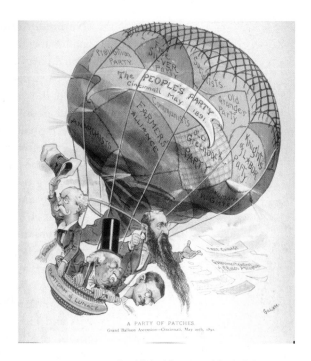

A PARTY OF PATCHES.
Grand Balloon Ascension—Cincinnati, May 20th, 1891.

Established interests ridiculed the Populists unmercifully. This hostile cartoon depicts the People's Party as an odd assortment of radical dissidents committed to a "Platform of Lunacy."
Kansas State Historical Society

19–5
The People's Party Platform (1892)

National Action.   Populists soon realized that successful reform would require national action. They met in Omaha, Nebraska, on July 4, 1892, to organize a national party and nominated former Greenbacker James B. Weaver for president. The party platform, known as the **Omaha Platform,** rejected the laissez-faire policies of the old parties: "We believe that the powers of government, in other words, of the people, should be expanded . . . to the end that oppression, injustice, and poverty shall eventually cease in the land." It demanded government ownership of the railroads and the telegraph and telephone systems, a national currency issued by the government rather than by private banks, the subtreasury system, free silver, a graduated income tax, and the redistribution to settlers of land held by railroads and speculative corporations. Accompanying resolutions endorsed the popular election of senators, the secret ballot, and other electoral reforms to make government more democratic and responsive to popular wishes.

The Populists left Omaha to begin an energetic campaign. Weaver toured the western states and with Mary Lease invaded the Democratic stronghold of the South where some Populists, such as Tom Watson of Georgia, tried to mobilize black voters. Southern Democrats, however, used violence and fraud to intimidate Populist voters and cheat Populist candidates of office. Some local Populist leaders were murdered, and Weaver was driven from the South. One Democrat confessed that Alabama's Populist gubernatorial candidate "carried the state, but was swindled out of his victory . . . with unblushing trickery and corruption."

Elsewhere, too, Populists met disappointment. Midwestern farmers unfamiliar with Alliance ideas and organization ignored Populist appeals and stood by their traditional political allegiances. So did most eastern working-class voters, who learned little of the Populist program beyond its demand for inflation, which they feared would worsen their own conditions.

The Populists lost the election but showed impressive support. They garnered more than a million votes, carried several western states, and won hundreds of state offices throughout the West and in pockets of the South, such as Texas and North Carolina. Populist leaders immediately began working to expand their support, to the alarm of both southern Democrats and northern Republicans.

THE CHALLENGE OF THE DEPRESSION

The emergence of a significant third-party movement was but one of many developments that combined by the mid-1890s to produce a national political crisis. A harsh and lengthy depression began in 1893, cruelly worsening conditions not only for farmers but for most other Americans. Labor unrest and violence engulfed the nation, reflecting workers' distress but frightening more comfortable Americans. The persistent failure of the major parties to respond to serious problems contributed mightily to the growing popular discontent. Together these developments constituted an important challenge to America's new industrial society and government.

Although the Populists lost in 1892, the election nonetheless reflected the nation's spreading dissatisfaction. Voters decisively rejected President Harrison and the incumbent Republicans in Congress, putting the Democrats in control of Congress and Grover Cleveland back in the White House. But the conservative Cleveland was almost oblivious to the mounting demand for reform, delivering an inaugural address championing laissez-faire and rejecting government action to solve social or economic problems.

Cleveland's resolve was immediately tested when the economy collapsed in the spring of 1893. Railroad overexpansion, a weak banking system, tight credit, and plunging agricultural prices all contributed to the disaster. Hundreds of banks

---

QUICK REVIEW

The Depression of 1893

- Harsh and lengthy depression began in 1893.
- By winter 1893, 20 percent of the labor force was unemployed.
- Most state governments offered little relief.

Omaha Platform   The 1892 platform of the Populist Party repudiating laissez-faire and demanding economic and political reforms to aid distressed farmers and workers.

Jacob Coxey's "Army" of the unemployed marches to Washington, D.C., in 1894. Many such "industrial armies" were organized during the depressed 1890s, revealing dissatisfaction with traditional politics and limited government.

Courtesy Library of Congress

closed, and thousands of businesses, including the nation's major railroads, went bankrupt. By winter, 20 percent of the labor force was unemployed, and the jobless scavenged for food in a country that had no public unemployment or welfare programs.

Churches, local charity societies, and labor unions tried to provide relief but were overwhelmed. Most state governments offered little relief beyond encouraging private charity to the homeless. In Kansas, however, the Populist governor insisted that traditional laissez-faire policies were inadequate: "It is the duty of government to protect the weak, because the strong are able to protect themselves." (See American Views: A Populist Views American Government.) Cleveland disagreed and showed little sympathy for the struggling. The functions of the government, he said, "do not include the support of the people."

Appeals for Federal Action. If Cleveland and Congress had no idea how the federal government might respond to the depression, other Americans did. Jacob Coxey, a Populist businessman from Ohio, proposed a government public-works program for the unemployed to be financed with paper money. This plan would improve the nation's infrastructure, create jobs for the unemployed, and provide an inflationary stimulus to counteract the depression's deflationary effects. In short, Coxey advocated positive government action to combat the depression.

Coxey organized a march of the unemployed to Washington as "a petition with boots on" to support his ideas. **Coxey's Army** of the unemployed, as the excited press dubbed it, marched through the industrial towns of Ohio and Pennsylvania and into Maryland, attracting attention and support. Other armies formed in eastern cities from Boston to Baltimore and set out for the capital. Some of the largest armies organized in the western cities of Denver, San Francisco, and Seattle. Three hundred men in an army from Oakland elected as their

Coxey's Army A protest march of unemployed workers, led by Populist businessman Jacob Coxey, demanding inflation and a public works program during the depression of the 1890s.

AMERICAN VIEWS

A POPULIST VIEWS AMERICAN GOVERNMENT

An educator, merchant, and former editor, Lorenzo D. Lewelling became one of the most articulate champions of the Populist Party and its principles. Elected governor of Kansas in 1892, he headed what was heralded as "The First People's Party Government on Earth." On January 9, 1893, Lewelling delivered his inaugural address, in which he declared, "I appeal to the people of this great commonwealth to array themselves on the side of humanity and justice." The following passages from the speech sketch out Lewelling's views of the 1890s and his "dream of the future."

- How does Lewelling's rhetoric reflect the deep divisions of the 1890s?
- What is Lewelling's view of the proper role of government?
- For what does Lewelling criticize the government of the 1890s?
- What does Lewelling mean by his statement that "the rich have no right to the property of the poor"?

The survival of the fittest is the government of brutes and reptiles, and such philosophy must give place to a government which recognizes human brotherhood. It is the province of government to protect the weak, but the government today is resolved into a struggle of the masses with the classes for supremacy and bread, until business, home, and personal integity are trembling in the face of possible want in the family. Feed a tiger regularly and you tame and make him harmless, but hunger makes tigers of men. If it be true that the poor have no right to the property of the rich let it also be declared that the rich have no right to the property of the poor.

It is the mission of Kansas to protect and advance the moral and material interests of all its citizens. It is its especial duty at the present time to protect the producer from the ravages of combined wealth. National legislation has for twenty years fostered and protected the interests of the few, while it has left the South and West to supply the products with which to feed and clothe the world, and thus to become the servants of wealth.

The demand for free coinage has been refused. The national banks have been permitted to withdraw their circulation, and thus the interests of the East and West have been diverged until the passage of the McKinley bill culminated in their diversement. The purchasing power of the dollar has become so great [that] corn, wheat, beef, pork, and cotton have scarcely commanded a price equal to the cost of production.

The instincts of patriotism have naturally rebelled against these unwarranted encroachments of the power of money. Sectional hatred has also been kept alive by

---

commander Anna Smith. "I'm not afraid of anything," Smith explained. "I have a woman's heart and a woman's sympathy, and these lead me to do what I have done for these men, even though it may not be just what a woman is expected to do."

The sympathy and assistance with which Americans greeted these industrial armies reflected more than anxiety over the depression and unemployment. As one economist noted, what distinguished the Populists and Coxeyites from earlier reformers was their appeal for federal action. Their substantial public support suggested a deep dissatisfaction with the failure of the government to respond to social and economic needs.

Nonetheless, the government acted to suppress Coxey. When he reached Washington with 600 marchers, police and soldiers arrested him and his aides, beat sympathetic bystanders in a crowd of 20,000, and herded the marchers into

the old powers, the better to enable them to control the products and make the producer contribute to the millionaire; and thus, while the producer labors in the field, the shop, and the factory, the millionaire usurps his earnings and rides in gilded carriages with liveried servants. . . .

The problem of today is how to make the State subservient to the individual, rather than become his master. Government is a voluntary union for the common good. It guarantees to the individual life, liberty, and the pursuit of happiness. The government then must make it possible for the citizen to enjoy liberty and pursue happiness. If the government fails of these things, it fails in its mission. . . . If old men go to the poorhouse and young men go to prison, something is wrong with the economic system of the government.

What is the State to him who toils, if labor is denied him and his children cry for bread? What is the State to the farmer who wearily drags himself from dawn till dark to meet the stern necessities of the mortgage on the farm? What is the State to him if it sanctions usury and other legal forms by which his home is destroyed and his innocent ones become a prey to the fiends who lurk in the shadow of civilization? What is the State to the business man, early grown gray, broken in health and spirit by successive failures; anxiety like a boding owl his constant companion by day and the disturber of his dreams by night? How is life to be sustained, how is liberty to be enjoyed, how is happiness to be pursued under such adverse conditions as the State permits if it does not sanction? Is the State powerless against these conditions?

This is the generation which has come to the rescue. Those in distress who cry out from the darkness shall not be heard in vain. Conscience is in the saddle. We have leaped the bloody chasm and entered a contest for the protection of home, humanity, and the dignity of labor.

The grandeur of civilization shall be emphasized by the dawn of a new era in which the people shall reign, and if found necessary they will "expand the powers of government to solve the enigmas of the times." The people are greater than the law or the statutes, and when a nation sets its heart on doing a great and good thing it can find a legal way to do it.

I have a dream of the future. I have the evolution of an abiding faith in human government, and in the beautiful vision of a coming time I behold the abolition of poverty. A time is foreshadowed when the withered hand of want shall not be outstretched for charity; when liberty, equality, and justice shall have permanent abiding places in the republic.

Source: *People's Party Paper* (Atlanta), January 20, 1893.

detention camps. Unlike the lobbyists for business and finance, Coxey was not permitted to reach Congress to deliver his statement urging the government to assist "the poor and oppressed."

Protecting Big Business.   The depression also provoked labor turmoil. In 1894, there were some 1,400 industrial strikes, involving nearly 700,000 workers, the largest number of strikers in any year in the nineteenth century. Cleveland had no response except to call for law and order. One result was the government's violent suppression of the Pullman strike (see Chapter 18).

In a series of decisions in 1895, the Supreme Court strengthened the bonds between business and government. First, it upheld the use of a court-ordered injunction to break the Pullman strike. As a result, injunctions became a major weapon for courts and corporations against labor unions, until Congress finally

William Jennings Bryan in 1896. A powerful orator of great human sympathies, Bryan was adored by his followers as "the majestic man who was hurling defiance in the teeth of the money power." Nominated three times for the presidency by the Democrats, he was never elected.

Culver Pictures, Inc.

---

limited their use in 1932. Next, in *United States v. E. C. Knight Company,* the Court gutted the Sherman Antitrust Act by ruling that manufacturing, as opposed to commerce, was beyond the reach of federal regulation. Finally, the Court invalidated an income tax that agrarian Democrats and Populists had maneuvered through Congress. The conservative Court rejected the reform as an "assault upon capital." A dissenting justice noted that the decision gave vested interests "a power and influence" dangerous to the majority of Americans.

Surveying these developments, farmers and workers increasingly concluded that the government protected powerful interests while ignoring the plight of ordinary Americans. Certainly the callous treatment shown workers contrasted sharply with Cleveland's concern for bankers as he managed the government's monetary policy in the depression. Cleveland blamed the economic collapse on the Sherman Silver Purchase Act. He persuaded Congress in 1893 to repeal the law, enraging southern and western members of his own party. These Silver Democrats condemned Cleveland for betraying the public good to "the corporate interests."

Cleveland's policy failed to end the depression. By 1894, the Treasury began borrowing money from Wall Street to bolster the gold reserve. These transactions benefited a syndicate of bankers headed by J. P. Morgan. It seemed to critics that an indifferent Cleveland was helping rich bankers profit from the nation's economic agony. "A set of vampires headed by a financial trust has control of our destiny," cried one rural newspaper.

THE BATTLE OF THE STANDARDS AND THE ELECTION OF 1896

The government's unpopular actions, coupled with the unrelenting depression, alienated workers and farmers from the Cleveland administration and the Democratic Party. In the off-year elections of 1894, the Democrats suffered the greatest loss of congressional seats in American history. Populists increased their vote by 42 percent, making especially significant gains in the South, but the real beneficiaries of the popular hatred of Cleveland and his policies were the Republicans, who gained solid control of Congress as well as state governments across the North and West.

As hard times persisted, the silver issue came to overshadow all others. Populist leaders, hoping to broaden the party's appeal, emphasized silver rather than the more radical planks of the Omaha Platform. Both to distance themselves and their party from the despised Cleveland, Democratic leaders in the South and West began using the silver issue to reorganize their party.

McKinley and the Republicans. William McKinley, governor of Ohio and author of the McKinley Tariff Act of 1890, emerged as the front-runner of a crowd of hopeful Republican presidential candidates. His candidacy benefited particularly from the financial backing and political management of Mark Hanna, a wealthy Ohio industrialist. Hanna thought that McKinley's passion for high tariffs as the key to revived prosperity would appeal to workers as well as to industry and business. As governor, McKinley had reached out to workers by supporting pro-labor legislation and by avoiding the anti-Catholic positions that alienated immigrants from the Republican Party.

The Republicans nominated McKinley on the first ballot at their 1896 convention. Their platform called for high tariffs but also endorsed the gold standard, placating eastern delegates but prompting several western Silver Republicans to withdraw from the party.

Bryan and the Silverites. The Democratic convention met shortly thereafter. With a fervor that conservatives likened to "scenes of the French Revolution," the Silver Democrats revolutionized their party. They adopted a platform repudiating Cleveland and his policies and endorsing free silver, the income tax, and tighter regulation of trusts and railroads. A magnificent speech supporting this platform by William Jennings Bryan helped convince the delegates to nominate him for president.

Holding their convention last, the Populists now faced a terrible dilemma. The Democratic nomination of Bryan on a silver platform undercut their hopes of attracting disappointed reformers from the major parties. Bryan, moreover, had already worked closely with Nebraska Populists, who now urged the party to endorse him rather than split the silver vote and ensure the victory of McKinley and the gold standard. Other Populists argued that fusing—joining with the Democrats—would cost the Populists their separate identity and subordinate their larger political principles to the issue of free silver. After anguished discussion, the Populists nominated Bryan for president.

Money and Oratory. The campaign was intense and dramatic, with each side demonizing the other. Eastern financial and business interests contributed millions of dollars to Hanna's campaign for McKinley. Standard Oil alone provided $250,000, about the same amount as the Democrats' total national expenses. Hanna used these funds to organize an unprecedented campaign. Shifting the emphasis from parades to information, Republicans issued 250 million campaign documents in a dozen languages, warning of economic disaster should Bryan be elected and the bimetallic standard be restored, but promising that McKinley's election would finally end the depression. Republicans were aided by a national press so completely sympathetic that many newspapers not only shaped their editorials but distorted their news stories to Bryan's disadvantage.

Lacking the Republicans' superior resources, the Democrats relied on Bryan's superb speaking ability and youthful energy. Bryan was the first presidential candidate to campaign systematically, speaking hundreds of times to millions of voters. By contrast, McKinley stayed home in Canton, Ohio, where he conducted a "front porch" campaign. Hanna brought groups of Republicans from all over the country to visit McKinley every day, and McKinley reiterated his simple promise of prosperity.

In the depression, that appeal proved enough. As the Democratic candidate, Bryan was, ironically, burdened with the legacy of the hated Cleveland administration. The intense campaign brought a record voter turnout. McKinley won decisively by capturing the East and Midwest as well as Oregon and California (see Map 20–2). Bryan carried the traditionally Democratic South and the mountain and plains states, where Populists and silverites dominated. He failed to gain support in either the Midwest or the cities of the East.

Bryan immediately wrote a personal account of the campaign, which he optimistically titled *The First Battle.* But Bryan and the Democrats would not win subsequent battles, at least not on the issues of the 1890s. The elections of 1894 and 1896 ended the close balance between the major parties. Cleveland's failures, coupled with an economic recovery in the wake of the election of 1896,

MAP EXPLORATION

To explore an interactive version of this map, go to
http://www.prenhall.com/goldfield3/map20.2

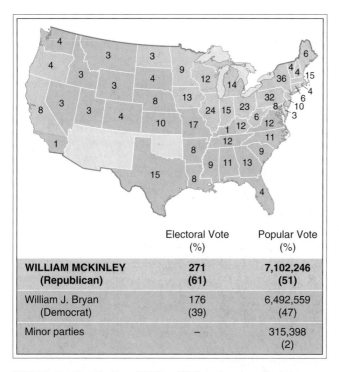

	Electoral Vote (%)	Popular Vote (%)
WILLIAM MCKINLEY (Republican)	**271 (61)**	**7,102,246 (51)**
William J. Bryan (Democrat)	176 (39)	6,492,559 (47)
Minor parties	–	315,398 (2)

MAP 20–2   The Election of 1896   William Jennings Bryan carried most of the rural South and West, but his free silver campaign had little appeal to more urban and industrial regions, which swung strongly to Republican candidate William McKinley.

WAS THE election of 1896 closer than the electoral vote would suggest?

QUICK REVIEW

McKinley's Program
- Tariff protection.
- Sound money.
- Overseas expansion.

W   WHERE TO LEARN MORE

★ Fairview, Lincoln, Nebraska
www.bryanlgh.org/aboutus/
fairviewhistory.htm

gained the Republicans a reputation as the party of prosperity and industrial progress, firmly establishing them in power for years to come. By contrast, the Democratic Party receded into an ineffectual sectional minority dominated by southern conservatives, despite Bryan's liberal views.

The People's Party simply dissolved. Demoralized by fusion with the Democrats, who had earlier violently repressed them, many southern Populists dropped out of politics. The Democrats' disfranchisement laws, directed at discontented poor white southerners as well as poor black southerners, further undermined the Populists in the South. In the West, the silver tide of 1896 carried many Populists into office, but with their party collapsing, they had no hope of reelection. By 1898, the Populist Party had virtually disappeared. Its reform legacy, however, proved more enduring. The issues it raised would continue to shape state and national politics.

McKinley plunged into his presidency. Unlike his predecessors, he had a definite, if limited, program, consisting of tariff protection, sound money, and overseas expansion. He worked actively to see it through Congress and to shape public opinion, thereby helping establish the model of the modern presidency. He had promised prosperity, and it returned, although not because of his policies. Prosperity returned, instead, because of reviving markets and a monetary inflation that resulted from the discovery of vast new deposits of gold in Alaska, Australia, and South Africa. Ironically, the new inflation was greater than the inflation that would have resulted from free silver. With the return of prosperity and the decline of social tensions, McKinley easily won reelection in 1900, defeating Bryan a second time.

CONCLUSION

*I*n late-nineteenth-century America, closely balanced political parties commanded the zealous support of their constituents and wielded power and influence. The institutions of government, by contrast, were limited in size, scope, and responsibility. A weakened presidency and an inefficient Congress, hampered by a restrictive judiciary, were often unable to resolve the very issues that were so dramatically raised in the political arena. The persistent disputes over tariff and monetary policy illustrate this impasse. But the issue that most reflected it was civil service reform. The patronage system provided the lifeblood of politics but also disrupted government business.

Localism, laissez-faire, and other traditional principles that shaped both politics and government were becoming increasingly inappropriate for America's industrializing society. New challenges were emerging that state and local governments could not effectively solve on their own. Both the depression of the

1890s and the popular discontent articulated most clearly by the Populist rejection of laissez-faire underscored the need for change and discredited the limited government of the Cleveland administration.

By the end of the decade, the political system had changed. The Republicans had emerged as the dominant party, ending the two-party stalemate of previous decades. Campaign hoopla in local communities had given way to information-based campaigns directed by national organizations. A new, activist presidency was emerging. Still greater changes were on the horizon. The depression and its terrible social and economic consequences undermined traditional ideas about the responsibilities of government and increased public support for activist policies. The stage was set for the Progressive Era.

SUMMARY

The Structure and Style of Politics Politics in the late nineteenth century expressed social values as it determined who held the reins of government. While the two major political parties dominated, third parties sought to activate those the Democrats and Republicans left unserved. Virtually all men participated in politics; the voter turnout of that era has never been equaled. Religious, ethnic, and regional factors determined party ties, but third parties, such as the Populists, emerged around issues. Women also participated in politics and some states now allowed full or partial suffrage.

The Limits of Government Government in the late nineteenth century was neither active nor productive by present standards; localism and laissez-faire policies were resurgent. Congress and a presidency divided between the two political parties, a small and inefficient federal bureaucracy, and judicial restraints joined powerful private interests to limit the size and objectives of the federal government.

Public Policies and National Elections The spoils system, the system for selecting and supervising federal employees, was finally reformed as a result of the assassination of President Garfield. The Pendleton Civil Service Act emphasized merit and skill; it also opened new opportunities for women. Americans heatedly debated the tariff policies; popular pressure compelled Congress to take the first steps toward the regulation of business; the most divisive political issue of the era was monetary policies with inflationists wanting more money, especially silver, in circulation.

The Crisis of the 1890s Protests from Midwestern farmers over freight rates, tariffs, and the money supply resulted in popular movements of protest and reform. The Populists, a third party, funneled the discontent into politics; their emergence was but one of the many developments combining to produce a national political crisis. A severe economic depression, labor unrest, and government inaction, along with the silver issue, underscored the need for change. The presidential election of 1896 was an intense campaign with record voter turnout; with William McKinley's victory over William Jennings Bryan, the Republicans became established as the party of prosperity and individual progress.

IMAGE KEY
for pages 574–575

a. 1892 Benjamin Harrison presidential campaign poster sponsored by the Republican Club.

b. Presidential Campaign, 1888. Grover Cleveland and Allen G. Thurman as the Democratic party candidates for President and Vice President on a lithograph campaign poster by Kurz & Allison, 1888.

c. McKinley-Roosevelt campaign paraphernalia.

d. "Tilden and Hendricks have been elected" ribbon.

e. William Jennings Bryan (1860–1925)-Democratic Convention, 1896, in which he made the "Cross of Gold" speech.

f. New Yorkers outside the Madison Square Garden during the Democratic National Convention of 1888, engraving from a contemporary American newspaper.

g. Meeting of the National Woman Suffrage Association.

h. Benjamin Harrison 1888 Presidential campaign paraphernalia.

i. Susan B. Anthony medal. created for the 1906 NY State Suffrage Association Convention, honoring Susan B. Anthony in the year of her death.

j. Coxey's Army with band passing a lumber yard.

k. "Bosses of the Senate" by Joseph Keppler. Giant corpulent (steel, copper, oil, sugar) trust figures loom over the deliberations of the US Senate in a nineteenth century political cartoon.

REVIEW QUESTIONS

1. What social and institutional factors shaped the disorderly nature of elections in the late nineteenth century? How did they operate in American politics?

2. What social and institutional factors determined the role of government? How and why did the role of government change during this period?

3. What factors determined the party affiliation of American voters? Why did so many third parties develop during this era?

4. How might the planks of the Omaha Platform have helped solve farmers' troubles?

5. What factors shaped the conduct and outcome of the election of 1896? How did that contest differ from earlier elections?

KEY TERMS

Coxey's Army (p. 593)
Farmers' Alliance (p. 590)
Free silver (p. 589)
Granger laws (p. 581)
Greenback Party (p. 581)
Interstate Commerce Act (p. 588)

Interstate Commerce Commission (ICC) (p. 588)
Laissez-faire (p. 583)
Mugwumps (p. 581)
National American Woman Suffrage Association (p. 582)

Omaha Platform (p. 592)
Pendleton Civil Service Act (p. 586)
Populist Party (p. 581)
Prohibition Party (p. 581)
Sherman Antitrust Act (p. 588)
Sound money (p. 588)

WHERE TO LEARN MORE

🛡 **Rest Cottage, Evanston, Illinois.** Frances Willard's home, from which she directed the Woman's Christian Temperance Union, is carefully preserved as a museum. The Willard Memorial Library contains more memorabilia and papers of Willard and the WCTU. **www.wctu.org/house.html**

🛡 **President Benjamin Harrison's Home, Indianapolis, Indiana.** President Harrison's brick Italianate mansion, completed in 1875, has been completely restored with the family's furniture and keepsakes. The former third-floor ballroom serves as a museum with exhibits of many artifacts of the Harrisons' public and private lives. **www.presidentbenjaminharrison.org/**

🛡 **Fairview, Lincoln, Nebraska.** A National Historic Landmark, Fairview was the home of William Jennings Bryan, who described it as "the Monticello of the West." Faithfully restored to depict the Bryan family's life in the early 1900s, it includes a museum and interpretive center. **www.bryanlgh.org/aboutus/fairviewhistory.htm**.

🛡 **Susan B. Anthony House National Historic Landmark, Rochester, New York.** This modest house was the home of the prominent suffragist and contains Anthony's original furnishings and personal photographs. **www.susanbanthonyhouse.org/main.html**

Rutherford B. Hayes Presidential Center, Fremont, Ohio. This complex contains President Hayes's home, office, and extensive grounds together with an excellent library and museum holding valuable collections of manuscripts, artifacts, and photographs illustrating his personal interests and political career. **www.rbhayes.org/**

 James A. Garfield Home, Mentor, Ohio. Operated by the Western Reserve Historical Society as a museum, Garfield's home is the site of his successful 1880 front-porch campaign for president. **www.nps.gov/jaga/index.htm**

U.S. History Documents CD-ROM
For primary sources related to this chapter, refer to the document CD-ROM.

www.prenhall.com/goldfield
For study resources related to this chapter, visit the *Companion Website*™.

21 The Progressive Era 1900-1917

CHAPTER HIGHLIGHTS

The Ferment of Reform The diversity of progressivism reflected the diverse impulses of reform. Clergy, journalists, business leaders, industrial workers, and women participated in reform movements. Nearly every movement encountered fierce opposition.

Reforming Society Progressives tried to transform society by improving living conditions, educational opportunities, family life, and social and industrial relations. Their vision of "social justice" sometimes shaded into social control. Racism permeated the Progressive Era.

Reforming Politics and Government Progressives pushed for the reform of politics and government, but they did not always agree on their objectives. All saw government reform as a necessary step in the alignment of government with the nation's new needs and priorities.

Theodore Roosevelt and the Progressive Presidency Theodore Roosevelt believed in a strong presidency and used the mass media to mold public opinion. Roosevelt was a conservationist, but not a preservationist. His reputation as a "trust buster" was built on relatively modest accomplishments.

Woodrow Wilson and Progressive Reform Elected president in 1912 and in 1916, Woodrow Wilson mediated differing progressive views to achieve a strong reform program, to enlarge the power of the executive branch, and to make the White House the center of national politics.

CHAPTER QUESTIONS

WHAT VALUES and beliefs bound progressives together?

WHAT ROLE did women play in progressive reform movements?

WHAT STEPS were taken toward woman suffrage during the Progressive Era?

HOW DID Theodore Roosevelt envision the power of the president?

HOW DID Woodrow Wilson's vision of reform differ from Theodore Roosevelt's?

CHAPTER OUTLINE

- The Ferment of Reform
- Reforming Society
- Reforming Politics and Government
- Theodore Roosevelt and the Progressive Presidency
- Woodrow Wilson and Progressive Reform

IMAGE KEY
for pages 602–603 is on page 634.

Five thousand women, marching in the woman suffrage pageant yesterday, practically fought their way foot by foot up Pennsylvania avenue, through a surging mass of humanity that completely defied the Washington police, swamped the marchers, and broke their procession into little companies. The women, trudging stoutly along under great difficulties, were able to complete their march only when troops of cavalry from Fort Myer were rushed into Washington to take charge of Pennsylvania avenue. No inauguration has ever produced such scenes, which in many instances amounted to little less than riots. . . .

The parade in itself, in spite of the delays, was a great success. . . . As a spectacle the pageant was entrancing. Beautiful women, posing in classic robes, passed in a bewildering array, presenting an irresistible appeal to the artistic, and completely captivating the hundred thousand spectators. . . .

Miss Margaret Foley, bearing aloft a large "Votes for Women" flag, and Mrs. G. Farquhar, carrying an American flag, led the procession. . . . After the float reading, "We Demand an Amendment to the United States Constitution Enfranchising the Women of This Country," came a body of ushers clad in light blue capes. . . . Two large floats . . . represented the countries in which women are working for equal rights, followed by a large body of women on foot dressed in street clothes, who bore the banners and pennants of scores of suffrage associations throughout the world. . . . The Homemakers . . . were dressed in long purple robes over their street clothes. Following them came a float, "In Patriotic Service," . . . and Miss Lillian Wald, the walking leader of a large body of women who followed the float, dressed as trained nurses, with gray caps and coats.

Miss Margaret Gage and Maurice Cohen, wearing college gowns with mortar boards, represented "Education," which was followed by nearly 1,000 women of the college section. . . . A group of young girls in blue capes represented the wage-earners, followed by "A Labor Story," which depicted the crowded condition of tenements, with women and children bendng over sewing machines, dirty and disheveled, in squalid quarters. . . . [Then followed] the women in the government section, all wearing light blue capes, . . . the business women, dressed in similar manner. . . . the teachers, . . . the social workers, . . . the white and pink costumed delegation of "writers," . . . club women and women clergy.

The greatest ovation was given to "General" Rosalie Jones, who led her little band of hikers from New York over rough roads and through snow and rain to march for the "cause." . . .

But there were hostile elements in the crowd through which the women marched. . . . Passing through two walls of antagonistic humanity, the marchers for the most part kept their temper. They suffered insult and closed their ears to jibes and jeers. . . .

The pageant moved up Pennsylvania avenue with great difficulty and surrounded with some danger. Crowds surged into the streets, completely overwhelming the police and stopping the pageant's progress. Mounted police charged into the crowds, but failed at times to drive them back, even with the free use of clubs. In more than an hour the pageant had moved only ten blocks. . . .

When the surging multitude was driven back in one place it flowed back into the street at another. The pageant slowly moved along, sometimes not more than a dozen feet at a time. . . .

As a result of the unruly spirit of the biggest crowd that ever witnessed a parade on Pennsylvania avenue, or of the inactivity of the police, who seemed powerless to protect the marching suffragists, the Emergency Hospital last night was filled to overflowing. . . .

Washington Post, March 4, 1913.

"GENERAL" ROSALIE JONES'S march and the jumbled news accounts from the *Washington Post* reporters convey the intensity of the dramatic woman suffrage parade on March 3, 1913. But the women's difficult journey down Pennsylvania Avenue that day, suggestive of the much longer journey to achieve woman suffrage, illustrated critical features of life in the **Progressive Era.**

Important movements challenged traditional relationships and attitudes—here involving women's role in American life—and often met strong resistance. "Progressives" seeking reforms organized their supporters across lines of class, education, occupation, geography, gender, and, at times, race and ethnicity—as the variety of groups in the suffrage parade demonstrates. Rather than rely on traditional partisan politics, reformers adopted new political techniques, including lobbying and demonstrating, as nonpartisan pressure groups. Reform work begun at the local and state levels—where the suffrage movement had already met some success—and inexorably moved to the national level as the federal government expanded its authority and became the focus of political interest. Finally, this suffrage demonstration reveals the exceptional diversity of the progressive movement, for the women were marching, in part, against Woodrow Wilson, who had campaigned for the presidency as a progressive.

Progressivism had no unifying organization, central leadership, or consensus on objectives. Instead, it represented the coalescing of different and sometimes even contradictory movements that sought changes in the nation's social, economic, and political life. But reformers did share certain convictions. They believed that remedying the social disorders produced by industrialization and urbanization required new ideas and methods. In particular, they rejected the ideology of individualism in favor of broader concepts of social responsibility, and they sought to achieve social order through organization and efficiency. Finally, most progressives believed that government itself, as the organized agent of public responsibility, should address social and economic problems.

Progressive Era   An era in the United States (roughly between 1900 and 1917) in which important movements challenged traditional relationships and attitudes.

Chronology

1893–1898	Depression grips the nation.
1898	South Dakota adopts initiative and referendum.
	National Consumers' League is organized.
1899	Anti-Cigarette League of America is established.
1900	Robert La Follette is elected governor of Wisconsin.
	President William McKinley is assassinated; Theodore Roosevelt becomes president.
	Socialist Party of America is organized.
	New York Tenement House Law is enacted.
	Galveston, Texas, initiates the city commission plan.
1902	Antitrust suit is filed against Northern Securities Company.
	McClure's initiates muckraking journalism.
	Mississippi enacts the first direct-primary law.
	National Reclamation Act is passed.
	Roosevelt intervenes in coal strike.
1903	Women's Trade Union League is organized.
	Women's Social and Political Union is organized in England.
1904	National Child Labor Committee is formed.
	Roosevelt is elected president.
1905	Industrial Workers of the World is organized.
1906	Hepburn Act strengthens the Interstate Commerce Commission.
	Meat Inspection Act extends government regulation.
	Pure Food and Drug Act is passed.
1908	*Muller v. Oregon* upholds maximum workday for women.
	William Howard Taft is elected president.
1910	National Association for the Advancement of Colored People is organized.
	Ballinger-Pinchot controversy erupts.
	Progressive Party organizes and nominates Roosevelt.
	Woodrow Wilson is elected president.
1913	Sixteenth and Seventeenth Amendments are ratified.
	Underwood-Simmons Tariff Act establishes an income tax.
	Federal Reserve Act creates the Federal Reserve System.
1914	Federal Trade Commission is established.
	Harrison Act criminalizes narcotics.
1915	National Birth Control League is formed.
1916	Keating-Owen Act prohibits child labor.
1917	Congress enacts literacy test for immigrants.
1918	Woman Suffrage is adopted in England.
1919	Eighteenth Amendment is ratified.
1920	Nineteenth Amendment is ratified.

THE FERMENT OF REFORM

WHAT VALUES and beliefs bound progressives together?

The diversity of progressivism reflected the diverse impulses of reform. Reformers responded to the tensions of industrialization and urbanization by formulating programs according to their own interests and priorities. Nearly every movement for change encountered fierce opposition. But in raising new issues and proposing new ideas, progressives helped America grapple with the problems of industrial society. (See the Overview table, "Major Progressive Organizations and Groups.")

OVERVIEW   MAJOR PROGRESSIVE ORGANIZATIONS AND GROUPS

Group	Activity
Social Gospel movement	Urged churches and individuals to apply Christian ethics to social and economic problems
Muckrakers	Exposed business abuses, public corruption, and social evils through investigative journalism
Settlement House movement	Attempted through social work and public advocacy to improve living and working conditions in urban immigrant communities
National Consumers' League (1898)	Monitored businesses to ensure decent working conditions and safe consumer products
Women's Trade Union League (1903)	United workingwomen and their middle-class "allies" to promote unionization and social reform
National Child Labor Committee (1904)	Campaigned against child labor
Country Life movement	Attempted to modernize rural social and economic conditions according to urban-industrial standards
National American Woman Suffrage Association	Led the movement to give women the right to vote
Municipal reformers	Sought to change the activities and structure of urban government to promote efficiency and control
Conservationists	Favored efficient management and regulation of natural resources rather than uncontrolled development or preservation

THE CONTEXT OF REFORM: INDUSTRIAL AND URBAN TENSIONS

The origins of progressivism lay in the crises of the new urban-industrial order that emerged in the late nineteenth century. The severe depression and consequent mass suffering of the 1890s, the labor violence and industrial armies, the political challenges of Populism and an obviously ineffective government shattered the complacency many middle-class Americans had felt about their nation. Many Americans began to question the validity of social Darwinism and the laissez-faire policies that had justified unregulated industrial growth. They began to reconsider the responsibilities of government and, indeed, of themselves for social order and betterment.

By 1900, returning prosperity had eased the threat of major social violence, but the underlying problems intensified. Big business, which had disrupted traditional economic relationships in the late nineteenth century, suddenly became bigger in a series of mergers between 1897 and 1903, resulting in huge new business combinations. Such gigantic corporations threatened to squeeze opportunities for small firms and workers, dominate markets, and raise social tensions. They also inspired calls for public control.

QUICK REVIEW

Triangle Shirtwaist Fire
- 1911: Fire kills 146 workers.
- Managers had locked the exits.
- The United States had the highest rate of industrial accidents in the world.

WHERE TO LEARN MORE

National Museum of American History, Smithsonian Institution, Washington, D.C.

Overcome with grief, families of the victims of the Triangle Shirtwaist fire later received from the factory owners $75 for each life lost. Still mourning, family members asked, "Justice, what justice?"

Kheel Center, Cornell University, Ithaca, NY 14853-3901

WHERE TO LEARN MORE

Lowell National Historic Park, Lowell, Massachusetts
www.nps.gov/lowe/

Social Gospel movement
Movement created by reform-minded Protestant ministers seeking to introduce religious ethics into industrial relations and appealing to churches to meet their social responsibilities.

Industrial growth affected factory workers most directly. Working conditions were difficult and often dangerous. Most workers still toiled nine to ten hours a day. Wages were minimal and family survival often required women and children to work, often in the lowest-paid, most exploited positions. Southern cotton mills employed children as young as seven; coal mines paid 12-year-old slate pickers 39 cents for a ten-hour day. Poor ventilation, dangerous fumes, open machinery, and the absence of safety programs threatened not only workers' health but their lives as well. Such conditions were gruesomely illustrated in 1911, when a fire killed 146 workers, most of them young women, trapped inside the factory of the Triangle Shirtwaist Company in New York because management had locked the exits. The United States had the highest rate of industrial accidents in the world. Half a million workers were injured and 30,000 killed at work each year.

Other Americans saw additional social problems in the continuing flood of immigrants who were transforming America's cities. From 1900 to 1917, more than 14 million immigrants entered the United States, and most became urban dwellers. Most of the arrivals were so-called new immigrants from southern and eastern Europe, rather than the British, Irish, Germans, and Scandinavians who had arrived earlier. Several hundred thousand Japanese also arrived, primarily in California, as did increasing numbers of Mexicans. Crowding into urban slums, immigrants overwhelmed municipal sanitation, education, and fire protection services. One Russian described his new life as "all filth and sadness."

Many native-born Americans associated the immigrants with rampant urban crime and disease and with city bosses and government corruption. Americans of the "Old Stock" often considered the predominantly Catholic and Jewish newcomers a threat to social stability and cultural identity and so demanded programs to reform either the urban environment or the immigrants themselves.

CHURCH AND CAMPUS

Many groups, drawing from different traditions and inspirations, responded to these economic and social issues. Reform-minded Protestant ministers were especially influential, creating the **Social Gospel movement,** which sought to introduce religious ethics into industrial relations and appealed to churches to meet their social responsibilities. Washington Gladden, a Congregational minister in Columbus, Ohio, was one of the earliest Social Gospelers. Shocked in 1884 by a bloody strike crushed by wealthy members of his own congregation, Gladden began a ministry to working-class neighborhoods that most churches ignored. He endorsed unions and workers' rights and proposed replacing a cruelly competitive wage system with profit sharing.

A more profound exponent of the Social Gospel was Walter Rauschenbusch, a Baptist minister who had served impoverished immigrants in New York's slums. In his book *Christianity and the Social Crisis* (1907), he argued that Christians should support social reform to alleviate poverty, slums, and labor exploitation. He attacked low wages for transforming workers "into lean, sallow, hopeless, stupid, and vicious young people, simply to enable some group of stockholders to earn 10 percent."

The Social Gospel movement flowered mainly among Episcopalian, Congregationalist, and Methodist Protestants. It climaxed in 1908 in the formation of the Federal Council of Churches of Christ in America. The council, representing thirty-three religious groups, adopted a program that endorsed welfare and regulatory legislation to achieve social justice. By linking reform with religion, the Social Gospel movement gave progressivism a powerful moral drive that affected much of American life.

Scholars in the social sciences also gradually helped turn public attitudes in favor of reform by challenging the laissez-faire views of the social Darwinists and traditional academics. In *Applied Sociology* (1906), Lester Ward called for social progress through rational planning and government intervention rather than through unrestrained and unpredictable competition. Economists rejected laissez-faire principles in favor of state action to accomplish social evolution. Industrialization, declared economist Richard T. Ely, "has brought to the front a vast number of social problems whose solution is impossible without the united efforts of church, state, and science."

MUCKRAKERS

Journalists also spread reform ideas by developing a new form of investigative reporting known as **muckraking.** Samuel S. McClure sent his reporters to uncover political and corporate corruption for *McClure's Magazine*. Sensational exposés sold magazines, and soon *Cosmopolitan, Everybody's,* and other journals began publishing investigations of business abuses, dangerous working conditions, and the miseries of slum life.

Muckraking novels also appeared. *The Octopus* (1901), by Frank Norris, dramatized the Southern Pacific Railroad's stranglehold on California's farmers, and *The Jungle* (1906), by Upton Sinclair, exposed the nauseating conditions in Chicago's meatpacking industry.

THE GOSPEL OF EFFICIENCY

Many progressive leaders believed that efficiency and expertise could control or resolve the disorders of industrial society. President Theodore Roosevelt praised the "gospel of efficiency." Like many other progressives, he admired the success of corporations in applying management techniques to guide economic growth. Drawing from science and technology as well as from the model of the corporation, many progressives attempted to manage or direct change efficiently. They used scientific methods to collect extensive data and relied on experts for analysis and recommendations. "Scientific management," a concept often used interchangeably with "sound business management," seemed the key to eliminating waste and inefficiency in government, society, and industry. Rural reformers thought that "scientific agriculture" could bring prosperity to the impoverished southern countryside; urban reformers believed that improvements in medical science and the professionalization of physicians through uniform state-licensing standards could eradicate the cities' wretched health problems.

Industrialists were drawn to the ideas of Frederick Taylor, a proponent of scientific management, for cutting factory labor costs. Taylor proposed to increase worker efficiency through imposed work routines, speedups, and mechanization. By assigning workers simple and repetitive tasks on machines, Taylorization made their skills expendable and enabled managers to control production, the pace of work, and hiring and firing of personnel. When labor complained, one business leader declared that unions failed "to appreciate the progressivism of the age."

Sophisticated managers of big business saw some forms of government intervention as another way to promote order and efficiency. In particular, they favored regulations that could bring about safer and more stable conditions in society and the economy. Government regulations, they reasoned, could reassure potential consumers, open markets, mandate working conditions that smaller competitors could not provide, or impose systematic procedures that competitive pressures would otherwise undercut.

LABOR'S DEMAND FOR RIGHTS

Industrial workers with different objectives also hastened the ferment of reform. Workers resisted the new rules of efficiency experts and called for improved wages and working conditions and reduced work hours. They and their middle-class sympathizers sought to achieve some of these goals through state intervention, demanding laws to compensate workers injured on the job, curb child labor, and regulate the employment of women. After the Triangle Shirtwaist fire, for example, urban politicians with working-class constituencies created the New York State Factory Commission and enacted dozens of laws dealing with fire hazards, machine safety, and wages and hours for women.

Workers also organized unions to improve their lot. The American Federation of Labor (AFL) claimed 4 million members by 1920, recruiting mainly skilled workers, particularly native-born white males. New unions organized the factories and sweatshops where most immigrants and women worked. Despite strong employer resistance, the International Ladies Garment Workers Union (1900) and the Amalgamated Clothing Workers (1914) organized the garment trades, developed programs for social and economic reforms, and led their members—mostly young Jewish and Italian women—in spectacular strikes. The "Uprising of the 20,000," a 1909 strike in New York City, included months of massive rallies, determined picketing, and police repression.

A still more radical union tried to organize miners, lumberjacks, and Mexican and Japanese farm workers in the West, black dockworkers in the South, and immigrant factory hands in New England. Founded in 1905, the Industrial Workers of the World (IWW), whose members were known as "**Wobblies,**" used sit-down strikes, sit-ins, and mass rallies, tactics adopted by other industrial unions in the 1930s and the civil rights movement in the 1960s. Private employers and public officials used every method, legal and illegal, to destroy the Wobblies, but broader labor unrest nonetheless stimulated the reform impulse.

EXTENDING THE WOMAN'S SPHERE

Women reformers and their organizations played a key role in progressivism. Women responded not merely to the human suffering caused by industrialization and urbanization but also to related changes in their own status and role. By the early twentieth century, more women than before were working outside the home. In 1910, more than one-fourth of all workers were women, increasing numbers of them married. Their importance in the workforce and participation in unions and strikes challenged assumptions that woman's "natural" role was to be a submissive housewife.

The women's clubs that had begun multiplying in the late nineteenth century became seedbeds of progressive ideas in the early twentieth century. Often

QUICK REVIEW

Unions

- American Federation of Labor recruited skilled workers, particularly native-born white males.
- Ladies Garment Workers Union and Amalgamated Clothing Workers organized garment trades.
- Industrial Workers of the World used innovative tactics and sought to organize a diverse set of workers.

Wobblies   Popular name for the members of the Industrial Workers of the World (IWW).

founded for cultural purposes, women's clubs soon adopted programs for social reform and gave their members a route to public influence. In 1914, an officer of the General Federation of Women's Clubs proudly declared that every cause for social reform had "received a helpful hand from the clubwomen."

Women also joined or created other organizations that pushed beyond the limits of traditional domesticity. By threatening healthy and happy homes, urban problems required that women become "social housekeepers" in the community. The National Congress of Mothers, organized in 1897, worried about crime and disease and championed kindergartens, foster-home programs, juvenile courts, and compulsory school attendance.

Led by the crusading Florence Kelley, the National Consumers' League, founded in 1898, tried to protect both women wage earners and middle-class housewives by monitoring stores and factories to ensure decent working conditions and safe products. The Women's Trade Union League (WTUL, founded in 1903) united working women and their self-styled middle-class "allies" to unionize women workers and eliminate sweatshop conditions. Its greatest success came in the 1909 garment workers' strike when the allies assisted strikers with relief funds, bail money, food supplies, and a public-relations campaign.

Although most progressive women stressed women's special duties and responsibilities as social housekeepers, others began to demand women's equal rights. In 1914, for example, critics of New York's policy of dismissing women teachers who married formed a group called the Feminist Alliance and demanded "the removal of all social, political, economic and other discriminations which are based upon sex, and the award of all rights and duties in all fields on the basis of individual capacity alone." With these new organizations and ideas, women gave important impetus and direction to the reform sentiments of the early twentieth century.

TRANSATLANTIC INFLUENCES

A major source of America's progressive impulse lay outside its borders. European nations were already grappling with many of the problems that stemmed from industrialization and urbanization, and they provided guidance, examples, and possible solutions. Progressive reformers soon learned that America's particular political, economic, and social structures made it necessary to modify, adapt, or even abandon these imported ideas, but their influence was obvious.

International influences were especially strong in the Social Gospel movement, symbolized by William T. Stead, a British social evangelist, whose idea of a "Civic Church" (a partnership of churches and reformers) captured great attention in the United States. Stead himself went to Chicago to promote "a broad and clear social programme," and his book *If Christ Came to Chicago* inspired many Americans. Foreign development similarly influenced muckraking journalists. *McClure's* sent Ray Stannard Baker to Europe in 1900 "to see why Germany is making such progress."

Institutional connections also linked progressives with European reformers. The American Association for Labor Legislation, for example, was founded in 1905 as an offshoot of the International Association for Labor Legislation, founded in 1900 by French, Belgian, and German social economists. By 1912, American consumer activists, trade unionists, factory inspectors, and feminists regularly participated in international conferences on labor legislation, child welfare, social insurance, and housing reform and returned home with new ideas and strategies.

State governments organized commissions to analyze European policies and agencies for lessons that might be applicable in the United States.

SOCIALISM

The growing influence of socialist ideas also promoted the spirit of progressivism. American socialists condemned social and economic inequities, criticized limited government, and demanded public ownership of railroads, utilities, and communications. They also campaigned for tax reforms, better housing, factory inspections, and recreational facilities for all.

The most prominent socialist was the dynamic and engaging Eugene V. Debs. An Indiana labor leader, Debs decried what he saw as the dehumanization produced by industrial capitalism and hoped for an egalitarian society where everyone would have the opportunity "to develop the best there is in him for his own good as well as the good of society." In 1901, Debs helped organize the Socialist Party of America; thereafter he worked tirelessly to attract followers to a vision of socialism deeply rooted in American political and religious traditions. In the next decade, the party won many local elections, especially in Wisconsin and New York.

Most progressives considered socialist ideas too drastic. Nevertheless, socialists contributed importantly to the reform ferment, not only by providing support for reform initiatives but often also by prompting progressives to push for changes to undercut increasingly attractive radical alternatives.

OPPONENTS OF REFORM

Not all Americans supported progressive reforms, and many people regarded as progressives on some issues opposed change in other areas. Social Gospeler Rauschenbusch, for instance, opposed expanding women's rights. More typically, opponents of reform held consistently traditional attitudes.

Social Gospelers themselves faced opposition. Quite strong among evangelical denominations with rural roots, Protestant **fundamentalists** stressed personal salvation rather than social reform. Indeed, the urban and industrial crises that inspired Social Gospelers to preach reform drove many evangelical leaders to endorse social and political conservatism. The most famous evangelist, the crude but spellbinding Billy Sunday, scorned all reforms but prohibition and denounced labor unions, women's rights, and business regulation as violating traditional values. Declaring that the Christian mission was only to save individual souls, he condemned the Social Gospel as "godless social service nonsense" and attacked its advocates as "infidels and atheists."

Business interests, angered by exposés of corporate abuse and corruption, attacked the muckrakers. Major corporations like Standard Oil created public relations bureaus to improve their image and identify business, not its critics, with the public interest. Advertising boycotts discouraged magazines from running critical stories, and credit restrictions forced some muckraking journals to suspend publication. By 1910, the heyday of muckraking was over.

Labor unions likewise encountered resistance. Led by the National Association of Manufacturers, business groups denounced unions as corrupt and radical, hired thugs to disrupt them, organized strikebreaking agencies, and used blacklists to eliminate union activists. The antiunion campaign peaked in Ludlow, Colorado, in 1914, when John D. Rockefeller's Colorado Fuel and Iron Company used armed guards and the state militia to shoot and burn striking workers and their families. The courts aided employers by issuing injunctions

Fundamentalists Religious conservatives who believe in the literal accuracy and divine inspiration of the Bible.

against strikes and prohibiting unions from using boycotts, one of their most effective weapons.

Progressives campaigning for government intervention and regulation also met stiff resistance. Many Americans objected to what they considered unwarranted interference in private economic matters. Again, the courts often supported these attitudes. In *Lochner v. New York* (1905), the Supreme Court even overturned a maximum-hours law on the grounds that it deprived employers and employees of their "freedom of contract." Progressives continually struggled against such opponents, and progressive achievements were limited by the persistence and influence of their adversaries.

REFORMING SOCIETY

With their varied motives and objectives, progressives worked to transform society by improving living conditions, educational opportunities, family life, and social and industrial relations. (See the Overview table, "Major Laws and Constitutional Amendments of the Progressive Era.") They sought what they called social justice, but their plans for social reform sometimes also smacked of social control. Organized women dominated the movement to reform society, but they were supported, depending on the goal, by Social Gospel ministers, social scientists, urban immigrants, labor unions, and even some conservatives eager to regulate personal behavior.

SETTLEMENT HOUSES AND URBAN REFORM

The spearheads for social reform were settlement houses—community centers in urban immigrant neighborhoods. Reformers created 400 settlement houses, largely modeled after Hull House in Chicago, founded in 1889 by Jane Addams. Settlement houses often reflected the ideals of the Social Gospel. Yet most were secular institutions, avoiding religion to gain the trust of Catholic and Jewish immigrants.

Most settlements were led and staffed primarily by middle-class young women, seeking to alleviate poverty and do useful professional work when most careers were closed to them. Settlement work did not immediately violate prescribed gender roles because it initially focused on the "woman's sphere"—family, education, domestic skills, and cultural "uplift."

However, settlement workers soon saw that the root problem for immigrants was widespread poverty that required more than changes in individual behavior. Unlike earlier reformers, they regarded many of the evils of poverty as products of the social environment rather than of moral weakness. Slum dwellers, Addams sadly noted, suffered from "poisonous sewage, contaminated water, infant mortality, adulterated food, smoke-laden air, juvenile crime, and unwholesome crowding." Thus, settlement workers campaigned for stricter building codes to improve slums, better urban sanitation systems to enhance public health, public parks to revive the urban environment, and laws to protect women and children.

Their crusades for sanitation and housing reform demonstrated the impact that social reformers often had on urban life. Lawrence Veiller was convinced by his work at the University Settlement in New York City that "the improvement of the homes of the people was the starting point for everything." Organizing pressure groups to promote tenement house reform, Veiller relied on settlement workers to investigate housing conditions, prepare public exhibits depicting rampant disease in congested slums, and agitate for improvements. Based on their findings,

WHAT ROLE did women play in progressive reform movements?

21–6
Jane Addams, Twenty Years at Hull House (1910)

WHERE TO LEARN MORE

Hull House, Chicago, Illinois
www.uic.edu/jaddams/hull/hull_house.html

OVERVIEW

MAJOR LAWS AND CONSTITUTIONAL AMENDMENTS OF THE PROGRESSIVE ERA

Legislation	Effect
New York Tenement House Law (1901)	Established a model housing code for safety and sanitation
Newlands Act (1902)	Provided for federal irrigation projects
Hepburn Act (1906)	Strengthened authority of the Interstate Commerce Commission
Pure Food and Drug Act (1906)	Regulated the production and sale of food and drug products
Meat Inspection Act (1906)	Authorized federal inspection of meat products
Sixteenth Amendment (1913)	Authorized a federal income tax
Seventeenth Amendment (1913)	Mandated the direct popular election of senators
Underwood-Simmons Tariff Act (1913)	Lowered tariff rates and levied the first regular federal income tax
Federal Reserve Act (1913)	Established the Federal Reserve System to supervise banking and provide a national currency
Federal Trade Commission Act (1914)	Established the FTC to oversee business activities
Harrison Act (1914)	Regulated the distribution and use of narcotics
Smith-Lever Act (1914)	Institutionalized the county agent system
Keating-Owen Act (1916)	Indirectly prohibited child labor
Eighteenth Amendment (1919)	Instituted prohibition
Nineteenth Amendment (1920)	Established woman suffrage

WHERE TO LEARN MORE

Lower East Side Tenement Museum, New York City, New York
www.tenement.org/

Veiller drafted a new housing code limiting the size of tenements and requiring toilet facilities, ventilation, and fire protection. In 1901, the New York Tenement House Law became a model for other cities.

PROTECTIVE LEGISLATION FOR WOMEN AND CHILDREN

While settlement workers initially undertook private efforts to improve society, many reformers eventually concluded that only government power could achieve social justice. As Veiller insisted, it was "unquestionably the duty of the state" to enforce justice in the face of "greed on the part of those who desire to secure for themselves an undue profit."

The National Child Labor Committee, organized in 1904, led the campaign to curtail child labor. Stiff resistance came from manufacturers who used child labor, conservatives who opposed government action as an intrusion into family life, and some poor parents who needed their children's income. Reformers documented the problem with extensive investigations and also benefited from the public outrage stirred by socialist John Spargo's muckraking book *The Bitter Cry of the Children* (1906). In 1900, most states had no minimum working age; by 1914, every state but one had such a law. Effective regulation, however, required national action, for many state laws were weak or poorly enforced.

Social reformers also lobbied for laws regulating the wages, hours, and working conditions of women and succeeded in having states from New York to Oregon pass maximum-hours legislation. After the Supreme Court upheld such laws in *Muller v. Oregon* (1908), 39 states enacted new or stronger laws on women's maximum hours between 1909 and 1917. Fewer states established minimum wages for women.

Protective legislation for women posed a troubling issue for reformers. In California, for example, middle-class clubwomen favored protective legislation on the grounds of women's presumed weakness. More radical progressives, as in the socialist-led Women's Trade Union League of Los Angeles, supported such legislation to help secure economic independence and equality in the labor market for women, in-crease the economic strength of the working class, and serve as a precedent for laws improving conditions for all workers.

The famous photographer Lewis Hine used his camera to document child labor. The eight-year-old girl on the right in this 1911 photograph of women and children working in an Alabama canning factory had been shucking oysters for three years.

Courtesy National Archives, photo no. 102-LH-1986

Progressive Era lawmakers adopted the first viewpoint. They limited pro-tective legislation to measures reflecting the belief that women needed paternal-ist protection, even by excluding them from certain occupations. Laws establishing a minimum wage for women, moreover, usually set a wage level below subsistence rates. Protective legislation thus ensured women, not economic independence, but continued dependence on husbands or fathers.

Protective legislation for male workers scarcely existed. Both lawmakers and judges rebuffed demands for the protection of all workers while approving reforms that endorsed inequality. Only in very dangerous industries did male workers gain much protection, due primarily to the relentless efforts of labor unions. The West-ern Federation of Miners persuaded several states that the extraordinary occupa-tional hazards of mining required laws regulating hours and conditions of work.

Prompted by both humanitarian and paternalistic urgings, many states began in 1910 to provide "mothers' pensions" to indigent widows with dependent children. Twenty-one states, led by Wisconsin in 1911, enacted workers' compensation pro-grams, ending the custom of holding workers themselves liable for injuries on the job.

Compared to the social insurance programs in western Europe, however, these were feeble responses to the social consequences of industrialization. Pro-posals for health insurance, unemployment insurance, and old-age pension pro-grams went nowhere. Business groups and other conservative interests curbed the movement toward state responsibility for social welfare.

RESHAPING PUBLIC EDUCATION

Concerns about child labor overlapped with increasing attention to the public schools. The rapid influx of immigrants, as well as the demands of the new cor-porate workplace, generated interest in education not only as a means of ad-vancement but also as a tool for assimilation and the training of future workers.

Between 1880 and 1920, compulsory school attendance laws, kindergartens, age-graded elementary schools, professional training for teachers, vocational

education, parent-teacher associations, and school nurses became standard elements in American education. School reformers believed these measures to be both educationally sound and important for countering slum environments. As Jacob Riis contended, the kindergartner would "rediscover . . . the natural feelings that the tenement had smothered." Others supported the kindergarten as "the earliest opportunity to catch the little Russian, the little Italian, the little German, Pole, Syrian, and the rest and begin to make good American citizens of them."

Public education in the South lagged behind the North. Northern philanthropy and southern reformers brought some improvements after 1900, as per capita expenditures for education doubled, school terms were extended, and high schools spread across the region. But the South frittered away its limited resources on a segregated educational system that shortchanged both races. Black southerners particularly suffered, for the new programs increased the disparity in funding for white and black schools.

Racism also underlay important changes in the schooling of American Indians. The earlier belief that education would promote equality and facilitate assimilation gave way to a conviction that Indians were inferior and fit merely for manual labor. Educators now rejected the notion of a common school education for Indian children in favor of manual training which would enable Indians to fill menial jobs. Educators also renounced the practice of integrating Indian children into previously all-white classrooms, a policy begun in 1891. The superintendent of the Chilocco, Oklahoma, school believed that the new commitment to practical vocational education "solved the Indian problem," but critics noted that limiting Indian children to a rudimentary and segregated education merely doomed them to the margins of American society.

CHALLENGING GENDER RESTRICTIONS

Most progressives held fairly conservative, moralistic views about sexuality and gender roles. Margaret Sanger, however, radically challenged conventional ideas about the social role of women. Despite great opposition, she initiated the modern birth control movement. A public-health nurse and an IWW organizer, she soon made the struggle for reproductive rights her personal crusade. Sanger saw in New York's immigrant neighborhoods the plight of poor women worn out from repeated pregnancies or injured or dead from self-induced knitting-needle abortions. Despite federal and state laws against contraceptives, Sanger began promoting birth control as a way to avert such tragedies. In 1914, Sanger published a magazine, *Woman Rebel*, in which she argued that "a woman's body belongs to herself alone. It does not belong to the United States of America or any other government on the face of the earth." Sanger declared that "Women cannot be on an equal footing with men until they have full and complete control over their reproductive function."

Sanger's crusade attracted support from many women's and labor groups, but it also infuriated those who regarded birth control as a threat to the family and morality. Indicted for distributing information about contraception, Sanger fled to Europe. Other women took up the cause, forming the National Birth Control League in 1915.

REFORMING COUNTRY LIFE

Although most progressives focused on the city, others sought to reform rural life, both to modernize its social and economic conditions and to integrate it more fully into the larger society. They worked to improve rural health and sanitation, to replace inefficient one-room schools with modern consolidated ones under professional control, and to extend new roads and communication services into the countryside. To further these goals, President Theodore Roosevelt created the Country Life Commission in 1908. The country lifers had a broad program for social and economic change, involving expanded government functions, activist government agencies staffed by experts, and the professionalization of rural social services.

Agricultural scientists, government officials, and many business interests also sought to promote efficient, scientific, and commercial agriculture, especially by the new county-agent system. This program placed an agent in each county to teach farmers new techniques and to encourage changes in the rural social values that had spawned the Populist radicalism that most progressives decried.

Few farmers, however, welcomed these efforts. As one Illinois county agent said in 1915, "Farmers, as a whole, resent exceedingly those forces which are at work with missionary intent trying to uplift them." Most farmers believed that their problems stemmed, not from rural life, but from industrial society and its nefarious trusts, banks, and middlemen.

Even so, rural people were drawn into the larger urban-industrial society during the Progressive Era. Government agencies, agricultural colleges, and railroads and banks steadily tied farmers to urban markets. Telephones and rural free delivery of mail lessened countryside isolation but quickened the spread of city values. Improved roads and the coming of the automobile eliminated many rural villages and linked farm families directly with towns and cities. Consolidated schools wiped out the social center of rural neighborhoods and carried children out of their communities, eventually encouraging an ever-growing migration to the city.

SOCIAL CONTROL AND MORAL CRUSADES

The tendency toward social control evident in the movements to pass protective legislation and transform country life also marked other less attractive progressive efforts. These efforts, moreover, often meshed with the restrictive attitudes that conservative Americans held about race, religion, immigration, and morality. The result was widespread attempts to restrict certain groups and control behavior.

Controlling Immigrants.   Many Americans wanted to limit immigration. Californians targeted Japanese and Mexican immigrants while others tried to restrict immigrants from southern and eastern Europe. Some labor leaders believed that immigration held down wages and impeded unionization; many sociologists thought it created serious social problems; other Americans disliked the newcomers on racial, religious, cultural, or ethnic grounds. As early as 1894, nativists had organized the Immigration Restriction League, which lobbied for a literacy test for admission, sure that it would "bear most heavily upon the Italians, Russians, Poles, Hungarians, Greeks, and Asiatics, and very lightly or not at all upon English-speaking immigrants or Germans, Scandinavians, and French." Congress enacted a literacy law in 1917.

Other nativists demanded the "Americanization" of immigrants already in the country. The Daughters of the American Revolution sought to inculcate loyalty, patriotism, and conservative values. Settlement workers and Social Gospelers promoted a gentler kind of Americanization through English classes and home mission campaigns, but they too attempted to transfer their own values to the newcomers.

Prohibition.   Closely linked to progressives' worries about immigrants was their campaign for **prohibition.** This movement engaged many of the progressives' basic impulses. Social workers saw liquor as a cause of crime, poverty, and family violence; employers blamed it for causing industrial accidents and inefficiency; Social Gospel ministers condemned the "spirit born of hell" because it impaired moral judgment and behavior. But also important was native-born Americans' fear of new immigrants—"the dangerous classes, who are readily dominated by the saloon." Many immigrants, in fact, viewed liquor and the neighborhood saloon as vital parts of daily life, and so prohibition became a focus of nativist hostility, cultural conflict, and Americanization pressures. In the South, racism also figured prominently. Alexander McKelway, the southern secretary for the National Child Labor Committee, helped organize the North Carolina Anti-Saloon League to deny alcohol to African Americans, whom he considered naturally "criminal and degenerate."

Protestant fundamentalists also stoutly supported prohibition, working through the Anti-Saloon League, founded in 1893. With most urban Catholics and Jews opposing prohibition, the Anti-Saloon League justified imposing its reform on city populations against their will: "Our nation can only be saved by turning the pure stream of country sentiment . . . to flush out the cesspools of cities and so save civilization from pollution."

With these varied motivations, prohibitionists campaigned for local and state laws against the manufacture and sale of alcohol. Beginning in 1907, they proved increasingly successful, especially in the South, Midwest, and Far West. By 1917, 26 states had prohibition laws. Congress then approved the **Eighteenth Amendment,** which made prohibition the law of the land by 1920.

Less controversial were drives to control or prohibit narcotics and cigarettes. Fears that drug addiction was spreading, particularly among black people and immigrants, prompted Congress in 1914 to pass the Harrison Act, prohibiting the distribution and use of narcotics for other than medicinal purposes. The Anti-Cigarette League of America, organized in 1899 and having 300,000 members by 1901, led the charge against cigarettes. Many states prohibited the manufacture, sale, or use of cigarettes, but such restrictive laws were rarely enforced and often repealed within a few years.

Suppressing Prostitution.   Reformers also sought to suppress the "social evil" of prostitution. Like crowded slums, sweatshops, and child labor, the "vice districts" where prostitution flourished were seen as part of the exploitation and disorder in the industrial cities. Women's low wages as factory workers and domestic servants explained some of the problem, as a muckraking article entitled "The Daughters of the Poor" pointed out. But nativism spurred public concern, as when New York officials insisted that most prostitutes and brothel owners, some of whom "have been seducers of defenseless women all their lives," were foreign-born. The progressive solution emerged in state and municipal action abolishing the "red light" districts previously tolerated and in a federal law, the Mann Act of 1910, prohibiting the interstate transport of women "for immoral purposes."

California provided other examples of progressives' interest in social control and moral reform. The state assembly prohibited gambling, cardplaying, and prizefighting. Los Angeles—influenced by the aptly named Morals Efficiency League—banned premarital sex and introduced censorship of art.

Prohibition   A ban on the production, sale, and consumption of liquor, achieved temporarily through state laws and the Eighteenth Amendment.

Eighteenth Amendment   Constitutional revision, adopted in 1919, that prohibited the production and sale of alcohol in the United States.

FOR WHITES ONLY?

Racism permeated the Progressive Era. In the South, progressivism was built on black disfranchisement and segregation. Like most white southerners, progressives believed that racial control was necessary for social order and that it enabled reformers to address other social problems. Such reformers also invoked racism to gain popular support for their objectives. In Georgia, for instance, child labor reformers warned that while white children worked in the Piedmont textile mills, black children were going to school: child labor laws and compulsory school attendance laws were necessary to maintain white supremacy.

The Flanner House, a black settlement house in Indianapolis, provided the black community with many essential services, including health care. In addition to this baby clinic, pictured in 1918, it established a tuberculosis clinic at a time when the city's public hospitals refused to treat black citizens afflicted with the disease.

Indiana Historical Society

Governors Hoke Smith of Georgia and James Vardaman, "the White Chief," of Mississippi typified the link between racism and reform in the South. These men supported progressive reforms but their racist demagogy incited antiblack violence throughout the South.

Even in the North, where relatively few black people lived, race relations deteriorated. Civil rights laws went unenforced, black customers were excluded from restaurants and hotels, and schools were segregated. A reporter in Pennsylvania found that "this disposition to discriminate against Negroes has greatly increased within the past decade." Antiblack race riots exploded in New York in 1900 and in Springfield, Illinois—Abraham Lincoln's hometown—in 1908.

Black Activism.   Although most white progressives promoted or accepted racial discrimination, and most black southerners had to adapt to it, black progressive activism was growing. Even in the South, some African Americans struggled to improve conditions. In Atlanta, for example, black women created established settlement houses, kindergartens, and day care centers. The women of the Neighborhood Union, organized in 1908, even challenged the discriminatory policies of Atlanta's board of education, demanding equal facilities and appropriations for the city's black schools. They had only limited success, but their efforts demonstrated a persisting commitment to reform society.

In the North, African Americans more openly criticized discrimination and rejected Booker T. Washington's philosophy of accommodation. In 1905, W. E. B. Du Bois and other black activists met in Niagara Falls, Canada, to make plans to promote political and economic equality. In 1910, the **Niagara Movement** joined with a small group of white reformers, including Jane Addams, to organize the National Association for the Advancement of Colored People. The NAACP sought to overthrow segregation and establish equal justice and educational opportunities. As its director of publicity and research, Du Bois launched an influential magazine, *The Crisis,* to shape public opinion. "Agitate," he counseled, "protest, reveal the truth, and refuse to be silenced."

Niagara Movement African-American group organized in 1905 to promote racial integration, civil and political rights, and equal access to economic opportunity.

WHAT STEPS were taken toward woman suffrage during the Progressive Era?

QUICK REVIEW

Votes for Women

- Woman suffrage movement began in the mid-nineteenth century.
- Early twentieth-century leaders adopted activist tactics.
- Nineteenth Amendment ratified in 1920.

Carrying ballot boxes on a stretcher to ridicule American pretensions to a healthy democracy without woman suffrage, these activists marched in a dramatic parade in New York City in 1915. Combining such tactics with traditional appeals to patriotism and women's moral purity, woman suffragists eventually achieved the greatest democratic reform of the Progressive Era.

Courtesy Library of Congress

REFORMING POLITICS AND GOVERNMENT

Progressives of all kinds clamored for the reform of politics and government. But their political activism was motivated by different concerns, and they sometimes pursued competing objectives. Many wanted to change procedures and institutions to promote greater democracy and responsibility. Others hoped to improve the efficiency of government, eliminate corruption, or increase their own influence. All justified their objectives as necessary to adapt the political system to the nation's new needs.

WOMAN SUFFRAGE

One of the most important achievements of the era was woman suffrage. The movement had began in the mid-nineteenth century, but suffragists had been frustrated by the prevailing belief that women's "proper sphere" was the home and the family. Woman suffrage, especially when championed as a step toward women's equality, seemed to challenge the natural order of society, and it generated much opposition, not only among men but among traditionalist-minded women as well.

In the early twentieth century, suffragists began to outflank the opposition. Under a new generation of leaders, such as Carrie Chapman Catt and Harriot Stanton Blatch, they adopted activist tactics, including parades, mass meetings, and "suffrage tours" by automobile. They also organized by political districts and attracted workingwomen and labor unions. By 1917, the National American Woman Suffrage Association had over 2 million members.

Some suffrage leaders adopted new arguments to gain more support. Rather than insist on the justice of woman suffrage or emphasize equal rights, they spoke of the special moral and maternal instincts women could bring to politics if allowed to vote. The suffrage movement now appeared less a radical, disruptive force than a vehicle for extending traditional female benevolence and service to society. Many suffragists, particularly in working-class groups, remained committed to the larger possibilities of suffrage, but the new image of the movement increased public support by appealing to conventional views of women (see Map 21–1).

In 1910, Washington became the first state since the mid-1890s to approve woman suffrage, followed by California in 1911 and Arizona, Kansas, and Oregon in 1912. Suffragists also mounted national actions, such as the dramatic inaugural parade in March 1913 described at the beginning of this chapter. The violence surrounding that event outraged public opinion, revived interest in a federal constitutional amendment to grant women the vote, and prompted women to send petitions and organize pilgrimages to Washington from across the country. (See Global Perspectives: "British Suffragettes.") By 1919, thirty-nine states had established full or partial woman suffrage,

MAP EXPLORATION

To explore an interactive version of this map, go to **http://www.prenhall.com/goldfield3/map21.1**

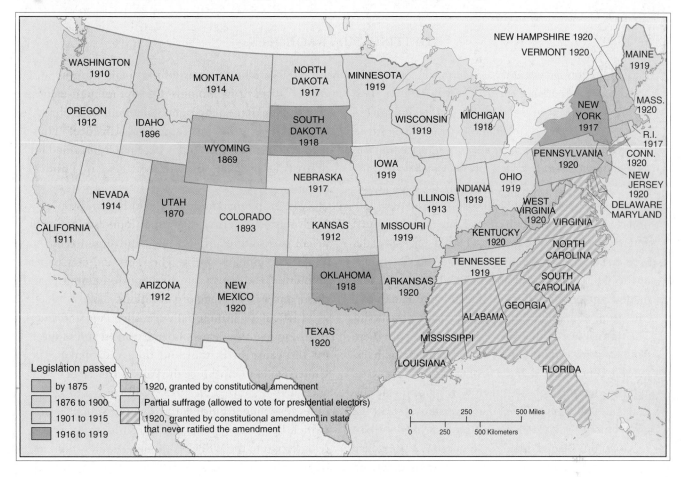

MAP 21–1   Woman suffrage in the United States before the ratification of the Nineteenth Amendment.
Beginning with Wyoming in 1869, woman suffrage slowly gained acceptance in the West, but women in the South and much of the East got the ballot only when the Nineteenth Amendment was ratified in 1920.

HOW might you explain the relatively early dates at which women in the West got the right to vote? Why was woman suffrage slower in coming to the East and South?

and Congress finally approved an amendment. Ratified by the states in 1920, the **Nineteenth Amendment** marked a critical advance in political democracy.

ELECTORAL REFORM

Other electoral reforms changed the election process and the meaning of political participation. The so-called **Australian ballot** adopted by most states during the 1890s provided for official ballots and secret voting, freeing voters from intimidation and discouraging vote buying and other corruption. Public regulation of other parts of the electoral process previously controlled by parties soon followed. Beginning with Mississippi in 1902, nearly every state provided for direct primaries to remove nominations from the boss-ridden caucus and convention system. Many states also reformed campaign practices.

Nineteenth Amendment
Constitutional revision that in 1920 established women citizens' right to vote.

Australian ballot   Secret voting and the use of official ballots rather than party tickets.

GLOBAL PERSPECTIVES

BRITISH SUFFRAGETTES

The movement for woman suffrage was an international one. In Great Britain the effort began in the nineteenth century, and women gained the right to vote for local officials in 1869. But the struggle to secure woman suffrage in elections for Parliament encountered great opposition from conservative interest groups and won little support from the major parties.

Frustrated that polite appeals to reason and petitions to Parliament had no effect, Emmeline Pankhurst and her daughters, Christabel and Sylvia, organized the Women's Social and Political Union in 1903. Members of the WSPU embarked on a militant campaign that made England, in the words of Emmeline Pankhurst, "the storm centre of the worldwide women's movement." The suffragettes (as they were called to distinguish them from conventional suffragists) disrupted meetings, heckled speakers, picketed Parliament, refused to pay taxes, and paraded through the streets wearing dramatic costumes and carrying bold signs urging voters to reject the government. Such activities often provoked violent reprisals; on "Black Friday," November 18, 1910, police viciously assaulted them for six hours. Eventually the suffragettes turned to the destruction of public and private property, smashing windows and setting fires. When arrested and jailed as ordinary criminals rather than political prisoners, they went on hunger strikes and were brutally force-fed. Suffragettes used the resulting publicity to further mobilize women, win public sympathy, and embarrass the government.

The Pankhursts insisted that male hostility and conservatism drove women to adopt militant tactics. "For women denied the right of petition," said Christabel Pankhurst, "the only thing left is violence." Thus, they maintained, suffragettes were not imprisoned for destroying property but for engaging in political protest.

The Pankhursts and other British suffragettes regularly toured America, where they found suffragists in a "curious state of quiescence" and urged them to adopt "the militant spirit." The tours and newspaper accounts of the British campaign spurred American activism and new suffrage organizations.

Particularly influential were Alice Paul and Lucy Burns, young Americans who had worked and suffered for the cause in Britain and then returned to the United States to introduce the Pankhursts' tactics. Paul and Burns organized the 1913 Washington suffrage parade and then founded the Congressional Union (which became the Woman's Party) as an American counterpart to the WSPU. Although certainly militant, the Woman's Party was nonviolent and never engaged in property destruction. Its members, instead, sacrificed themselves—most famously in 1917, when hundreds daily picketed the White House, the first group to do so, and were regularly beaten, arrested, and imprisoned, and endured both prolonged hunger strikes and brutal forced feeding in grotesque repetition of the British experience.

These reforms weakened the influence of political parties. Their decreasing ability to mobilize voters was reflected in a steady decline in voter participation, from 79 percent in 1896 to 49 percent in 1920. These developments had ominous implications, for parties and voting had traditionally linked ordinary Americans to their government. As parties contracted, nonpartisan organizations and pressure groups, promoting narrower objectives, gained influence. Many of these special-interest groups represented the same middle- or upper-class interests that had led the attack on parties. Their organized lobbying would steadily give them greater influence over government and contribute to the declining popular belief in the value of voting or participation in politics.

Disfranchisement more obviously undermined American democracy. In the South, Democrats—progressive and conservative alike—eliminated not only black voters but also many poor white voters from the electorate through poll taxes, literacy tests, and other restrictions. Republicans in the North adopted educational or literacy tests in ten states, enacted strict registration laws, and gradually abolished the right of aliens to vote. Such electoral reforms reduced the political power of ethnic and working-class Americans, often stripping them of their political rights and means of influence.

MUNICIPAL REFORM

Antiparty attitudes also affected progressives' efforts to reform municipal government, which they regarded as inefficient and corrupt, at least partly because of the power of urban political machines. Muckrakers had exposed crooked alliances between city bosses and business leaders that resulted in wasteful or inadequate municipal services. In some cities, urban reformers attempted to break these alliances and improve conditions for those suffering most from municipal misrule. For example, in Toledo, Ohio, Mayor Samuel "Golden Rule" Jones opened public playgrounds, established the eight-hour day for city workers, and improved public services. Other reforming mayors fought municipal corruption, limited the political influence of corporations, and championed public ownership of utilities.

More elitist progressives changed the structure of urban government by replacing ward elections, which could be controlled by the neighborhood-based city machine, with at-large elections. To win citywide elections required greater resources and therefore helped swell middle-class influence at the expense of the working class. So did nonpartisan elections, which reformers introduced to weaken party loyalties.

Urban reformers developed two other structural innovations: the city commission and the city manager. Both attempted to institutionalize efficient, businesslike government staffed by professional administrators. By 1920, hundreds of cities had adopted one of the new plans, which business groups often promoted. Again, then, reform often shifted political power from ethnic and working-class voters, represented however imperfectly by partisan elections, to smaller groups with greater resources.

PROGRESSIVE STATE GOVERNMENT

Progressives also reshaped state government. Some tried to democratize the legislative process, regarding the legislature—the most important branch of state government in the nineteenth century—as ineffective and even corrupt, dominated by party bosses and corporate influences. Populists had first raised such charges in the 1890s and proposed two novel solutions. The **initiative** enabled reformers to propose legislation directly to the electorate, bypassing an unresponsive legislature; the **referendum** permitted voters to approve or reject legislative measures. South Dakota Populists established the first system of "direct legislation" in 1898, and progressives adopted these innovations in twenty other states between 1902 and 1915.

Other innovations also expanded the popular role in state government. The **Seventeenth Amendment,** ratified in 1913, provided for the election of U.S. senators directly by popular vote instead of by state legislatures. Beginning with Oregon in 1908, ten states adopted the **recall,** enabling voters to remove unsatisfactory public officials from office.

As state legislatures and party machines were curbed, dynamic governors pushed progressive programs into law. Elected governor in 1900, "Fighting Bob" La Follette turned Wisconsin into "the laboratory of democracy." La Follette established direct primaries, railroad regulation, the first state income tax, workers' compensation, and other important measures before being elected to the U.S. Senate

---

QUICK REVIEW

Municipal Reform

- Urban reformers sought to break alliances between city bosses and business leaders.
- Urban reformers developed the concept of the city commission and the city manager.
- Business groups often promoted these reforms.

Initiative   Procedure by which citizens can introduce a subject for legislation, usually through a petition signed by a specific number of voters.

Referendum   Submission of a law, proposed or already in effect, to a direct popular vote for approval or rejection.

Seventeenth Amendment Constitutional change that in 1913 established the direct popular election of U.S. senators.

Recall   The process of removing an official from office by popular vote, usually after using petitions to call for such a vote.

in 1906. La Follette also stressed efficiency and expertise. He used regulatory commissions to oversee railroads, banks, and other interests. Most states followed suit, and expert commissions became an important feature of state government.

"Experts" were presumed to be disinterested and therefore committed to the general welfare. In practice, however, regulators were subject to pressures from competing interest groups, and some commissions became captives of the very industries they were supposed to control. This irony was matched by the contradiction between the expansion of democracy through the initiative and referendum and the increasing reliance on nonelected professional experts to set and implement public policy.

THEODORE ROOSEVELT AND THE PROGRESSIVE PRESIDENCY

HOW DID Theodore Roosevelt envision the power of the president?

WHERE TO LEARN MORE

Sagamore Hill, Oyster Bay, New York
www. nps.gov/sahi/

When a crazed anarchist assassinated William McKinley in 1901, Theodore Roosevelt entered the White House, and the progressive movement gained its most prominent leader. The son of a wealthy New York family, Roosevelt had pursued a career in Republican politics, serving as a New York legislator, U.S. civil service commissioner, and assistant secretary of the navy. After his exploits in the Spanish-American War (see chapter 22), he was elected governor of New York in 1898 and vice president in 1900.

Roosevelt's frenetic activity, aggressive personality, and penchant for self-promotion worried some Americans. Mark Twain fretted that "Mr. Roosevelt is the Tom Sawyer of the political world of the twentieth century; always showing off; always hunting for a chance to show off; in his frenzied imagination the Great Republic is a vast Barnum circus with him for a clown and the whole world for audience." But Roosevelt's flamboyance and ambitions made him the most popular politician of the time and enabled him to dramatize the issues of progressivism and to become the first modern president.

TR AND THE MODERN PRESIDENCY

Roosevelt rejected the limited role of Gilded Age presidents. He believed that the president could do anything to meet national needs that the Constitution did not specifically prohibit. Indeed, the expansion of government power and its consolidation in the executive branch were among his most significant accomplishments. Rather than defer to Congress, Roosevelt exerted legislative leadership so vigorously that critics complained of "executive arrogance." Roosevelt generally avoided direct challenges to the conservative Old Guard Republicans who controlled Congress, but his activities helped shift the balance of power within the national government.

Roosevelt also reorganized the executive branch. He believed in efficiency and expertise, which he attempted to institutionalize in special commissions and administrative procedures. To promote rational policymaking and public management, he staffed the expanding federal bureaucracy with able professionals. Here, too, he provoked opposition. The president, complained one Republican, was "trying to concentrate all power in Washington . . . and to govern the people by commissions and bureaus."

Finally, Roosevelt encouraged the development of a personal presidency by exploiting the public's interest in their exuberant young president. He established the first White House press room and skillfully handled the mass media. His endless and well-reported activities, from playing with his children in the White House to wrestling, hiking, and horseback-riding with various notables, made him a celebrity, known as "TR" or "Teddy." The publicity not only kept TR in the spotlight but also enabled him to mold public opinion.

ROOSEVELT AND LABOR

One sign of TR's vigorous new approach to the presidency was his handling of a coal strike in 1902. Members of the United Mine Workers Union walked off their jobs, demanding higher wages, an eight-hour day, and recognition of their union. The mine owners closed the mines and waited for the union to collapse. But led by John Mitchell, the strikers held their ranks. The prospect of a freezing winter frightened consumers. Management's stubborn arrogance contrasted with the workers' orderly conduct and willingness to negotiate and hardened public opinion against the owners.

Although his legal advisers told him that the government had no authority to intervene, Roosevelt invited both the owners and the union leaders to the White House and declared that the national interest made government action necessary. Mitchell agreed to negotiate with the owners or to accept an arbitration commission appointed by the president. The owners, however, refused even to speak to the miners and demanded that Roosevelt use the army to break the union, as Cleveland had done in the Pullman strike in 1894.

Roosevelt was not a champion of labor. But as president, he believed his role was to mediate social conflict for the public good. Roosevelt announced that he would use the army to seize and operate the mines, not to crush the union. Questioned about the constitutionality of such an action, Roosevelt bellowed, "To hell with the Constitution when the people want coal." Reluctantly, the owners accepted the arbitration commission they had previously rejected. The commission gave the miners a 10 percent wage increase and a nine-hour day but not union recognition, and permitted the owners to raise coal prices by 10 percent. Roosevelt described his intervention as simply giving both labor and management a "square deal. It also set important precedents for an active government role in labor disputes and a strong president acting as a steward of the public.

MANAGING NATURAL RESOURCES

Federal land policy had helped create farms and develop transportation, but it had also ceded to speculators and business interests much of the nation's forests, mineral deposits, waterpower sites, and grazing lands. Reckless exploitation of these resources alarmed a new generation that believed the public welfare required the **conservation** of natural resources through efficient and scientific management. Conservationists achieved early victories in the Forest Reserve Act (1891) and the Forest Management Act (1897), which authorized the federal government to withdraw timberlands from development and to regulate grazing, lumbering, and hydroelectric sites in the forests.

Roosevelt built on these beginnings to make conservation a major focus of his presidency. Aided by Gifford Pinchot, the head of the Forest Service, TR used presidential authority to triple the size of the forest reserves to 150 million acres, set aside another 80 million acres valuable for minerals and petroleum, and establish dozens of wildlife refuges. In 1908, Roosevelt held a White House conference of state and federal officials that led to the creation of the National Conservation Commission, 41 state conservation commissions, and widespread public support for the conservation movement.

Conservation The efficient management and use of natural resources, such as forests, grasslands, and rivers, as opposed to preservation or uncontrolled exploitation.

WHERE TO LEARN MORE

John Muir National Historic Site,
Martinez, California
www.nps. gov/jomu/

Not everyone, of course, agreed with TR's conservationist policies. Some favored **preservation,** hoping to set aside land as permanent wilderness. Preservationists won some victories, saving a stand of California's giant redwoods and helping create the National Park Service in 1916, but more Americans favored the utilitarian emphasis of the early conservationists.

Other interests opposed conservation completely. While some of the larger timber and mineral companies supported conservation as a way to guarantee long-run profits, smaller western entrepreneurs often cared only about quick returns. Many westerners, moreover, resented having easterners make key decisions about western growth and saw conservation as a perpetuation of this colonial subservience.

But westerners were happy to take federal money for expensive irrigation projects that private capital would not underwrite. They favored the 1902 National Reclamation Act, which established what became the **Bureau of Reclamation.** Its engineers were to construct dams, reservoirs, and irrigation canals, and the government was to sell the irrigated lands in tracts no larger than 160-acres. With massive dams and networks of irrigation canals, it reclaimed fertile valleys from the desert. Unfortunately, the bureau did not enforce the 160-acre limitation and thus helped create powerful corporate farms in the West.

Westerners also welcomed Roosevelt's conservationist emphasis on relational development when it restricted Indian control of land and resources. He favored policies breaking up many reservations to open the land to whites for "efficient" development and diverting Indian waters to growing cities like Phoenix. Tribal protests were ignored.

CORPORATE REGULATION

Nothing symbolized Roosevelt's active presidency better than his popular reputation as a "trust buster." TR regarded the formation of large business combinations favorably, but he realized he could not ignore the public anxiety about corporate power. To satisfy popular clamor, ensure social stability, and still retain the economic advantages of big modern corporations, TR proposed to "develop an orderly system, and such a system can only come through the gradually exercised right of efficient government control." Rather than invoking "the foolish antitrust law," he favored government regulation to prevent corporate abuses and defend the public interest. "Misconduct," not size, was the issue.

But Roosevelt did file some antitrust suits, including one against the Northern Securities Company, a holding company organized by J. P. Morgan to control the railroad network of the Northwest. For TR, this suit was an assertion of government power that reassured a worried public and encouraged corporate responsibility. In 1904, the Supreme Court ordered the dissolution of the Northern Securities Company.

Elected president in his own right in 1904 over the colorless and conservative Democratic candidate, Judge Alton B. Parker, Roosevelt responded to the growing popular demand for reform by pushing further toward a regulatory government. He proposed legislation "to work out methods of controlling the big corporations without paralyzing the energies of the business community." In 1906, Congress passed the Hepburn Act, the Pure Food and Drug Act, and the Meat Inspection Act. All three were compromises between reformers seeking serious government control of the industries and political defenders and lobbyists of the industries involved.

The Hepburn Act authorized the Interstate Commerce Commission to set maximum railroad rates. The two other laws aimed at consumer protection in food and drugs. In part, this legislation reflected public demand, but many business leaders also supported government regulation, convinced that it would expand their

Preservation   Protecting forests, land, and other features of the natural environment from development or destruction, often for aesthetic appreciation.

Bureau of Reclamation
Federal agency established in 1902 providing public funds for irrigation projects in arid regions.

markets by certifying the quality of their products and drive their smaller competitors out of business. Thus the laws extended government supervision and regulation over business to protect the public health and safety, but they also served some corporate purposes.

Despite the compromises and weaknesses in the three laws, TR contended that they marked "a noteworthy advance in the policy of securing federal supervision and control over corporations." In 1907 and 1908, he pushed for an eight-hour workday, stock market regulation, and inheritance and income taxes. Republican conservatives in Congress blocked such reforms, and tensions increased between the progressive and conservative wings of the party. Old Guard Republicans thought Roosevelt had extended government powers dangerously, but in fact his accomplishments had been relatively modest. As La Follette noted, Roosevelt's "cannonading filled the air with noise and smoke, which confused and obscured the line of action, but, when the battle cloud drifted by and the quiet was restored, it was always a matter of surprise that so little had really been accomplished."

Roosevelt enjoyed this cartoon illustrating his distinction between good trusts, retrained by government regulations for public welfare, and bad trusts. On those he put his foot down.

The Granger Collection, New York

TAFT AND THE INSURGENTS

TR handpicked his successor as president: a loyal lieutenant, William Howard Taft. Taft had been a federal judge, governor-general of the Philippines, and secretary of war. Later he would serve as chief justice of the United States. But Taft's election in 1908, over Democrat William Jennings Bryan in his third presidential campaign, led to a Republican political disaster.

Taft did preside over important progressive achievements. His administration pursued a more active and successful antitrust program than Roosevelt's. Taft set aside more public forest lands and oil reserves than Roosevelt had. He also supported a constitutional amendment authorizing an income tax, which went into effect in 1913 under the **Sixteenth Amendment.** One of the most important accomplishments of the Progressive Era, the income tax would provide the means for the government to expand its activities and responsibilities.

Nevertheless, Taft soon alienated progressives and floundered into a political morass. His problems were twofold. First, the Republicans were divided between conservatives and reformers. Second, Taft was politically inept. He was unable to mediate between the two Republican factions, and the party split apart.

Reformers wanted to restrict the power of the speaker of the House, "Uncle Joe" Cannon, a reactionary who systematically blocked progressive measures. After seeming to promise support, Taft backed down when conservatives threatened to

Sixteenth Amendment
Constitutional revision that in 1913 authorized a federal income tax.

WHERE TO LEARN MORE

William Howard Taft National
Historic Site, Cincinnati, Ohio

defeat important legislation. The insurgents in Congress eventually restricted the speaker's powers, but they never forgave what they saw as Taft's betrayal. The tariff also alienated progressives from Taft. He had campaigned in 1908 for a lower tariff to curb inflation, but when they introduced tariff reform legislation, the president failed to support them. Taft justified his inaction as avoiding presidential interference with congressional business, but this position clashed with TR's example and the reformers' expectations. Progressives concluded that Taft had sided with the Old Guard against real change.

This perception solidified when Taft stumbled into a controversy over conservation. Gifford Pinchot had become embroiled in a complex struggle with Richard Ballinger, Taft's secretary of the interior. When Pinchot challenged Ballinger's role in a questionable sale of public coal lands in Alaska to a J. P. Morgan syndicate, Taft upheld Ballinger and fired Pinchot. Progressives concluded that Taft had repudiated Roosevelt's conservation policies.

In 1911, the National Progressive League organized to champion La Follette for the Republican nomination in 1912. Roosevelt rejected an appeal for support, convinced that a challenge to the incumbent president was both doomed and divisive. But Taft's political blunders increasingly angered Roosevelt. Condemning Taft as "disloyal to our past friendship," TR began to campaign for the Republican nomination himself. In 13 state primaries, he won 278 delegates to only 46 for Taft. But most states did not then have primaries; as a result, Taft was able to dominate the Republican convention and win renomination. Roosevelt's forces formed a third party—the Progressive Party—and nominated the former president. The Republican split almost guaranteed victory for the Democratic nominee, Woodrow Wilson.

Woodrow Wilson and Progressive Reform

E lected president in 1912 and 1916, Woodrow Wilson mediated among differing progressive views to achieve a strong reform program, enlarge the power of the executive branch, and make the White House the center of national politics.

HOW DID Woodrow Wilson's vision of reform differ from Theodore Roosevelt's?

The Election of 1912

Despite the prominence of Roosevelt and La Follette, progressivism was not simply a Republican phenomenon. Congressional Democrats more consistently supported reform measures than Republicans did. As the Republicans quarreled during Taft's administration, Democrats pushed progressive remedies and achieved major victories in the state and congressional elections of 1910. To improve the party's chances in 1912, William Jennings Bryan announced that he would step aside. The Democratic spotlight shifted to the governor of New Jersey, Woodrow Wilson.

Wilson first entered public life as a conservative, steeped in the limited-government traditions of his native South. As president of Princeton University, beginning in 1902, he became a prominent representative of middle-class respectability and conservative causes. In 1910, New Jersey's Democratic bosses selected him for governor to head off the progressives. But once in office, Wilson championed popular reforms and immediately began to campaign as a progressive for the party's 1912 presidential nomination.

Wilson's progressivism differed from that of Roosevelt in 1912. TR emphasized a strong government to promote economic and social order. He defended big business as inevitable and healthy provided that government control ensured that it would benefit the entire nation. Roosevelt called this program the **New Nationalism,** reflecting his belief in a powerful state and a national interest. He also supported demands for social welfare, including workers' compensation and the abolition of child labor.

Wilson was horrified by Roosevelt's vision. His **New Freedom** program rejected what he called TR's "regulated monopoly." Wilson wanted "regulated competition," with the goverment's role limited to breaking up monopolies through antitrust action and preventing artificial barriers like tariffs from blocking free enterprise. Wilson opposed social welfare legislation as "paternalistic."

Roosevelt's endorsement of social legislation attracted many women into politics. As Jane Addams observed, "their long concern for the wreckage of industry has come to be considered politics." (see American Views: "Jane Addams and the Progressive Party.") The Progressive party also endorsed woman suffrage and promised women equal representation on party comittees.

Despite his personal popularity, however, TR was unable to add progressive Democrats to the Republicans who followed him into the Progressive Party, and thus was doomed to defeat. Other reform voters embraced the Socialist candidate, Eugene V. Debs, who captured 900,000 votes—6 percent of the total. Taft played little role in the campaign. "I might as well give up as far as being a candidate," he lamented. "There are so many people in the country who don't like me."

Wilson won an easy electoral college victory, though he received only 42 percent of the popular vote (see Map 21–2). Roosevelt came in second, Taft third. The Democrats also gained control of Congress, giving Wilson the opportunity to enact his New Freedom program.

IMPLEMENTING THE NEW FREEDOM

As president, Wilson built on Roosevelt's precedent to strengthen executive authority. Wilson proposed a full legislative program and worked forcefully to secure its approval. When necessary, he appealed to the public for support or doled out patronage and compromised with conservatives. With such methods and a solid Democratic majority, Wilson gained approval of important laws.

Wilson turned first to the traditional Democratic goal of reducing the high protective tariff, the symbol of special privileges for industry. He forced through the **Underwood-Simmons Tariff Act** of 1913, the first substantial reduction in duties since before the Civil War. The act also levied the first income tax under the recently ratified Sixteenth Amendment.

Wilson next reformed the nation's banking and currency system, which was inadequate for a modernizing economy. He skillfully maneuvered a compromise measure through Congress, balancing the demands of agrarian progressives for government control with the bankers' desires for private control. The **Federal Reserve Act** of 1913 created 12 regional Federal Reserve banks that, although privately controlled, were to be supervised by the Federal Reserve Board, appointed by the president. The law also provided for a flexible national currency and improved access to credit. Serious problems remained, but the new system promoted the progressive goals of order and efficiency and fulfilled Wilson's New Freedom principle of introducing limited government regulation while preserving private business control.

Wilson's third objective was new legislation to break up monopolies. To this end, he initially supported the Clayton antitrust bill, which prohibited unfair trade practices and sharply restricted holding companies. But when business leaders and other progressives strenuously objected, Wilson reversed himself. Opting for

New Nationalism Theodore Roosevelt's 1912 program calling for a strong national government to foster, regulate, and protect business, industry, workers, and consumers.

New Freedom Woodrow Wilson's 1912 program for limited government intervention in the economy to restore competition by curtailing the restrictive influences of trusts and protective tariffs, thereby providing opportunities for individual achievement.

Underwood-Simmons Tariff Act The 1913 reform law that lowered tariff rates and levied the first regular federal income tax.

Federal Reserve Act The 1913 law that revised banking and currency by extending limited government regulation through the creation of the Federal Reserve System.

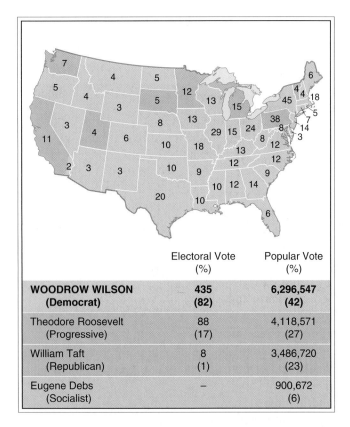

	Electoral Vote (%)	Popular Vote (%)
WOODROW WILSON (Democrat)	**435 (82)**	**6,296,547 (42)**
Theodore Roosevelt (Progressive)	88 (17)	4,118,571 (27)
William Taft (Republican)	8 (1)	3,486,720 (23)
Eugene Debs (Socialist)	–	900,672 (6)

MAP 21–2   The Election of 1912   The split within the Republican Party enabled Woodrow Wilson to carry most states and become president even though he won only a minority of the popular vote.

HOW IS it possible that Woodrow Wilson received 82 percent of the electoral vote but only 42 percent of the popular vote?

Federal Trade Commission
Government agency established in 1914 to provide regulatory oversight of business activity.

continuous federal regulation rather than for the dissolution of trusts, Wilson endorsed the creation of the **Federal Trade Commission (FTC)** to oversee business activity and prevent illegal restrictions on competition.

The Federal Trade Commission Act of 1914 dismayed many of Wilson's early supporters because it embraced the New Nationalism's emphasis on positive regulation. However, Wilson's conservative appointments to the FTC ensured that the agency would not seriously interfere with business, and by the 1920s, the FTC had become virtually a junior partner of the business community.

Wilson now announced that no further reforms were necessary—astonishing many progressives whose objectives had been completely ignored. Wilson refused to support woman suffrage and helped kill legislation abolishing child labor and expanding credits to farmers. He demonstrated his indifference to issues of social justice by supporting the introduction of racial segregation within the government itself. Government offices, shops, restrooms, and restaurants were all segregated; employees who complained were fired.

THE EXPANSION OF REFORM

Wilson had won in 1912 only because the Republicans had split. By 1916, Roosevelt had returned to the GOP, and Wilson realized that he had to attract some of TR's former followers. Wilson therefore abandoned his opposition to social and economic reforms and promoted measures he had previously condemned. But he had also grown in the White House and now recognized that some problems could be resolved only by positive federal action.

To assist farmers, Wilson in 1916 convinced Congress to pass the Federal Farm Loan Act, which provided farmers with federally financed long-term agricultural credits. The Warehouse Act of 1916 improved short-term agricultural credit. The Highway Act of 1916 provided funds to construct and improve rural roads.

Wilson and the Democratic Congress also reached out to labor. Wilson signed the Keating-Owen Act prohibiting the interstate shipment of products made by child labor. In 1902, Wilson had denounced Roosevelt's intervention in the coal strike, but in 1916 he broke a labor-management impasse and averted a railroad strike by helping pass the Adamson Act establishing an eight-hour day for railroad workers. Wilson also pushed the Kern-McGillicuddy Act, which achieved the progressive goal of a workers' compensation system for federal employees.

Wilson also promoted activist government when he nominated Louis Brandeis to the Supreme Court. Known as the "people's lawyer," Brandeis had successfully defended protective labor legislation before the conservative judiciary. Brandeis was the first Jew nominated to the court, and anti-Semitism motivated some of his opponents. Wilson overcame a vicious campaign against Brandeis and secured his confirmation.

By these actions, Wilson brought progressivism to a culmination of sorts and consolidated reformers behind him for a second term. Less than a decade earlier, Wilson the private citizen had assailed government regulation and social legislation; by

1916, he had guided an unprecedented expansion of federal power. His own transformation symbolized the development of progressivism.

CONCLUSION

*I*n the early twentieth century, progressive reformers responded to the tensions of industrial and urban development by organizing to promote social change and an interventionist state. Programs and laws to protect women, children, and injured workers testified to their compassion; the creation of new agencies and political techniques indicated their interest in order and efficiency; campaigns to end corruption, whether perceived in urban political machines, corporate influence, drunkeness, or "inferior" immigrants, illustrated their self-assured vision of the public good.

Progressivism had its ironies and paradoxes. It called for democratic reforms "and did achieve woman suffrage, direct legislation, and popular election of senators" but helped disfranchise black southerners and northern immigrants. It advocated social justice but often enforced social control. It demanded responsive government but helped create bureaucracies largely removed from popular control. It endorsed regulation of business in the public interest but forged regulatory laws and commissions that tended to aid businesses. Some of the these seeming contradictions reflected the persistence of traditional attitudes and the need to accommodate conservative opponents; others revealed the progressives' own limitations in vision, concern, or nerve.

Americans had come to accept that government action could resolve social and economic problems, and the role and power of government expanded accordingly. The emergence of an activist presidency, capable of developing programs, mobilizing public opinion, directing Congress, and taking forceful action, epitomized this key development.

These important features would be crucial when the nation fought World War I, which brought new challenges and dangers to the United States. The Great War would expose many of the limitations of progressivism and the naiveté of the progressives' optimism.

U.S. President Woodrow Wilson sits at his desk in an oil painting on canvas by Edmund Charles Tarbell.

The Granger Collection, New York

AMERICAN VIEWS

Jane Addams and the Progressive Party

Jane Addams, the founder of Hull House in Chicago, was active not merely in a range of social reform movements but also in nearly every facet of progressive politics. An ardent suffragist, Addams seconded the presidential nomination of Theodore Roosevelt at the founding convention of the Progressive Party in 1912, while a "Jane Addams Chorus" sang "Onward, Christian Soldiers" and "The Battle Hymn of the Republic." In this reminiscence from her second autobiography, Addams describes the convention and her part in the party's campaign that year.

- Why did settlement workers like Addams see the Progressive Party as the climax to their struggle for social justice?
- How did Addams's political interests fit into Roosevelt's program of the New Nationalism?
- How does Addams's rhetoric reflect the moral impulses underlying much of progressive reform?
- Why does Addams believe that women were attracted to the Progressive Party?

It was in August, 1912, that the Progressive Party was organized.

Suddenly, as if by magic, the city of Chicago became filled with men and women from every state in the Union who were evidently haunted by the same social compunctions and animated by like hopes; they revealed to each other mutual sympathies and memories. They urged methods which had already been tried in other countries, for righting old wrongs and for establishing standards in industry. For three days together they defined their purposes and harmonized their wills into gigantic cooperation. . . .

They believed that the program of social legislation placed before the country by the Progressive Party was of great significance to the average voter quite irrespective of the party which might finally claim his allegiance.

The platform, in the hope that the political organization of the nation might never again get so far away from the life of the people, advocated equal suffrage, direct primaries, the initiative and referendum. . . . In spite of our belief in our leader [Theodore Roosevelt], I was there, and I think the same was true of many others, because the platform expressed the social hopes so long ignored by the politicians; although we appreciated to the full our good fortune in securing on their behalf the magnetic personality of the distinguished candidate. Perhaps we felt so keenly the uplifting sense of comradeship with old friends and coworkers not only because we had all realized how inadequate we were in small groups but because the very sentiments of compassion and desire for social justice were futile unless they could at last find expression as an integral part of . . . government. At any rate, it was evident that measures of industrial amelioration and demands for social justice, so long discussed by small

SUMMARY

The Ferment of Reform Progressivism was a diverse movement; reformers responded to the tensions of industrialization and urbanization by developing programs to give women the right to vote, expose business abuses, end child labor, make government more efficient, manage natural resources, and bring about social reform. The Social Gospel movement sought to introduce religious ethics into industrial relations. As businesses adopted Taylorization to improve workplace efficiency, workers resisted these new rules of efficiency. Opponents of reform held to traditional values and religious fundamentalism; businesses, angered by muckraking, used public relations as well as less desirable tactics to counter their critics.

groups, were at last thrust into the stern arena of political action. . . .

The Progressive Convention has been described many times, and perhaps never quite adequately. It was a curious moment of release from inhibitions, and it did not seem in the least strange that reticent men and women should speak aloud of their religious and social beliefs, confident that they would be understood.

The women who identified themselves with the Progressive Convention inevitably experienced moments of heart searching and compunction. It is hard to understand it now, after we have possessed the ballot for a decade and have come to deem it a virtue "to enter politics," but at the moment we felt it necessary to give to the public our reasons for thus identifying ourselves with a political party. We said that when a great party pledges itself to the protection of children, to the care of the aged, to the relief of overworked girls, to the safeguarding of burdened men, it is inevitable that it should appeal to women and should seek to draw upon the great reservoir of their moral energy so long undesired and unutilized in practical politics; that one is the corollary of the other; a program of human welfare, the necessity for women's participation.

The real interest in the measures advocated in the party platform came however during the campaign itself when it was possible to place them before many groups throughout the country. Sometimes the planks in our platform were sharply challenged, but more often regarded with approval and occasionally with enthusiasm. I recall a meeting in Leadville, Colorado, made up altogether of miners who were much surprised to find that politics had anything to do with such affairs. They had always supposed that hours of labor were matters to be fought for and not voted upon. It was very exhilarating to talk to them, and it seemed to me that I had never before realized how slow we had been to place the definite interests of the workingmen in such shape that they could be voted upon. As a campaign speaker I was sent from town to town in both Dakotas, in Iowa, Nebraska, Oklahoma, Colorado, Kansas, and Missouri. The comradeship which a like-minded group always affords, combined with the heartiness of western good will, kept my spirits at high tide in spite of the fatigue of incessant speaking. . . .

The campaign renewed one's convictions that if the community as a whole were better informed as to the ethical implications of industrial wrongs whole areas of life could be saved from becoming brutalized or from sinking into hard indifference. . . . At moments we believed that we were witnessing a new pioneering of the human spirit, that we were in all humility inaugurating an exploration into the moral resources of our fellow citizens.

Source: Jane Addams, *The Second Twenty Years at Hull-House.* (New York: Macmillan Co., 1930).

Reforming Society Progressives worked to transform society by improving living conditions, educational opportunities, family life, and social and industrial relations. Settlement houses were the spearheads of social reform in urban immigrant neighborhoods, while the country lifers worked to transform rural society. Other progressives sought government intervention to limit immigration, impose prohibition, or improve schools. The Niagara Movement sought to extend equal justice to African Americans, who often suffered from the hostility or indifference of white progressives.

Reforming Politics and Government Progressives clamored for the reform of politics and the government; many wanted to change procedures and institutions

to promote greater democracy; others hoped to improve the efforts of government and eliminate corruption. One of the most important achievements was woman suffrage; the Nineteenth Amendment gave women across America the right to vote. The initiative, referendum, recall, and direct election of senators were all introduced into the American political landscape during this period.

Theodore Roosevelt and the Progressive Presidency
Progressive proponent Theodore Roosevelt entered the White House upon the assassination of President McKinley in 1901. He rejected the limited role of the Gilded Age presidents and expanded executive authority. Called the first "modern president," Roosevelt's flamboyance and ambitions made him the most popular president of the time and enabled him to take aggressive approaches toward a coal strike, conservation, "busting" trusts, and regulating business abuses.

Woodrow Wilson and Progressive Reform Progressivism was not limited to the Republican party; Democrats also pushed progressive remedies. President Woodrow Wilson, elected in 1912, introduced the New Freedom program; though he believed government's role should be more limited, he took steps to reduce the high protective tariff, create the Federal Reserve, regulate business through the Federal Trade Commission, assist farmers, help workers, and build highways. Wilson's Progressivism resulted in an unprecedented expansion of federal power.

IMAGE KEY
for pages 602–603

a. Woodrow Wilson (1856–1924). Oil on canvas.

b. Cover of "The Jungle" by Upton Sinclair, featuring a factory.

c. Photo of a women's suffrage parade in Washington D.C., 1913.

d. Dorothy Newell has "Votes for Women" written on her back.

e. Illustration "A Woman's Work Is Never Done".

f. Child labor in a canning factory.

g. American cartoon showing President Theodore Roosevelt slaying those trusts he considered 'bad' for the public interest while restraining those whose business practices he considered 'good' for the country.

h. Flanner House Baby Clinic, about 1918. The old Flanner house building on Indianapolis's Colton Street was soon abandoned for better quarters.

i. Striking garment workers in New York City.

j. Bull Moose party campaign paraphernalia.

k. Detail of a photo of a women's suffrage parade in Washington D.C., 1913.

REVIEW QUESTIONS

1. How and why did the presidency change during the Progressive Era?

2. How did the progressive concern for efficiency affect social reform efforts, public education, government administration, and rural life?

3. How and why did the relationship between business and government change during this time?

4. Why did social reform and social control often intermingle in the Progressive Era? Can such objectives be separate?

5. What factors, old and new, stimulated the reform movements of progressivism?

6. How did the role of women change during the Progressive Era? How did the changes affect progressivism?

7. Why did the demand for woman suffrage provoke such determined support and such bitter opposition, as illustrated by the 1913 parade and riot in Washington, D.C., and the experiences of the British suffragettes?

KEY TERMS

Australian ballot p. 621
Bureau of Reclamation p. 626
Conservation p. 625
Eighteenth Amendment p. 618

Federal Reserve Act p. 629
Federal Trade Commission (FTC) p. 630
Fundamentalists p. 612

Initiative p. 623
Muckraking p. 609
New Freedom p. 629
New Nationalism p. 629

WHERE TO LEARN MORE

John Muir National Historic Site, Martinez, California. The architecture and furnishings of this 17 room house reflect the interests of John Muir, the writer and naturalist who founded the Sierra Club and led the preservationists in the Progressive Era. **www.nps. gov/jomu/**

National Museum of American History, Smithsonian Institution, Washington, D.C. A permanent exhibition, "Parlor to Politics: Women and Reform, 1890–1925," uses design, artifacts, and recent scholarship to vividly illustrate the changing role of women in the Progressive Era. It effectively emphasizes their work in settlement houses and their growing politicization and demonstrates the importance of the work of black women's organizations.

Sewall-Belmont House National Historic Site, Washington, D.C. Headquarters of the National Woman's Party, this 200-year-old house on Capitol Hill has memorabilia of the woman suffrage movement, including posters, flags, and photographs of the early marches, and an extensive feminist library focused on the struggle for equal suffrage. Beginning in 1923 Alice Paul campaigned from this building for the Equal Rights Amendment.

Hull House, Chicago, Illinois. This pioneering settlement house is now a museum on the campus of the University of Illinois, Chicago. **www.uic.edu/jaddams/ hull/hull_house.html**

Lowell National Historic Park, Lowell, Massachusetts. "The Working People," a permanent exhibition, uses artifacts and photographs to chart the activities of immigrant workers at different times in the past, particularly during the Progressive Era. **www.nps.gov/lowe/**

Lower East Side Tenement Museum, New York City, New York. A six-story tenement building containing 22 apartments, this museum vividly illustrates the congested and unhealthy living conditions of urban immigrants from the 1870s to the early twentieth century. See **www.tenement.org/** for a virtual tour.

Sagamore Hill, Oyster Bay, New York. Theodore Roosevelt's home is now a National Historic Site and open to the public. **www. nps.gov/sahi/**

William Howard Taft National Historic Site, Cincinnati, Ohio. Taft was born in this house, the only national Taft memorial. An informative tour focuses on Taft's public and private life.

Staunton, Virginia. The birthplace and childhood home of Woodrow Wilson, restored with period furnishings, reveals many of the influences that shaped Wilson's career.

U.S. History Documents CD-ROM
For primary sources related to this chapter, refer to the document CD-ROM.

www.prenhall.com/goldfield
For study resources related to this chapter, visit the *Companion Website*™.

22 Creating an Empire 1865-1917

CHAPTER HIGHLIGHTS

The Roots of Imperialism The tradition of expansion across the continent contributed to overseas expansion in the late nineteenth century. Supporters of expansion made ideological, religious, and economic arguments in favor of American imperialism.

First Steps America pursued a generally passive foreign policy until the 1890s. The purchase of Alaska, growing influence in Hawaii, and the assertion of American dominance in Latin America were all steps toward the assertive national policies of the end of the century.

The Spanish-American War Victory in the Spanish-American War gave the United States a colonial empire. The United States gained Puerto Rico, Guam, and eventually the Philippines. Acquisition of overseas colonies sparked a debate in the United States over the wisdom and morality of imperialism.

Imperial Ambitions: The United States and East Asia, 1899-1917 The United States betrayed Filipinos' hopes for independence and, after a brutal war, established a colonial government in the Philippines. America pursued an "Open Door" policy in China, creating tension with Russia and Japan.

Imperial Power: The United States and Latin America, 1899-1917 After the Spanish-American War, the United States frequently intervened to promote its interests in Latin America. U.S. presidents used military force on numerous occasions to maintain or enhance U.S. control of the region.

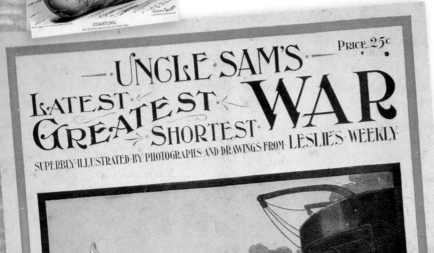

PRICE 25c

UNCLE SAM'S LATEST GREATEST SHORTEST WAR

SUPERBLY ILLUSTRATED BY PHOTOGRAPHS AND DRAWINGS FROM LESLIE'S WEEKLY

Copyright, 1898, by Arkell Publishing Company, 410 Fifth Avenue, New York.

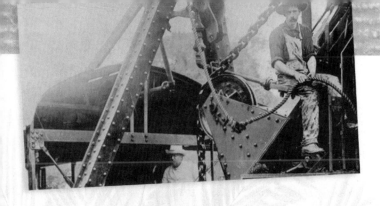

CHAPTER QUESTIONS

WHAT ARGUMENTS were made in favor of American expansion in the late nineteenth century?

WHAT ROLE did public opinion play in the emergence of American imperialism?

WHAT WERE the most important consequences of the Spanish-American War?

WHAT WAS the nature of U.S. involvement in Asia?

HOW DID Latin Americans respond to U.S. intervention in the region?

CHAPTER OUTLINE

IMAGE KEY
for pages 636–637 is on page 662.

Havana, Cuba

October 1901

When the Spanish-American war was declared the United States . . . assumed a position as protector of the interests of Cuba. It became responsible for the welfare of the people, politically, mentally, and morally. The mere fact of freeing the island from Spanish rule has not ended the care which this country should give. . . . The effect will be to uplift the people, gaining their permanent friendship and support and greatly increasing our own commerce. At present there are two million people requiring clothing and food, for but a small proportion of the necessaries of life are raised on the island. It is folly to grow food crops when sugar and tobacco produce such rich revenues in comparison. The United States should supply the Cubans with their breadstuffs, even wine, fruit, and vegetables, and should clothe the people. . . . The money received for their crops will be turned over in a great measure in buying supplies from the United States. . . .

Naturally the manufacturers of the United States should have precedence in furnishing machinery, locomotives, cars, and rails, materials for buildings and bridges, and the wide diversity of other supplies required, as well as fuel for their furnaces. With the present financial and commercial uncertainty at an end the people of the island will . . . come into the American market as customers for products of many kinds.

The meeting of the Constitutional Convention on November 5th will be an event in Cuban history of the greatest importance, and much will depend upon the action and outcome of this convention as to our future control of the island. . . . I considered it unwise to interfere, and I have made it a settled policy to permit the Cubans to manage every part of their constitution-making. This has been due to my desire to prevent any possible charge of crimination being brought against the United States in the direction of their constitutional affairs. . . .

There is no distrust of the United States on the part of the Cubans, and I know of no widespread antipathy to this country, its people, or its institutions. There are, of course, a handful of malcontents, as there must be in every country. . . . I could not well conceive how the Cubans could be otherwise than grateful to the United States for its efforts in their behalf. . . . In the brief time since the occupation of the island by American troops the island has been completely rehabilitated—agriculturally, commercially, financially, educationally, and governmentally. This improvement has been so rapid and so apparent that no Cuban could mistake it. To doubt in the face of these facts that their liberators were not still their faithful friends would be impossible.

Major-General Leonard Wood, "The Future of Cuba," *The Independent* 54 (January 23, 1902): 193–194; idem, "The Cuban Convention," *The Independent* 52 (November 1, 1900): 265–266.

GENERAL LEONARD WOOD'S reports on Cuba, then under his control as military governor, captured the complex mixture of attitudes and motives that underlay the journey of the United States from a developing nation to a world power. Plans for economic expansion, a belief in national mission, a sense of responsibility to help others, scarcely hidden religious impulses and racist convictions—all combined in an uneasy mixture of self-interest and idealism.

Wood himself had taken a symbolic journey in American expansionism. His earlier career had been with the troops chasing the Apache under Geronimo, but in 1898 he and Theodore Roosevelt organized the Rough Riders cavalry to participate in the Spanish-American War in Cuba. Upon Spain's surrender, Cuba came under United States military occupation, and Wood was appointed military governor of the island.

Wood's support for the war was reflected in his activities as a colonial administrator. Convinced of the superiority of American institutions, he favored their expansion. The United States had a responsibility, he believed, to uplift those less able. But expansion would promote American interests as well. Thus, Wood brought improved sanitation, schools, and transportation to Cuba, but he regarded Cubans as backward and incapable of self-government. And at the same time, he expected that American business interests would "naturally" be the beneficiaries of his reorganization of Cuban life. Thus Wood combined changes that satisfied paternalistic or humanitarian instincts with attempts to incorporate Cuba into America's new commercial empire.

His claim that he was not interfering with Cuba's constitutional convention was disingenuous, for he had already undertaken to limit those who could participate as voters or delegates and was even then devising means to restrict the convention's autonomy. And in his repeated insistence that the Cubans were "grateful" for the intervention of "their faithful friends," the Americans, Wood obviously protested too much: Cubans, as well as Filipinos, Puerto Ricans, and others, rarely perceived American motives or American actions as positively as did Wood and other proponents of American expansion. Victory in the Spanish-American War had provided the United States with an extensive empire, status as a world power, and opportunities and problems that would long shape American foreign policy.

THE ROOTS OF IMPERIALISM

The United States had a long-established tradition of expansion across the continent. Through purchase, negotiation, or conquest, the vast Louisiana Territory, Florida, Texas, New Mexico, California, and Oregon had become U.S. territory. Indeed, by the 1890s, Republican Senator Henry Cabot Lodge of Massachusetts boasted that Americans had "a record of conquest, colonization, and territorial expansion unequalled by any people in the nineteenth century." Lodge now urged the country to build an overseas empire, emulating the European model of **imperialism** based on the acquisition and exploitation of colonial possessions. Other Americans favored a less formal empire, in which United States interests and influence would be ensured through extensive trade and investments rather than through military occupation. Still others advocated a cultural expansionism in which the nation exported its ideals and institutions.

WHAT ARGUMENTS were made in favor of American expansion in the late nineteenth century?

Imperialism The policy and practice of exploiting nations and peoples for the benefit of an imperial power either directly through military occupation and colonial rule or indirectly through economic domination of resources and markets.

Chronology

1861–1869	Seward serves as secretary of state.
1867	United States purchases Alaska from Russia.
1870	Annexation of the Dominican Republic is rejected.
1879	France conquers Algeria.
1881	Naval Advisory Board is created.
1882	Great Britain occupies Egypt.
1887	United States gains naval rights to Pearl Harbor.
1889	First Pan-American Conference is held.
1890	Alfred Thayer Mahan publishes *The Influence of Sea Power upon History.*
1893	Harrison signs but Cleveland rejects a treaty for the annexation of Hawaii.
1893–1897	Depression increases interest in economic expansion abroad.
1894–1895	Sino-Japanese War is fought.
1895	United States intervenes in Great Britain–Venezuela boundary dispute.
	Cuban insurrection against Spain begins.
1896	William McKinley is elected president on an imperialist platform.
1898	Spanish-American War is fought.
	Hawaii is annexed.
	Anti-Imperialist League is organized.
	Treaty of Paris is signed.

1899–1902	Filipino-American War is fought.
1899	Open Door note is issued.
1900	Boxer Rebellion against foreign influence breaks out in China.
1901	Theodore Roosevelt becomes president.
1903	Platt Amendment restricts Cuban autonomy.
	Panama "revolution" is abetted by the United States.
1904	United States acquires the Panama Canal Zone.
	Roosevelt Corollary is announced.
1904–1905	Russo-Japanese War is fought.
1905	Treaty of Portsmouth ends the Russo-Japanese War through U.S. mediation.
1906–1909	United States occupies Cuba.
1907–1908	Gentlemen's Agreement restricts Japanese immigration.
1909	United States intervenes in Nicaragua.
1912–1933	United States occupies Nicaragua.
1914	Panama Canal opens.
1914–1917	United States intervenes in Mexico.
1915–1934	United States occupies Haiti.
1916–1924	United States occupies the Dominican Republic.
1917	Puerto Ricans are granted U.S. citizenship.
1917–1922	United States occupies Cuba.

IDEOLOGICAL AND RELIGIOUS ARGUMENTS

Scholars, authors, politicians, and religious leaders provided interlocking ideological arguments for the new imperialism (see the Overview table, "Rationales for Imperialism"). Some intellectuals, for example, invoked social Darwinism, maintaining that the United States should engage in a competitive struggle for wealth and power with other nations. As European nations expanded into Asia and Africa in the 1880s and 1890s, seeking colonies, markets, and raw materials, these advocates argued, the United States had to adopt similar policies to ensure national success.

Related to social Darwinism was a pervasive belief in racial inequality and, particularly, in the superiority of people of English, or Anglo-Saxon, descent.

To many Americans, the industrial progress, military strength, and political development of England and the United States were proof of an Anglo-Saxon superiority that carried with it a responsibility to extend the blessings of their rule to less able people. As a popular expression put it, colonialism was the "white

OVERVIEW   RATIONALES FOR IMPERIALISM

Category	Beliefs
Racism and Social Darwinism	The conviction that "Anglo-Saxons" were racially superior and should dominate other peoples, either to ensure national success, establish international stability, or benefit the "inferior" races by imposing American ideas and institutions on them.
Righteousness	The conviction that Christianity, and a supporting American culture, should be aggressively spread among the benighted peoples of other lands.
Mahanism	The conviction, following the ideas advanced by Alfred Thayer Mahan, that U.S. security required a strong navy and economic and territorial expansion.
Economics	A variety of arguments holding that American prosperity depended on acquiring access to foreign markets, raw materials, and investment opportunities.

man's burden," carrying with it a duty to aid and uplift other peoples. Such attitudes led some expansionists to favor imposing American ideas and practices on other cultures regardless of those cultures' own values and customs. The political scientist John W. Burgess, for example, concluded that Anglo-Saxons "must have a colonial policy" and "righteously assume sovereignty" over "incompetent" or "barbaric races" in other lands.

Reflecting this aggressiveness, as well as Darwinian anxieties, some Americans endorsed expansion as consistent with their ideals of masculinity. Forceful expansion would be a manly course, relying upon and building strength and honor among American males. "Pride of race, courage, manliness," predicted one enthusiast, would be both the causes and the consequences of an assertive foreign policy.

American missionaries also promoted expansionist sentiment. Hoping to evangelize the world, American religious groups increased the number of Protestant foreign missions sixfold from 1870 to 1900. Women in particular organized foreign missionary societies and served in the missions. Once abroad, missionaries pursued a religious transformation that often resembled a cultural conversion, for they promoted trade, developed business interests, and encouraged westernization through technology and education as well as religion.

Indeed, the American religious press endlessly repeated the themes of national destiny, racial superiority, and religious zeal. The Reverend J. H. Barrows in early 1898 lectured on the "Christian conquest of Asia," suggesting that American Christianity and commerce would cross the Pacific to fulfill "the manifest destiny of the Christian Republic." Thus, while missionaries were motivated by what they considered to be idealism and often brought real benefits to other lands, especially in education and health, religious sentiments reinforced the ideology of American expansion.

20–3
Albert Beveridge, "The March of the Flag" (1898)

STRATEGIC CONCERNS

America's location in the Western Hemisphere, its coastlines on two oceans, and the ambitions and activities of other nations, particularly Germany and Britain, convinced some Americans that the United States had to develop new policies to

Emily Hartwell, an American missionary, and her Chinese converts ("Bible Women") in the Foochow Mission in 1902. American missionaries wanted to spread the Gospel abroad but inevitably spread American influence as well. Hartwell used the ethnocentric and militant rhetoric of the imperialism of righteousness in appealing to Americans for money and prayers for her "picket duty on the very outskirts of the army of the Lord."

Courtesy Library of Congress

protect and promote its national security and interests. Alfred Thayer Mahan, a naval officer and president of the Naval War College, emphasized the importance of a strong navy for national greatness in his book *The Influence of Sea Power Upon History*. To complement the navy, Mahan proposed that the United States build a canal across the isthmus of Panama to link its coasts, acquire naval bases in the Caribbean and the Pacific to protect the canal, and annex Hawaii and other Pacific islands to promote trade and service the fleet.

Mahanism found a receptive audience. President Benjamin Harrison declared in 1891 that "as to naval stations and points of influence, we must look forward to a departure from the too conservative opinions which have been held heretofore." Still more vocal advocates of Mahan's program were a group of nationalistic Republicans, predominantly from the Northeast.

Theodore Roosevelt promoted Mahan's ideas when he became assistant secretary of the navy in 1897, but he was even more militaristic. Praising "the most valuable of all qualities, the soldierly virtues," Roosevelt declared in 1897: "No triumph of peace is quite so great as the supreme triumphs of war." One British observer concluded on the eve of the Spanish-American War that Mahan's influence had transformed the American spirit, serving "as oil to the flame of 'colonial expansion' everywhere leaping into life" (see American Views: "An Imperialist Views the World").

Even so, Mahan was not solely responsible for the large-navy policy popular among imperialists. Its origins went back to 1881, when Congress established the Naval Advisory Board, which successfully lobbied for bigger naval appropriations. The United States soon possessed the formidable navy the expansionists wanted. This larger navy, in turn, demanded strategic bases and coaling stations.

ECONOMIC DESIGNS

Nearly all Americans favored economic expansion through foreign trade. Such a policy promised national prosperity: more markets for manufacturers and farmers, greater profits for merchants and bankers, more jobs for workers. Far fewer favored the acquisition of colonies that was characteristic of European imperialism (see Global Perspectives: "European Colonial Imperialism"). As one diplomat declared in 1890, the nation was more interested in the "annexation of trade" than in the annexation of territory.

The United States had long aggressively fostered American trade, especially in Latin America and East Asia. As early as 1844, the United States had negotiated a trade treaty with China, and ten years later a squadron under Commodore Matthew Perry had forced the Japanese to open their ports to American products. Alabama Senator John Morgan had the cotton and textiles produced in the New South in mind when he warned in 1882: "Our home market is not equal to the demands of our producing and manufacturing classes and to the capital which

Mahanism The ideas advanced by Alfred Thayer Mahan, stressing U.S. naval, economic, and territorial expansion.

AMERICAN VIEWS

AN IMPERIALIST VIEWS THE WORLD

heodore Roosevelt, Henry Cabot Lodge, Alfred Thayer Mahan, and other influential imperialists frequently corresponded with one another, expressing their views forcefully if not always in depth. The following excerpts are from Roosevelt's private letters to Lodge and Mahan in 1897, while he was assistant secretary of the navy and before the Spanish-American War.

- In what ways does Roosevelt reflect the influence of Mahan?
- What is Roosevelt's view of war?
- How does Roosevelt view European nations?
- How does he view the independence of other nations in the Western Hemisphere?

I suppose that I need not tell you that as regards Hawaii I take your views absolutely, as indeed I do on foreign policy generally. If I had my way we would annex those islands tomorrow. If that is impossible I would establish a protectorate over them. I believe we should build the Nicaraguan canal at once, and in the meantime that we should build a dozen new battleships, half of them on the Pacific Coast; and these battleships should have a large coal capacity and a consequent increased radius of action. . . . I think President Cleveland's action [in rejecting the annexation of Hawaii] was a colossal crime, and we should be guilty of aiding him after the fact if we do not reverse what he did. I earnestly hope we can make the President [McKinley] look at things our way. Last Saturday night Lodge pressed his views upon him with all his strength.

I agree with all you say as to what will be the result if we fail to take Hawaii. It will show that we either have lost, or else wholly lack, the masterful instinct which alone can make a race great. I feel so deeply about it I hardly dare express myself in full. The terrible part is to see that it is the men of education who take the lead in trying to make us prove traitors to our race.

I fully realize the importance of the Pacific coast. . . . But there are big problems in the West Indies also. Until we definitely turn Spain out of those islands (and

if I had my way that would be done tomorrow), we will always be menaced by trouble there. We should acquire the Danish Islands [in the West Indies], and by turning Spain out should serve notice that no strong European power, and especially not Germany, should be allowed to gain a foothold by supplanting some weak European power. I do not fear England; Canada is a hostage for her good behavior.

I wish we had a perfectly consistent foreign policy, and that this policy was that every European power should be driven out of America, and every foot of American soil, including the nearest islands in both the Pacific and the Atlantic, should be in the hands of independent American states, and so far as possible in the possession of the United States or under its protection.

To speak with a frankness which our timid friends would call brutal, I would regard a war with Spain from two standpoints: first, the advisability on the grounds both of humanity and self-interest of interfering on behalf of the Cubans, and of taking one more step toward the complete freeing of America from European dominion; second, the benefit done our people by giving them something to think of which isn't material gain, and especially the benefit done our military forces by trying both the Navy and the Army in actual practice. I should be very sorry not to see us make the experiment of trying to land, and therefore feed and clothe, an expeditionary force [on Cuba], if only for the sake of learning from our own blunders. I should hope that the force would have some fighting to do. It would be a great lesson, and we would profit much by it.

I wish there was a chance that the [U.S. battleship] Maine was going to be used against some foreign power; by preference Germany—but I am not particular, and I'd take even Spain if nothing better offered.

Source: Reprinted by permission of the publisher from *The Letters of Theodore Roosevelt*, Vol. I, 1868–1898, selected and edited by Elting E. Morison (Cambridge: Harvard University Press, 1951)

GLOBAL PERSPECTIVES

EUROPEAN COLONIAL IMPERIALISM

The United States was not alone in expanding its role in the world. Beginning in the 1870s, leading European nations engaged in a competitive struggle to partition much of Africa and Asia in pursuit of their imperial ambitions. Like Americans, Europeans advanced many justifications for imperialism. Many favored colonies to acquire markets, resources, and investment opportunities; others saw in colonies strategic advantages or international prestige. Some interwove racist and religious attitudes to justify European empire building as "an instrument for the good of humanity."

But advanced industrialization, more than the questionable blessings of religion and race, accounted for European success. Railroads, steamships, and ocean cables facilitated transportation and communication, and modern weaponry easily overcame native resistance. In the Battle of Omdurman in 1898, a British expedition armed with machine guns massacred 11,000 Sudanese tribesmen trying to defend their independence. The British suffered only 28 casualties. Said one observer: "It was not a battle but an execution."

Before the 1870s Africa had largely escaped European colonialism, but within thirty years European powers divided much of the continent. France gained most of northwestern Africa, conquering Algeria in 1879, oc-

cupying Tunisia in 1881, and dividing Morocco with Spain. Britain acquired territory from the Mediterranean Sea to the Cape. To control the area around the Suez Canal, viewed as the empire's lifeline to India, the British occupied Egypt in 1882 and then seized the Sudan. With unimaginable brutality, Belgium's King Leopold colonized the Congo in central Africa. Germany established colonies in southwest Africa and, like Italy, in East Africa.

European powers also advanced on Asia. To its earlier control of India Great Britain added Burma and Malay. France extended its authority over Indochina in the 1880s and 1890s by gaining control of Vietnam and Laos. Russia expanded its empire into contiguous territories, securing Turkestan in Central Asia and then reaching toward East Asia, particularly the Manchurian region of China. Other nations also sought spheres of influence in China, acquiring ports, naval stations, and railroad and mining concessions.

Competitive imperialism risked conflict between expansive nations as well as with colonized peoples, but such risks did not deter aspiring imperialists. In 1887 the Japanese foreign minister insisted: "We have to establish a new, European-style empire on the edge of Asia." And in 1895 an American leader declared of European imperialism: "the United States must not fall out of the line of march."

is seeking employment. . . . We must either enlarge the field of our traffic, or stop the business of manufacturing just where it is." More ominous, a naval officer trying to open Korea to U.S. products declared in 1878, "At least one-third of our mechanical and agricultural products are now in excess of our wants, and we must *export* these products or *deport* the people who are creating them."

In the depression of the 1890s, with the secretary of state seeing "symptoms of revolution" in the Pullman strike and Coxey's Army of unemployed workers (see Chapter 20), the interest in foreign trade became obsessive. More systematic government efforts to promote trade seemed necessary, a conclusion strengthened by new threats to existing American markets. In that tumultuous decade, European nations raised tariff barriers against American products, and Japan and the European imperial powers began to restrict commercial opportunities in the areas of China that they controlled. Many American leaders decided that the United States had to adopt decisive new policies or face economic catastrophe.

FIRST STEPS

*B*efore the mid-1890s, the United States did not pursue a policy of isolationism from international affairs, for the nation maintained normal diplomatic and trade ties and at times vigorously intervened in Latin America and East Asia. But in general the government deferred to the initiative of private interests, reacted haphazardly to outside events, and did little to create a professional foreign service. In a few bold if inconsistent steps, however, the United States moved to expand its influence.

SEWARD AND BLAINE

Two secretaries of state, William H. Seward, secretary under Presidents Abraham Lincoln and Andrew Johnson (1861–1869), and James G. Blaine, secretary under Presidents James Garfield and Benjamin Harrison (1881, 1889–1892), laid the foundation for a larger and more aggressive American role in world affairs. Seward possessed an elaborate imperial vision, based on his understanding of commercial opportunities, strategic necessities, and national destiny. His interest in opening East Asia to American commerce and establishing American hegemony over the Caribbean anticipated the subsequent course of American expansion. He purchased Alaska from Russia in 1867, approved the navy's occupation of the Midway Islands in the Pacific, pushed American trade on a reluctant Japan, and repeatedly tried to acquire Caribbean naval bases (see Map 22–1). His policy of expansion, however, as one observer noted, "went somewhat too far and too fast for the public," and many of his plans fizzled.

Blaine was an equally vigorous, if inconsistent, advocate of expansion. He worked to extend what he called America's "commercial empire" in the Pacific. And he sought to ensure U.S. sovereignty over any canal in Panama, insisting that it be "a purely American waterway to be treated as part of our own coastline." In an effort to induce Latin American nations to import manufactured products from the United States rather than Europe, Blaine called for the establishment of a customs union to reduce trade barriers. The Latin American nations, however, wary of economic subordination to the colossus of the north, rejected Blaine's plan. Instead, they supported the establishment of what eventually came to be known as the **Pan American Union.** Based in Washington, it helped to promote hemispheric understanding and cooperation.

If U.S. officials were increasingly assertive toward Latin America and Asia, however, they remained little involved in Europe and were wholly indifferent to Africa. In short, despite some important precedents for the future, much of American foreign policy remained undeveloped, sporadic, and impulsive.

HAWAII

Blaine regarded Hawaii as "indispensably" part of "the American system." Hawaii was a key way station in the China trade, and American missionaries and merchants were soon active in the islands. Although Hawaii continued to be ruled by native monarchs, American influence grew, particularly as other Americans arrived to establish sugar plantations and eventually dominate the economy.

Treaties in 1875 and 1887 integrated the islands into the American economy. In 1887, the United States rejected a proposal from Britain and France for a joint guarantee of Hawaii's independence and endorsed a new Hawaiian constitution that gave political power to wealthy white residents.

WHAT ROLE did public opinion play in the emergence of American imperialism?

WHERE TO LEARN MORE

Seward House, Auburn, New York.

WHERE TO LEARN MORE

James G. Blaine House, Augusta, Maine

Pan American Union
International organization originally established as the Commercial Bureau of American Republics by Secretary of State James Blaine's first Pan-American Conference in 1889 to promote cooperation among nations of the Western Hemisphere through commercial and diplomatic negotiations.

MAP EXPLORATION
To explore an interactive version of this map, go to **http://www.prenhall.com/goldfield3/map22.1**

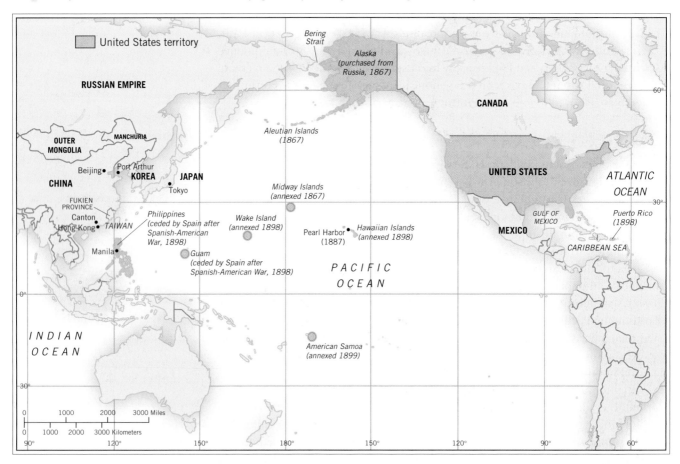

MAP 22–1   United States Expansion in the Pacific, 1867–1899   Pursuing visions of a commercial empire in the Pacific, the United States steadily expanded its territorial possessions as well as its influence there in the late nineteenth century.

WHAT DID the United States gain from its expansion in the Pacific?

A combination of factors soon impelled American planters to bid for annexation. The McKinley Tariff Act of 1890 effectively closed the U.S. market to Hawaiian sugar producers, threatening their economic ruin. At the same time, Queen Liliuokalani moved to restore native control of Hawaiian affairs. To ensure market access and protect their political authority, the American planters decided to seek annexation to the United States. In 1893, the American planters overthrew the queen. John Stevens, the American diplomatic representative, ordered U.S. marines to help the rebels and declared an American protectorate over the new Hawaiian government. A delegation from the new provisional government, which did not include any native Hawaiians, went to Washington to draft a treaty for annexation. President Harrison signed the pact but could not get Senate approval before the new Cleveland administration took office.

Grover Cleveland immediately called for an investigation of the whole affair. Soon convinced that "the undoubted sentiment of the people is for the Queen, against the provisional Government, and against annexation," Cleveland apologized to the queen for the "flagrant wrong" done her by the reprehensible conduct of American diplomats and troops. But the American-dominated provisional government refused to step down, and Cleveland's rejection of annexation set off a noisy debate in the United States.

Many Republicans strongly supported annexation, which they regarded as merely part of a larger plan of expansion. One eastern Republican manufacturer called for the annexation of Hawaii as the first step toward making the Pacific "an American ocean, dominated by American commercial enterprise for all time." Democrats generally opposed annexation. They doubted, as Missouri Senator George Vest declared, whether the United States should desert its traditional principles and "venture upon the great colonial system of the European powers." The Hawaiian episode of 1893 thus foreshadowed the arguments over imperialism at the end of the century and emphasized the policy differences between Democrats and the increasingly expansionist Republicans.

CHILE AND VENEZUELA

American reactions to developments in other countries in the 1890s also reflected an increasingly assertive national policy and excitable public opinion. In 1891, American sailors on shore leave in Chile became involved in a drunken brawl that left two of them dead, 17 injured, and dozens in jail. Encouraged by a combative navy, President Harrison threatened military retaliation against Chile, provoking an outburst of bellicose nationalism in the United States. Harrison relented only when Chile apologized and paid an indemnity.

A few years later, the United States again threatened war over a minor issue but against a more formidable opponent. In 1895, President Cleveland intervened in a boundary dispute between Great Britain and Venezuela over British Guiana. Cleveland was motivated not only by the long-standing U.S. goal of challenging Britain for Latin American markets but also by ever more expansive notions of the Monroe Doctrine and the authority of the United States. Secretary of State Richard Olney sent Britain a blunt note (a "twenty-inch gun," Cleveland called it) demanding arbitration of the disputed territory and stoutly asserting American supremacy in the Western Hemisphere. Cleveland urged Congress to establish a commission to determine the boundary and enforce its decision by war if necessary. As war fever swept the United States, Britain agreed to arbitration, recognizing the limited nature of the issue that so convulsed Anglo-American relations.

Cleveland's assertion of U.S. hemispheric dominance angered Latin Americans, and their fears deepened when the United States decided arbitration terms with Britain without consulting Venezuela, which protested before bowing to American pressure. The United States had intervened less to protect Venezuela from the British bully than to advance its own hegemony.

THE SPANISH-AMERICAN WAR

*T*he forces pushing the United States toward imperialism and international power came to a head in the Spanish-American War. Cuba's quest for independence from the oppressive colonial control of Spain activated Americans' long-standing interest in the island. But few foresaw that the war that finally erupted in 1898 would dramatically change America's relationships with the rest of the world and give it a colonial empire.

WHERE TO LEARN MORE

Mission Houses, Honolulu, Hawaii
www.missionhouses.org/

WHAT WERE the most important consequences of the Spanish-American War?

THE CUBAN REVOLUTION

Cuba was the last major European colony in Latin America, with an economic potential that attracted American business interests and a strategic significance for any Central American canal. In the late nineteenth century American investors expanded their economic influence in Cuba, while Cubans themselves rebelled repeatedly but unsuccessfully against increasingly harsh Spanish rule. Cuban discontent erupted again in 1895, when the Cuban patriot José Martí launched another revolt.

The rebellion was a classic guerrilla war, with the rebels controlling the countryside and the Spanish army the towns and cities. The Cleveland administration, motivated as much by a desire to protect American property and establish a safe environment for further investments as by a concern for Cuban rights, urged Spain to adopt reforms. But the brutality with which Spain attempted to suppress the revolt promoted American sympathy for the Cuban insurgents. Determined to cut the rebels off from their peasant supporters, the Spanish herded most civilians into "reconcentration camps," where tens of thousands died of starvation and disease.

American sympathy was further aroused by the sensationalist **yellow press.** A circulation war between William Randolph Hearst's *New York Journal* and Joseph Pulitzer's *New York World* helped stimulate interest in Cuban war. "Blood on the roadsides, blood on the fields, blood on the doorsteps, blood, blood, blood! The old, the young, the weak, the crippled—all are butchered without mercy," the *World* feverishly reported of Cuba. "Is there no nation wise enough, brave enough to aid this blood-smitten land?" Failure to intervene to protect the innocent from Spanish lust and cruelty, insisted the yellow journalists, would be dishonorable and cowardly.

The nation's religious press, partly because it reflected the prejudice of many Protestants against Catholic Spain, also advocated American intervention. One religious newspaper endorsed an American war against Spain as God's instrument for attacking "that system of iniquity, the papacy." Another promised that if war came, "every Methodist preacher will be a recruiting officer" for the military.

As the Cuban rebellion dragged on, more and more Americans advocated intervention to stop the carnage, protect U.S. investments, or curtail colonialism. In the election of 1896, both major parties endorsed Cuban independence.

GROWING TENSIONS

In 1897 President William McKinley grew increasingly concerned that chronic disorder in Cuba disrupted America's investments and agitated public opinion. Personally opposed to military intervention, he first used diplomacy to press Spain to adopt reforms that would settle the rebellion. Following his instructions, the U.S. minister to Spain warned the Spanish government that if it did not quickly establish peace, the United States would take whatever steps it "should deem necessary to procure this result." In late 1897, Spain modified its brutal military tactics and offered limited autonomy to Cuba. But Cubans insisted on complete independence, a demand that Spain refused to grant.

Relations between the United States and Spain deteriorated. In early 1898, the *New York Journal* published a private letter from a Spanish diplomat that mocked McKinley as "weak and a bidder for the admiration of the crowd." McKinley was troubled by the letter's intimation that Spain was not negotiating in good faith. Only days later, on February 15, 1898, the U.S. battleship *Maine* blew up in Havana harbor, killing 260 men. The Spanish were not responsible for the tragedy, which a modern naval inquiry has attributed to an internal accident. But many Americans agreed with Theodore Roosevelt, the assistant secretary of the navy, who called it "an act of dirty treachery on the part of the Spaniards" and told McKin-

Yellow Press A deliberately sensational journalism of scandal and exposure designed to attract an urban mass audience and increase advertising revenues.

ley that only war was "compatible with our national honor." Others demanded war, in the words of an Illinois politician, "if we would uphold our manhood." Thus understandings of appropriate male conduct also influenced decisions as to how the nation should act.

Other pressures soon began to build on the president. Increasingly, business interests favored war as less disruptive than a volatile peace that threatened their investments. Senator Lodge reported a consensus "that this situation must end. We cannot go on indefinitely with this strain, this suspense, and this uncertainty, this tottering upon the verge of war. It is killing to business." Further, McKinley feared that a moderate policy would endanger Republican congressional candidates. Again Senator Lodge, although hesitant to suggest "war for political reasons," nevertheless advised McKinley, "If the war in Cuba drags on through the summer with nothing done, we shall go down in the greatest [election] defeat ever known."

At the end of March 1898, McKinley sent Spain an ultimatum. He demanded an armistice in Cuba, an end to the reconcentration policy, and the acceptance of American arbitration, which implied Cuban independence. Desperately, Spain made concessions, abolishing reconcentration and declaring a unilateral armistice. But McKinley had already begun war preparations. He submitted a war message to Congress on April 11, asking for authority to use force against Spain "in the name of humanity, in the name of civilization, in behalf of endangered American interests." Congress declared war on Spain on April 25, 1898.

A few national leaders welcomed the war as a step toward imperialism, but there was little popular support for an imperialist foreign policy. Most interventionists were not imperialists, and Congress added the **Teller Amendment** to the war resolution, disclaiming any intention of annexing Cuba and promising that Cubans would govern themselves. Nevertheless, the Spanish-American War did turn the nation toward imperialism.

WAR AND EMPIRE

The decisive engagement of the war took place not in Cuba but in another Spanish colony, the Philippines, and it involved the favored tool of the expansionists, the new navy (see Map 22–2). In 1897, McKinley had approved plans for an attack on the Philippines in the event of war with Spain. Once war was declared, Commodore George Dewey led the U.S. Asiatic squadron into Manila Bay and destroyed the much weaker Spanish fleet on May 1, 1898. This dramatic victory galvanized expansionist sentiment in the United States. With Dewey's triumph, exulted one expansionist, "We are taking our proper rank among the nations of the world. We are after markets, the greatest markets now existing in the world." To expand this foothold in Asia, McKinley ordered troops to the Philippines, postponing the military expedition to Cuba.

Dewey's victory also precipitated the annexation of Hawaii, which had seemed unlikely only weeks before. Annexationists now pointed to the islands' strategic importance as stepping stones to Manila. McKinley himself privately declared, "We need Hawaii just as much and a good deal more than we did California. It is Manifest Destiny." In July, Congress approved annexation, a decision welcomed by Hawaii's white minority. Native Hawaiians solemnly protested this step. Filipinos would soon face the same American imperial impulse.

Military victory also came swiftly in Cuba, despite bureaucratic bungling in the War Department, which left the American army poorly led, trained, and supplied. More than 5,000 Americans died of diseases and accidents brought on by such mismanagement; only 379 were killed in battle. State militias supplemented

QUICK REVIEW

Pressure on McKinley to Go to War

- Spain was reluctant to modify oppressive policies in Cuba.
- Destruction of the *Maine* inflamed public opinion.
- Political advisors warned of election defeats if action were not taken.

 WHERE TO LEARN MORE

Funston Memorial Home, Iola, Kansas **http://skyways.lib.ks.us/ museums/funston/**

QUICK REVIEW

Dewey's Victory

- May 1, 1898: Dewey's squadron destroys Spanish fleet in Manila Bay.
- Expansionists saw victory as an opportunity for greater U.S. presence in the region.
- McKinley followed up Dewey's victory by sending troops to the Philippines.

Teller Amendment   A congressional resolution adopted in 1898 renouncing any American intention to annex Cuba.

✨ MAP EXPLORATION

To explore an interactive version of this map, go to **http://www.prenhall.com/goldfield3/map22.2**

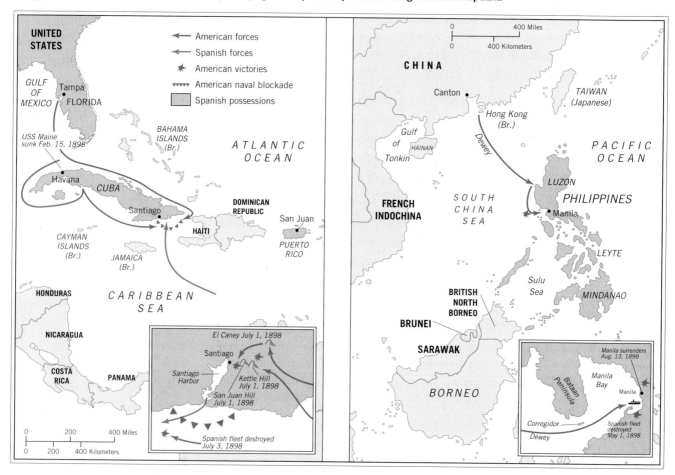

MAP 22–2 The Spanish-American War The United States gained quick victories in both theaters of the Spanish-American War. Its naval power proved decisive, with Commodore Dewey destroying one enemy fleet in the Philippines, and a second U.S. naval force defeating the Spanish in Cuba.

WHY DID the United States want to control the Philippines?

WHERE TO LEARN MORE

Rough Riders Memorial and City Museum, Las Vegas, New Mexico.
www.arco-iris.com/teddy/index.htm

the small regular army, as did volunteer units, such as the famous Rough Riders, a cavalry regiment of cowboys and eastern dandies organized by Leonard Wood and Theodore Roosevelt.

While the Rough Riders captured public attention, other units were more effective. The 10th Negro Cavalry, for example, played the crucial role in capturing San Juan Hill, a battle popularly associated with the Rough Riders. One war correspondent wrote of the black soldiers' charge: "They followed their leaders up the terrible hill from whose crest the desperate Spaniards poured down a deadly fire of shell and musketry. They never faltered. . . . Their aim was splendid, their coolness was superb. . . . The war had not shown greater heroism." Nevertheless, the Rough Riders gained the credit, thanks in part to Roosevelt's self-serving and well-promoted account of the conflict, which one humorist proposed retitling *Alone in Cuba.*

U.S. naval power again proved decisive. In a lopsided battle on July 3, the Spanish squadron in Cuba was destroyed, isolating the Spanish army and guaranteeing its defeat. U.S. forces then seized the nearby Spanish colony of Puerto Rico without serious opposition. Humbled, Spain signed an armistice ending the war on August 12.

THE TREATY OF PARIS

The armistice required Spain to accept Cuban independence, cede Puerto Rico and Guam (a Pacific island between Hawaii and the Philippines), and allow the Americans to occupy Manila, pending the final disposition of the Philippines at a formal peace conference. The acquisition of Puerto Rico and Guam indicated the expansionist nature the conflict had assumed for the United States. So did the postponement of the Philippine issue. McKinley knew that delay would permit the advocates of expansion to build public support for annexation.

McKinley defended his decision to acquire the Philippines with self-righteous imperialist rhetoric, promising to extend Christian influence and American values. But he was motivated primarily by a determination to use the islands to strengthen America's political and commercial position in East Asia. Moreover, he believed the Filipinos poorly suited to self-rule, and he feared that Germany or Japan might seize the Philippines if the United States did not. Meeting in Paris in December, American and Spanish negotiators settled the final terms for peace. Spain agreed—despite Filipino demands for independence—to cede the Philippines to the United States.

The decision to acquire the Philippines sparked a dramatic debate over the ratification of the Treaty of Paris. Imperialists invoked the familiar arguments of economic expansion, national destiny, and strategic necessity, while asserting that Americans had religious and racial responsibilities to advance civilization by uplifting backward peoples.

Opponents of the treaty raised profound questions about national goals and ideals. The Anti-Imperialist League campaigned against the treaty, distributing pamphlets, petitioning Congress, and holding rallies. The acquisition of overseas colonies, they argued, conflicted with the nation's commitment to liberty and its claim to moral superiority.

But other arguments were less high-minded. Many anti-imperialists objected to expansion on the racist grounds that Filipinos were inferior and unassimilable. Labor leader Samuel Gompers feared that cheap Asian labor would undercut the wages and living standards of American workers. The *San Francisco Call*, representing California-Hawaiian sugar interests, wanted no competition from the Philippines.

The debate over the treaty became bitter. Furious at the opponents of empire, Roosevelt called them "little better than traitors." Carl Schurz, a former Cabinet member and civil service reformer, responded that McKinley himself had earlier termed territorial annexation through conquest "a criminal act of aggression"; the president's seizure of the Philippines, Puerto Rico, and Hawaii, said Schurz, had perverted a legitimate concern for Cuba into "a war of selfish ambition and conquest."

Finally, on February 6, 1899, the Senate narrowly ratified the treaty. All but two Republicans supported the pact; most Democrats opposed it, although several voted in favor after William Jennings Bryan suggested that approval was necessary to end the war and detach the Philippines from Spain. Thereafter, he hoped, a congressional resolution would give the Filipinos their independence. But by a single vote, the Republicans defeated a Democratic proposal for Philippine independence once a stable government had been established; the United States would keep the islands.

Bryan attempted to make the election of 1900 a referendum on "the paramount issue" of imperialism, promising to free the Philippines if the Democrats won. But other issues determined the outcome. Some of the most ardent anti-imperialists were conservatives who remained loyal to McKinley because they could not tolerate

Most Americans enthusiastically greeted the declaration of war against Spain. Rallies and parades, such as this "Off to War Parade" in Denver, encouraged the war spirit.

20–5
William McKinley, "Decision on the Philippines" (1900)

QUICK REVIEW

The Anti-Imperialist League

- Central to campaign against the Treaty of Paris (ratified 1899).
- League members saw treaty as a repudiation of American moral and political traditions.
- Many anti-imperialists objected to expansion on racist grounds.

Bryan's economic policies. Republicans also benefited from the prosperity the country experienced under McKinley after the hard 1890s, and they played on the nationalist emotions evoked by the war, especially by nominating the "hero of San Juan Hill," Theodore Roosevelt, for vice president. Bryan lost again, as in 1896, and under Republican leadership, the United States became an imperial nation.

WHAT WAS the nature of U.S. involvement in Asia?

IMPERIAL AMBITIONS: THE UNITED STATES AND EAST ASIA, 1899–1917

*I*n 1899, as the United States occupied its new empire, Assistant Secretary of State John Bassett Moore observed that the nation had become "a world power. . . . Where formerly we had only commercial interests, we now have territorial and political interests as well." American policies to promote these expanded interests focused first on East Asia and Latin America, where the Spanish-American War had provided the United States with both opportunities and challenges. In Asia, the first issue concerned the fate of the Philippines, but looming beyond it were American ambitions in China, where other imperial nations had their own goals.

THE FILIPINO-AMERICAN WAR

Filipino nationalists, like the Cuban insurgents, were already fighting Spain for their independence before the sudden American intervention. The Filipino leader, Emilio Aguinaldo, welcomed Dewey's naval victory as the sign of a *de facto* alliance with the United States; he then issued a declaration of independence and proclaimed the Philippine Republic. His own troops captured most of Luzon, the Philippines' major island, before the U.S. Army arrived. But the Filipinos' optimism declined as American officials acted in an increasingly imperious manner toward them. When the Treaty of Paris provided for U.S. ownership rather than independence, Filipinos felt betrayed. Mounting tensions erupted in a battle between American and Filipino troops outside Manila on February 4, 1899, sparking a long and brutal war.

Ultimately, the United States used nearly four times as many soldiers to suppress the Filipinos as it had to defeat Spain in Cuba and, in a tragic irony, employed many of the same brutal methods for which it had condemned Spain. Recognizing that "the Filipino masses are loyal to Aguinaldo and the government which he heads," U.S. military commanders adopted ever harsher measures, often directed at civilians, who were crowded into concentration camps in which perhaps 200,000 died. American troops often made little effort to distinguish between soldiers and noncombatants, viewing all Filipinos with racial antagonism.

Before the military imposed censorship on war news, reporters confirmed U.S. atrocities; one wrote that "American troops have been relentless, have killed to exterminate men, women, and children, prisoners and captives, active insurgents and suspected people, from lads of 10 and up." A California newspaper defended such actions with remarkable candor: "There has been too much hypocrisy about this Philippine business. . . . Let us all be frank. WE DO NOT WANT THE FILIPINOS. WE DO WANT THE PHILIPPINES. All of our troubles in this annexation matter have been caused by the presence in the Philippine Islands of the Filipinos. . . . The more of them killed the better. It seems harsh. But they must yield before the superior race."

The overt racism of the war repelled African Americans. John Mitchell, a Virginia editor, condemned all the talk of "white man's burden" as deceptive rhetoric for brutal acts that could not be "defended either in moral or international

QUICK REVIEW

Filipino-American War
- Filipinos felt betrayed by Treaty of Paris.
- February 4, 1899: fighting between American and Filipino troops sparked war.
- 1902: U.S. colonial rule is established after a brutal war.

The Filipino-American War was documented extensively by photographers. "First Position near Manila" shows soldiers of the 20th Kansas Infantry Regiment deployed early in what would become a lengthy and brutal war.

National Archives and Records Administration

law." Mitchell argued that white southerners needed missionary work more than freedom-loving Filipinos.

Other Americans also denounced the war. The Anti-Imperialist League revived, citing the war as proof of the corrosive influence of imperialism on the nation's morals and principles. Women figured prominently in mass meetings and lobbying efforts to have the troops returned, their moral stature further undercutting the rationale for colonial wars. By 1902, the realities of imperial policy—including the many American casualties—disillusioned most of those who had clamored to save Cuba.

By that time, however, the American military had largely suppressed the rebellion, and the United States had established a colonial government headed by an American governor general appointed by the president. Filipino involvement in the government was limited on educational and religious grounds. Compared to the brutal war policies, U.S. colonial rule was relatively benign, though paternalistic. William Howard Taft, the first governor general, launched a program that brought the islands new schools and roads, a public health system, and an economy tied closely to both the United States and a small Filipino elite. Independence would take nearly half a century.

CHINA AND THE OPEN DOOR

America's determined involvement in the Philippines reflected its preoccupation with China. By the mid-1890s, other powers threatened prospects for American commercial expansion in China. Japan, after defeating China in 1895, annexed Formosa (Taiwan) and secured economic privileges in the mainland province of Fukien (Fujian); the major European powers then competed aggressively to claim other areas of China as their own **spheres of influence** In Manchuria, Russia won control of Port Arthur (Lüshun) and the right to construct a railway. Elsewhere in China, Germany, Britain, and France also gained control of parts and obtained exclusive commercial privileges.

These developments alarmed the American business community. It was confident that, given an equal opportunity, the United States would prevail in international trade because of its efficient production and marketing systems. But the creation of exclusive spheres of influence would limit the opportunity to compete. In early 1898, business leaders organized the Committee on American Interests in China to lobby Washington to promote American trade in the shrinking Chinese market. The committee persuaded the nation's chambers of commerce to petition the McKinley administration to act. The State Department soon reported that, given overproduction for the home market, "the United States has important interests at stake in the partition of commercial facilities in regions which are likely to offer developing markets for its goods. Nowhere is this consideration of more interest than in its relation to the Chinese Empire."

In 1899, the government moved to advance those interests. Without consulting the Chinese, Secretary of State John Hay asked the imperial powers to maintain an **Open Door** for the commercial and financial activities of all nations within their Chinese spheres of influence. Privately, Hay had already approved a plan to seize a Chinese port for the United States, and if necessary to join in the partition of China, but equal opportunity for trade and investment would serve American interests far better. It would avoid the expense of military occupation, avert further domestic criticism of U.S. imperialism, and guarantee a wider sphere for American business.

The other nations replied evasively, except for Russia, which rejected the Open Door concept. In 1900, an antiforeign Chinese nationalist movement known as the Boxers laid siege to the diplomatic quarter in Beijing. The defeat of the Boxer Rebellion by a multinational military force, to which the United States contributed troops, again raised the prospect of a division of China among the colonial powers. Hay sent a second Open Door note, reaffirming "the principle of equal and impartial trade" and respect for China's territorial integrity.

The Open Door became a cardinal doctrine of American foreign policy in the twentieth century, a means by which the United States sought to dominate foreign markets. The United States promoted an informal or economic empire, as opposed to the traditional territorial colonial empire identified with European powers. Henceforth, American economic interests expected the U.S. government to oppose any developments that threatened to close other nations' economies to American penetration and to advance "private enterprise" abroad.

RIVALRY WITH JAPAN AND RUSSIA

At the turn of the twentieth century, both the Japanese and the Russians were more deeply involved in East Asia than the United States. Japan and Russia expressed little support for the Open Door, which they correctly saw as favoring American interests over their own. But in pursuing their ambitions in China, the two countries came into conflict with each other. Alarmed at the threat of Russian expansion in Manchuria and Korea, Japan in 1904 attacked the Russian fleet at Port Arthur and defeated the Russian army in Manchuria.

American sympathies in the Russo-Japanese War lay with Japan, for the Russians were attempting to close Manchuria to foreign trade. President Theodore

QUICK REVIEW

Trade with China
- American business interests lobbied for access to China's markets.
- 1899: Secretary of State John Hay calls for an Open Door policy.
- Open Door became a central doctrine of American foreign policy.

Spheres of Influence Regions dominated and controlled by an outside power.

Open Door American policy of seeking equal trade and investment opportunities in foreign nations or regions.

Roosevelt welcomed the Japanese attack in the belief that "Japan is playing our game." But he soon began to fear that an overwhelming Japanese victory would threaten American interests as much as Russian expansionism did, so he skillfully mediated an end to the war. In the Treaty of Portsmouth in 1905, Japan won control of Russia's sphere of influence in Manchuria, half the Russian island of Sakhalin, and recognition of its domination of Korea.

The treaty marked Japan's emergence as a great power, but, ironically, it worsened relations with the United States. Anti-American riots broke out in Tokyo. The Japanese people blamed Roosevelt for obstructing further Japanese gains and blocking a Russian indemnity that would have helped Japan pay for the war. Tensions were further aggravated by San Francisco's decision in 1906 to segregate Asian and white schoolchildren. Japan regarded this as a racist insult, and Roosevelt worried that "the infernal fools in California" would provoke war. Finally he persuaded the city to rescind the school order in exchange for his limiting Japanese immigration, which lay at the heart of California's hostility. Under the **Gentlemen's Agreement,** worked out through a series of diplomatic notes in 1907 and 1908, Japan agreed to deny passports to workers trying to come to the United States, and the United States promised not to prohibit Japanese immigration overtly or completely.

A FAIR FIELD AND NO FAVOR.
UNCLE SAM: "I'm out for commerce, not conquest."

The United States usually preferred the "annexation of trade" to the annexation of territory. The Open Door policy promised to advance American commercial expansion, but Uncle Sam had to restrain other imperialists with colonial objectives.

© Stock Montage, 2004

The United States and Japan entered into other agreements aimed at calming their mutual suspicions in East Asia but failed to mend the deteriorating relationship.

Increasingly, Japan began to exclude American trade from its territories in East Asia and to press for further control over China. Elihu Root, Roosevelt's secretary of state, insisted that the Open Door and American access had to be maintained but asserted also that the United States did not want to be "a protagonist in a controversy in China with Russia and Japan or with either of them." The problem was that the United States could not sustain the Open Door without becoming a protagonist in China. This paradox, and the unwillingness to commit military force, would plague American foreign policy in Asia for decades.

IMPERIAL POWER: THE UNITED STATES AND LATIN AMERICA, 1899–1917

*I*n Latin America, where no major powers directly challenged American objectives as Japan and Russia did in Asia, the United States was more successful in exercising imperial power (see Map 22–3). In the two decades after the Spanish-American War, the United States intervened militarily in Latin America no fewer than 20 times to promote its own strategic and economic interests (see the Overview Table, "U.S. Interventions in Latin America, 1891–1933"). Policymakers believed that these goals required restricting the influence of European nations in the region, building an isthmian canal under American control, and establishing the order thought necessary for American trade and investments to expand. Intervention at times achieved these goals, but it often ignored the wishes and interests of Latin Americans, provoked resistance and disorder, and aroused lasting ill will.

HOW DID Latin Americans respond to U.S. intervention in the region?

Gentlemen's Agreement A diplomatic agreement in 1907 between Japan and the United States curtailing but not abolishing Japanese immigration.

MAP EXPLORATION

To explore an interactive version of this map, go to **http://www.prenhall.com/goldfield3/map22.3**

MAP 22–3   The United States in the Caribbean   For strategic and economic reasons, the United States repeatedly intervened in the Caribbean in the first three decades of the twentieth century. Such interventions protected the U.S. claim to dominance but often provoked great hostility among Latin Americans.

WHAT WERE the arguments for and against the repeated United States interventions in the Caribbean?

U.S. RULE IN PUERTO RICO

Well before 1898, expansionists like James G. Blaine had advocated acquiring Puerto Rico because of its strategic location in the Caribbean. During the Spanish-American War, Roosevelt urged Washington, "Do not make peace until we get" Puerto Rico. Military invasion and the Treaty of Paris brought the island under American control, with mixed consequences. A military government improved transportation and sanitation and developed public health and education. But to the dismay of Puerto Ricans, their political freedoms were curtailed. "We have suffered everything. No liberty, no rights," said José Henna, a physician who had led the resistance to Spanish colonialism. "We are Mr. Nobody from Nowhere." In 1900, the United States established a civil government, but it was under U.S. control, and popular participation was even less than under Spain. In the so-called *Insular Cases* (1901), the Supreme Court upheld the authority of Congress to establish an inferior status for Puerto Rico as an "unincorporated territory" without promise of statehood. In 1917, the United States granted citizenship and greater political rights to Puerto Ricans, but their island remained an unincorporated territory under an American governor appointed by the president.

Economic development also disappointed most islanders, for American investors quickly gained control of the best land and pursued large-scale sugar production for the U.S. market. The landless peasants struggled to survive as workers on large plantations. By 1929, the new governor—ironically, Theodore Roosevelt, Jr.—found that under the domination of American capital, "poverty was widespread and hunger, almost to the verge of starvation, common." A subsequent investigation concluded that while "the influx of capital has increased the efficiency of production and promoted general economic development," the benefits had gone largely to Americans, not to ordinary Puerto Ricans, whose conditions were "deplorable." Increasingly, they left their homes to seek work in the United States.

CUBA AS A U.S. PROTECTORATE

Despite the Teller Amendment, the Spanish-American War did not leave Cuba independent. McKinley opposed independence and distrusted the Cuban rebels. Accordingly, a U.S. military government was established in the island. Only in 1900, when the Democrats made an issue of imperialism, did the McKinley administration move toward permitting a Cuban government and withdrawing American troops. McKinley summoned a Cuban convention to draft a constitution under the direction of the American military governor, General Leonard Wood. Reflecting the continuing U.S. fear of Cuban autonomy, the constitution restricted suffrage on the basis of property and education, leaving few Cubans with the right to vote.

Even so, before removing its troops, the United States wanted to ensure its control over Cuba. It therefore made U.S. withdrawal contingent on Cuba's adding to its constitution the provisions of the **Platt Amendment,** drawn up in 1901 by the U.S. secretary of war. The Platt Amendment restricted Cuba's autonomy in diplomatic relations with other countries and in internal financial policies, required Cuba to lease naval bases to the United States, and authorized U.S. intervention to maintain order and preserve Cuban independence. Cubans resented this restriction on their sovereignty. As General Wood correctly observed, "There is, of course, little or no independence left Cuba under the Platt Amendment."

The United States prevented Cuba from extending the same trade privileges to the British that U.S. merchants enjoyed. The Open Door would not apply in the Caribbean, which was to be an American sphere of influence. To preserve that influence, the United States sent troops into Cuba three times between 1906 and 1917. Meanwhile, American property interests in Cuba increased more than fourfold, and American exports to the island increased eightfold from 1898 to 1917.

During their occupations of Cuba, the Americans modernized its financial system, built roads and public schools, and developed a public-health and sanitation program that eradicated the deadly disease of yellow fever. But most Cubans thought that these material benefits did not compensate for their loss of political and economic independence. The Platt Amendment remained the basis of American policy toward Cuba until 1934.

Platt Amendment A stipulation the United States had inserted into the Cuban constitution in 1901 restricting Cuban autonomy and authorizing U.S. intervention and naval bases.

OVERVIEW U.S. INTERVENTIONS IN LATIN AMERICA, 1891–1933

Country	Type of Intervention	Year
Chile	Ultimatum	1891–1892
Colombia	Military intervention	1903
Cuba	Occupation	1898–1902, 1906–1909, 1912, 1917–1922
Dominican Republic	Military and administrative intervention	1905–1907
	Occupation	1916–1924
Haiti	Occupation	1915–1934
Mexico	Military intervention	1914, 1916–1917
Nicaragua	Occupation	1912–1925, 1927–1933
Panama	Acquisition of Canal Zone	1904
Puerto Rico	Military invasion and territorial acquisition	1898

QUICK REVIEW

Acquisition of the Canal Zone

- Possible canal sites were located in Nicaragua and Panama (then part of Colombia).
- 1903: Colombia rejects Roosevelt's offer to purchase canal zone in Panama.
- 1903–1904: U.S. forces support Panamanian rebellion against Colombia and take control of canal zone.

20–6
Theodore Roosevelt, Third Annual Message to Congress (1903)

THE PANAMA CANAL

The Spanish-American War intensified the long American interest in a canal through Central America to eliminate the lengthy and dangerous ocean route around South America. Its commercial value seemed obvious, but the war emphasized its strategic importance. McKinley declared that a canal was now "demanded by the annexation of the Hawaiian Islands and the prospective expansion of our influence and commerce in the Pacific."

Theodore Roosevelt moved quickly to implement McKinley's commitment to a canal after becoming president in 1901. He was convinced that a strong presidential role was at least as important in foreign affairs as in domestic politics. Roosevelt's canal diplomacy helped establish the assertive presidency that has largely characterized U.S. foreign policy ever since.

First, Roosevelt persuaded Britain to renounce its treaty right to a joint role with the United States in any canal venture. Britain's willingness reflected a growing friendship between the two nations, both wary of Germany's increasing aggressiveness. Where to build the canal was a problem. One possibility was Nicaragua, where a sea-level canal could be built. Another was Panama, then part of Colombia. A canal through Panama would require an elaborate system of locks. But the French-owned Panama Canal Company had been unsuccessfully trying to build a canal in Panama and was now eager to sell its rights to the project before they expired in 1904.

In 1902, Congress directed Roosevelt to purchase the French company's claims for $40 million and build the canal in Panama if Colombia ceded a strip of land across the isthmus on reasonable terms. Otherwise, Roosevelt was to negotiate with Nicaragua for the alternative route. In 1903, Roosevelt pressed Colombia to sell a canal zone to the United States for $10 million and an annual payment of $250,000. Colombia, however, rejected the proposal.

Roosevelt was furious and began working with Philippe Bunau-Varilla, a French official of the Panama Canal Company, to exploit long-smoldering Panamanian discontent with Colombia. Roosevelt's purpose was to get the canal zone,

Bunau-Varilla's to get the American money. Roosevelt ordered U.S. naval forces to Panama; from New York, Bunau-Varilla coordinated a revolt against Colombian authority directed by officials of the Panama Railroad, owned by Bunau-Varilla's canal company. The bloodless "revolution" succeeded when U.S. forces prevented Colombian troops from landing in Panama, although the United States was bound by treaty to maintain Colombian sovereignty in the region. Bunau-Varilla promptly signed a treaty accepting Roosevelt's original terms for a canal zone and making Panama a U.S. protectorate, which it remained until 1939. Panamanians themselves denounced the treaty for surrendering sovereignty in the zone to the United States, but the United States took formal control of the canal zone in 1904 and completed construction of the Panama Canal in 1914. Roosevelt liked to boast, "I took the Canal Zone and let Congress debate," but his actions generated resentment among Latin Americans that rankled for decades.

THE ROOSEVELT COROLLARY

To protect the security of the canal, the United States increased its authority in the Caribbean. The objective was to establish conditions there that would both eliminate any pretext for European intervention and promote American control over trade and investment.

In his 1904 annual message to Congress, Roosevelt announced a new policy, the so-called **Roosevelt Corollary** to the Monroe Doctrine. "Chronic wrongdoing," he declared, would cause the United States to exercise "an international police power" in Latin America. The Monroe Doctrine had expressed American hostility to European intervention in Latin America; the Roosevelt Corollary attempted to justify U.S. intervention and authority in the region. Roosevelt invoked his corollary immediately, imposing American management of the debts and customs duties of the Dominican Republic in 1905. Commercial rivalries and political intrigue in that poor nation had created disorder, which Roosevelt suppressed for both economic and strategic reasons. Financial insolvency was averted, popular revolution prevented, and possible European intervention forestalled.

Latin Americans vigorously resented the United States' unilateral claim to authority. By 1907, the so-called Drago Doctrine (named after Argentina's foreign minister) was incorporated into international law, prohibiting armed intervention to collect debts. Still, the United States would continue to invoke the Roosevelt Corollary to advance its interests in the hemisphere.

DOLLAR DIPLOMACY

Roosevelt's successor as president, William Howard Taft, hoped to promote U.S. interests without such combative rhetoric and naked force. He proposed "substituting dollars for bullets"—using government action to encourage private American investments in Latin America to supplant European interests, promote development and stability, and gain profits for American bankers. Under this **dollar diplomacy,** American investments in the Caribbean increased dramatically during Taft's

Roosevelt's aggressive foreign policy, including the acquisition of the Canal Zone and the Roosevelt Corollary in 1904, worried many Americans even more than his expansion of presidential authority in domestic policy. Here a partisan cartoon offers a choice between TR and the Democratic presidential candidate, Alton Parker, in 1904.

Courtesy Library ofCongress

Roosevelt Corollary President Theodore Roosevelt's policy asserting U.S. authority to intervene in the affairs of Latin American nations; an expansion of the Monroe Doctrine.

Dollar Diplomacy The U.S. policy of using private investment in other nations to promote American diplomatic goals and business interests.

presidency from 1909 to 1913, and the State Department helped arrange for American bankers to establish financial control over Haiti and Honduras.

But Taft did not shrink from employing military force to protect American property or to establish the conditions he thought necessary for American investments. In fact, Taft intervened more frequently than Roosevelt had, with Nicaragua a major target. In 1909, Taft sent U.S. troops there to aid a revolution fomented by an American mining corporation and to seize the Nicaraguan customs houses. Under the new government, American bankers then gained control of Nicaragua's national bank, railroad, and customs service. To protect these arrangements, U.S. troops were again dispatched in 1912. To control popular opposition to the American client government, the marines remained in Nicaragua for two decades. Military power, not the social and economic improvement promised by dollar diplomacy, kept Nicaragua's minority government stable and subordinate to the United States.

Dollar diplomacy increased American power and influence in the Caribbean and tied underdeveloped countries to the United States economically and strategically. By 1913, American investments in the region reached $1.5 billion, and Americans had captured more than 50 percent of the foreign trade of Costa Rica, Cuba, the Dominican Republic, Guatemala, Haiti, Honduras, Nicaragua, and Panama. But this policy failed to improve conditions for most Latin Americans. U.S. officials remained primarily concerned with promoting American control and extracting American profits from the region, not with the well-being of its population. Not surprisingly, dollar diplomacy proved unpopular in Latin America.

WILSONIAN INTERVENTIONS

Taking office in 1913, the Democrat Woodrow Wilson repudiated the interventionist policies of his Republican predecessors. He promised that the United States would "never again seek one additional foot of territory by conquest" but would instead work to promote "human rights, national integrity, and opportunity" in Latin America. Wilson named as his secretary of state the Democratic symbol of anti-imperialism, William Jennings Bryan. Their generous intentions were apparent when Bryan signed a treaty with Colombia apologizing for Roosevelt's seizure of the Panama Canal Zone.

Nonetheless, Wilson soon became the most interventionist president in American history. Convinced that the United States had to expand its exports and investments abroad and that U.S. dominance of the Caribbean was strategically necessary, he also held the racist belief that Latin Americans were inferior and needed paternalistic guidance from the United States. His self-righteousness and determination to transform the behavior of other peoples led his policies to be dubbed "missionary diplomacy," but they also contained elements of Roosevelt's commitment to military force and Taft's reliance on economic power.

Caribbean Interventions.   In 1915, Wilson ordered U.S. marines to Haiti. They went, explained Bryan, to restore order and preserve "gravely menaced" American interests. The U.S. Navy selected a new Haitian president, granting him nominal authority over a client government. Real authority, however, rested with the American military, which controlled Haiti until 1934, protecting the small elite who cooperated with American interests and exploited their own people. As usual, American military rule improved the country's transportation, sanitation, and educational systems, but the forced-labor program that the United States adopted to build such public works provoked widespread resentment. In 1919, marines suppressed a revolt against American domination, killing more than 3,000 Haitians.

Wilson also intervened elsewhere in the Caribbean. In 1916, when the Dominican Republic refused to cede control of its finances to U.S. bankers, Wilson ordered the marines to occupy the country. The marines ousted Dominican officials, installed a military government to rule "on behalf of the Dominican government," and ran the nation until 1924. In 1917, the United States intervened in Cuba, which remained under American control until 1922.

Interfering with Mexico.   Wilson also involved himself in the internal affairs of Mexico. The lengthy dictatorship of Porfirio Díaz had collapsed in 1911 in revolutionary disorder. The popular leader Francisco Madero took power and promised democratic and economic reforms that alarmed both wealthy Mexicans and foreign investors, particularly Americans. In 1913, General Victoriano Huerta seized control in a brutal counterrevolution backed by the landed aristocracy and foreign interests. Wilson was appalled by the violence of Huerta's power grab and was aware that opponents had organized to reestablish constitutional government.

Wilson hoped to bring the Constitutionalists to power and "to secure Mexico a better government under which all contracts and business and concessions will be safer than they have been." He authorized arms sales to the forces led by Venustiano Carranza, pressured Britain and other nations to deprive Huerta of foreign support, and blockaded the Mexican port of Vera Cruz. In April 1914 Wilson exploited a minor incident to have the marines attack and occupy Vera Cruz. This assault damaged his image as a promoter of peace and justice, and even Carranza and the Constitutionalists denounced the American occupation as unwarranted aggression. By August, Carranza had toppled Huerta, and Wilson shifted his support to Francisco ("Pancho") Villa, who seemed more susceptible to American guidance. But Carranza's growing popular support in Mexico and Wilson's preoccupation with World War I in Europe finally led the United States to grant de facto recognition to the Carranza government in October 1915.

Villa then began terrorizing New Mexico and Texas, hoping to provoke an American intervention that would undermine Carranza. In 1916, Wilson ordered troops under General John J. Pershing to pursue Villa into Mexico, leading Carranza to fear a permanent U.S. occupation of northern Mexico. Soon the American soldiers were fighting the Mexican army rather than Villa's bandits. On the brink of full-fledged war, Wilson finally ordered U.S. troops to withdraw in January 1917 and extended full recognition to the Carranza government. His aggressive tactics had not merely failed but also embittered relations with Mexico.

CONCLUSION

By the time of Woodrow Wilson's presidency, the United States had been expanding its involvement in world affairs for half a century. Several themes had emerged from this activity: increasing American domination of the Caribbean, continuing interest in East Asia, the creation of an overseas empire, and the evolution of the United States into a major world power. The American involvement in the world reflected a traditional, if often misguided, sense of national rectitude and mission. Generous humanitarian impulses vied with ugly racist prejudices as Americans sought both to help other peoples and to direct them toward U.S. concepts of religion, sanitation, capitalist development, and public institutions. American motives ranged from ensuring national security and competing with European colonial powers to the conviction that the United States

had to expand its economic interests abroad. But if imperialism, both informal and at times colonial, brought Americans greater wealth and power, it also increased tensions in Asia and contributed to anti-American hostility and revolutionary ferment in Latin America. It also entangled the United States in the Great Power rivalries that would ultimately result in two world wars.

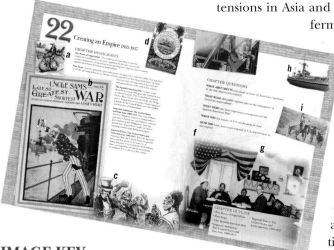

IMAGE KEY
for pages 636–637

a. Uncle Sam rides a bicycle with globes of the western and eastern hemisphere for wheels.

b. Cover of an American magazine, 1898, commemorating the country's swift victory in the Spanish-American War.

c. Cartoon concerning the Open Door Policy, 1899. "A Fair Field and No Favor. Uncle Sam: I'm out for commerce, not conquest."

d. A colorful poster for the Panama-California Exhibition in San Diego.

e. Theodore Roosevelt on a steam shovel during the Panama Canal construction.

f. Catalog Illustration of a Date Palm Tree ca. 1900.

g. An American missionary and her Chinese converts study the Bible in Manchuria.

h. Grey and red battle ship.

i. Charles Post, "Spanish Civil War."

SUMMARY

The Roots of Imperialism The United States had a long tradition of expansion across the continent; now America embarked on building an overseas empire. Some Americans favored acquiring and exploiting colonies; others wanted an empire based on trade and investments; still others advocated the United States exporting its ideas and institutions. Social Darwinism, Protestant evangelism, and naval expansion were all rationales for America becoming a world power.

First Steps Despite the growing pro-imperialist arguments, America was generally passive toward foreign affairs until the end of the nineteenth century. The purchase of Alaska from Russia, the growing American commercial influence in Hawaii, and the assertion of hemispheric domination in Latin America demonstrated America's increasingly assertive national policy throughout the late 1800s.

The Spanish-American War The war originated in Cuba's quest for independence from Spain. Spain's brutality in suppressing the revolt prompted American sympathy; the sensationalist yellow press fanned the flames for war. The Spanish-American War made America an imperialist nation; the Battle of Manila Bay gave America a foothold in the Philippines; Hawaii was annexed as part of America's "Manifest Destiny"; and a short campaign in Cuba resulted in the defeat of Spanish troops there. The Treaty of Paris gave America Puerto Rico and Guam and set the stage for the acquisition of the Philippines; anti-imperialists questioned national goals and America's commitment to liberty and freedom.

Imperial Ambitions: The United States and East Asia, 1899–1917 The Filipino-American War resulted from the betrayed hope of the Filipino people for independence following the Treaty of Paris. A brutal war fought to put down rebellion resulted in America's establishing a colonial government in the Philippines. America's involvement in the Philippines reflected its interest in China; European nations and Japan claimed areas of influence in China, limiting America's options to develop trade. Involvement in China brought the United States into conflict with Japan and Russia; Japan's emergence as a great power saw growing discord between the two countries.

Imperial Power: The United States and Latin America, 1899–1917 Following the Spanish-American War, America often intervened in Latin America to promote its own strategic and economic interests; trade expanded and ill will increased. Puerto Rico became a territory, Cuba, a U.S. protectorate, and land in Panama was acquired to build a canal; each was part of America's exercise of imperial power. President Theodore Roosevelt's Corollary to the Monroe Doctrine announced America's role as a policeman and debt collector; President Taft attempted dollar diplomacy; President Wilson intervened in the Caribbean, and his tactics in Mexico created lasting ill will.

REVIEW QUESTIONS

1. After the Spanish-American War, General Leonard Wood asserted that Cubans believed that their American "liberators" were "still their faithful friends." Why might Cubans not have agreed with Wood?

2. What factors, old and new, shaped American foreign policy in the late nineteenth century? How were they interrelated?

3. How were individual politicians and diplomats able to affect America's foreign policy? How were they constrained by governmental institutions, private groups, and public opinion?

4. To what extent was the United States' emergence as an imperial power a break from, as opposed to a culmination of, its earlier policies and national development?

5. How effective were U.S. interventions in Latin America? What were the objectives and consequences?

6. In what ways did the policies of other nations shape the development of American foreign policy?

KEY TERMS

Dollar diplomacy   (p. 659)
Gentlemen's Agreement   (p. 655)
Imperialism   (p. 639)
Mahanism   (p. 642)

Open Door   (p. 654)
Pan American Union   (p. 645)
Platt Amendment   (p. 657)
Roosevelt Corollary   (p. 659)

Spheres of Influence   (p. 654)
Teller Amendment   (p. 649)
Yellow Press   (p. 648)

WHERE TO LEARN MORE

Mission Houses, Honolulu, Hawaii. Built between 1821 and 1841, these buildings were homes and shops of missionaries sent to Hawaii by the American Board of Commissioners for Foreign Missions. Their exhibits include furnishings and memorabilia of a group important in developing American ties with Hawaii. www. missionhouses.org/

Funston Memorial Home, Iola, Kansas. Operated as a museum by the Kansas State Historical Society, this is the boyhood home of General Frederick Funston, prominent in the Spanish-American War and the Filipino-American War. For a virtual tour, together with military information, political cartoons, Roosevelt correspondence, and Funston links, see http://skyways.lib.ks.us/museums/funston/

James G. Blaine House, Augusta, Maine. The Executive Mansion of Maine's governor since 1919, this house was formerly Blaine's home and still contains his study and furnishings from the time he served as secretary of state and U.S. senator.

Rough Riders Memorial and City Museum, Las Vegas, New Mexico. Together with the nearby Castaneda Hotel, this site provides intriguing information on Roosevelt's volunteer cavalry, recruited primarily from the Southwest. www .arco-iris.com/teddy/index.htm

Seward House, Auburn, New York. The home of William H. Seward contains furniture and mementos from his career as secretary of state.

 U.S. History Documents CD-ROM
For primary sources related to this chapter, refer to the document CD-ROM.

 www.prenhall.com/goldfield
For study resources related to this chapter, visit the *Companion Website*™.

23 America and the Great War 1914–1920

CHAPTER HIGHLIGHTS

Waging Neutrality Few Americans believed that the United States would, or should, become involved in World War I. Despite the U.S. policy of neutrality, economic, political, and cultural ties bound the United States to the Allies. Germany's decision to wage unrestricted submarine warfare contributed to U.S. entry into the war in 1917.

Waging War in America Once involved in the war, the government reorganized the economy and took steps to control public opinion and suppress dissent. Labor shortages allowed women and minorities to enter the workforce in growing numbers.

Waging War and Peace Abroad American involvement ensured Allied victory. President Wilson hoped to build a peace based on his Fourteen Points. The competing agendas of other Allied leaders undermined his plans. A desire for vengeance against Germany and fear of Bolshevism shaped the Treaty of Versailles.

Waging Peace at Home Despite widespread public support for the Versailles treaty, Wilson failed to win approval for the treaty in the Senate. An influenza epidemic, economic problems, and the Red Scare left Americans wanting a return to "normalcy." Warren Harding's landslide victory in 1920 reflected this feeling.

Beat back the HUN with LIBERTY BONDS

CHAPTER QUESTIONS

WHY WERE Americans so reluctant to get involved in World War I?

HOW DID the war effort threaten civil liberties?

WHAT HOPES did Wilson have for the Treaty of Versailles?

WHAT CHALLENGES did America face in the aftermath of the war?

CHAPTER OUTLINE

- Waging Neutrality
- Waging War in America
- Waging War and Peace Abroad
- Waging Peace at Home

IMAGE KEY

for pages 664–665 is on page 689.

I have been traveling for nearly three weeks through six Middle Western States, talking about the war, with all classes of people: farmers, labor leaders, newspaper editors, college professors, business men, and state officials. I have been trying to get at the bedrock sentiment of the people regarding it, and to set it down exactly as I find it.

Almost without exception, even among those who favor the war most vigorously, the people I have talked with have commented upon the lack of popular enthusiasm for the war. The more closely these people were connected with the farmers or the workingmen, the more sweeping and positive were their statements.

The attitude of the people is wholly different from what it was at the opening of our Spanish War in 1898. There are no heroic slogans, no boast-fulness, no excitement, no glamour of war. There is still a great deal of haziness about the real issues and a great deal of doubt about how far America should go beyond mere defensive measures. One of the foremost political leaders of the West, himself an ardent supporter of the war, told me that if a secret ballot were taken as to whether American armies should be sent to France, the vote would be overwhelmingly against it. It is noteworthy, also, that the newspapers are full of a-b-c explanations of the reasons why we are at war and why we should go forward with it. . . . And finally, there are nowhere as yet any evidences of the passions and the hatred which war engenders. People do not hate Germans or Austrians or Turks; nor do they love the British.

On the other hand, if there is little enthusiasm, the people everywhere are taking the war as a grim necessity, feeling that they have been forced into it by events beyond their control, and they are going forward, more or less reluctantly, with the preparations; but they are really going forward. The draft was not popular; people wished it might have been done in some other way; and in some groups of population it was hated and feared, and yet, through all this country, there has been a wonderful and complete compliance with the law. In the same way the liberty loan is not popular. There is no popular rush to subscribe, and it has required an enormous amount of organization, advertising, and pressure to sell the bonds, and yet they are being sold and will be sold. . . . And there have been no signs of any popular rush to enlist, and men have been obtained only by dint of the most vigorous advertising and pressure. It is significant also that more than half of those registered in Chicago are demanding exemption.

The only real enthusiasm that I could find was in such campaigns as that of the Red Cross, the Y.M.C.A., and here and there in work for the American Ambulance in France. The work of women everywhere for the Red Cross is remarkably organized and well supported. . . . Of the value of these activities, no matter what happens, the people are convinced.

Ray Stannard Baker, "West in Grim Business of War Without Passion," *St. Louis Post-Dispatch,* June 17, 1917.

RAY STANNARD BAKER, the famous journalist, thus described his journey across the Midwest in 1917, three years after World War I began in Europe and two months after the United States had joined the conflict by declaring war on Germany. The American people were reluctant participants in the war, unconvinced that national interests were really involved.

But as the perceptive Baker also discovered, the nation's leaders were determined to whip up popular support for the war effort through "organization, advertising, and pressure." The goal would be not only to train soldiers to fight in Europe but to demonize Germany, mobilize the economy, and transform social attitudes.

The Great War was the United States' first major military conflict on foreign soil, and it changed American life. Government authority increased sharply. Business organizations, labor unions, farmers, ministers were all incorporated into the war effort. Women's organizational activities expanded dramatically beyond those noted by Baker and often developed in new and unexpected ways. Journalists, too, had their skills put to new and sometimes unfortunate uses; Baker himself, who had initially opposed the war as a threat to progress, eventually went to Europe to file confidential reports for the State Department and then to organize the Press Department and control news at the Versailles Peace Conference.

Many of the changes in American life, from increased efficiency to Americanization, reflected prewar progressivism. But the war also diverted reform energies into new channels, subordinated generous impulses to attitudes that were more coercive, and strengthened the conservative opposition to reform. The results were often reactionary and contributed to a postwar mood that not only curtailed further reform but also helped defeat the peace treaty upon which so much had been gambled.

WAGING NEUTRALITY

Few Americans were prepared for the Great War that erupted in Europe in August 1914, but fewer still foresaw that their own nation might become involved in it. With near unanimity, they supported neutrality. But American attitudes, decisions, and actions, both public and private, undercut neutrality, and the policies of governments in Berlin, London, and Washington drew the United States into the war.

WHY WERE Americans so reluctant to get involved in World War I?

THE ORIGINS OF CONFLICT

Since the 1870s, the competing imperial ambitions of the European powers had led to economic rivalries, military expansion, diplomatic maneuvering, and international tensions. A complex system of alliances divided the continent into two opposing blocs. In central Europe, the expansionist Germany of Kaiser Wilhelm II allied itself with the multinational Austro-Hungarian Empire. Confronting them, Great Britain and France entered into alliances with tsarist Russia. A succession of crises threatened this precarious balance of power.

On June 28, a Serbian terrorist assassinated Archduke Franz Ferdinand, the heir to the Austro-Hungarian throne, in Sarajevo. With Germany's support, Austria declared war on Serbia on July 28. Russia then mobilized its army against Austria to aid Serbia, its Slavic client state. To assist Austria, Germany declared war on Russia and then on Russia's ally, France. Hoping for a quick victory, Germany struck at France through neutral Belgium; in response, Britain declared war on Germany on August 4. Soon Turkey and Bulgaria joined Germany and Austria to form the

Chronology

1914	World War I begins in Europe.
	President Woodrow Wilson declares U.S. neutrality.
1915	Germany begins submarine warfare.
	Lusitania is sunk.
	Woman's Peace Party is organized.
1916	Sussex Pledge is issued.
	Preparedness legislation is enacted.
	Woodrow Wilson is reelected president.
1917	The February Revolution ends tsarist regime in Russia.
	Germany resumes unrestricted submarine warfare.
	The United States declares war on Germany.
	Selective Service Act establishes the military draft.
	Espionage Act is passed.
	Committee on Public Information, War Industries Board, Food Administration, and other mobilization agencies are established.
	American Expeditionary Force arrives in France.
	East St. Louis race riot erupts.
	Bolshevik Revolution occurs in Russia.
1918	Wilson announces his Fourteen Points.
	Sedition Act is passed.
	Eugene Debs is imprisoned.
	The United States intervenes militarily in Russia.
	Armistice ends World War I.
1919	Paris Peace Conference is held.
	Steel, coal, and other strikes occur.
	Red Scare breaks out.
	Prohibition amendment is adopted.
	Wilson suffers a massive stroke.
1920	Palmer Raids round up radicals.
	League of Nations is defeated in the U.S. Senate.
	Woman suffrage amendment is ratified.
	U.S. troops are withdrawn from Russia.
	Warren Harding is elected president.
1921	United States signs a separate peace treaty with Germany.

Central Powers Germany and its World War I allies in Austria, Turkey, and Bulgaria.

Allies In World War I, Britain, France, Russia, and other nations fighting against the Central Powers but not including the United States.

Central Powers. The **Allies**—Britain, France, and Russia—were joined by Italy and Japan. Britain drew on its empire for resources, using troops from India, Canada, Australia, New Zealand, and South Africa. The war had become a global conflict, waged not only in Europe but also in Africa, the Middle East, and East Asia.

Mass slaughter enveloped Europe as huge armies battled to a stalemate. The British and French faced the Germans along a line of trenches stretching across France and Belgium from the English Channel to Switzerland. Little movement occurred despite great efforts and terrible casualties from artillery, machine guns, and poison gas. The belligerents subordinated their economies, politics, and cultures to military demands. The Great War, said one German soldier, had become "the grave of nations."

AMERICAN ATTITUDES

Most believed that the United States had no vital interest in the war and would not become involved. "Our isolated position and freedom from entangling alliances," noted the *Literary Digest*, "inspire our press with the cheering assurance that we are in no peril of being drawn into the European quarrel." President Wilson issued a proclamation of neutrality and urged Americans to be "neutral in fact as well as in name . . . impartial in thought as well as in action."

However, neither the American people nor their president stayed strictly neutral. Most Americans sympathized with the Allies. Ethnic, cultural, and economic ties bound most Americans to the British and French. Politically, too, most Americans felt a greater affinity for the democratic Western Allies—tsarist Russia repelled them—than for Germany's more authoritarian government and society. And whereas Britain and the United States had enjoyed a rapprochement since 1895, Germany had repeatedly appeared as a potential rival.

Wilson himself admired Britain's culture and government and distrusted Germany's imperial ambitions. Like other influential Americans, Wilson believed that a German victory would threaten America's economic, political, and perhaps even strategic interests. Most officials favored the Allies. Robert Lansing, counselor of the State Department; Walter Hines Page, the ambassador to England; and Colonel Edward House, Wilson's closest adviser on foreign affairs—all assisted British diplomats, undercut official U.S. protests against British violations of American neutrality, and encouraged Wilson's suspicions of Germany.

British propaganda bolstered American sympathies. British writers, artists, and lecturers depicted the Allies as fighting for civilization against a brutal Germany that mutilated nuns and babies. Although German troops, like most other soldiers, did commit outrages, they were not guilty of the systematic barbarity claimed by Allied propagandists. Britain, however, shaped America's view of the conflict.

Sympathy for the Allies, however, did not mean that Americans favored intervention. Indeed, few Americans doubted that neutrality was the appropriate course and peace the proper goal. The carnage in France solidified their convictions. Wilson was determined to pursue peace as long as his view of national interests allowed.

THE ECONOMY OF WAR

Economic issues soon threatened American neutrality. International law permitted neutral nations to sell or ship war matériel to belligerents, and with the economy mired in a recession when the war began, many Americans looked to war orders to spur economic recovery. But the British navy prevented trade with the Central Powers. Only the Allies could buy American goods. Their orders for steel, explosives, uniforms, wheat, and other products, however, pulled the country out of the recession.

Other Americans worried that this one-sided war trade undermined genuine neutrality. Congress even considered an embargo on munitions. But few Americans supported the idea. Whatever its justification, however, the war trade strengthened U.S. ties with the Allies and embittered Germany.

A second economic issue complicated matters. To finance their war purchases, the Allies borrowed from American bankers. Initially, Secretary of State Bryan persuaded Wilson to prohibit loans to the belligerents as "inconsistent with the true spirit of neutrality." But as the importance of the war orders to both the Allies and the American economy became clear, Wilson ended the ban. Secretary of the Treasury William McAdoo argued that it would be "disastrous" not to finance the Allies' purchases, on which "our prosperity is dependent." By April 1917, American loans to the Allies exceeded $2 billion, nearly a hundred times the amount lent to Germany.

THE DIPLOMACY OF NEUTRALITY

The same imbalance characterized American diplomacy. Wilson insisted on American neutral rights but acquiesced in British violations of those rights, while sternly refusing to yield on German actions. Wilson argued that while British violations

President Woodrow Wilson reads his war message to Congress, April 2, 1917. He predicted "many months of fiery trial and sacrifice ahead of us."

Courtesy Library of Congress

Declaration of London
Statement drafted by an international conference in 1909 to clarify international law and specify the rights of neutral nations.

of international law cost Americans property, markets, and time, German violations cost lives. As the *Boston Globe* noted, the British were "a gang of thieves" and the Germans "a gang of murderers. On the whole, we prefer the thieves, but only as the lesser of two evils."

When the war began, the United States asked belligerents to respect the 1909 **Declaration of London** on neutral rights. Germany agreed to do so; the British refused. Instead, skirting or violating established procedures, Britain blockaded Germany, mined the North Sea, and forced neutral ships into British ports to search their cargoes and confiscate material deemed useful to the German war effort. These British actions infringed on U.S. trading rights. Wilson branded Britain's blockade illegal and unwarranted, but by October he had conceded many of America's neutral rights in order to avoid conflict with Britain.

The British then prohibited food and other products that Germany had imported during peacetime, thereby interfering further with neutral shipping. But when the Wilson administration finally protested, it undermined its own position by noting that "imperative necessity" might justify a violation of international law. This statement virtually authorized the British to violate American rights. In January 1915, Wilson yielded further by observing that "no very important questions of principle" were involved in the Anglo-American quarrels over ship seizures and that they could be resolved after the war.

Submarine Warfare. This policy tied the United States to the British war effort and provoked a German response. With its army stalemated on land and its navy no match for Britain's, Germany decided in February 1915 to use its submarines against Allied shipping in a war zone around the British Isles. Neutral ships risked being sunk by mistake, partly because British ships illegally flew neutral flags.

Submarines could not readily follow traditional rules of naval warfare. These rules had been drawn up for surface ships and required them to identify enemy merchant ships and ensure the safety of passengers before attacking. But small and fragile submarines depended on surprise attacks. They could not surface without risking attack, and they were too small to rescue victims of their sinkings. Yet Wilson refused to see the same "imperative necessity" in German tactics that he found in British tactics, and he warned that he would hold Germany responsible for any loss of American lives or property.

In May 1915, a German submarine sank a British passenger liner, the *Lusitania*. It had been carrying arms, and the German embassy had warned Americans against traveling on the ship, but the loss of life—1,198 people, including 128 Americans—caused Americans to condemn Germany. "To speak of technicalities and the rules of war, in the face of such wholesale murder on the high seas, is a waste of time," trumpeted one magazine. Yet only six of a thousand editors surveyed called for war, and even the combative Theodore Roosevelt estimated that 98 percent of Americans still opposed war. Wilson saw that he had to "carry out the double wish of our people, to maintain a firm front in respect of what we demand of Germany and yet do nothing that might by any possibility involve us in the war."

This was a difficult stance. Wilson demanded that Germany abandon its submarine campaign. His language was so harsh that Bryan resigned, warning that by requiring more of Germany than of Britain, the president violated neutrality and threatened to draw the nation into war. Bryan argued that "Germany has a right to prevent contraband from going to the Allies," and he protested Britain's use of American passengers as shields to protect contraband cargo. Bryan proposed prohibiting Americans from traveling on belligerent ships. His proposal gained support in the South and West and was introduced as a resolution in both the Senate and the House in February 1916.

Wilson moved to defeat the resolutions, insisting that they impinged on presidential control of foreign policy and on America's neutral rights. In truth, the resolutions abandoned no vital national interest and offered to prevent another provocative incident. Moreover, neither law nor tradition gave Americans the right to travel safely on belligerent ships. Wilson's assertion of such a right committed him to a policy that could only lead to conflict. Of the nation's "double wish," then, Wilson placed more priority on confronting what he saw as a German threat than on meeting the popular desire for peace.

In April 1916, a German submarine torpedoed the French ship *Sussex,* injuring four Americans. Wilson threatened to break diplomatic relations if Germany did not abandon unrestricted submarine warfare against all merchant vessels, enemy as well as neutral. This threat implied war. Germany promised not to sink merchant ships without warning but made its *Sussex* **Pledge** contingent on the United States' requiring Britain also to adhere to "the rules of international law universally recognized before the war." Wilson's diplomatic victory, then, was hollow. Peace for America would depend on the British adopting a course they had already rejected. As Wilson saw it, however, "any little German lieutenant can put us into the war at any time by some calculated outrage." Wilson's diplomacy had left the nation's future at the mercy of others.

THE BATTLE OVER PREPAREDNESS

The threat of war sparked a debate over military policy. Theodore Roosevelt and a handful of other politicians, mostly northeastern Republicans convinced that Allied victory was in the national interest, advocated what they called **preparedness,** a program to expand the armed forces and establish universal military training. Conservative business groups also joined the agitation, combining demands for preparedness with attacks on progressive reforms.

But most Americans opposed expensive military preparations. Leading feminists, such as Jane Addams, Charlotte Perkins Gilman, and Carrie Chapman Catt, formed the Woman's Peace Party in 1915, and other organizations, such as the American League to Limit Armaments, also campaigned against preparedness. William Jennings Bryan condemned preparedness as a program for turning the nation into "a vast armory with skull and crossbones above the door."

Wilson also opposed preparedness initially, but he reversed his position when the submarine crisis with Germany intensified. In early 1916, an election year, he made a speaking tour to generate public support for enlarging the armed forces.

***Sussex* Pledge**   Germany's pledge during World War I not to sink merchant ships without warning, on the condition that Britain also observe recognized rules of international laws.

Preparedness   Military buildup in preparation for possible U.S. participation in World War I.

A preparedness parade winds its way through Mobile, Alabama, on July 4, 1916. By 1916, President Wilson, invoking the spirit of patriotism, had given his support to the preparedness program of military expansion.

University of South Alabama Achives.

The National Defense Act and the Naval Construction Act increased the strength of the army and authorized a naval construction program. Draped in the flag, Wilson marched at the head of a huge preparedness parade in Washington to celebrate the military program.

THE ELECTION OF 1916

Wilson's preparedness plans stripped the Republicans of one issue in 1916, and his renewed support of progressive reforms (see Chapter 21) helped to hold Bryan Democrats in line. Wilson continued his balancing act in the campaign itself, at first stressing "Americanism" and preparedness but then emphasizing peace. The slogan "He Kept Us Out of War" appealed to the popular desire for peace, and the Democratic campaign became one long peace rally.

The Republicans were divided. They had hoped to regain their progressive members after Roosevelt urged the Progressive Party to follow him back into the GOP. But many joined the Democratic camp instead. The GOP nominated Charles Evans Hughes, a Supreme Court justice and former New York governor. The platform denounced Wilson's "shifty expedients" in foreign policy and promised "strict and honest neutrality." Unfortunately for Hughes, Roosevelt's attacks on Wilson for not pursuing a war policy persuaded many voters that the GOP was a war party. The link with Roosevelt kept Hughes from exploiting qualms about Wilson's own lack of neutrality. "If Hughes is defeated," wrote one observer, "he has Roosevelt to thank for it."

The election was the closest in decades (see Map 23–1). When California narrowly went for Wilson, it decided the contest. The desire for peace, all observers concluded, had determined the election.

DESCENT INTO WAR

Still, Wilson knew that war loomed, and he made a last effort to avert it. In January 1917, he sketched out the terms of what he called a "peace without victory." Anything else, he warned, would only lead to another war. The new world order should be based on national equality and **self-determination,** arms reductions, freedom of the seas, and an international organization to ensure peace. It was a distinctly American vision.

But both the Allies and the Central Powers had sacrificed too much to settle for anything short of outright victory. Germany wanted to annex territory in eastern Europe, Belgium, and France and to take over Belgian and French colonies in Africa; Austria sought Balkan territory. The Allies wanted to destroy German military and commercial power, weaken the Austro-Hungarian Empire, take Germany's colonies in Africa, and supplant Turkish influence in the Middle East. Wilson's initiative failed.

To break the deadlock, Germany resumed unrestricted submarine warfare. German generals believed that even if the United States declared war, it could do

Self-determination The right of a people or a nation to decide its own political allegiance or form of government without external influence.

little more in the short run to injure Germany than it was already doing. German submarines, they hoped, would end the war by cutting the Allies off from U.S. supplies before the United States could send an army to Europe.

Wilson Commits to War.   Wilson was now virtually committed to a war many Americans opposed. He broke diplomatic relations with Germany and asked Congress to arm American merchant vessels. When the Senate refused, Wilson invoked an antipiracy law of 1819 and armed the ships anyway. Although no American ships had yet been sunk, he also ordered the naval gun crews to fire at submarines on sight. The secretary of the navy warned Wilson that these actions violated international law and were a step toward war; Wilson called his policy "armed neutrality." Huge rallies across America demanded peace.

Several developments soon shifted public opinion. On March 1, Wilson released an intercepted message from the German foreign minister, Arthur Zimmermann, to the German minister in Mexico. It proposed that in the event of war between the United States and Germany, Mexico should ally itself with Germany; in exchange, Mexico would recover its "lost territory in Texas, New Mexico, and Arizona." The Zimmermann note produced a wave of hostility toward Germany and increased support for intervention in the war. In addition, a revolution in Russia overthrew the tsarist regime and established a provisional government. Russia was now "a fit partner" for the United States, said Wilson. When submarines sank four American freighters in mid-March, anti-German feeling broadened.

On April 2, 1917, Wilson delivered his war message, declaring that neutrality was no longer possible. To build support for joining a war that most people had long regarded with revulsion and as alien to American interests, Wilson set forth the nation's war goals as simple and noble. The United States would not fight for conquest or domination but for "the ultimate peace of the world and for the liberation of its peoples. . . . The world must be made safe for democracy."

After vigorous debate, the Senate passed the war resolution 82 to 6 and the House 373 to 50. On April 6, 1917, the United States officially entered the Great War—what House Democratic leader Claude Kitchin of North Carolina predicted would be "one vast drama of horrors and blood, one boundless stage upon which will play all the evil spirits of earth and hell."

	Electoral Vote (%)	Popular Vote (%)
WOODROW WILSON (Democrat)	**277 (52)**	**9,127,695 (49.4)**
Charles E. Hughes (Republican)	254 (48)	8,533,507 (46.2)
A.L. Benson (Socialist)	–	585,113 (3.2)
Other parties (Socialist Labor, Prohibition)	–	233,909 (1.3)

MAP 23–1   The Election of 1916   Woodrow Wilson won reelection in 1916, despite a reunified Republican Party, by sweeping the South and West on campaign appeals to peace and progressive reform.

HOW WAS Woodrow Wilson able to win reelection in 1916 despite the reunification of the Republican party?

WHERE TO LEARN MORE

National Infantry Museum, Fort Benning, Georgia
www.benningmwr.com/index.cfm

WAGING WAR IN AMERICA

*M*obilizing for military intervention was a massive undertaking. The government reorganized the economy to emphasize centralized management, developed policies to control public opinion and suppress dissent, and transformed the role of government itself. Mobilization often built on the progressives' moralism and sense of mission and their efforts to resolve social

HOW DID the war effort threaten civil liberties?

OVERVIEW   MAJOR GOVERNMENT WARTIME AGENCIES

Agency	Purpose
War Industries Board	Reorganized industry to maximize wartime production
Railroad Administration	Modernized and operated the nation's railroads
Food Administration	Increased agricultural production, supervised food distribution and farm labor
National War Labor Board	Resolved labor-management disputes, improved labor conditions, and recognized union rights as means to promote production and efficiency
Committee on Public Information	Managed propaganda to build public support for the war effort

and economic problems by government intervention. In other respects, however, the war experience undercut progressive achievements and withered the spirits of reformers. People on the home front, like the soldiers in Europe, would participate in the Great War in many different ways; all would find their lives changed.

MANAGING THE WAR ECONOMY

Federal and state governments developed a complex structure of agencies and controls for every sector of the economy, from industry and agriculture to transportation and labor (see the Overview table, "Major Government Wartime Agencies"). Supervised by the Council of National Defense, these agencies shifted resources to war-related enterprises, increased production of goods and services, and improved transportation and distribution.

Organizing Industry.   The most important agency was the **War Industries Board (WIB),** established in July 1917 to set industrial priorities, coordinate military purchasing, and supervise business. Led by financier Bernard Baruch, the WIB exercised unprecedented power over industry by setting prices, allocating scarce materials, and standardizing products and procedures to boost efficiency. Yet Baruch was not an industrial dictator; he aimed at business-government integration. The WIB promoted major business interests, helped suspend antitrust laws, and guaranteed huge corporate profits. One corporate executive admitted, "We are all making more money out of this war than the average human being ought to." Some progressives began to see the dangers, and business leaders the advantages, of government economic intervention.

The Railroad Administration also linked business ambitions to the war economy. Under William McAdoo, it operated the nation's railroads as a unified system to move supplies and troops efficiently. Centralized management eliminated competition, permitted improvements in equipment, and brought great profits to the owners but higher prices to the general public.

Ensuring Food Supplies.   Equally effective and far more popular was the Food Administration, headed by Herbert Hoover. Hoover persuaded millions of Americans to accept meatless and wheatless days, so that the Food Administration could feed military and foreign consumers. Half a million women went door to door to secure food-conservation pledges from housewives. City residents planted victory gardens in parks and vacant lots, and President Wilson even pastured sheep on the White House lawn.

QUICK REVIEW

The War Industries Board
- Promoted business interests.
- Helped suspend anti-trust laws.
- Guaranteed huge profits.

War Industries Board (WIB)
The federal agency that reorganized industry for maximum efficiency and productivity during World War I.

Hoover also worked closely with agricultural processors and distributors, ensuring profits in exchange for cooperation. Farmers profited from the war, too. To encourage production, Hoover established high prices for commodities, and agricultural income rose by 30 percent. State and federal governments provided commercial farmers with sufficient farm labor despite the military draft and competition from high-wage war industries. The Food Administration organized the Woman's Land Army to work in the fields. Most states formed units of the Boys' Working Reserve for agricultural labor. Agribusinesses in the Southwest persuaded the federal government to permit them to import Mexicans to work under government supervision and be housed in special camps.

Overseeing Labor Relations.   In exchange for labor's cooperation, the National War Labor Board guaranteed the rights of unions to organize and bargain collectively. The labor board also encouraged improved working conditions, higher wages, and shorter hours. These improvements limited labor disputes during the war, and Secretary of War Baker praised labor as "more willing to keep in step than capital." But when such unions as the Industrial Workers of the World did not keep in step, the government suppressed them.

Although these and other government regulatory agencies were dismantled when the war ended, they set a precedent for governmental activism that would prove valuable during the crises of the 1930s and 1940s.

WOMEN AND MINORITIES: NEW OPPORTUNITIES, OLD INEQUITIES

Women and War Work.   The reorganization of the economy also had significant social consequences, especially for women and African Americans. In response to labor shortages, public officials and private employers exhorted women to join the work force. Women now took jobs previously closed to them. More than 100,000 women worked in munitions plants and 40,000 in the steel industry. Harriot Stanton Blatch, a suffragist active in the Food Administration, estimated that a million women had replaced men in industry, where "their drudgery is for the first time paid for."

Many working women simply shifted to other jobs, where their existing skills earned better wages and benefits. The reshuffling of jobs among white women opened new vacancies for black women in domestic, clerical, and industrial employment. As black women replaced white women in the garment and textile industries, social reformers spoke of "a new day for the colored woman worker." But their optimism was unwarranted. Racial as well as gender segregation continued to mark employment, and wartime improvements were temporary.

Woman Suffrage and Prohibition.   The war did help middle-class women reformers achieve two long-sought objectives: woman suffrage and prohibition. Women's support for the war effort prompted more Americans to support woman suffrage. Emphasizing the national cooperation needed to wage the war, one magazine noted that "arbitrarily to draw the line at voting, at a time when every man and woman must share in this effort, becomes an absurd anomaly." Congress approved the suffrage amendment, which was ratified in 1920. Convinced that abstaining from alcohol would save grain and make workers and soldiers more efficient, Congress also passed the Prohibition amendment, which was ratified in 1919.

Mobilization opened new jobs for women, but subordination and segregation persisted. Black women, seen here working in a brickyard for wartime construction, often performed the hardest and least desirable work.

National Archives and Records Administration

African Americans and War Work. The war also changed the lives of African Americans. The demand for industrial labor caused a huge migration of black people from the rural South to northern cities, where they worked in shipyards, steel mills, and packing houses. Half a million African Americans moved north during the war, doubling and tripling the black populations of Chicago, Detroit, and other industrial cities.

Unfortunately, black people often encountered the kind of racial discrimination and violence in the North that they had hoped to leave behind in the South. Fearful and resentful, white people started race riots in northern cities. In East St. Louis, Illinois, where thousands of black southerners sought defense work, a white mob, in July 1917, murdered at least 39 black people, sparing, as an investigating committee reported, "neither age nor sex in their blind lust for blood."

FINANCING THE WAR

To finance the war, the government borrowed money and raised taxes. Business interests favored the first course, but southern and western progressives argued that taxation was more efficient and equitable and would minimize war profiteering. Despite conservative and business opposition to progressive taxation, the tax laws of 1917 and 1918 established a graduated tax structure with higher taxes on large incomes, corporate profits, and wealthy estates.

The government raised two-thirds of the war costs by borrowing. Most of the loans came from banks and wealthy investors, but the government also campaigned to sell **Liberty Bonds** to the general public. Celebrities went to schools, churches, and rallies to persuade Americans to buy bonds as their patriotic duty. "Every person who refuses to subscribe," Secretary of the Treasury McAdoo told a California audience, "is a friend of Germany."

CONQUERING MINDS

The government also tried to promote a war spirit among the American people by establishing propaganda agencies and enacting legislation to control social attitudes and behavior. The Wilson administration adopted this program of social mobilization because many Americans opposed the war: German Americans with ethnic ties to the Central Powers, Irish Catholics and Russian Jews who condemned the Allies for persecution and repression, Scandinavian immigrants averse to military service, pacifists who recoiled from what Wilson himself called "the most terrible and disastrous of all wars," radicals who denounced the war as capitalist and imperialist, and many others, especially among the rural classes of the South and Midwest, who saw no reason to participate in the distant war.

Government Propaganda.   To rally Americans behind the war effort, Wilson established the **Committee on Public Information (CPI)** under the journalist

Liberty Bonds   Interest-bearing certificates sold by the U.S. government to finance the American World War I effort.

Committee on Public Information (CPI)   Government agency during World War I that sought to shape public opinion in support of the war effort through newspapers, pamphlets, speeches, films, and other media.

George Creel. Despite its title, the CPI sought to manipulate, not inform, public opinion. Creel described his goal as winning "the fight for the minds of men, for the 'conquest of their convictions.'" The CPI flooded the country with press releases, advertisements, cartoons, and canned editorials. The CPI made newsreels and war movies to capture public attention. It scheduled 75,000 speakers, who delivered a million speeches to 400 million listeners. Its women's division targeted American women in stereotyped emotional terms. It hired artists to design posters, professors to write pamphlets in 23 languages, and poets to compose war poems for children. Other government agencies launched similar campaigns.

Government propaganda had three themes: national unity, the loathsome character of the enemy, and the war as a grand crusade for liberty and democracy. Obsessed with national unity and conformity, Creel promoted fear, hatred, and prejudice in the name of a triumphant Americanism. Germans were depicted as brutal, even subhuman, rapists and murderers. The campaign suggested that any dissent was unpatriotic, if not treasonous, and dangerous to national survival. This emphasis on unreasoning conformity helped prompt hysterical attacks on German Americans, radicals, and pacifists.

Police forcibly break up an antidraft protest by 5,000 women at New York City Hall on June 16, 1917. Insisting upon what President Wilson called "patriotic devotion," officials at all levels vigorously suppressed dissent during the Great War.

National Archives 165-W W481 A-6

SUPPRESSING DISSENT

The Wilson administration also suppressed dissent, now officially branded disloyalty. For reasons of their own, private interests helped shape a reactionary repression that tarnished the nation's professed idealistic war goals.

Congress rushed to stifle antiwar sentiment. The **Espionage Act** provided heavy fines and up to 20 years in prison for obstructing the war effort, a vague phrase but one "omnipotently comprehensive," warned an Idaho senator who opposed the law. In fact, the Espionage Act became a weapon to crush dissent and criticism. Eventually, Congress passed the still more sweeping **Sedition Act of 1918,** which provided severe penalties for speaking or writing against the draft, bond sales, and war production and for criticizing government personnel or policies. Senator Hiram Johnson lamented, "It is war. But, good God, . . . when did it become war upon the American people?"

Postmaster General Albert Burleson banned antiwar or radical newspapers and magazines from the mail, suppressing literature so indiscriminately that one observer said he "didn't know socialism from rheumatism." The reactionary attorney general, Thomas Gregory, made little distinction between traitors and pacifists, war critics, and radicals. Eugene Debs was sentenced to ten years in prison for a "treasonous" speech in which he declared it "extremely dangerous to exercise the right of free speech in a country fighting to make democracy safe in the world." By war's end, a third of the Socialist Party's national leadership was in prison, leaving the party in a shambles.

Gregory also enlisted the help of private vigilantes, including the several hundred thousand members of the reactionary American Protective League, which sought to purge radicals and reformers from the nation's economic and political life. They wiretapped telephones, intercepted private mail, burglarized union offices, broke up German-language newspapers, harassed immigrants, and staged

Espionage Act Law whose vague prohibition against obstructing the nation's war effort was used to crush dissent and criticism during World War I.

Sedition Act of 1918 Broad law restricting criticism of America's involvement in World War I or its government, flag, military, taxes, or officials.

"Beat Back the Hun," a poster to induce Americans to buy Liberty Bonds, demonizes the enemy in a raw, emotional appeal. Liberty bond drives raised the immense sum of $23 billion.

The Granger Collection, New York

mass raids, seizing thousands of people who they claimed were not doing enough for the war effort.

State and local authorities established 184,000 investigative and enforcement agencies, known as councils of defense or public-safety committees. They encouraged Americans to spy on one another, required people to buy Liberty Bonds, and prohibited teaching German in schools or using the language in religious services and telephone conversations. Germanic names of towns, streets, and people were changed; sauerkraut became liberty cabbage, and the hamburger the liberty sandwich. In Tulsa, a member of the council of defense killed someone for making allegedly pro-German remarks. The council declared its approval, and community leaders applauded the killer's patriotism.

Members of the business community exploited the hysteria to promote their own interests at the expense of farmers, workers, and reformers. On the Great Plains from Texas to North Dakota, the business target was the Nonpartisan League, a radical farm group demanding state control or ownership of banks, grain elevators, and flour mills. Although the League supported the war, oversubscribed bond drives, and had George Creel affirm its loyalty, conservatives depicted it as seditious to block its advocacy of political and economic reforms, including the confiscation of large fortunes to pay for the war. Public officials and self-styled patriots broke up the League's meetings and whipped and jailed its leaders.

In the West, business interests targeted labor organizations, especially the Industrial Workers of the World. In Arizona, for example, the Phelps-Dodge Company broke a mine strike in 1917 by depicting the Wobblie miners as bent on war-related sabotage. A vigilante mob, armed and paid by the mining company, seized 1,200 strikers, many of them Wobblies and one-third of them Mexican Americans, and herded them into the desert without food or water. Federal investigators found no evidence of sedition among the miners and reported that the company and its thugs had been inspired, not by "patriotism," but by "ordinary strike-breaking motives." Corporate management was merely "raising the false cry of 'disloyalty'" to suppress workers' complaints.

Nonetheless, the government itself used the army to break loggers' support for the IWW in the Pacific Northwest, and it raided IWW halls across the country in September 1917. The conviction of nearly 200 Wobblies on charges of sedition in three mass trials in Illinois, California, and Kansas crippled the nation's largest industrial union.

In the end, the government was primarily responsible for the war hysteria. It encouraged suspicion and conflict through inflammatory propaganda, repressive laws, and violation of basic civil rights, by supporting extremists who used the war for their own purposes, and by tolerating mob violence against German Americans.

WAGING WAR AND PEACE ABROAD

WHAT HOPES did Wilson have for the Treaty of Versailles?

*W*hile mobilizing the home front, the Wilson administration undertook an impressive military effort to help the Allies defeat the Central Powers. Wilson also struggled to secure international acceptance for his plans for a just and permanent peace.

THE WAR TO END ALL WARS

When the United States entered the war, the Allied position was dire. The losses from three years of trench warfare had sapped military strength and civilian morale. On the eastern front, the Russian army had collapsed, and the Russian government had gradually disintegrated after the overthrow of the tsarist regime.

What the Allies needed, said French Marshal Joseph Joffre in April 1917, was simple: "We want men, men, men." In May, Congress passed the **Selective Service Act of 1917,** establishing conscription. More than 24 million men eventually registered for the draft, and nearly 3 million entered the army when their numbers were drawn in a national lottery. Almost 2 million more men volunteered, as did more than 10,000 women, who served in the navy. Nearly one-fifth of America's soldiers were foreign-born; 367,000 were black. Many Native Americans served with distinction as well; in recognition, Indian veterans were made citizens in 1919, a status extended to all Native Americans five years later.

Civilians were transformed into soldiers in hastily organized training camps, operated according to progressive principles. Prohibition prevailed in the camps; the poorly educated and largely working-class recruits were taught personal hygiene and immigrants were taught English and American history.

Racial segregation was the rule, not only in training camps and military units but in assignments as well. The navy assigned black sailors to menial positions, and the army similarly used black soldiers primarily as gravediggers and laborers. But one black combat division was created, and four black regiments fought under French command. France decorated three of these units with its highest citations for valor.

More than 40,000 women were recruited as noncombatant personnel, such as clerks, translators, and switchboard operators, thereby enabling more men to be assigned to combat duty. On the eve of a major battle in France, Merle Egan in the U.S. Army Signal Corps, feverishly training soldiers to operate switchboards to help coordinate the massive military buildup, found that some of the men resented taking instructions from a woman. But "when I reminded them that any soldier could carry a gun but the safety of a whole division might depend on the switchboard one of them was operating, I had no more trouble."

Into Action in France.   The first American troops landed in France in June 1917. The American Expeditionary Force (AEF) was commanded by General John J. Pershing. Full-scale American intervention began in the late spring of 1918 (see Map 23–2). The influx of American troops in June and July tipped the balance toward Allied victory. By July 18, the German chancellor later acknowledged, "even the most optimistic among us knew that all was lost. "

The Russian Front.   In July, Wilson also agreed to commit 15,000 American troops to intervene in Russia. Russia's provisional government had collapsed when the radical **Bolshevik** faction of the communist movement had seized power in November 1917. Under V. I. Lenin, the Bolsheviks signed an armistice with Germany in early 1918, which freed German troops for the summer offensive in France. The Allied interventions were initially designed to reopen the eastern front and later to help overthrow the Bolshevik government.

Lenin's call for the destruction of capitalism and imperialism alarmed the Allied leaders. One Wilson adviser urged the "eradication" of the Russian government. Soon, American and British troops were fighting Russians in an effort

WHERE TO LEARN MORE

Fort George G. Meade Museum, Fort Meade, Maryland

22–5
Eugene Kennedy, A "Doughboy" Describes the Fighting Front (1918)

WHERE TO LEARN MORE

General John J. Pershing Boyhood Home, Laclede, Missouri
**www.mostateparks.com/pershingsite
.htm.**

Selective Service Act of 1917
The law establishing the military draft for World War I.

Bolshevik   Member of the Communist movement in Russia that established the Soviet government after the 1917 Russian Revolution.

MAP EXPLORATION

To explore an interactive version of this map, go to **http://www.prenhall.com/goldfield3/map23.2**

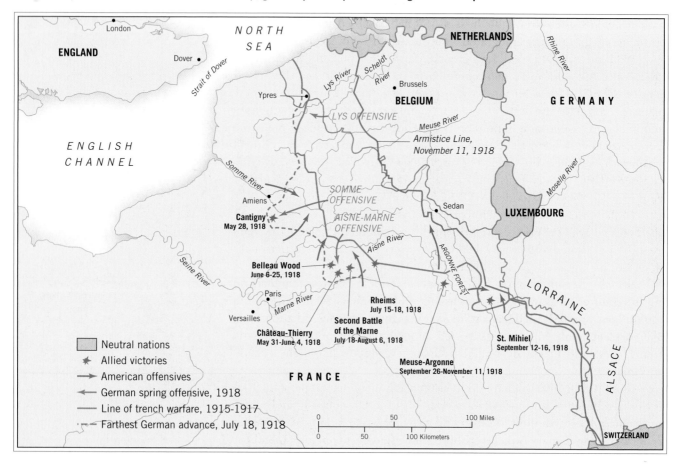

MAP 23–2 The Western Front, 1918 After three years of trench warfare, the arrival of large numbers of American troops in 1918 enabled the Allies to launch an offensive that drove back the Germans and forced an armistice.

AT THE time of the armistice, how far back had the Germans been forced to retreat from their farthest advance?

to influence Russia's internal affairs. U.S. forces remained in Russia until 1920, but these military interventions failed.

The Western Front. The Allies were more successful on the western front. Having stopped the German offensive in July, they launched their own advance. The decisive battle began in late September when an American army over 1 million strong attacked German trenches in the Argonne Forest. Lieutenant Maury Maverick (later a Texas congressman) described the shelling: "We were simply in a big black spot with streaks of screaming red and yellow, with roaring giants in the sky tearing and whirling and roaring." An exploding shell terrified him: "There is a great swishing scream, a smash-bang, and it seems to tear everything loose from you. The intensity of it simply enters your heart and brain, and tears every nerve to pieces."

The battle for the Argonne raged for weeks. But ultimately, the Allies' massive assault overwhelmed the Germans (see American Views: "Letter from Albert Smith, Oct. 15, 1918"). With its allies surrendering, its own army in retreat, and revolution breaking out among the war-weary residents of its major cities, Germany asked for peace. On November 11, 1918, an armistice ended the Great War. More than 115,000 Americans were among the 8 million soldiers and 7 million civilians dead.

THE FOURTEEN POINTS

The armistice was only a step toward final peace. President Wilson had already enunciated America's war objectives on January 8, 1918, in a speech outlining what became known as the Fourteen Points. In his 1917 war message, Wilson had advocated a more democratic world system, and this new speech spelled out how to achieve it. But Wilson also had a political purpose. The Bolsheviks had published the Allies' secret treaties dividing up the expected economic and territorial spoils of the war. Lenin had called for an immediate peace based on the liberation of all colonies, self-determination for all peoples, and the rejection of annexations and punitive indemnities. Wilson's Fourteen Points reassured the American and Allied peoples that they were fighting for more than imperialist gains and offered an alternative to what he called Lenin's "crude formula" for peace.

Eight of Wilson's points proposed creating new nations, shifting old borders, or ensuring self-determination for peoples previously subject to the Austrian, German, or Russian empire. The point about Russia would haunt Wilson after the Allied interventions there began, for it called on all nations to evacuate Russian territory and permit Russia "an unhampered and unembarrassed opportunity for the independent determination of her own political development" under "institutions of her own choosing." Another five points invoked principles to guide international relations: freedom of the seas, open diplomacy instead of secret treaties, reduction of armaments, free trade, and the fair settlement of colonial claims. Wilson's fourteenth and most important point proposed a league of nations to carry out these ideals and ensure international stability.

Wilson and the German government had these principles in mind when negotiating the armistice. The Allies, however, had never explicitly accepted the Fourteen Points, and framing a final peace treaty would be difficult. After their human and economic sacrifices, Britain and France wanted tangible compensation, not pious principles.

Convinced of the righteousness of his cause, Wilson decided to attend the peace conference in Paris himself. But Wilson weakened his position before he even set sail. First, he urged voters to support Democratic candidates in the November 1918 elections to indicate approval of his peace plan. But the electorate, responding primarily to domestic problems like inflation, gave the Republicans control of both houses of Congress. This meant that any treaty would have to be approved by Senate Republicans angry that Wilson had tried to use war and peace for partisan purposes. Second, Wilson refused to consult with Senate Republicans on plans for the peace conference and failed to name important Republicans to the Paris delegation. It was going to be Wilson's treaty, and Republicans would feel no responsibility to approve it.

 22–6 Newton D. Baker, "The Treatment of German-Americans" (1918)

 **WHERE TO LEARN MORE** Wisconsin Veterans Museum, Madison, Wisconsin

 23–2 The Sahara of the Bozart (1920)

QUICK REVIEW

Wilson's Fourteen Points
- Wilson articulated U.S. war aims in his Fourteen Points.
- The Allies did not explicitly support Wilson's program.
- Domestic political failures undermined Wilson's position at the Paris peace conference.

AMERICAN VIEWS

LETTER FROM ALBERT SMITH, OCTOBER 15, 1918

Ultimately numbering over 2 million men, the American troops sent to Europe were organized as the American Expeditionary Forces (AEF) under the command of General Pershing. By August 1918, Pershing had enough troops to form the American First Army, which fought on its own front. In this letter to his brother, Albert Smith describes the largest campaign of the American forces—the Meuse-Argonne campaign—which proved both decisive and costly for the Allies. In the struggle, the AEF cooperated with an African-American unit under French command, and the campaign produced one of the greatest heroes of World War I: Private Alvin York of Pall Mall, Tennessee, who would receive the Medal of Honor and promotion to sergeant for personally killing 20 Germans and destroying 35 German machine guns.

Smith's letter glowingly refers to the heroic actions of American doughboys—both white and black. Moreover, even as he discourages his own brother from joining the war, he also takes great pride in his own role on the front lines.

- What does Smith's letter illustrate about the impact of total war on soldiers and civilians?
- How does Smith suggest both his confidence about defeating the Germans and his war weariness?

- How did Smith adapt to the new tools of war, especially the use of gas and machine guns?

France
Oct, 15, 1918
Mr. Mcgregor Smith
Cookeville, Tenn.
Dear "Greg";

I received a letter from you a few weeks ago but have not had time to answer for we have been exceedingly busy. We are speedy clearing France of the Huns and making Europe safe for you Kids to come over next spring. This will be the most peaceable country in the world in about sixty days. You just think that you want to come over here we wont need you. I wanted to come over pretty badly and was happy as a lark the day we left New York but that will be nothing to the state of my feeling when I start back to the states. If the Statue of liberty ever sees me again it will have to about face and come down south to find me after she sees me pass going into the harbor at New York on my way home. This is the wettest muddiest country I ever saw, it has been raining steadily for seven weeks. I stepped in a mud hole the other night and went up to my waist in mud and didnt get to change clothes and in fact I

THE PARIS PEACE CONFERENCE

The peace conference opened on January 18, 1919. Meeting at the Palace of Versailles, the delegations were dominated by the principal Allied leaders: Wilson of the United States, David Lloyd George of Britain, Georges Clemenceau of France, and Vittorio Orlando of Italy. The Central Powers and Bolshevik Russia were excluded. The treaty would be one-sided except to the extent that Wilson could insist on the liberal terms of the Fourteen Points against French and British intransigence.

Under protest, Germany signed the **Treaty of Versailles** on June 28, 1919. Its terms were far more severe than Wilson had proposed or Germany had anticipated. Germany had to accept sole responsibility for starting the war, a stipulation that all Germans bitterly resented. It was required to pay huge reparations to the Allies, give up land to France, Poland, Belgium, and Denmark, cede

Treaty of Versailles The treaty ending World War I and creating the League of Nations.

haven't changed yet. I haven't changed for over two month and haven't even had my clothes off for that length of time. I have not had a bath for six weeks and none in sight for I haven't the slightest idea of using what little drinking water I get in my canteen for bathing purposes. I shave as often as possible for the beard on my face keeps my Gas mask from being effective and the germans use quite a bit of gas. Gas and machine gun is their only effective weapons. I have been on every front in France. You cant imagine how torn up this country really is. Every where there are wire entanglements and trenches and dug outs. Even out of the war zone there are entanglements and dugouts to protect the civilians from air raids. . . . The hardest fight we were in was in the Argenne [Argonne] Forest. Our batteries were the one that destroyed the machine gun nest at Montfaucon. I was at the Forward observation post the night the barrage was laid during the big drive of the last few weeks. The barrage that night was the heaviest one ever laid in France. I saw every bit of it and saw the infantry go over the top. That certainly was a night that I will always remember. Our doughboy are the greatest men in the world, they certainly have "Fritz" bluffed. During Aug. When we were in a drive against mount Sac [Montsec] the strongest fortified hill in France we supported a regiment of Negro infantry

and when they went over the top and up the hill they were saying to them germans "take yo hats off white folks no Kazerade to late now." They sure did slaughter the Huns. The southern boys are certainly hard fighters. The third Tenn. Infantry is the hardest fighting regiment over here. I understand that they have been cited by the British for bravery. At Cambrai they were the Americans that advanced thru the heart of the city and cleared the place of machine guns.

Don't worry about coming over here stay in school that is your service to your country. I am in good health and ready to come home after the war but not before, I will do my bit here. I was appointed for the officers, training camp this month for the third time but refused it, I will go later on in the year I want to stay on the front as long as the war lasts. Be good and study HARD have a good time and write often,

Love to all,

Albert

Corp. Albert P. Smith

Hq. Co. 115 F.A. American Expdt. France

Source: www.historychannel.com/letters/albert_smith.html

its colonies, limit its army and navy to small self-defense forces, destroy military bases, and promise not to manufacture or purchase armaments.

Wilson gained some acceptance of self-determination. As the German, Austro-Hungarian, Turkish, and Russian empires had collapsed at the end of the war, nationalist groups had proclaimed their independence. On one hand, the peace settlement formally recognized these new nation-states: Poland, Finland, Estonia, Latvia, and Lithuania in eastern Europe and Austria, Hungary, Czechoslovakia, and Yugoslavia in central Europe. On the other hand, France, Italy, Romania, and Japan all annexed territory regardless of the wishes of the inhabitants.

The Allied leaders endorsed the changes in eastern Europe in part because the new states there were anticommunist and would constitute a barrier against Bolshevism. Communist movements in early 1919 in Germany, Austria, and

23–1
F. J. Grimke, "Address of Welcome to the Men Who Have Returned from the Battlefront" (1919)

Hungary caused the Allies to fear that "the Russian idea was still rising in power," and they hoped to isolate and weaken Bolshevik Russia. Allied armies were in Russia during the peace conference, and Wilson and the other leaders agreed to provide further aid to fight the Bolsheviks. This hostility to Russia, like the punitive terms for Germany and the concessions to imperial interests, boded ill for a stable and just postwar order. (See Global Perspectives, "War and Revolution! The Bolsheviks and the International Community".)

But Wilson hoped that the final section of the Versailles treaty would resolve the flaws of the agreement by establishing his great international organization to preserve peace: the **League of Nations.** The Covenant, or constitution, of the League was built into the treaty. Its crucial feature, Article Ten, bound the member nations to guarantee each other's independence—a provision that was Wilson's concept of collective security.

WAGING PEACE AT HOME

Wilson was determined to defeat the opposition to the peace treaty. But many Americans were engaged in their own struggles with the new conditions of a nation suddenly at peace but riven by economic, social, and political conflict. Wilson's battle for the League of Nations would fail tragically. The other conflicts would rage until the election of 1920 restored a normalcy of sorts.

BATTLE OVER THE LEAGUE

Most Americans favored the Versailles treaty. A survey of 1,400 newspapers found fewer than 200 opposed. Thirty-three governors and 32 state legislatures endorsed the League of Nations. But when Wilson called for the Senate to accept "the moral leadership . . . and confidence of the world" by ratifying the treaty, he met resistance. Nearly all Democrats favored the treaty, but they were a minority; some Republicans would have to be converted for the treaty to be approved.

Progressive Republican senators, such as Robert La Follette and Hiram Johnson, led one group of opponents. Called the **Irreconcilables,** they opposed participation in the League of Nations, which they saw as designed to perpetuate the power of imperialist countries. Article Ten, they feared, would require the United States to help suppress rebellions in Ireland against British rule or to enforce disputed European borders. Most of the Irreconcilables gave priority to restoring civil liberties and progressive reform at home.

A larger group of opponents had reservations about the treaty's provisions. These **Reservationists** were led by Henry Cabot Lodge, the chairman of the Senate Foreign Relations Committee. They regarded Article Ten as eroding congressional authority to declare war. They also fretted that the League might interfere with domestic questions, such as immigration laws. Many progressives criticized the treaty's compromises on self-determination, reparations, and colonies. Linking these failures with Wilson's domestic policies, one former supporter concluded; "The administration has become reactionary, and deserves no support from any of us."

Lodge's own opposition was shaped by both partisanship and deep personal hostility. "I never expected to hate anyone in politics with the hatred I feel toward Wilson," Lodge confessed. Wilson reciprocated, and when Lodge proposed reservations or amendments to the treaty, Wilson refused to compromise. If they wanted war, he said, he would "give them a belly full." In early September 1919, Wilson set out across the country to win popular support for the League. In three weeks, he traveled 8,000 miles and delivered 37 speeches.

WHAT CHALLENGES did America face in the aftermath of the war?

League of Nations
International organization created by the Versailles Treaty after World War I to ensure world stability.

Irreconcilables Group of U.S. senators adamantly opposed to ratification of the Treaty of Versailles after World War I.

Reservationists Group of U.S. senators opposing approval of the Treaty of Versailles, without significant amendments.

GLOBAL PERSPECTIVES

WAR AND REVOLUTION: THE BOLSHEVIKS AND THE INTERNATIONAL COMMUNITY

 n uneasy amalgam of distinctive nationalities, the Russian Empire at the start of World War I covered vast territories and included 178 million people. A poor, agrarian country, Russia suffered from autocratic tsarist rule. Long-standing economic problems and political aspirations, especially among land-starved peasants, combined to make Russia a cauldron of tensions inflamed by its involvement in the Great War. The Russian army reflected the discontent that plagued the empire; 400,000 soldiers were killed during the first six months of war, and thereafter desertion became a significant problem.

Food shortages provoked protests among peasants and workers—all challenging tsarist rule. Uprisings in February 1917 immobilized Petrograd, the capital, and persuaded the military to mutiny. The February Revolution ended the Romanov dynasty and brought to power a Provisional Government dominated by liberal reformers. Despite recognition and financial aid from its Allies—the United States, France, and Britain—the new government was politically vulnerable and unable to solve the country's pressing problems.

As frustrations mounted, support for the Bolshevik faction of the Communist Party grew. The Bolsheviks envisioned a world without classes or war—a vision that appealed to a war-weary society with a disintegrating economy. In October 1917, the Provisional Government collapsed and the Bolsheviks came to power.

Promising peace, land, and workers' control, the Bolsheviks were led by V. I. Lenin, a lawyer who had worked for a socialist revolution in Russia since the turn of the century. On March 3, 1918, Russia and Ger-

many signed the Treaty of Brest-Litovsk, an armistice that cost Russia significant territory. But Lenin defended the treaty, because Germany still occupied large parts of Russia and the counterrevolutionary, or "White," forces were gathering momentum.

The Allies decried both the Bolshevik revolution and the separate peace with Germany, which enabled Germany to strengthen its forces on the western front. Russia's withdrawal from the war emboldened the "Whites," the opponents of the Bolshevik "Reds," and encouraged the Allies to assist them with financial support and troops. But the Allied invasions of Russia were failures, serving only to convince Lenin that the Allies were imperialists bent on overthrowing the world's only socialist state. In the tumultuous postwar period, Lenin's call for workers to overthrow their governments, European and American leaders believed, fed the postwar labor unrest that wracked industrialized nations. Woodrow Wilson fumed that the "poison" of Bolshevism was "running through the veins of the world." Wilson feared that returning African-American troops would serve as the "greatest medium in conveying bolshevism to America," but other policymakers targeted aliens, immigrants, and labor activists, culminating in the "Red Scare."

The fears stirred by the Bolshevik Revolution, however, did not provoke similar governmental extremism in either Great Britain or France, both of which would recognize the Soviet Union by 1924. But America, as the British ambassador noted, was singularly "frightened" of the revolution, and the United States would withhold recognition until 1933.

In poor health following a bout with influenza, Wilson collapsed in Pueblo, Colorado. Taken back to Washington, Wilson on October 2 suffered a massive stroke that paralyzed his left side and left him psychologically unstable and temporarily blind. Wilson's physician and his wife, Edith Galt Wilson, kept the nature of his illness secret from the public, Congress, and even the vice president and cabinet. Rumors circulated that Edith Wilson was running the administration, but she was not. Instead, it was immobilized.

By February 1920, Wilson had partially recovered, but he remained suspicious and quarrelsome. Bryan and other Democratic leaders urged him to accept

QUICK REVIEW

Defeat of the Treaty

- Most Democrats favored the treaty.
- Republicans led by Henry Cabot Lodge wanted amendments.
- Wilson's refusal to compromise doomed the treaty.

With the defeat of Germany, Americans wanted their soldiers home. And although many returning African-American soldiers were denied celebratory homecomings and would face discrimination and hostility, their role in World War I brought fresh confidence and respect to the African-American community. Few units stirred the patriotism and pride as did the valiant 369th Infantry Regiment, decorated by the French government for heroism and "gallantry under fire." Here African-American friends and families turn out to welcome home the "Men of Bronze," as they were also called.

Lodge's reservations to gain ratification of the treaty. Wilson refused. Isolated and inflexible, he ordered Democratic senators to vote with the Irreconcilables against the treaty as amended by Lodge. On March 19, 1920, the Senate killed the treaty.

ECONOMIC READJUSTMENT AND SOCIAL CONFLICT

The League was not the only casualty of the struggle to conclude the war. Grave problems shook the United States in 1919 and early 1920. An influenza epidemic had erupted in Europe in 1918 among the massed armies. It now hit the United States, killing perhaps 700,000 Americans, far more than had died in combat.

Meanwhile, the Wilson administration had no plans for an orderly reconversion of the wartime economy, and chaos ensued. The government canceled war contracts and dissolved the regulatory agencies. Bernard Baruch abolished the War Industries Board as of January 1, 1919. Other agencies followed in such haste that turmoil engulfed the economy. The government also demobilized the armed forces. With no planning or assistance, veterans were hustled back into civilian life. There they competed for scarce jobs with workers recently discharged from the war industries.

As unemployment mounted, the removal of wartime price controls brought runaway inflation. The cost of food, clothing, and other necessities more than doubled over prewar rates. The return of the soldiers caused a serious housing shortage, and rents skyrocketed. Farmers also suffered from economic readjustments. Net farm income declined by 65 percent between 1919 and 1921.

Postwar Battles: Gender and Race. Women also lost their wartime economic advances. Returning soldiers took away their jobs. One New York union maintained that "the same patriotism which induced women to enter industry during the war should induce them to vacate their positions after the war." "During the war they called us heroines," one woman complained, "but they throw us on the scrapheap now." Indeed, state legislatures passed laws prohibiting women from working in many of the occupations they had successfully filled during the war. By 1920, women constituted a smaller proportion of the work force than they had in 1910.

The postwar readjustments also left African Americans disappointed. During the war, they had agreed with W. E. B. Du Bois to "forget our special grievances and close our ranks shoulder to shoulder with our own white fellow citizens." Participation in the war effort, they had hoped, might be rewarded by better treatment thereafter. Now, the meagerness of their reward became clear.

Housing shortages and job competition interacted with racism in 1919 to produce race riots in 26 towns and cities, resulting in at least 120 deaths. In Chicago, 38 people were killed and more than 500 injured in a five-day riot that began when white thugs stoned to death a black youth swimming too near "their" beach. White rioters then fired a machine gun from a truck hurtling through black neighborhoods. But black residents fought back. The new militancy reflected both their experiences in the military and in industry and their exposure to propaganda about freedom and democracy. In recognition of both the persistence of white racism and the changed attitudes among African Americans, Du Bois revised his pre-war stance, affirming, "We return. We return from fighting. We return fighting."

Fighting for Industrial Democracy. Even more pervasive discontents roiled as America adjusted to the post-war world. More than 4 million angry workers launched a wave of 3,600 strikes in 1919. They were reacting not only to the soaring cost of living, which undermined the value of their wages, but also to employers' efforts to reassert their authority and destroy the legitimacy labor had won by its participation in the war effort. The abolition of government controls on industry enabled employers not only to raise prices but also to rescind their recognition of unions, reimpose objectionable working conditions, and freeze wages. In response, strikers demanded higher wages, better conditions, and recognition of unions and the right of collective bargaining.

Postwar labor unrest met determined suppression. Here, mounted police attack striking steelworkers in Pittsburgh in 1919. The strikers were seeking union recognition and an end to twelve-hour days.

Corbis/Bettman

The greatest strike involved the American Federation of Labor's attempt to organize steelworkers, who endured dangerous conditions and 12-hour shifts. When the steel companies refused to recognize the union or even discuss issues, 365,000 workers went out on strike in September 1919. Strikers in Pennsylvania pointed out that they had worked "cheerfully, without strikes or trouble of any kind" during the war to "make the world safe for democracy" and that they now sought "industrial democracy." Employers hired thugs to beat the strikers, used strikebreakers to take their jobs, and exploited ethnic and racial divisions. To undercut support for the workers, management portrayed the strikers as disruptive radicals influenced by Bolshevism. After four months, the strike failed.

Employers used the same tactic to defeat striking coal miners. Refusing to negotiate with the United Mine Workers, coal operators claimed that Russian Bolsheviks had financed the strike to destroy the American economy. Attorney General Mitchell Palmer secured an injunction against the strike under the authority of wartime legislation. Because the government no longer controlled coal prices or enforced protective labor rules, miners complained bitterly that the war had ended for corporations but not for workers.

In Boston, the police commissioner fired police officers for trying to organize a union to improve their inadequate pay. In response, the police went on strike. Newspapers, politicians, and business leaders attributed the strike to Bolshevism, and Wilson denounced the strike as "a crime against civilization." Massachusetts Governor Calvin Coolidge mobilized the National Guard and gained nationwide acclaim when he stated, "There is no right to strike against the public safety by anybody, anywhere, anytime." The entire police force was fired; many of their replacements were war veterans.

QUICK REVIEW

Labor Unrest
- Efforts to roll back war-time gains upset workers.
- 4 million workers launched 3,600 strikes in 1919.
- The largest strike involved efforts to organize steelworkers.

THE RED SCARE

The strikes contributed to an anti-Bolshevik hysteria that swept the country in 1919. The **Red Scare** reflected fears that the Bolshevik revolution in Russia might spread to the United States. Steeped in the antiradical propaganda of the war years, many Americans were appalled by Russian Bolshevism, described by the *Saturday Evening Post* as a "compound of slaughter, confiscation, anarchy, and universal disorder." Their alarm grew in 1919 when Russia established the Third International to foster revolution abroad and a few American socialists formed the American Communist Party. But the Red Scare also reflected the willingness of antiunion employers, ambitious politicians, sensational journalists, zealous veterans, and racists to exploit the panic to advance their own purposes.

Fed by misleading reports about Russian Bolshevism and its influence in the United States, the Red Scare reached panic levels by mid-1919. Bombs mailed anonymously to several prominent people on May Day seemed proof enough that a Bolshevik conspiracy threatened America. The Justice Department, Congress, and patriotic organizations like the American Legion joined with business groups to suppress radicalism, real and imagined. The government continued to enforce the repressive laws against Wobblies, socialists and other dissenters. Indeed, Wilson and Attorney General Mitchell Palmer called for more stringent laws and refused to release political prisoners jailed during the war.

Palmer created a new agency, headed by J. Edgar Hoover, to suppress radicals and impose conformity. Its war on radicalism became the chief focus of the Justice Department. As an ambitious and ruthless bureaucrat, Hoover had participated in the government's assault on aliens and radicals during the war. Now he collected files on labor leaders and other "radical agitators" from Senator Robert La Follette to Jane Addams, issued misleading reports on communist influence in labor strikes and race riots, and contacted all major newspapers "to acquaint people like you with the real menace of evil-thinking, which is the foundation of the Red Movement."

In November 1919, Palmer and Hoover began raiding groups suspected of subversion. A month later, they deported 249 alien radicals, including the anarchist Emma Goldman, to Russia. Rabid patriots endorsed such actions. In January 1920, Palmer and Hoover rounded up more than 4,000 suspected radicals in 33 cities. Often without warrants, they broke into union halls, club rooms, and private homes, assaulting and arresting everyone in sight. People were jailed without access to lawyers; some were beaten into signing false confessions. The *Washington Post* declared, "There is no time to waste on hairsplitting over infringement of liberty."

Other Americans began to recoil from the excesses and illegal acts. Assistant Secretary of Labor Louis Post stopped further deportations by demonstrating that most of the arrested were "working men of good character, who are not anarchists or revolutionists, nor politically or otherwise dangerous in any sense." Support for the Red Scare withered. Palmer's attempt to inflame public emotion backfired. When his predictions of a violent attempt to overthrow the government on May 1, 1920, came to naught, most Americans realized that no menace had ever existed. But if the Red Scare faded in mid-1920, the hostility to immigrants, organized labor, and dissent it reflected would endure for a decade.

THE ELECTION OF 1920

The Democratic coalition that Wilson had cobbled together on the issues of progressivism and peace came apart after the war. Americans were weary of great crusades and social sacrifices; in the words of Kansas journalist William Allen White,

Red Scare Post-World War I public hysteria over Bolshevik influence in the United States directed against labor activism, radical dissenters, and some ethnic groups.

they were "tired of issues, sick at heart of ideals, and weary of being noble." They yearned for what the Republican presidential candidate, Warren Harding of Ohio, called "normalcy."

The Republican ticket in 1920 symbolized the reassurance of simpler times. Harding, an Old Guard conservative, was a genial politician who devoted more time to golf and poker than to public policy. His running mate, Calvin Coolidge, governor of Massachusetts, owed his nomination to his handling of the Boston police strike.

Harding won in a landslide reflecting the nation's dissatisfaction with Wilson and the Democratic Party. "The Democrats are inconceivably unpopular," wrote Walter Lippmann, a prominent journalist. Harding received 16 million popular votes to Cox's 9 million. Running for president from his prison cell, Socialist Eugene Debs polled nearly a million votes.

22–9
Warren G. Harding, Campaign Speech, at Boston (1920)

CONCLUSION

The Great War disrupted the United States and much of the rest of the world. The initial American policy of neutrality yielded to sentimental and substantive links with the Allies and the pressure of German submarine warfare. Despite popular opposition, America joined the conflict when its leaders concluded that national interests demanded it. Using both military and diplomatic power, Woodrow Wilson sought to bring about a more stable and prosperous world order, with an expanded role for the United States. But the Treaty of Versailles only partly fulfilled his hopes, and the Senate refused to ratify the treaty and its League of Nations. The postwar world order would be unstable and dangerous.

Participation in the war, moreover, had changed the American government, economy, and society. Some of these changes, including the centralization of the economy and an expansion of the regulatory role of the federal government, were already under way; some offered opportunities to implement progressive principles or reforms. Woman suffrage and prohibition gained decisive support because of the war spirit. But other consequences of the war betrayed both progressive impulses and the democratic principles the war was allegedly fought to promote. The suppression of civil liberties, manipulation of human emotions, repression of radicals and minorities, and exploitation of national crises by narrow interests helped disillusion the public. The repercussions of the Great War would linger for years, at home and abroad.

IMAGE KEY
for pages 664–665

a. British Prime Minister Lloyd George, French Prime Minister George Clemenceau, and U.S. President Wilson in Versailles, Paris in 1919.
b. Women war workers working in an engineering shop, 1917.
c. Women draft protesters demonstrate in front of New York's City Hall on June 16, 1917.
d. President Woodrow Wilson reads his war message to Congress.
e. American World War I Liberty Bonds poster.
f. British Biplane.
g. A policeman on horseback swings a truncheon at strikers on a Pittsburgh street.
h. *The New York Times* front page reports the sinking of the Lusitania in 1915.
i. Female African-American workers stack bricks.

SUMMARY

Waging Neutrality Few Americans were prepared for the Great War that erupted in Europe in 1914; fewer still envisioned the United States becoming involved in the war. The Central Powers and the Allies were involved in mass slaughter and stalemate in Europe; America had no vital interest in the war, but it did not stay strictly neutral. The economy of America became closely tied with Britain and the Allies, the President sympathized with the Allied cause, and German submarine warfare tied the United States to the British war effort. The desire for peace determined the results of the 1916 election; in 1917 America entered the war as Germany decided to resume unrestricted submarine warfare and the contents of the Zimmermann note, linking Germany to Mexico's recovering the Southwest, were exposed.

Waging War in America In addition to mobilizing for military invention, the government reorganized the economy to emphasize centralized management and developed policies to control public opinion and suppress dissent. In response to labor shortages women and minorities entered the work force, obtaining jobs which had previously been closed to them; individual citizens planted victory gardens and bought Liberty Bonds to help the war effort. Government propaganda to rally Americans painted the enemy as subhuman; dissent was viewed as unpatriotic; Americans were encouraged to spy on one another; basic civil rights were violated.

Waging War and Peace Abroad The American involvement in the Great War turned the tide and ensured Allied victory. Having stopped the German advance on the Western Front, the Allies, with fresh American troops, began a counteroffensive that ended the war with an armistice on November 11, 1918. President Wilson envisioned the postwar world based on the Fourteen Points and attended the Paris Peace Conference convinced of the righteousness of his peace plans. The Allied leaders were more interested in revenge and retribution than righteousness. The Treaty of Versailles imposed harsh restrictions on Germany; the specter of Bolshevism hung over the peace conference; fear of communism influenced decisions made by the delegates.

Waging Peace at Home While most Americans favored the Versailles treaty, the senators who had to vote on the treaty were largely opposed to it. The Irreconcilables opposed participation in the League of Nations, and the Reservationists feared the power of the League and the erosion of Congressional authority. The Treaty of Versailles was never approved by the United States. The vote in the Senate was not the only war casualty: An influenza epidemic, the reconversion to a peacetime economy, housing shortages, unemployment, labor unrest, and the Red Scare wearied Americans. By 1920, Americans wanted a return to "normalcy" and elected Warren Harding as president in a landslide victory.

REVIEW QUESTIONS

1. What might have been the consequences, positive and negative, if the "deliberate and passionless method of doing what is regarded as a disagreeable duty" that Ray Stannard Baker found in 1917 had continued to characterize the U.S. war effort?

2. What were the major arguments for and against U.S. entry into the Great War? What position do you find most persuasive? Why?

3. How and why did the United States shape public opinion in World War I? What were the consequences, positive and negative, of the propaganda of the Committee on Public Information, the Food Administration, and other government agencies?

4. How did other groups exploit the war crisis and the government's propaganda and repression?

5. What was the impact of the Bolshevik revolution on the war and peace? How did the Allies respond to the Bolsheviks who came to power in Russia in October 1917?

6. Evaluate the role of Woodrow Wilson at the Paris Peace Conference. What obstacles did he face? How successful was he in shaping the settlement?

7. Discuss the arguments for and against American ratification of the Treaty of Versailles.

KEY TERMS

Allies (p. 668)
Bolshevik (p. 679)
Central Powers (p. 668)
Committee on Public Information (CPI) (p. 676)
Declaration of London (p. 670)
Espionage Act (p. 677)

Irreconcilables (p. 684)
League of Nations (p. 684)
Liberty Bonds (p. 676)
Preparedness (p. 671)
Red Scare (p. 688)
Reservationists (p. 684)
Sedition Act of 1918 (p. 677)

Selective Service Act of 1917 (p. 679)
Self-determination (p. 672)
Sussex **Pledge** (p. 671)
Treaty of Versailles (p. 682)
War Industries Board (WIB) (p. 674)

WHERE TO LEARN MORE

National Infantry Museum, Fort Benning, Georgia. This sprawling collection of weapons, uniforms, and equipment includes exhibits on World War I. **www.benningmwr.com/index.cfm**.

Fort George G. Meade Museum, Fort Meade, Maryland. This museum contains unparalleled exhibits depicting U.S. military life during World War I, including artifacts, photographs, and French and American tanks designed for trench warfare.

General John J. Pershing Boyhood Home, Laclede, Missouri. Maintained by the Missouri State Park Board, Pershing's restored nineteenth-century home exhibits some of his personal belongings and papers. **www.mostateparks.com/pershingsite.htm**

Sgt. Alvin C. York Homeplace and State Historic Site, Pall Mall, Tennessee. The home of America's greatest military hero of World War I contains fascinating artifacts, including York's letters written in the trenches. **www.alvincyork.org**

Wisconsin Veterans Museum, Madison, Wisconsin. The most stunning museum of its size in the United States, this large building combines impressive collections of artifacts ranging from uniforms to tanks, with substantive exhibits and video programs based on remarkable historical research. It both documents and explains the participation of Wisconsin soldiers in the nation's wars, including the Spanish-American War and World War I.

 U.S. History Documents CD-ROM
For primary sources related to this chapter, refer to the document CD-ROM.

 www.prenhall.com/goldfield
For study resources related to this chapter, visit the *Companion Website*™.

24 Toward a Modern America the 1920s

CHAPTER HIGHLIGHTS

The Economy that Roared The American economy boomed throughout most of the 1920s. Mechanization, investment, and new industries drove the economy. Oligopolies eliminated competition. Not all Americans shared in the prosperity and the gap between rich and poor widened.

The Business of Government The Republican alliance with big business led to pro-business policies. The Harding administration was marked by corruption. Progressivism lost much of its energy and focus.

Cities and Suburbs By 1920, more Americans lived in urban than rural areas. Urbanization affected all regions of the country. The Great Migration brought large numbers of blacks to Northern cities. The automobile contributed to the growth of suburbs.

Mass Culture in the Jazz Age Urbanization and the automobile joined with new systems of distribution, marketing, and communications to create a new mass culture. Not all Americans participated in this culture and some were hostile to it.

Culture Wars Cultural conflicts divided social groups. Unease with new currents in American life contributed to these struggles. The forces underlying the culture wars would resurface repeatedly in the future.

A New Era in the World? Americans sought peace and economic order at home and abroad. In the 1920s the United States took an enhanced role in international diplomacy.

Herbert Hoover and the Triumph of the New Era Herbert Hoover symbolized the policies of prosperity and the New Era. His election in 1928, however, was the last Republican triumph for many years. By the end of the 1920s, America was moving closer to economic catastrophe.

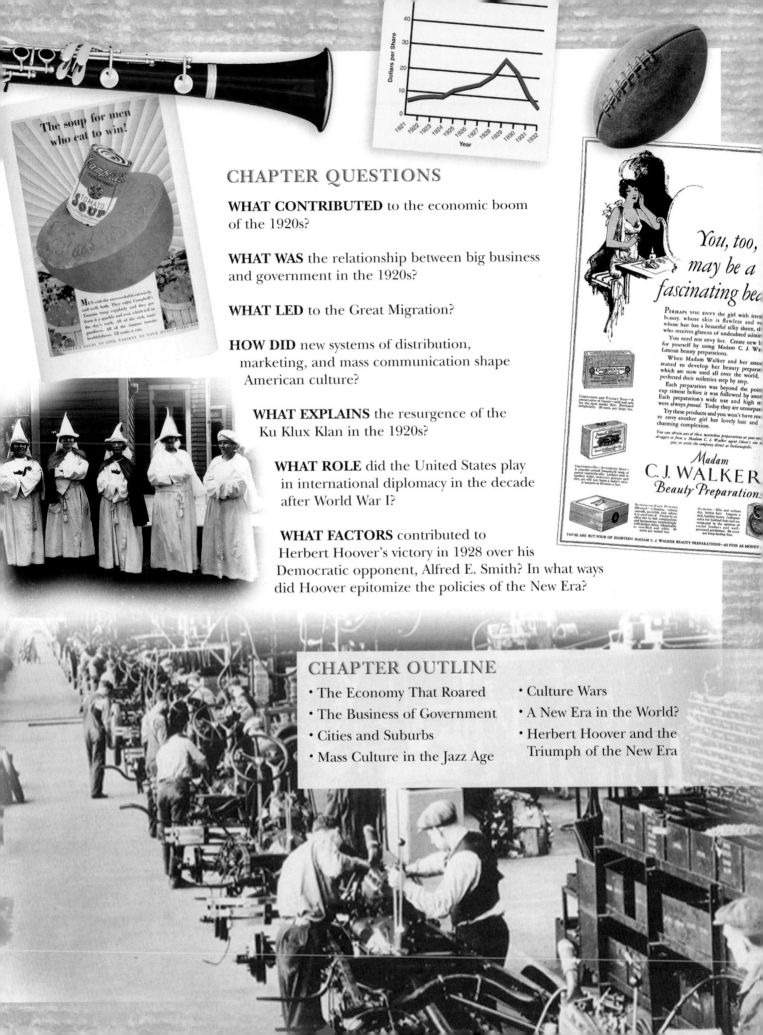

CHAPTER QUESTIONS

WHAT CONTRIBUTED to the economic boom of the 1920s?

WHAT WAS the relationship between big business and government in the 1920s?

WHAT LED to the Great Migration?

HOW DID new systems of distribution, marketing, and mass communication shape American culture?

WHAT EXPLAINS the resurgence of the Ku Klux Klan in the 1920s?

WHAT ROLE did the United States play in international diplomacy in the decade after World War I?

WHAT FACTORS contributed to Herbert Hoover's victory in 1928 over his Democratic opponent, Alfred E. Smith? In what ways did Hoover epitomize the policies of the New Era?

CHAPTER OUTLINE

- The Economy That Roared
- The Business of Government
- Cities and Suburbs
- Mass Culture in the Jazz Age
- Culture Wars
- A New Era in the World?
- Herbert Hoover and the Triumph of the New Era

IMAGE KEY
for pages 692–693 is on page 717.

> *Happy times were here again. American industry, adopting Henry Ford's policy of mass production and low prices, was making it possible for everybody to have his share of everything. The newspapers, the statesmen, the economists, all agreed that American ingenuity had solved the age-old problem of poverty. There could never be another depression. . . .*
>
> *The war had done something to Henry, it had taught him a new way to deal with his fellow men. . . . He became more abrupt in his manner, more harsh in his speech. "Gratitude?" he would say. "There's no gratitude in business. Men work for money." . . . From now on he was a business man, and held a tight rein on everything. This industry was his, he had made it himself, and what he wanted of the men he hired was that they should do exactly as he told them. . . .*
>
> *Every worker had to be strained to the uttermost limit, every one had to be giving the last ounce of energy he had in his carcass. . . . They were tired when they started in the morning, and when they quit they were grey and staggering with fatigue, they were empty shells out of which the last drop of juice had been squeezed. . . .*
>
> *Henry Ford was now getting close to his two million cars a year goal. . . . From the moment the ore was taken out of the ship at the River Rouge plant [in Detroit], through all the processes turning it into steel and shaping it into automobile parts with a hundred-ton press, and putting five thousand parts together into a car which rolled off the assembly line under its own power—all those processes were completed in less than a day and a half!*
>
> *Some forty-five thousand different machines were now used in the making of Ford cars, in sixty establishments scattered over the United States. . . . Henry Ford was remaking the roads of America, and in the end he would remake the roads of the world—and line them all with filling stations and hot-dog stands of the American pattern.*
>
> Upton Sinclair, *The Flivver King: A Story of Ford-America* (Chicago: Charles H. Kerr, 1999).

UPTON SINCLAIR, one of America's most famous muckraking journalists, won his greatest recognition with the 1906 publication of his novel, *The Jungle*, which graphically depicted the wretched conditions endured by Chicago's immigrant meatpacking workers. In *The Flivver King*, Sinclair again demonstrates his extraordinary ability to weave together a dramatic and historical account of industrial America, as embodied in the rise of the automobile industry and the revolutionizing vision of Henry Ford, the entrepreneur who captured the American mind and symbolized modern America to the world.

"Machinery," proclaimed Henry Ford, "is the new Messiah." Ford had introduced the assembly line at his automobile factory on the eve of World War I, and by 1925 it was turning out a Model T car every ten seconds. The term "mass production" originated in Henry Ford's 1926 description of the system of flow-production techniques popularly called "Fordism." The system symbolized the nation's booming economy: in the 1920s, Europeans used the word *Fordize* as a synonym for *Americanize*. Ford coupled machines and technology with managerial innovations. He established the "five-dollar day," twice the prevailing wage in Detroit's auto industry, and slashed the workweek from 48 to 40 hours. These changes, Ford argued, would reduce the costs of labor turnover and boost consumer purchasing power, leading to further profits from mass production.

The assembly line, however, alienated workers, and even Ford himself conceded that the repetitive operations on the line were "so monotonous that it scarcely seems possible that any man would care to continue long at the same job." Ford first tried to adapt his mostly immigrant workers to these conditions through an Americanization program. His "Education Department" taught classes in English, sobriety, obedience, and industrial efficiency to the unskilled laborers entering the factory. After the course, they participated in a symbolic pageant: they climbed into a huge "melting pot," 15 feet across and 7 feet deep. After Ford managers stirred the pot with ten-foot ladles, the workers emerged wearing new clothes and waving American flags—new Americans made for the factory. When the labor market became more favorable to management in the early 1920s, Ford abolished the Education Department and relied on discipline to control workers. To maximize profits and increase efficiency, Ford even prohibited talking, whistling, sitting, or smoking on the job. In keeping with the actions of other employers, Ford also joined the assault on labor organization, banning unions altogether and enlisting the aid of spies and informants to guard against their formation.

But even greater control and higher profits did not satisfy Henry Ford, for, like the 1920s itself, he remained conflicted about the progress he championed—the changes he saw and had helped facilitate. Cars and cigarettes were among the most intensively advertised goods in the 1920s, and for some they signaled rebellion and freedom. Women in short skirts and the rise of the Jazz Age—all contributed to what Ford saw as the evils of the "new America." Embracing nativism and Protestantism, Ford, an ardent anti-Semite, targeted Jewish Americans in his diatribes, blaming them for radicalism and labor organization, and he singled out the "International Jew" for allegedly controlling the international financial community.

Henry Ford and Fordism reflected the complexity of the 1920s. Economic growth and technological innovation were paired with social conflict as traditions were destroyed, values were displaced, and new people were incorporated into a society increasingly industrialized, urbanized, and dominated by big business. Industrial production and national wealth soared, buoyed by new techniques and markets for consumer goods. Business values pervaded society, and government promoted business interests.

But not all Americans prospered. Many workers were unemployed, and the wages of still more were stagnant or falling. Farmers endured grim conditions and worse prospects. Social change brought pleasure to some and

Chronology

1915	Ku Klux Klan is founded anew.
1919	Volstead Act is passed.
1920	Urban population exceeds rural population for the first time.
	Warren Harding is elected president.
	Prohibition takes effect.
	First commercial radio show is broadcast.
	Sinclair Lewis publishes *Main Street*.
1921	Sheppard-Towner Maternity and Infancy Act is passed.
	Washington Naval Conference limits naval armaments.
1922	Fordney-McCumber Act raises tariff rates.
	Sinclair Lewis publishes *Babbitt*.
	Country Club Plaza in Kansas City opens.
1923	Harding dies; Calvin Coolidge becomes president.
1924	National Origins Act sharply curtails immigration.
	Coolidge is elected president.
1925	Scopes trial is held in Dayton, Tennessee.
	F. Scott Fitzgerald publishes *The Great Gatsby*.
1927	Charles A. Lindbergh flies solo across the Atlantic.
1928	Kellogg-Briand Pact is signed.
	Herbert Hoover is elected president.
1929	Ernest Hemingway publishes *A Farewell to Arms*.

deep concern to others. City factories like the Ford Works attracted workers from the countryside, increasing urbanization; rapid suburbanization opened other horizons. Leisure activities flourished, and new mass media promoted modern ideas and stylish products. Workers would have to achieve personal satisfaction through consumption and not production. But such experiences often proved unsettling, and some Americans sought reassurance by imposing their cultural or religious values on everyone around them. The tumultuous decade thus had many unresolved issues, much like the complex personality of Henry Ford himself. And Ford so dominated the age that when college students were asked to rank the greatest people of all time, Ford came in third, behind Christ and Napoleon.

THE ECONOMY THAT ROARED

*F*ollowing a severe postwar depression in 1920 and 1921, the American economy boomed through the remainder of the decade. Although the prosperity was not evenly distributed and some sectors of the economy were deeply troubled, most Americans welcomed the industrial expansion and business principles of the New Era.

BOOM INDUSTRIES

WHAT CONTRIBUTED to the economic boom of the 1920s?

WHERE TO LEARN MORE

Henry Ford Museum and Greenfield Village, Dearborn, Michigan **www.hfmgv.org**.

Many factors spurred the economic expansion of the 1920s. The huge wartime and postwar profits provided investment capital that enabled business to mechanize. Mass production spread quickly in American industry; machine-made standardized parts and the assembly line increased efficiency and production. The nation more than doubled its capacity to generate electricity during the decade, further bolstering the economy. In factories, electric motors cut costs and improved manufacturing; in homes, electricity spurred demand for new products. Although not one in ten farm families had access to electric power, most other families did by 1929, and many bought electric sewing machines, vacuum cleaners, washing machines, and other labor-saving appliances.

The automobile industry drove the economy. Its productivity increased constantly, and sales rose from about 1.9 million vehicles in 1920 to nearly 5 million by 1929. The automobile industry also employed one of every 14 manufacturing workers and stimulated other industries, from steel to rubber and glass. It created a huge new market for the petroleum industry and fostered oil drilling in Oklahoma, Texas, and Louisiana. It launched new businesses, from service stations (over 120,000 by 1929) to garages. Large increases in road building and residential housing, prompted by growing automobile ownership and migration to cities and suburbs, provided construction jobs, markets for lumber and other building materials, and profits.

New industries also sprang up. The aviation industry grew rapidly during the 1920s, with government support. The U.S. Post Office subsidized commercial air service by providing air mail contracts to private carriers. Congress then authorized commercial passenger service over the mail routes, with regular traffic opening in 1927 between Boston and New York. By 1930, more than 100 airlines crisscrossed America.

The Great War also stimulated the chemical industry. The government confiscated chemical patents from German firms that had dominated the field and transferred them to U.S. companies like DuPont. With this advantage, DuPont in the 1920s became one of the nation's largest industrial firms, a chemical empire producing plastics, finishes, dyes, and organic chemicals. Led by such successes, the chemical industry became a $4 billion giant employing 300,000 workers by 1929.

The new radio and motion picture industries also flourished. Commercial broadcasting began with a single station in 1920. By 1927, there were 732 stations, and Congress created the Federal Radio Commission to prevent wave-band interference. Corporations quickly dominated the new industry. Westinghouse, RCA, and General Electric began opening strings of stations in the early 1920s.

The motion-picture industry became one of the nation's five largest businesses, with 20,000 movie theaters selling 100 million tickets a week. Hollywood studios were huge factories, hiring directors, writers, camera crews, and actors to produce films on an assembly-line basis. The advent of talking movies later in the decade brought still greater profits and power to the major studios, which alone could afford the increased engineering and production costs.

An Assembly Line
of the
Ford Motor Company

Ford Motor Company's assembly line at the River Rouge plant in Detroit. The increasing mechanization of work, linked to managerial and marketing innovations, boosted productivity in the 1920s and brought consumer goods within the reach of far more Americans than before.

State Historical Society of Wisconsin

CORPORATE CONSOLIDATION

Great corporations swallowed up thousands of small firms. Particularly significant was the spread of **oligopoly**—the control of an entire industry by a few giant firms. For example, only three companies—Ford, General Motors, and Chrysler—produced 83 percent of the nation's cars. By 1929, the nation's 200 largest corporations controlled nearly half of all nonbanking corporate wealth.

Oligopolies also dominated finance and marketing. By 1929, a mere 1 percent of the nation's banks controlled half its banking resources. In marketing, national chain stores, such as A&P and Woolworth's, displaced local retailers.

The corporate consolidation of the 1920s provoked little public fear or opposition. Independent retailers campaigned for local zoning regulations and laws to restrict chain stores, but for the most part, Americans accepted the idea that size brought efficiency and productivity.

OPEN SHOPS AND WELFARE CAPITALISM

Business also launched a vigorous assault on labor. In 1921, the National Association of Manufacturers organized an **open-shop** campaign to break union-shop contracts, which required all employees to be union members. Denouncing collective bargaining as un-American, businesses described the open shop, in which union membership was not required and usually prohibited, as the "American plan." They forced workers to sign so-called **yellow-dog contracts** that bound them to reject unions to keep their jobs. Business also used boycotts to force employers into a uniform antiunion front. Bethlehem Steel, for example, refused to sell steel to companies employing union labor. Where unions existed, corporations tried to crush them, using spies or hiring strikebreakers.

Some companies advocated a paternalistic system called **welfare capitalism** as an alternative to unions. Eastman Kodak, General Motors, U.S. Steel, and other firms provided medical services, insurance programs, pension plans, and vacations for their workers and established employee social clubs and sports teams.

Oligopoly An industry, such as steel making or automobile manufacturing, that is controlled by a few large companies.

Open-shop Factory or business employing workers whether or not they are union members; in practice, such a business usually refuses to hire union members and follows antiunion policies.

Yellow-dog Contracts Employment agreements binding workers not to join a union.

Welfare Capitalism A paternalistic system of labor relations emphasizing management responsibility for employee well-being.

These policies were designed to undercut labor unions and persuade workers to rely on the corporation. Welfare capitalism, however, covered scarcely 5 percent of the workforce and often benefited only skilled male workers already tied to the company through seniority.

Corporations in the 1920s also promoted company unions, management-sponsored substitutes for labor unions. But company unions were usually forbidden to handle wage and hour issues. Their function was to implement company policies and undermine real unionism.

Partly because of these pressures, membership in labor unions fell from 5.1 million in 1920 to 3.6 million in 1929. But unions also contributed to their own decline. Conservative union leaders neglected ethnic and black workers in mass-production industries. Nor did they try to organize women, by 1930 nearly one-fourth of all workers. And they failed to respond effectively to other changes in the labor market. The growing numbers of white-collar workers regarded themselves as middle class and beyond the scope of union action.

With increasing mechanization and weak labor unions, workers suffered from job insecurity and stagnant wages. Real wages (purchasing power) did improve, but most of the improvement came before 1923 and reflected falling prices more than rising wages. After 1923, American wages stabilized. The failure to raise wages when productivity was increasing threatened the nation's long-term prosperity. In short, rising national income largely reflected salaries and dividends, not wages.

Some workers fared worse than others. Unskilled workers, especially southern and eastern Europeans, black migrants from the rural South, and Mexican immigrants, saw their already low wages decline relative to those of skilled workers. Southern workers earned much less than northerners, even in the same industry, and women were paid much less than men even for the same jobs. By 1929, fully 71 percent of American families earned less than what the U.S. Bureau of Labor Statistics regarded as necessary for a decent living standard. The maldistribution of income meant that eventually Americans would be unable to purchase the products they made.

Consumer credit, rare before the 1920s, expanded during the decade. Credit offered temporary relief by permitting consumers to buy goods over time. By 1929, providing consumer credit had become the nation's tenth-largest business. Nevertheless, installment loans did not in the long run raise the purchasing power of an income; they simply added interest charges to the price of products.

SICK INDUSTRIES

Despite the general appearance of prosperity, several "sick" industries dragged on the economy. Coal mining, textile and garment manufacturing, and railroads suffered from excess capacity (too many mines and factories), shrinking demand, low returns, and management-labor conflicts. Unemployment in the coal industry approached 30 percent; by 1928, a reporter found "thousands of women and children literally starving to death" in Appalachia and the remaining miners held in "industrial slavery."

Similarly, the textile industry coped with overcapacity and declining demand by shifting operations from New England to the cheap-labor South, employing girls and young women for 56-hour weeks at 18 cents an hour. The textile industry, despite substandard wages and repressive policies, remained barely profitable.

American agriculture never recovered from the 1921 depression. Agricultural surpluses and shrinking demand forced down prices. After the war, foreign markets

QUICK REVIEW

Sick Industries
- Coal mining
- Textiles
- Railroads
- Agriculture

dried up, and domestic demand for cotton slackened. Moreover, farmers' wartime expansion left them heavily mortgaged in the 1920s. Many small farmers lost their land and became tenants or farm hands.

By the end of the 1920s, the average per capita income for people on the nation's farms was only one-fourth that of Americans off the farm.

THE BUSINESS OF GOVERNMENT

*T*he Republican surge in national politics also shaped the economy. In the 1920 election, the Republican slogan was "Less government in business, more business in government." By 1924, Calvin Coolidge, the decade's second Republican president, proclaimed, "This is a business country . . . and it wants a business government." Under such direction, the federal government advanced business interests at the expense of other objectives (see American Views: The Cult of Business).

WHAT WAS the relationship between big business and government in the 1920s?

REPUBLICAN ASCENDANCY

Republicans in 1920 had retained control of Congress and put Warren Harding in the White House. Harding was neither capable nor bright. But he had a genial touch that contrasted favorably with Wilson. He pardoned Eugene Debs, whom Wilson had refused to release from prison, and he spoke out against racial violence. He also helped shape the modern presidency by supporting the Budget and Accounting Act of 1921, which gave the president authority over the budget and created the Budget Bureau and the General Accounting Office. Some of his cabinet appointees were highly accomplished, and two of them, Secretary of Commerce Herbert Hoover and Secretary of the Treasury Andrew Mellon, shaped economic policy throughout the 1920s.

A self-described progressive dedicated to efficiency, Hoover made the Commerce Department the government's most dynamic office. He cemented its ties with the leading sectors of the economy, expanded its collection and distribution of industrial information, pushed to exploit foreign resources and markets, and encouraged innovation. Thanks to his spreading influence, he was often called the secretary of commerce and "assistant secretary of everything else." Hoover's goal was to foster prosperity by making business efficient, responsive, and profitable.

Andrew Mellon had a narrower goal. A wealthy banker and industrialist, he pressed Congress to reduce taxes on businesses and the rich. But Mellon's hope that favoring the rich would cause prosperity to trickle down to the working and middle classes proved ill-founded. Nevertheless, despite the opposition of progressives in Congress, Mellon succeeded in lowering maximum tax rates and eliminating wartime excess-profits taxes in 1921.

The Harding administration promoted business interests in other ways, too. The tariff of 1922 raised import rates to protect industry from foreign competition. But high tariffs made it difficult for European nations to earn the dollars to repay their war debts to the United States. High rates also impeded American farm exports and raised consumer prices.

The Harding administration aided the business campaign against unions. Attorney General Harry Daugherty secured an injunction against a railroad strike in 1922 and promised to "use the power of the government to prevent the labor unions of the country from destroying the open shop."

The Republicans also curtailed government regulation. By appointing advocates of big business to the Federal Trade Commission and the Federal Reserve

WHERE TO LEARN MORE

Warren G. Harding House, Marion, Ohio www.ohiohistory.org/places/harding

WHERE TO LEARN MORE

George Norris Home, McCook, Nebraska www.nebraskahistory.org/sites/norris/index.htm

AMERICAN VIEWS

THE CULT OF BUSINESS

During the 1920s, publicists and politicians joined manufacturers and merchants in proclaiming that business promoted not only material but also social and even spiritual well-being. In his best-seller The Man Nobody Knows *(1924), advertising executive Bruce Barton portrayed Jesus Christ as the founder of modern business. The following excerpt from an article by Edward E. Purinton, a popular lecturer on business values and efficiency, makes even more extensive claims for business.*

- How accurate are Purinton's claims of great opportunity in the corporate world of the 1920s? Of occupational mobility in the factory economy?
- What does this view of business imply about the role of government in American life?
- How do you think Protestant fundamentalists might have viewed the cult of business?

Among the nations of the earth today America stands for one idea: Business. National opprobrium? National opportunity. For in this fact lies, potentially, the salvation of the world.

Through business, properly conceived, managed, and conducted, the human race is finally to be redeemed. How and why a man works foretells what he will do, think, have, give, and be. And real salvation is in doing, thinking, having, giving, and being—not in sermonizing and theorizing. . . .

What is the finest game? Business. The soundest science? Business. The truest art? Business. The fullest education? Business. The fairest opportunity? Business. The cleanest philanthropy? Business. The sanest religion? Business. You may not agree. That is because you judge business by the crude, mean, stupid, false imitation of business that happens to be located near you.

The finest game is business. The rewards are for everybody, and all can win. There are no favorites—Providence always crowns the career of the man who is worthy. And in this game there is no "luck"—you have the fun of taking chances but the sobriety of guaranteeing certainties. The speed and size of your winnings are for you alone to determine. . . .

The soundest science is business. All investigation is reduced to action, and by action proved or disproved.

The idealistic motive animates the materialistic method. . . . Capital is furnished for the researches of "pure science"; yet pure science is not regarded pure until practical. Competent scientists are suitably rewarded—as they are not in the scientific schools. . . .

The fullest education is business. A proper blend of study, work and life is essential to advancement. The whole man is educated. Human nature itself is the open book that all business men study; and the mastery of a page of this educates you more than the memorizing of a dusty tome from a library shelf. In the school of business, moreover, you teach yourself and learn most from your own mistakes. What you learn here you live out, the only real test.

The fairest opportunity is business. You can find more, better, quicker chances to get ahead in a large business house than anywhere else on earth. . . . Recognition of better work, of keener and quicker thought, of deeper and finer feeling, is gladly offered by the men higher up, with early promotion the rule for the man who justifies it. There is, and can be, no such thing as buried talent in a modern business organization. . . .

The sanest religion is business. Any relationship that forces a man to follow the Golden Rule rightfully belongs amid the ceremonials of the church. A great business enterprise includes and presupposes this relationship. I have seen more Christianity to the square inch as a regular part of the office equipment of famous corporation presidents than may ordinarily be found on Sunday in a verbalized but not vitalized church congregation. . . . You can fool your preacher with a sickly sprout or a wormy semblance of character, but you can't fool your employer. I would make every business house a consultation bureau for the guidance of the church whose members were employees of the house. . . .

The future work of the businessman is to teach the teacher, preach to the preacher, admonish the parent, advise the doctor, justify the lawyer, superintend the statesman, fructify the farmer, stabilize the banker, harness the dreamer, and reform the reformer.

Source: Edward E. Purinton, "Big Ideas from Big Business," *Independent*, April 16, 1921. National Weekly Corp., New York.

Board, among others, Harding made government the collaborator rather than the regulator of business.

Finally, Harding reshaped the Supreme Court into a still more aggressive champion of business. He named the conservative William Howard Taft as chief justice and matched him with three other justices. The Court struck down much of the government economic regulation adopted during the Progressive Era, invalidated restraints on child labor and a minimum wage law for women, and approved restrictions on labor unions.

GOVERNMENT CORRUPTION

The green light that Harding Republicans extended to private interests led to corruption and scandals. Harding appointed many friends and cronies who saw public service as an opportunity for graft. Attorney General Daugherty's associates in the Justice Department took bribes in exchange for pardons and government jobs. Albert Fall, the secretary of the interior, leased petroleum reserves set aside by progressive conservationists to oil companies in exchange for cash, bonds, and cattle for his New Mexico ranch. Exposed for his role in the Teapot Dome scandal, named after a Wyoming oil reserve, Fall became the first cabinet officer in history to go to jail. Daugherty escaped a similar fate by destroying records and invoking the Fifth Amendment.

Harding was appalled by the scandals. "My God, this is a hell of a job!" he told William Allen White. "I have no trouble with my enemies. . . . But my damned friends, . . . they're the ones that keep me walking the floor nights!" Harding died shortly thereafter, probably of a heart attack.

COOLIDGE PROSPERITY

On August 3, 1923, Vice President Calvin Coolidge was sworn in as president by his father while visiting his birthplace in rural Vermont, thereby reaffirming his association with traditional values. This image reassured Americans troubled by the Harding scandals.

Coolidge supported business with ideological conviction. He cultivated a deliberate inactivity calculated to lower expectations about government. He endorsed Secretary of the Treasury Mellon's ongoing efforts to reverse the progressive tax policies of the Wilson years and backed Secretary of Commerce Hoover's persistent efforts on behalf of the business community.

Like Harding, Coolidge installed business supporters in the regulatory agencies. To chair the Federal Trade Commission he appointed an attorney who had condemned the agency as "an instrument of oppression and disturbance and injury instead of help to business." The *Wall Street Journal* crowed, "Never before, here or anywhere else, has a government been so completely fused with business."

"Coolidge prosperity" determined the 1924 election. The Democrats, hopelessly divided, took 103 ballots to nominate the colorless, conservative Wall Street lawyer John W. Davis. A more interesting opponent for Coolidge was Robert La Follette, nominated by discontented farm and labor organizations that formed a new Progressive Party. La Follette campaigned against "the power of private monopoly over the political and economic life of the American people." The Republicans, backed by immense contributions from business, denounced La Follette as an agent of Bolshevism. The choice, Republicans insisted, was "Coolidge or Chaos." Thus instructed, Americans chose Coolidge, though barely half the electorate bothered to vote.

THE FATE OF REFORM

But progressive reform was not completely dead. A small group in Congress, led by La Follette and George Norris, attacked Mellon's regressive tax policies and supported measures regulating agricultural processors, protecting workers' rights, and maintaining public ownership of a hydroelectric dam at Muscle Shoals, Alabama, that conservative Republicans wanted to privatize. Yet the reformers' successes were few and often temporary.

The fate of women's groups illustrates the difficulties reformers faced in the 1920s. At first, the adoption of woman suffrage prompted politicians to champion women's reform issues. In 1920, both major parties endorsed many of the goals of the new **League of Women Voters.** Within a year, many states had granted women the right to serve on juries, several enacted equal-pay laws, and Wisconsin adopted an equal-rights law. Congress passed the **Sheppard-Towner Maternity and Infancy Act,** the first federal social-welfare law, in 1921. It provided federal funds for infant and maternity care, precisely the type of protective legislation that the suffragists had described as women's special interest.

But thereafter women reformers gained little. As it became clear that women did not vote as a bloc but according to their varying social and economic backgrounds, Congress lost interest in women's issues. In 1929, Congress killed the Sheppard-Towner Act. Nor could reformers gain ratification of a child-labor amendment after the Supreme Court invalidated laws regulating child labor. Conservatives attacked women reformers as Bolsheviks.

CITIES AND SUBURBS

*T*he 1920 census was the first to report that more Americans lived in urban than in rural areas. The trend toward urbanization accelerated in the 1920s as millions of Americans fled the depressed countryside for the booming cities. This massive population movement interacted with technological innovations to reshape cities, build suburbs, and transform urban life (see Map 24–1).

EXPANDING CITIES

Urbanization affected every region of the country. The older industrial cities of the Northeast and upper Midwest attracted migrants from the rural South and distressed Appalachia. Migrants from the countryside poured into Atlanta, Birmingham, Memphis, and Houston. Little more than jungle before 1914, Miami became the fastest-growing city in the United States during the 1920s—"the Magic City."

In the West, Denver, Portland, Seattle (each a regional economic hub), and several California cities grew rapidly. Los Angeles grew by 115 percent and by 1930 was the nation's fifth-largest city, with over 1.2 million people.

The population surge transformed the urban landscape. As land values soared, developers built skyscrapers, giving Cleveland, Kansas City, San Francisco, and many other cities modern skylines. By the end of the decade, American cities had nearly 400 skyscrapers taller than 20 stories. The tallest, New York's 102-story Empire State Building, symbolized the urban boom.

THE GREAT BLACK MIGRATION

A significant feature of the rural-to-urban movement was the **Great Migration** of African Americans from the South. Like other migrants, they were responding chiefly to economic factors. Southern segregation and violence made migration attractive, but job opportunities made it possible. Prosperity created jobs, and with

---

WHAT LED to the Great Migration?

League of Women Voters
League formed in 1920 advocating for women's rights, among them the right for women to serve on juries and equal pay laws.

Sheppard-Towner Maternity and Infancy Act   The first federal social welfare law, passed in 1921, providing federal funds for infant and maternity care.

Great Migration   The mass movement of African Americans from the rural South to the urban North, spurred especially by new job opportunities during World War I and the 1920s.

MAP EXPLORATION

To explore an interactive version of this map, go to **http://www.prenhall.com/goldfield3/map24.1**

Very strong population growth
Moderate population growth
Population loss
African-American migration

MAP 24–1   Population Shifts, 1920–1930   Rural Americans fled to the cities during the 1920s, escaping a declining agricultural economy to search for new opportunities. African Americans in particular left the rural South for eastern and midwestern cities, but the urban population also jumped in the West and in the South itself.

WHY DID certain states and areas gain population during this period and why did others see population decreases?

the decline in European immigration, black workers filled the positions previously given to new immigrants. Black men worked as unskilled or semiskilled laborers; black women became domestics in white homes. The migrants often found adjustment to their new environment difficult. Still, more than 1.5 million African Americans moved to northern cities in the 1920s.

Although African Americans, like European immigrants, often wanted to live together to sustain their culture, racist restrictions meant that segregation, not congregation, most shaped their urban community. With thousands of newcomers limited to certain neighborhoods, rapacious landlords charged ever-increasing rents for ever-declining housing. Racism exacerbated urban poverty; black workers earned less than working-class white workers but had to spend 50 percent more for housing. High rents and low wages forced black families to share inferior and unsanitary housing that threatened their health and safety. In

WHERE TO LEARN MORE

Smithsonian Institution, Washington, D.C.

Harlem Renaissance A new African-American cultural awareness that flourished in literature, art, and music in the 1920s.

QUICK REVIEW

The Universal Negro Improvement Association
- Led by Marcus Garvey.
- Rejected goal of integration.
- Promoted black nationalism.
- Organized numerous black enterprises.

Making tortillas—the staple of the Mexican diet—these Mexican American women used stone mortars in the 1920s to grind the corn by hand at the El Sol del Mayo tortilla plant in East Los Angeles. Spurned by Anglo society, Mexican Americans found support, jobs, and community in the barrios where they lived and worked. The barrios also enabled some Mexican Americans, like plant owner Maria Quevedo, to become small business owners. They provided products and services that satisfied the traditional cultural values of the Mexican community.

Los Angeles Public Library LAPL

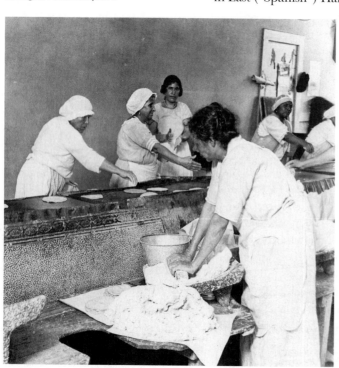

Pittsburgh, only 20 percent of black houses had bathtubs, and only 50 percent had indoor toilets. Continual migration disrupted efforts to develop a stable community; Harlem, said one social worker, was a "perpetual frontier."

However, the Great Migration also increased African Americans' racial consciousness, autonomy, and power. In 1928, for instance, black Chicagoans elected the first black man to Congress since the turn of the century. Mutual-aid societies and fraternal orders proliferated. Churches were very influential.

Another organization also appealed to poor black ghetto dwellers. The Universal Negro Improvement Association (UNIA), organized by Marcus Garvey, a Jamaican immigrant to New York, rejected the NAACP's goal of integration. A black nationalist espousing racial pride, Garvey exhorted black people to migrate to Africa to build a "free, redeemed, and mighty nation." In the meantime, he urged them to support black businesses. UNIA organized many enterprises, including groceries, restaurants, laundries, a printing plant, and the Black Star Steamship Line. UNIA attracted half a million members, the first black mass movement in American history. When Garvey was convicted of mail fraud and deported, however, the movement collapsed.

Racial pride also found expression in the **Harlem Renaissance,** an outpouring of literature, painting, sculpture, and music. Inspired by African-American culture and black urban life, writers and artists created works of power and poignancy. The poetry of Langston Hughes reflected the rhythm and mood of jazz and the blues. Other leading authors of the Harlem Renaissance who asserted their independence included Claude McKay, who wrote of the black working class in *Home to Harlem* (1928), Zora Neale Hurston, James Weldon Johnson, and Dorothy West.

BARRIOS

Hispanic migrants also entered the nation's cities in the 1920s, creating their own communities, or barrios. Fifty thousand Puerto Ricans settled in New York, mostly in East ("Spanish") Harlem, where they found low-paying jobs. Far more migrants arrived from Mexico. Although many worked as migrant farm laborers, they often lived in cities in the off-season. Others permanently joined the expanding urban economy in industrial and construction jobs. The barrios, with their own businesses, churches, and cultural organizations, created a sense of permanency.

These communities enabled the newcomers to preserve their cultural values and build social institutions, such as *mutualistas* (mutual aid societies), that helped them obtain credit, housing, and health care. But the barrios also reflected the hostility that Hispanics encountered in American cities, for racism often restricted them to such districts. The number of Mexicans in Los Angeles tripled during the 1920s to nearly 100,000, but segregation confined them to East Los Angeles. Other areas of the city, such as El Segundo and Lynwood, boasted of being "restricted to the white race" and having "no Negroes or Mexicans."

Some Hispanics fought discrimination. La Orden de Hijos de America ("The Order of the Sons of America"), organized in San Antonio in 1921, campaigned against inequities in schools and the jury system. In 1929, it helped launch the larger League of United Latin American Citizens (LULAC), which would help advance civil rights for all Americans.

THE ROAD TO SUBURBIA

As fast as the cities mushroomed in the 1920s, the suburbs grew twice as fast. The automobile created the modern suburb for it enabled people to live in formerly remote areas. A single-family house surrounded by a lawn became the social ideal, a pastoral escape from the overcrowded and dangerous city. Many suburbs excluded African Americans, Hispanics, Jews, and working-class people.

Suburbanization and the automobile brought other changes. The government provided federal money to states to build highways, and by the end of the decade, road construction was the largest single item in the national budget. Autos and suburbs also stimulated the growth of new industries. In 1922, J. C. Nichols opened the Country Club Plaza, the first suburban shopping center, in Kansas City; it provided free off-street parking. Department stores and other large retailers began leaving the urban cores for the suburbs, where both parking and more affluent customers were waiting. Drive-in restaurants began with Royce Hailey's Pig Stand in Dallas in 1921. That same year, the first fast-food franchise chain, White Castle, appeared, with its standardized menu and building.

MASS CULTURE IN THE JAZZ AGE

*T*he White Castle chain symbolized a new society and culture. Urbanization and the automobile joined with new systems of distributing, marketing, and communications to mold a mass culture of standardized experiences and interests. Not all Americans participated equally in the new culture, however, and some attacked it.

ADVERTISING THE CONSUMER SOCIETY

Advertising and its focus on increasing consumption shaped the new society. Advertisers exhorted consumers via newspapers, billboards, streetcar signs, junk mail, radio, movies, and even skywriting. They sought to create a single market where everyone, regardless of region and ethnicity, consumed brand-name products. Advertisers attempted to stimulate new wants by ridiculing previous models or tastes as obsolete, acclaiming the convenience of a new brand, or linking the latest fashion with status or sex appeal. "If I wear a certain brand of underwear," observed one critic, "I have the satisfaction of knowing that my fellow-men not so fortunately clad are undoubtedly fouled swine."

The home became a focus of consumerism. Middle- and upper-class women purchased mass-produced household appliances, such as electric irons, toasters, vacuum cleaners, washing machines, and refrigerators. Working-class women bought packaged food, ready-made clothing, and other consumer goods to lighten their workload. Advertisers attempted to redefine the housewife's role as primarily that of a consumer, purchasing goods for her family.

A shifting labor market also promoted mass consumption. The increasing number of white-collar workers had more time and money for leisure and consumption. Factory workers, whose jobs often provided little challenge, less satisfaction, and no prospect for advancement, found in consumption not only material rewards but, thanks to advertisers' claims, some self-respect and fulfillment as stylish and attractive people worthy of attention. Women clerical workers,

HOW DID new systems of distribution, marketing, and mass communication shape American culture?

Advertisements for brand-name products, like this 1929 ad for Campbell's tomato soup, often tried to link simple consumption with larger issues of personal success and achievement.

By permission of Campbell Soup Company

Violinist Carroll Dickerson, at the Sunset Café in 1922, led one of the jazz bands that flourished in Chicago's many clubs, pointing up the central role of African Americans in the Jazz Age. *Variety* magazine dubbed Chicago the "hottest café town" in the United States, but the Illinois Vigilance Association despaired that "in Chicago alone" it had "traced the fall of 1,000 girls to jazz music" in just two years.

Getty Images Inc.

Jazz Age   The 1920s, so called for the popular music of the day as a symbol of the many changes taking place in the mass culture.

the fastest-growing occupational group, found in the purchase of clothes and cosmetics a sign of social status and an antidote to workplace monotony.

Under the stimulus of advertising, consumption increasingly displaced the traditional virtues of thrift, prudence, and avoidance of debt. By 1928, fully 85 percent of furniture, 80 percent of radios, and 75 percent of washing machines were bought on credit. But with personal debt rising more than twice as fast as incomes, even aggressive advertising and the extension of credit could not indefinitely prolong the illusion of a healthy economy.

LEISURE AND ENTERTAINMENT

During the 1920s, Americans also spent more on recreation and leisure, important features of the new mass society. Millions of people packed into movie theaters whose ornate style symbolized their social importance.

Movies helped to spread common values and to set national trends in dress, language, and behavior. Studios made films to attract the largest audiences and fit prevailing stereotypes. Cecil B. De Mille titillated audiences while reinforcing conventional standards with religious epics like *The Ten Commandments* (1923) and *The King of Kings* (1927). Set in ancient times, such movies depicted both sinful pleasures and the eventual triumph of moral order.

Radio also helped to mold popular culture. The first radio network, the National Broadcasting Company (NBC), was formed in 1926. Soon it was charging $10,000 to broadcast a commercial to a national market. Networks provided standardized entertainment, personalities, and news to Americans across the nation. Radio incorporated listeners into a national society. Rural residents, in particular, welcomed the "talking furniture" for giving them access to the speeches, sermons, and business information available to city dwellers.

The phonograph, another popular source of entertainment, allowed families to listen to music of their choice in their own homes. Record companies promoted dance crazes, such as the Charleston, and developed regional markets for country, or "hillbilly," music in the South and West, as well as a "race market" for blues and jazz among the growing urban population, black and white. The popularity of the trumpet player Louis Armstrong and other jazz greats gave the decade its nickname, the **Jazz Age** (See Global Perspectives, "The International Journey of Jazz").

Jazz derived from African-American musical traditions. The Great Migration spread it from New Orleans and Kansas City to cities throughout the nation. Its improvisational and rhythmic characteristics differed sharply from older and more formal music and were often condemned by people who feared that jazz would undermine conventional restraints on behavior. A group in Cincinnati, ar-

GLOBAL PERSPECTIVES

THE INTERNATIONAL JOURNEY OF JAZZ

central part of American culture in the 1920s, jazz expanded its global reach in the decade known for mass production and mass consumerism. Just as Henry Ford sold his Model T cars abroad, jazz musicians took their distinctively American form of music south to Latin America and east to England, France, the Soviet Union, and China.

Jazz caught the imagination of the world. For many at home and abroad, the jarring spontaneity of jazz signaled a new age. It was, according to George Gershwin, the result of "energy stored up in America." For the composer John Alden Carpenter, it represented "the first art innovation originating in America to be accepted seriously in Europe." A German critic could not have agreed more, exclaiming, "Jazz is the expression of a Kultur epoch . . . Jazz is a musical revelation, a religion, a philosophy of the world, just like Expressionism and Impressionism."

Jazz also had its detractors—both in the United States and abroad. At home, one of the principal architects of mass production, Henry Ford, labeled jazz "musical slush" that encouraged the youth to imitate the "drivel of morons." A noted French poet called jazz "a triumph of barbaric folly," and an English observer worried that jazz—the "aboriginal music of the Negro"—might threaten American music.

Still, the enthusiasm for jazz was so strong that white jazz musicians claimed credit for its origins—at least until the 1930s, when the historical role of African Americans in creating jazz was more fully acknowledged in the United States and Europe. Black musicians had given Europe its first taste of jazz during World War I with James Reese Europe's 369th Division Band. Throughout the 1920s, other African-American bands and performers traveled abroad, spreading the international message of jazz while escaping the racism of their home country. Sam Wooding's orchestra toured Europe and the Soviet Union; Herb Flemming's band, the Red Devils, and Benny Peyton's band along with remarkable performers like Josephine Baker dazzled audiences with dance and music in Buenos Aires, Paris, and London.

Jazz underscored to America and the world that an important part of the American heritage derived from an African—not European—heritage. But as the popularity of jazz grew internationally, the music no longer belonged exclusively to Americans, or even African Americans. Other countries appropriated the music and shaped it on their own terms. Still, the origins of jazz—this movement that captured the world's attention—belonged to black musicians who regarded jazz as a special expression of the African-American community.

guing that the music would implant "jazz emotions" in babies, won an injunction against its performance near hospitals.

Professional sports also became more commercialized. Millions of Americans, attracted by the popularity of such celebrities as Babe Ruth of the New York Yankees, crowded into baseball parks to follow major league teams. Ruth treated himself as a commercial commodity, hiring an agent, endorsing Cadillacs and alligator shoes, and defending a salary in 1932 that dwarfed that of President Hoover by declaring, "I had a better year than he did."

Another celebrity who captured popular fascination was the aviator Charles Lindbergh, who flew alone across the Atlantic in 1927. In the *Spirit of St. Louis,* a tiny airplane built on a shoestring budget and nearly outweighed by the massive amount of fuel it had to carry, Lindbergh fought bad weather and fatigue for 34 hours before landing to a hero's welcome in Paris. Named its first "Man of the Year" by *Time*, one of the new mass-circulation magazines, Lindbergh won adulation and awards from Americans who still valued the image of individualism.

THE NEW MORALITY

The promotion of consumption and immediate gratification weakened traditional self-restraint and fed a desire for personal fulfillment. The failure of wartime sacrifices to achieve promised glories deepened Americans' growing disenchantment with traditional values. The social dislocations of the war years and growing urbanization accelerated moral and social change. Sexual pleasure became an increasingly open objective, as the growing availability of birth-control information enabled women to enjoy sex with less fear of pregnancy; and movie stars like Clara Bow, known as "the It Girl," and Rudolph Valentino, flaunted sexuality to mass audiences. Traditionalists worried as divorce rates, cigarette consumption, and hemlines went up while respect for parents, elders, and clergy went down.

Young people seemed to embody the new morality. Rejecting conventional standards, they embraced the era's frenzied dances, bootleg liquor, smoking, more revealing clothing, and sexual experimentation. They welcomed the freedom from parental control that the automobile afforded. The "flapper"—a frivolous young woman with short hair and a skimpy skirt who danced, smoked, and drank in oblivious self-absorption—was a major obsession.

But the new morality was neither as new nor as widespread as its advocates and critics believed. Signs of change had appeared before the Great War in the popularity of new clothing fashions, social values, and public amusements among working-class and ethnic groups. And if it now became fashionable for the middle class to adopt such attitudes and practices, most Americans still adhered to traditional beliefs and values. Moreover, the new morality offered only a limited freedom. It certainly did not promote social equality for women, who remained subject to traditional double standards, with marriage and divorce laws, property rights, and employment opportunities biased against them.

THE SEARCHING TWENTIES

Many writers rejected what they considered the materialism, conformity, and provincialism of mass culture. Their criticism made the postwar decade one of the most creative periods in American literature. The brutality and hypocrisy of the war stimulated the critics' disillusionment and alienation. What Gertrude Stein called the Lost Generation considered, in the words of F. Scott Fitzgerald, "all Gods dead, all wars fought, all faiths in man shaken." Ernest Hemingway, wounded as a Red Cross volunteer during the war, rejected idealism in his novel *A Farewell to Arms* (1929), declaring that he no longer saw any meaning in "the words sacred, glorious, and sacrifice."

Novelists also turned their attention to American society. In *The Great Gatsby* (1925), Fitzgerald traced the self-deceptions of the wealthy. Sinclair Lewis ridiculed middle-class society and its narrow business culture in *Babbitt* (1922), whose title character provided a new word applied to the smug and shallow. In 1930, Lewis became the first American to win the Nobel Prize in literature.

Other writers condemned the mediocrity and intolerance of mass society. The critic Harold Stearns edited *Civilization in the United States* (1922), a book of essays depicting a repressive society sunk in hypocrisy, conformity, and material-ism. H. L. Mencken made his *American Mercury* the leading magazine of cultural dissenters. Conventional and conservative himself, Mencken heaped vitriol on the "puritans," "peasants," and "prehensile morons" he saw everywhere in Amer-ican life.

CULTURE WARS

*D*espite the blossoming of mass culture and society in the 1920s, conflicts divided social groups. Some of these struggles involved reactions against the new currents in American life, including technological and scientific innovations, urban growth, and materialism. But movements to restrict immigra-tion, enforce prohibition, prohibit the teaching of evolution, and even sustain the Ku Klux Klan did not have simple origins, motives, or consequences. The forces underlying the culture wars of the 1920s would surface repeatedly in the fu-ture (see the Overview table, "Issues in the Culture Wars of the 1920s").

NATIVISM AND IMMIGRATION RESTRICTION

Renewed immigration after the war revived the anti-immigration movement, and the propaganda of the war and the Red Scare years generated public support for more restriction. Depicting immigrants as radicals, racial inferiors, religious sub-versives, or criminals, nativists clamored for congressional action. The Emergency Quota Act of 1921 reduced immigration by about two-thirds and established quotas for nationalities on the basis of their numbers in the United States in 1910. Re-strictionists, however, demanded more stringent action, especially against the largely Catholic and Jewish immigrants from southern and eastern Europe. Coolidge himself urged that America "be kept American," by which he meant white, Anglo-Saxon, and Protestant.

Congress adopted this racist rationale in the **National Origins Act of 1924,** which proclaimed its objective to be the maintenance of the "racial preponder-ance" of "the basic strain of our population." This law restricted immigration quo-tas to 2 percent of the foreign-born population of each nationality as recorded in the 1890 census, which was taken before the mass immigration from southern and eastern Europe. Another provision, effective in 1929, restricted total annual immigration to 150,000, with quotas that nearly eliminated southern and eastern Europeans. The law also completely excluded Japanese immigrants.

Other actions targeted Japanese residents in America. California, Oregon, Washington, Arizona, and other western states prohibited them from owning or leasing land, and in 1922, the Supreme Court ruled that, as nonwhites, they could never become naturalized citizens. A Japanese newspaper in Los Angeles criti-cized such actions as betraying America's own ideals. Dispirited by the prejudice of the decade, Japanese residents hoped for fulfillment through their children, the *Nisei,* who were American citizens by birth.

Ironically, the Philippines, as a U.S. territory, was not subject to the National Origins Act, and Filipino immigration increased ninefold during the 1920s. Most Filipino newcomers became farm laborers, especially in California, or worked in Alaskan fisheries. Similarly, because the law did not apply to immigrants from the Western Hemisphere, Mexican immigration also grew. Nativists lobbied to ex-clude Mexicans, but agribusiness interests in the Southwest blocked any restrictions on low-cost migrant labor.

WHAT EXPLAINS the resurgence of the Ku Klux Klan in the 1920s?

National Origins Act of 1924 Law sharply restricting immigra-tion on the basis of immigrants' national origins and discriminat-ing against southern and eastern Europeans and Asians.

Nisei   U.S. citizens born of immigrant Japanese parents.

OVERVIEW   ISSUES IN THE CULTURE WARS OF THE 1920S

Issue	Proponent view	Opponent view
The new morality	Promotes greater personal freedom and opportunities for fulfillment	Promotes moral collapse
Evolutionism	A scientific advance linked to notions of progress	A threat to religious belief
Jazz	Modern and vital	Unsettling, irregular, vulgar, and primitive
Immigration	A source of national strength from ethnic and racial diversity	A threat to the status and authority of old-stock white Protestants
Great Migration	A chance for African Americans to find new economic opportunities and gain autonomy and pride	A threat to traditional white privilege, control, and status
Prohibition	Promotes social and family stability and reduces crime	Restricts personal liberty and increases crime
Fundamentalism	An admirable adherence to traditional religious faith and biblical injunctions	A superstitious creed given to intolerant interference in social and political affairs
Ku Klux Klan	An organization promoting communal responsibility, patriotism, and traditional social, moral, and religious values	A group of religious and racial bigots given to violent vigilantism and fostering moral and public corruption
Mass culture	Increases popular participation in national culture; provides entertainment	Promotes conformity, materialism, mediocrity, spectacle, and relaxation
Consumerism	Promotes material progress and higher living standards	Promotes waste, sterility, and self-indulgence

THE KU KLUX KLAN

Nativism was also reflected in the popularity of the revived Ku Klux Klan, the goal of which, according to its leader, was to protect "the interest of those whose fore-fathers established the nation." Founded in Georgia in 1915 and modeled on its Reconstruction predecessor, the new Klan was a national, not only a southern, movement and claimed several million members by the mid-1920s. Admitting only native-born white Protestants, the Klan embodied the fears of a traditional culture threatened by social change.

In part, the Klan was a fraternal order, providing entertainment, assistance, and community for its members. Its picnics, parades, charity drives, and other so-cial and family-oriented activities—perhaps a half-million women joined the Women of the Ku Klux Klan—sharply distinguished the organization from both the small, secretive Klan of the nineteenth century and the still smaller, extrem-ist Klan of the later twentieth century. Regarding themselves as reformers, Klan members supported immigration restriction and Prohibition.

But the Klan also exploited racial, ethnic, and religious prejudices and cam-paigned against many social groups and what it called "alien creeds." It attacked African Americans in the South, Mexicans in Texas, Japanese in California, and

Catholics and Jews everywhere. A twisted religious impulse ran through much of the Klan's organization and activities. One Klan leader maintained that "the Klan stood for the same things as the Church, but we did the things the Church wouldn't do." This included publishing anti-Catholic newspapers, boycotting Catholic and Jewish businesses, and lobbying for laws against parochial schools and for compulsory Bible reading in the public schools. The Klan also resorted to violence. In 1921, for example, a Methodist minister who belonged to the Klan murdered a Catholic priest on his own doorstep, and other Klansmen burned down Catholic churches. The leader of the Oregon Klan insisted that "the only way to cure a Catholic is to kill him."

Appealing to traditional values and racist sentiments, the KKK also embraced the technological innovation and commercialism characteristic of the 1920s.

To the Klan, Catholics and Jews symbolized not merely subversive religions but also the ethnic diversity and swelling urban population that challenged traditional Protestant culture. To protect that culture, the Klan attempted to censor or disrupt "indecent" entertainment, assaulted those it accused of adultery, and terrorized doctors who performed abortions.

While the Klan's appeal seemed rooted in the declining countryside, it also attracted urban residents. Chicago had the largest Klan organization in the nation, with 50,000 members, and Houston, Dallas, Portland, Indianapolis, Denver, and the satellite communities ringing Los Angeles were also Klan strongholds. Urban Klansmen were largely lower or lower middle class, many recently arrived from the country and retaining its attitudes; others were long-term urban residents who feared being marginalized by social changes, especially by competition from immigrants and new ideas.

The Klan also ventured into politics, with some success. But eventually it encountered resistance. In the North, Catholic workers disrupted Klan parades. In the South, too, Klan excesses provoked a backlash. After the Klan in Dallas flogged 68 people in a "whipping meadow" along the Trinity River in 1922, respect turned to outrage. Newspapers demanded that the Klan disband, district attorneys began to prosecute Klan thugs, and in 1924 Klan candidates were defeated by a ticket headed by Miriam "Ma" Ferguson, whose gubernatorial campaign called for anti-Klan laws and for the loss of tax exemptions for churches used for Klan meetings. By 1930, the Klan had nearly collapsed.

PROHIBITION AND CRIME

Reformers had long believed that prohibiting the sale of alcohol would improve social conditions, reduce crime and family instability, increase economic efficiency, and purify politics. They rejoiced in 1920 when the Eighteenth Amendment, prohibiting the manufacture, sale, or transportation of alcoholic beverages, took effect. Congress then passed the **Volstead Act,** which defined the forbidden liquors and established the Prohibition Bureau to enforce the law. But many social groups,

Volstead Act   The 1920 law defining the liquor forbidden under the Eighteenth Amendment and giving enforcement responsibilities to the Prohibition Bureau of the Department of the Treasury.

especially in urban ethnic communities, opposed Prohibition, and the government could not enforce the law where public opinion did not endorse it.

Evasion was easy. By permitting alcohol for medicinal, sacramental, and industrial purposes, the Volstead Act gave doctors, priests, and druggists a huge loophole through which to satisfy their friends' needs. Hearing that the use of sacramental wines had increased by 800,000 gallons under Prohibition, one Protestant leader complained that "not more than one-quarter of this is sacramental—the rest is sacrilegious." Scofflaws frequented the "speakeasies" that replaced saloons or bought liquor from bootleggers and rumrunners, who imported it from Canada, Cuba, or Mexico. The limited resources of the Prohibition Bureau often allowed bootleggers to operate openly.

The ethics and business methods of bootleggers soon shocked Americans, however. The huge profits encouraged organized crime, which had previously concentrated on gambling and prostitution, to develop elaborate liquor-distribution networks. Operating outside the law, crime "families" used violence to enforce contracts, suppress competition, and attack rivals. Using the profits from bootlegging and new tools like the automobile and the submachine gun, organized crime corrupted city governments and police forces.

Gradually, even many "drys"—people who had initially favored Prohibition—dropped their support, horrified by the boost the amendment gave organized crime and worried about the general disrespect for law that it promoted. A 1926 poll found that four-fifths of Americans wanted to repeal or modify Prohibition. Yet it remained in force because it was entangled in party politics and social conflict. Many rural Protestant Americans saw Prohibition as a symbolic cultural issue. Prohibition represented the ability of rural Protestants to control the newcomers in the expanding cities. Democrats called for repeal in their 1928 and 1932 platforms, and in 1933, 36 states ratified an amendment repealing what Herbert Hoover had called a "noble experiment."

OLD-TIME RELIGION AND THE SCOPES TRIAL

Religion provided another fulcrum for traditionalists attempting to stem cultural change. Protestant fundamentalism, which emphasized the infallibility of the Bible, including the creation story, emerged at the turn of the century as a conservative reaction to religious modernism and the social changes brought by the mass immigration of Catholics and Jews, the growing influence of science and technology, and the secularization of public education. But the fundamentalist crusade to reshape America became formidable only in the 1920s.

Fundamentalist groups, colleges, and publications sprang up throughout the nation, especially in the South. The anti-Catholic sentiment exploited by the Klan was but one consequence of fundamentalism's insistence on strict biblical Christianity. A second was the assault on Darwin's theory of evolution, which contradicted literal interpretations of biblical Creation. Fundamentalist legislators tried to prevent the teaching of evolution in public schools in at least 20 states. In 1923, Oklahoma banned textbooks based on Darwinian theory, and Florida's legislature denounced teaching evolution as "subversive." In 1925, Tennessee forbade teaching any idea contrary to the biblical account of human origins.

Social or political conservatism, however, was not an inherent part of old-time religion. The most prominent antievolution politician, William Jennings Bryan, continued to campaign for political, social, and economic reforms. Bryan feared that Darwinism promoted political and economic conservatism. The survival of the fittest, he complained, elevated force and brutality, ignored spiritual values and democracy, and discouraged altruism and reform. How could a person fight for social justice "unless he believes in the triumph of right?"

The controversy over evolution came to a head when the American Civil Liberties Union (ACLU) responded to Tennessee's violation of the constitutional separation of church and state by offering to defend any teacher who tested the antievolution law. John Scopes, a high school biology teacher in Dayton, Tennessee, did so and was arrested. The Scopes trial attracted national attention after Bryan agreed to assist the prosecution and Clarence Darrow, a famous Chicago lawyer and prominent atheist, volunteered to defend Scopes.

Millions of Americans tuned their radios to hear the first trial ever broadcast. Though the local jury took only eight minutes to convict Scopes, fundamentalists suffered public ridicule from reporters, including H. L. Mencken, who sneered at the "hillbillies" and "yokels" of Dayton.

But fundamentalism was hardly destroyed, and antievolutionists continued their campaign. New organizations, such as the Bryan Bible League, lobbied for state laws and an antievolution amendment to the Constitution. Three more states forbade teaching evolution, but by 1929 the movement had faltered. Even so, fundamentalism retained religious influence and would again challenge science and modernism in American life (see From Then to Now, "The Culture Wars").

23–2
The Sahara of the Bozart (1920)

A NEW ERA IN THE WORLD?

*A*broad and at home, Americans in the 1920s sought peace and economic order. Rejection of the Treaty of Versailles and the League of Nations did not foreshadow isolationism. Indeed, in the 1920s, the United States became more deeply involved in international matters than ever before in peacetime.

WAR DEBTS AND ECONOMIC EXPANSION

The United States was the world's dominant economic power in the 1920s, changed by the Great War from a debtor to a creditor nation. The loans the United States had made to its allies during the war troubled the nation's relations with Europe throughout the decade. American insistence on repayment angered Europeans, who saw the money as a U.S. contribution to the joint war effort against Germany. Moreover, high American tariffs blocked Europeans from exporting goods to the United States and earning dollars to repay their debts. Eventually, the United States readjusted the terms for repayment, and American bankers extended large loans to Germany, which used the money to pay reparations to Britain and France, whose governments then used the same money to repay the United States. This unstable system depended on a continuous flow of money from the United States.

America's global economic role expanded in other ways as well. Exports, especially of manufactured goods, soared; by 1929, the United States was the world's largest exporter, responsible for one-sixth of all exports. American investment abroad more than doubled between 1919 and 1930. To expand their markets and avoid foreign tariffs, many U.S. companies became **multinational corporations,** establishing branches or subsidiaries abroad.

Other companies gained control of foreign supply sources. American oil companies invested in foreign oil fields, especially in Latin America, where they controlled more than half of Venezuelan production. The United Fruit Company developed such huge operations in Central America that it often dominated national economies.

WHAT ROLE did the United States play in international diplomacy in the decade after World War I?

QUICK REVIEW

America's Economic Power

- U.S. was the world's dominant economic power in the 1920s.
- U.S. war-time loans to European countries were a trouble spot throughout the decade.
- To expand their markets and avoid tariffs, many U.S. companies became multinational corporations.

Multinational Corporations
Firms with direct investments, branches, factories, and offices in a number of countries.

The government worked to open doors for American businesses in foreign countries, helping them to secure access to trade, investment opportunities, and raw materials. Hoover's Bureau of Foreign Commerce opened 50 offices around the world to boost American business. Hoover also pressed the British to give U.S. corporations access to rubber production in the British colony of Malaya. Secretary of State Charles Evans Hughes negotiated access to Iraqi oil fields for U.S. oil companies. The government also authorized bankers and manufacturers to form combinations, exempt from antitrust laws, to exploit foreign markets.

REJECTING WAR

Although government officials cooperated with business leaders to promote American strategic and economic interests, they had little desire to use force abroad. Popular reaction against the Great War, strengthened by a strong peace movement, constrained policymakers. Having repudiated collective security as embodied in the League of Nations, the United States nonetheless sought to minimize international conflict and promote its national security. In particular, the State Department sought to restrict the buildup of armaments among nations.

At the invitation of President Harding, delegations from nine nations met in Washington at the Washington Naval Conference in 1921 to discuss disarmament. The conference drafted a treaty to reduce battleship tonnage and suspend the building of new ships for a decade. The terms virtually froze the existing balance of naval power, with the first rank assigned to Britain and the United States, followed by Japan and then France and Italy. The U.S. Senate ratified it with only one dissenting vote.

The United States made a more dramatic gesture in 1928, when it helped draft the **Kellogg-Briand Pact.** Signed by 64 nations, the treaty renounced aggression and outlawed war. Without provisions for enforcement, however, it was little more than symbolic.

MANAGING THE HEMISPHERE

The United States continued to dominate the hemisphere to promote its own interests. It exerted its influence through investments, control of the Panama Canal, invocation of the Monroe Doctrine, and, when necessary, military intervention.

In response to American public opinion, the peace movement, and Latin American nationalism, the United States retreated from the extreme gunboat diplomacy of the Progressive Era, withdrawing troops from the Dominican Republic and Nicaragua. But Haiti remained under U.S. occupation throughout the decade, American troops stayed in Cuba and Panama, and the United States directed the financial policies of other Latin American countries. Moreover, it sent the marines into Honduras in 1924 and back to Nicaragua in 1926. Such interventions could establish only temporary stability while provoking further Latin American hostility.

Latin American resentment led to a resolution at the 1928 Inter-America Conference denying the right of any nation "to intervene in the internal affairs of another." The U.S. delegation rejected the measure, but the anger of Latin Americans prompted the Hoover administration to decline support for the Roosevelt Corollary (see chapter 22), and J. Reuben Clark, chief legal officer of the State Department, drafted the Clark Memorandum. Not published until 1930, this document stated that the Roosevelt Corollary was not a legitimate extension of the Monroe Doctrine and thereby helped prepare the way for the so-called Good Neighbor Policy toward Latin America.

Kellogg-Briand Pact A 1928 international treaty that denounced aggression and war but lacked provisions for enforcement.

HERBERT HOOVER AND THE FINAL TRIUMPH OF THE NEW ERA

As the national economy steamed ahead in 1928, the Republicans chose as their presidential candidate Herbert Hoover, a man who symbolized the policies of prosperity and the New Era. Hoover was not a politician—he had never been elected to office—but a successful administrator who championed rational and efficient economic development. Hoover's stiff managerial image was softened by his humanitarian record and his roots in rural Iowa.

The Democrats, by contrast, chose a candidate who evoked the cultural conflicts of the 1920s. Alfred E. Smith, a four-term governor of New York, was a Catholic, an opponent of Prohibition, and a Tammany politician tied to the immigrant constituency of New York City. His nomination plunged the nation into the cultural strife that had divided the Democrats in 1924. Rural fundamentalism, anti-Catholicism, Prohibition, and nativism were crucial factors in the campaign. The fundamentalist assault was unrelenting. A Baptist minister in Oklahoma City warned his congregation, "If you vote for Al Smith, you're voting against Christ and you'll all be damned."

But Hoover was, in fact, the more progressive candidate. Sympathetic to labor, sensitive to women's issues, hostile to racial segregation, and favorable to the League of Nations, Hoover had always distanced himself from what he called "the reactionary group in the Republican party." By contrast, despite supporting state welfare legislation to benefit his urban working-class constituents, Smith was essentially conservative and opposed an active government. Moreover, he was as parochial as his most rural adversaries and never attempted to reach out to them.

Although many Americans voted against Smith because of his social background, the same characteristics attracted others. Millions of urban and ethnic voters, previously Republican or politically uninvolved, voted for Smith and laid the basis for the new Democratic coalition that would emerge in the 1930s. In 1928, however, with the nation still enjoying the economic prosperity so closely associated with Hoover and the Republicans, the Democrats were routed.

CONCLUSION

The New Era of the 1920s changed America. Technological and managerial innovations produced giant leaps in productivity, new patterns of labor, a growing concentration of corporate power, and high corporate profits. Government policies, from protective tariffs and regressive taxation to the relaxation of regulatory laws, reflected and reinforced the triumphs of the business elite over traditional cautions and concerns.

The decade's economic developments, in turn, stimulated social change, drawing millions of Americans from the countryside to the cities, creating an urban nation, and fostering a new ethic of materialism, consumerism, and leisure and a new mass culture. This social transformation swept up many Americans but left others unsettled by the erosion of traditional practices and values. The concerns of traditionalists found expression in campaigns for prohibition and against immigration, the revival of the Ku Klux Klan, and the rise of religious fundamentalism. Intellectuals denounced the materialism and conformity they saw in the new social order and fashioned new artistic and literary trends.

WHAT FACTORS contributed to Herbert Hoovers victory in 1928 over his Democratic opponent, Alfred E. Smith? In what ways did Hoover epitomize the policies of the New Era?

WHERE TO LEARN MORE

Herbert Hoover National Historic Site, West Branch, Iowa

One 1920s cartoon depicting a "View of Washington," showed Herbert Hoover everywhere at once. In fact, the talented and ambitious secretary of commerce was not a politician but a successful engineer, businessman, and administrator who symbolized to many Americans the best of the New Era.

The Granger Collection, New York.

THE CULTURE WARS

Cultural conflict raged through American society in the 1920s as people reacted to great social changes, including new roles for women, increasing ethnic and racial diversity, rapid urbanization, and the "new morality." Such conflicts are rooted in the moral systems that give people identity and purpose. As a result, the challenges of the Great Depression and World War II dampened but did not extinguish them. Beginning in the 1960s, fueled as before by challenges to traditional values and beliefs, cultural conflict flared again and continues to burn.

In the 1920s, nativists succeeded in curtailing immigration with the passage of the National Origins Act of 1924. In 1994, the people of California approved Proposition 187, which barred undocumented aliens from public schools and social services. Again, as in the 1920s, fundamentalists are mounting an attack against the teaching of evolution in public schools, sometimes seeking to persuade local school boards to give equal time to the pseudoscience of creationism. And today rap and rock 'n' roll provoke the same kind of worried condemnation that jazz provoked in the 1920s.

The central battleground of today's culture wars, however, is women's rights, and especially abortion rights. Ever since the Supreme Court ruled in *Roe v. Wade* in 1973 that women had a right to an abortion, opponents, primarily religious conservatives, have sought to curtail or abolish that right in the name of family values. Antiabortion protests became increasingly violent in the 1980s and 1990s. Although the Supreme Court has upheld *Roe v. Wade* and laws restraining demonstrations at abortion clinics, it has also upheld state laws imposing limits on abortion rights. Abortions have become harder to obtain in many parts of the country.

Further complicating the issue of abortion rights is the recent challenge to fetal-tissue research. Even as advocates, including former first lady Nancy Reagan, argue that fetal-tissue research promises possible cures for such diseases as Alzheimer's and Parkinson's, their opponents passionately object to what they fear as biomedical engineering and continue to seek legislation prohibiting all fetal-tissue research.

Gay rights is another battleground in the culture wars. Religious conservatives, again in the name of family values, have sought to counter efforts to extend civil rights protections to gays and lesbians. Same-sex marriage, authorized in Massachusetts in 2004 and performed elsewhere by some religious leaders and public officials, has produced a volatile struggle, igniting public debate and provoking protest and legal challenges. Opponents, led by President George W. Bush, are calling for a constitutional amendment defining marriage as a bond for heterosexual couples only. Both sides believe the stakes are high, and the battle threatens to rage in the streets and the courts.

The hostility to the Catholic Church and Catholic immigrants that was long characteristic of American nativism has been largely absent from the current culture wars. On the contrary, conservative Catholics have joined forces with evangelical Protestants on many fronts, particularly on abortion, gay rights, school prayer, and publicly funded vouchers for parochial schools. The last issue has ignited the opposition of organized public school teachers, whereas school prayer has divided communities, as in Pontotoc, Mississippi, where it produced a searing controversy now chronicled in an Emmy-award winning film titled *School Prayer: A Community At War*. For a fuller discussion of the battles continuing to rage over school prayer and vouchers, see Chapter 30.

According to one popular analysis, the antagonists in today's culture wars are, on one side, those who find authority in religious traditions, and, on the other, those who find authority in society and human reason. Republican leader Tom DeLay of Texas, for example, declared in 1999 that the impeachment debate over former President Clinton was "about relativism versus absolute truth," and with the failure to convict Clinton, another Republican lamented, "we probably have lost the culture war." But the reelection of President Bush, who has declared his opposition to fetal-tissue research and rallied those who support family values, suggests that the war is not over and that cultural conflict, motivated by deeply rooted convictions, is likely to remain a persistent undercurrent in American life.

But the impact of the decade's trends was uneven. Mechanization increased the productivity of some workers but cost others their jobs; people poured into the cities while others left for the suburbs; Prohibition, intended to stabilize society, instead produced conflict, crime, and corruption; government policies advanced some economic interests but injured others. Even the notion of a "mass" culture obscured the degree to which millions of Americans were left out of the New Era. With no disposable income and little access to electricity, rural Americans scarcely participated in the joys of consumerism; racial and ethnic minorities were often isolated in ghettos and barrios; and many workers faced declining opportunities. Although living standards rose for many Americans and the rich expanded their share of the national wealth, more than 40 percent of the population fell below the established poverty level. The unequal distribution of wealth and income made the economy unstable and vulnerable to a disastrous collapse.

IMAGE KEY
for pages 692–693

a. Herbert Hoover.
b. Silent film star Gertrude Olmstead wears a ruffled flapper dress with a striped hat in 1925.
c. 1920s Ford poster.
d. A clarinet.
e. An old football.
f. African American assembly line at the Rouge Plant of the Ford Motor Company.
g. The price of stocks through the 1920s and early 1930s.
h. A African American family from the south arrives in Chicago, ca. 1910.
i. Campbell's Tomato Soup ad.
j. Women dressed in the white robes and hoods of the Ku Klux Klan in 1924.

SUMMARY

The Economy that Roared Following a postwar depression in 1920 and 1921, the American economy boomed through the rest of the decade. Mechanization of production, investment, new industries such as broadcasting and motion pictures and the automobile industry drove the economy. Oligopoly eliminated competition; Americans accepted the idea that size brought efficiency and productivity. While many businesses boomed, "sick" industries such as textiles, coal mining, agriculture and railroads dragged the economy down. Not all Americans shared in the economic boom; the gap between rich and poor widened.

The Business of Government The Republican surge in national politics also shaped the economy; a business government went hand in hand with a business country. Government regulation was curtailed, business supporters were installed in regulatory agencies, and the Supreme Court became a champion of business. While the Progressive party had little impact on politics, progressivism was not dead but had lost much of its energy and focus.

Cities and Suburbs By 1920 more Americans lived in urban than rural areas; the massive population movement interacted with technological innovations to reshape cities, build automobile-accessible suburbs, and transform urban life. The South was the most rapidly urbanizing region; however, African Americans left the South for job opportunities in Midwestern and Northern cities; increased racial pride found expression in the Harlem Renaissance. Puerto Ricans and Mexicans moved into U.S. cities creating their own communities. Suburbs grew more rapidly than cities as middle-class enclaves created by automobiles.

Mass Culture in the Jazz Age Fast food chains symbolized a new society and culture; advertising and its focus on increasing consumption shaped the new society. Brand-name goods, mass consumption, and buying on credit became hallmarks of the new American economy. People also spent more on recreation and leisure; radio, the phonograph, and the movies competed with college football, professional baseball, and boxing during the Jazz Age. The social dislocations and America's

growing disenchantment with traditional values fueled the new morality among the young; writers of the Lost Generation critized the new era.

Culture Wars Despite the new mass culture of the 1920's, conflicts divided social groups. Some of these struggles involved reactions against the new currents in American life, including technical and scientific innovation, urban growth, and materialism. Nativism, racism, religion, dislike of modernism and the expanding role of science, and the desire to return to and strengthen traditional rural values were all underlying issues in the culture wars.

A New Era in the World? The United States was changed by the Great War into a creditor nation. The loans made to the Allies troubled America's relations with Europe as America insisted on repayment; however, high tariffs blocked Europe exporting goods and earning money to repay those debts. America's global economic role expanded and companies became multinational corporations; Europe and Latin America resented this economic invasion. Reaction to the Great War resulted in America, along, with sixty-four other nations, outlawing war in 1928.

Herbert Hoover and the Triumph of the New Era Herbert Hoover's election as president in 1928 seemed the "final triumph over poverty"; in 1929, the Great Depression would begin.

REVIEW QUESTIONS

1. How did the automobile industry affect the nation's economy and society in the 1920s? In the excerpt from *The Flivver King,* how does Upton Sinclair illustrate the tension between workers and technology even as they both served Henry Ford's vision of mass production and mass consumerism?

2. What factors characterized the boom industries of the 1920s? The sick industries? How accurate is it to label the 1920s the decade of prosperity?

3. What were the underlying issues in the election of 1924? Of 1928? What role did politics play in the public life of the 1920s?

4. What were the chief points of conflict in the culture wars of the 1920s? What were the underlying issues in these clashes? Why were they so hard to compromise?

5. In what ways did the World War experience shape developments in the 1920s?

6. What were the chief features of American involvement in world affairs in the 1920s? To what extent did that involvement constitute a new role for the United States? And how did the influence of jazz music throughout the world affect America's role in cultural expansionism?

KEY TERMS

Great Migration (p. 702)
Harlem Renaissance (p. 704)
Jazz Age (p. 706)
Kellogg-Briand Pact (p. 714)
League of Women Voters (p. 702)
Multinational corporations
  (p. 713)

National Origins Act of 1924
  (p. 709)
Nisei (p. 709)
Oligopoly (p. 697)
Open-shop (p. 697)
Sheppard-Towner Maternity
  and Infancy Act (p. 702)

Volstead Act (p. 711)
Welfare capitalism (p. 697)
Yellow-dog contracts (p. 697)

WHERE TO LEARN MORE

F. Scott and Zelda Fitzgerald Museum, Montgomery, Alabama. The novelist and his wife lived a short while in this house in her hometown. **www.alabamatravel.org/central/szfm.html**.

Smithsonian Institution, Washington, D.C. "From Farm to Factory," a permanent exhibition at the National Museum of American History, splendidly portrays the human side of the Great Migration.

Herbert Hoover National Historic Site, West Branch, Iowa. Visitors may tour Hoover's birthplace cottage, presidential library, and museum.

Henry Ford Museum and Greenfield Village, Dearborn, Michigan. Among many fascinating exhibits, "The Automobile in American Life" superbly demonstrates the importance of the automobile in American social history. **www.hfmgv.org**.

George Norris Home, McCook, Nebraska. This museum, operated by the Nebraska State Historical Society, is dedicated to a leading progressive Republican of the 1920s. **www.nebraskahistory.org/sites/norris/index.htm**.

Warren G. Harding House, Marion, Ohio. Harding's home from 1891 to 1921 is now a museum with period furnishings. **www.ohiohistory.org/places/harding**.

Rhea County Courthouse and Museum, Dayton, Tennessee. The site of the Scopes Trial; the courtroom appears as it did in 1925, the museum contains memorabilia related to the trial.

Calvin Coolidge Homestead, Plymouth, Vermont. Operated by the Vermont Division of Historic Sites, the homestead preserves the exact interiors and furnishings from when Coolidge took the presidential oath of office there in 1923. **www.calvin-coolidge.org/pages/homestead** and **www.dhca.state.vt.us/HistoricSites/sites.htm**.

 U.S. History Documents CD-ROM
For primary sources related to this chapter, refer to the document CD-ROM.

 www.prenhall.com/goldfield
For study resources related to this chapter, visit the *Companion Website*™.

Visualizing The Past...

Advertising and the Modern Woman

DURING the 1920s, for the first time in American history, consumer demand was the chief impetus to economic growth. As a direct consequence, the 1920s witnessed the emergence of advertising as a major industry. Most of the ads from this period promoted benefits that had little to do with product. Why? The simplest explanation is that the ad agency and the manufacturer believed that youth and feminine beauty would sell. By the late twenties, advertisements for all sorts of products touted the "modern young woman" as the arbiter of taste and beauty. In so doing, the advertisers signaled a deep shift in American culture. Which specific feminine characteristics are promoted in the advertisements shown here?

The image of a young, attractive woman in this Lucky Strike ad from the 1920s is much more prominent than the product she is promoting. How does the ad make the connection between cigarettes and feminine beauty? What is the underlying message of the command to "reach for a Lucky—instead of a sweet?"

ADS-TOBACCO

"Reach for a Lucky - instead of a sweet"

LUCKY STRIKE "IT'S TOASTED"

CIGARETTES

"A flavor that completely satisfies"

Billie Burke
Popular American Actress

"It's toasted"

No Throat Irritation-No Cough.

© 1929, The American Tobacco Co., Manufacturers

The Wonder of Creole Hair

CREOLE charm has been as much admired in aristocratic European circles as in America. Empress Josephine, wife of Napoleon, was a Creole. Queen Hortense of Holland and Prince Eugene, Viceroy of Italy, were Creoles. The glorious Creole hair has always been especially admired. The hair is a special pride and care of the Creoles and for generations La Creole Hair Dressing has been favorite among them. It preserves the youthful color and beauty of the hair even through advanced years.

La Creole Ends Gray Hair

La Creole not alone prevents gray hair. La Creole treatment will bring back to its youthful color and beauty, hair that has become gray, gray-streaked, or faded. La Creole contains no dyes. It promotes the youthfully vigorous healthy condition of hair and scalp which nature intended. Its effect on the hair is gradual but certain. Two to five weeks treatment is required to bring back any shade—lightest brown to deepest black—whatever the natural color was. After that an occasional application will preserve the vigorous healthy color permanently.

Good taste and good breeding approve the use of La Creole and there is no reason for making any secret of its use, though it can never be detected.

La Creole must not be confused with dyes—it can not give a dyed look and there is nothing to stain the scalp or to wash or rub off. It makes the hair soft, wavy, lustrous and beautiful. Eliminates dandruff.

Absolutely guaranteed to bring back the hair's color or money refunded.

Send coupon for booklet "La Creole—Hair Beautiful." Shows style of hair dressing best suited to each type of face.

At Drug Stores and Toilet Counters, Price $1.00
If your Dealer can't supply you, send his name and address.
We will see that you are supplied.

VAN VLEET-MANSFIELD LABORATORIES
132 Tenth Street, Memphis, Tenn.

Van Vleet-Mansfield Laboratories
132 Tenth St., Memphis, Tenn.

Please send booklet "La Creole-Hair Beautiful," teaching the hair dress most becoming to each individual.

Name ....
Address ....
City .... State ....

▲

Virtually all ads during this period, except those aimed explicitly at African Americans, avoided any ethnic or racial references. "La Creole" ads are exceptions. The product name itself referred to a specific Community of people in Louisiana, descendants of French settlers. But the term was also used to refer to individuals of mixed racial background. How does the "La Creole" ad deal with this? What does that suggest for how you might interpret the other ads?

This ad is for a line of hair products created and manufactured by Madam C.J. Walker, one of the first African-American millionaires. The ad promises "fascinating beauty" to users of its product.

▼

You, too, may be a fascinating beauty

PERHAPS YOU ENVY the girl with irresistible beauty, whose skin is flawless and velvety, whose hair has a beautiful silky sheen, the girl who receives glances of undoubted admiration.

You need not envy her. Create new beauty for yourself by using Madam C. J. Walker's famous beauty preparations.

When Madam Walker and her associates started to develop her beauty preparations, which are now used all over the world, they perfected their toiletries step by step.

Each preparation was beyond the point of experiment before it was followed by another. Each preparation's wide use and high merit were always *proved*. Today they are unsurpassed.

Try these products and you won't have reason to envy another girl her lovely hair and her charming complexion.

You can obtain any of these marvelous preparations at your nearest druggist or from a Madam C. J. Walker agent (there's one near you) or write the company direct at Indianapolis.

Madam **C.J. WALKER'S** *Beauty Preparations*

THESE ARE BUT FOUR OF EIGHTEEN MADAM C. J. WALKER BEAUTY PREPARATIONS—AS FINE AS MONEY CAN BUY

25 The Great Depression and the New Deal 1929–1939

CHAPTER HIGHLIGHTS

Hard Times in Hooverville The prosperity of the 1920s ended in a stock market crash that revealed the flaws in the American economy. As America slid into depression, some protested, taking action to call attention to their plight.

Herbert Hoover and the Depression Hoover took unprecedented steps to resolve the country's economic crisis. However, his unwillingness to resort to interventionist policies and his reliance on voluntarism doomed his efforts and led to his defeat in 1932.

Launching the New Deal Franklin D. Roosevelt drew on a variety of sources for inspiration for his New Deal. The early New Deal had successes, but also had limitations and drew criticism from both the right and the left.

Consolidating the New Deal In 1935 Roosevelt launched policies that some have called the Second New Deal. The new phase reflected the persistence of the depression, growing political pressure, and the progressive inclinations of Roosevelt and his followers.

The New Deal and American Life Roosevelt won a landslide victory in 1936. New Deal policies had a mixed impact on women and minorities. Government programs changed daily life and ordinary people helped shape the new policies.

Ebbing of the New Deal Roosevelt was committed to further reform after 1936. However, determined opposition, continuing economic problems, and the president's own misjudgments undermined his plans.

Good Neighbors and Hostile Forces FDR worked to expand trade with the Soviet Union and with Latin America. Despite the rise of fascism, most Americans remained committed to peace at all costs. After the Munich agreement in 1938, Roosevelt moved toward preparedness for war.

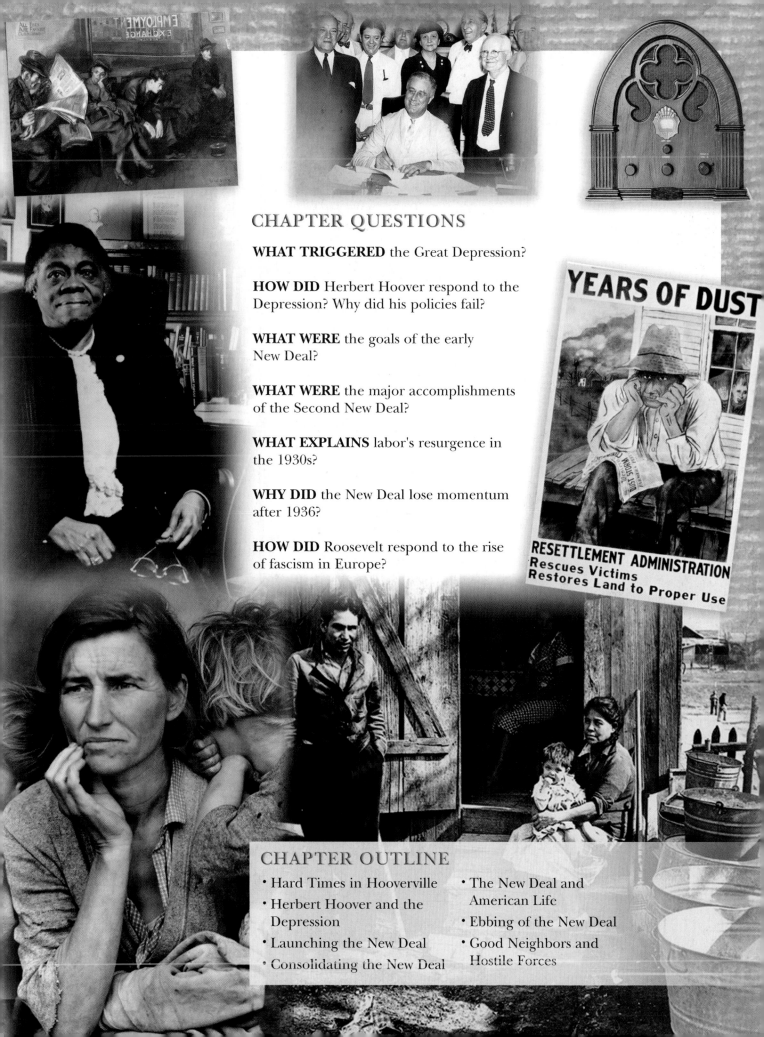

CHAPTER QUESTIONS

WHAT TRIGGERED the Great Depression?

HOW DID Herbert Hoover respond to the Depression? Why did his policies fail?

WHAT WERE the goals of the early New Deal?

WHAT WERE the major accomplishments of the Second New Deal?

WHAT EXPLAINS labor's resurgence in the 1930s?

WHY DID the New Deal lose momentum after 1936?

HOW DID Roosevelt respond to the rise of fascism in Europe?

YEARS OF DUST

RESETTLEMENT ADMINISTRATION
Rescues Victims
Restores Land to Proper Use

CHAPTER OUTLINE

- Hard Times in Hooverville
- Herbert Hoover and the Depression
- Launching the New Deal
- Consolidating the New Deal
- The New Deal and American Life
- Ebbing of the New Deal
- Good Neighbors and Hostile Forces

IMAGE KEY
for pages 722–723 is on page 752.

My mother had two small babies on her hands. When I became sickly, Grandmother Josefa took me home with her, and I never returned to my parents. . . . My grandmother's house was located on the "American" side of town, but there was nothing they could do about it because she was there before anybody else. . . . My grandmother worked very hard; I grew up in the Depression.

When it was time for me to go to school I was assigned to [the] Mexican side of town. We were segregated; [the] Anglo children were sent to Roosevelt and the Mexican children who lived closer to Roosevelt [still] had to go down to Harding. I'll admit, there was a lot of discrimination in those years.

During the Depression my grandmother sewed piecework for the WPA. My dad helped out when he could [and] Uncle Ernesto also worked. He used to dig graves.

The Depression years were very, very hard. I remember seeing the people passing on their way to California. . . .

It hurt me to see the people in their rickety old cars, their clothes in tatters, escaping from the drought and the dust bowls.

Oral Testimony,
Carlotta Silvas Martin

On April 27 [1933], according to the New York Times, *Paul Schneider, aged forty-four, a sick and crippled Chicago school teacher, shot himself to death. His widow, left with three children, stated that he had not been paid for eight months. . . . Less than a month after Paul Schneider's discouragement drove him to suicide, the militant action of Chicago teachers—patient no more . . . resulted in the payment of $12,000,000 due them for the last months of 1932. Their pay for the five months of 1933 is still owed them. Five hundred of them are reported to be in asylums and sanitariums as a result of the strain. . . .*

These are the conditions facing teachers fortunate enough to be employed. What of the unemployed? . . . "We are always hungry," wrote [one unemployed teacher]. "We owe six months' rent. . . . We live every hour in fear of eviction. . . . My sister, a typist, and I . . . have been out of work for two years. . . . We feel discouraged . . . and embittered. We are drifting, with no help from anyone."

Eunice Langdon,
The Nation, *August 16, 1933*

I am sitting in the city free employment bureau. It's the women's section. We have been sitting here now for hours. We sit here every day, waiting for a job. There are no jobs. . . .

. . . [W]e don't talk much. . . . There is a kind of humiliation. . . . We look away from each other. We look at the floor.

Meridel LeSueur, "Women on the Breadlines," 1932

Dear Mrs. Roosevelt,

I am now 15 years old and in the 10th grade. I have always been smart but I never had a chance as all of us is so poor. I hope to complete my education, but I will have to quit school I guess if there is no clothes can be bought. (Don't think that we are on the relief.) Mother has been a faithful servant for us to keep us together. I don't see how she has made it.

Mrs. Roosevelt, don't think I am just begging, but that is all you can call it I guess. . . . Do you have any old clothes you have throwed back. You don't realize how honored I would feel to be wearing your clothes.

Your friend,

M.I.

Star Route One

Albertville, Ala.

January 1, 1936

"Carlotta Silvas Martin: A Mexican American Childhood during the Depression" and "Meridel LeSueur: The Despair of Unemployed Women," both from Susan Ware, *Modern American Women: A Documentary History* (New York: McGraw-Hill Higher Education, 2002), pp. 162–165, 145–146, respectively; Eunice Langdon, "The Teacher Faces the Depression," *Nation* 137 (August 16, 1933): 182–187; Letter to Eleanor Roosevelt, January 1, 1936, www.newdeal.feri.org/eleanor/mi0136.htm.

CARLOTTA SILVAS MARTIN, Eunice Langdon, and Meridel LeSueur convey some of the trauma of the Great Depression, but no one voice can capture its devastating effect on Americans. The American economy utterly collapsed, leaving millions of people jobless, homeless, or in continual fear of foreclosure, eviction, even starvation. Men, women, children everywhere saw their families and dreams shattered and felt the sting of humiliation as they stood in bread lines or begged for clothes or food scraps. The winter of 1932–1933 was particularly cruel: unemployment soared and stories of malnutrition and outright starvation made headlines in newspapers throughout the nation.

Natural disaster accompanied economic crisis in the drought-stricken states of the Great Plains, forcing families to leave their farms. They packed up their meager belongings and took to the road to escape the darkened skies of the "Dust Bowl" in search of anything better.

The election of Franklin D. Roosevelt, however, lifted spirits and hopes of jobless Americans throughout the nation. They enthusiastically responded to his **New Deal,** taking jobs, as did Carlotta's grandmother, with such programs as the Works Progress Administration (WPA). In unprecedented numbers, they also wrote to both FDR and Eleanor Roosevelt, asking for advice and for assistance for everything from a month's rent money to tide them over to old clothes to wear to school, as did the 15-year-old girl from Alabama. And they also wrote to thank the president and first lady for their compassionate support and leadership. Throughout all such letters ran a common theme: the belief among poor and unemployed Americans that for the first time there were people in the White House who were interested in their welfare.

The collapse hit hardest those industries dominated by male workers, leaving mothers and wives with new roles as the family breadwinners, sometimes straining family relationships and men's sense of purpose and respect. Some families

New Deal The economic and political policies of the Roosevelt administration in the 1930s.

drifted apart, while others coped simply by making do. As Carlotta Silvas noted, her "dad helped out when he could."

Race and ethnicity further complicated the problems of joblessness and relief. Southern states routinely denied African Americans relief assistance, as did southwestern states for Hispanic Americans. The New Deal failed to overcome most of the traditional attitudes and practices that targeted women and minorities and reinforced local prejudice and segregation. For Carlotta Silvas, that meant walking farther to school—a daily journey that she remembered throughout her life.

Hard times, then, both united and divided the American people. Franklin and Eleanor Roosevelt and the programs of the New Deal brought fresh hope and connected Americans to the White House as never before. And although the federal activism of the 1930s achieved neither full recovery nor systematic reform, it restored confidence to many Americans and permanently transformed the nation's responsibility for the welfare of its citizens. By the end of the decade, President Roosevelt was no longer worried that the economy—indeed the whole of society—teetered on the edge of catastrophe; his gaze now fixed abroad, where even more ominous developments, he believed, threatened the nation's future and security.

HARD TIMES IN HOOVERVILLE

*T*he prosperity of the 1920s ended in a stock-market crash that revealed the flaws honeycombing the economy. As the nation slid into a catastrophic depression, factories closed, employment and incomes tumbled, and millions lost their homes, hopes, and dignity. Some protested and took direct action; others looked to the government for relief.

CRASH!

The buoyant prosperity of the New Era, more apparent than real by the summer of 1929, collapsed in October, when the stock market crashed. During the preceding two years, the market had hit record highs, stimulated by optimism, easy credit, and speculators' manipulations. But after peaking in September, it suffered several sharp checks, and on October 29, "Black Tuesday," panicked investors dumped their stocks, wiping out the previous year's gains in one day. Confidence in the economy disappeared, and the slide continued for months, and then years. The market hit bottom in July 1932. Much of the paper wealth of America had evaporated, and the nation sank into the **Great Depression.**

The Wall Street crash marked the beginning of the depression, but it did not cause it. The depression stemmed from weaknesses in the New Era economy. Most damaging was the unequal distribution of wealth and income. Workers' wages and farmers' incomes had fallen far behind industrial productivity and corporate profits; by 1929, the richest 0.1 percent of American families had as much total income as the bottom 42 percent. With more than half the nation's people living at or below the subsistence level, there was not enough purchasing power to maintain the economy.

A second factor was that oligopolies dominated American industries. By 1929, the 200 largest corporations (out of 400,000) controlled half the corporate wealth. Their power led to "administered prices," prices kept artificially high and rigid rather than determined by supply and demand. Because it did not respond to purchasing power, this system not only helped bring on economic collapse but also dimmed prospects for recovery.

Weaknesses in specific industries had further unbalanced the economy. Agriculture suffered from overproduction, declining prices, and heavy debt; so

WHAT TRIGGERED the Great Depression?

Great Depression   The nation's worst economic crisis, extending through the 1930s, producing unprecedented bank failures, unemployment, and industrial and agricultural collapse.

Chronology

1929 Stock market crashes.

1932 Farmers' Holiday Association organizes rural protests in the Midwest.

Reconstruction Finance Corporation is created to assist financial institutions.

Bonus Army is routed in Washington, D.C.

Franklin D. Roosevelt is elected president.

1931 Japan invades Manchuria.

1933 Adolf Hitler comes to power in Germany.

Emergency Banking Act is passed.

The United States recognizes the Soviet Union.

Agricultural Adjustment Administration (AAA) is created to regulate farm production.

National Recovery Administration (NRA) is created to promote industrial cooperation and recovery.

Federal Emergency Relief Act provides federal assistance to the unemployed.

Civilian Conservation Corps (CCC) is established to provide work relief in conservation projects.

Public Works Administration (PWA) is created to provide work relief on large public construction projects.

Civil Works Administration (CWA) provides emergency winter relief jobs.

Tennessee Valley Authority (TVA) is created to coordinate regional development.

1934 Securities and Exchange Commission (SEC) is established.

Indian Reorganization Act reforms Indian policy.

Huey Long organizes the Share-Our-Wealth Society.

Democrats win midterm elections.

1935 Supreme Court declares NRA unconstitutional.

Italy attacks Ethiopia.

National Labor Relations Act (Wagner Act) guarantees workers' rights to organize and bargain collectively.

Social Security Act establishes a federal social insurance system.

Banking Act strengthens the Federal Reserve.

Revenue Act establishes a more progressive tax system.

Resettlement Administration is created to aid dispossessed farmers.

Rural Electrification Administration (REA) is created to help provide electric power to rural areas.

Soil Conservation Service is established.

Emergency Relief Appropriation Act authorizes public relief projects for the unemployed.

Works Progress Administration (WPA) is created.

Huey Long is assassinated.

1936 Supreme Court declares AAA unconstitutional.

Roosevelt is reelected president.

Hitler remilitarizes the Rhineland.

Roosevelt sails to South America as part of Good Neighbor Policy.

Sit-down strikes begin.

1937 Chicago police kill workers in Memorial Day Massacre.

FDR tries but fails to expand the Supreme Court.

Farm Security Administration (FSA) is created to lend money to small farmers to buy and rehabilitate farms.

National Housing Act is passed to promote public housing projects.

"Roosevelt Recession" begins.

1938 Congress of Industrial Organizations (CIO) is founded.

Germany annexes Austria.

Fair Labor Standards Act establishes minimum wage and maximum hours rules for labor.

Roosevelt fails to "purge" the Democratic Party.

Republicans make gains in midterm elections.

Munich agreement reached, appeasing Hitler's demand for Sudetenland.

Kristallnacht, violent pogrom against Jews, occurs in Germany.

did the coal and textile industries. Increased mechanization in key industries had resulted in significant unemployment even during the 1920s. Banking presented other problems. Poorly managed and regulated, banks had contributed to the instability of prosperity; they now threatened to spread the panic and depression.

International economic difficulties spurred the depression as well. Shut out from U.S. markets by high tariffs, Europeans had depended on American investments to manage their debts and reparation payments from the Great War. The stock market crash dried up the flow of American dollars to Europe, causing financial panics and industrial collapse and making the Great Depression global. In turn, European nations curtailed their imports of American goods and defaulted on their debts, further debilitating the U.S. economy. American exports fell by 70 percent from 1929 to 1932 (See Global Perspectives, "The Worldwide Collapse").

Government policies also bore some responsibility for the crash and depression. Failure to enforce antitrust laws had encouraged oligopolies and high prices; failure to regulate banking and the stock market had permitted financial recklessness and irresponsible speculation. Reducing tax rates on the wealthy had also encouraged speculation and contributed to the maldistribution of income. Opposition to labor unions and collective bargaining helped keep workers' wages and purchasing power low. The absence of an effective agricultural policy and the high tariffs that inhibited foreign trade and reduced markets for agricultural products hurt farmers. In short, the same governmental policies that shaped the booming 1920s economy also led to economic disaster.

State and local fiscal policies also pointed to economic problems for the 1930s. The expansion of public education and road construction led to higher property taxes in communities throughout the nation. Indeed, state and local taxes rose faster than personal incomes in the 1920s.

But the crash did more than expose the weaknesses of the economy. Business lost confidence and refused to make investments that might have brought recovery. Instead, banks called in loans and restricted credit, and depositors tried to withdraw their savings, which were uninsured. The demand for cash caused banks to fail, dragging the economy down further. And the Federal Reserve Board prolonged the depression by restricting the money supply.

THE DEPRESSION SPREADS

By early 1930, the effects of financial contraction were painfully evident. Factories shut down or cut back, and industrial production plummeted; by 1932, it was scarcely 50 percent of its 1929 level. Unemployment skyrocketed and, by 1932, one-fourth of the labor force was out of work. Personal income dropped by more than half between 1929 and 1932. Moreover, the depression began to feed on itself in a vicious circle: Shrinking wages and employment cut into purchasing power, causing business to slash production again and lay off workers, thereby further reducing purchasing power.

The depression particularly battered farmers. Commodity prices fell by 55 percent between 1929 and 1932, stifling farm income. Unable to pay their mortgages, many farm families lost their homes and fields. "We have no security left," cried one South Dakota farm woman. "Foreclosures and evictions at the point of sheriff's guns are increasing daily." The dispossessed roamed the byways, highways, and railways of a troubled country.

Urban families were also evicted when they could not pay their rent. Some moved in with relatives; others lived in **Hoovervilles**—the name reflects the bitterness directed at the President—shacks where people shivered, suffered, and starved.

Soup kitchens became standard features of the urban landscape, with lines of the hungry stretching for blocks. But charities and local communities could not meet the massive needs, and neither the states nor federal government had welfare or unemployment compensation programs. To survive, people planted

Hoovervilles Shantytowns, sarcastically named after President Hoover, in which unemployed and homeless people lived in makeshift shacks, tents, and boxes.

gardens in vacant lots and back alleys and tore apart empty houses or tapped gas lines for fuel. In immigrant neighborhoods, social workers found a primitive "communism" in which people shared food, clothing, and fuel.

"WOMEN'S JOBS" AND "MEN'S JOBS"

The depression affected wage-earning women in complex ways. Although they suffered 20 percent unemployment by 1932, women were less likely than men to be fired. Gender segregation had concentrated women in low-paid service, sales, and clerical jobs that were less vulnerable than the heavy industries where men predominated. But while traditional attitudes somewhat insulated working women, they also reinforced opposition to female employment, especially that of married women. As one Chicago civic organization complained, "They are holding jobs that rightfully belong to the God-intended providers of the household." Nearly every state considered restricting the employment of married women. Many private employers, especially banks and insurance companies, fired married women. Despite such hostility, the proportion of married women in the workforce increased in the 1930s as women took jobs to help their families survive, and about one-third of working married women provided the sole support for their families.

Homeless Americans gathered in squalid Hoovervilles like this one in Seattle and struggled to survive.

University of Washington Libraries, Special Collections,

FAMILIES IN THE DEPRESSION

"I have watched fear grip the people in our neighborhood around Hull House," wrote Jane Addams as the depression deepened in 1931 and family survival itself seemed threatened. Divorce declined because it was expensive, but desertion increased, and people postponed marriage. Birthrates fell. Husbands and fathers, the traditional breadwinners, were often humiliated and despondent when laid off from work. A social worker observed in 1931, "Like searing irons, the degradation, the sheer terror and panic which loss of job brings, the deprivation and the bitterness have eaten into men's souls."

The number of female-headed households increased sharply. Not only did some women become wage earners, but their traditional role as homemakers also gained new significance. To make ends meet, many women sewed their own clothing and raised and canned vegetables, reversing the trend toward consumerism.

Some parents sacrificed their own well-being to protect their children. One witness described "the uncontrolled trembling of parents who have starved themselves for weeks so that their children might not go hungry." But children felt the tension and fear, and many went without food. In New York City, 139 people, most of them children, died of starvation and malnutrition in 1933. Boys and girls stayed home from school and church because they lacked shoes or clothing; others gave up their plans for college. As hope faded, family conflicts increased. The California Unemployment Commission concluded that the depression had left the American family "morally shattered. There is no security, no foothold, no future."

QUICK REVIEW

Gendered Attitudes About Work

• Women were concentrated in low-paid service, sales, and clerical jobs.

• Traditional attitudes reinforced opposition to female employment.

• Few men sought work in fields associated with women.

GLOBAL PERSPECTIVES

THE WORLDWIDE COLLAPSE

he Wall Street crash did not immediately provoke widespread alarm at home or abroad. One French observer commented that an "abscess" had been "lanced." British commentators dismissed it as an isolated event and predicted continuing prosperity. President Hoover remained confident well into 1930, even telling a group of religious leaders requesting relief for the unemployed, "You have come sixty days too late. The depression is over."

Still, the stock market collapse did have consequences: It made European borrowing more difficult, especially hurting Germany's failing economy. Without loans from the United States, Germany defaulted on its war debts and faced near bankruptcy. Moreover, the United States accounted for 40 percent of the world's manufactured goods—twice the figure for Germany and England combined in 1929. When the United States slid into depression, the global repercussions were staggering.

The international crisis required global cooperation, but the world's nations responded with various forms of economic nationalism. The United States rejected its role as the lender of the last resort for destitute countries and constructed trade barriers by passing the Smoot-Hawley tariff in 1930. Within months Canada, Mexico, France, Spain, and New Zealand raised their tariffs against American goods. World trade came to a standstill; its volume plummeted by two-thirds between 1929 and 1933.

As the depression deepened, world leaders pointed to external causes and turned to conventional solutions. In the United States, Herbert Hoover claimed that "the hurricane that swept our shores was of European origin" and affirmed the need to balance the budget in hard times. French leaders blamed British monetary policies and blasted the United States for "exporting unemployment" through "mechanization"

that replaced workers with machines. The French also regarded a balanced budget as inviolable. In Britain, however, the socialist prime minister, Ramsay Mac-Donald, faulted capitalism for the collapse, adding "we are not on trial, it is the system under which we live." Britain provided unemployment insurance and public relief. But even the socialist prime minister refused to unbalance the budget to meet the needs of all the jobless. The Japanese finance minister also objected to increased spending for the unemployed.

By 1932, the international crisis had worsened, and the United States and Germany had unemployment rates of 25 and 40 percent, respectively. The German banking system had collapsed in 1931, and the depression helped facilitate the political success of the Nazi Party in 1932. Jobless Germans looted stores and coal yards for food and fuel. As in the United States, working women were targeted as a cause of the depression. One German newspaper declared that "Germany will perish if the women are working and the men are unemployed."

The shockingly high rates of unemployment throughout the world created unprecedented conditions of poverty and despair. And although Americans did not leap from windows during the collapse of the stock market, suicide rates went up in both Germany and the United States during the 1930s. Cases of malnutrition were found in New York, Budapest, and Vienna, among other cities, and relief agencies everywhere were overwhelmed by the needs of the jobless. People lost jobs and homes, creating Hoovervilles in the United States, *bidonvilles* ("tin cities") in France, and the Hungry Mile in Australia. The Great Depression had indeed become global, and, without international cooperation, the unemployed looked to their governments for solutions and support.

"LAST HIRED, FIRST FIRED"

The depression particularly harmed racial minorities. With fewer resources and opportunities, they were less able than other groups to absorb the economic pain. African Americans were caught in a double bind, reported a sociologist at Howard University in 1932: They were "the last to be hired and the first to be fired." Black unemployment rates were more than twice the white rate, reflecting increased job competition and persistent racism. In Atlanta, white citizens paraded with banners denouncing the hiring of black workers "Until Every White Man Has a Job."

Racism also limited the assistance African Americans received. Religious and charitable organizations often refused to care for black people. Local and state governments set higher relief eligibility requirements for black people than for white people and provided them with less aid. One Memphis resident saw the result of such policies: "Colored men and women with rakes, hoes, and other digging tools, with buckets and baskets, digging around in the garbage and refuse for food." In 1931, African-American women in Harlem joined together as the Harlem Housewives League to challenge New York City's race-based unequal distribution of relief. An African-American social worker described the despair and poverty of Harlem's residents: "Packed in damp, rat-ridden dungeons, they existed in squalor not too different from that of Arkansas sharecroppers."

Hispanic Americans also suffered. As mostly unskilled workers, they faced increasing competition for decreasing jobs paying declining wages. They were displaced even in the California agricultural labor force, which they had dominated. By the mid-1930s, they made up only a tenth of the state's migratory labor force, which increasingly consisted of white people who had fled the South and the Great Plains.

Economic woes and racism drove nearly half a million Mexican immigrants and their American-born children from the United States. Local authorities in the Southwest, with the blessing of the Department of Labor, urged all Mexicans, regardless of their citizenship status, to return to Mexico and free up jobs and relief assistance for white Americans. To intimidate Mexican residents, the U.S. Immigration Service conducted several raids, rounding up people and demanding immediate proof of citizenship. In 1931, a Los Angeles official announced that tens of thousands of Mexicans "have been literally scared out of southern California."

PROTEST

Bewildered and discouraged, most Americans reacted to the crisis without protest. Influenced by traditional individualism, many blamed themselves for their plight. But others did act, especially to protect their families. Protests ranged from small desperate gestures like stealing food and coal to more dramatic deeds. In Louisiana, women seized a train to call attention to the needs of their families; in New Jersey, in the "bloodless battle of Pleasantville," 100 women held the city council hostage to demand assistance.

Communists, socialists, and other radicals organized more formal protests. Communists led the jobless into "unemployment councils" that staged hunger marches, demonstrated for relief, and blocked evictions. Mothers facing eviction in Chicago told their children: "Run quick and find the Reds." Socialists built similar organizations, including the People's Unemployment League in Baltimore. However, local officials often suppressed their protests. In 1932, police fired on the Detroit Unemployment Council as it marched to demand food and jobs, killing four marchers and wounding many more.

Rural protests also broke out. Again, communists organized some of them, as in Alabama, where the Croppers' and Farm Workers' Union mobilized black agricultural laborers in 1931 to demand better treatment. In the Midwest, the Farmers' Holiday Association, organized among family farmers in 1932, stopped the shipment of produce to urban markets, hoping to drive up prices. A guerrilla war broke out as farmers blocked roads and halted freight trains, dumped milk in ditches, and fought bloody battles with deputy sheriffs. In Iowa, farmers beat sheriffs and mortgage agents and nearly lynched a judge conducting foreclosure proceedings.

HOW DID Herbert Hoover respond to the Depression? Why did his policies fail?

WHERE TO LEARN MORE

Herbert Hoover National Historic Site, West Branch, Iowa. **www.nps.gov/heho**; **www.hoover.archives.gov**

HERBERT HOOVER AND THE DEPRESSION

The Great Depression challenged the optimism, policies, and philosophy that Herbert Hoover had carried into the White House in 1929. The president took unprecedented steps to resolve the crisis but shrank back from the interventionist policies activists urged. His failures, personal as well as political and economic, led to his repudiation and to a major shift in government policies.

THE FAILURE OF VOLUNTARISM

Hoover fought the economic depression more vigorously than any previous president, but he believed that voluntary private relief was preferable to federal intervention. The role of the national government, he thought, was to advise and encourage the voluntary efforts of private organizations, individual industries, or local communities. After the crash, he tried to apply this voluntarism to the depression.

Hoover obtained pledges from business leaders to maintain employment and wage levels. But most corporations soon repudiated these pledges, slashed wages, and laid off workers. Hoover himself said, "You know, the only trouble with capitalism is capitalists; they're too damn greedy." Still, he rejected government action.

Hoover also depended on voluntary efforts to relieve the misery caused by massive unemployment. He created the President's Organization for Unemployment Relief to help raise private funds for voluntary relief agencies. Charities and local authorities, he believed, should help the unemployed; direct federal relief would expand government power and undermine the recipients' character. He vetoed congressional attempts to aid the unemployed.

The depression rendered Hoover's beliefs meaningless. Private programs to aid the unemployed scarcely existed. Company plans for unemployment compensation covered less than 1 percent of workers, revealing the charade of the welfare capitalism of the 1920s. Private charitable groups like the Salvation Army, church associations, and ethnic societies quickly exhausted their resources. By 1931, the director of Philadelphia's Federation of Jewish Charities conceded, "Private philanthropy is no longer capable of coping with the situation." Tens of thousands of Philadelphians, he noted, had been reduced to "the status of a stray cat prowling for food. . . . What this does to the innate dignity of the human soul is not hard to guess."

Nor could local governments cope, and their efforts declined as the depression deepened. New York City provided relief payments of $2.39 a week for an entire family, and other cities much less. By 1932, more than 100 cities made no relief appropriations at all, and the commissioner of charity in Salt Lake City reported that people were sliding toward starvation. Only eight state governments provided even token assistance.

As the depression worsened, Hoover adopted more activist policies. He persuaded Congress to cut taxes to boost consumers' buying power, and he increased the public works budget. The Federal Farm Board lent money to cooperatives and spent millions trying to stabilize crop prices. Unable to control production, however, the board conceded failure by late 1931. More successful was the Reconstruction Finance Corporation (RFC). Established in January 1932, the RFC lent federal funds to banks, insurance companies, and railroads so that their recovery could "trickle down" to ordinary Americans.

But these programs satisfied few Americans. "While children starve," cried Pennsylvania's governor, Hoover "intends to let us have just as little relief as possible after the longest delay possible." Far more action was necessary, but Hoover remained committed to voluntarism and a balanced budget. Hoover's ideological limitations

QUICK REVIEW

The Limits of Voluntarism
- Business leaders failed to live up to pledges to maintain employment and wage levels.
- Private programs to aid the unemployed scarcely existed.
- Local governments were not equipped to deal with the magnitude of the crisis.

infuriated Americans who saw him as indifferent to their suffering and a reactionary protector of privileged business interests—an image his political opponents encouraged.

REPUDIATING HOOVER: THE 1932 ELECTION

Hoover's treatment of the **Bonus Army of 1932** symbolized his unpopularity and set the stage for the 1932 election. In 1932, unemployed veterans of World War I gathered in Washington, demanding payment of service bonuses not due until 1945. Hoover refused to meet with them, and Congress rejected their plan. But 10,000 veterans erected a shantytown at the edge of Washington and camped in vacant public buildings. Hoover decided to evict the veterans, but General Douglas MacArthur exceeded his cautious orders and on July 28 led cavalry, infantry, and tanks against the ragged Bonus Marchers. The troops cleared the buildings and assaulted the shantytown, dispersing the veterans and their families and setting their camp on fire.

This assault provoked widespread outrage. "What a pitiful spectacle is that of the great American Government, mightiest in the world, chasing unarmed men, women, and children with army tanks," commented the *Washington News*. The administration tried to brand the Bonus Marchers as communists and criminals, but subsequent investigations refuted such claims.

In the summer of 1932, with no prospects for victory, Republicans renominated Hoover. Confident Democrats selected Governor Franklin D. Roosevelt of New York, who promised "a new deal for the American people." Born into a wealthy family in 1882, FDR had been educated at Harvard, trained in the law, and schooled in politics as a state legislator, assistant secretary of the navy under Wilson, and the Democratic vice presidential nominee in 1920. In 1921, Roosevelt contracted polio, which paralyzed him from the waist down. His struggle with this ordeal gave him greater maturity, compassion, and determination. His continued involvement in politics, meanwhile, owed much to his wife, Eleanor. A social reformer, she became a Democratic activist, organizing women's groups and campaigning across New York. In a remarkable political comeback, FDR was elected governor in 1928 and reelected in 1930.

The 1932 campaign gave scant indication of what Roosevelt's New Deal might involve. The Democratic platform differed little from that of the Republicans, and Roosevelt spoke in vague or general terms. Still, observers found clues in Roosevelt's record in New York, where he had created the first state system of unemployment relief and supported social welfare and conservation. More important was his outgoing personality, which radiated warmth and hope in contrast to Hoover's gloom.

FDR carried every state south and west of Pennsylvania. It was the worst rout of a Republican candidate ever (except in 1912, when the party had split). Yet Hoover would remain president for four more months, and in those four months, the depression worsened, with rising unemployment, collapsing farm prices, and spreading misery. The final blow came in February 1933, when panic struck the banking system. Nearly 6,000 banks had already failed, robbing 9 million depositors of their savings. Desperate Americans rushed to withdraw their funds from the remaining banks, pushing them to the brink. With the federal government under Hoover immobilized, state governments shut the banks to prevent their failure.

Bonus Marchers battling police in Washington, D.C., in 1932. Police and army assaults on these homeless veterans infuriated Americans and prompted Democratic presidential nominee Franklin D. Roosevelt to declare, "Well, this will elect me."

National Archives and Records Administration

QUICK REVIEW

The 1932 Election

- Republicans renominated Hoover.
- The Democratic platform differed little from the Republican platform.
- Franklin D. Roosevelt's victory was a repudiation of Hoover.

25–1
Herbert Hoover,
Speech at New York
City (1932)

Bonus Army Unemployed veterans of World War I gathering in Washington in 1932 demanding payment of service bonuses not due until 1945.

WHAT WERE the goals of the early New Deal?

WHERE TO LEARN MORE

Center for New Deal Studies, Roosevelt University, Chicago, Illinois

Fireside Chats Speeches broadcast nationally over the radio in which President Franklin D. Roosevelt explained complex issues and programs in plain language, as though his listeners were gathered around the fireside with him.

Federal Deposit Insurance Corporation (FDIC) Government agency that guarantees bank deposits, thereby protecting both depositors and banks.

Securities and Exchange Commission (SEC) Federal agency with authority to regulate trading practices in stocks and bonds.

LAUNCHING THE NEW DEAL

*I*n the midst of this national anxiety, Franklin D. Roosevelt pushed forward an unprecedented program to resolve the crises of a collapsing financial system, crippling unemployment, and agricultural and industrial breakdown and to promote reform.

ACTION NOW!

On March 4, 1933, Franklin Delano Roosevelt became president and immediately reassured the American people. He insisted that "the only thing we have to fear is fear itself—nameless, unreasoning, unjustified terror, which paralyzes needed efforts to convert retreat into advance." And he promised "action, and action now!" Summoning Congress, Roosevelt pressed forward on a broad front. In the first three months of his administration, the famous Hundred Days of the New Deal, the Democratic Congress passed many important laws (see the Overview table, "Major Laws of the Hundred Days").

Roosevelt's program reflected a mix of ideas, some from FDR himself, some from a diverse group of advisers, including academic experts dubbed the "brain trust," politicians, and social workers. It also incorporated principles from the progressive movement, precedents from the Great War mobilization, and even plans from the Hoover administration. Above all, the New Deal was a practical response to the depression. FDR had set its tone in his campaign when he declared, "The country needs, and, unless I mistake its temper, the country demands bold, persistent experimentation. . . . Above all, try something."

FDR first addressed the banking crisis. On March 5, he proclaimed a national bank holiday, closing all remaining banks. Congress then passed his Emergency Banking Act, a conservative measure that extended government assistance to sound banks and reorganized weak ones. Prompt government action, coupled with a reassuring **fireside chat** over the radio by the president, restored popular confidence in the banks. When they reopened on March 13, deposits exceeded withdrawals. "Capitalism," said Raymond Moley of the brain trust, "was saved in eight days." In June, Congress created the **Federal Deposit Insurance Corporation (FDIC)** to guarantee bank deposits up to $2,500.

The financial industry was also reformed. The Glass-Steagall Act separated investment and commercial banking to curtail risky speculation. The Securities Act reformed the sale of stocks to prevent the insider abuses that had characterized Wall Street, and in 1934 the **Securities and Exchange Commission (SEC)** was created to regulate the stock market. Two other financial measures in 1933 created the Home Owners Loan Corporation and the Farm Credit Administration, which enabled millions to refinance their mortgages.

CREATING JOBS

Roosevelt also provided relief for the unemployed. The Federal Emergency Relief Administration (FERA) furnished funds to state and local agencies. Harry Hopkins, who had headed Roosevelt's relief program in New York, became its director and one of the New Deal's most important members. FERA spent over $3 billion before it ended in 1935, and by then Hopkins and FDR had developed new programs that provided work rather than just cash. In the winter of 1933–1934, Hopkins spent nearly $1 billion to create jobs for 4 million men and women through the Civil Works Administration (CWA). The Public Works Administration (PWA) provided work relief on useful projects to stimulate the economy

OVERVIEW   MAJOR LAWS OF THE HUNDRED DAYS

Law	Objective
Emergency Banking Act	Stabilized the private banking system
Agricultural Adjustment Act	Established a farm recovery program based on production controls and price supports
Emergency Farm Mortgage Act	Provided for the refinancing of farm mortgages
National Industrial Recovery Act	Established a national recovery program and authorized a public works program
Federal Emergency Relief Act	Established a national system of relief
Home Owners Loan Act	Protected homeowners from mortgage foreclosure by refinancing home loans
Glass-Steagall Act	Separated commercial and investment banking and guaranteed bank deposits
Tennessee Valley Authority Act	Established the TVA and provided for the planned development of the Tennessee River Valley
Civilian Conservation Corps Act	Established the CCC to provide work relief on reforestation and conservation projects
Farm Credit Act	Expanded agricultural credits and established the Farm Credit Administration
Securities Act	Required full disclosure from stock exchanges
Wagner-Peyser Act	Created a U.S. Employment Service and encouraged states to create local public employment offices

through public expenditures. Directed by Harold Ickes, the PWA spent billions from 1933 to 1939 to build schools, hospitals, courthouses, dams, and bridges.

One of FDR's personal ideas, the Civilian Conservation Corps (CCC), combined work relief with conservation. Launched in 1933, the CCC employed 2.5 million young men to work on reforestation and flood-control projects, build roads and bridges in national forests and parks, restore Civil War battlefields, and fight forest fires.

HELPING SOME FARMERS

Besides providing relief, the New Deal promoted economic recovery. In May 1933, Congress established the Agricultural Adjustment Administration (AAA) to combat the depression in agriculture caused by crop surpluses and low prices. The AAA subsidized farmers who agreed to restrict production. The objective was to boost farm prices to parity, a level that would restore farmers' purchasing power to what it had been in 1914. In the summer of 1933, the AAA paid southern farmers to plow up 10 million acres of cotton and midwestern farmers to bury 9 million pounds of pork.

Agricultural conditions improved. Farm prices rose from 52 percent of parity in 1932 to 88 percent in 1935, and gross farm income rose by 50 percent. Not until 1941, however, would income exceed the level of 1929, a poor year for farmers. Moreover, some of the decreased production and increased prices stemmed from devastating droughts and dust storms on the Great Plains. The AAA itself harmed poor farmers while aiding larger commercial growers. As southern planters restricted their acreage, they dismissed tenants and sharecroppers, and with AAA payments, they bought new farm machinery, reducing their need for farm labor.

WHERE TO LEARN MORE

★ Civilian Conservation Corps Interpretive Center, Whidbey Island, Washington

New Deal agricultural programs stabilized the farm economy, but not all farmers benefited. Landowners who received AAA payments evicted these black sharecroppers huddled in a makeshift roadside camp in Missouri in 1935.

Corbis/Bettmann

WHERE TO LEARN MORE

W

Labor Museum and Learning Center of Michigan, Flint, Michigan

The Supreme Court declared the AAA unconstitutional in 1936, but new laws established the farm subsidy program for decades to come. Increasing mechanization and scientific agriculture kept production high and farmers dependent on government intervention.

THE FLIGHT OF THE BLUE EAGLE

The New Deal attempted to revive American industry with the National Industrial Recovery Act (NIRA), which created the National Recovery Administration (NRA). The NRA sought to halt the slide in prices, wages, and employment by suspending antitrust laws and authorizing industrial and trade associations to draft codes setting production quotas, price policies, wages and working conditions, and other business practices. The codes promoted the interests of business generally and big business in particular, but Section 7a of the NIRA guaranteed workers the rights to organize unions and bargain collectively—a provision that John L. Lewis of the United Mine Workers called an Emancipation Proclamation for labor.

Hugh Johnson became director of the NRA. He persuaded business leaders to cooperate in drafting codes and the public to patronize participating companies. The NRA Blue Eagle insignia and its slogan "We Do Our Part" covered workplaces, storefronts, and billboards. Blue Eagle parades marched down the nation's main streets and climaxed in a massive demonstration in New York City.

Support for the NRA waned, however. Corporate leaders used it to advance their own goals and to discriminate against small producers, consumers, and labor.

Businesses also violated the labor rights specified in Section 7a. Defiant employers viewed collective bargaining as infringing their authority. Employers even used violence to smother unions. The NRA did little to enforce Section 7a, and Johnson, strongly probusiness, denounced all strikes. Workers felt betrayed. Roosevelt tried to reorganize the NRA, but the act remained controversial until the Supreme Court declared it unconstitutional in 1935.

CRITICS RIGHT AND LEFT

The early New Deal did not end the depression. Recovery was fitful and uneven; millions of Americans remained unemployed. Nevertheless, the New Deal's efforts to grapple with problems, its successes in reducing suffering and fear, and Roosevelt's own skills carried the Democratic Party to victory in the 1934 elections. But New Deal policies also provoked criticism, from both those convinced that too little had been achieved and those alarmed that too much had been attempted.

Despite the early New Deal's probusiness character, conservatives complained that the expansion of government activity and its regulatory role weakened the autonomy of American business. They also condemned the efforts to aid nonbusiness groups as socialistic, particularly the "excessive" spending on unemployment relief and the "instigation" of labor organizing. These critics attracted little popular support, however, and their selfishness antagonized Roosevelt.

More realistic criticism came from the left. In 1932, FDR had campaigned for "the forgotten man at the bottom of the economic pyramid," and some radicals argued that the early New Deal had forgotten the forgotten man. Communists and socialists focused public attention on the poor, especially in the countryside. In California, communists organized Mexican, Filipino, and Japanese farm workers into the Cannery and Agricultural Workers Union; in Arkansas and Tennessee, socialists in 1934 helped organize sharecroppers into the Southern Tenant Farmers Union, protesting the "Raw Deal" they had received from the AAA. Both unions encountered violent reprisals. This terrorism, however, created sympathy for farmworkers.

Even without the involvement of socialists or communists, labor militancy in 1934 pressed Roosevelt. The number of workers participating in strikes leaped from 325,000 in 1932 (about the annual average since 1925) to 1.5 million in 1934.

Rebuffing FDR's pleas for fair treatment, employers moved to crush the strikes, often using complaisant police and private strikebreakers. In Minneapolis, police shot 67 teamsters, almost all in the back, as they fled an ambush arranged by employers; in Toledo, company police and National Guardsmen attacked autoworkers with tear gas, bayonets, and rifle fire; in the textile strike, police killed six picketers in South Carolina, and soldiers wounded another 50 in Rhode Island. Against such powerful opponents, workers needed help to achieve their rights. Harry Hopkins and other New Dealers realized that labor's demands could not be ignored.

Four prominent individuals mobilized popular discontent to demand government action to assist groups neglected by the New Deal. Representative William Lemke of North Dakota, an agrarian radical leader of the Nonpartisan League, called attention to rural distress. Lemke objected to the New Deal's limited response to farmers crushed by the depression. In his own state, nearly two-thirds of the farmers had lost their land through foreclosures.

Francis Townsend, a California physician, proposed to aid the nation's elderly, many of whom were destitute. The Townsend Plan called for a government pension to every American over the age of 60, provided that the recipient retired from work and spent the entire pension. This scheme promised to extend relief to the elderly, open jobs for the unemployed, and stimulate economic recovery. Over 5,000 Townsend Clubs lobbied for government action to help the elderly poor.

Father Charles Coughlin, a Catholic priest in the Detroit suburb of Royal Oak, threatened to mobilize another large constituency against the limitations of the early New Deal. Thirty million Americans listened eagerly to his weekly radio broadcasts, which mixed religion with anti-Semitism and demands for social justice and financial reform. Coughlin had condemned Hoover for assisting banks but ignoring the unemployed, and initially he welcomed the New Deal as "Christ's Deal." But after concluding that FDR's policies favored "the virile viciousness of business and finance," Coughlin organized the National Union for Social Justice to lobby for his goals. With support among lower-middle-class, heavily Catholic, urban ethnic groups, Coughlin posed a real challenge to Roosevelt's Democratic party.

Roosevelt found Senator Huey P. Long of Louisiana still more worrisome. Alternately charming and autocratic, Long had modernized his state with taxation and educational reforms and an extensive public-works program after his election as governor in 1928. Moving to the Senate and eyeing the White House, Long proposed more comprehensive social-welfare policies than the New Deal had envisaged. In 1934, he organized the Share-Our-Wealth Society. His plan to end poverty and unemployment called for confiscatory taxes on the rich to provide every family with a decent income, health coverage, education, and old-age pensions. Long's appeal was enormous. Within months, his organization claimed more than 27,000 clubs and 7 million members.

These dissident movements raised complex issues and simple fears. Their programs were often ill-defined or impractical and some of the leaders, like Cough-

QUICK REVIEW

Critique of the New Deal

- Conservative critics of the expansion of government gained little support.
- Many on the left saw the early New Deal as a "Raw Deal."
- Popular pressure mounted for more aggressive policies.

lin and Long, approached demagoguery. Nevertheless, their popularity warned Roosevelt that government action was needed to satisfy reform demands and ensure his reelection in 1936.

CONSOLIDATING THE NEW DEAL

WHAT WERE the major accomplishments of the Second New Deal?

Responding to the persistence of the depression and political pressures, Roosevelt in 1935 undertook economic and social reforms that some observers have called the Second New Deal. The new measures shifted government action more toward reform even as they still addressed relief and recovery. Nor did FDR's interest in reform simply reflect cynical politics. He had frequently championed progressive measures in the past, and many of his advisers had deep roots in reform movements.

WEEDING OUT AND LIFTING UP

"In spite of our efforts and in spite of our talk," Roosevelt told the new Congress in 1935, "we have not weeded out the overprivileged and we have not effectively lifted up the underprivileged." To do so, he developed "must" legislation. One of the new laws protected labor's rights to organize and bargain collectively. The Wagner National Labor Relations Act, dubbed "Labor's Magna Carta," guaranteed workers the right to organize unions and prohibited employers from adopting unfair labor practices, such as firing union activists and forming company unions.

Social Security.　Of greater long-range importance was the Social Security Act. The law was a compromise, framed by a nonpartisan committee of business, labor, and public representatives and then weakened by congressional conservatives. It provided unemployment compensation, old-age pensions, and aid for dependent mothers and children and the blind.

This photograph by Dorothea Lange of an eighteen-year-old mother and her child in a migrant labor camp in 1937 illustrates both despair and detachment and conveys the hardship of homelessness and deprivation in the Great Depression.

Courtesy of the Library of Congress.

The conservative nature of the law appeared in its stingy benefit payments, its lack of health insurance, and its exclusion of more than one-fourth of all workers, including many in desperate need of protection, such as farm laborers and domestic servants. Moreover, unlike in other nations, the old-age pensions were financed through a regressive payroll tax on both employees and employers rather than through general tax revenues. Thus the new system was more like a compulsory insurance program.

Despite its weaknesses, the Social Security Act was one of the most important laws in American history. It provided, Roosevelt pointed out, "at least some measure of protection to the average citizen and to his family against the loss of a job and against poverty-ridden old age." Moreover, by establishing federal responsibility for social welfare, it inaugurated a welfare system that subsequent generations would expand.

Money, Tax, and Land Reform.　Another reform measure, the Banking Act of 1935, increased the authority of the Federal Reserve Board over the nation's currency and credit system and decreased the power of the private bankers whose irresponsible behavior had contributed to the depression and the appeal of Father Coughlin. The Revenue Act of 1935, passed after Roosevelt assailed the "unjust concentration of wealth and economic power," provided for graduated income taxes and increased estate and corporate taxes.

The Second New Deal also responded belatedly to the environmental catastrophe that had turned much of the Great Plains from Texas to the Dakotas into a Dust Bowl (see Map 25–1). Since World War I, farmers had stripped marginal land of its native grasses to plant wheat. When drought and high winds hit the plains in 1932, crops failed, and nothing was left to hold the soil. Dust storms blew away millions of tons of topsoil, despoiling the land and darkening the sky a thousand miles away. Families abandoned their farms in droves. Many of these poor "Okies" headed for California, their plight captured in John Steinbeck's novel, *The Grapes of Wrath* (1939).

In 1935, Roosevelt established the Resettlement Administration to focus on land reform and help poor farmers. This agency initiated soil erosion projects and attempted to resettle impoverished farmers on better land, but the problem exceeded its resources. Congress moved to save the land, if not its people, by creating the Soil Conservation Service in 1935.

EXPANDING RELIEF

If reform gained priority in the Second New Deal, relief remained critical. With millions still unemployed, Roosevelt pushed through Congress in 1935 the Emergency Relief Appropriation Act, authorizing $5 billion—at the time the largest single appropriation in American history—for emergency public employment. Roosevelt created the Works Progress Administration (WPA) under Hopkins, who set up work relief programs to assist the unemployed and boost the economy. Before its end in 1943, the WPA gave jobs to 9 million people (more than a fifth of the labor force) and spent nearly $12 billion. Three-fourths of its expenditures went on construction projects that could employ manual labor: the WPA built 125,000 schools, post offices, and hospitals; 8,000 parks; nearly 100,000 bridges; and enough roads and sewer systems to circle the earth 30 times. The WPA laid much of the basic infrastructure on which the nation still relies.

The WPA also developed work projects for unemployed writers, artists, musicians, and actors. The Federal Art Project hired artists to teach art in night schools, prepare exhibits at museums, and paint murals on post office walls. The Federal Theatre Project organized theatrical productions and drama companies that in four years played to 30 million Americans. The Federal Music Project hired musicians to collect and perform folk songs. These WPA programs allowed people to use their talents while surviving the depression, increased popular access to cultural performances, and established a precedent for federal support of the arts.

The National Youth Administration (NYA), another WPA agency, gave part-time jobs to students, enabling 2 million high school and college students to stay in school, learn skills, and do productive work.

MAP EXPLORATION

To explore an interactive version of this map, go to
http://www.prenhall.com/goldfield3/map25.1

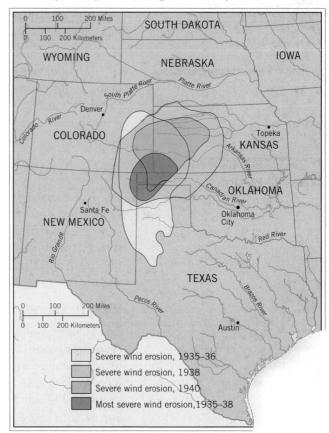

MAP 25–1   The Dust Bowl   Years of overcultivation, drought, and high winds created the Dust Bowl, which most severely affected the southern Great Plains. Federal relief and conservation programs provided assistance, but many residents fled the area, often migrating to California.

WHY WAS this drought particularly damaging to people in the region?

THE ROOSEVELT COALITION AND THE ELECTION OF 1936

The 1936 election gave Americans an opportunity to judge FDR and the New Deal. Conservatives alarmed at the expansion of government, business people angered by regulation and labor legislation, and wealthy Americans furious with tax reform decried the New Deal. But they were a minority. Even the presidential candidate they supported, Republican Governor Alf Landon of Kansas, endorsed much of the New Deal, criticizing merely the inefficiency and cost of some of its programs.

The programs and politicians of the New Deal had created an invincible coalition behind Roosevelt. Despite ambivalence about large-scale government intervention, the New Deal's agricultural programs reinforced the traditional Democratic allegiance of white southerners while attracting many western farmers. Labor legislation clinched the active support of the nation's workers. Middle-class voters, whose homes had been saved and whose hopes had been raised, also joined the Roosevelt coalition.

So did urban ethnic groups, who had benefited from welfare programs and appreciated the unprecedented recognition Roosevelt's administration gave them. FDR named the first Italian American to the federal judiciary, for example, and appointed five times as many Catholics and Jews to government positions as the three Republican presidents had during the 1920s. African Americans voted overwhelmingly Democratic for the first time. Women, too, were an important part of the Roosevelt coalition, and Eleanor often attracted their support as much as Franklin did.

This political realignment produced a landslide. Roosevelt polled 61 percent of the popular vote and the largest electoral vote margin ever recorded, 523 to 8. Roosevelt's political coalition reflected a mandate for himself and the New Deal; it would enable the Democrats to dominate national elections for three decades.

THE NEW DEAL AND AMERICAN LIFE

*T*he landslide of 1936 revealed the impact of the New Deal on Americans. Industrial workers mobilized to secure their rights, women and minorities gained increased, if still limited, opportunities to participate in American society, and southerners and westerners benefited from government programs they turned to their own advantage. Government programs changed daily life, and ordinary people often helped shape the new policies.

LABOR ON THE MARCH

The labor revival in the 1930s reflected both workers' determination and government support. Workers wanted to improve their wages and benefits as well as to gain union recognition and union contracts that would allow them to limit arbitrary managerial authority and achieve some control over the workplace.

The Second New Deal helped. By guaranteeing labor's rights to organize and bargain collectively, the Wagner Act sparked a wave of labor activism. But if the government ultimately protected union rights, the unions themselves had to form locals, recruit members, and demonstrate influence in the workplace.

At first, those tasks overwhelmed the American Federation of Labor (AFL). Its reliance on craft-based unions and reluctance to organize immigrant, black, and women workers left it unprepared for the rush of industrial workers seeking unionization. More progressive labor leaders saw that industry-wide unions were more appropriate for unskilled workers in mass-production industries. Forming the Committee for Industrial Organization (CIO) within the AFL, they campaigned to unionize workers in the steel, auto, and rubber industries, all notoriously hostile

---

WHERE TO LEARN MORE

Franklin D. Roosevelt Home and Presidential Library, Hyde Park, New York **www.fdrlibrary.marist.edu**

WHAT EXPLAINS labor's resurgence in the 1930s?

to unions. AFL leaders tried to make the CIO disband and then in 1937 expelled its unions. The militants reorganized as the separate **Congress of Industrial Organizations.** (In 1955, the two groups merged as the AFL-CIO.)

The split roused the AFL to increase its own organizing activities, but it was primarily the new CIO that put labor on the march. It inspired workers previously neglected by organized labor. The CIO's interracial union campaign in the Birmingham steel mills, said one organizer, was "like a second coming of Christ" for black workers, who welcomed the union as a chance for social recognition as well as economic opportunity. The CIO also employed new and aggressive tactics, particularly the sit-down strike, in which workers, rather than picketing outside the factory, simply sat inside the plant, thereby blocking both production and the use of strikebreakers.

The CIO won major victories despite bitter opposition from industry and its allies. The issue was not wages but labor's right to organize and bargain with management. Sit-down strikes paralyzed General Motors in 1937 after it refused to recognize the United Auto Workers. GM tried to force the strikers out of its Flint, Michigan, plants by turning off the heat, using police and tear gas, threatening strikers' families, and obtaining court orders to clear the plant by military force. But the governor refused to order National Guardsmen to attack, and the strikers held out, aided by the Women's Emergency Brigade. After six weeks, GM signed a contract with the UAW. Chrysler soon followed suit. Ford refused to recognize the union until 1941, often violently disrupting organizing efforts.

Steel companies also used violence against unionization. In the Memorial Day Massacre in Chicago in 1937, police guarding a plant of the Republic Steel Company fired on strikers and their families, killing ten people as they tried to flee. A Senate investigation found that Republic and other companies had hired private police to attack workers seeking to unionize, stockpiled weapons and tear gas, and corrupted officials. Federal court orders finally forced the companies to bargain collectively.

New Deal labor legislation, government investigations and court orders, and the federal refusal to use force against strikes helped the labor movement secure basic rights for American workers. Union membership leaped from under 3 million in 1932 to 9 million by 1939, and workers won higher wages, better working conditions, and more economic democracy.

WOMEN AND THE NEW DEAL

New Deal relief programs had a mixed impact on working women. Formal government policy required equal consideration for women and men, but local officials flouted this requirement. Women on relief were restricted to women's work—more than half worked on sewing projects, regardless of their skills—and were paid scarcely half what men received. WPA training programs also reinforced traditional ideas about women's work; black women, for example, were trained to be maids, dishwashers, and cooks. Although women constituted nearly one-fourth of the labor force, they obtained only 19 percent of the jobs created by the WPA, 12 percent of those created by the FERA, and 7 percent of those created by the CWA. The CCC excluded women altogether. Still, relief agencies provided crucial assistance to women during the depression.

Other New Deal programs also had mixed benefits for women. Despite demands by the League of Women Voters and the Women's Trade Union League for "equal pay for equal work and equal opportunity for equal ability regardless of sex," many NRA codes mandated lower wage scales for women than for men. But by raising minimum wages, the NRA brought relatively greater improvement to women, who were concentrated in the lowest-paid occupations, than to male

25–3
Mrs. Henry Weddington, Letter to President Roosevelt (1938)

Congress of Industrial Organizations An alliance of industrial unions that spurred the 1930s organizational drive among the mass-production industries.

WHERE TO LEARN MORE

Eleanor Roosevelt National Historic Site, Hyde Park, New York
www.nps.gov/elro

QUICK REVIEW

Impact of the New Deal on Women

- Despite their numbers in the workforce, women received proportionately fewer New Deal jobs than men.

- The increase in the minimum wage brought relatively greater improvements to workers in the lowest-paying jobs, most of whom were women.

- Women gained political influence under the New Deal.

---

workers. The Social Security Act did not cover domestic servants, waitresses, or women who worked in the home, but it did help mothers with dependent children.

Still more significant, the Social Security Act reflected and reinforced prevailing notions about proper roles for men and women. The system was based on the idea that men should be wage earners and women should stay at home as wives and mothers. Accordingly, if a woman worked outside the home and her husband was eligible for benefits, she would not receive her own retirement pension. And if a woman had no husband but had children, welfare authorities would remove her from work-relief jobs regardless of whether she wanted to continue to work, and would give her assistance from the Aid to Dependent Children (ADC) program, which was also created under the Social Security Act. These new programs, then, institutionalized a modern welfare system that segregated men and women in separate spheres and reaffirmed the then popular belief that the success of the family depended on that separation.

Women also gained political influence under the New Deal. Molly Dewson, the director of the Women's Division of the Democratic party, exercised considerable political power and helped to shape the party's campaigns. Around Dewson revolved a network of women, linked by friendships and experiences in the National Consumers' League, Women's Trade Union League, and other progressive reform organizations. Appointed to many positions in the Roosevelt administration, they helped develop and implement New Deal social legislation.

Eleanor Roosevelt was their leader. Described by a Washington reporter as "a cabinet member without portfolio," she roared across the social and political landscape of the 1930s, pushing for women's rights, demanding reforms, traveling across the country, writing newspaper columns and speaking on the radio, developing plans to help unemployed miners in West Virginia and abolish slums in Washington, and lobbying both Congress and her husband. Indeed, Eleanor Roosevelt had become not merely the most prominent first lady in history but a force in her own right and a symbol of the growing importance of women in public life.

MINORITIES AND THE NEW DEAL

Although Roosevelt deplored racial abuses, he never pushed for civil rights legislation, fearing to antagonize southern congressional Democrats whose support he needed. For similar reasons, many New Deal programs discriminated against African Americans. In addition, racist officials discriminated in allocating federal relief. Atlanta, for instance, provided average monthly relief checks of $32.66 to white people but only $19.29 to black people.

Nonetheless, disproportionately poor and unemployed African Americans did benefit from the New Deal's welfare and economic programs. W.E.B. DeBois affirmed that the New Deal sharpened their sense of the value of citizenship by making clear the "direct connection between politics and industry, between government and work, [and] between coting and wages." And key New Dealers campaigned against racial discrimination. Eleanor Roosevelt prodded FDR to appoint black officials, wrote articles supporting racial equality, and flouted segregationist laws. Harry Hopkins and Harold Ickes also promoted equal rights. Ickes, a former president of Chicago's NAACP chapter, insisted that African Americans receive PWA relief jobs in proportion to their share of the population and ended segregation in the Department of the Interior, prompting other cabinet secretaries to follow suit. As black votes in northern cities became important, pragmatic New Dealers also began to pay attention to black needs.

African Americans themselves pressed for reforms. Civil rights groups protested discriminatory policies, including the unequal wage scales in the NRA codes and the CCC's limited enrollment of black youth. African Americans demonstrated against racial discrimination in hiring and their exclusion from federally financed construction projects.

In response, FDR took more interest in black economic and social problems. He prohibited discrimination in the WPA in 1935, and the NYA adopted enlightened racial policies. Roosevelt also appointed black people to important positions, including the first black federal judge.

The New Deal improved economic and social conditions for many African Americans. Black illiteracy dropped because of federal education projects, and the number of black college students and graduates more than doubled, in part because the NYA provided student aid to black colleges. New Deal relief and public health programs reduced black infant mortality rates and raised life expectancy rates. Conditions for black people continued to lag behind those for white people, and discrimination persisted, but the black switch to the Roosevelt coalition reflected the New Deal's benefits.

Native Americans also benefited from the New Deal. The depression had imposed further misery on a group already suffering from poverty, wretched health conditions, and the nation's lowest educational level. Many New Deal programs had limited applicability to Indians, but the CCC appealed to their interests and skills. More than 80,000 Native Americans received training in agriculture, forestry, and animal husbandry, along with basic academic subjects. CCC projects, together with those undertaken by the PWA and the WPA, built schools, hospitals, roads, and irrigation systems on reservations.

New Deal officials also refocused government Indian policy. Appointed commissioner of Indian affairs in 1933, John Collier prohibited interference with Native American religious or cultural life, directed the Bureau of Indian Affairs to employ more Native Americans, and prevented Indian schools from suppressing native languages and traditions.

Collier also persuaded Congress to pass the Indian Reorganization Act of 1934, often called the Indians' New Deal. The act guaranteed religious freedom, reestablished tribal self-government, and halted the sale of tribal lands. It also provided funds to expand Indian landholdings, support Indian students, and establish tribal businesses. White missionaries and business interests attacked Collier's reforms as atheistic and communistic. And not all Native Americans supported Collier's reforms, asserting that he, too, stereotyped Indians and their culture, and labeling his efforts as "back-to-the-blanket" policies designed to make Native American cultures historical commodities (see American Views: "The Commissioner of the Bureau of Indian Affairs on the New Deal for Native Americans").

Hispanic Americans received less assistance from the New Deal. Relief programs aided many Hispanics in California and the Southwest but ignored those who were not citizens. Moreover, local administrators often discriminated against Hispanics, especially by providing higher relief payments to Anglos. Finally, by excluding agricultural workers, neither the Social Security Act nor the Wagner Act gave Mexican Americans much protection or hope. Farm workers remained largely unorganized, exploited, and at the mercy of agribusinesses.

THE NEW DEAL: NORTH, SOUTH, EAST, AND WEST

"We are going to make a country," President Roosevelt declared, "in which no one is left out." And with that statement, along with his belief that the federal government must take the lead in building a new "economic constitutional order," FDR ensured that his New Deal programs and policies fanned out throughout

With an appointment in the National Youth Administration, the educator Mary McLeod Bethune was the highest-ranking African-American woman in the Roosevelt administration. She advised FDR on all racial matters and envisioned "dozens of Negro women coming after me, filling positions of trust and strategic importance."

Courtesy of the Library of Congress

WHERE TO LEARN MORE

★ Bethune Museum and Archives National Historic Site, Washington, D.C.

The Great Depression made more desperate the plight of Mexican Americans; they faced discrimination and feared deportation. As migrant laborers, they also struggled with the forces of nature as they traveled from field to field in search of work. This Mexican migrant worker holds his new baby with his wife standing at door's edge. They lived in this shack on the edge of a frozen pea field in California.

National Archives and Records Administration

Tennessee Valley Authority (TVA) Federal regional planning agency established to promote conservation, produce electric power, and encourage economic development in seven southern states.

the nation, bolstering the stock market and banking in New York, constructing public housing for poor white and African-American families in most major cities, and building schools, roads, and bridges in every region of the United States.

The New Deal in the South.   The New Deal's agricultural program boosted farm prices and income more in the South than any other region. By controlling cotton production, it also promoted diversification; its subsidies financed mechanization. The resulting modernization helped replace an archaic sharecropping system with an emergent agribusiness. The rural poor were displaced, but the South's agricultural economy advanced.

The New Deal also improved southern cities. FERA and WPA built urban sewer systems, airports, bridges, roads, and harbor facilities. Whereas northern cities had already constructed such facilities themselves—and were still paying off the debts these had incurred—the federal government largely paid for such modernization in the South, giving its cities an economic advantage.

Federal grants were supposed to be awarded to states in proportion to their own expenditures, but while southern politicians welcomed New Deal funds, they refused to contribute their share of the costs. Nationally, the federal proportion of FERA expenditures was 62 percent; in the South, it was usually 90 percent and never lower than 73 percent.

Federal money enabled southern communities to balance their budgets, preach fiscal orthodoxy, and maintain traditional claims of limited government. Federal officials complained about the South's "parasitic" behavior, and even southerners acknowledged the hypocrisy of the region's invocation of state's rights. "We recognize state boundaries when called on to give," noted the *Houston Press*, "but forget them when Uncle Sam is doing the giving."

The federal government had a particularly powerful impact on the South with the **Tennessee Valley Authority (TVA),** launched in 1933 (see Map 25–2). Coordinating activities across seven states, the TVA built dams to control floods and generate hydroelectric power, produced fertilizer, fostered agricultural and forestry development, encouraged conservation, improved navigation, and modernized school and health systems. Its major drawback was environmental damage that only became apparent later. Over a vast area of the South, it provided electricity for the first time.

The New Deal further expanded access to electricity by establishing the Rural Electrification Administration (REA) in 1935. Private companies had refused to extend power lines into the countryside because it was not profitable consigning 90 percent of the nation's farms to drudgery and darkness. The REA revolutionized farm life by sponsoring rural nonprofit electric cooperatives. By 1941, 35 percent of American farms had electricity; by 1950, 78 percent.

The New Deal in the West.   The New Deal also changed the West. Westerners received the most federal money per capita in welfare, relief projects, and loans. Western farmers and cattle raisers were saved by federal payments, and even refugees from the Dust Bowl depended on relief assistance and medical care in federal camps.

The Bureau of Reclamation, established in 1902, emerged as one of the most important government agencies in the West. It built huge dams to control the western river systems, promote large-scale development, and prevent flooding, and it

AMERICAN VIEWS

THE COMMISSIONER OF THE BUREAU OF INDIAN AFFAIRS ON THE NEW DEAL FOR NATIVE AMERICANS.

John Collier, refomer and social worker, served as commissioner of the Bureau of Indian Affairs (BIA) from 1933 until 1945. During his tenure, he radically transformed the agency—long known to be corrupt and hostile to Native Americans—into an organization committed to the preservation of tribal cultures and the restoration of Indian lands. Like other New Dealers, Collier attempted to use the power of the federal government to protect those who had no political power or economic influence—in this case Native Americans.

Collier was extraordinarily successful in promoting the restoration of tribal rights and autonomy and helped ensure that future generations of Indians could reclaim their lands. Yet he was frustrated by Congress' unwillingness to fund the programs he believed necessary for a genuine New Deal for Native Americans. In his 1938 annual report, he calls for greater economic support, arguing that it would be a good investment for the nation. Most important, even as he acknowledges that real changes have occurred since 1933, he points out that there is still much to be done to achieve political autonomy and economic self-sufficiency for American Indians.

- How did Collier describe the treatment of Native Americans, and why did white Americans regard Indians as a "problem" to be eliminated?
- What were the new goals of the Bureau of Indian Affairs?
- How did Collier regard the role of land in Native American society? Why?
- What was the greatest challenge Collier saw for Native Americans in 1938?

For nearly 300 years white Americans, in our zeal to carve out a nation made to order, have dealt with the Indians on the erroneous, yet tragic, assumption that the Indians were a dying race—to be liquidated. We took away their best lands; broke treaties, promises; tossed them the most nearly worthless scraps of a continent that had once been wholly theirs. But we did not liquidate their spirit. The vital spark which kept them alive was hardy. So hardy, indeed, that we now face an astounding and heartening fact.

Actually, the Indians, on the evidence of federal census rolls of the past eight years, are increasing almost twice the rate of the population as a whole.

With this fact before us, our whole attitude toward the Indians has necessarily undergone a profound change. Dead is the centuries-old notion that the sooner we eliminate this doomed race, preferably humanely, the better. . . . No longer can we naively talk of or think of the "Indian problem."

We, therefore, define our Indian policy somewhat as follows: So productively to use the moneys appropriated by the Congress for Indians as to enable them, on good, adequate land of their own, to earn decent livelihoods and lead self-respecting, organized lives in harmony with their own aims and ideals, as an integral part of American life. This will not happen tomorrow; perhaps not in our lifetime; but with the revitalization of Indian hope due to the actions and attitudes of this government during the last few years, that aim is a probability, and a real one. . . .

So intimately is all of Indian life tied up with the land and its utilization that to think of Indians is to think of land. The two are inseparable. Upon the land and its intelligent use depends the main future of the American Indian.

The Indian feels toward his land, not a mere ownership but a devotion and veneration befitting that what is not only a home but a refuge. . . . Not only does the Indian's major source of livelihood derive from the land but his social and political organizations are rooted in soil.

Since 1933, the Indian Service has made a concerted effort—an effort which is as yet but a mere beginning—to help the Indian to build back his landholdings to a point where they will provide an adequate basis for a self-sustaining economy, a self-satisfying social organization.

Source: John Collier. *Annual Report of the Secretary of the Interior for the Fiscal Year Ended June 30, 1938.* From www.historymatters.gmu.edu.

745

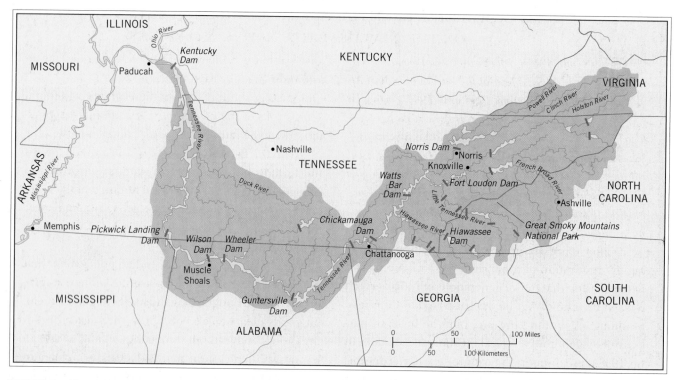

MAP 25–2   The Tennessee Valley Authority   By building dams and hydroelectric power plants, the TVA controlled flooding and soil erosion and generated electricity that did much to modernize a large region of the Upper South.

WHAT ECONOMIC and social impact did the Tennessee Valley Authority have on the Upper South?

produced cheap hydroelectric power and created reservoirs and canal systems to bring water to farms and cities. By furnishing capital and expertise, the government subsidized and stimulated western economic development, particularly the growth of agribusiness.

Westerners welcomed such assistance but rarely shared the federal goals of rational resource management. Instead, they often wanted to continue to exploit the land and resented federal supervision as colonial control. In practice, however, the government worked in partnership with the West's agribusinesses and timber and petroleum industries.

THE NEW DEAL AND PUBLIC ACTIVISM

Despite Hoover's fear that government responsibility would discourage local initiative, the 1930s witnessed an upsurge in activism. New Deal programs, in fact, often encouraged or empowered groups to shape public policy and social and economic behavior. Moreover, because the administration worried about centralization, some federal agencies fostered what New Dealers called "grassroots democracy." The AAA set up committees that ultimately included more than 100,000 people to implement agricultural policy and held referendums on crop controls; local advisory committees guided the various federal arts projects; federal management of the West's public grasslands mandated cooperation with associations of livestock raisers.

At times, local administration of national programs enabled groups to exploit federal policy for their own advantage. But federal programs often allowed previously unrepresented groups to contest traditionally dominant interests. Often seeing greater opportunities for participation and influence in federal programs than in city and state governments, community groups campaigned to expand federal authority. In short, depression conditions and New Deal programs actually increased citizen involvement in public affairs.

EBBING OF THE NEW DEAL

After his victory in 1936, Roosevelt committed himself to further reforms. "I see one-third of a nation ill-housed, ill-clad, ill-nourished," he declared in his second inaugural address. "The test of our progress is not whether we add more to the abundance of those who have much; it is whether we provide enough for those who have too little." But determined opponents, continuing economic problems, and the president's own misjudgments blocked his reforms and deadlocked the New Deal.

WHY DID the New Deal lose momentum after 1936?

CHALLENGING THE COURT

Roosevelt regarded the Supreme Court as his most dangerous opponent. During his first term, the Court had declared several important measures unconstitutional. FDR complained that the justices held "horse-and-buggy" ideas about government that prevented the president and Congress from responding to changes.

Emboldened by the 1936 landslide, Roosevelt decided to restructure the federal judiciary. In early 1937, he proposed legislation authorizing the president to name a new justice for each one serving past the age of 70. His goal was to appoint new justices more sympathetic to the New Deal.

His Court plan led to a divisive struggle. The proposal was perfectly legal: Congress had the authority, which it had used repeatedly, to change the number of justices on the Court. But Republicans and conservative Democrats attacked the plan as a scheme to "pack" the Court and subvert the separation of powers among the three branches of government and even many liberals expressed reservations about the plan or FDR's lack of candor in proposing it.

The Court itself undercut support for FDR's proposal by upholding the Social Security and Wagner acts and minimum-wage legislation. Moreover, the retirement of a conservative justice allowed Roosevelt to name a sympathetic successor. Congress rejected Roosevelt's plan.

Roosevelt's challenge to the Court hurt the New Deal. It worried the public, split the Democratic Party, and revived conservatives. Opponents promptly attacked other New Deal policies, from support for unions to progressive taxation. Henceforth, a conservative coalition of Republicans and southern Democrats in Congress blocked FDR's reforms.

A symbol of progress and prosperity in the 1920s, automobility became something very different during the Great Depression. People fleeing the Dust Bowl, such as this family in Oklahoma, packed up their few tattered possessions and headed for California in hopes of getting a "little bit of this good dirt" for their own.

MORE HARD TIMES

A sharp recession, beginning in August 1937, added to Roosevelt's problems. As the economy improved in 1936, Roosevelt decided to cut federal expenditures and balance the budget. But private investment and employment remained stagnant, and the economy plunged. A record decline in

More Oklahomans reach Calif. via the cotton fields of Ariz.

industrial production canceled the gains of the preceding two years, and unemployment leaped from 7 million to 11 million within a few months.

In 1938, Roosevelt reluctantly increased spending. His decision was based on the principles of the British economist John Maynard Keynes. As Marriner Eccles of the Federal Reserve Board explained, the federal government had to serve as the "compensatory agent" in the economy—it would use deficit spending to increase demand and production when private investment declined, and would raise taxes to pay its debt and cool the economy when business activity became excessive. New appropriations for the PWA and other government programs revived the faltering economy, but neither FDR nor Congress would spend what was necessary to end the depression. Only the vast expenditures for World War II would bring full recovery.

POLITICAL STALEMATE

The recession interrupted the momentum of the New Deal and strengthened its opponents. In late 1937, their leaders in Congress issued a "conservative manifesto" decrying New Deal fiscal, labor, and regulatory policies. Holding seniority in a Congress malapportioned in their favor, they blocked most of Roosevelt's reforms. None of his must legislation passed a special session of Congress in December. In 1938, Congress rejected tax reforms and reduced corporate taxes.

The few measures that passed were heavily amended. The Fair Labor Standards Act established maximum hours and minimum wages for workers but authorized so many exemptions that one New Dealer asked "whether anyone is subject to this bill."

To protect the New Deal, Roosevelt turned again to the public, with whom he remained immensely popular. In the 1938 Democratic primaries, he campaigned against the New Deal's conservative opponents. But FDR could not transfer his personal popularity to the political newcomers he supported. Roosevelt lost further political leverage when the Republicans gained 75 seats in the House, seven in the Senate, and 13 governorships.

With Roosevelt in the White House and his opponents controlling Congress, the New Deal ended in political stalemate.

GOOD NEIGHBORS AND HOSTILE FORCES

HOW DID Roosevelt respond to the rise of fascism in Europe?

Even before FDR's conservative opponents derailed the New Deal, the president felt their impact in the area of foreign policy. Isolationists in Congress counseled against any U.S. involvement in world affairs and appealed to the growing national disillusionment with America's participation in the Great War to support their position.

Responding to the spreading popular belief that World War I had been fought to protect the fortunes of financiers and munitions makers, Republican Senator Gerald Nye established a committee in 1934 to investigate the origins of U.S. involvement in what many Americans now termed the European War. For two years, the Nye Committee sensationally exposed the greed of big business and intimated that President Woodrow Wilson had gone to war to save profits for capitalists—and not democracy for the world. Jobless and homeless Americans reacted angrily to the committee's findings, and public sentiment against fighting another foreign war hardened. Moreover, Roosevelt himself believed that the gravity of the nation's economic depression warranted a primary focus on domestic recovery, and in the early years of his presidency, took few international initiatives.

The actions he did take related directly to salvaging America's desperate economy. As the depression worsened in 1933, American businesses searched for new markets throughout the world, and key business leaders informed FDR that they would welcome the opportunity to expand trade to the Soviet Union. Moscow was also eager to renew ties to the United States, and President Roosevelt extended formal recognition of the Soviet Union in November 1933.

Enhancing trade opportunities and rescuing the economy from the damage wrought by high tariffs figured prominently in Roosevelt's policies in the Western Hemisphere. In large measure, Roosevelt merely extended the Good Neighbor policy begun by his predecessor. Still, the Great Depression strained U.S.-Latin American relations, sending economic shock waves throughout Central and South America and, in several instances, helping propel to power ruthless dictators who ruled with iron fists and U.S. support. Moreover, although FDR continued the policy of military nonintervention, his displeasure with the 1933 election of a radical as president of Cuba led him to support a coup there that resulted in the coming to power of the infamous dictator Fulgencio Batista. The Batista era lasted until he was overthrown by Fidel Castro in 1959.

In 1936, FDR broke new ground by becoming the first U.S. president to sail to South America. He also worked to encourage trade by reducing tariffs. Between 1929 and 1933, the volume of trade worldwide had collapsed by 40 percent and American exports had plummeted by 60 percent. Secretary of State Cordell Hull finalized trade agreements with numerous Latin American nations that allowed "most favored nation" status and resulted in sharply increasing U.S. exports to its southern neighbors. Good neighbors were also good trading partners.

NEUTRALITY AND FASCISM

Outside the hemisphere, during his first term as president, Roosevelt generally followed the policy of avoiding involvement in Europe's political, economic, and social problems. But the aggressive actions of Adolf Hitler in Germany ultimately led Roosevelt to a different position, and in the latter part of the decade, he faced the task of educating the American public about the fascist danger that was spreading in Europe.

Hitler came to power in 1933, shortly before FDR entered the White House. As the leader of the National Socialist Workers Party, or Nazis, Hitler established a **fascist government**—a one-party dictatorship closely aligned with corporate interests, committed to a "biological world evolution," and determined to establish a new empire, the Third Reich. He vowed to eliminate Bolshevik radicalism and purify the German "race" through the elimination of those he deemed undesirable, especially targeting Jews, the group Hitler blamed for most, if not all, Germany's ills.

Others aided the spread of fascism. Italian leader Benito Mussolini, who had assumed power in 1922 and envisaged emulating the power and prestige of the Roman Empire, brutally attacked Ethiopia in 1935. The following year, a young fascist military officer, Francisco Franco, led an uprising in Spain, and with the assistance of Italy and Germany, successfully ousted the Spanish Republic and its loyalist supporters by 1939 to create an authoritarian government. Meanwhile, Hitler implemented his plan of conquest: he remilitarized the Rhineland in 1936, and in 1938 he annexed Austria.

The aggressive actions of Germany and Italy failed to eclipse American fears of becoming involved in another European war. Congress passed four Neutrality Acts designed to continue America's trade with its world partners but prohibit the president from taking sides in the mounting European crisis.

Appeasement and More Neutrality.   After annexing Austria, Hitler pushed again in 1938 when he demanded the Sudetenland from Czechoslovakia. Meeting

Fascist Government   A government subscribing to a philosophy of dictatorship that merges the interests of the state, armed forces, and big business.

in Munich in September 1938, the leaders of England and France abandoned their security obligations to the Czechs, yielding the Sudetenland to Hitler in exchange for a weak promise of no more annexations.

In America, too, the sentiment was for peace at all costs, and isolationism permeated the halls of Congress. Indeed, Hitler himself did not regard the United States as a threat to his expansionist plan. Hitler held FDR in low esteem and denounced America as a racially mixed nation of intellectual inferiors.

Isolationism compounded by anti-Semitism and by the divisions among leaders of the American Jewish community combined to ensure that the United States would not become a haven for Jews suffering under Nazi brutality. News of Nazi atrocities against Austrian Jews in 1938 shocked the American press, and Hitler's violent pogrom, known as *Kristallnacht* ("Night of the Broken Glass"), conducted against Jews throughout Germany in November 1938, added fresh proof of Nazi cruelty. Although the United States recalled its ambassador from Berlin to protest the pogrom, it did not alter its restrictive immigration-quota system to provide refuge for German Jews.

As Europe edged closer to war, the relationship between the United States and Japan, periodically tense in the twentieth century, became more strained. The United States regarded Japan's desires for empire as threatening but also needed Japan as a trading partner, especially in the economically depressed 1930s. Consequently, in September 1931, when Japan seized Manchuria, the United States did little more than denounce the action. Again in 1937, after Japanese troops attacked Chinese forces north of Beijing and outright war began between Japan and China, the United States merely condemned the action.

EDGING TOWARD INVOLVEMENT

After the Munich agreement, President Roosevelt moved away from domestic reform toward preparedness for war, fearful that conflict in Europe was unavoidable and determined to revise the neutrality laws. In his State of the Union address in January 1939, FDR explained that America's neutrality laws might "actually give aid to an aggressor and deny it to the victim." By the fall of that year, he had won support for eliminating the prohibition on arms sales and adding armaments to the list of cash-and-carry items—a revision that would enable the United States to provide important assistance to Britain and France in the winter of 1939–1940. Hitler's defiance of the Munich agreement, overrunning Prague, by March 1939, merely anticipated his next move toward Poland and also convinced the British and the French that war was imminent.

CONCLUSION

The Great Depression and the New Deal mark a major divide in American history. The depression cast doubt on the traditional practices, policies, and attitudes that underlay not only the nation's economy but also its social and political institutions and relationships. The New Deal brought only partial economic recovery. However, its economic policies, from banking and securities regulation to unemployment compensation, farm price supports, and minimum wages, created barriers against another depression. The gradual adoption of compensatory spending policies expanded the government's role in the economy. Responding to the failures of both private organizations and state and local governments, the federal government assumed the obligation to provide social welfare. "Better the occasional faults of a Government that lives in a spirit of charity," Roosevelt warned, "than the constant omission of a Government frozen in the ice of its own indifference."

Roosevelt expanded the role of the presidency and made the federal government, rather than state or local governments, the focus of public interest and expectations.

Roosevelt and the New Deal also revitalized the Democratic Party, drawing minorities, industrial workers, and previously uninvolved citizens into a coalition with white southerners that made the Democrats the dominant national party.

Political constraints explain some of the New Deal's failures. Conservative southern Democrats and northern Republicans limited its efforts to curtail racial discrimination or protect the rural and urban poor. But Roosevelt and other New Dealers were often constrained by their own vision, refusing to consider the massive deficit spending necessary to end the depression or not recognizing the need to end gender discrimination. But if the New Deal did not bring the revolution its conservative critics claimed, it did change American life.

By the end of the 1930s, FDR cautiously led the nation toward war—this time against an enemy far more threatening than the Great Depression. Ironically, only then would President Roosevelt end the depression that had ravaged the nation for nearly a decade.

SUMMARY

Hard Times in Hooverville The prosperity of the 1920s ended in a stock market crash that revealed the flaws in the economy. As the nation slid into a catastrophic depression, factories closed, employment and incomes tumbled, and millions lost their homes, hopes, and dignity. Some protested and took direct action; others looked to the government for relief. The stock market crash of 1929 marked the beginning of the Great Depression but did not cause it. Contributing factors were the uneven distribution of wealth and income; industries dominated by oligarchies; overproduction in agriculture and other industries; declining prices; government policies; and European debts.

Herbert Hoover and the Depression President Hoover took unprecedented steps to resolve the growing economic crises, but he believed that voluntary private relief was preferable to federal intervention. The scope of the depression overwhelmed anything that private individuals and agencies could manage; Hoover blundered by refusing to admit a more activist approach was needed. The Reconstruction Finance Corporation lent funds that could "trickle down" to the public. The treatment of the Bonus Army symbolized Hoover's unpopularity and set the stage for the election of Franklin D. Roosevelt.

Launching the New Deal In the midst of national anxiety, Franklin D. Roosevelt pushed forward an unprecedented program to resolve the crisis of a collapsing financial system, crippling unemployment, and agricultural and industrial breakdown and to promote reform. After initially addressing the banking crisis, the New Deal went on to establish relief agencies and promote economic recovery. The New Deal achieved successes and attracted support but it also had limitations and generated criticism that suggested the need for still greater innovations.

Consolidating the New Deal In 1935 Roosevelt undertook additional economic and social reforms. Labor's right to organize and bargain collectively was addressed, the path-breaking Social Security Act was passed, and the Works

Progress Administration was created. The administration also responded to the environmental crises that had turned the Great Plains into a dustbowl and driven the "Okies" to California. The 1936 election gave Americans an opportunity to judge the New Deal and Roosevelt. Political realignment resulted: Former Republican constituents voted Democratic and produced a landslide victory for the president.

The New Deal and American Life   The election of 1936 revealed the impact the New Deal had on Americans. Industrial workers mobilized to secure their rights; women and minorities gained increased, if still limited, opportunities to participate in American society; and Southerners and Westerners benefited from government programs like the TVA that they turned to their own advantage. Government programs changed daily life, and ordinary people often helped shape the new policies.

Ebbing of the New Deal   After his 1936 election, Roosevelt committed himself to further reforms, but his misjudgment blocked some efforts and deadlocked others. Regarding the Supreme Court as an adversary, Roosevelt attempted to restructure the federal judiciary; his attempt to "pack" the court hurt the New Deal. A 1937 recession caused by the New Deal's lack of aggressiveness caused the administration to adopt Keynesian economic theories and have the government use deficient spending to increase demand and production.

Good Neighbors and Hostile Forces   While isolationists in Congress counseled against involvement in foreign affairs, fascism was spreading in Europe and Asia. In his first term Roosevelt followed a policy of neutrality; after the Munich crisis, Hitler's intentions toward the world and Germany's Jewish citizens had become more defined and threatening. America's relationship with Japan continued to deteriorate; by 1939, the "epidemic of world lawlessness" was edging the United States toward involvement.

IMAGE KEY

for pages 722–723

a. The National Recovery Agency seal with an eagle holding a cog in one talon and lightning bolts in the other over the slogan "We Do Our Part."

b. Hungry men stand in a bread line in New York City.

c. A Works Progress Administration poster, depicting a farmer and a miner shaking hands.

d. Anxious citizens crowd along Wall Street sidewalks while automobiles edge down the street on Black Tuesday October 29, 1929.

e. The Civilian Conservation Corps Emblem.

f. Isaac Soyer, "Employment Agency." Oil on canvas, 34 1/2" × 45".

g. Mary McLeod Bethune.

h. A photo symbolizing the Great Depression for many people.

i. Mexican farm workers, in San Antonio, TX.

j. FDR signs the Social Security Act.

k. An old fashioned radio in a wooden cabinet.

l. Ben Shahn, "Years of Dust," 1936. Poster for the Resettlement Administration.

REVIEW QUESTIONS

1. What were the international consequences of the stock market crash in 1929? How did world leaders respond to the global depression? With what results?

2. Why did President Hoover's emphasis on voluntarism fail to resolve the problems of the Great Depression in the United States?

3. Describe the relief programs of the New Deal. What were they designed to accomplish? What were their achievements and their limitations?

4. What were the major criticisms of the early New Deal? How accurate were those charges?

5. How did the policies of the New Deal shape the constituency and the prospects of the Democratic Party in the 1930s?

6. Describe the conflict between management and labor in the 1930s. What were the major issues and motivations? How did the two sides differ in resources and tactics, and how and why did these factors change over time?

7. How did the role of the federal government change in the 1930s? What factors were responsible for the changes?

KEY TERMS

Bonus Army   (p. 733)
Congress of Industrial Organizations   (p. 741)
Fascist government   (p. 749)
Federal Deposit Insurance Corporation (FDIC)   (p. 734)

Fireside chat   (p. 734)
Great Depression   (p. 726)
Hoovervilles   (p. 728)
New Deal   (p. 725)

Securities and Exchange Commission (SEC)   (p. 734)
Tennessee Valley Authority (TVA)   (p. 744)

WHERE TO LEARN MORE

Center for New Deal Studies, Roosevelt University, Chicago, Illinois. The center contains political memorabilia, photographs, papers, and taped interviews dealing with Franklin D. Roosevelt and the New Deal; it also sponsors an annual lecture series about the Roosevelt legacy.

Herbert Hoover National Historic Site, West Branch, Iowa. This 186-acre site contains the birthplace cottage and grave of Herbert Hoover as well as his presidential library and museum, which contains a reconstruction of Hoover's White House office. **www.nps.gov/heho**; **www.hoover.archives.gov**

Labor Museum and Learning Center of Michigan, Flint, Michigan. Exhibits trace the history of the labor movement, including the dramatic "Sit-Down Strike" of 1936–1937.

Franklin D. Roosevelt Home and Presidential Library, Hyde Park, New York. The Roosevelt home, furnished with family heirlooms, and the spacious grounds, where FDR is buried, personalize the president and provide insights into his career. The nearby library has displays and exhibitions about Roosevelt's presidency, and the Eleanor Roosevelt Wing is dedicated to her career. **www.fdrlibrary.marist.edu**

Eleanor Roosevelt National Historic Site, Hyde Park, New York. These two cottages, where Eleanor Roosevelt worked and, after 1945, lived, contain her furniture and memorabilia. Visitors can also watch a film biography of ER and tour the grounds of this retreat where she entertained personal friends and world leaders. **www.nps.gov/elro**

Civilian Conservation Corps Interpretive Center, Whidbey Island, Washington. This stone and wood structure, built as a CCC project, now houses exhibits and artifacts illustrating the history of the CCC.

Bethune Museum and Archives National Historic Site, Washington, D.C. This four-story townhouse was the home of Mary McLeod Bethune, a friend of Eleanor Roosevelt and the director of the New Deal's Division of Negro Affairs, and the headquarters of the National Council of Negro Women, which Bethune founded in 1935. Exhibits feature the contributions of black activist women and activities of the civil rights movement.

 U.S. History Documents CD-ROM
For primary sources related to this chapter, refer to the document CD-ROM.

 www.prenhall.com/goldfield
For study resources related to this chapter, visit the *Companion Website*™.

26

World War II 1939–1945

"above and beyond the call of duty"

DORIE MILLER
Received the Navy Cross
at Pearl Harbor, May 7...

CHAPTER HIGHLIGHTS

The Dilemmas of Neutrality Even as German aggression escalated in the late 1930s, most Americans wanted to stay out of war in Europe. Roosevelt's challenge was to aid Britain and the Soviet Union and to prepare the country for war without provoking widespread resistance. The Japanese attack on Pearl Harbor brought the United States into World War II.

Holding the Line The Allies planned to defeat Germany first and Japan second. By the end of 1942, the tide of battle was turning in favor of the Allies. In mid-1943 the Allies could begin to plan for victory.

Mobilizing for Victory World War II brought on unprecedented expansion of the federal government. The war penetrated every facet of everyday life. Women and minorities changed the composition of the industrial workforce. Japanese Americans were interned in camps throughout the West. Women and minorities faced discrimination in the armed forces.

War and Peace Plans for ending the war were drawn up at Casablanca and Tehran. Allied operations in North Africa, Italy, and France, along with Soviet advances on the Eastern Front, made German defeat a certainty. As the Allies advanced, the nature and extent of the Holocaust became clear. The American strategy of island hopping pushed back Japanese forces in the Pacific. American use of the atomic bomb in 1945 ended the war with Japan. The Yalta and Potsdam conferences determined the fate of postwar Europe.

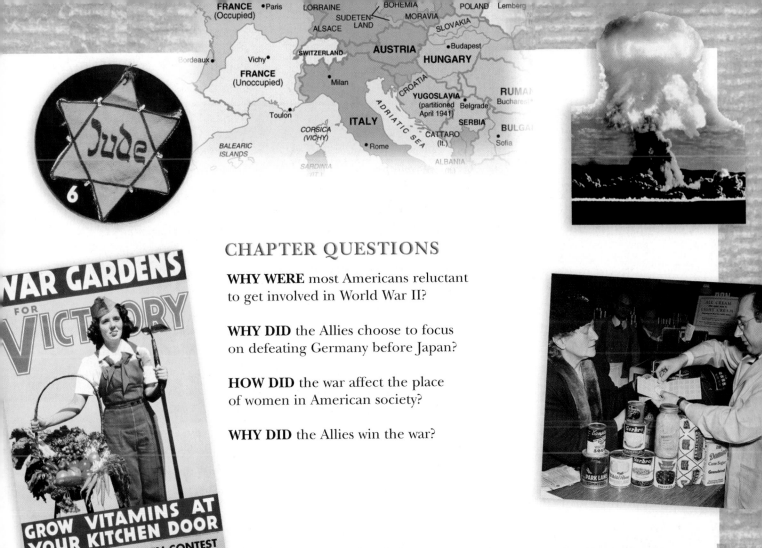

CHAPTER QUESTIONS

WHY WERE most Americans reluctant to get involved in World War II?

WHY DID the Allies choose to focus on defeating Germany before Japan?

HOW DID the war affect the place of women in American society?

WHY DID the Allies win the war?

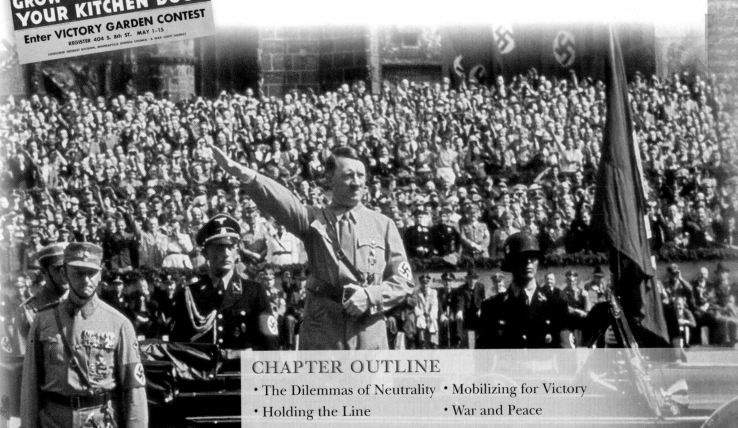

CHAPTER OUTLINE

- The Dilemmas of Neutrality
- Holding the Line
- Mobilizing for Victory
- War and Peace

IMAGE KEY
for pages 754–755 is on page 784.

December, 1942

> *The scene [under the stadium] at The University of Chicago would have been confusing to an outsider, if he could have eluded the security guards and gained admittance. He would have seen only what appeared to be a crude pile of black bricks and wooden timbers. . . .*
>
> *Finally, the day came when we were ready to run the experiment. We gathered on a balcony about 10 feet above the floor of the large room in which the structure had been erected. Beneath us was a young scientist, George Weil, whose duty it was to handle the last control rod that was holding the reaction in check. . . .*
>
> *Finally, it was time to remove the control rods. Slowly, Weil started to withdraw the main control rod. On the balcony, we watched the indicators which measured the neutron count and told us how rapidly the disintegration of the uranium atoms under their neutron bombardment was proceeding.*
>
> *At 11:35 A.M., the counters were clicking rapidly. Then, with a loud clap, the automatic control rods slammed home. The safety point had been set too low.*
>
> *It seemed a good time to eat lunch. During lunch everyone was thinking about the experiment but nobody talked much about it.*
>
> *At 2:30, Weil pulled out the control rod in a series of measured adjustments. Shortly after, the intensity shown by the indicators began to rise at a slow but ever-increasing rate. At this moment we knew that the self-sustaining [nuclear] reaction was under way.*
>
> *The event was not spectacular, no fuses burned, no lights flashed. But to us it meant that release of atomic energy on a large scale would be only a matter of time.*

Enrico Fermi, in *The First Reactor* (Washington: U.S. Department of Energy, 1982).

ENRICO FERMI was describing the first controlled nuclear chain reaction—the critical experiment from which atomic weapons and atomic power would soon develop. Fermi himself had emigrated to escape the growing political repression of Fascist Italy. After the United States entered World War II, Fermi, other atomic scientists, and their families moved to Los Alamos, a science city that the government built hurriedly on a high plateau in northern New Mexico, where isolation was supposed to ensure secrecy and help the United States win the race with Nazi Germany to develop atomic weapons.

The Fermis were not the only family to give Los Alamos a multinational flavor. British and Canadians worked alongside U.S. scientists. So did refugees from Europe, their presence making Los Alamos the most distinguished assemblage of physicists in the world. Niels Bohr had fled Denmark to escape the Nazis. Edward Teller was a Hungarian who had studied in Germany. Hans Bethe had left Germany, and Stanislaus Ulam was the only member of his family to survive the Nazi conquest of Poland. Absent were scientists from the Soviet Union, which was bearing the worst of the fighting against Germany but was carefully excluded from the secret of the atomic bomb.

The scientists racing to perfect the atomic bomb knew that victory was far from certain. Germany and Japan had piled one conquest on another since the late 1930s, and they continued to seize new territories in 1942. Allied defeat in a few key battles could have resulted in a standoff or an Axis victory. A new weapon might end the war more quickly or make the difference between victory and defeat.

The war's domestic impacts were as profound as its international consequences. The race to build an atomic bomb was only one part of a vast effort to harness the resources of the United States to the war effort. The war highlighted racial inequalities, gave women new opportunities, and fostered growth in the South and West. By devastating the nation's commercial rivals, compelling workers to retrain and factories to modernize, World War II left the United States dominant in the world economy. It also increased the size and scope of the federal government and built an alliance among the armed forces, big business, and science that helped shape postwar America.

The Dilemmas of Neutrality

Americans in the 1930s wanted no part of another overseas war. Despite two years of German victories and a decade of Japanese aggression against China, opinion polls in the fall of 1941 showed that a majority of voters still hoped to avoid war. President Roosevelt's challenge was to lead the United States toward rearmament and support for Great Britain and China without alarming a reluctant public.

WHY WERE most Americans reluctant to get involved in World War II?

The Roots of War

The roots of World War II can be found in the after effects of World War I. The peace settlement created a set of small new nations in eastern Europe that were vulnerable to aggression by their much larger neighbors, Germany and the Soviet Union (more formally, the Union of Soviet Socialist Republics, or USSR). Italy and Japan thought that the Treaty of Versailles had not recognized their stature as world powers. Many Germans were convinced that Germany had been betrayed rather than defeated in 1918. In the 1930s, economic crisis undermined an already shaky political order. Unemployment rose in every country, and the level of international trade dropped by two-thirds. Economic hardship and political instability fueled the rise of right-wing dictatorships that offered territorial expansion by military conquest as the way to redress old rivalries, dominate trade, and gain access to raw materials.

Japanese nationalists believed that the United States, Britain, and France had treated Japan unfairly after World War I despite its participation against Germany. They believed that Japan should expel the French, British, Dutch, and Americans from Asia and create a **Greater East Asia Co-Prosperity Sphere,** in which Japan gave the orders and other Asian peoples complied. Seizing the Chinese province of Manchuria to expand an East Asian empire that already included Korea and Taiwan emboldened Japan's military in 1931. A full-scale invasion of China followed in 1937. Japan took many of the key cities and killed tens of thousands of civilians in the "rape of Nanking," but failed to dislodge the government of Jiang Jieshi (Chiang Kai-shek) and settled into a war of attrition.

Greater East Asia Co-Prosperity Sphere Japanese nationalists believed that Japan should expel the French, British, Dutch, and Americans from Asia and create this sphere in which Japan would give the orders and other Asian peoples would comply.

Chronology

1931	Japan invades Manchuria.
1933	Hitler takes power in Germany.
1935	Congress passes first of three neutrality acts.
	Italy invades Ethiopia.
1936	Germany and Italy form the Rome-Berlin Axis.
	Civil war erupts in Spain.
1937	Japan invades China.
1938	Germany absorbs Austria.
	Munich agreement between Germany, Britain, and France.
1939	Germany and the Soviet Union sign a nonagression pact.
	Germany absorbs Czechoslovakia.
	Germany invades Poland; Great Britain and France declare war on Germany.
1940	Germany conquers Denmark, Norway, Belgium, the Netherlands, and France.
	Japan, Germany, and Italy sign the Tripartite Pact.
	Germany bombs England in the Battle of Britain.
	The United States begins to draft men into the armed forces.
	Franklin Roosevelt wins an unprecedented third term.
1941	The United States begins a lend-lease program to make military equipment available to Great Britain and later the Soviet Union.
	The Fair Employment Practices Committee is established.
	Germany invades the Soviet Union.
	Roosevelt and Churchill issue the Atlantic Charter.
	Japan attacks U.S. military bases in Hawaii.
1942	American forces in the Philippines surrender to Japan.
	President Roosevelt authorizes the removal and internment of Japanese Americans living in four western states.

	Naval battles in the Coral Sea and off the island of Midway blunt Japanese expansion. U.S. forces land in North Africa.
	Soviet forces encircle a German army Stalingrad.
	The first sustained and controlled nuclear chain reaction takes place at the University of Chicago.
1943	U.S. and British forces invade Italy, which makes terms with the Allies.
	Race conflict erupts in riots in Detroit, New York, and Los Angeles.
	The landing of Marines on Tarawa initiates the island-hopping strategy.
	U.S. war production peaks.
	Roosevelt, Churchill, and Stalin confer at Tehran.
1944	Allied forces land in Normandy.
	The U.S. Navy destroys Japanese sea power in the battles of the Philippine Sea and Leyte Gulf.
	The Battle of the Bulge is the last tactical setback for the Allies.
1945	Roosevelt, Stalin, and Churchill meet at Yalta to plan the postwar world.
	The United States takes the Pacific islands of Iwo Jima and Okinawa.
	Franklin Roosevelt dies; Harry S Truman becomes president.
	Germany surrenders to the United States, Great Britain, and the Soviet Union.
	The United Nations is organized at an international meeting in San Francisco.
	Allies meet at Potsdam Conference.
	Japan surrenders after the detonation of atomic bombs over Hiroshima and Nagasaki.

Italian aggression embroiled Africa and the Mediterranean. The Fascist dictator Benito Mussolini had sent arms and troops to aid General Francisco Franco's right-wing rebels in Spain. The three-year civil war, which ended with Franco's victory in 1939, became a bloody testing ground for new German military tactics and German and Italian ambitions against democratic Europe.

In Germany, Adolf Hitler mixed the desire to reassert national pride and power after the defeat of World War I with an ideology of racial hatred. Proclaiming the start of a thousand-year Reich ("empire"), he combined the historic German interest in eastward expansion with a long tradition of racialist thought about German superiority. In the Nazi scheme, Germany and other northern European nations ranked above the Slavs of eastern Europe, who were to be pushed aside to provide more territory for a growing German population.

Special targets of Nazi hatred were the Jews, who were prominent in German business and professional life but soon faced persecution aimed at driving them from the country. In l935, the Nuremberg Laws denied civil rights to Jews and the campaign against them intensified. The Nazi government began expropriating Jewish property and excluded Jews from most employment.

Germany and Italy formed the Rome-Berlin Axis in October 1936 and the Tripartite Pact with Japan in 1940, leading to the term **Axis Powers** to describe the aggressor nations. Political dissidents in all three nations were suppressed, but Hitler's Germany was the most repressive. The Nazi concentration camp began as a device for political terrorism. Hitler decreed that opponents should disappear into "night and fog." Soon the systematic discrimination and concentration camps would evolve into massive forced-labor camps and then into hellish extermination camps.

HITLER'S WAR IN EUROPE

After annexing Austria through a coup and seizing and slicing up Czechoslovakia, Germany demonstrated the worthlessness of the Munich agreement by invading Poland on September 1, 1939. Britain and France, Poland's allies, declared war on Germany but could not stop the German war machine. Western journalists covering the three-week conquest of Poland coined the term *Blitzkrieg,* or "lightning war," to describe the German tactics. Armored divisions with tanks and motorized infantry supported by air power punched holes in defensive positions and raced forward 30 or 40 miles per day.

Hitler's greatest advantage was the ability to attack when and where he chose. From September 1939 to October 1941, Germany marched from victory to victory (see Map 26–1). Striking from a central position against scattered enemies, Hitler chose the targets and timing of each new front. Hitler also launched the Battle of Britain in the second half of l940. German planes bombarded Britain mercilessly, in an unsuccessful effort to pound the British into submission.

Hitler gambled once too often in June 1941. Having failed to knock Britain out of the war, he invaded the Soviet Union. The attack caught the Red Army off guard. From June until December 1941, more than 4 million Germans, Italians, Hungarians, and Romanians pushed through Belarus, Ukraine, and western Russia. They encircled and captured entire Soviet armies. Before desperate Soviet counterattacks and a bitter winter stopped the German columns, they had reached the outskirts of Moscow and expected to finish the job in the spring.

TRYING TO KEEP OUT

"We Must Keep Out!" shouted the September 7, 1939, *Chicago Daily News.* As war erupted in Europe, most Americans wanted to avoid foreign quarrels. For more than two years after the invasion of Poland, strong sentiment against intervention shaped public debate and limited President Roosevelt's ability to help Britain and its allies.

Much of the emotional appeal of neutrality came from disillusionment with the American crusade in World War I, which had failed to make the world safe for democracy. Many opponents of intervention wanted the United States to protect its traditional spheres of interest in Latin America and the Pacific. Like George Washington, whose Farewell Address they quoted, they wanted to avoid becoming entangled in the perpetual quarrels of the European nations.

Axis Powers   The opponents of the United States and its allies in World War II.

Blitzkrieg   German war tactic in World War II ("lightning war") involving the concentration of air and armored firepower to punch and exploit holes in opposing defensive lines.

MAP EXPLORATION

To explore an interactive version of this map, go to **http://www.prenhall.com/goldfield3/map26.1**

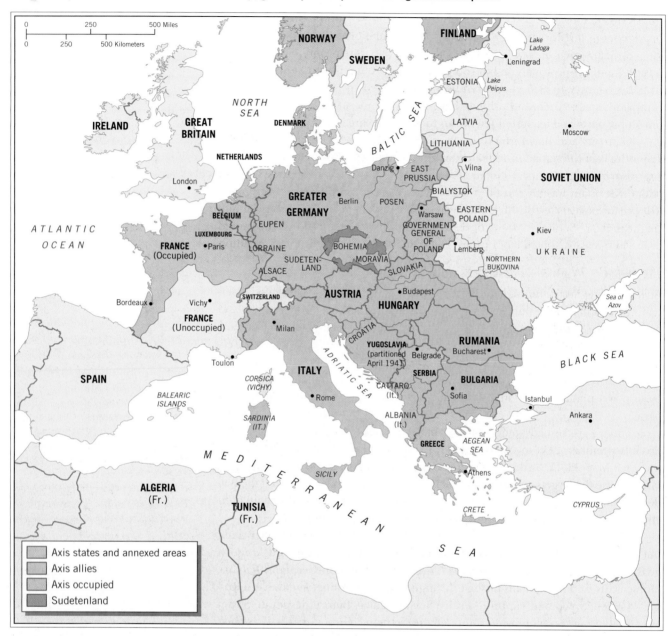

MAP 26–1 Axis Europe, 1941, on the Eve of Hitler's Invasion of the Soviet Union After almost two years of war, the Axis powers controlled most of Europe, from the Atlantic Ocean to the Soviet border through annexation, military conquest, and alliances. Failure to force Britain to make peace caused Hitler to look eastward in 1941 to attempt the conquest of the Soviet Union.

HOW WAS Germany's central location in Europe both a strength and a weakness?

Congressional hearings by the Nye committee on munitions manufacturers and financiers had strengthened antiwar leanings. Between 1935 and 1937, Congress had passed five neutrality acts, which forbade arms sales and limited economic relations with nations at war. Noninterventionists spanned the political spectrum from left-leaning labor unions to conservative business tycoons like Henry Ford. Any move to intervene in Europe had to take these different views into account, meaning that Roosevelt had to move slowly and carefully in his effort to align the United States on the side of Britain.

EDGING TOWARD INTERVENTION

Because 85 percent of the American people agreed that the nation should fight only if it was directly attacked, Roosevelt had to chip away at neutrality, educating, arguing, and taking one step at a time. The first step came in October 1939. A month-long congressional debate inspired millions of letters and telegrams in favor of keeping the arms embargo against warring nations. Nevertheless, the lawmakers reluctantly allowed arms sales to belligerent nations on a "cash-and-carry" basis, to avoid expanding European debts. In control of the Atlantic, France and Britain were the only expected customers.

Isolationism and anti-Semitism help to explain why the United States accepted only a few thousand Jewish refugees. In 1939, officials turned the passenger ship *St. Louis* away from Miami and forced its 950 German Jewish refugees back to Europe. FDR made small gestures, such as allowing 15,000 German and Austrian refugees, including many scientists and artists, to remain in the United States on visitor permits, but the public supported restrictions on immigration. The consequences of these restrictions would prove tragic later in the war, as the Nazis began systematic genocide of European Jews.

The Collapse of France and U.S. Rearmament. Despite the efforts of noninterventionists, in 1940 the United States edged closed to involvement in the war. The sudden defeat of France, which had survived four years of German attacks in World War I, made the new war seem far more serious. In the summer of 1940, Congress voted to expand the army to 2 million men, build 19,000 new warplanes, and add 150 ships to the navy. Lawmakers approved the nation's first peacetime draft in September, requiring 16.5 million men between the ages of 21 and 35 to register for military service on October 16.

In the same month, the United States concluded a destroyer deal with Britain. The British were desperate for small, maneuverable warships to guard imports of food and war materials against German submarines. The Americans had long wanted additional air and naval bases to guard the approaches to North America. Roosevelt met both needs by trading 50 old destroyers for the use of bases on British territories in the Caribbean, Bermuda, and Newfoundland.

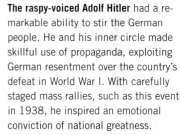

25.2
Charles Lindbergh, Radio Address (1941)

25.3
Franklin Delano Roosevelt, Annual Message to Congress (1941)

The raspy-voiced Adolf Hitler had a remarkable ability to stir the German people. He and his inner circle made skillful use of propaganda, exploiting German resentment over the country's defeat in World War I. With carefully staged mass rallies, such as this event in 1938, he inspired an emotional conviction of national greatness.

Bildrchiv Preubisher Kulterbesitz, Berlin

The Election of 1940.   In the presidential election of 1940 the big campaign issue was whether FDR's unprecedented try for a third term represented arrogance or a legitimate concern for continuity in a time of peril. The election was tighter than in 1932 or 1936, but Roosevelt defeated Republican Wendell Wilkie and received 55 percent of the vote. The president pledged that no Americans would fight in a foreign war. But if the United States were attacked, he said privately, the war would no longer be "foreign."

THE BRINK OF WAR

After the election, FDR and his advisers edged the United States toward stronger support of Britain and put pressure on Japan. In January 1941, Roosevelt proposed the lend-lease program, which allowed Britain to "borrow" military equipment for the duration of the war. Roosevelt compared the program to lending a garden hose to a neighbor whose house had caught fire.

The **Lend-Lease Act** triggered intense political debate. The Committee to Defend America by Aiding the Allies argued the administration's position. In opposition, the strongly isolationist America First Committee claimed that lend-lease would allow the president to declare anything a "defense article." Congress finally passed the measure in March 1941, authorizing the president to lease, lend, or otherwise dispose of arms and other equipment to any country whose defense was considered vital to the security of the United States.

FDR soon began an undeclared war in the North Atlantic, instructing the navy to report sightings of German submarines to the British. In September, the U.S. destroyer *Greer* clashed with a German submarine. Portraying the incident as German aggression, Roosevelt proclaimed a "shoot on sight" policy for German subs and ordered American ships to escort British convoys to within 400 miles of Britain. In reply, German submarines torpedoed the destroyer *Kearny* on October 17 and sank the destroyer *Reuben James,* with the loss of more than 100 lives, on October 30. The United States was now approaching outright naval war with Germany.

The Atlantic Charter.   With U.S. ships on a war footing in the North Atlantic, Roosevelt and the British prime minister, Winston Churchill, met secretly off Newfoundland in August 1941 to map out military strategy and postwar goals. They agreed that the defeat of Germany was their first priority, and Japan was secondary. Their joint proclamation, known as the **Atlantic Charter,** provided a political umbrella for American involvement in the war.

Roosevelt's intent in the North Atlantic remains uncertain. Some historians think that he hoped the United States could support Britain short of war. Others believe that he accepted the inevitability of war but hesitated to outpace public opinion. In this second interpretation, FDR wanted to eliminate Hitler without going to war if possible, with war if necessary. "I am waiting to be pushed into the situation," he told his secretary of the treasury.

Events in the Pacific.   The final shove came in the Pacific rather than the Atlantic. In 1940, as part of its rearmament program, the United States decided to build a "two-ocean navy." This decision antagonized Japan, prodding it toward a war that most U.S. leaders hoped to postpone or avoid. Through massive investment and national sacrifice, Japan had achieved roughly 70 percent of U.S. naval strength by late 1941. However, America's buildup promised to reduce the ratio to only 30 percent by 1944. Furthermore, the United States was restricting Japan's vital imports of steel, iron ore, and aluminum in an effort to curb its military ag-

---

QUICK REVIEW

Undeclared War

- March 1941: Lend-lease program approved by Congress.
- FDR ordered Navy to offer support to Britain.
- August 1941: Atlantic Charter lays out British and American war aims.

Lend-Lease Act   Program begun in 1941 through which the U.S. transferred military equipment to Britain and other World War II allies.

Atlantic Charter   Statement of common principles and war aims developed by President Franklin Roosevelt and British Prime Minister Winston Churchill at a meeting in August 1941.

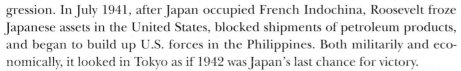

gression. In July 1941, after Japan occupied French Indochina, Roosevelt froze Japanese assets in the United States, blocked shipments of petroleum products, and began to build up U.S. forces in the Philippines. Both militarily and economically, it looked in Tokyo as if 1942 was Japan's last chance for victory.

Japanese war planners never seriously considered an invasion of the United States or expected a decisive victory. They hoped that attacks on American Pacific bases would shock the United States into letting Japan have its way in Asia or at least win time to create impenetrable defenses in the central Pacific.

DECEMBER 7, 1941

It seems likely that Roosevelt wanted to restrain the Japanese with bluff and intimidation, so that the United States could focus on defeating Germany. American moves were intended to be aggressive but measured in the Atlantic, firm but defensive in the Pacific. After July, however, Washington expected a confrontation with Japan over the oil fields and rubber plantations of Southeast Asia. Because the United States had cracked the Japanese codes, it knew by November that Japanese military action was imminent but expected the blow to come in Southeast Asia.

Instead, the Japanese navy launched a surprise attack on American bases in Hawaii. Before dawn on December 7, 1941, six Japanese aircraft carriers launched 351 planes in two bombing strikes against Pearl Harbor. When the smoke cleared, Americans counted their losses: eight battleships, eleven other warships, and nearly all military aircraft damaged or destroyed, and 2,403 people killed. They could also count their good fortune. Dockyards, drydocks, and oil storage tanks remained intact because the Japanese admiral had refused to order a third attack. And the American aircraft carriers, at sea on patrol, were unharmed.

Speaking to Congress the following day, Roosevelt proclaimed December 7, 1941, "a date which will live in infamy." He asked for and got a declaration of war against Japan. Hitler and Mussolini declared war on the United States on December 11, following their obligation under the Tripartite Pact. On January 1, 1942, the United States, Britain, the Soviet Union, and 23 other nations subscribed to the principles of the Atlantic Charter and pledged not to negotiate a separate peace.

HOLDING THE LINE

When Japan was considering war with the United States and Great Britain in 1940, Admiral Isoroku Yamamoto, the commander of Japan's Combined Fleet, weighed the chances of victory: "If I am told to fight regardless of the consequences, I shall run wild for the first six months or a year, but I have utterly no confidence for the second or third year." The admiral was right. As it turned out, Japan's conquests reached their limit after six months, but in early 1942, this was far from clear. At the same time, in Europe, Allied fortunes went from bad to worse. Decisive turning points did not come until November 1942, a year after the United States entered the war, and not until the middle of 1943 could the **Allies**—the United States, Britain, the Soviet Union, China, and other nations at war with Germany, Japan, and Italy—begin with confidence to plan for victory.

STOPPING GERMANY

In December 1941, the United States plunged into a truly global war that was being fought on six distinct fronts (see Map 26–2). In North Africa, the British were battling Italian and German armies that were trying to seize the Suez Canal, a

WHY DID the Allies choose to focus on defeating Germany before Japan?

Allies In World War I, these were Britain, France, Russia, and other belligerent nations (but not the United States, which insisted upon being merely an associated nation.) fighting against the **Central Powers** In World War II, the Allies fighting the **Axis Powers** included the United States as well as the Soviet Union, Great Britain, France, China, and other nations.

MAP EXPLORATION

To explore an interactive version of this map, go to **http://www.prenhall.com/goldfield3/map26.2**

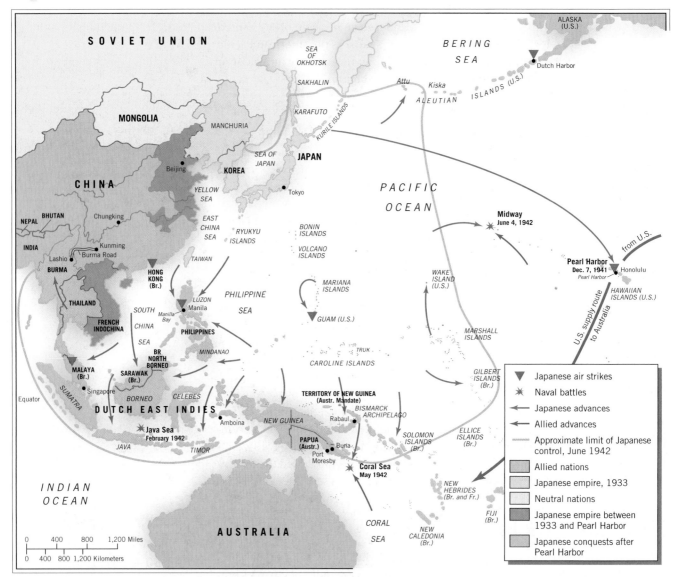

MAP 26–2   World War II in the Pacific, from Pearl Harbor to Midway   The first six months after the Japanese attack on Pearl Harbor brought a string of Japanese victories and conquests in the Pacific, the islands southeast of Asia, and the British colonies of Malaya and Burma. Japan's advance was halted by a standoff battle in the Coral Sea, a decisive U.S. naval victory at Midway, and the length and vulnerability of Japanese supply lines to the most distant conquests.

HOW WAS Japan able to mount a series of victories in the Pacific after their attack?

critical transportation link to Asia. Along the 1,000-mile **Eastern Front,** Soviet armies held defensive positions as German forces, pushing deeply into Soviet territory, reached the outskirts of Moscow and Leningrad (now St. Petersburg). In the North Atlantic, German submarines stalked merchant ships carrying supplies to Britain. In China, Japan controlled the most productive provinces but could not crush Chinese resistance. In Southeast Asia, Japanese troops attacked the Philippines, the Dutch East Indies (now Indonesia), New Guinea, Malaya, and Burma. In the central Pacific, the Japanese fleet confronted the U.S. Navy.

Despite the popular desire for revenge against Japan, the Allies had already decided to defeat Germany first. The reasoning was simple: Germany, with its huge armies, massive industrial capacity, and technological expertise, was far stronger than Japan. Defeat of Japan would not ensure the defeat of Germany, especially if it crushed the Soviet Union or starved Britain into submission. By contrast, a strategy that helped the Soviets and British survive and then destroyed German military power would doom Japan.

The Eastern Front and the Battle of Stalingrad.

The Eastern Front held the key to Allied hopes. In 1941, Germany had seized control of 45 percent of the Soviet population, 47 percent of its grain production, and more than 60 percent of its coal, steel, and aluminum industries. Hitler next sought to destroy the Soviet capacity to wage war, targeting southern Russia, an area rich in grain and oil.

The scheme was easier to plot on a map than to carry out in the fields of Russia. The German offensive opened with stunning success. Every day's advance, however, stretched supply lines. The turning point of the war in Europe came at Stalingrad (present-day Volgograd), an industrial center on the western bank of the Volga River. In September and October, 1942, German, Italian, and Romanian soldiers fought their way house by house into the city. For both Hitler and Stalin, the city became a test of will that outweighed even its substantial military importance.

The Red Army delivered a counterstroke on November 18 that cut off 290,000 Axis soldiers. Airlifts kept the Germans fighting for more than two additional months, but they surrendered in February 1943. This was the first German mass capitulation, and it came at immense human cost to both sides. The Soviet army suffered more deaths in this battle than the United States did in the entire war.

Behind the victory was an extraordinary revival of the Soviet capacity to make war. In the desperate months of 1941, the Soviets dismantled nearly 3,000 factories and rebuilt them far to the east of the German advance in the midst of Siberian winter. As many as 25 million workers and their families followed the factories eastward. By the time the two armies clashed at Stalingrad, the Soviets were producing four times as many tanks and warplanes as the Germans.

THE SURVIVAL OF BRITAIN

After the failure of German air attacks in 1940, the British struggled to save their empire and supply themselves with food and raw materials. From bases in France, greatly improved U-boats intercepted shipments of oil from Nigeria, beef from Argentina, minerals from Brazil, and weapons from the United States. Through the end of 1941, German "tonnage warfare" sank British, Allied, and neutral merchant vessels faster than they could be replaced.

The Battle of the Atlantic.

The British fought back in what came to be known as the **Battle of the Atlantic.** At sea, the British organized protected convoys.

Eastern Front The area of military operations in World War II located east of Germany in eastern Europe and the Soviet Union.

Battle of the Atlantic The long struggle between German submarines and the British and U.S. navies in the North Atlantic from 1940 to 1943.

Roosevelt's destroyer deal of 1940 and U.S. naval escorts in the western Atlantic in 1941 contributed directly to Britain's survival.

Nevertheless, German submarines dominated the Atlantic in 1942. In June 1942, U-boats sank 144 ships, and U-boats operating in "wolfpacks" continued to decimate convoys into 1943. The balance shifted only when Allied aircraft began to track submarines with radar, spot them with searchlights as they maneuvered to the surface, and attack them with depth charges. By the spring of 1943, American shipyards were launching ships faster than the Germans could sink them.

North Africa.　British ground fighting in 1942 centered in North Africa, where the British operated out of Egypt and the Italians and Germans from the Italian colony of Libya. By October 1942, Field Marshal Erwin Rommel's German and Italian forces were within striking distance of the Suez Canal. At El Alamein, however, General Bernard Montgomery forced the enemy to retreat in early November and lifted the danger to the Middle East.

RETREAT AND STABILIZATION IN THE PACIFIC

Reports from eastern Asia after Pearl Harbor were appalling. The Japanese attack on the Philippines (see Map 26–2) had been another tactical surprise that destroyed most American air power on the ground and isolated U.S. forces. In February, a numerically inferior Japanese force seized British Singapore, until then considered an anchor of Allied strength, and then pushed the British out of Burma. In a three-month siege, they overwhelmed Filipino and U.S. defensive positions on the Bataan peninsula outside Manila. The Japanese fleet was virtually undamaged at the end of April, and the Japanese army was triumphant in conquest of European and American territories in Southeast Asia.

The Battles of the Coral Sea and Midway.　The first check to Japanese expansion came on May 7–8, 1942, in the Battle of the Coral Sea, where U.S. aircraft carriers halted a Japanese thrust toward Australia and confirmed that the U.S. Navy could fight effectively. In June, the Japanese struck at the island of Midway, 1,500 miles northwest of Honolulu. Their goal was to destroy American carrier forces. On the morning of June 4, the Japanese and American carrier fleets faced off across 175 miles of ocean, each sending planes to search out the other. U.S. Navy dive bombers found the Japanese fleet and sank or crippled three aircraft carriers in five minutes; another damaged Japanese carrier sank later in the day. The Battle of Midway ended Japanese efforts to expand in the Pacific.

MOBILIZING FOR VICTORY

*W*ar changed the lives of most Americans. Millions of men and women served in the armed forces, and millions more worked in defense factories. In order to keep track of this staggering level of activity, the number of civilian employees of the federal government quadrupled to 3.8 million, a much greater increase than during the New Deal. Meanwhile, youngsters saved tin foil, collected scrap metal, and followed the freedom-fighting stories of Wonder Woman in the comics. College science students might be recruited to work at scientific espionage against the Nazis. The breadth of involvement in the war effort gave Americans a common purpose that softened the divisions of region, class, and national origin while calling attention to continuing inequalities of race.

HOW DID the war affect the place of women in American society?

ORGANIZING THE ECONOMY

The need to fight a global war brought a huge expansion of the federal government. Congress authorized the president to reorganize existing government departments and create new agencies. The War Manpower Commission allocated workers among vital industries and the military. The War Production Board invested $17 billion for new factories and managed $181 billion in war-supply contracts, favoring existing corporations because they had experience in large-scale production.

The Office of Price Administration (OPA) fought inflation with price controls and rationing. "Use it up, wear it out, make it do or do without" was the OPA's slogan. By slowing price increases, the OPA helped convince Americans to buy the war bonds that financed half the war spending. Americans also felt the bite of the first payroll deductions for income taxes as the government secured a steady flow of revenues and soaked up some of the high wages that would have pushed inflation. In total, the federal budget in 1945 was $98 billion, eleven times as large as in 1939, and the national debt had increased more than sixfold.

Industry had reluctantly begun to convert from consumer goods to defense production in 1940 and 1941. By the time of the attack on Pearl Harbor, 25 percent of the national economy was devoted to military needs. Existing factories retooled to make war equipment, and huge new facilities turned out thousands of planes and ships.

The United States applied mass-production technology to aircraft production at a time when Japan was building warplanes one at a time and Germany in small batches. The most spectacular example was the new Ford plant at Willow Run, Michigan, designed to adapt assembly-line approaches to manufacturing B-24 bombers. By 1943, the plant was delivering ten planes a day. American aircraft workers were twice as productive as their German counterparts and four times more productive than Japanese.

Most defense contracts went to such established industrial states as Michigan, New York, and Ohio, but the relative impact was greatest in the South and West, where the war marked the takeoff of what Americans would later call the Sunbelt. Albuquerque, New Mexico, more than doubled in population during the 1940s. War-boom cities, such as San Diego (up 92 percent in population in the 1940s) and Mobile (up 68 percent), bustled with activity and hummed with tension.

The output of America's war industries was staggering. One historian estimates that 40 percent of the world's military production was coming from the United States by 1944. Equally impressive is the 30 percent increase in the productivity of U.S. workers between 1939 and 1945. Surging farm income pulled agriculture out of its long slump. The rich certainly got richer, but overall per capita income doubled, and the poorest quarter of Americans made up some of the ground lost during the Great Depression.

THE ENLISTMENT OF SCIENCE

The war reached into scientific laboratories as well as shops and factories. "There wasn't a physicist able to breathe who wasn't doing war work," remembered Professor Philip Morrison. At the center of the scientific enterprise was Vannevar Bush, former dean at the Massachusetts Institute of Technology. As head of the newly established Office of Scientific Research and Development, Bush guided spending to develop new drugs such as antibiotics, blood-transfusion procedures, weapons systems, radar, sonar, and dozens of other military technologies. The

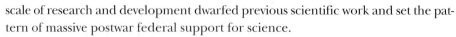

Manhattan Project The effort, using the code name Manhattan Engineer District, to develop an atomic bomb under the management of the U.S. Army Corps of Engineers during World War II.

WHERE TO LEARN MORE

Los Alamos County Historical Museum and Bradbury Science Museum, Los Alamos, New Mexico
www.lanl.gov/museum/

25–5
A. Philip Randolph, "Why Should We March?" (1942)

African American soldiers served in the full range of military roles, including this signal corps company set up in an ancient ruin in Italy.

National Archives and Records

scale of research and development dwarfed previous scientific work and set the pattern of massive postwar federal support for science.

In late 1941, Roosevelt established the **Manhattan Project.** By December 2, 1942, scientists proved that it was possible to create and control a sustained nuclear reaction. The Manhattan Project moved from theory to practice in 1943. The physicist J. Robert Oppenheimer directed the young scientists at Los Alamos in designing a nuclear-fission bomb. Engineers in other new science cities tried two approaches to producing the fissionable material. Richland, Washington, on the dusty banks of the Columbia River, burgeoned from a handful of peach farmers into a sprawling metropolis that supported the creation of plutonium at the Hanford Engineer Works. Oak Ridge, Tennessee, near Knoxville, was built around gaseous-diffusion plants that separated rare and vital uranium-235 from the more common uranium-238.

The Manhattan Project ushered in the age of atomic energy. Plutonium from Hanford fueled the first bomb tested at the Trinity site in New Mexico on July 16, 1945. The explosion astonished even the physicists; Oppenheimer quoted from Hindu scriptures in trying to comprehend the results: "Now I am become Death, destroyer of worlds."

MEN AND WOMEN IN THE MILITARY

World War II required a more than thirtyfold expansion of the U.S. armed forces from their 1939 level of 334,000 soldiers, sailors, and marines. By 1945, 8.3 million men and women were on active duty in the army and army air forces and 3.4 million in the navy and Marine Corps, totals exceeded only by the Soviet Union. In total, some 350,000 women and more than 16 million men served in the armed forces; 292,000 died in battle, 100,000 survived prisoner-of-war camps, and 671,000 returned wounded.

Native Americans in the Military. Twenty-five thousand American Indians served in the armed forces. Most were in racially integrated units, and Harvey Natcheez, of the Ute tribe, was the first American to reach the center of conquered Berlin. Because the Navajo were one of the few tribes that had not been studied by German anthropologists, the Army Signal Corps decided that their language would be unknown to the Axis armies. More than 300 members of the tribe were "code-talkers" who served in radio combat-communication teams in the Pacific theater, transmitting vital information in Navajo.

African Americans in the Military. Approximately 1 million African Americans served in the armed forces during World War II. As it had since the Civil War, the army organized black soldiers in segregated units and often assigned them to the menial jobs, such as construction work, and excluded them from combat until manpower shortages forced changes in policy.

The average black soldier encountered discrimination on and off the base. Private Charles Wilson wrote President Roosevelt that Davis-Monthan Army Air Force

Base in Tucson was color-coded: barracks for African Americans were coated with black tar paper, and those for white soldiers sported white paint. Military courts were quick to judge and harshly punish black GIs. Despite the obstacles, all-black units, such as the 761st Tank Battalion and the 99th Pursuit Squadron, earned distinguished records. More broadly, the war experience helped to invigorate postwar efforts to achieve equal rights, as had also been true after World War I.

Women in the Military. The nation had a different—but also mixed—reaction to the women who joined the armed forces as army and navy nurses and as members of the WACS (Women's Army Corps), WAVES (Navy), SPARS (Coast Guard), and Marine Corps Women's Reserve. The armed services tried not to change established gender roles. Military officials told Congress that women in uniform could free men for combat. Many of the women hammered at typewriters, worked switchboards, inventoried supplies. Others, however, worked close to combat zones as photographers, code analysts, and nurses.

During the course of World War II, the government limited the consumption of a number of products to reserve supplies of products for the war effort and to prevent demand from pushing up the prices of scarce consumer goods. Shoppers, like this woman at a grocery store counter used ration stamps to obtain their share of controlled products.

Bettmann/Corbis

THE HOME FRONT

The war inexorably penetrated everyday life. Residents in war-production cities had to cope with throngs of new workers. Especially in 1941 and 1942, many were unattached males—young men waiting for their draft call and older men without their families. Military and defense officials worried about sexually transmitted diseases and pressured cities to shut down their vice districts.

Families in Wartime. Americans put their lives on fast forward. Couples who had postponed marriage because of the depression could afford to marry as the economy picked up. Altogether, the war years brought 1.2 million "extra" marriages, compared to the rate for the period 1920–1939.

The war's impact on families was gradual. The draft started with single men, then called up married men without children, and finally tapped fathers in 1943. Left at home were millions of "service wives," whose compensation from the government was $50 per month.

The war had mixed effects on children. "Latchkey children" of working mothers often had to fend for themselves, but middle-class kids whose mothers stayed home could treat the war as an interminable scout project, with salvage drives and campaigns to sell war bonds. Between the end of the school day and suppertime, children listened as Captain Midnight, Jack Armstrong, and Hop Harrigan ("America's ace of the airways") fought the Nazis and Japanese on the radio.

War Propaganda and Censorship. The federal government tried to keep civilians of all ages committed to the war. It encouraged scrap drives and backyard victory gardens and created colorful posters to warn against espionage, inspire women to join the effort, and promote rationing and car-pooling. The government also managed news about the fighting. Censors screened soldiers' letters. Early in the war, they blocked publication of most photographs of war casualties. Worried about flagging commitment, censors later authorized photographs of enemy atrocities to motivate the public.

War films revealed the nation's racial attitudes, often drawing distinctions between "good" and "bad" Germans but uniformly portraying Japanese as subhuman and repulsive. The most successful films dramatized the courage of the Allies.

WOMEN AND ETHNIC MINORITIES IN THE WORKFORCE

As draft calls took men off the assembly line, women changed the composition of the industrial workforce. The war gave them new job opportunities that were embodied in the image of Rosie the Riveter. Women made up one-quarter of West Coast shipyard workers and nearly half of Dallas and Seattle aircraft workers. Most women in the shipyards were clerks and general helpers. The acute shortage of welders and other skilled workers, however, opened thousands of lucrative journeyman positions to them.

By July 1944, 19 million women held paid jobs, up 6 million in four years. Women's share of government jobs increased from 19 to 38 percent, and their share of manufacturing jobs from 22 to 33 percent. Mirroring the sequence in which the military draft took men, employers recruited single women before turning to married women in 1943 and 1944. The federal government assisted female entry into the labor force by funding day-care programs that served 600,000 children. Some women worked out of patriotism. Many others, however, needed to support their families and already had years of experience in the workforce. As one of the workers recalled of herself and a friend, "We both had to work, we both had children, so we became welders, and if I might say so, damn good ones."

Americans did not know how to respond to the growing numbers of working women. The country needed their labor, but many worried that their employment would undermine families. Men and women commonly assumed that women would want to return to the home after victory.

Mexican American workers made special contributions to the war effort. As defense factories and the military absorbed workers, western farms and railroads faced an acute shortage of workers. In 1942 the United States and Mexico negotiated the *bracero* program, under which the Mexican government recruited workers to come to the United States on six-to-twelve month contracts. More than 200,000 Mexicans worked on U.S. farms under the program, and more than 100,000 worked for western railroads.

The war was a powerful force for the assimilation of Native Americans. Forty thousand moved to off-reservation jobs; they were a key labor force for military supply depots throughout the West. The average cash income of Indian households tripled during the war. Many stayed in cities at its end. The experience of the war accelerated the fight for full civil rights. Congress had made Indians citizens in 1924, in part to recognize their contributions in World War I, but several states continued to deny them the vote. Activists organized the National Congress of American Indians in 1944 and began the efforts that led the U.S. Supreme Court in 1948 to require states to grant voting rights.

African Americans, too, found economic advancement through war jobs. Early in the mobilization, labor leader A. Philip Randolph of the Brotherhood of Sleeping Car Porters worked with Walter White of the NAACP to plan a "Negro March on Washington" to protest racial discrimination by the federal government. To head off a major embarrassment, Roosevelt issued Executive Order 8802 in June 1941, barring racial discrimination in defense contracts and creating the **Fair Employment Practices Committee** (FEPC).

The FEPC's small staff resolved fewer than half of the employment-discrimination complaints, and white resistance to black coworkers remained

Fair Employment Practices Committee (FEPC)   Federal agency established in 1941 to curb racial discrimination in war production jobs and government employment.

strong. In Mobile, New Orleans, and Jacksonville, agreements between shipyards and segregated unions blocked skilled black workers from high-wage jobs. Attempts to overturn discrimination sometimes led to violence. Nevertheless, African American membership in labor unions doubled, and wartime prosperity raised the average black income from 41 percent of the white average in 1939 to 61 percent by 1950.

CLASHING CULTURES

As men and women migrated in search of work, they also crossed or collided with traditional boundaries of race and region. White southerners and black northerners with different ideas of racial etiquette found themselves side by side in West Coast shipyards. In the Midwest, black migrants from the South and white migrants from Appalachia crowded into cities such as Cincinnati and Chicago, competing for the same high-wage jobs and scarce apartments.

Tensions between black and white residents exploded in at least 50 cities in 1943 alone. New York's Harlem neighborhood erupted in a riot after rumors of attacks on black servicemen. In Detroit, the issue was the boundary between white and black territory. In June 1943, an argument over the use of Detroit's Belle Isle Park set off three days of violence: Twenty-five black people and nine white people died in the most serious racial riot of the war.

Tensions were simultaneously rising between Mexican Americans and Anglos. As the Mexican community in Los Angeles swelled to an estimated 400,000, newspapers published anti-Mexican articles. On June 6, 1943, off-duty sailors and soldiers attacked Latinos on downtown streets and invaded Mexican-American neighborhoods. The main targets were so-called *pachucos*—young Chicanos who wore flamboyant "zoot suits" with long, wide-shouldered jackets and pleated, narrow-cuffed trousers, whom the rioters considered delinquents or draft dodgers. The assaults were poignantly ironic because 750,000 Mexican Americans served in the armed forces and were the most decorated group relative to their numbers.

In 1942, the federal government removed Japanese Americans from parts of four western states and interned them in isolated camps scattered throughout the West.

INTERNMENT OF JAPANESE AMERICANS

On February 19, 1942, President Roosevelt authorized the secretary of war to define restricted areas and remove civilian residents who were threats to national security. The primary targets were 112,000 Japanese Americans in California and parts of Washington, Oregon, and Arizona. Japanese immigrants and their children in the western states had experienced 40 years of hostility because of racial prejudice, fear of the growing power of Japan, and jealousy of their business success. The outbreak of war triggered anti-Japanese hysteria and gave officials an excuse to take action against enemy aliens (immigrants who retained Japanese citizenship) and their American-born

AMERICAN VIEWS

THE INTERNMENT OF JAPANESE AMERICANS IN 1942

In the spring of 1942, the U.S. Army ordered Japanese Americans in four western states relocated to internment camps distant from the Pacific Coast. Monica Itoe Stone describes the experience of her Seattle family as they were transferred to temporary quarters—at the state fairgrounds, renamed "Camp Harmony" by the military—before they were moved again to Idaho.

- How do the expectations of *issei* (immigrants who had been born in Japan) differ from those of *nisei* (their American-born children, including the author of this memoir)?
- Why did the U.S. Army wait five months after Pearl Harbor before beginning the internment?
- Does the management of the assembly and internment suggest anything about stereotypes of Japanese Americans?

General DeWitt kept reminding us that E day, evacuation day, was drawing near. "E day will be announced in the very near future. If you have not wound up your affairs by now, it will soon be too late."

. . . On the twenty-first of April, a Tuesday, the general gave us the shattering news. "All the Seattle Japanese will be moved to Puyallup by May 1. Everyone must be registered Saturday and Sunday between 8 A.M. and 5 P.M. Up to that moment, we had hoped against hope that something or someone would intervene for us.

Now there was no time for moaning. A thousand and one details must be attended to in this one week of grace. Those seven days sputtered out like matches struck in the wind, as we rushed wildly about. Mother distributed sheets, pillowcases and blankets, which we stuffed into seabags. Into the two suitcases, we packed heavy winter overcoats, plenty of sweaters, woolen slacks and skirts, flannel pajamas and scarves. Personal toilet articles, one tin plate, tin cup and silverware completed our luggage. The one seabag and two suitcases apiece were going to be the backbone of our future home, and we planned it carefully.

Henry went to the Control Station to register the family. He came home with twenty tags, all numbered "10710," tags to be attached to each piece of baggage, and one to hang from our coat lapels. From then on, we were known as Family #10710. [On the day set for relocation] we climbed into the truck. . . . As we coasted down Beacon Hill bridge for the last time, we fell silent, and stared out at the delicately flushed, morning sky of Puget Sound. We drove through bustling Chinatown, and in a few minutes arrived on the corner of Eighth and Lane. This area was ordinarily lonely and deserted but now it was gradually filling up with silent, labeled Japanese. . . .

Finally at ten o'clock, a vanguard of Greyhound busses purred in and parked themselves neatly along the curb. The crowd stirred and murmured. The bus

children. As the general commanding on the West Coast put it, "A Jap is a Jap. It makes no difference whether he is an American citizen or not."

At the end of April 1942, Japanese in the coastal states were given a week to organize their affairs and report to assembly centers at fairgrounds and armories, where they were housed for several weeks before being moved again to ten internment camps in isolated locations in the western interior (see American Views: "The Internment of Japanese Americans in 1942: Life in Camp Harmony"). Here, they were housed in tar-paper barracks, hemmed in by barbed-wire fences, and guarded by military police.

Although the U.S. Supreme Court sanctioned the removals in *Korematsu* v. *United States* (1944), the nation officially recognized its liability for lost property with the Japanese Claims Act of 1948. The nation acknowledged its broader moral

doors opened and from each, a soldier with rifle in hand stepped out and stood stiffly at attention by the door. The murmuring died. It was the first time I had seen a rifle at such close range and I felt uncomfortable. . . .

Newspaper photographers with flash-bulb cameras pushed busily through the crowd. One of them rushed up to our bus, and asked a young couple and their little boy to step out and stand by the door for a shot. They were reluctant, but the photographers were persistent and at length they got out of the bus and posed, grinning widely to cover their embarrassment. We saw the picture in the newspaper shortly after and the caption underneath it read, "japs good-natured about evacuation." Our bus quickly filled to capacity. . . . The door closed with a low hiss. We were now the Wartime Civil Control Administration's babies.

About noon we crept into a small town . . . and we noticed at the left of us an entire block filled with neat rows of low shacks, resembling chicken houses. Someone commented on it with awe, "Just look at those chicken houses. They sure go in for poultry in a big way here." Slowly the bus made a left turn, drove through a wire-fenced gate, and to our dismay, we were inside the oversized chicken farm. . . .

The apartments resembled elongated, low stables about two blocks long. Our home was one room, about 18 by 20 feet, the size of a living room. There was one small window in the wall opposite the one door. It was bare except for a small, tinny wood-burning stove crouching in the center. The flooring consisted of two by fours laid directly on the earth, and dandelions were already pushing their way up through the cracks. . . .

I stared at our little window, unable to sleep. I was glad Mother had put up a makeshift curtain on the window for I noticed a powerful beam of light sweeping across it every few seconds. The lights came from high towers placed around the camp where guards with Tommy guns kept a twenty-four hour vigil. I remembered the wire fence encircling us, and a knot of anger tightened in my breast. What was I doing behind a fence like a criminal? If there were accusations to be made, why hadn't I been given a fair trial? Maybe I wasn't considered an American anymore. My citizenship wasn't real, after all. Then what was I? I was certainly not a citizen of Japan as my parents were. On second thought, even Father and Mother . . . had little tie with their mother country. In their twenty-five years in America, they had worked and paid their taxes to their adopted government as any other citizen.

Of one thing I was sure. The wire fence was real. I no longer had the right to walk out of it. It was because I had Japanese ancestors. It was also because some people had little faith in the ideas and ideals of democracy.

Source: Monica Itoi Sone, *Nisei Daughter* (Seattle: University of Washington Press, 1979).

responsibility in 1988, when Congress approved redress payments to each of the 60,000 surviving evacuees.

The internment of West Coast Japanese contrasted with the treatment of Japanese Americans by the military government of Hawaii. Despite the greater threat that Japan posed to Hawaii than to California, local residents and officials avoided panic. Hawaii's long history as a multiethnic society made residents disinclined to look for a racial scapegoat. Fewer than 1 percent of Hawaii's Japanese-American population of 160,000 were interned. The treatment of mainland Japanese Americans also contrasted with the situation of German Americans and Italian Americans. The government interned approximately 11,000 German nationals and German Americans who were explicitly seen as individual threats. Until November 1942, it imposed curfews and travel restrictions on Italians and

Italian Americans on the West Coast, but it interned fewer than 2,000. Both numbers were tiny fractions of the total populations.

THE END OF THE NEW DEAL

Roosevelt's New Deal ran out of steam in 1938. The war had reinvigorated his political fortunes by focusing national energies on foreign policy, over which presidents have the greatest power. After the 1942 election left Congress in the hands of Republicans and conservative southern Democrats, lawmakers ignored proposals that war emergency housing be used to improve the nation's permanent housing stock, abolished the National Resources Planning Board, curtailed rural electrification, and crippled the Farm Security Administration.

The presidential election of 1944 raised few new issues of substance. The Republicans nominated Governor Thomas Dewey of New York. The Democrats renominated Roosevelt for a fourth term. Missouri Senator Harry S Truman replaced liberal New Dealer Henry Wallace as Roosevelt's running mate. The move appeased southern Democrats and moved the ticket toward the political center.

The most important issue was a fourth term for Roosevelt. Supporters argued that the nation could not afford to change leaders in the middle of a war. Voters gave Roosevelt 432 electoral votes to 99, but the narrowing gap in the popular vote—54 percent for Roosevelt and 46 percent for Dewey—made the Republicans eager for 1948.

WHY DID the Allies win the war?

WAR AND PEACE

*I*n January 1943, the U.S. War Department completed the world's largest office building, the Pentagon. The building housed 23,000 workers along 17.5 miles of corridors. The building provided the space in which military planners could coordinate the tasks of raising and equipping the armed forces that would strike directly at Germany and Japan. Indeed, while Congress was chipping away at federal programs, the war effort was massively expanding the government presence in American life.

TURNING THE TIDE IN EUROPE

The unanswered military question of 1942 and 1943 was when the United States and Britain would open a second front against Germany by attacking across the English Channel. U.S. leaders wanted to justify massive mobilization with a war-winning campaign and to strike across Europe to occupy the heart of Germany. Stalin needed a full-scale invasion of western Europe to divert German forces from the Eastern Front, where Soviet troops were inflicting 90 percent of German battle casualties.

The Allies spent 1943 hammering out war aims and strategies. Meeting in Casablanca in January 1943, Roosevelt and Churchill demanded the unconditional surrender of Italy, Germany, and Japan. The phrase meant that there would be no deals that kept the enemy governments or leaders in power and was an effort to avoid the mistake of ending World War I with Germany intact. Ten months later, the Allied leaders huddled again in Tehran. At Tehran, the United States and Britain promised to invade France within six months. "We leave here," said the three leaders, "friends in fact, in spirit, in purpose."

The superficial harmony barely survived the end of the war. The Soviets had shouldered the brunt of the war for nearly two and a half years, suffering millions of casualties and seeing their nation devastated. Stalin and his generals scoffed at the small scale of early U.S. efforts. Roosevelt's ideal of self-determination for all peoples, embodied in the Atlantic Charter, seemed naive to Churchill, who wanted the major powers to carve out realistic spheres of influence in Europe. Stalin wanted control of eastern Europe.

The Campaign in North Africa.

The United States entered the ground war in Europe with Operation TORCH. Soon after the British victory at El Alamein, British and American troops under General Dwight Eisenhower landed in French Morocco and Algeria on November 8, 1942 (see Map 26–3). German troops that remained in North Africa taught U.S. forces hard lessons in tactics and leadership, but their stubborn resistance ended in May 1943, leaving all of Africa in Allied hands.

As millions of men entered the armed forces, millions of women went to work. By 1943, federal agencies were actively recruiting women workers. Those who took production-line jobs in shipyards and aircraft factories, such as the woman shown here, received the greatest attention.

Courtesy Library of Congress

Eisenhower had already demonstrated his ability to handle the politics of military leadership, skills he perfected commanding a multinational army for the next two and one-half years. He also chose the right subordinates, giving operational command to Generals Omar Bradley and George Patton.

The Invasion of Italy.

The central Mediterranean remained the focus of U.S. and British action for the next year. U.S. Army Chief of Staff George Marshall and President Roosevelt agreed to invade Italy in 1943, in part so that U.S. troops could participate in the ground fighting in Europe. Allied forces overran Sicily in July and August, but the Italian mainland proved more difficult. When Sicily fell, the Italian king and army forced Mussolini from power. In September, the Allies announced an armistice with Italy, and Eisenhower's troops landed south of Naples on September 9. Germany responded by occupying the rest of Italy.

Just as American military planners had feared, the Italian campaign soaked up Allied resources. The mountainous Italian peninsula was one long series of defensive positions, and the Allies repeatedly bogged down. Despite months of bitter fighting, the Allies managed to gain control of only two-thirds of Italy before German resistance crumbled in the final weeks of the war.

Soviet Advances and the Battle of Kursk.

Meanwhile, the Soviets recruited, rearmed, and upgraded new armies, despite enormous losses. As Soviet soldiers recaptured western Russia and Ukraine, they marched in 13 million pairs of American-made boots and ate U.S. rations. They traveled in 78,000 jeeps and 350,000 Studebaker, Ford, and Dodge trucks. "Just imagine how we could have advanced from Stalingrad to Berlin without [lend-lease vehicles]," future Soviet premier Nikita Khrushchev later commented.

The climactic battle of the German-Soviet war erupted on July 5, 1943. The Germans sent 3,000 tanks against the Kursk salient, a huge wedge that the Red Army had pushed into their lines. With 1 million men actively engaged on each side for more than two weeks, Kursk was the largest pitched battle of the war. It

QUICK REVIEW

Allied Collaboration
- 1943: U.S. and Soviet leaders prepare for a full-scale invasion of Europe.
- Soviet advances made possible by U.S. equipment and materials.
- November 1943: Allied leaders leave Tehran with a time-table for invasion of Europe.

MAP EXPLORATION
To explore an interactive version of this map, go to **http://www.prenhall.com/goldfield3/map26.3**

MAP 26–3 World War II in Europe, 1942–1945 Nazi Germany had to defend its conquests on three fronts. Around the Mediterranean, American and British forces pushed the Germans out of Africa and southern Italy, while guerrillas in Yugoslavia pinned down many German troops. On the Eastern Front, Soviet armies advanced hundreds of miles to drive the German Army out of the Soviet Union and eastern Europe. In June 1944, U.S. and British landings opened the Western Front in northern France for a decisive strike at the heart of Germany.

WHAT WERE the turning points in the war in Europe?

marked the end of the last great German offensive, leaving Germany capable of a fighting retreat but too weak to have any hope of winning the war.

OPERATION OVERLORD

On **D-Day**—June 6, 1944—the western Allies landed on the coast of Normandy in northwestern France. Six divisions went ashore from hundreds of attack transports carrying 4,000 landing craft. Dozens of warships and 12,000 aircraft provided support. One British and two American airborne divisions dropped behind German positions. When the sun set on the "longest day," the Allies had a tenuous toehold in France.

The next few weeks brought limited success. The Allies secured their beachheads and poured more than a million men and hundreds of thousands of vehicles ashore in the first six weeks. However, the German defenders kept them pinned along a narrow coastal strip. **Operation OVERLORD,** the code name for the entire campaign across northern France, met renewed success in late July and August. U.S. troops improved their fighting skills through "experience, sheer bloody experience." They finally broke through the German lines around the town of St.-Lô and then drew a ring around the Germans that slowly closed on the town of Falaise. The Germans lost a quarter of a million troops. The German command chose to regroup closer to Germany rather than fight in France. The Allies liberated Paris on August 25.

The story was similar on the Eastern Front, where the Soviets relentlessly battered one section of the German lines after another. By the end of 1944, the Red Army had entered the Balkans and reached central Poland. The Soviets had suffered as many as 27 million military and civilian deaths and sustained by far the heaviest burden in turning back Nazi tyranny.

VICTORY AND TRAGEDY IN EUROPE

In the last months of 1944, massive air strikes finally began to reduce German war production, which had actually increased during 1943 and much of 1944. P-51 escort fighters helped B-17s overfly Germany in relative safety after mid-1944. Thousand-bomber raids on railroads and oil facilities began to cripple the German economy. The raids forced Germany to devote 2.5 million workers to air defense and damage repair and to divert fighter planes from the front lines. The air raids cut German military production by one-third through 1944 and destroyed the transportation system. Politics, rather than military need, governed the final great action of the European air war. British and U.S. bombers in February 1945 staged a terror raid on the nonindustrial city of Dresden, packed with refugees, filled with great art, and undefended by the Germans; a firestorm fueled by incendiary bombs and rubble from blasted buildings killed tens of thousands of civilians.

The Battle of the Bulge and the Collapse of Germany.   Hitler struck a last blow in the Ardennes Forest of Belgium on December 16, 1944. He hoped to split

American, British, and Canadian forces opened the long-awaited second front against Germany on June 6, 1944—D-Day—when tens of thousands of troops landed on the coast of Normandy in France. The landings were the largest amphibious operation ever staged. Although the Germans had expected the landings farther north, their defenses pinned the Allies to a narrow beachhead for several weeks.

QUICK REVIEW

The Beginning of the End
- Allies gained footholds in North Africa.
- Allies took control of much of Italy.
- German's last offensive in Russia turned back.

D-Day   June 6, 1944, the day of the first paratroop drops and amphibious landings on the coast of Normandy, France, in the first stage of Operation OVERLORD during World War II.

Operation OVERLORD   U.S. and British invasion of France in June 1944 during World War II.

WHERE TO LEARN MORE

★ National Museum of the Air Force, Dayton, Ohio **www.wpafb.af.mil/ museum/**

WHERE TO LEARN MORE

★ United States Holocaust Memorial Museum, Washington, D.C. **http://www.ushmm.org**

WHERE TO LEARN MORE

★ National Museum of the Pacific War, Fredericksburg, Texas **www.nimitz-museum.org/**

Holocaust The systematic murder of millions of European Jews and others deemed undesirable by Nazi Germany.

Island Hopping The Pacific campaigns of 1944 that were the American naval versions of the *Blitzkrieg.*

U.S. and British forces by capturing the Belgian port of Antwerp. The attack surprised the Americans, and taking advantage of snow and fog that grounded Allied aircraft, the Germans drove a 50-mile bulge into U.S. lines. Although the Americans took substantial casualties, the German thrust literally ran out of gas beyond the town of Bastogne and the Battle of the Bulge never seriously threatened the outcome of the war.

The Nazi empire collapsed in the spring of 1945. American and British divisions crossed the Rhine in March and enveloped Germany's industrial core. The Soviets drove through eastern Germany toward Berlin. On April 25, American and Soviet troops met on the Elbe River. Hitler committed suicide on April 30 in his concrete bunker deep under devastated Berlin, which surrendered to the Soviets on May 2. The Nazi state formally capitulated on May 8.

The Holocaust. The defeat of Germany revealed appalling evidence of the evil at the heart of the Nazi ideology of racial superiority. After occupying Poland in 1939, the Nazis had transformed concentration camps into forced-labor camps, where overwork, starvation, and disease killed hundreds of thousands of Jews, Gypsies, Poles, Russians, and others the Nazis classed as subhuman. As many as 7 million labor conscripts from eastern and western Europe provided forced labor in fields, factories, mines, and repair crews, often dying on the job from overwork and starvation.

The "final solution" to what Hitler thought of as the "Jewish problem" went far beyond slave labor. In the fall of 1941, Hitler decided on the total elimination of Europe's Jews. The elite SS, Hitler's personal army within the Nazi Party, in 1942 set out to do his bidding. At Auschwitz, Treblinka, and several other death camps, the SS organized the efficient extermination of up to 6 million Jews and 1 million Poles, Gypsies, and others who failed to fit the Nazi vision of the German master race.

The evidence of genocide—systematic racial murder—is irrefutable. At Dachau in southwestern Germany, American forces found 10,000 bodies and 32,000 prisoners near death through starvation. Soviet troops who overran the camps in Poland found even more appalling sights—gas chambers as big as barns, huge ovens, the dead stacked like firewood. For more than half a century, the genocide that we now call the **Holocaust** has given the world its most vivid images of inhumanity.

THE PACIFIC WAR

Washington divided responsibilities in the Pacific theater. General Douglas MacArthur operated in the islands that stretched between Australia and the Philippines. Admiral Chester Nimitz commanded in the central Pacific. The Allies planned to isolate Japan from its southern conquests. The British moved from India to retake Burma. The Americans advanced along the islands of the southern Pacific to retake the Philippines. With Japan's army still tied down in China, the Americans then planned to bomb Japan into submission.

Racial hatred animated both sides in the Pacific war and fueled a "war without mercy." Americans often characterized Japanese soldiers as vermin. In turn, the Japanese viewed Americans as racial mongrels and called them demons. Each side expected the worst of the other and frequently lived up to expectations.

The Pacific campaigns of 1944 are often called **island hopping.** Planes from American carriers controlled the air, allowing the navy and land forces to isolate and capture the most strategically located Japanese-held islands while bypassing the rest (see Map 26–4).

MacArthur used a version of the bypass strategy in the Solomon Islands and New Guinea, leapfrogging past Japanese strong points. The invasion of the Philippines repeated the approach by landing on Leyte, in the middle of the island chain. The Philippine campaign also destroyed the last offensive capacity of the

 MAP EXPLORATION
To explore an interactive version of this map, go to **http://www.prenhall.com/goldfield3/map26.4**

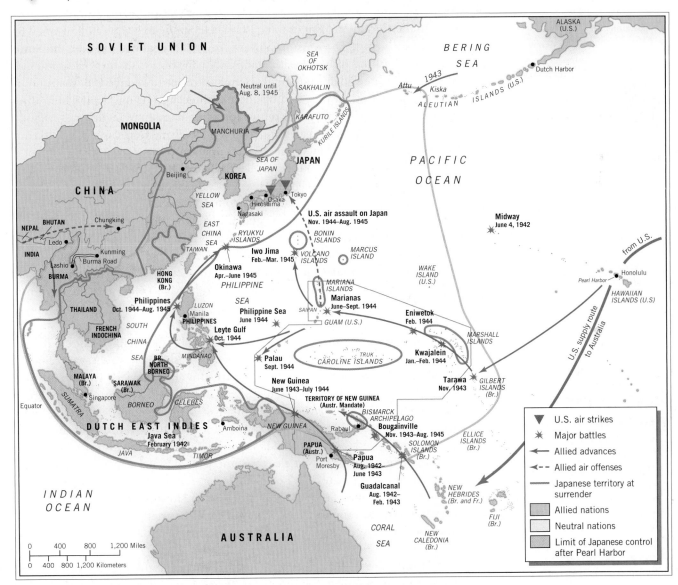

MAP 26–4 World War II in the Pacific, 1942–1945 The Allied strategy against Japan was to cut off Japan's southern conquests by retaking the central Pacific islands, the Philippines, and Burma and then to strike at the Japanese home islands. Submarine warfare and massive air attacks from November 1944 to August 1945 crippled Japan's capacity to wage war. The detonation of atomic bombs over Hiroshima and Nagasaki then forced surrender on August 15, 1945.

WHY WAS Japan unable to maintain its conquests in the Pacific?

Japanese fleet. The Japanese home islands were left with no defensive screen against an expected invasion.

During 1943 and 1944, the United States also savaged the Japanese economy. By 1945, imports to Japan were one-eighth of the 1940 level. Heavy bombing of Japan began in early 1944, using the new long-range B-29. Overall, conventional bombing destroyed 42 percent of Japan's industrial capacity. By the time the United States captured the islands of Iwo Jima and Okinawa in fierce fighting (April–June 1945) and neared the Japanese home islands, Japan's position was hopeless.

SEARCHING FOR PEACE

At the beginning of 1945, the Allies sensed victory. Conferring from February 4 to 11 in the Ukrainian town of Yalta, Roosevelt, Stalin, and Churchill planned for the postwar world. The most important American goal was to enlist the Soviet Union in finishing off the Pacific war. Americans hoped that a Soviet attack on Manchuria would tie down enough Japanese troops to reduce U.S. casualties in invading Japan. Stalin repeated his intent to declare war on Japan within three months of victory in Europe, in return for a free hand in Manchuria.

In Europe, the Allies had decided in 1944 to divide Germany and Austria into French, British, American, and Soviet occupation zones and to share control of Berlin. The Red Army already controlled Bulgaria, Romania, and Hungary, countries that had helped the Germans; Soviet officials were installing sympathetic regimes there. Soviet armies also controlled Poland. The most that Roosevelt could coax from Stalin was a vague pledge to allow participation of non-communists in coalition governments in eastern Europe.

Conservative critics later charged that the western powers "gave away" eastern Europe at the **Yalta Conference.** In fact, the Soviet Union gained little that it did not already control. In East Asia as well, the Soviets could seize the territories the agreement granted them.

Truman and Potsdam. On April 12, two months after Yalta, Roosevelt died of a cerebral hemorrhage. Harry Truman, the new president, was a shrewd politician, but his experience was limited. Deeply distrustful of the Soviets, Truman first ventured into personal international diplomacy in July 1945 at a British-Soviet-American conference at Potsdam, near Berlin. Most of the sessions debated the future of Germany. The leaders endorsed the expulsion of ethnic Germans from eastern Europe and moved the borders of Poland 100 miles west into historically German territory. Truman also made it clear that the United States expected to dominate the occupation of Japan. The **Potsdam Declaration** on July 26 summarized U.S. policy and gave Japan an opening for surrender. However, the declaration failed to guarantee that Emperor Hirohito would not be tried as a war criminal. The Japanese response was so cautious that Americans read it as rejection.

The Atomic Bomb. Secretary of State James Byrnes now urged Truman to use the new atomic bomb, tested just weeks earlier. Japan's ferocious defense of Okinawa had confirmed American fears that the Japanese would fight to the death. Prominent Americans were wondering if unconditional surrender was worth another six or nine months of bitter fighting. In contrast, using the bomb to end the conflict quickly would ensure that the United States could occupy Japan without Soviet participation, and the bomb might intimidate Stalin (see the Overview table, "The Decision to Use the Atomic Bomb"). In short, a decision not to use atomic weapons was never a serious alternative in the summer of 1945.

QUICK REVIEW

Preparations for Victory

- February 1945: Allies debate plans for postwar world at Yalta.
- Soviets solidified their hold on Eastern Europe.
- July 26, 1945: Potsdam Declaration fails to produce a definitive response from Japan.

Yalta Conference Meeting of U.S. President Franklin Roosevelt, British Prime Minister Winston Churchill, and Soviet Premier Joseph Stalin held in February 1945 to plan the final stages of World War II and postwar arrangements.

Potsdam Declaration Statement issued by the United States during a meeting of U.S. President Harry Truman, British Prime Minister Winston Churchill, and Soviet Premier Joseph Stalin in which the United States declared its intention to democratize the Japanese political system and reintroduce Japan into the international community.

OVERVIEW   THE DECISION TO USE THE ATOMIC BOMB

Americans have long argued about whether the use of atomic bombs on the Japanese cities of Hiroshima and Nagasaki was necessary to end the war. Several factors probably influenced President Truman's decision to use the new weapon.

Military necessity	After the war, Truman argued that the use of atomic bombs was necessary to avoid an invasion of Japan that would have cost hundreds of thousand of lives. Military planners expected Japanese soldiers to put up the same kind of suicidal resistance in defense of the home islands as they had to American landings in the Philippines, Iwo Jima, and Okinawa. More recently, historians have argued that the Japanese military was near collapse and an invasion would have met far less resistance than feared.
Atomic diplomacy	Some historians believe that Truman used atomic weapons to overawe the Soviet Union and induce it to move cautiously in expanding its influence in Europe and East Asia. Truman and his advisers were certainly aware of how the bomb might influence the Soviet leadership.
Domestic politics	President Roosevelt and his chief military advisers had spent billions on the secret atomic bomb project without the full knowledge of Congress or the American public. The managers of the Manhattan Project may have believed that only proof of its military value would quiet critics and justify the huge cost.
Momentum of war	The United States and Britain had already adopted wholesale destruction of German and Japanese cities as a military tactic. Use of the atomic bomb looked like a variation on fire bombing, not the start of a new era of potential mass destruction. In this context, some historians argue, President Truman's choice was natural and expected.

In early August, the United States dropped two of the three available nuclear bombs on Japan. On August 6, at Hiroshima, the first bomb killed at least 80,000 people and poisoned thousands more with radiation. A second bomb, three days later at Nagasaki, took another 40,000 lives. Japan ceased hostilities on August 14 and surrendered formally on September 2. The world has wondered ever since whether the United States might have defeated Japan without resorting to atomic bombs, but recent research shows that the bombs were the shock that allowed the emperor and peace advocates to overcome military leaders who wanted to fight to the death.

HOW THE ALLIES WON

The Allies won with economic capacity, technology, and military skill. The ability to outproduce the enemy made victory certain in 1944 and 1945, but it was the ability to outthink and outmaneuver the Axis powers that staved off defeat in 1942 and 1943.

The ruins of Hiroshima in the aftermath of the atomic bomb. Atomic bombs, dropped first on Hiroshima and then on Nagasaki in August 1945, instantly destroyed most of each city.

Getty Images, Inc.

Jewish residents of Cracow, Poland, boarding cattle cars under the eye of the German SS; their destination was one of the extermination camps where Germans systematically killed millions of people.

United States Holocaust Museum

In the spring of 1942, an unbroken series of conquests had given the Axis powers control of roughly one-third of the world's production of industrial raw materials. But while Germany and Japan struggled to turn these resources into military strength, the Soviet Union accomplished wonders in relocating and rebuilding its manufacturing capacity after the disasters of 1941. The United States, meanwhile, rearmed with astonishing swiftness, accomplishing in one year what Germany had thought would take three.

The United States and the Soviet Union not only built more planes and tanks than the Axis nations, but they also built better ones. The Soviets developed and mass-produced the T-34, the world's most effective tank. American aircraft designers soon jumped ahead of the Germans. The United States and Britain gained the lead in communication systems, radar, code-breaking capability, and, of course, atomic weapons.

The Allies learned hard lessons from defeat and figured out how to outfight the Axis. The Russians reexamined every detail of their military procedures and devised new tactics that kept the vast German armies off guard and on the defensive. New ways to fight U-boats in the Atlantic devastated the German submarine service and staved off defeat. Americans in the Pacific utilized the full capacity of aircraft carriers, while Japanese admirals still dreamed of confrontations between lines of battleships.

Finally, the Allies had the appeal of democracy and freedom. The Axis nations were clearly the aggressors. Germany and Japan made bitter enemies by exploiting and abusing the people of the countries they conquered, from Yugoslavia and France to Malaya and the Philippines, and incited local resistance movements. The Allies were certainly not perfect, but they fought for the ideals of political independence and were welcomed as liberators as they pushed back the Axis armies.

CONCLUSION

World War II changed the lives of tens of millions of Americans. It made and unmade families. It gave millions of women new responsibilities and then sent them back to the kitchen. It put money in pockets that had been emptied by the Great Depression and turned struggling business owners into tycoons. In war zones and behind the lines, it introduced millions of men and women in the armed forces to people and places outside the United States.

The war unified the nation in new ways, while confirming old divisions. People of all backgrounds shared a common cause. Farm boys mixed with city slickers, northerners with southerners. "When I woke up the first morning on the troop train in Fulton, Kentucky," recalled one midwesterner, "I thought I was in Timbuktu." The war narrowed the distance between native-born, small-town Americans and recent European immigrants from the big cities. The chasms between Protestant, Catholic, and Jewish Americans were far narrower in 1945 than they had been in 1940.

But nothing broke the barriers that separated white and black Americans. Unequal treatment in a war for democracy outraged black soldiers, who returned to fight for civil rights. The uprooting of Japanese Americans was another reminder of racial prejudice. After the war, however, memories of the contrast between the nation's fight against Axis tyranny and the unequal treatment of American citizens fueled a gradual shift of public attitudes that climaxed in the civil rights movements of the 1950s and 1960s.

The United States ended the war as the world's overwhelming economic power. Having suffered almost no direct destruction, the United States was able to dictate a postwar economic trading system that favored its interests.

Nevertheless, the insecurities of the war years influenced the United States for decades. Even though the United States ended 1945 with the world's mightiest navy, biggest air force, and only atomic bomb, memories of the instability that had followed World War I made its leaders nervous about the shape of world politics.

One result in the postwar era was conflict between the United States and the Soviet Union, whose only common ground had been a shared enemy. After Germany's defeat, their wartime alliance gave way to hostility and confrontation in the Cold War. At home, international tensions fed the pressure for social and political conformity. The desire to enjoy the fruits of victory after 15 years of economic depression and sacrifice made the postwar generation sensitive to perceived threats to steady jobs and stable families. For the next generation, the unresolved business of World War II would haunt American life.

SUMMARY

The Dilemmas of Neutrality In the late 1930s President Roosevelt's challenge was to lead the United States toward rearmament and support nations at war with fascism without alarming the public. The roots of World War II were to be found in the after-effects of the first World War; as Germany marched from victory to victory from 1939 to 1941, strong isolationist sentiment in America shaped public

debate and limited attempts to help Britain and the Soviet Union. The swift collapse of France and radio broadcasts describing the bombing of London frightened Americans; the Lend Lease Act, an undeclared naval war, and the Atlantic Charter drew America closer to war. The final shove came in the Pacific with the attack on Pearl Harbor; in December 1941 America entered World War II.

Holding the Line Despite the popular desire to defeat Japan, the Allies planned to defeat Germany first. The Soviet Union held the Eastern front in the Battle of Stalingrad; the British fought back in the Battle of the Atlantic; German troops in North Africa were forced to retreat; Japanese expansion came to a halt at the Battle of the Coral Sea and Battle of Midway. By the end of 1942 the tide was turning; in mid-1943 the Allies could begin to plan for victory with confidence.

Mobilizing for Victory The need to fight a global war brought a huge expansion of the federal government; price controls and rationing fought inflation, industry mobilized for defense production, and the Manhattan Project ushered in the age of atomic energy. The war penetrated every facet of everyday life; women and minorities changed the composition of the industrial work force. The government saw Japanese Americans as threats and interned them in camps throughout the West. The war required more than a thirtyfold expansion of the U.S. military; soldiers came from across the American spectrum. While women in the military received unequal treatment, African Americans fared worse.

War and Peace Plans for ending the war were drawn up at Casablanca and Tehran; Italy was invaded in 1943; Operation Overlord opened the second front in Europe; in 1944 Germany was being battered from the east and west. As Allied troops entered Germany and discovered the death camps, the extent of what is now called the Holocaust became clear. Through the island hopping campaign in the Pacific, American forces neared the Japanese home islands; in 1945 President Truman chose to use the atomic bomb to end the war with Japan. The postwar world would prove to be a challenge; the Yalta and Potsdam conferences divided Europe into spheres that would last for almost fifty years.

IMAGE KEY
for pages 754–755

a. Dorie Miller, a mess attendant on the battleship *West Virginia,* received the Navy Cross for "extraordinary courage" during the Japanese attack on Pearl Harbor.

b. Unusually addressed letters to Winston Churchill.

c. American soldiers landing on the coast of France at Normandy on 6 June 1944 (D-Day).

d. Attack on Pearl Harbor.

e. All POWs had to carry indentification tags with them at all times.

f. A cloth patch with a yellow Star of David that all Jews had to wear under the Nazi regime.

g. Victory Garden poster.

h. Adolf Hitler speaks at a 1938 rally.

i. Map of Central Europe.

j. The explosion of an atomic bomb.

k. A wartime shopper uses ration coupons to purchase groceries.

REVIEW QUESTIONS

1. What motivated German, Italian, and Japanese aggression in the 1930s? How did Great Britain, the USSR, and other nations respond to the growing conflict?

2. What arguments did Americans make against involvement in the war in Europe, and how deep was anti-intervention sentiment? Why did President Roosevelt and many others believe it necessary to block German and Japanese expansion? What steps did Roosevelt take to increase U.S. involvement short of war?

3. What was the military balance in early 1942? What were the chief threats to the United States and its allies? Why did the fortunes of war turn in late 1942?

4. Assess how mobilization for World War II altered life in the United States. How did the war affect families? How did it shift the regional balance of the economy? What opportunities did it open for women?

5. Did World War II help or hinder progress toward racial equality in the United States? How did the experiences of Japanese Americans, African Americans, and Mexican Americans challenge American ideals?

6. What factors were decisive in the defeat of Germany? How important were Soviet efforts on the Eastern Front, the bomber war, and the British-American landings in France?

7. What was the U.S. strategy against Japan, and how well did it work? What lay behind President Truman's decision to use atomic bombs against Japanese cities?

8. What role did advanced science and technology play in World War II? How did the scientific lead of the United States affect the war's outcome?

KEY TERMS

Allies (p. 763)
Atlantic Charter (p. 762)
Axis Powers (p. 759)
Battle of the Atlantic (p. 765)
Blitzkrieg (p. 759)
D-Day (p. 777)

Eastern Front (p. 765)
Fair Employment Practices
  Committee (FEPC) (p. 770)
Greater East Asia Co-Prosperity
  Sphere (p. 757)
Holocaust (p. 778)

Island hopping (p. 778)
Lend-Lease Act (p. 762)
Manhattan Project (p. 768)
Operation OVERLORD (p. 777)
Potsdam Declaration (p. 780)
Yalta Conference (p. 780)

WHERE TO LEARN MORE

National Museum of the Air Force, Dayton, Ohio. Visitors can walk among World War II fighter planes and bombers, including the B-29 that dropped the atomic bomb on Nagasaki, and learn about the role of aviation in the war. **www.wpafb.af.mil/museum/**

National Museum of the Pacific War, Fredericksburg, Texas. In the birthplace of Admiral Chester Nimitz, this new museum is an excellent introduction to the war with Japan. **www.nimitz-museum-org/**

Los Alamos County Historical Museum and **Bradbury Science Museum, Los Alamos, New Mexico.** The museum traces the origins of atomic energy for military and civilian uses. Nearby is the Los Alamos County Historical Museum, which gives the feel of everyday life in the atomic town. **www.lanl.gov/museum/**

United States Holocaust Memorial Museum, Washington, D.C. The Holocaust Museum gives visitors a deeply moving depiction of the deadly impact of Nazi ideas in the 1930s and 1940s. The museum's website at **http://www.ushmm.urlorg** also explores virtually every facet of the Holocaust experience for Jews during World War II.

 U.S. History Document CD-ROM
For primary sources related to this chapter, refer to the document CD-ROM.

 www.prenhall.com/goldfield
For study resources related to this chapter, visit the *Companion Website*™.

27 The Cold War at Home and Abroad
1946–1952

CHAPTER HIGHLIGHTS

Launching the Great Boom The end of the war ushered in economic expansion that would last a quarter century. Federal programs helped alleviate a housing shortage and send veterans to college. The first steps toward civil rights were taken by the federal government.

Truman, Republicans, and the Fair Deal Americans wanted to retain the gains of the New Deal, but were unwilling to risk new experiments. Truman's energetic campaign, combined with Dewey's missteps, resulted in Truman's victory in the 1948 presidential campaign. Truman's Fair Deal, an effort to build on the gains of the New Deal, was only partially implemented by Congress.

Confronting the Soviet Union After World War II, the United States and the Soviet Union entered into the Cold War. Mistrust on both sides contributed to escalating tensions and massive military buildups. The Marshall Plan committed the United States to rebuilding Western Europe. U.S. policy was encapsulated in the Truman Doctrine.

Cold War and Hot War The Soviet Union and China developed nuclear weapons, starting an arms race and fueling fears of nuclear war. NSC-68 argued that the United States should use force to counter communist aggression. The first expression of this policy was U.S. involvement in the war in Korea.

The Second Red Scare The Korean War reinforced the second Red Scare, an assault of civil liberties that lasted from the mid–1940s to the mid–1950s. National and state governments established loyalty programs. Courts punished members of suspect organizations. Congressional and state legislative investigations searched for communists in all areas of public life.

CHAPTER QUESTIONS

WHAT WAS the catalyst for the economic boom that began in 1947?

HOW WAS Harry Truman able to win the 1948 presidential election?

WHAT WERE the origins of the Cold War?

HOW DID the Korean War shape American domestic politics?

WHY DID fear of communism escalate in the years following World War II?

CHAPTER OUTLINE

- Launching the Great Boom
- Truman, Republicans, and the Fair Deal
- Confronting the Soviet Union
- Cold War and Hot War
- The Second Red Scare

IMAGE KEY
for pages 786–787 is on page 810.

> *My eyes popped when I got to town hall because the lobby and the stairs leading up to the hearing room were loaded with people. The upstairs hallway was jammed and the room was packed. People were standing along the walls. I remember there were a lot of children, toddlers—some in strollers—and many babies held by men and women. We expected there would be quite a turnout. But the extent of the crowd was a big surprise to me. . . . The meeting itself was rather brief. There were some speeches. No screaming and yelling the way people do at town meetings today. Everyone was quiet, anxious. I remember one guy in uniform, holding a baby, made a strong statement. These people were desperate. It was very moving. When the decision was announced, the crowd broke into applause.*
>
> *Levittown was the last place on the planet I thought I would be living. But, as it turned out, we moved there because the house was such a good buy. . . . We loved living there. I came into work and told [Newsday managing editor Alan] Hathway that I would be eating crow for the rest of my days.*
>
> Bernadette Rischer Wheeler, in "Levittown at Fifty: Long Island Voices," at www.lihistory.com/specsec/hsvoices.htm; originally published in *Newsday*.

BERNADETTE WHEELER WAS a reporter for *Newsday*, the daily newspaper for the Long Island suburbs of New York, who covered the birth of the new community of Levittown. She remembers the meeting on May 21, 1947, when the local governing board approved construction of the new subdivision. The size of the crowd indicated the severity of the housing shortage after World War II and the intense desire of Americans to return to normal life. Over the next decade, the residents who moved to Levittown and thousands of other new subdivisions would start the baby boom and rekindle the economy with their purchases of automobiles, appliances, and televisions.

This compelling desire to enjoy the promise of American life after years of sacrifice helps explain why Americans reacted so fiercely to new challenges and threats. The confrontation with the Soviet Union was soon being called the **Cold War.** By the time real war broke out in Korea in 1950, many Americans were venting their frustration by blaming international setbacks on internal subversion and trying to root out suspected "reds."

The Cold War began in the late 1940s, but it would shape the United States and the world for another generation. Massive rearmament allowed U.S. presidents to act as international policemen in the name of democratic values. Defense spending also reshaped American industry and helped stimulate 25 years of economic growth. The Cold War narrowed the range of political discussion, making many of the left-wing ideas of the 1930s taboo by the 1950s. It also made racial segregation and limits on immigration into international embarrassments and thus nudged the nation to live up to its ideals.

Cold War The political and economic confrontation between the Soviet Union and the United States that dominated world affairs from 1946 to 1989.

Chronology

LAUNCHING THE GREAT BOOM

When World War II ended, Americans feared that demobilization would bring a return of the inflation and unemployment that had followed World War I. Indeed, in the first 18 months of peace, rising prices, strife between labor and management, and shortages of everything from meat to automobiles confirmed their anxiety. But in fact, 1947 and 1948 ushered in an economic expansion that lasted for a quarter-century. The resulting prosperity would finance a military buildup and an activist foreign policy. It also supported continuity in domestic politics from the late 1940s to the mid-1960s.

RECONVERSION CHAOS

Japan's sudden surrender took the United States by surprise. The Pentagon, already scaling back defense spending, canceled $15 billion in war contracts in the first two days after the Japanese surrender. Public pressure demanded that the military release the nation's 12 million service personnel as rapidly as possible.

Veterans came home to shortages of food and consumer goods. Meanwhile, producers, consumers, and retailers scrambled to evade price restrictions and scarcities. Farmers sold meat on the black market, bypassing the big packing companies. Automobiles were extremely scarce.

A wave of strikes made it hard to retool factories for civilian products. Inflation squeezed factory workers, who had accepted wage controls during the war effort. Since 1941, prices had risen twice as fast as base wages. In the fall of 1945, more and more workers went on strike to redress the balance. By January 1946, some 1.3 million auto, steel, electrical, and packinghouse workers were off the job.

WHAT WAS the catalyst for the economic boom that began in 1947?

QUICK REVIEW

Post-war Economic Problems

- Military spending and military service came to an abrupt halt.
- Veterans came home to shortages in food and consumer goods.
- Inflation contributed to labor unrest.

Strikes in these basic industries shut other factories down for lack of supplies. Presidential committees crafted settlements that allowed steel and auto workers to make up ground lost during the war, but they also allowed corporations to pass on higher costs to consumers. One Republican senator complained of "unionists who fatten themselves at the expense of the rest of us." Bill Nation, who inspected window moldings at a GM plant in Detroit, wondered who the senator was talking about. The strike gave him an hourly raise of 18 cents, pushing his weekly income to $59. After paying for food, housing, and utilities, Bill was left with $13.44 for himself, his wife, and five children to spend on clothes, comic books, and doctor bills.

ECONOMIC POLICY

The economic turmoil of 1946 set the stage for two major and contradictory efforts to deal more systematically with peacetime economic readjustment. The Employment Act of 1946 and the **Taft-Hartley Act** of 1947 represented liberal and conservative approaches to the peacetime economy.

The Employment Act was an effort by congressional liberals to ward off economic crisis by fine-tuning government taxation and spending. It started as a proposal for a full-employment bill. Watered down in the face of business opposition, it still defined economic growth and high employment as national goals. It also established the **Council of Economic Advisers** to assist the president.

In the short term, the Employment Act aimed at a problem that did not materialize. Economists had predicted that the combination of returning veterans and workers idled by canceled defense work would bring depression-level unemployment of 8 to 10 million. In fact, more than 2 million women provided some slack by leaving the labor force outright. In addition, a savings pool of $140 billion in bank accounts and war bonds created a huge demand for consumer goods and workers to produce them. Total employment rose rather than fell with the end of the war.

From the other end of the political spectrum, the Taft-Hartley Act climaxed a ten-year effort by conservatives to reverse the gains made by organized labor in the 1930s. The act passed in 1947 because of anger about continuing strikes. In November 1946, Republicans capitalized on the problems of reconversion chaos, labor unrest, and dissatisfaction with Truman. Their election slogan was simple: "Had enough?" The GOP won control of Congress for the first time since the election of 1928, continuing the political trend toward the right that had been apparent since 1938.

Adopted by the now firmly conservative Congress, the Taft-Hartley Act was a serious counterattack by big business against large unions. It outlawed several union tools as "unfair labor practices." It barred the closed shop (the requirement that all workers hired in a given company or plant be union members) and blocked secondary boycotts (strikes against suppliers or customers of a targeted business). The federal government could postpone a strike by imposing a cooling-off period, which gave companies time to stockpile their products. Officers of national unions had to swear that they were not Communists or Communist sympathizers, even though corporate executives had no similar obligation. The bill passed over Truman's veto.

THE GI BILL

The Servicemen's Readjustment Act of 1944 was designed to ease veterans back into the civilian mainstream. Popularly known as the **GI Bill of Rights,** it was one of the federal government's most successful public assistance programs. Rather than pay cash bonuses to veterans, as after previous wars, Congress tied benefits to specific public goals. The GI Bill guaranteed loans of up to $2,000 for buying a house or farm or start-

Taft-Hartley Act Federal legislation of 1947 that substantially limited the tools available to labor unions in labor-management disputes.

Council of Economic Advisers Board of three professional economists established in 1946 to advise the president on economic policy.

GI Bill of Rights Legislation in June 1944 that eased the return of veterans into American society by providing educational and employment benefits.

ing a business, a substantial sum at a time when a new house cost $6,000. The program encouraged veterans to attend college with money for tuition and books plus monthly stipends.

The GI Bill democratized American higher education by making college degrees accessible to men with working-class backgrounds. In the peak year of 1947, veterans made up half of all college students. "We're all trying to get where we would have been if there hadn't been a war," one veteran attending Indiana University told *Time* magazine. However, an unfortunate side effect of the GI tide was to crowd women out of classrooms. Cornell University made room for veterans by limiting women to 20 percent of its entering class; the University of Wisconsin closed its doors to women from out of state. Women's share of bachelor's degrees dropped from 40 percent in 1940 to 25 percent in 1950.

The Best Years of Our Lives dealt realistically with the problems facing veterans trying to readjust to civilian life. Director William Wyler strove for a feeling of accuracy, shooting on location in Cincinnati and costuming the actors in clothing bought in local stores.

RKO Radio Pictures/Hulton Archive

ASSEMBLY-LINE NEIGHBORHOODS

Americans faced a housing shortage after the war. In 1947, fully 3 million married couples were unable to set up their own households.

The solution started with the federal government and its Veterans Administration (VA) mortgage program. By guaranteeing repayment, the VA allowed veterans to get home-purchase loans from private lenders without a down payment. Eyeing the mass market created by the federal programs, innovative private builders devised their own solution. In 1947, William Levitt, a New York builder who had developed defense housing projects, built 2,000 houses for veterans on suburban Long Island. His basic house had 800 square feet of living space in two bedrooms, living room, kitchen, and a bath. It was only one-third the size of the typical new house 50 years later, but it gave new families a place to start. There were 6,000 **Levittown** houses by the end of 1948 and more than 17,000 by 1951.

Other successful builders worked on the same scale. Floor plans were square, simple, and easy for semiskilled workers to construct. For the first time, kitchens across America were designed for preassembled cabinets and appliances in standard sizes. "On-site fabrication" was mass production without an assembly line. Work crews in the Los Angeles suburb of Lakewood started a hundred houses a day as they moved down one side of the street and back up the other.

From 1946 through 1950, the federal government backed $20 billion in VA and Federal Housing Administration (FHA) loans, approximately 40 percent of all home-mortgage debt. Housing starts neared 2 million in the peak year of 1950. By the end of the 1940s, 55 percent of American households owned their homes. All during this time, the suburban population grew much faster than the population of central cities, and the population outside of metropolitan areas actually declined.

Isolation and Discrimination. Unfortunately, the suburban solution to the housing shortage had some costs. The vast new housing tracts tended to isolate women and children from traditional community life. And, as the migration of black workers and their families to northern and western cities continued after the war, discrimination excluded them from new housing. As late as 1960, the 82,000 residents of Levittown had no African-American neighbors. Federal housing agencies and private industry worsened the problem by **redlining** older neighborhoods, which involved withholding home-purchase loans and insurance coverage from inner-city areas.

QUICK REVIEW

Housing Shortages
- Americans faced housing shortages after the war.
- The VA mortgage program allowed veterans to purchase homes without a down payment.
- Builders responded with mass-produced housing.

Levittown   Suburban Long Island community of postwar rental houses built by William Levitt for veterans of World War II.

Redlining   The withholding of home purchase loans and insurance coverage from innercity older neighborhoods by federal housing agencies and private industry.

Jackie Robinson, the first black player in modern major league baseball, joined the Brooklyn Dodgers in 1947. He was both personally courageous and an outstanding player. Here he steals home against the Chicago Cubs in 1952.

Corbis/Bettmann

Public and private actions kept African Americans in deteriorating inner-city ghettos. In Chicago, where an estimated 27,000 black migrants were arriving each year, landlords squeezed them into run-down buildings, subdividing larger apartments into one-room "kitchenette" units, with sinks and hot plates but no private bathrooms. Families who tried to find new homes in white neighborhoods on the edge of black ghettos often met violence in the form of rocks thrown through their windows, firebombs, and angry white mobs.

STEPS TOWARD CIVIL RIGHTS

The urgent need for decent housing helped to motivate African Americans to demand full rights as citizens. The wartime experience of fighting for freedom abroad while suffering discrimination at home steeled a new generation of black leaders to close the gap between America's ideal of equality and its performance. As had also been true after World War I, some white Americans held the opposite view, and a wave of racist violence surged across the South after the war; special targets were black veterans who tried to register to vote. However, many white Americans felt uneasy about the contradiction between a crusade for freedom abroad and racial discrimination at home.

In this era of rapid change and racial tension, the Truman administration recognized the importance of upholding civil rights for all Americans. Caught between pressure from black leaders and the fear of alienating southern Democrats, the president in 1946 appointed the Committee on Civil Rights, whose report developed an agenda for racial justice that would take two decades to put into effect. The NAACP had already begun a campaign of antisegregation lawsuits, which the Justice Department now began to support.

The president also ordered "equality of treatment and opportunity" in the armed services in July 1948. The army in particular dragged its feet, hoping to limit black enlistees to 10 percent of the total. Manpower needs and the record of integrated units in the war in Korea from 1950 to 1953 persuaded the reluctant generals. Over the next generation, African Americans would find the military an important avenue for career opportunities.

More Americans were interested in lowering racial barriers in professional team sports. The center of attention was Jack Roosevelt ("Jackie") Robinson, a gifted African-American athlete, who opened the 1947 baseball season as a member of the Brooklyn Dodgers. Robinson broke the color line that had reserved the modern major leagues for white players. In the segregated society of the 1940s, Robinson found himself a powerful symbol of racial change.

CONSUMER BOOM AND BABY BOOM

The housing boom was a product of both pent-up demand and a postwar "family boom." Americans celebrated the end of the war with weddings; the marriage rate in 1946 surpassed even its wartime high. Many women who left the labor force opted for marriage, and at increasingly younger ages. By 1950, the median age at which women married would be just over 20 years—lower than at any previous time in the twentieth century. The United States ended the 1940s with 7 million more married couples than at the decade's start.

New marriages jump-started the "baby boom," as did already married couples who decided to catch up after postponing childbearing during the war. In the early 1940s, an average of 2.9 million children per year were born in the United States; in 1946–1950, the average was 3.6 million. Those 3.5 million "extra" babies needed diapers, swing sets, lunch boxes, bicycles, and schoolrooms. Fast-growing families also needed to stock up on household goods. Out of an average household income of roughly $4,000 in 1946 and 1947, a family of four had $300 to $400 a year for furnishings and appliances.

TRUMAN, REPUBLICANS, AND THE FAIR DEAL

From new radios to new homes to new jobs, the economic gains of the postwar years propelled Americans toward the political center. After 15 years of economic crisis and world war, they wanted to enjoy prosperity. William Levitt tried to humorously capture the American satisfaction with the fruits of free enterprise when he said in 1948 that "no man who owns his house and lot can be a Communist; he has too much to do."

Recognizing this attitude, Harry Truman and his political advisers tried to define policies acceptable to moderate Republicans as well as to Democrats. This meant creating a bipartisan coalition to block Soviet influence in western Europe and defending the core of the New Deal's social and economic agenda at home.

This political package is known as the strategy of the "vital center," after the title of a 1949 book by Arthur Schlesinger, Jr. The book linked anti-communism in foreign policy with efforts to enact inclusive social and economic policies to extend freedom abroad and at home. The vital center reflected the political reality of the Cold War years, when Democrats had to prove that they were tough on communism before they could enact domestic reforms.

TRUMAN'S OPPOSITION

Besides the Republicans, Truman faced new fringe parties on the far right and far left that allowed him to position himself in the moderate center. The blunt, no-nonsense Missourian entered the campaign an underdog, but he soon looked like the country's best option for steering a steady course.

Truman's opponents represented the left-leaning American Progressive Party, the **Dixiecrats** (officially the States' Rights Democrats), and the Republicans. The Progressive candidate was Henry Wallace, who had been FDR's vice president from 1941 to 1945. The Dixiecrat, Governor Strom Thurmond of South Carolina, had bolted the Democratic Party over civil rights. The most serious challenger was the Republican, Thomas Dewey, who had run against Roosevelt in 1944.

Wallace cast himself as the prophet for "the century of the common man" and argued that the United States was forcing the Cold War on the Soviet Union and undermining American ideals by diverting attention from poverty and racism at home. He wanted to repeal the draft and destroy atomic weapons. His arguments had merit, for the United States was becoming a militarized society, but Wallace struck most voters as a kook rather than a statesman, and he made skepticism about the Cold War increasingly vulnerable to right-wing attack.

At the other political extreme were the southerners who walked out when the 1948 Democratic National Convention called for full civil rights for African

HOW WAS Harry Truman able to win the 1948 presidential election?

 WHERE TO LEARN MORE

★ Harry S Truman National Historical Site, Library, and Museum, Independence, Missouri **www.nps.gov/hstr/**

QUICK REVIEW

1948: Candidates for President
- Harry Truman (Democrat).
- Thomas Dewey (Republican).
- Henry Wallace (Progressive).
- Strom Thurmond (States' Rights Democrat, or Dixiecrat).

Dixiecrats States' Rights Democrats.

Harry Truman greets supporters and rail-road workers in Pittsburgh at the start of an 18-state campaign tour in June 1948. Truman's grassroots campaign and down-home style helped him pull out an unexpected victory in November 1948.

AP Wide World Photos

Americans. Mayor Hubert Humphrey of Minneapolis challenged the Democratic Party "to get out of the shadow of states' rights and walk forthrightly into the bright sunshine of human rights." When the angry southerners met to nominate their own candidate, however, the South's important politicians stayed away. Strom Thurmond claimed that the Dixiecrats were really trying to defend Americans against government bureaucracy, not fighting to preserve racial segregation, but few listened outside the deep South.

Tom Dewey had been an effective governor of New York and represented the moderate eastern establishment within the Republican Party. Fortunately for Truman, Dewey lacked the common touch. He was an arrogant campaigner, refusing to interrupt his morning schedule to talk to voters. He acted like a snob and looked like the groom on a wedding cake.

Dewey was also saddled with the results of the Republican-controlled "do-nothing" 80th Congress (1947–1948). Truman used confrontation with Congress to rally voters who had supported the New Deal. Vote for me, Truman argued, to protect the New Deal, or vote Republican to bring back the days of Herbert Hoover. After his nomination in July 1948, Truman called Congress back into session and dared Republicans to enact all the measures for which their party claimed to stand. Congress did nothing, and Truman had more proof that the Republicans were all talk and no show.

WHISTLE-STOPPING ACROSS AMERICA

The 1948 presidential campaign mixed old and new. For the last time, a major candidate crisscrossed the nation by rail and made hundreds of speeches from the rear platforms of trains. For the first time, national television broadcast the two party conventions, although the primitive cameras showed the handful of viewers little more than talking heads. The Republican campaign issued a printed T-shirt that read "Dew-It With Dewey," the earliest advertising T-shirt in the collections of the Smithsonian Institution.

Truman was a widely read and intelligent man who cultivated the image of a backslapper. Crowds across the country greeted him with "Give 'em hell, Harry!" He covered 31,700 miles in his campaign train and gave ten speeches a day. Republicans belittled the small towns and cities he visited, calling them "whistle stops." Democrats made the term a badge of pride for places like Laramie, Wyoming, and Pocatello, Idaho.

Truman brought the campaign home to average Americans. He tied Dewey to inflation, housing shortages, and fears about the future of Social Security. In industrial cities, he hammered at the Taft-Hartley Act. In the West, he pointed out that Democratic administrations had built dams and helped to turn natural resources into jobs. He called the Republicans the party of privilege and arrogance. The Democrats, he said, offered opportunity for farmers, factory workers, and small business owners.

Truman got a huge boost from Dewey's unwillingness to fight. Going into the fall with a huge lead in the public opinion polls, Dewey sought to avoid mistakes and failed to counter Truman's attacks. The results astounded the poll takers, who had stopped sampling opinion in mid-October just as a swing to Truman gathered strength. Wallace and Thurmond each took just under 1.2 million votes. Dewey received nearly 22 million popular votes and 189 electoral votes, but Truman won more than 24 million popular votes and 303 electoral votes (see Map 27–1).

TRUMAN'S FAIR DEAL

Truman hoped to build on the gains of the New Deal. In his State of the Union address in January 1949, he called for a Fair Deal for all Americans. He promised to extend the New Deal and ensure "greater economic opportunity for the mass of the people." Over the next four years, however, conservative Republicans and southern Democrats forced Congress to choose carefully among Truman's proposals. The result was a set of disconnected measures rather than the consistent program that Truman had advocated.

With the Housing Act of 1949, the federal government reaffirmed its concern about families who had been priced out of the private market. The act provided money for local housing agencies to buy, clear, and resell land for housing. The program never worked as intended because of scanty appropriations and poor design of the replacement housing, but it established the goal of decent housing for all Americans.

In 1950, Congress revitalized the weak Social Security program. Benefits went up by an average of 80 percent, and 10.5 million additional people received old-age and survivors' insurance. Most of the new coverage went to rural and small-town people, thus consolidating the broad support that has made it politically difficult to change Social Security ever since, even in the face of projected shortages in the twenty-first century.

Congress rejected other Fair Deal proposals that would remain on the national agenda for decades. A plan to alter the farm subsidy system to favor small farmers rather than agribusiness went nowhere. A Senate filibuster killed a permanent Fair Employment Practices Commission to fight racial discrimination in hiring, halting progress toward civil rights. The medical establishment blocked a proposal for national health insurance as "socialistic." The overall message from Truman's second term was clear: Americans liked what the New Deal had given them but were hesitant about new initiatives.

CONFRONTING THE SOVIET UNION

*I*n 1945, the United States and the Soviet Union were allies, victorious against Germany and planning the defeat of Japan. By 1947, they were engaged in a diplomatic and economic confrontation and soon came close to war over the city of Berlin.

MAP EXPLORATION
To explore an interactive version of this map, go to
http://www.prenhall.com/goldfield3/map27.1

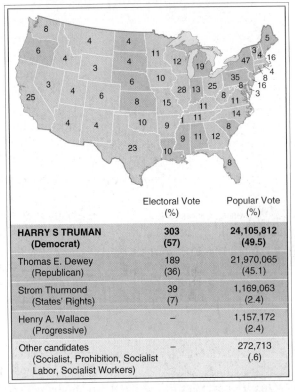

	Electoral Vote (%)	Popular Vote (%)
HARRY S TRUMAN (Democrat)	**303** **(57)**	**24,105,812** **(49.5)**
Thomas E. Dewey (Republican)	189 (36)	21,970,065 (45.1)
Strom Thurmond (States' Rights)	39 (7)	1,169,063 (2.4)
Henry A. Wallace (Progressive)	–	1,157,172 (2.4)
Other candidates (Socialist, Prohibition, Socialist Labor, Socialist Workers)	–	272,713 (.6)

MAP 27–1 The Election of 1948 Harry Truman won a narrow victory in the presidential election of 1948 by holding many of the traditionally Democratic states of the South and West and winning key industrial states in the Middle West. His success depended on the coalition of rural and urban interests that Franklin Roosevelt had pulled together in the 1930s.

WHY DO you think industrial states in the Midwest supported Harry S Truman in the 1948 presidential election?

WHAT WERE the origins of the Cold War?

Over the next 40 years, the United States and the Soviet Union contested for economic, political, and military influence around the globe. The heart of Soviet policy was control of eastern Europe as a buffer zone against Germany. The centerpiece of American policy was to link the United States, western Europe, and Japan into an alliance of overwhelming economic power. Both sides spent vast sums on conventional military forces and atomic weapons that held the world in a "balance of terror."

Americans and Soviets frequently interpreted each other's actions in the most threatening terms, turning miscalculations and misunderstandings into crises. A U.S. public that had suffered through nearly two decades of economic depression and war reacted to international problems with frustration and anger.

THE END OF THE GRAND ALLIANCE

The Yalta Conference of February 1945 had recognized military realities by marking out rough spheres of influence. The Soviet defeat of Germany on the Eastern Front had made the Soviet Union the only military power in eastern Europe. The American and British attacks through Italy and France had made the Western allies dominant in western Europe and the Mediterranean. The Western allies had the better of the bargain. Defeated Italy and Japan, whose reconstruction was firmly in Western hands, had far greater economic potential than Soviet-controlled Bulgaria, Romania, or Hungary.

As the victorious powers tried to put their broad agreements into operation, they argued bitterly about Germany and eastern Europe. Facing Soviet intransigence over eastern Europe, Truman decided that the United States should "take the lead in running the world in the way the world ought to be run." One technique was economic pressure. The State Department "mislaid" a Soviet request for redevelopment loans. The United States also tried to involve the Soviet Union and eastern Europe in new international organizations. The Senate approved American membership in the newly organized United Nations (UN). The Washington-based **International Monetary Fund (IMF)** and the **World Bank** were designed to revive international trade. These organizations ensured that the reviving world economy would revolve around the industrial and technological power of the United States. American leaders were increasingly convinced of Soviet aggressiveness. In February 1946, George Kennan, a senior American diplomat in Moscow, sent a "long telegram" to the State Department. He depicted a Soviet Union driven by expansionist Communist ideology. The Soviets, he argued, would constantly probe for weaknesses in the capitalist world. The best response was firm resistance to protect the Western heartlands.

The British encouraged the same tough stand. Lacking the strength to shape Europe on its own, Great Britain repeatedly nudged the United States to block Soviet influence. Speaking at Westminster College in Missouri in March 1946, Winston Churchill warned that the Soviet Union had dropped an "iron curtain" across the middle of Europe and urged a firm Western response.

Truman's foreign-policy advisers shared the belief in an aggressive Soviet Union. Administration leaders did not fear an immediate Soviet military threat to the United States, for they knew that World War II had exhausted the Soviet Union. But they knew that the Soviets were strong enough to brush aside the U.S. occupation forces in Germany. Added to military apprehension were worries about political and economic competition. In Asia and Africa, the allegiance of nationalists who were fighting for independence from European powers remained in

WHERE TO LEARN MORE

★ United Nations Headquarters, New York, New York **www.un.org**

27–1
George F. Kennan, "Long Telegram" (1946)

International Monetary Fund (IMF) International organization established in 1945 to assist nations in maintaining stable currencies.

World Bank Designed to revive postwar international trade, it drew on the resources of member nations to make economic development loans to governments for such projects as new dams or agricultural modernization.

doubt. America's leaders worried that much of the Eastern Hemisphere might fall under Soviet control.

In their determination to avoid another Munich, Truman and his foreign-policy circle ignored examples of Soviet caution and conciliation. The Soviets withdrew troops from Manchuria in northern China and acquiesced in America's control of defeated Japan. They allowed a neutral but democratic government in Finland. They demobilized much of their huge army and reduced their forces in eastern Europe.

However, the Soviet regime also did more than enough to justify American fears. The Soviet Union could not resist exerting influence in the Middle East. It pressured Turkey to give it partial control of the exit from the Black Sea. It retained troops in northern Iran until warned out by the United States. The Soviets were ruthless in support of Communist control in Eastern Europe in 1946 and 1947. U.S. policymakers read these Soviet actions as a rerun of Nazi aggression and determined not to let a new totalitarian threat undermine Western power.

THE TRUMAN DOCTRINE AND THE MARSHALL PLAN

Whatever restraint the Soviet Union showed was too late or too little. Early in 1947, Truman and his advisers acted decisively. The British could no longer afford to back the Greek government that was fighting Communist rebels, and U.S. officials feared that a Communist takeover in Greece would threaten the stability of Italy, France, and the Middle East. On March 12, he told Congress that the United States faced a "fateful hour" and requested $400 million to fight Communism in Greece and Turkey and secure the free world. Congress agreed, and the United States became the dominant power in the eastern Mediterranean.

In a sweeping declaration that became known as the **Truman Doctrine,** the president pledged to use U.S. economic power to help free nations everywhere resist internal subversion or aggression. "It must be the policy of the United States," he said, "to support free peoples who are resisting attempted subjugation by armed minorities or by outside pressures. . . . I believe that our help should be primarily through economic and financial aid, which is essential to economic stability and orderly political processes."

Meanwhile, Europe was sliding toward chaos. Germany was close to famine after the bitter winter of 1946–1947. Western European nations were bankrupt and unable to import raw materials for their factories. Overstressed medical systems could no longer control tuberculosis and other diseases. Communist parties had gained in Italy, France, and Germany.

Secretary of State George C. Marshall announced the European Recovery Plan on June 5, 1947. What the press quickly dubbed the **Marshall Plan** committed the United States to help rebuild Europe. Aid totaled $13.5 billion over four years. It met many of Europe's economic needs and quieted class conflict. Because Europeans spent much of the aid on U.S. goods and machinery, and because economic recovery promised markets for U.S. products, business and labor both supported it. In effect, the Marshall Plan created an "empire by invitation," in which Americans and Europeans jointly planned Europe's recovery.

U.S. policy in Japan followed the pattern set in Europe. As supreme commander of the Allied Powers, General Douglas MacArthur acted as Japan's postwar dictator. He tried to change the values of the old war-prone Japan through social reform, democratization, and demilitarization. At the end of 1947, however, the

Truman Doctrine President Harry Truman's statement in 1947 that the United States should assist other nations that were facing external pressure or internal revolution.

Marshall Plan Secretary of State George C. Marshall's European Recovery Plan of June 5, 1947, committing the United States to help in the rebuilding of post-World War II Europe.

Berlin was still a devastated city in 1948. When the Soviet Union closed off ground access to the British, French, and American occupation zones, the city became a symbol of the West's Cold War resolve. Allied aircraft lifted in food, fuel, and other essentials for West Berliners for nearly a year until the Soviets ended the blockade.

TimePix

Containment The policy of resisting further expansion of the Soviet bloc through diplomacy and, if necessary, military action, developed in 1947–1948.

Berlin blockade Three-hundred-day Soviet blockade of land access to United States, British, and French occupation zones in Berlin, 1948–1949.

Central Intelligence Agency (CIA) Agency established in 1947 that coordinates the gathering and evaluation of military and economic information on other nations.

National Security Council (NSC) The formal policymaking body for national defense and foreign relations, created in 1947 and consisting of the president, the secretary of defense, the secretary of state, and others appointed by the president.

United States decided that democracy and pacifism could go too far. Policymakers were fearful of economic collapse and political chaos, just as in Europe. The "reverse course" in occupation policy aimed to make Japan an economic magnet for other nations in East Asia, pulling them toward the American orbit and away from the Soviet Union. MacArthur reluctantly accepted the new policy of "economic crankup" by preserving Japan's corporate giants and encouraging American investment. At American insistence, the new Japan accepted American bases and created its own "self-defense force" (with no capacity for overseas aggression).

George Kennan summed up the new American policies in the magazine *Foreign Affairs* in July 1947. Writing anonymously as "X," Kennan argued that the proper posture of the United States should be a patient commitment to "firm and vigilant **containment** of Russian expansive tendencies." Kennan warned that the emerging Cold War would be a long conflict, with no quick fixes.

SOVIET REACTIONS

The bold American moves in the first half of 1947 put the Soviet Union on the defensive. East of the Iron Curtain, Hungarian Communists expelled other political parties from a coalition government. Bulgarian Communists shot opposition leaders. Romania, Bulgaria, and Hungary signed defense pacts with the Soviet Union.

In early 1948, the Soviets targeted Czechoslovakia. For three years, a neutral coalition government there on the model of Finland had balanced trade with the West with a foreign policy friendly to the Soviet Union. In February 1948, while Russian forces assembled on the Czech borders, local Communists pushed aside Czechoslovakia's democratic leadership and turned the nation into a dictatorship and Soviet satellite within a week.

The climax of the Soviet reaction came in divided Berlin, located 110 miles inside the Soviet Union's East German occupation zone. The city was divided into four sectors: one controlled by the Soviets and three by the United States, Britain, and France. On June 4, 1948, Soviet troops blockaded surface traffic into Berlin, cutting off the U.S., British, and French sectors. Rather than abandon 2.5 million Berliners or shoot their way through, the Western nations responded to the **Berlin blockade** by airlifting supplies to the city. Stalin decided not to intercept the flights. After 11 months, the Soviets abandoned the blockade, making the Berlin airlift a triumph of American resolve.

AMERICAN REARMAMENT

The coup in Czechoslovakia and the Berlin blockade shocked American leaders and backfired on the Soviets. Congress responded in 1948 by reinstating the military draft and increasing defense spending.

The National Security Act of July 1947 created the **Central Intelligence Agency (CIA)** and the **National Security Council (NSC).** The CIA handled intelligence gathering and covert operations. The NSC assembled top diplomatic and military advisers in one committee. In 1949, legislation also created the Department of Defense to oversee the army, navy, and air force (independent from the army since 1947).

In April 1949, ten European nations, the United States, and Canada signed the North Atlantic Treaty as a mutual defense pact. American commitments to the **North Atlantic Treaty Organization (NATO)** included military aid and the deployment of U.S. troops in western Europe. In short, NATO was a sort of marriage contract between Europe and the previously standoffish United States. After 1955, its counterpart would be the Warsaw Pact for mutual defense among the Soviet Union and its European satellites.

Two years later, the United States signed similar but less comprehensive agreements in the western Pacific: the ANZUS Pact with Australia and New Zealand and a new treaty with the Philippines. The alliances reassured Pacific allies that were nervously watching the United States negotiate a unilateral peace treaty with Japan (ignoring the Soviet Union). Taken together, peacetime rearmament and mutual defense pacts amounted to a revolution in American foreign policy.

COLD WAR AND HOT WAR

*T*he first phase of the Cold War reached a crisis in the autumn of 1949. Two key events seemed to tilt the world balance against the United States and its allies. In September, Truman announced that the Soviet Union had tested its own atomic bomb. A month later, the Communists under Mao Zedong (Mao Tse-tung) took power in China. The following summer, civil war in Korea sucked the United States into a fierce war with Communist North Korea and China.

THE NUCLEAR SHADOW

Experts in Washington had known that the Soviets were working on an A-bomb, but the news dismayed the average citizen. In 1946, advocates of civilian control had won a small victory when Congress gave control of atomic energy to the new Atomic Energy Commission (AEC). The AEC tried to balance research on atomic power with continued testing of new weapons. Now Truman told the AEC to double the output of fissionable uranium and plutonium for "conventional" nuclear weapons. Nuclear weapons proliferated in the early 1950s. The United States exploded the first hydrogen bomb in the South Pacific in November 1952. Releasing 100 times the energy of the Hiroshima bomb, the detonation tore a mile-long chasm in the ocean floor. Great Britain became the third nuclear power in the same year. The Soviet Union tested its own hydrogen bomb only nine months after the U.S. test.

The nuclear arms race and the gnawing fear of nuclear war multiplied the apprehensions of the Cold War. Under the guidance of the Federal Civil Defense Administration, Americans learned that they should always keep a battery-powered radio and tune to 640 or 1240 on the AM dial for emergency information when they heard air raid sirens.

More insidiously, nuclear weapons development generated new environmental and health problems. Soldiers were exposed to post-test radiation with minimal protection. Nuclear tests in the South Pacific dusted fishing boats with radioactivity and forced islanders to abandon contaminated homes. Las Vegas promoted tests in southern Nevada as tourist attractions, but radioactive fallout contaminated large sections of the West and increased cancer rates among "downwinders" in Utah. Weapons production and atomic experiments contaminated vast tracts in Nevada, Washington, and Colorado and left huge environmental costs for later generations.

THE COLD WAR IN ASIA

Communist victory in China's civil war was as predictable as the Soviet nuclear bomb but no less controversial. The collapse of Jiang Jieshi's Nationalist regime was nearly inevitable, given its corruption and narrow support. Nevertheless, Americans looked for a scapegoat when Jiang's anti-Communist government and remnants of the Nationalist army fled to the island of Taiwan off China's southern coast.

Advocates for Jiang, mostly conservative Republicans from the Midwest and West, were certain that Truman's administration had done too little. Critics looked for scapegoats. Foreign Service officers who had honestly analyzed the weakness of the Nationalists were accused of Communist sympathies and hounded from their jobs. The results were tragedy for those unfairly branded as traitors and damage to the State Department, a weakness that would haunt the United States as it became entangled in southeast Asia in the 1950s and 1960s.

NSC-68 AND AGGRESSIVE CONTAINMENT

The turmoil of 1949 led to a comprehensive statement of American strategic goals. In April 1950, the State Department prepared a sweeping report known as **National Security Council Paper 68 (NSC-68).** The document described a world divided between the forces of "slavery" and "freedom" and assumed that the Soviet Union was actively aggressive, motivated by greed for territory and a "fanatic faith" in Communism. To defend civilization itself, said the experts, the United States should use as much force as needed to resist Communist expansion anywhere and everywhere.

The authors of NSC-68 thought in terms of military solutions. NSC-68 argued that the United States needed to press friendly nations to rearm and make its former enemies into military allies. It also argued that the nation needed expensive conventional forces to defend Europe on the ground and to react to crises as a "world policeman." NSC-68 thus advocated nearly open-ended increases in the defense budget (which, in fact, tripled between 1950 and 1954).

Although it was not a public document, NSC 68's portrait of implacable Communist expansion would have made sense to most Americans; it certainly did to Harry Truman. The outbreak of war in Korea at the end of June 1950 seemed to confirm that Communism was a military threat. The thinking behind the report led the United States to approach the Cold War as a military competition and to view political changes in Africa and Asia as parts of a Soviet plan.

WAR IN KOREA, 1950–1953

The success of Mao and the Chinese Communists forced the Truman administration to define national interests in eastern Asia and the western Pacific. The most important U.S. interest was Japan, still an industrial power despite its devastating defeat. Protected by American armed forces, Japan would be part of a crescent of offshore strong points that included Alaska, the Philippines, Australia, and New Zealand.

Two questions remained at the start of 1950 (and were still troublesome at the end of the century). One was the future of Taiwan and the remnants of Jiang's regime. The other question was Korea, whose own civil war would soon bring the world to the brink of World War III.

The Korean peninsula is the closest point on the Asian mainland to Japan. With three powerful neighbors—China, Russia, and Japan—Korea had always had to fight for its independence. From 1910 to 1945, it was an oppressed colony of the Japanese Empire. As World War II ended, Soviet troops moved down the peninsula from the north and American forces landed in the south, creating a situation similar to that in Germany. The 38th parallel, which Russians and Americans set as the dividing line between their zones of occupation, became a *de facto* border. The United States in 1948 recognized an independent South Korea, with its capital at Seoul, under a conservative government led by Syngman Rhee. The So-

27–3
National Security Council Memorandum Number 68 (1950)

National Security Council Paper 68 (NSC-68) Policy statement that committed the United States to a military approach to the Cold War.

viets recognized a separate North Korea, whose Communist leader, Kim Il Sung, advocated radical social and political change. Both leaders saw the 38th parallel as a temporary barrier and hoped to unify all Koreans under their own rule.

As early as 1947, the United States had decided that Korea was not essential to American military strategy. But Korea remained politically important as the only point of direct confrontation with the Soviet Union in Asia.

On June 25, 1950, North Korea, helped by Soviet equipment and Chinese training, attacked South Korea. The invasion began the **Korean War,** which lasted until 1953 (see Map 27–2). Truman and Secretary of State Dean Acheson believed that Moscow lay behind the invasion. They worried that the attack was a ploy to suck America's limited military resources into Asia before a bigger war came in Europe or the Middle East. The war was really an intensification of an ongoing civil war that Stalin was willing to exploit. Kim originated the invasion plan because he seemed to be losing the civil war in the south, and he spent a year persuading Stalin to agree to it. Stalin hoped that the conquest of South Korea would force Japan to sign a favorable treaty with the USSR.

As the South Korean army collapsed, Truman committed American ground troops from Japan on June 30. The United States also had the good fortune of securing an endorsement from the United Nations. Because the Soviet Union was boycotting the UN, it could not use its veto when the Security Council asked UN members to help South Korea. The Korean conflict remained officially a United Nations action. Although U.S. Generals Douglas MacArthur, Matthew Ridgway, and Mark Clark ran the show as the successive heads of the UN command, 21 other nations committed military resources in a true multinational coalition.

THE POLITICS OF WAR

Fortunes in the first year of the Korean conflict seesawed three times. The first U.S. combat troops were outnumbered, outgunned, and poorly trained. By early August, the Americans clung to a narrow toehold around the port of Pusan on the tip of the Korean peninsula. As reinforcements arrived, however, MacArthur transformed the war with a daring amphibious counterattack at Inchon, 150 miles behind North Korean lines. The North Korean army was already overextended and exhausted. It collapsed and fled north.

MacArthur and Washington officials disregarded warnings by China that it would enter the war if the United States tried to reunite Korea by force. U.S. and South Korean troops rolled north, drawing closer and closer to the boundary between North Korea and China.

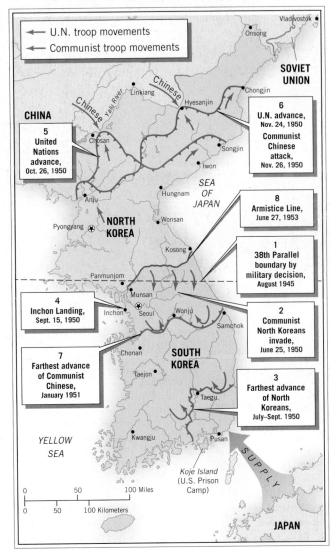

MAP EXPLORATION
To explore an interactive version of this map, go to
http://www.prenhall.com/goldfield3/map27.2

MAP 27–2 The Korean War After rapid reversals of fortune in 1950 and early 1951, the war in Korea settled into stalemate. Most Americans agreed with the need to contain Communist expansion but found it deeply frustrating to fight for limited objectives rather than total victory.

WAS A stalemate the inevitable end to the Korean War? Why or why not?

Korean War Pacific war started on June 25, 1950, when North Korea, helped by Soviet equipment and Chinese training, attacked South Korea.

United Nation forces in Korea fought the weather as well as Communist North Koreans and Chinese. Baking summer heat alternated with fierce winters. Snow and cold were a major help to the Chinese when they surprised United States forces in November 1950 and drove American troops such as these southward.

National Archives and Records Administration

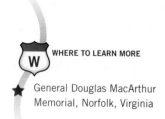

WHERE TO LEARN MORE

General Douglas MacArthur Memorial, Norfolk, Virginia

On November 26, the Chinese struck the overextended American columns. They had massed 300,000 troops without detection by American aviation. Their assault drove the UN forces into a two-month retreat that again abandoned Seoul.

In March 1951, with the UN forces again pushing north, Truman prepared to offer a cease-fire that would have preserved the separate nations of South and North Korea. MacArthur tried to preempt the president by demanding that China admit defeat or suffer the consequences. He then published a direct attack on the administration's policy of limiting the Asian war to ensure the security of Europe. President Truman had no choice. To protect civilian control of the armed forces, he relieved MacArthur of his command on April 11, 1951.

In Korea itself, U.S. and South Korean forces stabilized a strong defensive line that cut diagonally across the 38th parallel. What had started as a civil war was now an international conflict between the two sides in the larger Cold War. For two years, boredom alternated with fierce inch-by-inch battles for territory with such names as Heartbreak Ridge and Pork Chop Hill. Meanwhile, white and black soldiers learned to work together under the pressure of combat (See American Views: "Integrating the Army in Korea").

Stabilization of the Korean front ushered in two years of truce negotiations beginning in July 1951, for none of the key actors wanted a wider war. The Chinese were careful to keep their warplanes north of the ground combat zone. The Russians stayed out of the war. The United States learned a painful lesson in 1950 and was willing to accept a divided Korea. The war was a decisive factor behind the Republican victory in the November 1952 elections and dragged on until June 1953, when an armistice returned the peninsula roughly to its prewar political division.

The blindly ambitious attack into North Korea was one of the great failures of intelligence and strategic leadership in American military history. Nearly everyone in Washington shared the blame. Civilian leaders could not resist the desire to roll back Communism. Truman hoped for a striking victory before the 1950 congressional elections. The Joint Chiefs of Staff failed to adequately question a general with MacArthur's heroic reputation. MacArthur himself allowed ambition and wishful thinking to jeopardize his army.

Consequences of the Korean War.   The war in Korea was a preview of Vietnam 15 years later. American leaders propped up an undemocratic regime to defend democracy. American soldiers found it hard to distinguish between allied and enemy Koreans. American emphasis on massive firepower led U.S. forces to demolish entire villages to kill single snipers. The air force tried to break North Korean resistance by pouring bombs on cities, power stations, factories, and dams.

AMERICAN VIEWS

INTEGRATING THE ARMY IN KOREA

Racial integration of the armed forces became official policy in 1948, but President Truman's directive was not fully implemented until after the war in Korea. Two veterans of that war—white G.I. Harry Summers and black officer Beverly Scott—recall some of the steps toward integration.

- What do these recollections say about the pervasiveness of racism in mid-century American life?
- How has the experience of minority soldiers changed from the 1950s to the 1990s?

Harry Summers: When they first started talking about integration, white soldiers were aghast. They would say, How can you integrate the army? How do you know when you go to the mess hall that you won't get a plate or a knife or a spoon that was used by a Negro? Or when you go to the supply room and draw sheets, you might get a sheet that a Negro had slept on? . . .

I remember a night when your rifle company was scheduled to get some replacements. I was in a three-man foxhole with one other guy, and they dropped this new replacement off at our foxhole. The other guy I was in the foxhole with was under a poncho, making coffee. It was bitterly cold. And pitch dark. He got the coffee made, and he gave me a drink, and he took a drink, and then he offered some to this new replacement, who we literally couldn't see, it was that dark.

And the guy said, "No, I don't want any."

"What the hell are you talking about, you don't want any? You got to be freezing to death. Here, take a drink of coffee."

"Well," he said, "you can't tell it now, but I'm black. And tomorrow morning when you find out I was drink-

ing out of the same cup you were using, you ain't gonna be too happy."

Me and this other guy kind of looked at each other.

"You silly son of a bitch," we told him, "here, take the goddam coffee."

Beverly Scott: The 24th Regiment was the only all-black regiment in the division, and as a black officer in an all-black regiment commanded by whites I was always super sensitive about standing my ground. Being a man. Being honest with my soldiers. . . .

Most of the white officers were good. Taken in the context of the times, they were probably better than the average white guy in civilian life. But there was still that patronizing expectation of failure. White officers came to the 24th Regiment knowing or suspecting or having been told that this was an inferior regiment.

[In September 1951, members of the regiment were integrated into other units.]

I was transferred to the 14th [Regiment] and right away I experienced some problems. People in the 14th didn't want anybody from the 24th. I was a technically qualified communications officer, which the 14th said they needed very badly, but when I got there, suddenly they didn't need any commo officers.

Then their executive officer said, "We got a rifle platoon for you. Think you can handle a rifle platoon?"

What the hell do you mean, can I handle a rifle platoon? I was also trained as an infantry officer. He know that. I was a first lieutenant, been in the army six years . . . If I had been coming in as a white first lieutenant the question never would have been asked.

Source: Rudy Tomedi, *No Bugles, No Drums: An Oral History of the Korean War* (New York: John Wiley, 1993).

The Korean War helped to legitimize the United Nations and set a precedent for its peace-keeping role in places like the Middle East. In Washington, it confirmed the ideas underlying NSC-68, with its call for the United States to expand its military and to lead an anti-Communist alliance. Two days after the North Korean invasion, President Truman ordered the Seventh Fleet to interpose between mainland China and the Nationalist Chinese on Taiwan, a decision that guaranteed 20 years of hostility between the United States and the People's Republic of China. In the same month, the United States began to aid France's struggle to retain control over its Southeast Asian colony of Indochina, which included Laos, Cambodia, and Vietnam.

In Europe, the United States now pushed to rearm West Germany as part of a militarized NATO and sent troops to Europe as a permanent defense force. It increased military aid to European governments and secured a unified command for the national forces allocated to NATO. The unified command made West German rearmament acceptable to France and the smaller nations of western Europe. Rearmament also stimulated German economic recovery and bound West Germany to the political and economic institutions of the North Atlantic nations.

THE SECOND RED SCARE

The Korean War reinforced the second Red Scare, an assault on civil liberties that stretched from the mid-1940s to the mid-1950s and dwarfed the Red Scare of 1919–1920. The Cold War fanned fears of Communist subversion on American soil. The scare was also a weapon that the conservative wing of the Republican Party used against the men and women who had built Roosevelt's New Deal (see the Overview table, "The Second Red Scare").

Efforts to root out suspected subversives operated on three tracks. National and state governments established loyalty programs to identify and fire suspect employees. The courts punished members of suspect organizations. Congressional and state legislative investigations followed the whims of committee chairs. Anti-Communist crusaders often relied on dubious evidence and eagerly believed the worst. They also threatened basic civil liberties.

OVERVIEW THE SECOND RED SCARE

Type of Anti-Communist Effort	Key Tools	Results
Employee loyalty programs	U.S. attorney general's list of subversive organizations	Thousands of federal and state workers fired, careers damaged
Congressional investigations	HUAC McCarran Committee Army-McCarthy hearings	Employee blacklists, harassment of writers and intellectuals, Hollywood Ten
Criminal prosecutions	Trials for espionage and conspiracy to advocate violent overthrow of the U.S. government	Convictions of Communist Party leaders (1949), Alger Hiss (1950), and Rosenbergs (1951)

THE COMMUNIST PARTY AND THE LOYALTY PROGRAM

The Communist Party in the United States was in rapid decline after World War II. Many intellectuals had left the party over the Nazi-Soviet Pact in 1939. In 1946, Walter Reuther defeated a Communist for the presidency of the huge United Auto Workers union, and other CIO unions froze Communists out of leadership positions. Communist support for Henry Wallace reduced the party's influence and separated it from the increasingly conservative mainstream of American politics.

Nevertheless, Republicans used Red-baiting as a campaign technique in 1944 and 1946, setting the stage for a national loyalty program. In 1944 they tried to frighten voters about "commydemocrats" by linking FDR, CIO labor unions, and Communism. Democrats slung their own mud by trying to convince voters that Hitler preferred the Republicans. Two years later, Republican campaigners told the public that the basic choice was "between Communism and Republicanism." Starting a 30-year political career, a young navy veteran named Richard Nixon won a southern California congressional seat by hammering on his opponent's connections to supposedly Communist-dominated organizations.

President Truman responded to the Republican landslide with Executive Order 9835 in March 1947, initiating a loyalty program for federal employees. Order 9835 was a blunt instrument. It authorized the attorney general to prepare a list of "totalitarian, Fascist, Communist, or subversive" organizations and made membership or even "sympathetic association" with such groups grounds for dismissal.

Federal employees worked under a cloud of fear. Would the cooperative store they had once patronized or the protest group they had joined in college suddenly appear on the attorney general's list? Would someone complain that they had disloyal books on their shelves? Loyalty boards asked about religion, racial equality, and a taste for foreign films; they also tried to identify homosexuals, who were thought to be targets for blackmail by foreign agents. The loyalty program resulted in 1,210 firings and 6,000 resignations under Truman and comparable numbers during Dwight Eisenhower's first term from 1953 to 1956.

NAMING NAMES TO CONGRESS

Congress was even busier than the executive branch. The congressional hunt for subversives had its roots in 1938, when Congressman Martin Dies, a Texas Democrat, created the Special Committee on Un-American Activities. Originally intended to ferret out pro-Fascists, the Dies Committee evolved into the permanent **House Un-American Activities Committee (HUAC)** in 1945. It investigated "un-American propaganda" that attacked constitutional government.

One of HUAC's juiciest targets was Hollywood. In the last years before television, the movie industry stood at the height of its capacity to influence public opinion. In 1946, Americans bought an average of 90 million tickets every week. But Hollywood's reputation for loose morals, foreign-born directors, Jewish producers, and left-leaning writers aroused the suspicions of many congressmen. HUAC sought to make sure that no un-American messages were being peddled through America's most popular entertainment.

When the hearings opened in October 1947, studio executives, such as Jack Warner of Warner Brothers and Louis B. Mayer of MGM, assured HUAC of their anti-Communism. So did the popular actors Gary Cooper and Ronald Reagan. By contrast, eight screenwriters and two directors—the so-called Hollywood Ten—

House Un-American Activities Committee (HUAC) Originally intended to ferret out pro-Fascists, it later investigated "un-American propaganda" that attacked constitutional government.

26–6
Ronald Reagan,
Testimony before the
House Un-American
Activities Committee
(1947)

refused to discuss their past political associations, citing the free-speech protections of the First Amendment to the Constitution. HUAC countered with citations for contempt of Congress. The First Amendment defense failed when it reached the Supreme Court, and the Ten went to jail in 1950.

HUAC changed the politics of Hollywood. Before 1947, it had been fashionable to lean toward the left. After the hearings, it was imperative to tilt the other way. The government refused to let British-born Charlie Chaplin reenter the United States in 1952 because of his left-wing views. Other actors, writers, and directors found themselves on the Hollywood blacklist, banned from jobs where they might insert Communist propaganda into American movies.

At the start of 1951, the new Senate Internal Security Subcommittee joined the sometimes bumbling HUAC. The McCarran Committee, named for the Nevada senator who chaired it, targeted diplomats, labor union leaders, professors, and schoolteachers. Both committees turned their investigations into rituals. The real point of the investigations was not to force personal confessions from witnesses but to badger them into identifying friends and associates who might have been involved in suspect activities.

The only sure way to avoid "naming names" was to respond to every question by citing the Fifth Amendment to the Constitution, which protects Americans from testifying against themselves. Many Americans assumed that citing the amendment was a sure sign of guilt, not a matter of principle, and talked about Fifth Amendment Communists.

State legislatures imitated Congress by searching for "Reducators" among college faculty in such states as Oklahoma, Washington, and California. College presidents frequently fired faculty who took the Fifth Amendment. The experience of an economics professor fired from the University of Kansas City after testifying before the McCarran Committee was typical. He found it hard to keep any job once his name had been in the papers. A local dairy fired him because it thought its customers might be uneasy having a radical handle their milk bottles.

SUBVERSION TRIALS

In 1948, the Justice Department indicted the leaders of the American Communist Party under the Alien Registration Act of 1940. Eleven men and women were convicted in 1949 of conspiring to advocate the violent overthrow of the United States government through their speech and publications.

In 1948, a former Communist, Whittaker Chambers, named Alger Hiss as a Communist with whom he had associated in the 1930s. Hiss denied any involvement with Communists and sued Chambers for slander. As proof, Chambers revealed microfilms that he had hidden inside a pumpkin on his Maryland farm, and Congressman Richard Nixon quickly announced the discovery. Tests seemed to show that the "pumpkin papers" were State Department documents that had been copied on a typewriter Hiss had once owned. With the new evidence, the Justice Department indicted Hiss for perjury—lying under oath. A first perjury trial ended in deadlock, but a second jury convicted Hiss in January 1950.

For more than 40 years, the essence of his case was a matter of faith, not facts. Even his enemies agreed that any documents he might have stolen were of limited importance. What was important, they said, was the sort of disloyalty and "weak thinking" that Hiss represented. To his opponents, Hiss stood for every wrong turn the nation had taken since 1932. In contrast, his supporters found a virtue in every trait his enemies hated. Many supporters believed that he had been framed. Both sides claimed support from Soviet records that became public in the 1990s; the weight of evidence seems to confirm that he did pass information to the Soviets from the mid-1930s through 1945.

The case of Julius and Ethel Rosenberg represented a similar test of belief. In 1950, the British arrested nuclear physicist Klaus Fuchs, who confessed to passing atomic secrets to the Soviets when he worked at Los Alamos in 1944 and 1945. The "Fuchs spy ring" soon implicated the Rosenbergs. Convicted in 1951 on the vague charge of conspiring to commit espionage, they were sent to the electric chair in 1953 after refusing to buy a reprieve by naming other spies.

As with Alger Hiss, the government had a plausible but not airtight case. There is no doubt that Julius Rosenberg was a convinced Communist. It is likely that he was a minor participant in a Soviet spy ring, but he probably did not pass atomic secrets. Ethel Rosenberg was charged, in the words of FBI director J. Edgar Hoover, "as a lever" to pressure her husband into naming his confederates.

SENATOR MCCARTHY ON STAGE

The best-remembered participant in the second Red Scare was Senator Joseph McCarthy of Wisconsin. Crude, sly, and ambitious, McCarthy had ridden to victory in the Republican landslide of 1946. He burst into national prominence on February 9, 1950. In a rambling speech in Wheeling, West Virginia, he latched on to the issue of Communist subversion. Although no transcript of the speech survives, he supposedly stated; "I have here in my hand a list of 205 that were known to the Secretary of State as being members of the Communist Party and who, nevertheless, are still working and shaping the policy of the State Department." In the following days, the 205 Communists changed quickly to 57, to 81, to 10, to 116. Over the next several years, his speeches were aimed at moving targets, full of multiple untruths. He threw out so many accusations, true or false, that the facts could never catch up.

The Senate disregarded McCarthy, but the public heard only the accusations, not the lack of evidence. Senators treated McCarthy as a crude outsider in their exclusive club, but voters in 1950 turned against his most prominent opponents. In 1951, McCarthy even called George Marshall, then serving as secretary of defense, an agent of Communism. The idea was ludicrous. Marshall was one of the most upright Americans of his generation, the architect of victory in World War II, and a key contributor to the stabilization of Europe. That fall, the Republican presidential candidate, Dwight Eisenhower, appeared on the same campaign platform with McCarthy and conspicuously failed to defend George Marshall, who had been chiefly responsible for Eisenhower's fast-track career.

McCarthy's personal crudeness made him a media star but eventually undermined him. Given control of the Senate Committee on Government Operations in 1953, he investigated dozens of agencies from the Government Printing Office to the Army Signal Corps. Early in 1954, he investigated an army dentist with a supposedly subversive background. The back-and-forth confrontation led to two months of televised hearings. The cameras brought political debates into living rooms and put McCarthy's bullying style on trial. "Have you no decency?" asked the army's lawyer, Joseph Welch, at one point.

The end came quickly. McCarthy's "favorable" rating in the polls plummeted. The comic strip *Pogo* began to feature a foolishly menacing figure with McCarthy's face named Simple J. Malarkey. The U.S. Senate finally voted 67 to 22 in December 1954 to condemn McCarthy for conduct "unbecoming a Member of the Senate." When he died in 1957, he had been repudiated by the Senate and ignored by the media that had built him up.

Senator Joe McCarthy used press releases and carefully managed congressional committee hearings to attack suspected Communists, although he had almost no hard information. At the Army-McCarthy hearings in June 1954, he clashed with attorney Joseph Welch. Here Welch listens as McCarthy points to Oregon on a map that supposedly showed Communist Party organization in the United States.

UPI/Corbis/Bettman

McCarthyism   Anti-Communist attitudes and actions associated with Senator Joe McCarthy in the early 1950s, including smear tactics and innuendo.

UNDERSTANDING MCCARTHYISM

The antisubversive campaign that everyone now calls **McCarthyism,** however, died a slower death. Legislation, such as the Internal Security Act (1950) and the Immigration and Nationality Act (1952), remained as tools of political repression. HUAC continued to mount investigations as late as the 1960s.

Fear of Communist subversion reached deep into American society. In retrospect, at least four factors made Americans afraid of Communist subversion. One was a legitimate but exaggerated concern about atomic spies. A second was an undercurrent of anti-Semitism and nativism, for many labor organizers and Communist Party members (like the Rosenbergs) had Jewish and eastern European backgrounds. Third was southern and western resentment of the nation's Ivy League elite. Most general, finally, was a widespread fear that the world was spinning out of control. Many people sought easy explanations for global tensions. It was basically reassuring if Soviet and Chinese Communist successes were the result of American traitors rather than of Communist strengths.

Partisan politics mobilized the fears and resentments into a political force. From 1946 through 1952, the conservative wing of the Republican Party used the Red Scare to attack New Dealers and liberal Democrats. HUAC, the McCarran Committee, and McCarthy were all tools for bringing down the men and women who had been moving the United States toward a more active government at home and abroad.

The broader goal of the second Red Scare was conformity of thought. Many of the professors and bureaucrats targeted for investigation had indeed been Communists or interested in Communism, usually in the 1930s and early 1940s. Most saw it as a way to increase social justice, and they sometimes excused the failures of Communism in the Soviet Union. Unlike the handful of real spies, however, they were targeted not for actions but for ideas. The investigations and loyalty programs were efforts to ensure that Americans kept any left-wing ideas to themselves.

Conclusion

*I*n the face of confrontation over Berlin, fighting in Korea, and growing numbers of nuclear weapons, the Cold War stayed cool because each side achieved its essential goals. The Soviet Union controlled eastern Europe, while the United States built increasingly strong ties with the NATO nations and Japan. Though the result was a stalemate, it nevertheless absorbed huge shares of Soviet and American resources and conditioned the thinking of an entire generation.

The shift from prewar isolationism to postwar internationalism was one of the most important changes in the nation's history. To many of its advocates, internationalism represented a commitment to spread political democracy to other nations. Even as the results overseas fell short of the ideal, however, the new internationalism highlighted and helped change domestic racial attitudes.

The Truman years saw the implementation of a national security policy that dominated the next half-century. The armed forces were strong but subordinate to the civilian administration through the National Security Council and Department of Defense. The expansion of the close alliance between scientific research and defense needs that had begun with World War II augmented the national defense capacity. The United States led an international system of collective security based on mutual defense treaties, contributing financial assistance and sophisticated weapons while its allies helped to provide the military manpower.

These same years also brought increasing stability within the nation. Americans in the early 1950s could be confident that New Deal and Fair Deal programs to expand economic opportunity and increase economic security were permanent, if incomplete, setting the stage for new social activism in the 1960s. If the Republicans had won in 1948, they might have dismantled the New Deal. By 1952, both presidential candidates affirmed the consensus that placed economic opportunity at the center of the national agenda.

Despite the turmoil and injustice of the second Red Scare and deep worries about nuclear war, the United States emerged from the Truman years remarkably prosperous. The years from 1946 to 1952 set the themes for a generation that believed that the United States could do whatever it set its mind to: end poverty, land an astronaut on the moon, thwart Communist revolutions in other countries. As the world moved slowly toward greater stability in the 1950s, Americans were ready for a decade of confidence.

Summary

Launching the Great Boom Americans feared demobilization would bring inflation and unemployment, but the immediate postwar years ushered in an economic expansion that would last a quarter century; the resulting prosperity would finance a military buildup and activist foreign policy. Veterans benefited from VA mortgages and the GI Bill of Rights; the need for family housing fueled a boom and suburbs expanded; the housing boom was a product of the consumer and baby booms. The first steps toward civil rights for African Americans were taken; the crusade for freedom abroad had contrasted with the racial discrimination faced at home.

Truman, Republicans, and the Fair Deal   The economic gains of the postwar years propelled Americans toward the political center; after depression and war they wanted prosperity. In his campaign for a full term as president in 1948, Truman faced third-party candidates in addition to Republican Thomas Dewey. Truman appealed to average Americans and his victory astounded the pollsters. The Fair Deal showed that Americans liked what the New Deal had given them but were hesitant about major new initiatives.

Confronting the Soviet Union   By 1947 the former allies were involved in a conflict that came to be known as the Cold War. Both sides assumed the other's ill will, spent vast amounts on military forces and atomic weapons, and competed for political advantage around the globe. As the "iron curtain" divided Europe, the Marshall Plan committed the United States to aid European recovery. The announcement of the Truman Doctrine brought Soviet reactions climaxing in the Berlin blockade; the formation of the CIA, NSC, and signing mutual defense pacts such as NATO amounted to a revolution in American foreign policy.

Cold War and Hot War   The news that the Soviet Union and China had developed nuclear bombs helped begin the "arms race" and the fear of nuclear war multiplied the apprehensions of the Cold War. America's strategic goals were outlined in NSC-68: America would use force to counter communist aggression: The first use of this policy was in Korea. North Korea, helped by Soviet equipment and Chinese training, attacked South Korea. The Korean War, which lasted until 1953, had global consequences and was a preview of another war to come.

The Second Red Scare   The Korean War reinforced the second Red Scare, an assault on civil liberties that dwarfed the Red Scare of 1919–1920. The Cold War fanned fears of Communist subversion on American soil. Legitimate concerns about espionage mixed with suspicions that Communist sympathizers in high places were helping China and the Soviet Union. Loyalty programs and the Congressional hunt for subversives such as that by Senator Joseph McCarthy showed how deep the fear of Communists was in the country.

IMAGE KEY

for pages 786–787

a. Man reads "The Mirror" which features Lucille Ball.

b. Mother, father, and 3 children in fallout shelter.

c. North Atlantic Treaty Organization document.

d. The 1946 movie *"The Best Years of Our Life."*

e. Civilians atop bombed out ruins of buildings watching American C-54 cargo plane fly overhead during Allied airlift to bring food & supplies to beseiged citizens of Soviet controlled Berlin.

f. Unidentified model displaying a kitchen interior, photo 1950s.

g. American President Harry Truman shakes hands with supporters from a train car during a rally in the 1948 presidential campaign.

h. "Fallout shelter" sign.

i. Senator Joseph McCarthy points to Oregon on a organizational map implying Communist Party organization in the United States.

j. Air lifting food and supplies to West Berliners.

REVIEW QUESTIONS

1. As described in the opening of the chapter, what housing choices were available after World War II? How did these choices reshape American cities? How did the postwar readjustment create a suburban society?

2. What were the key differences between Harry Truman and congressional Republicans about the legacy of the New Deal? Why did regulating labor unions become a central domestic issue in the late 1940s? Why did Truman manage to win the presidential election of 1948 despite starting as an underdog?

3. How did the postwar years expand opportunity for veterans and members of the working class? How did they limit opportunities for women? How did they begin to challenge racial inequities in American society?

4. What foreign policy priorities did the United States set after 1945? To what extent did the United States achieve its most basic objectives? How did mutual mistrust fuel and deepen the Cold War?

5. How did the Cold War change character in 1949 and 1950? What were key actions by the Soviet Union and China, and how did the United States respond? What was the effect of the chaotic fighting in Korea on U.S. domestic politics and diplomacy?

6. What factors motivated an increasingly frantic fear of domestic subversion in the late 1940s and early 1950s? Who were the key actors in the second Red Scare? What was its long-term impact on American society?

7. How did the continuation and expansion of the nation's global commitments after 1945 affect life in the United States?

KEY TERMS

Berlin blockade   (p. 798)
Central Intelligence Agency (CIA)
  (p. 798)
Cold War   (p. 788)
Containment   (p. 798)
Council of Economic Advisers
  (p. 790)
Dixiecrats   (p. 793)
GI Bill of Rights   (p. 790)

House Un-American Activities
  Committee (HUAC)   (p. 805)
International Monetary Fund (IMF)
  (p. 796)
Korean War   (p. 801)
Levittown   (p. 791)
Marshall Plan   (p. 797)
McCarthyism   (p. 808)
National Security Council

(NSC)   (p. 798)
National Security Council Paper 68
  (NSC-68)   (p. 800)
North Atlantic Treaty Organization
  (NATO)   (p. 799)
Redlining   (p. 791)
Taft-Hartley Act   (p. 790)
Truman Doctrine   (p. 797)
World Bank   (p. 796)

WHERE TO LEARN MORE

 Harry S Truman National Historical Site, Library, and Museum, Independence, Missouri. The museum has exhibits on Truman's political career and U.S. history during his administration. Also in Independence is the Harry S Truman Courtroom and Office, with exhibits on his early career. **www.nps.gov/hstr/**

 General Douglas MacArthur Memorial, Norfolk, Virginia. The MacArthur Memorial in downtown Norfolk commemorates the career of a key figure in shaping the postwar world.

 United Nations Headquarters, New York, New York. A tour of the United Nations complex in New York is a reminder of the new organizations for international cooperation that emerged from World War II. **www.un.org**

 U.S. History Document CD-ROM
For primary sources related to this chapter, refer to the document CD-ROM.

 www.prenhall.com/goldfield
For study resources related to this chapter, visit the *Companion Website*™.

28 The Confident Years
1953–1964

CHAPTER HIGHLIGHTS

A Decade of Affluence President Eisenhower presided over the prosperity of the 1950s. Suburbs and the "car culture" grew. Families were seen as part of the anti-Communist crusade. A new "youth culture" emerged. The conformity and confidence of mainstream culture masked considerable inequality and dissatisfaction.

Facing Off with the Soviet Union The policies of the United States and Soviet Union created a bipolar world. The Soviet launch of Sputnik shook the certainty of many Americans about U.S. technological superiority. Overseas intervention and "brinksmanship" characterized this period of the Cold War.

John F. Kennedy and the Cold War Television played a key role in Kennedy's defeat of Richard Nixon in the 1960 presidential election. The Kennedy administration made a number of mistakes that contributed to growing tension between the United States and the Soviet Union. The Cuban missile crisis brought the world to the brink of nuclear war. Kennedy committed the United States to landing a man on the moon.

Righteousness Like a Mighty Stream: The Struggle for Civil Rights The Supreme Court's *Brown* decision made the effort to secure civil rights for African Americans a challenge to American society. The first phase of the struggle for civil rights culminated in the March on Washington in 1963. African Americans used a variety of tactics to push for integration of schools and public facilities, voting rights, and legal equality.

"Let Us Continue" After Kennedy's assassination, Lyndon Johnson pursued a domestic agenda centered on economic betterment and racial equality. The legislation underlying his War on Poverty and Great Society was passed before the escalation of the war in Vietnam eroded his political standing.

MISSILE EQUIPMENT
MARIEL PORT FACILITY
4 NOVEMBER 1962

CHAPTER QUESTIONS

HOW DID the "Decade of Affluence" alter social and religious life in America?

WHAT IMPACT did Dwight Eisenhower's foreign policy have on U.S. relations with the Soviet Union?

WHAT WAS John F. Kennedy's approach to dealing with the Soviet Union?

WHAT WAS the significance of *Brown v. Board of Education of Topeka*?

HOW DID Lyndon B. Johnson continue the domestic agenda inherited from the Kennedy Administration? In what ways did he depart from it?

TV *happiness shared by all the family!*

CHAPTER OUTLINE

- A Decade of Affluence
- Facing Off with the Soviet Union
- John F. Kennedy and the Cold War
- Righteousness Like a Mighty Stream: The Struggle for Civil Rights
- "Let Us Continue"

IMAGE KEY
for pages 812–813 is on page 840.

The first day I was able to enter Central High School [in Little Rock, Arkansas, September 23, 1957], what I felt inside was terrible, wrenching, awful fear. On the car radio I could hear that there was a mob. I knew what a mob meant and I knew that the sounds that came from the crowd were very angry. So we entered the side of the building, very, very fast. Even as we entered there were people running after us, people tripping other people. . . . There has never been in my life any stark terror or any fear akin to that. I'd only been in the school a couple of hours and by that time it was apparent that the mob was just overrunning the school. Policemen were throwing down their badges and the mob was getting past the wooden sawhorses because the police would no longer fight their own in order to protect us. So we were all called into the principal's office, and there was great fear that we would not get out of this building. We were trapped. And I thought, Okay, so I'm going to die here, in school. . . . Even the adults, the school officials, were panicked, feeling like there was no protection. . . . [A] gentleman, who I believed to be the police chief, said . . . "I'll get them out." And we were taken to the basement of this place. And we were put into two cars, grayish blue Fords. And the man instructed the drivers, he said, "Once you start driving, do not stop." And he told us to put our heads down. This guy revved up his engine and he came up out of the bowels of this building, and as he came up, I could just see hands reaching across this car, I could hear the yelling, I could see guns, and he was told not to stop. "If you hit somebody, you keep rolling, 'cause the kids are dead." And he did just that, and he didn't hit anybody, but he certainly was forceful and aggressive in the way he exited this driveway, because people tried to stop him and he didn't stop. He dropped me off at home. And I remember saying, "Thank you for the ride," and I should've said, "Thank you for my life."

Melba Pattillo Beals, in Henry Hampton and Steve Frayer, eds., *Voices of Freedom: An Oral History of the Civil Rights Movement from the 1950s through the 1980s* (New York: Bantam, 1990).

MELBA PATTILLO WAS one of the nine African-American students who entered previously all-white Central High in the fall of 1957. Her enrollment in the high school, where she managed to last through a year of harassment and hostility, was a symbolic step in the journey toward greater racial equality in American society. School integration in Little Rock implemented the U.S. Supreme Court decision in the case of *Brown v. Board of Education* in 1954, which declared that racially segregated schools violated the mandate that all citizens receive equal protection of the law. The violence with which some white residents of Little Rock responded, and the courage of the students, marked one of the key episodes in the civil rights revolution that spanned roughly a decade from the *Brown* decision to the Voting Rights Act of 1965.

The struggle for full civil rights for all Americans was rooted in national ideals, but it was also shaped by the continuing tensions of the Cold War. President Dwight Eisenhower acted against his own inclinations and sent federal troops to keep the peace in Little Rock in part because he worried about public opinion in other nations. As the United States and the Soviet Union maneuvered for influence in Africa and Asia, domestic events sometimes loomed large in foreign relations.

Melba Pattillo's life after Little Rock also reveals something about the increasing economic opportunities available to most Americans. She graduated from San Francisco State University, earned a master's degree from Columbia University, and worked as a television reporter and writer. San Francisco State was part of the great expansion of higher education that helped millions of Americans move into middle-class jobs and neighborhoods. The prosperous years from 1953 to 1964 spread the economic promise of the 1940s across American society. Young couples could afford large families and new houses. Labor unions grew conservative because cooperation with big business offered immediate gains for their members.

Despite challenges at home and abroad, Americans were fundamentally confident during the decade after the Korean War. They expected corporations to use scientific research to craft new products for eager customers and medical researchers to conquer diseases. When the USSR challenged U.S. preeminence and launched the first artificial space satellite in 1957, Americans responded with shock followed by redoubled efforts to regain what they considered their rightful world leadership in science and technology.

A DECADE OF AFFLUENCE

HOW DID the "Decade of Affluence" alter social and religious life in America?

Americans in the 1950s believed in the basic strength of the United States. Television's *General Electric Theater* was third in the ratings in 1956–1957. Every week, its host, Ronald Reagan, a popular Hollywood lead from the late 1930s, stated, "At General Electric, progress is our most important product." It made sense to his viewers. Large, technologically sophisticated corporations were introducing new marvels: Orlon sweaters and Saran Wrap, long-playing records and Polaroid cameras. As long as the United States defended free enterprise, Reagan told audiences on national speaking tours, the sky was the limit.

Many Americans valued free enterprise and family life as part of the anti-Communist crusade. Social and intellectual conformity ensured a united front. Congress established Loyalty Day in 1955. National leaders argued that strong families were bulwarks against Communism and that churchgoing inoculated people against subversive ideas. Under the lingering cloud of McCarthyism, the range of political ideas that influenced government policy was narrower than in the 1930s and 1940s. Nevertheless, critics began to voice the discontents that exploded in the 1960s and 1970s.

WHAT'S GOOD FOR GENERAL MOTORS

Dwight Eisenhower presided over the prosperity of the 1950s. In 1952 he easily defeated the Democratic candidate, Adlai Stevenson, the moderately liberal governor of Illinois. Over the next eight years, Eisenhower claimed the political middle for Republicans. Publicists tried a variety of labels for his domestic views: "progressive moderation," "New Republicanism," "dynamic conservatism." Satisfied

Chronology

1953	CIA-backed coup returns Shah Reza Pahlevi to power in Iran.
	Soviet Union detonates hydrogen bomb.
1954	Vietnamese defeat the French; Geneva conference divides Vietnam.
	United States and allies form SEATO.
	Supreme Court decides *Brown v. Board of Education of Topeka*.
	CIA overthrows the government of Guatemala.
	China provokes a crisis over Quemoy and Matsu.
1955	Salk polio vaccine is announced.
	Black citizens boycott Montgomery, Alabama, bus system.
	Soviet Union forms the Warsaw Pact.
	AFL and CIO merge.
1956	Interstate Highway Act is passed.
	Soviets repress Hungarian revolt.
	Israel, France, and Britain invade Egypt.
1957	U.S. Army maintains law and order in Little Rock after violent resistence to integration of Central High School.
	Soviet Union launches *Sputnik,* world's first artificial satellite.
1958	United States and Soviet Union voluntarily suspend nuclear tests.
1959	Fidel Castro takes power in Cuba.
	Nikita Khrushchev visits the United States.
1960	U-2 spy plane shot down over Russia.
	Sit-in movement begins in Greensboro, North Carolina.

1961	Bay of Pigs invasion fails.
	Kennedy establishes the Peace Corps.
	Vienna summit fails.
	Freedom rides are held in the Deep South.
	Berlin crisis leads to construction of the Berlin Wall.
1962	John Glenn orbits the earth.
	Cuban missile crisis brings the world to the brink of nuclear war.
	Michael Harrington publishes *The Other America*.
1963	Civil rights demonstrations rend Birmingham.
	Civil rights activists march in Washington.
	Betty Friedan publishes *The Feminine Mystique*.
	Limited Test Ban Treaty is signed.
	Ngo Dinh Diem is assassinated in South Vietnam.
	President Kennedy is assassinated.
1964	Civil Rights Act is passed.
	Freedom Summer is organized in Mississippi.
	Office of Economic Opportunity is created.
	Gulf of Tonkin Resolution is passed.
	Wilderness Act marks new direction in environmental policy.
1965	Medical Care Act establishes Medicare and Medicaid.
	Elementary and Secondary Education Act extends direct federal aid to local schools.
	Selma-Montgomery march climaxes era of nonviolent civil rights demonstrations.
	Voting Rights Act suspends literacy tests for voting.

with postwar America, Eisenhower accepted much of the New Deal but saw little need for further reform.

Eisenhower's first secretary of defense, "Engine Charlie" Wilson, had headed General Motors. At his Senate confirmation hearing, he proclaimed, "For years, I thought what was good for the country was good for General Motors and vice versa." Wilson's statement captured a central theme of the 1950s. Not since the 1920s had Americans been so excited about the benefits of big business.

The New Prosperity. Between 1950 and 1964, output grew by a solid 3.2 percent per year. American workers in the 1950s had more disposable income than ever before. Their productivity, or output per worker, increased steadily. Average compensation per hour of work rose faster than consumer prices in nine of eleven years from 1953 to 1964. Rising productivity made it easy for corporations to share gains with large labor unions. The steel and auto industries set the pace with contracts that gave their workers a middle-class way of life. In turn, labor leaders lost interest in making radical changes in American society.

For members of minority groups with regular industrial and government jobs, the 1950s were also economically rewarding. Detroit, Dayton, Oakland, and other industrial cities offered them factory jobs at wages that could support a family. However, there were never enough family-wage jobs for all of the African-American and Latino workers who continued to move to northern and western cities. Many Mexican Americans were still migrant farm laborers and workers in nonunionized sweatshops. Minority workers were usually the first to suffer from the erosion of industrial jobs that began in the 1960s, and black unemployment crept upward to twice the white rate.

Native Americans faced equally daunting prospects. To cut costs and accelerate assimilation, Congress pushed the policy of termination between 1954 and 1962. The government sold tribal land and assets, distributed the proceeds among tribal members, and terminated its treaty relationship with the tribe. Applied to such tribes as the Klamaths in Oregon and the Menominees in Wisconsin, termination gave thousands of Indians one-time cash payments but cut them adrift from the security of tribal organizations. The Bureau of Indian Affairs encouraged Indians to move to large cities, but jobs were often unavailable.

RESHAPING URBAN AMERICA

If Eisenhower's administration opted for the status quo on many issues, it nevertheless reshaped American cities around an agenda of economic development. In 1954, Congress transformed the public housing program into urban renewal. Cities used federal funds to replace low-rent businesses and run-down housing on the fringes of their downtowns with new hospitals, civic centers, sports arenas, office towers, and luxury apartments. Urban renewal temporarily revitalized older cities in the Northeast and Midwest that were already feeling the competition of the fast-growing South and West. *Fortune* in 1956 concluded that some of the largest cities were the best run—Cincinnati, New York, Philadelphia, Detroit, Milwaukee.

Only a decade later, the same cities would top the list of urban crisis spots, in part because of accumulating social costs from urban renewal. The bulldozers often leveled minority neighborhoods in the name of downtown expansion. Urban renewal displaced Puerto Ricans in New York, African Americans in Atlanta and Norfolk, Mexican Americans in Denver. Los Angeles demolished the seedy Victorian mansions of Bunker Hill, just northwest of downtown, for a music center and bank towers.

The Eisenhower administration also revolutionized American transportation. The **Federal Highway Act of 1956** created a national system of interstate and defense highways. The legislation wrapped a program to build 41,000 miles of freeways in the language of the Cold War. The roads would be wide and strong enough for trucks hauling military hardware; they were also supposed to make it easy to evacuate cities in case of a Soviet attack. Interstates halved the time of city-to-city travel. They were good for General Motors, the steel industry, and the concrete industry, requiring the construction equivalent of 60 Panama Canals. The highways promoted long-distance trucking at the expense of railroads. They also wiped out hundreds of homes per mile when they plunged through large cities. As with urban renewal, the bulldozers most often plowed through African-American or Latino neighborhoods, where land was cheap and white politicians could ignore protests. Some cities, such as Miami, used the highways as barriers between white and black neighborhoods. At the same time, interstates accelerated suburbanization. The beltways or perimeter highways that began to ring most large cities made it easier and more profitable to develop new subdivisions and factory sites than to reinvest in city centers.

COMFORT ON CREDIT

Prosperity transformed spending habits. The 1930s had taught Americans to avoid debt. The 1950s taught them to buy on credit. Families financed their new houses with 90 percent Federal Housing Administration (FHA) mortgages and 100 percent Veterans Administration (VA) mortgages. They filled the rooms by signing installment contracts at furniture and appliance stores and charging the drapes and carpeting on department-store credit cards. The value of consumer debt, excluding home mortgages, tripled from 1952 to 1964.

New forms of marketing facilitated credit-based consumerism. The first large-scale suburban shopping center was Northgate in Seattle. By the end of the decade, developers were building malls with 1 million square feet of shopping floor. At the start of the 1970s, the universal credit card (Visa, MasterCard) made shopping even easier.

Surrounding the new malls were the servants and symbols of America's car culture. Where cities of the early twentieth century had been built around public transportation—streetcars and subways—those of the 1950s depended on private automobiles. Interstate highways sucked retail business from small-town main streets to interchanges on the edge of town. Nationally franchised motels and fast-food restaurants sprang up along suburban shopping strips, pioneered by Holiday Inn (1952) and McDonald's (nationally franchised in 1955). By shopping along highways rather than downtown, suburban whites also opted to minimize contact with people of other races.

More extreme than the mall were entirely new environments for high-intensity consumption and entertainment that appeared in the Southwest, such as Las Vegas with its hotel-casinos. Opening in Orange County, California, in 1955, Disneyland offered a carefully tended environment that was as safe as a shopping mall and as artificial as Las Vegas—a never-ending state fair without the smells and dust.

THE NEW FIFTIES FAMILY

Family life in the Eisenhower years departed from historic patterns. Prosperity allowed children to finish school and young adults to marry right after high school. The proportion of single adults reached its twentieth-century low in 1960. At all social levels, young people married quickly and had an average of three children spaced closely together, adding to the number of baby boomers whose needs would influence American society into the twenty-first century. Family activities replaced the street corner for kids and the neighborhood tavern for men. Strong families, said experts, defended against communism by teaching American values.

The Impact of Television.   Popular entertainment had been a communal activity; people saw movies as part of a group, cheered baseball teams as part of a crowd. Television was made to order for the family-centered fifties. By 1960, fully 87 percent of households had sets. TV was watched in the privacy of the home. Situation comedies were the most successful programs. Viewers liked continuing characters who resolved everyday problems in half an hour. Most successful shows depicted the ideal of family togetherness. Lucille Ball and Desi Arnaz in *I Love Lucy* (1951–1955) started a family and left New York for suburbia. The families on *The Adventures of Ozzie and Harriet* (1952–1966), *Father Knows Best* (1954–1962), and *Leave It to Beaver* (1957–1962) were white, polite, and happy.

Television sets were major pieces of living room furniture in the 1950s. This 1951 Motorola ad from Woman's Home Companion emphasizes television as a source of family togetherness, a popular theme in the 1950s.

Gaslight Advertising Archives, Inc. NY.

Stay-at-Home Moms and Working Women.   The 1950s extended the stay-at-home trend of the postwar years. Women gave up some of their earlier educational gains. Their share of new college degrees and professional jobs fell. Magazines proclaimed that proper families maintained distinct roles for dad and mom, and mom was urged to find fulfillment in a well-scrubbed house and children.

In fact, far from allowing women to stay home as housewives, family prosperity in the 1950s often depended on their earnings. The number of employed women reached new highs. By 1960, nearly 35 percent of all women held jobs, including 7.5 million mothers with children under 17.

INVENTING TEENAGERS

Teenagers in the 1950s joined adults as consumers of movies, clothes, and automobiles. Advertisers tapped and expanded the growing youth market by promoting a distinct "youth culture," an idea that became omnipresent in the 1960s and 1970s. While psychologists pontificated on the special problems of adolescence, many cities matched their high schools to the social status of their students: college-prep curricula for middle-class neighborhoods, vocational and technical schools for future factory workers, and separate schools or tracks for African Americans and Latinos.

All teenagers shared rock-and-roll, a new music of the mid-1950s that adapted black urban rhythm-and-blues for a white mass market. Record producers played up the association between rock music and youthful rebellion. The 1955 movie *Blackboard Jungle* depicted juvenile delinquency to the music of Bill Haley's "Rock Around the Clock." Elvis Presley's meteoric career, launched in 1956 with "Heartbreak Hotel," depended both on his skill at blending country music with rhythm-and-blues and the sexual suggestiveness of his stage act.

Technological changes helped rock split off from adult pop music. Portable phonographs and 45-rpm records let kids listen to rock-and-roll in their own rooms. Car radios and transistor radios (first marketed around 1956) let disc jockeys reach teenagers outside the home. The result was separate music for young listeners and separate advertising for teenage consumers, the roots of the teenage mall culture of the next generation.

QUICK REVIEW

Teenagers
- Teenagers became consumers in the 1950s.
- Advertisers directed their message at the youth market.
- Teenagers developed a shared culture.

The United States exhibit at a technology exposition in Moscow in 1959 displayed a wide range of American consumer goods, from soft-drink dispensers to sewing machines. It included a complete six-room ranch house with an up-to-date kitchen where, in a famous encounter dubbed the "kitchen debate," Vice President Richard Nixon and Soviet Communist Party chairman Nikita Khrushchev disputed the merits of capitalism and Communism.

Corbis/Bettmann

TURNING TO RELIGION

Leaders from Dwight Eisenhower to FBI Director J. Edgar Hoover advocated churchgoing as an antidote for Communism. Regular church attendance grew from 48 percent of the population in 1940 to 63 percent in 1960. *Newsweek* talked about the "vast resurgence of Protestantism," and *Time* claimed that "everybody knows that church life is booming in the U.S." The situation was more complex. Growing church membership looked impressive at first, but the total barely kept pace with population growth. In some ways, the so-called return to religion was new. Congress created new connections between religion and government when it added "under God" to the Pledge of Allegiance in 1954 and required currency to bear the phrase "In God We Trust" in 1955.

Radio and television preachers added a new dimension to religious life. Bishop Fulton J. Sheen brought vigorous anti-communism and Catholic doctrine to millions of TV viewers who would never have entered a Catholic church. Norman Vincent Peale blended popular psychology with Protestantism, presenting Jesus Christ as "the greatest expert on human nature who ever lived." His book *The Power of Positive Thinking* (1952) sold millions of copies.

Another strand in the religious revival was found in the revitalized evangelical and fundamentalist churches. During the 1950s, the theologically and socially conservative Southern Baptists passed the Methodists as the largest Protestant denomination. The evangelist Billy Graham continued the grand American tradition of the mass revival meeting. Graham was a pioneer in the resurgence of evangelical Christianity that gradually shifted the tone of American religious life by stressing an individual approach to belief and social issues.

African-American churches were community institutions as well as religious organizations. With limited options for enjoying their success, the black middle class joined prestigious churches. Black congregations in northern cities swelled in the postwar years. Prestigious black churches thrived and often supported extensive social service programs. In southern cities, churches were centers for community pride and training grounds for the emerging civil rights movement.

Other important changes to come in American religion had their roots in the 1950s and early 1960s. Boundaries between many Protestant denominations blurred as church leaders emphasized national unity, paving the way for the ecumenical movement and denominational mergers. In *Engel v. Vitale* (1962), the Supreme Court ruled that public schools could not require children to start the school day with group prayer. *Abington Township v. Schempp* (1963) prohibited devotional Bible reading in the schools. Such decisions alarmed many evangelicals; within two decades, school prayer would be a central issue in national politics.

THE GOSPEL OF PROSPERITY

Writers and intellectuals often marveled at the prosperity of Eisenhower's America. For scholars and journalists who had grown up during the Great Depression, the lack of economic hardship was the big story. At times in these years, production and consumption outweighed democracy in the American's message to the world. Officially, Americans argued that abundance was a natural by-product of a free society. In fact, it was easy to present prosperity as a goal in itself, as Vice President Richard Nixon did when he represented the United States at a technology exposition in Moscow in 1959. The American exhibit included 21 models of automobiles and a complete six-room ranch house. In its "miracle kitchen," Nixon engaged Soviet Communist Party chairman Nikita Khrushchev in a carefully planned "kitchen debate." The vice president claimed that the "most important thing" for Americans was "the right to choose": "We have so many different manufacturers and many different kinds of washing machines so that the housewives have a choice."

THE UNDERSIDE OF AFFLUENCE

The most basic criticism of the ideology of prosperity was the simplest—that affluence concealed vast inequalities. Michael Harrington had worked among the poor before writing *The Other America* (1962). He reminded Americans about the "underdeveloped nation" of 40 to 50 million poor people who had missed the last two decades of prosperity.

C. Wright Mills found dangers in the way that the Cold War distorted American society at the top. *The Power Elite* (1956) described an interlocking alliance of big government, big business, and the military. The losers in a permanent war economy, said Mills, were economic and political democracy.

Other critics targeted the alienating effects of consumerism and the conformity of homogeneous suburbs. Sociologist David Riesman saw suburbia as the home of "other-directed" individuals who lacked inner convictions.

There was far greater substance to the increasing dissatisfaction among women, who faced conflicting images of the perfect woman in the media. On one side was the comforting icon of Betty Crocker, the fictional spokeswoman for General Mills who made housework and cooking look easy. On the other side were sultry sexpots, like Marilyn Monroe and the centerfold women of *Playboy* magazine, which first appeared in 1953. In 1963, Betty Friedan's book *The Feminine Mystique* recognized that thousands of middle-class housewives were seething behind their picture windows. What Friedan called "the problem that has no name" was a sense of personal emptiness. "I got up one morning," remembered Geraldine Bean, "and I got my kids off to school. I went in to comb my hair and wash my face, and I stood in front of the bathroom mirror crying . . . because at eight-thirty in the morning I had my children off to school. I had my housework done. There was absolutely nothing for me to do the rest of the day." She went on to earn a Ph.D. and win election to the board of regents of the University of Colorado.

FACING OFF WITH THE SOVIET UNION

Americans got a reassuring new face in the White House in 1953, but not new policies toward the world. As had been true since 1946, the nation's leaders weighed every foreign policy decision for its effect on

WHAT IMPACT did Dwight Eisenhower's foreign policy have on U.S. relations with the Soviet Union?

School children in the 1950s regularly practiced taking cover in case of atomic attack. If there was warning, they were to file into interior hallways, crouch against the walls, and cover their heads with their jackets as protection against flying glass. If they saw the blinding flash of an atomic explosion without warning, they were to "duck and cover" under their school desks.

the Cold War. The United States pushed ahead in an arms race with the Soviet Union, stood guard on the borders of China and the Soviet empire, and judged political changes in Latin America, Africa, and Asia for their effect on the global balance of power.

WHY WE LIKED IKE

In the late twentieth century, few leaders were able to master both domestic policy and foreign affairs. Some presidents, such as Lyndon Johnson, were more adept at social problems than diplomacy. By contrast, Richard Nixon and George H. W. Bush were more interested in the world outside the United States.

Dwight Eisenhower was also a "foreign-policy president." As a general, he had understood that military power should serve political ends. He had helped to hold together the alliance that defeated Nazi Germany and built NATO into an effective force in 1951–1952. He then sought the Republican nomination, he said, to ensure that the United States would keep its international commitments. He sealed his victory in 1952 by emphasizing his foreign-policy expertise.

What makes Eisenhower's administration hard to appreciate is that many of its accomplishments were things that did not happen. Eisenhower refused to dismantle the social programs of the New Deal. He exerted American political and military power around the globe but avoided war. Preferring to work behind the scenes, he knew how to delegate authority and keep disagreements private.

In his "hidden-hand" presidency, Eisenhower sometimes masked his intelligence. It helped his political agenda if Americans thought of him as a smiling grandfather. The "Ike" whose face smiled from "I Like Ike" campaign buttons and who gave rambling, incoherent answers at White House press conferences knew exactly what he was doing. When his press secretary advised him to duck questions at one press conference, Ike replied, "Don't worry, I'll just confuse them." He was easily reelected in 1956.

A BALANCE OF TERROR

The backdrop for U.S. foreign policy was the growing capacity for mutual nuclear annihilation. The rivalry between the United States and the USSR was played out within a framework of deterrence, the knowledge that each side could launch a devastating nuclear attack. The old balance of power had become a balance of terror.

WHERE TO LEARN MORE

Kansas Cosmosphere, Hutchinson, Kansas **www.cosmo.org**

The Eisenhower administration's doctrine of **massive retaliation** took advantage of America's superior technology while economizing on military spending. Eisenhower compared uncontrolled military spending to crucifying humankind on a "cross of iron." "Every gun that is fired," he warned, "every warship launched, every rocket fired signifies . . . a theft from those who hunger and are not fed, those who are cold and not clothed." The administration concentrated military spending where the nation already had the greatest advantage—on atomic weapons. In response to any serious attack, the United States would direct maximum force against the homeland of the aggressor.

The massive-retaliation doctrine treated nuclear weapons as ordinary or even respectable. It put European and American cities on the frontline in the defense of Germany, for it meant that the United States would react to a Soviet conventional attack on NATO by dropping nuclear bombs on the Soviet Union, which would presumably retaliate in kind.

The doctrine grew even more fearful as the Soviet Union developed its own hydrogen bombs. Dozens of nuclear weapons tests in the late 1950s made the atomic threat immediate. So did signs for air-raid shelters posted on downtown buildings and city-wide air-raid drills. Radioactivity carried by fallout from the tests appeared in milk supplies in the form of the isotope strontium 90. Stories about handfuls of survivors groping through the ruins of atomic war filled popular literature.

The Soviet Union added to the worries about atomic war by launching the world's first artificial satellite. On the first Sunday of October 1957, Americans discovered that *Sputnik*—Russian for "satellite"—was orbiting the earth. Americans wondered if the United States had lost its edge. Schools beefed up science courses and began to introduce the "new math," Congress passed the National Defense Education Act to expand college and postgraduate education, and the new **National Aeronautics and Space Administration (NASA)** took over the satellite program in 1958.

The crisis was more apparent than real. The combination of Soviet rocketry and nuclear capacity created alarm about a missile gap. The Soviet Union was said to be building hundreds of intercontinental ballistic missiles (ICBMs) to overwhelm American air defenses designed to intercept piloted bombers. Although there was no such gap, Eisenhower was unwilling to reveal secret information that might have allayed public anxiety.

CONTAINMENT IN ACTION

Someone who heard only the campaign speeches in 1952 might have expected sharp foreign-policy changes under Eisenhower, but there was more continuity than change. In fact, Eisenhower viewed the Cold War in the same terms as Truman. Around the periphery of the Communist nations, from eastern Asia to the Middle East to Europe, the United States accepted the existing sphere of Communist influence but attempted to block its growth, a policy most Americans accepted.

The American worldview assumed both the right and the need to intervene in the affairs of other nations, especially countries in Latin America, Asia, and Africa. Policymakers saw these nations as markets for U.S. products and sources of vital raw materials. When political disturbances arose in these states, the United States blamed Soviet meddling to justify U.S. intervention. If Communism could not be rolled back in eastern Europe, the CIA could still undermine anti-American

WHERE TO LEARN MORE

National Air and Space Museum, Washington, D.C. **www.nasm.edu**

Massive Retaliation Popular name for the military doctrine adopted in the 1950s, whereby the U.S. promised to respond to any attack on itself or its allies with massive force, including nuclear weapons.

National Aeronautics and Space Administration (NASA) Federal agency created in 1958 to manage American space flights and exploration.

MAP EXPLORATION

To explore an interactive version of this map, go to **http://www.prenhall.com/goldfield3/map28.1**

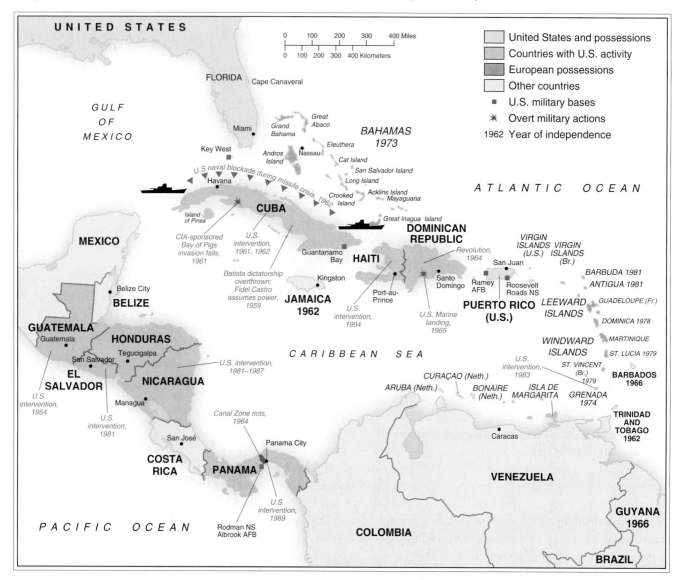

MAP 28-1 U.S. Intervention around the Caribbean since 1954 The United States has long kept a careful eye on the politics of neighboring nations to the south. In the second half of the twentieth century, the United States frequently used military assistance or force to influence or intervene in Caribbean and Central American nations. The purpose has usually been to counter or undermine left-leaning governments; some interventions, as in Haiti, have been intended to stabilize democratic regimes.

WHAT WAS the effect of U.S. involvement in the Caribbean?

governments in the third world. The Soviets themselves took advantage of local revolutions even when they did not instigate them; in doing so they confirmed Washington's belief that the developing world was a game board on which the superpowers carried on their rivalry by proxy.

Twice during Eisenhower's first term, the CIA subverted democratically elected governments that seemed to threaten U.S. interests. In Iran, which had nationalized British and U.S. oil companies in an effort to break the hold of Western corporations, the CIA in 1953 backed a coup that toppled the government and helped the young shah, as the reigning monarch was called, to gain control. In Guatemala, the leftist government was threatening the United Fruit Company. When the Guatemalans accepted weapons from the Communist bloc in 1954, the CIA imposed a regime friendly to U.S. business (see Map 28–1).

For most Americans in 1953, democracy in Iran was far less important than ending the war in Korea and stabilizing relations with China. Eisenhower declined to escalate the Korean War by blockading China and sending more U.S. ground forces. Instead he positioned atomic bombs on Okinawa, only 400 miles from China. The nuclear threat, along with the continued cost of the war on both sides, brought the Chinese to a truce that left Korea divided into two nations.

Halfway around the world, there was a new crisis when three American friends—France, Britain, and Israel—ganged up on Egypt. France was angry at Egyptian support for revolutionaries in French Algeria. Britain was even angrier at Egypt's nationalization of the British-dominated Suez Canal. And Israel wanted to weaken its most powerful Arab enemy. On October 29, 1956, Israel attacked Egypt. A week later, British and French forces attempted to seize the canal. The United States forced a quick cease-fire, partly to maintain its standing with oil-producing Arab nations. Because Egypt blocked the canal with sunken ships, the war left Britain and France dependent on American oil that Eisenhower would not provide until they left Egypt.

In Europe, Eisenhower accepted the status quo because conflicts there could result in nuclear war. In 1956, challenges to Communist rule arose in East Germany, Poland, and Hungary and threatened to break up the Soviet empire. The Soviets replaced liberal Communists in East Germany and Poland with hard-liners. In Hungary, however, reformers took the fatal step of proposing to quit the Warsaw Pact. Open warfare broke out when the Soviet army rolled across the border to preserve the Soviet empire. Hungarian freedom fighters in Budapest used rocks and firebombs against Soviet tanks for several days, while pleading in vain for Western aid. Tens of thousands of Hungarians died, and 200,000 fled when the Soviets crushed the resistance.

GLOBAL STANDOFF

The Soviet Union, China, and the United States and its allies were all groping in the dark as they maneuvered for influence in the 1950s and 1960s. In one international crisis after another, each player misinterpreted the other's motivations and diplomatic signals.

A good example is the U-2 spy plane affair of 1960, which derailed progress toward nuclear disarmament. The United States and the Soviet Union voluntarily suspended nuclear tests in 1958 and prepared for a June 1960 summit meeting in Paris, where Eisenhower intended to negotiate a test ban treaty. But on May 1, 1960, Soviet air defenses shot down an American U-2 aircraft over the heart of Russia and captured the pilot, Francis Gary Powers. The cover story for the U-2 was weather research, but the frail-looking black plane was a CIA operation. Designed to soar above the range of Soviet antiaircraft missiles, information obtained by U-2s had assured American officials that there was no missile gap.

When Moscow trumpeted the news of the plane's downing, Eisenhower took personal responsibility in hopes that Khrushchev would accept the U-2 as an unpleasant reality of international espionage. Unfortunately, the planes meant something very different to the Soviets, touching their festering sense of inferiority. They had stopped protesting the flights in 1957, because they saw complaints as de-

QUICK REVIEW

The U-2 Spy Plane Incident

- May 1, 1960: Soviets shot down American U-2 spy plane
- Eisenhower took responsibility, hoping to reassure the Soviets
- The Soviets responded with renewed distrust and hostility
- The incident set back efforts at disarmament for years

New Frontier John F. Kennedy's domestic and foreign policy initiatives, designed to reinvigorate a sense of national purpose and energy.

meaning. The Americans thought their silence signaled acceptance. Khrushchev had staked his future on good relations with the United States; when Eisenhower refused to apologize in Paris, Khrushchev stalked out. Disarmament was set back for years because the two sides had such different understandings of the same events.

The most important aspect of Eisenhower's foreign policy was continuity. Despite militant rhetoric, the administration pursued containment as defined under Truman. The Cold War consensus, however, prevented the United States from seeing the nations of the developing world on their own terms. By viewing every independence movement and social revolution as part of the competition with Communism, American leaders created unnecessary problems. In the end, Eisenhower left troublesome and unresolved issues for his successor, John Kennedy, who wanted to confront international Communism even more vigorously (see American Views: "Two Presidents Assess the Implications of the Cold War").

JOHN F. KENNEDY AND THE COLD WAR

WHAT WAS John F. Kennedy's approach to dealing with the Soviet Union?

John Kennedy was a man of contradictions. A Democrat who promised to get the country moving again, he presided over policies whose direction was set under Eisenhower. Despite stirring rhetoric about leading the nation toward a **New Frontier** of scientific and social progress, he recorded his greatest failures and successes in the continuing Cold War.

THE KENNEDY MYSTIQUE

Kennedy won the presidency over Richard Nixon in a cliffhanging election that was more about personality and style than about substance (see Map 28–2). Both candidates were determined not to yield another inch to Communism. The charming and eloquent Kennedy narrowly skirted scandal in his personal life. Nixon had wider experience and was a shrewd tactician, but he was also self-righteous and awkward. Eisenhower had wanted to drop Nixon as vice president in 1956 and gave him only lukewarm support in 1960—when a reporter asked Eisenhower to cite important decisions to which Nixon had contributed, Ike replied, "Give me a week and I might think of one."

The campaign featured the first televised presidential debates. In the first session, Nixon actually gave better replies, but his nervousness and a bad makeup job turned off millions of viewers, who admired Kennedy's energy. Nixon never overcame the setback, but the race was tight, with tiny margins in crucial states giving Kennedy the victory. His televised inauguration was the perfect setting for

MAP EXPLORATION

To explore an interactive version of this map, go to
http://www.prenhall.com/goldfield3/map28.2

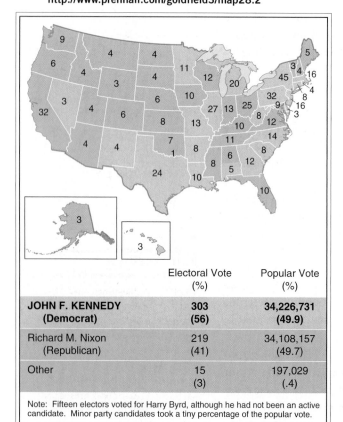

	Electoral Vote (%)	Popular Vote (%)
JOHN F. KENNEDY (Democrat)	**303 (56)**	**34,226,731 (49.9)**
Richard M. Nixon (Republican)	219 (41)	34,108,157 (49.7)
Other	15 (3)	197,029 (.4)

Note: Fifteen electors voted for Harry Byrd, although he had not been an active candidate. Minor party candidates took a tiny percentage of the popular vote.

MAP 28–2 The Election of 1960 The presidential election of 1960 was one of the closest in American history. John Kennedy's victory depended on his appeal in northern industrial states with large Roman Catholic populations and his ability to hold much of the traditionally Democratic South. Texas, the home state of his vice-presidential running mate, Lyndon Johnson, was vital to the success of the ticket.

WHY DID most Western states not support Kennedy?

AMERICAN VIEWS

TWO PRESIDENTS ASSESS THE IMPLICATIONS OF THE COLD WAR

I n speeches two days apart in January 1961, outgoing President Dwight Eisenhower and incoming President John Kennedy offered contrasting interpretations of America's Cold War crusade. Eisenhower spoke with concern about the effects of defense spending on American society. Kennedy promised an unlimited commitment of resources to achieve national goals.

- Why did Kennedy define the American mission to the world so broadly?
- What changes in the 1950s led Eisenhower to warn about the dangers of pursuing that mission?
- Do the selections show basic agreement or disagreement about the goals of national policy?

Dwight D. Eisenhower
Farewell Address, January 18, 1961

Our military organization today bears little relation to that known by any of my predecessors in peacetime. . . . This conjunction of an immense military establishment and a large arms industry is new in the American experience. The total influence—economic, political, even spiritual—is felt in every city, every State house, every office of the federal government. We recognize the imperative need for this development. Yet we must not fail to comprehend its grave implications. . . .

In the councils of government, we must guard against the acquisition of unwarranted influence, whether sought or unsought, by the military-industrial complex. The potential for the disastrous rise of misplaced power exists and will persist.

We must never let the weight of this combination endanger our liberties or democratic processes. We should take nothing for granted. Only an alert and knowledgeable citizenry can compel the proper meshing of the huge industrial and military machinery of defense with our peaceful methods and goals.

John F. Kennedy
Inaugural Address, January 20, 1961

Let the word go forth from this time and place, to friend and foe alike, that the torch has been passed to a new generation of Americans—born in this century, tempered by war, disciplined by a hard and bitter peace, proud of our ancient heritage—and unwilling to witness or permit the slow undoing of those human rights to which this nation has always been committed, and to which we are committed today at home and around the world.

Let every nation know, whether it wishes us well or ill, that we shall pay any price, bear any burden, meet any hardship, support any friends, oppose any foe to assure the survival and the success of liberty.

an impassioned plea for national unity: "My fellow Americans," he challenged, "ask not what your country can do for you—ask what you can do for your country."

Kennedy brought dash to the White House. People began to talk about Kennedy's "charisma," his ability to lead by sheer force of personality.

Behind the glamorous façade, Kennedy remained a puzzle. One day, Kennedy could propose the Peace Corps, which gave thousands of idealistic young Americans a chance to help developing nations; another day, he could approve plots to assassinate Fidel Castro. Visitors who expected a shallow glad-hander were astonished to meet a sharp, hard-working man who was eager to learn about the world.

KENNEDY'S MISTAKES

Kennedy and Khrushchev perpetuated similar problems. Talking tough to satisfy their more militant countrymen, they repeatedly pushed each other into a corner, continuing the problems of mutual misunderstanding that had marked the 1950s.

WHERE TO LEARN MORE

John F. Kennedy Library and Museum, Boston, Massachusetts
www.cs.umb.edu/jfklibrary/

Kennedy fed Soviet fears of American aggressiveness by sponsoring an invasion of Cuba. At the start of 1959, Fidel Castro had toppled the corrupt dictator Fulgencio Batista, who had made Havana infamous for Mafia-run gambling and prostitution. Castro then nationalized American investments, and thousands of Cubans fled to the United States.

When 1,400 anti-Castro Cubans landed at Cuba's **Bay of Pigs** on April 17, 1961, they were following a plan prepared by the Eisenhower administration. The CIA had trained and armed the invaders and convinced Kennedy that the landing would trigger spontaneous uprisings. But when Kennedy refused to commit American armed forces to support them, Cuban forces captured the attackers.

Kennedy followed the Bay of Pigs debacle with a hasty and ill-thought-out summit meeting with Khrushchev in Vienna in June. Poorly prepared and nearly incapacitated by agonizing back pain, Kennedy made little headway. Coming after Kennedy's refusal to salvage the Bay of Pigs by military intervention, the meeting left the Soviets with the impression that the president was weak and dangerously erratic.

To exploit Kennedy's perceived vulnerability, the Soviet Union renewed tension over Berlin, deep within East Germany. The divided city served as an escape route from Communism for hundreds of thousands of East Germans. Khrushchev now threatened to transfer the Soviet sector in Berlin to East Germany, which had no treaty obligations to France, Britain, or the United States. If the West had to deal directly with East Germany for access to Berlin, it would have to recognize a permanently divided Germany. Rather than confront the United States directly, however, the Soviets and East Germans on August 13, 1961, built a wall around the western sectors of Berlin while leaving the access route to West Germany open. The **Berlin Wall** thus isolated East Germany without challenging the Western allies in West Berlin itself. In private, Kennedy accepted the wall as a clever way to stabilize a dangerous situation.

GETTING INTO VIETNAM

American involvement in Vietnam, located in Southeast Asia on the southern border of China, dated to the mid-1950s. After World War II ended, France had fought to maintain its colonial rule there against rebels who combined Communist ideology with fervor for national independence under the leadership of Ho Chi Minh. The United States picked up three-quarters of the costs, but the French military position collapsed in 1954 after Vietnamese forces overran the French stronghold at Dien Bien Phu. A Geneva peace conference "temporarily" divided Vietnam into a Communist north and a non-Communist south and scheduled elections for a single Vietnamese government.

The United States then replaced France as the supporter of the pro-Western Vietnamese in the south. Washington's client was Ngo Dinh Diem, an anti-Communist from South Vietnam's Roman Catholic elite. U.S. officials encouraged Diem to put off the elections and backed his efforts to construct an independent South Vietnam. Ho meanwhile consolidated the northern half as a communist state that claimed to be the legitimate government for all Vietnam. The United States further reinforced containment in Asia by bringing Thailand, the Philippines, Pakistan, Australia, New Zealand, Britain, and France together in the **Southeast Asia Treaty Organization (SEATO)** in 1954.

Another indirect consequence of the Vienna summit was the growing American entanglement in South Vietnam, where Kennedy saw a chance to take a firm stand and reassert America's commitment to containment. In the countryside, Communist insurgents known as the **Viet Cong** were gaining strength. The anti-Communist leader, Diem, controlled the cities with the help of a large army and a Vietnamese elite that had worked with the French. The United States stepped up its supply of weapons and sent advisers, including members of one of Kennedy's military innovations, the Army Special Forces Group (Green Berets).

U.S. aid did not work. Despite overoptimistic reports and the help of 16,000 American troops, Diem's government by 1963 was losing the loyalty—the "hearts and minds"—of many South Vietnamese. North Vietnamese support for the Viet Cong canceled the effect of U.S. assistance. Diem courted a second civil war by violently crushing opposition from Vietnamese Buddhists. Kennedy's administration tacitly approved a coup on November 1 that killed Diem and his brother and installed an ineffective military junta.

For many Americans in the early 1960s, John and Jacqueline Kennedy and their two children represented the ideal family, although the carefully posed pictures with happy smiles concealed the president's severe health problems and deep rifts in the marriage.

John F. Kennedy Library

MISSILE CRISIS: A LINE DRAWN IN THE WAVES

On October 15 1962, reconnaissance photos revealed Soviets at work on launching sites from which nuclear missiles could hit the United States. Top officials spent five exhausting and increasingly desperate days sorting through the options. Secretary of Defense Robert McNamara suggested demanding removal of the missiles and declaring a naval "quarantine" against the arrival of further offensive weapons. A blockade would buy time for diplomacy.

Kennedy imposed the blockade in a terrifying speech on Monday, October 22. He emphasized the "deceptive" deployment of the Russian missiles and raised the specter of nuclear war. While Khrushchev hesitated, Soviet ships circled outside the quarantine line. On Friday, Khrushchev offered to withdraw the missiles in return for an American pledge not to invade Cuba. On Saturday, a second communication nearly dashed this hopeful opening by raising a new complaint about American missiles on the territory of NATO allies. Kennedy decided to accept the first letter and ignore the second. The United States pledged not to invade Cuba and secretly promised to remove obsolete Jupiter missiles from Turkey. Khrushchev accepted these terms on Sunday, October 28.

Why did Khrushchev risk the Cuban gamble? One reason was to protect Castro as a symbol of Soviet commitment to anti-Western regimes in the developing world. Kennedy had tried to preempt Castroism in 1961 by launching the **Alliance for Progress,** an economic-development program for Latin America that tied aid

The Cuban Missile Crisis

- October 15, 1962: U.S. acquires evidence of construction of missile launching sites in Cuba.

- In response, Kennedy imposed a blockade.

- The Soviets removed the launchers in exchange for removal of U.S. missiles from Turkey and a U.S. promise not to invade Cuba.

Viet Cong   Communist rebels in South Vietnam who fought the pro-American government established in South Vietnam in 1954.

Alliance for Progress   Program of economic aid to Latin America during the Kennedy administration.

to social reform. However, the United States had also orchestrated the Bay of Pigs invasion and funded a CIA campaign to sabotage Cuba. High American officials were not contemplating a full-scale invasion, but Castro and Khrushchev had reason to fear the worst.

Khrushchev also hoped to redress the strategic balance. As Kennedy discovered on taking office, the United States actually led the world in the deployment of strategic missiles. The strategic imbalance had sustained NATO during the Berlin confrontation, but 40 launchers in Cuba with two warheads each would have doubled the Soviet capacity to strike at the United States.

Soviet missiles in Cuba thus flouted the Monroe Doctrine and posed a real military threat. In the end, both sides were cautious. Khrushchev backed down rather than fight. Kennedy fended off hawkish advisers who wanted to destroy Castro. The world had trembled, but neither nation wanted war over "the missiles of October."

28-2
John F. Kennedy,
Cuban Missile Address
(1962)

SCIENCE AND FOREIGN AFFAIRS

The two superpowers competed through science as well as diplomacy. When Kennedy took office, the United States was still playing catch-up in space technology. A Russian, Yuri Gagarin, was the first human to orbit the earth, on April 12, 1961. American John Glenn did not match Gagarin's feat until February 1962. Kennedy committed the United States to placing an American astronaut on the moon by 1970.

The Soviet Union and the United States were also fencing about nuclear weapons testing. After the three-year moratorium, both resumed tests in 1961–1962. Renewed testing let the Russians show off huge hydrogen bombs. Both nations worked on multiple-targetable warheads, antiballistic missiles, and other innovations that might destabilize the balance of terror.

After the missile crisis showed his toughness, however, Kennedy had enough political maneuvering room to give priority to disarmament. In July 1963, the United States, Britain, and the USSR signed the **Limited Test Ban Treaty,** which outlawed nuclear testing in the atmosphere, in outer space, and under water, and invited other nations to join in. France and China, the other nuclear powers, refused to sign, and the treaty did not halt weapons development, but it was the most positive achievement of Kennedy's foreign policy and a step toward later disarmament treaties.

WHAT WAS the significance of
Brown v. Board of Education of Topeka?

Limited Test Ban Treaty Treaty, signed by the United States, Britain, and the Soviet Union, outlawing nuclear testing in the atmosphere, in outer space, and under water.

Brown v. Board of Education of Topeka Supreme Court decision in 1954 that declared that "separate but equal" schools for children of different races violated the Constitution.

RIGHTEOUSNESS LIKE A MIGHTY STREAM: THE STRUGGLE FOR CIVIL RIGHTS

Linda Brown of Topeka, Kansas, was a third-grader whose parents were fed up with sending her past an all-white public school to attend an all-black school a mile away. The Browns volunteered to help the NAACP challenge Topeka's school segregation by trying to enroll Linda in their neighborhood school, beginning a legal case that reached the Supreme Court. On May 17, 1954, the Court decided *Brown v. Board of Education of Topeka,* opening a new civil rights era. Led by the persuasive power of the new chief justice, Earl Warren, the Court unanimously reversed the 1896 case of *Plessy v. Ferguson* by ruling that sending black children to "separate but equal" schools denied them equal treatment under the Constitution.

OVERVIEW   CIVIL RIGHTS: THE STRUGGLE FOR RACIAL EQUALITY

Area of Concern	Key Actions	Results
Public school integration (1954)	Federal court cases	*Brown v. Board of Education of Topeka* (1954)
		Enforcement by presidential action, Little Rock (1957)
		Follow-up court decisions, including mandatory busing programs
Equal access to public facilities	Montgomery bus boycott (1955)	Civil Rights Act of 1964
	Lunch counter sit-ins (1960)	
	Freedom rides (1961)	
	Birmingham demonstrations (1963)	
	March on Washington (1963)	
Equitable voter registration	Voter registration drives, including Mississippi Summer Project (1964)	Voting Rights Act of 1965
	Demonstrations and marches, including Selma to Montgomery march (1965)	

GETTING TO THE SUPREME COURT

The *Brown* decision climaxed a 25-year campaign to reenlist the federal courts on the side of equal rights (see the Overview table, "Civil Rights: The Struggle for Racial Equality"). The work began in the 1930s when Charles Hamilton Houston, dean of Howard University's law school, trained a corps of civil rights lawyers. Working on behalf of the NAACP, he hoped to erode *Plessy* by suits focused on interstate travel and professional graduate schools (the least defensible segregated institutions, because states seldom provided alternatives). In 1938, Houston's student Thurgood Marshall, a future Supreme Court justice, took over the NAACP job.

Efforts in the 1940s and early 1950s, often fueled by the experience of World War II soldiers, had important successes. In *Smith v. Allwright* (1944), the Supreme Court invalidated the all-white primary, a decision that led to increased black voter registration in many southern communities. With new political power, and often with the cooperation of relatively progressive white leaders, blacks fought for specific improvements, such as equal pay for teachers or the hiring of black police officers.

The *Brown* case combined lawsuits from Delaware, Virginia, South Carolina, the District of Columbia, and Kansas. In each instance, students and families braved community pressure to demand equal access to a basic public service. Viewing public education as central for the equal opportunity that lay at the heart of

Elizabeth Eckford, one of the first black students to attend Central High in Little Rock, Arkansas, in 1957, enters the school amid taunts from white students and bystanders.

American values, the Court weighed the consequences of segregated school systems and concluded that separate meant unequal.

Brown also built on efforts by Mexican Americans in the Southwest to assert their rights of citizenship. After World War II, Latino organizations such as the League of United Latin American Citizens battled job discrimination and ethnic segregation. In 1946, the federal courts had prohibited segregation of Mexican-American children in California schools. Eight years later, the Supreme Court forbade Texas from excluding Mexican Americans from juries. These cases provided precedents for the Court's decision in *Brown* and subsequent civil rights cases.

DELIBERATE SPEED

Racial segregation by law was largely a southern problem, the legacy of Jim Crow laws (see Chapter 17). The civil rights movement therefore focused first on the South, allowing Americans elsewhere to think of racial injustice as a regional issue.

Southern responses to *Brown* revealed regional differences. Few southern communities desegregated schools voluntarily, for to do so undermined the entrenched principle of a dual society. Their reluctance was bolstered in 1955 when the Supreme Court allowed segregated states to carry out the 1954 decision "with all deliberate speed" rather than immediately. Thurgood Marshall later commented, "I've finally figured out what 'all deliberate speed' means. It means slow."

The following year, 101 southern congressmen and senators issued the **Southern Manifesto,** which asserted that the Court decision was unconstitutional. President Eisenhower privately deplored the desegregation decision, which violated his sense of states' rights and upset Republican attempts to gain southern votes. At the same time, many in Washington knew that racial discrimination offered, in the words of Dean Acheson, "the most effective kind of ammunition" for Soviet propaganda.

In September 1957 the city school board of Little Rock, Arkansas, admitted nine African Americans, including Melba Pattillo, to Central High, while segre-

WHERE TO LEARN MORE

National Afro-American Museum and Cultural Center, Wilberforce, Ohio www.ohiohistory.org/places/afroam/

Southern Manifesto A document signed by 101 members of Congress from Southern states in 1956 that argued that the Supreme Court's decision in *Brown v. Board of Education of Topeka* itself contradicted the Constitution.

grationist groups, such as the White Citizens Council, stirred up white fears. Claiming he feared violence, Governor Orval Faubus surrounded Central High with the National Guard and turned the new students away. Under intense national pressure, Faubus withdrew the Guard. The black students entered the school, but a howling mob forced the police to sneak them out after two hours. Fuming at the governor's defiance of federal authority, Eisenhower reluctantly nationalized the National Guard and sent in the 101st Airborne Division to keep order. Eight of the students endured a year of harassment in the hallways of Central.

The breakthrough in school integration did not come until the end of the 1960s, when the courts rejected further delays, and federal authorities threatened to cut off education funds. As late as 1968, only 6 percent of African-American children in the South attended integrated schools. By 1973, the figure was 90 percent. Attention thereafter shifted to northern communities, whose schools were segregated, not by law, but by the divisions between white and black neighborhoods and between white suburbs and multiracial central cities, a situation known as *de facto* segregation.

PUBLIC ACCOMMODATIONS

The civil rights movement also sought to integrate public accommodations. Most southern states separated the races in bus terminals and movie theaters. They required black riders to take rear seats on buses. They labeled separate restrooms and drinking fountains for "colored" users. Hotels denied rooms to black people, and restaurants refused them service.

The struggle to end segregated facilities started in Montgomery, Alabama. On December 1, 1955, Rosa Parks, a seamstress who worked at a downtown department store, refused to give up her bus seat to a white passenger and was arrested. Parks acted spontaneously, but she was part of a network of civil rights activists who wanted to challenge segregated buses and was the secretary of the Montgomery NAACP. As news of her action spread, the community institutions that enriched southern black life went into action. The Women's Political Council, a group of college-trained black women, initiated a mass boycott of the privately owned bus company. Martin Luther King, Jr., a 26-year-old pastor, led the boycott. He galvanized a mass meeting with a speech that quoted the biblical prophet Amos: "We are determined here in Montgomery to work and fight until justice runs down like water, and righteousness like a mighty stream."

Montgomery's African Americans organized their boycott in the face of white outrage. A car pool substituted for the buses despite police harassment. As the boycott survived months of pressure, the national media began to pay attention. After nearly a year, the Supreme Court agreed that the bus segregation law was unconstitutional.

Victory in Montgomery depended on steadfast African-American involvement. Success also revealed the discrepancy between white attitudes in the Deep South and national opinion. For white southerners, segregation was a local concern best defined as a legal or constitutional matter. For other Americans, it was increasingly an issue of the South's deviation from national moral norms.

QUICK REVIEW

The Montgomery Bus Boycott
- December 1, 1955: Rosa Parks refused to give up her bus seat to a white passenger and was arrested
- The Women's Political Council organized a boycott of the bus company
- After nearly a year, the Supreme Court ruled the bus segregation law unconstitutional

28–3
John Lewis, Address at the March on Washington (1963)

The Montgomery boycott won a local victory and made King famous, but it did not propel immediate change. King formed the **Southern Christian Leadership Conference (SCLC)** and sparred with the NAACP about community-based versus court-based civil rights tactics, but four African-American college students in Greensboro, North Carolina, started the next phase of the struggle. On February 1, 1960, they put on jackets and ties and sat down at the segregated lunch counter in Woolworth's, waiting through the day without being served. Their patient courage brought more demonstrators; within two days, 85 students packed the store. Nonviolent sit-ins spread throughout the South.

The sit-ins had both immediate and long-range effects. In such comparatively sophisticated border cities as Nashville, Tennessee, sit-ins integrated lunch counters. Elsewhere, they precipitated white violence and mass arrests. King welcomed nonviolent confrontation. SCLC leader Ella Baker helped the students form a new organization, the **Student Nonviolent Coordinating Committee (SNCC).**

The year 1961 brought "freedom rides" to test the segregation of interstate bus terminals. The idea came from James Farmer of the **Congress of Racial Equality (CORE).** Two buses carrying black and white passengers met only minor problems in Virginia, the Carolinas, and Georgia, but Alabamians burned one of the buses and attacked the riders in Birmingham, where they beat demonstrators senseless and clubbed a Justice Department observer. The governor and police refused to protect the freedom riders. The riders traveled into Mississippi under National Guard protection but were arrested at the Jackson bus terminal. Despite Attorney General Robert Kennedy's call for a cooling-off period, freedom rides continued through the summer. The rides proved that African Americans were in charge of their own civil rights revolution.

THE MARCH ON WASHINGTON, 1963

John Kennedy was a tepid supporter of the civil rights movement and entered office with no civil rights agenda. He appointed segregationist judges to mollify southern congressmen and would have preferred that African Americans stop disturbing the fragile Democratic Party coalition. As Eisenhower did at Little Rock, Kennedy intervened at the University of Mississippi in 1962 because of a state challenge to federal authority, not to further racial justice.

In the face of the slow federal response, the SCLC concentrated for 1963 on rigidly segregated Birmingham. Birmingham's commissioner of public safety, Bull Connor, used fire hoses to blast demonstrators against buildings and roll children down the streets. When demonstrators fought back, his men chased them with dogs. Continued marches brought the arrest of hundreds of children. King's "Letter from Birmingham City Jail" stated the case for protest: "We have not made a single gain in civil rights without determined legal and nonviolent pressure. . . . Freedom is never voluntarily given by the oppressor; it must be demanded by the oppressed."

The Birmingham demonstrations were inconclusive. White leaders accepted minimal demands on May 10 but delayed enforcing them. Antiblack violence continued, including a bomb that killed four children in a Birmingham church. Meanwhile, the events in Alabama had forced President Kennedy to board the freedom train with an eloquent June 11 speech and to send a civil rights bill to Congress. "Are we to say . . . that this is the land of the free, except for Negroes, that we have

---

QUICK REVIEW

Civil Rights During the Kennedy Administration

- Kennedy was a tepid supporter of the civil rights movement.
- 1963: activists focused their attention on segregation in Birmingham.
- August 28, 1963: quarter of a million people marched to the Lincoln Memorial in support of civil rights.

Southern Christian Leadership Conference (SCLC) Black civil rights organization founded in 1957 by Martin Luther King, Jr., and other clergy.

Student Nonviolent Coordinating Committee (SNCC) Black civil rights organization founded in 1960 and drawing heavily on younger activists and college students.

Congress of Racial Equality (CORE) Civil rights group formed in 1942 and committed to nonviolent civil disobedience.

no second-class citizens, except Negroes . . .? Now the time has come for the nation to fulfill its promise."

On August 28, 1963, a rally in Washington transformed African-American civil rights into a national cause. A quarter of a million people, black and white, marched to the Lincoln Memorial. The day gave Martin Luther King, Jr., a national pulpit. His call for progress toward Christian and American goals had immense appeal.

The March on Washington demonstrated the mass appeal of civil rights and its identification with national values.

"Let Us Continue"

*T*he two years that followed King's speech mingled despair and accomplishment. The optimism of the March on Washington shattered with the assassination of John Kennedy in November 1963. In 1964 and 1965, however, President Lyndon Johnson pushed through Kennedy's legislative agenda and much more. Federal legislation brought victory to the first phase of the civil rights revolution, launched the **War on Poverty,** expanded health insurance and aid to education, and opened an era of environmental protection.

Dallas, 1963

In November 1963, President Kennedy visited Texas to raise money and patch up feuds among Texas Democrats. On November 22, the president's motorcade took him near the Texas School Book Depository building in Dallas, where Lee Harvey Oswald had stationed himself at a window on the sixth floor. When Kennedy's open car swung into the sights of his rifle, Oswald fired three shots that wounded Texas Governor John Connally and killed the president. Dallas police quickly arrested Oswald. Two days later, as Oswald was being led to a courtroom, Jack Ruby, a Texas nightclub owner, killed him with a handgun in full view of TV cameras.

Lee Oswald was a 24-year-old misfit. He had served in the Marines and worked maintaining U-2 spy planes before defecting to the Soviet Union, which he found to be less than a workers' paradise. He returned to the United States after three years with a Russian wife and a fervent commitment to Fidel Castro's Cuban revolution. He visited the Soviet and Cuban embassies in Mexico City in September trying to drum up a job, but neither country thought him worth hiring.

Some Americans believe there is more to the story. The sketchy job done by the Warren Commission, appointed to investigate the assassination, bred doubts. The commission hurried to complete its work before the 1964 election. It also sought to assure Americans that Kennedy had not been killed as part of a Communist plot. The Warren Commission calmed fears in the short run but left loose ends that have fueled conspiracy theories.

All of the theories remain unproved. Until they are, logic holds that the simplest explanation is usually the best. Oswald was a social misfit with a grievance against American society. Ruby was an impulsive man who told his brother on his deathbed that he thought he had done the country a favor. Like Presidents

HOW DID Lyndon B. Johnson continue the domestic agenda inherited from the Kennedy administration? In what ways did he depart from it?

W **WHERE TO LEARN MORE**

Sixth Floor Museum, Dallas, Texas
www.jfk.org

War on Poverty   Set of programs introduced by Lyndon Johnson between 1963 and 1966 designed to break the cycle of poverty by providing funds for job training, community development, nutrition, and supplementary education.

Garfield and McKinley before him, Kennedy died at the hands of one unbalanced man acting alone.

WAR ON POVERTY

Five days after the assassination, Lyndon Johnson claimed Kennedy's progressive aura for his new administration. "Let us continue," he told the nation, promising to implement Kennedy's policies. In fact, Johnson was vastly different from Kennedy. He was a professional politician who, as Senate majority leader during the 1950s, had built a web of political obligations and friendships. Johnson's presence on the ticket in 1960 had helped to elect Kennedy by attracting southern voters, but the Kennedy entourage loathed him. He lacked Kennedy's polish and easy relations with the eastern elite. Johnson's upbringing in rural Texas shaped a man who was endlessly ambitious, ruthless, and often personally crude, but also deeply committed to social equity. He had entered public life with the New Deal in the 1930s and believed in its principles. Johnson, not Kennedy, was the true heir of Franklin Roosevelt.

Johnson inherited a domestic agenda that the Kennedy administration had defined but not enacted. Kennedy's farthest-reaching initiative was rooted in the acknowledgment that poverty was a persistent American problem. Michael Harrington's study *The Other America* became an unexpected bestseller. As poverty captured public attention, Kennedy's economic advisers devised a community action program that emphasized education and job training, a national service corps, and a youth conservation corps.

Johnson made Kennedy's antipoverty package his own. Adopting Cold War rhetoric, he declared "unconditional war on poverty." The core of Johnson's program was the **Office of Economic Opportunity (OEO).** Established under the direction of Kennedy's brother-in-law R. Sargent Shriver in 1964, the OEO operated the Job Corps for school dropouts, the Neighborhood Youth Corps for unemployed teenagers, the Head Start program to prepare poor children for school, and VISTA (Volunteers in Service to America), a domestic Peace Corps. OEO's biggest effort went to Community Action Agencies. By 1968, more than 500 such agencies provided health and educational services. Despite flaws, the War on Poverty improved life for millions of Americans.

CIVIL RIGHTS, 1964–1965

Johnson's passionate commitment to economic betterment accompanied a commitment to civil rights. In Johnson's view, segregation not only deprived African Americans of access to opportunity but also distracted white southerners from their own poverty and underdevelopment. As he complained in a speech in New Orleans, southern leaders ignored the region's economic needs in favor of racial rabble-rousing.

One solution was the **Civil Rights Act of 1964,** which Kennedy had introduced but which Johnson got enacted. The law prohibited segregation in public accommodations, such as hotels, restaurants, gas stations, theaters, and parks, and outlawed employment discrimination on federally assisted projects. It also created the Equal Employment Opportunity Commission (EEOC) and included gender in the list of categories protected against discrimination, a provision whose consequences were scarcely suspected in 1964.

WHERE TO LEARN MORE

National Civil Rights Museum, Memphis, Tennessee
http://www.civilrightsmuseum.org

Office of Economic Opportunity (OEO)　Federal agency that coordinated many programs of the War on Poverty between 1964 and 1975.

Civil Rights Act of 1964
Federal legislation that outlawed discrimination in public accommodations and employment on the basis of race, skin color, sex, religion, or national origin.

Even as Congress was debating the 1964 law, **Freedom Summer** moved political power to the top of the civil rights agenda. Organized by SNCC, the Mississippi Summer Freedom Project was a voter-registration drive that sent white and black volunteers to the small towns and back roads of Mississippi. Local black activists had laid the groundwork for a registration effort with years of courageous effort through the NAACP and voter leagues. Now an increasingly militant SNCC took the lead. The explicit goal was to increase the number of African-American voters. The tacit intention was to attract national attention by putting middle-class white college students in the line of fire. Freedom Summer gained 1,600 new voters and taught 2,000 children in SNCC-run Freedom Schools at the cost of beatings, bombings, church arson, and the murder of three project workers.

Another outgrowth of the SNCC effort was the Mississippi Freedom Democratic Party (MFDP), a biracial coalition that bypassed Mississippi's all-white Democratic Party, followed state party rules, and sent its own delegates to the 1964 Democratic convention. To preserve party harmony, President Johnson refused to expel the "regular" Mississippi Democrats and offered instead to seat two MFDP delegates and enforce party rules for 1968. The MFDP walked out, seething with anger.

Freedom Summer and political realities both focused national attention on voter registration. Lyndon Johnson and Martin Luther King, Jr., agreed on the need for federal voting legislation when King visited the president in December 1964 after winning the Nobel Peace Prize. For King, power at the ballot box would help black southerners to take control of their own communities. For Johnson, voting reform would fulfill the promise of American democracy. It would also benefit the Democratic Party by replacing with black voters the white southerners who were drifting toward the anti-integration Republicans.

The target for King and the SCLC was Dallas County, Alabama, where only 2 percent of eligible black residents were registered, compared with 70 percent of white residents. Peaceful demonstrations started in January 1965. By early February, jails in the county seat of Selma held 2,600 black people whose offense was marching to the courthouse to demand the vote. The campaign climaxed with a march from Selma to the state capital of Montgomery.

On Sunday, March 7, 500 marchers crossed the bridge over the Alabama River, to meet a sea of state troopers. The troopers gave them two minutes to disperse and then attacked on foot and horseback "as if they were mowing a big field." The attack drove the demonstrators back in bloody confusion while television cameras rolled.

As violence continued, Johnson addressed a joint session of Congress to demand a voting-rights law. By opening the political process to previously excluded citizens, the Voting Rights Act was as revolutionary and far-reaching as the Nineteenth Amendment, which guaranteed women the right to vote, and the Labor Relations Act of 1935, which recognized labor unions as the equals of corporations.

Johnson signed the **Voting Rights Act** on August 6, 1965. The law outlawed literacy tests and provided for federal voting registrars in states where registration or turnout in 1964 was less than 50 percent of the eligible population. It applied initially in seven southern states. Black registration in these states jumped from 27 percent to 55 percent within the first year. In 1975, Congress extended coverage to Hispanic voters in the Southwest. The Act required new moderation

Freedom Summer Voter registration effort in rural Mississippi organized by black and white civil rights workers in 1964.

Voting Rights Act Legislation in 1965 that overturned a variety of practices by which states systematically denied voter registration to minorities.

Students from North Carolina A&T, an all-black college, began the lunch-counter sit-in movement in February 1960. Here four students sit patiently in the Greensboro Woolworth's without being served. Participants wore their best clothes and suffered politely through days of verbal and sometimes physical abuse.

News and Records Library

Gulf of Tonkin Resolution
Request to Congress from President Lyndon Johnson in response to North Vietnamese torpedo boat attacks in which he sought authorization for "all necessary measures" to protect American forces and stop further aggression.

from white leaders, who had to satisfy black voters, and it opened the way for black and Latino candidates to win positions at every level of state and local government. In the long run, the Voting Rights Act climaxed the battle for civil rights and shifted attention to the continuing problems of economic opportunity and inequality.

WAR, PEACE, AND THE LANDSLIDE OF 1964

Lyndon Johnson was the peace candidate in 1964. Johnson had maintained Kennedy's commitment to South Vietnam. On the advice of such Kennedy holdovers as Defense Secretary Robert McNamara, he stepped up commando raids and naval shelling of North Vietnam. On August 2, North Vietnamese torpedo boats attacked the U.S. destroyer *Maddox* in the Gulf of Tonkin while it was eavesdropping on North Vietnamese military signals. Two days later, the *Maddox* and the *C. Turner Joy* reported another torpedo attack (probably false sonar readings). Johnson ordered a bombing raid in reprisal and asked Congress to authorize "all necessary measures" to protect American forces and stop further aggression. Congress passed the **Gulf of Tonkin Resolution** with only two nay votes, effectively authorizing the president to wage undeclared war.

Johnson's militancy palled beside that of his Republican opponent, Senator Barry Goldwater of Arizona. Goldwater wanted minimal government interference in free enterprise and aggressive confrontation with Communism. Goldwater's campaign made Johnson look moderate. Johnson pledged not "to send American boys nine or ten thousand miles from home to do what Asian boys ought to be doing for themselves" while Goldwater proposed an all-out war.

The election was a landslide. Johnson's 61 percent of the popular vote was the greatest margin ever recorded in a presidential election. Democrats racked up two-to-one majorities in Congress. For the first time in decades, liberal Democrats could enact their domestic program without begging votes from conservative southerners or Republicans, and Johnson could achieve his goal of a **Great Society** based on freedom and opportunity for all.

The result was a series of measures that Johnson pushed through Congress before the Vietnam War eroded his political standing and distracted national attention. The National Endowment for the Arts and the National Endowment for the Humanities seemed uncontroversial at the time but would later become the focus of liberal and conservative struggles over the character of American life. The Wilderness Act (1964), which preserved 9.1 million acres from development, would prove another political battlefield in the face of economic pressures in the next century.

The goal of increasing opportunity for all Americans stirred the president most deeply. As he told a July 1965 news conference, "When I was young, poverty was so common that we didn't know it had a name. An education was something that you had to fight for. . . . It is now my opportunity to help every child get an education, to help every Negro and every American citizen have an equal opportunity, to have every family get a decent home, and to help bring healing to the sick and dignity to the old." The Elementary and Secondary Education Act was the first general federal aid program for public schools, allocating $1.3 billion for textbooks and special education. The Higher Education Act funded low-interest student loans and university research facilities. The Medical Care Act created **Medicare,** federally funded health insurance for the elderly, and **Medicaid,** which helped states offer medical care to the poor. The Appalachian Regional Development Act funded economic development in the depressed mountain counties of 12 states from Georgia to New York and proved a long-run success.

It is sometimes said that the United States declared war on poverty and lost. In fact, the nation came closer to winning the war on poverty than it did the war in Vietnam. New or expanded social insurance and income-support programs, such as Medicare, Medicaid, Social Security, and food stamps, cut the proportion of poor people from 22 percent of the American population in 1960 to 13 percent in 1970. Infant mortality dropped by a third because of improved nutrition and better access to health care for mothers and children. Taken together, the political results of the 1964 landslide moved the United States much closer to the vision of an end to poverty and racial injustice

CONCLUSION

*T*he era commonly remembered as the 1950s stretched from 1953 to 1964. Consistent goals guided American foreign policy through the entire period, including vigilant anti-communism and the confidence to intervene in trouble spots around the globe. At home, the Supreme Court's *Brown* decision

WHERE TO LEARN MORE
Birmingham Civil Rights Institute Museum, Birmingham, Alabama
www.bcri.bham.al.us

WHERE TO LEARN MORE
Martin Luther King, Jr., National Historical Site, Atlanta, Georgia
http://www.nps.gov/malu/

Great Society Theme of Lyndon Johnson's administration, focusing on poverty, education, and civil rights.

Medicare Basic medical insurance for the elderly, financed through the federal government; program created in 1965.

Medicaid Supplementary medical insurance for the poor, financed through the federal government; program created in 1965.

introduced a decade-long civil rights revolution that reached its emotional peak with the March on Washington and its political climax with the Civil Rights Act (1964) and Voting Rights Act (1965). However, many patterns of personal behavior and social relations remained unchanged. Women faced similar expectations from the early fifties to the early sixties. Churches showed more continuity than change.

In retrospect, it is remarkable how widely and deeply the Cold War shaped U.S. society. Fundamental social institutions, such as marriage and religion, got extra credit for their contributions to anti-communism. The nation's long tradition of home-grown radicalism was virtually silent in the face of the Cold War consensus. Even economically meritorious programs like more money for science and better roads went down more easily if linked to national defense.

But the consistency and stability of the 1950s were fragile and the national consensus splintered after 1964. Some members of minority groups turned their backs on integration. Some younger Americans dropped out of mainstream society to join the aptly named counterculture. Others sought the security of religious commitment and community. Perhaps most divisively, "hawks" battled "doves" over Vietnam. If civil rights and Cold War had been the defining issues for the fifties, Vietnam would define the sixties, which stretched from 1965 to 1974.

IMAGE KEY

for pages 812–813

a. A drawing of the Sputnik satellite appears on a playing card from a card game about the space race.
b. Elvis Presley.
c. Russian nuclear missiles photographed at Mariel Port facility in Cuba, with illustrative tags describing various equipment.
d. 1960 Presidential candidates Richard Milhous Nixon and John F. Kennedy during a televised debate.
e. The album cover of "We Insist!" by Max Roach depicts African-American men at a lunch counter during a sit-in.
f. Elizabeth Eckford is heckled by a white student while integrating Central High School in Little Rock, Arkansas in 1957.
g. LBJ takes the oath of office on the ride back to Washington, D.C. from Dallas, after the assassination of JFK.
h. President Kennedy's TV address on the Cuban Missile Crisis.
i. Suburban family standing in front of their Levittown house in 1950.
j. Children huddle below their desks in an elementary school classroom during an air raid drill.

SUMMARY

A Decade of Affluence President Eisenhower presided over the prosperity of the 1950s. He claimed the "political middle" and accepted much of the New Deal but saw little need for further reform. During his administration, workers had more disposable income and credit-based consumerism expanded; suburbs and the "car culture" grew. Families were seen as part of the anti-Communist crusade. The "youth culture" emerged, but religious affiliation, the belief in prosperity, and social conformity characterized the era. Vast inequalities were concealed; many had missed out on "affluent America" and many women were unhappy in their "perfect" world.

Facing Off with the Soviet Union The actions of the United States and Soviet Union created a bipolar world: Each was a magnetic pole with countries aligning themselves or attempting to remain neutral. The Soviet launching of the *Sputnik* satellite concerned Americans who thought they were technologically superior. America's worldview of the right and need to intervene in areas that were possible Communist takeover targets resulted in an expansion of containment. "Brinksmanship" characterized this period in the Cold War.

John F. Kennedy and the Cold War John F. Kennedy won over Richard Nixon in a close election in 1960; television was a critical element. Kennedy's administration dealt with the Bay of Pigs invasion, a new Berlin crisis and the building of the Berlin Wall, growing American involvement in Vietnam, and the Cuban Missile crisis. Kennedy supported science as well as diplomacy; he committed the United

States to placing an American astronaut on the moon and signed the Limited Test Ban Treaty which was a step toward later disarmament treaties.

Righteousness Like a Mighty Stream: The Struggle for Civil Rights The Supreme Court's *Brown* decision made the growing effort to secure equal legal treatment for African Americans a challenge to American society. The first phase of the civil rights struggle built from the Supreme Court's decision in 1954 to a vast gathering at the Lincoln Memorial in 1963. In between African Americans chipped away at racial segregation of schools, universities, and public facilities with boycotts, sit-ins, and lawsuits, forcing segregationists to choose between integration and violent defiance.

"Let Us Continue" After President Kennedy's assassination, Lyndon Johnson inherited a domestic agenda that was based on the knowledge that poverty was a widespread American problem. Johnson's passionate commitment to economic betterment accompanied a commitment to civil rights. War on Poverty and Great Society measures were passed before Johnson's enlargement of the Vietnam War eroded his political standing; the United States moved closer to addressing the effects of poverty and racial injustice than ever before.

REVIEW QUESTIONS

1. What were the sources of prosperity in the 1950s and 1960s? How did prosperity shape cities, family life, and religion? What opportunities did it create for women and for young people? How did it affect the American role in the world? Why did an affluent nation still need a war on poverty in the 1960s?

2. What assumptions about the Soviet Union shaped U.S. foreign policy? What assumptions about the United States shaped Soviet policy? What did American leaders think was at stake in Vietnam, Berlin, and Cuba?

3. Who initiated and led the African-American struggle for civil rights? What role did the federal government play? What were the goals of the civil rights movement? Where did it succeed, and in what ways did it fall short?

4. How did the growth of nuclear arsenals affect international relations? How did the nuclear shadow affect American politics and society?

5. In what new directions did Lyndon Johnson take the United States? Were there differences between the goals of the New Frontier and the Great Society?

6. Why was school integration the focus of such strong conflict? How did the work of Mexican Americans and African Americans support the same goal of equal access to education?

7. How did religious belief shape American society in the Eisenhower and Kennedy years?

KEY TERMS

Alliance for Progress   (p. 829)
Bay of Pigs   (p. 828)
Berlin Wall   (p. 828)
Brown v. Board of Education of Topeka
    (p. 830)
Civil Rights Act of 1964   (p. 836)
Congress of Racial Equality
    (CORE)   (p. 834)
Federal Highway Act of 1956
    (p. 817)
Freedom Summer   (p. 837)
Great Society   (p. 839)

Gulf of Tonkin Resolution
    (p. 838)
Limited Test Ban Treaty   (p. 830)
Massive retaliation   (p. 823)
Medicaid   (p. 839)
Medicare   (p. 839)
National Aeronautics and Space
    Administration (NASA)
    (p. 823)
New Frontier   (p. 826)
Office of Economic Opportunity
    (OEO)   (p. 836)

Southeast Asia Treaty Organization
    (SEATO)   (p. 828)
Southern Christian Leadership
    Conference (SCLC)   (p. 834)
Southern Manifesto   (p. 832)
Student Nonviolent Coordinating
    Committee (SNCC)   (p. 834)
Viet Cong   (p. 828)
Voting Rights Act   (p. 837)
War on Poverty   (p. 835)

WHERE TO LEARN MORE

⬡ **National Air and Space Museum, Washington, D.C.** Part of the Smithsonian Institution's complex of museums in Washington, the Air and Space Museum is the richest source for artifacts and discussion of the American space program. **www.nasm.edu**.

⬡ **Kansas Cosmosphere, Hutchinson, Kansas.** A rich collection of artifacts and equipment from the U.S. space program. **www.cosmo.org**.

⬡ **Sixth Floor Museum, Dallas, Texas.** Occupying the sixth floor of the former Texas School Book Depository building, exhibits examine the life, death, and legacy of John F. Kennedy. **www.jfk.org**.

⬡ **Birmingham Civil Rights Institute Museum, Birmingham, Alabama.** This museum and archive deal with the background of southern racial segregation, civil rights activism, and the 1963 demonstrations in Birmingham. **www.bcri. bham.al.us**.

⬡ **Martin Luther King, Jr., National Historical Site, Atlanta, Georgia.** The birthplace and grave of Reverend King are the nucleus of a park set in the historic black neighborhood of Auburn. **http://www.nps.gov/malu/**.

⬡ **National Civil Rights Museum, Memphis, Tennessee.** Located in the Lorraine Motel, where Martin Luther King, Jr., was killed, the museum traces the participants, background, and effects of key events in the civil rights movement. **http://www.civilrightsmuseum.org**.

⬡ **National Afro-American Museum and Cultural Center, Wilberforce, Ohio.** The exhibit "From Victory to Freedom: Afro-American Life in the Fifties" looks at home, family, music, and religion. **www.ohiohistory.org/places/afroam/**.

⬡ **John F. Kennedy Library and Museum, Boston, Massachusetts.** Exhibits offer a sympathetic view of Kennedy's life and achievements. **www.cs. umb.edu/ jfklibrary/**.

U.S. History Document CD-ROM
For primary sources related to this chapter, refer to the document CD-ROM.

 www.prenhall.com/goldfield
For study resources related to this chapter, visit the *Companion Website*™.

29

Shaken to the Roots
1965–1980

CHAPTER HIGHLIGHTS

The End of Consensus The failure to win an easy victory in Vietnam eroded the nation's confidence and fueled bitter debate about the nation's goal. The antiwar movement reflected growing grassroots activism on college campuses, among women, and in the counterculture.

Cities Under Stress
Cities gained a reputation as centers of violence, pollution, and poverty. Many urban problems were associated with the creation of "second ghettos." Race riots reflected the anger and frustration of the urban poor. Some members of minority groups responded to the same pressures by developing separatist movements. As the cities deteriorated, the suburbs grew.

The Year of the Gun, 1968
After the Tet offensive, mainstream America turned against the war in Vietnam. LBJ chose not to run for reelection. The violence outside of the 1968 Democratic convention was an indicator of growing division within the country.

Nixon, Watergate, and the Crisis of the Early 1970s In July 1969, President Nixon shifted the emphasis of U.S. support for South Vietnam from soldiers to money and weapons. His secret war against Cambodia extended the military stalemate in the region. Nixon made overtures to China and inaugurated a period of easing tensions with the Soviet Union. Revelations about Nixon's abuse of power to cover up his role in the Watergate affair led to his resignation.

Jimmy Carter: Idealism and Frustration in the White House Jimmy Carter brought both the advantages and disadvantages of an outsider to the White House. His greatest successes were in foreign policy. Economic problems and the Iranian hostage crisis undermined his presidency.

CHAPTER QUESTIONS

WHY DID the national consensus of the 1950s and early 1960s unravel?

WHAT CHALLENGES did cities face in the late 1960s and 1970s?

HOW DID the Tet offensive change American public opinion about the war in Vietnam?

WHAT WAS the legacy of Richard Nixon's presidency?

WHAT FACTORS limited Jimmy Carter's effectiveness as president?

CHAPTER OUTLINE

- The End of Consensus
- Cities Under Stress
- The Year of the Gun, 1968
- Nixon, Watergate, and the Crisis of the Early 1970s
- Jimmy Carter: Idealism and Frustration in the White House

IMAGE KEY

for pages 844–845 is on page 874.

Contact light! O.K., engine stop. . . . Houston, Tranquility Base here. The Eagle has landed! . . . We opened the hatch and Neil, with me as navigator, began backing out of the tiny opening [in the Lunar Module Eagle]. It seemed like a small eternity before I heard Neil say, "That's one small step for man . . . one giant leap for mankind." In less than fifteen minutes I was backing awkwardly out of the hatch onto the surface to join Neil, who, in the tradition of all tourists, had his camera ready to photograph my arrival.

I took off jogging to test my maneuverability. The exercise gave me an odd sensation and looked even more odd when I later saw the films of it. With bulky suits on, we seemed to be moving in slow motion. . . . At one point, I remarked that the surface was "Beautiful, beautiful. Magnificent desolation." I was struck by the contrast between the starkness of the shadows and the desert-like barrenness of the rest of the surface. It ranged from dusty gray to light tan and was unchanging except for one startling sight: our LM sitting there with its black, silver and bright yellow-orange thermal coating shining brightly in the otherwise colorless landscape.

During a pause in experiments, Neil suggested we proceed with the flag. . . . To our dismay the staff of the pole wouldn't go far enough into the lunar surface. . . . I dreaded the possibility of the American flag collapsing into the lunar dust in front of the television camera.

Edgar Cortright, ed., *Apollo Expeditions to the Moon* (Washington: NASA SP 350, 1975).

Buzz Aldrin and Neil Armstrong, on July 20, 1969, completed the longest journey that anyone had yet taken. Landing the *Apollo 11* lunar module on the surface of the moon climaxed a five-day trip across the quarter million miles separating the earth from the moon.

The *Apollo 11* expedition combined science and Cold War politics. The American flag waving on the lunar surface was a symbol of victory in one phase of the space race between the United States and the Soviet Union. NASA had been working since 1961 to meet John F. Kennedy's goal of a manned trip to the moon before the end of the decade.

Even with the excitement of *Apollo's* success, however, the United States was increasingly shaken and divided in the later 1960s and 1970s. Stalemate in Southeast Asia, political changes in third world countries, and an oil supply crisis in the 1970s challenged U.S. influence in the world. Frustrated by the slow progress toward racial equality, many minority Americans advocated separation rather than integration, helping to plunge the nation's cities into crisis, while other Americans began to draw back from some of the objectives of racial integration

Political scandals, summarized in three syllables, "Watergate," undercut faith in government. Fifteen years of turmoil forced a grudging recognition of the limits to American military power, economic capacity, governmental prerogatives, and even the ideal of a single American dream.

Chronology

1962	Rachel Carson publishes *Silent Spring*.
	Port Huron Statement launches Students for a Democratic Society.
1965	Congress approves Wilderness Act.
	Malcolm X is assassinated.
	Residents of Watts neighborhood in Los Angeles riot.
1967	African Americans riot in Detroit and Newark.
1968	Viet Cong launches Tet Offensive.
	James Earl Ray kills Martin Luther King, Jr.
	Lyndon Johnson declines to run for reelection.
	SDS disrupts Columbia University.
	Sirhan Sirhan kills Robert Kennedy.
	Peace talks start between the United States and North Vietnam.
	Police riot against antiwar protesters during the Democratic National Convention in Chicago.
	Richard Nixon is elected president.
1969	Neil Armstrong and Buzz Aldrin walk on the moon.
1970	United States invades Cambodia.
	National Guard units kill students at Kent State and Jackson State universities.
	Earth Day is celebrated.
	Environmental Protection Agency is created.
1971	*New York Times* publishes the secret Pentagon Papers.
	President Nixon freezes wages and prices.
	Plumbers unit is established in the White House.
1972	Nixon visits China.
	United States and Soviet Union adopt SALT I.
	Operatives for Nixon's reelection campaign break into Democratic headquarters in the Watergate complex in Washington, D.C.

1973	Paris accords end direct U.S. involvement in South Vietnamese war.
	United States moves to all-volunteer armed forces.
	Watergate burglars are convicted.
	Senate Watergate hearings reveal the existence of taped White House conversations.
	Spiro Agnew resigns as vice president, is replaced by Gerald Ford.
	Arab states impose an oil embargo after the third Arab-Israeli War.
1974	Nixon resigns as president, is succeeded by Gerald Ford.
1975	Communists triumph in South Vietnam.
	United States, USSR, and European nations sign the Helsinki Accords.
1976	Jimmy Carter defeats Gerald Ford for the presidency.
1978	Carter brings the leaders of Egypt and Israel to Camp David for peace talks.
	U.S. agrees to transfer control of the Panama Canal to Panama.
1979	SALT II agreement is signed but not ratified.
	OPEC raises oil prices.
	Three Mile Island nuclear plant comes close to disaster.
	Iranian militants take U.S. embassy hostages.
1980	Iranian hostage rescue fails.
	Soviet troops enter Afghanistan.
	Ronald Reagan defeats Jimmy Carter for the presidency.

THE END OF CONSENSUS

WHY DID the national consensus of the 1950s and early 1960s unravel?

Pleiku is a town in Vietnam 240 miles north of Saigon (now Ho Chi Minh City). In 1965, Pleiku was the site of a South Vietnamese army headquarters and American military base. At 2:00 A.M. on February 7, Viet Cong attacked the U.S. base, killing eight Americans and wounding a hundred. President Johnson ordered a retaliatory air strike against North Vietnam, and navy bombers roared off aircraft carriers in Operation FLAMING DART. A month later, Johnson ordered a full-scale air offensive code-named ROLLING THUNDER.

The attack at Pleiku triggered plans that were waiting to be put into effect since the Gulf of Tonkin resolution the previous summer. As the South Vietnamese government lost control of the countryside, air strikes on North Vietnam looked like an easy way to redress the balance. In the back of President Johnson's mind were the need to prove his toughness and the mistaken assumption that China was aggressively backing North Vietnam.

The air strikes pushed the United States over the line from propping up the South Vietnamese government to leading the war effort. Eventually, the war in Vietnam would distract the United States from the goals of the Great Society and drive Johnson from office. It hovered like a shadow over the next two presidents, set back progress toward global stability, and divided the American people.

DEEPER INTO VIETNAM

Lyndon Johnson faced limited options in Vietnam (see Map 29–1). The pervasive American determination to contain Communism and Kennedy's previous commitments there hemmed Johnson in. Advisers persuaded him that controlled military escalation—a middle course between withdrawal and all-out war—could secure Vietnam. They failed to understand the extent of popular opposition to the official government in Saigon and the willingness of North Vietnam to sacrifice to achieve national unity.

Because ROLLING THUNDER required ground troops to protect bases in South Vietnam, U.S. Marines landed on March 8. Over the next four months, General Westmoreland wore away Johnson's desire to contain American involvement. More bombs, a pause, an offer of massive U.S. aid—nothing brought North Vietnam to the negotiating table. Meanwhile, defeat loomed. Johnson dribbled in new forces and expanded their mission from base security to combat. On July 28, he finally gave Westmoreland doubled draft calls and an increase in U.S. combat troops from 75,000 to 275,000 by 1966. Johnson's decision turned a South Vietnamese war into an American war. At the end of 1967, American forces in South Vietnam totaled 485,000; they reached their maximum of 543,000 in August 1969.

The U.S. strategy on the ground was **search and destroy.** As conceived by Westmoreland, it used sophisticated surveillance and heavily armed patrols to locate enemy detachments, which could then be destroyed by air strikes, artillery, and reinforcements carried in by helicopter. The approach made sense when the opposition consisted of North Vietnamese troops and large Viet Cong units.

However, most opponents were not North Vietnamese divisions but South Vietnamese guerrillas. The enemy was difficult for Americans to recognize among farmers and workers, making South Vietnamese society itself the target. The American penchant for massive firepower killed thousands of Vietnamese and made millions refugees. Because the South Vietnamese government was unable to secure areas after American sweeps, the Viet Cong often reappeared after the Americans had crashed through a district.

The American air war also had limited results. Pilots dropped a vast tonnage of bombs on the Ho Chi Minh Trail, a network of supply routes from North Vietnam to South Vietnam through the mountains of neighboring Laos. Despite the bombing, thousands of workers converted rough paths into roads that were repaired as soon as they were damaged. The air assault on North Vietnam itself remained "diplomatic," intended to force North Vietnam to stop intervening in the

WHERE TO LEARN MORE

Vietnam Veterans Memorial, Washington, D.C. **www.nps.gov/vive/**

Search and Destroy U.S. military tactic in South Vietnam, using small detachments to locate enemy units and then massive air, artillery, and ground forces to destroy them.

MAP EXPLORATION

To explore an interactive version of this map, go to **http://www.prenhall.com/goldfield3/map29.1**

MAP 29–1   The War in Vietnam   The United States attacked North Vietnam with air strikes but confined large-scale ground operations to South Vietnam and Cambodia. In South Vietnam, U.S. forces faced both North Vietnamese army units and Viet Cong rebels, all of whom received supplies by way of the so-called Ho Chi Minh Trail, named for the leader of North Vietnam. The coordinated attacks on cities and towns throughout South Vietnam during the Tet Offensive in 1968 surprised the United States.

WHAT WERE the shortcomings of American military strategy in Vietnam?

OVERVIEW   WHY WERE WE IN SOUTH VIETNAM?

American leaders offered a number of justifications for American military involvement in Vietnam. Here are some of the key arguments, with points that supported or questioned the explanation.

To Prop Up a Domino: Communist success in South Vietnam would undermine pro-American regimes in adjacent nations, which would topple like a row of dominoes,

Pro   The firm U.S. stand contributed to an anti-Communist coup in Indonesia in 1965 and encouraged pro-American interests in Thailand and the Philippines.

Con   Close examination of each nation in Southeast Asia shows that their own histories and internal issues were far more important in determining their futures than was American action in Vietnam.

To Contain China: China's Communist regime wanted to expand its control throughout Asia.

Pro   The People's Republic of China was hostile to the United States, as shown in the Korean War, and had a long history of trying to control Vietnam.

Con   North Vietnam had closer ties to the Soviet Union than to China and played the two communist nations against each other to preserve its independence from China.

To Defeat Aggression: South Vietnam was an independent nation threatened by invasion.

Pro   The major military threat to South Vietnam after 1965 came from the growing presence of the North Vietnamese army, and U.S. military intervention was necessary to counter that invasion.

Con   The conflict in South Vietnam originated as a civil war within South Vietnam. Moreover, South and North Vietnam were a single nation, artificially divided in 1954, so that North Vietnam was trying to reunify rather than invade South Vietnam.

To Protect Democracy: South Vietnam was a democratic nation that deserved American support.

Pro   South Vietnam had an emerging middle class and an opportunity to develop democratic institutions.

Con   South Vietnam was never a true democracy, ruled first by civilian dictator Ngo Dinh Diem and then a series of military strongmen.

South Vietnamese civil war. Since North Vietnam's leadership considered North and South to be one country, the American goal was unacceptable. Attacking North Vietnam's poorly developed economy, the United States soon ran out of targets.

VOICES OF DISSENT

At home, protest against the war quickly followed the commitment of American combat forces. The first national antiwar march took place in Washington on April 17, 1965. Twenty-five thousand people picketed the White House, assembled at the Washington Monument for speeches by Senator Ernest Gruening of Alaska (one of the two dissenting votes on the Gulf of Tonkin Resolution) and African-American leaders, and walked up the Mall to the Capitol.

One group of opponents consisted of "realists" who argued that the war was a mistake. Respected figures like the Cold War strategist George Kennan joined in the dissent. Senator J. William Fulbright held well-publicized hearings in 1966 and 1967, at which respectable critics of the war could state their case to a national audience, and published *The Arrogance of Power* (1967), a book arguing that even the United States needed to recognize limits on its vast political and military power.

If the realists thought that the United States was simply being stupid, more radical critics found the roots of the war in basic flaws in the American character and system. Novelist Norman Mailer compared the American military to big-game trophy hunters in Alaska in *Why Are We in Vietnam?* (1967). Others called the war an example of economic imperialism that showed the power of multinational corporations to control American foreign policy.

Antiwar protests were simultaneously symbolic and disruptive. Some activists dumped jars of animal blood over draft-board records. Others tried to block munitions trains. In October 1967, a hundred thousand people marched on the Pentagon and surrounded it with the light of burning draft cards. Some in front stuck flowers in the rifle barrels of the soldiers ringing the building; others kicked and spat. The troops and police cleared the grounds with tear gas and clubs.

Corbis/Bettmann

From Protest to Confrontation.   In 1966 and 1967, antiwar activity changed from respectful protest to direct confrontations with what protesters called the war machine. Protesters lay down in front of trains carrying munitions. Representatives of Women Strike for Peace journeyed to North Vietnam to explore possible solutions. Religious groups such as the American Friends Service Committee tried to dispense medical and humanitarian aid even-handedly in both North Vietnam and South Vietnam.

The tone of the debate became nastier. Johnson and his associates ridiculed the dissenters. Protesters chanted "Hey, hey, LBJ! How many kids did you kill today?" Much of the anger was directed at the military draft administered by the **Selective Service System.** As the war expanded, the administration tried to hold the allegiance of the middle class by finding ways to exempt their sons from service in Vietnam. Full-time college enrollment was good for a deferment; so was the right medical diagnosis from the right doctor. As a result, draftees and enlistees tended to be small-town and working-class youth. Women who served as military nurses tended to come from the same small-town and working-class backgrounds where patriotism was unquestioned. The resentment created by the draft was an important wedge that began to erode the long-standing alliance between working-class Americans and the Democratic Party.

Military service also deepened the gap between blacks and whites. In 1965, when African Americans made up 11 percent of the nation's population, 24 percent of the soldiers who died in Vietnam were black. This disparity forced the Defense Department to revise its combat assignments so that the racial impact was more equal in later years.

Draft resistance provided a direct avenue for protest against the war. Some young men burned the small paper cards that indicated their selective service classification, causing Congress to enact steep penalties for the act. Several thousand moved to Canada, to spend a decade or more in exile. Thousands of others described their religious and ethical opposition to war in applications for conscientious-objector classification. Much smaller numbers went to jail for refusing to cooperate in any way with the Selective Service System. Resistance mounted throughout the decade. By the end of 1969, over half the men drafted in California were refusing to show up, and prosecutions for draft evasion would peak in 1972 at nearly 5,000.

The popular media portrayed the conflicting visions of the Vietnam War. Barry McGuire's "Eve of Destruction" climbed the charts. Folksinger Phil Ochs sang "I Ain't Marching Anymore." Supporters countered with an aging John Wayne in the movie *The Green Berets*. Country singer Merle Haggard spoke for many small-town Americans who supported the war in "Okie from Muskogee" (where they didn't burn draft cards).

New Left and Community Activism

The antiwar movement was part of a growing grassroots activism that took much of its tone from the university-based **Students for a Democratic Society (SDS)**. Its Port Huron Statement, adopted in 1962, called for grassroots action and participatory democracy. Building on the ideas of such 1950s dissenters as C. Wright Mills, SDS tried to harness youthful disillusionment about consumerism, racism, and imperialism. It wanted to counter the trends that seemed to be turning Americans into tiny cogs in the machinery of big government, corporations, and universities. SDS thought of itself as a "New Left" that was free from the doctrinal squabbles that hampered the old left of the 1930s and 1940s.

Many of the original SDS leaders were also participants in the civil rights movement. The same was true of Mario Savio, founder of the **Free Speech Movement (FSM)** at the University of California at Berkeley in 1964. Savio hoped to build a multi-issue "community of protest" around the idea of "a free university in a free society." FSM protests climaxed with a December sit-in that led to 773 arrests and stirred protest on other campuses.

What SDS wanted to do with its grassroots organizing resembled the federal community-action programs associated with the war on poverty. The **Model Cities Program** (1966) invited residents of poor neighborhoods to write their own plans for using federal funds to improve local housing, education, health services, and job opportunities. Model Cities assemblies challenged the racial bias in programs like urban renewal and helped train community leaders.

In the 1970s and 1980s, the lessons of grassroots reform were visible in alternative organizations and political movements that strengthened democracy from the bottom up. Activists staffed food cooperatives, free clinics, women's health groups, and drug-counseling centers across the country. Community-based organization was a key element in self-help efforts by African Americans, Asian Americans, and Latinos. Neighborhood associations and community-development corporations that provided affordable housing and jobs extended the "backyard revolution" into the 1980s and beyond. Social conservatives, such as antiabortionists, used the same techniques on behalf of their own agendas.

Youth Culture and Counterculture

The popular context for the serious work of the New Left was the growing youth culture and **counterculture**. Millions of young people in the second half of the 1960s expressed their alienation from American society by sampling drugs or chasing the rainbow of a youth culture. Some just smoked marijuana, grew long hair,

Students for a Democratic Society (SDS) The leading student organization of the New Left of the early and mid-1960s.

Free Speech Movement (FSM) Student movement at the University of California, Berkeley, formed in 1964 to protest limitations on political activities on campus.

Model Cities Program Effort to target federal funds to upgrade public services and economic opportunity in specifically defined urban neighborhoods between 1966 and 1974.

Counterculture Various alternatives to mainstream values and behaviors that became popular in the 1960s, including experimentation with psychedelic drugs, communal living, a return to the land, Asian religions, and experimental art.

and listened to psychedelic rock. Others plunged into ways of life that scorned their middle-class backgrounds.

The youth culture took advantage of the nation's prosperity. It was consumerism in a tie-dyed T-shirt. A high point was the 1969 Woodstock rock festival in New York State, a weekend of "sex, drugs, and rock-and-roll" for 400,000 young people. But Woodstock was an excursion, not a life-altering commitment. Members of the Woodstock Generation were consumers in a distinct market niche, dressing but not living like social reformers or revolutionaries.

Within the youth culture was a smaller and more intense counterculture that added Eastern religion, social radicalism, and evangelistic belief in the drug LSD. Rock lyrics began to reflect the drug culture in 1966 and 1967, and young people talked about Harvard professor Timothy Leary's advice to "tune in, turn on, and drop out." San Francisco's Haight–Ashbury district became a national mecca for hippies in 1967's "Summer of Love," and hippie districts sprang up around university campuses across the country.

The cultural rebels of the late 1950s and early 1960s had been trying to combine personal freedom with new social arrangements. Many hippies were more interested in altering their minds with drugs than with politics or poetry. Serious exploration of societal alternatives was left for the minority who devoted themselves to the political work of the New Left, communal living, women's liberation, and other movements.

SOUNDS OF CHANGE

The youth culture was shaped by films and philosophers, by pot and poets, but above all by music. Many changes in American society are mirrored in the abrupt shift from the increasingly complacent rock-and-roll of the early 1960s to the more provocative albums of mid-decade: Bob Dylan's *Highway 61 Revisited* (1965), the Beatles *Rubber Soul* (1965) and *Sergeant Pepper's Lonely Hearts Club Band* (1967), the Jefferson Airplane's *Surrealistic Pillow* (1967). The songs were still aimed at popular success, but the musicians were increasingly self-conscious of themselves as artists and social critics.

At the start of the decade, the African-American roots of rock-and-roll were unmistakable, but there was no social agenda. Elvis Presley and the Everly Brothers kept the messages personal. Music that criticized American society initially found a much smaller audience through the folk-music revival in a few big cities and university campuses.

Then, in an artistic revolution, the doors opened to a new kind of rock music. The Beatles capitalized on their immense popularity to begin a career of artistic experimentation. They also opened the way for such hard-edged British bands as the Rolling Stones and The Who to introduce social criticism and class consciousness into rock lyrics. San Francisco's new psychedelic-rock

Writer Ken Kesey and the self-defined Merry Pranksters toured the country in a brightly painted bus, parked here in San Francisco's Golden Gate Park. They sometimes threw open parties where they served punch laced with psychedelic drugs in the hope of inciting radical social change.

Black Star

scene took its name from drugs, such as LSD, and centered on shows at the Fillmore Auditorium, where performers in 1966 included the Jefferson Airplane, the Grateful Dead, and Buffalo Springfield. The Texan Janis Joplin came to San Francisco to draw on black musical styles after reading the Beat writers who had celebrated the city's jazz and racial openness.

Bob Dylan, a folksinger with an acoustic guitar, "went electric" at the Newport, Rhode Island, folk festival in 1965 and further transformed the music scene. Songs like "Blowin' in the Wind" and "Like a Rolling Stone" were personal and political at the same time; Dylan's music was musically exciting and socially critical in a way that expressed much of the discontent of American young people. Dylan paved the way for later singers like Bruce Springsteen and Kurt Cobain.

The transformation of rock in the mid-1960s invited far more explicit treatment of sex and illegal drugs than was previously accepted in pop music. Jim Morrison and The Doors, Lou Reed and the Velvet Underground, and Jimi Hendrix exploded onto the scene in 1967. Their driving rhythms and sexually aggressive stage personalities blended the tensions of big cities with influences from white rock and roll and black rhythm and blues.

COMMUNES AND CULTS

Out of the half-secular, half-spiritual vision of the counterculture came people who not only dropped out of mainstream institutions but also tried to drop into miniature societies built on new principles. Thousands of Americans in the late 1960s and 1970s formed "intentional communities" or "communes." Their members usually tried to combine individual freedom and spontaneity with cooperative living. Communes were artificial families, financed by inheritances, food stamps, and handicraft sales. Many suffered from the same inequality between men and women that was fueling the feminist revolt. Like natural families, they were emotional hothouses that often most collapsed because their members had incompatible goals.

However, a number of communes were serious endeavors. Some tried to follow spiritual leadings from Christianity or Buddhism. Thousands of smaller and less conspicuous urban communes whose members occupied large old houses pursued experiments in socialism, environmentalism, or feminism. Such efforts helped to spread the ideas of organic farming, cooperative land ownership, and low-consumption environmentalism. Similar to communes but far more organized were exotic religious communities. Following an American tradition, they offered tightly knit group membership and absolute answers to basic questions of human life.

THE FEMINIST CRITIQUE

The growing dissatisfaction of many women with their domestic roles helped set the stage for a revived feminism that was another result of the ferment of the 1960s. Important steps in this revival included the Presidential Commission on the Status of Women in 1961, the addition of gender as one of the categories protected by the Civil Rights Act of 1964 (see Chapter 28), and creation of the National Organization for Women (NOW) in 1966.

Mainstream feminism targeted unequal opportunity in the job market. Newspapers in the early 1960s segregated help-wanted ads by sex. College-educated baby boomers encountered "glass ceilings" and job discrimination. Throughout the mid-1960s and 1970s, activists battled to open job categories to women, who battled for equal pay for everyone with equal qualifications and responsibilities.

Changes in sexual behavior paralleled efforts to equalize treatment in the workplace. More reliable methods of contraception, especially birth-control pills

29-4
National Organization for Women, Statement of Purpose (1966)

introduced in the early 1960s, gave women greater control over childbearing. In some ways a replay of ideas from the 1920s, a new sexual revolution eroded the double standard that expected chastity of women but tolerated promiscuity among men.

More radical versions of the feminist message came from women who had joined the civil rights and antiwar movements only to find themselves working the copy machine and the coffeemaker while men plotted strategy. Radicals caught the attention of the national media with a demonstration against the 1968 Miss America pageant. Protesters crowned a sheep as Miss America and encouraged women to make a statement by tossing their bras and makeup in the trash.

The feminist movement, and specific policy measures related to it, put equal rights and the fight against sexism (a word no one knew before 1965) on the national agenda and gradually changed how Americans thought about the relationships between men and women. Feminists focused attention on rape as a crime of violence and called attention to the burdens the legal system placed on rape victims. In the 1980s and 1990s, they also challenged sexual harassment in the workplace, gradually refining the boundaries between acceptable and unacceptable behavior.

COMING OUT

The new militancy among gay men and lesbians drew on several of the social changes of the late 1960s and 1970s. Willingness to acknowledge and talk about nonstandard sexual behavior was part of a change in public values. Tactics of political pressure came from the antiwar and civil rights movements. The timing, with a series of key events from 1969 to 1974, coincided with that of women's liberation.

Gay activism spread from big cities to small communities, from the coasts to Middle America. New York police had long harassed gay bars and their customers. When police raided Manhattan's Stonewall Inn in June 1969, however, patrons fought back in a weekend of disorder. The **Stonewall Rebellion** was a catalyst for homosexuals to assert themselves as a political force. San Francisco also became a center of gay life. By the late 1970s, the city had more than 300 business and social-gathering places identified as gay and lesbian.

With New Yorkers and San Franciscans as examples, more and more gay men and lesbians "came out," or went public about their sexual orientation. They published newspapers, organized churches, and lobbied politicians for protection of basic civil rights such as equal access to employment, housing, and public accommodations. They staged "gay pride" days and marches. In 1974, the American Psychiatric Association eliminated homosexuality from its official list of mental disorders.

CITIES UNDER STRESS

By the 1970s, slums and squalid back streets dominated popular imagery of the big city. *The French Connection* (1971) followed a drug dealer from Fifth Avenue to empty and menacing warehouses. *Klute* (1971) and *Taxi Driver* (1976) took moviegoers through the twilight world of prostitution. *Blade Runner* (1982) showed a Los Angeles driven mad by corporate violence and social isolation. Television cop shows repeated the message that cities had become places of random and frequent violence.

DIAGNOSING AN URBAN CRISIS

Popular entertainment reflected Americans' growing discomfort with their cities. The nation entered the 1960s with the assumption that urban problems were growing pains. In mid-decade, however, TV networks and news magazines began

WHAT CHALLENGES did cities face in the late 1960s and 1970s?

Stonewall Rebellion   On June 27, 1969, patrons fought back when police raided the gay Stonewall Inn in New York; the name refers to that event and to the increase in militancy by gay Americans that it symbolizes.

to run stories about "Battlefield, USA" and "Crisis in the Cities" that described cities as sinking under racial violence, crime, and unemployment.

Central cities had a special burden in caring for the domestic poor. Impoverished and often fragmented, many urban families needed schools to serve as social-work agencies as well as educational institutions. Poor people with no other access to health care treated city hospital emergency rooms as the family doctor.

Many urban problems were associated with the "second ghettos" created by the migration of 2.5 million African Americans from southern farms to northern and western cities in the 1950s and 1960s. By 1970, one-third of all African Americans lived in the 12 largest cities, crowding into ghetto neighborhoods dating from World War II.

Postwar black migrants found systems of race relations that limited their access to decent housing, the best schools, and many unionized jobs. Many families arrived just in time to face the consequences of industrial layoffs and plant closures in the 1970s and 1980s. Already unneeded in the South because of the mechanization of agriculture, the migrants found themselves equally unwanted in the industrial North, caught in decaying neighborhoods and victimized by crime.

Central cities faced additional financial problems unrelated to poverty and race. Many of their roads, bridges, fire stations, and water mains were 50 to 100 years old by the 1960s and 1970s, and they were wearing out. Decay of urban utility and transportation systems was a by-product of market forces and public policy. Private developers often borrowed money saved through northeastern bank accounts, insurance policies, and pension funds to finance new construction in the suburbs. The defense budget pumped tax dollars from the old industrial cities into the South and West.

High local taxes in older cities was one result, for the American system of local government demands that cities and the poor help themselves. By the early 1970s, the average resident of a central city paid roughly twice the state and local taxes per $1,000 of income as the average suburbanite.

RACIAL RIOTING

African Americans and Hispanics who rioted in city streets in the mid-1960s were fed up with the lack of job opportunities, with substandard housing, and with crime. Riots in Rochester, Harlem, and Brooklyn in July 1964 opened four years of racial violence. Before they subsided, the riots had scarred most big cities and killed 200 people, most of them African Americans.

The explosion of the Watts neighborhood in Los Angeles fixed the danger of racial unrest in the public mind. Trouble started on August 11, 1965, when a white highway-patrol officer arrested a young African American for drunken driving. Loud complaints drew a crowd, and the arrival of Los Angeles police turned the bystanders into an angry mob that attacked passing cars. Rioting, looting, and arson spread through Watts for two days until the National Guard cordoned off the trouble spots and occupied the neighborhood on August 14 and 15.

The outburst frightened white Americans. In most previous race riots, whites had used violence to keep blacks "in their place." In Watts, blacks were the instigators. The primary targets were the police and ghetto businesses that had reputations for exploiting their customers. The National Advisory Commission on Civil Disorders concluded in 1968 that most property damage was the "result of deliberate attacks on white-owned businesses characterized in the Negro community as unfair or disrespectful." In short, the riots were protests about the problems of ghetto life.

QUICK REVIEW

Urban Problems

- Minorities and the poor were concentrated in urban centers.
- Postwar black migrants to the north found themselves with limited access to better houses, schools, and jobs.
- Cities faced decaying infrastructure and high taxes.

28–2
Stokely Carmichael and Charles Hamilton, from Black Power (1968)

Scores of cities suffered riots in 1966, including a riot by Puerto Ricans in Chicago that protested the same problems blacks faced. The following year, the worst violence was in Newark, New Jersey, and in Detroit, where 43 deaths and blocks of blazing buildings stunned television viewers.

Few politicians wanted to admit that African Americans and Hispanics had serious grievances. Their impulse was to blame riffraff and outside agitators—"lawbreakers and mad dogs," to quote future California governor Ronald Reagan. This theory was wrong. Almost all participants were neighborhood residents. Except that they were younger, they were representative of the African-American population, and their violence came from the frustration of rising expectations. Despite the political gains of the civil rights movement, unemployment remained high, and the police still treated all blacks as potential criminals. The urban riots were political actions to force the problems of African Americans onto the national agenda.

Some members of the Black Panther Party raised funds to pay the legal fees of those arrested and charged with various offenses, such as Bobby Seale and Ericka Huggins. The Panthers advocated a radical economic, social, and educational agenda that made the group the target of a determined campaign of suppression by the police and the FBI.

Leonard Freed/MAGNUM Photos

Minority Separatism

Minority separatism tapped the same anger that fueled the urban riots. Separatists challenged the central goal of the civil rights movement, which sought full participation in American life. The phrase **Black Power** summed up the new alternative. The term came from frustrated SNCC leader Stokely Carmichael in 1966: "We've been saying freedom for six years—and we ain't got nothing. What we're going to start saying now is 'Black Power'!"

The slogans of Black Power, Brown Power, and Red Power spanned goals that ran from civil rights to cultural pride to revolutionary separatism. They were all efforts by minorities to define themselves through their own heritage and backgrounds, not simply by looking in the mirror of white society.

Expressions of Black Power. Black power translated many ways—control of one's own community through the voting machine, celebration of the African-American heritage, creation of a parallel society that shunned white institutions. At the personal level, it was a synonym for black pride.

Black Power also meant increased interest in the **Nation of Islam,** or Black Muslims, who combined a version of Islam with radical separatism. They called for self-discipline, support of black institutions and businesses, and total rejection of whites. The Nation of Islam appealed to blacks who saw no future in integration.

In the early 1960s, Malcolm X emerged as a leading Black Muslim. Malcolm preached that blacks should stop letting whites set the terms by which they judged their appearance, communities, and accomplishments. He emphasized the African cultural heritage and economic self-help and proclaimed himself an extremist for black rights. In the last year of his life, however, he returned from a pilgrimage to Mecca willing to consider limited acceptance of whites. Rivals within the movement assassinated him in February 1965, but his ideas lived on in *The Autobiography of Malcolm X.*

The **Black Panthers** pursued similar goals. Bobby Seale and Huey Newton saw African-American ghettos as internal colonies in need of self-determination. They created the Panthers in 1966 in Oakland, California, began to carry firearms, and recruited Eldridge Cleaver as the group's chief publicist.

Black Power Philosophy emerging after 1965 that real economic and political gains for African Americans could come only through self-help, self-determination, and organizing for direct political influence.

Nation of Islam Religious movement among black Americans that emphasizes self-sufficiency, self-help, and separation from white society.

Black Panthers Political and social movement among black Americans, founded in Oakland, California, in 1966 and emphasizing black economic and political power.

Dolores Huerta and César Chávez confer at the 1973 convention of the United Farm Workers. Chávez and Huerta tried to build a union that welcomed workers of all ethnic backgrounds, but the UFW leaders were largely Hispanic, and the union took much of its symbolism from the Mexican heritage shared by most of its members.

Walter P. Reuther Library, Wayne State University

The Panthers asserted their equality. They shadowed police patrols to prevent mistreatment of African Americans and carried weapons into the California State Legislature in May 1967 to protest gun control. The Panthers also promoted community-based self-help efforts, such as a free-breakfast program for school children and medical clinics, and ran political candidates.

In contrast to the rioters in Watts, the Panthers had a political program, if not the ability to carry it through. The movement was shaken when Newton was convicted of manslaughter for killing a police officer, Cleaver fled to Algeria, and an unjustified police raid killed Chicago Panther leader Fred Hampton. Panther chapters imploded when they attracted thugs and shakedown artists as well as visionaries. Nevertheless, the Panthers survived as a political party into the 1970s.

Hispanic Activism in the Southwest. Latinos in the Southwest developed a their own Brown Power movement in the late 1960s. Led by Reies López Tijerina, Hispanics in rural New Mexico demanded the return of lands that had been lost to Anglo Americans despite the guarantees of the Treaty of Guadalupe Hidalgo in 1848. Mexican Americans in the 1970s organized for political power in southern Texas communities where they were a majority. In Denver, Rodolfo Gonzales established the Crusade for Justice. His "Plan for the Barrio" emphasized Hispanic cultural traditions, community control of schools, and economic development.

The best-known Hispanic activism combined social protest with the crusading spirit of earlier labor union organizing campaigns. César Chávez organized the multiracial United Farm Workers (UFW) among Mexican-American agricultural workers in California in 1965. Because farm workers were not covered by the National Labor Relations Act of 1935, the issue was whether farm owners would recognize the union as a bargaining agent and sign a contract. Chávez supplemented work stoppages with national boycotts against table grapes, lettuce, and certain brands of wine, making *la huelga* ("the strike") into *la causa* for urban liberals. Rival organizing by the Teamsters Union and the short attention span of the national public gradually undermined the UFW's initial success. Nevertheless, Chávez's dogged toughness and self-sacrifice gave both Chicanos and the country a new hero.

Latino political activism had strong appeal for young people. Ten thousand young Chicanos stormed out of Los Angeles high schools in March 1968 to protest poor education and racist teachers. Some students organized as Brown Berets to demand more relevant education and fairer police treatment. Many rejected assimilation in favor of community self-determination and began to talk about *la raza* ("the people"), whose language and heritage descended from centuries of Mexican history.

Native Americans Assert Their Identity. Native Americans also fought both for equal access to American society and to preserve cultural traditions through tribal institutions. Congress in 1968 restored the authority of tribal law on reservations. A few years later, it granted native Alaskans 40 million acres to settle claims for their ancestral lands. Legally sophisticated tribes sued for compensation and enforcement of treaty provisions, such as fishing rights in the Pacific Northwest. Larger tribes established their own colleges, such as Navajo Community College (1969) and Oglala Lakota College (1971).

A second development was newly media-oriented protest that asserted Red Power. Indians in Minneapolis created the **American Indian Movement (AIM)** in 1968 to increase economic opportunity, stop police mistreatment, and to assert their distinctiveness within American society.

SUBURBAN INDEPENDENCE: THE OUTER CITY

In the mid-1960s, the United States became a suburban nation. The 1970 census found more people living in the suburban counties of metropolitan areas (37 percent) than in central cities (31 percent) or in small towns and rural areas (31 percent). Just after World War II, most new suburbs had been bedroom communities that depended on the jobs, services, and shopping of central cities. By the late 1960s, suburbs were evolving into "outer cities," whose inhabitants had little need for the old central city.

Suburban Economic Growth and Political Influence.   Suburbs captured most new jobs, leaving the urban poor with few opportunities for employment. In the 15 largest metropolitan areas, the number of central city jobs fell by 800,000 in the 1960s, while the number of suburban jobs rose by 3.2 million. The shift from rail to air for business travel accentuated suburban job growth. By the 1970s, every major airport had a fringe of hotels, office parks, and corporate offices. Around many cities, suburban retailing, employment, and services fused into so-called edge cities, such as the Galleria Post Oak district in Houston and the Tysons Corner area in northern Virginia. Suburban rings gained a growing share of public facilities intended to serve the entire metropolitan area. As pioneered in California, community colleges served the suburban children of the baby boom. Many of the new four-year schools that state university systems added in the 1960s and early 1970s were also built for suburbanites.

Suburban political power grew along with economic clout. In 1962, the Supreme Court handed down a landmark decision in the case of *Baker v. Carr.* Overturning laws that treated counties or other political subdivisions as the units to be represented in state legislatures, *Baker* required that legislative seats be apportioned on the basis of population. This principle of "one person, one vote" broke the stranglehold of rural counties on state governments, but the big beneficiaries were not older cities, but fast-growing suburbs. By 1975, suburbanites held the largest block of seats in the House of Representatives. Reapportionment in 1982, based on the 1980 census, produced a House that was even more heavily suburban.

School Busing Controversies.   School integration controversies in the 1970s reinforced a tendency for suburbanites to separate themselves from city problems. In *Swann v. Charlotte-Mecklenburg Board of Education* (1971), the U.S. Supreme Court held that crosstown busing was an acceptable solution to the *de facto* segregation that resulted from residential patterns within a single school district. When school officials around the country failed to achieve racial balance, federal judges ordered their own busing plans. Although integration through busing occurred peacefully in dozens of cities, many white people resented the practice. Working-class students who depended on public schools found themselves on the front lines of integration, while many middle-class families switched to private education.

American Indian Movement (AIM)   Group of Native-American political activists who used confrontations with the federal government to publicize their case for Indian rights.

Baker v. Carr   U.S. Supreme Court decision in 1962 that allowed federal courts to review the appointment of state legislative districts and established the principle that such districts should have roughly equal populations ("one person, one vote").

Swann v. Charlotte-Mecklenburg Board of Education   U.S. Supreme Court decision in 1971 that upheld cross-city busing to achieve the racial integration of public schools.

Because the Supreme Court also ruled that busing programs normally stopped at school-district boundaries, suburbs with independent districts escaped school integration. One result was to make busing self-defeating, for it led white families to move out of the integrating school district, or place their children in private academies. Busing also caused suburbanites to defend their political independence fiercely. In Denver, for example, a bitter debate over busing produced by-products that included incorporation or expansion of several large suburbs and a state constitutional amendment that blocked further expansion of the city boundaries (and thus of the Denver school district).

THE YEAR OF THE GUN, 1968

Some years are turning points that force society to reconsider its basic assumptions. In 1914, the violence of World War I undermined Europe's belief in progress. In 1933, Americans had to rethink the role of government. In 1968, mainstream Americans increasingly turned against the war in Vietnam, student protest and youth counterculture turned ugly, and political consensus shattered.

THE TET OFFENSIVE

The longer the Vietnam War continued and the less interest that China or the Soviet Union showed in it, the less valid the conflict seemed to the American people. It looked more and more like a war for pride, not national security.

The Viet Cong's Tet Offensive on January 30, 1968, undermined that pride. At the end of 1967, U.S. officials were overconfidently predicting victory. Then, at the beginning of Tet, the Vietnamese New Year, the Viet Cong attacked 36 of 44 provincial capitals and the national capital, Saigon. They hit the U.S. embassy and reached the runways of Tan Son Nhut air base. If the United States was winning, the Tet offensive should not have been possible.

As a military effort, the attacks failed. U.S. and South Vietnamese troops repulsed the attacks and cleared the cities. But the offensive was a psychological blow that convinced the American public that the war was quicksand. Television coverage of the Tet battles made the bad publicity worse. A handful of images stayed in people's memories—a Buddhist monk burning himself to death in protest; a child with flesh peeled off by napalm; a South Vietnamese official executing a captive on the streets of Saigon.

In the wake of the Tet crisis, General Westmoreland's request for 200,000 more troops forced a political and military reevaluation. Twenty "wise men"—the big names of the Cold War—told the president that the war was unwinnable on terms acceptable to America's allies and to many Americans. By devouring resources and souring relations with other nations, it endangered rather than enhanced American security. Most scholars have agreed with this assessment. Tet and its aftermath had shown American military superiority but highlighted the nation's inability to translate tactical advantage into political success in South Vietnam or the United States. The best option, the wise men told LBJ, was disengagement.

LBJ's EXIT

The president was already in political trouble. After other prominent Democrats held back, Minnesota's liberal Senator Eugene McCarthy had decided to challenge Johnson in the presidential primaries. With enthusiastic college students staffing his campaign, McCarthy won a startling 42 percent of the popular vote and 20 of 24 delegates in the New Hampshire primary. The vote proved that the political middle would no longer hold.

HOW DID the Tet offensive change American public opinion about the war in Vietnam?

QUICK REVIEW

The Tet Offensive
- January 30, 1968: Viet Cong attacked cities across Vietnam.
- As a military effort, the offensive failed.
- The attack shook American confidence that the war was winnable.

WHERE TO LEARN MORE

Lyndon B. Johnson National Historical Park, Johnson City, Texas
www.nps.gov/lypo/

By showing Johnson's vulnerability, New Hampshire also drew Robert Kennedy into the race. The younger brother of the former president, Kennedy inspired both fervent loyalty and strong distaste. In the 1950s, he had worked for Senator Joe McCarthy and had initially been a reluctant supporter of civil rights during his brother's administration. More than other mainstream politicians of the 1960s, he touched the hearts of Hispanic and African-American voters as well as the white working class. He had left his position as attorney general to win election to the Senate from New York in 1964. Now he put the Kennedy mystique on the line against a man he despised.

Facing political challenges and an unraveling war, on March 31, 1968, Johnson announced a halt to most bombing of North Vietnam, opening the door for peace negotiations that formally began in May 1969. He then astounded the country by withdrawing from the presidential race. It was a statesmanlike act by a man who had been consumed by a war he did not want, had never understood, and could not end.

VIOLENCE AND POLITICS: KING, KENNEDY, AND CHICAGO

Johnson's dramatic withdrawal was followed by the violent disruption of American politics through assassination and riot. On April 4, 1968, an ex-convict, James Earl Ray, shot and killed Martin Luther King, Jr., as he stood on the balcony of a Memphis motel. King's death was the product of pure racial hatred, and it triggered a climactic round of violence in black ghettos.

The shock of King's death was still fresh when another political assassination stunned the nation. On June 5, Robert Kennedy won California's primary election. He was still behind Vice President Hubert Humphrey in the delegate count but coming on strong. As Kennedy walked out of the ballroom at his headquarters in the Ambassador Hotel in Los Angeles, a Jordanian immigrant named Sirhan Sirhan put a bullet in his brain. Sirhan may have wanted revenge for America's tilt toward Israel in that country's victorious Six-Day War with Egypt and Jordan in 1967.

Kennedy's death ensured the Democratic nomination for Humphrey, a liberal who had loyally supported Johnson's war policy. After his nomination, Humphrey faced the Republican Richard Nixon and the Independent George Wallace. Nixon positioned himself as the candidate of the political middle. Wallace appealed to southern whites and working-class northerners who feared black militancy and hated "the ivory-tower folks with pointy heads."

Both got great help from the Democratic Convention, held in Chicago on August 26–29. While Democrats feuded among themselves, Chicago Mayor Richard Daley and his police department monitored antiwar protesters. The National Mobilization Committee to End the War in Vietnam drew from the New Left and from older peace activists—sober and committed people who had fought against nuclear weapons in the 1950s and the Vietnam War throughout the 1960s. They wanted to embarrass the Johnson-Humphrey administration by marching to the convention hall on nomination night. Mixed in were the Yippies (the term supposedly stood for Youth International Party). The Yippies planned to attract young people to Chicago with the promise of street theater, media events, and confrontation that would puncture the pretensions of the power structure.

On August 28, the same night that Democratic delegates were nominating Humphrey, tensions exploded in a police riot. Protesters and Yippies had congregated in Grant Park, across Michigan Avenue from downtown hotels. Undisciplined police waded into the crowds with clubs and tear gas. Young people fought back with rocks and bottles. Television caught the hours of violence that ended when the National Guard separated police from demonstrators. On the convention floor,

Dr. Martin Luther King, Jr.
Corbis/Bettman

Senator Abraham Ribicoff of Connecticut decried "Gestapo tactics" on the streets of Chicago. Mayor Daley shouted back obscenities. For Humphrey, the convention was a catastrophe, alienating liberal Democrats and associating Democrats with disorder in the public mind.

Election day gave Wallace 13.5 percent of the popular vote, Humphrey 42.7 percent of the popular vote and 191 electoral votes, and Nixon 43.4 percent of the popular vote and 301 electoral votes (see Map 29–2). The national media saw Wallace in terms of bigotry and a backlash against civil rights, getting only part of the story. Many of Wallace's northern backers were unhappy with both parties. Liberal on economic issues but conservative on family and social issues, many of these working-class voters evolved into "Reagan Democrats" by the 1980s.

WHAT WAS the legacy of Richard Nixon's presidency?

NIXON, WATERGATE, AND THE CRISIS OF THE EARLY 1970S

The new president was an unlikely politician, ill at ease in public and consumed by a sense of inferiority. A product of small-town California, he felt rejected by the eastern elite. After losing a 1962 race for governor of California, he announced that he was quitting politics and that the press would no longer have Dick Nixon "to kick around." In 1968, he skillfully sold a "new Nixon" to the media. Seven years later, the press was his undoing as it uncovered the Watergate scandal.

GETTING OUT OF VIETNAM, 1969–1975

Nixon had no secret plan to end the war. Opposition intensified with the revelation that U.S. soldiers in March 1968 had slaughtered hundreds of men, women, and children in the South Vietnamese village of My Lai after failing to find any Vietcong. Protests at home culminated in 1969 with the Vietnam Moratorium on October 15, when 2 million protesters joined rallies across the country.

Disaffection also mounted in Vietnam. Racial tensions sapped morale on the front lines. Troops lost discipline, took drugs, and hunkered down waiting for their tours of duty to end, and the high command had to adapt its code of justice to keep an army on the job.

Nixon and Vice President Spiro Agnew responded by trying to isolate the antiwar opposition, but Nixon also reduced the role of U.S. ground forces. He claimed that his policies represented "the great silent majority of my fellow Americans." The administration arranged for a "spontaneous" attack by construction workers on antiwar protesters in New York. The hard-hat counterattack was a cynically manipulated symbol, but Nixon and Agnew tapped genuine anger about failure in Asia and rapid change in American society.

The New Left had already split into factions. About a hundred angry SDS members declared themselves the

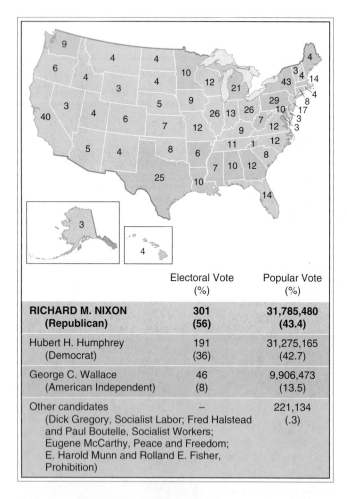

	Electoral Vote (%)	Popular Vote (%)
RICHARD M. NIXON (Republican)	**301 (56)**	**31,785,480 (43.4)**
Hubert H. Humphrey (Democrat)	191 (36)	31,275,165 (42.7)
George C. Wallace (American Independent)	46 (8)	9,906,473 (13.5)
Other candidates (Dick Gregory, Socialist Labor; Fred Halstead and Paul Boutelle, Socialist Workers; Eugene McCarthy, Peace and Freedom; E. Harold Munn and Rolland E. Fisher, Prohibition)	–	221,134 (.3)

MAP 29–2 The Election of 1968 Richard Nixon won the presidency with the help of George Wallace, the American Independent Party candidate. Wallace won several southern states, offering an alternative to white southerners unhappy with the Democratic Party but not yet prepared to vote Republican. He also drew northern working-class votes away from Hubert Humphrey and thus helped Nixon to take several midwestern states.

WHAT ROLE did opposition to the war in Vietnam play in determining the outcome of the 1968 election?

Weather Underground. Three Weatherpeople accidentally blew themselves up with a homemade bomb in New York in 1970. Others robbed a Boston bank to get money for the revolution. Still others bombed a University of Wisconsin building and killed a student.

"Vietnamization" and the Secret War against Cambodia.

Nixon's secretary of defense, Melvin Laird, responded to the antiwar sentiment with "Vietnamization," withdrawing U.S. troops as fast as possible without undermining the South Vietnamese government. In July 1969, the president announced the **Nixon Doctrine.** The United States would help other countries fight their wars with weapons and money but not with soldiers. The policy substituted machines for men. Americans rearmed and enlarged the South Vietnamese army and surreptitiously bombed Communist bases in neutral Cambodia.

The secret war against Cambodia culminated on April 30, 1970, with an invasion. The aim was to smash Vietcong and North Vietnamese bases to allow time to rebuild the South Vietnamese army. Americans who had hoped that the war was fading away were outraged. At Kent State University in Ohio, the National Guard was called in to maintain order. Taunts, tossed bottles, and the recent record of violence put them on edge. On May 4, one unit fired on a group of young people and killed four of them.

Stalemate and Cease-fire.

The Cambodian "incursion" extended the military stalemate in Vietnam to U.S. policy. In December 1970, Congress repealed the Gulf of Tonkin Resolution and prohibited the use of U.S. ground troops outside South Vietnam. Cambodia, however, was already devastated. The U.S. invasion had destabilized its government and opened the way for the bloodthirsty Khmer Rouge, who killed millions of Cambodians in the name of a working-class revolution. Vietnamization continued; only 90,000 U.S. ground troops were still in Vietnam by early 1972. A final air offensive in December smashed Hanoi into rubble and helped to force four and a half years of peace talks to a conclusion.

The cease-fire began on January 27, 1973. It confirmed America's withdrawal from Vietnam. North Vietnamese and Viet Cong forces would remain in control of the territory they occupied in South Vietnam, but they were not to be reinforced or substantially reequipped. The United States promised not to increase its military aid to South Vietnam. There were no solid guarantees for the South Vietnamese government. Immediately after coming to terms with North Vietnam, Nixon suspended the draft in favor of an all-volunteer military.

In 1975, South Vietnam collapsed. Only the American presence had kept its political, ethnic, and religious factions together. For the first two years after the Paris agreement, North Vietnam quietly rebuilt its military capacity. In the spring of 1975, it opened an offensive. Resistance crumbled so rapidly that the United States had to evacuate its embassy in Saigon by helicopter while frantic Vietnamese tried to join the flight.

NIXON AND THE WIDER WORLD

Nixon and Henry Kissinger, his national security adviser (and later secretary of state), shared what they considered a realistic view of foreign affairs. For both men, foreign policy was not about crusades or moral stands. It was about the balance of world economic and military power and securing the most advantageous agreements, alliances, and military positions. In particular, they hoped to trade improved relations with China and the Soviet Union for help in settling the Vietnam War.

Nixon Doctrine President Nixon's new American policy (1969) toward Asia in which the United States would honor treaty commitments but would gradually disengage and expect Asian nations to handle military defense on their own.

WHERE TO LEARN MORE

Richard Nixon Library and
Birthplace, Yorba Linda, California
www.nixonfoundation.org/index.shtml

WHERE TO LEARN MORE

Titan Missile Museum, Green Valley,
Arizona
www.pimaair.org/titan_01.htm

SALT (Strategic Arms Limitation Treaty)   Treaty signed in 1972 by the United States and the Soviet Union to slow the nuclear arms race.

Détente   (French for "easing of tension") Used to describe the new U.S. relations with China and the Soviet Union in 1972.

New Federalism   President Richard Nixon's policy to shift responsibilities of government programs from the federal level to the states.

Since 1950, the United States had acted as if China did not exist, refusing economic relations and insisting that the Nationalist regime on Taiwan was the legitimate Chinese government. But the People's Republic of China was increasingly isolated within the Communist world. In 1969, it almost went to war with the Soviet Union. Nixon was eager to take advantage of Chinese-Soviet tension. Secret talks led to an easing of the American trade embargo in April 1971 and a tour of China by a U.S. table-tennis team. Kissinger then arranged for Nixon's startling visit to Mao Zedong in Beijing in February 1972.

Playing the "China card" helped to improve relations with the Soviet Union. The Soviets needed increased trade with the United States and a counterweight to China, the United States was looking for help in getting out of Vietnam, and both countries wanted to limit nuclear armaments. In 1969, the Senate came within one vote of stopping the development of defensive antiballistic missiles (ABMs). Nixon treated the ABM program as a bargaining chip. Protracted negotiations led to arms agreements known as **SALT (Strategic Arms Limitation Treaty)** that Nixon signed in Moscow in May 1972.

Diplomats used the French word *détente* to describe the new U.S. relations with China and the Soviet Union. *Détente* means an easing of tensions, not friendship or alliance. It facilitated travel between the United States and China. It allowed U.S. farmers to sell wheat to the Soviets. More broadly, détente implied that the United States and China recognized mutual interests in Asia and that the United States acknowledged the Soviet Union as an equal in world affairs. Détente made the world safer.

COURTING MIDDLE AMERICA

Nixon designed domestic policy to help him win reelection. His goal was to solidify his "Middle American" support. The strategy targeted the growing populations of the South and the suburbs, as well as blue-collar voters who were ready to abandon the Democrats for law-and-order Republicans.

The Nixon White House preferred to ignore troubled big cities. Spokesmen announced that the urban crisis was over and dismantled the urban initiatives of Johnson's Great Society. Instead, Nixon tilted federal assistance to the suburbs. The centerpiece of his **New Federalism** was General Revenue Sharing (1972), which passed federal funds directly to local governments with no limits on use. By 1980, it had transferred more than $18 billion to the states and more than $36 billion to local governments. Revenue sharing was a suburban-aid program. Its no-strings grants supplemented the general funds of every full-service government, whether a city of 2 million or a suburban town of 500.

Nixon pursued the southern strategy through the symbolism of Supreme Court nominations. His first nominees were Clement Haynsworth of Florida and G. Harrold Carswell of Alabama. Although the Senate rejected both as unqualified, the nominations nonetheless gave Nixon a reputation as a champion of the white South.

OIL, OPEC, AND STAGFLATION

One of the most troublesome domestic issues was inflation. The cost of living began to outpace wages in the late 1960s. Economists saw the situation as a classic example of "demand-pull" inflation, in which too many dollars from government and consumer spending were chasing too few goods and services. One of the causes was LBJ's decision to fight in Vietnam without tax increases until 1968. An income tax cut in 1969, supported by both parties, made the situation worse. Inflation eroded the value of savings and pensions. It also made U.S. goods too expensive for foreign buyers and generated a trade deficit that placed pressures on the international value of the dollar.

The U.S. economy took another hit from inflation in 1973–74. This time it was "cost-push" inflation, in which a price increase for one key product raises the cost of producing other items. The main cause was the sharp increase in the price of energy, an input to every product and service. Angry at American support for Israel in the Arab-Israeli War of October 1973, Arab nations imposed an embargo on oil exports that lasted from October 1973 to March 1974. Shortages of gasoline and heating oil eased when the embargo ended, but the **Organization of Petroleum Exporting Countries (OPEC)** had challenged the ability of the industrial nations to dictate world economic policy.

While Nixon searched for short-term political advantage, underlying problems of the American economy went untreated. After 30 years at the top, the United States could no longer dominate the world economy by itself. The newly found power of OPEC was obvious. Just as important was the surging industrial capacity of Germany and Japan, which now had economies as modern as that of the United States. Declining rates of saving and investment in industrial capacity seemed to put the United States in danger of following the British road to economic obsolescence and second-level status. Indeed, a new term entered the popular vocabulary in 1971: *stagflation* was the painful combination of stagnant economic growth, high unemployment, and inflation that matched no one's economic theory but everyone's daily experience.

AMERICANS AS ENVIRONMENTALISTS

In the turbulent 1970s, Americans found one issue they could agree on. In the 1970s, resource conservation grew into a multifaceted environmental movement.

After the booming 1950s, Americans had started to pay attention to "pollution," a catchall for the damage that advanced technologies and industrial production did to natural systems. Rachel Carson's *Silent Spring* in 1962 pushed pollution onto the national agenda. Carson, a well-regarded science writer, described the side effects of DDT and other pesticides on animal life. In her imagined future, spring was silent because all the birds had died of pesticide poisoning.

Environmentalism gained strength among Americans in 1970. On April 22, 10,000 schools and 20 million other people took part in Earth Day, an occasion first conceived by Wisconsin Senator Gaylord Nelson. Earth Day gained a grassroots following in towns and cities across the country. New York closed Fifth Avenue to automobiles for the day. Companies touted their environmental credentials.

The American establishment had been looking for a safe and respectable crusade to divert the idealism and discontent of the 1960s. Now the mainstream media discovered the ravaged planet. So did a politically savvy president. An expedient proenvironmental stance might attract some of the antiwar constituency. Nixon had already signed the National Environmental Policy Act on January 1, 1970, and later in the year created the **Environmental Protection Agency (EPA)** to enforce environmental laws. The rest of the Nixon years brought legislation on clean air, clear water, pesticides, hazardous chemicals, and endangered species (see the Overview table, "The Environmental Decades") that made environmental management and protection part of governmental routine.

The first Earth Day in 1970 tapped growing concern about the environment. It helped turn the technical field of pollution control into the broad-based environmental movement.

QUICK REVIEW

Environmentalism

- In the 1970s resource conversation grew into an environmental movement.
- Nixon created the Environmental Protection Agency (EPA) in 1970.
- Low-income and minority communities had a disproportionate share of environmental problems.

Organization of Petroleum Exporting Countries (OPEC) Cartel of oil-producing nations in Asia, Africa, and Latin America that gained substantial power over the world economy in the mid- to late- 1970s by controlling the production and price of oil.

Environmental Protection Agency (EPA) Federal agency created in 1970 to oversee environmental monitoring and cleanup programs.

As Americans became more aware of human-caused environmental hazards, they realized that minority and low-income and communities had more than their share of problems. In the Louisiana petrochemical belt along the Mississippi River, African Americans often lived downstream and downwind. Landfills and waste disposal sites were frequently located near minority neighborhoods. In Buffalo, white working-class residents near the Love Canal industrial site discovered in 1978 that an entire neighborhood was built on land contaminated by decades of chemical dumping. Activists sought to understand the health effects and force compensation, paving the way for the Superfund cleanup legislation (see American Views: "Grassroots Community Action").

FROM DIRTY TRICKS TO WATERGATE

The **Watergate** crisis pivoted on Richard Nixon's character. Despite his solid political standing, Nixon saw enemies everywhere and overestimated their strength. In 1972 and 1973, dirty tricks grew from a scandal into a constitutional crisis when Nixon abused the power of his office to cover up wrongdoing and hinder criminal investigations.

The chain of events that undermined Nixon's presidency started with the **Pentagon Papers.** In his last year as secretary of defense, Robert McNamara had commissioned a report on America's road to Vietnam. The documents showed that the country's leaders had planned to expand the war even while they claimed to be looking for a way out. In June 1971, one of the contributors to the report, Daniel Ellsberg, leaked it to the *New York Times.* Its publication infuriated Nixon.

In response, the White House compiled a list of journalists and politicians who opposed Nixon. Nixon set up a special investigations unit in the White House. Two former CIA employees, E. Howard Hunt and G. Gordon Liddy, became the chief "plumbers," as the group was known because its job was to prevent leaks of information. They cooked up schemes to embarrass political opponents and ransacked the office of Ellsberg's psychiatrist.

Early in 1972, Hunt went to work for CREEP—the Committee to Re-Elect the President. On June 17, 1972, five inept burglars hired with CREEP funds were caught breaking into the Democratic National Committee office in Washington's Watergate apartment building. Nixon felt too insecure to ride out what would probably have been a small scandal. Instead, he initiated a coverup.

The coverup worked in the short run. Nixon's opponent in the 1972 election was South Dakota Senator George McGovern, an impassioned opponent of the Vietnam War. McGovern was honest, intelligent, and well to the left of center. He did not appeal to the white southerners and blue-collar northerners whom Nixon and Agnew were luring from the Democrats.

The coverup began to come apart with the trial of the Watergate burglars in January 1973. Federal Judge John Sirica used the threat of heavy sentences to pressure one burglar into a statement that implied that higher-ups had been involved. Meanwhile, the *Washington Post* was linking Nixon's people to dirty tricks and illegal campaign contributions. The White House scrambled to find a defensible story. Nixon was aware of many of the actions that his subordinates had undertaken. He now began to coach people on what they should tell investigators, claimed his staff had lied to him, and tried to set up White House staffer John Dean to take the fall.

In the late spring and early summer, attention shifted to the televised hearings of the Senate's Select Committee on Presidential Campaign Activities. A parade of White House and party officials described their parts in the affair, often

Watergate A complex scandal involving attempts to cover up illegal actions taken by administration officials and leading to the resignation of President Richard Nixon in 1974.

Pentagon Papers Classified Defense Department documents on the history of the United States' involvement in Vietnam, prepared in 1968 and leaked to the press in 1971.

OVERVIEW	THE ENVIRONMENTAL DECADES

Administration	Focus of Concern	Legislation
Johnson	Wilderness and wildlife	Wilderness Act (1964) National Wildlife Refuge System (1966) Wild and Scenic Rivers Act (1968)
Nixon	Pollution control and endangered environments	National Environmental Policy Act (1969) Environmental Protection Agency (1970) Clean Air Act (1970) Occupational Safety and Health Act (1970) Water Pollution Control Act (1972) Pesticide Control Act (1972) Coastal Zone Management Act (1972) Endangered Species Act (1973)
Ford	Energy and hazardous materials	Toxic Substances Control Act (1976) Resource Conservation and Recovery Act (1976)
Carter	Energy and hazardous materials	Energy Policy and Conservation Act (1978) Comprehensive Emergency Response, Compensation, and Liability Act (Superfund) (1980)

accusing each other and revealing the plumbers and the enemies list. The real questions, it became obvious, were what the president knew and when he knew it.

A bombshell turned the scandal into a constitutional crisis. A mid-level staffer told the committee that Nixon had made tape recordings of his White House conversations. Both the Senate and the Watergate special prosecutor, Archibald Cox, subpoenaed the tapes. Nixon refused to give them up, citing executive privilege and the separation of powers. In April 1974, he finally released edited transcripts of the tapes, with foul language deleted and key passages missing; he claimed that his secretary had accidentally erased crucial material. Finally, on July 24, 1974, the U.S. Supreme Court ruled unanimously that Nixon had to deliver 64 tapes to the new special prosecutor.

Opposition to the president now spanned the political spectrum from Barry Goldwater to liberal Democrats, and Congress began impeachment proceedings. On July 27, the House Judiciary Committee took up the specific charges. Republicans joined Democrats in voting three articles of impeachment: for hindering the criminal investigation of the Watergate break-in, for abusing the power of the presidency by using federal agencies to deprive citizens of their rights, and for ignoring the committee's subpoena for the tapes. Before the full House could vote on the articles of impeachment and send them to the Senate for trial, Nixon delivered the tapes. One of them contained the "smoking gun," direct evidence that Nixon had participated in the coverup on June 23, 1972, and had been lying ever since. On August 8 he announced his resignation, effective the following day.

THE FORD FOOTNOTE

Gerald Ford was Nixon's appointee to replace Spiro Agnew, who had resigned and pleaded no contest to charges of bribery and income tax evasion in 1973 as Watergate was gathering steam. Ford was competent but unimaginative. His first

AMERICAN VIEWS

GRASSROOTS COMMUNITY ACTION

I n the 1950s, a major chemical company closed a waste dump in Niagara Falls, New York. The site, known as Love Canal, was soon surrounded by a park, school, and hundreds of modest homes. Residents put up with noxious odors and seepage of chemical wastes until 1978, when they learned that the state health department was concerned about the health effects on small children and pregnant women. Over the next two years, residents battled state and federal bureaucracies and reluctant politicians for accurate information about the risks they faced and then for financial assistance to move from the area (often their homes represented their only savings). In October 1980, President Carter signed a bill to move all of the families permanently from the Love Canal area.

One of the leaders of the grassroots movement was housewife Lois Gibbs. The following excerpts from her story show her increasing sophistication as a community activist, starting by ringing doorbells in 1978 and ending with national television exposure in 1980. Although the Love Canal case itself was unusual, community-based organizations in all parts of the country learned the tactics of effective action in the 1960s and 1970s.

- What public programs in the 1960s and 1970s gave citizens experience in grassroots action?
- How might the Internet change the tactics of community organizing?

KNOCKING ON DOORS

I decided to go door-to-door with a petition. It seemed like a good idea to start near the school, to talk to the mothers nearest it. I had already heard that a lot of the residents near the school had been upset about the chemicals for the past couple of years. I thought they might help me. I had never done anything like this. . . . I was afraid a lot of doors would be slammed in my face, that people would think I was some crazy fanatic. But I decided to do it anyway . . . and knocked on my first door. There was no answer. I just stood there, not knowing what to do. It was an usually warm June day and I was perspiring. I thought: What am I doing here? I must be crazy. People are going to think I am. Go home, you fool! And that's just what I did.

It was one of those times when I had to sit down and face myself. I was afraid of making a fool of myself, I had scared myself, and I had gone home. When I got there,

---

major act was his most controversial—the pardon of Nixon for "any and all crimes" committed while president. Since Nixon had not yet been indicted, the pardon saved him from future prosecution. To many Americans, the act looked like a payoff. Ford insisted that the purpose was to clear the decks so that the nation could think about the future rather than the past. He also offered clemency to thousands of draft resisters.

Ford's administration presided over the collapse of South Vietnam in 1975, but elsewhere in the world, *détente* continued. American diplomats joined the Soviet Union and 30 other European nations in the capital of Finland to sign the **Helsinki Accords.** The agreements called for increased commerce between the Eastern and Western blocs and for human-rights guarantees. They also legitimized the national boundaries that had been set in eastern Europe in 1945. At home, the federal government did little new during Ford's two and a half years in office. The economy slid into recession, unemployment climbed above 10 percent, inflation diminished the value of savings and wages. Ford beat back Ronald Reagan for the Republican presidential nomination, but he was clearly vulnerable.

Helsinki Accords Agreement in 1975 among NATO and Warsaw Pact members that recognized European national boundaries as set after World War II and included guarantees of human rights.

I sat at the kitchen table with my petition in my hand, thinking. Wait. What if people do slam doors in your face? People may think you're crazy. But what's more important—what people think or your child's health? Either you're going to do something or you're going to have to admit you're a coward and not do it. . . . The next day, I went out on my own street to talk to people I knew. It was a little easier to be brave with them. If I could convince people I knew—friends—maybe it would be less difficult to convince others. . . . I went to the back door, as I always did when I visited a neighbor. Each house took about twenty or twenty-five minutes. . . .

PHIL DONAHUE AND POLITICAL ACTION

The *Phil Donahue Show* called. They wanted us to appear on their June 18 show. The reaction in the office was different this time, compared to the show in October 1978. In October, everyone was excited. "Phil Donahue—wow!" Now, residents reacted differently. "Donahue. That's great press. Now we'll get the politicians to move!" . . . Now our people looked at the show as a tool to use in pushing the government to relocate

us permanently. By this time we understood how politicians react to public pressure, how to play the political game. We eagerly agreed to go, and found forty other residents to go with us. . . .

[After arriving in Chicago] We then planned how we would handle the *Phil Donahue Show*. . . . We had to get the real issues across. Each resident was assigned an issue. One told of the chromosome tests. Another was to concentrate on her multiple miscarriages. Another was to ask for telegrams from across the country to the White House in support of permanent relocation. I coached them to get their point in, no matter the question asked. For example, if Donahue asked what you thought of the mayor, and your assignment was to discuss miscarriages, you should answer: "I don't like the mayor because I have had three miscarriages and other health problems, and he won't help us." Or: "My family is sick, and the mayor won't help us. That's why we need people to send telegrams to the White House for permanent relocation." . . . The residents were great! Each and every one followed through with our plan.

Source: Lois Marie Gibbs, as told to Murray Levine, *Love Canal: My Story* (Albany: State University of New York Press, 1982), pp. 12–13, 161–64.

His Democratic opponent, James Earl Carter, Jr., had been a navy officer, a farmer, and the governor of Georgia. He was one of several new-style politicians who transformed southern politics in the 1970s. Carter and the others left race-baiting behind to talk like modern New Dealers, emphasizing that whites and blacks both needed better schools and economic growth. He appealed to Democrats as someone who could reassemble LBJ's political coalition and return the South to the Democratic Party. In his successful campaign, Carter presented himself as an alternative to party hacks and Washington insiders.

JIMMY CARTER: IDEALISM AND FRUSTRATION IN THE WHITE HOUSE

WHAT FACTORS limited Jimmy Carter's effectiveness as president?

Carter was an outsider, a stranger to the national policy establishment that revolves around Washington think tanks and New York law firms. As such, Carter had one great advantage: freedom from the narrow mind-set of experts who talk only to each other. However, he lacked both the knowledge of key political players and the experience to resolve legislative gridlock.

Even had he been the most skilled of politicians, however, Carter took office with little room to maneuver. Watergate bequeathed him a powerful and self-satisfied Congress and a combative press. OPEC oil producers, Islamic fundamentalists, and Soviet generals followed their own agendas. The American people themselves were fractionalized and quarrelsome, uneasy with the new advocacy of equality for women, uncertain as a nation whether they shared the same values and goals.

CARTER, ENERGY, AND THE ECONOMY

Carter's approach to politics reflected his training as an engineer. He was analytical, logical, and given to breaking a problem into its component parts. He was better at working with details than at defining broad goals. He filled his cabinet with experts rather than with political operators. He failed to understand the importance of personalities and was uncomfortable with compromise. He did not seem to understand the basic rules of Washington politics. For example, he and his cabinet officers developed policies and made appointments without consulting key congressional committee chairs.

The biggest domestic problem remained the economy, which slid into another recession in 1978. Another jump in oil prices helped make 1979 and 1980 the worst years for inflation in the postwar era. Interest rates surged past 20 percent as the Federal Reserve tried to reduce inflation by squeezing business and consumer credit. Carter himself was a fiscal conservative whose impulse was to cut federal spending. This course worsened unemployment and alienated liberal Democrats, who wanted to revive the Great Society.

Carter simultaneously proposed a comprehensive energy policy. He asked Americans to make energy conservation the moral equivalent of war—to accept individual sacrifices for the common good. Congress created the Department of Energy but refused to raise taxes on oil and natural gas to reduce consumption. However, the Energy Policy and Conservation Act (1978) did encourage alternative energy sources to replace foreign petroleum.

However, antinuclear activism blocked one obvious alternative to fossil fuels. The antinuclear movement had started with concern about the ability of the Atomic Energy Commission to monitor the safety of nuclear-power plants and about the disposal of spent fuel rods. In the late 1970s, activists staged sit-ins at the construction sites of nuclear plants. A near-meltdown at the Three Mile Island nuclear plant in Pennsylvania in March 1979 stalemated efforts to expand nuclear-power capacity.

CLOSED FACTORIES AND FAILING FARMS

Ford and Carter both faced massive problems of economic transition that undercut their efforts to devise effective government programs. Industrial decay stalked such "gritty cities" as Allentown, Pennsylvania; Trenton, New Jersey; and Gary, Indiana. Communities whose workers had made products in high volume for a mass market found that technological revolutions made them obsolete. Critics renamed the old manufacturing region of the Northeast and Middle West the Rustbelt in honor of its abandoned factories.

Stories of **deindustrialization** were similar in small cities like Springfield, Ohio, and large cities like Cleveland. Springfield lost 10,000 manufacturing jobs and 4,000

29–3
Jimmy Carter, The "Malaise" Speech (1979)

Deindustrialization The process of economic change involving the disappearance of outmoded industries and the transfer of factories to new low-wage locations, with devastating effects in the Northeast and Middle West, especially in the 1970s and 1980s.

people during the 1970s, suffered unemployment of 17 percent, and needed $30 million in public subsidies to keep its largest factory going in 1982. Cleveland had built a century of prosperity on oil refining, steel, and metalworking. As high-paying jobs in unionized industries disappeared, sagging income undermined small businesses and neighborhoods. Falling tax revenue brought the city to the verge of bankruptcy in 1978; bankers forced public service cuts and tax increases, which meant further job losses.

Plant closures were only one facet of business efforts to increase productivity by substituting machinery for employees. Between 1947 and 1977, American steelmakers doubled output while cutting their workforce from 600,000 to 400,000. High interest rates and a strong dollar made U.S. exports too expensive and foreign imports cheap, forcing American manufacturers to cut costs or perish.

Despite the despairing headlines, some older industries and their workers found new roles in the sink-or-swim environment of technological and international competition. Buffalo, New York, lost much of its steel industry but retained smaller and more flexible factories making diverse products. The auto industry went through a similar cycle of crisis and response. Booming imports of well-made Toyotas and Hondas and customer demand for smaller cars destroyed the complacency of U.S. automakers in the fuel-short 1970s. In response, Ford, Chrysler, and finally General Motors remade themselves on the Japanese model as lean and flexible manufacturers.

Parallel to the decline of heavy industry was the continuing transformation of American agriculture from small family enterprises to corporate agribusinesses. The early 1970s brought an unexpected boom in farming. Crop failures and food shortages around the world in 1972 and 1973 expanded markets and pushed up prices for U.S. farm products. For a few years, agriculture looked like the best way for the United States to offset the high cost of imported oil. But the boom was over by the 1980s, when global commodity prices slumped. Farmers found themselves with debts they could not cover. The number of farms slid from 4 million in 1960 to 2.4 million in 1980 and 1.9 million in 2000. By 2000, fewer than 2 percent of American workers made their living from farming.

BUILDING A COOPERATIVE WORLD

Despite troubles on the home front, Carter's first two years brought foreign-policy successes that reflected a new vision of a multilateral world. As a relative newcomer to international politics, Carter was willing to work with African, Asian, and Latin American nations on a basis of mutual respect. He appointed Andrew Young—an African American from Georgia with long experience in the civil rights movement—as ambassador to the United Nations, where he worked effectively to build bridges to third-world nations. He convinced the Senate in 1978 to approve treaties to transfer control of the Panama Canal to Panama by 2000, removing a sore point in relations with Latin America.

Carter's moral convictions were responsible for a new concern with human rights around the globe. He criticized the Soviet Union for prohibiting free speech and denying its citizens the right to emigrate. Carter was also willing to criticize some (but not all) American allies. He withheld economic aid from South Africa, Guatemala, Chile, and Nicaragua, which had long records of human rights abuses.

The triumph of the new foreign policy was the **Camp David Agreement** between Egypt and Israel. Carter risked his reputation and credibility in September

1978 to bring Egyptian President Anwar al-Sadat and Israeli Prime Minister Menachem Begin together at Camp David, the presidential retreat. He refused to admit failure and dissuaded the two leaders from walking out. A formal treaty was signed in Washington on March 26, 1979. The pact normalized relations between Israel and its most powerful neighbor and led to Israel's withdrawal from the Sinai Peninsula.

NEW CRISES ABROAD

In the last two years of Carter's administration, the Cold War sprang back to life around the globe and smothered the promise of a new foreign policy. The Soviets ignored the human-rights provisions of the Helsinki Accords. Soviet advisers or Cuban troops intervened in African civil wars. At home, Cold Warriors who had never accepted détente found it easier to attack Carter than Nixon.

The Failure of SALT II.   Carter inherited negotiations for SALT II—a strategic arms-limitation treaty that would have reduced both the American and Soviet nuclear arsenals—from the Ford administration. SALT II met stiff resistance in the Senate. Opponents claimed it would create a "window of vulnerability" in the 1980s that would invite the Soviets to launch a nuclear first strike.

Hopes for SALT II vanished on December 24, 1979, when Soviet troops entered Afghanistan, a technically neutral Muslim nation on the southern border of the Soviet Union. The situation resembled the American involvement in South Vietnam. Similar, too, was the inability of Soviet forces to suppress the Afghan guerrillas, who had American weapons and controlled the mountains. In the end, it took the Soviets a decade to find a way out.

The Iranian Hostage Crisis.   The final blow to Carter's foreign policy came in Iran. Since 1953, the United States had strongly backed Iran's monarch, Shah Reza Pahlevi. The shah modernized Iran's economy, but his feared secret police jailed and tortured political opponents. U.S. aid and oil revenues helped him build a large army, but the Iranian middle class despised his authoritarianism, and Muslim fundamentalists opposed the Westernizing influence of modernization. A revolution toppled the shah at the start of 1979.

The upheaval installed a nominally democratic government, but the Ayatollah Ruhollah Khomeini, a Muslim cleric who hated the United States, exercised real power. Throughout 1979, Iran grew increasingly anti-American. After the United States allowed the exiled shah to seek medical treatment in New York, a mob stormed the U.S. embassy in Tehran on November 4, 1979, and took more than 60 Americans hostage. They demanded that Carter surrender the shah. The administration tried economic pressure and diplomacy, but Khomeini had no desire for accommodation. When Iran announced in April 1980 that the hostages would remain in the hands of the militants rather than be transferred to the government, Carter ordered an airborne rescue. Hampered by lack of coordination among the military services, the attempt misfired when three of the eight helicopters malfunctioned and one crashed in the Iranian desert. The fiasco added to the national embarrassment. The United States and Iran finally reached agreement on the eve of the 1980 election. The hostages gained their freedom after 444 days, at the moment Ronald Reagan took office as the new president.

After 30 years in which the United States had viewed the entire world as a Cold War battlefield, Carter was willing to accept the developing world on its own terms. His human-rights efforts showed that evangelical religious convictions could

Camp David Agreement
Agreement to reduce points of conflict between Israel and Egypt, hammered out in 1977 with the help of U.S. President Jimmy Carter.

be tied to progressive aims. He wanted to avoid supporting oppressive regimes, but the past was too burdensome. Iranian rage at past policies of the sort Carter hoped to change destroyed his ability to direct a new course. After he left office, his continuing work for peace and humanitarian efforts would earn him the Nobel Peace Prize in 2002.

CONCLUSION

*I*n the mid-1970s, Americans encountered real limits to national capacity. From 1945 to 1973, they had enjoyed remarkable prosperity. That ended in 1974. Long lines at gas stations showed that prosperity was fragile. Cities and regions felt the costs of obsolete industries. Environmental damage caused many Americans to reconsider the goal of economic expansion.

Ruined factory Outmoded facilities and foreign competition undermined the competitiveness of much of the nation's heavy manufacturing in the 1970s and 1980s. Many older factories were closed and abandoned, lending the name Rustbelt to the old industrial heartland.

Corbis-NY

The nation also had to recognize that it could not run the world. American withdrawal from Vietnam in 1973 and the collapse of the South Vietnamese government in 1975 were defeats; the United States ended up with little to show for a long and painful war. SALT I stabilized the arms race, but it also recognized that the Soviet Union was an equal. The American nuclear arsenal might help deter a third world war, but it could not prevent the seizure of hostages in Iran.

These challenges came amid deep economic changes in the United States. The ways Americans made their livings and the range of opportunities they faced were in flux. The nation finished the 1970s more egalitarian than it had been in the early 1960s but also more divided. More citizens had the opportunity to advance economically and to seek political power, but there were deepening fissures between social liberals and cultural conservatives, old and new views about roles for women, rich and poor, whites and blacks.

SUMMARY

The End of Consensus The failure to win an easy victory in Vietnam eroded the nation's confidence and fueled bitter division about the nation's goals. Operation Rolling Thunder in the air and search and destroy missions on the ground were not "wining" the war; protest against the war at home quickly followed America's decision to use combat forces. The tone of the debate over Vietnam turned nastier, much of the anger directed at the draft. The antiwar movement reflected a growing grass-roots activism on college campuses, among women, and the Woodstock generation counterculture.

Cities Under Stress Exploding metropolitan areas needed money for streets, schools, and sewers. Many urban problems were associated with the creation of "second ghettos" due to immigration in the 1950s and 1960s. A series of riots scarred most big cities during the 1960s; the riots were protests about the problems of ghetto life but were often blamed on "outsiders." Minority separatism tapped into the same anger that caused the riots. The Black Power movement, Hispanic activism in the Southwest, and the American Indian Movement all questioned the American assumption that everyone wanted to be a part of the same homogeneous society, a society increasingly becoming "suburbanized."

The Year of the Gun, 1968 1968 was a watershed year that forced American society to rethink the role of government. Mainstream Americans began questioning the war in Vietnam after the Tet Offensive; President Johnson was advised that the war was unwinnable on acceptable terms. Facing political challenges, Johnson announced a halt to the bombing of North Vietnam and his withdrawal from the presidential race. The assassinations of Martin Luther King Jr. and Robert Kennedy and the riots at the Democratic National Convention captured America's attention. Richard Nixon gained the presidency in 1968 with a secret plan to end the war and an appeal to middle America.

Nixon and Watergate President Nixon had no plan to end the Vietnam War and antiwar sentiment grew; while the Nixon Doctrine and "Vietnamization" made it appear the United States was withdrawing from Southeast Asia, the bombing of Cambodia intensified. The 1973 cease-fire confirmed American withdrawal from Vietnam; in 1975 South Vietnam collapsed. To his credit, Nixon took American foreign policy in new directions, improving relations with the Soviet Union and China, and the president signed numerous laws relating to environmental issues. Nixon abused the power of his office in the Watergate scandal and resigned before he could be impeached; Gerald Ford, who had been appointed vice president, succeeded him.

Jimmy Carter: Idealism and Frustration in the White House Washington outsider Jimmy Carter's major domestic challenge was the economy. A recession, an energy crisis, the deindustrization of America, and the transformation of the family farm to agribusiness challenged the president upon his election. Carter's moral convictions brought attention to human rights issues abroad. The signing of the Camp David Agreement between Egypt and Israel was a high point; hopes for reducing nuclear arsenals ended when the Soviet Union invaded Afghanistan. The Iranian hostage crisis consumed the Carter administration and helped contribute to Ronald Reagan's 1980 victory.

IMAGE KEY
for pages 844–845

a. Damaged tape evocative of the Watergate scandal.
b. Daisies represent the "Flower Power" mindset.
c. A weeping young woman kneels beside the body of a protester during the 1970 riots at Kent State University in Ohio.
d. Caeser Chávez.
e. Antiwar peace button.
f. Crowds gather to hear Martin Luther King, Jr. speak.
g. Vietnamese refugees.
h. President Nixon announces he will resign on August 9, 1974 during a broadcast from the Oval Room of the White House.
i. Egyptian president Anwar el-Sadat, US President Jimmy Carter, and Israeli Prime Minister Menachem Begin share a three-way handshake after signing an Arab-Israeli peace treaty on March 26, 1979. The three leaders agreed on the terms of the treaty at Camp David in September 1978.
j. Vietnamese flee napalm attack.

REVIEW QUESTIONS

1. Why did the United States fail to achieve its objectives in Vietnam? What factors limited President Johnson's freedom of action there? How did the Tet Offensive affect U.S. policy? How did antiwar protests in the United States influence national policy?

2. How did racial relations change between 1965 and 1970? What were the relationships between the civil rights movement and minority separatism? What were the similarities and differences between African-American, Latino, and Native American activism?

3. In what ways was 1968 a pivotal year for American politics and society? How was it influenced by global events?

4. What were the implications of *détente*? Why did the Cold War reappear in the late 1970s? How and why did U.S. influence over the rest of the world change during the 1970s?

5. How did Richard Nixon's political strategy respond to the growth of the South and West? How did it respond to the shift of population from central cities to suburbs?

6. How did the backgrounds of Presidents Johnson, Nixon, and Carter shape their successes and failures as national leaders?

7. What political and constitutional issues were at stake in the Watergate scandal? How did it change American politics?

8. Why was the space race important for the United States? How did it strengthen the alliance between American science, government, and industry?

KEY TERMS

American Indian Movement (AIM) (p. 859)

Baker v. Carr (p. 859)

Black Panthers (p. 857)

Black Power (p. 857)

Camp David Agreement (p. 872)

Counterculture (p. 852)

Deindustrialization (p. 870)

Détente (p. 864)

Environmental Protection Agency (p. 865)

Free Speech Movement (FSM) (p. 852)

Helsinki Accords (p. 868)

Model Cities Program (p. 852)

Nation of Islam (p. 857)

New Federalism (p. 864)

Nixon Doctrine (p. 863)

Organization of Petroleum Exporting Countries (OPEC) (p. 865)

Pentagon Papers (p. 866)

SALT (Strategic Arms Limitation Treaty) (p. 864)

Search and destroy (p. 848)

Selective Service System (p. 851)

Stonewall Rebellion (p. 855)

Students for a Democratic Society (SDS) (p. 852)

Swann v. Charlotte-Mecklenburg Board of Education (p. 859)

Watergate (p. 866)

WHERE TO LEARN MORE

☐ **Lyndon B. Johnson National Historical Park, Johnson City, Texas.** Johnson's ranch, southwest of Austin, gives visitors a feeling for the open landscape in which Johnson spent his early years. **www.nps. gov/lypo/**

☐ **Vietnam Veterans Memorial, Washington, D.C.** A simple wall engraved with the names of the nation's Vietnam War dead is testimony to one of the nation's most divisive wars. **www.nps.gov/vive/**

☐ **Richard Nixon Library and Birthplace, Yorba Linda, California.** Exhibits trace Nixon's political career and related world events with a sympathetic interpretation. **www.nixonfoundation.org/index.shtml**

☐ **Titan Missile Museum, Green Valley, Arizona.** The Green Valley complex near Tucson held 18 Titan missiles. They were deactivated after SALT I, and the complex is now open to visitors. **www.pimaair.org/titan_01.htm**

 U.S. History Documents CD-ROM
For primary source documents related to this chapter, refer to the document cd-rom.

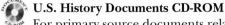 **www.prenhall.com/goldfield**
For study resources related to this chapter, visit the *Companion Website*™.

Visualizing The Past...
Iconic Images of the Vietnam Era

PRESIDENTS HAVE their picture taken shaking hands with visitors countless times. Usually they are of interest only to the visitors. What do you think made the photograph of President Nixon with Elvis Presley of interest to so many? During the late 1960s and early 1970s violence at home and overseas was distressingly commonplace. What do you think made the photographs of Mary Vecchio and Kim Phuc so memorable?

Television famously brought the Vietnam War "into the living room." Nonetheless some of the most memorable images of the era were photographs. What is it about particular images that turn them into iconic representations of a moment of history? Pictured here are three such photographs. The first shows Richard Nixon and Elvis Presley in the Oval Office. Fifteen years earlier, Presley had scandalized the "older generation" with his uninhibited gyrations. Nixon, then and later, always campaigned for "family values." Next is a photograph of a young woman reacting to the killing of a student on May 4, 1970 at Kent State University in Ohio. The preceeding week Nixon had ordered U.S. troops into Cambodia to destroy North Vietnamese supply routes and command centers. Campuses across the country erupted and in Ohio, the governor called in the National Guard to quell the demonstrations at Kent State. Guard soldiers fired on the students, killing the young man shown this photograph. The third photograph shows the impact on an American napalm attack upon the children of a South Vietnamese village.

◄ **This is the single most requested item in the National Archives which contain, among other national treasures, originals of the Declaration of Independence, the Constitution, and the Bill of Rights.** President Nixon and Elvis Presley met at the singer's request. He had volunteered to work in the administration's anti-drug crusade. The president, looking for a way to reach out to young people, readily agreed. He appointed Presley a "deputy" in the anti-drug war. Presley was, at the time, addicted to a variety of uppers, downers, and other medications.

◀ **Mary Vecchio reacting to the death of fellow student Jeff Miller.** John Filo, a Kent State student and photographer for the yearbook, won a Pulitzer Prize for the picture. It appeared on the cover of *Newsweek* magazine with the caption "Nixon's Home Front."

© John Paul Filo/Getty Images - Hulton Archive

This Pulitzer Prize-winning photograph of 9-year-old Kim Phuc, center, running after an aerial napalm attack on her village in 1972 was taken by Associated Press photographer Nick Ut (Cong Ut). Kim suffered burns over 65% of her body. She survived and is now a peace activist. ▶

AP/Wide World Photos

30 The Reagan Revolution and a Changing World
1981–1992

CHAPTER HIGHLIGHTS

Reagan's Domestic Revolution Ronald Reagan presided over revolutionary change in American government and policies. The consequences of his two terms included an altered role for government, powerful but selective economic growth, and a shift of domestic policy toward lifestyle concerns. Reaganomics brought prosperity to some, but also brought large budget deficits and a widening gap between rich and poor.

The Second (Short) Cold War Ronald Reagan's policies helped reignite the Cold War. Gorbachev's reforms convinced Reagan to engage in a new round of arms control. By 1991, Eastern Europe had rejected communism and the Soviet Union had disintegrated. President George H. W. Bush invaded Iraq in response to Iraq's invasion of Kuwait. A quick American military victory restored the prewar status quo.

Growth in the Sunbelt Military and defense spending fueled growth in the Sunbelt. Conservative voters in the Sunbelt were a crucial source of Republican political strength. The rise of the Sunbelt reflected the leading economic trends of the 1970s and 1980s.

Values in Collision The cultural conflicts of the 1980s and 1990s were rooted in the social and cultural changes of the 1960s and 1970s. Abortion rights and the conservative backlash, the increase of women in the workplace, a new openness about homosexuality, and the new "culture wars" were part of modern America.

CHAPTER QUESTIONS

WHAT GROUPS of traditionally Democratic voters were attracted to Ronald Reagan's message? Why?

WHAT WERE the goals of the Reagan administration's policies in Central America?

HOW DID growth in the Sunbelt shape national politics in the 1980s and 1990s?

WHAT KEY social and cultural issues divided Americans in the 1980s and 1990s?

CHAPTER OUTLINE

- Reagan's Domestic Revolution
- The Second (Short) Cold War
- Growth in the Sunbelt
- Values in Collision

IMAGE KEY
for pages 878–879 is on page 909.

The Khmer Rouge marched into the city [Phnom Penh, the capital of Cambodia], dressed in black. . . . Young Khmer Rouge [Marxist revolutionary] soldiers, eight or ten years old, were dragging their rifles, which were taller than them. . . . The whole city, more than two million people was forced out of their homes into the streets. My family walked until we reached Mao Tse-Tung Boulevard, the main boulevard in Phnom Penh. All the population of the city was gathered there. The Khmer Rouge were telling everyone to leave the city.

Although my two middle children were safe in France, my oldest and youngest daughters were close beside me. Parika was only seven. Mealy, who was nineteen, carried her infant son. I kept my children huddled together. As soon as a parent let go, a child would be lost in the huge crowd. . . . And the Khmer Rouge kept ordering everybody, "You must go forward." They shot their guns in the air. Even during the middle of the night the procession was endless. The Khmer Rouge kept shooting and we kept moving forward. . . .

Recently I saw the movie Doctor Zhivago, *about the Russian Revolution. If you compare that to what happened in Phnom Penh, the movie is only on a very small scale. Even* Killing Fields *only gives you part of the idea of what happened in Cambodia. The reality was much more incredible. . . .*

Each night, when we came back to the village from working in the fields, Mom would say, "Children, let's all go to sleep." She would quietly warn me that the wood had eyes and ears. She'd say, "It's nine o'clock now. Go to sleep. . . . There is nothing else to do but work. All the men are gone in our family." Mom was actually saying for the Khmer Rouge spies to hear, "They are only girls. Don't kill them. We are the only members left of the family.". . . We were lying to them about our identity. It was a horrible game.

If you hid your identity, that meant you wanted your past forgotten. We had changed from people who were intellectual, who used to think independently. . . . You became humiliated, allowed to live only as a slave. . . . We were accepted into the United States thanks to my husband's military service. . . . My daughters and I flew to the United States on July 4, 1979. . . . As we landed, I thought, "This is real freedom.". . .

I've found that America is a country where people have come from all over the world. You do your job, you get paid like anybody else, and you're accepted. But Cambodians I know in France, like my sister, feel differently. People are not accepted if they are not French. But in America you're part of the melting pot. . . . In 1983, I came to Los Angeles for my daughter Monie's wedding. I decided to stay. . . . Long Beach has the largest concentration of Cambodians in the country. I called the community center in Long Beach. They said they had no job openings. So I decided to get involved in running a store. . . . Donut shops are very American. . . .

All that refugees have is our work, our dreams. Do I still hurt from what happened in the past? When I opened my mouth to tell you my story, I don't know where my tears came from.

. . . My daughters don't like to talk about the past in Cambodia. They want to forget and think about their future. They ask me why I would talk about the past with anybody. I said, "The past cannot be erased from my memory."

Celia Noup, in Al Santoli, *New Americans: An Oral History* (New York, 1988).

CELIA NOUP TAUGHT school for 20 years in Cambodia, which borders on South Vietnam. In 1975, after a long civil war, the Communist Khmer Rouge insurgents took over Cambodia's capital, Phnom Penh, and forced its inhabitants into the countryside to work in the fields. Four years later, Noup managed to make her way to a refugee camp in neighboring Thailand and then to the United States. Here she joined hundreds of thousands of other refugees who arrived in the later 1970s and 1980s from war-devastated nations such as Cambodia, Vietnam, Laos, Ethiopia, and Afghanistan. Within a decade, she was working in her own donut shop near Los Angeles airport and worrying about helping her children buy houses.

Celia Noup's life shows some of the ways that new waves of immigration from Asia, Latin America, and Africa have changed the United States over the last generation. Immigrants fueled economic growth in the 1980s and 1990s with their labor and their drive to succeed in business. They revitalized older neighborhoods in cities from coast to coast and changed the ethnic mix of major cities. And they created new racial tensions that found their way into national political debates about immigration and into open conflict in places such as Miami and Los Angeles.

Noup's story is also a reminder of the drawn-out consequences of the U.S. involvement in Vietnam and the long shadow of the Cold War. The Cambodian civil war was fueled by reactions to the Vietnamese war and the American invasion of Cambodia in 1969. American refugee policy was humanitarian but also political, opening the door to people fleeing Communist regimes but holding it shut against refugees from right-wing dictatorships. In Washington, foreign policy decisions in the 1980s started with the desire of a new administration to reaffirm American toughness after failures in Vietnam and ended with the astonishing evaporation of the Cold War.

By the end of Ronald Reagan's presidency (1981–89), new rules governed domestic affairs as well as international relations. In the 1980s Americans decided to reverse the growth of federal government responsibilities that had marked both Republican and Democratic administrations since the 1930s. By the 1990s, the center of U.S. politics had shifted substantially to the right.

The backdrop to the political changes were massive readjustments in the American economy that began in the 1970s with the decline of heavy industry and then continued to shift employment from factory jobs to service jobs in the 1980s. The ideology of unregulated markets celebrated economic success and made "yuppies," or young urban professionals, the center of media attention. But behind the lifestyle stories was a troubling reality: a widening gap between the

Chronology

1973	*Roe v. Wade:* Supreme Court struck down state laws banning abortion in the first trimester of pregnancy.
1980	Ronald Reagan is elected president.
1981	Economic Recovery and Tax Act, reducing personal income tax rates, is passed.
	Reagan breaks strike by air traffic controllers.
	AIDS is recognized as a new disease.
1982	Nuclear freeze movement peaks.
	United States begins to finance Contra rebels against the Sandinista government in Nicaragua.
	Equal Rights Amendment fails to achieve ratification.
1983	241 Marines are killed by a terrorist bomb in Beirut, Lebanon.
	Strategic Defense Initiative introduced.
	U.S. invades Grenada.
1984	Reagan wins reelection.
1985	Mikhail Gorbachev initiates economic and political reforms in the Soviet Union.
1986	Tax Reform Act is adopted.

1987	Congress holds hearings on the Iran-Contra scandal.
	Reagan and Gorbachev sign the Intermediate Nuclear Force treaty.
1988	George H. W. Bush is elected president.
1989	Communist regimes in Eastern Europe collapse; Germans tear down Berlin Wall.
	Financial crisis forces federal bailout of many savings and loans.
	United States invades Panama to capture General Manuel Noriega.
1990	Iraq invades Kuwait; United States sends forces to the Persian Gulf.
	West Germany and East Germany reunite.
	Americans with Disabilities Act is adopted.
1991	Persian Gulf War: Operation Desert Storm drives the Iraqis from Kuwait.
	Soviet Union dissolves into independent nations.
	Strategic Arms Reduction Treaty (START) is signed.
1992	Acquittal of officers accused of beating Rodney King triggers Los Angeles riots.

rich and poor. The result by 1992 was a nation that was much more secure in the world than it had been in 1980, but also more divided against itself.

WHAT GROUPS of traditionally Democratic voters were attracted to Ronald Reagan's message? Why?

REAGAN'S DOMESTIC REVOLUTION

Political change began in 1980, when Ronald Reagan and running his mate, George H. W. Bush, rode American discontent to a decisive victory in the presidential election (see Map 30–1). Building on a conservative critique of American policies and developing issues that Jimmy Carter had placed on the national agenda, Reagan presided over revolutionary changes in American government and policies. The consequences of his two terms included an altered role for government, powerful but selective economic growth, and a shift of domestic politics away from bread-and-butter issues toward moral or lifestyle concerns.

REAGAN'S MAJORITY

A product of small-town Illinois, Ronald Reagan succeeded in Hollywood in the late 1930s as a romantic lead actor while adopting the liberal politics common at the time. After World War II, he moved rapidly to the political right as a spokesman for General Electric. He entered politics with a rousing conservative speech at the 1964 Republican convention and then accepted the invitation of wealthy California Republicans to run for governor in 1966. In two terms in that office, he offered

WHERE TO LEARN MORE

Ronald Reagan Boyhood Home, Dixon, Illinois

little formal leadership but spoke for a state and then a nation that were drifting toward more conservative values and expectations.

With a common touch that made him a favorite for a sizable segment of the public, Reagan tapped into the nostalgia for a simpler America. His Hollywood background made it easy for him to use popular films to make his points. He once threatened to veto legislation by challenging Congress with Clint Eastwood's "Make my day." Many blockbuster movies reinforced two of Reagan's messages. One was the importance of direct confrontation with bad guys, ranging from terrorists (*Die Hard*) to drug dealers (*Lethal Weapon*). The second was the incompetence of government bureaucracies, whose elitist mistakes could only be set right by tough individuals like the movie heroes Dirty Harry Callahan and John Rambo.

Some of Reagan's most articulate support came from anti-Communist stalwarts of both parties, who feared that the United States was losing influence in the world. Soviet military buildup, charged the critics, was creating a "window of vulnerability," a dangerous period when the Soviet Union might threaten the United States with a first strike by nuclear weapons.

Other Reagan voters directed their anger at government bureaucracies. Christian conservatives worried that social activists were using the federal courts to alter traditional values. Wealthy entrepreneurs from the fast-growing South and West believed that Nixon-era federal offices, such as the Environmental Protection Agency and the Occupational Safety and Health Administration, were choking their businesses in red tape. Many of these critics had amassed new fortunes in oil, real estate, and retailing and hated the taxes that funded social programs.

Foreign policy activists and opponents of big government would have been unable to elect Reagan without disaffected blue-collar and middle-class voters who deserted the Democrats. Democrats faced a special dilemma with the deepening tension between working-class white voters and black voters. They needed both groups to win but found white blue-collar voters deeply alienated by affirmative action and busing for school integration. The same sorts of voters worried about inflation and blamed their difficulties on runaway government spending.

A further Democratic challenge was Ronald Reagan's personal appeal. Reagan's popularity compounded the Democrats' inability to excite younger voters. The mid-1980s consistently showed that roughly two-thirds of people in their twenties and early thirties were choosing the Republicans as the party of energy and new ideas, leaving the Democrats to the middle-aged and elderly.

In the election of 1984, Democrats sealed their fate by nominating Walter Mondale, who had been vice president under Carter. Mondale was earnest, honest, and dull. Reagan ran on the theme "It's Morning in America," with the message that a new age of pride and prosperity had begun. Mondale assumed that Americans cared enough about the exploding federal deficit that Reagan's defense

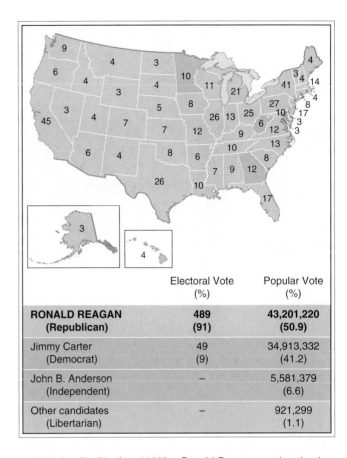

	Electoral Vote (%)	Popular Vote (%)
RONALD REAGAN (Republican)	**489 (91)**	**43,201,220 (50.9)**
Jimmy Carter (Democrat)	49 (9)	34,913,332 (41.2)
John B. Anderson (Independent)	–	5,581,379 (6.6)
Other candidates (Libertarian)	–	921,299 (1.1)

MAP 30–1   The Election of 1980   Ronald Reagan won in a landslide in 1980. Independent candidate John Anderson took more votes from Jimmy Carter than from Reagan, but Reagan's personal magnetism was a powerful political force. His victory confirmed the shift of the South to the Republican Party.

WHAT DID Reagan's victory tell about voters' desire for change in 1980?

Ronald Reagan and his wife, Nancy, celebrate Reagan's inauguration as president.

Corbis/Bettmann

30–1
Ronald Reagan, First
Inaugural Address
(1981)

spending had produced to accept an across-the-board tax increase. With the economy growing and inflation now in check, most voters did not want Mondale to remind them of long-range financial realities, and Reagan won reelection with 98 percent of the electoral votes.

THE NEW CONSERVATISM

Reagan's approach to public policy drew on conservative intellectuals who offered a coherent critique of the New Deal–New Frontier approach to American government. Some of the leading figures were journalists and academics who had embraced the ideas of the "vital center" a generation earlier (see Chapter 27). Now they feared that the antiwar movement had undermined the anti-Communist stance and that social changes were corrupting mainstream values.

Downsizing the Great Society.   Worries about big government permeated the critique of domestic policy. Edward Banfield's radical ideas about the failures of the Great Society set the tone of the neoconservative analysis. In *The Unheavenly City* (1968), he questioned the basic idea of public solutions for social problems. He argued that inequality is based on human character and rooted in the basic structure of society; government action can only solve problems that require better engineering, such as pollution control, better highways, or the delivery of explosives to military targets. Government's job, said Banfield, was to preserve public order, not to right wrongs or encourage unrealistic expectations.

Free Market Utopians.   Another strand of conservative argument came from free market utopians. After years of stagflation, Americans were eager to hear that unleashing free markets would trigger renewed prosperity. The common themes of the conservative critique were simple: free markets work better than government programs; government intervention does more harm than good; government assistance saps the initiative of the poor. In 1964, three-quarters of Americans had trusted Washington "to do what is right." By 1980, three-quarters were convinced that the federal government wasted tax money. The neoconservatives offered the details to support Reagan's own summary: "Government is not the solution to our problems; government is the problem." The cumulative effect of the neoconservative arguments was to trash the word "liberal" and convince many Americans that labor unions and minorities were "special interests" but that oil tycoons, defense contractors, and other members of Reagan's coalition were not.

The conservative cause found support in new "think tanks" and political lobbying organizations. Many conservatives were convinced that university faculty members were hopelessly liberal. In response, wealthy businesspeople funded alternative organizations, such as the Manhattan Institute, the Heritage Foundation, and the American Enterprise Institute, where conservative analysts could develop policy proposals and opinion pieces for newspapers. The cumulative effect was to shift the terms of political discussion substantially in a conservative direction between 1975 and 1990.

Conservative Political Savvy.   Conservatives promoted their ideology with new political tactics. Targeted mailings raised funds and mobilized voters with emo-

---

QUICK REVIEW

The Conservative Critique
- Free markets work better than government programs.
- Government intervention does more harm than good.
- Government assistance saps the initiative of the poor.

tional appeals while bypassing the mass media, with their supposed preference for mainstream or liberal policies. Conservative organizers also knew how to use radio call-in shows to spread their message. Through the 1980s, Democrats repeatedly found themselves blindsided by creative Republican campaign tactics.

REAGANOMICS: DEFICITS AND DEREGULATION

The heart of the 1980s revolution was the **Economic Recovery and Tax Act of 1981 (ERTA),** which reduced personal income tax rates by 25 percent over three years. The explicit goal was to stimulate business activity by lowering taxes overall and slashing rates for the rich. Cutting the government's total income by $747 billion over five years, ERTA meant less money for federal programs and more money in the hands of consumers and investors to stimulate economic growth.

Reagan's first budget director, David Stockman, later revealed a second goal. ERTA would lock in deficits by "pulling the revenue plug." Because defense spending and Social Security were untouchable, Congress would find it impossible to create and fund new programs without cutting old ones. The first year's tax reductions were accompanied by cuts of $40 billion in federal aid to mass transit, school lunches, and similar programs.

The second part of the economic agenda was to free capitalists from government regulations, in the hope of increasing business innovation and efficiency. The **deregulation** revolution built on a head start from the 1970s. A federal antitrust case had split the unified Bell System of AT&T and its subsidiaries into seven regional telephone companies and opened long-distance service to competition. Congress also deregulated air travel in 1978.

Environmental Regulation and Federal Lands.
Corporate America used the Reagan administration to attack environmental legislation as "strangulation by regulation." Reagan's new budgets sliced funding for the Environmental Protection Agency. Vice President Bush headed the White House Task Force on Regulatory Relief, which delayed or blocked regulations on hazardous wastes, automobile emissions, and exposure of workers to chemicals on the job.

Most attention, however, went to the controversial appointment of a Colorado lawyer, James Watt, as secretary of the interior. Watt had long worked to open up federal lands in the West to more intensive development. He was sympathetic to a western movement known as the **Sagebrush Rebellion,** which wanted the vast federal land holdings in the West transferred to the states for less environmental protection and more rapid economic use. Federal resource agencies sold trees to timber companies at a loss to the Treasury, expanded offshore oil drilling, and expedited exploration for minerals.

Deregulation of the Banking Industry.
The early 1980s also transformed American financial markets. Savings and loans had traditionally been conservative financial institutions that funneled individual savings into safe home mortgages. Under new rules, they began to compete for deposits by offering high interest rates and reinvesting the money in much riskier commercial real estate. By 1990, the result was a financial crisis in which bad loans destroyed hundreds of S&Ls, especially in the Southwest. American taxpayers were left to bail out depositors to the tune of hundreds of billions of dollars to prevent a collapse of the nation's financial and credit system.

With the deregulation of financial markets, corporate consolidations and mergers flourished. The merger mania channeled capital into paper transactions

30–2
Ronald Reagan, Speech to the House of Commons (1982)

QUICK REVIEW

Key Components of Reaganomics
- Lower personal income tax rates.
- Increase defense spending.
- Deregulate industry.

Economic Recovery and Tax Act of 1981 (ERTA)   A major revision of the federal income tax system.

Deregulation   Reduction or removal of government regulations and encouragement of direct competition in many important industries and economic sectors.

Sagebrush Rebellion   Political movement in the Western states in the early 1980s that called for easing of regulations on the economic issue of federal lands and the transfer of some or all of those lands to state ownership.

rather than investments in new equipment and products. Another effect was to damage the economies of small and middle-sized communities by transferring control of local companies to outside managers.

In the short term, the national economy boomed in the mid-1980s. Deregulated credit, tax cuts, and massive deficit spending on defense fueled exuberant growth. The decade as a whole brought nearly 20 million new jobs, especially for professional and managerial workers, office support staff, salespeople, and workers providing personal services. Inflation dipped to 3 percent per year. The stock market mirrored the overall prosperity; the Dow Jones average of blue-chip industrial stock prices more than tripled from August 1982 to August 1987.

CRISIS FOR ORGANIZED LABOR

The flip side of the economic boom was another round in the Republican offensive against labor unions. Reagan set the tone when he fired more than 11,000 members of the Professional Air Traffic Controllers Organization for violating a no-strike clause in their hiring agreements. For many years, corporations had hesitated to hire permanent replacements for striking workers. With Reagan's example, large companies, such as Hormel and Phelps-Dodge, chose that option, undercutting the strike as an effective union strategy. During the Reagan administration, the National Labor Relations Board and other federal agencies also weakened collective bargaining by their interpretation of labor-management regulations.

Decline of Union Membership and Blue-Collar Jobs.   Organized labor counted a million fewer members at the end of Reagan's administration in 1989 than in 1964, even though the number of employed Americans had nearly doubled. As union membership declined and unions struggled to cope with the changing economy, corporations seized the opportunity to demand wage rollbacks and concessions on working conditions as trade-offs for continued employment. Workers in the 1970s and 1980s faced the threat that employers might move a factory to a new site elsewhere in the United States or overseas. Or a company might sell out to a new owner, who could close a plant and reopen without a union contract.

Another cause for shrinking union membership was the overall decline of blue-collar jobs, from 36 percent of the American workforce in 1960 to roughly 25 percent at the end of the 1990s. Unionization of white-collar workers made up only part of the loss from manufacturing. Unions were most successful in recruiting government workers, such as police officers, teachers, and bus drivers. In the private sector, however, many white-collar jobs were in small firms that were difficult to organize.

Impact of Economic Restructuring.   In the 1950s and 1960s, increasing productivity, expanding markets for U.S. goods, and strong labor unions had made it possible for factory workers to enter the middle class. In an era of deindustrialization, however, companies replaced blue-collar workers with machinery or shifted production to nonunion plants. The corporate merger mania of the 1980s added to instability when takeover specialists loaded old companies with new debt, triggering efforts to cut labor costs, sell off plants, or raid pension funds for cash to pay the interest. Manufacturing employment in the 1980s declined by nearly 2 million jobs, with the expansion of high-tech manufacturing concealing much higher losses in traditional industries.

AN ACQUISITIVE SOCIETY

The national media in the early 1980s discovered yuppies, or young urban professionals, who were both a marketing category and a symbol of social change. These upwardly mobile professionals supposedly defined themselves by elitist consumerism. Middle-line retailers like Sears had clothed Americans for decades and furnished their homes. With the help of catalog shopping, status-seeking consumers now flocked to such upscale retailers as Neiman-Marcus and Bloomingdale's.

Far richer than the typical yuppy were wheeler-dealers who made themselves into media stars of finance capitalism. The autobiography of Lee Iacocca, who had helped revive the fortunes of the Chrysler Corporation, was a bestseller in 1984, portraying the corporate executive as a hero. *Forbes* magazine began to publish an annual list of the nation's 400 richest people. Long before his television show, real-estate developer Donald Trump made himself a celebrity with a well-publicized personal life and a stream of projects crowned with his name: office tower, hotel, casino. Before he admitted to violating the law against profiting from insider information, the corporate-merger expert Ivan Boesky had told a business-school audience, "Greed is all right. . . . You shouldn't feel guilty," epitomizing an era of big business takeovers driven by paper profits rather than underlying economic fundamentals.

The superficial glamour of this era of acquisitiveness and corporate greed had its underside of loneliness and despair. Young novelists in the 1980s explored the emptiness of life among the privileged, repeating some of the themes of the 1920s in the process. Bret Easton Ellis in *Less Than Zero* (1985) dissected the despair and drug habits of college students from the affluent west side of Los Angeles. *In Bright Lights, Big City* (1986), Jay McInerney took on the same problems of glamour and depression among young professionals in New York. In his bestselling novel *The Bonfire of the Vanities* (1987), Tom Wolfe depicted a New York where the art dealers and stockbrokers of glitzy Manhattan meet the poor of the devastated South Bronx only through an automobile accident, to their mutual incomprehension and ruin.

New movements in popular music reacted to the acquisitive 1980s. Punk rock pared rock-and-roll to its basics, lashing out at the emptiness of 1970s disco sound. Hip-hop originated among African Americans and Latinos in New York, soon adding the angry and often violent lyrics of rap. Rap during the 1980s was about personal power and sex, but it also dealt with social inequities and deprivation and tapped some of the same anger and frustration that had motivated black power advocates in the 1960s. When it crossed into mainstream entertainment, it retained a hard-edged "attitude" that undercut any sense of complacency about an inclusive American society.

MASS MEDIA AND FRAGMENTED CULTURE

On June 1, 1980, CNN, Cable News Network, gave television viewers their first chance to watch news coverage 24 hours a day. Newscasters Bernard Shaw and Mary Alice Williams brought instant information to an initial audience of 1.7 million subscribers; a decade later, CNN had hundreds of millions of viewers in more than 75 countries.

Fourteen months after CNN went on the air, another new cable channel, MTV. Music Television, started broadcasting. By the time it reached the key New York and Los Angeles markets in January 1983, MTV's round-the-clock programming of music videos had created a new form of popular art and advertising. With

QUICK REVIEW

Greed is Good?
- Yuppies: young urban professionals.
- Corporate dealmakers made themselves into media stars.
- New movements in music emerged in response to the acquisitive 1980s.

its own programming aimed at viewers aged 18 to 34, MTV inspired Nickelodeon for kids and VH-1 for baby boomers.

CNN, MTV, and the rest of cable television reflected both the fragmentation of American society in the 1980s and 1990s and the increasing dependence on instant communication. As late as 1980, ordinary Americans had few choices for learning about their nation and world: virtually identical newscasts on NBC, CBS, and ABC and similar stories in *Time* and *Newsweek* helped to create a common understanding. Fifteen years later, they had learned to surf through dozens of cable channels in search of specialized programs and were beginning to explore the amazing variety of the World Wide Web (see Chapter 31). Hundreds of magazines for niche markets had replaced the general-circulation periodicals of the postwar generation. Vast quantities of information were more easily available, but much of it was packaged for a subdivided marketplace of specialized consumers.

POVERTY AMID PROSPERITY

Federal tax and budget changes had different effects on the rich and poor. Those in the top fifth increased their share of after-tax income relative to everyone else during the 1980s, and the richest 1 percent saw their share of all privately held wealth grow from 31 percent to 37 percent. The 1981 tax cuts also came with sharp increases in the Social Security tax, which hit lower-income workers the hardest. The tax changes meant that the average annual income of households in the bottom 20 percent *declined* and that many actually paid higher taxes.

The budget changes that fueled conspicuous consumption put pressure on American cities. Cities and their residents absorbed approximately two-thirds of the cuts in the 1981–1982 federal budget. Provisions for accelerated depreciation (tax write-offs) of factories and equipment in the 1981 tax act encouraged the abandonment of center-city factories in favor of new facilities in the suburbs. One result was a growing jobs-housing mismatch. There were often plenty of jobs in the suburbs, but the poorer people who most needed the jobs were marooned in city slums and dependent on public transit that seldom served suburban employers.

Federal tax and spending policies in the 1980s decreased the security of middle-class families. As the economy continued to struggle through deindustrialization, average wage rates fell in the 1980s when measured in real purchasing. The squeeze put pressure on traditional family patterns and pushed into the workforce women who might otherwise have stayed home. Even with two incomes, many families found it hard to buy a house because of skyrocketing prices in urban markets and sky-high interest rates. Many Americans no longer expected to surpass their parents' standard of living.

Corporate Downsizing and White-Collar Jobs.   Lower-paying office jobs fell under the same sorts of pressure as factory jobs with the growing reliance of banks, telephone companies, and credit card companies on automation. Increasing numbers of clerical and office workers were "temps" who shifted from job to job. The shift toward temporary and part-time workers not only kept wages low but also allowed less spending on health insurance and other benefits.

The chill of corporate downsizing hit white-collar families most heavily toward the end of the 1980s. Big business consolidations delivered improved profits by squeezing the ranks of middle managers as well as assembly-line workers. Takeovers sometimes meant the elimination of the entire management and support staff of target companies. Those white-collar workers whose jobs survived clung to them more firmly than ever. The combined result was to clog the ladder of economic opportunity for college graduates.

Increase in the Poverty Rate.   At the lower end of the economic ladder, the proportion of Americans living in poverty increased. After declining steadily from 1960 to a low of 11 percent in 1973, the poverty rate climbed back to the 13 to 15 percent range. Conservative critics began to talk about an underclass of Americans permanently outside the mainstream economy because of poor education, drug abuse, or sheer laziness. In fact, talk of an underclass was a way to avoid confronting the realities of limited economic opportunity. Most of the nation's millions of poor people lived in households with employed adults. In 1992, fully 18 percent of all full-time jobs did not pay enough to lift a family of four out of poverty, a jump of 50 percent over the proportion of underpaid jobs in 1981.

The Wage Gap and the Feminization of Poverty.   Nor could most women, even those working full-time, expect to earn as much as men. In the 1960s and 1970s, the average working woman earned just 60 percent of the earnings of the average man. Only part of the wage gap could be explained by measurable factors, such as education or experience. The gap narrowed in the 1980s and 1990s, with women's earnings rising to 75 percent of men's by 2003. About half of the change was the result of bad news—the decline of earnings among men as high-wage factory jobs disappeared. The other half was the positive result of better-educated younger women finding better jobs. Indeed, women earned 57 percent of the four-year college degrees awarded in 2002 (up from 38 percent in 1960) and 47 percent of first professional degrees (up from 3 percent).

Nevertheless, the low earning capacity of women with limited educations meant that women were far more likely than men to be poor. Women constituted nearly two-thirds of poor adults at the end of the 1980s. The feminization of poverty and American reliance on private support for child rearing also meant that children had a higher chance of living in poverty than adults and that poor American children were worse off than their peers in other advanced nations.

Homelessness in America.   Falling below even the working poor were growing numbers of homeless Americans. In the 1980s, several factors made homelessness more visible and pressing. A new approach to the treatment of the mentally ill reduced the population of mental hospitals from 540,000 in 1960 to only 140,000 in 1980. Deinstitutionalized patients were supposed to receive community-based treatment, but many ended up on the streets and in overnight shelters. New forms of self-destructive drug abuse, such as crack addiction, joined alcoholism. A boom in downtown real estate destroyed old skid-row districts with their bars, missions, and dollar-a-night hotels.

These factors tripled the number of permanently homeless people during the early and middle 1980s, from 200,000 to somewhere between 500,000 and 700,000. Twice or three times that many may have been homeless for part of a given year. For every person in a shelter on a given night, two people were sleeping on sidewalks, in parks, in cars, and in abandoned buildings.

W WHERE TO LEARN MORE

★ The Causes of Homelessness in America **http://www.stanford.edu/ class/e297c/poverty_prejudice/soc_ sec/hcauses.htm**

CONSOLIDATING THE REVOLUTION: GEORGE BUSH

In 1988 George H. W. Bush, Reagan's vice-president for eight years, won the presidential election with 56 percent of the popular vote and 40 out of 50 states. Bush's view of national and world politics reflected a background in which personal connections counted. He was raised as part of the New England elite, built an oil business in Texas, and then held a series of high-level federal appointments.

Michael Dukakis, the Democratic nominee in 1988, was a dry-as-dust, by-the-numbers manager who offered the American people "competence." The Bush campaign director, Lee Atwater, looked for hot-button issues that could fit onto a three-by-five card. He found that Dukakis as governor of Massachusetts had delayed cleanup of Boston Harbor, favored gun control, and vetoed a bill requiring schoolchildren to recite the Pledge of Allegiance (arguing correctly that it would be overturned in the courts). Even more damaging, Massachusetts officials had allowed a murderer named Willie Horton a weekend furlough from prison, during which he committed a brutal rape. Pro-Bush advertisements tapped into real worries among the voters—fear of crime, racial tension (Horton was black), eroding social values.

The ads locked Bush into a rhetorical war on crime and drugs that was his major domestic policy. Americans had good cause to be worried about public safety, but most were generally unaware that the likelihood of becoming the target of a violent crime had leveled off and would continue to fall in the 1990s or that crime was far worse in minority communities than elsewhere, in part due to gang- and drug-related activities.

The Bush administration stepped up the fight against illegal drugs, and the federal drug-control budget tripled. In the early 1980s, a quarter of federal prison inmates were in jail for drug offenses. Longer sentences, mandatory jail time, and tougher parole terms for drug crimes pushed the proportion over 50 percent by 1990.

George Bush believed that Americans wanted government to leave them alone. The major legislation from the Bush administration was a transportation bill that shifted federal priorities from highway building toward mass transit and the **Americans with Disabilities Act** (1990) to prevent discrimination against people with physical handicaps. In the areas of crime and health care, however, Bush's lack of leadership left continuing problems.

The same attitude produced weak economic policies. The national debt had amounted to 50 percent of personal savings in 1980 but swelled to 125 percent by 1990. The massive budget deficits of the 1980s combined with growing trade deficits to turn the United States from an international creditor to a debtor nation. When Reagan took office, foreigners owed the United States and its citizens the equivalent of $2,500 for every American family. When Bush took office, the United States had used up its foreign assets and become the world's biggest debtor, with liabilities that averaged $7,000 per family. After pledging no new taxes in his campaign, Bush backed into a tax increase in 1990.

The most conspicuous domestic event of the Bush administration—the "Rodney King riot" of April 1992 in Los Angeles—was a reminder of the nation's inattention to the problems of race and poverty. Rodney King was a black motorist who had been savagely clubbed and kicked by police officers while being arrested after a car chase on March 3, 1991. A nearby resident captured the beating on videotape from his apartment. The grainy pictures shocked the nation and confirmed African Americans' worst fears about biased police behavior. The televised trial and the unexpected verdict of not guilty from a suburban jury on April 29 stirred deep anger that escalated into four days of rioting.

The disorder revealed multiple tensions among ethnic groups and was far more complex than the Watts outbreak of 1965 (see Chapter 29). African Americans from south-central Los Angeles participated, but so did Central American and Mexican immigrants in adjacent districts, who accounted for about one-third

Americans with Disabilities Act
Legislation in 1992 that banned discrimination against physically handicapped persons in employment, transportation, and public accommodations.

of the 12,000 arrests. As in 1965, some targets were white passers-by and symbols of white authority. But members of competing minority groups were also victims as angry black people targeted hundreds of Korean-owned and Vietnamese-owned shops as symbols of economic discrimination.

The Second (Short) Cold War

Ronald Reagan entered office determined to reassert U.S. leadership in world affairs and not to lose the Cold War. He considered the Soviet Union not a coequal nation with legitimate world interests but an "evil empire." After the era of détente, global tensions had started to mount in the late 1970s. They were soon higher than they had been since the 1960s. But by the end of Reagan's two terms, unexpected changes were rapidly bringing the Cold War to an end, and George Bush faced a radically new set of foreign policy issues.

Confronting the Soviet Union

Who renewed the Cold War after Nixon's diplomacy of détente and Carter's early efforts at negotiation? The Soviets had pursued military expansion in the 1970s, and in 1980 were supporting Marxist regimes in civil wars in Angola, Ethiopia, Nicaragua, and especially Afghanistan, where its 1980 intervention led to a decade of costly and futile military occupation. Were these actions parts of a careful plan? Or did they result from the Cold War inertia of a rudderless nation that reacted to situations one at a time? Given the aging Soviet leadership and the economic weaknesses revealed in the late 1980s, it makes more sense to see the Soviets as muddling along rather than executing a well-planned global strategy.

On the American side, Reagan's readiness to confront "the focus of evil in the modern world" reflected the views of many conservative supporters that the Soviet Union was a monolithic and ideologically motivated foe bent on world conquest. In hindsight, some Reaganites claim that the administration's foreign policy and massive increases in defense spending were part of a deliberate and coordinated scheme to check a Soviet offensive and bankrupt the Soviet Union by pushing it into a new arms race. It is just as likely, however, that the administration's defense and foreign policy initiatives were a set of discrete but effective decisions.

The Reagan administration reemphasized central Europe as the focus of superpower rivalry, just as it had been in the 1950s and early 1960s. To counter improved Soviet armaments, the United States began to place cruise missiles and mid-range Pershing II missiles in Europe in 1983. NATO governments approved the action, but it frightened millions of their citizens. By the mid-1980s, many Europeans saw the United States as the dangerous and aggressive force in world affairs and the Soviet Union as the voice of moderation—international attitudes that continue to this day.

The controversy over new missiles was part of new thinking about nuclear strategy. National Security Directive D-13 (1981) set forth a new doctrine that it might be possible to fight and win a nuclear war despite its enormous costs. A reactivated civil defense program also suggested that the United States was serious about nuclear war.

Escalation of the nuclear arms race reinvigorated the antiwar and antinuclear movement in the United States as well as Europe. The nuclear-freeze campaign sought to halt the manufacture and deployment of new atomic weapons by the great powers. Nearly a million people turned out for a nuclear-freeze rally in New York in 1982. Hundreds of local communities endorsed the freeze or took the symbolic step of declaring themselves nuclear-free zones.

WHAT WERE the goals of the Reagan administration's policies in Central America?

QUICK REVIEW

The New Arms Race

- The Reagan administration reemphasized central Europe as the focus of superpower rivalry.
- Pershing II missiles were placed in Europe in 1983.
- A National Security Directive stated that the U.S. might be able to win a nuclear war.

In response, Reagan announced the **Strategic Defense Initiative (SDI),** or Star Wars program, in 1983. SDI was to deploy new defenses that could intercept and destroy ballistic missiles as they rose from the ground and arced through space. Few scientists thought that SDI could work. Many arms control experts thought that defensive systems were dangerous and destabilizing, because strong defenses suggested that a nation might be willing to risk a nuclear exchange.

RISKY BUSINESS: FOREIGN POLICY ADVENTURES

Reagan asserted America's right to intervene anywhere in the world to support local groups fighting against Marxist governments. The assumption underlying this assertion, which later became known as the **Reagan Doctrine,** was that Soviet-influenced governments in Asia, Africa, and Latin America needed to be eliminated if the United States was to win the Cold War.

Nevertheless, Reagan kept the United States out of a major war and backed off in the face of serious trouble. Foreign interventions were designed to achieve symbolic victories rather than change the global balance of power. The exception was the Caribbean and Central America.

Intervention and Covert Activities in Central America. The Reagan administration attributed political turmoil in Central America to Soviet influence and to arms and agitators from Soviet-backed Cuba. Central America became the focus of a secret foreign policy operated by the CIA and then by National Security Council (NSC) staff, since a Democratic Congress was not convinced of the danger. The CIA and the NSC engaged not just in espionage but in direct covert operations. The chief target was Nicaragua, the Central American country where leftist Sandinista rebels had overthrown the Somoza dictatorship in 1979. In the early 1980s, Reagan approved CIA plans to arm and organize approximately 10,500 so-called Contras, from the remnants of Somoza's national guard. From bases in Honduras, the Contras harassed the Sandinistas with sabotage and raids.

The Reagan administration bent the law to support its covert effort to overthrow the Sandinista regime. An unsympathetic Congress blocked U.S. funding for the Contras. In response, CIA director William Casey directed Lieutenant Colonel Oliver North of the National Security Council staff to illegally organize aid from private donors. The arms pipeline operated until a supply plane was shot down in 1986. The Contras failed as a military effort, but the civil war and international pressure persuaded the Sandinistas to allow free elections that led to a democratic, centrist government.

The War against Drugs. The American war against drugs was simultaneously shaping U.S. policy in the Caribbean and straining relations with Latin America. As president, George Bush parlayed the war on drugs into war on Panama during his first year in office. General Manuel Noriega, the Panamanian strongman, had once been on the CIA payroll. On December 20, 1989, American troops invaded Panama, hunted down Noriega, and brought him back to stand trial in the United States on drug-trafficking charges. A handful of Americans and thousands of Panamanians died, many of them civilians caught in the crossfire.

Intervention in the Middle East. If the results of intervention in Nicaraugua and Panama were mixed, intervention in the Middle East was a failure. In 1982 Israel invaded Lebanon, a small nation to its north, to clear Palestinian guerrillas from its borders and set up a friendly Lebanese government. The Israeli army

QUICK REVIEW

Small-scale Military Intervention
- Marines were sent into Lebanon to help stabilize the Lebanese state and allow the Israelis to withdraw.
- The U.S. invaded Grenada to prevent the possible creation of a Cuban military base.
- Nicaragua and El Salvador were the targets of secret foreign policy operated by the CIA and later the National Security Council staff.

Strategic Defense Initiative (SDI) President Reagan's program, announced in 1983, to defend the United States against nuclear missile attack with untested weapons systems and sophisticated technologies.

Reagan Doctrine The policy assumption that Soviet-influenced governments in Asia, Africa, and Latin America needed to be eliminated if the United States was to win the Cold War.

bogged down in a civil war between Christian Arabs and Muslims. Reagan sent U.S. Marines to preserve the semblance of a Lebanese state and provide a face-saving exit for Israel. The presence of the Marines angered Arabs and motivated terrorist actions against Israel and the United States by Islamic radicals. In October 1983, a terrorist car bomb killed 241 marines in their barracks. The remainder were soon gone. The debacle in Lebanon undermined U.S.-backed peace initiatives in the Middle East.

The Iran-Contra Affair.   Even less effective were the Reagan administration's secret efforts to sell weapons to Iran in return for Iranian help in securing the release of Americans held hostage by pro-Iranian Islamic radicals in Lebanon. The United States in 1985 joined Israel in selling 500 antitank missiles to Iran, then embroiled in a long, bitter war with Iraq. The deal violated the official trade embargo against Iran, which had been in place since the U.S. embassy seizure in 1980. The pro-Iranian radicals released several hostages, but others were soon taken. When the deals came to light in 1986 and congressional hearings were held in the summer of 1987, Americans were startled to learn that Colonel North had funneled millions of dollars from the arms sales to the Nicaraguan Contras in a double evasion of the law.

As had been true with Watergate, the Iran-Contra affair was a two-sided scandal. First was the blatant misjudgment of operating a secret, bumbling, and unlawful foreign policy that depended on international arms dealers and ousted Nicaraguan military officers. Second was a concerted effort to cover up the illegal and unconstitutional actions. North shredded relevant documents and lied to Congress. In his final report in 1994, Special Prosecutor Lawrence Walsh found that President Reagan and Vice President Bush were aware of much of what had gone on and had participated in efforts to withhold information and mislead Congress.

U.S. Policy in Asia.   American policy in Asia was a refreshing contrast with practices in Central America and the Middle East. In the Philippines, American diplomats helped push corrupt President Ferdinand Marcos out and opened the way for a popular uprising to put Corazon Aquino in office. In South Korea, the United States similarly helped ease out an unpopular dictator by firmly supporting democratic elections that brought in a more popular but still pro-American government.

EMBRACING PERESTROIKA

Thaw in the Cold War started in Moscow. Mikhail Gorbachev became general secretary of the Communist Party in 1985. A master of public relations who charmed western Europe's leaders and public, he was also a modernizer in a long Russian tradition that stretched back to Tsar Peter the Great in the eighteenth century. Gorbachev startled Soviet citizens by urging *glasnost,* or political openness, with free discussion of issues and relaxation of controls on the press. He followed by setting the goal of *perestroika,* or restructuring of the painfully bureaucratic Soviet economy that was falling behind capitalist nations. His hope was that market-oriented reforms would help the Soviet Union keep up with the United States.

Gorbachev decided that he needed to reduce the crushing burden of Soviet defense spending if the Soviet Union was to have any chance of modernizing. During Reagan's second term, the Soviets offered one concession after another in a drive for arms control. They agreed to cut the number of land-based strategic

WHERE TO LEARN MORE

The Intermediate Nuclear Force Agreement (INF)
http://www.state.gov/www/global/arms/treaties/inf1.html

Glasnost   Russian for "openness" applied to Mikhail Gorbachev's encouragement of new ideas and easing of political repression in the Soviet Union.

Perestroika   Russian for "restructuring," applied to Mikhail Gorbachev's efforts to make the Soviet economic and political systems more modern, flexible, and innovative.

The wall that divided East from West Berlin from 1962 to 1989 was a hated symbol of the Cold War. When the Communist government of East Germany collapsed in November 1989, jubilant Berliners celebrated the opening of the wall and the reuniting of the divided city.

Corbis/Sygma

Intermediate Nuclear Force Agreement (INF)   Disarmament agreement between the United States and the Soviet Union under which an entire class of missiles would be removed and destroyed and on-site inspections would be permitted.

weapons in half. They gave up their demand for an end to SDI research. In negotiations on conventional forces in Europe, they accepted bigger cuts for the Warsaw Pact nations than for NATO. They even agreed to on-site inspections to control chemical weapons.

Reagan had the vision (or audacity) to cast off decades of belief in the dangers of Soviet Communism and take Gorbachev seriously. One of his reasons for SDI had been his personal belief that the abolition of nuclear weapons was better than fine-tuning the balance of terror. Now he was willing to forget his own rhetoric. He frightened his own staff when he met with Gorbachev in the summer of 1986 and accepted the principle of deep cuts in strategic forces.

In the end, Reagan negotiated the **Intermediate Nuclear Force Agreement (INF)** over the strong objections of the CIA and the Defense Department. INF was the first true nuclear-disarmament treaty (see the Overview table, "Controlling Nuclear Weapons: Four Decades of Effort"). Previous agreements had only slowed the growth of nuclear weapons; they were "speed limits" for the arms race. The new pact matched Soviet SS-20s with American cruise missiles as an entire class of weapons that would be destroyed, with on-site inspections for verification.

CRISIS AND DEMOCRACY IN EASTERN EUROPE

As a believer in personal diplomacy, George Bush based much of his foreign policy on his changing attitudes toward Mikhail Gorbachev. He started lukewarm, talking tough to please the Republican right wing. Bush feared that Gorbachev, by instituting reforms that challenged the entrenched Communist Party leaders, was being imprudent: one of the worst things he could say about another leader. Before 1989 was over, however, the president had decided that Gorbachev was OK. For the next two years, the United States pushed the prodemocratic transformation of eastern Europe while being careful not to gloat in public or damage Gorbachev's position at home. Bush tried not to push the Soviet Union too hard and infuriate Russian hard-liners. "I don't want to do something that would inadvertently set back the progress," Bush said.

The End of Communist Regimes in Eastern Europe.   The people of eastern Europe overcame both American and Soviet caution. Gorbachev had urged his eastern European allies to emulate *perestroika* to free their economies from stifling controls. Each Communist nation could introduce reforms without fearing the Soviet tanks that had crushed change in Hungary in 1956 and Czechoslovakia in

OVERVIEW   CONTROLLING NUCLEAR WEAPONS: FOUR DECADES OF EFFORT

Limiting the Testing of Nuclear Weapons	Limited Test Ban Treaty (1963)	Banned Nuclear Testing in the Atmosphere, Ocean, and Outer Space
	Comprehensive Test Ban Treaty (1996)	Banned all nuclear tests, including underground tests. Rejected by U.S. Senate in 1999.
Halting the spread of nuclear weapons	Nuclear Non-Proliferation Treaty (1968)	Pledged five recognized nuclear nations (United States, Soviet Union, Britain, France, China) to pursue disarmament in good faith, and 140 other nations not to acquire nuclear weapons.
	Strategic Arms Limitation Treaty (SALT I, 1972)	Limited the number of nuclear-armed missiles and bombers maintained by the United States and Soviet Union. Closely associated with U.S. Soviet agreement to limit deployment of antiballistic missile systems to one site each.
	Strategic Arms Limitation Treaty (SALT II, 1979)	Further limited the number of nuclear-armed missiles and bombers. Not ratified but followed by Carter and Reagan administrations.
Reducing the number of nuclear weapons	Intermediate Nuclear Force Agreement (1987)	Required the United States to eliminate 846 nuclear armed cruise missiles, and the Soviet Union to eliminate 1,846 SS-20 missiles.
	Strategic Arms Reduction Treaty (START I, 1991)	By July 1999, led to reductions of approximately 2,750 nuclear warheads by the United States and 3,725 warheads by the nations of the former USSR.
	Strategic Arms Reduction Treaty (START II, 1993)	Set further cuts in nuclear arsenals. Ratified by Russia in April 2000. Russia withdrew in 2002 after the U.S. abandoned the Anti-Ballistic Missile Treaty.
	Strategic Offensive Reductions (2002)	Russia and the United States each agree to deploy no more than 1,700–2,200 strategic nuclear warheads.

Data Source: Arms Control Association.

1968. Instead of careful economic liberalization, the Warsaw Pact system collapsed. Poland held free elections in June 1989, Hungary adopted a democratic constitution in October, and prodemocracy demonstrations then forced out Communist leaders in other eastern European countries. When East Germans began to flee westward through Hungary, the East German regime bowed to mounting pressure and opened the Berlin Wall on November 9. By the end of 1989, there were new democratic or non-Communist governments in Czechoslovakia, Romania, Bulgaria, and East Germany. These largely peaceful revolutions destroyed the military and economic agreements that had harnessed the satellites to the Soviet economy (the Warsaw Pact and Comecon). The Soviet Union swallowed hard, accepted the loss of its satellites, and slowly withdrew its army from eastern Europe.

WHERE TO LEARN MORE

★ A Concrete Curtain: The Life and Death of the Berlin Wall **http:www .wall-berlin.org/gb/berlin.htm**

German Reunification and the Dissolution of the Soviet Union.   By July 1990, the United States and the Soviet Union had agreed that a reunited Germany

QUICK REVIEW

The Fall of Gorbachev and the Soviet Union

- August 1991: old-line communists attempt a coup against Gorbachev.
- Boris Yeltsin organized the successful resistance to the plotters.
- Gorbachev resigned and all fifteen Soviet republics declared their independence.

would belong to NATO. In October, the two Germanies completed their political unification, although it would be years before their mismatched economies functioned as one. Reunification was the last step in the diplomatic legacy of World War II.

The final act in the transformation of the Soviet Union began with a failed coup against Mikhail Gorbachev in August 1991. Gorbachev had scheduled a vote on a new constitution that would decrease the power of the central government. Old-line Communist bureaucrats, who feared the change, arrested Gorbachev in his vacation house and tried to take over the government apparatus in Moscow. Boris Yeltsin, president of the Russian Republic, organized the resistance to the plotters. Muscovites flocked to support Yeltsin and defied tank crews in front of the Russian parliament building. Within three days, the plotters themselves were under arrest.

The coup hastened the fragmentation of the Soviet Union. Before the month was out, the Soviet parliament banned the Communist Party. Gorbachev soon resigned. Previously suppressed nationalist feelings caused all 15 component republics of the Soviet Union to declare their independence. The superpower Union of Soviet Socialist Republics ceased to exist. Russia remained the largest and strongest of the new states, followed by Ukraine and Kazakhstan.

Analysts agree that the relentless pressure of American defense spending helped bankrupt and undermine the Soviet Union. It is an open question whether this defense spending also weakened the U.S. economy and America's ability to compete in the world marketplace. Some scholars see the demise of the Soviet empire as ultimate justification for forty years of Cold War. Dissenters argue the opposite—that the collapse of European Communism shows that American leaders had magnified its threat. Before we can choose among these views, we need to wait for scholars to explore Russian archives and develop a fuller history of Soviet Cold War policy to place alongside our understanding of U.S. policy (see the Overview table, "Why Did the Cold War End?").

THE PERSIAN GULF WAR

On August 2, 1990, President Saddam Hussein of Iraq seized the small neighboring oil-rich country of Kuwait. The quick conquest gave Iraq control of 20 percent of the world's oil production and reserves. President Bush demanded unconditional withdrawal, enlisted European and Arab allies in an anti-Iraq coalition, and persuaded Saudi Arabia to accept substantial U.S. forces to protect it against Iraqi invasion. Within weeks, the Saudis were host to tens of thousands of U.S. soldiers and hundreds of aircraft.

The background for Iraq's invasion was a simmering dispute over border oil fields and islands in the Persian Gulf. Iraq was a dictatorship that had just emerged from an immensely costly eight-year war with Iran. Saddam Hussein had depended on help from the United States and Arab nations in this war, but Iraq was now economically exhausted. Kuwait was a small, rich nation whose ruling dynasty enjoyed few friends but plenty of oil royalties. The U.S. State Department had signaled earlier in 1990 that it might support some concessions by Kuwait in its dispute with Iraq. Saddam Hussein read the signal as an open invitation to do what he wanted.

The Iraqis gave George Bush a golden opportunity to assert America's world influence. The Bush administration was concerned that Iraq might target oil-rich Saudi Arabia. The importance of Middle Eastern oil helped to enlist France and Britain as military allies and to secure billions of dollars from Germany and Japan.

30–3
George Bush, Address to the Nation Announcing Allied Military Action in the Persian Gulf (1991)

OVERVIEW   WHY DID THE COLD WAR END?

Commentators have offered a number of explanations for the rapid failure of the USSR and the collapse of Soviet power at the end of the 1980s. All of these factors made contributions to the complex unraveling of the Cold War.

Economic exhaustion:	The United States in the late 1970s embarked on a great modernization and expansion of its military forces. The USSR exhausted its economy and revealed its technical backwardness by trying to keep pace. Gorbachev's policy of *perestroika* was an attempt to reduce the bureaucratic inertia of the economy.
Failure of leadership:	The Soviet Union in the 1970s and early 1980s was governed by unimaginative bureaucrats. A closed elite that thought only of preserving their privileges and authority could not adapt to a changing world. The policy of *glasnost* was an effort to encourage new ideas.
Intervention in Afghanistan:	The disastrous intervention in Afghanistan revealed the limits of Soviet military power. It alienated the large Muslim population of the USSR and brought disillusionment with the incompetence of Soviet leaders.
Triumph of democratic ideas:	As political discussion became more free, the appeal of democratic ideas took on its own momentum, especially in eastern European satellite nations such as East Germany, Czechoslovakia, and Poland.
Power of nationalism:	The collapse of the Soviet empire was triggered by the resurgence of national sentiments throughout the Soviet empire. National sentiments fueled the breakaway of the eastern European satellite nations such as Hungary, Romania, and Poland. Nationalism also broke up the USSR itself as 14 smaller socialist republics declared independence of the Russian-dominated Union.

The collapse of Soviet power and Gorbachev's interest in cooperating with the United States meant that the Soviets would not interfere with U.S. plans.

Bush and his advisers offered a series of justifications for American actions. First, and most basic, were the desire to punish armed aggression and the presumed need to protect Iraq's other neighbors. In fact, there was scant evidence of Iraqi preparations against Saudi Arabia. The buildup of American air power plus effective economic sanctions would have accomplished both protection and punishment. Sanctions and diplomatic pressure might also have brought withdrawal from most or all of Kuwait. However, additional American objectives—to destroy Iraq's capacity to create nuclear weapons and to topple Saddam's regime—would require direct military action.

Bush probably decided on war in October, eventually increasing the number of American troops in Saudi Arabia to 580,000. The United States stepped up diplomatic pressure by securing a series of increasingly tough United Nations resolutions that culminated in November 1990 with Security Council Resolution 678, authorizing "all necessary means" to liberate Kuwait. The president convinced Congress to agree to military action under the umbrella of the UN. The United States ignored compromise plans floated by France and last-minute concessions from Iraq.

War began one day after the UN's January 15 deadline for Iraqi withdrawal from Kuwait. **Operation Desert Storm** opened with massive air attacks on command centers, transportation facilities, and Iraqi forward positions. The air war

W **WHERE TO LEARN MORE**

The Gulf War. **http://www.pbs.org/ wgbh/pages/frontline/gulf/**

Operation Desert Storm   Code name for the successful offensive against Iraq by the United States and its allies in the Persian Gulf War (1991).

MAP EXPLORATION

To explore an interactive version of this map, go to
http://www.prenhall.com/goldfield3/map30.2

MAP 30–2 The Persian Gulf War Ground operations against Iraq in the Persian Gulf War followed six weeks of aerial bombardment. The ground attack, which met quick success, was a multinational effort by the United States, Britain, France, Saudi Arabia, and other Arab nations threatened by an aggressive Iraq. The war freed Kuwait from Iraqi occupation but stopped before forcing a change in Iraq's government.

WHY DID So many people, including many in the military, believe that the Persian Gulf War would be a protracted conflict with high casualties on the U.S. side?

HOW DID growth in the Sunbelt shape national politics in the 1980s and 1990s?

Sunbelt The states of the American South and Southwest.

destroyed 40 to 50 percent of Iraqi tanks and artillery by late February. The attacks also seriously hurt Iraqi civilians by disrupting utilities and food supplies.

The 40-day rain of bombs was the prelude to a ground attack. (see Map 30–2). On February 24, 1991, U.S. and allied forces swept into Iraq in a great arc. Americans, Saudis, Syrians, and Egyptians advanced directly to liberate Kuwait. A cease-fire came 100 hours after the start of the ground war. Allied forces suffered only 240 deaths in action, compared to perhaps 100,000 for the Iraqis.

Bush directed Desert Storm with the "Vietnam syndrome" in mind, believing that Americans were willing to accept war only if it involved overwhelming U.S. force and ended quickly. The desire for a quick war, however, posed a problem. The United States hoped to replace Saddam Hussein without disrupting Iraqi society. Instead, the 100-hour war incited armed rebellions against Saddam in southern Iraq by Shi'ites, a group with in the Muslim religion whose adherents comprise a majority in Iraq, and in the north by the ethnically distinct Kurds. Because Bush and his advisers were unwilling to get embroiled in a civil war or commit the United States to occupy all of Iraq, they stood by while Saddam crushed the uprisings. In one sense, the United States won the war but not the peace. Saddam Hussein became a hero to many in the Islamic world simply by remaining in power. In another sense, Bush had accomplished exactly what he wanted: the restoration of the status quo. In 2002, however, President George W. Bush (his son, elected in 2000), made a change in the Iraqi regime a centerpiece of U.S. foreign policy.

GROWTH IN THE SUNBELT

The rise in military and defense spending from the late 1970s through the early 1990s and the Persian Gulf War was one of the most powerful sources of growth in the **Sunbelt,** the southern and western regions of the United States. Kevin Phillips's book *The Emerging Republican Majority* (1969) first popularized the term "Sunbelt." Phillips pointed out that people and economic activity had been flowing southward and westward since World War II, shifting the balance of power away from the Northeast. Sections of the South and West, historically controlled from the northeastern industrial core, have developed as independent centers of economic change.

The Sunbelt was a region of conservative voting habits where Republicans solidified their status as a majority party, a process continuing to the present. In the 1990s, the region's economic power was reflected in a conservative tone in both the Republican and Democratic parties and in the prominence of southern political leaders. (see Map 30–2).

The rise of the Sunbelt, which is anchored by Florida, Texas, and California, reflected the leading economic trends of the 1970s and 1980s, including military spending, immigration from Asia and Latin America, and recreation and retirement spending. Corporations liked the business climate of the South, which had weak labor laws, low taxes, and generally low costs of living and doing business.

New factories dotted the southern landscape, often in smaller towns rather than cities. General Motors closed factories in Flint, Michigan, but invested in a new Saturn plant in Spring Hill, Tennessee. In contrast to troubled industrial cities in the Northeast and Midwest, cities like Orlando, Charlotte, Atlanta, Dallas, and Phoenix enjoyed headlong prosperity.

George P. Bush, son of Jeb Bush and his Mexican-American wife Columba, and nephew of President George W. Bush, marches in New York's Puerto Rican Day Parade in June 2002. Both George W. Bush in Texas and Jeb Bush in Florida were more successful than many Republicans in winning the approval of Hispanic voters. George P. Bush appeared in television ads during the 2000 campaign saying, "I am a young Latino and very proud of my bloodline."

AP Wide World Photos

THE DEFENSE ECONOMY

The Vietnam buildup and reinvestment in the military during the Carter (1977–1981) and Reagan (1981–1989) administrations fueled the growth of the Sunbelt. Military bases and defense contractors remolded the economic landscape, as mild winters and clear skies for training and operations helped the South and West attract more than 75 percent of military payrolls.

Big cities and small depended on defense spending. Southern California thrived on more than 500,000 jobs in the aircraft industry. A thousand miles away, visitors to Colorado Springs could drive past sprawling Fort Carson and visit the new Air Force Academy, opened in 1958. Sunk deep from view was the North American Air Defense Command headquarters beneath Cheyenne Mountain west of the city. Malmstrom Air Force Base transformed Great Falls, Montana, from a manufacturing and transportation center into a coordinating center for Minuteman missiles targeted at Moscow and Beijing.

Defense spending underwrote the expansion of American science and technology. Nearly one-third of all engineers worked on military projects. Large universities, such as MIT, the University of Michigan, the California Institute of Technology, and Stanford, were leading defense contractors. The modern electronics business started in New York, Boston, and the San Francisco Bay area with research and development for military uses, such as guided-missile controls. California's Silicon Valley grew with military sales long before it turned to consumer markets.

AMERICANS FROM AROUND THE WORLD

Few Americans anticipated the effects of the **Immigration and Nationality Act of 1965,** which transformed the ethnic mix of the United States and helped to stimulate the Sunbelt boom. The new law initiated a change in the composition of the American people by abolishing the national quota system in effect since 1924. Quotas had favored immigrants from western Europe and limited those from other parts of the world. The new law gave preference to family reunification and welcomed immigrants from all nations equally.

Immigration reform opened the doors to Mediterranean Europe, Latin America, and Asia. Legal migration to the United States surged from 1.1 million in 1960–1964 to nearly 4 million for 1990–1994. Nonlegal immigrants may have

Immigration and Nationality Act of 1965 Federal legislation that replaced the national quota system for immigration with new limits for each hemisphere.

doubled the total number of newcomers in the 1970s and early 1980s. Not since World War I had the United States absorbed so many new residents.

Immigration changed the nation's ethnic mix. Members of officially defined ethnic and racial minorities accounted for 25 percent of Americans in 1990 and 30 percent in 2000 (see Table 30–1). Roughly 28 million Americans had been born in other countries according to the 2000 census, or 10.4 percent of the population. This was lower than the high of 14.7 percent in 1910 but a great increase from the low of 4.7 percent in 1970. One-third of the foreign born were from Latin America and one-fourth were from Asia.

The largest single group of new Americans came from Mexico. The long border has facilitated easy movement from south to north. Mexican Americans were the largest minority group in many southwestern and western states in the later twentieth century. They were transforming neighborhoods in Chicago and other midwestern cities and changing everything from politics to the Catholic Church.

The East Coast has especially welcomed migrants from the West Indies and Central America. Many Puerto Ricans, who hold U.S. citizenship, came to Philadelphia and New York in the 1950s and 1960s. Other countries sending large numbers of immigrants include Haiti, the Dominican Republic, Guatemala, Honduras, Nicaragua, El Salvador, and Jamaica. Cuban refugees from Castro's regime concentrated in Miami and in major cities such as Chicago and New York. Another great immigration has occurred eastward across the Pacific. Chinese, Filipinos, Koreans, Samoans, and other Asians and Pacific Islanders constituted only 6 percent of newcomers to the United States in 1965 but nearly half of all arrivals in 1990. The number of ethnic Chinese in the United States jumped from a quarter of a million in 1965 to 1,645,000 in 1990. Immigrants from Taiwan, Hong Kong, and the People's Republic created new Chinatowns in Houston and San Diego and crowded into the historic Chinatowns of New York and San Francisco.

The most publicized Asian immigrants were refugees from Indochina after the Communist victory in 1975. The first arrivals tended to be highly educated professionals who had worked with the Americans. Another 750,000 Vietnamese, Laotians, and Cambodians arrived after 1976 by way of refugee camps in Thailand, as did Celia Noup. Most settled on the West Coast. The San Francisco Bay area, for example, had more than a dozen Vietnamese-language newspapers, magazines, and cable television programs.

In addition to southeast Asians, political conflicts and upheavals sent other waves of immigrants to the United States. Many Iranians fled the religious regime

Table 30–1 Major Racial and Ethnic Minorities in the United States

	1960 Population (in millions)	Percentage of total	2000 Population (in millions)	Percentage of total
American Indians	0.5	0.3	2.5	0.9
Asians and Pacific Islanders	1.1	0.6	10.6	3.7
African Americans	18.9	10.5	34.7	12.3
Hispanics	not available		35.3	12.5

that took power in their country in the late 1970s, at the same time that Ethiopians were fleeing a nation shattered by drought, civil war, and doctrinaire Marxism. To escape repression in the Soviet Union, Jews and conservative Christians came to the United States in the 1980s, and the collapse of Communism in the Soviet Union opened the door for Russians, Ukrainians, Romanians, and other eastern Europeans in the 1990s to emigrate to the United States.

Recent immigrants have found both economic possibilities and problems. On the negative side, legal and illegal immigration has added to the number of nonunion workers. But a positive contrast was the abundance of opportunities for talent and ambition in the expanding economy of the mid-1980s and 1990s. The 130,000 Vietnamese immigrants of 1975 now have an average adjusted income above the national average. Asians and Pacific islanders by 2000 constituted 22 percent of the students in California's public universities. Like earlier European immigrants, many newcomers have opened groceries, restaurants, and other businesses that serve their own group before expanding into larger markets.

OLD GATEWAYS AND NEW

The new immigration from Asia, Latin America, and the Caribbean had its most striking effects in coastal and border cities. New York again became a great mixing bowl of the American population. By 1990, some 28 percent of the population of New York City was foreign-born, compared to 42 percent at the height of European immigration in 1910.

Just as important was the transformation of southern and western cities into gateways for immigrants from Latin America and Asia. Los Angeles emerged as "the new Ellis Island" that rivaled New York's historic role in receiving immigrants. In 1960, a mere 1 percent of the Los Angeles County population was Asian and 11 percent was Hispanic. By 2000, the figures for the area's population of 9.5 million were 12 percent Asian and 45 percent Hispanic. The sprawling neighborhoods of East Los Angeles make up the second-largest Mexican city in the world. One hundred languages are spoken among students entering Los Angeles schools.

New York and Los Angeles are world cities as well as immigrant destinations. Like London and Tokyo, they are capitals of world trade and finance, with international banks and headquarters of multinational corporations. They have the country's greatest concentrations of international lawyers, accounting firms, and business consultants. The deregulation of international finance and the explosive spread of instant electronic communication in the 1980s confirmed their importance as global decision centers.

Similar factors have turned Miami into the economic capital of the Caribbean. A quarter-million Cuban businessmen, white-collar workers, and their families moved to the United States between 1959 and 1962 to escape Castro's new socialist government. New "freedom flights" carried 150,000 additional Cubans to the United States from 1966 to 1973, and a third round added 125,000 in 1980. Most of the newcomers stayed in South Florida. Their success in business made Miami a major Latino market and helped to attract 2 million Latin American tourists and shoppers to its stores and hotels during the 1980s. Access to the Caribbean and South America also made Miami an international banking and commercial center with hundreds of offices for corporations engaged in U.S.–Latin American trade.

Cross-border communities in the Southwest, such as El Paso, Texas, and Juarez, Mexico, or San Diego, California, and Tijuana, Mexico, are "Siamese twins joined at the cash register." Both nations have promoted the cross-border economy.

The Mexican government in the mid-1960s began to encourage a "platform economy" by allowing companies on the Mexican side of the border to import components and inputs duty-free as long as 80 percent of the items were reexported and 90 percent of the workers were Mexicans. The intent was to encourage American corporations to locate assembly plants south of the border. Such *maquila* industries were able to employ lower-wage workers and avoid strict antipollution laws (leading to serious threats to public health on both sides of the border). From the Gulf of Mexico to the Pacific Ocean, 1,800 *maquiladora* plants employed half a million workers. North of the border, U.S. factories supplied components under laws that meshed with the Mexican regulations.

THE GRAYING OF AMERICA

Between 1965 and 2000, the number of Americans aged 65 and over jumped from 18.2 million to 35 million, or 12.4 percent of the population. For the first time, most Americans could expect to survive into old age. The "young old" are people in their sixties and seventies who remain sharp, vigorous, and financially secure because of private pensions, Social Security, and Medicare. The "old old" are the 9 million people in their eighties and nineties who often require daily assistance, although data show that improved medical services have made such Americans healthier and more self-sufficient than they were ten or twenty years ago.

Older Americans have become a powerful voice in public affairs. They tend to vote against local taxes but fight efforts to slow the growth of Social Security. By the 1990s, observers noted increasing resentment among younger Americans, who fear that public policy is biased against the needs of those in their productive years. In turn, the elderly fiercely defend the programs of the 1960s and 1970s that have kept many of them from poverty. Protecting Medicare and Social Security was one of the Democrats' best campaign issues in 1996 and 2000, after Republicans suggested cuts in spending growth.

Retired Americans changed the social geography of the United States. Much growth in the South and Southwest has been financed by money earned in the Northeast and Midwest and transferred by retirees. Florida in the 1980s absorbed nearly 1 million new residents aged 60 or older. California, Arizona, Texas, the Carolinas, and the Ozark Mountains of Missouri and Arkansas have all attracted retirees.

VALUES IN COLLISION

In 1988, two very different religious leaders sought a presidential nomination. Pat Robertson's campaign for the Republican nomination tapped deep discontent with the changes in American society since the 1960s. A television evangelist, Robertson used the mailing list from his *700 Club* program to mobilize conservative Christians and push the Republican Party further to the right on family and social issues. Jesse Jackson, a civil rights leader and minister from Chicago, mounted a grassroots campaign with the opposite goal of moving the Democratic Party to the left on social and economic policy. Drawing on his experience in the black civil rights movement, he assembled a "Rainbow Coalition" that included labor unionists, feminists, and others whom Robertson's followers feared. Both Jackson and Robertson used their powerful personalities and religious convictions to inspire support from local churches and churchgoers.

QUICK REVIEW

Older Americans

- 2000: 35 million Americans were aged 65 or older.
- Older Americans were a powerful political force.
- Retired Americans changed the social geography of the United States.

WHAT KEY social and cultural issues divided Americans in the 1980s and 1990s?

In diagnosing social ills, Robertson pointed to the problems of individual indulgence, while Jackson pointed to racism and economic inequality. Their sharp divergence expressed differences in basic values that divided Americans in the 1980s and beyond. In substantial measure, the conflicts were rooted in the social and cultural changes of the 1960s and 1970s. Changes in roles and expectations among women and new openness about gay and lesbian sexuality were particularly powerful in dividing American churches and politics.

WOMEN'S RIGHTS AND PUBLIC POLICY

The women's liberation movement of the 1960s achieved important gains when Congress wrote many of its goals into law in the early 1970s. Title IX of the Educational Amendments (1972) to the Civil Rights Act prohibited discrimination by sex in any educational program receiving federal aid. The legislation expanded athletic opportunities for women and slowly equalized the balance of women and men in faculty positions. In the same year, Congress sent the Equal Rights Amendment (ERA) to the states for ratification. The amendment read, "Equal rights under the law shall not be denied or abridged by the United States or by any state on account of sex." More than 20 states ratified in the first few months. As conservatives who wanted to preserve traditional family patterns rallied strong opposition, however, the next dozen states ratified only after increasingly tough battles in state legislatures. The ERA then stalled, three states short, until the time limit for ratification expired in 1982.

Abortion Rights and the Conservative Reaction.   In January 1973, the U.S. Supreme Court expanded the debate about women's rights with the case of *Roe v. Wade.* Voting 7 to 2, the Court struck down state laws forbidding abortion in the first three months of pregnancy and set guidelines for abortion during the remaining months. Drawing on the earlier decision of *Griswold v. Connecticut,* which dealt with birth control, the Court held that the Fourteenth Amendment includes a right to privacy that blocks states from interfering with a woman's right to terminate a pregnancy. The Supreme Court later upheld congressional limitations on the use of federal funds for abortion in *Webster v. Reproductive Health Services* (1989) and allowed some state restrictions in *Planned Parenthood v. Casey* (1992). Nevertheless, the *Roe* decision remained in place.

These changes came in the context of increasingly sharp conflict over the feminist agenda. Both the ERA and *Roe* stirred impassioned support and equally passionate opposition. Behind the rhetoric were male fears of increased job competition during a time of economic contraction and concern about changing families. Also fueling the debate was a deep split between the mainstream feminist view of women as fully equal individuals and the contrary conservative belief that women had a special role as anchors of families. The debate about abortion drew on the same issue of women's relationship to families but added strong religious voices, particularly the formal opposition of the Roman Catholic Church to abortion. The arguments tapped such deep emotion that the two sides could not even agree on a common language, juxtaposing a right to life against rights to privacy and freedom of choice.

Women in the Workforce.   The most sweeping change in the lives of American women did not come from federal legislation or court cases, but from the growing

Roe v. Wade   U.S. Supreme Court decision (1973) that disallowed state laws prohibiting abortion during the first three months (trimester) of pregnancy and established guidelines for abortion in the second and third trimesters.

likelihood that a woman would work outside the home. In 1960, some 32 percent of married women were in the labor force; 40 years later, 61 percent were working or looking for work (along with 69 percent of single women). Federal and state governments slowly responded to the changing demands of work and family with new policies, such as a federal child care tax credit.

More women entered the workforce as inflation in the 1970s and declining wages in the 1980s eroded the ability of families to live comfortable lives on one income. Between 1979 and 1986, fully 80 percent of married households saw the husband's income fall in constant dollars.

A second reason for the increase in working women from 29 million in 1970 to 66 million in 2000 was the broad shift from manufacturing to service jobs, reducing demand for factory workers and manual laborers and increasing the need for such "women's jobs" as data-entry clerks, reservation agents, and nurses. Indeed, the American economy still divides job categories by sex. There was some movement toward gender-neutral hiring in the 1970s because of legal changes and the pressures of the women's movement. Women's share of lawyers more than quadrupled, of economists more than tripled, and of police detectives more than doubled. Nevertheless, job types were more segregated by sex than by race in the 1990s.

AIDS AND GAY ACTIVISM

After the increasing openness about sexual orientation in the 1970s, the character of life in gay communities took an abrupt turn in the 1980s when a new worldwide epidemic emerged. Scientists identified a new disease pattern, **acquired immune deficiency syndrome (AIDS),** in 1981. The name described the symptoms resulting from infection by the human immunodeficiency virus (HIV), which destroys the body's ability to resist disease. HIV is transferred through blood and semen. In the 1980s, the most frequent American victims were gay men and intravenous drug users.

A decade later, it was clear that HIV/AIDS was a national and even global problem. By the end of 2003, AIDS had been responsible for 500,000 deaths in the United States, and transmission to heterosexual women was increasing. The U.S. Centers for Disease Control and Prevention estimated roughly 40,000 new cases of HIV infection per year at the beginning of the twenty-first century, bringing the total of infected Americans to around 900,000. Once a problem of big cities, HIV infection had spread to every American community. Meanwhile, the toll of AIDS deaths in other parts of the world, particularly eastern Africa, dwarfed that in the United States and made it a world health crisis.

By the 1990s, Americans were accustomed to open discussion of gay sexuality, if not always accepting of its reality. On the issue of gays in the military, however, Congress and the Pentagon were more cautious, accepting a policy that made engaging in homosexual acts, though not sexual orientation itself, grounds for discharge.

CHURCHES IN CHANGE

Between 1980 and 1984, efforts to develop the oil-shale resources of western Colorado pushed the population of Grand Junction from 60,000 to 80,000. Newcomers to Grand Junction, a fast-changing city within a rapidly evolving society, searched for family stability and a sense of community by joining established congregations and organizing new churches. The telephone book in 1985 listed 28

Acquired Immune Deficiency Syndrome (AIDS) A complex of deadly pathologies resulting from infection with the human immunodeficiency virus (HIV).

mainline Protestant and Catholic churches, 24 Baptist churches, five more liberal churches (e.g., Unitarian), and more than 50 Pentecostal, Bible, and Evangelical churches. Nearly a dozen Christian schools supplemented the public schools.

Grand Junction's religious bent is typical of the contemporary United States, where religion is prominent in daily lives, institutions, and public policy debates. Americans take their search for spiritual grounding much more seriously than do citizens of other industrial nations. Roughly half of privately organized social activity (such as charity work) is church related. In the mid-1970s, 56 percent of Americans said that religion was "very important" to them, compared to only 27 percent of Europeans. Moreover, religious belief is an important source of political convictions and basis for political action (see American Views: "The Religious Imperative in Politics").

As the Grand Junction statistics also suggest, the mainline Protestant denominations that traditionally defined the center of American belief were struggling after 1970. The United Methodist Church, the Presbyterian Church U.S.A., the United Church of Christ, and the Episcopal Church battled internally over the morality of U.S. foreign policy, the role of women in the ministry, and the reception of gay and lesbian members. They were strengthened by an ecumenical impulse that united denominational branches divided by ethnicity or regionalism. However, they gradually lost their position among American churches, perhaps because ecumenism diluted the certainty of their message.

By contrast, evangelical Protestant churches have benefitted from the direct appeal of their message and from strong roots in the booming Sunbelt. Members of evangelical churches (25 percent of white Americans) now outnumber the members of mainline Protestant churches (20 percent).

Evangelical churches emphasized religion as an individual experience focused on personal salvation. Unlike many of the secular and psychological avenues to fulfillment, however, they also offered communities of faith that might stabilize fragmented lives. The conservative nature of their theology and social teaching in a changing society offered certainty that was especially attractive to many younger families.

Another important change in national religious life has been the continuing Americanization of the Roman Catholic Church following the Second Vatican Council in 1965, in which church leaders sought to respond to postwar industrial society. Even as the tight connection between Catholicism and membership in European immigrant communities gradually faded, Asian and Latino immigrants brought new vigor to many parishes, and many inner-city churches have been centers for social action. Traditional and nontraditional Catholics disagree about whether priests should be allowed to marry and other adaptations to American culture.

The new globalization of American society simultaneously increased the nation's religious diversity and confirmed the dominant position of Christianity.

The AIDS Quilt, displayed in Washington in October 1992, combined individual memorials to AIDS victims into a powerful communal statement. The quilt project reminded Americans that AIDS had penetrated every American community.

Black Star

AMERICAN VIEWS

THE RELIGIOUS IMPERATIVE IN POLITICS

*T*he strong religious faith of many Americans frequently drives them to different stands on political issues. The first of these two documents, a letter by Jerry Falwell to potential supporters of the Moral Majority, reflects the politically conservative outlook of many evangelical Christians. Falwell is pastor of the Thomas Road Baptist Church in Lynchburg, Virginia. He founded the Moral Majority, a conservative religious lobbying and educational organization, in 1979 and served as its president until 1987, the year he wrote the letter reprinted here. The second document, from an open letter issued by the Southside United Presbyterian Church in Tucson in 1982, expresses the conviction of other believers that God may sometimes require civil disobedience to oppose oppressive government actions. The letter explains the church's reasons for violating immigration law to offer sanctuary to refugees from repressive Central American regimes supported by the United States.

- How do Falwell and the Southside Presbyterian Church define the problems that demand a religious response?
- Are there any points of agreement?
- How does each statement balance the claims of God and government?

FROM THE REVEREND JERRY FALWELL

I believe that the overwhelming majority of Americans are sick and tired of the way that amoral liberals are trying to corrupt our nation from its commitment to freedom, democracy, traditional morality, and the free enterprise system.

And I believe that the majority of Americans agree on the basic moral values which this nation was founded upon over 200 years ago.

Today we face four burning crises as we continue in this Decade of Destiny—the 1980s—loss of our freedom by giving in to the Communists; the destruction of the family unit; the deterioration of the free enterprise system; and the crumbling of basic moral principles which has resulted in the legalizing of abortion, wide-spread pornography, and a drug problem of epidemic proportions.

That is why I went to Washington, D.C., in June of 1979, and started a new organization The Moral Majority.

Right now you may be wondering: "But I thought Jerry Falwell was the preacher on the Old-Time Gospel Hour television program?"

Many immigrants from Asia and Africa have come with their native religious beliefs. There are now hundreds of Hindu temples and thousands of Buddhist centers. More than a million Muslims now worship in mosques that are found in every major city. In total, the proportion of Americans who identify themselves with non-Christian religions grew from 3 percent in 1990 to 4 percent in 2001. Over the same period, however, the proportion identifying with a Christian group or denomination grew from 86 to 87 percent.

CULTURE WARS

In the 1950s and 1960s, Americans argued most often over foreign policy, racial justice, and the economy. Since the 1980s, they have also quarreled over beliefs and values, especially as the patterns of family life have become more varied. In the course of these quarrels, religious belief has heavily influenced politics as individuals and groups try to shape America around their own, and often mutually conflicting, ideas of the godly society. Americans who are undogmatic in religion are often liberal in politics as well. Religious and political conservatism also tend to go together.

You are right. For over twenty-four years I have been calling the nation back to God from the pulpit on radio and television.

But in recent months I have been led to do more than just preach. I have been compelled to take action.

I have made the commitment to go right into the halls of Congress and fight for laws that will save America. . . .

I will still be preaching every Sunday on the Old-Time Gospel Hour and I still must be a husband and father to my precious family in Lynchburg, Virginia.

But as God gives me the strength, I must do more. I must go into the halls of Congress and fight for laws that will protect the grand old flag . . . for the sake of our children and grandchildren.

FROM SOUTHSIDE UNITED PRESBYTERIAN CHURCH

We are writing to inform you that Southside Presbyterian Church will publicly violate the Immigration and Nationality Act, Section 274 (A). . . .

We take this action because we believe the current policy and practice of the United States Government with regard to Central American refugees is illegal and immoral. We believe our government is in violation of the 1980 Refugee Act and international law by continuing to arrest, detain, and forcibly return refugees to the terror, persecution, and murder in El Salvador and Guatemala.

We believe that justice and mercy require the people of conscience actively assert our God-given right to aid anyone fleeing from persecution and murder. . . .

We beg of you, in the name of God, to do justice and love mercy in the administration of your office. We ask that "extended voluntary departure" be granted to refugees from Central America and that current deportation proceedings against these victims be stopped.

Until such time, we will not cease to extend the sanctuary of the church. . . . Obedience to God requires this of us all.

Sources: Gary E. McCuen, ed., *The Religious Right* (Hudson, WI, G. E. McCuen, 1989); Ann Crittenden, *Sanctuary* (New York Weidenfeld & Nicolson, 1988).

The division on social issues is related to theological differences within Protestantism. The "conservative" emphasis on personal salvation and the literal truth of the Bible expresses itself in a desire to restore "traditional" social patterns. Conservatives worry that social disorder occurs when people follow personal impulses and pleasures. In contrast, the "liberal" or "modern" emphasis on the universality of the Christian message restates the Social Gospel with its call to build the Kingdom of God through social justice and may recognize divergent pathways toward truth. Liberals worry that greed in the unregulated marketplace creates disorder and injustice.

Conservatives have initiated the culture wars, trying to stabilize what they fear is an American society spinning out of control because of sexual indulgence. In fact, the evidence on the sexual revolution is mixed. Growing numbers of teenagers reported being sexually active in the 1970s, but the rate of increase tapered off in the 1980s. The divorce rate began to drop after 1980. Births to teenagers dropped after 1990, and the number of two-parent families increased. Most adults remained monogamous, according to data from 1994.

In December 1993, the U.S. Supreme Court heard arguments on whether states could require protesters to remain a certain distance from abortion clinics. These antiabortion and proabortion protesters revealed the deep divisions over this and other issues in the culture wars.

AP/Wide World Photos

The explosion of explicit attention to sexual behavior set the stage for religiously rooted battles over two sets of issues. One cluster revolves around so-called family values, questioning the morality of access to abortion, the acceptability of homosexuality, and the roles and rights of women. A second set of concerns has focused on the supposed role of public schools in undermining morality through sex education, unrestricted reading matter, non-biblical science, and the absence of prayer.

Not all issues of the culture wars carry the same weight. Censorship of art exhibits and library collections has mostly been an issue for political grandstanding. Efforts to restrict legal access to abortion mobilized thousands of right to life advocates in the late 1980s and early 1990s, but illegal acts remained the work of a radical fringe.

A culturally conservative issue with great popular appeal in the early 1990s was an effort to prevent states and localities from protecting homosexuals against discrimination. Under the slogan "No special rights," antigay measures passed in Cincinnati, Colorado, and communities in Oregon in 1993 and 1994, only to have the Supreme Court overturn the Colorado law in *Romer v. Evans* (1996). It is important to note that public support for lesbian and gay civil rights varies with different issues (strong support for equal employment opportunity, much less for granting marriage rights to same-sex couples) and whether the issues are framed in terms of specified rights for gays or in terms of the right of everyone, including gays, to be free from government interference with personal decisions, such as living arrangements and sexual choices.

CONCLUSION

*A*mericans entered the 1980s searching for stability. The 1970s had brought unexpected and uncomfortable change. Ronald Reagan's presidential campaign played to these insecurities by promising to revitalize the older ways of life and restore the United States to its former influence.

Taken as a whole, the years from 1981 through 1992 brought transformations that redirected the course of American life. Because many changes were associated with national policy choices, it is fair to call this the era of the Reagan revolution. The astonishing collapse of the Soviet Union ended 40 years of Cold War. New political leadership in Washington reversed the 50-year expansion of federal government programs to deal with economic and social inequities. Prosperity alternated with recessions that shifted the balance between regions. Economic inequality increased after narrowing for a generation at the same time that more and more leaders proclaimed that unregulated markets could best meet social needs. Middle-class Latinos and African Americans made substantial gains, while many other minority Americans sank deeper into poverty.

At the same time, it is important to recognize that every revolution has its precursors. Intellectuals have been clarifying the justifications for Reagan administration actions since the 1960s. The Reagan-Bush years extended changes that began in the 1970s, particularly the conservative economic policies and military buildup of the troubled Carter administration. Intervention in the Persian Gulf amplified American policies that had been in place since the CIA intervened in Iran in 1953. The outbreak of violence in Los Angeles after the Rodney King verdict showed that race relations were as tense as they had been in the 1960s.

In 1992, the United States stood as the undisputed world power. Its economy was poised for a surge of growth at the same time that rivals such as Japan were mired in economic crisis. It was the leader in scientific research and the development of new technologies. Its military capacities far surpassed those of any rival and seemed to offer a free hand in shaping the world—capacities that would be tested and utilized in the new century.

SUMMARY

Reagan's Domestic Revolution Political change began in 1980, when Ronald Reagan and his running mate George H. W. Bush, rode American discontent to a decisive victory in the presidential election. Building on a neoconservative critique of American public policies and issues from the Carter administration, Reagan presided over revolutionary changes in American government and policies. The consequences of his two terms included an altered role for government, powerful but selected economic growth, and a shift of domestic policy toward lifestyle concerns. Reaganomics and a new prosperity contrasted with corporate "downsizing" and an increase in the poverty rate.

The Second (Short) Cold War Reagan regarded the Soviet Union as an "evil empire." By the end of 1991 the Soviet Union was gone, Communist regimes had ended in Eastern Europe, and the Berlin Wall had come down. Reagan's foreign policy was marked by the invasion of Granada, assistance to Nicaraguan Contras, and the revelation of the Iran-Contra affair. In 1991, President George H. W. Bush intervened in the Persian Gulf in response to Iraq's invasion of Kuwait; the war fascinated millions who watched it live on television; America won the war but not the peace.

Growth in the Sunbelt The emergence of the Sunbelt as a center of population and source of conservative voting strength, the immigration "boom," the demographic and ethnic changes in American cities, and the graying of America are all characteristics of America since 1981. Much of the Sunbelt growth has come from retired Americans and new job seekers. Older Americans have now become a powerful voice in public affairs. Immigration has significantly changed the American ethnic mix; while the largest single group of immigrants is Hispanic, immigrants from Asia, Russia, Eastern Europe, and the Middle East are reflected in the 10.4 percent of the population that is foreign-born.

Values in Collision In the 1950s and 1960s Americans argued most often about foreign policy, racial injustice, and the economy. Since that time, they have also quarreled over beliefs and values, especially as patterns in family life have become more varied. In substantial measure these conflicts were rooted in the social and cultural changes of the 1960s and 1970s that had altered traditional institutions.

IMAGE KEY
for pages 878–879

a. A piece of the fallen Berlin Wall.
b. President Ronald Reagan and First Lady Nancy Reagan dance at his first inaugural at the Smithsonian on January 21, 1981.
c. Nesting dolls of Communist and/or Russian leaders Boris Yeltsin, Mikhail Gorbechev, Leonid Brezhnev, Nikita Khruschev, Joseph Stalin, Vladimir Lenin, and Czar Nicholas II.
d. The black flying wing design of the stealth bomber resembles a bat.
e. Abortion rights advocate Inga Coulter stands next to pro life protester Elizabeth McGee during clashing demonstrations outside the Supreme Court building.
f. Affluent family pedals by a group of homeless people.
g. AIDS quilt displayed in Washington.
h. Mikhail Gorbachev and Ronald Reagan sign INF treaty at the White House.
i. Hispanic female student raises her hand in class.
j. Traders on the floor of the new York Stock Exchange work frantically as panic selling swept Wall Street, Monday, October 19, 1987. The Dow Jones Industrial average plunged more than 500 points for the biggest one-day loss in history.

Changes in roles and expectations among women and new openness about gay and lesbian sexuality were particularly powerful in dividing American churches and politics. Abortion rights and the conservative backlash, the increase of women in the work force, and the new "culture wars" were part of modern America.

REVIEW QUESTIONS

1. Is it accurate to talk about a Reagan Revolution in American politics? Did Reagan's presidency change the economic environment for workers and business corporations? How did economic changes in the 1980s affect the prospects of the richest and poorest Americans?

2. How did American ideas about the proper role of government change during the 1980s? What were the basis of these changes?

3. What caused the breakup of the Soviet Union and the end of the Cold War? Did U.S. foreign policy under Reagan and Bush contribute significantly to the withdrawal of Soviet power from eastern Europe? Did the collapse of the USSR show the strength of the United States and its allies or the weakness of Soviet Communism?

4. How did the United States use military force during the Reagan and Bush administrations? Did military actions achieve the expected goals?

5. What were some of the important economic trends that shifted American growth toward the Sunbelt (South and West)? How has immigration from other nations affected the different American regions?

6. What changes in family roles and sexual behavior became divisive political issues? How have churches responded to cultural changes? What are some of the ways in which churches and religious leaders have tried to influence political decisions?

7. How did U.S. military involvement in southeast Asia in the 1960s continue to affect American society for decades to come?

KEY TERMS

Acquired immune deficiency syndrome (AIDS) (p. 904)

Americans with Disabilities Act (p. 890)

Deregulation (p. 885)

Economic Recovery and Tax Act of 1981 (ERTA) (p. 885)

Glasnost (p. 893)

Immigration and Nationality Act of 1965 (p. 899)

Intermediate Nuclear Force Agreement (p. 894)

Operation Desert Storm (p. 897)

Perestroika (p. 893)

Reagan Doctrine (p. 892)

Roe v. Wade (p. 903)

Sagebrush Rebellion (p. 885)

Strategic Defense Initiative (SDI) (p. 892)

Sunbelt (p. 898)

WHERE TO LEARN MORE

Ronald Reagan Boyhood Home, Dixon, Illinois. The home where Reagan lived from 1920 to 1923 tells relatively little about Reagan himself but a great deal about the small-town context that shaped his ideas.

The Causes of Homelessness in America. Social and political policies since the 1980s that have contributed to the gap between rich and poor and the rise of homelessness. **http://www. stanford.edu/class/e297c/poverty_prejudice/soc_sec/ hcauses.htm**

The Intermediate Nuclear Force Agreement (INF). The full-text document of the INF agreement between the United States and the Soviet Union, the first true nuclear-disarmament treaty. **http://www.state.gov/www/global/arms/treaties/ inf1.html**

The Gulf War. Read about the Persian Gulf war commanders, see testimony of American combat soldiers, and learn about the events leading up to the invasion. **http://www.pbs.org/wgbh/pages/frontline/gulf/**

A Concrete Curtain: The Life and Death of the Berlin Wall. Traces the wall from its creation in the 1960s to its destruction after the collapse of Communist East Germany. **Http:www.wall-berlin.org/gb/berlin.htm**

 U.S. History Documents CD-ROM
For primary sources related to this chapter, refer to the document CD-ROM.

 www.prenhall.com/goldfield
For study resources related to this chapter, visit the *Companion Website*™.

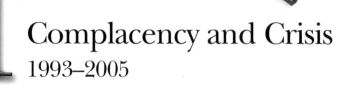

31 Complacency and Crisis
1993–2005

CHAPTER HIGHLIGHTS

Politics of the Center Bill Clinton's two terms as president underscored the importance of the political center. Clinton clashed with Republicans in Congress. Republicans pursued his impeachment over the Lewinsky scandal, but were unable to secure a conviction in the Senate.

A New Economy? By the 1990s, the service sector accounted for 70 percent of American jobs. Technological innovation helped support a decade-long economic boom. Strong economic growth led to federal budget surpluses. America's economy was increasingly tied to the global marketplace.

Broadening Democracy Between 1990 and 2000, the United States experienced the largest 10-year population rise in its history. Women and minorities gained increased prominence in national politics. Immigration policy and affirmative action programs sparked heated public debate.

Edging into a New Century
The 2000 election came down to a contested vote in Florida that was not resolved until the Supreme Court voted 5–4 to halt additional recounts. The new George W. Bush administration opted out of numerous international agreements and pursued many of the elements of Ronald Reagan's domestic agenda.

Paradoxes of Power
Despite the power of the United States, the country remained vulnerable to terrorist attack. In response to the attacks of September 11, 2001, the United States invaded Afghanistan in an effort to capture Osama bin Laden. The threat of terrorism precipitated changes in the organization of the federal government and the passage of laws that gave authorities new capacities for the conduct of criminal investigations. In March 2003 the United States invaded Iraq with the stated purpose of eliminating that country's potential to use or disseminate weapons of mass destruction. Military victory proved easier than the creation of a stable peace.

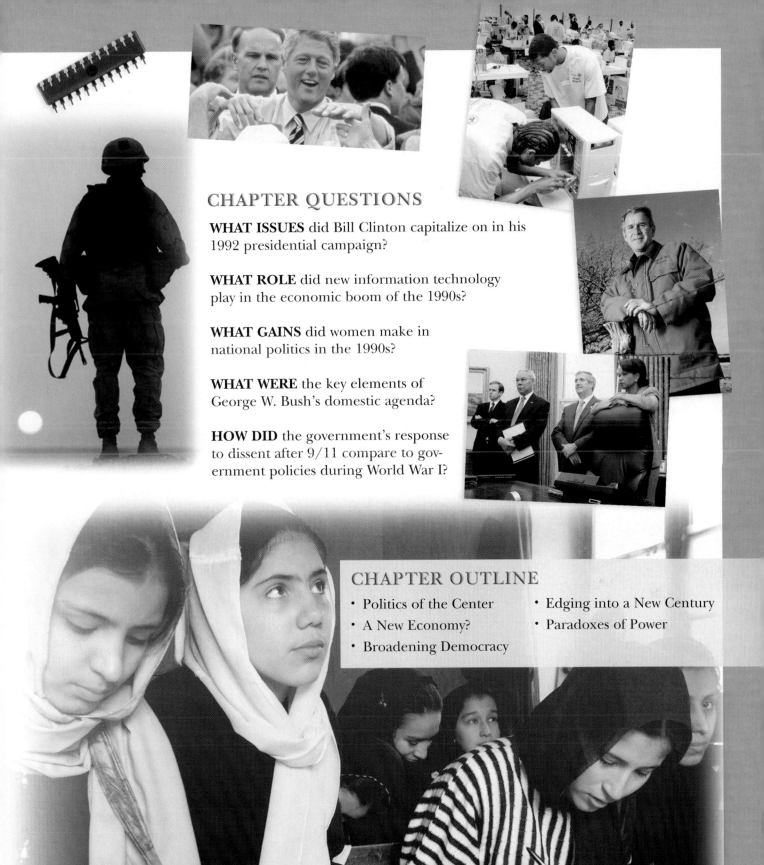

CHAPTER QUESTIONS

WHAT ISSUES did Bill Clinton capitalize on in his 1992 presidential campaign?

WHAT ROLE did new information technology play in the economic boom of the 1990s?

WHAT GAINS did women make in national politics in the 1990s?

WHAT WERE the key elements of George W. Bush's domestic agenda?

HOW DID the government's response to dissent after 9/11 compare to government policies during World War I?

CHAPTER OUTLINE

- Politics of the Center
- A New Economy?
- Broadening Democracy
- Edging into a New Century
- Paradoxes of Power

IMAGE KEY

for pages 912–913 is on page 941.

> *I'm a firefighter for the FDNY [Fire Department New York]. I had gotten off the night before. . . . My friend woke me up early that morning to borrow my car to take his sick cat to the vet. . . . I was up so I went to my local bagel store for my coffee and paper . . . when I heard a lady scream a plane had hit the Trade Center. . . . I thought since it was a beautiful day that perhaps a Cessna with the pilot having a heart attack had accidentally done this. . . . I ran home to put the TV on. . . . as soon as I saw what damage was done I knew this wasn't any Cessna. . . . my god people were jumping . . . phone rang it was a fellow from my station and he hadn't turned his TV on yet. . . . I screamed to him to turn his #*#* TV on. . . .*
>
> *When the second plane hit . . . I said goodbye and told him I was going in. . . . I jumped in my car and was off to the races. . . . the highway was closed . . . but open for us.*
>
> *. . . I had the gas pedal to the floor as I headed toward the city looking out my window I see both towers burning . . . when I hear a rumble and see the south tower #2 fall. . . . I have to get my gear so I pull off the highway going down the on ramp . . . arriving at the firehouse everyone's in shock and we know we gotta get there now to help. . . . as we're getting ready to leave the 2nd tower fell. . . . we commandeer a bus and we're off. . . .*
>
> *We arrived at a staging area and then finally got the ok to go in. . . . who's in charge? . . . Shoes, papers, and dust are everywhere. . . . we wait til [building] 7 collapses. . . . chief gets us into the site by going thru the financial center and bam there we are. . . . pieces of the outside wall sticking out of the highway. . . . cars on fire . . . buses gutted. . . . I saw numerous acts of courage that day both civilian and uniformed. . . . the looks on the faces of the people coming out of the city that day will haunt me forever . . . everyone was the same color. . . . dust white. . . . women crying. . . . men crying. . . . we must never forget the men and women that died that day. . . . their sacrifice will live on for generations to come. . . .*

John McNamara, Story #400, The September 11 Digital Archive, 13 April 2002, http://911digitalarchive.org/stories/details/400

JOHN MCNAMARA WAS one of the many off-duty New York City fire fighters who rushed to the World Trade Center after the terrorist attack on September 11, 2001. Hijacking four commercial jetliners, the terrorists crashed one plane into the Pentagon and one into each of the twin towers of the World Trade Center, 110-story buildings that housed 50,000 workers at the peak of the workday. Like John McNamara, tens of millions of Americans were jolted out of morning routines by riveting television coverage of the burning towers and watched in horror as first one tower and then the other disintegrated into itself. September 11 was an occasion for terror and courage. Passengers on the fourth plane fought the hijackers and made sure that it crashed in the Pennsylvania mountains rather than hit a fourth target. Altogether, 479 police officers, fire fighters, and other emergency workers died in the collapse of the towers. Thousands of volunteers rushed to assist rescue efforts or contribute to relief efforts. As of November 2003 the total confirmed death toll was 2,752 in New York, 184 at the Pentagon, and 40 in Pennsylvania.

The attacks, masterminded by the Al-Qaeda network of Muslim extremists, ended a decade of prosperity at home and complacency about the place of the United States in the world. In their aftermath, as Americans noticed millions of Muslim neighbors and tried to balance civil liberties against national security, they realized how diverse the nation had become. For most of the 1990s, prosperity had allowed politics to focus on social issues, such as health care and education, as well as on bitterly partisan but often superficial battles over personalities and presidential behavior. However, the terrorists attacked buildings that were symbols of the nation's economic and military power. The aftermath of the attacks deepened a business recession that had followed a decade of growth spurred by new technologies. At the same time, the vulnerability of the targets undermined Americans' sense of security and isolation from world problems, underscored the global reach of terrorism, and made understanding its sources more necessary than ever.

The Politics of the Center

*I*n Bill Clinton's race for president in 1992, the "war room" was the decision center where Clinton and his staff planned tactics and countered Republican attacks. On the wall was a sign with a simple message: "It's the economy, stupid." The short sentence was a reminder that victory lay in emphasizing everyday problems that George H. W. Bush had neglected. What mattered most were down-to-earth issues, not the distant problems of foreign policy, which seemed to have little urgency after the end of the Cold War. As voters worried about the changing economy and its social consequences, they were eager for leaders who promised practical responses. As had happened time and again, the nation's two-party system punished extremes and rewarded practical leaders who claimed the middle of the road with such issues as economic growth.

The Election of 1992: A New Generation

Every 15 to 20 years, a new group of voters and leaders comes to power, driven by the desire to fix the mess that the previous generation left behind. The conservative agenda for Ronald Reagan's and George H. W. Bush's administrations arose from the disillusion and crises of the late 1960s and 1970s, shaping leaders who believed that the answer was to turn the nation's social and economic problems over to the market while asserting America's influence and power around the world.

The mid-1990s brought another generation into the political arena. The members of "Generation X" came of voting age with deep worries about the foreclosing of opportunities. They worried that previous administrations had ignored growing economic divisions and let the competitive position of the United States deteriorate.

This generational change made 1992 one of the most volatile national elections in decades. A baby boomer and successful governor of Arkansas who was not widely known nationally, Democrat Bill Clinton, decided that George Bush was vulnerable when more senior Democrats opted to pass on the contest. Clinton made sure that the Democrats fielded a full baby boomer (and southern) ticket by choosing as his running mate the equally youthful Tennessean Albert Gore, Jr., who had served in the Senate for two terms and was widely known for his book on the environment, *Earth in the Balance.*

WHAT ISSUES did Bill Clinton capitalize on in his 1992 presidential campaign?

QUICK REVIEW

Candidates for President in 1992

- Republican George H.W. Bush seeking a second term.
- Democrat Bill Clinton: little known governor of Arkansas.
- Independent Ross Perot: Texas billionaire and political maverick.

Chronology

1969	First version of Internet (ARPAnet) launched.
1980	CNN begins broadcasting.
1991	World Wide Web launched.
1992	Bill Clinton elected president.
1993	Congress approves the North American Free Trade Agreement (NAFTA).
	Congress adopts Family Leave Act.
1994	Independent Counsel Kenneth Starr begins investigation of Bill and Hillary Clinton. Paula Jones files sexual harassment lawsuit against Bill Clinton.
	Republicans sweep to control of Congress.
	Federal government temporarily shuts down for lack of money.
1995	United States sends troops to Bosnia.
1996	Clinton wins a second term as president.
1998	Paula Jones lawsuit dismissed.
	House of Representatives impeaches Clinton.
1999	Senate acquits Clinton of impeachment charges.
	United States leads NATO intervention in Kosovo.
2000	George W. Bush defeats Al Gore in nation's closest presidential election.

2001	Congress passes massive ten-year tax reduction.
	United States refuses to agree to Kyoto Treaty to limit global warming.
	Terrorists crash airliners into World Trade Center and Pentagon.
	U.S. military operations eliminate Taliban regime in Afghanistan.
	Congress passes U.S. Patriot Act to combat domestic terror.
2002	United States and Russia agree to cut number of deployed nuclear warheads.
	Congress creates Department of Homeland Security.
	United Nations Security Council passes resolution requiring Iraq to allow open inspections of weapons systems.
2003	U.S. and British troops invade Iraq and topple government of Saddam Hussein.
	Supreme Court allows limited forms of affirmative action in university admissions.
2004	George W. Bush reelected as president.

Bush, the last politician of the World War II generation to gain the White House, won renomination by beating back the archconservative Patrick Buchanan. The Republican National Convention in Houston showed how important cultural issues had become to the Republican Party. The party platform conformed to the beliefs of the Christian right. Buchanan delivered a startling speech that called for right-thinking Americans to crusade against unbelievers. Buchanan's divisive comments were a reminder of the multiple ways that religious belief was reshaping American politics.

The wild card was the Texas billionaire Ross Perot, whose independent campaign started with an appearance on a television talk show. Perot loved flip charts, distanced himself from professional politicians, and claimed to talk sense to the American people. He also tried to occupy the political center, appealing to the middle of the middle-class—small business owners, middle managers, and professionals who had approved of Reagan's antigovernment rhetoric but distrusted his corporate cronies.

Bush expected voters to reward him for the end of the Cold War, but he ignored anxieties about the nation's direction at home. His popularity had surged immediately after the victorious Persian Gulf War, only to fall rapidly as the country became mired in a recession. Clinton hammered away at economic concerns, appealing to swing voters, such as suburban independents and blue-collar Reagan

Democrats. He presented himself as the leader of new, pragmatic, and livelier Democrats.

Election day gave the Clinton-Gore ticket 43 percent of the popular vote, Bush 38 percent, and Perot 19 percent. Clinton held the Democratic core of northern and midwestern industrial states and loosened the Republican hold on the South and West (see Map 31–1). Clinton ran best among voters over 65, who remembered FDR and Harry Truman, and voters under 30.

POLICING THE WORLD

Clinton inherited a confused expectation that the United States could use its military and economic power to keep the world on an even keel and counter ethnic hatred without incurring serious risks to itself. During the administration's first years, U.S. diplomats helped broker an Israel-PLO accord that gave Palestinians self-government in Gaza and the West Bank, only to watch extremists on both sides undermine the accords and plunge Israel into a near–civil war by 2002. The United States in 1994 used diplomatic pressure to persuade North Korea to suspend building nuclear weapons, temporarily calming a potentially explosive trouble spot. The world also benefitted from a gradual reduction of nuclear arsenals and from a 1996 treaty to ban the testing of nuclear weapons. Elsewhere in the world, Clinton used military power with caution.

Bosnia and Kosovo. Clinton reluctantly committed the United States to a multinational effort to end the bloody civil war in ethnically and religiously divided Bosnia in 1995. In the early 1990s, the former Communist nation of Yugoslavia, in southeastern Europe, fragmented into five independent nations: Slovenia, Macedonia, Croatia, Bosnia, and Yugoslavia (the name retained by the predominantly Serbian nation with its capital at Belgrade). Bosnia, divided both ethnically and religiously between Christians and Muslims, erupted in bitter civil war. Christian Serbs, supported by Belgrade, engaged in massacres and deportations of Muslim Bosnians with the goal of creating "ethnically clean" Serbian districts. Too late to stop most bloodshed, NATO eventually intervened in 1995.

The American military revisited the same part of Europe in 1999, when the United States and Britain led NATO's intervention in Kosovo. The overwhelming majority of people in this Yugoslav province were ethnic Albanians who had chafed under the control of the Serb-controlled Yugoslav government. When a Kosovar independence movement began a rebellion, Yugoslav president Slobodan Milosevic responded with brutal repression that threatened to drive over 1 million ethnic Albanians out of the province. To protect the Kosovars, NATO in March 1999 began a bombing campaign that targeted Yugoslav military bases and forces in Kosovo. In June, Yugoslavia agreed to withdraw its troops and make way for a multinational NATO peacekeeping force, marking a measured success for U.S. policy.

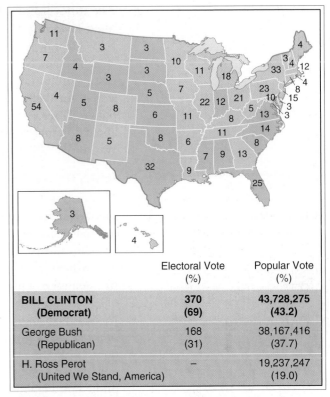

	Electoral Vote (%)	Popular Vote (%)
BILL CLINTON (Democrat)	**370 (69)**	**43,728,275 (43.2)**
George Bush (Republican)	168 (31)	38,167,416 (37.7)
H. Ross Perot (United We Stand, America)	–	19,237,247 (19.0)

MAP 31–1 The Election of 1992 Bill Clinton defeated George Bush in 1992 by reviving the Democratic Party in the industrial Northeast and enlisting new Democratic voters in the western states, where he appealed both to Hispanic immigrants and to people associated with fast-growing high-tech industries. He won reelection in 1996 with the same pattern of support. However, the coalition was an unstable combination of "Old Democrats," associated with older industries and labor unions, and "New Democrats," favoring economic change, free trade, and globalization.

WHAT FACTORS led to George H. W. Bush's downfall in the election of 1992?

The Reinvention of NATO. To satisfy Russia, the peacekeeping force that entered Kosovo in June was technically a U.S. operation, but it was a reinvented NATO that negotiated with Yugoslavia.

The new NATO is a product of the new Europe of the 1990s. A key step was expansion into the former Soviet sphere in eastern Europe. At the anniversary summit in 1999, NATO formally admitted Poland, Hungary, and the Czech Republic. Three years later, NATO agreed to give Russia a formal role in discussions about a number of its policy decisions, further eroding the barriers of the Cold War, and it added another seven nations of eastern Europe in 2004.

CLINTON'S NEOLIBERALISM

The heart of Clinton's agenda was an effort to make the United States economy more equitable domestically and more competitive internationally. These goals marked Clinton as a **neoliberal** who envisioned a partnership between a leaner government and a dynamic private sector. Steps to "reinvent" government cut federal employment below Reagan administration levels. A new tax bill reversed some of the inequities of the 1980s by increasing taxes on the well-off (the top 1.2 percent of households). At the other end of the income scale was expansion of the Earned Income Tax Credit, a Nixon-era program that helped lift working Americans out of poverty. An improved college student-aid program spread benefits to more students by allowing direct federal loans. The National and Community Service Trust Act created a pilot program for a domestic Peace Corps. In early 1993, Clinton pushed through the Family and Medical Leave Act, which provided up to 12 weeks of unpaid leave for workers with newborns or family emergencies.

Clinton's biggest setback was the failure of comprehensive health-care legislation. The goals seemed simple at first: containment of health care costs and extension of basic medical insurance from 83 percent of Americans under age 65 to 100 percent. In the abstract, voters agreed that something needed to be done.

The plan that emerged from the White House ran to 1,342 pages of complex regulations, with something for everyone to dislike. Senior citizens worried about limits on Medicare spending. Insurance companies did not want more regulations. Businesses did not want the costs of insuring their workers. Taxpayers liked the idea of wider medical insurance coverage but not the idea of paying for it through higher taxes or rationing of medical services. Thus the reform effort went nowhere.

If Reagan avoided blame for mistakes, Clinton in his first two years in office seemed to avoid credit for successes. Despite his legislative accomplishments, the press emphasized his difficulty in reaching decisions. Both the president and his wife attracted extreme and bitter hatred from the far right, of a sort previously reserved for Franklin and Eleanor Roosevelt and the Kennedy family. Indeed, Hillary Rodham Clinton became a symbol of discomfiting changes in American families.

CONTRACT WITH AMERICA AND THE ELECTION OF 1996

Conservative political ideology and personal animosity against the Clintons were both part of the background for an extraordinary off-year election in 1994, in which voters defeated dozens of incumbents and gave Republicans control of Congress. For most of 1995, the new speaker of the House, Newt Gingrich of Georgia, dominated political headlines as he pushed the **Contract with America,** the official Republican campaign platform for the 1994 elections, which called for a revolutionary reduction in federal responsibilities.

Clinton lay low and let the new Congress attack environmental protections, propose cuts in federal benefits for the elderly, and try to slice the capital-gains tax

Neoliberal Advocate or participant in the effort to reshape the Democratic Party for the 1990s around a policy emphasizing economic growth and competitiveness in the world economy.

Contract with America
Platform proposing a sweeping reduction in the role and activities of the federal government on which many Republican candidates ran for Congress in 1994.

to help the rich. As Congress and president battled over the budget, congressional Republicans refused to authorize interim spending and forced the federal government to shut down for more than three weeks between November 1995 and January 1996. Gingrich was the clear loser in public opinion, both for the shutdowns and for his ideas. Democrats painted Gingrich and his congressional allies as a radical fringe who wanted to gut Medicare and Medicaid, undermine education, punish legal immigrants, and sell off national parks.

Hillary Rodham Clinton's mastery of policy details seemed to some critics to be inappropriate for a first lady, but it helped her be an effective senator from New York beginning in 2001.

SIPA Press

After the budget confrontations, 1996 brought a series of measures to reward work—a centrist position acceptable to most Americans. The minimum wage increased. Congress made pension programs easier for employers to create and made health insurance portable when workers changed jobs. After tough negotiations, Clinton signed bipartisan legislation to "end welfare as we know it." The new program of **Temporary Assistance to Needy Families (TANF)** replaced Aid to Families with Dependent Children (AFDC). TANF had strict requirements that aid recipients be seeking work or be enrolled in schooling, and it set a time limit on assistance. By 2001, the number of public-assistance recipients had declined 58 percent from its 1994 high, but there are doubts that many of the former recipients have found jobs adequate to support their families.

Clinton's reelection in 1996 was a virtual replay of 1992. His opponent, Robert Dole, represented the World War II generation of politicians. The Republican Party was uncertain whether to stress free markets or morality. Evangelicals dominated many state parties, but they made many traditional party regulars uncomfortable and carried few statewide elections. The Republicans thus displayed many of the internal fractures that characterized American society as a whole.

Clinton became the first Democratic president to be elected to a second term since Franklin Roosevelt. The Clinton-Gore ticket took 70 percent of the electoral votes and 49 percent of the popular vote (versus 41 percent for Dole and 9 percent for a recycled Ross Perot). Clinton easily won the Northeast, the industrial Midwest, and the Far West; Hispanic voters alienated by anti-immigrant rhetoric from the Republicans helped Clinton also take the usually Republican states of Florida and Arizona.

The election confirmed that voters liked the pragmatic center. What voters wanted was to continue the reduction of the federal role in domestic affairs that had begun in the 1980s without damaging social insurance programs.

THE DANGERS OF EVERYDAY LIFE

Part of the background for the sometimes vicious politics of mid-decade was a sense of individual insecurity and fear of violence that coexisted with an economy that was booming in some sectors but still leaving many Americans behind.

Temporary Assistance for Needy Families (TANF)
Federal program, utilizing work requirements for and time limits on benefits, created in 1996 to replace earlier welfare programs to aid families and children.

WHERE TO LEARN MORE

Oklahoma City National Memorial Center Museum, Oklahoma City, OK
Exhibits about the federal building bombing and its impacts on the community.
www.oklahomacitynationalmemorial.org.

Random Violence and Domestic Terrorism. One after another, headlines and news flashes proclaimed terrifying random acts of violence. The greatest losses of life came in Waco, Texas, and in Oklahoma City. On April 19, 1993, federal agents raided the fortified compound of the Branch Davidian cult outside Waco after a 51-day siege. The raid triggered a fire, probably set from inside, that killed more than 80 people. On the second anniversary of the Waco raid, Timothy McVeigh packed a rented truck with explosive materials and detonated it in front of the federal office building in downtown Oklahoma City, presumably as revenge against what he considered an oppressive government. The blast collapsed the entire front of the nine-story building and killed 169 people.

In April 1999, two high school students in Littleton, Colorado, took rifles and pipe bombs into Columbine High School to kill 12 classmates and a teacher. A national manhunt in 1997 captured Ted Kaczynski, the so-called Unabomber, who since 1978 had mailed more than a dozen bombs to college professors and airlines as protest against an industrialized economy.

Gun Control. Work-place assassins, schoolroom murders, and domestic terrorism invigorated efforts to monitor access to firearms. The Brady Handgun Violence Prevention Act, passed in 1994, set up a waiting period and background checks for purchases of firearms from retailers, pawnshops, and licensed firearm dealers. But gun control was political dynamite, for Americans have drastically differing understandings of the Second Amendment, which states: "A well regulated militia, being necessary to the security of a free State, the right of the people to keep and bear arms, shall not be infringed." The powerful National Rifle Association, the major lobby for gun owners and manufacturers, now argued that the amendment establishes an absolute individual right. Until the 1980s, in contrast, federal courts consistently interpreted the amendment to apply to the possession of weapons in connection with citizen service in a government-organized militia, and federal courts have yet to strike down any gun-control law for violating the Second Amendment.

Crime and the War on Drugs. Conservatives, including many gun-ownership absolutists, put their faith in strict law enforcement as the best route to pubic security. The 1990s saw numerous states adopt "three-strike" measures that drastically increased penalties for individuals convicted of a third crime. One result was an explosive growth of the prison industry. Mandatory minimum sentencing caused Louisiana's prison population to grow by 50 percent between 1994 and 2001. Mississippi legislation that severely restricted the possibility of parole caused an even greater jump in the state's prison population from 10,700 in 1994 to 37,700 in 2001. States diverted funds from education and health care to build and staff more prisons. The number of people serving sentences of a year or longer in state and federal prisons grew from 316,000 in 1980 to 740,000 in 1990 and 1,368,000 in 2002, with another 658,000 being held for shorter periods in local jails.

The war on drugs, begun in the 1980s, was the biggest contributor to the prison boom. Aggressive enforcement of domestic laws against drug possession or sales filled American prison cells. The antidrug campaign fell most heavily on minorities. Connecticut, for example, required mandatory sentences for selling or possessing drugs within two-thirds of a mile of a school, day-care center, or public housing project. Because these criteria encompassed nearly all the neighborhoods in Hartford and New Haven with large minority populations, minority offenders arrested on drug charges were nine times more likely than white offenders to end up in jail.

In fact, crime fell steadily for a decade after reaching a peak in 1991. The rate of violent crime (murder, rape, robbery, aggravated assault) fell by 33 percent from 1991 to 2000, including a 36 percent drop in the number of murders. The rate of major property crimes (burglary, larceny-theft, and motor vehicle theft) fell by 30 percent over the same period. Easing fears combined with escalating costs to cause some states to rethink the reliance on prison terms. California voters adopted a measure that provides for treatment rather than prison for many drug offenders.

Debating the Death Penalty. Governor George Ryan of Illinois was elected in 1998 as a conservative Republican. In January 2003, this small-town businessman emptied death row in the Illinois prison system by commuting the death sentences of 167 convicted murderers to prison terms of life or less. He asserted that his review of individual cases had led him to doubt the justice of the death-penalty system as a whole, which he said is "haunted by the demons of error—error in determining guilt and error in determining who among the guilty deserves to die."

Specific discussion of flaws in the application of the death penalty reveals basic disagreements about the best approach to public order. Thirty-eight of the 50 states impose the death penalty, although seven have not carried out an execution since 1976. The majority of Americans have accepted capital punishment as a flawed but necessary defense for society.

In contrast, a passionate minority thinks that capital punishment is a tool so bent and blunted as to be worse than useless. They point out that the deterrent effect of capital punishment is weak at best; murder rates are often higher in death-penalty states than in similar states without the penalty. They note that African Americans and Latinos receive the death penalty far more often than whites charged with the same crimes. The debate about capital punishment exemplifies the fault lines that divide Americans as they try to balance the demands of justice and public order.

MORALITY AND PARTISANSHIP

In 1998 and 1999, the United States was riveted by revelations about the president's sex life, doubts about his integrity, and debates about his fitness for high office. Years of rumors, innuendos, and lawsuits culminated in 1999 in the nation's second presidential impeachment trial. To his enemies, Clinton's behavior seemed one more example of disregard for law and morality, while his supporters found the entire issue to be nothing but partisan politics.

The attacks on President Clinton were accompanied by unprecedented assaults on the reputation of Hillary Clinton, attacks which showed that tension over social values remained an important dimension of American life. Both her active role in shaping policy and her stands on social issues made her a symbol of changes in American families and values that distressed many conservatives. Talk-show hosts and ultraconservative activists tried repeatedly to link her to scandals and wrongdoing.

The president's problems began in 1994 with the appointment of a special prosecutor to investigate possible fraud in the **Whitewater** development, an Arkansas land promotion in which Bill and Hillary Clinton had invested in the 1980s. The probe by Kenneth Starr, the independent counsel, however, expanded into a wide-ranging investigation that encompassed the firing of the White House travel-office staff early in 1993, the suicide of White House aide Vincent Foster, and the sexual behavior of the president. Meanwhile, Paula Jones had brought a lawsuit

Whitewater Arkansas real estate development in which Bill and Hillary Clinton were investors; several fraud convictions resulted from investigations into Whitewater, but evidence was not found that the Clinton's were involved in wrongdoing.

claiming sexual harassment by then-governor Clinton while she was a state worker in Arkansas. The investigation of Whitewater brought convictions of several friends and former associates of the Clintons, but no evidence pointing decisively at either Bill or Hillary Clinton.

The legal landscape changed in January 1998, when allegations surfaced about an affair between the president and Monica Lewinsky, a former White House intern. Lewinsky admitted to the relationship privately and then to Starr's staff after the president had denied it in a sworn deposition for the Paula Jones case. This opened Clinton to charges of perjury and obstruction of justice. The Lewinsky affair certainly revealed deep flaws in Clinton's character and showed his willingness to shade the truth. Newspaper editorials, radio talk shows, and politicians debated whether such flaws were relevant to his ability to perform his constitutional duties.

In the fall of 1998, the Republican leaders who controlled Congress decided that Clinton's statements and misstatements justified them in initiating the process of impeachment. In December, the Republican majority on the House Judiciary Committee recommended four articles of impeachment, or specific charges against the president, to the House of Representatives. By a partisan vote, the full House approved two of the charges and forwarded them to the Senate. Moderate Republicans joined Democrats, thereby ensuring that the Senate would fall far short of the two-thirds majority required for conviction and removal from office.

Why did Congressional Republicans pursue impeachment to the bitter end? It was clear by the end of 1998 that a majority of Americans strongly disapproved of Clinton's conduct but did not think that his personal behavior merited removal from office (see Overview table, "Presidential Impeachment"). The 1998 election, which reduced the Republican majority in the House and resulted in the resignation of Newt Gingrich, confirmed the opinion polls. At the same time, 25 to 30 percent of Americans remained convinced that Clinton was a disgrace whose presence in the White House demeaned the nation. It was not so much that they disliked his policies, which were often quite conservative, but that they felt that his personal flaws and sins made him unfit to lead and represent the nation and deprived him of the moral authority necessary to inspire its people. In other words, although anti-Clinton people were a powerful force within the Republican Party and impeachment was certainly motivated by politics, it was also another battle in America's continuing culture wars.

A NEW ECONOMY?

In the closing months of 1999, many people stocked up on canned food and kerosene, powdered milk, ammunition, and cash. They were preparing to survive, not foreign invasion or natural disaster, but rather the possible collapse of the global computer network. Europeans called the problem the "millennium bug," Americans the "Y2K" problem (for Year 2000). In the early years of computers, memory space was precious, causing programmers to designate dates with only the last two digits of the year (thus, "82" for 1982). In the mid-1990s, many realized that such programs might treat the year 2000 as 1900, or might choke in electronic confusion, throwing information systems into chaos.

In fact, almost nothing happened. In larger perspective, the Y2K worries illustrate how much the American economy had changed in the preceding decade, and how mysterious the changes seemed. More than ever, it was a global economy. And, unlike any time in the past, it was an economy that depended on electronic computing to manage and transmit vast quantities of data.

WHAT ROLE did new information technology play in the economic boom of the 1990s?

QUICK REVIEW

Boom Times

- U.S. enjoyed nine years of economic expansion between 1992 and 2000.
- Unemployment fell to 4.0 percent in 2000.
- The economic boom resulted in increased government revenues.

OVERVIEW   PRESIDENTIAL IMPEACHMENT

Andrew Johnson, 1868	Charges:	Failure to comply with Tenure of Office Act requiring congressional approval to fire cabinet members.
	Political Lineup:	Radical Republicans against Johnson; Democrats and moderate Republicans for him.
	Actions:	Tried and acquitted by Senate.
	Underlying Issues:	Johnson's opposition to Republican plans for reconstruction of southern states after the Civil War.
Richard Nixon, 1974	Charges:	Obstruction of justice in Watergate investigation, abuse of power of federal agencies for political purposes, refusal to recognize congressional subpoena.
	Political Lineup:	Democrats and many Republicans against Nixon.
	Actions:	Charges approved by House committee; Nixon resigned before action by the full House of Representatives.
	Underlying Issues:	Nixon's construction of a secret government and his efforts to undermine integrity of national elections.
Bill Clinton, 1999	Charges:	Perjury and obstruction of justice in the investigation of sexual-misconduct allegations by Paula Jones.
	Political Lineup:	Conservative Republicans against Clinton; Democrats and some moderate Republicans for him.
	Actions:	Tried and acquitted by Senate.
	Underlying Issues:	Republican frustration with Clinton's ability to block their agenda; deep concern about Clinton's character and moral fitness for presidency.

THE PROSPEROUS 1990S

From 1992 through 2000, Americans enjoyed nine years of continuous economic expansion. Unemployment dropped from 7.2 percent in 1992 to 4.0 percent at the start of 2000 as American businesses created more than 12 million new jobs. The stock market soared during the nineties; rising demand for shares in established blue-chip companies and new **Internet** firms swelled the value of individual portfolios, retirement accounts, and pension funds. The proportion of Americans in poverty dropped to 12 percent in 1999, and the gap between rich and poor began to narrow (slightly) for the first time in two decades.

The economic boom was great news for the federal budget. Tight spending and rising personal income turned perennial deficits into surpluses for 1998, 1999, and 2000. Reduced borrowing by the U.S. Treasury resulted in low interest rates, which further fueled corporate expansion and consumer spending. In 1997, Clinton signed a deficit-reduction bill that seemed to promise fiscal stability.

Behind the statistics were substantial gains in the efficiency of the American economy. By the end of the decade the productivity of manufacturing workers was increasing more than 4 percent per year, the highest rate in a generation. Part of the gain was the payoff from the painful business restructuring and downsizing of the 1970s and 1980s. Another cause was improvements in efficiency from the full incorporation of personal computers and electronic communication into everyday life and business practice.

Internet The system of interconnected computers and servers that allows the exchange of e-mail, posting of Web sites, and other means of instant communication.

THE SERVICE ECONOMY

At the beginning of the twenty-first century, the United States was an economy of services. The service sector includes everyone not directly involved in producing and processing physical products. Service workers range from lawyers to hair stylists, from police officers who write traffic tickets to theater employees who sell movie tickets. In 1965, services already accounted for more than half of American jobs. By the end of the 1990s, their share rose to more than 75 percent.

Service jobs vary greatly. At the bottom of the scale are minimum-wage jobs held mostly by women, immigrants, and the young, such as cleaning people, child-care workers, hospital orderlies, and fast-food workers. In contrast, many of the best new jobs are in information industries. Teaching, research, government, advertising, mass communications, and professional consulting depend on producing and manipulating information. All of these fields have grown.

The rise of the service economy had political consequences. Rapid expansion of jobs in state and local government triggered popular revolts against state taxes that started in 1978 with passage of California's Proposition 13, which limited property taxes, and continued into the 1990s. Another growth industry was health care. Spending on medical and health services amounted to 15 percent of the gross domestic product in 2000, up from 5 percent in 1960. The need to share this huge expense fairly was the motivation for Medicare and Medicaid in the 1960s and the search for a national health insurance program in the 1990s.

THE HIGH-TECH SECTOR

The epitome of the "sunrise" economy was electronics, which grew hand-in-glove with the defense budget. The first computers in the 1940s were derived in part from wartime code-breaking efforts. In the 1950s, IBM got half its revenues from air defense computers and guidance systems for B-52 bombers. California's **Silicon Valley,** north of San Jose, took off with corporate spinoffs and civilian applications of military technologies and benefitted equally from proximity to Stanford University.

Invention of the microprocessor in 1971 kicked the industry into high gear. The farmlands of Santa Clara County, California, became a "silicon landscape" of neat one-story factories and research campuses. In 1950, the county had 800 factory workers. In 1980, it had 264,000 manufacturing workers and 3,000 electronics firms; 20 years later, San Jose had the highest average annual pay of any metropolitan area. Related hardware and microchip factories spread the industry throughout the West, to such cities as Austin, Phoenix, Portland, Boise, and Salt Lake City.

The electronics boom was driven by extraordinary improvements in computing capacity. At the start of the microcomputer era, Intel co-founder Gordon Moore predicted that the number of transistors on a microchip would double every 18 months, with consequent increases in performance and drops in price. "Moore's Law" worked at least until the opening of the new century as producers moved from chips with 5,000 transistors to ones with 50,000,000. The practical result was a vast increase in the capacities and portability of computers.

Personal computers and consumer electronics became part of everyday life in the 1990s. In 2003, 79 percent of adults reported that they had Internet access at home or work, up from around 14 percent in 1996, and nearly all of them had used it in the previous month. It took radio 38 years and television 13 years before 50 million Americans tuned in; the Internet reached the same level of use in four years.

The electronics boom was part of a larger growth of high-technology industries. If the term *high-tech* is applied to industries that devote a substantial portion of their income to research and development, it also covers chemicals,

Silicon Valley The region of California between San Jose and San Francisco that holds the nation's greatest concentration of electronics firms.

synthetic materials, cosmetics, aircraft and space satellites, drugs, measuring instruments, and many other products. Pharmaceuticals, medical imaging and diagnosis, bioengineering, and genetic engineering were all areas of rapid advance. In fundamental ways, they were all examples of activities based on the acquisition and processing of information.

AN INSTANT SOCIETY

The spread of consumer electronics helped to create an "instant society." Americans in the 1990s learned to communicate by e-mail and to look up information on the **World Wide Web.** The United States was increasingly a society that depended on instant information and expected instant results.

The Internet grew out of concerns about defense and national security. Its prototype was ARPAnet (for Advanced Research Projects Administration of the Defense Department), intended to be a communication system that could survive nuclear attack. As the Internet evolved into a system that connected universities and national weapons laboratories, the Pentagon gave up control in 1984. Through the 1980s, it was used mainly by scientists and academics to share data and communicate by e-mail. The World Wide Web, created in 1991, expanded the Internet's uses by allowing organizations and companies to create websites that placed political and commercial information only a few clicks away from wired consumers. The equally rapid expansion of bandwidth allowed web pages filled with pictures and graphics to replace the text-only sites of the 1980s.

Mobile telephones, or cell phones, were part of the same instant society. They exploited underutilized radio bands and communication satellites to allow wireless conversations among cells—geographic areas linked by special microwave broadcasting towers. Wireless phone companies originally sold their phones as emergency backups and business necessities, just as wired telephones had been sold in the first years of the twentieth century. The 5 million cell phone subscribers of 1990 had exploded to 159 million in 2003.

IN THE WORLD MARKET

Instant access to business and financial information accelerated the globalizing of the American economy. With the help of national policy and booming economies overseas, the value of American imports and exports more than doubled, from 7 percent of the gross domestic product in 1965 to 16 percent in 1990—the largest percentage since World War I. Americans in the 1970s began to worry about a "colonial" status, in which the United States exported food, lumber, and minerals and imported automobiles and television sets. By the 1980s, foreign economic competitiveness and trade deficits, especially with Japan, became issues of national concern which continued into the new century.

The effects of international competition were more complex than "Japan-bashers" acknowledged. Mass-production industries, such as textiles and aluminum, suffered from cheaper and sometimes higher-quality imports, but many specialized industries and services, such as Houston's oil equipment and exploration firms, thrived. Globalization also created new regional winners and losers. In 1982, the United States began to do more business with Pacific nations than with Europe.

The Politics of Trade.   More recent steps to expand the global reach of the American economy were the **North American Free Trade Agreement (NAFTA)** in 1993 and a new worldwide General Agreement on Tarrifs and Trade (GATT) approved in 1994. NAFTA combined 25 million Canadians, 90 million Mexicans,

RELIEF WORK IN AFRICA

In the early twenty-first century, thousands of Americans work in other countries for relief and reconstruction organizations such as the Peace Corps, CARE, and Mercy Corps, and thousands more do similar work under the sponsorship of religious groups. In 2003, Peggy Senger Parsons, an evangelical Quaker minister and trauma counselor from "far off Planet America" spent several months in the small African nation of Burundi, trying to help residents develop strategies for dealing with the impacts of civil war and endemic criminal violence. Here are some excerpts from her blog.

- What does Peggy Parsons's experience suggest about the spread of American culture around the world?
- How does the level of personal safety in a nation such as Burundi compare to that in the United States?
- What questions does Parsons's experience raise about the challenges of building peace and democracy in troubled and divided nations?
- How might religiously based work in other countries differ from efforts sponsored by the U.S. government, such as with the Peace Corps? How might it be the same?

We function in Swahili and French, mine bad and hers good. . . . I have been in the company of four children who have been giving me language and cultural tutorials, which I exchanged for introducing them to the Beatles.

Pavement is a subjective concept in Burundi. Traffic is extremely real. We fly in a zig zag pattern through cars, trucks, bicycles, and lots of little children. If you notice a lack of angels in America, it is because they are all in Burundi keeping the babies from being killed on the road. . . . And in four days I am totally immune to the sight of guys with automatic weapons. My host says that he cannot tell a rebel from a Burundi soldier and sometimes neither can they.

We have a night watchman . . . we live in a walled compound and he is there to keep us safe. His only weapon is a whistle. The children tell me that if there is trouble he whistles, and all the nearby watchmen

whistle and then come running to help. Then I met Gadi the moneychanger. He walks around with rolls of money as big as softballs in every pocket and he does not carry a gun. He has a quiet gentle confidence that reminds me of every wiseguy I ever met in Chicago. I do not know what happens if you jump a moneychanger—but it must be bad enough that nobody tries. Some things are very familiar.

My traumatology students are amazing. They have come from great distances and at great sacrifice to study with me. . . . Many of the terms I need to use have no equivalent. I have learned the face that my translator makes when I give her a hard one. She signals for me to stop, and the students confer and when a consensus is reached about a newly coined phrase someone shouts *Voila!* And we have a new psychological term. My students were interviewed on Burundi National Radio. The reporter came on the second day to do a quick filler piece and stayed all afternoon and then asked to join the class. He carries a huge reel to reel recorder. The voices of these students went out to 22 million listeners this morning in Burundi, Congo, Rwanda, and Tanzania. They were fabulous explaining the effects of trauma and how they themselves had been helped in the class. On Friday my class thanked me for telling them the truth and for bringing them the best of myself. They compared me to a Jonah "who did not run away but ran towards her call," can't get better pay than that.

I was not prepared for the fact that my trauma class students would be such recent victims [many bearing fresh wounds from beatings or torture]. Thursday there was a bit of shooting outside of the teaching compound. I had to be told what it was—a "thump" and then a "tat, tat. tat." But it was quiet after that and we resume. After a long morning of brain physiology and learning about the left brain functions, my translator said, "Peggy have mercy on them—they say they need to sing." And so they did, all Christian music. I taught them "We Shall Overcome" and told them about Dr. King and we marched around the room singing that "I do believe, deep in my heart, that Burundi will have peace one day."

and 250 million U.S. consumers in a single "common market" similar to that of western Europe. This enlarged free-trade zone was intended to open new markets and position the United States to compete more effectively against the European Community and Japan.

NAFTA was a hard pill for many Democrats, and it revived the old debate between free traders and protectionists. Support was strongest from businesses and industries that sought foreign customers, including agriculture and electronics. Opponents included organized labor, communities already hit by industrial shutdowns, and environmentalists worried about lax controls on industrial pollution in Mexico.

The **World Trade Organization (WTO),** which replaced GATT in 1996, became the unexpected target of a global protest movement. Fifty thousand protesters converged on the WTO meeting, held in Seattle from November 30 to December 4, 1999. Most demonstrators were peaceful, but several hundred started a rampage through downtown that triggered a massive overreaction by unprepared police.

The battle of Seattle was part of an international movement. Protesters were convinced that the WTO is a tool of transnational corporations that flout local labor and environmental protections in the name of "free trade" that benefits only the wealthy nations and their businesses. WTO defenders pointed to the long-term effects of open trade in raising net production in the world economy and thereby making more wealth available for developing nations. Opponents asserted, in turn, that such wealth never reaches the workers and farmers in those nations.

Seattle in the 1980s and 1990s prospered from the globalizing economy and the rise of the information industries. Only old-timers noticed the disappearance of fish canneries and lumber mills. Taking their place were Boeing, which fueled an international travel revolution; Microsoft, which made Seattle a high-tech capital; and the many foreign companies that used Seattle's port for access to the U.S. market.

Corbis Digital Stock

BROADENING DEMOCRACY

Closely related to the changes in the American economy were the changing composition of the American people and the continued emergence of new participants in American government. Bill Clinton's first cabinet, in which three women and four minority men balanced seven white men, recognized the make-up of the American population and marked the maturing of minorities and women as distinct political constituencies. The first cabinet appointed by George W. Bush in 2001 included four minority men and four women, one of whom was Asian American. In both administrations, the new prominence of women and minorities in the national government followed years of growing success in cities and states.

AMERICANS IN 2000

The federal census for the year 2000 found 281,400,000 Americans in the 50 states, District of Columbia, and Puerto Rico (and probably 2–3 million more residents were not counted). The increase from 1990 was 13.2 percent, or 32,700,000. It was the largest ten-year population increase in U.S. history, evidence of the nation's prosperity and its attractiveness for immigrants (Table 31–1). One third of all Americans lived in four states: California, Texas, New York, and Florida.

WHAT GAINS did women make in national politics in the 1990s?

World Trade Organization (WTO) International organization that sets standards and practices for global trade, and the focus of international protests over world economic policy in the late 1990s.

Table 31–1 Immigrants 1991–2002, by Continent and by Twenty Most Important Countries of Origin

Total	11,223,000
North America	4,730,000
Mexico	2,677,000
Dominican Republic	385,000
El Salvador	280,000
Cuba	237,000
Haiti	229,000
Jamaica	204,000
Canada	179,000
Guatemala	133,000
Asia	4,730,000
Philippines	610,000
China	542,000
India	525,000
Vietnam	490,000
Korea	213,000
Pakistan	155,000
Iran	136,000
Europe	1,661,000
Poland	194,000
Ukraine	184,000
United Kingdom	171,000
Russia	169,000
South America	683,000
Colombia	167,000
Africa	497,000
Oceania	60,000

Source: Statistical Abstract of the United States, 2004-2005, Table 8.

The West grew the fastest. The super boom states were Nevada (66 percent growth), Arizona (40 percent), Colorado (31 percent), Utah (30 percent), and Idaho (29 percent). Fast growth implies young populations, and the states with the lowest average ages were all western: Utah, Alaska, Idaho, and Texas. The Southwest and South also had the fastest-growing metropolitan areas. Among large metro areas with over 500,000 people in 2000, all 20 of the fastest growing of were in the West and Southeast.

In contrast, parts of the American midlands grew slowly. No state lost population, but North Dakota and West Virginia had ten year gains of only 1 percent. Another important trend was increasing ethnic and racial diversity (Table 31–2). Hispanics were the fastest-growing group in the American population. Although immigrants concentrated in the coastal and border states, Hispanics and Asian Americans were also spreading into interior states. Asians and Hispanics who had been in the United States for some time showed substantial economic success. Non-Hispanic whites are now a minority in California at 47 percent, in the District of Columbia, in Hawaii, and in New Mexico. Over the coming decades, the effects of ethnic change will be apparent not only in schools but also in the workplace, popular culture, and politics.

WOMEN FROM THE GRASSROOTS TO CONGRESS

The increasing prominence of women and family issues in national politics was a steady, quiet revolution that bore fruit in the 1990s, when the number of women in Congress more than doubled. In 1981, President Reagan appointed Arizona judge Sandra Day O'Connor to be the first woman on the United States Supreme Court. In 1984, Walter Mondale chose New York Congresswoman Geraldine Ferraro as his vice presidential candidate. In 1993 Clinton appointed the second woman to the Supreme Court, U.S. Appeals Court judge Ruth Bader Ginsburg. Clinton appointee Janet Reno was the first woman to serve as attorney general, and Madeleine K. Albright the first to serve as secretary of state. George W. Bush continued to break new ground by naming Condoleezza Rice as his national security advisor in 2001 and as secretary of state in 2005.

Political gains for women at the national level reflected their growing importance in grassroots politics. The spreading suburbs of postwar America were "frontiers" that required concerted action to solve immediate needs like adequate schools and decent parks. Because pursuit of such community services was often viewed as "woman's work" (in contrast to the "man's work" of economic development), postwar metropolitan areas offered numerous opportunities for women to engage in volunteer civic work, learn political skills, and run for local office. Moreover, new cities and suburbs had fewer established political institutions, such as political machines and strong parties; their politics were open to energetic women. Most women in contemporary politics have been more liberal than men— a difference that political scientists attribute to women's interest in the practical problems of schools, neighborhoods, and two-earner families. But women's grassroots mobilization, especially through evangelical churches, has also strengthened groups committed to conservative social values.

Regional differences have affected women's political gains. The West has long been the part of the country most open to women in state and local government and in business. Many of the skills learned from politics were also useful as women played a growing role in professional and managerial occupations Westerners have been more willing than voters in the East or South to choose women as mayors of major cities and as members of state legislatures.

In 1991, the nomination of Judge Clarence Thomas, an African American, to the U.S. Supreme Court ensured that everyone knew that the terms of American politics were changing. Because of his conservative positions on social and civil rights issues, Thomas was a controversial nominee. Controversy deepened when law professor Anita Hill accused Thomas of harassing her sexually while she served on his staff at the Equal Employment Opportunity Commission. Critics tried to discredit Hill with vicious attacks on her character, and the committee failed to call witnesses who could have supported her claims. The public was left with Hill's plausible but unproved allegations and Thomas's equally vigorous but unproved denials. The Senate confirmed Thomas to the Supreme Court. Partisans on each side continued to believe the version that best suited their preconceptions and agendas.

Whatever the merits of her charges, Hill's badgering by skeptical senators angered millions of women. In the shadow of the hearings, women made impressive gains in the 1992 election, which pushed women's share of seats in the 50 state legislatures above 20 percent (it was 22 percent in 1999). The number of women in the U.S. Senate jumped from two to seven (and grew further to nine Democrats and five Republicans in 2005).

Women have influenced national politics as voters as well as candidates and cabinet members. Since the 1980s, voting patterns have shown a widening gender gap. Women in the 1990s identified with the Democratic Party and voted for its candidates at a higher rate than men. The reasons include concerns about the effect of government spending cuts and interest in measures to support families rather than in conservative rhetoric. This gender gap has helped keep Democrats competitive and dampened the nation's conservative swing on social issues.

MINORITIES AT THE BALLOT BOX

The changing makeup of the American populace also helped black and Latino candidates for public office to increased success. After the racial violence of the 1960s, many black people turned to local politics to gain control of their own communities. The first black mayor of a major twentieth-century city was Carl Stokes in Cleveland in 1967. The 1973 election brought victories for Tom Bradley in Los Angeles, Maynard Jackson in Atlanta, and Coleman Young in Detroit. By 1983, three of the nation's four largest cities had black mayors. In 1989, Virginia made Douglas Wilder the first black governor in any state since Reconstruction.

Table 31–2 States with Highest Proportions of Minority Residents in 2000 (percentage of total population)

Hispanic	
New Mexico	42%
California	32%
Texas	32%
Arizona	25%
Nevada	20%
Asian and Pacific Islander	
Hawaii	51%
California	11%
Washington	6%
New Jersey	6%
New York	6%
Black	
Mississippi	36%
Louisiana	33%
South Carolina	30%
Georgia	29%
Maryland	28%
American Indian	
Alaska	16%
New Mexico	10%
South Dakota	8%
Oklahoma	8%
Montana	6%

The election of a minority mayor was sometimes more important for its symbolism than for the transfer of real power. Efforts to restructure the basis of city council elections, however, struck directly at the balance of power. Most mid-sized cities stopped electing city councils by wards or districts during the first half of the twentieth century. Voting at large shifted power away from geographically concentrated ethnic groups. It favored business interests that claimed to speak for the city as a whole but could assign most of the costs of economic growth to older and poorer neighborhoods.

In the 1970s, minority leaders and community activists realized that a return to district voting could convert neighborhood segregation from a liability to a political resource. As amended in 1975, the federal Voting Rights Act allowed minorities to use the federal courts to challenge at-large voting systems that diluted the impact of their votes. Blacks and Mexican Americans used the act to reestablish city council districts in the late 1970s and early 1980s in city after city across the South and Southwest. The political rebalancing meant that local leaders faced strong pressures to ensure equitable distribution of the benefits and burdens of growth. Newly empowered minorities began to press for a fair share of an expanding economic pie.

At the national level, minorities gradually increased their representation in Congress. Ben Nighthorse Campbell of Colorado, a Cheyenne, brought a Native American voice to the U.S. Senate in 1992. The number of African Americans in the House of Representatives topped 40 after 1992, with the help of districts drawn to concentrate black voters. Even after a series of Supreme Court cases invalidated districts drawn with race as the "predominant factor," however, African Americans held most of their gains, while the number of Latino members of Congress rose to 26 by 2005.

In struggling for political influence, recent immigrants have added new panethnic identities to their national identities. Hispanic activists revived the term "Chicano" to bridge the gap between recent Mexican immigrants and Latinos whose families had settled in the Southwest before the American conquest in 1848. Great gaps of experience and culture separated Chinese, Koreans, Filipinos, and Vietnamese, but they gained political recognition and influence if they dealt with other Americans as "Asians." Native Americans have similarly downplayed tribal differences in efforts to secure better opportunities for Indians as a group.

RIGHTS AND OPPORTUNITIES

The increasing presence of Latinos and African Americans in public life highlighted a set of troublesome questions about the proper balance between equal rights and equal opportunities. Was government justified in seeking to equalize outcomes as well as starting points? More broadly, was the United States to be a unitary society in which everyone assimilated to a single culture and adhered to a single set of formal and informal rules, or might it be a plural society in which different groups accepted different goals and behaviors? The debates at the end of the twentieth century replayed many of the questions that European immigration raised at the century's beginning.

Illegal Immigration and Bilingual Education.   One issue is the economic impact of illegal immigration. Advocates of tight borders assert that illegal immigrants take jobs away from legal residents and eat up public assistance. Many studies, however, find that illegal immigrants fill jobs that nobody else wants. Over the long run, high employment levels among immigrants mean that their tax contributions through sales taxes and Social Security taxes and payroll deductions more than pay for their use of welfare, food stamps, and unemployment benefits, which illegal immigrants are often afraid to claim for fear of calling attention to themselves. Nevertheless, high immigration can strain local government budgets even if it benefits the nation as a whole.

A symbolic issue was the degree to which American institutions should accommodate non–English speakers. Referendums in Alaska (1996) and Utah (2000) raised to 26 the number of states that declared English their official language. The measures ranged from general statements to specific prohibitions on printing forms and ballots in multiple languages. California voters in 1998 banned bilingual public education, a system under which children whose first language was Spanish or another "immigrant" tongue were taught for several years in that language before shifting to English-language classrooms. Advocates of bilingual education claimed that it eased the transition into American society, but opponents said that it blocked immigrant children from fully assimilating into American life.

Affirmative Action.   A more encompassing issue was a set of policies that originated in the 1960s as **affirmative action,** a phrase that first appeared in executive orders issued by Presidents Kennedy and Johnson. The initial goal was to require businesses that received federal contracts to "take affirmative action to ensure that applicants are employed, and that employees are treated during employment without regard for their race, creed, color, or national origin." By the 1970s, many states and cities had adopted similar policies for hiring their own employees and choosing contractors and extended affirmative action to women as well as minorities. Colleges and universities used affirmative-action policies in recruiting faculty and admitting students.

As these efforts spread, the initial goal of nondiscrimination evolved into expectations and requirements for active ("affirmative") efforts to achieve greater diversity among employees, students, or contractors. Government agencies began to set aside a small percentage of contracts for woman-owned or minority-owned firms. Cities actively worked to hire more minority police officers and firefighters. Colleges made special efforts to attract minority students. The landmark court case about affirmative action was *University of California v. Bakke* (1978). Alan Bakke was an unsuccessful applicant to the medical school at the University of California at Davis. He argued that the university had improperly set aside 16 of 100 places in its entering class for minority students, thereby engaging in reverse discrimination against white applicants. In a narrow decision, the U.S. Supreme Court ordered Bakke admitted because the only basis for his rejection had been race. At the same time, the Court stated that race or ethnicity could legally be one of several factors considered in college and university admissions as long as a specific number of places were not reserved for minorities.

In 1996, California voters approved a ballot measure to eliminate state-sponsored affirmative action. One effect was to prohibit state-funded colleges and universities from using race or ethnicity as a factor in deciding which applicants to admit. In the same year, the Supreme Court let stand a lower-court ruling in *Hopwood v. Texas,* which had forbidden the University of Texas to consider race in admission decisions. The number of black freshmen in the University Texas dropped by half in 1997 and the number of blacks and Hispanics among first-year law students by

As leadership opportunities for African Americans have increased in recent decades, they have gained positions of influence in a growing range of activities. During his first term, for example, President George W. Bush chose Colin Powell as secretary of state and Condoleezza Rice as national security advisor. Later Rice became Secretary of State.

Getty Images Inc.

Affirmative Action   A set of policies to open opportunities in business and education for members of minority groups and women by allowing race and sex to be factors included in decisions to hire, award contracts, or admit students to higher education programs.

University of California v. Bakke   U.S. Supreme Court case in 1978 that allowed race to be used as one of several factors in college and university admission decisions but made rigid quotas unacceptable.

two-thirds. The results were similar at the University of California at Berkeley, where the number of blacks among entering law students dropped from twenty to one.

Affirmative action has come under such close scrutiny and attack because it is a lightning rod for disagreements about the character of American society. The problem is that the goal of diversity seems to conflict with the fundamental American value of individual opportunity. In opinion polls, a majority of Americans reject the idea that past injustice and unequal opportunity can justify special consideration for all members of a group. Instead, they believe that individual merit and qualifications should be the sole basis for getting into school or getting a job, and that such factors as SAT scores and civil service exams can measure such qualifications. Others argue that the merit system is severely flawed, that students from poor families lack the advantages at home and at school that give upper-middle-class and wealthy students a head start for success. Affirmative action, they argue, helps to level the field. Nevertheless, many minorities worry that affirmative action undermines their success by suggesting that they received jobs or contracts by racial preference rather than merit.

In 2003, the Supreme Court affirmed the basic principle of affirmative action in two cases involving admission to the University of Michigan. Aided by supporting statements filed by major corporations and by members of the U.S. military, the Court found that promoting ethnic and racial diversity among students constitutes a compelling state interest, and it approved narrowly tailored affirmative-action programs that weigh race and ethnicity along with other admissions criteria on an individual basis.

EDGING INTO A NEW CENTURY

On the evening of November 7, 2000, CBS-TV made the kind of mistake that journalists dread. Relying on questions put to a sample of voters after they cast their ballots in the presidential contest between Albert Gore, Jr. and George W. Bush, the CBS newsroom first projected that Gore would win Florida and likely the election, then reversed itself and called the election for Bush, only to find that it would be days or even weeks before the votes in several pivotal states, including Florida, could be certified.

The inability to predict the outcome in 2000 was an indication of the degree to which Americans were split down the middle in their political preferences and their visions for the future. The United States entered the twenty-first century both divided and balanced, with extremes of opinion revolving around a center of basic goals and values.

THE 2000 ELECTION

On November 8, 2000, the day after their national election, Americans woke up to the news that neither Republican George W. Bush nor Democrat Albert Gore, Jr., had a majority of votes in the electoral college. Although Gore held a lead in the popular vote (about 340,000 votes out of more than 100 million cast), both candidates needed a majority in Florida to win its electoral votes and the White House. After protracted protests about voting irregularities and malfunctioning voting equipment, politically divided Floridians engaged in an on-again off-again recount in key counties. The U.S. Supreme Court finally preempted the state process and ordered a halt to recounting on December 12 by the politically charged margin of 5 to 4. The result was to make Bush the winner in Florida by a few hundred votes and the winner nationwide by 271 electoral votes to 267 (see Map 31–2).

WHAT WERE the key elements of George W. Bush's domestic agenda?

QUICK REVIEW

Election Controversy
- Al Gore secured a majority of the popular vote.
- Both sides needed Florida's contested electoral votes to secure election.
- The U.S. Supreme Court voted 5–4 to end the recount in Florida, making George W. Bush the new president.

It is difficult to know who "really" won Florida. There is good evidence that African-American voters, who strongly favored Gore, were turned away in disproportionate numbers because of technical challenges to their registration. In one county, a ballot with a particularly poor design probably caused several thousand mistaken votes for a minor candidate rather than Gore. But recounts by teams of newspaper reporters came to different conclusions about who might have won, depending on what criteria were used to accept or reject disputed punchcard ballots.

The outcome of the election showed a nation that was paradoxically divided around a strong center. The votes showed basic differences between the parties. Gore appealed especially to residents of large cities, to women, to African Americans, and to families struggling to make it economically. Bush appealed to people from small towns, to men, and to members of households that had benefitted the most from the prosperity of the Clinton era. These were divisions that had marked the two parties since the 1930s, and their persistence was a reminder of the nation's diversity of opinions and values. The nation also divided regionally, with Gore strong in the Northeast, upper Middle West, and Pacific Coast, Bush in the South, Ohio Valley, Great Plains, and Rocky Mountain states.

At the same time, both Bush, governor of Texas and son of President George H. W. Bush (1989–93), and Gore, vice president for the previous eight years, targeted their campaigns at middle Americans. Each offered to cut taxes, down size the federal government, and protect Social Security, differing in the details rather than the broad goals. In trying to claim the political middle, they reflected the successful political message of the Clinton administration. Voters also shaved the Republican control of Congress to razor-thin margins, further undermining any chance of radical change in either a conservative or a liberal direction. To those on the political left and right who had hoped for new directions for the nation, it looked like a formula for paralysis; for the majority of Americans, it looked like stability.

REAGANOMICS REVISITED

Despite the message of stability, the Bush administration took the Republican return to executive power as opportunity to tilt domestic policy abruptly to the right. Following the example of Ronald Reagan, Bush made massive tax cuts the centerpiece of his first months in office. By starting with proposals for ten-year cuts so large that two generations of federal programs were threatened, Bush and congressional Republicans forced the Democrats to "compromise" on reductions far higher than the economy could probably support. The resulting cuts to income taxes and estate taxes were projected to total $1,350 billion over the decade, with one-third of the benefits going to families earning more than $200,000. The federal budget quickly plunged into the red, undoing the careful political balancing and fiscal discipline of the Clinton administration. Deficits were $158 billion in 2002, $374 billion in 2003, and $412 billion in 2004, with more of the same forecast for the rest of the decade.

The Bush team also moved quickly to deregulate the economy. It opened many of the environmental and business regulations of the last two decades to reconsideration—from arsenic standards in drinking water to protection for wetlands to the pollution

George W. Bush awaits the results of the 2000 Presidential Election recount at his ranch in Texas. The controversial Florida recount was part of the closest election in U.S. history, finally granting Bush the presidency one month after election day.

Corbis/Bettmann

MAP EXPLORATION

To explore an interactive version of this map, go to
http://www.prenhall.com/goldfield3/map31.2

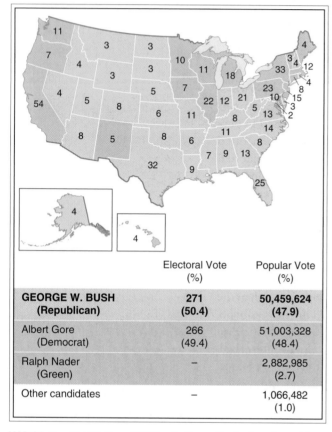

	Electoral Vote (%)	Popular Vote (%)
GEORGE W. BUSH (Republican)	**271** **(50.4)**	**50,459,624** **(47.9)**
Albert Gore (Democrat)	266 (49.4)	51,003,328 (48.4)
Ralph Nader (Green)	–	2,882,985 (2.7)
Other candidates	–	1,066,482 (1.0)

MAP 31–2   The Election of 2000   In the nation's closest presidential election, Democrat Al Gore was most successful in the Northeast and Far West, while George W. Bush swept the South and won most of the Great Plains states. Green Party candidate Ralph Nader took most of his votes from Gore, and, in an ironic twist, helped to swing the election to Bush.

WHAT DO the 2000 election results reveal about the divisions that separate Americans today?

controls required of electric utilities. In many cases, the administration proposed to rely on the market through voluntary compliance and incentives to replace regulations. Vice President Dick Cheney developed a new production-oriented energy policy in consultation with energy companies but not with environmental or consumer groups. The collapse of the energy-trading company Enron in a hailstorm of criticism over deceptive accounting and shady market manipulations to create an energy crisis in California in early 2000 slowed the push to deregulate. In turn, Enron proved to the first of many companies that had to restate earnings in 2002, depressing the stock market and raising questions about the ethics of big business and business accounting practices. Stock market declines and the evaporation of retirement savings for many workers raised doubts about the solidity of the 1990s boom and helped to hold down economic growth for the third year.

Education policy, a centerpiece of Bush's image as an innovator from his service as governor of Texas, was another legislative front. Tough battles with Congress resulted in compromise legislation, reminiscent of the 1990s, that included national testing standards, as Bush wanted, balanced by more federal funding. More important for both education and religion was the narrow decision by the Supreme Court in *Zelman v. Simmons-Harris* (2002) to uphold the use of taxpayer-funded assistance, or vouchers, to help students attend religious schools. By declaring that both religious and secular institutions can compete for government money as long as it is channeled through individuals who made "true private choices" about how to spend it, the court continued a two-decade trend to narrow the constitutional prohibition on the "establishment of religion."

DOWNSIZED DIPLOMACY

The new Bush administration brought a revolutionary approach to foreign affairs, repeatedly adopting unilateral or bilateral policies in preference to the complexities of negotiations with an entire range of nations.

In his first 18 months, Bush opted out of a series of treaties and negotiations on global issues, sometimes despite years of careful bargaining. The administration undercut efforts to implement the Convention on Biological Warfare because of possible adverse effects on drug companies. It refused to sign on to efforts to reduce the international trade in armaments, declined to acknowledge a new International Criminal Court that is designed to try war criminals, and ignored an international compact on the rights of women in deference to cultural conservatives. Most prominently, it refused to accept the Kyoto Agreement, aimed at combating the threat of massive environmental change through global warming resulting from the carbon dioxide released by fossil fuels, dismissing a growing scientific consensus on the problem.

In the field of arms control, Bush entered office with the intention of ending the 1972 treaty that had limited the deployment of antimissile defenses by the United States and Russia in order to stabilize the arms race. The treaty had been a cornerstone of national security policy. Despite the objection of Russia, however, he formally withdrew from the treaty in December 2001. In its place he revived Ronald Reagan's idea of a Strategic Defense Initiative with proposals for new but unproven technologies to protect the United States against nuclear attacks by "rogue states." Bush also decided not to implement the START II treaty, which had been one of the major accomplishments of his father's term as president. In its place, he worked directly to improve relations with Russia and negotiated a bilateral agreement to reduce substantially the number of nuclear warheads that Russia and the United States actively deploy (while pressing for the development of new tactical nuclear weapons). A new U.S. policy that explicitly claimed the right to act militarily to preempt potential threats confirmed the go-it-alone approach.

PARADOXES OF POWER

The United States in the twenty-first century faced the paradox of power: the enormous economic, military, and technological capacity that allowed it to impose its will on other nations did not extend to an ability to prevent anti-American actions by deeply enraged individuals.

In the 1990s, the U.S. economy had surged while Japan stagnated, Europe marked time, and Russia verged on economic collapse. The American economy in the early twenty-first century was twice the size of Japan's; California alone had economic capacity equal to France or Britain. America's lead was nurtured by research and development spending equal to that of the next six countries combined. The American military budget exceeded the total military spending of the next dozen nations. The United States had the world's only global navy and a huge edge in military technology.

But the United States remained vulnerable. Huge trade deficits, massive oil imports, and a falling dollar in the early years of the new century underlined its economic vulnerability. Overseas, terrorist attacks by Islamic radicals killed 19 American soldiers at military housing in Saudi Arabia in 1996 and 17 sailors on the destroyer *Cole* while in port in the Arab nation of Yemen in 2000. Bombs at the U.S. embassies in Kenya and Tanzania in 1998 killed more than 200 people. These bombings followed the detonation of explosives in basement garage of the World Trade Center in New York in February 1993, killing six people. New acts of terror remained a constant threat—realized in an appalling manner on September 11, 2001.

9-11-01

The men who hijacked four commercial jetliners on the morning of September 11 were part of the Al-Qaeda network of terrorists coordinated by Osama Bin-Laden. A Saudi Arabian businessman who had turned against the United States because of its role in the Gulf War and its support for Israeli, Bin-Laden was probably the brains behind the attacks on the U.S. military and on diplomats overseas and the earlier blast at the World Trade Center. The first hijacked plane hit the North Tower of the World Trade Center at 8:46 A.M. eastern time, and the second plane hit the South Tower at 9:30. As flames billowed upward, the South Tower disintegrated at 10:05 and the North Tower at 10:28.

The events of September 11 were an enormous shock to the American people, but worries about escalating terrorism were not new. Security specialists such as Defense Secretary William Cohen had been sounding the alarm through the 1990s. The U.S. Commission on National Security/21st Century, appointed by President Clinton, had included detailed warnings in its February 2001 report, although the new administration had ignored its recommendations to reorganize federal homeland security. The problem, however, had been to connect broad concerns to specific threats. After September 11, there were reports of information-gathering failures by the FBI and CIA. However, it is always enormously difficult to separate and correlate key points in the vast flood of information that flows through law-enforcement and intelligence agencies. It is much easier to read the warnings after an event has occurred than to pick out the essential data before the unexpected happens—something as true about the attack on Pearl Harbor, for example, as about the attack of 9-11.

SECURITY AND CONFLICT

On September 12, President George W. Bush called the Pentagon and World Trade Center attacks "acts of war." Three days later, Congress passed a Joint Resolution that gave the president sweeping powers "to use all necessary and appropriate force against those nations, organizations, or persons he determines planned, authorized, committed, or aided the terrorist attacks that occurred on September 11, 2001." Only one member voted against the resolution—the same level of agreement that the nation showed after December 7, 1941.

The government response in the United States was a hodge-podge of security measures and arrests. Air travelers found endless lines and stringent new screening procedures, watched over by army reservists called to duty by the president. Members of Congress and journalists received letters containing potentially deadly anthrax spores, heightening fears of biological warfare (the source of the letters remained a mystery four years later). Federal agents detained more than 1,000 terrorist suspects, mostly men from the Middle East, releasing some but holding hundreds without charges, evidence, or legal counsel. President Bush also declared that "enemy combatants" could be tried by special military tribunals, although domestic and international protest caused the administration to agree to more legal safeguards than originally planned. Congress passed the **Patriot Act** (Providing Appropriate Tools Required to Intercept and Obstruct Terrorists) in late October, which gave federal authorities substantial new capacity to conduct criminal investigations, in most provisions for the next three to five years.

These measures raised a number of concerns about the protection of civil liberties, as noted by the several dozen members of Congress who voted against the act, and it was subject to increasing criticism for threatening basic constitutional and political rights before its renewal in 2006.

In November 2002, Congress approved a massive reorganization of the federal government to improve security at home. The new Department of Homeland Security includes the Immigration and Naturalization Service, Customs Service, Coast Guard, Secret Service, federal airport security workers, bioterrorism experts, and many others. With 170,000 employees, it is the second-largest federal agency, after the Defense Department. In 2004 Congress adopted a pack-

Patriot Act   Federal legislation adopted in 2001, in response to the terrorist attacks of September 11, intended to facilitate antiterror actions by federal law enforcement and intelligence agencies.

age of reforms to improve intelligence gathering and analysis, creating the position of director of national intelligence to oversee the CIA and report directly to the president.

In contrast to the suppression of dissent during World War I or the internment of Japanese Americans during World War II, Americans in 2001 and 2002 were careful on the home front. The leaders and supporters of the War on Terror reacted to dissenting voices, particularly those from a pacifist tradition, with caustic remarks rather than repression. Censorship consisted of careful management of the news and stonewalling of requests under the Freedom of Information Act rather than direct censorship of speech and the press. Violations of civil liberties

Firefighters work in the rubble of one of the World Trade Center towers soon after its destruction on September 11, 2001.

have affected individuals rather than entire groups. President Bush made an important gesture soon after September 11 by appearing at a mosque and arguing against blanket condemnation of Muslims. Ethnic profiling has resulted in heightened suspicion and surveillance of Muslims, selective enforcement of immigration laws on visitors from 20 Muslim nations, and detention of several hundred U.S. residents of Middle Eastern origin, rather than incarceration of entire ethnic groups.

In the months after 9-11, the military response overseas focused on Afghanistan, where the ruling Taliban regime was harboring Bin-Laden. American bombing attacks on Taliban forces began in early October 2001, and internal opposition groups in Afghanistan threw the Taliban out of power by December. Bin-Laden, however, apparently escaped with the aid of mountainous terrain and the confusion of war, leaving the United States with an uncertain commitment to rebuild a stable Afghanistan. The Al-Qaeda network and sympathetic groups remained active around the world with bombings in places as distant as Indonesia and Kenya.

IRAQ AND CONFLICTS IN THE MIDDLE EAST

Even while the United States was intervening in Afghanistan, the administration was extending its attention to other nations that supported or condoned anti-American terrorists or had the potential to produce chemical, biological, or nuclear weapons of mass destruction. George Bush named North Korea, Iran, and Iraq as an "axis of evil" for these reasons, and then focused on Iraq. After the Gulf War, Iraq had grudgingly accepted a United Nations requirement that it eliminate such weapons, but gradually made UN inspections impossible. This resistance caused Bush to make the overthrow of Iraq's ruthless dictator, Saddam Hussein, the center of foreign policy. In effect, he declared one small, possibly dangerous nation to be the greatest menace the United States faced. In the meantime, North Korea created a further crisis by actively pursuing its atomic weapons program with the threat of additional war, although in 2005 it did enter into talks with China, Japan, Russia, South Korea, and the United States that held a chance of peaceful resolution.

In addition to the direct fallout from the Persian Gulf War, the background to the deep-seated tensions in the Middle East included U.S. support of Israel amidst the deterioration of relations between Israel and the Arab Palestinians in territories occupied by Israel since 1967. The United States has consistently backed Israel since the 1960s. The United States helped to broker an Israel-Egypt peace agreement in 1977 and agreements pointing toward an independent Palestinian state in the 1990s. But hardline Israeli governments have repeatedly taken advantage of U.S. support from the 1980s in Lebanon (see Chapter 30) to the present.

In 2001–2002, the United States watched from the sidelines as the Israeli-Palestinian agreements for transition to a Palestinian state fell apart. Palestinian extremists and suicide bombers and an Israeli government that favored military responses locked each other into a downward spiral that turned into civil war. As a result, many Arabs identify the United States as an enemy of Arab nations and peoples. Israel's decision in 2005 to withdraw from the Gaza Strip and transfer authority there to the Palestinian government was a step toward resolution, but the deep and long unsoluable Israel-Palestinian conflict helps to explain anti-American terrorism among Arabs, and sometimes other Muslims.

In the spring and summer of 2002, the administration escalated threats of unilateral intervention to change the Iraqi regime and began preparations for a second war in the Persian Gulf region. On October 10, Congress authorized pre-emptive military action against Iraq. However, international pressure from unenthusiastic allies and from other Arab nations persuaded Bush to put diplomacy ahead of war and devote two months to making his case at the United Nations. On November 8, the UN Security Council unanimously adopted a compromise resolution that gave Iraq three and a half months to allow full and open inspections before military action might be considered. In the following months, UN inspectors searched Iraqi military sites while the United States built up forces in the Middle East in preparation for war. On March 17, 2003, Bush suspended further diplomatic efforts, and on March 19 a full scale U.S.-British invasion of Iraq began.

The Iraq War was a military success and, on May 1, 2003, President Bush declared that U.S. and British forces now controlled Iraq and major combat operations in Iraq were over. Peace proved more difficult than war. Reconstruction of damaged bridges, roads, water systems, and electrical systems took far longer than expected. Meanwhile, American troops and relief workers were the continuing targets of car bombs, booby-trapped highways, mortar attacks, and similar guerrilla resistance. By April 2006, more than 2,300 American soldiers had died in Iraq, over 90 percent of them after the president declared victory.

The aftermath of the war also created political problems for George Bush. A systematic search found no active production facilities or stockpiles for chemical, nuclear,

Soldiers in combat in Iraq.

Getty Images, Inc.

or biological weapons of mass destruction, refuting one of the basic justifications for the war. The continuing necessity to mobilize National Guard and reserve units because of the need to keep an occupying army or more than 100,000 in Iraq met heavy criticism.

THE 2004 ELECTION

Wars past and present were the pivotal issue in the 2004 election. George W. Bush argued for staying the course with the same administration. Democratic candidate John Kerry had a liberal voting record as a Massachusetts senator and decorations for meritorious service in Vietnam, but central to the Republican campaign were attacks on the veracity of his war record. A wild card was the issue of same-sex marriage. Courts in Massachusetts and politicians in Oregon and San Francisco decided that legal marriage could not be denied to same-sex couples. Their actions mobilized religious and cultural conservatives and led to successful ballot measures banning same-sex marriage in 11 states.

Bush won a solid although not overwhelming victory that helped Republicans extend their lead in Congress. Commentators liked to talk about a nation divided on issues of morality between Democratic "blue states" and Republican "red states." In fact, many states remained closely divided. Pundits also claimed that Bush used the issue of "moral values," including opposition to same-sex marriage, to mobilize voters, but he did not do any better among regular churchgoers in 2004 than in 2000.

After the election, Bush reaffirmed his commitment to an American presence in Iraq, where a deeply divided nation held elections for a new government early in 2005. Kurds from northern Iraq and Shiite Muslims from southern Iraq voted in large numbers and formed a coalition government. Participation was much lower among Sunni Muslims in central Iraq, who had benefitted most from Saddam Hussein's regime and who were the heart of guerrilla resistance to the United States occupation forces. The same divisions were evident in Octover when Iraqis approved a new constitution that met Shiite and Kurdish desires for greater autonomy but left many Sunnis dissatisfied.

As the nation worried about the open-ended commitment in Iraq, it received a devastating reminded of vulnerability. At the end of August 2005, hurricane Katrina devastated the Gulf Coast. It first seemed to spare new Orleans, much of which lies below sea level, but its backlash breached levees that protected the city. Much of the city and its surroundings flooded. Tens of thousands of residents who had not evacuated found themselves trapped in homes or huddled in the Superdome. The slowness and inadequacy of the emergency response raised serious doubts about the effectiveness of the Department of Homeland Security and revealed the deep fault line that still separate the poor from the larger society. Behind the growing discussion about whether and how to rebuild New Orleans on its vulnerable site was a larger problem of continuing inequality.

CONCLUSION

*I*f there was a dominant theme that ran through the changes and challenges of the 1990s and early 2000s, it was interconnection. The Internet, e-mail, and cell phones brought instant communication. The national economy was more and more deeply engaged with the rest of the world through trade, investment, travel, and immigration. Corporate mismanagement affected far more people than before because of pensions and savings invested in the stock market.

AMERICA'S MISSION TO THE WORLD

On April 2, 1917, President Woodrow Wilson addressed an extraordinary session of Congress and asked for a declaration of war against Germany. For nearly three years, the United States had avoided direct involvement in the great war raging in Europe, and Wilson had won reelection in 1916 on a platform of continued peace. Now, Wilson said, Germany's decision to engage in unrestricted submarine warfare had made than nation the enemy of international law and morality.

Wilson argued the need for the United States to protect its citizens, but he also proclaimed a crusade to make "the world safe for democracy." The United States, in other words, would engage in overseas war to carry out a mission to the world. The nation's goal, he said, was "to vindicate the principles of peace and justice in the life of the world" and "to fight thus for the ultimate peace of the world and for the liberation of its peoples." Wilson's idealism echoed repeatedly through the twentieth century—in Franklin Roosevelt's proclamation of the Four Freedoms, in John Kennedy's claim that Americans would "bear any burden" in the defense of liberty, in Jimmy Carter's emphasis on advancing human rights in other nations.

But the clearest echo came in January 2005, in the second inaugural address of George W. Bush. Like Wilson, Bush proclaimed that the United States has a mission and destiny to actively and tirelessly extend democracy throughout the world. "It is the policy of the United States to seek and support the growth of democratic movements and institutions in every nation and culture, with the ultimate goal of ending tyranny in our world. . . . America's influence is considerable and we will use it confidently." Later in the speech, he repeated, "We go forward with complete confidence . . . history also has a visible direction, set by liberty and the author of Liberty."

Bush's reference to "the author of Liberty" reveals the religious foundations of his policy. Both Wilson and Bush drew on deep religious beliefs that have provided continuity for American foreign policy. Wilson's flinty, fierce Presbyterianism made him adamant in his conviction that God had given the United States a mandate to change the world and reluctant to compromise to political realities. Bush's evangelical Christianity similarly helps to give certainty to his goals and decisions.

In 1918 and 1919, Wilson's idealism crashed on the rocks of European power politics and the weakness of the new League of Nations, which Congress spurned. Later in the twentieth century, U.S. policy balanced uneasily between democratic idealism and expedient compromises to combat Nazism and Communism. For example, the Truman administration helped democracy flourish in previously repressive nations like Japan and Italy, but after World War II the United States just as often made common cause with dictators who opposed the Soviet Union but had little interest in the freedom of their own people. In the twenty-first century, George W. Bush has rearticulated Wilson's absolute idealism as the standard for foreign policy. In practice, however, Bush's doctrine has taken the form not only of diplomacy but also of preemptive war, leaving the nation to see whether its new crusade for freedom depends on the old tactics of power politics.

The nation's growing diversity—closely connected to its internationalized economy—was reflected in the political gains of African Americans and Hispanics, as well as women. The same diversity fueled battles over affirmative action and language politics. It underlay the effort to increase security against terrorism without endangering the civil liberties of Muslim Americans.

Despite what some might have wished, Americans also found that they could not always isolate the nation from the problems and conflicts that wracked much of the rest of the world. The Clinton administration joined international peacekeeping efforts in Bosnia and Kosovo. The Bush administration chose to ignore several international agreements, but still sought United Nations approval for action against Iraq.

Beyond its growing military commitments, the United States in the first years of the twenty-first century was deeply connected to the world. Travel, work and study abroad—and foreign tourists, workers, and students in the United States—improved American understanding of other nations. But the ease and volume of travel and trade also brought problems and fears. Many Americans had long worried that the United States was being flooded by illegal immigrants, and the revelation that some of the 9-11 terrorists had learned to fly in U.S. training schools compounded fears of a porous border. A ballooning national debt and fast-growing trade deficits reduced the purchasing power of the dollar and made the economy dependent on investment from abroad.

The events of September 11 sparked a renewed sense of national unity, at least in the short run. Stories of heroism were inspiring, as was the outpouring of volunteers and contributions for rescue and relief efforts. As the nation slowly settled back into routines, however, the devastation of hurricane Katrina revealed continuing divisions that undercut the full promise of American life. The question that remained was whether Americans could sustain and build an inclusive and unified nation under the pressures of economic uncertainty, threats of terrorism, and war.

IMAGE KEY
for pages 912–913

a. Computer chips.
b. A cell phone like those used by many in the stricken World Trade Center Towers to call for help or give their families their last good-byes.
c. Black smoke billowing through lower Manhattan during the collapse of the World Trade Center.
d. A paper voting card like those used in Florida in the contentious 2000 presidential election.
e. A gas mask used as protection from a chemical or biological attack.
f. A soldier stops to watch the sunset during military exercises in Kuwait, November 18, 2002.
g. Bill Clinton campaigning in 1992.
h. The overthrow of the Taliban re-opens opportunities for women in Afghanistan.
i. S.V. Marshall High School students join other Mississippi teens in building more than 125 new high-speed multimedia computers during a Computer Blitz Build at Jackson State University e-Center.
j. George W. Bush awaits results from 2000 Presidental Elections recount.
k. Leadership opportunities for African Americans have increased in recent decades.
l. Computer chips have come to symbolize the boom of the 1990s.

SUMMARY

Politics of the Center In 1992 voters ranked the economy as their first concern, and Bill Clinton hammered at this in his campaign messages. His elections in 1992 and 1996 showed a move toward the political center; Clinton emerged as a neoliberal. Conservative political ideology and animosity toward the Clintons dominated the headlines; the Contract with America, the budget battle that shut down the federal government, Whitewater, the Clinton scandals, and impeachment filled the political headlines. Domestic terrorism (Waco, Oklahoma City, and Columbine) also grabbed the national spotlight. In foreign affairs, the United States became involved in a multinational effort to restore peace in Bosnia and Kosovo.

A New Economy? At the end of the millennium, America had a new worry, the "Y2K" problem, that did not materialize. In the 1990s Americans enjoyed nine years of continuous economic expansion; services became the new underpinning of the economy; and an instant society based on twenty-four hour access gave people immediate satisfaction. The American economy also expanded internationally. The controversial North American Free Trade Agreement went into effect and

protestors took on the World Trade Organization in the streets of Seattle which demonstrated as part of a larger worldwide debate over free trade and the role of transnational corporations.

Broadening Democracy The changing composition of the American people is related to the changes in the economy. The growing West, the concentration of one-third of the population in four states, the largest ten-year population increase in history, and racial and ethnic diversity, are all significance trends. As women have become more influential in national politics, so have minorities; both have contributed to a political rebalancing. Questions about equal rights and equal opportunities (Proposition 187, bilingual education, and affirmative action) have become part of the American dialogue.

REVIEW QUESTIONS

1. Was the American political system more polarized and divided in 1992 than in 1980? How did religiously conservative Americans understand issues of foreign relations and economic policy? How did religiously liberal Americans understand the same issues? What was the gender gap in national politics in the 1990s? Why were Republicans unable to appeal to most black and Hispanic voters in 1992?

2. What were Bill Clinton's major policy accomplishments? Do these represent liberal, moderate, or conservative positions?

3. What was the Contract with America? What are other examples of a conservative political trend in the 1990s?

4. What issues were involved in Clinton's impeachment? How does the impeachment compare with the challenges to Presidents Andrew Johnson and Richard Nixon?

5. Did the American economy undergo fundamental changes in the 1990s? What has been the impact of the computer revolution? Of the growing importance of world markets?

6. What new directions did George W. Bush establish for U.S. domestic and foreign policy?

7. How did the terrorist attacks of September 11, 2001 change life in the United States? How did ordinary Americans respond at the time and since the attacks?

KEY TERMS

Affirmative action (p. 931)
Contract with America (p. 918)
Internet (p. 923)
Neoliberal (p. 918)
North American Free Trade Agreement (NAFTA) (p. 925)

Patriot Act (p. 936)
Silicon Valley (p. 924)
Temporary Assistance for Needy Families (TANF) (p. 919)
University of California v. Bakke (p. 931)

Whitewater (p. 921)
World Trade Organization (WTO) (p. 927)
World Wide Web (p. 925)

WHERE TO LEARN MORE

 Oklahoma City National Memorial Center Museum, Oklahoma City, OK.
Exhibits about the federal building bombing and its impacts on the community.
www.oklahomacitynationalmemorial.org

 U.S. History Documents CD-ROM
For primary sources related to this chapter, refer to the document CD-ROM.

www.prenhall.com/goldfield
For study resources related to this chapter, visit the *Companion Website*™.

CHAPTER 12

1790 Samuel Slater opens the first permanent cotton mill in Rhode Island.

1793 Eli Whitney patents the first cotton gin.

1807 Robert Fulton's steamboat, the Clermont, makes its pioneering voyage up the Hudson River.

1814 The Boston Associates opens its Waltham mill, the first textile factory to mechanize all phases of production.

1817 Construction of the Erie Canal begins. American Colonization Society is founded.

1819–1823 Economic depression.

1824 In *Gibbons v. Ogden*, the Supreme Court strikes down a state monopoly over steamboat navigation.

1825 Erie Canal is completed.

1826 American Temperance Society launches its crusade.

1828 The Baltimore and Ohio, the most important of the early railroads, is chartered.

1829 David Walker publishes Appeal to the Colored Citizens of the World.

1830 Joseph Smith founds the Church of Jesus Christ of Latter-day Saints.

1830–1831 Evangelical revivals are held in northern cities.

1831 William Lloyd Garrison begins publishing the *Liberator*.

1833 Slaves in the British Empire are emancipated. American Anti-Slavery Society is organized.

1834 New York Female Reform Society is founded. Female workers at the Lowell Mills stage their first strike.

1836 Congress passes gag rule.

1837 Horace Mann begins campaign for school reform in Massachusetts. Antiabolitionist mob kills Elijah P. Lovejoy.

1839–1843 Economic depression.

1840 Abolitionists split into Garrisonian and anti-Garrisonian societies. Political abolitionists launch the Liberty party.

1841 Brook Farm is established. Dorothea Dix begins her work to improve conditions for the mentally ill.

1842 Massachusetts Supreme Court in Commonwealth v. Hunt strengthens the legal right of workers to organize trade unions.

1845 Potato famine in Ireland sets off a mass migration of Irish to the United States.

1846–1848 Mormons migrate to the West.

1847 John Humphrey Noyes establishes the Oneida Community.

1848 Seneca Falls Convention outlines a program for women's rights.

CHAPTER 13

1803–1806 Lewis and Clark travel up the Missouri River in search of a water route to the Pacific.

1816 Settlers surge into the trans-Appalachian region.

1821 Santa Fe Trail opens. Stephen F. Austin establishes the first American colony in Texas.

1824 Rocky Mountain Fur Company begins the rendezvous system.

1830 Congress creates the Indian Territory.

1834 Protestant missions are established in Oregon. Santa Anna seizes power in Mexico.

1836 Texas wins its independence from Mexico.

1837 Smallpox epidemic hits the Plains Indians.

1842 First large parties of migrants set out on the Oregon Trail.

1845 United States annexes Texas. Democrats embrace Manifest Destiny. The Great Irish Famine begins.

1846 Mexican War breaks out. United States and Britain reach an agreement in Oregon.

1847 Mormons begin settlement of Utah.

1848 Oregon Territory is organized. Treaty of Guadalupe Hidalgo ends the Mexican War.

1851 Fort Laramie Treaty with the Plains Indians is signed.

CHAPTER 14

1846 Wilmot Proviso is submitted to Congress but is defeated.

1848 Gold is discovered in California. Whig Party candidate Zachary Taylor defeats Democrat Lewis Cass and Free-Soiler Martin Van Buren for the presidency.

1850 California applies for statehood. President Taylor dies; Vice President Millard Fillmore succeeds him. Compromise of 1850 is passed.

1851 Harriet Beecher Stowe publishes *Uncle Tom's Cabin*.

1852 Democrat Franklin Pierce is elected president in a landslide over Whig candidate Winfield Scott. Whig Party disintegrates.

1853 National Black Convention opens in Rochester, New York, to demand repeal of the Fugitive Slave Act.

1854 Kansas-Nebraska Act repeals the Missouri Compromise. Know-Nothing and Republican parties are formed.

1855 Civil war erupts in "Bleeding Kansas."

1856 "Sack of Lawrence" occurs in Kansas; John Brown makes a retaliatory raid at Pottawatomie Creek. Democratic congressman Preston Brooks of South Carolina canes Massachusetts senator Charles Sumner in the U.S. Senate. Democrat James Buchanan is elected president over Republican John C. Frémont and American (Know-Nothing) candidate Millard Fillmore.

1857 Supreme Court issues Dred Scott decision. Kansas territorial legislature passes the proslavery Lecompton Constitution. Panic of 1857 begins.

1858 Senatorial candidates Abraham Lincoln and Stephen A. Douglas hold series of debates in Illinois.

1859 John Brown's raid fails at Harpers Ferry, Virginia.

1860 Constitutional Union Party forms. Democratic Party divides into northern and southern factions. Republican candidate Abraham Lincoln is elected president over southern Democratic candidate John C. Breckinridge, northern Democratic candidate Stephen A. Douglas, and Constitutional Unionist candidate John Bell. South Carolina secedes from the Union.

1861 The rest of the Lower South secedes from the Union. Crittenden Plan and Tyler's Washington peace conference fail. Jefferson Davis assumes presidency of the Confederate States of America. Lincoln is inaugurated. Fort Sumter is bombarded; Civil War begins. Several Upper South states secede.

CHAPTER 15

1861 Confederates fire on Fort Sumter; Civil War begins. First Battle of Bull Run.

1862 Forts Henry and Donelson fall to Union forces. Peninsula Campaign begins. Battle of Glorieta Pass, New Mexico. Battle of Shiloh. New Orleans falls to Federal forces. Union captures Corinth, Mississippi. Seven Days' Battles end. Congress passes the Confiscation Act. Second Battle of Bull Run. Battle of Antietam. Battle of Fredericksburg.

1863 Emancipation Proclamation takes effect. Battle of Chancellorsville. Stonewall Jackson is mortally wounded. Battle of Gettysburg. Vicksburg falls to Union forces. New York Draft Riot occurs. Black troops of the 54th Massachusetts Volunteer Infantry Regiment assault Fort Wagner outside Charleston. Battle of Chickamauga. Battle of Chattanooga.

1864 Battle of the Wilderness. Battle of Cold Harbor. Sherman captures Atlanta. President Lincoln is reelected. Sherman begins his march to the sea.

1865 Congress passes Thirteenth Amendment to the Constitution, outlawing slavery (ratified December 1865). Charleston surrenders. Confederate Congress authorizes enlistment of black soldiers. Federal troops enter Richmond. Lee surrenders to Grant at Appomattox Court House. Lincoln is assassinated.

CHAPTER 16

1863 Lincoln proposes his Ten Percent Plan.

1864 Congress proposes the Wade-Davis Bill.

1865 Sherman issues Field Order No. 15. Freedmen's Bureau is established. Andrew Johnson succeeds to the presidency, unveils his Reconstruction plan. Massachusetts desegregates all public facilities. Black citizens in several southern cities organize Union Leagues. Former Confederate states begin to pass black codes.

1866 Congress passes Southern Homestead Act, Civil Rights Act of 1866. Ku Klux Klan is founded. Fourteenth Amendment to the Constitution is passed (ratified in 1868).

1867 Congress passes Military Reconstruction Acts, Tenure of Office Act.

1868 President Johnson is impeached and tried in the Senate for defying the Tenure of Office Act. Republican Ulysses S. Grant is elected president.

1869 Fifteenth Amendment passed (ratified 1870).

1870 Congress passes Enforcement Act. Republican regimes topple in North Carolina and Georgia.

1871 Congress passes Ku Klux Klan Act.

1872 Freedmen's Bureau closes down. Liberal Republicans emerge as a separate party. Ulysses S. Grant is reelected.

1873 Severe depression begins. Colfax Massacre occurs. U.S. Supreme Court's decision in the Slaughterhouse cases weakens the intent of the Fourteenth Amendment. Texas falls to the Democrats in the fall elections.

1874 White Leaguers attempt a coup against the Republican government of New Orleans. Democrats win off-year elections across the South amid wide spread fraud and violence.

1875 Congress passes Civil Rights Act of 1875.

1876 Supreme Court's decision in United States v. Cruikshank nullifies Enforcement Act of 1870. Outcome of the presidential election between Republican Rutherford B. Hayes and Democrat Samuel J. Tilden is contested.

1877 Compromise of 1877 makes Hayes president and ends Reconstruction.

CHAPTER 17

1872 Texas and Pacific Railway connects Dallas to eastern markets.

1880 First southern local of the Women's Christian Temperance Union is formed in Atlanta.

1881 Booker T. Washington establishes Tuskegee Institute.

1882 Agricultural Wheel is formed in Arkansas.

1883 Laura Haygood founds the home mission movement in Atlanta.

1884 James B. Duke automates his cigarette factory.

1886 Dr. John Pemberton creates Coca-Cola. Southern railroads conform to national track gauge standards.

1887 Charles W. Macune expands the Southern Farmer's Alliance from its Texas base to the rest of the South.

1888 The Southern Farmers' Alliance initiates a successful boycott of jute manufacturers.

1890 Mississippi becomes the first state to restrict black suffrage with literacy tests.

1892 The Populist Party forms.

1894 United Daughters of the Confederacy is founded. Populist and Republican fusion candidates win control of North Carolina.

1895 Booker T. Washington delivers his "Atlanta Compromise" address.

1896 Populists endorse the Democratic presidential candidate and fade as a national force. In Plessy v. Ferguson, the Supreme Court permits segregation by law.

1898 North Carolina Mutual Life Insurance is founded. Democrats regain control of North Carolina.

1903 W. E. B. Du Bois publishes *The Souls of Black Folk*.

1905 James B. Duke forms the Southern Power Company. Thomas Dixon publishes *The Clansman*.

1906 Bloody race riots break out in Atlanta.

1907 Pittsburgh-based U.S. Steel takes over Birmingham's largest steel producer.

CHAPTER 18

1869 The Knights of Labor is founded in Philadelphia.

1870 John D. Rockefeller organizes the Standard Oil Company. Congress passes the Naturalization Act barring Asians from citizenship.

1876 The Centennial Exposition opens in Philadelphia. Beginning of the rule of dictator Porfirio Diaz in Mexico, whose regime is ended by the Mexican Revolution.

1877 Execution of ten Molly Maguires in Pennsylvania. The Great Uprising railroad strike, the first nation-wide work stoppage in the United States, provokes violent clashes between workers and federal troops.

1879 Thomas Edison unveils the electric light bulb.

1880 Founding of the League of American Wheelmen helps establish bicycling as one of urban America's favorite recreational activities.

1881 Assassination of Tsar Alexander II begins a series of pogroms that triggers a wave of Russian Jewish immigration to the United States.

1882 Congress passes the Chinese Exclusion Act. First country club in the United States founded in Brookline, Massachusetts.

1883 National League merges with the American Association and opens baseball to working-class fans.

1886 The Neighborhood Guild, the nation's first settle-ment house, opens in New York City. Riot in Chicago's Haymarket Square breaks the Knights of Labor. American Federation of Labor is formed.

1887 Anti-Catholic American Protective Association is formed.

1888 Wanamaker's department store introduces a "bargain room," and competitors follow suit.

1889 Jane Addams opens Hull House, the nation's most celebrated settlement house, in Chicago.

1890 Jacob A. Riis publishes *How the Other Half Lives*.

1891 African-American Chicago physician Daniel Hale Williams establishes Provident Hospital, the nation's first interracially staffed hospital.

1892 General Electric opens the first corporate research and development division in the United States. Strike at Andrew Carnegie's Homestead steelworks fails.

1894 Pullman Sleeping Car Company strike fails. Immigration Restriction League is formed.

1895 American-born Chinese in California form the Native Sons of the Golden State to counter nativism.

1897 George C. Tilyou opens Steeplechase Park on Coney Island in Brooklyn, New York.

1898 Congress passes the Erdman Act to provide for voluntary mediation of railroad labor disputes.

CHAPTER 19

1858 Gold is discovered in Colorado, Nevada, and British Columbia.

1860 Gold is discovered in Idaho.

1862 Homestead Act is passed. Gold is discovered in Montana.

1864 Militia slaughters Cheyennes at Sand Creek, Colorado.

1867 Cattle drives make Abilene the first cow town.

1868 Fort Laramie Treaty is signed.

1869 First transcontinental railroad is completed.

1874 Gold is discovered in the Black Hills. Barbed wire is patented.

1876 Indians devastate U.S. troops in the Battle of the Little Bighorn.

1879 "Exodusters" migrate to Kansas.

1885 Chinese massacred at Rock Springs, Wyoming.

1887 Dawes Act is passed.

1890 Government troops kill 200 Sioux at Wounded Knee, South Dakota.

1892 Mining violence breaks out at Coeur d'Alene, Idaho.

1893 Western Federation of Miners is organized.

CHAPTER 20

1867 Patrons of Husbandry (the Grange) is founded.

1869 Massachusetts establishes the first state regulatory commission.

1873 Silver is demonetized in the "Crime of '73."

1874 Woman's Christian Temperance Union is organized.

1875 U.S. Supreme Court, in Minor v. Happersett, upholds denial of suffrage to women.

1876 Greenback Party runs presidential candidate.

1877 Rutherford B. Hayes becomes president after dis-puted election. Farmers' Alliance is founded. Supreme Court, in Munn v. Illinois, upholds state regulatory authority over private property.

1878 Bland-Allison Act obliges the government to buy silver.

1880 James A. Garfield is elected president.

1881 Garfield is assassinated; Chester A. Arthur becomes president.

1883 Pendleton Civil Service Act is passed.

1884 Grover Cleveland is elected president.

1886 Supreme Court, in Wabash v. Illinois, rules that only the federal government, not the states, can regulate interstate commerce.

1887 Interstate Commerce Act is passed.

1888 Benjamin Harrison is elected president.

1890 Sherman Antitrust Act is passed. McKinley Tariff Act is passed. Sherman Silver Purchase Act is passed. National American Woman Suffrage Association is organized. Wyoming enters the Union as the first state with woman suffrage.

1892 People's Party is organized. Grover Cleveland is elected to his second term as president.

1893 Depression begins. Sherman Silver Purchase Act is repealed.

1894 Coxey's Army marches to Washington. Pullman strike ends in violence.

1895 Supreme Court, in *Pollock v. Farmers' Loan and Trust Company*, invalidates the federal income tax. Supreme Court, in *United States v. E. C. Knight Company*, limits the Sherman Antitrust Law to commerce, excluding industrial monopolies.

1896 William Jennings Bryan is nominated for president by Democrats and Populists. William McKinley is elected president.

1900 Currency Act puts U.S. currency on the gold standard.

CHAPTER 21

1893–1898 Depression grips the nation.

1898 South Dakota adopts initiative and referendum. National Consumers' League is organized.

1899 Anti-Cigarette League of America is established.

1901 United States Steel Corporation is formed, the world's largest business at the time. President William McKinley is assassinated; Theodore Roosevelt becomes president. Socialist Party of America is organized. New York Tenement House Law is enacted. Galveston, Texas, initiates the city commission plan.

1902 Antitrust suit is filed against Northern Securities Company. McClure's initiates muckraking journalism. Mississippi enacts the first direct-primary law. National Reclamation Act is passed. Roosevelt intervenes in coal strike.

1903 Women's Trade Union League is organized.

1904 National Child Labor Committee is formed. Roosevelt is elected president.

1905 Industrial Workers of the World is organized.

1906 Hepburn Act strengthens the Interstate Commerce Commission. Meat Inspection Act extends govern-ment regulation. Pure Food and Drug Act is passed.

1908 Muller v. Oregon upholds maximum workday for women. William Howard Taft is elected president.

1910 National Association for the Advancement of Colored People is organized. Ballinger-Pinchot controversy erupts.

1912 Children's Bureau is established. Progressive Party organizes and nominates Theodore Roosevelt. Woodrow Wilson is elected president.

1913 Sixteenth and Seventeenth Amendments are rati-fied. Underwood-Simmons Tariff Act establishes an income tax. Federal Reserve Act creates the Federal Reserve System.

1914 Federal Trade Commission is established. Harrison Act criminalizes narcotics.

1915 National Birth Control League is formed.

1916 Keating-Owen Act prohibits child labor.

1917 Congress enacts literacy test for immigrants.

1919 Eighteenth Amendment is ratified.

1920 Nineteenth Amendment is ratified.

CHAPTER 22

1861–1869 Seward serves as secretary of state.
1867 United States purchases Alaska from Russia.
1881 Naval Advisory Board is created.
1887 United States gains naval rights to Pearl Harbor.
1889 First Pan-American Conference is held.
1893 Harrison signs but Cleveland rejects a treaty for the annexation of Hawaii.
1894–1895 Sino-Japanese War is fought.
1895 United States intervenes in Great Britain–Venezuelan boundary dispute.
1896 William McKinley is elected president on an imperialist platform.
1898 Spanish-American War is fought. Hawaii is annexed. Anti-Imperialist League is organized. Treaty of Paris is signed.
1899–1902 Filipino-American War is fought.
1899 Open Door note is issued.
1900 Boxer Rebellion against foreign influence breaks out in China.
1901 Theodore Roosevelt becomes president.
1903 Platt Amendment restricts Cuban autonomy. Panama "revolution" is abetted by the United States.
1904 United States acquires the Panama Canal Zone. Roosevelt Corollary is announced.
1905 Treaty of Portsmouth ends the Russo-Japanese War through U.S. mediation.
1906–1909 United States occupies Cuba.
1907–1908 Gentlemen's Agreement restricts Japanese immigration.
1909 United States intervenes in Nicaragua.
1912–1933 United States occupies Nicaragua.
1914 Panama Canal opens.
1914–1917 United States intervenes in Mexico.
1915–1934 United States occupies Haiti.
1916–1924 United States occupies the Dominican Republic.
1917 Puerto Ricans are granted U.S. citizenship.
1917–1922 United States occupies Cuba.

CHAPTER 23

1914 World War I begins in Europe. President Woodrow Wilson declares U.S. neutrality.
1915 Germany begins submarine warfare. Lusitania is sunk. Woman's Peace Party is organized.
1916 Gore-McLemore resolutions are defeated. Sussex Pledge is issued. Preparedness legislation is enacted. Woodrow Wilson is reelected president.
1917 The United States declares war on Germany. Selective Service Act establishes the military draft. Espionage Act is passed. Committee on Public Information, War Industries Board, Food Administration, and other mobilization agencies are established. American Expeditionary Force arrives in France. East St. Louis race riot erupts.
1918 Wilson announces his Fourteen Points. Sedition Act is passed. Eugene Debs is imprisoned. The United States intervenes militarily in Russia. Armistice ends World War I.
1919 Paris Peace Conference is held. Steel, coal, and other strikes occur. Red Scare breaks out. Prohibition amendment is adopted. Wilson suffers a massive stroke.
1920 Palmer Raids round up radicals. League of Nations is defeated in the U.S. Senate. Woman suffrage amendment is ratified. U.S. troops are withdrawn from Russia. Warren Harding is elected president.
1921 United States signs a separate peace treaty with Germany.

CHAPTER 24

1915 Ku Klux Klan is founded anew.
1919 Volstead Act is passed.
1920 Urban population exceeds rural population for the first time. Warren Harding is elected president. Prohibition takes effect. First commercial radio show is broadcast. Sinclair Lewis publishes Main Street.
1921 Sheppard-Towner Maternity and Infancy Act is passed. Washington Naval Conference limits naval armaments.
1922 Fordney-McCumber Act raises tariff rates. Sinclair Lewis publishes *Babbitt*. Country Club Plaza in Kansas City opens.
1923 Warren Harding dies; Calvin Coolidge becomes president.
1924 National Origins Act sharply curtails immigration. Calvin Coolidge is elected president.
1925 Scopes trial is held in Dayton, Tennessee. F. Scott Fitzgerald publishes *The Great Gatsby*.
1927 Charles A. Lindbergh flies solo across the Atlantic.
1928 Kellogg-Briand Pact is signed. Herbert Hoover is elected president.
1929 Ernest Hemingway publishes *A Farewell to Arms*.

CHAPTER 25

1929 Stock market crashes.
1932 Farmers' Holiday Association organizes rural protests in the Midwest. Reconstruction Finance Corporation is created to assist financial institutions. Bonus Army is routed in Washington, D.C. Franklin D. Roosevelt is elected president.
1933 Emergency Banking Act is passed. The United States recognizes the Soviet Union. Agricultural Adjustment Administration (AAA) is created to regulate farm production. National Recovery Administration (NRA) is created to promote industrial cooperation and recovery. Federal Emergency Relief Act provides federal assistance to the unemployed. Civilian Conservation Corps (CCC) is established to provide work relief in conservation projects. Public Works Administration (PWA) is created to provide work relief on large public construction projects. Civil Works Administration (CWA) provides emergency winter relief jobs. Tennessee Valley Authority (TVA) is created to coordinate regional development.
1934 Securities and Exchange Commission (SEC) is established. Indian Reorganization Act reforms Indian policy. Huey Long organizes the Share-Our-Wealth Society. Democrats win midterm elections.
1935 Supreme Court declares NRA unconstitutional. National Labor Relations Act (Wagner Act) guarantees workers' rights to organize and bargain collectively. Social Security Act establishes a federal social insurance system. Banking Act strengthens the Federal Reserve. Revenue Act establishes a more progressive tax system. Resettlement Administration is created to aid dispossessed farmers. Rural Electrification Administration (REA) is created to help provide electric power to rural areas. Soil Conservation Service is established. Emergency Relief Appropriation Act authorizes public relief projects for the unemployed. Works Progress Administration (WPA) is created. Huey Long is assassinated.
1936 Supreme Court declares AAA unconstitutional. Roosevelt is reelected president. Roosevelt sails to South America as part of Good Neighbor Policy.
1937 Chicago police kill workers in Memorial Day Massacre. FDR tries but fails to expand the Supreme Court. Farm Security Administration (FSA) is created to lend money to small farmers to buy and rehabilitate farms. National Housing Act is passed to promote public housing projects. "Roosevelt Recession" begins.
1938 Congress of Industrial Organizations (CIO) is founded. Fair Labor Standards Act establishes minimum wage and maximum hours rules for labor. Roosevelt fails to "purge" the Democratic Party. Republicans make gains in midterm elections.

CHAPTER 26

1935 Congress passes first of three neutrality Acts.
1939 Germany and the Soviet Union sign a non-aggression pact. Germany absorbs Czechoslovakia. Germany invades Poland; Great Britain and France declare war on Germany.
1940 Germany conquers Denmark, Norway, Belgium, the Netherlands, and France. Japan, Germany, and Italy sign the Tripartite Pact. Germany bombs England in the Battle of Britain. The United States begins to draft men into the armed forces. Franklin Roosevelt wins an unprecedented third term.
1941 The United States begins a lend-lease program to make military equipment available to Great Britain and later the Soviet Union. The Fair Employment Practices Committee is established. Germany invades the Soviet Union. Roosevelt and Churchill issue the Atlantic Charter. Japan attacks U.S. military bases in Hawaii.
1942 American forces in the Philippines surrender to Japan. President Roosevelt authorizes the removal and internment of Japanese Americans living in four western states. Naval battles in the Coral Sea and off the island of Midway blunt Japanese expansion. U.S. forces land in North Africa. Soviet forces encircle a German army at Stalingrad. The first sustained and controlled nuclear chain reaction takes place at the University of Chicago.
1943 U.S. and British forces invade Italy, which makes terms with the Allies. Race conflict erupts in riots in Detroit, New York, and Los Angeles. The landing of Marines on Tarawa initiates the island-hopping strategy. U.S. war production peaks. Roosevelt, Churchill, and Stalin confer at Tehran.
1944 Allied forces land in Normandy. The U.S. Navy destroys Japanese sea power in the battles of the Philippine Sea and Leyte Gulf. The Battle of the Bulge is the last tactical setback for the Allies.
1945 Roosevelt, Stalin, and Churchill meet at Yalta to plan the postwar world. The United States takes the Pacific islands of Iwo Jima and Okinawa. Franklin Roosevelt dies; Harry S Truman becomes president. Germany surrenders to the United States, Great Britain, and the Soviet Union. The United Nations is organized at an international meeting in San Francisco. Potsdam Conference. Japan surrenders after the detonation of atomic bombs over Hiroshima and Nagasaki.

CHAPTER 7

1776 States begin writing the first constitutions.
1777 Articles of Confederation proposed.
1781 Articles ratified.
1783 Americans celebrate independence and the peace treaty with Britain. British West Indies closed to U.S. traders.

1784 Onset of the postwar depression. Opening of China trade by the United States. Spain closes the Mississippi. Treaty of Fort Stanwix.
1785 Land Ordinance of 1785. Treaty of Fort McIntosh.
1786 Shay's Rebellion breaks out. Jay-Gardoqui Treaty defeated. Annapolis Convention.

1787 Constitutional Convention at Philadelphia. Northwest Ordinance.
1788 Constitution ratified and goes into effect. Publication of *The Federalist*.

CHAPTER 8

1789 Inauguration of George Washington. Congress establishes he first federal departments.
1790 Alexander Hamilton submits the first of his financial reports to Congress.
1791 Bill of Rights ratified. Congress charters the Bank of the United States.
1792 St. Clair's defeat along the Wabash. Reelection of Washington.
1793 Genêt Mission. Washington issues Proclamation

of Neutrality.
1794 Ohio is opened with the victory of General Anthony Wayne at the Battle of Fallen Timbers. Suppression of the Whiskey Rebellion in western Pennsylvania.
1795 Jay's Treaty with Britain ratified. Treaty of Greenville with Ohio Indians.
1796 Pinckney's Treaty with Spain ratified. John Adams elected president.

1797 Beginning of the Quasi-War with France.
1798 XYZ Affair. Alien and Sedition Acts. Provisional army and direct tax. Virginia and Kentucky Resolutions.
1799 Fries's Rebellion in Pennsylvania.
1800 Franco-American Accord. Thomas Jefferson elected president.

CHAPTER 9

1801 Thomas Jefferson is inaugurated. John Marshall becomes chief justice.
1802 Congress repeals the Judiciary Act of 1801.
1803 Marbury v. Madison sets the precedent of judicial review by the Supreme Court. Louisiana Purchase. Lewis and Clark expedition begins.
1804 Vice President Aaron Burr kills Alexander Hamilton in a duel.
1806 Britain and France issue orders restricting neutral shipping. Betrayal of the Burr conspiracy.
1807 Chesapeake affair. Congress passes the Embargo Act. Congress prohibits the African slave trade.
1808 James Madison elected president.
1809 Repeal of the Embargo Act. Passage of the Nonintercourse Act.
1810 Macon's Bill No. 2 reopens trade with Britain and France. United States annexes part of West Florida.

Georgia state law invalidated by the Supreme Court in Fletcher v. Peck.
1811 Battle of Tippecanoe and defeat of the Indian confederation. Charter of the Bank of the United States expires.
1812 Congress declares war on Britain. American loss of Detroit.
1813 Perry's victory at Battle of Put-in-Bay. Battle of the Thames and death of Tecumseh.
1814 Andrew Jackson crushes the Creeks at the Battle of Horseshoe Bend. British burn Washington, D.C., and attack Baltimore. Macdonough's naval victory on Lake Champlain turns back a British invasion. Hartford Convention meets. Treaty of Ghent signed.
1815 Jackson routs British at the Battle of New Orleans.
1816 Congress charters the Second Bank of the United States and passes a protective tariff. James Monroe

elected president.
1817 Rush-Bagot Treaty demilitarizes the Great Lakes.
1818 Anglo-American Accords on trade and boundaries. Jackson's border campaign in Spanish East Florida.
1819 Trans-Continental Treaty between United States and Spain. Beginning of the Missouri controversy. Financial panic sends economy into a depression. McCulloch v. Maryland upholds constitutionality of the Bank of the United States.
1820 Missouri Compromise on slavery in the Louisiana Purchase. Monroe reelected.
1822 The United States extends diplomatic recognition to the new nations of Latin America.
1823 Monroe Doctrine proclaims Western Hemisphere closed to further European colonization.
1825 John Quincy Adams elected president by the House of Representatives

CHAPTER 10

1827 Emergence of the Anti-Masons, the first third party.
1828 Andrew Jackson elected president. John C. Calhoun writes The South Carolina Exposition and Protest.
1830 Congress passes the Indian Removal Act.
1832 Jackson vetoes bill for rechartering the Second Bank of the United States; Bank War begins. South Carolina nullifies the Tariffs of 1828 and 1832. Jackson reelected.

1833 Congress passes the Force Act and the Compromise Tariff. American Anti-Slavery Society established.
1834 Whig party begins to organize.
1836 Texas War of Independence and establishment of the Republic of Texas. Congress passes first gag rule on abolitionist petitions. Van Buren elected president.
1837 Panic of 1837 sets off a depression.
1840 Independent Treasury Act passes. William Henry

Harrison elected first Whig president.
1841 John Tyler succeeds to presidency on death of Harrison.
1842 United States and Britain sign the Webster-Ashburton Treaty.
1844 James K. Polk elected president. Gag rule repealed.
1845 Texas admitted to the Union.

CHAPTER 11

1790s Large-scale conversions of slaves to Christianity begin.
1793 Eli Whitney patents the cotton gin.
1800 Gabriel Prosser leads a rebellion in Richmond, Virginia.
1807 Britain abolishes the slave trade.
1808 Congress prohibits the African slave trade.
1811 Slaves rebel in Louisiana.

1816–1819 First cotton boom in the South.
1822 Denmark Vesey's Conspiracy fails in Charleston, South Carolina.
1831 Nat Turner leads a rebellion in Southampton County, Virginia.
1831–1832 Virginia legislature debates and rejects gradual emancipation.
1832 Thomas R. Dew publishes the first full-scale defense of slavery.

1837–1845 Slavery issue divides Presbyterians, Methodists, and Baptists into separate sectional churches.
1845 Florida and Texas, the last two slave states, are admitted to the Union.
1850s Cotton production doubles.
1857 Hinton R. Helper publishes *The Impending Crisis of the South*.

CHAPTER 1

c. 40,000–8,000 b.c. Ancestors of Native Americans cross Bering land bridge.

c. 10,000–9000 b.c. Paleo-Indians expand through the Americas.

c. 9000 b.c. Extinction of large land mammals in North America.

c. 8000–1500 b.c. Archaic Indian era.

c. 3000 b.c. Beginnings of agriculture in Mesoamerica.

c. 1500 b.c. Earliest mound-building culture begins.

c. 500 b.c.–a.d. 400 Adena-Hopewell mound-building culture.

c. a.d. 700–1600 Rise of West African empires.

c. 900 First mounds built at Cahokia. Ancestral Puebloan expansion.

c. 1000 Spread of Islam in West Africa.

c. 1000–1015 First Viking voyages to North America

c. 1000–1500 Last mound-building culture, the Mississippian.

c. 1290s Ancestral Puebloan dispersal into smaller villages.

1430s Beginnings of Portuguese slave trade in West Africa.

1492 End of reconquista in Spain. Columbus's first voyage.

1494 Treaty of Tordesillas.

1497 John Cabot visits Nova Scotia and Newfoundland.

1519–1521 Hernán Cortés conquers the Aztec empire.

1532–1533 Francisco Pizarro conquers the Inca empire.

1534–1542 Jacques Cartier explores eastern Canada for France.

1540–1542 Coronado explores southwestern North America.

1542–1543 Roberval's failed colony in Canada.

1558 Elizabeth I becomes queen of England.

1565 Spanish establish outpost at St. Augustine in Florida.

1587 Founding of "Lost Colony" of Roanoke.

1598 Spanish found colony at New Mexico.

CHAPTER 2

1602 Founding of Dutch East India Company

1607 Founding of English colonies at Jamestown and Sagadahoc.

1619 First Africans arrive in Jamestown. Virginia's House of Burgesses meets for the first time.

1620 Founding of Plymouth Colony in New England. Mayflower Compact signed.

1624 Dutch found colony of New Netherland.

1625 Virginia becomes a royal colony. Fort Amsterdam founded.

1630 Massachusetts Bay Colony founded.

1630–1642 Great Migration to New England.

1634 Lord Baltimore (Cecilius Calvert) founds proprietary colony of Maryland.

1635–1636 Roger Williams banished from Massachusetts, founds Providence, Rhode Island.

1637 Anne Hutchinson banished from Massachusetts. Pequot War in New England.

1638 New Haven colony founded.

1640s Sugar cultivation and slavery established in West Indies.

1649 Maryland's Act for Religious Toleration.

1654 Jewish emigrants from Brazil move to New Amsterdam, creating North America's first permanent Jewish community.

1663 Founding of Carolina colony.

1664 New Netherland conquered by the English, becomes New York. New Jersey established.

1673 French explorers reach the Mississippi River.

1681 Founding of Pennsylvania.

CHAPTER 3

c. 1450 Iroquois form Great League of Peace and Power.

1610–1614 First war between English settlers and Powhatan Indians.

1619 First Africans arrive in Virginia.

1622–1632 Second war between English settlers and Powhatan Indians.

1640s Slave labor begins to dominate in the West Indies. First phase of the Beaver Wars.

1651 First "praying town" established at Natick, Massachusetts.

1661 Maryland law defines slavery as lifelong, inheritable status.

1670 Virginia law defines status of slaves.

1675–1676 King Philip's War in New England.

1676 Bacon's Rebellion in Virginia.

1680 Pueblo Revolt in New Mexico.

1680s Second phase of Beaver Wars begins.

1690s Shift from white indentured servants to black slaves as principal labor force in the Chesapeake.

1701 Iroquois adopt policy of neutrality toward French and English.

1711–1713 Tuscarora War in Carolina.

1713 Beginnings of substantial Scottish, Scots-Irish, and German immigration to colonies.

1715–1716 Yamasee War in Carolina.

1732 Georgia established.

1739 Stono Rebellion in South Carolina.

1741 Slave conspiracy discovered in New York City.

1750 Slavery legalized in Georgia.

1760–1775 Peak of European and African immigration to English colonies.

CHAPTER 4

1651–1733 Parliament passes series of Navigation Acts to regulate imperial trade.

1662 Halfway Covenant adopted by Massachusetts clergy.

1686–1689 Dominion of New England.

1689 Leisler's Rebellion begins in New York.

1689–1697 King William's War in America.

1691–1692 Witchcraft trials in Salem, Massachusetts.

1698 First French settlements near mouth of Mississippi River.

1701 Iroquois adopt policy of neutrality toward France and Britain.

1702–1713 Queen Anne's War in America.

1718 San Antonio, Texas, and New Orleans founded.

1734–1735 Jonathan Edwards leads religious revival in Northampton, Massachusetts.

1739 Great Awakening begins in Middle Colonies with George Whitefield's arrival.

1744–1748 King George's War in America.

1754–1763 Seven Years' War in America.

1760s Spanish begin establishing missions in California.

CHAPTER 5

1759–1761 Cherokee War takes place.

1761–1762 Writs of Assistance case in Massachusetts.

1763 Peace of Paris ends French and Indian War. Proclamation Line of 1763 limits western expansion of colonial settlement. Pontiac's Rebellion begins. Paxton Boys murder peaceful Indians. Virginia Court decides Parson's Cause.

1764 Sugar Act passed. Currency Act passed.

1765 Quartering Act passed. Stamp Act passed. Stamp Act Congress meets in New York.

1766 Stamp Act repealed; Declaratory Act passed. New York Assembly refuses to comply with Quartering Act.

1767 Townshend duties imposed. Regulator movements begin in North and South Carolina.

1769 James Watt, a British inventor, patents a steam engine.

1770 Boston Massacre takes place. Tea duty retained, other Townshend duties repealed.

1771 North Carolina Regulator movement defeated.

1772 Gaspee burned. Committees of Correspondence formed.

1773 Boston Tea Party takes place.

1774 Coercive Acts passed. Quebec Act passed. First Continental Congress meets and agrees to boycott British imports.

CHAPTER 6

1775 Battles of Lexington and Concord. Second Continental Congress meets. Battle of Bunker Hill. American attack on Quebec.

1776 Thomas Paine's Common Sense. Declaration of Independence. British take New York City. Battle of Trenton.

1777 Battle of Princeton. Battle of Brandywine Creek. American victory at Saratoga. Runaway inflation begins. Continental Army winters at Valley Forge.

1778 George Rogers Clark captures British position in the Mississippi Valley. British capture Savannah.

1779 Spain declares war on Britain. Americans devastate the Iroquois country. John Paul Jones captures the British ship Serapis.

1780 Fall of Charleston, South Carolina. Americans win Battle of Kings Mountain. Nathanael Greene takes command in the South.

1781 Americans defeat British at Battle of Cowpens. Battle of Guilford Court House. Cornwallis surrenders at Yorktown.

1783 Washington quells the Newburgh "Conspiracy." Peace of Paris signed. British begin evacuating New York. Quakers present first anti-slavery petition to the British parliament.

1784 United States vessel opens trade with Canton, China.

CHAPTER 27

1944   Servicemen's Readjustment Act (GI Bill) is passed.
1945   United Nations is established.
1946   Employment Act creates Council of Economic Advisers. George Kennan sends his "long telegram." Winston Churchill delivers his "iron curtain" speech.
1947   Truman Doctrine is announced. Truman establishes a federal employee loyalty program.Kennan explains containment policy in an anonymous article in Foreign Affairs. Marshall Plan begins providing economic aid to Europe. HUAC holds hearings on Hollywood. Taft-Hartley Act rolls back gains of organized labor. National Security Act creates National Security Council and Central Intelligence Agency.
1948   Communists stage coup in Czechoslovakia. Berlin airlift overcomes Soviet blockade. Truman orders desegregation of the armed forces. Selective Service is reestablished. Truman wins reelection.
1949   North Atlantic Treaty Organization is formed. Communist Chinese defeat Nationalists. Soviet Union tests an atomic bomb. Department of Defense is established.
1950   Senator McCarthy begins his Red hunt. Alger Hiss is convicted of perjury. NSC-68 is drafted and accepted as U.S. policy. Korean War begins.
1951   Senate Internal Security Subcommittee begins hearings.Truman relieves MacArthur of his command. Julius and Ethel Rosenberg are convicted of conspiring to commit espionage.Truce talks begin in Korea.
1952   United States tests the hydrogen bomb. Dwight Eisenhower is elected president

CHAPTER 28

1953   CIA-backed coup returns Shah Reza Pahlevi to power in Iran. Soviet Union detonates hydrogen bomb.
1954   Vietnamese defeat the French; Geneva conference divides Vietnam. United States and allies form SEATO. Supreme Court decides *Brown v. Board of Education of Topeka.* CIA overthrows the government of Guatemala.
1955   Salk polio vaccine is announced. Black citizens boycott Montgomery, Alabama bus system. Soviet Union forms the Warsaw Pact. AFL and CIO merge.
1956   Interstate Highway Act is passed.
1957   U.S. Army maintains law and order in Little Rock after violent resistence to integration of Central High School. Soviet Union launches Sputnik, world's first artificial satellite.
1958   United States and Soviet Union voluntarily suspend nuclear tests.
1959   Fidel Castro takes power in Cuba. Nikita Khrushchev visits the United States.
1960   U-2 spy plane shot down over Russia. Sit-in move ment begins in Greensboro, North Carolina.
1961   Bay of Pigs invasion fails. Kennedy establishes the Peace Corps. Vienna summit fails. Freedom rides are held in the Deep South. Berlin crisis leads to construction of the Berlin Wall.
1962   John Glenn orbits the earth. Cuban missile crisis brings the world to the brink of nuclear war. Michael Harrington publishes *The Other America.*
1963   Civil rights demonstrations rend Birmingham. Civil rights activists march in Washington. Betty Friedan publishes *The Feminine Mystique.* Limited Test Ban Treaty is signed. Ngo Dinh Diem is assassinated in South Vietnam. President John F. Kennedy is assassinated.
1964   Civil Rights Act is passed. Freedom Summer is organized in Mississippi. Office of Economic Opportunity is created. Gulf of Tonkin Resolution is passed. Wilderness Act marks new direction in environmental policy.
1965   Medical Care Act establishes Medicare and Medicaid.Elementary and Secondary Education Act extends direct federal aid to local schools. Selma-Montgomery march climaxes era of nonviolent civil rights demonstrations. Voting Rights Act suspends literacy tests for voting.

CHAPTER 29

1962   Rachel Carson publishes Silent Spring. Port Huron Statement launches Students for a Democratic Society.
1965   Congress approves Wilderness Act. Malcolm X is assassinated. Residents of Watts neighborhood in Los Angeles riot.
1967   African Americans riot in Detroit and Newark.
1968   Viet Cong launches Tet Offensive. James Earl Ray kills Martin Luther King, Jr. Lyndon Johnson declines to run for reelection. SDS disrupts Columbia University. Sirhan Sirhan kills Robert Kennedy. Peace talks start between the United States and North Vietnam. Police riot against antiwar protesters during the Democratic National Convention in Chicago. Richard Nixon is elected president.
1969   Neil Armstrong and Buzz Aldrin walk on the moon.
1970   United States invades Cambodia. National Guard units kill students at Kent State and Jackson State universities. Earth Day is celebrated. Environmental Protection Agency is created.
1971   New York Times publishes the secret Pentagon Papers. President Nixon freezes wages and prices. Plumbers unit is established in the White House.
1972   Nixon visits China. United States and Soviet Union adopt SALT I. Operatives for Nixon's reelection campaign break into Democratic headquarters in the Watergate complex in Washington, D.C.
1973   Paris accords end direct U.S. involvement in South Vietnamese war. United States moves to all-volunteer armed forces. Watergate burglars are convicted. Senate Watergate hearings reveal the existence of taped White House conversations. Spiro Agnew resigns as vice president, is replaced by Gerald Ford. Arab states impose an oil embargo after the third Arab-Israeli War.
1974   Nixon resigns as president, is succeeded by Gerald Ford.
1975   Communists triumph in South Vietnam. United States, USSR, and European nations sign the Helsinki Accords.
1976   Jimmy Carter defeats Gerald Ford for the presidency.
1978   Carter brings the leaders of Egypt and Israel to Camp David for peace talks. U.S. agrees to transfer control of the Panama Canal to Panama.
1979   SALT II agreement is signed but not ratified. OPEC raises oil prices. Three Mile Island nuclear plant comes close to disaster. Iranian militants take U.S. embassy hostages.
1980   Iranian hostage rescue fails. Soviet troops enter Afghanistan. Ronald Reagan defeats Jimmy Carter for the presidency.

CHAPTER 30

1973   Roe v. Wade: Supreme Court struck down state laws banning abortion in the first trimester of pregnancy.
1980   Ronald Reagan is elected president.
1981   Economic Recovery and Tax Act, reducing personal income tax rates, is passed. Reagan breaks strike by air traffic controllers. AIDS is recognized as a new disease.
1982   Nuclear freeze movement peaks. United States begins to finance Contra rebels against the Sandinista government in Nicaragua. Equal Rights Amendment fails to achieve ratification.
1983   241 Marines are killed by a terrorist bomb in Beirut, Lebanon.Strategic Defense Initiative introduced. U.S. invades Grenada.
1984   Reagan wins reelection.
1986   Tax Reform Act is adopted.
1987   Congress holds hearings on the Iran-Contra scandal. Reagan and Gorbachev sign the Intermediate Nuclear Force treaty.
1988   George H.W. Bush is elected president.
1989   Communist regimes in eastern Europe collapse; Germans tear down Berlin Wall. Financial crisis forces federal bailout of many savings and loans.
United States invades Panama to capture General Manuel Noriega.
1990   Iraq invades Kuwait; and United States sends forces to the Persian Gulf. West Germany and East Germany reunite. Americans with Disabilities Act is adopted.
1991   Persian Gulf War: Operation Desert Storm drives the Iraqis from Kuwait. Soviet Union dissolves into independent nations. Strategic Arms Reduction Treaty (START) is signed.
1992   Acquittal of officers accused of beating Rodney King triggers Los Angeles riots.

CHAPTER 31

1969   First version of Internet (ARPAnet) launched.
1980   CNN begins broadcasting.
1991   World Wide Web launched.
1992   Bill Clinton elected president.
1993   Congress approves the North American Free Trade Agreement (NAFTA). Congress adopts Family Leave Act.
1994   Independent Counsel Kenneth Starr begins investigation of Bill and Hillary Clinton. Paula Jones files sexual harassment lawsuit against Bill Clinton. Republicans sweep to control of Congress. Federal government temporarily shuts down for lack of money.
1995   United States sends troops to Bosnia.
1996   Clinton wins a second term as president.
1998   Paula Jones lawsuit dismissed. House of Representatives impeaches Clinton.
1999   Senate acquits Clinton of impeachment charges. United States leads NATO intervention in Kosovo.
2000   George W. Bush defeats Al Gore in nation's closest presidential election.
2001   Congress passes massive ten-year tax reduction. United States refuses to agree to Kyoto Treaty to limit global warning. Terrorists crash airliners into World Trade Center and Pentagon. U.S. military operations eliminate Taliban regime in Afghanistan.
Congress passes U.S. Patriot Act to combat domestic terror.
2002   United States and Russia agree to cut number of deployed nuclear warheads. Congress creates Department of Homeland Security. United Nations Security Council passes resolution requiring Iraq to allow open inspections of weapons systems.
2003   U.S. and British troops invade Iraq and topple government of Saddam Hussein. Supreme Court allows limited forms of affirmative action in university admissions.
2004   George W. Bush reelected president.

The Declaration of Independence

When in the course of human events it becomes necessary for one people to dissolve the political bands which have connected them with another and to assume, among the powers of the earth, the separate and equal station to which the laws of nature and of nature's God entitle them, a decent respect to the opinions of mankind requires that they should declare the causes which impel them to the separation.

We hold these truths to be self-evident, that all men are created equal; that they are endowed by their Creator with certain unalienable rights; that among these are life, liberty, and the pursuit of happiness. That, to secure these rights, governments are instituted among men, deriving their just powers from the consent of the governed; that, whenever any form of government becomes destructive of these ends, it is the right of the people to alter or to abolish it, and to institute a new government, laying its foundation on such principles, and organizing its powers in such form, as to them shall seem most likely to effect their safety and happiness. Prudence, indeed, will dictate that governments long established should not be changed for light and transient causes; and, accordingly, all experience hath shown that mankind are more disposed to suffer, while evils are sufferable, than to right themselves by abolishing the forms to which they are accustomed. But when a long train of abuses and usurpations, pursuing invariably the same object, evinces a design to reduce them under absolute despotism, it is their right, it is their duty, to throw off such government and to provide new guards for their future security. Such has been the patient sufferance of these colonies, and such is now the necessity which constrains them to alter their former systems of government. The history of the present King of Great Britain is a history of repeated injuries and usurpations, all having, in direct object, the establishment of an absolute tyranny over these States. To prove this, let facts be submitted to a candid world:

He has refused his assent to laws the most wholesome and necessary for the public good.

He has forbidden his governors to pass laws of immediate and pressing importance, unless suspended in their operation till his assent should be obtained; and, when so suspended, he has utterly neglected to attend to them.

He has refused to pass other laws for the accommodation of large districts of people, unless those people would relinquish the right of representation in the legislature, a right inestimable to them and formidable to tyrants only.

He has called together legislative bodies at places unusual, uncomfortable, and distant from the depository of their public records, for the sole purpose of fatiguing them into compliance with his measures.

He has dissolved representative houses, repeatedly for opposing, with manly firmness, his invasions on the rights of the people.

He has refused, for a long time after such dissolutions, to cause others to be elected; whereby the legislative powers, incapable of annihilation, have returned to the people at large for their exercise; the state remaining, in the meantime, exposed to all the danger of invasion from without and convulsions within.

He has endeavored to prevent the population of these States; for that purpose, obstructing the laws for naturalization of foreigners, refusing to pass others to encourage their migration hither, and raising the conditions of new appropriations of lands.

He has obstructed the administration of justice by refusing his assent to laws for establishing judiciary powers.

He has made judges dependent on his will alone for the tenure of their offices and the amount and payment of their salaries.

He has erected a multitude of new offices and sent hither swarms of officers to harass our people and eat out their substance.

He has kept among us, in time of peace, standing armies, without the consent of our legislatures.

He has affected to render the military independent of, and superior to, the civil power.

He has combined with others to subject us to a jurisdiction foreign to our Constitution and unacknowledged by our laws, giving his assent to their acts of pretended legislation—

For quartering large bodies of armed troops among us;

For protecting them by mock trial, from punishment for any murders which they should commit on the inhabitants of these States;

For cutting off our trade with all parts of the world;

For imposing taxes on us without our consent;

For depriving us, in many cases, of the benefit of trial by jury;

For transporting us beyond seas to be tried for pretended offences;

For abolishing the free system of English laws in a neighboring province, establishing therein an arbitrary government, and enlarging its boundaries, so as to render it at once an example and fit instrument for introducing the same absolute rule into these colonies;

For taking away our charters, abolishing our most valuable laws, and altering, fundamentally, the powers of our governments.

For suspending our own legislatures and declaring themselves invested with power to legislate for us in all cases whatsoever.

He has abdicated government here by declaring us out of his protection and waging war against us.

He has plundered our seas, ravaged our coasts, burnt our towns, and destroyed the lives of our people.

He is, at this time, transporting large armies of foreign mercenaries to complete the works of death, desolation, and tyranny already begun with circumstances of cruelty and perfidy scarcely paralleled in the most barbarous ages, and totally unworthy the head of a civilized nation.

He has constrained our fellow citizens, taken captive on the high seas, to bear arms against their country, to become the executioners of their friends and brethren, or to fall themselves by their hands.

He has excited domestic insurrections amongst us and has endeavored to bring on the inhabitants of our frontiers, the merciless Indian savages, whose known rule of warfare is an undistinguished destruction of all ages, sexes, and conditions.

In every stage of these oppressions, we have petitioned for redress in the most humble terms; our repeated petitions have been answered only by repeated injury. A prince whose character is thus marked by every act which may define a tyrant is unfit to be the ruler of a free people.

Nor have we been wanting in attention to our British brethren. We have warned them, from time to time, of attempts made by their legislature to extend an unwarrantable jurisdiction over us. We have reminded them of the circumstances of our emigration and settlement here. We have appealed to their native justice and magnanimity, and we have conjured them, by the ties of our common kindred, to disavow these usurpations, which would inevitably interrupt our connections and correspondence. They, too, have been deaf to the voice of justice and consanguinity. We must, therefore, acquiesce in the necessity which denounces our separation, and hold them, as we hold the rest of mankind, enemies in war, in peace, friends.

We, therefore, the representatives of the United States of America, in general Congress assembled, appealing to the Supreme Judge of the world for the rectitude of our intentions, do, in the name and by the authority of the good people of these colonies, solemnly publish and declare, that these united colonies are, and of right ought to be, free and independent states: that they are absolved from all allegiance to the British Crown, and that all political connection between them and the state of Great Britain is, and ought to be, totally dissolved; and that, as free and independent states, they have full power to levy war, conclude peace, contract alliances, establish commerce, and to do all other acts and things which independent states may of right do. And, for the support of this declaration, with a firm reliance on the protection of Divine Providence, we mutually pledge to each other our lives, our fortunes, and our sacred honor.

The Articles of Confederation and Perpetual Union*

Between the states of New Hampshire, Massachusetts-bay Rhode Island and Providence Plantations, Connecticut, New York, New Jersey, Pennsylvania, Delaware, Maryland, Virginia, North Carolina, South Carolina, and Georgia.

Article 1

The Stile of this Confederacy shall be "The United States of America."

Article 2

Each state retains its sovereignty, freedom, and independence, and every power, jurisdiction, and right, which is not by this Confederation expressly delegated to the United States, in Congress assembled.

Article 3

The said States hereby severally enter into a firm league of friendship with each other, for their common defense, the security of their liberties, and their mutual and general welfare, binding themselves to assist each other, against all force offered to, or attacks made upon them, or any of them, on account of religion, sovereignty, trade, or any other pretense whatever.

Article 4

The better to secure and perpetuate mutual friendship and intercourse among the people of the different States in this Union, the free inhabitants of each of these States, paupers, vagabonds, and fugitives from justice excepted, shall be entitled to all privileges and immunities of free citizens in the several States; and the people of each State shall have free ingress and regress to and from any other State, and shall enjoy therein all the privileges of trade and commerce, subject to the same duties, impositions, and restrictions as the inhabitants thereof respectively, provided that such restrictions shall not extend so far as to prevent the removal of property imported into any State, to any other State of which the owner is an inhabitant; provided also that no imposition, duties or restriction shall be laid by any State, on the property of the United States, or either of them.

If any person guilty of, or charged with, treason, felony, or other high misdemeanor in any State, shall flee from justice, and be found in any of the United States, he shall, upon demand of the Governor or executive power of the State from which he fled, be delivered up and removed to the State having jurisdiction of his offense.

Full faith and credit shall be given in each of these States to the records, acts, and judicial proceedings of the courts and magistrates of every other State.

_____

*Agreed to in Congress November 15, 1777; ratified March 1781.

ARTICLE 5

For the most convenient management of the general interests of the United States, delegates shall be annually appointed in such manner as the legislatures of each State shall direct, to meet in Congress on the first Monday in November, in every year, with a power reserved to each State to recall its delegates, or any of them, at any time within the year, and to send others in their stead for the remainder of the year.

No State shall be represented in Congress by less than two, nor by more than seven members; and no person shall be capable of being a delegate for more than three years in any term of six years; nor shall any person, being a delegate, be capable of holding any office under the United States, for which he, or another for his benefit, receives any salary, fees or emolument of any kind.

Each State shall maintain its own delegates in a meeting of the States, and while they act as members of the committee of the States.

In determining questions in the United States in Congress assembled, each State shall have one vote.

Freedom of speech and debate in Congress shall not be impeached or questioned in any court or place out of Congress, and the members of Congress shall be protected in their persons from arrests or imprisonments, during the time of their going to and from, and attendence on Congress, except for treason, felony, or breach of the peace.

ARTICLE 6

No State, without the consent of the United States in Congress assembled, shall send any embassy to, or receive any embassy from, or enter into any conference, agreement, alliance or treaty with any King, Prince or State; nor shall any person holding any office of profit or trust under the United States, or any of them, accept any present, emolument, office or title of any kind whatever from any King, Prince or foreign State; nor shall the United States in Congress assembled, or any of them, grant any title of nobility.

No two or more States shall enter into any treaty, confederation or alliance whatever between them, without the consent of the United States in Congress assembled, specifying accurately the purposes for which the same is to be entered into, and how long it shall continue.

No State shall lay any imposts or duties, which may interfere with any stipulations in treaties, entered into by the United States in Congress assembled, with any King, Prince or State, in pursuance of any treaties already proposed by Congress, to the courts of France and Spain.

No vessel of war shall be kept up in time of peace by any State, except such number only, as shall be deemed necessary by the United States in Congress assembled, for the defense of such State, or its trade; nor shall any body of forces be kept up by any State in time of peace, except such number only, as in the judgement of the United States in Congress assembled, shall be deemed requisite to garrison the forts necessary for the defense of such State; but every State shall always keep up a well-regulated and disciplined militia, sufficiently armed and accoutered, and shall provide and constantly have ready for use, in public stores, a due number of filed pieces and tents, and a proper quantity of arms, ammunition and camp equipage.

No State shall engage in any war without the consent of the United States in Congress assembled, unless such State be actually invaded by enemies, or shall have received certain advice of a resolution being formed by some nation of Indians to invade such State, and the danger is so imminent as not to admit of a delay, till the United States in Congress assembled can be consulted; nor shall any State grant commissions to any ships or vessels of war, nor letters of marque or reprisal, except it be after a declaration of war by the United States in Congress assembled, and then only against the King-dom or State and the subjects thereof, against which war has been so declared, and under such regulations as shall be established by the United States in Congress assembled, unless such State be infested by pirates, in which case vessels of war may be fitted out for that occasion, and kept so long as the danger shall continue, or until the United States in Congress assembled shall determine otherwise.

ARTICLE 7

When land forces are raised by any State for the common defense, all officers of or under the rank of colonel, shall be appointed by the legislature of each State respectively, by whom such forces shall be raised, or in such manner as such State shall direct, and all vacancies shall be filled up by the State which first made the appointment.

ARTICLE 8

All charges of war, and all other expenses that shall be incurred for the common defense or general welfare, and allowed by the United States in Congress assembled, shall be defrayed out of a common treasury, which shall be supplied by the several States in proportion to the value of all land within each State, granted to or surveyed for any person, as such land and the buildings and improvements thereon shall be estimated according to such mode as the United States in Congress assembled, shall from time to time direct and appoint.

The taxes for paying that proportion shall be laid and levied by the authority and direction of the legislatures of the several States within the time agreed upon by the United States in Congress assembled.

ARTICLE 9

The United States in Congress assembled, shall have the sole and exclusive right and power of determining on peace and war, except in the cases mentioned in the sixth article; of sending and receiving ambassadors; entering into treaties and alliances, provided that no treaty of commerce shall be made whereby the legislative power of the respective States shall be restrained from imposing such imposts and duties on foreigners, as their own people are subjected to, or from prohibiting the exportation or importation of any species of goods or commodities whatsoever; of establishing rules for deciding in all cases, what captures on land or water shall be legal, and in what manner prizes taken by land or naval forces in the service of the United States shall be divided or appropriated; of granting letters of marque and reprisal in times of peace; appointing courts for the trial of piracies and felonies committed on the high seas and establishing courts for receiving and determining finally appeals in all cases of captures, provided that no member of Congress shall be appointed a judge of any of the said courts.

The United States in Congress assembled shall also be the last resort on appeal in all disputes and differences now subsisting or that hereafter may arise between two or more States concerning boundary, jurisdiction or any other causes whatever; which authority shall always be exercised in the manner following. Whenever the legislative or executive authority or lawful agent of any State in controversy with another shall present a petition to Congress stating the matter in question and praying for a hearing, notice thereof shall be given by order of Congress to the legislative or executive authority of the other State in controversy, and a day assigned for the appearance of the parties by their lawful agents, who shall then be directed to appoint by joint consent, commissioners or judges to constitute a court for hearing and determining the matter in question: but if they cannot agree, Congress shall name three persons out of each of the United States, and from the list of such persons each party shall alternately strike out one, the petitioners beginning, until the number shall be reduced to thirteen; and from that number not less than seven, nor more than nine names as Congress shall direct, shall in the presence of Congress be drawn out by lot, and the persons whose names shall be so drawn or any five of them, shall be commissioners or judges, to hear and finally determine the controversy, so always as a major part of the judges who shall hear the cause shall agree in the determination: and if either party shall neglect to attend at the day appointed, without showing reasons, which Congress shall judge sufficient, or being present shall refuse to strike, the Congress shall proceed to nominate three persons out of each State, and the secretary of Congress shall strike in behalf of such party absent or refusing; and the judgement and sentence of the court to be appointed, in the manner before prescribed, shall be final and conclusive; and if any of the parties shall refuse to submit to the authority of such court, or to appear or defend their claim or cause, the court shall nevertheless proceed to pronounce sentence, or judgement, which shall in like manner be final and decisive, the judgement or sentence and other proceedings being in either case transmitted to Congress, and lodged among the acts of Congress for the security of the parties concerned: provided that every commissioner, before he sits in judgement, shall take an oath to be administered by one of the judges of the supreme or superior court of the State, where the cause shall be tried, "well and truly to hear and determine the matter in question, according to the best of his judgement, without favor, affection or hope of reward:" provided also, that no State shall be deprived of territory for the benefit of the United States.

All controversies concerning the private right of soil claimed under different grants of two or more States, whose jurisdictions as they may respect such lands, and the States which passed such grants are adjusted, the said grants or either of them being at the same time claimed to have originated antecedent to such settlement of jurisdiction, shall on the petition of either party to the Congress of the United States, be finally determined as near as may be in the same manner as is before prescribed for deciding disputes respecting territorial jurisdiction between different States.

The United States in Congress assembled shall also have the sole and exclusive right and power of regulating the alloy and value of coin struck by their own authority, or by that of the respective States; fixing the standards of weights and measures throughout the United States; regulating the trade and managing all affairs with the Indians not members of any of the States; provided that the legislative right of any State within its own limits be not infringed or violated; establishing or regulating post offices from one State to another, throughout all the United States, and exacting such postage on the papers passing through the same as may be requisite to defray the expenses of the said office; appointing all officers of the land forces in the service of the United States, excepting regimental officers; appointing all the officers of the naval forces, and commissioning all officers whatever in the service of the United States; making rules for the government and regulation of the said land and naval forces, and directing their operations.

The United States in Congress assembled shall have authority to appoint a committee, to sit in the recess of Congress, to be denominated "A Committee of the States," and to consist of one delegate from each State; and to appoint such other committees and civil officers as may be necessary for managing the general affairs of the United States under their direction; to appoint one of their members to preside, provided that no person be allowed to serve in the office of president more than one year in any term of three years; to ascertain the necessary sums of money to be raised for the service of the United States, and to appropriate and apply the same for defraying the public expenses; to borrow money, or emit bills on the credit of the United States, transmitting every half year to the respective States an account of the sums of money so borrowed or emitted; to build and equip a navy; to agree upon the number of land forces, and to make requisitions from each State for its quota, in proportion to the number of white inhabitants in such State; which requisition shall be binding, and thereupon the legislature of each State shall appoint the regimental officers, raise the men and cloath, arm and equip them in a soldierlike manner, at the expense of the United States; and the officers and men so cloathed, armed and equipped shall march to the place appointed, and within the time agreed on by the United States in Congress assembled; but if the United States in Congress assembled shall, on consideration of circumstances judge proper that any State should not raise men, or should raise a smaller number of men than the quota thereof, such extra number shall be raised, officered, cloathed, armed and equipped in the same manner as the quota of each State, unless the legislature of such State shall judge that such extra number cannot be safely spared out in the same, in which case they shall raise, officer, cloath, arm and equip as many of such extra number as they judge can be safely spared. And the officers and men so cloathed, armed, and equipped, shall march to the place appointed, and within the time agreed on by the United States in Congress assembled.

The United States in Congress assembled shall never engage in a war, nor grant letters of marque or reprisal in time of peace, nor enter into any treaties or alliances, nor coin money, nor regulate the value thereof, nor ascertain the sums and expenses necessary for the defense and welfare of the United States, or any of them, nor emit bills, nor borrow money on the credit of the United States, nor appropriate money, nor agree upon the number of vessels of war, to be built or purchased, or the number of land or sea forces to be raised, nor appoint a commander in chief of the army or navy, unless nine States assent to the same: nor shall a question on any other point, except for adjourning from day to day be determined, unless by the votes of the majority of the United States in Congress assembled.

The Congress of the United States shall have power to adjourn to any time within the year, and to any place within the United States, so that no period of adjournment be for a longer duration than the space of six months, and shall publish the journal of their proceedings monthly, except such parts thereof relating to treaties, alliances or military operations, as in their judge-ment require secrecy; and the yeas and nays of the delegates of each State on any question shall be entered on the journal, when it is desired by any delegates of a State, or any of them, at his or their request shall be furnished with a transcript of the said journal, except such parts as are above excepted, to lay before the legislatures of the several States.

ARTICLE 10

The Committee of the States, or any nine of them, shall be authorized to execute, in the recess of Congress, such of the powers of Congress as the United States in Congress assembled, by the consent of the nine States, shall from time to time think expedient to vest them with; provided that no power be delegated to the said Committee, for the exercise of which, by the Articles of Confederation, the voice of nine States in the Congress of the United States assembled is requisite.

ARTICLE 11

Canada acceding to this confederation, and adjoining in the measures of the United States, shall be admitted into, and entitled to all the advantages of this Union; but no other colony shall be admitted into the same, unless such admission be agreed to by nine States.

ARTICLE 12

All bills of credit emitted, monies borrowed, and debts contracted by, or under the authority of Congress, before the assembling of the United States, in pursuance of the present confederation, shall be deemed and considered as a charge against the United States, for payment and satisfaction whereof the said United States, and the public faith are hereby solemnly pledged.

ARTICLE 13

Every State shall abide by the determination of the United States in Congress assembled, on all questions which by this confederation are submitted to them. And the Articles of this Confederation shall be inviolably observed by every State, and the Union shall be perpetual; nor shall any alteration at any time hereafter be made in any of them; unless such alteration be agreed to in a Congress of the United States, and be afterwards confirmed by the legislatures of every State.

These articles shall be proposed to the legislatures of all the United States, to be considered, and if approved of by them, they are advised to authorize their delegates to ratify the same in the Congress of the United States; which being done, the same shall become conclusive.

THE CONSTITUTION OF THE UNITED STATES OF AMERICA

We the people of the United States, in order to form a more perfect union, establish justice, insure domestic tranquillity, provide for the common defense, promote the general welfare, and secure the blessings of liberty to ourselves and our posterity, do ordain and establish this Constitution for the United States of America.

Note: This version of the Constitution has been edited to conform to present-day punctuation and usage standards. In addition, paragraphs within sections have been numbered for ease of reference.

ARTICLE I

SECTION 1. All legislative powers herein granted shall be vested in a Congress of the United States, which shall consist of a Senate and House of Representatives.

SECTION 2. 1. The House of Representatives shall be composed of members chosen every second year by the people of the several States, and the electors in each State shall have the qualifications requisite for electors of the most numerous branch of the State legislature.

2. No person shall be a representative who shall not have attained to the age of twenty-five years, and been

seven years a citizen of the United States, and who shall not, when elected, be an inhabitant of that State in which he shall be chosen.

3. Representatives and direct taxes[1] shall be apportioned among the several States which may be included within this Union, according to their respective numbers, which shall be determined by adding to the whole number of free persons, including those bound to service for a term of years, and excluding Indians not taxed, three fifths of all other persons.[2] The actual enumeration shall be made within three years after the first meeting of the Congress of the United States, and within every subsequent term of ten years, in such manner as they shall by law direct. The number of representatives shall not exceed one for every thirty thousand, but each State shall have at least one representative; and until such enumeration shall be made, the State of New Hampshire shall be entitled to choose three, Massachusetts eight, Rhode Island and Providence Plantations one, Connecticut five, New York six, New Jersey four, Pennsylvania eight, Delaware one, Maryland six, Virginia ten, North Carolina five, South Carolina five, and Georgia three.

4. When vacancies happen in the representation from any State, the executive authority thereof shall issue writs of election to fill such vacancies.

5. The House of Representatives shall choose their speaker and other officers; and shall have the sole power of impeachment.

SECTION 3. 1. The Senate of the United States shall be composed of two senators from each State, chosen by the legislature thereof,[3] for six years; and each senator shall have one vote.

2. Immediately after they shall be assembled in consequence of the first election, they shall be divided as equally as may be into three classes. The seats of the senators of the first class shall be vacated at the expiration of the second year, of the second class at the expiration of the fourth year, and of the third class at the expiration of the sixth year, so that one third may be chosen every second year; and if vacancies happen by resignation, or otherwise, during the recess of the legislature of any State, the executive thereof may make temporary appointments until the next meeting of the legislature, which shall then fill such vacancies.[4]

3. No person shall be a senator who shall not have attained to the age of thirty years, and been nine years a citizen of the United States, and who shall not, when elected, be an inhabitant of that State for which he shall be chosen.

4. The Vice President of the United States shall be President of the Senate, but shall have no vote, unless they be equally divided.

5. The Senate shall choose their other officers, and also a president pro tempore, in the absence of the Vice

President, or when he shall exercise the office of the President of the United States.

6. The Senate shall have the sole power to try all impeachments. When sitting for that purpose, they shall be on oath or affirmation. When the President of the United States is tried, the chief justice shall preside: and no person shall be convicted without the concurrence of two thirds of the members present.

7. Judgment in cases of impeachment shall not extend further than to removal from office, and disqualification to hold and enjoy any office of honor, trust or profit under the United States: but the party convicted shall nevertheless be liable and subject to indictment, trial, judgment and punishment, according to law.

SECTION 4. 1. The times, places, and manner of holding elections for senators and representatives, shall be prescribed in each State by the legislature thereof; but the Congress may at any time by law make or alter such regulations, except as to the places of choosing senators.

2. The Congress shall assemble at least once in every year, and such meeting shall be on the first Monday in December, unless they shall by law appoint a different day.

SECTION 5. 1. Each House shall be the judge of the elections, returns and qualifications of its own members, and a majority of each shall constitute a quorum to do business; but a smaller number may adjourn from day to day, and may be authorized to compel the attendance of absent members, in such manner, and under such penalties as each House may provide.

2. Each House may determine the rules of its proceedings, punish its members for disorderly behavior, and, with the concurrence of two thirds, expel a member.

3. Each House shall keep a journal of its proceedings, and from time to time publish the same, excepting such parts as may in their judgment require secrecy; and the yeas and nays of the members of either House on any question shall, at the desire of one fifth of those present, be entered on the journal.

4. Neither House, during the session of Congress, shall, without the consent of the other, adjourn for more than three days, nor to any other place than that in which the two Houses shall be sitting.

SECTION 6. 1. The senators and representatives shall receive a compensation for their services, to be ascertained by law, and paid out of the Treasury of the United States. They shall in all cases, except treason, felony, and breach of the peace, be privileged from arrest during their attendance at the session of their respective Houses, and in going to and returning from the same; and for any speech or debate in either House, they shall not be questioned in any other place.

2. No senator or representative shall, during the time for which he was elected, be appointed to any civil office under the authority of the United States, which shall have been created, or the emoluments whereof shall have been increased, during such time; and no

---

[1]See the Sixteenth Amendment.
[2]See the Fourteenth Amendment.
[3]See the Seventeenth Amendment.
[4]See the Seventeenth Amendment.

person holding any office under the United States shall be a member of either House during his continuance in office.

SECTION 7. 1. All bills for raising revenue shall originate in the House of Representatives; but the Senate may propose or concur with amendments as on other bills.

2. Every bill which shall have passed the House of Representatives and the Senate, shall, before it become a law, be presented to the President of the United States; If he approves he shall sign it, but if not he shall return it, with his objections, to that House in which it shall have originated, who shall enter the objections at large on their journal, and proceed to reconsider it. If after such reconsideration two thirds of that House shall agree to pass the bill, it shall be sent, together with the objections, to the other House, by which it shall likewise be reconsidered, and if approved by two thirds of that House, it shall become a law. But in all such cases the votes of both Houses shall be determined by yeas and nays, and the names of the persons voting for and against the bill shall be entered on the journal of each House respectively. If any bill shall not be returned by the President within ten days (Sundays excepted) after it shall have been presented to him, the same shall be a law, in like manner as if he had signed it, unless the Congress by their adjournment prevent its return, in which case it shall not be a law.

3. Every order, resolution, or vote to which the concurrence of the Senate and the House of Representatives may be necessary (except on a question of adjournment) shall be presented to the President of the United States; and before the same shall take effect, shall be approved by him, or being disapproved by him, shall be repassed by two thirds of the Senate and House of Representatives, according to the rules and limitations prescribed in the case of a bill.

SECTION 8. 1. The Congress shall have the power

1. To lay and collect taxes, duties, imposts, and excises, to pay the debts and provide for the common defense and general welfare of the United States; but all duties, imposts, and excises shall be uniform throughout the United States.

2. To borrow money on the credit of the United States;

3. To regulate commerce with foreign nations, and among the several States, and with the Indian tribes;

4. To establish a uniform rule of naturalization, and uniform laws on the subject of bankruptcies throughout the United States;

5. To coin money, regulate the value thereof, and of foreign coin, and fix the standard of weights and measures;

6. To provide for the punishment of counterfeiting the securities and current coin of the United States;

7. To establish post offices and post roads;

8. To promote the progress of science and useful arts, by securing for limited times to authors and inventors the exclusive right to their respective writings and discoveries;

9. To constitute tribunals inferior to the Supreme Court;

10. To define and punish piracies and felonies committed on the high seas, and offenses against the law of nations;

11. To declare war, grant letters of marque and reprisal, and make rules concerning captures on land and water;

12. To raise and support armies, but no appropriation of money to that use shall be for a longer term than two years;

13. To provide and maintain a navy;

14. To make rules for the government and regulation of the land and naval forces;

15. To provide for calling forth the militia to execute the laws of the Union, suppress insurrections and repel invasions;

16. To provide for organizing, arming, and disciplining the militia, and for governing such part of them as may be employed in the service of the United States, reserving to the States respectively, the appointment of the officers, and the authority of training the militia according to the discipline prescribed by Congress;

17. To exercise exclusive legislation in all cases whatsoever, over such district (not exceeding ten miles square) as may, by cession of particular States, and the acceptance of Congress, become the seat of the government of the United States, and to exercise like authority over all places purchased by the consent of the legislature of the State in which the same shall be, for the erection of forts, magazines, arsenals, dockyards, and other needful buildings; and

18. To make all laws which shall be necessary and proper for carrying into execution the foregoing powers, and all other powers vested by this Constitution in the government of the United States, or any department or officer thereof.

SECTION 9. 1. The migration or importation of such persons as any of the States now existing shall think proper to admit, shall not be prohibited by the Congress prior to the year one thousand eight hundred and eight, but a tax or duty may be imposed on such importation, not exceeding ten dollars for each person.

2. The privilege of the writ of habeas corpus shall not be suspended, unless when in cases of rebellion or invasion the public safety may require it.

3. No bill of attainder or ex post facto law shall be passed.

4. No capitation, or other direct, tax shall be laid, unless in proportion to the census or enumeration herein-before directed to be taken.[5]

5. No tax or duty shall be laid on articles exported from any State.

6. No preference shall be given by any regulation of commerce or revenue to the ports of one State over those of another: nor shall vessels bound to, or from, one State be obliged to enter, clear, or pay duties in another.

---

[5]See the Sixteenth Amendment.

7. No money shall be drawn from the treasury, but in consequence of appropriations made by law; and a regular statement and account of the receipts and expenditures of all public money shall be published from time to time.

8. No title of nobility shall be granted by the United States: and no person holding any office of profit or trust under them, shall, without the consent of the Congress, accept of any present, emolument, office, or title, of any kind whatever, from any king, prince, or foreign State.

SECTION 10. 1. No State shall enter into any treaty, alliance, or confederation; grant letters of marque and reprisal; coin money; emit bills of credit; make any thing but gold and silver coin a tender in payment of debts; pass any bill of attainder, ex post facto law, or law impairing the obligation of contracts, or grant, any title of nobility.

2. No State shall, without the consent of the Congress, lay any imposts or duties on imports or exports, except what may be absolutely necessary for executing its inspection laws: and the net produce of all duties and imposts laid by any State on imports or exports, shall be for the use of the treasury of the United States; and all such laws shall be subject to the revision and control of the Congress.

3. No State shall, without the consent of the Congress, lay any duty of tonnage, keep troops, or ships of war in time of peace, enter into any agreement or compact with another State, or with a foreign power, or engage in war, unless actually invaded, or in such imminent danger as will not admit of delay.

ARTICLE II

SECTION 1. 1. The executive power shall be vested in a President of the United States of America. He shall hold his office during the term of four years, and, together with the Vice President, chosen for the same term, be elected, as follows:

2. Each State shall appoint, in such manner as the legislature thereof may direct, a number of electors, equal to the whole number of senators and representatives to which the State may be entitled in the Congress: but no senator or representative, or person holding any office of trust or profit under the United States, shall be appointed an elector.

The electors shall meet in their respective States, and vote by ballot for two persons, of whom one at least shall not be an inhabitant of the same State with themselves. And they shall make a list of all the persons voted for, and of the number of votes for each; which list they shall sign and certify, and transmit sealed to the seat of the government of the United States, directed to the president of the Senate. The president of the Senate shall, in the presence of the Senate and House of Representatives, open all the certificates, and the votes shall then be counted. The person having the greatest number of votes shall be the President, if such number be a majority of the whole number of electors appointed; and if there be more than one who have such majority, and have an equal number of votes, then the House of Representatives shall immediately choose by ballot one of them for President; and if no person have a majority, then from the five highest on the list the said House shall in like manner choose the President. But in choosing the President, the votes shall be taken by States, the representation from each State having one vote; a quorum for this purpose shall consist of a member or members from two thirds of the States, and a majority of all the States shall be necessary to a choice. In every case after the choice of the President, the person having the greatest number of votes of the electors shall be the Vice President. But if there should remain two or more who have equal votes, the Senate shall choose from them by ballot the Vice President.[6]

3. The Congress may determine the time of choosing the electors, and the day on which they shall give their votes; which day shall be the same throughout the United States.

4. No person except a natural born citizen, or a citizen of the United States, at the time of the adoption of this Constitution, shall be eligible to the office of President; neither shall any person be eligible to the office who shall not have attained to the age of thirty-five years, and been fourteen years a resident within the United States.

5. In case of the removal of the President from office, or of his death, resignation, or inability to discharge the powers and duties of the said office, the same shall devolve on the Vice President, and the congress may by law provide for the case of removal, death, resignation or inability, both of the President and Vice President, declaring what officer shall then act as President, and such officer shall act accordingly until the disability be removed, or a President shall be elected.

6. The President shall, at stated times, receive for his services a compensation which shall neither be increased nor diminished during the period for which he shall have been elected, and he shall not receive within that period any other emolument from the United States, or any of them.

7. Before he enter on the execution of his office, he shall take the following oath or affirmation:—"I do solemnly swear (or affirm) that I will faithfully execute the office of President of the United States, and will to the best of my ability, preserve, protect and defend the Constitution of the United States."

SECTION 2. 1. The President shall be commander in chief of the army and navy of the United States, and of the militia of the several States, when called into the actual service of the United States; he may require the opinion in writing, of the principal officer in each of the executive departments, upon any subject relating to the duties of their respective offices, and he shall have power to grant reprieves and pardons for offenses against the United States, except in cases of impeachment.

2. He shall have power, by and with the advice and consent of the Senate, to make treaties, provided two

---

[6]Superseded by the Twelfth Amendment.

thirds of the senators present concur; and he shall nominate, and by and with the advice and consent of the Senate, shall appoint ambassadors, other public ministers and consuls, judges of the Supreme Court, and all other officers of the United States, whose appointments are not herein otherwise provided for, and which shall be established by law; but the Congress may by law vest the appointment of such inferior officers, as they think proper, in the President alone, in the courts of laws, or in the heads of departments.

3. The President shall have power to fill up all vacancies that may happen during the recess of the Senate, by granting commissions which shall expire at the end of their next session.

SECTION 3. He shall from time to time give to the Congress information of the state of the Union, and recommend to their consideration such measures as he shall judge necessary and expedient; he may, on extraordinary occasions, convene both Houses, or either of them, and in case of disagreement between them with respect to the time of adjournment, he may adjourn them to such time as he shall think proper; he shall receive ambassadors and other public ministers; he shall take care that the laws be faithfully executed, and shall commission all the officers of the United States.

SECTION 4. The President, Vice President, and all civil officers of the United States, shall be removed from office on impeachment for, and conviction of, treason, bribery, or other high crimes and misdemeanors.

ARTICLE III

SECTION 1. The judicial power of the United States shall be vested in one Supreme Court, and in such inferior courts as the Congress may from time to time ordain and establish. The judges, both of the Supreme and inferior courts, shall hold their offices during good behavior, and shall, at stated times, receive for their services, a compensation, which shall not be diminished during their continuance in office.

SECTION 2. 1. The judicial power shall extend to all cases, in law and equity, arising under this Constitution, the laws of the United States, and treaties made, or which shall be made, under their authority;—to all cases of admiralty and maritime jurisdiction;—to controversies to which the United States shall be a party;[7]—to controversies between two or more States;—between a State and citizens of another State;—between citizens of different States;—between citizens of the same State claiming lands under grants of different States, and between a State, or the citizens thereof, and foreign States, citizens or subjects.

2. In all cases affecting ambassadors, other public ministers and consuls, and those in which a State shall be party, the Supreme Court shall have original jurisdiction. In all the other cases before mentioned, the Supreme Court shall have appellate jurisdiction, both as to law and fact, with such exceptions, and under such regulations as the Congress shall make.

3. The trial of all crimes, except in cases of impeachment, shall be by jury; and such trial shall be held in the State where the said crimes shall have been committed; but when not committed within any State, the trial shall be such place or places as the congress may by law have directed.

SECTION 3. 1. Treason against the United States shall consist only in levying war against them, or in adhering to their enemies, giving them aid and comfort. No person shall be convicted of treason unless on the testimony of two witnesses to the same overt act, or on confession in open court.

2. The Congress shall have power to declare the punishment of treason, but no attainder of treason shall work corruption of blood, or forfeiture except during the life of the person attained.

ARTICLE IV

SECTION 1. Full faith and credit shall be given in each State to the public acts, records, and judicial proceedings of every other State. And the Congress may by general laws prescribe the manner in which such acts, records and proceedings shall be proved, and the effect thereof.

SECTION 2. 1. The citizens of each State shall be entitled to all privileges and immunities of citizens in the several States.[8]

2. A person charged in any State with treason, felony, or other crime, who shall flee from justice, and be found in another State, shall on demand of the executive authority of the State from which he fled, be delivered up to be removed to the State having jurisdiction of the crime.

3. No person held to service or labor in one State under the laws thereof, escaping into another, shall, in consequence of any law or regulation therein, be discharged from such service or labor, but shall be delivered up on claim of the party to whom such service or labor may be due.[9]

SECTION 3. 1. New States may be admitted by the Congress into this Union; but no new State shall be formed or erected within the jurisdiction of any other State, nor any State be formed by the junction of two or more States, or parts of States, without the consent of the legislatures of the States concerned as well as of the Congress.

2. The Congress shall have power to dispose of and make all needful rules and regulations respecting the territory or other property belonging to the United States; and nothing in this Constitution shall be so construed as to prejudice any claims of the United States, or of any particular State.

SECTION 4. The United States shall guarantee to every State in this Union a republican form of government, and shall protect each of them against invasion; and on application of the legislature, or of the executive (when the legislature cannot be convened) against domestic violence.

---

[7]See the Eleventh Amendment.

[8]See the Fourteenth Amendment, Sec. 1.
[9]See the Thirteenth Amendment.

ARTICLE V

The Congress, whenever two thirds of both Houses shall deem it necessary, shall propose amendments to this Constitution, or, on the application of the legislatures of two thirds of the several States, shall call a convention for proposing amendments, which in either case shall be valid to all intents and purposes, as part of this Constitution, when ratified by the legislatures of three fourths of the several States, or by conventions in three fourths thereof, as the one or the other mode of ratification may be proposed by the Congress; Provided that no amendment which may be made prior to the year one thousand eight hundred and eight shall in any manner affect the first and fourth clauses in the ninth section of the first article; and that no State, without its consent, shall be deprived of its equal suffrage in the Senate.

ARTICLE VI

1. All debts contracted and engagements entered into, before the adoption of this Constitution, shall be as valid against the United States under this Constitution, as under the Confederation.[10]

2. This Constitution, and the laws of the United States which shall be made in pursuance thereof; and all treaties made, or which shall be made, under the authority of the United States, shall be the supreme law of the land; and the judges in every State shall be bound thereby, any thing in the Constitution or laws of any State to the contrary notwithstanding.

3. The senators and representatives before mentioned, and the members of the several State legislatures, and all executive and judicial officers, both of the United States and of the several States, shall be bound by oath or affirmation to support this Constitution; but no religious test shall ever be required as a qualification to any office or public trust under the United States.

ARTICLE VII

The ratification of the conventions of nine States shall be sufficient for the establishment of this Constitution between the States so ratifying the same.

Done in Convention by the unanimous consent of the States present the seventeenth day of September in the year of our Lord one thousand seven hundred and eighty-seven, and of the independence of the United States of America the twelfth. In witness whereof we have hereunto subscribed our names.

[Signatories' names omitted]

Articles in addition to, and amendment of, the Constitution of the United States of America, proposed by Congress, and ratified by the legislatures of the several States, pursuant to the fifth article of the original Constitution.

Amendment I

[First ten amendments ratified December 15, 1791] Congress shall make no law respecting an establishment of religion, or prohibiting the free exercise thereof; or abridging the freedom of speech, or of the press; or the right of the people peaceably to assemble, and to petition the government for a redress of grievances.

Amendment II

A well regulated militia, being necessary to the security of a free State, the right of the people to keep and bear arms, shall not be infringed.

Amendment III

No soldier shall, in time of peace be quartered in any house, without the consent of the owner, nor in time of war, but in a manner to be prescribed by law.

Amendment IV

The right of the people to be secure in their persons, houses, papers, and effects, against unreasonable searches and seizures, shall not be violated, and no warrants shall issue, but upon probable cause, supported by oath or affirmation, and particularly describing the place to be searched, and the persons or things to be seized.

Amendment V

No person shall be held to answer for a capital or otherwise infamous crime, unless on a presentment or indictment of a grand jury, except in cases arising in the land or naval forces, or in the militia, when in actual service in time of war or public danger; nor shall any person be subject for the same offense to be twice put in jeopardy of life or limb; nor shall be compelled in any criminal case to be a witness against himself, nor be deprived of life, liberty, or property, without due process of law; nor shall private property be taken for public use, without just compensation.

Amendment VI

In all criminal prosecutions, the accused shall enjoy the right to a speedy and public trial, by an impartial jury of the State and district wherein the crime shall have been committed, which district shall have been previously ascertained by law, and to be informed of the nature and cause of the accusation; to be confronted with the witnesses against him; to have compulsory process for obtaining witnesses in his favor, and to have the assistance of counsel for his defense.

Amendment VII

In suits at common law, where the value in controversy shall exceed twenty dollars, the right of trial by jury shall be preserved, and no fact tried by a jury shall be otherwise reexamined in any court of the United States, than according to the rules of the common law.

Amendment VIII

Excessive bail shall not be required, nor excessive fines imposed, nor cruel and unusual punishments inflicted.

Amendment IX

The enumeration in the Constitution of certain rights shall not be construed to deny or disparage others retained by the people.

---

[10]See the Fourteenth Amendment, Sec. 4.

Amendment X

The powers not delegated to the United States by the Constitution, nor prohibited by it to the States, are reserved to the States respectively, or to the people.

Amendment XI [January 8, 1798]

The judicial power of the United States shall not be construed to extend to any suit in law or equity, commended or prosecuted against one of the United States by citizens of another State, or by citizens or subjects of any foreign State.

Amendment XII [September 25, 1804]

The electors shall meet in their respective States, and vote by ballot for President and Vice President, one of whom, at least, shall not be an inhabitant of the same State with themselves; they shall name in their ballots the person voted for as President, and in distinct ballots, the person voted for as Vice President, and they shall make distinct lists of all persons voted for as President and of all persons voted for as Vice President, and of the number of votes for each, which lists they shall sign and certify, and transmit sealed to the seat of the government of the United States, directed to the President of the Senate;—The President of the Senate shall, in the presence of the Senate and House of Representatives, open all the certificates and the votes shall then be counted;—The person having the greatest number of votes for President, shall be the President, if such number be a majority of the whole number of electors appointed; and if no person have such majority, then from the persons having the highest numbers not exceeding three on the list of those voted for as President, the House of Representatives shall choose immediately, by ballot, the President. But in choosing the President, the votes shall be taken by States, the representation from each State having one vote; a quorum for this purpose shall consist of a member or members from two thirds of the States, and a majority of all the States shall be necessary to a choice. And if the House of Representatives shall not choose a President whenever the right of choice shall devolve upon them, before the fourth day of March next following, then the Vice President shall act as President, as in the case of the death or other constitutional disability of the President. The person having the greatest number of votes as Vice President shall be the Vice President, if such number be a majority of the whole number of electors appointed, and if no person have a majority, then from the two highest numbers on the list, the Senate shall choose the Vice President; a quorum for the purpose shall consist of two thirds of the whole number of Senators, and a majority of the whole number shall be necessary to a choice. But no person constitutionally ineligible to the office of President shall be eligible to that of Vice President of the United States.

Amendment XIII [December 18, 1865]

SECTION 1. Neither slavery nor involuntary servitude, except as a punishment for crime whereof the party shall have been duly convicted, shall exist within the United States, or any place subject to their jurisdiction.

SECTION 2. Congress shall have power to enforce this article by appropriate legislation.

Amendment XIV [July 28, 1868]

SECTION 1. All persons born or naturalized in the United States, and subject to the jurisdiction thereof, are citizens of the United States and of the State wherein they reside. No State shall make or enforce any law which shall abridge the privileges or immunities of citizens of the United States; nor shall any State deprive any person of life, liberty, or property, without due process of law; nor deny to any person within its jurisdiction the equal protection of the laws.

SECTION 2. Representatives shall be apportioned among the several States according to their respective numbers, counting the whole number of persons in each State, excluding Indians not taxed. But when the right to vote at any election for the choice of electors for President and Vice President of the United States, representatives in Congress, the executive and judicial officers of a State, or the members of the legislature thereof, is denied to any of the male inhabitants of such State, being twenty-one years of age, and citizens of the United States, or in any way abridged, except for participating in rebellion, or other crime, the basis of representation there shall be reduced in the proportion which the number of such male citizens shall bear to the whole number of male citizens twenty-one years of age in such State.

SECTION 3. No person shall be a senator or representative in Congress, or elector of President and Vice President, or hold any office, civil or military, under the United States, or under any State, who having previously taken an oath, as a member of Congress, or as an officer of the United States, or as a member of any State legislature, or as an executive or judicial officer of any State, to support the Constitution of the United States, shall have engaged in insurrection or rebellion against the same, or given aid or comfort to the enemies thereof. But Congress may by a vote of two thirds of each House, remove such disability.

SECTION 4. The validity of the public debt of the United States, authorized by law, including debts incurred for payment of pensions and bounties for services in suppressing insurrection or rebellion; shall not be questioned. But neither the United States nor any State shall assume or pay any debt or obligation incurred in aid of insurrection or rebellion against the United States, or any claim for the loss or emancipation of any slave; but all such debts, obligations, and claims shall be held illegal and void.

SECTION 5. The Congress shall have the power to enforce, by appropriate legislation, the provisions of this article.

Amendment XV [March 30, 1870]

SECTION 1. The right of citizens of the United States to vote shall not be denied or abridged by the United States or by any State on account of race, color, or previous condition of servitude.

SECTION 2. The Congress shall have power to enforce this article by appropriate legislation.

Amendment XVI [February 25, 1913]

The Congress shall have power to lay and collect taxes on incomes, from whatever source derived, without apportionment among the several States, and without regard to any census or enumeration.

Amendment XVII [May 31, 1913]

The Senate of the United States shall be composed of two senators from each State, elected by the people thereof, for six years; and each senator shall have one vote. The electors in each State shall have the qualifications requisite for electors of the most numerous branch of the State legislature.

When vacancies happen in the representation of any State in the Senate, the executive authority of such State shall issue writs of election to fill such vacancies: Provided, That the legislature of any State may empower the executive thereof to make temporary appointments until the people fill the vacancies by election as the legislature may direct.

This amendment shall not be so construed as to affect the election or term of any senator chosen before it becomes valid as part of the Constitution.

Amendment XVIII[11] [January 29, 1919]

After one year from the ratification of this article, the manufacture, sale, or transportation of intoxicating liquors within, the importation thereof into, or the exportation thereof from the United States and all territory subject to the jurisdiction thereof for beverage purposes is thereby prohibited.

The Congress and the several States shall have concurrent power to enforce this article by appropriate legislation.

This article shall be inoperative unless it shall have been ratified as an amendment to the Constitution by the legislatures of the several States, as provided in the constitution, within seven years from the date of the submission hereof to the States by Congress.

Amendment XIX [August 26, 1920]

The right of citizens of the United States to vote shall not be denied or abridged by the United States or by any State on account of sex.

Congress shall have the power to enforce this article by appropriate legislation.

Amendment XX [January 23, 1933]

SECTION 1. The terms of the President and Vice President shall end at noon on the 20th day of January and the terms of Senators and Representatives at noon on the

---

[11]Repealed by the Twenty-first Amendment

3d day of January, of the years in which such terms would have ended if this article had not been ratified; and the terms of their successors shall then begin.

SECTION 2. The Congress shall assemble at least once in every year, and such meeting shall begin at noon on the 3d day of January, unless they shall by law appoint a different day.

SECTION 3. If, at the time fixed for the beginning of the term of President, the President-elect shall have died, the Vice President-elect shall become President. If a President shall not have been chosen before the time fixed for the beginning of his term, or if the President-elect shall have failed to qualify, then the Vice President-elect shall act as President until a President shall have qualified; and the Congress may by law provide for the case wherein neither a President-elect nor a Vice President-elect shall have qualified, declaring who shall then act as President, or the manner in which one who is to act shall be selected, and such person shall act accordingly until a President or Vice President shall have qualified.

SECTION 4. The Congress may by law provide for the case of the death of any of the persons from whom, the House of Representatives may choose a President whenever the right of choice shall have devolved upon them, and for the case of the death of any of the persons from whom the Senate may choose a Vice President whenever the right of choice shall have devolved upon them.

SECTION 5. Sections 1 and 2 shall take effect on the 15th day of October following the ratification of this article.

SECTION 6. This article shall be inoperative unless it shall have been ratified as an amendment to the Constitution by the legislatures of three-fourths of the several States within seven years from the date of its submission.

Amendment XXI [December 5, 1933]

SECTION 1. The Eighteenth Article of amendment to the Constitution of the United States is hereby repealed.

SECTION 2. The transportation or importation into any State, Territory, or possession of the United States for delivery or use therein of intoxicating liquors in violation of the laws thereof, is hereby prohibited.

SECTION 3. This article shall be inoperative unless it shall have been ratified as an amendment to the Constitution by conventions in the several States, as provided in the Constitution, within seven years from the date of the submission thereof to the States by the Congress.

Amendment XXII [March 1, 1951]

No person shall be elected to the office of the President more than twice, and no person who has held the office of President, or acted as President, for more than two years of a term to which some other person was elected President shall be elected to the office of the President more than once.

But this article shall not apply to any person holding the office of President when this article was proposed by the Congress, and shall not prevent any person who may be holding the office of President, or acting as President, during the term within which this article becomes operative from holding the office of President or acting as President during the remainder of such term.

This article shall be inoperative unless it shall have been ratified as an amendment to the Constitution by the legislatures of three-fourths of the several States within seven years from the date of its submission to the States by the Congress.

Amendment XXIII [March 29, 1961]

SECTION 1. The District constituting the seat of Government of the United States shall appoint in such manner as the Congress may direct.

A number of electors of President and Vice President equal to the whole number of Senators and Representatives in Congress to which the District would be entitled if it were a State, but in no event more than the least populous State; they shall be in addition to those appointed by the States, but they shall be considered, for the purposes of the election of President and Vice President, to be electors appointed by a State; and they shall meet in the District and perform such duties as provided by the twelfth article of amendment.

SECTION 2. The Congress shall have power to enforce this article by appropriate legislation.

Amendment XXIV [January 23, 1964]

SECTION 1. The right of citizens of the United States to vote in any primary or other election for President or Vice President, for electors for President or Vice President, or for Senator or Representative in Congress, shall not be denied or abridged by the United States or any State by reason of failure to pay any poll tax or other tax.

SECTION 2. The Congress shall have power to enforce this article by appropriate legislation.

Amendment XXV [February 10, 1967]

SECTION 1. In case of the removal of the President from office or of his death or resignation, the Vice President shall become President.

SECTION 2. Whenever there is a vacancy in the office of the Vice President, the President shall nominate a Vice President who shall take office upon confirmation by a majority of both Houses of Congress.

SECTION 3. Whenever the President transmits to the President pro tempore of the Senate and the Speaker of the House of Representatives his written declaration that he is unable to discharge the powers and duties of his office, and until he transmits to them a written declaration to the contrary, such powers and duties shall be discharged by the Vice President as Acting President.

SECTION 4. Whenever the Vice President and a majority of either the principal officers of the executive departments or of such other body as Congress may by law provide, transmit to the President pro tempore of the Senate and the Speaker of the House of Representatives their written declaration that the President is unable to discharge the powers and duties of his office, the Vice President shall immediately assume the powers and duties of the office as Acting President.

Thereafter, when the President transmits to the President pro tempore of the Senate and the Speaker of the House of Representatives his written declaration that no inability exists, he shall resume the powers and duties of his office unless the Vice President and a majority of either the principal officers of the executive departments or of such other body as Congress may by law provide, transmit within four days to the President pro tempore of the Senate and the Speaker of the House of Representatives their written declaration that the President is unable to discharge the powers and duties of his office. Thereupon Congress shall decide the issue, assembling within forty-eight hours for that purpose if not in session. If the Congress, within twenty-one days after receipt of the latter written declaration, or, if Congress is not in session, within twenty-one days after Congress is required to assemble, determines by two-thirds vote of both Houses that the President is unable to discharge the powers and duties of his office, the Vice President shall continue to discharge the same as Acting President; otherwise, the President shall resume the powers and duties of his office.

Amendment XXVI [June 30, 1971]

SECTION 1. The right of citizens of the United States who are eighteen years of age or older to vote shall not be denied or abridged by the United States or by any State on account of age.

SECTION 2. The Congress shall have power to enforce this article by appropriate legislation.

Amendment XXVII[12] [May 7, 1992]

No law, varying the compensation for services of the Senators and Representatives, shall take effect until an election of Representatives shall have intervened.

---

[12]James Madison proposed this amendment in 1789 together with the ten amendments that were adopted as the Bill of Rights, but it failed to win ratification at the time. Congress, however, had set no deadline for its ratification, and over the years—particularly in the 1980s and 1990s—many states voted to add it to the Constitution. With the ratification of Michigan in 1992 it passed the threshold of 3/4ths of the states required for adoption, but because the process took more than 200 years, its validity remains in doubt.

PRESIDENTIAL ELECTIONS

Year	Number of States	Candidates	Party	Popular Vote*	Electoral Vote†	Percentage of Popular Vote
1789	11	GEORGE WASHINGTON	No party designations		69	
		John Adams			34	
		Other Candidates			35	
1792	15	GEORGE WASHINGTON	No party designations		132	
		John Adams			77	
		George Clinton			50	
		Other Candidates			5	
1796	16	JOHN ADAMS	Federalist		71	
		Thomas Jefferson	Democratic-Republican		68	
		Thomas Pinckney	Federalist		59	
		Aaron Burr	Democratic-Republican		30	
		Other Candidates			48	
1800	16	THOMAS JEFFERSON	Democratic-Republican		73	
		Aaron Burr	Democratic-Republican		73	
		John Adams	Federalist		65	
		Charles C. Pinckney	Federalist		64	
		John Jay	Federalist		1	
1804	17	THOMAS JEFFERSON	Democratic-Republican		162	
		Charles C. Pinckney	Federalist		14	
1808	17	JAMES MADISON	Democratic-Republican		122	
		Charles C. Pinckney	Federalist		47	
		George Clinton	Democratic-Republican		6	
1812	18	JAMES MADISON	Democratic-Republican		128	
		DeWitt Clinton	Federalist		89	
1816	19	JAMES MONROE	Democratic-Republican		183	
		Rufus King	Federalist		34	
1820	24	JAMES MONROE	Democratic-Republican		231	
		John Quincy Adams	Independent-Republican		1	
1824	24	JOHN QUINCY ADAMS	Democratic-Republican	108,740	84	30.5
		Andrew Jackson	Democratic-Republican	153,544	99	43.1
		William H. Crawford	Democratic-Republican	46,618	41	13.1
		Henry Clay	Democratic-Republican	47,136	37	13.2
1828	24	ANDREW JACKSON	Democrat	647,286	178	56.0
		John Quincy Adams	National Republican	508,064	83	44.0
1832	24	ANDREW JACKSON	Democrat	687,502	219	55.0
		Henry Clay	National Republican	530,189	49	42.4
		William Wirt	Anti-Masonic	33,108	7	2.6
		John Floyd	National Republican		11	

* Percentage of popular vote given for any election year may not total 100 percent because candidates receiving less than 1 percent of the popular vote have been omitted.

† Prior to the passage of the Twelfth Amendment in 1904, the electoral college voted for two presidential candidates; the runner-up became Vice-President. Data from Historical Statistics of the United States, Colonial Times to 1957 (1961), pp. 682–683, and The World Almanac.

PRESIDENTIAL ELECTIONS   (CONTINUED)

Year	Number of States	Candidates	Party	Popular Vote	Electoral Vote	Percentage of Popular Vote
1836	26	MARTIN VAN BUREN	Democrat	765,483	170	50.9
		William H. Harrison	Whig		73	
		Hugh L. White	Whig	739,795	26	
		Daniel Webster	Whig		14	49.1
		W. P. Mangum	Whig		11	
1840	26	WILLIAM H. HARRISON	Whig	1,274,624	234	53.1
		Martin Van Buren	Democrat	1,127,781	60	46.9
1844	26	JAMES K. POLK	Democrat	1,338,464	170	49.6
		Henry Clay	Whig	1,300,097	105	48.1
		James G. Birney	Liberty	62,300		2.3
1848	30	ZACHARY TAYLOR	Whig	1,360,967	163	47.4
		Lewis Cass	Democrat	1,222,342	127	42.5
		Martin Van Buren	Free Soil	291,263		10.1
1852	31	FRANKLIN PIERCE	Democrat	1,601,117	254	50.9
		Winfield Scott	Whig	1,385,453	42	44.1
		John P. Hale	Free Soil	155,825		5.0
1856	31	JAMES BUCHANAN	Democrat	1,832,955	174	45.3
		John C. Frémont	Republican	1,339,932	114	33.1
		Millard Fillmore	American ("Know Nothing")	871,731	8	21.6
1860	33	ABRAHAM LINCOLN	Republican	1,865,593	180	39.8
		Stephen A. Douglas	Democrat	1,382,713	12	29.5
		John C. Breckinridge	Democrat	848,356	72	18.1
		John Bell	Constitutional Union	592,906	39	12.6
1864	36	ABRAHAM LINCOLN	Republican	2,206,938	212	55.0
		George B. McClellan	Democrat	1,803,787	21	45.0
1868	37	ULYSSES S. GRANT	Republican	3,013,421	214	52.7
		Horatio Seymour	Democrat	2,706,829	80	47.3
1872	37	ULYSSES S. GRANT	Republican	3,596,745	286	55.6
		Horace Greeley	Democrat	2,843,446	*	43.9
1876	38	RUTHERFORD B. HAYES	Republican	4,036,572	185	48.0
		Samuel J. Tilden	Democrat	4,284,020	184	51.0
1880	38	JAMES A. GARFIELD	Republican	4,453,295	214	48.5
		Winfield S. Hancock	Democrat	4,414,082	155	48.1
		James B. Weaver	Greenback-Labor	308,578		3.4
1884	38	GROVER CLEVELAND	Democrat	4,879,507	219	48.5
		James G. Blaine	Republican	4,850,293	182	48.2
		Benjamin F. Butler	Greenback-Labor	175,370		1.8
		John P. St. John	Prohibition	150,369		1.5
1888	38	BENJAMIN HARRISON	Republican	5,447,129	233	47.9
		Grover Cleveland	Democrat	5,537,857	168	48.6
		Clinton B. Fisk	Prohibition	249,506		2.2
		Anson J. Streeter	Union Labor	146,935		1.3

* Because of the death of Greeley, Democratic electors scattered their votes.

PRESIDENTIAL ELECTIONS (CONTINUED)

Year	Number of States	Candidates	Party	Popular Vote	Electoral Vote	Percent- age of Popular Vote
1892	44	GROVER CLEVELAND	Democrat	5,555,426	277	46.1
		Benjamin Harrison	Republican	5,182,690	145	43.0
		James B. Weaver	People's	1,029,846	22	8.5
		John Bidwell	Prohibition	264,133		2.2
1896	45	WILLIAM MCKINLEY	Republican	7,102,246	271	51.1
		William J. Bryan	Democrat	6,492,559	176	47.7
1900	45	WILLIAM MCKINLEY	Republican	7,218,491	292	51.7
		William J. Bryan	Democrat; Populist	6,356,734	155	45.5
		John C. Woolley	Prohibition	208,914		1.5
1904	45	THEODORE ROOSEVELT	Republican	7,628,461	336	57.4
		Alton B. Parker	Democrat	5,084,223	140	37.6
		Eugene V. Debs	Socialist	402,283		3.0
		Silas C. Swallow	Prohibition	258,536		1.9
1908	46	WILLIAM H. TAFT	Republican	7,675,320	321	51.6
		William J. Bryan	Democrat	6,412,294	162	43.1
		Eugene V. Debs	Socialist	420,793		2.8
		Eugene W. Chafin	Prohibition	253,840		1.7
1912	48	WOODROW WILSON	Democrat	6,296,547	435	41.9
		Theodore Roosevelt	Progressive	4,118,571	88	27.4
		William H. Taft	Republican	3,486,720	8	23.2
		Eugene V. Debs	Socialist	900,672		6.0
		Eugene W. Chafin	Prohibition	206,275		1.4
1916	48	WOODROW WILSON	Democrat	9,127,695	277	49.4
		Charles E. Hughes	Republican	8,533,507	254	46.2
		A. L. Benson	Socialist	585,113		3.2
		J. Frank Hanly	Prohibition	220,506		1.2
1920	48	WARREN G. HARDING	Republican	16,143,407	404	60.4
		James M. Cox	Democrat	9,130,328	127	34.2
		Eugene V. Debs	Socialist	919,799		3.4
		P. P. Christensen	Farmer-Labor	265,411		1.0
1924	48	CALVIN COOLIDGE	Republican	15,718,211	382	54.0
		John W. Davis	Democrat	8,385,283	136	28.8
		Robert M. La Follette	Progressive	4,831,289	13	16.6
1928	48	HERBERT C. HOOVER	Republican	21,391,993	444	58.2
		Alfred E. Smith	Democrat	15,016,169	87	40.9
1932	48	FRANKLIN D. ROOSEVELT	Democrat	22,809,638	472	57.4
		Herbert C. Hoover	Republican	15,758,901	59	39.7
		Norman Thomas	Socialist	881,951		2.2
1936	48	FRANKLIN D. ROOSEVELT	Democrat	27,752,869	523	60.8
		Alfred M. Landon	Republican	16,674,665	8	36.5
		William Lemke	Union	882,479		1.9
1940	48	FRANKLIN D. ROOSEVELT	Democrat	27,307,819	449	54.8
		Wendell L. Willkie	Republican	22,321,018	82	44.8

PRESIDENTIAL ELECTIONS   (CONTINUED)

Year	Number of States	Candidates	Party	Popular Vote	Electoral Vote	Percentage of Popular Vote
1944	48	FRANKLIN D. ROOSEVELT	Democrat	25,606,585	432	53.5
		Thomas E. Dewey	Republican	22,014,745	99	46.0
1948	48	HARRY S. TRUMAN	Democrat	24,105,812	303	49.5
		Thomas E. Dewey	Republican	21,970,065	189	45.1
		J. Strom Thurmond	States' Rights	1,169,063	39	2.4
		Henry A. Wallace	Progressive	1,157,172		2.4
1952	48	DWIGHT D. EISENHOWER	Republican	33,936,234	442	55.1
		Adlai E. Stevenson	Democrat	27,314,992	89	44.4
1956	48	DWIGHT D. EISENHOWER	Republican	35,590,472	457*	57.6
		Adlai E. Stevenson	Democrat	26,022,752	73	42.1
1960	50	JOHN F. KENNEDY	Democrat	34,227,096	303†	49.9
		Richard M. Nixon	Republican	34,108,546	219	49.6
1964	50	LYNDON B. JOHNSON	Democrat	42,676,220	486	61.3
		Barry M. Goldwater	Republican	26,860,314	52	38.5
1968	50	RICHARD M. NIXON	Republican	31,785,480	301	43.4
		Hubert H. Humphrey	Democrat	31,275,165	191	42.7
		George C. Wallace	American Independent	9,906,473	46	13.5
1972	50	RICHARD M. NIXON‡	Republican	47,165,234	520	60.6
		George S. McGovern	Democrat	29,168,110	17	37.5
1976	50	JIMMY CARTER	Democrat	40,828,929	297	50.1
		Gerald R. Ford	Republican	39,148,940	240	47.9
		Eugene McCarthy	Independent	739,256		
1980	50	RONALD REAGAN	Republican	43,201,220	489	50.9
		Jimmy Carter	Democrat	34,913,332	49	41.2
		John B. Anderson	Independent	5,581,379		
1984	50	RONALD REAGAN	Republican	53,428,357	525	59.0
		Walter F. Mondale	Democrat	36,930,923	13	41.0
1988	50	GEORGE BUSH	Republican	48,901,046	426	53.4
		Michael Dukakis	Democrat	41,809,030	111	45.6
1992	50	BILL CLINTON	Democrat	43,728,275	370	43.2
		George Bush	Republican	38,167,416	168	37.7
		H. Ross Perot	United We Stand, America	19,237,247		19.0
1996	50	BILL CLINTON	Democrat	45,590,703	379	49.0
		Robert Dole	Republican	37,816,307	159	41.0
		H. Ross Perot	Reform	7,866,284		8.0
2000	50	GEORGE W. BUSH	Republican	50,459,624	271	47.9
		Albert Gore, Jr.	Democrat	51,003,328	266	49.4
		Ralph Nader	Green	2,882,985		2.7

* *Walter B. Jones received 1 electoral vote.*

† *Harry F. Byrd received 15 electoral votes.*

‡ *Resigned August 9, 1974: Vice President Gerald R. Ford became President.*

** *John Hospers received 1 electorial vote.*

*** *Ronald Reagan received 1 electorial vote.*

*** *Lloyd Bentsen received 1 electorial vote.*

SUPREME COURT JUSTICES

Name*	Years on Court	Appointing President
JOHN JAY	1789–1795	Washington
James Wilson	1789–1798	Washington
John Rutledge	1790–1791	Washington
William Cushing	1790–1810	Washington
John Blair	1790–1796	Washington
James Iredell	1790–1799	Washington
Thomas Johnson	1792–1793	Washington
William Paterson	1793–1806	Washington
JOHN RUTLEDGE†	1795	Washington
Samuel Chase	1796–1811	Washington
OLIVER ELLSWORTH	1796–1800	Washington
Bushrod Washington	1799–1829	J. Adams
Alfred Moore	1800–1804	J. Adams
JOHN MARSHALL	1801–1835	J. Adams
William Johnson	1804–1834	Jefferson
Brockholst Livingston	1807–1823	Jefferson
Thomas Todd	1807–1826	Jefferson
Gabriel Duvall	1811–1835	Madison
Joseph Story	1812–1845	Madison
Smith Thompson	1823–1843	Monroe
Robert Trimble	1826–1828	J. Q. Adams
John McLean	1830–1861	Jackson
Henry Baldwin	1830–1844	Jackson
James M. Wayne	1835–1867	Jackson
ROGER B. TANEY	1836–1864	Jackson
Philip P. Barbour	1836–1841	Jackson
John Cartron	1837–1865	Van Buren
John McKinley	1838–1852	Van Buren
Peter V. Daniel	1842–1860	Van Buren
Samuel Nelson	1845–1872	Tyler
Levi Woodbury	1845–1851	Polk
Robert C. Grier	1846–1870	Polk
Benjamin R. Curtis	1851–1857	Fillmore
John A. Campbell	1853–1861	Pierce
Nathan Clifford	1858–1881	Buchanan
Noah H. Swayne	1862–1881	Lincoln
Samuel F. Miller	1862–1890	Lincoln
David Davis	1862–1877	Lincoln
Stephen J. Field	1863–1897	Lincoln
SALMON P. CHASE	1864–1873	Lincoln
William Strong	1870–1880	Grant
Joseph P. Bradley	1870–1892	Grant
Ward Hunt	1873–1882	Grant
MORRISON R. WAITE	1874–1888	Grant
John M. Harlan	1877–1911	Hayes
William B. Woods	1881–1887	Hayes
Stanley Matthews	1881–1889	Garfield
Horace Gray	1882–1902	Arthur
Samuel Blatchford	1882–1893	Arthur

SUPREME COURT JUSTICES   (CONTINUED)

Name*	Years on Court	Appointing President
Lucious Q. C. Lamar	1888–1893	Cleveland
MELVILLE W. FULLER	1888–1910	Cleveland
David J. Brewer	1890–1910	B. Harrison
Henry B. Brown	1891–1906	B. Harrison
George Shiras, Jr.	1892–1903	B. Harrison
Howell E. Jackson	1893–1895	B. Harrison
Edward D. White	1894–1910	Cleveland
Rufus W. Peckham	1896–1909	Cleveland
Joseph McKenna	1898–1925	McKinley
Oliver W. Holmes	1902–1932	T. Roosevelt
William R. Day	1903–1922	T. Roosevelt
William H. Moody	1906–1910	T. Roosevelt
Horace H. Lurton	1910–1914	Taft
Charles E. Hughes	1910–1916	Taft
EDWARD D. WHITE	1910–1921	Taft
Willis Van Devanter	1911–1937	Taft
Joseph R. Lamar	1911–1916	Taft
Mahlon Pitney	1912–1922	Taft
James C. McReynolds	1914–1941	Wilson
Louis D. Brandeis	1916–1939	Wilson
John H. Clarke	1916–1922	Wilson
WILLIAM H. TAFT	1921–1930	Harding
George Sutherland	1922–1938	Harding
Pierce Butler	1923–1939	Harding
Edward T. Sanford	1923–1930	Harding
Harlan F. Stone	1925–1941	Coolidge
CHARLES E. HUGHES	1930–1941	Hoover
Owen J. Roberts	1930–1945	Hoover
Benjamin N. Cardozo	1932–1938	Hoover
Hugo L. Black	1937–1971	F. Roosevelt
Stanley F. Reed	1938–1957	F. Roosevelt
Felix Frankfurter	1939–1962	F. Roosevelt
William O. Douglas	1939–1975	F. Roosevelt
Frank Murphy	1940–1949	F. Roosevelt
HARLAN F. STONE	1941–1946	F. Roosevelt
James F. Brynes	1941–1942	F. Roosevelt
Robert H. Jackson	1941–1954	F. Roosevelt
Wiley B. Rutledge	1943–1949	F. Roosevelt
Harold H. Burton	1945–1958	Truman
FREDERICK M. VINSON	1946–1953	Truman
Tom C. Clark	1949–1967	Truman
Sherman Minton	1949–1956	Truman
EARL WARREN	1953–1969	Eisenhower
John Marshall Harlan	1955–1971	Eisenhower
William J. Brennan, Jr.	1956–1990	Eisenhower
Charles E. Whittaker	1957–1962	Eisenhower
Potter Stewart	1958–1981	Eisenhower
Byron R. White	1962–1993	Kennedy
Arthur J. Goldberg	1962–1965	Kennedy

SUPREME COURT JUSTICES   (CONTINUED)

Name*	Years on Court	Appointing President
Abe Fortas	1965–1970	L. Johnson
Thurgood Marshall	1967–1991	L. Johnson
WARREN E. BURGER	1969–1986	Nixon
Harry A. Blackmun	1970–1994	Nixon
Lewis F. Powell, Jr.	1971–1987	Nixon
William H. Rehnquist	1971–1986	Nixon
John Paul Stevens	1975–	Ford
Sandra Day O'Connor	1981–2006	Reagan
WILLIAM H. REHNQUIJST	1986–2005	Reagan
Antonin Scalia	1986–	Reagan
Anthony Kennedy	1988–	Reagan
David Souter	1990–	Bush
Clarence Thomas	1991–	Bush
Ruth Bader Ginsburg	1993–	Clinton
Stephen Breyer	1994–	Clinton
John Roberts	2005–	Bush, G.W.
Samuel A. Alito	2006–	Bush, G.W.

Capital letters designate Chief Justices

† Never confirmed by the Senate as Chief Justice

ADMISSION OF STATES INTO THE UNION

State	Date of Admission	State	Date of Admission
1. Delaware	December 7, 1787	26. Michigan	January 26, 1837
2. Pennsylvania	December 12, 1787	27. Florida	March 3, 1845
3. New Jersey	December 18, 1787	28. Texas	December 29, 1845
4. Georgia	January 2, 1788	29. Iowa	December 28, 1846
5. Connecticut	January 9, 1788	30. Wisconsin	May 29, 1848
6. Massachusetts	February 6, 1788	31. California	September 9, 1850
7. Maryland	April 28, 1788	32. Minnesota	May 11, 1858
8. South Carolina	May 23, 1788	33. Oregon	February 14, 1859
9. New Hampshire	June 21, 1788	34. Kansas	January 29, 1861
10. Virginia	June 25, 1788	35. West Virginia	June 20, 1863
11. New York	July 26, 1788	36. Nevada	October 31, 1864
12. North Carolina	November 21, 1789	37. Nebraska	March 1, 1867
13. Rhode Island	May 29, 1790	38. Colorado	August 1, 1876
14. Vermont	March 4, 1791	39. North Dakota	November 2, 1889
15. Kentucky	June 1, 1792	40. South Dakota	November 2, 1889
16. Tennessee	June 1, 1796	41. Montana	November 8, 1889
17. Ohio	March 1, 1803	42. Washington	November 11, 1889
18. Louisiana	April 30, 1812	43. Idaho	July 3, 1890
19. Indiana	December 11, 1816	44. Wyoming	July 10, 1890
20. Mississippi	December 10, 1817	45. Utah	January 4, 1896
21. Illinois	December 3, 1818	46. Oklahoma	November 16, 1907
22. Alabama	December 14, 1819	47. New Mexico	January 6, 1912
23. Maine	March 15, 1820	48. Arizona	February 14, 1912
24. Missouri	August 10, 1821	49. Alaska	January 3, 1959
25. Arkansas	June 15, 1836	50. Hawaii	August 21, 1959

DEMOGRAPHICS OF THE UNITED STATE

POPULATION GROWTH

Year	Population	Percent Increase
1630	4,600	
1640	26,600	478.3
1650	50,400	90.8
1660	75,100	49.0
1670	111,900	49.0
1680	151,500	35.4
1690	210,400	38.9
1700	250,900	19.2
1710	331,700	32.2
1720	466,200	40.5
1730	629,400	35.0
1740	905,600	43.9
1750	1,170,800	29.3
1760	1,593,600	36.1
1770	2,148,100	34.8
1780	2,780,400	29.4
1790	3,929,214	41.3
1800	5,308,483	35.1
1810	7,239,881	36.4
1820	9,638,453	33.1
1830	12,866,020	33.5
1840	17,069,453	32.7
1850	23,191,876	35.9
1860	31,443,321	35.6
1870	39,818,449	26.6
1880	50,155,783	26.0
1890	62,947,714	25.5
1900	75,994,575	20.7
1910	91,972,266	21.0
1920	105,710,620	14.9
1930	122,775,046	16.1
1940	131,669,275	7.2
1950	151,325,798	14.5
1960	179,323,175	18.5
1970	203,302,031	13.4
1980	226,542,199	11.4
1990	248,718,301	9.8
2000	281,421,906	13.1

Source: *Historical Statistics of the United States* (1975); *Statistical Abstract by the United States* (2001).
Note: Figures for 1630–1780 include British colonies within limits of present United States only; Native American population included only in 1930 and thereafter. Figures before 1790 are estimates.

WORK FORCE

Year	Total Number Workers (1000s)	Farmers as % of Total	Women as % of Total	% Workers in Unions
1810	2,330	84	(NA)	(NA)
1840	5,660	75	(NA)	(NA)
1860	11,110	53	(NA)	(NA)
1870	12,506	53	15	(NA)
1880	17,392	52	15	(NA)
1890	23,318	43	17	(NA)
1900	29,073	40	18	3
1910	38,167	31	21	6
1920	41,614	26	21	12
1930	48,830	22	22	7
1940	53,011	17	24	27
1950	59,643	12	28	25
1960	69,877	8	32	26
1970	82,049	4	37	25
1980	106,940	3	43	23
1990	125,840	3	45	16
2000	140,863	2	47	12

Source: *Historical Statistics of the United States* (1975); *Statistical Abstract of the United States* (2001).

VITAL STATISTICS (IN THOUSANDS)

Year	Births	Deaths	Marriages	Divorces
1800	55	(NA)	(NA)	(NA)
1810	54.3	(NA)	(NA)	(NA)
1820	55.2	(NA)	(NA)	(NA)
1830	51.4	(NA)	(NA)	(NA)
1840	51.8	(NA)	(NA)	(NA)
1850	43.3	(NA)	(NA)	(NA)
1860	44.3	(NA)	(NA)	(NA)
1870	38.3	(NA)	9.6 (1867)	0.3 (1867)
1880	39.8	(NA)	9.1 (1875)	0.3 (1875)
1890	31.5	(NA)	9.0	0.5
1900	32.3	17.2	9.3	0.7
1910	30.1	14.7	10.3	0.9
1920	27.7	13.0	12.0	1.6
1930	21.3	11.3	9.2	1.6
1940	19.4	10.8	12.1	2.0
1950	24.1	9.6	11.1	2.6
1960	23.7	9.5	8.5	2.2
1970	18.4	9.5	10.6	3.5
1980	15.9	8.8	10.6	5.2
1990	16.7	8.6	9.8	4.7
1997	14.6	8.6	8.9	4.3

Source: *Historical Statistics of the United States* (1975); *Statistical Abstract of the United States* (1999).

POPULATIONS BY RACIAL GROUPS AND HISPANIC ORIGINS (IN THOUSANDS)

Year	White	Black	Indian	Asian/Pacific Islander	Other Race*	Hispanic Origin*
1790	3,172	757	(NA)	(NA)	(NA)	(NA)
1800	4,306	1,002	(NA)	(NA)	(NA)	(NA)
1820	7,867	1,772	(NA)	(NA)	(NA)	(NA)
1840	14,196	2,874	(NA)	(NA)	(NA)	(NA)
1860	26,923	4,442	(NA)	(NA)	(NA)	(NA)
1880	43,403	6,581	(NA)	(NA)	(NA)	(NA)
1900	66,809	8,834	(NA)	(NA)	(NA)	(NA)
1910	81,732	9,828	(NA)	(NA)	(NA)	(NA)
1920	94,821	10,463	(NA)	(NA)	(NA)	(NA)
1930	110,287	11,891	(NA)	(NA)	(NA)	(NA)
1940	118,215	12,866	(NA)	(NA)	(NA)	(NA)
1950	134,942	15,042	(NA)	(NA)	(NA)	(NA)
1960	158,832	18,872	(NA)	(NA)	(NA)	(NA)
1970	178,098	22,581	(NA)	(NA)	(NA)	(NA)
1980	194,713	26,683	1,420	3,500	6,758	14,609
1990	208,727	30,511	1,959	7,273	9,805	22,354
2000	211,461	34,658	2,476	10,642	22,185	35,603

Source: U.S. Bureau of the Census, U.S. Census of Population: 1940, vol. II, part 1, and vol. IV, part 1; 1950, vol. II, part 1; 1960, vol. I, part 1; 1970, vol. I, part B; and Current Population Reports, P25-1095 and P25-1104; Statistical Abstract of the United States (2001). *Other or multiple race as self-identified. **Hispanic population may be of any race.

THE ECONOMY AND FEDERAL SPENDING

Year	Gross National Product (GNP) (in billions)	Foreign Trade (in millions) Exports	Imports	Balance of Trade	Federal Budget (in billions)	Federal Surplus/Deficit (in billions)	Federal Debt (in billions)
1790	(NA)	$ 20	$ 23	$ −3	$ 0.004	$ +0.00015	$ 0.076
1800	(NA)	71	91	−20	0.011	+0.0006	0.083
1810	(NA)	67	85	−18	0.008	+0.0012	0.053
1820	(NA)	70	74	−4	0.018	−0.0004	0.091
1830	(NA)	74	71	+3	0.015	+0.100	0.049
1840	(NA)	132	107	+25	0.024	−0.005	0.004
1850	(NA)	152	178	−26	0.040	+0.004	0.064
1860	(NA)	400	362	−38	0.063	−0.01	0.065
1870	$ 7.4	451	462	−11	0.310	+0.10	2.4
1880	11.2	853	761	+92	0.268	+0.07	2.1
1890	13.1	910	823	+87	0.318	+0.09	1.2
1900	18.7	1,499	930	+569	0.521	+0.05	1.2
1910	35.3	1,919	1,646	+273	0.694	−0.02	1.1
1920	91.5	8,664	5,784	+2,880	6.357	+0.3	24.3
1930	90.7	4,013	3,500	+513	3.320	+0.7	16.3
1940	100.0	4,030	7,433	−3,403	9.6	−2.7	43.0
1950	286.5	10,816	9,125	+1,691	43.1	−2.2	257.4
1960	506.5	19,600	15,046	+4,556	92.2	+0.3	286.3
1970	992.7	42,700	40,189	+2,511	195.6	−2.8	371.0
1980	2,631.7	220,783	244,871	+24,088	590.9	−73.8	907.7
1990	5,524.5	394,030	494,042	−101,012	1,251.8	−220.5	3,233.3
2000	9,958.7	1,068,397	1,438,086	−369,689	1,788.8	+236.4	5,629.0

Source: U.S. Office of Management and Budget, Budget of the United States Government, annual; Statistical Abstract of the United States, 2001.

Immigration to the United States Since 1820 (by decade)

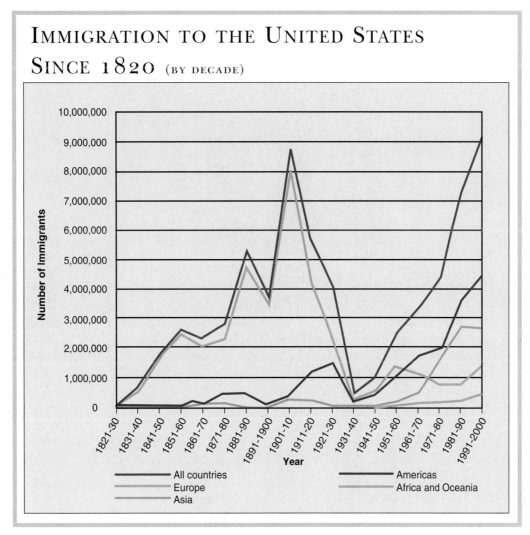

Source: *Statistical Yearbook of the Immigration and Naturalization Service,* 2001.

Act for Religious Toleration The first law in America to call for freedom of worship for all Christians. It was enacted in Maryland in 1649 to quell disputes between Catholics and Protestants, but it failed to bring peace.

Actual representation The practice whereby elected representatives normally reside in their districts and are directly responsive to local interests.

Affirmative Action A set of policies to open opportunities in business and education for members of minority groups and women by allowing race and sex to be factors included in decisions to hire, award contracts, or admit students to higher education programs.

Age of Enlightenment Major intellectual movement occurring in western Europe in the late seventeenth and early eighteenth centuries. Inspired by recent scientific advances, thinkers emphasized the role of human reason in understanding the world and directing its events. Their ideas placed less emphasis on God's role in ordering worldly affairs.

Agricultural Wheel One of several farmer organizations that emerged in the South during the 1880s. It sought federal legislation to deal with credit and currency issues.

AIDS (Acquired immune deficiency syndrome) A complex of deadly pathologies resulting from infection with the human immunodeficiency virus (HIV).

Alamo Franciscan mission at San Antonio, Texas, that was the site in 1836 of a siege and massacre of Texans by Mexican troops.

Albany Plan of Union Plan put forward in 1754 by Massachusetts Governor William Shirley, Benjamin Franklin, and other colonial leaders, calling for an intercolonial union to manage defense and Indian affairs. The plan was rejected by participants at the Albany Congress.

Alien and Sedition Acts Collective name given to four acts passed by Congress in 1798 that curtailed freedom of speech and the liberty of foreigners resident in the United States.

Alien Friends Act Law passed by Congress in 1798 authorizing the president during peacetime to expel aliens suspected of subversive activities; one of the **Alien and Sedition Acts**.

Alliance for Progress Program of economic aid to Latin America during the Kennedy administration.

Allies In World War I, Britain, France, Russia, and other belligerent nations fighting against the **Central Powers** but not including the United States, which insisted upon being merely an associated nation. In World War II, the Allies fighting the **Axis Powers** included the United States as well as the Soviet Union, Great Britain, France, China, and other nations.

American Anti-Slavery Society The first national organization of abolitionists, founded in 1833.

American Colonization Society Organization, founded in 1817 by antislavery reformers, that called for gradual emancipation and the removal of freed blacks to Africa.

American Federation of Labor (AFL) Union formed in 1886 that organized skilled workers along craft lines and emphasized a few workplace issues rather than a broad social program.

American Female Moral Reform Society Organization founded in 1839 by female reformers that established homes of refuge for prostitutes and petitioned for state laws that would criminalize adultery and the seduction of women.

American Indian Movement (AIM) Group of Native American political activists who used confrontations with the federal government to publicize their case for Indian rights.

American Liberty League Business group organized to sway popular opinion against the **New Deal**.

American Revenue Act See **Sugar Act**.

Americans with Disabilities Act Legislation in 1992 that banned discrimination against physically handicapped persons in employment, transportation, and public accommodations.

American System The program of government subsidies favored by Henry Clay and his followers to promote American economic growth and protect domestic manufacturers from foreign competition.

American system of manufacturing A technique of production pioneered in the United States in the first half of the nineteenth century that relied on precision manufacturing with the use of interchangeable parts.

American Temperance Society National organization established in 1826 by evangelical Protestants that campaigned for total abstinence from alcohol and was successful in sharply lowering per capita consumption of alcohol.

Anarchist A person who believes that all government interferes with individual liberty and should be abolished by whatever means.

Anglican Of or belonging to the Church of England, a Protestant denomination.

Anglo–American Accords Series of agreements reached in the British–American Convention of 1818 that fixed the western boundary between the United States and Canada at the 49th parallel, allowed for the joint occupation of the Oregon Country, and restored to Americans fishing rights off Newfoundland.

Anglo-Saxon Broadly, a person of English descent.

Annapolis Convention Conference of state delegates at Annapolis, Maryland, that issued a call in September 1786 for a convention to meet at Philadelphia in May 1787 to consider fundamental changes to the **Articles of Confederation**.

Antifederalist An opponent of the **Constitution** in the debate over its ratification.

Anti-Masons Third party formed in 1827 in opposition to the presumed power and influence of the Masonic order.

Archaic Period The period roughly between 8000 and 1500 B.C., during which time Native Americans adapted to a changed continental climate, developed larger communities, and, in several regions, adopted agriculture.

Articles of Confederation Written document setting up the loose confederation of states that comprised the first national government of the United States from 1781 to 1788.

Atlanta Compromise Booker T. Washington's policy accepting segregation and **disfranchisement** for African Americans in exchange for white assistance in education and job training.

Atlantic Charter Statement of common principles and war aims developed by President Franklin Roosevelt and British Prime Minister Winston Churchill at a meeting in August 1941.

Australian ballot Secret voting and the use of official ballots rather than party tickets.

Axis Powers The opponents of the United States and its allies in World War II. The Rome–Berlin Axis was formed between Germany and Italy in 1936 and included Japan after 1940.

Aztecs A warrior people who dominated the Valley of Mexico from about 1100 until their conquest in 1519–21 by Spanish soldiers led by Hernán Cortés.

Bacon's Rebellion Violent conflict in Virginia (1675–1676), beginning with settler attacks on Indians but culminating in a rebellion led by Nathaniel Bacon against Virginia's government.

Baker v. Carr U.S. Supreme Court decision in 1962 that allowed federal courts to review the apportionment of state legislative districts and established the principle that such districts should have roughly equal populations ("one person, one vote").

Bank War The political struggle between President Andrew Jackson and the supporters of the **Second Bank of the United States**.

Battle of the Atlantic The long struggle between German submarines and the British and U.S. navies in the North Atlantic from 1940 to 1943.

Bay of Pigs Site in Cuba of an unsuccessful landing by fourteen hundred anti-Castro Cuban refugees in April 1961.

Beaver Wars Series of bloody conflicts, occurring between 1640s and 1680s, during which the Iroquois fought the French and their Indian allies for control of the fur trade in eastern North America and the Great Lakes region.

Benevolent empire Network of reform associations affiliated with Protestant churches in the early nineteenth century dedicated to the restoration of moral order.

Berlin blockade Three-hundred-day Soviet blockade of land access to United States, British, and French occupation zones in Berlin, 1948–1949.

Berlin Wall Wall erected by East Germany in 1961 and torn down in 1989 that isolated West Berlin from the surrounding areas in Communist-controlled East Berlin and East Germany.

Bill of Rights A written summary of inalienable rights and liberties.

Black codes Laws passed by states and municipalities denying many rights of citizenship to free blacks before the Civil War. Also, during the **Reconstruction era**, laws passed by newly elected southern state legislatures to control black labor, mobility, and employment.

Black Hawk's War Short 1832 war in which federal troops and Illinois militia units defeated the Sauk and Fox Indians led by Black Hawk.

Black Panthers Political and social movement among black Americans, founded in Oakland, California, in 1966 and emphasizing black economic and political power.

Black Power Philosophy emerging after 1965 that real economic and political gains for African-Americans could come only through self-help, **self-determination**, and organizing for direct political influence. Latinos and Native Americans developed their own versions as Brown Power and Red Power, respectively.

"Bleeding Kansas" Violence between pro- and antislavery forces in Kansas Territory after the passage of the **Kansas-Nebraska Act** in 1854.

Blitzkrieg German war tactic in World War II ("lightning war") involving the concentration of air and armored firepower to punch and exploit holes in opposing defensive lines.

Bolshevik Member of the communist movement in Russia that established the Soviet government after the 1917 Russian Revolution; hence, by extension, any radical or disruptive person or movement seeking to transform economic and political relationships.

Bosnia A nation in southeast Europe that split off from Yugoslavia and became the site of bitter civil war and religious war, requiring NATO and U.S. intervention in the 1990s.

Boston Tea Party Incident that occurred on December 16, 1773, in which Bostonians, disguised as Indians, destroyed £9,000 worth of tea belonging to the British East India Company in order to prevent payment of the duty on it.

British Constitution The principles, procedures, and precedents that governed the operation of the British government. These could be found in no single written document; Parliament and the king made the Constitution by their actions.

Brook Farm A utopian community and experimental farm established in 1841 near Boston.

Brown v. Board of Education of Topeka Supreme Court decision in 1954 that declared that "separate but equal" schools for children of different races violated the **Constitution**.

Bureau of Reclamation Federal agency established in 1902 providing public funds for irrigation projects in arid regions; played a major role in the development of the West by constructing dams, reservoirs, and irrigation systems, especially beginning in the 1930s.

Cahokia Located near modern St. Louis, this was one of the largest urban centers created by Mississippian peoples, containing perhaps 30,000 residents in 1250.

Camp David Agreement Agreement to reduce points of conflict between Israel and Egypt, hammered out in 1977 with the help of U.S. President Jimmy Carter.

Central Intelligence Agency (CIA) Agency that coordinates the gathering and evaluation of military and economic information on other nations, established in 1947.

Central Powers Germany and its World War I allies Austria, Turkey, and Bulgaria.

Chain migration Process common to many immigrant groups whereby one family member brings over other family members, who in turn bring other relatives and friends and occasionally entire villages.

Charles River Bridge v. Warren Bridge Supreme Court decision of 1837 that promoted economic competition by ruling that the broader rights of the community took precedence over any presumed right of monopoly granted in a corporate charter.

Cherokee War Conflict (1759–1761) on the southern frontier between the Cherokee Indians and colonists from Virginia southward. It caused South Carolina to request the aid of British troops and resulted in the surrender of more Indian land to white colonists.

***Chesapeake* Incident** Attack in 1807 by the British ship *Leopard* on the American ship *Chesapeake* in American territorial waters that nearly provoked an Anglo-American war.

Chisholm Trail The route followed by Texas cattle raisers driving their herds north to markets at Kansas railheads.

Church of Jesus Christ of Latter-day Saints *See* **Mormon Church.**

Civil Rights Act of 1866 Law that defined national citizenship and specified the civil rights to which all national citizens were entitled.

Civil Rights Act of 1875 Law that prohibited racial discrimination in jury selection, public transportation, and public accommodations; declared unconstitutional by the U.S. Supreme Court in 1883.

Civil Rights Act of 1964 Federal legislation that outlawed discrimination in public accommodations and employment on the basis of race, skin color, sex, religion, or national origin.

Claims club A group of local settlers on the nineteenth-century frontier who banded together to prevent the price of their land claims from being bid up by outsiders at public land auctions.

Coercive Acts Legislation passed by Parliament in 1774; included the Boston Port Act, the Massachusetts Government Act, the Administration of Justice Act, and the **Quartering Act** of 1774.

Cold War The political and economic confrontation between the Soviet Union and the United States that dominated world affairs from 1946 to 1989.

Collective bargaining Representatives of a union negotiating with management on behalf of all members.

Colored Farmers' Alliance An organization of southern black farmers formed in Texas in 1886 in response to the **Southern Farmers' Alliance**, which did not accept black people as members.

Columbian exchange The transatlantic exchange of plants, animals, and diseases that occurred after the first European contact with the Americas.

Committees of correspondence Committees formed in Massachusetts and other colonies in the pre-Revolutionary period to keep Americans informed about British measures that would affect the colonies.

Committee of Safety Any of the extralegal committees that directed the Revolutionary movement and carried on the functions of government at the local level in the period between the breakdown of royal authority and the establishment of regular governments under the new state constitutions. Some Committees of Safety continued to function throughout the Revolutionary War.

Committee on Public Information (CPI) Government agency during World War I that sought to shape public opinion in support of the war effort through newspapers, pamphlets, speeches, films, and other media.

Communism A social structure based on the common ownership of property.

Conciliatory Proposition Plan proposed by Lord North and adopted by the House of Commons in February 1775 whereby Parliament would "forbear" taxation of Americans in colonies whose assemblies imposed taxes considered satisfactory by the British government. The Continental Congress rejected this plan on July 31, 1775.

Confederate States of America Nation proclaimed in Montgomery, Alabama, in February 1861 after the seven states of the Lower South seceded from the United States.

Confiscation Act of 1862 Second confiscation law passed by Congress, ordering the seizure of land from disloyal Southerners and the emancipation of their slaves.

Congressional Reconstruction Name given to the period 1867–1870 when the Republican-dominated Congress controlled **Reconstruction Era** policy. It is sometimes known as Radical Reconstruction, after the radical faction in the **Republican party**.

Congress of Industrial Organizations An alliance of industrial unions that spurred the 1930s organizational drive among the mass-production industries.

Congress of Racial Equality (CORE) Civil rights group formed in 1942 and committed to nonviolent civil disobedience, such as the 1961 "freedom rides."

Conservation The efficient management and use of natural resources, such as forests, grasslands, and rivers, as opposed to **preservation** or uncontrolled exploitation.

Constitutional Convention Convention that met in Philadelphia in 1787 and drafted the **Constitution of the United States**.

Constitutional Union party National party formed in 1860, mainly by former **Whigs**, that emphasized allegiance to the Union and strict enforcement of all national legislation.

Constitution of the United States The written document providing for a new central government of the United States, drawn up at the **Constitutional Convention** in 1787 and ratified by the states in 1788.

Containment The policy of resisting further expansion of the Soviet bloc through diplomacy and, if necessary, military action, developed in 1947–48.

Continental Army The regular or professional army authorized by the Second Continental Congress and commanded by General George Washington during the Revolutionary War. Better training and longer service distinguished its soldiers from the state militiamen.

Continental Association Agreement, adopted by the **First Continental Congress** in 1774 in response to the **Coercive Acts**, to cut off trade with Britain until the objectionable measures were repealed. Local committees were established to enforce the provisions of the association.

Contract theory of government The belief that government is established by human beings to protect certain rights—such as life, liberty, and property—that are theirs by natural, divinely sanctioned law and that when government protects these rights, people are obligated to obey it. But when government violates its part of the bargain (or contract) between the rulers and the ruled, the people are no longer required to obey it and may establish a new government that will do a better job of protecting them. Elements of this theory date back to the ancient Greeks; John Locke used it in his *Second Treatise on Government* (1682), and Thomas Jefferson gave it memorable expression in the Declaration of Independence, where it provides the rationale for renouncing allegiance to King George III.

Contract with America Platform on which many Republican candidates ran for Congress in 1994.

Associated with House Speaker Newt Gingrich, it proposed a sweeping reduction in the role and activities of the federal government.

Copperheads A term Republicans applied to Northern war dissenters and those suspected of aiding the Confederate cause during the Civil War.

Council of Economic Advisers Board of three professional economists established in 1946 to advise the president on economic policy.

Counterculture Various alternatives to mainstream values and behaviors that became popular in the 1960s, including experimentation with psychedelic drugs, communal living, a return to the land, Asian religions, and experimental art.

Country (Real Whig) ideology Strain of thought first appearing in England in the late seventeenth century in response to the growth of governmental power and a national debt. Main ideas stressed the threat to personal liberty posed by a standing army and high taxes and emphasized the need for property holders to retain the right to consent to taxation.

Coureur de bois French for "woods runner," an independent fur trader in New France.

Coxey's Army A protest march of unemployed workers, led by Populist businessman Jacob Coxey, demanding inflation and a public works program during the depression of the 1890s.

Cult of domesticity The belief that women, by virtue of their sex, should stay home as the moral guardians of family life.

Currency Act Law passed by Parliament in 1764 to prevent the colonies from issuing **legal tender** paper money, which often depreciated.

Dartmouth College v. Woodward Supreme Court decision of 1819 that prohibited states from interfering with the privileges granted to a private corporation.

Dawes Act An 1887 law terminating tribal ownership of land and allotting some parcels of land to individual Indians with the remainder opened for white settlement.

D-Day June 6, 1944, the day of the first paratroop drops and amphibious landings on the coast of Normandy, France, in the first stage of **Operation OVERLORD** during World War II.

Declaration of Independence The document by which the Second Continental Congress announced and justified its decision (reached July 2, 1776) to renounce the colonies' allegiance to the British government. Drafted mainly by Thomas Jefferson and adopted by Congress on July 4, the declaration's indictment of the king provides a remarkably full catalog of the colonists' grievances, and Jefferson's eloquent and inspiring statement of the **contract theory of government** makes the document one of the world's great state papers.

Declaration of London Statement drafted by an international conference in 1909 to clarify international law and specify the rights of neutral nations.

Declaration of Rights and Grievances Resolves, adopted by the **Stamp Act Congress** at New York in 1765, asserting that the **Stamp Act** and other taxes imposed on the colonists without their consent, given through their colonial legislatures, were unconstitutional.

Declaration of Sentiments The resolutions passed at the **Seneca Falls Convention** in 1848 calling for full female equality, including the right to vote.

Declaration of the Causes and Necessity of Taking Up Arms Document, written mainly by John Dickinson of Pennsylvania and adopted on July 6, 1775, by which the Second Continental Congress justified its armed resistance against British measures.

Declaratory Act Law passed in 1766 to accompany repeal of the **Stamp Act** that stated that Parliament had the authority to legislate for the colonies "in all cases whatsoever." Whether "legislate" meant tax was not clear to Americans.

Deindustrialization The process of economic change involving the disappearance of outmoded industries and the transfer of factories to new low-wage locations, with devastating effects in the Northeast and Middle West, especially in the 1970s and 1980s.

Deism Religious orientation that rejects divine revelation and holds that the workings of nature alone reveal God's design for the universe.

Democratic Party Political party formed in the 1820s under the leadership of Andrew Jackson; favored states' rights and a limited role for the federal government, especially in economic affairs.

Denmark Vesey's Conspiracy The most carefully devised slave revolt, named after its leader, a free black in Charleston. The rebels planned to seize control of Charleston in 1822 and escape to freedom in Haiti, a free black republic, but they were betrayed by other slaves, and seventy-five conspirators were executed.

Deregulation Reduction or removal of government regulations and encouragement of direct competition in many important industries and economic sectors.

Disfranchisement The use of legal means to bar individuals or groups from voting.

Dollar diplomacy The U.S. policy of using private investment in other nations to promote American diplomatic goals and business interests.

Dominion of New England James II's failed plan of 1686 to combine eight northern colonies into a single large province, to be governed by a royal appointee (Sir Edmund Andros) with an appointed council but no elective assembly. The plan ended with James's ouster from the English throne and rebellion in Massachusetts against Andros's rule.

***Dred Scott* decision** Supreme Court ruling, in a lawsuit brought by Dred Scott, a slave demanding his freedom based on his residence in a free state and a free territory with his master, that slaves could not be U.S. citizens and that Congress had no jurisdiction over slavery in the territories.

Eastern Front The area of military operations in World War II located east of Germany in eastern Europe and the Soviet Union.

Economic Recovery and Tax Act of 1981 (ERTA) A major revision of the federal income tax system.

Eighteenth Amendment Constitutional revision, ratified in 1919 and repealed in 1933, that prohibited the manufacture or sale of alcohol in the United States.

Emancipation Proclamation Decree announced by President Abraham Lincoln in September 1862 and formally issued on January 1, 1863, freeing slaves in all Confederate states still in rebellion.

Embargo Act of 1807 Act passed by Congress in 1807 prohibiting American ships from leaving for any foreign port.

Empresario An agent who received a land grant from the Spanish or Mexican government in return for organizing settlements.

Encomienda In the Spanish colonies, the grant to a Spanish settler of a certain number of Indian subjects, who would pay him tribute in goods and labor.

Enumerated products Items produced in the colonies and enumerated in acts of Parliament that could be legally shipped from the colony of origin only to specified locations, usually England and other destinations within the British empire.

Environmental Protection Agency (EPA) Federal agency created in 1970 to oversee environmental monitoring and cleanup programs.

Era of Good Feelings The period from 1817 to 1823 in which the disappearance of the **Federalists** enabled the **Republicans** to govern in a spirit of seemingly nonpartisan harmony.

Espionage Act of 1917 Law whose vague prohibition against obstructing the nation's war effort was used to crush dissent and criticism during World War I.

Fair Employment Practice Committee (FEPC) Federal agency established in 1941 to curb racial discrimination in war production jobs and government employment.

Farmers' Alliance A broad mass movement in the rural South and West during the late nineteenth century, encompassing several organizations and demanding economic and political reforms; helped create the **Populist party**.

Fascist Subscribing to a philosophy of governmental dictatorship that merges the interests of the state, armed forces, and big business; associated with the dictatorship of Italian leader Benito Mussolini between 1922 and 1943 and also often applied to Nazi Germany.

Federal Deposit Insurance Corporation (FDIC) Government agency that guarantees bank deposits, thereby protecting both depositors and banks.

Federal Highway Act of 1956 Measure that provided federal funding to build a nationwide system of interstate and defense highways.

Federalism The sharing of powers between the national government and the states.

Federalist A supporter of the **Constitution** who favored its ratification.

Federal Reserve Act The 1913 law that revised banking and currency by extending limited government regulation through the creation of the Federal Reserve System.

Federal Trade Commission (FTC) Government agency established in 1914 to provide regulatory oversight of business activity.

Field Order No. 15 Order by General William T. Sherman in January 1865 to set aside abandoned land along the southern Atlantic coast for forty-acre grants to freedmen; rescinded by President Andrew Johnson later that year.

Fireside chats Speeches broadcast nationally over the radio in which President Franklin Roosevelt explained complex issues and programs in plain language, as though his listeners were gathered around the fireside with him.

First Continental Congress Meeting of delegates from most of the colonies held in 1774 in response to the **Coercive Acts**. The Congress endorsed the **Suffolk Resolves**, adopted the **Declaration of Rights and Grievances**, and agreed to establish the **Continental Association** to put economic pressure on Britain to repeal its objectionable measures. The Congress also wrote addresses to the king, the people of Britain, and the American people.

Fletcher v. Peck Supreme Court decision of 1810 that overturned a state law by ruling that it violated a legal contract.

Fort Sumter Begun in the late 1820s to protect Charleston, South Carolina, it became the center of national attention in April 1861 when President Lincoln attempted to provision federal troops at the fort, triggering a hostile response from on-shore Confederate forces, opening the Civil War.

Fourierist communities Short-live utopian communities in the 1840s based on the ideas of economic cooperation and self-sufficiency popularized by the Frenchman Charles Fourier.

Fourteenth Amendment Constitutional amendment passed by Congress in April 1866 incorporating some of the features of the **Civil Rights Act of 1866**. It prohibited states from violating the civil rights of its citizens and offered states the choice of allowing black people to vote or losing representation in Congress.

Franco-American Accord of 1800 Settlement reached with France that brought an end to the **Quasi-War** and released the United States from its 1778 alliance with France.

Freedmen's Bureau Agency established by Congress in March 1865 to provide social, educational, and economic services, advice, and protection to former slaves and destitute whites; lasted seven years.

Freedom Summer Voter registration effort in rural Mississippi organized by black and white civil rights workers in 1964.

Free silver Philosophy that the government should expand the money supply by purchasing and coining all the silver offered to it.

Free Speech Movement (FSM) Student movement at the University of California, Berkeley, formed in 1964 to protest limitations on political activities on campus.

French and Indian War The last of the Anglo-French colonial wars (1754–1763) and the first in which fighting began in North America. The war (which merged with the European conflict known as the Seven Years' War) ended with France's defeat and loss of its North American empire.

Fugitive Slave Act Law, part of the Compromise of 1850, that required that authorities in the North to assist southern slave catchers and return runaway slaves to their owners.

Fundamental Constitutions of Carolina A complex plan for organizing the colony of Carolina, drafted in 1669 by Anthony Ashley Cooper and John Locke. Its provisions included a scheme for creating a hierarchy of nobles who would own vast amounts of land and wield political power; below them would be a class of freedmen and slaves. The provisions were never implemented by the Carolina colonists.

Fundamentalists Religious conservatives who believe in the literal accuracy and divine inspiration of the Bible; the name derives from an influential series of pamphlets, *The Fundamentals* (1909–1914).

Gabriel Prosser's Rebellion Slave revolt that failed when Gabriel Prosser, a slave preacher and blacksmith, organized a thousand slaves for an attack on Richmond, Virginia, in 1800. A thunderstorm upset the timing of the attack, and a slave informer alerted the whites. Prosser and twenty-five of his followers were executed.

Gang system The organization and supervision of slave field hands into working teams on southern plantations.

General Union for Promoting the Observance of the Christian Sabbath See **Sabbatarian movement.**

Gentlemen's Agreement A diplomatic agreement in 1907 between Japan and the United States curtailing but not abolishing Japanese immigration.

Ghent, Treaty of Treaty signed in December 1814 between the United States and Britain that ended the **War of 1812.**

GI Bill of Rights Legislation in June 1944 that eased the return of veterans into American society by providing educational and employment benefits.

Gibbons v. Ogden Supreme Court decision of 1824 involving coastal commerce that overturned a steamboat monopoly granted by the state of New York on the grounds that only Congress had the authority to regulate interstate commerce.

Gilded Age Term applied to late-nineteenth-century America that refers to the shallow display and worship of wealth characteristic of the period.

Glasnost Russian for "openness," applied to Mikhail Gorbachev's encouragement of new ideas and easing of political repression in the Soviet Union.

Glorious Revolution Bloodless revolt that occurred in England in 1688 when parliamentary leaders invited William of Orange, a Protestant, to assume the English throne and James II fled to France. James's ouster was prompted by fears that the birth of his son would establish a Catholic dynasty in England.

Gospel of Wealth Thesis that hard work and perseverance lead to wealth, implying that poverty is a character flaw.

Grandfather clause Rule that required potential voters to demonstrate that their grandfathers had been eligible to vote; used in some southern states after 1890 to limit the black electorate, as most black men's grandfathers had been slaves.

Grand Settlement of 1701 Separate peace treaties negotiated by Iroquois diplomats at Montreal and Albany that marked the beginning of Iroquois neutrality in conflicts between the French and the British in North America.

Grange The National Grange of the Patrons of Husbandry, a national organization of farm owners formed after the Civil War.

Granger laws State laws enacted in the Midwest in the 1870s that regulated rates charged by railroads, grain elevator operators, and other middlemen.

Great Awakening Tremendous religious revival in colonial America. Sparked by the tour of the English evangelical minister George Whitefield, the Awakening struck first in the Middle Colonies and New England in the 1740s and eventually spread to the southern colonies by the 1760s.

Great Compromise Plan proposed by Roger Sherman of Connecticut at the 1787 **Constitutional Convention** for creating a national bicameral legislature in which all states would be equally represented in the Senate and proportionally represented in the House.

Great Depression The nation's worst economic crisis, extending throughout the 1930s, producing unprecedented bank failures, unemployment, and industrial and agricultural collapse and prompting an expanded role for the federal government.

Great Migration The mass movement of African Americans from the rural South to the urban North, spurred especially by new job opportunities during World War I and the 1920s.

Great Society Theme of Lyndon Johnson's administration, focusing on poverty, education, and civil rights.

Great Uprising Unsuccessful railroad strike of 1877 to protest wage cuts and the use of federal troops against strikers; the first nationwide work stoppage in American history.

Greenback party A third party of the 1870s and 1880s that garnered temporary support by advocating currency inflation to expand the economy and assist debtors.

Greenville, Treaty of Treaty of 1795 in which Native Americans in the Old Northwest were forced to cede most of the present state of Ohio to the United States.

Halfway Covenant Plan adopted in 1662 by New England clergy to deal with the problem of declining church membership. It allowed adults who had been baptized because their parents were church members but who had not yet experienced conversion to have their own children baptized. Without the Halfway Covenant, these third-generation children would remain unbaptized until their parents experienced conversion.

Harlem Renaissance A new African-American cultural awareness that flourished in literature, art, and music in the 1920s.

Helsinki Accords Agreement in 1975 among NATO and Warsaw Pact members that recognized European national boundaries as set after World War II and included guarantees of human rights.

Holocaust The systematic murder of millions of European Jews and others deemed undesirable by Nazi Germany.

Homestead Act Law passed by Congress in May 1862 providing homesteaders (mainly in the West) with 160 acres of free land in exchange for improving the land (as by cultivating it and erecting a house) within five years of the grant.

Hooverville Shantytown, sarcastically named after President Hoover, in which unemployed and homeless people lived in makeshift shacks, tents, and boxes. Hoovervilles cropped up in many cities in 1930 and 1931.

House of Burgesses The legislature of colonial Virginia. First organized in 1619, it was the first institution of representative government in the English colonies.

Hull House Chicago **settlement house** that became part of a broader neighborhood revitalization project led by Jane Addams.

Immigration and Nationality Act of 1965 Federal legislation that replaced the national quota system for immigration with overall limits of 170,000 immigrants per year from the Eastern Hemisphere and 120,000 per year from the Western Hemisphere.

Imperialism The policy and practice of exploiting nations and peoples for the benefit of an imperial power either directly through military occupation and colonial rule or indirectly through economic domination of resources and markets.

Impressment The British policy of forcibly enlisting American sailors into the British navy.

Indentured servant An individual—usually male but occasionally female—who contracted to serve a master for a period of four to seven years in return for payment of the servant's passage to America. Indentured servitude was the primary labor system in the Chesapeake colonies for most of the seventeenth century.

Independent Treasury System Fiscal arrangement first instituted by President Martin Van Buren in which the federal government kept its money in regional vaults ("pet banks") and transacted its business entirely in hard money.

Initiative Procedure by which citizens can introduce a subject for legislation, usually through a petition signed by a specific number of voters.

Intermediate Nuclear Force Agreement (INF) Disarmament agreement between the United States and the Soviet Union under which an entire class of missiles would be removed and destroyed and on-site inspections would be permitted for verification.

International Monetary Fund (IMF) International organization established in 1945 to assist nations in maintaining stable currencies.

Internet The system of interconnected computers and servers that allows the exchange of e-mail, posting of web sites, and other means of instant communication.

Interstate and Defense Highways Federal legislation in 1956 committed the federal government to finance more than 40,000 miles of new limited access freeways to criss-cross the United States.

Interstate Commerce Act The 1887 law that expanded federal power over business by prohibiting pooling and discriminatory rates by railroads and establishing the first federal regulatory agency, the **Interstate Commerce Commission**.

Interstate Commerce Commission (ICC) The first federal regulatory agency, established in 1887 to oversee railroad practices.

Intolerable Acts American term for the **Coercive Acts** and the **Quebec Act**.

Iroquois League The union of five Indian nations (Mohawks, Oneidas, Onondagas, Cayugas, and Senecas) formed around 1450, also known as the League of Five Nations. Essentially a religious organization, its purpose was to maintain peace among the five nations and unite them to fight against other enemies. After the Tuscarora War (1713–1715), the Tuscaroras joined the league, thereafter known as the League of Six Nations.

Irreconcilables Group of U.S. senators adamantly opposed to ratification of the **Treaty of Versailles** after World War I.

Jacksonian Democrats *See* **Democratic Party**.

Jay's Treaty Treaty with Britain negotiated in 1794 in which the United States made major concessions to avert a war over the British seizure of American ships.

Jazz Age The 1920s, so called for the popular music of the day as a symbol of the many changes taking place in the mass culture.

Jeffersonian Republicans *See* **Republican Party (Jeffersonian)**.

Jim Crow laws **Segregation** laws that became widespread in the South during the 1890s, named for a minstrel show character portrayed satirically by white actors in blackface.

John Brown's Raid New England abolitionist John Brown's ill-fated attempt to free Virginia's slaves with a raid on the federal arsenal at Harpers Ferry, Virginia, in 1859.

Joint-stock company Business enterprise in which a group of stockholders pooled their money to engage in trade or to fund colonizing expeditions. Joint-stock companies participated in the founding of the Virginia, Plymouth, and Massachusetts Bay colonies.

Judicial review A power implied in the **Constitution** that gives federal courts the right to review and determine the constitutionality of acts passed by Congress and state legislatures.

Judiciary Act of 1789 Act of Congress that implemented the judiciary clause of the **Constitution** by establishing the Supreme Court and a system of lower federal courts.

Kansas-Nebraska Act Law passed in 1854 creating the Kansas and Nebraska Territories but leaving the question of slavery open to residents, thereby repealing the **Missouri Compromise**.

Kellogg-Briand Pact 1928 international treaty that denounced aggression and war but lacked provisions for enforcement.

King George's War The third Anglo-French war in North America (1744–1748), part of the European conflict known as the War of the Austrian Succession. During the North American fighting, New Englanders captured the French fortress of Louisbourg, only to have it returned to France after the peace negotiations.

King Philip's War Conflict in New England (1675–1676) between Wampanoags, Narragansetts, and other Indian peoples against English settlers; sparked by English encroachments on native lands.

King William's War The first Anglo-French conflict in North America (1689–1697), the American phase of Europe's War of the League of Augsburg. Ended in negotiated peace that reestablished the balance of power.

Knights of Labor Labor union that included skilled and unskilled workers irrespective of race or gender; founded in 1869, peaked in the 1880s, and declined when its advocacy of the eight-hour workday led to violent strikes in 1886.

Know-Nothing Party Anti-immigrant party formed from the wreckage of the **Whig Party** and some disaffected northern Democrats in 1854.

Kosovo Province of Yugoslavia, in southeast Europe, where the U.S. and NATO intervened militarily in 1999 to protect ethnic Albanians from expulsion by Yugoslavia.

Ku Klux Klan Perhaps the most prominent of the vigilante groups that terrorized black people in the South during **Reconstruction Era**, founded by Confederate veterans in 1866.

Laissez-faire The doctrine that government should not intervene in the economy, especially through regulation.

Lancaster, Treaty of Negotiation in 1744 whereby Iroquois chiefs sold Virginia land speculators the right to trade at the Forks of the Ohio. Although the Iroquois had not intended this to include the right to settle in the Ohio Country, the Virginians assumed that it did. Ohio Valley Indians considered this treaty a great grievance against both the English and the Iroquois.

Land Grant College Act Law passed by Congress in July 1862 awarding proceeds from the sale of public lands to the states for the establishment of agricultural and mechanical (later engineering) colleges. Also known as the Morrill Act, after its sponsor, Congressman Justin Morrill of Vermont.

Land Ordinance of 1785 Act passed by Congress under the **Articles of Confederation** that created the grid system of surveys by which all subsequent public land was made available for sale.

League of Nations International organization created by the **Versailles Treaty** after World War I to ensure world stability.

Lecompton Constitution Proslavery draft written in 1857 by Kansas territorial delegates elected under questionable circumstances; it was rejected by two governors, supported by President Buchanan, and decisively defeated by Congress.

Legal tender An attribute of money that results from legislation declaring it to be, as in the case of modern United States currency, "legal tender for all debts public and private." Creditors must therefore accept it at face value.

Lend-Lease Program begun in 1941 through which the U.S. transferred military equipment to Britain and other World War II allies.

Liberal Republicans Members of a reform movement within the **Republican Party** in 1872 that promoted measures to reduce government influence in the economy and restore control of southern governments to local white elites.

Liberty Bonds Interest-bearing certificates sold by the U.S. government to finance the American World War I effort.

Liberty Party The first antislavery political party, formed in 1840.

Lincoln-Douglas debates Series of debates in the 1858 Illinois senatorial campaign during which Democrat Stephen A. Douglas and Republican Abraham Lincoln staked out their differing opinions on the issue of slavery in the territories.

Little Bighorn, Battle of the Battle in which Colonel George A. Custer and the Seventh Cavalry were defeated by the Sioux and Cheyennes under Sitting Bull and Crazy Horse in Montana in 1876.

Lost Cause The phrase many white Southerners applied to their Civil War defeat. They viewed the war as a noble cause but only a temporary setback in the South's ultimate vindication.

Lynching Execution, usually by a mob, without trial.

Mahanism The ideas advanced by Alfred Thayer Mahan, stressing U.S. naval, economic, and territorial expansion.

Manhattan Project The effort, using the code name Manhattan Engineer District, to develop an atomic bomb under the management of the U.S. Army Corps of Engineers during World War II.

Manifest Destiny Doctrine, first expressed in 1845, that the expansion of white Americans across the continent was inevitable and ordained by God.

Marbury v. Madison Supreme Court decision of 1803 that created the precedent of judicial review by ruling as unconstitutional part of the **Judiciary Act of 1789**.

Massive retaliation Popular name for the military doctrine adopted in the 1950s, whereby the U.S. promised to respond to any attack on itself or its allies with massive force, including nuclear weapons.

McCarthyism Anticommunist attitudes and actions associated with Senator Joe McCarthy in the early 1950s, including smear tactics and innuendo.

McCulloch v. Maryland Supreme Court decision of 1819 upholding the constitutionality of the Second Bank of the United States and the exercise of federal powers within a state.

Medicaid Supplementary medical insurance for the poor, financed through the federal government; program created in 1965.

Medicare Basic medical insurance for the elderly, financed through the federal government; program created in 1965.

Mercantilism Economic system whereby the government intervenes in the economy for the purpose of increasing national wealth. Mercantilists advocated possession of colonies as places where the mother country could acquire raw materials not available at home.

Middle Passage The voyage between West Africa and the New World slave colonies.

Minute Men Special companies of militia formed in Massachusetts and elsewhere beginning in late 1744.

These units were composed of men who were to be ready to assemble with their arms at a minute's notice.

Missouri Compromise   Sectional compromise in Congress in 1820 that admitted Missouri to the Union as a slave state and Maine as a free state and prohibited slavery in the **Louisiana Purchase** territory above 36°30´ north latitude.

Model Cities Program   Effort to target federal funds to upgrade public services and economic opportunity in specifically defined urban neighborhoods between 1966 and 1974.

Monroe Doctrine   Declaration by President James Monroe in 1823 that the Western Hemisphere was to be closed off to further European colonization and that the United States would not interfere in the internal affairs of European nations.

Mormon Church (Church of Jesus Christ of Latter-day Saints)   Church founded in 1830 by Joseph Smith and based on the revelations in a sacred book he called the Book of Mormon.

Muckraking   Journalism exposing economic, social, and political evils, so named by Theodore Roosevelt for its "raking the muck" of American society.

Mugwumps   Elitist and conservative reformers who favored **sound money** and limited government and opposed tariffs and the **spoils system**.

Multinational corporation   Firm with direct investments, branches, factories, and offices in a number of countries.

National Aeronautics and Space Administration (NASA)   Federal agency created in 1958 to manage American space flights and exploration.

National American Woman Suffrage Association   The organization, formed in 1890, that coordinated the ultimately successful campaign to achieve women's right to vote.

Nationalists   Group of leaders in the 1780s who spearheaded the drive to replace the **Articles of Confederation** with a stronger central government.

National Origins Act   A 1924 law sharply restricting immigration on the basis of immigrants' national origins and discriminating against southern and eastern Europeans and Asians.

National Security Council (NSC)   The formal policymaking body for national defense and foreign relations, created in 1947 and consisting of the president, the secretary of defense, the secretary of state, and others appointed by the president.

National Security Council Paper 68 (NSC-68)   Policy statement that committed the United States to a military approach to the **Cold War**.

National War Labor Board   Government agency that supervised labor relations during World War I, guaranteeing union rights in exchange for industrial stability.

Nation of Islam   Religious movement among black Americans that emphasizes self-sufficiency, self-help, and separation from white society.

Nativist/Nativism   Favoring the interests and culture of native-born inhabitants over those of immigrants.

Nat Turner's Rebellion   Uprising of slaves in Southampton County, Virginia, in the summer of 1831 led by Nat Turner that resulted in the death of fifty-five whites.

Natural rights   Political philosophy that maintains that individuals have an inherent right, found in nature and preceding any government or written law, to life and liberty.

Neoconservative   Advocate of or participant in the revitalized conservative politics of the 1980s and 1990s, calling for a strong government role in defense and foreign policy and a limited role in social and economic policy.

Neoliberal   Advocate of or participant in the effort to reshape the **Democratic party** for the 1990s around a policy emphasizing economic growth and competitiveness in the world economy.

New Deal   The economic and political policies of the Roosevelt administration in the 1930s.

New Federalism   President Richard Nixon's policy to shift responsibilities for government programs from the federal level to the states.

New Freedom   Woodrow Wilson's 1912 program for limited government intervention in the economy to restore competition by curtailing the restrictive influences of trusts and protective tariffs, thereby providing opportunities for individual achievement.

New Frontier   John F. Kennedy's domestic and foreign policy initiatives, designed to reinvigorate a sense of national purpose and energy.

New Harmony   Short-lived utopian community established in Indiana in 1825, based on the socialist ideas of Robert Owen, a wealthy Scottish manufacturer.

New Jersey Plan   Proposal of the New Jersey delegation at the 1787 **Constitutional Convention** for a strengthened national government in which all states would have equal representation in a **unicameral legislature**.

New Lights   People who experienced conversion during the revivals of the **Great Awakening**.

New Nationalism   Theodore Roosevelt's 1912 program calling for a strong national government to foster, regulate, and protect business, industry, workers, and consumers.

New Orleans, Battle of   Decisive American **War of 1812** victory over British troops in January 1815 that ended any British hopes of gaining control of the lower Mississippi River Valley.

New York Draft Riot   A mostly Irish-immigrant protest against conscription in New York City in July 1863 that escalated into class and racial warfare that had to be quelled by federal troops.

Niagara Movement African-American group organized in 1905 to promote racial integration, civil and political rights, and equal access to economic opportunity.

Nineteenth Amendment Constitutional revision that in 1920 established women citizens' right to vote.

Nisei U.S. citizens born of immigrant Japanese parents.

Nixon Doctrine In July, 1969, President Nixon described a new American policy toward Asia, in which the U.S. would honor treaty commitments but would gradually disengage and expect Asian nations to handle military defense on their own.

Nonimportation Movement A tactical means of putting economic pressure on Britain by refusing to buy its exports to the colonies. Initiated in response to the taxes imposed by the **Sugar** and **Stamp Acts**, it was used again against the **Townshend duties** and the **Coercive Acts**. The nonimportation movement popularized resistance to British measures and deepened the commitment of many ordinary people to a larger American community.

Nonintercourse Act Law passed by Congress in 1809 that prohibited American trade with Britain and France.

North American Free Trade Agreement (NAFTA) Agreement reached in 1993 by Canada, Mexico, and the United States to substantially reduce barriers to trade.

Northwest Ordinance of 1787 Legislation passed by Congress under the **Articles of Confederation** that prohibited slavery in the Northwest Territories and provided the model for the incorporation of future territories into the Union as coequal states.

Nullification A constitutional doctrine holding that a state has a legal right to declare a national law null and void within its borders.

Nullification crisis Sectional crisis in the early 1830s in which a **states' rights** party in South Carolina attempted to nullify federal law.

Office of Economic Opportunity (OEO) Federal agency that coordinated many programs of the **War on Poverty** between 1964 and 1975.

Oligopoly An industry, such as steel making or automobile manufacturing, that is controlled by a few large companies.

Olive Branch Petition Petition, written largely by John Dickinson and adopted by the Second Continental Congress on July 5, 1775, as a last effort of peace that avowed America's loyalty to George III and requested that he protect them from further aggressions. Congress continued military preparations, and the king never responded to the petition.

Omaha Platform The 1892 platform of the **Populist party** repudiating laissez-faire and demanding economic and political reforms to aid distressed farmers and workers.

Oneida Community Utopian community established in upstate New York in 1848 by John Humphrey Noyes and his followers.

Open Door American policy of seeking equal trade and investment opportunities in foreign nations or regions.

Open shop Factory or business employing workers whether or not they are union members; in practice, such a business usually refuses to hire union members and follows antiunion policies.

Operation Desert Storm Code name for the successful offensive against Iraq by the United States and its allies in the Persian Gulf War (1991).

Operation OVERLORD U.S. and British invasion of France in June 1944 during World War II.

Oregon Trail Overland trail of more than two thousand miles that carried American settlers from the Midwest to new settlements in Oregon, California, and Utah.

Organization of Petroleum Exporting Countries (OPEC) Cartel of oil-producing nations in Asia, Africa, and Latin America that gained substantial power over the world economy in the mid- to late 1970s by controlling the production and price of oil.

Pan American Union International organization originally established as the Commercial Bureau of American Republics by Secretary of State James Blaine's first Pan-American Conference in 1889 to promote cooperation among nations of the Western Hemisphere through commercial and diplomatic negotiations.

Panic of 1857 Banking crisis that caused a credit crunch in the North; it was less severe in the South, where high cotton prices spurred a quick recovery.

Pan-Indian resistance movement Movement calling for the political and cultural unification of Indian tribes in the late eighteenth and early nineteenth centuries.

Patriot Act Federal legislation adopted in 2001, in response to the terrorist attacks of September 11, intended to facilitate anti-terror actions by federal law enforcement and intelligence agencies.

Peace of Paris Treaties signed in 1783 by Great Britain, the United States, France, Spain, and the Netherlands that ended the Revolutionary War. First in a preliminary agreement and then in the final treaty with the United States, Britain recognized the independence of the United States, agreed that the Mississippi River would be its western boundary, and permitted it to fish in some Canadian waters. Prewar debts owed by the inhabitants of one country to those of the other were to remain collectible, and Congress was to urge the states to return property confiscated from Loyalists. British troops were to evacuate United States territory without removing slaves or other property. In a separate agreement, Britain relinquished its claim to East and West Florida to Spain.

Pendleton Civil Service Act A law of 1883 that reformed the **spoils system** by prohibiting government workers from making political contributions and creating the Civil Service Commission to oversee their appointment on the basis of merit rather than politics.

Pentagon Papers Classified Defense Department documents on the history of the United States' involvement in Vietnam, prepared in 1968 and leaked to the press in 1971.

People's Party *See* **Populist Party**.

Pequot War Conflict between English settlers (who had Narragansett and Mohegan allies) and Pequot Indians over control of land and trade in eastern Connecticut. The Pequots were nearly destroyed in a set of bloody confrontations, including a deadly English attack on a Mystic River village in May 1637.

Perestroika Russian for "restructuring," applied to Mikhail Gorbachev's efforts to make the Soviet economic and political systems more modern, flexible, and innovative.

Persian Gulf War War (1991) between Iraq and a U. S. led coalition that followed Iraq's invasion of Kuwait and resulted in the expulsion of Iraqi forces from that country.

Pietists Protestants who stress a religion of the heart and the spirit of Christian living.

Pilgrims Settlers of Plymouth Colony, who viewed themselves as spiritual wanderers.

Pinckney's Treaty Treaty with Spain in 1795 in which Spain recognized the 31st parallel as the boundary between the United States and Spanish Florida and opened the Mississippi River through the port of New Orleans to American shipping.

Platt Amendment A stipulation the United States had inserted into the Cuban constitution in 1901 restricting Cuban autonomy and authorizing U.S. intervention and naval bases.

Plattsburg, Battle of American naval victory on Lake Champlain in September 1814 in the **War of 1812** that thwarted a British invasion from Canada.

Pogroms Government-directed attacks against Jewish citizens, property, and villages in tsarist Russia beginning in the 1880s; a primary reason for Russian Jewish migration to the United States.

Poll tax A tax imposed on voters as a requirement for voting. Most southern states imposed poll taxes after 1900 as a way to disfranchise black people; the measures also restricted the white vote.

Pontiac's Rebellion Indian uprising (1763–1766) led by Pontiac of the Ottawas and Neolin of the Delawares. Fearful of their fate at the hands of the British after the French had been driven out of North America, the Indian nations of the Ohio River Valley and the Great Lakes area united to oust the British from the Ohio-Mississippi Valley. They failed and were forced to make peace in 1766.

Populist Party A major third party of the 1890s, also known as the **People's Party**. Formed on the basis of the **Southern Farmers' Alliance** and other reform organizations, it mounted electoral challenges against the Democrats in the South and the Republicans in the West.

Potsdam Declaration Statement issued by the United States during a meeting of U.S. President Harry Truman, British Prime Minister Winston Churchill, and Soviet Premier Joseph Stalin held at Potsdam, near Berlin, in July 1945 to plan the defeat of Japan and the future of eastern Europe and Germany. In it, the United States declared its intention to democratize the Japanese political system and reintroduce Japan into the international community and gave Japan an opening for surrender.

Predestination The belief that God decided at the moment of Creation which humans would achieve salvation.

Preparedness Military buildup in preparation for possible U.S. participation in World War I.

Preservation Protecting forests, land, and other features of the natural environment from development or destruction, often for aesthetic appreciation.

Proclamation Line Boundary, decreed as part of the **Proclamation of 1763**, that limited British settlements to the eastern side of the Appalachian Mountains, thereby threatening colonial expansionists and causing resentment. It proved unenforceable.

Proclamation of 1763 Royal proclamation setting the boundary known as the **Proclamation Line**.

Prohibition A ban on the production, sale, and consumption of liquor, achieved temporarily through state laws and the Eighteenth Amendment.

Prohibition Party A venerable third party still in existence that has persistently campaigned for the abolition of alcohol but has also introduced many important reform ideas into American politics.

Proposition 187 California legislation adopted by popular vote in California in 1994, which cuts off state-funded health and education benefits to undocumented or illegal immigrants.

Proprietary colony A colony created when the English monarch granted a huge tract of land to an individual or group of individuals, who became "lords proprietor." Many lords proprietor had distinct social visions for their colonies, but these plans were hardly ever implemented. Examples of proprietary colonies are Maryland, Carolina, New York (after it was seized from the Dutch), and Pennsylvania.

Pueblo Revolt Rebellion in 1680 of Pueblo Indians in New Mexico against their Spanish overlords, sparked by religious conflict and excessive Spanish demands for tribute.

Puritan An individual who believed that Queen Elizabeth's reforms of the Church of England had not gone far enough in improving the church, particularly in ensuring that church members were among the saved. Puritans led the settlement of Massachusetts Bay Colony.

Put-in-Bay, Battle of American naval victory on Lake Erie in September 1813 in the **War of 1812** that denied the British strategic control over the Great Lakes.

Putting-out system System of manufacturing in which merchants furnished households with raw materials for processing by family members.

Quakers Members of the Society of Friends, a radical religious group that arose in the mid-seventeenth century. Quakers rejected formal theology and an educated ministry, focusing instead on the importance of the "Inner Light," or Holy Spirit that dwelt within them. Quakers were important in the founding of Pennsylvania.

Quartering Acts Acts of Parliament requiring colonial legislatures to provide supplies and quarters for the troops stationed in America. Americans considered this taxation in disguise and objected. None of these acts passed during the pre-Revolutionary controversy required that soldiers be quartered in an occupied house without the owner's consent.

Quasi-War Undeclared naval war of 1797 to 1800 between the United States and France.

Quebec Act Law passed by Parliament in 1774 that provided an appointed government for Canada, enlarged the boundaries of Quebec southward to the Ohio River, and confirmed the privileges of the Catholic Church. Alarmed Americans termed this act and the **Coercive Acts** the **Intolerable Acts**.

Queen Anne's War American phase (1702–1713) of Europe's War of the Spanish Succession. At its conclusion, England gained Nova Scotia.

Radical Republicans A shifting group of Republican congressmen, usually a substantial minority, who favored the abolition of slavery from the beginning of the Civil War and later advocated harsh treatment of the defeated South.

Reagan Doctrine The policy assumption that Soviet-influenced governments in Asia, Africa, and Latin America needed to be eliminated if the United States was to win the Cold War.

Recall The process of removing an official from office by popular vote, usually after using petitions to call for such a vote.

Reconquista The long struggle (ending in 1492) during which Spanish Christians reconquered the Iberian peninsula from Muslim occupiers, who first invaded in the eighth century.

Reconstruction Era The era (1865–1877) when the resolution of two major issues—the status of the former slaves and the terms of the Confederate states' readmission into the Union—dominated political debate.

Redeemers Southern Democrats who wrested control of governments in the former Confederacy, often through electoral fraud and violence, from Republicans beginning in 1870.

Redemptioners Similar to **indentured servants**, except that redemptioners signed labor contracts in America rather than in Europe, as indentured servants did. Shipmasters sold redemptioners into servitude to recoup the cost of their passage if they could not pay the fare upon their arrival.

Red Scare Post–World War I public hysteria over **Bolshevik** influence in the United States directed against labor activism, radical dissenters, and some ethnic groups.

Referendum Submission of a law, proposed or already in effect, to a direct popular vote for approval or rejection.

Regulators Vigilante groups active in the 1760s and 1770s in the western parts of North and South Carolina. The South Carolina Regulators attempted to rid the area of outlaws; the North Carolina Regulators sought to protect themselves against excessively high taxes and court costs. In both cases, westerners lacked sufficient representation in the legislature to obtain immediate redress of their grievances. The South Carolina government eventually made concessions; the North Carolina government suppressed its Regulator movement by force.

Repartimiento In the Spanish colonies, the assignment of Indian workers to labor on public works projects.

Republicanism A complex, changing body of ideas, values, and assumptions, closely related to **country ideology**, that influenced American political behavior during the eighteenth and nineteenth centuries. Derived from the political ideas of classical antiquity, Renaissance Europe, and early modern England, republicanism held that self-government by the citizens of a country, or their representatives, provided a more reliable foundation for the good society and individual freedom than rule by kings. The benefits of monarchy depended on the variable abilities of monarchs; the character of republican government depended on the virtue of the people. Republicanism therefore helped give the American Revolution a moral dimension. But the nature of republican virtue and the conditions favorable to it became sources of debate that influenced the writing of the state and federal constitutions as well as the development of political parties.

Republican Party Party that emerged in the 1850s in the aftermath of the bitter controversy over the **Kansas-Nebraska Act**, consisting of former **Whigs**, some northern Democrats, and many **Know-Nothings**.

Republican Party (Jeffersonian) Party headed by Thomas Jefferson that formed in opposition to the financial and diplomatic policies of the **Federalist Party**; favored limiting the powers of the national government and placing the interests of farmers and planters over those of financial and commercial groups; supported the cause of the French Revolution.

Rescate Procedure by which Spanish colonists would pay ransom to free Indians captured by rival natives. The rescued Indians then became workers in Spanish households.

Reservationists   Group of U.S. senators favoring approval of the **Treaty of Versailles**, the peace agreement after World War I, after amending it to incorporate their reservations.

Rhode Island system   During the industrialization of the early nineteenth century, the recruitment of entire families for employment in a factory.

Roe v. Wade   U.S. Supreme Court decision in 1973 that disallowed state laws prohibiting abortion during the first three months (trimester) of pregnancy and established guidelines for abortion in the second and third trimesters.

Roosevelt Corollary   President Theodore Roosevelt's policy asserting U.S. authority to intervene in the affairs of Latin American nations; an expansion of the **Monroe Doctrine**.

Rush–Bagot Agreement   Treaty of 1817 between the United States and Britain that effectively demilitarized the Great Lakes by sharply limiting the number of ships each power could station on them.

Sabbatarian movement   Reform organization founded in 1828 by Congregationalist and Presbyterian ministers that lobbied for an end to the delivery of mail on Sundays and other Sabbath violations.

"Sack of Lawrence"   Vandalism and arson committed by a group of proslavery men in Lawrence, the free-state capital of Kansas Territory.

Sagebrush Rebellion   Political movement in the western states in the early 1980s that called for easing of regulations on the economic use of federal lands and the transfer of some or all of those lands to state ownership.

SALT   Strategic Arms Limitation Treaty signed in 1972 by the United States and the Soviet Union to slow the nuclear arms race.

Sand Creek Massacre   The near annihilation in 1864 of Black Kettle's Cheyenne band by Colorado troops under Colonel John Chivington's orders to "kill and scalp all, big and little."

San Jacinto, Battle of   Battle fought in eastern Texas on April 21, 1836, in which Texas troops under General Sam Houston overwhelmed a Mexican army and forced its commander, General Antonio López de Santa Anna, to recognize the independence of Texas.

San Lorenzo, Treaty of   *See* **Pinckney's Treaty**.

Scalawags   Southern whites, mainly small landowning farmers and well-off merchants and planters, who supported the southern **Republican Party** during **Reconstruction** for diverse reasons; a disparaging term.

Search and destroy   U.S. military tactic in South Vietnam, using small detachments to locate enemy units and then massive air, artillery, and ground forces to destroy them.

Second Bank of the United States   A national bank chartered by Congress in 1816 with extensive regulatory powers over currency and credit.

Second Continental Congress   An assemblage of delegates from all the colonies that convened in May 1775 after the outbreak of fighting in Massachusetts between British and American forces. It became the national government that eventually declared independence and conducted the Revolutionary War.

Second Great Awakening   Series of religious revivals in the first half of the nineteenth century characterized by great emotionalism in large public meetings.

Second party system   The national two-party competition between **Democrats** and **Whigs** from the 1830s through the early 1850s.

Second Treaty of Fort Laramie   The treaty acknowledging U.S. defeat in the Great Sioux War in 1868 and supposedly guaranteeing the Sioux perpetual land and hunting rights in South Dakota, Wyoming, and Montana.

Securities and Exchange Commission (SEC)   Federal agency with authority to regulate trading practices in stocks and bonds.

Sedition Act of 1918   Broad law restricting criticism of America's involvement in World War I or its government, flag, military, taxes, or officials.

Segregation   A system of racial control that separated the races, initially by custom but increasingly by law during and after **Reconstruction**.

Selective Service Act of 1917   The law establishing the military draft for World War I.

Selective Service System   Federal agency that coordinated military conscription before and during the Vietnam War.

Self-determination   The right of a people or nation to decide on its own political allegiance or form of government without external influence.

Seneca Falls Convention   The first convention for women's equality in legal rights, held in upstate New York in 1848. *See also* **Declaration of Sentiments**.

Separatist   Member of an offshoot branch of Puritanism. Separatists believed that the Church of England was too corrupt to be reformed and hence were convinced that they must "separate" from it to save their souls. Separatists helped found Plymouth Colony.

Settlement house   A multipurpose structure in a poor neighborhood that offered social welfare, educational, and homemaking services to the poor or immigrants; usually under private auspices and directed by middle-class women.

Seventeenth Amendment   Constitutional change that in 1913 established the direct popular election of U.S. senators.

Shakers   The followers of Mother Ann Lee, who preached a religion of strict celibacy and communal living.

Sharecropping   Labor system that evolved during and after **Reconstruction** whereby landowners furnished laborers with a house, farm animals, and tools and advanced credit in exchange for a share of the laborers' crop.

Shays's Rebellion   An armed movement of debt-ridden farmers in western Massachusetts in the winter of 1786–1787. The rebellion shut down courts and created a crisis atmosphere, strengthening the case of **nationalists** that a stronger central government was needed to maintain civil order in the states.

Sherman Antitrust Act   The first federal antitrust measure, passed in 1890; sought to promote economic competition by prohibiting business combinations in restraint of trade or commerce.

Silicon Valley   The region of California between San Jose and San Francisco that holds the nation's greatest concentration of electronics firms.

Sixteenth Amendment   Constitutional revision that in 1913 authorized a federal income tax.

Slaughterhouse **cases**   Group of cases resulting in one sweeping decision by the U.S. Supreme Court in 1873 that contradicted the intent of the **Fourteenth Amendment** by decreeing that most citizenship rights remained under state, not federal, control.

Slave codes   Sometimes known as "black codes." A series of laws passed mainly in the southern colonies in the late seventeenth and early eighteenth centuries to define the status of slaves and codify the denial of basic civil rights to them. Also, after American independence and before the Civil War, state laws in the South defining slaves as property and specifying the legal powers of masters over slaves.

Slave Power   A key concept in abolitionist and northern antislavery propaganda that depicted southern slaveholders as the driving force in a political conspiracy to promote slavery at the expense of white liberties.

Social Darwinism   The application of Charles Darwin's theory of biological evolution to society, holding that the fittest and the wealthiest survive, the weak and the poor perish, and government action is unable to alter this "natural" and beneficial process.

Socialism   A social order based on government ownership of industry and worker control over corporations as a way to prevent worker exploitation.

Solid South   The one-party (Democratic) political system that dominated the South from the 1890s to the 1950s.

Songhai empire   A powerful West African state that flourished between 1450 and 1591, when it fell to a Moroccan invasion.

Sons of Liberty   Secret organizations in the colonies formed to oppose the **Stamp Act**. From 1765 until independence, they spoke, wrote, and demonstrated against British measures. Their actions often intimidated stamp distributors and British supporters in the colonies.

Sound money   Misleading slogan that referred to a conservative policy of restricting the money supply and adhering to the gold standard.

Southeast Asia Treaty Organization (SEATO)   Mutual defense alliance signed in 1954 by the United States, Britain, France, Thailand, Pakistan, the Philippines, Australia, and New Zealand.

Southern Christian Leadership Conference (SCLC)   Black civil rights organization founded in 1957 by Martin Luther King, Jr., and other clergy.

Southern Farmers' Alliance   The largest of several organizations that formed in the post-Reconstruction South to advance the interests of beleaguered small farmers.

Southern Homestead Act   Largely unsuccessful law passed in 1866 that gave black people preferential access to public lands in five southern states.

Southern Manifesto   A document signed by 101 members of Congress from southern states in 1956 that argued that the Supreme Court's decision in Brown v. Board of Education of Topeka itself contradicted the **Constitution**.

Southwest Ordinance of 1790   Legislation passed by Congress that set up a government with no prohibition on slavery in U.S. territory south of the Ohio River.

Specie Circular   Proclamation issued by President Andrew Jackson in 1836 stipulating that only gold or silver could be used as payment for public land.

Sphere of influence   A region dominated and controlled by an outside power.

Spoils system   The awarding of government jobs to party loyalists.

Stamp Act   Law passed by Parliament in 1765 to raise revenue in America by requiring taxed, stamped paper for legal documents, publications, and playing cards. Americans opposed it as "taxation without representation" and prevented its enforcement. Parliament repealed it a year after its enactment.

Stamp Act Congress   October 1765 meeting of delegates sent by nine colonies, held in New York City, that adopted the **Declaration of Rights and Grievances** and petitioned against the **Stamp Act**.

States' rights   Favoring the rights of individual states over rights claimed by the national government.

Stonewall Rebellion   On June 27, 1969, patrons fought back when police raided the gay Stonewall Inn in New York; the name refers to that event and to the increase in militancy by gay Americans that it symbolizes.

Stono Rebellion   Uprising in 1739 of South Carolina slaves against whites; inspired in part by Spanish officials' promise of freedom for American slaves who escaped to Florida.

Strategic Defense Initiative (SDI)   President Reagan's program, announced in 1983, to defend the United States against nuclear missile attack with untested weapons systems and sophisticated technologies; also known as "Star Wars."

Student Nonviolent Coordinating Committee (SNCC) Black civil rights organization founded in 1960 and drawing heavily on younger activists and college students.

Students for a Democratic Society (SDS) The leading student organization of the New Left of the early and mid-1960s.

Subtreasury plan A program promoted by the **Southern Farmers' Alliance** in response to low cotton prices and tight credit. Farmers would store their crop in a warehouse (or "subtreasury") until prices rose, in the meantime borrowing up to 80 percent of the value of the stored crops from the government at a low interest rate.

Suffolk Resolves Militant resolves adopted in September 1774 in response to the **Coercive Acts** by representatives from the towns in Suffolk County, Massachusetts, including Boston. They termed the **Coercive Acts** unconstitutional, advised the people to arm, and called for economic sanctions against Britain. The **First Continental Congress** endorsed these resolves.

Suffrage The right to vote in a political election.

Sugar Act Law passed in 1764 to raise revenue in the American colonies. It lowered the duty from 6 pence to 3 pence per gallon on foreign molasses imported into the colonies and increased the restrictions on colonial commerce.

Sunbelt The states of the American South and Southwest.

Sussex **Pledge** Germany's pledge during World War I not to sink merchant ships without warning, on the condition that Britain also observe recognized rules of international law.

Swann v. Charlotte-Mecklenburg Board of Education U.S. Supreme Court decision in 1971 that upheld cross-city busing to achieve the racial integration of public schools.

Sweatshops Small, poorly ventilated shops or apartments crammed with workers, often family members, who pieced together garments.

Taft-Hartley Act Federal legislation of 1947 that substantially limited the tools available to labor unions in labor–management disputes.

Tammany Hall New York City's **Democratic party** organization, dating from well before the Civil War, that evolved into a powerful political machine after 1860, using patronage and bribes to maintain control of the city administration.

Taos Revolt Uprising of Pueblo Indians in New Mexico that broke out in January 1847 over the imposition of American rule during the Mexican War; the revolt was crushed within a few weeks.

Tariff Act of 1789 Apart from a few selected industries, this first tariff passed by Congress was intended primarily to raise revenue and not protect American manufacturers from foreign competition.

Tariff Act of 1798 Law placing a duty of 5 percent on most imported goods, designed primarily to generate revenue and not to protect American goods from foreign competition.

Tea Act of 1773 Act of Parliament that permitted the East India Company to sell tea through agents in America without paying the duty customarily collected in Britain, thus reducing the retail price. Americans, who saw the act as an attempt to induce them to pay the Townshend duty still imposed in the colonies, resisted this act through the **Boston Tea Party** and other measures.

Tejano A person of Spanish or Mexican descent born in Texas.

Teller Amendment A congressional resolution adopted in 1898 renouncing any American intention to annex Cuba.

Temperance Reform movement originating in the 1820s that sought to eliminate the consumption of alcohol.

Temporary Assistance for Needy Families (TANF) Federal program created in 1996 to replace earlier welfare programs to aid families and children; it involves explicit work requirements for receiving aid and places a time limit on benefits.

Tenement Four- to six-story residential dwelling, once common in New York and certain other cities, built on a tiny lot without regard to providing ventilation or light.

Tennessee Valley Authority (TVA) Federal regional planning agency established to promote **conservation**, produce electric power, and encourage economic development in seven southern states.

Thirteenth Amendment Constitutional amendment ratified in 1865 that freed all slaves throughout the United States.

Tonnage Act of 1789 Duty levied on the tonnage of incoming ships to U.S. ports; tax was higher on foreign-owned ships to favor American shippers.

Tordesillas, Treaty of Treaty negotiated by the pope in 1494 to resolve the territorial claims of Spain and Portugal. It drew a north–south line approximately 1,100 miles west of the Cape Verde Islands, granting all lands west of the line to Spain and all lands east of the line to Portugal. This limited Portugal's New World empire to Brazil but confirmed its claims in Africa and Asia.

Tories A derisive term applied to **Loyalists** in America who supported the king and Parliament just before and during the American Revolution. The term derived from late-seventeenth-century English politics when the Tory party supported the Duke of York's succession to the throne as James II. Later the Tory party favored the Church of England and the crown over dissenting denominations and Parliament.

Townshend Duty Act Act of Parliament, passed in 1767, imposing duties on colonial tea, lead, paint, paper, and glass. Designed to take advantage of the supposed American distinction between internal and external taxes, the Townshend duties were to help support government in America. The act prompted a successful colonial nonimportation movement.

Trail of Tears The forced march in 1838 of the Cherokee Indians from their homelands in Georgia to the Indian Territory in the West; thousands of Cherokees died along the way.

Transcendentalism A philosophical and literary movement centered on an idealistic belief in the divinity of individuals and nature.

Trans-Continental Treaty of 1819 Treaty between the United States and Spain in which Spain ceded Florida to the United States, surrendered all claims to the Pacific Northwest, and agreed to a boundary between the Louisiana Purchase territory and the Spanish Southwest.

Transportation revolution Dramatic improvements in transportation that stimulated economic growth after 1815 by expanding the range of travel and reducing the time and cost of moving goods and people.

Truman Doctrine President Harry Truman's statement in 1947 that the United States should assist other nations that were facing external pressure or internal revolution; an important step in the escalation of the **Cold War**.

Underground Railroad Support system set up by antislavery groups in the Upper South and the North to assist fugitive slaves in escaping the South.

Underwood-Simmons Tariff Act The 1913 reform law that lowered tariff rates and levied the first regular federal income tax.

Unicameral legislature A legislative body composed of a single house.

Union League A **Republican party** organization in northern cities that became an important organizing device among freedmen in southern cities after 1865.

University of California v. Bakke U.S. Supreme Court case in 1978 that allowed race to be used as one of several factors in college and university admission decisions but made rigid quotas unacceptable.

Valley Forge Area of Pennsylvania approximately 20 miles northwest of Philadelphia where General George Washington's continental troops were quartered from December 1777 to June 1778 while British forces occupied Philadelphia during the Revolutionary War. Approximately 2,500 men, about a quarter of those encamped there, died of hardship and disease.

Versailles, Treaty of The treaty ending World War I and creating the **League of Nations**.

Vertical integration The consolidation of numerous production functions, from the extraction of the raw materials to the distribution and marketing of the finished products, under the direction of one firm.

Viet Cong Communist rebels in South Vietnam who fought the pro-American government established in South Vietnam in 1954.

Virginia Plan Proposal of the Virginia delegation at the 1787 **Constitution Convention** calling for a national legislature in which the states would be represented according to population. The national legislature would have the explicit power to veto or overrule laws passed by state legislatures.

Virtual representation The notion, current in eighteenth-century England, that parliamentary members represented the interests of the nation as a whole, not those of the particular district that elected them.

Volstead Act The 1920 law defining the liquor forbidden under the Eighteenth Amendment and giving enforcement responsibilities to the Prohibition Bureau of the Department of the Treasury.

Voting Rights Act Legislation in 1965 that overturned a variety of practices by which states systematically denied voter registration to minorities.

Waltham system During the industrialization of the early nineteenth century, the recruitment of unmarried young women for employment in factories.

War Hawks Members of Congress, predominantly from the South and West, who aggressively pushed for a war against Britain after their election in 1810.

War Industries Board (WIB) The federal agency that reorganized industry for maximum efficiency and productivity during World War I.

War of 1812 War fought between the United States and Britain from June 1812 to January 1815 largely over British restrictions on American shipping.

War on Poverty Set of programs introduced by Lyndon Johnson between 1963 and 1966 designed to break the cycle of poverty by providing funds for job training, community development, nutrition, and supplementary education.

Watergate A complex scandal involving attempts to cover up illegal actions taken by administration officials and leading to the resignation of President Richard Nixon in 1974.

Webster–Ashburton Treaty Treaty signed by the United States and Britain in 1842 that settled a boundary dispute between Maine and Canada and provided for closer cooperation in suppressing the African slave trade.

Welfare capitalism A paternalistic system of labor relations emphasizing management responsibility for employee well-being. While providing some limited benefits, its function was primarily to forestall the formation of unions or public intervention.

Whig party Political party, formed in the mid-1830s in opposition to the **Jacksonian Democrats**, that favored a strong role for the national government in promoting economic growth.

Whigs The name used by advocates of colonial resistance to British measures during the 1760s and 1770s. The Whig party in England unsuccessfully attempted to exclude the Catholic Duke of York from succession to the throne as James II; victorious in the **Glorious Revolution**, the Whigs later stood for religious toleration and the supremacy of Parliament over the crown.

Whiskey Rebellion Armed uprising in 1794 by farmers in western Pennsylvania who attempted to prevent the collection of the excise tax on whiskey.

Whitewater Arkansas real estate development in which Bill and Hillary Clinton were investors; several fraud convictions resulted from investigations into Whitewater, but evidence was not found that the Clintons were involved in wrong-doing.

Wide Awakes Group of red-shirted, black-caped young men who paraded through city streets in the North extolling the virtues of the **Republican party** during the 1860 presidential election campaign.

Wobblies Popular name for the members of the Industrial Workers of the World (IWW).

Women's Christian Temperance Union (WCTU) National organization formed after the Civil War dedicated to prohibiting the sale and distribution of alcohol.

World Trade Organization International organization that sets standards and practices for global trade, and the focus of international protests over world economic policy in the late 1990s.

World Wide Web Since 1991, the Web has expanded the use of the Internet by allowing organizations and companies to create websites that place political and commercial information only a few clicks away from wired consumers.

Wounded Knee Massacre The U.S. Army's brutal winter massacre in 1890 of at least two hundred Sioux men, women, and children as part of the government's assault on the tribe's Ghost Dance religion.

Writs of assistance Documents issued by a court of law that gave British officials in America the power to search for smuggled goods wherever they wished. The legality of these writs became an important cause of controversy in Massachusetts in 1761 and 1762.

XYZ Affair Diplomatic incident in 1798 in which Americans were outraged by the demand of the French for a bribe as a condition for negotiating with American diplomats.

Yalta Conference Meeting of U.S. President Franklin Roosevelt, British Prime Minister Winston Churchill, and Soviet Premier Joseph Stalin held in February 1945 to plan the final stages of World War II and postwar arrangements.

Yellow-dog contracts Employment agreements binding workers not to join a union.

Yellow press A deliberately sensational journalism of scandal and exposure designed to attract an urban mass audience and increase advertising revenues.

Chapter 1 Image Key: A. Getty Images Inc.-Hulton Archive Photos; B. The Granger Collection, New York; C. The Bridgeman Art Library International Ltd.; D. Corbis/Bettmann; E. The Granger Collection, New York; F. The Granger Collection; G. Cahokia Mounds State Historic Site; I. James Stanfield, National Geographic Image Collection.

Chapter 2 Image Key: A. Getty Images Inc.-Hutton Archive Photo; B. Corbis/Bettmann; C. Getty Images Inc.-Photodisc; D. Courtesy American Antiquarian Society; E. Dorling Kindersley Media Library; F. Corbis/Bettmann; G. Pilgrim Society, Courtesy of Pilgrim Hall Museum, Plymouth Massachusetts; H. Jonathan Carver, A TREATISE ON THE CULTURE OF THE TOBACCO PLANT (London, 1779), Manuscript and Rare Books Division, Swem Library College of William and Mary; I. Fur traders and Indians, engraving 1777; J. The Granger Collection, New York.

Chapter 3 Image Key: A. The Granger Collection, New York; B. Courtesy of The Library of Congress; C. Courtesy, American Antiquarian Society; D. Royal Albert Memorial MuseumExeter, Devon, UK, Bridgeman Art Library, London/New York; E. Dorling Kindersley Media Library; F. Chronicles of Michoacan (by Beaumont); Collection Revillagigedo Historia; 18th-century manuscript (detail); Archivos General de la Nacion, Palacio National; G. The Granger Collection, New York; H. The Library of Congress; I. Corbis/Bettmann.

Chapter 4 Image Key: A. Liz McMacAulay, Dorling Kindersley/Worthing Museum; B. The Granger Collection, New York; C. Courtesy, Museum of Fine Arts Boston; D. Schalkwijk, Art Resource, NY; E. Dorling Kindersley Media Library; F. Frank Greenaway, Dorling Kindersley Media Library; G. Judith Miller & Dorling Kindersley; H. Courtesy, Museum of Fine Art Boston; I. Washington and Lee University, Lexington VA; J. North Wind Picture Archives; K. Davis Murray, Dorling Kindersley; L. Tina Chambers, Dorling Kindersley/National Maritime Museum; M. Benjamin West (1738-1820), "The Death of General Wolfe", 1770. Oil on canvas, 152.6 × 214.5cm. Transfer from the Canadian War Memorials, National Gallery of Canada, Ottawa, Ontario; N. Robert Feke portrait of Benjamin Franklin (1706-1790) Courtesy, Harvard University Portrait Collection. Bequest of Dr. John Collins Warren, 1856.

Chapter 5 Image Key: A. Dorling Kindersely Media Library; B. The Granger Collection, New York; C. Samual Adams about 1772, John Singleton Copley, American, 1738-1815, Oil on Canvas, 125.73 × 100.33 cm (49 1/2 × 39 1/2 in.), Deposited bythe City of Boston, L-R 30.76c. D. © Judith Miller & Dorling Kindersley; E. Steve Gorton, Dorling Kindersely Media Library; F. Getty Images, Inc. Hutton Archive Photos; G. © Christie's Images Inc. 2004; H. Courtesy, Library of Congress; I. Dorling Kindersely Media Library; J. Dave King, Dorling Kindersely Media Library.

Chapter 6 Image Key: A. Courtesy of the Library of Congress; B. Corbis/Bettmann; C. Yale University Art Gallery: D. Corbis/Bettmann; E. Battle of Lexington, April 19th 1775. OH: 13 3/4 "OW: 19". Courtesy Winterthur Museum." F. Courtesy of the Library of Congress; G. Joseph Sohm, Corbis/Bettmann; H. George Washington after the Battle of Princeton, January 3, 1777, 1779. Oil on canvas, 234.5 × 155 cm. Inv:MV 4560. Photo General Blot. Chateau de Versailles de Trianon, Versailles France; I. Independence National Historical Park; J. "Mezzotint", 1780–1800. Size: H. 7 3/8≤, W. 9 3/4≤. Courtesy, Winterthur Museum. K. Benjamin West, 1783 "American Commissioners of Preliminary Negotiations". Courtesy, Winterthur Museum. L. Photograph courtesy of the Concord Museum, Concord, MA and the archives of the Lexington Historical Society. David Bohl, photographer; M. "Paul Jones Shooting a sailor", color engraving from the Olds Collection #366, no. negative number. Collection of The New-York Historical Society.

Chapter 7 Image Key: A. Harry N. Abrams, Inc.; B. Courtesy of The Historical Society of Pennsylvania Collection, Atwater Kent Museum of Philadelphia. C. Corbis/Bettmann. D. Charles Allen Munn Collection, Fordham University Library, Bronx New York; E. Courtesy of the Library of Congress; F. The Granger Collection, New York; G. CORBIS; H. The Granger Collection, New York; I. Gallery of the Republic; J. The Granger Collection.

Chapter 8 Image Key: A. Courtesy of the Library of Congress; B. Abby Aldrich Rockefeller Folk Art Museum, Colonial Williamsburg Foundation, Williamsburg, VA; C. Museum of American Political Life; D. White House Collection, Courtesy White House Historical Association; E. Maentel, Jacob (American, 1778-1863). :General Schumacker's Daughter" c. 1812, pen and watercolor, sight size: 365 × 240 14 1/4 × 9 1/2). National Gallery of Art, Washington, DC. Gift of Edgar William and Bernice Garbisch. F. Painting: P & S—1914.0001; "The Treaty of Fort Greenville, Ohio;" 1795. Artist unknown, member of General Anthony Wayne's staff; G. "White House Historical Association (White House Collection)" (25). H. The Granger Collection, New York; I. Getty Images, Inc. Hutton Archive Photos

Chapter 9 Image Key: A. Corbis/Bettmann; B. From the collection of Mac G. and Janelle C. Morris Collection; C. Getty Images–Hutton Archive Photos; D. Getty Images Inc.-Hulton Archive Photos E. The Granger Collection; F. The Granger Collection, New York; G. North Wind Picture Archives; H. ©Bettmann/CORBIS; I. Corbis/Bettmann; J. Courtesy, CORBIS.

Chapter 10 Image Key: A. Courtesy of the Library of Congress; B. Corbis/Bettmann; C. National Numismatic Collection/Smithsonian Institution; D. Smithsonian Institution/Office of Imaging, Printing, and Photographic Services; E. The Bridgeman Art Library International Ltd.; F. The Granger Collection; G. Courtesy of the New York Historical Society: H. Courtesy of the Library of Congress; I. Getty Images, Inc.-Photodisc.

Chapter 11 Image Key: A. "Returning from the Cotton Fields in South Carolina", ca. 1860, stereograph by Barbard, negative number 47843. Collection of The New York Historical Society. B. Corbis/Bettmann; C. The Granger Collection, New York; D. Library of Congress; E. Dorling Kindersley Media Library; F. Tina Chambers, Dorling Kindersley Media Library; G. The Boston Athenaeum; H. William Gladstone; I. James Cameron (1817–1882), "Colonel and Mrs. James A. Whiteside, Son Charles and Servants", Oil on Canvas; c. 1858–1859. Hunter Museum of Art, Chattanooga, Tennessee, Gift of Mr. and Mrs. Whiteside; J. Courtesy of the Library of Congress; K. Courtesy of the Library of Congress; L. Courtesy of the Library of Congress.

Chapter 12 Image Key: A. The Granger Collection, New York; B. Courtesy of the New York Historical Society, New York City; C. The Granger Collection; D. Frederick Douglass (1817–95). Oil on canvas, c. 1844, attr. to E. Hammond. The Granger Collection; E. Omni-Photo Communications, Inc.; F. CORBIS; G. Courtesy of the Rhode Island Historical Society, negative number RHi •5 22; H. ©Bettmann/CORBIS; I. Courtesy of the Library of Congress.

Chapter 13 Image Key: A. Peter Anderson, Dorling Kindersley Media Library; B. Albert Bierstadt (1830–1902), "The Oregon Trail" (oil on canvas). Private Collection/Bridgeman Art Library International Ltd., New York; C. Getty Images Inc.-Hulton Archive Photos; D. Courtesy of the Lane County Historical Museum; E. Lynton Gardinier, Dorling Kindersely, Media Library; F. © Denver Art Museum, All rights reserved; G. © Christie's Images Inc. 2004; H. Art Resource, NY. H. Nathaniel Currier, "General Winfield Scott at the Siege of Vera Cruz, March 1847", 1847. Lithograph. The Granger Collection; I. Alfred Jacob Miller, "The Interior of Fort Laramie", 1858–60. The Walters Art Museum, Baltimore.

Chapter 14 Image Key: A. Corbis NY; B. Courtesy of the Library of Congress; C. Corbis NY. D. Getty Images, Inc.-Photodisc; E. Courtesy of Library of Congress; F. The Granger Collection, New York; G. Southworth, Albert Sands (1811-1894), and Hawes, Josiah Johnson (1808-1901), Harriet Beecher Stowe. Daguerreotype, 4 1/2 × 33/2 in. The Metropolitan Museum of Art, Gift of I. N. Phelps Stokes, Edward S. Hawes, Alice Mary Hawes, and Marion Augusta Hawes, 1937: H. Center of Military History, U.S. Army; I. Courtesy of Library of Congress; J. Corbis/Bettmann; K. Courtesy of the Library of Congress.

Chapter 15 Image Key: National Archives and Records Administration; George Hayward (American, born England, 1800-1872?), "Departure of the 7th Regiment, N.Y.S.M., April 19, 1861," April 19, 1861. Graphite pencil, transparent and opaque watercolor on paper, Sheet: 36.7 × 51.3 cm (14 7/16 × 20 3/16 in.). Museum of Fine Art; Boston Public Library / Rare Books Department-Courtesy of the Trustees; Corbis/Bettmann, (c)CORBIS,; Theodor Kaufmann (American, b. 1814), "On to Liberty," 1867. Oil on canvas, 36" × 56" (91.4 × 142); National Archives and Records Administration, 464; Center of Military History, U.S. Army; Corbis/Bettmann, (c)Bettmann/CORBIS; National Archives and Records Administration; Courtesy of the Library of Congress; Harper's Weekly, March 18, 1865. Courtesy of William C. Hine; Library of Congress.

Chapter 16 Image Key: A. Dorling Kindersley Media Library. B. Dorling Kindersley Media Library; C. Theo Kaufman, "On to Liberty, " 1867, oil on canvas, 36" × 56". The Metropolitan Museum of Art. Gift of Irving and Joyce Wolf, 1982 (1982, 443.3). Photograph © 1982 The Metropolitan Museum of Art; D. Library of Congress; E. Corbis/Bettmann; F. National Archives and Records Administration: G. Getty Images Inc.-Hulton Archive Photos; H. Corbis/Bettmann; I. Getty Images, Inc.-Photodisc; J. Dorling Kindersley Media Library.

Chapter 17 Image Key: A. The Granger Collection, New York; B. Courtesy of the Library of Congress; C. The Granger Collection; D. Library of Congress; E. The Granger Collection, New York; F. SHOMBURG CENTER Center/Art Resource, NY; G. Courtesy of The North Carolina Division of Archives and History; H. T. E. Armistead Collection, South Alabama Collection; I. Cincinnati, Hamilton and Dayton Railroad Advertisement, Lithograph poster, 1894. Strobridge Lithograph Company, from the Bella C. Landauer Collection, negative number 51391. Collection of The New York Historical Society; K. Getty Images Inc.-Hulton Archive Photos.

Chapter 18 Image Key: A. Courtesy of the Library of Congress; B. Lewis W. Hine, George Eastman House; C. The Granger Collection, New York; D. Ford Motor Company; E. The Granger Collection, New York; F. National Park Service, Edison National Site; Courtesy of the Library of Congress; G. Courtesy of the Library of Congress; H. Getty Images Inc.-Hulton Archive Photos; Corbis/Bettmann.

Chapter 19 Image Key: A. Frederick Remington, "The Cheyenne" 1901, cast 1904. Amon Carter Museum, Fort Worth, Texas, (1997.140); B. . The Granger Collection, New York; C. Courtesy of the Library of Congress; D. Frederick Remington, "The Rattlesnake," 1905, Amon Carter Museum; E. Library of Congress; F. Library of Congress; G. Dorling Kindersley Media Library; H. Chinese mining laborers, Idaho, 76-119.2/A, Idaho State Historical Society.

Chapter 20 Image Key: A. Picture Research Consultants; B. The Granger Collection, New York; C. Corbis/Bettmann; D. Courtesy of the Library of Congress; E. Culver Pictures, Inc. K. Corbis/Bettmann; F. The Granger Collection, New York; G. The Granger Collection; H. Corbis/Bettmann; I. Courtesy of the Library of Congress; J. Courtesy of the Library of Congress; K. Courtesy of the Library of Congress.

Chapter 21 Image Key: A. The Granger Collection, New York; B. The Granger Collection, New York C. Corbis/Bettmann; D. The Granger Collection, New York; Corbis/Bettmann; E. Kheel Center, Cornell University, Ithaca, NY 14853-3901; F. Courtesy National Archives, photo no. 102-LH-1986; G. The Granger Collection, New York; H. Indiana Historical Society, A70; I. Cornell University School of Industrial and Labor Relations; J. Corbis/Bettmann; K. Corbis/Bettmann.

Chapter 22 Image Key: A. Corbis/Bettmann; B. The Granger Collection, New York; C. © Stock Montage, 2004; D. Corbis/Bettmann; E. Theodore Roosevelt Collection, Harvard College Library; F. Corbis/Bettmann G. Photo reproduced with permission of Wider Church Ministries of the United Church of Christ by permission of the Houghton Library, Harward University; H. Jonathan Potter, Dorling Kindersley Media Library; I. © Stock Montage, 2004.

Chapter 23 Image Key: A. Corbis/Bettmann; B. Getty Images Inc.-Hulton Archive Photos; C. Corbis/Bettmann; D. Courtesy, Library of Congress; E. National Archives and Records Administration; F. the Granger Collection, New York; G. CORBIS; H. Richard Ward, Dorling Kindersley Media Library; I. National Archives and Records Administration.

Chapter 24 Image Key: A. Getty Images Inc.-Hulton Archive Photos; B. Corbis/Bettmann; C. Getty Images–Photodisc; D. C. Squared Studios, Getty Images, Inc. Photodisc E. Wisconsin Historical Society/WHi-5020; F. Prentice Hall Higher Education; G. Stock Montage, Inc./Historical Pictures Collection; H. By permission of the Campbell Soup Company; I. Courtesy W. A. Swift Photograph Collection, Archives and Special Collections, Ball State University.

Chapter 25 Image Key: A. Corbis/Bettmann; B. Super Stock, Inc.; C. Corbis/Bettmann; D. Brown Brothers; E. Corbis/Bettmann; F. Isaac Soyer, "Employment Agency". Oil on canvas, 34 1/2≤ • 45≤. The Whitney Museum of American Art; G. Courtesy, Library of Congress; H. Courtesy of the Library of Congress; I. National Archives and Records Administration; J. AP World Wide Photos; K. Getty Images, Inc.-Photodisc. L. The Granger Collection/© Estate Of Ben Shahn/Liscensed By Vaga, New York, NY.

Chapter 26 Image Key: A. Courtesy, The Library of Congress; B. Getty Images Inc.-Hulton Archive Photos; C. The Granger Collection, New York; D. Rieger Communications, Inc; E. Andy Crawford, Dorling Kindersley Media Library; F. Andy Crawford, Dorling Kindersley Media Library; G. Corbis/Bettmann; H. Bildarchiv Preubisher Kulterbesitz, Berlin; I. Prentice Hall Higher Education; J. Corbis/Bettmann; K. Bettnann/Corbis.

Chapter 27 Image Key: A. Corbis/Bettmann; B. Getty Images/Time Life Pictures; C. Corbis/Bettmann; D. Charles Fenno Jacobs, Getty Images Inc.; E. RKO Radio Pictures/HultonArchive; F. Corbis/Bettmann; G. AP/Wide World Photos; H. Getty Images Inc.-Hulton Archive Photos; I. Corbis/Bettmann; J. Getty Images/Time Life Pictures.

Chapter 28 Image Key: A. Getty Images Inc.-Hulton Archive Photos; B. Dorling Kindersley Media Library; C. Corbis/Bettmann; D. Bernard Hoffman/Life Magazine/©1950 TimePix; E. Getty Images, Inc.-Photodisc; F. AP/Wide World Photos; G. AP/Wide World Photos; H/ AP/Wide World Photos; I. Sondak, Getty Images, Inc.–Taxi; J. Ralph Crane, Getty Images/Time Life Pictures.

Chapter 29 Image Key: A. © Royalty-Free/CORBIS; B. © Royalty-Free/CORBIS; C. ©John Paul Filo/Hulton/Archive; D. Getty Images, Inc.-Photodisc; E. Bernard Hoffman/Life Magazine/©1950 TimePix; F. Sondak, Getty Images, Inc.–Taxi; G. Ralph Crane, Getty Images/Time Life Pictures; H. AP/Wide World Photos; I. AP/Wide World Photos J. AP/Wide World Photos.

Chapter 30 Image Key: A. © Royalty-Free/CORBIS; B. © Royalty-Free/CORBIS; C. ©John Paul Filo/Hulton/Archive; D. George Meany Memorial Archives; E. AP/Wide World Photos; F. P. F. Bentley, TimeMagazine © Timepix; G. Lisa Quinones/Black Star; H. AP/Wide World Photos; I. Philip Jones Griffith, Magnum Photos, Inc.; J. Corbis/Bettmann.

Chapter 31 Image Key: A. Dorling Kindersley Media Library; B. Author supplied; C. Doug Kanter, SIPA Press; D. Dorling Kindersley Media Library; E. Dorling Kindersley Media Library; F. Stephen Crowley, New York Times Pictures; G. Ira Wyman, Corbis/Sygma; H. AP World Wide Photos; I. Barbara Gauntt/The Clarion-Ledger; J. Corbis/Bettmann; K. AFP /Corbis, Photo by Stephen Jaffe.

SINGLE PC LICENSE AGREEMENT AND LIMITED WARRANTY

READ THIS LICENSE CAREFULLY BEFORE OPENING THIS PACKAGE. BY OPENING THIS PACKAGE, YOU ARE AGREEING TO THE TERMS AND CONDITIONS OF THIS LICENSE. IF YOU DO NOT AGREE, DO NOT OPEN THE PACKAGE. PROMPTLY RETURN THE UNOPENED PACKAGE AND ALL ACCOMPANYING ITEMS TO THE PLACE YOU OBTAINED THEM.

1. GRANT OF LICENSE AND OWNERSHIP: THE ENCLOSED COMPUTER PROGRAMS <<AND DATA>> ("SOFTWARE") ARE LICENSED, NOT SOLD, TO YOU BY PEARSON EDUCATION, INC. PUBLISHING AS PEARSON PRENTICE HALL ("WE" OR THE "COMPANY") AND IN CONSIDERATION OF YOUR PURCHASE OR ADOPTION OF THE ACCOMPANYING COMPANY TEXTBOOKS AND/OR OTHER MATERIALS, AND YOUR AGREEMENT TO THESE TERMS. WE RESERVE ANY RIGHTS NOT GRANTED TO YOU. YOU OWN ONLY THE DISK(S) BUT WE AND/OR OUR LICENSORS OWN THE SOFTWARE ITSELF. THIS LICENSE ALLOWS YOU TO USE AND DISPLAY YOUR COPY OF THE SOFTWARE ON A SINGLE COMPUTER (I.E., WITH A SINGLE CPU) AT A SINGLE LOCATION FOR ACADEMIC USE ONLY, SO LONG AS YOU COMPLY WITH THE TERMS OF THIS AGREEMENT. YOU MAY MAKE ONE COPY FOR BACK UP, OR TRANSFER YOUR COPY TO ANOTHER CPU, PROVIDED THAT THE SOFTWARE IS USABLE ON ONLY ONE COMPUTER.

2. RESTRICTIONS: YOU MAY NOT TRANSFER OR DISTRIBUTE THE SOFTWARE OR DOCUMENTATION TO ANYONE ELSE. EXCEPT FOR BACKUP, YOU MAY NOT COPY THE DOCUMENTATION OR THE SOFTWARE. YOU MAY NOT NETWORK THE SOFTWARE OR OTHERWISE USE IT ON MORE THAN ONE COMPUTER OR COMPUTER TERMINAL AT THE SAME TIME. YOU MAY NOT REVERSE ENGINEER, DISASSEMBLE, DECOMPILE, MODIFY, ADAPT, TRANSLATE, OR CREATE DERIVATIVE WORKS BASED ON THE SOFTWARE OR THE DOCUMENTATION. YOU MAY BE HELD LEGALLY RESPONSIBLE FOR ANY COPYING OR COPYRIGHT INFRINGEMENT THAT IS CAUSED BY YOUR FAILURE TO ABIDE BY THE TERMS OF THESE RESTRICTIONS.

3. TERMINATION: THIS LICENSE IS EFFECTIVE UNTIL TERMINATED. THIS LICENSE WILL TERMINATE AUTOMATICALLY WITHOUT NOTICE FROM THE COMPANY IF YOU FAIL TO COMPLY WITH ANY PROVISIONS OR LIMITATIONS OF THIS LICENSE. UPON TERMINATION, YOU SHALL DESTROY THE DOCUMENTATION AND ALL COPIES OF THE SOFTWARE. ALL PROVISIONS OF THIS AGREEMENT AS TO LIMITATION AND DISCLAIMER OF WARRANTIES, LIMITATION OF LIABILITY, REMEDIES OR DAMAGES, AND OUR OWNERSHIP RIGHTS SHALL SURVIVE TERMINATION.

4. LIMITED WARRANTY AND DISCLAIMER OF WARRANTY: COMPANY WARRANTS THAT FOR A PERIOD OF 60 DAYS FROM THE DATE YOU PURCHASE THIS SOFTWARE (OR PURCHASE OR ADOPT THE ACCOMPANYING TEXTBOOK), THE SOFTWARE, WHEN PROPERLY INSTALLED AND USED IN ACCORDANCE WITH THE DOCUMENTATION, WILL OPERATE IN SUBSTANTIAL CONFORMITY WITH THE DESCRIPTION OF THE SOFTWARE SET FORTH IN THE DOCUMENTATION, AND THAT FOR A PERIOD OF 30 DAYS THE DISK(S) ON WHICH THE SOFTWARE IS DELIVERED SHALL BE FREE FROM DEFECTS IN MATERIALS AND WORKMANSHIP UNDER NORMAL USE. THE COMPANY DOES NOT WARRANT THAT THE SOFTWARE WILL MEET YOUR REQUIREMENTS OR THAT THE OPERATION OF THE SOFTWARE WILL BE UNINTERRUPTED OR ERROR-FREE. YOUR ONLY REMEDY AND THE COMPANY'S ONLY OBLIGATION UNDER THESE LIMITED WARRANTIES IS, AT THE COMPANY'S OPTION, RETURN OF THE DISK FOR A REFUND OF ANY AMOUNTS PAID FOR IT BY YOU OR REPLACEMENT OF THE DISK. THIS LIMITED WARRANTY IS THE ONLY WARRANTY PROVIDED BY THE COMPANY AND ITS LICENSORS, AND THE COMPANY AND ITS LICENSORS DISCLAIM ALL OTHER WARRANTIES, EXPRESS OR IMPLIED, INCLUDING WITHOUT LIMITATION, THE IMPLIED WARRANTIES OF MERCHANTABILITY AND FITNESS FOR A PARTICULAR PURPOSE. THE COMPANY DOES NOT WARRANT, GUARANTEE OR MAKE ANY REPRESENTATION REGARDING THE ACCURACY, RELIABILITY, CURRENTNESS, USE, OR RESULTS OF USE, OF THE SOFTWARE.

5. LIMITATION OF REMEDIES AND DAMAGES: IN NO EVENT, SHALL THE COMPANY OR ITS EMPLOYEES, AGENTS, LICENSORS, OR CONTRACTORS BE LIABLE FOR ANY INCIDENTAL, INDIRECT, SPECIAL, OR CONSEQUENTIAL DAMAGES ARISING OUT OF OR IN CONNECTION WITH THIS LICENSE OR THE SOFTWARE, INCLUDING FOR LOSS OF USE, LOSS OF DATA, LOSS OF INCOME OR PROFIT, OR OTHER LOSSES, SUSTAINED AS A RESULT OF INJURY TO ANY PERSON, OR LOSS OF OR DAMAGE TO PROPERTY, OR CLAIMS OF THIRD PARTIES, EVEN IF THE COMPANY OR AN AUTHORIZED REPRESENTATIVE OF THE COMPANY HAS BEEN ADVISED OF THE POSSIBILITY OF SUCH DAMAGES. IN NO EVENT SHALL THE LIABILITY OF THE COMPANY FOR DAMAGES WITH RESPECT TO THE SOFTWARE EXCEED THE AMOUNTS ACTUALLY PAID BY YOU, IF ANY, FOR THE SOFTWARE OR THE ACCOMPANYING TEXTBOOK. BECAUSE SOME JURISDICTIONS DO NOT ALLOW THE LIMITATION OF LIABILITY IN CERTAIN CIRCUMSTANCES, THE ABOVE LIMITATIONS MAY NOT ALWAYS APPLY TO YOU.

6. GENERAL: THIS AGREEMENT SHALL BE CONSTRUED IN ACCORDANCE WITH THE LAWS OF THE UNITED STATES OF AMERICA AND THE STATE OF NEW YORK, APPLICABLE TO CONTRACTS MADE IN NEW YORK, EXCLUDING THE STATE'S LAWS AND POLICIES ON CONFLICTS OF LAW, AND SHALL BENEFIT THE COMPANY, ITS AFFILIATES AND ASSIGNEES. THIS AGREEMENT IS THE COMPLETE AND EXCLUSIVE STATEMENT OF THE AGREEMENT BETWEEN YOU AND THE COMPANY AND SUPERSEDES ALL PROPOSALS OR PRIOR AGREEMENTS, ORAL, OR WRITTEN, AND ANY OTHER COMMUNICATIONS BETWEEN YOU AND THE COMPANY OR ANY REPRESENTATIVE OF THE COMPANY RELATING TO THE SUBJECT MATTER OF THIS AGREEMENT. IF YOU ARE A U.S. GOVERNMENT USER, THIS SOFTWARE IS LICENSED WITH "RESTRICTED RIGHTS" AS SET FORTH IN SUBPARAGRAPHS (A)-(D) OF THE COMMERCIAL COMPUTER-RESTRICTED RIGHTS CLAUSE AT FAR 52.227-19 OR IN SUBPARAGRAPHS (C)(1)(II) OF THE RIGHTS IN TECHNICAL DATA AND COMPUTER SOFTWARE CLAUSE AT DFARS 252.227-7013, AND SIMILAR CLAUSES, AS APPLICABLE.

SHOULD YOU HAVE ANY QUESTIONS CONCERNING THIS AGREEMENT OR IF YOU WISH TO CONTACT THE COMPANY FOR ANY REASON, PLEASE CONTACT IN WRITING: LEGAL DEPARTMENT, PRENTICE HALL, 1 LAKE STREET, UPPER SADDLE RIVER, NJ 07450 OR CALL PEARSON EDUCATION PRODUCT SUPPORT AT 1-800-677-6337.